PETERSON'S
DISTANCE LEARNING PROGRAMS

SECOND EDITION

Published in cooperation with
the University Continuing Education Association

Peterson's
Princeton, New Jersey

About Peterson's

Peterson's is the country's largest educational information/communications company, providing the academic, consumer, and professional communities with books, software, and on-line services in support of lifelong education access and career choice. Well-known references include Peterson's annual guides to private schools, summer programs, colleges and universities, graduate and professional programs, financial aid, international study, adult learning, and career guidance. Peterson's Web site at petersons.com is the only comprehensive—and most heavily traveled—education resource on the Internet. The site carries all of Peterson's fully searchable major databases and includes financial aid sources, test-prep help, job postings, direct inquiry and application features, and specially created Virtual Campuses for every accredited academic institution and summer program in the U.S. and Canada that offers in-depth narratives, announcements, and multimedia features.

Visit Peterson's Education Center on the Internet (World Wide Web) at www.petersons.com

© 1997 by Peterson's
Previous edition published as *Peterson's Distance Learning*, © 1996.

All rights reserved. No part of this book may be reproduced, stored in a retrieval system, or transmitted, in any form or by any means—electronic, mechanical, photocopying, recording, or otherwise—except for citations of data for scholarly or reference purposes with full acknowledgment of title, edition, and publisher and written notification to Peterson's prior to such use.

ISBN 1-56079-875-0

Printed in the United States of America

10 9 8 7 6 5 4 3 2 1

EDITORIAL ADVISORY BOARD

Lisa DiChiara Platt, Executive Director, Burlington County Community College
Barry Howard, Director, Computer and Distance Learning Centers, NYNEX
Jerry Ice, Vice President and Provost, Thomas Edison State College
William Philipp Jr., Director, PBS Adult Learning Services
Eugene Rubin, Director, International University Consortium
Richard Vigilante, Director, Information Technology Institute, New York University

TABLE OF CONTENTS

Foreword, Kay Kohl, Executive Director, UCEA	v
STUDENT PROFILE: Ashlea Rogers	vi
What You Need to Know About Distance Learning— Questions & Answers	vii
STUDENT PROFILE: Gary and Bridgette Anderson	xii
Academic Advising for the Distance Learner	xiii
Finding a Program that is Right for You	xv
What Are My Financing Options?	xviii
STUDENT PROFILE: Lenora Everett	xix
How to Use this Guide	xx
Institution Profiles	1
In-Depth Descriptons	375
STUDENT PROFILE: Brenda Eades	532
Index of Institutions Offering Degree and Certificate Programs	533
STUDENT PROFILE: Gregory Hotchkiss	542
Index of Institutions Offering Individual Courses	543
STUDENT PROFILE: Samuel Krosney	608
Geographic Index	609

FOREWORD

by Kay Kohl

Executive Director, University Continuing Education Association

New communication technologies enable learning to take place beyond the classroom—in the workplace, car, or home. Increasing numbers of colleges and universities now offer courses electronically. As a consequence, someone pursuing an undergraduate degree or struggling to keep pace with new developments in a profession can often obtain the required learning without needing to enroll in a conventional campus-based course.

Remaining occupationally competent in today's knowledge economy necessitates continual learning. Use of technology often makes it easier to acquire new learning. Technology can provide highly individualized instruction and enhance communication between faculty members and students. When an individual chooses to pursue learning through an electronic course, this also tends to expand the person's knowledge of how to use technology and the person's capacity to draw upon the resources of the Internet. In today's digital era, these skills are increasingly important.

This edition of *Peterson's Distance Learning* brings together in a single volume an abundant selection of instructional programs available electronically from individual colleges, universities, and consortia of higher education institutions. The rapid growth of electronic higher education in evidenced by the fact that this guide lists the programs of some 700 accredited North American institutions. When the University Continuing Education Association, in partnership with Peterson's, prepared the first edition of this publication four years ago, there were fewer than 100 institutional listings.

Peterson's Distance Learning constitutes a valuable resource for any individual or employer interested in accessing electronic learning opportunities offered by accredited colleges and universities. The programs described in this guide rely on diverse distance education technologies, and together present a wide array of degree and certificate opportunities. All of the higher education institutions highlighted herein are committed to utilizing communication technologies to help students transcend significant time and geographical barriers and to supporting new approaches to teaching and learning.

Founded in 1915, the University Continuing Education Association represents some 425 accredited colleges and universities, public and private, dedicated to providing degree and nondegree instruction and the pre- and postbaccalaureate levels to students of all ages. The association is based in Washington, DC.

STUDENT PROFILE

Ashlea Rogers

Personal: Age 21, single

Home: Glennville, GA

College: Georgia Southern University

Courses Taken: Principles of marketing, buyer behavior

Academic/Professional Goals: Bachelor's degree in Public Relations with an emphasis in marketing

"Although I'm an on-campus student, I take distance learning courses to learn more about the technologies which are now prevalent in the workplace and the healthcare field which I hope to enter when I graduate. Since our professor travels to the remote site half the time, we on-campus students are distance learners as well.

"As Miss Tattnall County, I have been involved in the preliminary competitions for the Miss America Pageant. My platform—the cause that I help advance for the competition—is 'nontraditional learning.' I come from a rural area 45 miles from Statesboro and I see how great the need is for distance learning. When I traveled to the Miss Georgia Pageant this summer, it turned out to be a lifesaver for me since I was able to get video tapes of the classes I missed.

"The first time I walked into a distance learning classroom I was extremely intimidated by the microphones and cameras, but the interaction with the professors was wonderful—they held 'ice-breakers' to encourage you to speak up. We got to know the 30 students at the remote sites through class sessions and conversations during the breaks. Because you can see yourself on camera, it helps to build your media and public speaking skills as well as your self-esteem. I encourage anyone who has the opportunity to take a distance learning course."

WHAT YOU NEED TO KNOW ABOUT DISTANCE LEARNING—

Questions & Answers

What, Exactly, is Distance Learning?

Distance Learning is the delivery of educational programs to off-site students through the use of technologies such as cable or satellite television, video and audiotapes, fax, computer modem, computer and video conferencing, and other means of electronic delivery.

What Does this Mean to You?

It may mean that now you can find the resources of your state's top four-year university right next door at your local community college.

Or it may mean that you can walk down the hall at your place of work and spend your lunch hour taking a course with like-minded colleagues seeking career advancement.

Or it may mean that you can connect to your professor's e-mail with your home computer modem, exchange messages, and turn in a 10-page "paper" electronically.

Or it may mean that you will use your personal computer to locate library references and information.

Distance learning expands the reach of the classroom by using various technologies to deliver university resources to off-campus sites, transmit college courses into the work place, and enable students to view class lectures in the comfort of their homes.

Where and How Can I Take Distance Learning Courses?

The proliferation of new, cheaper telecommunications technologies and the demand for broader access to educational resources have prompted the development of diverse educational networks. Most states have established new distance learning systems to advance the delivery of instruction to schools, postsecondary institutions and state government agencies. Colleges and universities are collaborating with commercial telecommunications entities, including online information services—such as America Online®—cable, and telephone companies to provide education to far-flung student constituencies. Professions such as law, medicine, and accounting as well as knowledge-based industries are utilizing telecommunications networks for the transmission of customized higher education programs to working professionals, technicians and managers.

This guide lists course offerings from accredited colleges and universities including:

Credit courses. In general, if these credit courses are completed successfully, they may be applied towards a degree.

"Non-credit" courses and courses offered for professional certification. These programs can help you acquire specialized knowledge in a concentrated, time-efficient manner and stay on the top of the latest developments in your field. They provide a flexible way for you to prepare for a new career or study for professional licensure and certification. Many of these university programs are created in cooperation with professional and trade associations so that courses are based on real-life workforce needs and the practical skills learned are immediately applicable in the field.

What Does Distance Learning Offer?

Professional Certification

Certificate programs often focus on employment specializations, such as hazardous waste management or electronic publishing, and can be helpful to those seeking to advance or change careers. Also many states mandate continuing education for professionals such as teachers, nursing home administrators, or accountants. Distance learning offers a convenient way for many individuals to meet professional certification requirements. Health care, engineering, and education are just a few of the many professions that take advantage of the distance learning to help their professionals maintain certification.

Many colleges offer a sequence of distance learning courses in a specific field of a profession. For instance, within the engineering profession, certificate programs in *Computer Integrated Manufacturing Systems Engineering Test*

What You Need to Know About Distance Learning—Questions & Answers

& Evaluation, and *Waste Management Education & Research Consortium* are offered via distance learning.

Business offerings include distance learning certification in *Information Technology, Total Quality Management,* and *Health Services Management.*

Within the field of education, you'll find distance learning certificate programs in areas such as *Early Reading Instruction* or *Special Education for Learning Handicapped.*

Degree Programs

This book outlines opportunities for individuals to earn degrees at a distance at the associate, baccalaureate and graduate levels. Two-year community college students are now able to earn baccalaureate degrees—without relocating—by transferring to distance learning programs offered by four-year universities. Corporations are forming partnerships with universities to bring college courses to worksites and encourage employees to continue their education. Distance learning is especially popular among working adults who want to earn their degree part-time while continuing to work full-time. Although on-campus residencies are sometimes required for certain distance learning degree programs, they generally can be completed while employees are on short-term leave or vacation.

Continuing Education Units (CEUs)

If you choose to take a course on a non-credit basis, you may be able to earn Continuing Education Units (CEUs). The CEU system is a nationally recognized system to provide a standardized measure for accumulating, transferring, and recognizing participation in Continuing Education programs. One CEU is defined as 10 contact hours of participation in an organized continuing education experience under responsible sponsorship, capable direction, and qualified instruction. Some institutions in this book allow you to take distance education courses on a continuing education credit or noncredit course basis.

Who Is Learning at a Distance?

Most students who enroll in distance education courses are over 25 years old, employed and have previous college experience. Over half are female. As a group, distance learners are highly motivated. Their course completion rate exceeds that of students enrolled in traditional, on-campus courses. The successful distance learner is by definition a committed student. The individual must have the discipline to establish a regular study schedule each week and adhere to it without having to be reminded by an instructor or classmates to meet deadlines.

A wide range of employers—businesses, hospitals, government offices, military installations—which find it difficult to release employees for on-campus study, are discovering that it is a good investment to bring the classroom to their worksites. According to a survey conducted by the International Foundation of Employee Benefits Plans, employees rank continuing education as more important than childcare, flextime and family leave. "Convenience" is the single most cited factor influencing a student's decision to choose to learn at a distance rather than in a traditional classroom setting. For many, it is the only way they can fit continuing education into their schedules.

What's New in Distance Learning?

In the past few years, distance learning opportunities have grown exponentially thanks to technological advances and a growing number of public and private partnerships. A 1995 nationwide survey conducted by Washington State University revealed that "lifelong learning" has become a reality for most Americans; 81 percent of those surveyed said that gaining additional education is important for them to be successful at work. Interest did not vary by income level and seems to reflect the pressures of working in a knowledge-based economy. Distance learning can be an important solution to the problems of access that adult learners face. Many adults need highly focused, 'just-in-time' knowledge about a new theory or technique to use at work. Colleges and universities have found that telecommunications networks can make it possible to deliver education to adult learners when and where they need it.

Partnerships

Community colleges, four-year universities, cable, public broadcasting services and international consortia are forging numerous partnerships to expand distance learning services. The first edition of this guide (*The Electronic University: A Guide to Distance Learning, 1993*) contained programs from just 93 accredited four-year colleges and universities. This volume contains courses from more than 700 accredited institutions across the United States and Canada. Such partnerships are broadening the offerings, expanding the reach and improving the quality of programs available at a distance.

For example, the University of Delaware recently introduced an electronically delivered Bachelor's of Science Degree in Hotel, Restaurant & Institutional Management in partnership with community colleges and Mind Extension University. The program began delivery in 1996 and allows students to combine community college courses with distance learning courses to earn a four-year degree from UD. It is available through video tapes and MEU cable connections which reach some 25 million subscribers.

Eliminating Boundaries

Access to distance learning is expanding. Although some courses are still limited to certain states or regional areas, many programs are available to students nationwide and even internationally. For example, California State Fullerton's recently formed a partnership with Wescott, a Dallas based satellite communication company. Cal State-Fullerton's bachelor of science degree program in nursing is now available at 1200 hospitals and 1000 longterm care centers across the United States. Courses are delivered through two digitalized satellite networks—Health & Sciences Television Network and The Long Term Care Network. The students (diploma nurses who already hold two-year associate degrees) can interact with faculty members via two-way data and audio in real-time. Cal State's program joins numerous nursing programs offered statewide and regionally, however, because Fullerton's program is designed for students who have already met their clinical requirements for licensure it requires no travel to campus—although students must submit a videotape of themselves performing a physical assessment.

Internationally, distance learning opportunities are growing as well. For example, University of Maryland University College's program offers electronically delivered courses to military personnel and their families in Europe and Asia. U.S. troops on assignment in Croatia, Hungary, and Bosnia were able to choose from 14 undergraduate and graduate distance education courses. Areas of study included: government, history, management, sociology, speech, mathematics, English and Hungarian. Embry-Riddle Aeronautical University's program enables students anywhere in the world to earn a master's degree with specially prepared videotapes and print materials and by communicating with their professors and fellow students via a private forum on CompuServe. In 1997, Embry-Riddle added a specialization in aviation safety to its distance learning curriculum for a Master's Degree in Aeronautical Science.

A Changing Work Place Requires "Technology Literacy"

The spread of computer systems and the rise of global markets are rendering traditional workplace bureaucracies increasingly unwieldy. Rigid organizational hierarchies are being replaced by project-oriented, problem-solving work groups. Often employees in work groups are geographically dispersed and must collaborate in "virtual" workplaces created by networked computers.

Changes in higher education parallel those of the workplace. Even nontechnical workers are faced with the need to conform to decentralized and networked offices. Distance learning is helping individuals gain the collaborative and technical skills needed to work in such environments.

New York University's "Virtual College" involves a partnership with NYNEX and funding from the Sloan Foundation. The program is targeted to non-technical business generalists who must use computers in their work. All course work is conducted from the student's home or office PC, with *no* on-campus sessions. Students and faculty communicate via high-speed Integrated Service Digital Network (ISDN) lines. The program is unique in that *all* instruction materials—video, simulations, laboratories, readings, online libraries—are digital and interactively accessible through one common user interface. Special hardware and software is required and the system relies on the Lotus Notes— network for students to share information with instructors and classmates.

At the graduate degree level, two land grant universities—University of Tennessee, Knoxville and the University of Virginia—recently collaborated to deliver the first inter-institutional, degree program in Information Sciences available through distance learning. The program uses state of the art two-way television and is delivered to multiple sites in Tennessee and Virginia.

Is Distance Learning Right for Me?

Limitations of Distance Learning and This Guide

You should be aware that some Distance Learning courses are limited to certain geographical areas and/or times of offering. Others may have some on-campus requirements. Please read the listings of your preferred college or university carefully so that you are aware of any limitations before you enroll.

Consider the Instructional Environment

Some programs may connect students electronically to a live, real-time classroom setting. Other institutions offer students in remote areas the opportunity for periodic face-to-face interaction. In an asynchronous instructional environment, however, students typically interact with one another and the professor through computer conference and e-mail. The level of student-to-instructor and student-to-student interaction is a critical consideration for anyone involved in distance education.

Do You Have the Tools Required to Access Distance Learning?

Colleges and universities use multiple technologies for distance education. Some courses are based on telecourses, requiring a VCR and television set. Others require access to a computer and modem. If you do not own a computer with the proper specifications, you may be able to use one where you work. All distance learning programs rely on telephone connections for some services.

What You Need to Know About Distance Learning—Questions & Answers

ASSESSING QUALITY IN DISTANCE EDUCATION

Your work environment may help you decide which technology to choose for distance education. Even though you may be personally more comfortable with a videocassette course, you may decide it is important to take a course via online computer modem because your employer's long-range plan involves conducting research on the Internet. Likewise, many self-described "computer-phobic" school librarians are now proud holders of certificates and masters degrees in library computer science which they earned through distance education programs.

Whether the program is offered in a synchronous or asynchronous learning mode is an important consideration. Although, conference calls, online chat groups, and two-way video hook-ups provide opportunities for class interaction, they may not be available for all courses or for every assignment. It is important to know what you value most in a learning experience and select a course that is delivered by technologies that match your personal preferences.

Inform yourself about testing, evaluation, and assessment systems. It is important to ascertain before registering for a course whether such activities occur on campus or are also available close to home.

What are the qualifications of the faculty? What is the student-faculty ratio and is it important to the subject matter? For on-line courses that are very time intensive, it's probably best to have a low ratio of perhaps 20 students. For lecture classes, a much higher ratio may be acceptable. Find out who your classmates will be and how much peer-to-peer interaction you realistically expect to have with them—and through which media? What are the supporting student services? What library resources are available to you and how much lead time must you allow? Before signing up, you might ask to talk to other distance learning students who have already completed similar courses or degree programs.

Much of the Material in this Book is Time Sensitive

The distance learning field is constantly changing. You should contact the sponsoring institutions for the most recent information on any given course or subject area. In many cases, courses are added to or deleted from a given curriculum between printings of this catalog.

Although Distance Learning removes many barriers to education, the lack of a formal classroom environment necessitates student discipline and planning. Faculty who design instructional materials and guide your study will not be physically present to "breathe down your neck" to remind you to complete assignments. It's up to *you* to make sure you to set aside study time, to initiate the personal contact and feedback you need—whether its through e-mail, 800 number phone calls, two-way video or in writing—to have a successful learning experience.

How Does "Distance Learning" Differ From "Independent Study?"

Independent Study in the form of correspondence study is sometimes called "Distance Learning." But while correspondence study has been offered by colleges and universities for more than 100 years, distance learning today is *not* the same educational experience as independent study. While correspondence or "independent" study requires no attendance on campus and no "real time" interaction with professor or classmates, distance learning may require class participation via technology, short trips to the home campus or a satellite site, and off-site students may be required to work at the same pace as on-campus students. (If you decide that Independent Study is a better option for you, consult *UCEA/Peterson's The Independent Study Catalog*, a guide to 10,000 correspondence courses offered by accredited colleges and universities.)

Why It Is Important To Take Distance Learning Courses From A Regionally Accredited College or University?

Taking a course from an institution accredited by one of the six U.S. regional accrediting associations is an assurance of quality in terms of the curriculum and the instruction you will receive. Many employers will pay the tuition for an employee to complete a course that seems likely to improve job performance. Most organizations will insist, however, that an employee relying on employer-provided tuition assistance, pursue studies at an accredited college or university. Another important consideration is whether the institution is non-profit or proprietary, because credits from the latter may not be acknowledged by the former. For that matter, it is always wise to check with an academic advisor at the institution to which you intend to transfer the credits *before* enrolling in a course. This guide includes institutions whose distance learning programs have obtained accreditation by either a regional accrediting association or, in special circumstances, accreditation by another recognized body as noted in the institution's listing.

The Accrediting Council for Independent Colleges and Schools recommends that students ask the accredited institution questions regarding 1) the percentage of student/teacher interaction; 2) the objectives of the program; 3) the success rate of graduates; 4) the completion rate; and 5) how many graduates are placed in their fields of training.

STUDENT PROFILE

Gary and Bridgette Anderson

Personal: Age 38 and 37, married (no children)

Home: Norman, Oklahoma

College: University of Oklahoma

Courses Taken: Gary, a history major, has taken telecourses on the Pacific century, Japan, the changing tradition; and principles of management. Bridgette, an European studies major, has taken telecourses in introduction to archaeology, history 1865–present, and Western civilization I and II.

Academic/Professional Goals: Distance learning is helping both Andersons earn their baccalaureate degrees and prepare for the U.S. foreign service exam. Ultimately they would like to return to work overseas.

Originally from West Sussex, England, Bridgette was serving in the British Foreign Service when she met Gary, a Marine guard at the American Embassy in Warsaw. She currently works for the Oklahoma State Regents for Higher Education and Gary is a U.S. Postal Service employee.

"As mature students, both in full-time employment, we were keen to take accelerated undergraduate programs. CLEP tests were one way for us to gain advanced credits. We have also found that telecourses have eased the stress caused by sometimes conflicting work/school schedules and have given us access to courses not always available as evening classes. Being able to tape the courses from our local cable channel and review them later has been a great help. Not only has the quality of the telecourses to date been impressive, but our professors have consistently made themselves available for consultation, either via e-mail, over the phone or by appointment."

Distance Learning Programs

ACADEMIC ADVISING FOR THE DISTANCE LEARNING STUDENT

Can I Earn a Degree?

If you are contemplating entering a degree program, or taking a distance learning course to transfer credit to a program you are already in, it is important to take the time to inform yourself about the institution and its offerings in your field of interest *prior* to enrolling. Some institutions have formed partnerships that guaranteed transfer of credit. For example in 1995, two Big Ten universities—Penn State and the University of Iowa—formed such a distance learning partnership. Students who have earned an Extended-Access Associate Degree in Letters, Arts and Sciences from Penn State are guaranteed admission to UI's Bachelors of Liberal Studies external degree program.

Official information about the institution's programs is best obtained from the admissions office and the academic department offering the course you wish to take. If you are interested in earning academic credit, it is important for you to consult the institution's *academic advising service* before registering. The academic advising department can explain entrance requirements and application procedures. You should be able to register for a class electronically, by phone, or by mail from your home.

You may find it necessary to develop a portfolio of your past experiences and of your accomplishments that may have resulted in college-level learning. A detailed portfolio, properly assessed by an accredited institution, can help to award you credits towards your degree.

Applying Distance Learning Credits Toward a Traditional Degree

If you are interested in obtaining degree credit for a course, you should ask your academic advisor:

- Will the college of my choice accept the course credit and apply it toward my graduation?
- How many credits by distance learning will be accepted toward graduation from the institution of my choice?
- Will my institution accept credit for course work transferred from another institution?
- Will credits earned by distance learning be accepted in my area of concentration?

Applying Distance Learning Credits Toward Certification

If you plan to take the course for certification and not for degree purposes, you should ask the certifying agency:

- What are the certification requirements?
- Will the course be acceptable to the relevant certifying agency or professional association?
- How many credits can be earned or how much of the work can be done by distance learning?

What Options Are Available to Me If I Seek to Transfer Credit?

Institutions offer various ways to take their courses and/or earn degree credit. Important considerations here are:

- Is the pass-fail option acceptable to my college or certifying agency?
- Is credit by examination acceptable?
- Is credit for experiential (life experience) learning available and acceptable?
- Is the distance degree programs that I'm interested in acceptable to other colleges, employers, and certifying agencies?

Earning Credit for What You Know

Ninety-three percent of the nation's higher education institutions award credit for prior learning if students take examinations to assess their knowledge and skills.

Credit by Examination. If you are already knowledgeable in certain areas, rather than completing prerequisites for an individual course, or for degree or certificate programs, you may be able to "test out" of a course by taking and passing its final exam. College and university academic advising can also provide you with information on taking standardized Advanced Placement tests. You can receive degree credit for successful scores on the various tests of the College-Level Examination Program (CLEP, Box 6600, Princeton, NJ 08543), the American College Testing Program, Proficiency Examination Program (ACT-PEP, Box

168, Iowa City, Iowa 52243), or DANTES Standard Subject Tests (DANTES, DSSTs, 6490 Saufley Field Rd., Code 20A, Pensacola, FL 32509-5243; 904/452-1089).

Credits for Life Experience, "Portfolio" Development

To apply for possible award of credit through a college or university for life experience, you should assemble a file or "portfolio" of information about your work and accomplishments (writing samples, awards, taped presentations, copies of speeches) that may have resulted in college-level learning. With academic guidance, you can identify those activities resulting in learning that can be stated as education outcomes or curriculum-relevant "competencies." Your portfolio is then evaluated by an institution's faculty. Information about assessment opportunities for adult learners is available through the Council for Adult and Experiential Learning (CAEL, 243 South Wabash Ave., #800, Chicago, IL 60604).

Credit for Work Training. Since 1974, thousands of employees have been earning college credit for selected educational programs sponsored by businesses, industry, professional associations, labor unions, and government agencies. The American Council on Education's Program on Non-Collegiate Sponsored Instruction (ACE-PONSI, One Dupont Circle, Suite 250, Washington, DC 20036)

STUDY TIPS FOR SUCCESSFUL DISTANCE LEARNING

Tools. Before enrolling in a course, make sure you have access to the tools necessary to complete assignments. A word processor can help you to organize your work and communicate your thoughts more clearly. If your lessons appear through cable television, you'll want to know how to program your VCR to record the programs to refer back to. Access to a fax machine, computer with adequate hard disk space and modem for e-mail transmission are "musts" for many classes.

Schedule. Set aside a regularly scheduled time for study. If you have not been involved in academic pursuits recently, you may find that your career, family, hobbies, social and civic commitments leave little time for studying. To help you fit studying into your schedule, keep a record for a week of how you spend your time, and then decide what you are willing to give up. Schedule your studies for a time when you are mentally fresh and able to devote at least one hour to your work. Think of the hour as "reserved time." If you miss too many study periods, revise your schedule.

Where to Study. You will find it easier to focus in an appropriate environment for study. Find a place that is free from distractions. You might consider work—before or after hours and on your lunch hour—a public library, or a separate room in your home.

Reading Skills. You must comprehend and retain what you read for real learning to take place. Reading skills can be developed by concentrating on what you read and by taking frequent pauses to organize and review the material in your mind. At the end of a study session, review everything you have read, making special notes of important points. Reading a computer screen can be hard on your eyes; it may be necessary to download hard copies of reading assignments and communications from your instructor and co-workers.

Communication Skills. It can be intimidating to speak into a microphone in a video or conference call, but your communication skills are an important part of any assignment—on the job, at home, and at school. Distance learning provides the opportunity to enhance these skills. Pay careful attention to instructions and be certain that you understand what is being asked. It often helps to develop a brief outline before responding to questions whether they are submitted in writing, via e-mail, orally or on video/audio tape. Organization, grammar, and the appropriate style are important whichever medium you choose.

evaluates such programs according to established college-level criteria and recommends college credit for those programs that measure up to these standards.

Credit for Military Training. Your service in the military, specialized training, and occupational experience can potentially earn you college credit. Many military programs have already been evaluated in terms of their equivalency to college credit. The Institutions that belong to Servicemembers Opportunities Colleges (SOC) agree to assess student prior learning and accept each others credits in transfer. (Contact SOC, One Dupont Circle, Suite 680, Washington, DC 20036-1117, 202/667-0079 or 1-800-368-5622, and ask for *College Degrees Without Classrooms*, flyer #2122).

Credit for Volunteering, Working inside the Home. You may be able to reap college credit for skills you have learned as a volunteer or working at home. (Accrediting Women's Competencies, T-154, Educational Testing Service, Princeton, NJ 08541 offers information on this.)

FINDING A PROGRAM THAT IS RIGHT FOR YOU

Do I Have the Study Skills Required?

You should take the time to evaluate your own approach to work and study before you enroll. Assess how you spend your time and decide, with as much objectivity as possible, how well you think you can fit distance learning in your life.

Although distance learning can provide many advantages in terms of commuting time saved, often students find it to be more rigorous than regular classroom courses. If you can take responsibility for your own education, you will find distance learning rewarding and satisfying. Before enrolling, consider both the advantages and drawbacks of this method of continuing education.

Completing a distance learning course may or may not be easy for you, but the benefits can be significant. In addition to mastering the subject matter, the study skills you develop should enable you to undertake other difficult educational and work related tasks with heightened confidence.

How Do I Communicate with My Instructor?

Student/faculty exchanges occur using electronic communication (through, fax and e-mail). Many institutions offer their distance learning students access to toll-free "800" numbers so students can talk to their professors or teaching assistants without incurring any long-distance charges. Details about these and other types of electronic communication, including any cost to the student, appear in the institution's catalog and/or the course description.

Responses to your instructor's comments on your lessons, requests for clarification of comments, and all other exchanges between you and your instructor will take time. Interaction with your instructor—whether by computer, phone, or letter—is important and you must be willing to take the initiative.

How Does It Work?

Enrolling In A Course

Enrolling in a distance learning course may simply involve filling out a registration form, making sure that you have access to the equipment needed, and paying the tuition/fees listed in the catalog by check, money order, or credit card. In these cases your applications may be accepted without entrance examinations or proof of prior educational experience.

Other courses may involve educational prerequisites and access to equipment not found in all geographic locations. Usually such limitations are listed in the institution's profile.

After reviewing the course names shown in this guide, you can obtain registration forms and catalogs that will provide more detailed descriptions of the courses. Some institutions offer detailed information about individual courses, such as a course outline, upon request. To obtain these materials, contact the person whose name and address or telephone number appear at the end of each institution's entry in the "Institutions and Courses Offered" section of this guide. If you have access to the Internet computer network and simply wish to review course descriptions, you may be able to peruse an institution's course catalogs electronically by accessing the institution's homepage on the World Wide Web.

Time Requirements

Some courses allow you to enroll at your convenience and work at your own pace. Others closely adhere to a traditional classroom schedule. Specific policies and time limitations pertaining to withdrawals, refunds, transfers, and renewal periods can be are found in the institutional catalog.

Admission to a Degree Program

If you plan to enter a degree program, you should consult the academic advising department of the institution of your choice to learn of entrance requirements and application procedures. You may find it necessary to develop a portfolio of your past experiences and of your accomplish-

Distance Learning Programs

Finding a Program that is Right for You

ments that may have resulted in college-level learning. A detailed portfolio, properly assessed by an accredited institution, can help to award you credits towards a degree. (See previous section *Credit for Prior Learning*.)

Transferring Credit

If you wish to apply credit for a distance learning course(s), you should be aware that some institutions may impose certain requirements before they will accept the credit, and some courses or programs may require previous study or experience.

NOTE: If you wish to earn credit for a course and apply it to a degree program, be certain that it meets the requirements of the institution to which you want to transfer the credit, as well as the requirements of your specific program within that institution.

For example, if you want to earn three credits from College A's accounting course and apply those credits toward University B's bachelor-of-arts degree, check with University B and as well as its department of business before you enroll in the course, to ascertain whether the credits will be accepted. Most institutions' catalogs will list both the general admission requirements and the prerequisites for individual courses.

Most institutions limit the number and kinds of credits that they will accept. You can usually transfer credit earned in a distance learning course from one regionally accredited institution to another. As policies and degree requirements of colleges and universities vary markedly, you should consult the appropriate officials at the institution from which you expect to receive a degree to be sure that the credit is transferable. If you pursue course work at an institution that is not regionally accredited, it may be difficult for you to transfer the credit.

Credit for Distance Learning

College Credit

Academic credit is measured in semester or quarter hours. You should consult with the institution(s) to which you are transferring credits, because some institutions use different systems of conversion or do not accept partial hours of credit.

Enrollment in Credit Courses on a Noncredit Basis

Most universities and colleges accept enrollment in credit courses on a noncredit basis and take special interest in students who are studying for personal satisfaction or career advancement without regard to credit.

The Continuing Education Unit or CEU

The Continuing Education Unit (CEU) is used to recognize participation in noncredit courses. The CEU is defined as 10 contact hours of participation in an organized continuing education experience under responsible sponsorship, capable direction, and qualified instruction. If you are interested in receiving CEUs for noncredit courses listed in this guide, request information from the institutions offering the courses.

Grades and Transcripts for College Courses

Each institution follows its regular grading policies in evaluating the work of distant learning students. When you complete a course, the institution sends a grade report to you. The grade is also recorded at the institution, and a transcript will be sent to any address you designate in a written request, although most institutions charge for additional transcripts. Some institutions use special designations to indicate courses that have been taken by distance learning.

Course Materials

Course materials include a study guide, which is usually provided as part of the initial cost. A course may also require workbooks, procedure manuals, lab kits, video or audio tapes, slides, photographs, or other audiovisual materials, which you must purchase separately. The cost of these items varies from institution to institution. In some cases, you may borrow materials from the institution by paying a deposit that is partially refunded when you return the materials. Audiovisual materials are usually sent with the study guide, and you will be charged as indicated in the institution's catalog. Details about costs for course materials will be listed in the institution's catalog or in the study guide.

Textbooks

In most cases, the cost of textbooks is not included in the course fee. Depending upon the particular institution, you may purchase the required textbooks and other course materials in a number of ways. In general, you have three choices: 1) you can order the books at the time of enrollment and the institution will send them to you along with the study guide; or 2) you can order books from a designated bookstore after receiving the study guide; or 3) you can obtain the books from local sources. For some courses, the study guide also serves as the text.

The cost of textbooks varies widely, depending upon

Finding a Program that is Right for You

the number and kinds of texts. The institution's catalog or the course study guide will indicate where textbooks can be obtained and how much they will cost. It may also provide information on the selling of your used textbooks.

Fax, E-mail Communication and Access to Digital Libraries

Learning to navigate the Internet and its World Wide Web may be part of your distance learning experience. Some course learning guides are available over the Internet and you can register for courses by fax, phone or e-mail at many institutions listed in this Catalog. Course catalogs are also frequently available over commercial services like America Online®, Compuserve®, or Prodigy®.

Some universities have made their online "digital libraries" available to students learning from a distance. Recognizing that some off-campus students do not have access to computer modems, at least one school—Kansas State University—has instituted a unique outreach library. The library is available to students who live more than 30 miles from the main campus. By paying a small fee, these students can call upon the services of a special Library Services Facilitator who will conduct online and CD-ROM index searches, photocopy articles, and check out and mail books to students. In all cases, the extra research time long distance library services require must be planned for in advance when budgeting homework completion time.

Not all schools are equipped to accept lessons via fax or e-mail. Thus, if you want to submit your work electronically, check with the institution regarding its assignment submission policies *before* you enroll. In many situation, institutions will *not* accept exams (which must be administered by an authorized proctor) via fax.

Special Considerations for Students in Other Countries

If you plan to take a distance learning course from overseas, it is important to make sure you will have access to the proper computer equipment and wiring once you are out of the country. It is wise to enroll before you leave the United States, taking your textbooks and course materials with you to avoid both postage and tariff expenses. An institution's catalog will identify policies, costs and availability for international enrollments.

Handling and Special Fees

Some institutions charge a handling fee to help them defray the cost of processing materials and registration. In addition, rental fees may be charged for special course materials. Special fees are usually charged for course transfers and course extensions and sometimes for enrollment by out-of-state residents.

Distance Learning Programs

WHAT ARE MY FINANCING OPTIONS?

The costs vary from course to course and from one college or university to another. Each institution sets its own pricing structure. In general, you can expect direct charges for tuition, textbooks, and other necessary course materials and equipment as well as for any postage and handling.

Tuition

Tuition information is included based on 1997 pricing and is subject to change. Before enrolling, check the catalog of the institution for its current rates.

Payment Plans

Most institutions require full payment of all charges due at the time of registration. The preferred method of payment is a check or money order. In a few instances, textbooks are paid for separately. Some institutions accept charge cards and offer partial or deferred payment plans. You should consult the institution's catalog to determine payment policies.

Financial Aid

The list below identifies a few possible sources of financial aid, and students who require aid are encouraged to explore all applicable options.

Employers. Many employers provide educational benefits to their employees. These are generally administered through the personnel or benefits department of the organization. If you are a teacher or other public school employee, you may be able to receive reimbursement of fees taken for college credit. Contact the coordinator of staff development within your district for further information.

Unions. Unions often negotiate educational benefits into their contracts. The union's business manager would be the person to provide information.

Veterans' and Military Benefits. Federal veterans' assistance acts have had provisions for financial assistance for college and university study. The amount and type of assistance varies, and it is best to check with a local Veterans Administration office for specific details. If you are an active-duty military personnel, including a member of the National Guard and Armed Forces Reserve, you have two options available to you for financial assistance. The first consists of "in-service" benefits through the U.S. Department of Veteran Affairs. The second is "tuition assistance," which comes from the military person's respective service and is administered by DANTES (Defense Activity for Non-Traditional Educational Support). In either case, the Educational Service Officer of your base, post, or ship can provide information. In addition to the federal government's tuition assistance plans, some states have educational benefits for veterans and military personnel. Direct your questions and inquiries to the state veterans or military affairs offices.

Other Federal Programs. Although most federal programs providing grants or loans are directed to the resident student, some are applicable to the distance learning student as well. Under certain conditions, for example, Pell Grants may be available to a person studying at a distance. Because eligibility is limited to degree candidates, you should contact the financial aid office of the institution from which you are seeking your degree.

Vocational Rehabilitation. Nearly all states provide financial benefits for the education of persons with some form of handicap. Direct any questions to your state's department of vocational rehabilitation.

Institutional Aid. A small number of colleges and universities have a limited amount of financial aid available for distance learning students. You should carefully examine an institution's catalog for financial aid information or consult its office of financial aid.

Unfortunately, as a distance education student, you may find that you have more difficulty qualifying for financial aid than traditional full-time students—depending upon the institution you contact. However, at press time, Congress is considering legislation to remedy this situation. For free information on qualifying for financial aid, check out the Web site of the National Association of Student Financial Aid Administrators at www.nasfaa.org

STUDENT PROFILE

Lenora Everett

Personal: Age 42, married, mother of three children.

Home: Memphis, Tennessee

College: New York University

Courses Taken: "The Virtual College"

Academic/Professional Goals: To start her own consulting business

"After working for IBM for 16 years, I wanted to start my own consulting business. I decided to take NYU's Virtual College course to gain experience using the Lotus Notes system in context. I had experience as a team facilitator at IBM but I found it a very different situation to lead a team where all your contacts are on-line and it takes longer to coordinate deadlines. After a few false starts, I had everyone type in their schedules so that I could set realistic deadlines for project input. Lotus Notes allows you to see the entire thread of communication from all your colleagues, which is much better than just e-mail. We also had access to NYU's readings online. In addition to our group projects, we had a 'Virtual Cafe' chat group where we debated everything from the benefits of OS2 vs. Windows to whether Barney is good for kids or not. As long as you have a phone line for your computer, you can communicate on-line from anywhere. I even took my laptop with me on vacation in Puerto Rico. Another classmate plugged in from Japan.

"I invested a lot of time in the class and was on the computer perhaps more than my husband would have liked, but my one-year old loved having me home and would sit in my lap while I worked on the computer. I did miss the adult contact of the corporate environment but my NYU classmates became my new corporate family—making the transition to working from home a lot easier."

Three years after her course, Everett's consulting business is thriving. She is a certified Lotus Notes instructor and specializes in application development. "I now work fewer hours and make more money than I did at IBM."

Distance Learning Programs

HOW TO USE THIS GUIDE

NOTE If you have not already done so, please refer to the preceding pages for valuable insights on: *What You Need to Know about Distance Learning; Academic Advising for the Distance Learner; Finding a Program that is Right for You;* and the answer to the question: *What are My Financing Options?*

What's Inside

Institution profiles Here you'll find more than 800 institutions offering postsecondary education at a distance. Profiles provide a general overview of each institution and offer key information on:

For each institution, specific degree and certificate programs are described, followed by a list of subjects for which individual courses are offered (undergraduate, graduate, and noncredit).

In-Depth Descriptions Additional details on their distance learning offerings are provided by participating institutions and consortiums. Each two-page entry provides details on delivery media, programs of study, special programs, credit options, faculty, students, admission, tuition and fees, financial aid, and applying.

Student Profiles Get the inside scoop on distance learning from those who've experienced it first hand. Real-life students share their experience, offer advice, and relate how distance learning has worked for them.

Finding What You Want

If you simply want to get a sense of the variety of programs being offered in distance learning, you may want to just browse through the **Institutional Profiles** page by page.

If you are interested in locating a certificate or degree program in a specific field of study, refer to the **Certificate and Degree Programs Index.** Here you'll find institutions offering everything from Accounting to Theological & Ministerial Studies. More than 100 areas in all.

If it is individual courses you're looking for, the **Individual Courses Index** will guide you to institutions offering credit and noncredit courses at either the undergraduate or graduate level.

The **Geographic Index** lets you find programs that are offered by institutions that are located near you. Keep in mind that, most institution's offerings are available nationally, and sometimes internationally. See individual listings for details.

How Schools Get Into the Guide

This book profiles more than 800 institutions of higher education currently offering courses or entire programs at a distance. To be included, all U.S. institutions must have full accreditation or candidate-for-accreditation (preaccreditation) status granted by an institutional or specialized accrediting body recognized by the U.S. Department of Education or the Council for Higher Education Accreditation. Canadian and other non-U.S. institutions must be chartered and authorized to grant degrees by the provincial or national government, be affiliated with a chartered institution, or be accredited by a recognized U.S. accrediting body.*

In the research for this guide, the following definition of "distance learning" was used: a planned teaching/learning experience in which teacher and students are separated by physical distance, and use any of a wide spectrum of media. This definition is based on the one developed by the University of Wisconsin Extension.

Research Procedures

The information provided in these profiles was collected during the spring and summer of 1997 by way of a survey sent to colleges and universities. All data included in this edition have been submitted by officials at the schools themselves. All usable information received in time for publication has been included. The omission of any particular item from an index or profile listing signifies that the item is either not applicable to that institution or

---

*The six U.S. regional accrediting associations are: the New England Association of Schools and Colleges, Middle States Association of Colleges and Schools, North Central Association of Colleges and Schools, Northwest Association of Schools and Colleges, Southern Association of Colleges and Schools, and Western Association of Schools and Colleges, Inc.

In addition to the accreditation of UCEA institutions by these bodies, approval by state educational agencies is conferred separately on some distance education courses.

that data were not available. Although Peterson's has every reason to believe that the information presented in this guide is accurate, students should check with each college or university to verify such figures as tuition and fees, which may have changed since the publication of this volume.

Profiles

Institution profiles appear in alphabetical order in this guide.

Institutional information

The sections here describe overall characteristics of an institution and its distance learning offerings.

General information This section lists key facts and figures about the institution, including when it was founded, the type of accreditation it has, the number of students enrolled in distance learning and the number of course titles offered at a distance.

Course delivery sites This section lists the locations where distance learning students receive instruction: home, work, military bases, other colleges, off-campus centers, or other locations.

Media This section describes the kinds of media used to deliver the courses and for student-teacher interaction. The following media are listed: television (broadcast or cable), videocassettes, videoconferencing (a two-way video connection via satellite, fiber optics, or other connection), audiocassettes, radio broadcast, audioconferencing (a two-way audio connection via telephone or other means), computer software, World Wide Web, e-mail, print, telephone, and fax.

The lists of course delivery sites and media represent a summary of all options of all courses at the institution. Availability at particular sites and use of specific media will vary from course to course; contact the institution for details.

Restrictions This section outlines any geographical or other restrictions that may affect eligibility to enroll in the institution's distance learning courses. Many of the institutions listed in the guide serve only a local or in-state audience. Be sure to check this section before contacting a school.

Services This section lists the kinds of student services that are available at a distance through computer, phone, fax, or other means. These include library services, access to the campus computer network, e-mail services, tutoring, career placement assistance, and academic advising.

Credit earning options This section lists alternative means of earning college credit that are available to distance learning students at the institution. Among the possibilities are transfer from another college, standardized exams (such as CLEP or PEP), institutionally-developed exams, portfolio assessment, and military and business training programs evaluated by American Council on Education.

Typical costs This section lists the tuition and mandatory fees for distance learning courses—undergraduate, graduate, and non-credit–based on 1996–97 tuition figures. Where costs differ based on where a student resides, the different figures for in-district, in-state, and out-of-state students are given. This section also indicates whether institutionally-administered financial aid can be applied to courses or programs completed at a distance.

Registration The following means of registering for classes are listed here: mail, fax, phone, e-mail, and World Wide Web.

Contact This section lists the person or office to contact for more information about the institution's distance learning courses.

Degree and Certificate Programs

This part of the profile describes each program leading to a degree or certificate that can be completed entirely at a distance. Programs are grouped by the level of award: associates degrees, baccalaureate degrees, graduate degrees, undergraduate certificates, and graduate certificates.

General information This section identifies the degree awarded, the subjects in which it can be earned, the number of students enrolled in the program, and the number of degrees awarded in the last academic year.

Restrictions Some distance learning degree or certificate programs have enrollment requirements that differ from other programs at the same institution. If this is the case, the specific restrictions will be indicated here. Otherwise, refer to the similar sections of the institution profile for information.

Application requirements This section lists what is required when applying to the program. This might include standardized exam scores, high school or college transcripts, letters of recommendation, and application fees.

Completion requirements This section describes the course requirements for the program. The total number of credits or courses is indicated. Some programs are identified as degree completion programs, in which students are expected to have already completed a certain amount of undergraduate coursework. This section also lists any on-campus requirements for the program. These are usually in the form of brief orientations, weekend seminars, or short summer residencies.

Program contact If there are particular persons or offices to contact about specific programs, they are listed here. Otherwise contact the person or office given in the institution profile.

Individual Course Subject Areas

This part of the profile lists the general subject areas in which the institution offers individual courses at a distance. Subjects are divided into those offered for undergraduate credit, for graduate credit, and non-credit. (Note that this is not a listing of course titles; you will need to contact the institution for a detailed list of courses offered.) In addition, *Peterson's Independent Study Catalog* also contains lists or distance learning courses.

ABILENE CHRISTIAN UNIVERSITY

Abilene, Texas

Abilene Christian University, founded in 1906, is an independent-religious comprehensive institution affiliated with the Church of Christ. It is accredited by the Southern Association of Colleges and Schools. It first offered distance learning courses in 1995. In 1996–97, it offered 2 courses at a distance. In the fall of 1996, there was a total of 10 students enrolled in distance learning courses.
Course delivery sites Courses are delivered to your home, West Texas A&M University (Canyon), Trans Texas Video Network.
Media Courses are delivered via videotapes, videoconferencing, World Wide Web, e-mail. Students and teachers interact via videoconferencing, telephone.
Restrictions Programs are available to in-state students only.
Services Distance learners have access to academic advising, tutoring at a distance.
Typical costs Tuition of $274 per hour. Financial aid is available to distance learners.
Contact K. B. Massingill, Director of Instructional Technology, Abilene Christian University, ACU Box 29201, Abilene, TX 79699-9201. *Telephone:* 915-674-2833. *Fax:* 915-674-2834. *E-mail:* massingill@cte.acu.edu.

INDIVIDUAL COURSE SUBJECT AREAS

Undergraduate
Engineering/industrial management

Graduate
Philosophy and religion

Noncredit
Philosophy and religion

ACADIA UNIVERSITY

Wolfville, Nova Scotia, Canada

Center for Distance and Continuing Education

Acadia University, founded in 1838, is a province-supported comprehensive institution. It is provincially chartered. It first offered distance learning courses in 1968. In 1996–97, it offered 80 courses at a distance. In the fall of 1996, there was a total of 1,100 students enrolled in distance learning courses.
Course delivery sites Courses are delivered to your home, your workplace, military bases, 20 off-campus centers.
Media Courses are delivered via videotapes, videoconferencing, audiotapes, audioconferencing, computer software, World Wide Web, print. Students and teachers interact via videoconferencing, audioconferencing, mail, telephone, fax, e-mail. A computer is required for some courses.
Services Distance learners have access to library services, the campus computer network, e-mail services, academic advising, tutoring at a distance.
Credit-earning options Students may transfer credits from another institution or may earn credits through institutionally developed exams.
Typical costs *Undergraduate:* Tuition of $387.50 per hour. *Graduate:* Tuition of $437.50 per hour. *Noncredit courses:* $300 per course. Costs may vary by campus or location. Financial aid is available to distance learners enrolled full-time or part-time.
Registration Students may register by mail, fax, phone, World Wide Web.
Contact Continuing Education, Acadia University, 42 University Avenue, Wolfville, NS B0P 1X0, Canada. *Telephone:* 902-585-1434. *Fax:* 902-585-1068. *E-mail:* continuing.education@acadiau.ca. *Web site:* http://webster.acadiau.ca/conted/.

DEGREE & CERTIFICATE PROGRAMS

Undergraduate Certificates

▶ *Business Administration*
In the fall of 1996 there were 35 students enrolled in this program. In 1995–96, 5 certificates were earned at a distance through this program.
Application requirements *Prior education:* high school diploma or equivalent. *Other requirements:* high school transcript, an application fee of $25.
Completion requirements 30 credit hours are required. 24 credit hours must be completed through the institution. *Maximum time for completion:* five years.

▶ *Computer Science*
In the fall of 1996 there were 37 students enrolled in this program. In 1995–96, 6 certificates were earned at a distance through this program.
Application requirements *Prior education:* high school diploma or equivalent. *Other requirements:* high school transcript, an application fee of $25, high school academic math.
Completion requirements 30 credit hours are required. 24 credit hours must be completed through the institution. *Maximum time for completion:* five years.

INDIVIDUAL COURSE SUBJECT AREAS

Undergraduate
Art history and criticism; business; Classical languages and literatures; computer and information sciences; education; English language and literature; European languages and literatures; history; home economics and family studies; mathematics; philosophy and religion; physical sciences; psychology; social sciences; theological studies

See full description on page 376.

ADAMS STATE COLLEGE

Alamosa, Colorado

Division of Extended Studies

Adams State College, founded in 1921, is a state-supported comprehensive institution. It is accredited by the North Central Association of Colleges and Schools. It first offered distance learning courses in 1988. In 1996–97, it offered 40 courses at a distance. In the fall of 1996, there was a total of 120 students enrolled in distance learning courses.
Course delivery sites Courses are delivered to your home.
Media Courses are delivered via videotapes, print. Students and teachers interact via mail, telephone, fax, e-mail. A computer is required for some courses.
Services Distance learners have access to library services at a distance.
Typical costs *Undergraduate:* Tuition of $70 per semester hour. *Graduate:* Tuition of $70 per semester hour. Costs may vary by specific program of study, number of credits taken, course delivery options, term of enrollment. Financial aid is available to distance learners enrolled full-time or part-time.
Registration Students may register by mail, fax, phone.

Profiles: Adams State College

Contact Alberta Coolbaugh, Assistant Director, Adams State College, Division of Extended Studies, Alamosa, CO 81102. *Telephone:* 719-587-7671. *Fax:* 719-587-7974. *E-mail:* amcoolba@adams.edu. *Web site:* http://www.adams.edu.

INDIVIDUAL COURSE SUBJECT AREAS

Undergraduate
Accounting; business administration and management; business communications; business law; developmental and child psychology; economics; English composition; environmental science; finance; health and physical education/fitness; history; management information systems; mathematics; radio and television broadcasting; sociology; statistics

Graduate
Biology; health and physical education/fitness

ALLEGANY COLLEGE OF MARYLAND

Cumberland, Maryland

Advanced Technologies

Allegany College of Maryland, founded in 1961, is a state and locally supported two-year college. It is accredited by the Middle States Association of Colleges and Schools. It first offered distance learning courses in 1995. In 1996–97, it offered 12 courses at a distance. In the fall of 1996, there was a total of 150 students enrolled in distance learning courses.
Course delivery sites Courses are delivered to your home, your workplace, 2 off-campus centers in Everett (PA), Somerset (PA), local high schools.
Media Courses are delivered via television, videotapes, videoconferencing, computer software. Students and teachers interact via videoconferencing, mail, telephone, fax.
Services Distance learners have access to library services, the campus computer network, e-mail services, academic advising, tutoring, career placement assistance at a distance.
Credit-earning options Students may transfer credits from another institution or may earn credits through institutionally developed exams.
Typical costs Tuition of $73 per credit hour plus mandatory fees of $75 per semester for local area residents. Tuition of $93 per credit hour plus mandatory fees of $75 per semester for in-state residents. Tuition of $121 per credit hour plus mandatory fees of $75 per semester for out-of-state residents. *Noncredit courses:* $100 per course. Costs may vary by campus or location. Financial aid is available to distance learners enrolled full-time or part-time.
Registration Students may register by mail, fax.
Contact Ms. Catherine M. Nolan, Advanced Degrees Contact Person for Distance Learning, Allegany College of Maryland, Willowbrook Road, Cumberland, MD 21502. *Telephone:* 301-724-7700.

INDIVIDUAL COURSE SUBJECT AREAS

Undergraduate
Accounting; administrative and secretarial services; business; business administration and management; computer and information sciences; developmental and child psychology; economics; English composition; English language and literature; history; journalism; liberal arts, general studies, and humanities; library and information studies; mathematics; philosophy and religion; political science; social psychology; sociology

Noncredit
Administrative and secretarial services; business; business administration and management; computer and information sciences

ALLEGHENY UNIVERSITY OF THE HEALTH SCIENCES

Philadelphia, Pennsylvania

Allegheny University of the Health Sciences, founded in 1848, is an independent-nonprofit university. It is accredited by the Middle States Association of Colleges and Schools. It first offered distance learning courses in 1995. In 1996–97, it offered 15 courses at a distance. In the fall of 1996, there was a total of 120 students enrolled in distance learning courses.
Course delivery sites Courses are delivered to your home, your workplace, 1 off-campus center in Pittsburgh.
Media Courses are delivered via videoconferencing. Students and teachers interact via videoconferencing, telephone, e-mail.
Services Distance learners have access to library services, the campus computer network, e-mail services at a distance.
Credit-earning options Students may earn credits through standardized exams, institutionally developed exams.
Typical costs *Undergraduate:* Tuition of $315 per credit. *Graduate:* Tuition of $9000 per semester. Costs may vary by campus or location, specific program of study, number of credits taken. Financial aid is available to distance learners enrolled full-time.
Registration Students may register by mail.
Contact Gerald Kelliher, Vice Provost for Education, Allegheny University of the Health Sciences, 1505 Race Street, M-S 629, Philadelphia, PA 19102. *Telephone:* 215-762-6400. *Fax:* 215-762-6909. *E-mail:* kelliher@allegheny.edu.

DEGREE & CERTIFICATE PROGRAMS

Baccalaureate Degrees

▶ *Emergency Medical Services (BS)*
In the fall of 1996 there were 20 students enrolled in this program.
Restrictions Program is available to students in Philadelphia and Pittsburgh only.
Application requirements *Prior education:* high school diploma or equivalent. *Minimum age:* 18. *Other requirements:* SAT, ACT, high school transcript, CPR/EMT certification.
Completion requirements 134 credits are required. 100 credits must be completed through the institution.
Program contact John C. Lewis, Chair, Department of Liberal Arts and Applied Sciences, Allegheny University of the Health Sciences, 1505 Race Street, M-S 629, Philadelphia, PA 19102. Phone: 215-762-7910. E-mail: lewisj@allegheny.edu.

INDIVIDUAL COURSE SUBJECT AREAS

Undergraduate
Health professions and related sciences

Noncredit
Biological and life sciences

ALVIN COMMUNITY COLLEGE

Alvin, Texas

Alvin Community College, founded in 1949, is a state and locally supported two-year college. It is accredited by the Southern Association of Colleges and Schools. It first offered distance learning courses in

1995. In 1996–97, it offered 8 courses at a distance. In the fall of 1996, there was a total of 50 students enrolled in distance learning courses.
Course delivery sites Courses are delivered to your home.
Media Courses are delivered via television, videotapes, computer software, print. Students and teachers interact via mail, telephone, fax, e-mail. A computer is required for some courses.
Restrictions Students must be admitted to the college, and must be on campus for orientation.
Services Distance learners have access to library services, the campus computer network, e-mail services, academic advising, tutoring, career placement assistance at a distance.
Credit-earning options Students may transfer credits from another institution or may earn credits through examinations, portfolio assessment, military training, business training.
Typical costs Tuition of $84 per credit hour plus mandatory fees of $54 per credit hour for local area residents. Tuition of $84 per credit hour plus mandatory fees of $64 per credit hour for in-state residents. Tuition of $200 per credit hour plus mandatory fees of $64 per credit hour for out-of-state residents. Costs may vary by number of credits taken. Financial aid is available to distance learners enrolled full-time or part-time.
Registration Students may register by mail.
Contact Admissions Office, Alvin Community College, 3110 Mustang Road, Alvin, TX 77511-4898. *Telephone:* 281-388-4615.

INDIVIDUAL COURSE SUBJECT AREAS

Undergraduate
Biology; economics; European languages and literatures; geology; history; mathematics; political science; psychology

AMERICAN COLLEGE

Bryn Mawr, Pennsylvania

American College, founded in 1927, is an independent-nonprofit graduate institution. It is accredited by the Middle States Association of Colleges and Schools. It first offered distance learning courses in 1927.
Course delivery sites Courses are delivered to your home, your workplace, other colleges.
Media Courses are delivered via videotapes, audiotapes, print. Students and teachers interact via mail, telephone, fax.
Services Distance learners have access to library services, academic advising at a distance.
Credit-earning options Students may transfer credits from another institution or may earn credits through examinations.
Typical costs *Undergraduate:* Tuition of $275 per course. *Graduate:* Tuition of $490 per course. $60 matriculation fee, $125 admissions fee for graduate programs.
Registration Students may register by mail, fax, phone.
Contact Student Services, American College, 270 Bryn Mawr Avenue, Bryn Mawr, PA 19010. *Telephone:* 610-526-1490. *Fax:* 610-526-1465.

DEGREE & CERTIFICATE PROGRAMS

Graduate Degrees
▶ *Financial Services (MSFS)*
On-campus requirements Two 1-week residences.
▶ *Management (MSM)*
On-campus requirements Two 1-week residences.

Undergraduate Certificates
▶ *Chartered Financial Consultant*
▶ *Chartered Life Underwriter*
▶ *Registered Employee Benefit Consultant*
▶ *Registered Health Underwriter*

INDIVIDUAL COURSE SUBJECT AREAS

Undergraduate
Business

Graduate
Business

AMERICAN MILITARY UNIVERSITY

Manassas Park, Virginia

American Military University, founded in 1991, is a proprietary upper-level institution. It is accredited by the Distance Education and Training Council.
Course delivery sites Courses are delivered to your home.
Media Courses are delivered via World Wide Web, e-mail, print. Students and teachers interact via mail, telephone, e-mail.
Typical costs *Undergraduate:* Tuition of $400 per course. *Graduate:* Tuition of $600 per course. $35 admission fee.
Contact Jim Herhusky, Director of Development, American Military University, 9104-P Manassas Drive, Manassas Park, VA 22111. *Telephone:* 703-330-5398, Ext. 111.

DEGREE & CERTIFICATE PROGRAMS

Baccalaureate Degrees
▶ *Military History, Military Management, Intelligence Studies (BA)*

Graduate Degrees
▶ *Military Studies (MA)*

INDIVIDUAL COURSE SUBJECT AREAS

Undergraduate
Military studies

Graduate
Military studies

AMERICAN RIVER COLLEGE

Sacramento, California

American River College, founded in 1955, is a district-supported two-year college. It is accredited by the Western Association of Schools and Colleges, Inc. It first offered distance learning courses in 1975. In 1996–97, it offered 10 courses at a distance. In the fall of 1996, there was a total of 173 students enrolled in distance learning courses.
Course delivery sites Courses are delivered to your home.
Media Courses are delivered via television, videotapes. Students and teachers interact via on-campus meetings.

Profiles: American River College

Restrictions Programs are available to local area students only. Students must attend the mandatory on-campus class meetings for lectures and/or tests.
Services Distance learners have access to library services at a distance.
Credit-earning options Students may transfer credits from another institution.
Typical costs Tuition of $39 per course for local area residents. Tuition of $138 per course for in-state residents. Costs may vary by number of credits taken. Financial aid is available to distance learners.
Registration Students may register by phone.
Contact Debby Ondricka, Secretary, American River College, 4700 College Oak Drive, Sacramento, CA 95841. *Telephone:* 916-484-8456. *Fax:* 916-484-8018. *E-mail:* ondricd@mail.arc.losrios.cc.ca.us.

INDIVIDUAL COURSE SUBJECT AREAS

Undergraduate
Biology; business administration and management; health and physical education/fitness; marketing; philosophy and religion

ANGELINA COLLEGE

Lufkin, Texas

Continuing Education

Angelina College, founded in 1968, is a state and locally supported two-year college. It is accredited by the Southern Association of Colleges and Schools. It first offered distance learning courses in 1990. In 1996–97, it offered 4 courses at a distance.
Course delivery sites Courses are delivered to your home.
Media Courses are delivered via television. Students and teachers interact via telephone.
Restrictions Programs are available to local area students only.
Services Distance learners have access to library services at a distance.
Credit-earning options Students may transfer credits from another institution or may earn credits through standardized exams, institutionally developed exams, portfolio assessment, military training.
Typical costs Tuition of $14 per credit plus mandatory fees of $9 per credit for in-state residents. Tuition of $24 per credit plus mandatory fees of $9 per credit for out-of-state residents. *Noncredit courses:* $30 per course. Costs may vary by number of credits taken. Financial aid is available to distance learners enrolled full-time or part-time.
Contact Jill Hill, Registrar, Angelina College, PO Box 1768, Lufkin, TX 75902-1768. *Telephone:* 409-639-1301. *Fax:* 409-639-4299.

INDIVIDUAL COURSE SUBJECT AREAS

Undergraduate
History; political science; social psychology; sociology

ANNE ARUNDEL COMMUNITY COLLEGE

Arnold, Maryland

Distance Learning Center

Anne Arundel Community College, founded in 1961, is a state and locally supported two-year college. It is accredited by the Middle States Association of Colleges and Schools. It first offered distance learning courses in 1981. In 1996–97, it offered 50 courses at a distance. In the fall of 1996, there was a total of 1,400 students enrolled in distance learning courses.
Course delivery sites Courses are delivered to your home, institutions in Maryland Interactive Distance Learning network.
Media Courses are delivered via television, videotapes, videoconferencing, computer software, World Wide Web. Students and teachers interact via videoconferencing, audioconferencing, mail, telephone, fax, e-mail.
Services Distance learners have access to library services at a distance.
Credit-earning options Students may transfer credits from another institution or may earn credits through examinations, military training, business training.
Typical costs Tuition of $58 per credit hour plus mandatory fees of $35 per course for local area residents. Tuition of $106 per credit hour plus mandatory fees of $35 per course for in-state residents. Tuition of $202 per credit hour plus mandatory fees of $35 per course for out-of-state residents. All students pay a $20 registration fee. Financial aid is available to distance learners.
Registration Students may register by mail, fax, phone.
Contact Mary Barnes, Coordinator, Distance Learning, Anne Arundel Community College, 101 College Parkway, Arnold, MD 21012-1895. *Telephone:* 410-541-2465. *Fax:* 410-541-2874. *E-mail:* zmab@aacci.aacc.cc.md.us. *Web site:* http://www.aacc.cc.md.us/diseduc.

INDIVIDUAL COURSE SUBJECT AREAS

Undergraduate
Accounting; architecture; astronomy and astrophysics; business; business administration and management; chemistry; computer and information sciences; developmental and child psychology; economics; European languages and literatures; fine arts; health and physical education/fitness; history; home economics and family studies; hospitality services management; human resources management; law and legal studies; liberal arts, general studies, and humanities; library and information studies; mathematics; philosophy and religion; political science; social psychology; sociology; teacher education

ARAPAHOE COMMUNITY COLLEGE

Littleton, Colorado

Community Education Program

Arapahoe Community College, founded in 1965, is a state-supported two-year college. It is accredited by the North Central Association of Colleges and Schools. It first offered distance learning courses in 1985. In 1996–97, it offered 20 courses at a distance. In the fall of 1996, there was a total of 500 students enrolled in distance learning courses.
Course delivery sites Courses are delivered to your home, your workplace, other colleges.
Media Courses are delivered via videotapes, World Wide Web. Students and teachers interact via audioconferencing, mail, telephone, fax, e-mail. A computer is required for some courses.
Services Distance learners have access to library services at a distance.
Credit-earning options Students may transfer credits from another institution or may earn credits through standardized exams, institutionally developed exams, portfolio assessment, military training, business training.
Typical costs Tuition of $65.25 per credit for in-state residents. Tuition of $246.75 per credit for out-of-state residents. Costs may vary by campus or location, number of credits taken, course delivery options, term of enrollment. Financial aid is available to distance learners enrolled full-time or part-time.
Registration Students may register by mail, phone.

Contact Kim Larson-Cooney, Director of Community Education, Arapahoe Community College, 2500 West College Drive, Littleton, CO 80160. *Telephone:* 303-797-5723. *Fax:* 303-797-2647. *E-mail:* klcooney@arapahoe.edu.

INDIVIDUAL COURSE SUBJECT AREAS

Undergraduate
Biology; business; business administration and management; chemistry; computer and information sciences; economics; English composition; English language and literature; geology; history; liberal arts, general studies, and humanities; marketing; mathematics; political science; psychology; sociology

Noncredit
Business; business administration and management; computer and information sciences; fine arts; human resources management

ARIZONA STATE UNIVERSITY

Tempe, Arizona

Distance Learning Technology

Arizona State University, founded in 1885, is a state-supported university. It is accredited by the North Central Association of Colleges and Schools. It first offered distance learning courses in 1955. In 1996–97, it offered 161 courses at a distance. In the fall of 1996, there was a total of 1,606 students enrolled in distance learning courses.
Course delivery sites Courses are delivered to your home, your workplace, military bases, Arizona State University West (Phoenix), Northern Arizona University (Flagstaff), Paradise Valley Community College (Phoenix), Phoenix College (Phoenix), Scottsdale Community College (Scottsdale), South Mountain Community College (Phoenix), University of Arizona (Tucson), high schools in Arizona.
Media Courses are delivered via television, videotapes, World Wide Web, print. Students and teachers interact via videoconferencing, mail, telephone, fax, e-mail, computer conferencing. A computer is required for some courses.
Services Distance learners have access to library services, e-mail services, academic advising, tutoring at a distance.
Credit-earning options Students may transfer credits from another institution or may earn credits through examinations.
Typical costs *Undergraduate:* Tuition of $102 per credit hour. *Graduate:* Tuition of $102 per credit hour. Costs may vary by number of credits taken, course delivery options. Financial aid is available to distance learners.
Registration Students may register by mail, fax, phone.
Contact Brent Woodhouse, Distance Learning Technology, Arizona State University, PO Box 872904, Tempe, AZ 85287-2904. *Telephone:* 602-965-6738. *Fax:* 602-965-1371. *E-mail:* idbpw@asuvm.inre.asu.edu. *Web site:* http://www-distlearn.pp.asu.edu.

DEGREE & CERTIFICATE PROGRAMS

Graduate Degrees
▶ *Electrical Engineering (MSEE)*
Restrictions This program is available to local area students only.
Application requirements *Prior education:* baccalaureate degree. *Other requirements:* college transcripts.
Completion requirements 30 semester hours are required. 24 semester hours must be completed through the institution. *Maximum time for completion:* six years.
On-campus requirements For final comprehensive exam.

Program contact Darlene Mandt, Credentials Evaluator, Arizona State University, CEAS, PO Box 875706, Tempe, AZ 85287-5706. Phone: 602-965-3424. Fax: 602-965-3837. E-mail: eeinfo@enpop1.eas.asu.edu.

INDIVIDUAL COURSE SUBJECT AREAS

Undergraduate
Advertising; aerospace, aeronautical engineering; architecture; area, ethnic, and cultural studies; biology; botany; business administration and management; business law; chemical engineering; civil engineering; computer and information sciences; developmental and child psychology; educational psychology; electrical engineering; engineering; engineering-related technologies; engineering/industrial management; English language and literature; environmental engineering; fine arts; health and physical education/fitness; history; home economics and family studies; industrial engineering; journalism; law and legal studies; liberal arts, general studies, and humanities; library and information studies; marketing; mechanical engineering; Medieval/Renaissance studies; nursing; philosophy and religion; political science; women's studies; zoology

Graduate
Aerospace, aeronautical engineering; chemical engineering; civil engineering; computer and information sciences; education administration; educational psychology; electrical engineering; engineering; engineering-related technologies; engineering/industrial management; English language and literature; environmental engineering; health professions and related sciences; history; industrial engineering; instructional media; liberal arts, general studies, and humanities; mathematics; mechanical engineering; Medieval/Renaissance studies; nursing; public health; teacher education

Noncredit
Engineering

ARIZONA STATE UNIVERSITY WEST

Phoenix, Arizona

Office of Extended Instruction

Arizona State University West, founded in 1984, is a state-supported upper-level institution. It is accredited by the North Central Association of Colleges and Schools. It first offered distance learning courses in 1995. In 1996–97, it offered 5 courses at a distance. In the fall of 1996, there was a total of 50 students enrolled in distance learning courses.
Course delivery sites Courses are delivered to your home, your workplace, Arizona State University (Tempe), 1 off-campus center in Gila River.
Media Courses are delivered via television, World Wide Web, e-mail, print. Students and teachers interact via mail, telephone, fax, e-mail, World Wide Web.
Services Distance learners have access to library services, the campus computer network, e-mail services, academic advising, career placement assistance at a distance.
Typical costs *Undergraduate:* Tuition of $102 per credit for in-state residents. Tuition of $346 per credit for out-of-state residents. *Graduate:* Tuition of $102 per credit for in-state residents. Tuition of $346 per credit for out-of-state residents. Costs may vary by number of credits taken. Financial aid is available to distance learners enrolled full-time or part-time.
Registration Students may register by mail, phone.
Contact Christine Hall, Associate Vice Provost, Arizona State University West, PO Box 37100, Phoenix, AZ 85069-7100. *Telephone:* 602-543-4577. *Fax:* 602-543-7012.

Profiles: Arizona State University West

INDIVIDUAL COURSE SUBJECT AREAS

Undergraduate
Biology; environmental science; special education

Graduate
Special education

ARKANSAS TECH UNIVERSITY

Russellville, Arkansas

Arkansas Tech University, founded in 1909, is a state-supported comprehensive institution. It is accredited by the North Central Association of Colleges and Schools. It first offered distance learning courses in 1996. In 1996–97, it offered 5 courses at a distance. In the fall of 1996, there was a total of 77 students enrolled in distance learning courses.
Course delivery sites Courses are delivered to Westark Community College (Fort Smith).
Media Courses are delivered via videotapes, videoconferencing. Students and teachers interact via videoconferencing, telephone, e-mail. A computer is required for some courses.
Services Distance learners have access to library services, the campus computer network, e-mail services at a distance.
Credit-earning options Students may transfer credits from another institution or may earn credits through examinations.
Typical costs *Undergraduate:* Tuition of $951 per semester plus mandatory fees of $45 per semester for in-state residents. Tuition of $1902 per semester plus mandatory fees of $45 per semester for out-of-state residents. *Graduate:* Tuition of $86 per credit hour plus mandatory fees of $45 per semester for in-state residents. Tuition of $172 per credit hour plus mandatory fees of $45 per semester for out-of-state residents. Costs may vary by campus or location, number of credits taken. Financial aid is available to distance learners.
Contact Mr. Ron Harrell, Registrar, Arkansas Tech University, 209 Administration Building, Russellville, AR 72801. *Telephone:* 501-968-0272. *Fax:* 501-968-0683. *E-mail:* rgrh@atuvm.atu.edu.

INDIVIDUAL COURSE SUBJECT AREAS

Undergraduate
Computer and information sciences; special education; teacher education

ASSEMBLIES OF GOD THEOLOGICAL SEMINARY

Springfield, Missouri

Department of Extension and Continuing Education

Assemblies of God Theological Seminary, founded in 1972, is an independent-religious graduate institution. It is accredited by the North Central Association of Colleges and Schools. It first offered distance learning courses in 1980. In 1996–97, it offered 60 courses at a distance. In the fall of 1996, there was a total of 133 students enrolled in distance learning courses.
Course delivery sites Courses are delivered to your home, North Central Bible College (Minneapolis, MN), Northwest College of the Assemblies of God (Kirkland, WA), Southeastern College of the Assemblies of God (Lakeland, FL), Southwestern Assemblies of God University (Waxahachie, TX), Valley Forge Christian College (Phoenixville, PA).
Media Courses are delivered via audiotapes. Students and teachers interact via mail, telephone, fax, e-mail, site visits.
Services Distance learners have access to library services, academic advising, tutoring, career placement assistance at a distance.
Credit-earning options Students may transfer credits from another institution or may earn credits through examinations.
Typical costs Tuition of $230 per credit. *Noncredit courses:* $55 per credit. Financial aid is available to distance learners enrolled full-time.
Registration Students may register by mail, fax, phone, e-mail, World Wide Web.
Contact Gary A. Kellner, Director, Assemblies of God Theological Seminary, AGTS Extension Education Department, 1445 Boonville Avenue, Springfield, MO 65802. *Telephone:* 417-862-3344. *Fax:* 417-864-7165. *E-mail:* agts-ext@ag.org. *Web site:* http://www.agts.edu.

DEGREE & CERTIFICATE PROGRAMS

Graduate Degrees

▶ *Christian Ministries (MA)*
In the fall of 1996 there were 68 students enrolled in this program.
Application requirements *Prior education:* baccalaureate degree. *Other requirements:* college transcripts, an essay or personal statement, letter(s) of recommendation, an application fee of $35, statement of faith and ethics.
Completion requirements 36–48 credit hours are required. *Other requirements:* analytical reflection paper.
On-campus requirements Six 1-week courses at any of six sites across the country.

▶ *Divinity (MDiv)*
In the fall of 1996 there were 12 students enrolled in this program.
Application requirements *Prior education:* baccalaureate degree. *Minimum age:* 30. *Other requirements:* college transcripts, an essay or personal statement, letter(s) of recommendation, an application fee of $35, statement of faith and ethics.
Completion requirements 72–90 credit hours are required. 1 year must be completed through the institution. *Other requirements:* analytical reflection paper. *Maximum time for completion:* 10 years.
On-campus requirements Six 1-week courses at any of six sites across the country.

▶ *Theological Studies (MA)*
Application requirements *Prior education:* baccalaureate degree. *Other requirements:* college transcripts, an essay or personal statement, letter(s) of recommendation, an application fee of $35, statement of faith and ethics.
Completion requirements 36–48 credit hours are required. 1 year must be completed through the institution. *Other requirements:* analytical reflection paper.
On-campus requirements Six 1-week courses at any of six sites across the country.

INDIVIDUAL COURSE SUBJECT AREAS

Graduate
Business administration and management; Classical languages and literatures; communications; education; English language and literature; history; Jewish studies; liberal arts, general studies, and humanities; music; philosophy and religion; psychology; theological studies

Noncredit
Business administration and management; Classical languages and literatures; communications; education; English language and literature; history; Jewish studies; liberal arts, general studies, and humanities; music; philosophy and religion; psychology; theological studies

ATHABASCA UNIVERSITY

Athabasca, Alberta, Canada

Athabasca University, founded in 1970, is a province-supported comprehensive institution. It is provincially chartered. It first offered distance learning courses in 1972. In 1996–97, it offered 335 courses at a distance. In the fall of 1996, there was a total of 11,000 students enrolled in distance learning courses.

Course delivery sites Courses are delivered to your home, your workplace, several colleges throughout Canada.

Media Courses are delivered via television, videotapes, audiotapes, computer software, e-mail, print. Students and teachers interact via mail, telephone, fax, e-mail. A computer is required for some courses.

Services Distance learners have access to library services, the campus computer network, e-mail services, academic advising, tutoring at a distance.

Credit-earning options Students may transfer credits from another institution or may earn credits through examinations, business training.

Typical costs *Undergraduate:* Tuition of $358 per course for in-state residents. Tuition of $408 per course for out-of-state residents. *Graduate:* Tuition of $5600 per degree program for in-state residents. Tuition of $11,200 per degree program for out-of-state residents. MBA cost is $19,000 Canadian dollars for Canadian students, and $19,000 US dollars for non-Canadian students. $634 per course for undergraduate, non-Canadian students. Costs may vary by specific program of study, number of credits taken.

Registration Students may register by mail, fax, phone, e-mail, World Wide Web.

Contact Information Centre, Athabasca University, Box 10000, Athabasca, AB T9S 1A1, Canada. *Telephone:* 800-788-9041. *Fax:* 403-675-6145. *E-mail:* auinfo@admin.athabascau.ca. *Web site:* http://www.athabascau.ca.

DEGREE & CERTIFICATE PROGRAMS

Baccalaureate Degrees

▶ *Administration (BA)*

In the fall of 1996 there were 882 students enrolled in this program. In 1995–96, 42 degrees were earned at a distance through this program.

Application requirements *Prior education:* some undergraduate course work. *Other requirements:* Alberta Universities writing competence test, high school transcript, college transcripts, an application fee of $50.

Completion requirements 120 credits are required. 30 credits must be completed through the institution.

▶ *Commerce (BComm)*

In the fall of 1996 there were 304 students enrolled in this program. In 1995–96, 14 degrees were earned at a distance through this program.

Application requirements *Prior education:* some undergraduate course work. *Other requirements:* high school transcript, college transcripts, an application fee of $50, $55 evaluation fee.

Completion requirements 120 credits are required. 30 credits must be completed through the institution. This is a degree completion program. *Maximum time for completion:* eight years.

▶ *Communications, Criminal Justice (BPA)*

Restrictions This program is available to local area students only.

Application requirements *Prior education:* some undergraduate course work. *Minimum age:* 18. *Other requirements:* high school transcript, college transcripts, an application fee of $50.

Completion requirements 120 credits are required. 30 credits must be completed through the institution. This is a degree completion program.

On-campus requirements For collaborative agreements.

▶ *Computer and Information Systems (BS)*

Application requirements *Prior education:* some undergraduate course work. *Minimum age:* 18. *Other requirements:* high school transcript, college transcripts, an application fee of $50.

Completion requirements 120 credits are required. 30 credits must be completed through the institution.

▶ *General Studies (BGS)*

In the fall of 1996 there were 489 students enrolled in this program. In 1995–96, 88 degrees were earned at a distance through this program.

Application requirements *Prior education:* some undergraduate course work. *Other requirements:* high school transcript, college transcripts, an application fee of $50, two-year approved diploma from a college or institute of technology.

Completion requirements 90 credits are required.

▶ *Nursing (BN)*

In the fall of 1996 there were 522 students enrolled in this program. In 1995–96, 27 degrees were earned at a distance through this program.

Application requirements *Prior education:* graduation from an approved nursing diploma program. *Other requirements:* high school transcript, college transcripts, an application fee of $50, 60% average, current active registration within a provincial, territorial or state nursing association.

Completion requirements 69 credits are required. 30 credits must be completed through the institution. *Other requirements:* arrangements must be set for practicum to be completed.

▶ *Science (BS)*

In the fall of 1996 there were 211 students enrolled in this program.

Application requirements *Prior education:* graduation from a two-year science-oriented college program. *Minimum age:* 18. *Other requirements:* high school transcript, college transcripts, an application fee of $50.

Completion requirements 120 credits are required. 30 credits must be completed through the institution.

Graduate Degrees

▶ *Business Administration (MBA)*

In the fall of 1996 there were 154 students enrolled in this program.

Application requirements *Prior education:* a first degree from a recognized university, or hold an acceptable professional designation (e.g., CA, CGA, CMA). *Minimum age:* 18. *Other requirements:* high school transcript, college transcripts, an application fee of $100.

Completion requirements 48 credits are required.

On-campus requirements One-week summer school and 2 weekend schools.

▶ *Distance Education (MDE)*

In the fall of 1996 there were 106 students enrolled in this program.

Application requirements *Prior education:* baccalaureate degree. *Other requirements:* high school transcript, college transcripts, letter(s) of recommendation, an application fee of $50, up-to-date vita or resume, $100 admission fee.

Completion requirements 42 credits are required.

Undergraduate Certificates

▶ *Accounting*

In the fall of 1996 there were 347 students enrolled in this program. In 1995–96, 15 certificates were earned at a distance through this program.

Application requirements *Prior education:* none required. *Other requirements:* an application fee of $50.

Completion requirements 30 credits are required. 15 credits must be completed through the institution.

▶ *Administration*

In the fall of 1996 there were 197 students enrolled in this program. In 1995–96, 20 certificates were earned at a distance through this program.

Restrictions Students holding a BA in administration, communication, or a similar area cannot enroll in this program.

Profiles: Athabasca University

Application requirements *Prior education:* none required. *Minimum age:* 18. *Other requirements:* an application fee of $50.
Completion requirements 30 credits are required. 15 credits must be completed through the institution.

▶ *Advanced Accounting*
In the fall of 1996 there were 6 students enrolled in this program.
Application requirements *Prior education:* university certificate in Accounting or equivalent. *Minimum age:* 18. *Other requirements:* an application fee of $50, university certificate in accounting or equivalent.
Completion requirements 33 credits are required. 15 credits must be completed through the institution.

▶ *Career Development*
Application requirements *Prior education:* none required. *Minimum age:* 18. *Other requirements:* some work experience in the career development field.
Completion requirements 30 credits are required.

▶ *French Language*
Application requirements *Prior education:* none required. *Minimum age:* 18. *Other requirements:* an application fee of $50.
Completion requirements 30 credits are required. 15 credits must be completed through the institution.

▶ *Health Development*
In the fall of 1996 there were 40 students enrolled in this program. In 1995–96, 2 certificates were earned at a distance through this program.
Application requirements *Prior education:* none required. *Minimum age:* 18. *Other requirements:* an application fee of $50.
Completion requirements 60 credits are required. 30 credits must be completed through the institution. *Maximum time for completion:* two years.
On-campus requirements For practicums.

▶ *Home Health Nursing*
Application requirements *Prior education:* RN license. *Other requirements:* high school transcript, college transcripts, an application fee of $50, must have registered nurse certification.
Completion requirements 31 credits are required. 15 credits must be completed through the institution.

▶ *Information Systems*
In the fall of 1996 there were 157 students enrolled in this program. In 1995–96, 3 certificates were earned at a distance through this program.
Application requirements *Prior education:* none required. *Minimum age:* 18. *Other requirements:* an application fee of $50.
Completion requirements 33 credits are required. 18 credits must be completed through the institution.

▶ *Labor Relations*
In the fall of 1996 there were 57 students enrolled in this program. In 1995–96, 4 certificates were earned at a distance through this program.
Application requirements *Prior education:* none required. *Minimum age:* 18. *Other requirements:* an application fee of $50.
Completion requirements 30 credits are required. 9 credits must be completed through the institution.

▶ *Labor Studies*
Application requirements *Prior education:* none required. *Minimum age:* 18. *Other requirements:* an application fee of $50.
Completion requirements 30 credits are required. 15 credits must be completed through the institution.

▶ *Public Administration*
In the fall of 1996 there were 27 students enrolled in this program. In 1995–96, 7 certificates were earned at a distance through this program.
Restrictions Students holding a BA in administration, public administration, or a similar area cannot enroll in this program.
Application requirements *Prior education:* none required. *Minimum age:* 18. *Other requirements:* an application fee of $50.
Completion requirements 30 credits are required. 15 credits must be completed through the institution.

Graduate certificates

▶ *English Language Studies*
Restrictions Program is intended for students whose first language is not English.
Application requirements *Prior education:* college diploma, degree, or be at least 22 years of age with an understanding of the English language. *Minimum age:* 22. *Other requirements:* an application fee of $50, understanding of English language.
Completion requirements 30 credits are required. 9 credits must be completed through the institution.

▶ *Management (Advanced Graduate Diploma)*
In the fall of 1996 there were 89 students enrolled in this program. In 1995–96, 62 certificates were earned at a distance through this program.
Application requirements *Prior education:* a degree or an acceptable professional designation (e.g., CA, CGA, CMA). *Minimum age:* 18. *Other requirements:* letter(s) of recommendation, an application fee of $100.
Completion requirements 18 credits are required.

INDIVIDUAL COURSE SUBJECT AREAS

Undergraduate
Accounting; area, ethnic, and cultural studies; astronomy and astrophysics; biological and life sciences; biology; botany; business; business administration and management; chemistry; communications; computer and information sciences; conservation and natural resources; creative writing; developmental and child psychology; economics; educational psychology; English as a second language (ESL); English composition; English language and literature; European languages and literatures; geology; health professions and related sciences; history; law and legal studies; liberal arts, general studies, and humanities; mathematics; nursing; philosophy and religion; physical sciences; physics; political science; psychology; public administration and services; social psychology; social sciences; sociology

Graduate
Business administration and management

ATLANTIC COMMUNITY COLLEGE

Mays Landing, New Jersey

Atlantic Community College, founded in 1966, is a county-supported two-year college. It is accredited by the Middle States Association of Colleges and Schools. It first offered distance learning courses in 1984. In 1996–97, it offered 26 courses at a distance. In the fall of 1996, there was a total of 301 students enrolled in distance learning courses.
Course delivery sites Courses are delivered to your home, 1 off-campus center in Atlantic City, local high schools.
Media Courses are delivered via television, videoconferencing, World Wide Web, e-mail. Students and teachers interact via videoconferencing, mail, telephone, fax, e-mail, computer conferencing. A computer is required for some courses.
Services Distance learners have access to library services, tutoring at a distance.
Credit-earning options Students may transfer credits from another institution or may earn credits through standardized exams, institutionally developed exams, portfolio assessment, military training, business training.
Typical costs Tuition of $54.15 per credit plus mandatory fees of $8.50 per semester for local area residents. Tuition of $108.30 per credit plus mandatory fees of $8.50 per semester for in-state residents. Tuition of $188.90 per credit plus mandatory fees of $8.50 per semester for

out-of-state residents. Mandatory $30 fee for each distance education course. Financial aid is available to distance learners.
Registration Students may register by mail, fax, phone, World Wide Web.
Contact Dr. Mary B. Wall, Associate Dean, Business, English, Social Sciences, Computer Information Systems, Atlantic Community College, 5100 Black Horse Pike, Mays Landing, NJ 08330. *Telephone:* 609-343-4987. *Fax:* 609-343-5122. *E-mail:* wall@heron.atlantic.edu. *Web site:* http://www.atlantic.edu.

DEGREE & CERTIFICATE PROGRAMS

Associate Degrees

▶ *General Studies (AS)*
Application requirements *Prior education:* high school diploma or equivalent. *Other requirements:* Basic Skills Test, high school transcript.
Completion requirements 64 quarter credits are required. 32 semester credits must be completed through the institution.

INDIVIDUAL COURSE SUBJECT AREAS

Undergraduate

Accounting; anthropology; art history and criticism; business; business administration and management; business law; developmental and child psychology; English language and literature; European languages and literatures; health and physical education/fitness; history; human resources management; information sciences and systems; liberal arts, general studies, and humanities; nursing; oceanography; social psychology; sociology; statistics

ATLANTIC UNION COLLEGE

South Lancaster, Massachusetts

Adult Degree Program

Atlantic Union College, founded in 1882, is an independent-religious Seventh-day Adventist comprehensive institution. It is accredited by the New England Association of Schools and Colleges. It first offered distance learning courses in 1972. In the fall of 1996, there was a total of 101 students enrolled in distance learning courses.
Course delivery sites Courses are delivered to your home.
Media Courses are delivered via videotapes, print. Students and teachers interact via mail, telephone, fax, e-mail. A computer is required for some courses.
Restrictions Students must be 25 years of age or older.
Services Distance learners have access to library services, e-mail services, academic advising at a distance.
Credit-earning options Students may transfer credits from another institution or may earn credits through standardized exams, portfolio assessment, military training, business training.
Typical costs Tuition of $3300 per semester. Costs may vary by number of credits taken.
Contact Anne Gustafson, Assistant to the Director, Atlantic Union College, PO Box 1000, South Lancaster, MA 01561. *Telephone:* 508-368-2300. *Fax:* 508-368-2015.

DEGREE & CERTIFICATE PROGRAMS

Baccalaureate Degrees

▶ *Computer Science (BS)*
In the fall of 1996 there were 9 students enrolled in this program. In 1995–96, 3 degrees were earned at a distance through this program.

Application requirements *Prior education:* high school diploma or equivalent. *Minimum age:* 25. *Other requirements:* high school transcript, college transcripts, an essay or personal statement, letter(s) of recommendation, an application fee of $15.
Completion requirements 128 semester hours are required. 2 semesters for degree must be completed through the institution. This is a degree completion program.
On-campus requirements 8–10 days every six months.

▶ *Art, Behavioral Sciences, Early Childhood Education, Elementary Education, Interior Design, Psychology (BS)*
Application requirements *Prior education:* high school diploma or equivalent. *Minimum age:* 25. *Other requirements:* high school transcript, college transcripts, an essay or personal statement, letter(s) of recommendation, an application fee of $15, equivalent high school degree (GED) or admissions portfolio.
Completion requirements 128 semester hours are required. 2 semesters for degree must be completed through the institution. This is a degree completion program.
On-campus requirements 8–10 days every six months.

▶ *Art, Business Administration, Communications, English, History, Modern Languages, Philosophy (BA)*
Application requirements *Prior education:* high school diploma or equivalent. *Minimum age:* 25. *Other requirements:* high school transcript, college transcripts, an essay or personal statement, letter(s) of recommendation, an application fee of $15.
Completion requirements 128 semester hours are required. 2 semesters for degree must be completed through the institution. This is a degree completion program.
On-campus requirements 8–10 days every six months.

AUBURN UNIVERSITY

Auburn University, Alabama

Distance Learning and Outreach Technology

Auburn University, founded in 1856, is a state-supported university. It is accredited by the Southern Association of Colleges and Schools. It first offered distance learning courses in 1976. In 1996–97, it offered 175 courses at a distance. In the fall of 1996, there was a total of 350 students enrolled in distance learning courses.
Course delivery sites Courses are delivered to your home, your workplace, military bases, Auburn University at Montgomery (Montgomery), The University of Alabama (Tuscaloosa), The University of Alabama at Birmingham (Birmingham), The University of Alabama in Huntsville (Huntsville).
Media Courses are delivered via videotapes, videoconferencing, audiotapes, computer software, World Wide Web, print. Students and teachers interact via mail, telephone, fax, e-mail. A computer is required for some courses.
Services Distance learners have access to library services, e-mail services, academic advising, career placement assistance at a distance.
Credit-earning options Students may transfer credits from another institution.
Typical costs *Undergraduate:* Tuition of $210 per course plus mandatory fees of $17 per course. *Graduate:* Tuition of $1180 per course. *Noncredit courses:* $425 per course. Costs may vary by specific program of study, number of credits taken. Financial aid is available to distance learners enrolled full-time.
Registration Students may register by mail, fax, phone, e-mail, World Wide Web.
Contact Ernestine Morris, Student Services Coordinator, Auburn University, 204 Mell Hall, Auburn, AL 36849. *Telephone:* 334-844-

Profiles: Auburn University

3114. *Fax:* 334-844-4731. *E-mail:* ernestin@uce.auburn.edu. *Web site:* http://www.auburn.edu/outreach/dl.

DEGREE & CERTIFICATE PROGRAMS

Graduate Degrees

▶ *Aerospace Engineering (MS, MAE)*
In the fall of 1996 there were 11 students enrolled in this program. In 1995–96, 2 degrees were earned at a distance through this program.
Application requirements *Prior education:* baccalaureate degree. *Other requirements:* GRE, college transcripts, letter(s) of recommendation, an application fee of $25.
Completion requirements 45 quarter hours are required. *Maximum time for completion:* five years.
On-campus requirements One-day oral examination for MAE; one-year residency for MS.
Program contact Latisha Durroh, Marketing Coordinator, Auburn University, 202 Ramsay Hall, Auburn, AL 36849-5336. Phone: 888-844-5300. Fax: 334-844-2519. E-mail: durrocl@eng.auburn.edu.

▶ *Business Administration (MBA)*
In the fall of 1996 there were 200 students enrolled in this program. In 1995–96, 28 degrees were earned at a distance through this program.
Application requirements *Prior education:* baccalaureate degree. *Other requirements:* GMAT, college transcripts, letter(s) of recommendation, an application fee of $25, MBA application.
Completion requirements 58–87 quarter hours are required. *Maximum time for completion:* five years.
On-campus requirements 2–3 days to complete group projects.
Program contact Dr. Daniel Gropper, Director of MBA Program, Auburn University, College of Business, Auburn, AL 36849-5240. Phone: 334-844-4060. Fax: 334-844-4861. E-mail: dgropper@business.auburn.edu.

▶ *Chemical Engineering (MS, MChe)*
In the fall of 1996 there were 6 students enrolled in this program.
Application requirements *Prior education:* baccalaureate degree. *Other requirements:* GRE, college transcripts, letter(s) of recommendation, an application fee of $25.
Completion requirements 45 quarter hours are required. *Maximum time for completion:* five years.
On-campus requirements One-day oral examination for MChe; one-year residency for MS.
Program contact Latisha Durroh, Marketing Coordinator, Auburn University, 202 Ramsay Hall, Auburn, AL 36849-5336. Phone: 888-844-5300. Fax: 334-844-2519. E-mail: durrocl@eng.auburn.edu.

▶ *Civil Engineering (MS, MCE)*
In the fall of 1996 there were 13 students enrolled in this program. In 1995–96, 2 degrees were earned at a distance through this program.
Application requirements *Prior education:* baccalaureate degree. *Other requirements:* GRE, college transcripts, letter(s) of recommendation, an application fee of $25.
Completion requirements 45 quarter hours are required. *Maximum time for completion:* five years.
On-campus requirements One-day oral examination for MCE; one-year residency for MS.
Program contact Latisha Durroh, Marketing Coordinator, Auburn University, 202 Ramsay Hall, Auburn, AL 36849-5336. Phone: 888-844-5300. Fax: 334-844-2519. E-mail: durrocl@eng.auburn.edu.

▶ *Computer Science and Engineering (MS, MCSE)*
In the fall of 1996 there were 9 students enrolled in this program. In 1995–96, 8 degrees were earned at a distance through this program.
Application requirements *Prior education:* baccalaureate degree. *Other requirements:* GRE, college transcripts, letter(s) of recommendation, an application fee of $25.
Completion requirements 45 quarter hours are required. *Maximum time for completion:* five years.
On-campus requirements One-day oral examination for MCSE; one-year residency for MS.
Program contact Latisha Durroh, Marketing Coordinator, Auburn University, 202 Ramsay Hall, Auburn, AL 36849-5336. Phone: 888-844-5300. Fax: 334-844-2519. E-mail: durrocl@eng.auburn.edu.

▶ *Hotel and Restaurant Management (MS)*
In the fall of 1996 there were 11 students enrolled in this program.
Application requirements *Prior education:* baccalaureate degree. *Other requirements:* GRE, college transcripts, an application fee of $25.
Completion requirements 45 quarter hours are required. *Maximum time for completion:* five years.
On-campus requirements To defend master's project: 1–2 days for non-thesis option, 8 weeks for thesis option.
Program contact Ms. Braden Kuhlman, Program Developer, Auburn University, 204 Mell Hall, Auburn, AL 36849. Phone: 334-844-3198. Fax: 334-844-4731. E-mail: bradenk@uce.auburn.edu.

▶ *Industrial and Systems Engineering (MS, MISE)*
In the fall of 1996 there were 26 students enrolled in this program. In 1995–96, 4 degrees were earned at a distance through this program.
Application requirements *Prior education:* baccalaureate degree. *Other requirements:* GRE, college transcripts, letter(s) of recommendation, an application fee of $25.
Completion requirements 45 quarter hours are required. *Maximum time for completion:* five years.
On-campus requirements One-day oral examination for MISE; one-year residency for MS.
Program contact Latisha Durroh, Marketing Coordinator, Auburn University, 202 Ramsay Hall, Auburn, AL 36849-5336. Phone: 888-844-5300. Fax: 334-844-2519. E-mail: durrocl@eng.auburn.edu.

▶ *Materials Engineering (MS, MME)*
In the fall of 1996 there were 15 students enrolled in this program. In 1995–96, 1 degree was earned at a distance through this program.
Application requirements *Prior education:* baccalaureate degree. *Other requirements:* GRE, college transcripts, letter(s) of recommendation, an application fee of $25.
Completion requirements 45 quarter hours are required. *Maximum time for completion:* five years.
On-campus requirements One-day oral examination for MME; one-year residency for MS.
Program contact Latisha Durroh, Marketing Coordinator, Auburn University, 202 Ramsay Hall, Auburn, AL 36849-5336. Phone: 888-844-5300. Fax: 334-844-2519. E-mail: durrocl@eng.auburn.edu.

▶ *Mechanical Engineering (MS, MME)*
In the fall of 1996 there were 14 students enrolled in this program. In 1995–96, 5 degrees were earned at a distance through this program.
Application requirements *Prior education:* baccalaureate degree. *Other requirements:* GRE, college transcripts, letter(s) of recommendation, an application fee of $25.
Completion requirements 45 quarter hours are required. *Maximum time for completion:* five years.
On-campus requirements One-day oral examination for MME; one-year residency for MS.
Program contact Latisha Durroh, Marketing Coordinator, Auburn University, 202 Ramsay Hall, Auburn, AL 36849-5336. Phone: 888-844-5300. Fax: 334-844-2519. E-mail: durrocl@eng.auburn.edu.

Undergraduate Certificates

▶ *Dietary Management*
In the fall of 1996 there were 650 students enrolled in this program. In 1995–96, 150 certificates were earned at a distance through this program.
Restrictions Program requires health care setting.
Application requirements *Prior education:* high school diploma or equivalent. *Other requirements:* endorsement by clinical instructor (local mentor) and facility administrator.
Completion requirements 24 units are required. *Other requirements:* final exam. *Maximum time for completion:* 24 months.

INDIVIDUAL COURSE SUBJECT AREAS

Undergraduate
Biology; criminal justice; developmental and child psychology; economics; film studies; health and physical education/fitness; history; horticulture; hospitality services management; mathematics; political science; social psychology; sociology

Graduate
Business administration and management; engineering

See full description on page 380.

AURORA UNIVERSITY

Aurora, Illinois

New College

Aurora University, founded in 1893, is an independent-nonprofit comprehensive institution. It is accredited by the North Central Association of Colleges and Schools. It first offered distance learning courses in 1995. In 1996–97, it offered 1 course at a distance.
Course delivery sites Courses are delivered to Benedictine University (Lisle), Judson College (Elgin).
Media Courses are delivered via television. Students and teachers interact via videoconferencing, mail, telephone, fax, e-mail.
Services Distance learners have access to library services, the campus computer network, e-mail services, academic advising, career placement assistance at a distance.
Credit-earning options Students may transfer credits from another institution or may earn credits through standardized exams, institutionally developed exams, portfolio assessment, military training, business training.
Typical costs *Undergraduate:* Tuition of $392 per semester hour plus mandatory fees of $10 per semester. *Graduate:* Tuition of $392 per semester hour plus mandatory fees of $10 per semester. *Noncredit courses:* $75–$200 per course. Costs may vary by specific program of study, number of credits taken. Financial aid is available to distance learners enrolled full-time or part-time.
Registration Students may register by mail, fax, phone.
Contact Dr. Ron Ramer, Director of Continuing Education, Aurora University, 347 South Gladstone Avenue, Aurora, IL 60506. *Telephone:* 630-844-6517. *Fax:* 630-844-3852. *E-mail:* rramer@aurora.edu. *Web site:* http://www.aurora.edu.

INDIVIDUAL COURSE SUBJECT AREAS

Undergraduate
Information sciences and systems

AUSTIN COMMUNITY COLLEGE

Austin, Texas

Open Campus

Austin Community College, founded in 1972, is a district-supported two-year college. It is accredited by the Southern Association of Colleges and Schools. It first offered distance learning courses in 1979. In 1996–97, it offered 90 courses at a distance. In the fall of 1996, there was a total of 2,700 students enrolled in distance learning courses.
Course delivery sites Courses are delivered to your home, your workplace, 4 off-campus centers in Bastrop, Fredericksburg, Georgetown, San Marcos.
Media Courses are delivered via television, videotapes, computer software, World Wide Web, e-mail, print. Students and teachers interact via mail, telephone, fax, e-mail. A computer is required for some courses.
Restrictions Programs are available to local area students only.
Services Distance learners have access to library services, the campus computer network, e-mail services, academic advising at a distance.
Credit-earning options Students may transfer credits from another institution or may earn credits through standardized exams, institutionally developed exams.
Typical costs Tuition of $102 per course plus mandatory fees of $28 per course for local area residents. Tuition of $177 per course plus mandatory fees of $28 per course for in-state residents. Tuition of $405 per course plus mandatory fees of $28 per course for out-of-state residents. Costs may vary by number of credits taken. Financial aid is available to distance learners.
Registration Students may register by mail, phone.
Contact Student Hotline Open Campus, Austin Community College, 7748 Highway 290, W, Austin, TX 78736-3290. *Telephone:* 512-223-8028. *Fax:* 512-288-8111. *Web site:* http://www.opc.austin.cc.tx.us/.

INDIVIDUAL COURSE SUBJECT AREAS

Undergraduate
Accounting; administrative and secretarial services; American literature; anthropology; area, ethnic, and cultural studies; art history and criticism; biology; botany; business; business administration and management; business law; computer and information sciences; computer programming; developmental and child psychology; economics; engineering-related technologies; English composition; English language and literature; European languages and literatures; finance; fine arts; French language and literature; geography; geology; health and physical education/ fitness; history; human resources management; marketing; nursing; philosophy and religion; political science; social psychology; social work; sociology; Spanish language and literature; technical writing

BAKER COLLEGE

Flint, Michigan

Baker College On-Line

Baker College, founded in 1911, is an independent-nonprofit comprehensive institution. It is accredited by the North Central Association of Colleges and Schools. It first offered distance learning courses in 1994. In 1996–97, it offered 116 courses at a distance. In the fall of 1996, there was a total of 916 students enrolled in distance learning courses.
Course delivery sites Courses are delivered to your home.
Media Courses are delivered via computer software, World Wide Web, e-mail, print. Students and teachers interact via telephone, fax, e-mail. A computer is required for all courses. The institution provides assistance with acquiring computer equipment.
Services Distance learners have access to library services, the campus computer network, e-mail services, academic advising, tutoring, career placement assistance at a distance.
Credit-earning options Students may transfer credits from another institution or may earn credits through standardized exams, institutionally developed exams, portfolio assessment, military training, business training.
Typical costs *Undergraduate:* Tuition of $135 per quarter hour. *Graduate:* Tuition of $210 per quarter hour. *Noncredit courses:* $300 per course. Financial aid is available to distance learners enrolled full-time or part-time.

Distance Learning Programs

Profiles: Baker College

Registration Students may register by mail, fax, phone, e-mail, World Wide Web.
Contact Chuck Gurden, Director of Development, Baker College, Baker College On-Line, 1050 West Bristol Road, Flint, MI 48507. *Telephone:* 800-621-7440. *Fax:* 810-766-4399. *E-mail:* online@baker.edu. *Web site:* http://www.baker.edu.

DEGREE & CERTIFICATE PROGRAMS

Associate Degrees
▶ *Business Administration (ABA)*
Application requirements *Prior education:* high school diploma or equivalent. *Other requirements:* high school transcript, college transcripts, an essay or personal statement, letter(s) of recommendation, an application fee of $25.
Completion requirements 90 quarter hours are required. 45 quarter hours must be completed through the institution.

Baccalaureate Degrees
▶ *Business Administration (BBA)*
In the fall of 1996 there were 107 students enrolled in this program.
Application requirements *Prior education:* associate degree. *Other requirements:* college transcripts, an essay or personal statement, letter(s) of recommendation, an application fee of $25.
Completion requirements 180 quarter hours are required. 90 quarter hours must be completed through the institution. This is a degree completion program.

Graduate Degrees
▶ *Business Administration (MBA)*
In the fall of 1996 there were 618 students enrolled in this program. In 1995–96, 106 degrees were earned at a distance through this program.
Application requirements *Prior education:* baccalaureate degree. *Other requirements:* college transcripts, an essay or personal statement, letter(s) of recommendation, an application fee of $25, 3 years work experience and a GPA of 2.5.
Completion requirements 50 quarter hours are required. 34 quarter hours must be completed through the institution.

INDIVIDUAL COURSE SUBJECT AREAS

Undergraduate
Accounting; administrative and secretarial services; business; business administration and management; computer and information sciences; health professions and related sciences; human resources management

Graduate
Accounting; administrative and secretarial services; business; business administration and management; computer and information sciences; engineering-related technologies; health professions and related sciences; human resources management; international business; marketing

Noncredit
Accounting
See full description on page 382.

BAKERSFIELD COLLEGE

Bakersfield, California

Bakersfield College, founded in 1913, is a state and locally supported two-year college. It is accredited by the Western Association of Schools and Colleges, Inc. It first offered distance learning courses in 1980. In 1996–97, it offered 46 courses at a distance. In the fall of 1996, there was a total of 906 students enrolled in distance learning courses.
Course delivery sites Courses are delivered to your home, 1 off-campus center in Delano.
Media Courses are delivered via television, videotapes, videoconferencing. Students and teachers interact via mail, telephone, fax, e-mail.
Services Distance learners have access to library services, academic advising, tutoring, career placement assistance at a distance.
Typical costs Tuition of $13 per unit plus mandatory fees of $15 per semester for in-state residents. Tuition of $115 per unit plus mandatory fees of $15 per semester for out-of-state residents. Costs may vary by number of credits taken. Financial aid is available to distance learners.
Registration Students may register by phone.
Contact Kathleen Loomis-Tubbesing, Distance Learning Coordinator, Bakersfield College, 1801 Panorama Drive, Bakersfield, CA 93305. *Telephone:* 805-395-4202. *Fax:* 805-395-4690. *E-mail:* kloomis@bc.cc.ca.us. *Web site:* http://www.bc.kern.cc.ca.us.

INDIVIDUAL COURSE SUBJECT AREAS

Undergraduate
Agriculture; anthropology; astronomy and astrophysics; biology; business administration and management; child care and development; computer and information sciences; drama and theater; English as a second language (ESL); foods and nutrition studies; geology; health and physical education/fitness; history; mathematics; political science; psychology; sociology

BALL STATE UNIVERSITY

Muncie, Indiana

School of Continuing Education and Public Service

Ball State University, founded in 1918, is a state-supported university. It is accredited by the North Central Association of Colleges and Schools. It first offered distance learning courses in 1984. In 1996–97, it offered 65 courses at a distance. In the fall of 1996, there was a total of 465 students enrolled in distance learning courses.
Course delivery sites Courses are delivered to your home, your workplace, military bases, other colleges, 2 off-campus centers in Indianapolis, Westfield.
Media Courses are delivered via television, videoconferencing, World Wide Web. Students and teachers interact via videoconferencing, mail, telephone, fax, e-mail. A computer is required for some courses.
Restrictions Programs are primarily available to in-state students.
Services Distance learners have access to library services, the campus computer network, e-mail services, academic advising, career placement assistance at a distance.
Credit-earning options Students may transfer credits from another institution or may earn credits through standardized exams, institutionally developed exams, military training, business training.
Typical costs *Undergraduate:* Tuition of $120 per credit hour. *Graduate:* Tuition of $126 per credit hour. Financial aid is available to distance learners enrolled full-time or part-time.
Registration Students may register by mail, fax, phone.
Contact Kathryn McCartney, Director, Off-Campus Academic Support Services, Ball State University, School of Continuing Education and Public Service, CA 200, Muncie, IN 47306. *Telephone:* 765-285-1581. *Fax:* 765-285-7161. *E-mail:* kmccartn@bsu.edu. *Web site:* http://www.bsu.edu.

DEGREE & CERTIFICATE PROGRAMS

Associate Degrees

▶ *Business Administration (AA)*
In the fall of 1996 there were 10 students enrolled in this program. In 1995–96, 1 degree was earned at a distance through this program.
Restrictions This program is available to in-state students only.
Application requirements *Prior education:* high school diploma or equivalent. *Other requirements:* high school transcript, college transcripts, an application fee of $25.
Completion requirements 63 credits are required. 15 credits must be completed through the institution.

▶ *General Arts (AA)*
In the fall of 1996 there were 10 students enrolled in this program. In 1995–96, 1 degree was earned at a distance through this program.
Restrictions This program is available to in-state students only.
Application requirements *Prior education:* high school diploma or equivalent. *Other requirements:* high school transcript, college transcripts, an application fee of $25.
Completion requirements 63 credits are required. 15 credits must be completed through the institution.

Baccalaureate Degrees

▶ *Nursing (BSN)*
In the fall of 1996 there were 50 students enrolled in this program. In 1995–96, 5 degrees were earned at a distance through this program.
Restrictions This program is available to in-state students only.
Application requirements *Prior education:* RN license. *Other requirements:* high school transcript, college transcripts, an application fee of $25.
Completion requirements 126 credits are required. 30 credits must be completed through the institution. This is a degree completion program.
Program contact Patricia Mundy, Advisor, BSN Program, Ball State University, School of Continuing Education and Public Service, Muncie, IN 47306. Phone: 765-285-1581. Fax: 765-285-7161. E-mail: pmundy@bsu.edu.

Graduate Degrees

▶ *Business Administration (MBA)*
In the fall of 1996 there were 200 students enrolled in this program. In 1995–96, 35 degrees were earned at a distance through this program.
Application requirements *Prior education:* baccalaureate degree. *Other requirements:* GMAT, college transcripts, an essay or personal statement, an application fee of $15.
Completion requirements 30 credits are required.
Program contact Tamara Estep, Director, Graduate Programs, College of Business, Ball State University, College of Business, Muncie, IN 47306. Phone: 765-285-1931. Fax: 765-285-8818. E-mail: testep@bsu.edu.

▶ *Computer Science (MS)*
In the fall of 1996 there were 15 students enrolled in this program.
Restrictions This program is available to in-state students only. Students need a computer science background.
Application requirements *Prior education:* baccalaureate degree. *Other requirements:* college transcripts, an application fee of $15.
Completion requirements 30 credits are required. *Maximum time for completion:* five years.

▶ *Educational Administration and Supervision (MAE)*
In the fall of 1996 there were 45 students enrolled in this program. In 1995–96, 4 degrees were earned at a distance through this program.
Restrictions This program is available to in-state students only.
Application requirements *Prior education:* baccalaureate degree. *Other requirements:* college transcripts, an application fee of $15.
Completion requirements 30 credits are required. *Maximum time for completion:* five years.
On-campus requirements Some televised classes require a Saturday on-campus session.

▶ *Elementary Education (MAE)*
In the fall of 1996 there were 55 students enrolled in this program. In 1995–96, 5 degrees were earned at a distance through this program.
Restrictions This program is available to in-state students only.
Application requirements *Prior education:* baccalaureate degree. *Other requirements:* college transcripts, an application fee of $15.
Completion requirements 30 credits are required. *Maximum time for completion:* five years.
On-campus requirements Some televised classes require a Saturday on-campus session.

▶ *Executive Development (MA)*
In the fall of 1996 there were 5 students enrolled in this program.
Restrictions This program is available to in-state students only.
Application requirements *Prior education:* baccalaureate degree. *Other requirements:* college transcripts, an application fee of $15.
Completion requirements 30 credits are required. *Maximum time for completion:* five years.
On-campus requirements Some televised courses require a Saturday on-campus session.

▶ *Special Education (MAE)*
In the fall of 1996 there were 10 students enrolled in this program. In 1995–96, 1 degree was earned at a distance through this program.
Restrictions This program is available to in-state students only.
Application requirements *Prior education:* baccalaureate degree. *Other requirements:* college transcripts, an application fee of $15.
Completion requirements 30 credits are required. *Maximum time for completion:* five years.
On-campus requirements Some televised classes require a Saturday on-campus session.

INDIVIDUAL COURSE SUBJECT AREAS

Undergraduate
Accounting; administrative and secretarial services; advertising; area, ethnic, and cultural studies; astronomy and astrophysics; biological and life sciences; biology; business; business administration and management; economics; English composition; English language and literature; fine arts; geology; health and physical education/fitness; health professions and related sciences; history; home economics and family studies; journalism; liberal arts, general studies, and humanities; mathematics; nursing; philosophy and religion; physical sciences; physics; political science; psychology; public administration and services; public health; social psychology; social sciences; sociology; visual and performing arts

Graduate
Accounting; administrative and secretarial services; architecture; business; business administration and management; computer and information sciences; education; education administration; educational psychology; human resources management; special education; teacher education

BARCLAY COLLEGE

Haviland, Kansas

Barclay College, founded in 1917, is an independent-religious four-year college affiliated with the Society of Friends. It is accredited by the Accrediting Association of Bible Colleges. It first offered distance learning courses in 1993. In 1996–97, it offered 30 courses at a distance. In the fall of 1996, there was a total of 10 students enrolled in distance learning courses.

Profiles: Barclay College

Course delivery sites Courses are delivered to your home, Dodge City Community College (Dodge City), Pratt Community College and Area Vocational School (Pratt), 1 off-campus center.
Media Courses are delivered via television, print. Students and teachers interact via mail, telephone, fax, interactive television.
Restrictions Programs are available to in-state students only.
Services Distance learners have access to library services, academic advising at a distance.
Credit-earning options Students may transfer credits from another institution or may earn credits through standardized exams, portfolio assessment, military training.
Typical costs Tuition of $175 per semester hour plus mandatory fees of $37.50 per course. Financial aid is available to distance learners enrolled full-time.
Registration Students may register by mail, fax.
Contact Erik Ritschard, Academic Dean, Barclay College, PO Box 288, Haviland, KS 67059. *Telephone:* 316-862-5252. *Fax:* 316-862-5403.

INDIVIDUAL COURSE SUBJECT AREAS

Undergraduate
American literature; biology; English composition; religious studies

BASTYR UNIVERSITY

Bothell, Washington

Distance Learning

Bastyr University, founded in 1978, is an independent-nonprofit upper-level institution. It is accredited by the Northwest Association of Schools and Colleges. It first offered distance learning courses in 1992. In 1996–97, it offered 8 courses at a distance. In the fall of 1996, there was a total of 80 students enrolled in distance learning courses.
Course delivery sites Courses are delivered to your home.
Media Courses are delivered via print. Students and teachers interact via mail, telephone, fax, e-mail.
Services Distance learners have access to academic advising, tutoring, career placement assistance at a distance.
Credit-earning options Students may transfer credits from another institution or may earn credits through institutionally developed exams.
Typical costs Tuition of $162 per quarter hour. Students pay a one-time $25 registration fee. *Noncredit courses:* $20–$185 per course. Costs may vary by number of credits taken. Financial aid is available to distance learners.
Registration Students may register by mail, fax, phone, e-mail, World Wide Web.
Contact Distance Learning Manager, Bastyr University, 14500 Juanita Drive, NE, Bothell, WA 98011. *Telephone:* 425-602-3154. *Fax:* 425-823-6222. *E-mail:* dlcourses@bastyr.edu.

DEGREE & CERTIFICATE PROGRAMS

Undergraduate Certificates
▶ *Nutrition and Natural Health*
In the fall of 1996 there were 80 students enrolled in this program.
Application requirements *Prior education:* none required. *Other requirements:* high school transcript.

INDIVIDUAL COURSE SUBJECT AREAS

Undergraduate
Foods and nutrition studies; health professions and related sciences

BEAUFORT COUNTY COMMUNITY COLLEGE

Washington, North Carolina

Distance Education Center

Beaufort County Community College, founded in 1967, is a state-supported two-year college. It is accredited by the Southern Association of Colleges and Schools. It first offered distance learning courses in 1995.
Course delivery sites Courses are delivered to other colleges.
Media Courses are delivered via videoconferencing.
Restrictions Programs are available to in-state students only.
Services Distance learners have access to library services, academic advising, tutoring, career placement assistance at a distance.
Credit-earning options Students may transfer credits from another institution. Financial aid is available to distance learners.
Contact Dean of Institutional Development and Information Technology, Beaufort County Community College, PO Box 1069, Washington, NC 27889. *Telephone:* 919-946-6194. *Fax:* 919-975-0199.

INDIVIDUAL COURSE SUBJECT AREAS

Undergraduate
Accounting; history; mathematics; political science; social psychology; sociology

BELLEVUE COMMUNITY COLLEGE

Bellevue, Washington

Telecommunications Program–Distance Learning Department

Bellevue Community College, founded in 1966, is a state-supported two-year college. It is accredited by the Northwest Association of Schools and Colleges. It first offered distance learning courses in 1980. In 1996–97, it offered 32 courses at a distance. In the fall of 1996, there was a total of 380 students enrolled in distance learning courses.
Course delivery sites Courses are delivered to your home, your workplace.
Media Courses are delivered via television, videotapes, World Wide Web, e-mail, print. Students and teachers interact via mail, telephone, fax, e-mail. A computer is required for some courses.
Services Distance learners have access to library services, e-mail services, academic advising, tutoring at a distance.
Credit-earning options Students may transfer credits from another institution or may earn credits through institutionally developed exams.
Typical costs Tuition of $48 per credit. Financial aid is available to distance learners.
Registration Students may register by mail, phone.
Contact Thornton Perry, Director of Distance Learning, Bellevue Community College, 3000 Landerholm Circle, SE, Bellevue, WA 98007. *Telephone:* 425-641-2278. *Fax:* 425-649-3108. *E-mail:* tperry@bcc.ctc.edu. *Web site:* http://distance-ed.bcc.ctc.edu.

DEGREE & CERTIFICATE PROGRAMS

Associate Degrees
▶ *General Studies (AA)*
Application requirements *Prior education:* none required.

Completion requirements 90 quarter credits are required. 30 quarter credits must be completed through the institution.
On-campus requirements Some classes, like science labs and foreign languages, have some on-campus requirements.

INDIVIDUAL COURSE SUBJECT AREAS

Undergraduate
Astronomy and astrophysics; business administration and management; chemistry; computer and information sciences; conservation and natural resources; creative writing; developmental and child psychology; economics; English composition; English language and literature; European languages and literatures; fine arts; geography; geology; history; international relations; mathematics; oceanography; political science; psychology; sociology

BELLEVUE UNIVERSITY

Bellevue, Nebraska

Center for Distributed Learning

Bellevue University, founded in 1965, is an independent-nonprofit comprehensive institution. It is accredited by the North Central Association of Colleges and Schools. It first offered distance learning courses in 1985. In 1996–97, it offered 10 courses at a distance. In the fall of 1996, there was a total of 100 students enrolled in distance learning courses.
Course delivery sites Courses are delivered to your home, your workplace, military bases, other colleges, 3 off-campus centers in Columbus, Grand Island, Sioux City (IA), Tongsook College (Bangkok, Thailand).
Media Courses are delivered via videotapes, audioconferencing, computer software, World Wide Web, e-mail, print. Students and teachers interact via audioconferencing, mail, telephone, fax, e-mail. A computer is required for some courses.
Services Distance learners have access to library services, the campus computer network, e-mail services, academic advising, tutoring at a distance.
Credit-earning options Students may transfer credits from another institution or may earn credits through standardized exams, institutionally developed exams, portfolio assessment, military training, business training.
Typical costs Costs vary. Contact university for details. Financial aid is available to distance learners enrolled full-time.
Registration Students may register by mail, fax, phone, e-mail, World Wide Web.
Contact Diane Johnson, Admissions Counselor, Bellevue University, 1000 Galvin Road, S, Bellevue, NE 68005. *Telephone:* 800-756-7920. *Fax:* 402-293-2020. *E-mail:* dij@scholars.bellevue.edu. *Web site:* http://bruins.bellevue.edu.

DEGREE & CERTIFICATE PROGRAMS

Baccalaureate Degrees
▶ *Business Information Systems, Criminal Justice, International Business Management, Management, Management Information Systems (BS)*
Application requirements *Prior education:* associate degree. *Minimum age:* 23. *Other requirements:* high school transcript, college transcripts, an essay or personal statement, letter(s) of recommendation, an application fee of $100.
Completion requirements 127 credit hours are required. 36 must be completed through the institution. This is a degree completion program. *Maximum time for completion:* seven years.

Graduate Degrees
▶ *Business Administration (MBA)*
Application requirements *Prior education:* baccalaureate degree. *Other requirements:* GMAT, GRE or MAT, high school transcript, college transcripts, an essay or personal statement, letter(s) of recommendation, an application fee of $100, undergraduate business degree.
Completion requirements 36 semester hours are required. 27 semester hours must be completed through the institution. *Maximum time for completion:* five years.

▶ *Management (MAM)*
Application requirements *Prior education:* baccalaureate degree. *Other requirements:* GMAT, GRE or MAT, high school transcript, college transcripts, an essay or personal statement, letter(s) of recommendation, an application fee of $100, undergraduate business degree.
Completion requirements 36 semester hours are required. 27 semester hours must be completed through the institution. *Maximum time for completion:* five years.

INDIVIDUAL COURSE SUBJECT AREAS

Undergraduate
English language and literature; history; philosophy and religion
See full description on page 384.

BEMIDJI STATE UNIVERSITY

Bemidji, Minnesota

Center for Extended Learning

Bemidji State University, founded in 1919, is a state-supported comprehensive institution. It is accredited by the North Central Association of Colleges and Schools. It first offered distance learning courses in 1977. In 1996–97, it offered 141 courses at a distance. In the fall of 1996, there was a total of 500 students enrolled in distance learning courses.
Course delivery sites Courses are delivered to your home, Mesabi Range Community and Technical College (Virginia), Metropolitan State University (St. Paul), Rainy River Community College (International Falls), Vermilion Community College (Ely), 1 off-campus center in Hibbing, George Brown College (Toronto, ON).
Media Courses are delivered via videotapes, videoconferencing, audiotapes, World Wide Web, e-mail, print. Students and teachers interact via videoconferencing, mail, telephone, fax, e-mail. A computer is required for some courses.
Restrictions Availability varies by course, program, or delivery means.
Services Distance learners have access to library services, academic advising, career placement assistance at a distance.
Credit-earning options Students may transfer credits from another institution or may earn credits through standardized exams, portfolio assessment, military training.
Typical costs *Undergraduate:* Tuition of $52.50 per quarter credit plus mandatory fees of $8 per quarter credit for in-state residents. Tuition of $117.30 per quarter credit plus mandatory fees of $8 per quarter credit for out-of-state residents. *Graduate:* Tuition of $80.20 per quarter credit plus mandatory fees of $8 per quarter credit for in-state residents. Tuition of $120.30 per quarter credit plus mandatory fees of $8 per quarter credit for out-of-state residents. Financial aid is available to distance learners.

Profiles: Bemidji State University

Registration Students may register by phone.
Contact Edward G. Gersich, Director, Center for Extended Learning, Bemidji State University, 1500 Birchmont Drive, NE, Bemidji, MN 56601-2699. *Telephone:* 218-755-2068. *Fax:* 218-755-4048. *E-mail:* egersich@vax1.bemidji.msus.edu. *Web site:* http://bsuweb.bemidji.msus.edu/~cel/home.html.

DEGREE & CERTIFICATE PROGRAMS

Associate Degrees

▶ *Criminal Justice (AS)*
Application requirements *Prior education:* high school diploma or equivalent. *Other requirements:* high school transcript.
Completion requirements 102–107 quarter credits are required. 32 quarter credits must be completed through the institution.

▶ *Liberal Studies (AA)*
Application requirements *Prior education:* high school diploma or equivalent. *Other requirements:* high school transcript.
Completion requirements 96 quarter credits are required. 32 quarter credits must be completed through the institution.

Baccalaureate Degrees

▶ *Criminal Justice (BS)*
Application requirements *Prior education:* high school diploma or equivalent. *Other requirements:* high school transcript.
Completion requirements 192 quarter credits are required. 45 quarter credits must be completed through the institution.

▶ *History (BA)*
Application requirements *Prior education:* high school diploma or equivalent. *Other requirements:* high school transcript.
Completion requirements 192 quarter credits are required. 45 quarter credits must be completed through the institution.

▶ *Social Studies (BA)*
Application requirements *Prior education:* high school diploma or equivalent. *Other requirements:* high school transcript.
Completion requirements 192 quarter credits are required. 45 quarter credits must be completed through the institution.

INDIVIDUAL COURSE SUBJECT AREAS

Undergraduate
Area, ethnic, and cultural studies; chemistry; creative writing; English composition; English language and literature; history; liberal arts, general studies, and humanities; music; nursing; philosophy and religion; physical sciences; political science; protective services; psychology; social sciences; sociology; teacher education

Graduate
Teacher education

BEREAN UNIVERSITY OF THE ASSEMBLIES OF GOD

Springfield, Missouri

Berean University of the Assemblies of God, founded in 1948, is an independent-religious comprehensive institution affiliated with the Assemblies of God. It is accredited by the Distance Education and Training Council. It first offered distance learning courses in 1948. In 1996–97, it offered 139 courses at a distance. In the fall of 1996, there was a total of 12,000 students enrolled in distance learning courses.
Course delivery sites Courses are delivered to your home.
Media Courses are delivered via World Wide Web, print. Students and teachers interact via audioconferencing, mail, telephone, fax, e-mail. A computer is required for some courses.
Restrictions Courses are available to US students only.
Services Distance learners have access to library services, e-mail services, academic advising, tutoring, career placement assistance at a distance.
Credit-earning options Students may transfer credits from another institution or may earn credits through standardized exams, institutionally developed exams, portfolio assessment, military training.
Typical costs *Undergraduate:* Tuition of $69 per semester hour. *Graduate:* Tuition of $129 per semester hour. *Noncredit courses:* $45 per course. Financial aid is available to distance learners enrolled full-time or part-time.
Registration Students may register by mail, fax, phone, e-mail, World Wide Web.
Contact Mrs. Dilla Dawson, Director of Institutional Advancement, Berean University of the Assemblies of God, 1445 Boonville Avenue, Springfield, MO 65802. *Telephone:* 800-443-1083. *Fax:* 417-862-5318. *E-mail:* ddawson@affil.ag.org. *Web site:* http://www.berean.edu.

Special note
Berean University of the Assemblies of God has 5 decades of experience in distance education. Present enrollment is approximately 12,000 adults of varying ages and denominations.

The mission of Berean University is to provide accredited distance education for ministers and laypersons, based on a Christian worldview, utilizing current technologies to facilitate the evangelization of the world, the nurture of the church, and the well-being and improvement of society.

The University anticipates tremendous growth in educational technology. Some courses are already offered on-line. Students now have 24-hour access to the voice-mail boxes of their own student services representatives. This new phone system will eventually offer to students access to their own records and a convenient way to take tests and receive scores.

The University has a presence on the Internet (http://www.berean.edu) where students and prospective students can send in prayer requests, listen to chapel messages, send e-mail messages to Berean employees, access free on-line Bible reference materials, link up with a study partner or mentor, and much more. The Web page is regularly updated.

Local groups who desire to study together may register as a Berean Study Center. These groups should contact the school to receive a free copy of the *Study Center Guidelines* for establishing an authorized study group or to ask any questions about Berean's study programs.

Berean University is committed to providing convenient, high-quality distance education for students who must sandwich their studies between their families and their jobs or for anyone who desires to increase his or her biblical knowledge.

DEGREE & CERTIFICATE PROGRAMS

Associate Degrees

▶ *Bible and Theology, Church Ministries, Ministerial Studies (AA)*
In the fall of 1996 there were 750 students enrolled in this program. In 1995–96, 5 degrees were earned at a distance through this program.
Application requirements *Prior education:* high school diploma or equivalent. *Minimum age:* 20. *Other requirements:* high school transcript, an application fee of $35.
Completion requirements 64 semester hours are required. 32 semester credits must be completed through the institution.

Baccalaureate Degrees

▶ *Bible and Theology, Christian Counseling, Christian Education, Evangelism/Missions, Pastoral Ministries (BA)*
In the fall of 1996 there were 450 students enrolled in this program. In 1995–96, 6 degrees were earned at a distance through this program.
Application requirements *Prior education:* high school diploma or equivalent. *Minimum age:* 20. *Other requirements:* high school transcript, college transcripts, an application fee of $35.
Completion requirements 128 semester credits are required. 32 semester credits must be completed through the institution.

Graduate Degrees

▶ *Biblical Studies, Ministerial Studies (MA)*
Application requirements *Prior education:* baccalaureate degree. *Other requirements:* high school transcript, college transcripts, an essay or personal statement, letter(s) of recommendation, an application fee of $45, at least 24 semester hours of undergraduate bible and theology.
Completion requirements 36 credits are required. 30 credits must be completed through the institution.

▶ *Christian Counseling (MA)*
Application requirements *Prior education:* baccalaureate degree. *Other requirements:* high school transcript, college transcripts, an essay or personal statement, letter(s) of recommendation, an application fee of $45, at least 24 semester hours of undergraduate bible and theology and 15 credits of behavioral science.
Completion requirements 42 credits are required. 36 credits must be completed through the institution.
On-campus requirements Three 1-week periods in residence.

Undergraduate Certificates

▶ *Ministerial Studies (Diploma)*
Application requirements *Prior education:* none required. *Other requirements:* an application fee of $5.
Completion requirements 142 continuing education units are required. 71 continuing education units must be completed through the institution.

INDIVIDUAL COURSE SUBJECT AREAS

Undergraduate
Business; Classical languages and literatures; communications; conservation and natural resources; developmental and child psychology; educational psychology; English composition; English language and literature; history; law and legal studies; liberal arts, general studies, and humanities; music; philosophy and religion; physical sciences; radio and television broadcasting; social psychology; sociology; theological studies

Graduate
Theological studies

Noncredit
Theological studies

BERGEN COMMUNITY COLLEGE

Paramus, New Jersey

Center for Distance Learning

Bergen Community College, founded in 1965, is a county-supported two-year college. It is accredited by the Middle States Association of Colleges and Schools. It first offered distance learning courses in 1974. In 1996–97, it offered 8 courses at a distance. In the fall of 1996, there was a total of 184 students enrolled in distance learning courses.
Course delivery sites Courses are delivered to your home, your workplace, Ramapo College of New Jersey (Mahwah), local high schools.
Media Courses are delivered via television, videotapes. Students and teachers interact via mail, telephone, fax, on-campus meetings.
Restrictions Courses are available to students within television transmission area only.
Services Distance learners have access to library services at a distance.
Credit-earning options Students may earn credits through examinations, business training.
Typical costs Tuition of $63.50 per credit plus mandatory fees of $9.50 per credit for local area residents. Tuition of $132 per credit plus mandatory fees of $9.50 per credit for in-state residents. Tuition of $254 per credit plus mandatory fees of $9.50 per credit for out-of-state residents. Costs may vary by number of credits taken. Financial aid is available to distance learners enrolled full-time or part-time.
Registration Students may register by mail.
Contact Dr. Cheryl M. Smith, Dean of Instructional Support Services, Bergen Community College, 400 Paramus Road, Paramus, NJ 07652. *Telephone:* 201-612-5254.

INDIVIDUAL COURSE SUBJECT AREAS

Undergraduate
American (US) history; business administration and management; developmental and child psychology; finance; history; mathematics; psychology; sociology

BETHEL THEOLOGICAL SEMINARY

St. Paul, Minnesota

In-Ministry Programs

Bethel Theological Seminary, founded in 1871, is an independent-religious graduate institution. It is accredited by the North Central Association of Colleges and Schools. It first offered distance learning courses in 1994. In 1996–97, it offered 7 courses at a distance. In the fall of 1996, there was a total of 105 students enrolled in distance learning courses.
Course delivery sites Courses are delivered to your home, your workplace, military bases.
Media Courses are delivered via videotapes, videoconferencing, audiotapes, audioconferencing, World Wide Web, e-mail. Students and teachers interact via audioconferencing, e-mail. A computer is required for all courses.
Services Distance learners have access to library services, academic advising at a distance.
Credit-earning options Students may transfer credits from another institution or may earn credits through portfolio assessment.
Typical costs Tuition of $655 per course. Financial aid is available to distance learners enrolled full-time.
Registration Students may register by mail, fax, e-mail, World Wide Web.
Contact Morris Anderson, Director of Admissions and Financial Aid, Bethel Theological Seminary, 3949 Bethel Drive, St. Paul, MN 55112. *Telephone:* 612-638-6288. *Fax:* 612-638-6002. *E-mail:* jbakerbsem@aol.com. *Web site:* http://www.bethel.edu.

DEGREE & CERTIFICATE PROGRAMS

Graduate Degrees

▶ *Divinity/Ministry (MDiv)*
In the fall of 1996 there were 105 students enrolled in this program.
Application requirements *Prior education:* baccalaureate degree. *Other requirements:* college transcripts, an essay or personal statement, letter(s) of recommendation, an application fee of $20.

Profiles: Bethel Theological Seminary

Completion requirements 144 hours are required. 48 quarter credits must be completed through the institution. *Maximum time for completion:* seven years.
On-campus requirements Four 1-week intensives per year.

INDIVIDUAL COURSE SUBJECT AREAS

Graduate
Bible studies; religious studies; theological studies

BLACK HAWK COLLEGE

Moline, Illinois

Distance Learning

Black Hawk College, founded in 1946, is a state and locally supported two-year college. It is accredited by the North Central Association of Colleges and Schools. It first offered distance learning courses in 1993. In 1996–97, it offered 20 courses at a distance.
Course delivery sites Courses are delivered to your home, your workplace, other colleges, 5 off-campus centers.
Media Courses are delivered via television, videotapes, videoconferencing, World Wide Web, print. Students and teachers interact via videoconferencing, mail, telephone, fax, e-mail.
Services Distance learners have access to library services, e-mail services, academic advising, tutoring at a distance.
Credit-earning options Students may transfer credits from another institution or may earn credits through examinations, military training.
Typical costs Tuition of $49 per credit plus mandatory fees of $3 per credit. Financial aid is available to distance learners.
Registration Students may register by mail, fax, phone.
Contact Maureen Conway, Director of Electronic and Extended Learning Systems, Black Hawk College, 6600 34th Avenue, Moline, IL 61265. *Telephone:* 309-796-1311, Ext. 1307. *Fax:* 309-792-5976. *E-mail:* conwaym@bhc1.bhc.edu. *Web site:* http://www.bhc.edu.

DEGREE & CERTIFICATE PROGRAMS

Associate Degrees
▶*Banking (AAS)*
Program contact Dick Schallerd, Black Hawk College, 6600 34th Avenue, Moline, IL 61265. Phone: 309-796-1311, Ext. 2119.

▶*Legal Assistant (AA)*
Program contact Larry Lorenson, Department Chair, Black Hawk College, 6600 34th Avenue, Moline, IL 61265. Phone: 309-796-1311, Ext. 1412. Fax: 309-792-5976. E-mail: lorensonl@bhc1.bhc.edu.

Undergraduate Certificates
▶*Banking*
Program contact Dick Schallerd, Black Hawk College, 6600 34th Avenue, Moline, IL 61265. Phone: 309-796-1311, Ext. 2119.

▶*Inventory Control Systems*
Program contact Joyce Piechowski, Black Hawk College, 6600 34th Avenue, Moline, IL 61265. Phone: 309-755-2000, Ext. 239.

▶*Nursing (LPN)*
Program contact Sally Alesch, Black Hawk College, 6600 34th Avenue, Moline, IL 61265. Phone: 309-796-1311, Ext. 3319. Fax: 309-792-5976.

▶*Small Business Development*
Program contact Donna Scals, Black Hawk College, 6600 34th Avenue, Moline, IL 61265. Phone: 309-755-2200, Ext. 211.

INDIVIDUAL COURSE SUBJECT AREAS

Undergraduate
Administrative and secretarial services; agriculture; biological and life sciences; biology; business administration and management; computer and information sciences; economics; English composition; English language and literature; geology; health and physical education/fitness; history; law and legal studies; liberal arts, general studies, and humanities; mathematics; nursing; philosophy and religion; protective services; social psychology; sociology

BLACKHAWK TECHNICAL COLLEGE

Janesville, Wisconsin

Blackhawk Technical College, founded in 1968, is a district-supported two-year college. It is accredited by the North Central Association of Colleges and Schools. In 1996–97, it offered 30 courses at a distance. In the fall of 1996, there was a total of 200 students enrolled in distance learning courses.
Course delivery sites Courses are delivered to your home, your workplace, Lakeshore Technical College (Cleveland), Waukesha County Technical College (Pewaukee), 2 off-campus centers in Janesville, Monroe.
Media Courses are delivered via videotapes, videoconferencing, computer software, print, interactive television. Students and teachers interact via mail, telephone, fax.
Credit-earning options Students may transfer credits from another institution or may earn credits through standardized exams, institutionally developed exams, portfolio assessment, military training, business training.
Typical costs Tuition of $54.20 per credit plus mandatory fees of $5.50 per credit for in-state residents. Tuition of $427.20 per credit plus mandatory fees of $5.50 per credit for out-of-state residents. Costs may vary by number of credits taken. Financial aid is available to distance learners enrolled full-time or part-time.
Registration Students may register by mail.
Contact Student Services, Blackhawk Technical College, PO Box 5009, Janesville, WI 53547-5009. *Telephone:* 608-757-7654. *Fax:* 608-757-9407. *E-mail:* crichards@mail.blackhawk.tec.wi.us.

INDIVIDUAL COURSE SUBJECT AREAS

Undergraduate
Administrative and secretarial services; business; communications; health and physical education/fitness; health professions and related sciences; home economics and family studies; law and legal studies; mathematics; psychology

BLACK HILLS STATE UNIVERSITY

Spearfish, South Dakota

Extended Services and Instructional Technology

Black Hills State University, founded in 1883, is a state-supported comprehensive institution. It is accredited by the North Central Association of Colleges and Schools. It first offered distance learning courses in 1994. In 1996–97, it offered 14 courses at a distance. In the fall of 1996, there was a total of 117 students enrolled in distance learning courses.

Course delivery sites Courses are delivered to your home, military bases, South Dakota School of Mines and Technology (Rapid City), high schools.
Media Courses are delivered via television, videotapes, World Wide Web. Students and teachers interact via videoconferencing, mail, telephone, e-mail. A computer is required for some courses.
Restrictions Availability varies by course, program, or delivery means.
Credit-earning options Students may transfer credits from another institution or may earn credits through examinations, military training.
Typical costs *Undergraduate:* Tuition of $78.63 per credit for in-state residents. Tuition of $178.38 per credit for out-of-state residents. *Graduate:* Tuition of $112.18 per credit for in-state residents. Tuition of $251.15 per credit for out-of-state residents. Costs may vary by number of credits taken, course delivery options. Financial aid is available to distance learners.
Registration Students may register by mail, fax, phone, e-mail, World Wide Web.
Contact Verla Fish, Distance Learning Coordinator, Black Hills State University, 1200 University, USB #9508, Spearfish, SD 57799-9508. *Telephone:* 605-642-6771. *Fax:* 605-642-6031. *E-mail:* vfish@mystic.bhsu.edu. *Web site:* http://www.bhsu.edu.

INDIVIDUAL COURSE SUBJECT AREAS

Undergraduate
Accounting; conservation and natural resources; developmental and child psychology; drama and theater; education; English language and literature; genetics; teacher education

Graduate
Developmental and child psychology; education; teacher education

BLADEN COMMUNITY COLLEGE

Dublin, North Carolina

Information Systems

Bladen Community College, founded in 1967, is a state and locally supported two-year college. It is accredited by the Southern Association of Colleges and Schools. It first offered distance learning courses in 1995. In 1996–97, it offered 1 course at a distance. In the fall of 1996, there was a total of 10 students enrolled in distance learning courses.
Course delivery sites Courses are delivered to your home.
Media Courses are delivered via television. Students and teachers interact via audioconferencing, telephone, e-mail.
Services Distance learners have access to library services, the campus computer network, e-mail services, academic advising at a distance.
Credit-earning options Students may transfer credits from another institution or may earn credits through examinations, military training.
Typical costs Tuition of $20 per hour for in-state residents. Tuition of $163 per hour for out-of-state residents. *Noncredit courses:* $35 per course. Costs may vary by number of credits taken. Financial aid is available to distance learners enrolled full-time or part-time.
Registration Students may register by mail.
Contact David Perry, Director of Technology, Bladen Community College, PO Box 266, Dublin, NC 28332. *Telephone:* 910-862-2164. *Fax:* 910-862-7424. *E-mail:* dperry@encore.ncren.net. *Web site:* http://www.bcc.cc.nc.us.

INDIVIDUAL COURSE SUBJECT AREAS

Undergraduate
Business administration and management

Distance Learning Programs

BLINN COLLEGE

Brenham, Texas

Distance Education Center

Blinn College, founded in 1883, is a state and locally supported two-year college. It is accredited by the Southern Association of Colleges and Schools. It first offered distance learning courses in 1996. In 1996–97, it offered 7 courses at a distance. In the fall of 1996, there was a total of 240 students enrolled in distance learning courses.
Course delivery sites Courses are delivered to your home.
Media Courses are delivered via television, videotapes. Students and teachers interact via mail, telephone, fax, e-mail.
Restrictions Programs are available to local area students only.
Credit-earning options Students may transfer credits from another institution or may earn credits through standardized exams, military training.
Typical costs Tuition of $171.50 per course plus mandatory fees of $81.50 per course. *Noncredit courses:* $45 for 3 semester credit hour courses; $52 for 4 semester credit hour courses. Costs may vary by campus or location.
Contact Dr. Henry C. Hill, Director, Distance Education, Blinn College, PO Box 6030, Bryan, TX 77805. *Telephone:* 409-821-0201. *Fax:* 409-821-0209. *E-mail:* hhill@mailroom.blinncol.edu. *Web site:* http://www.blinncol.edu.

INDIVIDUAL COURSE SUBJECT AREAS

Undergraduate
Anthropology; history; political science; psychology; sociology

BLOOMSBURG UNIVERSITY OF PENNSYLVANIA

Bloomsburg, Pennsylvania

Division of Continuing and Distance Education

Bloomsburg University of Pennsylvania, founded in 1839, is a state-supported comprehensive institution. It is accredited by the Middle States Association of Colleges and Schools. It first offered distance learning courses in 1983.
Course delivery sites Courses are delivered to your home.
Media Courses are delivered via television. Students and teachers interact via telephone.
Restrictions Courses are available to students within broadcast range of Pennsylvania cable television only.
Services Distance learners have access to academic advising, tutoring, career placement assistance at a distance.
Credit-earning options Students may transfer credits from another institution or may earn credits through examinations, portfolio assessment, military training, business training.
Typical costs Tuition of $495.75 per course for in-state residents. Tuition of $1146.75 per course for out-of-state residents. Financial aid is available to distance learners.
Contact G. Michael Vavrek, Dean, Continuing and Distance Education, Bloomsburg University of Pennsylvania, 700 West Main Street, Bloomsburg, PA 17815. *Telephone:* 717-389-4420. *Fax:* 717-387-4358. *E-mail:* mvavrek@bloomu.edu. *Web site:* http://www.bloomu.edu.

Profiles: Bloomsburg University of Pennsylvania

INDIVIDUAL COURSE SUBJECT AREAS

Undergraduate
Economics; history; mathematics; philosophy and religion; psychology; sociology

BLUEFIELD STATE COLLEGE

Bluefield, West Virginia

Instructional Technology Center/Center for Extended Learning

Bluefield State College, founded in 1895, is a state-supported four-year college. It is accredited by the North Central Association of Colleges and Schools. It first offered distance learning courses in 1976. In 1996–97, it offered 35 courses at a distance. In the fall of 1996, there was a total of 300 students enrolled in distance learning courses.
Course delivery sites Courses are delivered to your home, your workplace, 2 off-campus centers in Beckley, Lewisburg.
Media Courses are delivered via television, videotapes, interactive television. Students and teachers interact via mail, telephone, fax, e-mail, interactive television. A computer is required for some courses. The institution provides assistance with acquiring computer equipment.
Restrictions Courses are available to regional area students only.
Services Distance learners have access to library services, the campus computer network, e-mail services, academic advising, tutoring, career placement assistance at a distance.
Credit-earning options Students may transfer credits from another institution or may earn credits through standardized exams, portfolio assessment, military training, business training.
Typical costs Tuition of $1022 per semester for in-state residents. Tuition of $2484 per semester for out-of-state residents. Costs may vary by number of credits taken. Financial aid is available to distance learners enrolled full-time or part-time.
Registration Students may register by mail, phone.
Contact Dr. Thomas E. Blevins, Director of Institutional Technology and Extended Learning, Bluefield State College, 219 Rock Street, Bluefield, WV 24701. *Telephone:* 304-327-4059. *Fax:* 304-327-4106. *E-mail:* tblevins@bscvax.wvnet.edu.

DEGREE & CERTIFICATE PROGRAMS

Associate Degrees
▶ **General Education (AS)**
In the fall of 1996 there were 200 students enrolled in this program.
Application requirements *Prior education:* high school diploma or equivalent. *Other requirements:* high school transcript.
Completion requirements 64 semester hours are required. 32 semester hours must be completed through the institution.
On-campus requirements Students must attend class sessions at one of three BSC campus sites.

INDIVIDUAL COURSE SUBJECT AREAS

Undergraduate
Astronomy and astrophysics; business law; computer and information sciences; criminal justice; developmental and child psychology; earth science; economics; English composition; English language and literature; ethics; European history; fine arts; geography; geology; gerontology; health and physical education/fitness; history; liberal arts, general studies, and humanities; mathematics; political science; sociology; teacher education; women's studies

BLUE MOUNTAIN COMMUNITY COLLEGE

Pendleton, Oregon

Blue Mountain Community College, founded in 1962, is a state and locally supported two-year college. It is accredited by the Northwest Association of Schools and Colleges. It first offered distance learning courses in 1982.
Course delivery sites Courses are delivered to your home, your workplace, other colleges.
Media Courses are delivered via television, videotapes, videoconferencing, audiographics conferencing, computer conferencing.
Restrictions Programs are available to local area students only.
Credit-earning options Students may transfer credits from another institution or may earn credits through examinations, portfolio assessment. Financial aid is available to distance learners.
Contact Program Coordinator, Blue Mountain Community College, Department of Continuing Education, PO Box 100, Pendleton, OR 97801. *Telephone:* 503-276-1260. *Fax:* 503-276-6523.

INDIVIDUAL COURSE SUBJECT AREAS

Undergraduate
Area, ethnic, and cultural studies; astronomy and astrophysics; biology; civil engineering; developmental and child psychology; economics; geology; health and physical education/fitness; music; psychology; public health

BOISE STATE UNIVERSITY

Boise, Idaho

Division of Continuing Education

Boise State University, founded in 1932, is a state-supported comprehensive institution. It is accredited by the Northwest Association of Schools and Colleges. It first offered distance learning courses in 1987. In 1996–97, it offered 61 courses at a distance. In the fall of 1996, there was a total of 465 students enrolled in distance learning courses.
Course delivery sites Courses are delivered to your home, your workplace, military bases, College of Southern Idaho (Twin Falls), 6 off-campus centers in Boise, Mountain Home, Nampa.
Media Courses are delivered via television, radio broadcast, computer software, World Wide Web. Students and teachers interact via telephone, e-mail, computer conferencing, interactive television. A computer is required for some courses.
Services Distance learners have access to e-mail services, academic advising at a distance.
Credit-earning options Students may transfer credits from another institution or may earn credits through standardized exams, military training.
Typical costs *Undergraduate:* Tuition of $1147 per semester for in-state residents. Tuition of $2940 per semester for out-of-state residents. *Graduate:* Tuition of $1408 per semester for in-state residents. Tuition of $1408 per semester for out-of-state residents. Costs may vary by number of credits taken. Financial aid is available to distance learners enrolled full-time.
Registration Students may register by fax, phone.
Contact Nancy Ness, Director, Telecommunications Courses, Boise State University, Division of Continuing Education, 1910 University Drive, Boise, ID 83725. *Telephone:* 208-385-1709. *Fax:* 208-385-3467. *E-mail:* aceness@bsu.idbsu.edu. *Web site:* http://www.idbsu.edu/conted.

DEGREE & CERTIFICATE PROGRAMS

Graduate Degrees

▶ *Instructional Performance Technology (MS)*
In the fall of 1996 there were 101 students enrolled in this program. In 1995–96, 15 degrees were earned at a distance through this program.
Application requirements *Prior education:* baccalaureate degree. *Other requirements:* MAT, college transcripts, an essay or personal statement, an application fee of $20, 3.0 GPA.
Completion requirements 36 credits are required. 27 credits must be completed through the institution.
Program contact JoAnn Fenner, Coordinator, IPT Program, Boise State University, 1910 University Drive, Boise, ID 83725-0399. Phone: 208-385-4457. Fax: 208-385-3467. E-mail: jofenner@micron.net.

INDIVIDUAL COURSE SUBJECT AREAS

Undergraduate

Accounting; astronomy and astrophysics; business; business administration and management; communications; computer and information sciences; developmental and child psychology; drama and theater; English language and literature; geography; geology; health professions and related sciences; history; human resources management; marketing; mathematics; philosophy and religion; physical sciences; political science; social sciences; sociology; teacher education; visual and performing arts

BOSTON UNIVERSITY

Boston, Massachusetts

Department of Manufacturing Engineering

Boston University, founded in 1839, is an independent-nonprofit university. It is accredited by the New England Association of Schools and Colleges. It first offered distance learning courses in 1989. In 1996–97, it offered 8 courses at a distance. In the fall of 1996, there was a total of 60 students enrolled in distance learning courses.
Course delivery sites Courses are delivered to your workplace.
Media Courses are delivered via videoconferencing. Students and teachers interact via videoconferencing, mail, telephone, fax, e-mail. A computer is required for some courses.
Services Distance learners have access to academic advising, tutoring at a distance.
Credit-earning options Students may transfer credits from another institution.
Typical costs Tuition of $643 per credit. Students pay a $40 registration fee.
Registration Students may register by mail, fax.
Contact Jennifer Pilton, Department Director, Boston University, Department of Manufacturing Engineering, 15 St. Mary's Street, Boston, MA 02215. *Telephone:* 617-353-2842. *Fax:* 617-353-5548. *E-mail:* jpilton@bu.edu. *Web site:* http://eng.bu.edu/MFG.

DEGREE & CERTIFICATE PROGRAMS

Graduate Degrees

▶ *Manufacturing Engineering (MS)*
In the fall of 1996 there were 60 students enrolled in this program. In 1995–96, 11 degrees were earned at a distance through this program.
Restrictions Program is designed for BS engineers who are working in manufacturing.
Application requirements *Prior education:* baccalaureate degree. *Other requirements:* GRE or GMAT, college transcripts, an essay or personal statement, letter(s) of recommendation, an application fee of $50.
Completion requirements 36 credits are required. 28 credits must be completed through the institution. *Maximum time for completion:* five years.

INDIVIDUAL COURSE SUBJECT AREAS

Graduate
Engineering

Noncredit
Engineering
See full description on page 386.

BRADLEY UNIVERSITY

Peoria, Illinois

Division of Continuing Education and Professional Development

Bradley University, founded in 1897, is an independent-nonprofit comprehensive institution. It is accredited by the North Central Association of Colleges and Schools. In 1996–97, it offered 67 courses at a distance. In the fall of 1996, there was a total of 50 students enrolled in distance learning courses.
Course delivery sites Courses are delivered to your workplace.
Media Courses are delivered via videotapes, videoconferencing, audioconferencing, World Wide Web. Students and teachers interact via videoconferencing, audioconferencing, mail, telephone, fax, e-mail. A computer is required for some courses.
Services Distance learners have access to library services, the campus computer network, e-mail services, academic advising, bookstore at a distance.
Credit-earning options Students may transfer credits from another institution or may earn credits through standardized exams.
Typical costs *Undergraduate:* Tuition of $380 per semester hour. *Graduate:* Tuition of $380 per semester hour. Shipping and handling charges may apply to some locations. Costs may vary by course delivery options. Financial aid is available to distance learners enrolled full-time.
Registration Students may register by mail, fax.
Contact Carla Rich Montez, Director of Summer, Interim and Off-Campus Courses, Bradley University, 1501 West Bradley Avenue, Peoria, IL 61625. *Telephone:* 309-677-2374. *Fax:* 309-677-3321. *E-mail:* cmontez@bradley.edu. *Web site:* http://www.bradley.edu/bucepd/.

Special note
Bradley University, founded in 1897, is a medium-sized independent institution of higher education located in Peoria, Illinois, serving approximately 6,000 graduate and undergraduate students. Its programs in distance education include the delivery of 2 graduate degrees via videotape.

The Master of Science degree in mechanical engineering is a 30-semester-hour program with concentrations available in mechanical systems or energy systems/thermosciences. Qualified applicants should have the equivalent of an undergraduate degree in mechanical engineering with a minimum overall GPA of 3.0/4.0. Other applicants may be admitted conditionally at the discretion of the department. All students must pass a comprehensive exam in their last semester.

The Master of Science in electrical engineering is a 33-semester-hour program designed to give the student a balanced technical background in core areas of modern electrical engineering and a

Distance Learning Programs

Profiles: Bradley University

significant experience in advanced design via a thesis or project. Applicants from non-ABET-accredited schools of engineering are required to take the General Test of the GRE. Qualified applicants should have the equivalent of an undergraduate degree in electrical or computer engineering. All students must pass a comprehensive exam in their last semester.

Tuition for the 1997–98 academic year is $380 per semester hour, with some additional fees related to shipping and handling. Application materials are available from the Division of Continuing Education and Professional Development, 1501 West Bradley Avenue, Peoria, Illinois 61625. Students should contact Carla Rich Montez (telephone: 309-677-2374; fax: 309-677-3321; e-mail: cmontez@bradley.edu).

DEGREE & CERTIFICATE PROGRAMS

Graduate Degrees

▶ *Electrical Engineering (MSEE)*
In the fall of 1996 there were 15 students enrolled in this program. In 1995–96, 2 degrees were earned at a distance through this program.
Application requirements *Prior education:* baccalaureate degree. *Other requirements:* GRE (if student is from a non-ABET school), college transcripts, an essay or personal statement, letter(s) of recommendation, an application fee of $35.
Completion requirements 33 semester hours are required. *Maximum time for completion:* five years, although some flexibility applies to working students.
On-campus requirements Students may be required to do their comprehensive exam on campus.

▶ *Mechanical Engineering (MSME)*
In the fall of 1996 there were 19 students enrolled in this program. In 1995–96, 2 degrees were earned at a distance through this program.
Application requirements *Prior education:* baccalaureate degree. *Other requirements:* GRE, college transcripts, an essay or personal statement, letter(s) of recommendation, an application fee of $35.
Completion requirements 30 semester hours are required. *Maximum time for completion:* five years, although some flexibility applies to working students.
On-campus requirements Students may be required to do their comprehensive exams on campus.

INDIVIDUAL COURSE SUBJECT AREAS

Undergraduate
Communications; electrical engineering

Graduate
Electrical engineering; mechanical engineering; nursing

BREVARD COMMUNITY COLLEGE

Cocoa, Florida

Distance Learning

Brevard Community College, founded in 1960, is a state-supported two-year college. It is accredited by the Southern Association of Colleges and Schools. It first offered distance learning courses in 1974. In 1996–97, it offered 65 courses at a distance. In the fall of 1996, there was a total of 1,280 students enrolled in distance learning courses.
Course delivery sites Courses are delivered to your home, your workplace, military bases, other colleges.
Media Courses are delivered via television, videotapes, computer software, World Wide Web, e-mail, print. Students and teachers interact via mail, telephone, fax, e-mail. A computer is required for some courses.
Services Distance learners have access to library services, e-mail services, academic advising, tutoring, career placement assistance at a distance.
Credit-earning options Students may transfer credits from another institution or may earn credits through examinations, portfolio assessment, military training, business training.
Typical costs Tuition of $37 per credit hour for in-state residents. Tuition of $135 per credit hour for out-of-state residents. *Noncredit courses:* $30–$100 per course. Costs may vary by course delivery options. Financial aid is available to distance learners.
Registration Students may register by mail, phone, World Wide Web.
Contact Tammy Ham Ronsisvalle, Assistant Director, Distance Learning, Brevard Community College, 1519 Clearlake Road, Cocoa, FL 32922. *Telephone:* 407-632-1111, Ext. 62326. *Fax:* 407-634-3724. *E-mail:* ham.t@a1.brevard.cc.fl.us. *Web site:* http://www.brevard.cc.fl.us/distlrn.

DEGREE & CERTIFICATE PROGRAMS

Associate Degrees

▶ *Criminal Justice (AS)*
Application requirements *Prior education:* high school diploma or equivalent. *Other requirements:* high school transcript, college transcripts, an application fee of $20.
Completion requirements 60 semester hours are required. 15 semester hours must be completed through the institution.
Program contact Bill Taylor, Dean, Student Development, Brevard Community College, 1519 Clearlake Road, Cocoa, FL 32922. Phone: 407-632-1111. Fax: 407-634-3752. E-mail: taylor.w@a1.brevard.cc.fl.us.

▶ *Drafting and Design (AS)*
Application requirements *Prior education:* high school diploma or equivalent. *Other requirements:* high school transcript, college transcripts, an application fee of $20.
Completion requirements 60 semester hours are required. 15 semester hours must be completed through the institution.
Program contact Bill Taylor, Dean, Student Development, Brevard Community College, 1519 Clearlake Road, Cocoa, FL 32922. Phone: 407-632-1111. Fax: 407-634-3752. E-mail: taylor.w@a1.brevard.cc.fl.us.

▶ *Electronic Engineering (AS)*
Application requirements *Prior education:* high school diploma or equivalent. *Other requirements:* high school transcript, college transcripts, an application fee of $20.
Completion requirements 60 semester hours are required. 15 semester hours must be completed through the institution.
Program contact Bill Taylor, Dean, Student Development, Brevard Community College, 1519 Clearlake Road, Cocoa, FL 32922. Phone: 407-632-1111. Fax: 407-634-3752. E-mail: taylor.w@a1.brevard.cc.fl.us.

▶ *Fire Science (AS)*
Application requirements *Prior education:* high school diploma or equivalent. *Other requirements:* high school transcript, college transcripts, an application fee of $20.
Completion requirements 60 semester hours are required. 15 semester hours must be completed through the institution.
Program contact Bill Taylor, Dean, Student Development, Brevard Community College, 1519 Clearlake Road, Cocoa, FL 32922. Phone: 407-632-1111. Fax: 407-634-3752. E-mail: taylor.w@a1.brevard.cc.fl.us.

▶ *General Studies (AA)*
Application requirements *Prior education:* high school diploma or equivalent. *Other requirements:* high school transcript, college transcripts, an application fee of $20.

Completion requirements 60 semester hours are required. 15 semester hours must be completed through the institution.
Program contact Bill Taylor, Dean, Student Development, Brevard Community College, 1519 Clearlake Road, Cocoa, FL 32922. Phone: 407-632-1111. Fax: 407-634-3752. E-mail: taylor.w@a1.brevard.cc.fl.us.

▶ *Hazardous Materials Technology (AS)*
Application requirements *Prior education:* high school diploma or equivalent. *Other requirements:* high school transcript, college transcripts.
Completion requirements 60 semester hours are required. 15 semester hours must be completed through the institution.
Program contact Bill Taylor, Dean, Student Development, Brevard Community College, 1519 Clearlake Road, Cocoa, FL 32922. Phone: 407-632-1111. Fax: 407-634-3752. E-mail: taylor.w@a1.brevard.cc.fl.us.

▶ *International Business Management (AS)*
Application requirements *Prior education:* high school diploma or equivalent. *Other requirements:* high school transcript, college transcripts, an application fee of $20.
Completion requirements 60 semester hours are required. 15 semester hours must be completed through the institution.
Program contact Bill Taylor, Dean, Student Development, Brevard Community College, 1519 Clearlake Road, Cocoa, FL 32922. Phone: 407-632-1111. Fax: 407-634-3752. E-mail: taylor.w@a1.brevard.cc.fl.us.

▶ *Legal Studies (AS)*
Application requirements *Prior education:* high school diploma or equivalent. *Other requirements:* high school transcript, college transcripts, an application fee of $20.
Completion requirements 60 semester hours are required. 15 semester hours must be completed through the institution.
Program contact Bill Taylor, Dean, Student Development, Brevard Community College, 1519 Clearlake Road, Cocoa, FL 32922. Phone: 407-632-1111. Fax: 407-634-3752. E-mail: taylor.w@a1.brevard.cc.fl.us.

▶ *Liberal Studies (AA)*
In the fall of 1996 there were 1,200 students enrolled in this program.
Restrictions Program is available to students in the broadcast area only.
Application requirements *Prior education:* high school diploma or equivalent. *Other requirements:* high school transcript, college transcripts, an application fee of $20.
Completion requirements 60 semester hours are required. 15 semester hours must be completed through the institution.
On-campus requirements For testing.

▶ *Marketing Management (AS)*
Application requirements *Prior education:* high school diploma or equivalent. *Other requirements:* high school transcript, college transcripts.
Completion requirements 60 semester hours are required. 15 semester hours must be completed through the institution.
Program contact Bill Taylor, Dean, Student Development, Brevard Community College, 1519 Clearlake Road, Cocoa, FL 32922. Phone: 407-632-1111. Fax: 407-634-3752. E-mail: taylor.w@a1.brevard.cc.fl.us.

▶ *Radio-TV Programming (AS)*
Application requirements *Prior education:* high school diploma or equivalent. *Other requirements:* high school transcript, college transcripts.
Completion requirements 60 semester hours are required. 15 semester hours must be completed through the institution.
Program contact Bill Taylor, Dean, Student Development, Brevard Community College, 1519 Clearlake Road, Cocoa, FL 32922. Phone: 407-632-1111. Fax: 407-634-3752. E-mail: taylor.w@a1.brevard.cc.fl.us.

▶ *Solar Energy Technology (AS)*
Application requirements *Prior education:* high school diploma or equivalent. *Other requirements:* high school transcript, college transcripts.
Completion requirements 60 semester hours are required. 15 semester hours must be completed through the institution.
Program contact Bill Taylor, Dean, Student Development, Brevard Community College, 1519 Clearlake Road, Cocoa, FL 32922. Phone: 407-632-1111. Fax: 407-634-3752. E-mail: taylor.w@a1.brevard.cc.fl.us.

INDIVIDUAL COURSE SUBJECT AREAS

Undergraduate
Accounting; administrative and secretarial services; advertising; area, ethnic, and cultural studies; Asian languages and literatures; astronomy and astrophysics; biological and life sciences; biology; business; business administration and management; chemical engineering; computer and information sciences; developmental and child psychology; economics; electrical engineering; English language and literature; geology; health and physical education/fitness; history; home economics and family studies; hospitality services management; journalism; law and legal studies; liberal arts, general studies, and humanities; mathematics; music; philosophy and religion; political science; social psychology; sociology; visual and performing arts

BRIGHAM YOUNG UNIVERSITY

Provo, Utah

Independent Study

Brigham Young University, founded in 1875, is an independent-religious university affiliated with the Church of Jesus Christ of Latter-day Saints. It is accredited by the Northwest Association of Schools and Colleges. It first offered distance learning courses in 1921. In 1996–97, it offered 500 courses at a distance.
Course delivery sites Courses are delivered to your home.
Media Courses are delivered via World Wide Web, print. Students and teachers interact via mail, telephone, fax, e-mail. A computer is required for some courses.
Restrictions Students must be able to visit campus several times throughout the program.
Services Distance learners have access to library services, e-mail services at a distance.
Typical costs Tuition of $78 per credit. *Noncredit courses:* $74 per course.
Registration Students may register by mail, fax, phone, e-mail, World Wide Web.
Contact Scott Howell, Assistant Director, Brigham Young University, 206 Harmon Building, Provo, UT 84602. *Telephone:* 801-378-7163. *Fax:* 801-378-5817. *E-mail:* scott_howell@byu.edu. *Web site:* http://coned.byu.edu/is/indstudy.htm.

INDIVIDUAL COURSE SUBJECT AREAS

Undergraduate
Abnormal psychology; accounting; algebra; American (US) history; American literature; animal sciences; anthropology; art history and criticism; astronomy and astrophysics; bible studies; biological and life sciences; biology; botany; business; calculus; chemistry; civil engineering; communications; community health services; creative writing; curriculum and instruction; developmental and child psychology; drama and theater; economics; education; educational psychology; engineering; English composition; English language and literature; English literature;

Profiles: Brigham Young University

European history; European languages and literatures; film studies; finance; fine arts; geography; German language and literature; health and physical education/fitness; health professions and related sciences; Hebrew language and literature; history; logic; marketing; mass media; mathematics; microbiology; music; organizational behavior studies; philosophy and religion; physical sciences; physics; political science; psychology; social sciences; sociology; Spanish language and literature; statistics; technical writing

See full description on page 388.

BRISTOL COMMUNITY COLLEGE

Fall River, Massachusetts

Continuing Education and Community Services

Bristol Community College, founded in 1965, is a state-supported two-year college. It is accredited by the New England Association of Schools and Colleges. It first offered distance learning courses in 1990. In 1996–97, it offered 8 courses at a distance. In the fall of 1996, there was a total of 100 students enrolled in distance learning courses.
Course delivery sites Courses are delivered to your home, Cape Cod Community College (West Barnstable), 1 off-campus center in New Bedford.
Media Courses are delivered via television, videoconferencing. Students and teachers interact via videoconferencing, e-mail.
Services Distance learners have access to academic advising at a distance.
Credit-earning options Students may transfer credits from another institution or may earn credits through standardized exams, institutionally developed exams, military training, business training.
Typical costs Tuition of $36 per credit plus mandatory fees of $46 per credit for in-state residents. Tuition of $184 per credit plus mandatory fees of $46 per credit for out-of-state residents. *Noncredit courses:* $50–$160 per course. Costs may vary by number of credits taken. Financial aid is available to distance learners enrolled full-time or part-time.
Registration Students may register by mail, fax, phone.
Contact John J. Gregory, Director of Administrative Services, Continuing Education, Bristol Community College, 777 Elsbree Street, Fall River, MA 02720. *Telephone:* 508-678-2811. *Fax:* 508-678-2876. *E-mail:* jgregory@bristol.mass.edu.

INDIVIDUAL COURSE SUBJECT AREAS

Undergraduate
Algebra; business administration and management; calculus; chemistry; European history; geography; psychology; public health; social sciences; sociology

BROCK UNIVERSITY

St. Catharines, Ontario, Canada

Faculty of Education, Continuing Studies

Brock University, founded in 1964, is a province-supported comprehensive institution. It is provincially chartered. It first offered distance learning courses in 1994.
Course delivery sites Courses are delivered to your workplace, military bases, other colleges.
Media Courses are delivered via videotapes. Students and teachers interact via mail, telephone, fax, e-mail.
Services Distance learners have access to library services, e-mail services, academic advising, tutoring, career placement assistance at a distance.
Credit-earning options Students may transfer credits from another institution or may earn credits through examinations, business training.
Typical costs Tuition of $900 per course. Cost given in Canadian dollars.
Contact Phyllis J. Stanley, Program Coordinator: BEd/ADED, Brock University, Faculty of Education, St. Catharines, ON L2S 3A1, Canada. *Telephone:* 905-688-5550, Ext. 3971. *Fax:* 905-688-0544. *E-mail:* pstanley@dewey.ed.brocku.ca.

DEGREE & CERTIFICATE PROGRAMS

Baccalaureate Degrees
▶*Adult Education (BEd)*
Application requirements Experience and/or interest in working with adults in a teaching/learning situation.

Undergraduate Certificates
▶*Adult Education*
Application requirements Experience and/or interest in working with adults in a teaching/learning situation.

INDIVIDUAL COURSE SUBJECT AREAS

Undergraduate
Education

BROOKDALE COMMUNITY COLLEGE

Lincroft, New Jersey

Telecourse Program–Division of Arts and Communication

Brookdale Community College, founded in 1967, is a county-supported two-year college. It is accredited by the Middle States Association of Colleges and Schools. It first offered distance learning courses in 1974. In 1996–97, it offered 18 courses at a distance. In the fall of 1996, there was a total of 239 students enrolled in distance learning courses.
Course delivery sites Courses are delivered to your home, your workplace, military bases.
Media Courses are delivered via television, audiotapes, radio broadcast. Students and teachers interact via mail, telephone.
Restrictions Programs are available to in-state students only.
Services Distance learners have access to tutoring at a distance.
Credit-earning options Students may transfer credits from another institution or may earn credits through institutionally developed exams, portfolio assessment, military training, business training.
Typical costs Tuition of $72.25 per credit plus mandatory fees of $15 per credit for local area residents. Tuition of $144.50 per credit plus mandatory fees of $15 per credit for in-state residents. Tuition of $289 per credit plus mandatory fees of $15 per credit for out-of-state residents. *Noncredit courses:* $155 for an entire day, $85 for a 3-hour seminar. Costs may vary by campus or location, number of credits taken. Financial aid is available to distance learners enrolled full-time.
Registration Students may register by mail.
Contact Ms. Cheryl A. Cummings, Manager, Broadcast Services, Brookdale Community College, 765 Newman Springs Road, Lincroft, NJ 07738. *Telephone:* 908-224-2765. *Fax:* 908-224-2494. *E-mail:* wbjb@shell.monmouth.com.

DEGREE & CERTIFICATE PROGRAMS

Associate Degrees

▶ *Business Administration (AA)*
In the fall of 1996 there were 239 students enrolled in this program.
Application requirements *Prior education:* none required. *Minimum age:* 18.
Completion requirements 60 credits are required. 30 credits must be completed through the institution.
On-campus requirements For orientation; some instructors require two or three on-campus review sessions.

▶ *Liberal Arts (AA)*
In the fall of 1996 there were 239 students enrolled in this program.
Application requirements *Prior education:* none required. *Minimum age:* 18.
Completion requirements 60 credits are required. 30 credits must be completed through the institution.

INDIVIDUAL COURSE SUBJECT AREAS

Undergraduate
Anthropology; biology; business; business administration and management; creative writing; developmental and child psychology; economics; English composition; English language and literature; European languages and literatures; health and physical education/fitness; history; liberal arts, general studies, and humanities; marketing; music; philosophy and religion; social psychology; sociology

Noncredit
Marketing

BROWARD COMMUNITY COLLEGE

Fort Lauderdale, Florida

Instructional Technology

Broward Community College, founded in 1960, is a state-supported two-year college. It is accredited by the Southern Association of Colleges and Schools. It first offered distance learning courses in 1978. In 1996–97, it offered 48 courses at a distance. In the fall of 1996, there was a total of 686 students enrolled in distance learning courses.
Course delivery sites Courses are delivered to your home, Edison Community College (Fort Myers), Tallahassee Community College (Tallahassee).
Media Courses are delivered via videotapes, videoconferencing, audiotapes, e-mail. Students and teachers interact via mail, telephone, fax, e-mail.
Restrictions Telecourses are available for local area students only.
Services Distance learners have access to library services, the campus computer network, e-mail services, academic advising, tutoring, career placement assistance at a distance.
Credit-earning options Students may transfer credits from another institution or may earn credits through standardized exams, institutionally developed exams, portfolio assessment, military training.
Typical costs Tuition of $36.75 per credit for in-state residents. Tuition of $134 per credit for out-of-state residents. Costs may vary by number of credits taken. Financial aid is available to distance learners enrolled full-time or part-time.
Registration Students may register by phone.
Contact Wanda Thomas, Director, Center for Health Sciences, Broward Community College, 3501 Southwest Davie Road, Davie, FL 33314. *Telephone:* 954-475-6767. *Fax:* 954-473-9037. *Web site:* http://www.broward.cc.fl.us.

Distance Learning Programs

INDIVIDUAL COURSE SUBJECT AREAS

Undergraduate
Accounting; astronomy and astrophysics; biology; business; business administration and management; computer and information sciences; developmental and child psychology; economics; English composition; English language and literature; geography; geology; health and physical education/fitness; health professions and related sciences; history; music; philosophy and religion; political science; sociology

BROWN UNIVERSITY

Providence, Rhode Island

Brown University Interactive Network (BRUIN)

Brown University, founded in 1764, is an independent-nonprofit university. It is accredited by the New England Association of Schools and Colleges. It first offered distance learning courses in 1994.
Course delivery sites Courses are delivered to your home.
Media Courses are delivered via e-mail. Students and teachers interact via e-mail. A computer is required for all courses.
Restrictions Courses are available to Brown University alumni only.
Typical costs *Noncredit courses:* $50 per course. Costs may vary by specific program of study.
Registration Students may register by mail, fax, phone, e-mail.
Contact James D. Rooney, Acting Director of Alumni Education, Brown University, Box 1859, Providence, RI 02912. *Telephone:* 401-863-3309. *Fax:* 401-863-7070. *E-mail:* continuing_college@brown.edu. *Web site:* http://www.brown.edu/Administration/Alumni/bruininfo.html.

INDIVIDUAL COURSE SUBJECT AREAS

Noncredit
Anthropology; business administration and management; political science; public health

BUCKS COUNTY COMMUNITY COLLEGE

Newtown, Pennsylvania

Distance Learning Office

Bucks County Community College, founded in 1964, is a county-supported two-year college. It is accredited by the Middle States Association of Colleges and Schools. It first offered distance learning courses in 1994. In 1996–97, it offered 56 courses at a distance. In the fall of 1996, there was a total of 560 students enrolled in distance learning courses.
Course delivery sites Courses are delivered to your home, your workplace, military bases.
Media Courses are delivered via television, videotapes, videoconferencing, audiotapes, computer software, World Wide Web, e-mail, print. Students and teachers interact via videoconferencing, audioconferencing, mail, telephone, fax, e-mail. A computer is required for some courses.
Services Distance learners have access to library services, the campus computer network, e-mail services, academic advising, tutoring, career placement assistance at a distance.
Credit-earning options Students may transfer credits from another institution or may earn credits through standardized exams, institutionally developed exams, portfolio assessment, military training, business training.

Profiles: Bucks County Community College

Typical costs Tuition of $66 per credit plus mandatory fees of $25 per semester for local area residents. Tuition of $132 per credit plus mandatory fees of $25 per semester for in-state residents. Tuition of $198 per credit plus mandatory fees of $25 per semester for out-of-state residents. Financial aid is available to distance learners enrolled full-time or part-time.
Registration Students may register by mail, fax, phone.
Contact Betty Kulick, Admissions Office, Bucks County Community College, Swamp Road, Newtown, PA 18940. *Telephone:* 215-968-8101. *E-mail:* kulicke@bucks.edu. *Web site:* http://www.bucks.edu.

DEGREE & CERTIFICATE PROGRAMS

Associate Degrees

▶*Business Administration (AA)*
Application requirements *Prior education:* high school diploma or equivalent. *Other requirements:* high school transcript.
Completion requirements 60 credits are required.

▶*Liberal Arts (AA)*
Application requirements *Prior education:* high school diploma or equivalent. *Other requirements:* high school transcript.
Completion requirements 60 credits are required.

INDIVIDUAL COURSE SUBJECT AREAS

Undergraduate
Abnormal psychology; accounting; advertising; algebra; American (US) history; American literature; art history and criticism; astronomy and astrophysics; biology; business; business administration and management; business law; chemistry; computer and information sciences; economics; education; English composition; English language and literature; English literature; ethics; foods and nutrition studies; history; human resources management; law and legal studies; marketing; mathematics; philosophy and religion; physical sciences; political science; psychology; social psychology; statistics

BUENA VISTA UNIVERSITY

Storm Lake, Iowa

Buena Vista University, founded in 1891, is an independent-religious comprehensive institution affiliated with the Presbyterian Church (U.S.A.). It is accredited by the North Central Association of Colleges and Schools. It first offered distance learning courses in 1975. In 1996–97, it offered 825 courses at a distance. In the fall of 1996, there was a total of 1,319 students enrolled in distance learning courses.
Course delivery sites Courses are delivered to 11 off-campus centers in Council Bluffs, Creston, Denison, Estherville, Fort Dodge, Iowa Falls, Marshalltown, Mason City, Ottumwa, Spencer, Spirit Lake.
Media Courses are delivered via television. Students and teachers interact via in-person meetings.
Restrictions Programs are available to in-state students only. Students must have 60 semester hours of credit.
Services Distance learners have access to library services at a distance.
Credit-earning options Students may transfer credits from another institution or may earn credits through standardized exams, military training.
Typical costs Tuition of $179 per credit hour. Financial aid is available to distance learners enrolled full-time or part-time.
Registration Students may register by mail, fax, phone.

Contact Dr. John Phillips, Associate Dean for Centers, Buena Vista University, 610 West Forth Street, Storm Lake, IA 50588. *Telephone:* 712-749-2247. *Fax:* 712-749-1410. *E-mail:* johnp@bvu.edu.

Special note
Buena Vista University (BVU) is a private, accredited, coeducational university in Storm Lake, Iowa. BVU offers more than 30 majors and 15 preprofessional programs to more than 1,150 students on the state-of-the-art residential campus and serves more than 1,350 students enrolled in branch campuses throughout Iowa. BVU is at the forefront of technology using the 2-way, fiber-optic Iowa Communication Network (ICN) and BVU's new 49,000-square-foot Information Technology Center (ITC). The ITC features 2 fully operational distance learning classrooms and hosts more than 125 of the nearly 500 computers on campus with access to on-line card catalogs, databases, and the Internet. Students off campus access the ITC and library resources via the Internet.
BVU is starting its 24th year as a national leader in distance learning through its Centers program on the community college campuses of Council Bluffs, Creston, Denison, Fort Dodge, Iowa Falls, Emmetsburg, Estherville, Marshalltown, Mason City, Ottumwa, Spencer, and Spirit Lake. Third and 4th years for degree completion in a variety of majors and education endorsements are offered. Graduate majors in education geared toward the practicing teacher are offered through BVU'S distance learning program. Educators have licensure options in school administration and leadership, guidance and counseling, and curriculum and instruction that accumulate credit over a 3-year period. Courses on the ICN and seminars on the BVU main campus result in a master's degree from BVU.

INDIVIDUAL COURSE SUBJECT AREAS

Undergraduate
Accounting; computer and information sciences; education; English language and literature; finance; history; human resources management; psychology; social sciences

BURLINGTON COUNTY COLLEGE

Pemberton, New Jersey

Burlington County College, founded in 1966, is a county-supported two-year college. It is accredited by the Middle States Association of Colleges and Schools. It first offered distance learning courses in 1978. In 1996–97, it offered 40 courses at a distance. In the fall of 1996, there was a total of 800 students enrolled in distance learning courses.
Course delivery sites Courses are delivered to your home, military bases, prisons.
Media Courses are delivered via television, videotapes, audiotapes, radio broadcast, computer software, World Wide Web, e-mail, print. Students and teachers interact via mail, telephone, fax, e-mail. A computer is required for some courses.
Credit-earning options Students may transfer credits from another institution or may earn credits through examinations.
Typical costs Tuition of $210 per course plus mandatory fees of $25 per course for local area residents. Tuition of $73.50 per credit plus mandatory fees of $25 per course for in-state residents. Tuition of $73.50 per credit plus mandatory fees of $25 per course for out-of-state residents. Costs may vary by number of credits taken. Financial aid is available to distance learners.
Registration Students may register by mail, phone.

Contact Sue Espenshade, Coordinator of Distance Learning, Burlington County College, County Route 530, Pemberton, NJ 08068. *Telephone:* 609-894-9311, Ext. 7790. *Fax:* 609-894-4189. *Web site:* http://www.bcc.edu.

DEGREE & CERTIFICATE PROGRAMS

Associate Degrees

▶ *Business Administration (AS)*
Application requirements *Prior education:* high school diploma or equivalent. *Other requirements:* NJ Basic Skills Test, high school transcript.
Completion requirements 64 semester credits are required.

▶ *Liberal Arts and Sciences (AA)*
Application requirements *Prior education:* high school diploma or equivalent. *Other requirements:* NJ Basic Skills Test, high school transcript.
Completion requirements 64 semester credits are required.

INDIVIDUAL COURSE SUBJECT AREAS

Undergraduate
Administrative and secretarial services; astronomy and astrophysics; biological and life sciences; biology; business; business administration and management; computer and information sciences; conservation and natural resources; developmental and child psychology; economics; English composition; European languages and literatures; geology; health and physical education/fitness; history; home economics and family studies; law and legal studies; liberal arts, general studies, and humanities; mathematics; music; political science; psychology; sociology

See full description on page 390.

BUTTE COLLEGE

Oroville, California

Information Services and Technology

Butte College, founded in 1966, is a district-supported two-year college. It is accredited by the Western Association of Schools and Colleges, Inc. It first offered distance learning courses in 1975. In 1996–97, it offered 40 courses at a distance. In the fall of 1996, there was a total of 1,200 students enrolled in distance learning courses.
Course delivery sites Courses are delivered to your home, 4 off-campus centers in Chico, Gridley, Paradise, Willows.
Media Courses are delivered via television, videoconferencing, World Wide Web. Students and teachers interact via videoconferencing, mail, telephone, fax, e-mail. A computer is required for some courses.
Services Distance learners have access to library services, the campus computer network, e-mail services, academic advising, tutoring, career placement assistance at a distance.
Credit-earning options Students may transfer credits from another institution or may earn credits through institutionally developed exams.
Typical costs Tuition of $13 per unit plus mandatory fees of $72 per semester for in-state residents. Tuition of $138 per unit plus mandatory fees of $72 per semester for out-of-state residents. *Noncredit courses:* $72.50 per unit. Costs may vary by number of credits taken. Financial aid is available to distance learners enrolled full-time.
Registration Students may register by phone.
Contact Robert Ellsworth, Media and Distance Learning Coordinator, Butte College, 3536 Butte Campus Drive, Oroville, CA 95965. *Telephone:* 916-895-2344. *Fax:* 916-895-2380. *E-mail:* ellsworthro@butte.cc.ca.us.

Distance Learning Programs

INDIVIDUAL COURSE SUBJECT AREAS

Undergraduate
Agriculture; area, ethnic, and cultural studies; astronomy and astrophysics; biological and life sciences; biology; business administration and management; developmental and child psychology; English as a second language (ESL); English composition; European languages and literatures; fine arts; health and physical education/fitness; history; home economics and family studies; liberal arts, general studies, and humanities; mathematics; philosophy and religion; political science; protective services; radio and television broadcasting; social psychology; social sciences

CABRILLO COLLEGE

Aptos, California

Cabrillo College, founded in 1959, is a district-supported two-year college. It is accredited by the Western Association of Schools and Colleges, Inc. It first offered distance learning courses in 1994. In 1996–97, it offered 10 courses at a distance. In the fall of 1996, there was a total of 300 students enrolled in distance learning courses.
Course delivery sites Courses are delivered to your home.
Media Courses are delivered via television, videotapes, audiotapes, computer software. Students and teachers interact via mail, telephone, fax, e-mail.
Restrictions Students must be able to travel to campus.
Services Distance learners have access to e-mail services at a distance.
Credit-earning options Students may earn credits through institutionally developed exams.
Typical costs Tuition of $13 per credit for in-state residents. Tuition of $125 per credit for out-of-state residents. Financial aid is available to distance learners enrolled full-time or part-time.
Registration Students may register by mail.
Contact Dr. Bette G. Hirsch, Dean of Transfer Education, Cabrillo College, Aptos, CA 95003. *Telephone:* 408-479-5075. *Fax:* 408-479-5092. *E-mail:* behirsch@cabrillo.cc.ca.us.

INDIVIDUAL COURSE SUBJECT AREAS

Undergraduate
Accounting; anthropology; business law; film studies; geography; political science; psychology; Spanish language and literature

CALDWELL COLLEGE

Caldwell, New Jersey

Center for Continuing Education

Caldwell College, founded in 1939, is an independent-religious Roman Catholic comprehensive institution. It is accredited by the Middle States Association of Colleges and Schools. It first offered distance learning courses in 1979. In 1996–97, it offered 210 courses at a distance. In the fall of 1996, there was a total of 440 students enrolled in distance learning courses.
Course delivery sites Courses are delivered to your home.
Media Courses are delivered via videotapes, audiotapes, computer software, e-mail, print. Students and teachers interact via mail, telephone, fax, e-mail. A computer is required for some courses.
Restrictions Students must be matriculating at Caldwell College and attend External Degree weekend (first weekend of each semester).

Profiles: Caldwell College

Services Distance learners have access to library services, the campus computer network, e-mail services, academic advising at a distance.
Credit-earning options Students may transfer credits from another institution or may earn credits through examinations, portfolio assessment, military training, business training.
Typical costs Tuition of $258 per credit. Students pay a $30 external degree fee. Financial aid is available to distance learners enrolled full-time or part-time.
Registration Students may register by mail, fax, e-mail.
Contact Jack Albalah, Corporate and Adult Admissions, Caldwell College, 9 Ryerson Avenue, Caldwell, NJ 07006. *Telephone:* 201-228-4424, Ext. 285. *Fax:* 201-228-2897. *E-mail:* caldwellad@aol.com.

DEGREE & CERTIFICATE PROGRAMS

Baccalaureate Degrees

▶*Accounting, Business, Computer Information Systems, International Business, Management, Marketing (BS)*
Application requirements *Prior education:* some undergraduate course work. *Minimum age:* 23. *Other requirements:* high school transcript, college transcripts, an application fee of $25, must declare a major.
Completion requirements 122 credits are required. 45 credits must be completed through the institution. This is a degree completion program.
On-campus requirements One day in the beginning of the semester.

▶*Communication Arts, Criminal Justice, English, Foreign Language, History, Political Science, Psychology, Religious Studies, Sociology (BA)*
Application requirements *Prior education:* some undergraduate course work. *Minimum age:* 23. *Other requirements:* high school transcript, college transcripts, an application fee of $25, must declare a major.
Completion requirements 122 credits are required. 45 credits must be completed through the institution. This is a degree completion program.
On-campus requirements One day in the beginning of the semester.
See full description on page 392.

CALIFORNIA COLLEGE FOR HEALTH SCIENCES

National City, California

California College for Health Sciences, founded in 1978, is a proprietary comprehensive institution. It is accredited by the Distance Education and Training Council. It first offered distance learning courses in 1978. In 1996–97, it offered 90 courses at a distance. In the fall of 1996, there was a total of 1,200 students enrolled in distance learning courses.
Course delivery sites Courses are delivered to your home, your workplace, military bases.
Media Courses are delivered via audiotapes, print. Students and teachers interact via mail, telephone, fax, e-mail. A computer is required for some courses.
Services Distance learners have access to academic advising, tutoring at a distance.
Credit-earning options Students may transfer credits from another institution or may earn credits through examinations, portfolio assessment, military training, business training.
Typical costs *Undergraduate:* Tuition of $100 per credit plus mandatory fees of $35 per course. *Graduate:* Tuition of $100 per credit plus mandatory fees of $35 per course.
Registration Students may register by mail, phone.
Contact Marita Gubbe, Registrar, California College for Health Sciences, 222 West 24th Street, National City, CA 91950. *Telephone:* 619-477-4800. *Fax:* 619-477-2257. *E-mail:* admissns@cchs.edu.

DEGREE & CERTIFICATE PROGRAMS

Associate Degrees

▶*Allied Health (AS)*
In the fall of 1996 there were 10 students enrolled in this program. In 1995–96, 1 degree was earned at a distance through this program.
Restrictions Students must currently be working in the health care field.
Application requirements *Prior education:* 30 credits of college training in a specific health related field such as Lab Technician, Medical Assisting, EMT, etc. *Other requirements:* high school transcript, college transcripts, an application fee of $35.
Completion requirements 60 semester credits are required. 30 semester credits must be completed through the institution.

▶*Early Childhood Education (AS)*
In the fall of 1996 there were 10 students enrolled in this program. In 1995–96, 2 degrees were earned at a distance through this program.
Application requirements *Prior education:* high school diploma or equivalent. *Other requirements:* high school transcript, an application fee of $35.
Completion requirements 60 semester credits are required. 30 semester credits must be completed through the institution.

▶*EEG Technology (AS)*
In the fall of 1996 there were 77 students enrolled in this program. In 1995–96, 14 degrees were earned at a distance through this program.
Restrictions Students must have access to a facility that performs EEGs.
Application requirements *Prior education:* high school diploma or equivalent. *Other requirements:* high school transcript, an application fee of $35, $65.00 enrollment fee.
Completion requirements 60 semester credits are required. 30 semester credits must be completed through the institution.

▶*Medical Transcription (AS)*
In the fall of 1996 there were 167 students enrolled in this program. In 1995–96, 2 degrees were earned at a distance through this program.
Application requirements *Prior education:* high school diploma or equivalent. *Other requirements:* high school transcript, an application fee of $35, $65.00 enrollment fee.
Completion requirements 60 semester credits are required. 30 semester credits must be completed through the institution.

▶*Respiratory Therapy (AS)*
In the fall of 1996 there were 546 students enrolled in this program. In 1995–96, 244 degrees were earned at a distance through this program.
Application requirements *Prior education:* graduate of an accredited Respiratory Technician program. *Other requirements:* high school transcript, completion of a respiratory technician program.
Completion requirements 60 semester credits are required. 30 semester credits must be completed through the institution.

Baccalaureate Degrees

▶*Health Sciences/Management (BS)*
In the fall of 1996 there were 200 students enrolled in this program. In 1995–96, 30 degrees were earned at a distance through this program.
Application requirements *Prior education:* associate degree or 60 semester credits. *Other requirements:* high school transcript, college transcripts, an application fee of $35.
Completion requirements 120 semester credits are required. 30 semester credits must be completed through the institution. This is a degree completion program.

▶*Health Services/Respiratory Care (BS)*
In the fall of 1996 there were 5 students enrolled in this program.

Application requirements *Prior education:* graduate of respiratory therapy program or an Associate degree. *Other requirements:* high school transcript, college transcripts, an application fee of $35.
Completion requirements 120 semester credits are required. 30 semester credits must be completed through the institution. This is a degree completion program.

Graduate Degrees

▶ *Community Health Administration and Wellness Promotion (MS)*

In the fall of 1996 there were 250 students enrolled in this program. In 1995–96, 50 degrees were earned at a distance through this program.
Application requirements *Prior education:* baccalaureate degree. *Other requirements:* high school transcript, college transcripts, an application fee of $35, resume, completion of psychology courses.
Completion requirements 36 semester credits are required. 27 semester credits must be completed through the institution.

INDIVIDUAL COURSE SUBJECT AREAS

Undergraduate
Business; chemistry; computer and information sciences; developmental and child psychology; education administration; educational psychology; English composition; health professions and related sciences; human resources management; law and legal studies; mathematics; microbiology; physics; social psychology; special education; teacher education

Graduate
Health professions and related sciences; human resources management; law and legal studies; public administration and services; social psychology; social work

CALIFORNIA INSTITUTE OF INTEGRAL STUDIES

San Francisco, California

Division of Transformative Learning

California Institute of Integral Studies, founded in 1968, is an independent-nonprofit graduate institution. It is accredited by the Western Association of Schools and Colleges, Inc. It first offered distance learning courses in 1992. In 1996–97, it offered 24 courses at a distance. In the fall of 1996, there was a total of 150 students enrolled in distance learning courses.
Course delivery sites Courses are delivered to your home.
Media Courses are delivered via World Wide Web, e-mail. Students and teachers interact via mail, telephone, e-mail. A computer is required for all courses.
Restrictions Students must have consistent access to computer and World Wide Web.
Services Distance learners have access to library services, the campus computer network, e-mail services, academic advising at a distance.
Credit-earning options Students may transfer credits from another institution.
Typical costs Tuition of $335 per unit plus mandatory fees of $82 per quarter. Costs may vary by specific program of study, number of credits taken. Financial aid is available to distance learners enrolled full-time or part-time.
Contact Division of Transformative Learning Admissions, California Institute of Integral Studies, 9 Peter Yorke Way, San Francisco, CA 94109. *Telephone:* 415-674-5500. *Fax:* 415-674-5555. *E-mail:* kimb@ciis.edu. *Web site:* http://www.ciis.edu.

Special note

The California Institute of Integral Studies (CIIS), with a tradition of innovative educational programs and a transformative approach to learning and change, offers accredited distance learning programs (PhD in transformative learning) for adults who are interested in change both on the level of the individual and of institutions—businesses, corporations, associations, schools, and governments. These programs provide a way for people who are dispersed in time and space to share interests, concerns, and ideas about personal and social change. The programs also allow students to individualize a course of study culminating in action research with practical results they can apply to their particular professional and personal concerns.

The distance learning program requires attendance at two 1-week seminars, one in August and one in March. Students take courses at a distance on the Institute's Web-based environment, which is supplemented by written, audio, and visual materials.

The monthly weekend residential learning community meets together for 3 academic years. Each year students also attend a weeklong seminar in August. Thereafter, students meet with their learning community in monthly 3-day weekend seminars (3 weekends each quarter for 3 academic years). This design facilitates collaborative small-group projects. In addition to the weekend seminars, students meet in small study groups either face-to-face or via computer conferencing.

DEGREE & CERTIFICATE PROGRAMS

Graduate Degrees

▶ *Learning and Change in Human Systems (PhD)*

In the fall of 1996 there were 150 students enrolled in this program. In 1995–96, 1 degree was earned at a distance through this program.
Application requirements *Prior education:* some graduate course work. *Other requirements:* college transcripts, letter(s) of recommendation, an application fee of $60, autobiography, resume/vita, goal statement, writing sample.
Completion requirements 130 units are required, 90 with advanced standing. 118 units must be completed through the institution. *Other requirements:* group and individual "Demonstration of Competency" is required in March of the third year.
On-campus requirements Weeklong seminar in August, four-day seminar in March.

INDIVIDUAL COURSE SUBJECT AREAS

Graduate
Interdisciplinary studies

Noncredit
Interdisciplinary studies

Profiles: California State University, Bakersfield

CALIFORNIA STATE UNIVERSITY, BAKERSFIELD

Bakersfield, California

Instructional Television Network

California State University, Bakersfield, founded in 1970, is a state-supported comprehensive institution. It is accredited by the Western Association of Schools and Colleges, Inc. It first offered distance learning courses in 1989.

Course delivery sites Courses are delivered to your home, other colleges.
Media Courses are delivered via videotapes, videoconferencing.
Restrictions Programs are available to local area students only.
Services Distance learners have access to library services at a distance.
Credit-earning options Students may transfer credits from another institution or may earn credits through examinations, portfolio assessment. Financial aid is available to distance learners.
Contact ITV Network, California State University, Bakersfield, 9001 Stockdale Highway, Bakersfield, CA 93311. *Telephone:* 805-664-2448.

DEGREE & CERTIFICATE PROGRAMS

Undergraduate Certificates
▶ *Environmental Resource Management*
Program contact Dr. Mark Evans, Professor, California State University, Bakersfield, 9001 Stockdale Highway, Bakersfield, CA 93311. Phone: 805-664-2461. Fax: 805-664-2049. E-mail: mevans@csubak.edu.

INDIVIDUAL COURSE SUBJECT AREAS

Undergraduate
Area, ethnic, and cultural studies; astronomy and astrophysics; biology; business administration and management; economics; fine arts; history; liberal arts, general studies, and humanities; philosophy and religion; political science

Graduate
Accounting

CALIFORNIA STATE UNIVERSITY, CHICO

Chico, California

Center for Regional and Continuing Education

California State University, Chico, founded in 1887, is a state-supported comprehensive institution. It is accredited by the Western Association of Schools and Colleges, Inc. It first offered distance learning courses in 1974. In 1996–97, it offered 60 courses at a distance. In the fall of 1996, there was a total of 700 students enrolled in distance learning courses.

Course delivery sites Courses are delivered to your workplace, military bases, other colleges, 38 off-campus centers in Alturas, Anderson, Beale AFB, Bishop, Blythe, Burney, Chester, Clearlake, Colusa, Covelo, Crescent City, Fort Bragg, Garden Valley, Healdsburg, Hoopa, Imperial, Kentfield, Lakeport, Marysville, Nevada City, Orland, Oroville, Paradise, Porterville, Quincy, Red Bluff, Redding, Seaside, South Lake Tahoe, Susanville, Taft, Tulelake, Victorville, Weaverville, Weed, Yreka.
Media Courses are delivered via videotapes, videoconferencing. Students and teachers interact via videoconferencing, mail, telephone, e-mail. A computer is required for some courses.
Restrictions Programs are available to in-state students only.
Services Distance learners have access to library services, academic advising, career placement assistance at a distance.
Credit-earning options Students may transfer credits from another institution or may earn credits through examinations, portfolio assessment.
Typical costs *Undergraduate:* Tuition of $1027 per semester. *Graduate:* Tuition of $1275 per course. Costs may vary by specific program of study, number of credits taken, course delivery options. Financial aid is available to distance learners.
Registration Students may register by mail, fax, phone.
Contact Jeffrey S. Layne, Telecommunications Specialist, California State University, Chico, Center for Regional and Continuing Education, Chico, CA 95929-0250. *Telephone:* 916-898-6105. *Fax:* 916-898-4020. *E-mail:* jlayne@oavax.csuchico.edu. *Web site:* http://www.csuchico.edu/cont/sat.

DEGREE & CERTIFICATE PROGRAMS

Baccalaureate Degrees

▶ *Liberal Studies (BA)*
Restrictions Program is available to students at established learning centers only.
Application requirements *Prior education:* associate degree. *Other requirements:* college transcripts.
Completion requirements 124 semester credits are required. 30 semester credits must be completed through the institution. This is a degree completion program. *Maximum time for completion:* seven years.
On-campus requirements Several courses which do not lend themselves to televised instruction will be offered on campus only, either in the regular session or summer session.

▶ *Political Science (BA)*
Restrictions Program is available to students at established learning centers only.
Application requirements *Prior education:* associate degree. *Other requirements:* college transcripts.
Completion requirements 124 semester credits are required. 30 semester credits must be completed through the institution. This is a degree completion program. *Maximum time for completion:* seven years.

▶ *Social Sciences (BA)*
Restrictions Program is available to students at established learning centers only.
Application requirements *Prior education:* associate degree. *Other requirements:* college transcripts.
Completion requirements 124 semester credits are required. 30 semester credits must be completed through the institution. This is a degree completion program. *Maximum time for completion:* seven years.

▶ *Sociology (BA)*
Restrictions Program is available to students at established learning centers only.
Application requirements *Prior education:* associate degree. *Other requirements:* college transcripts.
Completion requirements 124 semester credits are required. 30 semester credits must be completed through the institution. This is a degree completion program. *Maximum time for completion:* seven years.

Graduate Degrees

▶ *Computer Science (MS)*
In the fall of 1996 there were 220 students enrolled in this program.
Restrictions Only employees of participating companies may enroll.
Application requirements *Prior education:* baccalaureate degree.
Completion requirements 30 semester credits are required. 21 semester credits must be completed through the institution. *Maximum time for completion:* seven years.

INDIVIDUAL COURSE SUBJECT AREAS

Undergraduate
Computer and information sciences; liberal arts, general studies, and humanities; political science; social sciences; sociology

Graduate
Computer and information sciences

Noncredit
Computer and information sciences

CALIFORNIA STATE UNIVERSITY, DOMINGUEZ HILLS

Carson, California

Distance Learning

California State University, Dominguez Hills, founded in 1960, is a state-supported comprehensive institution. It is accredited by the Western Association of Schools and Colleges, Inc. It first offered distance learning courses in 1975. In 1996–97, it offered 45 courses at a distance. In the fall of 1996, there was a total of 2,500 students enrolled in distance learning courses.
Course delivery sites Courses are delivered to your home, your workplace, Coastline Community College (Fountain Valley), Mission College (Santa Clara), 4 off-campus centers in Los Angeles, Santa Ana.
Media Courses are delivered via television, videotapes, videoconferencing, audiotapes, World Wide Web, e-mail, print. Students and teachers interact via videoconferencing, mail, telephone, fax, e-mail. A computer is required for some courses.
Restrictions Availability varies by course, program, or delivery means.
Services Distance learners have access to library services, e-mail services, academic advising, tutoring at a distance.
Credit-earning options Students may transfer credits from another institution or may earn credits through examinations, business training.
Typical costs Tuition of $150 per semester hour. Costs may vary by specific program of study, course delivery options. Financial aid is available to distance learners.
Registration Students may register by mail, fax, phone, e-mail, World Wide Web.
Contact Warren Ashley, Director, Distance Learning, California State University, Dominguez Hills, 1000 East Victoria, Carson, CA 90747. *Telephone:* 310-243-2272. *Fax:* 310-516-4127. *E-mail:* washley@dhvx20.csudh.edu. *Web site:* http://www.csudh.edu/distance.

DEGREE & CERTIFICATE PROGRAMS

Baccalaureate Degrees
▶ *Nursing (BS)*
In the fall of 1996 there were 400 students enrolled in this program.
Application requirements *Prior education:* RN license. *Other requirements:* college transcripts, an application fee of $55, RN license.
Completion requirements 126 semester credits are required. 30 semester credits must be completed through the institution. *Maximum time for completion:* five years.
Program contact Kathleen Johnston, Coordinator, California State University, Dominguez Hills, Division of Nursing, 1000 East Victoria, Carson, CA 90747. Phone: 310-243-2021. Fax: 310-516-3542. E-mail: kjohnston@dhvx20.csudh.edu.

Graduate Degrees
▶ *Business Administration (MBA)*
In the fall of 1996 there were 100 students enrolled in this program. In 1995–96, 15 degrees were earned at a distance through this program.
Restrictions This program is available to in-state students only.
Application requirements *Prior education:* baccalaureate degree. *Other requirements:* GMAT, college transcripts, an application fee of $55.
Completion requirements 30 semester credits are required. 21 semester credits must be completed through the institution. *Maximum time for completion:* five years.
Program contact Lynn Hutcheson, Coordinator, California State University, Dominguez Hills, MBA Program, 1000 East Victoria, Carson, CA 90747. Phone: 310-243-3465. Fax: 310-516-4178. E-mail: lhutcheson@soma.csudh.edu.

▶ *Humanities (MA)*
In the fall of 1996 there were 600 students enrolled in this program. In 1995–96, 35 degrees were earned at a distance through this program.
Application requirements *Prior education:* baccalaureate degree. *Other requirements:* college transcripts, an essay or personal statement, an application fee of $55.
Completion requirements 30 semester credits are required. 21 semester credits must be completed through the institution. *Maximum time for completion:* five years.
Program contact Art Harshman, Coordinator, HUX, California State University, Dominguez Hills, 1000 East Victoria, Carson, CA 90747. Phone: 310-243-3743. Fax: 310-516-4399. E-mail: huxonline@dhux20.csudh.edu.

▶ *Negotiation and Conflict Management (MA)*
In the fall of 1996 there were 100 students enrolled in this program. In 1995–96, 30 degrees were earned at a distance through this program.
Restrictions This program is available to in-state students only.
Application requirements *Prior education:* baccalaureate degree. *Other requirements:* college transcripts, an application fee of $55.
Completion requirements 30 semester credits are required. 21 semester credits must be completed through the institution. *Maximum time for completion:* five years.

▶ *Quality Assurance (MS)*
In the fall of 1996 there were 100 students enrolled in this program.
Application requirements *Prior education:* baccalaureate degree. *Other requirements:* college transcripts, an application fee of $55.
Completion requirements 30 semester credits are required. 21 semester credits must be completed through the institution. *Maximum time for completion:* five years.
Program contact Scott Mackay, Director, California State University, Dominguez Hills, 1000 East Victoria, Carson, CA 90747. Phone: 310-243-3355. Fax: 310-516-3753. E-mail: smackay@dhvx20.csudh.edu.

INDIVIDUAL COURSE SUBJECT AREAS

Undergraduate
Area, ethnic, and cultural studies; drama and theater; liberal arts, general studies, and humanities; nursing; teacher education

Graduate
Business administration and management; education administration; teacher education

Noncredit
English as a second language (ESL)

Profiles: California State University, Fresno

CALIFORNIA STATE UNIVERSITY, FRESNO

Fresno, California

Academic Innovation Center

California State University, Fresno, founded in 1911, is a state-supported comprehensive institution. It is accredited by the Western Association of Schools and Colleges, Inc.
Course delivery sites Courses are delivered to other colleges.
Media Courses are delivered via television, videoconferencing, print.
Restrictions Programs are available to local area students only.
Services Distance learners have access to library services at a distance.
Credit-earning options Students may transfer credits from another institution or may earn credits through examinations, military training. Financial aid is available to distance learners.
Contact Administrative Coordinator, California State University, Fresno, 2225 East San Ramon Avenue, Fresno, CA 93740-0121. *Telephone:* 209-278-5766. *Fax:* 209-278-7026.

DEGREE & CERTIFICATE PROGRAMS

Baccalaureate Degrees

▶ *Liberal Studies (BA)*
Program contact Jaques Benninga, Coordinator, California State University, Fresno, 5005 North Maple Avenue, Fresno, CA 93740-0202. Phone: 209-278-0250. Fax: 209-278-0404. E-mail: jaques_benninga@csufresno.edu.

Graduate Degrees

▶ *Education Administration and Supervision (MS)*
Program contact Dr. Donald G. Coleman, Coordinator, California State University, Fresno, 5005 North Maple Avenue, Fresno, CA 93740-0303. Phone: 209-278-0350. Fax: 209-278-0404. E-mail: don_coleman@csufresno.edu.

Undergraduate Certificates

▶ *Cross-cultural Language and Academic Development (CLAD) Certificate Program*
On-campus requirements Two weekends.
Program contact Jaques Bennings, Chair, Department of Literacy and Early Education, California State University, Fresno, 5005 North Maple Avenue, Fresno, CA 93740-0202. Phone: 209-278-0250. Fax: 209-278-0404. E-mail: jaques_benninga@csufresno.edu.

INDIVIDUAL COURSE SUBJECT AREAS

Undergraduate
Area, ethnic, and cultural studies; biology; business administration and management; developmental and child psychology; economics; education; education administration; English as a second language (ESL); English language and literature; European languages and literatures; liberal arts, general studies, and humanities; music; nursing; psychology; social psychology; social sciences; teacher education; visual and performing arts

Graduate
Education; teacher education

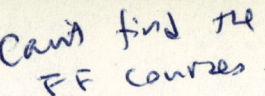
Can't find the FF courses.

CALIFORNIA STATE UNIVERSITY, FULLERTON

Fullerton, California

California State University, Fullerton, founded in 1957, is a state-supported comprehensive institution. It is accredited by the Western Association of Schools and Colleges, Inc.
Course delivery sites Courses are delivered to your workplace, other colleges.
Media Courses are delivered via television, videoconferencing.
Services Distance learners have access to library services, academic advising at a distance.
Credit-earning options Students may transfer credits from another institution or may earn credits through examinations. Financial aid is available to distance learners.
Contact Admissions, California State University, Fullerton, PO Box 34080, Fullerton, CA 92834-9480. Telephone: 714-773-2300. Fax: 714-773-2341. 714-278-2611

DEGREE & CERTIFICATE PROGRAMS

Baccalaureate Degrees

▶ *Nursing (BSN)*
Application requirements *Prior education:* AA in nursing.
Program contact Dr. Julia George, Chair, Department of Nursing, California State University, Fullerton, PO Box 34080, Fullerton, CA 92634-9480. Phone: 714-773-3308.

Graduate Degrees

▶ *Electrical Engineering (MSEE)*
Program contact Dr. Hamidian, Graduate Advisor, Electrical Engineering, California State University, Fullerton, 800 North State College Boulevard, Fullerton, CA 92634-9480. Phone: 714-773-3013. Fax: 714-449-7162.

INDIVIDUAL COURSE SUBJECT AREAS

Undergraduate
Advertising; electrical engineering; health and physical education/fitness; liberal arts, general studies, and humanities; nursing

Graduate
Accounting; business; business administration and management

CALIFORNIA STATE UNIVERSITY, HAYWARD

Hayward, California

Instructional Media Center

California State University, Hayward, founded in 1957, is a state-supported comprehensive institution. It is accredited by the Western Association of Schools and Colleges, Inc. It first offered distance learning courses in 1993.
Course delivery sites Courses are delivered to your home, other colleges.
Media Courses are delivered via television, videotapes, World Wide Web. Students and teachers interact via videoconferencing, audioconferencing, mail, telephone, fax, e-mail.
Services Distance learners have access to library services at a distance.
Credit-earning options Students may transfer credits from another institution or may earn credits through examinations.

Typical costs In-state students pay $378 for 1-6 units or $600 for 7 or more units. Non-residents pay in-state tuition plus an additional $164 per unit. Financial aid is available to distance learners.
Contact Enrollment Services, California State University, Hayward, Hayward, CA 94542. *Telephone:* 510-885-2624.

INDIVIDUAL COURSE SUBJECT AREAS

Undergraduate

Accounting; biology; business; business administration and management; computer and information sciences; fine arts; health professions and related sciences; history; industrial psychology; liberal arts, general studies, and humanities; library and information studies; nursing; philosophy and religion; political science; social psychology; teacher education

CALIFORNIA STATE UNIVERSITY, LONG BEACH

Long Beach, California

University College and Extension Services

California State University, Long Beach, founded in 1949, is a state-supported comprehensive institution. It is accredited by the Western Association of Schools and Colleges, Inc. It first offered distance learning courses in 1988. In 1996–97, it offered 15 courses at a distance. In the fall of 1996, there was a total of 110 students enrolled in distance learning courses.
Course delivery sites Courses are delivered to your home, your workplace, California State University, Chico (Chico), Humboldt State University (Arcata), Porterville College (Porterville), Taft College (Taft), 6 off-campus centers in Avalon, Bakersfield, Hi-Hill, Oakland, San Jose, Tracy.
Media Courses are delivered via television, videotapes, videoconferencing, audioconferencing, computer software, World Wide Web, e-mail, print. Students and teachers interact via videoconferencing, audioconferencing, mail, telephone, fax, e-mail. A computer is required for some courses.
Restrictions Availability varies by course, program, or delivery means.
Services Distance learners have access to library services, the campus computer network, e-mail services, academic advising at a distance.
Credit-earning options Students may transfer credits from another institution or may earn credits through portfolio assessment, military training, business training.
Typical costs *Undergraduate:* Tuition of $175 per unit. *Graduate:* Tuition of $200 per unit. *Noncredit courses:* $545 per course. Costs may vary by specific program of study, course delivery options. Financial aid is available to distance learners enrolled full-time.
Registration Students may register by mail, fax, phone, e-mail, World Wide Web.
Contact Wendy Ito, Distance Learning Specialist, California State University, Long Beach, 6300 State University Drive, Suite 104, Long Beach, CA 90815. *Telephone:* 562-985-7754. *Fax:* 562-985-8449. *E-mail:* ideas@uces.csulb.edu. *Web site:* http://www.uces.csulb.edu.

DEGREE & CERTIFICATE PROGRAMS

Baccalaureate Degrees
▶ *Vocational Education (BA)*
In the fall of 1996 there were 35 students enrolled in this program. In 1995–96, 5 degrees were earned at a distance through this program.
Restrictions This program is available to in-state students only. Program is offered only at specific locations.

Application requirements *Prior education:* some undergraduate course work. *Other requirements:* college transcripts, an application fee of $55, seven years full-time work experience or the equivalent.
Completion requirements 124 quarter credits are required. 30 semester credits must be completed through the institution.

Graduate Degrees
▶ *Social Work (MSW)*
In the fall of 1996 there were 40 students enrolled in this program.
Restrictions This program is available to in-state students only. Program is offered only at specific locations.
Application requirements *Prior education:* baccalaureate degree. *Other requirements:* SAT, college transcripts, an essay or personal statement, letter(s) of recommendation, an application fee of $55.
Completion requirements 60 semester hours are required. 54 semester hours must be completed through the institution. *Maximum time for completion:* seven years.
Program contact Ginger Wilson, Graduate Coordinator, Social Work, California State University, Long Beach, 1250 Bellflower Boulevard, Long Beach, CA 90840-0119. Phone: 562-985-5654. Fax: 562-985-5514.

INDIVIDUAL COURSE SUBJECT AREAS

Undergraduate
Educational psychology; finance; home economics and family studies

Graduate
Educational psychology; social work

CALIFORNIA STATE UNIVERSITY, LOS ANGELES

Los Angeles, California

Office of Continuing Education

California State University, Los Angeles, founded in 1947, is a state-supported comprehensive institution. It is accredited by the Western Association of Schools and Colleges, Inc. It first offered distance learning courses in 1987.
Course delivery sites Courses are delivered to your home, your workplace, other colleges.
Media Courses are delivered via television, videotapes, audioconferencing.
Services Distance learners have access to library services at a distance.
Credit-earning options Students may transfer credits from another institution or may earn credits through examinations. Financial aid is available to distance learners.
Contact Coordinator, California State University, Los Angeles, Office of Continuing Education, 5151 State University Drive, Room 3022 Library North, Los Angeles, CA 90032-8619. *Telephone:* 213-343-4916. *Fax:* 213-343-4954. *Web site:* http://bestla.calstatela.edu/www/lifelong/learning.html.

DEGREE & CERTIFICATE PROGRAMS

Baccalaureate Degrees
▶ *Fire Science (BS)*

INDIVIDUAL COURSE SUBJECT AREAS

Undergraduate
Accounting; anthropology; electrical engineering; industrial engineering; microbiology; political science; radio and television broadcasting; teacher education

Profiles: California State University, Los Angeles

Noncredit
Accounting; anthropology; electrical engineering; industrial engineering; microbiology; political science; radio and television broadcasting; teacher education

CALIFORNIA STATE UNIVERSITY, NORTHRIDGE

Northridge, California

Educational Technologies and Distance Learning Services

California State University, Northridge, founded in 1958, is a state-supported comprehensive institution. It is accredited by the Western Association of Schools and Colleges, Inc. It first offered distance learning courses in 1982. In 1996–97, it offered 40 courses at a distance. In the fall of 1996, there was a total of 200 students enrolled in distance learning courses.
Course delivery sites Courses are delivered to your home, your workplace, military bases, Antelope Valley College (Lancaster), 7 off-campus centers in China Lake, Edwards, El Segundo, Lancaster, Thousand Oaks, Woodland Hills.
Media Courses are delivered via television, videotapes, computer software, World Wide Web, e-mail, print. Students and teachers interact via videoconferencing, audioconferencing, mail, telephone, fax, e-mail. A computer is required for some courses. The institution provides assistance with acquiring computer equipment.
Restrictions Courses are available to students in northeast California only.
Services Distance learners have access to library services, the campus computer network, e-mail services, academic advising at a distance.
Credit-earning options Students may earn credits through examinations.
Typical costs Contact university for details. Financial aid is available to distance learners enrolled part-time.
Registration Students may register by phone, World Wide Web.
Contact Peg Auchterlonie, Executive Director, California State University, Northridge, 18111 Nordhoff Street, Northridge, CA 91330-8324. *Telephone:* 800-882-0128. *Fax:* 818-677-2316. *E-mail:* pauchterlonie@huey.csun.edu.

DEGREE & CERTIFICATE PROGRAMS

Baccalaureate Degrees
▶ *Communicative Disorders (BA)*
In the fall of 1996 there were 40 students enrolled in this program.
Application requirements *Prior education:* some undergraduate course work. *Other requirements:* college transcripts, an essay or personal statement, letter(s) of recommendation, an application fee of $50.

▶ *Engineering Management (BS)*
Application requirements *Prior education:* some undergraduate course work. *Other requirements:* college transcripts, an essay or personal statement, letter(s) of recommendation, an application fee of $50.

▶ *Special Education (BA)*
Application requirements *Prior education:* some undergraduate course work. *Other requirements:* college transcripts, an essay or personal statement, letter(s) of recommendation, an application fee of $50.

Graduate Degrees
▶ *Electrical Engineering (MS)*
In the fall of 1996 there were 90 students enrolled in this program.
Application requirements *Prior education:* baccalaureate degree. *Other requirements:* college transcripts, an essay or personal statement, letter(s) of recommendation, an application fee of $50.

▶ *Mechanical Engineering (MS)*
In the fall of 1996 there were 90 students enrolled in this program.
Application requirements *Prior education:* baccalaureate degree. *Other requirements:* college transcripts, an essay or personal statement, letter(s) of recommendation, an application fee of $50.

INDIVIDUAL COURSE SUBJECT AREAS

Undergraduate
Aerospace, aeronautical engineering; civil engineering; electrical engineering; engineering mechanics; mechanical engineering

Graduate
Aerospace, aeronautical engineering; civil engineering; electrical engineering; engineering mechanics; engineering/industrial management; mechanical engineering

CALIFORNIA STATE UNIVERSITY, SACRAMENTO

Sacramento, California

California State University, Sacramento, founded in 1947, is a state-supported comprehensive institution. It is accredited by the Western Association of Schools and Colleges, Inc. It first offered distance learning courses in 1987. In 1996–97, it offered 34 courses at a distance. In the fall of 1996, there was a total of 1,266 students enrolled in distance learning courses.
Course delivery sites Courses are delivered to your home, your workplace, California State University, Chico (Chico), California State University, Stanislaus (Turlock), Sierra College (Rocklin), Solano Community College (Suisun City), 1 off-campus center in Lodi, Nevada County Office of Education.
Media Courses are delivered via television, videoconferencing, World Wide Web. Students and teachers interact via videoconferencing, mail, telephone, fax, e-mail. A computer is required for some courses.
Restrictions Students must be able to travel to receive sites.
Services Distance learners have access to library services, the campus computer network, e-mail services, academic advising, tutoring, career placement assistance at a distance.
Credit-earning options Students may transfer credits from another institution.
Typical costs *Undergraduate:* Tuition of $975 per semester for in-state residents. *Graduate:* Tuition of $975 per semester for in-state residents. *Noncredit courses:* $69–$600 per course. Costs may vary by specific program of study, number of credits taken, term of enrollment. Financial aid is available to distance learners enrolled full-time or part-time.
Registration Students may register by mail, phone, World Wide Web.
Contact Regional and Continuing Education Office, California State University, Sacramento, 7750 College Town Drive, Suite 100, Sacramento, CA 95826. *Telephone:* 916-278-4433. *Fax:* 916-278-4602.

DEGREE & CERTIFICATE PROGRAMS

Graduate Degrees
▶ *Nursing (MS)*
In the fall of 1996 there were 23 students enrolled in this program.
Application requirements *Prior education:* baccalaureate degree. *Other requirements:* GRE, college transcripts, an essay or personal statement, letter(s) of recommendation, 2.5 GPA, prerequisite course work and undergraduate research and statistics.
Completion requirements 36 units are required. 21 units must be completed through the institution. *Maximum time for completion:* seven years.

INDIVIDUAL COURSE SUBJECT AREAS

Undergraduate
Anthropology; biology; business administration and management; business communications; computer and information sciences; conservation and natural resources; criminal justice; electrical engineering; environmental health; European history; French language and literature; German language and literature; health professions and related sciences; history; home economics and family studies; management information systems; philosophy and religion; social sciences; sociology; statistics

Graduate
Curriculum and instruction; nursing; special education; teacher education

CALIFORNIA STATE UNIVERSITY, STANISLAUS

Turlock, California

Provost's Office

California State University, Stanislaus, founded in 1957, is a state-supported comprehensive institution. It is accredited by the Western Association of Schools and Colleges, Inc. It first offered distance learning courses in 1981. In 1996–97, it offered 85 courses at a distance. In the fall of 1996, there was a total of 1,360 students enrolled in distance learning courses.
Course delivery sites Courses are delivered to San Joaquin Delta College (Stockton), 3 off-campus centers in Dos Palos, Manteca, Tracy.
Media Courses are delivered via television, videoconferencing. Students and teachers interact via videoconferencing, mail, telephone, fax, e-mail. A computer is required for some courses.
Restrictions Programs are available to local area students only.
Services Distance learners have access to library services, the campus computer network, e-mail services, academic advising, tutoring, career placement assistance at a distance.
Credit-earning options Students may transfer credits from another institution or may earn credits through portfolio assessment, military training.
Typical costs *Undergraduate:* Tuition of $1915 per year plus mandatory fees of $100 per unit for in-state residents. Tuition of $1915 per year plus mandatory fees of $100 per unit for out-of-state residents. *Graduate:* Tuition of $1915 per year plus mandatory fees of $100 per unit for in-state residents. Tuition of $1915 per year plus mandatory fees of $100 per unit for out-of-state residents. *Noncredit courses:* $125 per unit. Costs may vary by number of credits taken. Financial aid is available to distance learners.
Registration Students may register by phone.
Contact Samuel A. Oppenheim, Coordinator of Regional Distance Learning, California State University, Stanislaus, 801 West Monte Vista Avenue, Turlock, CA 95382. *Telephone:* 209-667-3319. *Fax:* 209-667-3299. *E-mail:* oppenhei@toto.csustan.edu.

DEGREE & CERTIFICATE PROGRAMS

Baccalaureate Degrees

▶ *Communication Studies (BA)*
In the fall of 1996 there were 266 students enrolled in this program.
Application requirements *Prior education:* some undergraduate course work. *Other requirements:* SAT or ACT, high school transcript, college transcripts, an application fee of $55, 3.6 GPA if out-of-state, in-state students must be in top 30% of graduating class.
Completion requirements 124 units are required.

Program contact Dr. Fred Hilpert, Communications Studies, California State University, Stanislaus, 801 West Monte Vista Avenue, Turlock, CA 95350. Phone: 209-667-3270. Fax: 209-667-3525. E-mail: fredh@toto.csustan.edu.

▶ *History (BA)*
In the fall of 1996 there were 254 students enrolled in this program.
Application requirements *Prior education:* some undergraduate course work. *Other requirements:* SAT or ACT, high school transcript, college transcripts, an application fee of $55, 3.6 GPA if out-of-state, in-state students must be in top 30% of graduating class.
Completion requirements 30 units are required. 30 units must be completed through the institution. This is a degree completion program.
Program contact Dr. Austin Ahanotu, Chair, History Department, California State University, Stanislaus, 801 West Monte Vista Avenue, Turlock, CA 95382. Phone: 209-667-3238. Fax: 209-667-3299. E-mail: aahanotu@toto.csustan.edu.

INDIVIDUAL COURSE SUBJECT AREAS

Undergraduate
Accounting; anthropology; area, ethnic, and cultural studies; biological and life sciences; business; business administration and management; chemistry; cognitive psychology; communications; computer and information sciences; economics; English language and literature; history; journalism; liberal arts, general studies, and humanities; mathematics; nursing; psychology; social sciences; sociology; visual and performing arts

Graduate
Accounting; business; business administration and management; computer and information sciences

CALVIN COLLEGE

Grand Rapids, Michigan

Calvin College, founded in 1876, is an independent-religious comprehensive institution affiliated with the Christian Reformed Church. It is accredited by the North Central Association of Colleges and Schools. It first offered distance learning courses in 1995.
Course delivery sites Courses are delivered to your home, other colleges.
Media Courses are delivered via videoconferencing, computer software, computer conferencing.
Services Distance learners have access to library services at a distance.
Contact Director of Graduate Studies, Calvin College, 3201 Burton, SE, Grand Rapids, MI 49546. *Telephone:* 616-957-8533. *Fax:* 616-957-6601.

INDIVIDUAL COURSE SUBJECT AREAS

Graduate
Biological and life sciences; communications; European languages and literatures; health professions and related sciences; liberal arts, general studies, and humanities; physical sciences; teacher education; visual and performing arts

Profiles: Camden County College

CAMDEN COUNTY COLLEGE

Blackwood, New Jersey

Extended Educational Services

Camden County College, founded in 1967, is a state and locally supported two-year college. It is accredited by the Middle States Association of Colleges and Schools. It first offered distance learning courses in 1995. In 1996–97, it offered 25 courses at a distance. In the fall of 1996, there was a total of 655 students enrolled in distance learning courses.
Course delivery sites Courses are delivered to your home, your workplace.
Media Courses are delivered via television, videoconferencing. Students and teachers interact via videoconferencing, mail, telephone, fax, e-mail.
Services Distance learners have access to library services, e-mail services at a distance.
Credit-earning options Students may transfer credits from another institution or may earn credits through standardized exams, institutionally developed exams, portfolio assessment, military training.
Typical costs Tuition of $56 per credit for local area residents. Tuition of $60 per credit for in-state residents. Tuition of $60 per credit for out-of-state residents. $25 per course telecourse fee; general service fee of $19 term (part-time), $32 term (full-time). *Noncredit courses:* $35–$50 per course. Costs may vary by specific program of study, number of credits taken, course delivery options. Financial aid is available to distance learners enrolled full-time or part-time.
Registration Students may register by mail, fax, phone.
Contact Anthony C. Cherby, Dean of Extended Educational Services, Camden County College, PO Box 200, Blackwood, NJ 08012-0200. *Telephone:* 609-227-7200, Ext. 4271. *Fax:* 609-374-4892. *E-mail:* cerbino@aol.com.

INDIVIDUAL COURSE SUBJECT AREAS

Undergraduate
Business; developmental and child psychology; economics; English language and literature; European languages and literatures; health and physical education/fitness; history; journalism; law and legal studies; liberal arts, general studies, and humanities; philosophy and religion; psychology; sociology

CAPE COD COMMUNITY COLLEGE

West Barnstable, Massachusetts

Distance Learning

Cape Cod Community College, founded in 1961, is a state-supported two-year college. It is accredited by the New England Association of Schools and Colleges. It first offered distance learning courses in 1993. In 1996–97, it offered 14 courses at a distance. In the fall of 1996, there was a total of 150 students enrolled in distance learning courses.
Course delivery sites Courses are delivered to your home, military bases.
Media Courses are delivered via videotapes, videoconferencing. Students and teachers interact via videoconferencing, mail, telephone, fax, e-mail.
Services Distance learners have access to library services at a distance.
Credit-earning options Students may transfer credits from another institution or may earn credits through standardized exams.
Typical costs Tuition of $118.50 per course plus mandatory fees of $141 per course. Costs may vary by number of credits taken. Financial aid is available to distance learners enrolled full-time or part-time.
Registration Students may register by mail, fax, phone.
Contact Steven Leclair, Director of Distance Learning, Cape Cod Community College, 2240 Iyanough Road, West Barnstable, MA 02668-1599. *Telephone:* 508-375-4040. *Fax:* 508-375-4041. *E-mail:* sleclair@ccsnet.com.

INDIVIDUAL COURSE SUBJECT AREAS

Undergraduate
Business administration and management; English composition; English language and literature; fine arts; mathematics; nursing; psychology; social psychology; sociology

CAPITOL COLLEGE

Laurel, Maryland

Capitol College, founded in 1964, is an independent-nonprofit comprehensive institution. It is accredited by the Middle States Association of Colleges and Schools. It first offered distance learning courses in 1995. In 1996–97, it offered 4 courses at a distance. In the fall of 1996, there was a total of 5 students enrolled in distance learning courses.
Course delivery sites Courses are delivered to your home, Charles County Community College (La Plata), Montgomery College–Rockville Campus (Rockville).
Media Courses are delivered via videoconferencing. Students and teachers interact via videoconferencing.
Restrictions Programs are available to local area students only.
Services Distance learners have access to tutoring at a distance.
Credit-earning options Students may transfer credits from another institution or may earn credits through standardized exams, military training.
Typical costs Tuition of $368 per credit. Costs may vary by campus or location. Financial aid is available to distance learners.
Registration Students may register by mail, fax.
Contact Robert Weiler, Department Chairperson, EE Department, Capitol College, 11301 Springfield Road, Laurel, MD 20708. *Telephone:* 301-953-3200. *Fax:* 301-953-3876. *E-mail:* rweiler@capitol-college.edu.

DEGREE & CERTIFICATE PROGRAMS

Baccalaureate Degrees
▶ *Engineering (BSEE)*
Application requirements *Prior education:* high school diploma or equivalent.
Completion requirements 136 credits are required. 40 credits must be completed through the institution.
Program contact Tony Miller, Director of Admission, Capitol College, 11301 Springfield Road, Laurel, MD 20708. Phone: 301-953-3200. Fax: 301-953-1442. E-mail: admissions@capitol-college edu.

INDIVIDUAL COURSE SUBJECT AREAS

Undergraduate
Electrical engineering

CARLETON UNIVERSITY

Ottawa, Ontario, Canada

Instructional Television

Carleton University, founded in 1942, is a province-supported university. It is provincially chartered. It first offered distance learning courses in 1978. In 1996–97, it offered 58 courses at a distance. In the fall of 1996, there was a total of 5,000 students enrolled in distance learning courses.
Course delivery sites Courses are delivered to your home.
Media Courses are delivered via television, videotapes, World Wide Web. Students and teachers interact via mail, telephone, e-mail.
Restrictions Certain courses require students to come to campus.
Services Distance learners have access to library services, e-mail services, academic advising, tutoring at a distance.
Credit-earning options Students may transfer credits from another institution or may earn credits through institutionally developed exams.
Typical costs Tuition of $650 per course. Mandatory fees or service charges for delivery and remote exam services extra. Financial aid is available to distance learners enrolled full-time or part-time.
Registration Students may register by mail, phone.
Contact Beverlae Buckland, Manager and Instructor of Student Services, Carleton University, Room 302, Robertson Hall, 1125 Col. By Drive, Ottawa, ON K1S 5B6, Canada. *Telephone:* 613-520-2600, Ext. 3509. *Fax:* 613-520-4456. *E-mail:* bbucklan@ccs.carleton.ca.

INDIVIDUAL COURSE SUBJECT AREAS

Undergraduate
Abnormal psychology; accounting; anthropology; architecture; astronomy and astrophysics; biological and life sciences; biology; business; chemistry; civil engineering; cognitive psychology; developmental and child psychology; economics; engineering; English language and literature; European languages and literatures; geography; geology; history; law and legal studies; liberal arts, general studies, and humanities; philosophy and religion; physical sciences; physics; political science; psychology; public administration and services; social psychology; social sciences; social work; sociology

CARL SANDBURG COLLEGE

Galesburg, Illinois

Carl Sandburg College, founded in 1967, is a state and locally supported two-year college. It is accredited by the North Central Association of Colleges and Schools. It first offered distance learning courses in 1986. In 1996–97, it offered 31 courses at a distance. In the fall of 1996, there was a total of 256 students enrolled in distance learning courses.
Course delivery sites Courses are delivered to your home, your workplace, Black Hawk College (Moline), 2 off-campus centers in Galesburg.
Media Courses are delivered via videoconferencing. Students and teachers interact via videoconferencing, in-person meetings.
Restrictions Programs are available to in-state students only.
Services Distance learners have access to library services, academic advising, tutoring, career placement assistance at a distance.
Credit-earning options Students may transfer credits from another institution or may earn credits through institutionally developed exams, portfolio assessment, military training, business training.
Typical costs Tuition of $47 per semester hour plus mandatory fees of $6 per semester hour for local area residents. Tuition of $116.25 per semester hour plus mandatory fees of $6 per semester hour for in-state residents. Tuition of $201.83 per semester hour plus mandatory fees of $6 per semester hour for out-of-state residents. *Noncredit courses:* $50 per course. Financial aid is available to distance learners enrolled full-time.
Registration Students may register by mail, fax, phone.
Contact Carol Kreider, Director of Admissions and Records, Carl Sandburg College, 2232 South Lake Storey Drive, Galesburg, IL 61401. *Telephone:* 309-341-5234. *Fax:* 309-344-3291. *E-mail:* cscaro@misslink.net.

INDIVIDUAL COURSE SUBJECT AREAS

Undergraduate
Accounting; administrative and secretarial services; agriculture; anthropology; art history and criticism; business; business administration and management; business law; child care and development; economics; educational psychology; English composition; English literature; geography; history; human resources management; mathematics; nursing; political science; psychology; public health; sociology; teacher education

CATAWBA VALLEY COMMUNITY COLLEGE

Hickory, North Carolina

Telecommunications Department

Catawba Valley Community College, founded in 1960, is a state and locally supported two-year college. It is accredited by the Southern Association of Colleges and Schools. It first offered distance learning courses in 1983. In 1996–97, it offered 26 courses at a distance. In the fall of 1996, there was a total of 300 students enrolled in distance learning courses.
Course delivery sites Courses are delivered to your home, North Carolina Information Highway Fiber Optics Network sites.
Media Courses are delivered via television, videotapes, computer software. Students and teachers interact via mail, telephone, fax.
Services Distance learners have access to library services, the campus computer network, academic advising, tutoring, career placement assistance at a distance.
Credit-earning options Students may transfer credits from another institution or may earn credits through institutionally developed exams.
Typical costs Tuition of $65 per course for in-state residents. Tuition of $492 per course for out-of-state residents. Costs may vary by number of credits taken. Financial aid is available to distance learners enrolled full-time or part-time.
Contact Dr. Linda Lutz, Coordinator, Distance Education, Catawba Valley Community College, 2550 Highway 70 SE, Hickory, NC 28602. *Telephone:* 704-327-7000, Ext. 130. *Fax:* 704-324-5130. *E-mail:* llutz@linus.cvcc.cc.nc.us.

DEGREE & CERTIFICATE PROGRAMS

Undergraduate Certificates
▶ *Business Administration, Health Care Management Technology*
On-campus requirements For orientation.

INDIVIDUAL COURSE SUBJECT AREAS

Undergraduate
Advertising; business; business administration and management; creative writing; developmental and child psychology; economics; English

Distance Learning Programs

Profiles: Catawba Valley Community College

composition; English language and literature; health professions and related sciences; history; mathematics; philosophy and religion; social psychology; sociology; teacher education

CATONSVILLE COMMUNITY COLLEGE

Catonsville, Maryland

Educational Communications and Technology (ECT)

Catonsville Community College, founded in 1957, is a county-supported two-year college. It is accredited by the Middle States Association of Colleges and Schools. It first offered distance learning courses in 1972. In 1996–97, it offered 56 courses at a distance. In the fall of 1996, there was a total of 650 students enrolled in distance learning courses.
Course delivery sites Courses are delivered to your home, Baltimore City Community College (Baltimore), Carroll Community College (Westminster), Dundalk Community College (Baltimore), Essex Community College (Baltimore), 2 off-campus centers in Hunt Valley, Owings Mills.
Media Courses are delivered via television, videotapes, videoconferencing, audiotapes, computer software, World Wide Web. Students and teachers interact via videoconferencing, mail, telephone, fax, e-mail. A computer is required for some courses.
Restrictions Telecourses require 3–4 on campus meetings which can be waived by professor.
Services Distance learners have access to library services, the campus computer network, e-mail services, tutoring at a distance.
Credit-earning options Students may transfer credits from another institution or may earn credits through standardized exams, portfolio assessment, military training, articulation agreements with public and private secondary schools.
Typical costs Tuition of $60 per credit plus mandatory fees of $5 per hour for local area residents. Tuition of $106 per credit plus mandatory fees of $5 per hour for in-state residents. Tuition of $166 per credit plus mandatory fees of $5 per hour for out-of-state residents. Financial aid is available to distance learners enrolled full-time or part-time.
Registration Students may register by mail.
Contact Joel C. Martin, Coordinator of Telecourses, Catonsville Community College, 800 South Rolling Road, Catonsville, MD 21228. *Telephone:* 410-455-4584. *Fax:* 410-455-6106. *E-mail:* aa19@catmus.cat.cc.md.us. *Web site:* http://www.cat.cc.md.us/ect.

INDIVIDUAL COURSE SUBJECT AREAS

Undergraduate

Abnormal psychology; accounting; African-American studies; American (US) history; anthropology; astronomy and astrophysics; business; business administration and management; business communications; business law; chemistry; community health services; creative writing; developmental and child psychology; earth science; economics; educational psychology; English composition; English literature; environmental science; fire science; French language and literature; geology; German language and literature; gerontology; health and physical education/fitness; history; individual and family development studies; information sciences and systems; Japanese language and literature; marketing; mathematics; oceanography; philosophy and religion; political science; psychology; Russian language and literature; social psychology; sociology; Spanish language and literature

CENTRAL ARIZONA COLLEGE

Coolidge, Arizona

Central Arizona College, founded in 1961, is a county-supported two-year college. It is accredited by the North Central Association of Colleges and Schools. In 1996–97, it offered 60 courses at a distance. In the fall of 1996, there was a total of 1,800 students enrolled in distance learning courses.
Course delivery sites Courses are delivered to your workplace, 2 off-campus centers in Winkelman, Apache Junction, Arizona Learning Systems Network.
Media Courses are delivered via television, World Wide Web, print. Students and teachers interact via videoconferencing, telephone, site visits. A computer is required for some courses.
Restrictions Programs are available to in-state students only.
Services Distance learners have access to library services, the campus computer network, tutoring at a distance.
Credit-earning options Students may transfer credits from another institution or may earn credits through standardized exams, institutionally developed exams.
Typical costs Tuition of $28 per credit for in-state residents. Tuition of $81 per credit for out-of-state residents. Costs may vary by specific program of study, number of credits taken. Financial aid is available to distance learners enrolled full-time or part-time.
Registration Students may register by mail, phone.
Contact Admissions Office, Central Arizona College, 8470 North Overfield Road, Coolidge, AZ 85228. *Telephone:* 520-426-4260.

INDIVIDUAL COURSE SUBJECT AREAS

Undergraduate

Algebra; American (US) history; American literature; anthropology; area, ethnic, and cultural studies; art history and criticism; biological and life sciences; business; business law; chemistry; child care and development; communications; education; English composition; foods and nutrition studies; health professions and related sciences; mathematics; music; protective services; psychology; sociology; Spanish language and literature; visual and performing arts

CENTRAL BAPTIST THEOLOGICAL SEMINARY

Kansas City, Kansas

Long Distance Learning

Central Baptist Theological Seminary, founded in 1901, is an independent-religious graduate institution. It is accredited by the North Central Association of Colleges and Schools. It first offered distance learning courses in 1989. In 1996–97, it offered 2 courses at a distance. In the fall of 1996, there was a total of 17 students enrolled in distance learning courses.
Course delivery sites Courses are delivered to your home, churches.
Media Courses are delivered via videotapes, audioconferencing. Students and teachers interact via videoconferencing, audioconferencing, telephone.
Credit-earning options Students may transfer credits from another institution.
Typical costs Tuition of $165 per credit hour plus mandatory fees of $45 per semester. *Noncredit courses:* $66 per credit hour.
Contact Tom Davis, Director of Student Life and Enrollment Services, Central Baptist Theological Seminary, 741 North 31st, Kansas City, KS 66102-3964. *Telephone:* 913-371-5313. *Fax:* 913-371-8110.

INDIVIDUAL COURSE SUBJECT AREAS

Graduate
Theological studies

Noncredit
Theological studies

CENTRAL COMMUNITY COLLEGE–GRAND ISLAND CAMPUS

Grand Island, Nebraska

Central Community College–Grand Island Campus, founded in 1976, is a state and locally supported two-year college. It is accredited by the North Central Association of Colleges and Schools. It first offered distance learning courses in 1992.
Course delivery sites Courses are delivered to your home, your workplace, other colleges.
Media Courses are delivered via television, videotapes, videoconferencing, audiotapes, audioconferencing, computer software, World Wide Web, e-mail, print. Students and teachers interact via videoconferencing, audioconferencing, mail, telephone, fax, e-mail.
Services Distance learners have access to library services, academic advising, career placement assistance at a distance.
Credit-earning options Students may transfer credits from another institution or may earn credits through portfolio assessment, military training, business training.
Typical costs Tuition of $42 per credit hour for in-state residents. Tuition of $57.90 per credit hour for out-of-state residents. Financial aid is available to distance learners.
Contact Sarah C. Cunningham, Instructional Advancement, Central Community College–Grand Island Campus, PO Box 4903, Grand Island, NE 68802-4903. *Telephone:* 308-389-6387. *Fax:* 308-389-6398. *E-mail:* cungacc@cccadm.cccneb.edu.

DEGREE & CERTIFICATE PROGRAMS

Associate Degrees
▶*Accounting (AAS)*
▶*Business Administration (AA, AAS)*
▶*General Studies (AA)*
▶*Information Services (AAS)*
On-campus requirements For lab requirements.

Undergraduate Certificates
▶*Accounting*
▶*Agricultural Marketing*
▶*Basic Electronics*
On-campus requirements For lab requirements.
▶*Business Administration*
▶*Information Technology*
▶*Legal Office*
▶*Management Assistant*
▶*Manufacturing Engineering*
On-campus requirements For lab requirements.

▶*Medical Office*

INDIVIDUAL COURSE SUBJECT AREAS

Undergraduate
Accounting; administrative and secretarial services; advertising; agriculture; area, ethnic, and cultural studies; astronomy and astrophysics; business; business administration and management; communications; computer and information sciences; creative writing; developmental and child psychology; economics; English composition; English language and literature; geology; history; industrial engineering; law and legal studies; liberal arts, general studies, and humanities; mathematics; nursing; social psychology; sociology; Spanish language and literature

CENTRAL FLORIDA COMMUNITY COLLEGE

Ocala, Florida

Central Florida Community College, founded in 1957, is a state and locally supported two-year college. It is accredited by the Southern Association of Colleges and Schools. It first offered distance learning courses in 1979. In 1996–97, it offered 15 courses at a distance. In the fall of 1996, there was a total of 100 students enrolled in distance learning courses.
Course delivery sites Courses are delivered to your home, your workplace.
Media Courses are delivered via television, videotapes, audiotapes, World Wide Web, e-mail. Students and teachers interact via mail, telephone, fax, e-mail. A computer is required for some courses.
Services Distance learners have access to library services, the campus computer network, e-mail services at a distance.
Credit-earning options Students may transfer credits from another institution or may earn credits through examinations.
Typical costs Tuition of $43.76 per credit for in-state residents. Tuition of $155.19 per credit for out-of-state residents. Financial aid is available to distance learners enrolled full-time.
Registration Students may register by phone.
Contact Pat Fleming, Media Services Coordinator/Distance Learning Facilitator, Central Florida Community College, PO Box 1388, Ocala, FL 34478. *Telephone:* 352-237-2111, Ext. 348. *Fax:* 352-237-7097. *E-mail:* flemingp@cfcc.cc.fl.us. *Web site:* http://www.cfcc.cc.fl.us.

INDIVIDUAL COURSE SUBJECT AREAS

Undergraduate
American (US) history; anthropology; business administration and management; computer programming; corrections; developmental and child psychology; earth science; economics; English composition; European languages and literatures; fire services administration; geology; health and physical education/fitness; history; horticulture; music; oceanography; sociology; Spanish language and literature

CENTRAL METHODIST COLLEGE

Fayette, Missouri

Central Methodist College, founded in 1854, is an independent-religious Methodist comprehensive institution. It is accredited by the North Central Association of Colleges and Schools. It first offered distance learning courses in 1993. In 1996–97, it offered 16 courses at

Profiles: Central Methodist College

a distance. In the fall of 1996, there was a total of 100 students enrolled in distance learning courses.
Course delivery sites Courses are delivered to your home, East Central College (Union), Mineral Area College (Park Hills), area high schools.
Media Courses are delivered via videoconferencing, audioconferencing. Students and teachers interact via videoconferencing, audioconferencing, fax.
Restrictions Programs are available to in-state students only.
Services Distance learners have access to library services, academic advising, tutoring, career placement assistance at a distance.
Credit-earning options Students may transfer credits from another institution or may earn credits through examinations.
Typical costs Costs may vary by campus or location, specific program of study. Financial aid is available to distance learners enrolled full-time or part-time.
Registration Students may register by mail, fax, e-mail.
Contact Kay Winegard, Registrar, Central Methodist College, 411 Central Methodist Square, Fayette, MO 65248. *Telephone:* 816-248-3392, Ext. 208. *Fax:* 816-248-2287.

INDIVIDUAL COURSE SUBJECT AREAS

Undergraduate
Algebra; American (US) history; anatomy; biology; chemistry; education administration; educational psychology; nursing; physiology; teacher education

Graduate
Education administration; educational psychology; teacher education

CENTRAL MICHIGAN UNIVERSITY

Mount Pleasant, Michigan

Independent Learning and Distance Delivery Center

Central Michigan University, founded in 1892, is a state-supported university. It is accredited by the North Central Association of Colleges and Schools. It first offered distance learning courses in 1993.
Course delivery sites Courses are delivered to your home, your workplace, military bases, other colleges.
Media Courses are delivered via television, videotapes, audiotapes, computer software, World Wide Web, e-mail, print. Students and teachers interact via mail, telephone, fax, e-mail.
Services Distance learners have access to library services, academic advising at a distance.
Credit-earning options Students may transfer credits from another institution or may earn credits through examinations, portfolio assessment, military training, business training.
Typical costs *Undergraduate:* Tuition of $140 per credit hour. *Graduate:* Tuition of $155 per credit hour. All students pay a $50 enrollment fee. Financial aid is available to distance learners.
Contact Independent Learning and Distance Delivery Center, Central Michigan University, Rowe 126, Mount Pleasant, MI 48859. *Telephone:* 800-950-1144. *E-mail:* infocntr@cmich.edu. *Web site:* http://www.cel.cmich.edu.

DEGREE & CERTIFICATE PROGRAMS

Baccalaureate Degrees
▶*Business Administration, Community Development (BS)*
Application requirements *Prior education:* high school diploma or equivalent. *Other requirements:* high school transcript, an application fee of $50.
Completion requirements 124 credits are required. 34 credits must be completed through the institution. This is a degree completion program.
▶*Health Administration (BAA)*
Application requirements *Prior education:* high school diploma or equivalent. *Other requirements:* high school transcript, an application fee.
Completion requirements 124 credits are required. 34 credits must be completed through the institution. This is a degree completion program.

INDIVIDUAL COURSE SUBJECT AREAS

Undergraduate
Accounting; astronomy and astrophysics; biology; business; business administration and management; economics; English language and literature; finance; geography; health professions and related sciences; home economics and family studies; human resources management; industrial psychology; journalism; marketing; mathematics; music; philosophy and religion; physics; political science; public administration and services; public health; radio and television broadcasting; sociology; Spanish language and literature; statistics; visual and performing arts

CENTRAL MISSOURI STATE UNIVERSITY

Warrensburg, Missouri

Extended Campus

Central Missouri State University, founded in 1871, is a state-supported comprehensive institution. It is accredited by the North Central Association of Colleges and Schools. It first offered distance learning courses in 1993. In 1996–97, it offered 19 courses at a distance. In the fall of 1996, there was a total of 250 students enrolled in distance learning courses.
Course delivery sites Courses are delivered to your workplace, Missouri Southern State College (Joplin), Missouri Western State College (St. Joseph), Penn Valley Community College (Kansas City), high schools.
Media Courses are delivered via television, videotapes, videoconferencing. Students and teachers interact via videoconferencing, fax.
Services Distance learners have access to library services, academic advising, career placement assistance at a distance.
Credit-earning options Students may transfer credits from another institution or may earn credits through examinations, military training.
Typical costs *Undergraduate:* Tuition of $114 per credit hour. *Graduate:* Tuition of $176 per credit hour. Dual-credit courses for high school students: $42 per credit hour. Financial aid is available to distance learners.
Registration Students may register by mail, fax, phone.
Contact Robyn Criswell-Bloom, Coordinator of Distance Learning, Central Missouri State University, 403 Humphreys, Warrensburg, MO 64093. *Telephone:* 816-543-4984. *Fax:* 816-543-8333. *E-mail:* criswell@cmsuvmb.cmsu.edu.

DEGREE & CERTIFICATE PROGRAMS

Graduate Degrees
▶*Aviation Safety (MS)*
▶*Criminal Justice (MS)*
In the fall of 1996 there were 37 students enrolled in this program.
Application requirements *Prior education:* baccalaureate degree. *Other requirements:* 2.75 GPA, BS in criminal justice or 15 hours of course work in criminal justice.
Completion requirements 36 semester credits are required. 24 semester credits must be completed through the institution. *Other requirements:* thesis. *Maximum time for completion:* eight years.

Profiles: Central Washington University

▶ *Industrial Safety Management (MS)*
In the fall of 1996 there were 83 students enrolled in this program.
Application requirements *Prior education:* baccalaureate degree. *Other requirements:* 2.5 GPA, 15 hours of senior-level safety courses or equivalent.
Completion requirements 36 semester credits are required. 24 semester credits must be completed through the institution. *Other requirements:* comprehensive exam. *Maximum time for completion:* eight years.

Undergraduate Certificates
▶ *Police Institute*
Completion requirements *Other requirements:* this program is designed for those who need to satisfy Missouri state certification for law enforcement.
Program contact Mike Wiggins, Director of Police Institute, Central Missouri State University, Humphreys Room 30, Warrensburg, MO 64093.

INDIVIDUAL COURSE SUBJECT AREAS

Undergraduate
Advertising; biology; education administration; engineering/industrial management; English as a second language (ESL); English composition; European languages and literatures; foods and nutrition studies; journalism; liberal arts, general studies, and humanities; library and information studies; mathematics; protective services; radio and television broadcasting; special education; teacher education

Graduate
Education administration; engineering/industrial management; special education; teacher education

Noncredit
Education administration; special education; teacher education
See full description on page 394.

CENTRAL PIEDMONT COMMUNITY COLLEGE

Charlotte, North Carolina

Distance Learning Services

Central Piedmont Community College, founded in 1963, is a state and locally supported two-year college. It is accredited by the Southern Association of Colleges and Schools. It first offered distance learning courses in 1977. In 1996–97, it offered 25 courses at a distance. In the fall of 1996, there was a total of 629 students enrolled in distance learning courses.
Course delivery sites Courses are delivered to your home, your workplace, other colleges, 3 off-campus centers in Charlotte, Huntersville, Matthews.
Media Courses are delivered via television, videotapes, World Wide Web. Students and teachers interact via mail, telephone, fax, e-mail. A computer is required for some courses.
Credit-earning options Students may transfer credits from another institution.
Typical costs Tuition of $20 per credit hour for in-state residents. Tuition of $163 per credit hour for out-of-state residents. Financial aid is available to distance learners enrolled full-time or part-time.
Registration Students may register by phone.
Contact Carole Schultz, Director, College Without Walls, Central Piedmont Community College, PO Box 35009, Charlotte, NC 28235-5009. *Telephone:* 704-330-6883. *Fax:* 704-330-6597.

INDIVIDUAL COURSE SUBJECT AREAS

Undergraduate
Abnormal psychology; accounting; administrative and secretarial services; algebra; astronomy and astrophysics; biology; business; business administration and management; communications; computer and information sciences; developmental and child psychology; economics; English composition; English language and literature; geography; health and physical education/fitness; history; liberal arts, general studies, and humanities; mathematics; philosophy and religion; political science; psychology; social sciences; sociology; statistics

CENTRAL VIRGINIA COMMUNITY COLLEGE

Lynchburg, Virginia

Learning Resources

Central Virginia Community College, founded in 1966, is a state-supported two-year college. It is accredited by the Southern Association of Colleges and Schools. It first offered distance learning courses in 1984. In 1996–97, it offered 16 courses at a distance. In the fall of 1996, there was a total of 278 students enrolled in distance learning courses.
Course delivery sites Courses are delivered to your home.
Media Courses are delivered via videotapes, videoconferencing, audiotapes, print. Students and teachers interact via videoconferencing, mail, fax.
Services Distance learners have access to library services, the campus computer network, academic advising at a distance.
Credit-earning options Students may transfer credits from another institution or may earn credits through examinations.
Typical costs Tuition of $46.65 per credit hour for in-state residents. Tuition of $156 per credit hour for out-of-state residents. Costs may vary by number of credits taken. Financial aid is available to distance learners enrolled full-time.
Registration Students may register by phone.
Contact Susan S. Beasley, Audiovisual Supervisor, Central Virginia Community College, 3506 Wards Road, Lynchburg, VA 24502. *Telephone:* 804-386-4634. *Fax:* 804-386-4677. *E-mail:* cvbeass@cv.cc.va.us.

INDIVIDUAL COURSE SUBJECT AREAS

Undergraduate
Biology; business; business administration and management; developmental and child psychology; economics; health and physical education/fitness; mathematics; sociology

CENTRAL WASHINGTON UNIVERSITY

Ellensburg, Washington

Central Washington University, founded in 1891, is a state-supported comprehensive institution. It is accredited by the Northwest Association of Schools and Colleges. It first offered distance learning courses in 1995. In 1996–97, it offered 20 courses at a distance. In the fall of 1996, there was a total of 82 students enrolled in distance learning courses.
Course delivery sites Courses are delivered to Big Bend Community College (Moses Lake), Pierce College (Lakewood), Wenatchee Valley College (Wenatchee), Yakima Valley Community College (Yakima), off-campus center(s) in Lynnwood.

Distance Learning Programs

Profiles: Central Washington University

Media Courses are delivered via television, computer software, World Wide Web, e-mail, print. Students and teachers interact via videoconferencing, mail, telephone, fax, e-mail.
Restrictions Programs are available to local area students only.
Services Distance learners have access to library services, academic advising, tutoring at a distance.
Credit-earning options Students may transfer credits from another institution or may earn credits through examinations, military training.
Typical costs Tuition of $781 per quarter for in-state residents. Tuition of $2763 per quarter for out-of-state residents. Advanced courses are $1247 for in-state students and $2763 for non-residents per quarter. Fees vary. Costs may vary by number of credits taken. Financial aid is available to distance learners.
Registration Students may register by World Wide Web.
Contact Academic Advising Office, Central Washington University, 400 East 8th Street, Mitchell Hall, First Floor, Ellensburg, WA 98926. *Telephone:* 509-963-3001. *Fax:* 509-963-1590. *E-mail:* lyndeg@cwu.edu.

DEGREE & CERTIFICATE PROGRAMS

Baccalaureate Degrees

▶*Business Administration (BS)*
Completion requirements This is a degree completion program.
On-campus requirements Requirements vary according to course.
Program contact Gary Lynde, Acting Dean, Continuing Education, Central Washington University, 400 East 8th Street, Ellensburg, WA 98926. Phone: 509-963-1504. Fax: 509-963-1590. E-mail: lyndeg@cwu.edu.

▶*Teacher Education (BA)*
On-campus requirements Requirements vary according to course.
Program contact Gary Lynde, Acting Dean, Continuing Education, Central Washington University, 400 East 8th Street, Ellensburg, WA 98926. Phone: 509-963-1504. Fax: 509-963-1590. E-mail: lyndeg@cwu.edu.

Undergraduate Certificates

▶*Teacher Education*
On-campus requirements Requirements vary according to course.
Program contact Gary Lynde, Acting Dean, Continuing Education, Central Washington University, 400 East 8th Street, Ellensburg, WA 98926. Phone: 509-963-1504. Fax: 509-963-1590. E-mail: lyndeg@cwu.edu.

INDIVIDUAL COURSE SUBJECT AREAS

Undergraduate
Business administration and management; creative writing; developmental and child psychology; engineering-related technologies; English composition; teacher education

CENTRAL WYOMING COLLEGE

Riverton, Wyoming

Extended Studies Division

Central Wyoming College, founded in 1966, is a state and locally supported two-year college. It is accredited by the North Central Association of Colleges and Schools. In 1996–97, it offered 30 courses at a distance.
Course delivery sites Courses are delivered to your home, your workplace, 5 off-campus centers in Dubois, Jackson, Lander, Thermopolis, prisons.
Media Courses are delivered via television, videotapes. Students and teachers interact via mail, telephone, fax, e-mail.
Services Distance learners have access to the campus computer network, e-mail services, academic advising, tutoring, career placement assistance at a distance.
Credit-earning options Students may transfer credits from another institution or may earn credits through standardized exams.
Typical costs Tuition of $39 per credit plus mandatory fees of $16.50 per credit for in-state residents. Tuition of $117 per credit plus mandatory fees of $16.50 per credit for out-of-state residents. Costs may vary by number of credits taken. Financial aid is available to distance learners enrolled full-time or part-time.
Registration Students may register by mail, fax, phone, e-mail.
Contact Office of Registration and Records, Central Wyoming College, 2660 Peck Avenue, Riverton, WY 82501-2273. *Telephone:* 307-855-2000. *Fax:* 307-855-2095.

DEGREE & CERTIFICATE PROGRAMS

Associate Degrees
▶*General Studies (AA, AS)*
Application requirements *Prior education:* none required.
On-campus requirements For science labs.

INDIVIDUAL COURSE SUBJECT AREAS

Undergraduate
Accounting; biology; business; English composition; European languages and literatures; geography; health and physical education/fitness; home economics and family studies; mathematics; nursing; political science; psychology; sociology; visual and performing arts; zoology

CENTURY COMMUNITY AND TECHNICAL COLLEGE

White Bear Lake, Minnesota

Customized Training Division

Century Community and Technical College, founded in 1970, is a state-supported two-year college. It is accredited by the North Central Association of Colleges and Schools. It first offered distance learning courses in 1982.
Course delivery sites Courses are delivered to your home, your workplace, prisons.
Media Courses are delivered via print. Students and teachers interact via mail, telephone, fax.
Restrictions Courses are available to US students only.
Services Distance learners have access to academic advising, tutoring at a distance.
Credit-earning options Students may transfer credits from another institution or may earn credits through examinations, military training, business training.
Typical costs Tuition varies. Contact school for information.
Contact Distance Learning Department-Customized Training, Century Community and Technical College, 3300 Century Avenue North, White Bear Lake, MN 55110. *Telephone:* 800-832-4916. *Fax:* 612-779-5779.

INDIVIDUAL COURSE SUBJECT AREAS

Undergraduate
Anatomy; business; engineering-related technologies; health professions and related sciences

Noncredit
Accounting; electronics

CERRITOS COLLEGE

Norwalk, California

Cerritos College, founded in 1956, is a state and locally supported two-year college. It is accredited by the Western Association of Schools and Colleges, Inc. It first offered distance learning courses in 1985. In 1996–97, it offered 20 courses at a distance. In the fall of 1996, there was a total of 2,000 students enrolled in distance learning courses.
Course delivery sites Courses are delivered to your home.
Media Courses are delivered via television, videotapes, videoconferencing, computer software, World Wide Web, e-mail. Students and teachers interact via videoconferencing, audioconferencing, telephone, fax, e-mail. A computer is required for some courses.
Services Distance learners have access to library services, the campus computer network, e-mail services at a distance.
Credit-earning options Students may transfer credits from another institution or may earn credits through examinations.
Typical costs Tuition of $13 per unit plus mandatory fees of $10 per semester for local area residents. Tuition of $13 per unit for in-state residents. Tuition of $121 per unit for out-of-state residents. *Noncredit courses:* $13 per unit. Costs may vary by number of credits taken. Financial aid is available to distance learners.
Registration Students may register by phone.
Contact Dr. Morgan Lynn, Dean, Humanities and Social Science, Cerritos College, 11110 Alondra Boulevard, Norwalk, CA 90650. *Telephone:* 562-860-2451, Ext. 2751. *Fax:* 562-467-5005. *E-mail:* lynn@cerritos.edu.

INDIVIDUAL COURSE SUBJECT AREAS

Undergraduate
Area, ethnic, and cultural studies; English composition; English language and literature; philosophy and religion; political science; psychology; sociology; teacher education

CHADRON STATE COLLEGE

Chadron, Nebraska

Regional Programs

Chadron State College, founded in 1911, is a state-supported comprehensive institution. It is accredited by the North Central Association of Colleges and Schools. It first offered distance learning courses in 1991. In 1996–97, it offered 80 courses at a distance. In the fall of 1996, there was a total of 400 students enrolled in distance learning courses.
Course delivery sites Courses are delivered to your home, Casper College (Casper, WY), Mid-Plains Community College (North Platte), Western Nebraska Community College (Scottsbluff), off-campus center(s) in Alliance, Sidney, Sutherland.
Media Courses are delivered via television, videotapes, audioconferencing, computer software, World Wide Web, e-mail, print. Students and teachers interact via videoconferencing, audioconferencing, mail, telephone, fax, e-mail. A computer is required for some courses.
Restrictions Courses are available to students in western Nebraska only.
Services Distance learners have access to library services, the campus computer network, e-mail services, academic advising, career placement assistance at a distance.
Credit-earning options Students may transfer credits from another institution or may earn credits through standardized exams, institutionally developed exams, portfolio assessment, military training.
Typical costs *Undergraduate:* Tuition of $55 per credit plus mandatory fees of $11 per credit for in-state residents. Tuition of $110 per credit plus mandatory fees of $11 per credit for out-of-state residents. *Graduate:* Tuition of $69 per credit plus mandatory fees of $11 per credit for in-state residents. Tuition of $137.50 per credit plus mandatory fees of $11 per credit for out-of-state residents. Costs may vary by number of credits taken. Financial aid is available to distance learners enrolled full-time or part-time.
Registration Students may register by mail, fax, phone.
Contact Annette Langford, Coordinator, Distance Learning, Chadron State College, 100 Main Street, Chadron, NE 69363. *Telephone:* 308-432-6211. *Fax:* 308-432-6274. *E-mail:* alangford@csc1.csc.edu. *Web site:* http://www.csc.edu.

DEGREE & CERTIFICATE PROGRAMS

Graduate Degrees

▶ *Business Administration (MBA)*
Application requirements *Prior education:* baccalaureate degree. *Other requirements:* GMAT, high school transcript, college transcripts, an essay or personal statement, letter(s) of recommendation, an application fee of $10.
Completion requirements 36 semester hours are required. 27 semester hours must be completed through the institution. *Maximum time for completion:* seven years.
Program contact Tim Anderson, Chair, Business, Chadron State College, 100 Main Street, Chadron, NE 69337. Phone: 308-432-6349.

INDIVIDUAL COURSE SUBJECT AREAS

Undergraduate
Accounting; administrative and secretarial services; agriculture; area, ethnic, and cultural studies; business; business administration and management; creative writing; developmental and child psychology; economics; education administration; educational psychology; English language and literature; health and physical education/fitness; history; home economics and family studies; human resources management; law and legal studies; liberal arts, general studies, and humanities; mathematics; philosophy and religion; political science; social work; sociology; special education; teacher education

Graduate
Accounting; administrative and secretarial services; business; business administration and management; creative writing; education administration; English language and literature; human resources management; teacher education

CHAMPLAIN COLLEGE

Burlington, Vermont

Continuing Education Division

Champlain College, founded in 1878, is an independent-nonprofit primarily two-year college. It is accredited by the New England Association of Schools and Colleges. It first offered distance learning courses in 1993. In 1996–97, it offered 35 courses at a distance.

Profiles: Champlain College

Course delivery sites Courses are delivered to your home, your workplace, military bases.
Media Courses are delivered via computer software, Internet. Students and teachers interact via telephone, fax, e-mail. A computer is required for all courses.
Services Distance learners have access to library services, academic advising, tutoring, career placement assistance at a distance.
Credit-earning options Students may transfer credits from another institution or may earn credits through institutionally developed exams, portfolio assessment, military training, business training.
Typical costs Tuition of $295 per credit. *Noncredit courses:* $195 for 8 hours of instruction. Costs may vary by number of credits taken. Financial aid is available to distance learners.
Registration Students may register by mail, fax, phone, World Wide Web.
Contact Diane Byrnes, Registrar, Champlain College, Continuing Education Division, 163 South Willard Street, Burlington, VT 05402. *Telephone:* 802-860-2777. *Fax:* 802-860-2774. *E-mail:* ced@champlain.edu. *Web site:* http://www.champlain.edu/success.

DEGREE & CERTIFICATE PROGRAMS

Associate Degrees

▶ *Accounting (AS)*
Application requirements *Prior education:* high school diploma or equivalent. *Other requirements:* high school transcript, college transcripts, an essay or personal statement, an application fee of $25, program is geared towards adults.
Completion requirements 60 credits are required. 30 credits must be completed through the institution.

▶ *Business (AS)*
Application requirements *Prior education:* high school diploma or equivalent. *Other requirements:* high school transcript, college transcripts, an essay or personal statement, an application fee of $25, program is geared towards adults.
Completion requirements 60 credits are required. 30 credits must be completed through the institution.

▶ *Computer Programming–PC Track (AS)*
Application requirements *Prior education:* high school diploma or equivalent. *Other requirements:* high school transcript, college transcripts, an essay or personal statement, an application fee of $25, program is geared towards adults.
Completion requirements 60 credits are required. 30 credits must be completed through the institution.

▶ *Management (AS)*
Application requirements *Prior education:* high school diploma or equivalent. *Other requirements:* high school transcript, college transcripts, an essay or personal statement, an application fee of $25, program is geared towards adults.
Completion requirements 60 credits are required. 30 credits must be completed through the institution.

Baccalaureate Degrees

▶ *Business, Professional Studies (BS)*
Application requirements *Prior education:* some courses of study require an Associate's degree in related field. *Other requirements:* high school transcript, college transcripts, an essay or personal statement, letter(s) of recommendation, an application fee of $25, program is geared towards adults.
Completion requirements 120 credits are required. 30 credits must be completed through the institution.

Undergraduate Certificates

▶ *Accounting*
Application requirements *Prior education:* high school diploma or equivalent. *Other requirements:* high school transcript, college transcripts, an essay or personal statement, an application fee of $25, program is geared towards adults.
Completion requirements 19–22 credits are required.

▶ *Business*
Application requirements *Prior education:* high school diploma or equivalent. *Other requirements:* high school transcript, college transcripts, an essay or personal statement, an application fee of $25, program is geared towards adults.
Completion requirements 22 credits are required.

▶ *Computer Programming–PC Track*
Application requirements *Prior education:* high school diploma or equivalent. *Other requirements:* high school transcript, college transcripts, an essay or personal statement, an application fee of $25, program is geared towards adults.
Completion requirements 19–22 credits are required.

▶ *Management*
Application requirements *Prior education:* high school diploma or equivalent. *Other requirements:* high school transcript, college transcripts, an essay or personal statement, an application fee of $25, program is geared towards adults.
Completion requirements 22 credits are required.

INDIVIDUAL COURSE SUBJECT AREAS

Undergraduate
Accounting; advertising; business; business administration and management; computer and information sciences; economics; English composition; English language and literature; history; human resources management; law and legal studies; liberal arts, general studies, and humanities; marketing; mathematics; philosophy and religion; political science; psychology; sociology; statistics

Noncredit
Computer and information sciences

See full description on page 396.

CHAPMAN UNIVERSITY

Orange, California

Department of Distance Learning

Chapman University, founded in 1861, is an independent-religious comprehensive institution affiliated with the Christian Church (Disciples of Christ). It is accredited by the Western Association of Schools and Colleges, Inc.
Course delivery sites Courses are delivered to your home, military bases.
Media Courses are delivered via videotapes, World Wide Web, e-mail. Students and teachers interact via mail, telephone, fax, e-mail, computer conferencing.
Services Distance learners have access to library services, academic advising, tutoring, career placement assistance at a distance.
Credit-earning options Students may transfer credits from another institution or may earn credits through examinations, military training.
Typical costs Tuition of $375 per credit. Fees vary. Financial aid is available to distance learners.
Contact Department of Distance Learning, Chapman University, 333 North Glassell Street, Orange, CA 92666. *Telephone:* 714-997-6980. *Fax:* 714-997-6641. *E-mail:* diener@chapman.edu. *Web site:* http://www.chapman.edu.

INDIVIDUAL COURSE SUBJECT AREAS

Undergraduate
Communications; economics; history; liberal arts, general studies, and humanities; mathematics; psychology; theological studies

CHARLES COUNTY COMMUNITY COLLEGE

La Plata, Maryland

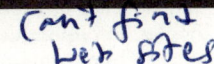
(can't find web sites.)

Charles County Community College, founded in 1958, is a state and locally supported two-year college. It is accredited by the Middle States Association of Colleges and Schools. It first offered distance learning courses in 1985. In 1996–97, it offered 22 courses at a distance.
Course delivery sites Courses are delivered to your home, your workplace, military bases, Anne Arundel Community College (Arnold), Chesapeake College (Wye Mills), Montgomery College–Rockville Campus (Rockville), 2 satellite centers in Calvert and St. Mary's counties.
Media Courses are delivered via television, videotapes, print. Students and teachers interact via mail, telephone, fax, e-mail.
Restrictions Programs are available to local area students only.
Credit-earning options Students may transfer credits from another institution or may earn credits through standardized exams, institutionally developed exams, portfolio assessment, military training, business training.
Typical costs Tuition of $65 per credit hour plus mandatory fees of $100 per semester for local area residents. Tuition of $130 per credit hour for in-state residents. Tuition of $195 per credit hour for out-of-state residents. Costs may vary by specific program of study, number of credits taken. Financial aid is available to distance learners.
Registration Students may register by mail, fax, phone.
Contact Jean Fuller, Director of Media Services, Charles County Community College, Box 910, La Plata, MD 20646. *Telephone:* 301-934-7615. *Fax:* 301-934-7699.

DEGREE & CERTIFICATE PROGRAMS

Associate Degrees
▶ *General Studies (AA)*
Restrictions Program is available to students in the local region only.
Application requirements *Prior education:* high school diploma or equivalent. *Minimum age:* 16. *Other requirements:* an application fee, GED or high school class graduation.
Completion requirements 60 credits are required.
On-campus requirements Lab courses require on-campus time.
Program contact William E. Montgomery, Chair, Biological and Physical Sciences, Charles County Community College, Box 910, Mitchell Road, LaPlata, MD 20646-0910. Phone: 301-934-7842. Fax: 301-934-7688. E-mail: billm@charles.cc.md.us.

INDIVIDUAL COURSE SUBJECT AREAS

Undergraduate
Accounting; administrative and secretarial services; American (US) history; art history and criticism; astronomy and astrophysics; biology; business administration and management; calculus; computer and information sciences; computer programming; creative writing; developmental and child psychology; economics; electrical engineering; English composition; English language and literature; ethics; European history; European languages and literatures; film studies; fine arts; French language and literature; history; journalism; liberal arts, general studies, and humanities; logic; mathematics; nursing; oceanography; philosophy and religion; physical therapy; political science; sociology; statistics; teacher education; technical writing

CHARLES STEWART MOTT COMMUNITY COLLEGE

Flint, Michigan

Distance Learning Office

Charles Stewart Mott Community College, founded in 1923, is a district-supported two-year college. It is accredited by the North Central Association of Colleges and Schools. It first offered distance learning courses in 1981.
Course delivery sites Courses are delivered to your home, your workplace.
Media Courses are delivered via videotapes, World Wide Web. Students and teachers interact via videoconferencing, telephone, fax, e-mail.
Services Distance learners have access to library services, academic advising, tutoring, career placement assistance at a distance.
Credit-earning options Students may transfer credits from another institution or may earn credits through examinations.
Typical costs Tuition of $450 per course plus mandatory fees of $35 per semester. Financial aid is available to distance learners.
Contact Lori France, Coordinator, Distance Learning, Charles Stewart Mott Community College, 1401 East Court Street, Flint, MI 48503. *Telephone:* 800-398-2715. *Fax:* 810-762-5610. *E-mail:* l.france@edtech.mcc.edu. *Web site:* http://edtech.mcc.edu.

DEGREE & CERTIFICATE PROGRAMS

Associate Degrees
▶ *General Business (AAS)*
Restrictions Program is marketed to employees through employers.
Completion requirements 62 credit hours are required. 30 credit hours must be completed through the institution.
▶ *General Studies (AA)*
Restrictions Program is marketed to employees through employers.
Completion requirements 62 credit hours are required. 30 credit hours must be completed through the institution.

INDIVIDUAL COURSE SUBJECT AREAS

Undergraduate
Administrative and secretarial services; advertising; area, ethnic, and cultural studies; biology; business; business administration and management; computer and information sciences; developmental and child psychology; engineering-related technologies; English composition; English language and literature; history; liberal arts, general studies, and humanities; mathematics; political science; social psychology; social work; sociology; technical writing

CHARTER OAK STATE COLLEGE

Newington, Connecticut

Charter Oak State College, founded in 1973, is a state-supported four-year college. It is accredited by the New England Association of Schools and Colleges. It first offered distance learning courses in 1992. In 1996–97, it offered 16 courses at a distance. In the fall of 1996, there was a total of 84 students enrolled in distance learning courses.
Course delivery sites Courses are delivered to your home.

Distance Learning Programs

Profiles: Charter Oak State College

Media Courses are delivered via videotapes, audiotapes, print. Students and teachers interact via mail, telephone, e-mail. A computer is required for some courses.
Services Distance learners have access to academic advising at a distance.
Credit-earning options Students may transfer credits from another institution or may earn credits through standardized exams, portfolio assessment, military training, business training.
Typical costs Tuition of $58 per credit for in-state residents. Tuition of $87 per credit for out-of-state residents. $12 registration fee for Independent Guided Study courses. Financial aid is available to distance learners enrolled part-time.
Registration Students may register by mail, fax, phone, e-mail.
Contact Ms. Marlene Woodman, Assistant to the President, Charter Oak State College, 66 Cedar Street, Newington, CT 06111. *Telephone:* 860-666-4595, Ext. 26. *Fax:* 860-666-4852. *E-mail:* mwoodman@commnet.edu. *Web site:* http://www.ctstateu.edu/~charteroak.

INDIVIDUAL COURSE SUBJECT AREAS

Undergraduate

Astronomy and astrophysics; biology; business administration and management; economics; English language and literature; history; liberal arts, general studies, and humanities; mathematics; philosophy and religion; sociology

See full description on page 398.

CHATTANOOGA STATE TECHNICAL COMMUNITY COLLEGE

Chattanooga, Tennessee

Distance Learning Program

Chattanooga State Technical Community College, founded in 1965, is a state-supported two-year college. It is accredited by the Southern Association of Colleges and Schools. It first offered distance learning courses in 1985. In 1996–97, it offered 90 courses at a distance. In the fall of 1996, there was a total of 1,050 students enrolled in distance learning courses.
Course delivery sites Courses are delivered to your home, your workplace, military bases, Milligan College (Milligan College), Southern Adventist University (Collegedale), prisons.
Media Courses are delivered via television, videotapes, audiotapes, computer software, World Wide Web, e-mail, print. Students and teachers interact via mail, telephone, fax, e-mail. A computer is required for some courses.
Services Distance learners have access to library services, e-mail services, academic advising, tutoring, career placement assistance at a distance.
Credit-earning options Students may transfer credits from another institution or may earn credits through standardized exams, institutionally developed exams, portfolio assessment, military training.
Typical costs Tuition of $45 per semester hour plus mandatory fees of $38 per semester hour for in-state residents. Tuition of $179 per semester hour plus mandatory fees of $38 per semester hour for out-of-state residents. Costs may vary by number of credits taken. Financial aid is available to distance learners enrolled full-time or part-time.
Registration Students may register by mail, fax, phone.
Contact Sue Hyatt, Director, Distance Learning, Chattanooga State Technical Community College, 4501 Amnicola Highway, Chattanooga, TN 37406. *Telephone:* 423-697-4408. *Fax:* 423-697-4479. *E-mail:* hyatt@cstcc.tn.us. *Web site:* http://cstcc.chattanooga.net.

DEGREE & CERTIFICATE PROGRAMS

Associate Degrees

▶ *Emergency Medical Care Concentrations, Emergency Service Administration, Fire Science Technology (AAS)*
In the fall of 1996 there were 30 students enrolled in this program.
Restrictions Students must bring EMT certification or Basic firefighter certification.
Application requirements *Prior education:* high school diploma or equivalent. *Other requirements:* high school transcript, an application fee of $5, evidence of work experience in field.
Completion requirements 67 semester hours are required. 20 semester hours must be completed through the institution.

▶ *Engineering Technology, Maintenance Technology (AAS)*
In the fall of 1996 there were 66 students enrolled in this program.
Restrictions This program is available to local area students only. Primarily delivered through companies.
Application requirements *Prior education:* high school diploma or equivalent. *Other requirements:* high school transcript, an application fee of $5.
Completion requirements 72 credits are required. Last 20 credits must be completed through the institution.
On-campus requirements In some courses students need to be present for exams.

Undergraduate Certificates

▶ *Forestry*
In the fall of 1996 there were 10 students enrolled in this program. In 1995–96, 8 certificates were earned at a distance through this program.
Application requirements *Prior education:* high school diploma or equivalent. *Other requirements:* high school transcript, college transcripts, an application fee of $5.
Completion requirements 19 semester hours are required.

INDIVIDUAL COURSE SUBJECT AREAS

Undergraduate

Accounting; advertising; agriculture; biological and life sciences; business; business administration and management; computer and information sciences; creative writing; developmental and child psychology; economics; education; educational psychology; electrical engineering; English composition; English language and literature; fine arts; health and physical education/fitness; history; journalism; liberal arts, general studies, and humanities; mathematics; music; philosophy and religion; political science; protective services; psychology; radio and television broadcasting; social psychology; social work; sociology; teacher education

See full description on page 400.

CHEMEKETA COMMUNITY COLLEGE

Salem, Oregon

Chemeketa Online

Chemeketa Community College, founded in 1955, is a state and locally supported two-year college. It is accredited by the Northwest Association of Schools and Colleges.
Course delivery sites Courses are delivered to your home, your workplace, other colleges.

Media Courses are delivered via television, videotapes, videoconferencing, World Wide Web, e-mail, print. Students and teachers interact via videoconferencing, audioconferencing, mail, telephone, fax, e-mail.
Services Distance learners have access to library services, academic advising, tutoring, career placement assistance at a distance.
Credit-earning options Students may transfer credits from another institution or may earn credits through examinations, portfolio assessment, military training, business training.
Typical costs Tuition of $35 per credit plus mandatory fees of $8 per credit. Financial aid is available to distance learners.
Contact Donna Carver, Coordinator, Distance Education, Chemeketa Community College, 4000 Lancaster Drive, NE, Salem, OR 97305. *Telephone:* 800-336-5191. *Fax:* 503-399-5214. *E-mail:* donnac@chemek.cc.or.us. *Web site:* http://www.chemek.cc.or.us/.

DEGREE & CERTIFICATE PROGRAMS

Associate Degrees

▶*Fire Prevention Technology (AAS)*
Completion requirements 100 quarter hours are required. 30 quarter hours must be completed through the institution.
Program contact Brian Bay, Director, Emergency Services, Physical Education and Athletics, Chemeketa Community College, 4000 Lancaster Drive, NE, Salem, OR 97305. Phone: 503-399-6240. Fax: 503-588-6438. E-mail: briane@chemek.cc.or.us.

▶*Fire Suppression Technology (AAS)*
Completion requirements 100 quarter hours are required. 30 quarter hours must be completed through the institution.
Program contact Brian Bay, Director, Emergency Services, Physical Education and Athletics, Chemeketa Community College, 4000 Lancaster Drive, NE, Salem, OR 97305. Phone: 503-399-6240. Fax: 503-588-6438. E-mail: briane@chemek.cc.or.us.

▶*General Studies (AGS)*
Completion requirements 90 quarter hours are required. 30 quarter hours must be completed through the institution.

▶*Liberal Arts (AA)*
Completion requirements 90 quarter hours are required. 30 quarter hours must be completed through the institution.

INDIVIDUAL COURSE SUBJECT AREAS

Undergraduate
Accounting; administrative and secretarial services; area, ethnic, and cultural studies; biological and life sciences; business; business administration and management; computer and information sciences; creative writing; developmental and child psychology; economics; English composition; English language and literature; geology; health and physical education/fitness; history; hospitality services management; liberal arts, general studies, and humanities; mathematics; philosophy and religion; physical sciences; social psychology

CHESAPEAKE COLLEGE

Wye Mills, Maryland

Chesapeake College, founded in 1965, is a state and locally supported two-year college. It is accredited by the Middle States Association of Colleges and Schools. It first offered distance learning courses in 1994. In 1996–97, it offered 23 courses at a distance. In the fall of 1996, there was a total of 133 students enrolled in distance learning courses.
Course delivery sites Courses are delivered to 4 off-campus centers in Cambridge, Chestertown, Denton, Ridgely.
Media Courses are delivered via television, videoconferencing. Students and teachers interact via videoconferencing, telephone, fax, e-mail. A computer is required for some courses.
Restrictions Fiber-optics programs are available to local area students only.
Services Distance learners have access to library services, academic advising, career placement assistance at a distance.
Credit-earning options Students may earn credits through examinations.
Typical costs Tuition of $62 per credit hour plus mandatory fees of $15 per credit hour. *Noncredit courses:* $62 per hour. Costs may vary by specific program of study. Financial aid is available to distance learners.
Registration Students may register by mail.
Contact Registration/Admissions Office, Chesapeake College, PO Box 8, Wye Mills, MD 21679. *Telephone:* 410-822-5400. *Fax:* 410-827-9466.

INDIVIDUAL COURSE SUBJECT AREAS

Undergraduate
Accounting; area, ethnic, and cultural studies; business; business administration and management; communications; computer and information sciences; education; English composition; English language and literature

CHESTNUT HILL COLLEGE

Philadelphia, Pennsylvania

Graduate Division

Chestnut Hill College, founded in 1924, is an independent-religious Roman Catholic comprehensive institution. It is accredited by the Middle States Association of Colleges and Schools. It first offered distance learning courses in 1996. In 1996–97, it offered 8 courses at a distance. In the fall of 1996, there was a total of 40 students enrolled in distance learning courses.
Course delivery sites Courses are delivered to your home.
Media Courses are delivered via videotapes, computer software, World Wide Web, e-mail, print. Students and teachers interact via mail, telephone, fax, e-mail. A computer is required for all courses.
Restrictions Programs are available to local area students only.
Services Distance learners have access to library services, e-mail services at a distance.
Credit-earning options Students may transfer credits from another institution or may earn credits through examinations, portfolio assessment.
Typical costs Tuition of $300 per credit plus mandatory fees of $25 per semester. *Noncredit courses:* $175 per course. Costs may vary by specific program of study. Financial aid is available to distance learners.
Registration Students may register by mail, phone.
Contact Dr. Louise Mayock, SND, Chair, Applied Technology, Chestnut Hill College, 9601 Germantown Avenue, Philadelphia, PA 19118-2693. *Telephone:* 215-248-7186. *Fax:* 215-248-7139. *E-mail:* lmayock@chc.edu.

INDIVIDUAL COURSE SUBJECT AREAS

Graduate
Business administration and management; curriculum and instruction; educational research; engineering-related technologies; instructional media

Profiles: Chippewa Valley Technical College

CHIPPEWA VALLEY TECHNICAL COLLEGE

Eau Claire, Wisconsin

Instructional Design

Chippewa Valley Technical College, founded in 1912, is a district-supported two-year college. It is accredited by the North Central Association of Colleges and Schools. It first offered distance learning courses in 1990. In 1996–97, it offered 50 courses at a distance.

Course delivery sites Courses are delivered to your home, your workplace, other colleges, off-campus center(s).

Media Courses are delivered via television, videotapes, videoconferencing, audiotapes, computer software, World Wide Web, e-mail, print. Students and teachers interact via videoconferencing, mail, fax, e-mail. A computer is required for some courses.

Services Distance learners have access to library services, e-mail services, academic advising, tutoring, career placement assistance at a distance.

Credit-earning options Students may transfer credits from another institution or may earn credits through examinations, portfolio assessment, business training.

Typical costs Tuition of $54.20 per credit. Costs may vary by specific program of study, number of credits taken, course delivery options. Financial aid is available to distance learners enrolled full-time.

Registration Students may register by mail.

Contact Tammy Moss, Admissions, Chippewa Valley Technical College, 620 West Clairemont Avenue, Eau Claire, WI 54701. *Telephone:* 715-833-6200. *Fax:* 715-833-6511. *E-mail:* tmoss@mail.chippewa.tec.wi.us. *Web site:* http://www.chippewa.tec.wi.us.

DEGREE & CERTIFICATE PROGRAMS

Graduate certificates

▶ *Legal Nurse Consulting*

Application requirements *Prior education:* associate degree. *Other requirements:* high school transcript, college transcripts, an application fee of $25, RN license, one year of experience, letter or resume that states 2000 hours of experience.

Completion requirements 12 credits are required. 12 credits must be completed through the institution.

Program contact Cynthia Weishapple, Paralegal Department Director, Chippewa Valley Technical College, 620 West Clairemont Avenue, Eau Claire, WI 54701. Phone: 715-833-6355. Fax: 715-833-6511. E-mail: cweishapple@mail.chippewa.tec.wi.us.

INDIVIDUAL COURSE SUBJECT AREAS

Undergraduate

Accounting; biology; business; business administration and management; chemistry; computer and information sciences; creative writing; developmental and child psychology; economics; education administration; English composition; health professions and related sciences; home economics and family studies; hospitality services management; law and legal studies; liberal arts, general studies, and humanities; mathematics; nursing; psychology; sociology; teacher education

Noncredit

Administrative and secretarial services; agriculture; biology; business administration and management; computer and information sciences; human resources management; teacher education

CHRISTOPHER NEWPORT UNIVERSITY

Newport News, Virginia

CNU Online

Christopher Newport University, founded in 1961, is a state-supported comprehensive institution. It is accredited by the Southern Association of Colleges and Schools. It first offered distance learning courses in 1993. In 1996–97, it offered 40 courses at a distance. In the fall of 1996, there was a total of 500 students enrolled in distance learning courses.

Course delivery sites Courses are delivered to your home, your workplace, military bases, Mountain Empire Community College (Big Stone Gap).

Media Courses are delivered via videotapes, computer software, World Wide Web, e-mail, print. Students and teachers interact via mail, telephone, fax, e-mail. A computer is required for all courses.

Services Distance learners have access to library services, academic advising at a distance.

Credit-earning options Students may transfer credits from another institution or may earn credits through examinations, portfolio assessment, military training, business training.

Typical costs Tuition of $139 per credit hour for in-state residents. Tuition of $331 per credit hour for out-of-state residents. Financial aid is available to distance learners.

Registration Students may register by mail, fax, phone.

Contact James Husband, Coordinator, CNU Online, Christopher Newport University, 50 Shoe Lane, Newport News, VA 23606. *Telephone:* 757-594-7607. *Fax:* 757-594-7481. *E-mail:* jhusband@cnuonline.cnu.edu. *Web site:* http://cnuonline.cnu.edu.

Special note

Christopher Newport University offers general education, elective, and major courses leading to the Bachelor of Science degree in governmental administration (BSGA) and the Bachelor of Arts in philosophy and religious studies entirely on-line. Degree concentrations for the BSGA program include public management, criminal justice, and international studies. The BA in philosophy also includes a concentration in religious studies and ethics in the professions. On-line courses may be used to fulfill requirements for many university degree programs, transfer credit to other institutions, or satisfy full degree requirements for the government and philosophy departments.

Students enjoy high levels of participation in the learning process with fellow students and instructors because of the interactive environment of computer-managed telecommunications. Participants learn the skills necessary to succeed in an increasingly computerized telecommunication environment. In addition to regular instruction in individual courses, students have access to experts in such areas as critical thinking and professional writing that fosters acquisition of skills and knowledge expected in the job market. Individualized interactive tutorials with instructors and discussions with other class members are available 24 hours a day, 7 days a week. Learners are not blocked from pursuing a college degree because of distance from the classroom, care of children, shift work, employment travel, or disability.

Prospective students can receive more information by calling 800-333-4CNU or via e-mail at info@cnuonline.cnu.edu or the World Wide Web at http://cnuonline.cnu.edu.

DEGREE & CERTIFICATE PROGRAMS

Baccalaureate Degrees

▶ *Philosophy, Religion (BA)*
In the fall of 1996 there were 15 students enrolled in this program.
Application requirements *Prior education:* high school diploma or equivalent. *Other requirements:* high school transcript.
Completion requirements 30 credit hours in Philosophy and Religion are required. This is a degree completion program.
Program contact George Teschner, Chair, Philosophy Department, Christopher Newport University, 50 Shoe Lane, Newport News, VA 23606. Phone: 757-594-7171.

▶ *Criminal Justice Administration, International Administration, Legal Studies, Public Management (BSGA)*
In the fall of 1996 there were 550 students enrolled in this program.
Application requirements *Prior education:* high school diploma or equivalent. *Other requirements:* high school transcript.
Completion requirements 120 credit hours are required. 60 credits must be completed through the institution.
Program contact Dr. Buck Miller, Department Chair, Christopher Newport University, 50 Shoe Lane, Newport News, VA 23606. Phone: 757-594-7821. Fax: 757-594-7481. E-mail: bmiller@cnu.edu.

Undergraduate Certificates

▶ *Mid-Atlantic Police Supervisory Institute (MAPSI)*
In the fall of 1996 there were 45 students enrolled in this program.
Restrictions Students must be current certified police officers with agency approval.
Application requirements *Prior education:* some undergraduate course work. *Other requirements:* high school transcript, police employment.
Completion requirements 12 credit hours are required. *Maximum time for completion:* three years.
Program contact Mr. Tom Dempsey, Director, MAPSI, Christopher Newport University, 50 Shoe Lane, Newport News, VA 23606. Phone: 757-594-7097. Fax: 757-594-7481. E-mail: tdempsey@cnu.edu.

INDIVIDUAL COURSE SUBJECT AREAS

Undergraduate
Accounting; American studies; business administration and management; business communications; business law; community services; corrections; creative writing, criminal justice; English composition; English language and literature; English literature; human resources management; marketing; nursing; philosophy and religion; physics; political science; public policy analysis; sociology; Spanish language and literature; statistics; teacher education; women's studies

Graduate
Teacher education

CINCINNATI BIBLE COLLEGE AND SEMINARY

Cincinnati, Ohio

Cincinnati Bible College and Seminary, founded in 1924, is an independent-religious comprehensive institution affiliated with the Church of Christ. It is accredited by the North Central Association of Colleges and Schools. It first offered distance learning courses in 1994. In 1996–97, it offered 6 courses at a distance. In the fall of 1996, there was a total of 5 students enrolled in distance learning courses.
Course delivery sites Courses are delivered to your home.
Media Courses are delivered via print. Students and teachers interact via mail, telephone, fax, e-mail.
Services Distance learners have access to e-mail services, academic advising at a distance.
Credit-earning options Students may transfer credits from another institution.
Typical costs Tuition of $165 per credit hour.
Registration Students may register by mail, fax, phone, e-mail.
Contact Priscilla Berry, Administrative Assistant for Academic Affairs, Cincinnati Bible College and Seminary, 2700 Glenway Avenue, PO Box 4320, Cincinnati, OH 45204-3200. *Telephone:* 513-244-8160. *Fax:* 513-244-8140. *E-mail:* priscilla.berry@cincybible.edu.

INDIVIDUAL COURSE SUBJECT AREAS

Undergraduate
Bible studies; philosophy and religion; theological studies

CITRUS COLLEGE

Glendora, California

Citrus College, founded in 1915, is a state and locally supported two-year college. It is accredited by the Western Association of Schools and Colleges, Inc. It first offered distance learning courses in 1996.
Course delivery sites Courses are delivered to your home, your workplace, military bases.
Media Courses are delivered via World Wide Web. Students and teachers interact via mail, telephone, e-mail.
Services Distance learners have access to library services, academic advising, tutoring, career placement assistance at a distance.
Credit-earning options Students may transfer credits from another institution.
Typical costs Tuition of $39 per course plus mandatory fees of $20 per semester for in-state residents. Tuition of $405 per course plus mandatory fees of $20 per semester for out-of-state residents. Financial aid is available to distance learners.
Contact James D. Williams, Dean of Faculty, Citrus College, 1000 West Foothill Boulevard, Glendora, CA 91741. *Telephone:* 818-914-8794. *Fax:* 818-963-2531. *E-mail:* jwilliams@citrus.cc.ca.us.

INDIVIDUAL COURSE SUBJECT AREAS

Undergraduate
English as a second language (ESL); history; mathematics; political science; psychology; sociology

CITY COLLEGE OF SAN FRANCISCO

San Francisco, California

Telecourses

City College of San Francisco, founded in 1935, is a state and locally supported two-year college. It is accredited by the Western Association of Schools and Colleges, Inc. It first offered distance learning courses in 1988. In 1996–97, it offered 31 courses at a distance.
Course delivery sites Courses are delivered to your home.
Media Courses are delivered via television. Students and teachers interact via mail, telephone, e-mail, computer conferencing.
Restrictions Programs are available to local area students only.
Services Distance learners have access to library services, the campus computer network, academic advising, tutoring, career placement assistance at a distance.

Profiles: City College of San Francisco

Credit-earning options Students may transfer credits from another institution or may earn credits through examinations.
Typical costs Tuition of $13 per unit. Financial aid is available to distance learners enrolled full-time or part-time.
Registration Students may register by mail, phone.
Contact Phillip Brown, Telecourse Coordinator, City College of San Francisco, 50 Phelan Avenue, San Francisco, CA 94112. *Telephone:* 415-239-3885. *Fax:* 415-239-3694.

INDIVIDUAL COURSE SUBJECT AREAS

Undergraduate
Area, ethnic, and cultural studies; astronomy and astrophysics; biological and life sciences; biology; business; business administration and management; English language and literature; European languages and literatures; health professions and related sciences; history; liberal arts, general studies, and humanities; music; physics; social psychology

CITY COLLEGES OF CHICAGO, HAROLD WASHINGTON COLLEGE

Chicago, Illinois

Center for Open Learning

City Colleges of Chicago, Harold Washington College, founded in 1962, is a state and locally supported two-year college. It is accredited by the North Central Association of Colleges and Schools. It first offered distance learning courses in 1956. In 1996–97, it offered 45 courses at a distance. In the fall of 1996, there was a total of 2,858 students enrolled in distance learning courses.
Course delivery sites Courses are delivered to your home, military bases.
Media Courses are delivered via television, videotapes, videoconferencing. Students and teachers interact via mail, telephone, fax, e-mail.
Restrictions Programs are available to local area students only.
Services Distance learners have access to the campus computer network at a distance.
Credit-earning options Students may earn credits through examinations, portfolio assessment, military training.
Typical costs Tuition of $45 per credit hour plus mandatory fees of $20 per course for local area residents. Tuition of $142.98 per credit hour plus mandatory fees of $20 per course for in-state residents. Tuition of $201.84 per credit hour plus mandatory fees of $20 per course for out-of-state residents. All students pay an additional $20 per semester fee. Costs may vary by number of credits taken. Financial aid is available to distance learners.
Registration Students may register by phone.
Contact Pamela C. Lattimore, Assistant Dean, Center for Open Learning, City Colleges of Chicago, Harold Washington College, 30 East Lake Street, Chicago, IL 60601. *Telephone:* 312-553-5980. *Fax:* 312-553-5987. *E-mail:* plattimore@ccc.edu.

INDIVIDUAL COURSE SUBJECT AREAS

Undergraduate
Accounting; algebra; Asian languages and literatures; astronomy and astrophysics; business administration and management; chemistry; Classical languages and literatures; creative writing; developmental and child psychology; economics; English composition; English language and literature; European languages and literatures; fine arts; geology; history; physics; political science; social work; sociology; statistics

CITY UNIVERSITY

Bellevue, Washington

Distance Learning Operations

City University, founded in 1973, is an independent-nonprofit comprehensive institution. It is accredited by the Northwest Association of Schools and Colleges. It first offered distance learning courses in 1985. In 1996–97, it offered 325 courses at a distance.
Course delivery sites Courses are delivered to your home, your workplace.
Media Courses are delivered via videotapes, computer software, World Wide Web, e-mail. Students and teachers interact via mail, telephone, fax, e-mail. A computer is required for all courses.
Services Distance learners have access to library services, e-mail services, academic advising, career placement assistance at a distance.
Credit-earning options Students may transfer credits from another institution or may earn credits through standardized exams, portfolio assessment, military training, business training.
Typical costs *Undergraduate:* Tuition of $150 per credit. *Graduate:* Tuition of $268 per credit.
Registration Students may register by mail, fax, phone, e-mail, World Wide Web.
Contact Advisor for Distance Learning, City University, Office of Admissions and Student Affairs, 919 Southwest Grady Way, 2nd Floor, Renton, WA 98055. *Telephone:* 800-426-5596. *Fax:* 206-277-2437. *E-mail:* bsmith@cityu.edu. *Web site:* http://www.cityu.edu.

DEGREE & CERTIFICATE PROGRAMS

Associate Degrees
▶ *General Studies, International Management, Management, Medical Laboratory Technology, Medical Office/Laboratory Technology, Office Technology–Accounting, Office Technology–General Office and Document Processing, Office Technology–Medical Transcription (AS)*
In the fall of 1996 there were 148 students enrolled in this program. In 1995–96, 17 degrees were earned at a distance through this program.
Application requirements *Prior education:* high school diploma or equivalent. *Other requirements:* an application fee of $75.
Completion requirements 90 credit hours are required.

Baccalaureate Degrees
▶ *Accounting, Business Administration, Computer Systems, Energy and Environmental Quality Management, General Studies, Law Enforcement Administration, Management Specialty, Marketing, Security Administration (BS)*
In the fall of 1996 there were 1,408 students enrolled in this program. In 1995–96, 75 degrees were earned at a distance through this program.
Application requirements *Prior education:* high school diploma or equivalent. *Other requirements:* high school transcript, an application fee of $75.
Completion requirements 180 credit hours are required.

▶ *General Studies, International Studies, Literature and Comparative Literature, Management, Marketing, Mass Communications/Journalism, Mathematics, Philosophy, Political Science, Psychology, Sciences, Sociology (BA)*
In the fall of 1996 there were 195 students enrolled in this program. In 1995–96, 1 degree was earned at a distance through this program.
Application requirements *Prior education:* high school diploma or equivalent. *Other requirements:* high school transcript, an application fee of $75.

Completion requirements 180 credit hours are required.

Graduate Degrees

▶ *Business Administration, Financial Management, Health Care Administration, Individual Financial Planning, Individualized Studies, Information Systems, Managerial Leadership, Marketing, Technology-Engineering Management, Telecommunications Management (MBA)*
In the fall of 1996 there were 980 students enrolled in this program. In 1995–96, 68 degrees were earned at a distance through this program.
Application requirements *Prior education:* baccalaureate degree. *Other requirements:* college transcripts, an application fee of $75.
Completion requirements 45 credit hours are required.

▶ *Business Administration (EMBA)*
Application requirements *Prior education:* baccalaureate degree. *Other requirements:* college transcripts, an application fee of $75.
Completion requirements 45 credit hours are required.

▶ *Curriculum and Instruction, Educational Administration, Educational Psychology, Educational Technology, ESL Instructional Methods, Guidance and Counseling, School Administration, School Psychology, Special Education (MEd)*
In the fall of 1996 there were 112 students enrolled in this program.
Application requirements *Prior education:* baccalaureate degree. *Other requirements:* college transcripts, an essay or personal statement, letter(s) of recommendation, an application fee of $75, admissions portfolio.
Completion requirements 33–90 credits are required.

▶ *Human Behavior, Management, Marriage and Family Counseling, Mental Health Counseling, Vocational Rehabilitation Counseling (MA)*
In the fall of 1996 there were 56 students enrolled in this program. In 1995–96, 2 degrees were earned at a distance through this program.
Application requirements *Prior education:* baccalaureate degree. *Other requirements:* college transcripts, an application fee of $75.
Completion requirements 45–74 credits are required.

▶ *Management and Leadership, Organizational and Human Systems Design (EMA)*
Application requirements *Prior education:* baccalaureate degree. *Other requirements:* college transcripts, an application fee of $75.
Completion requirements 45 credit hours are required.

▶ *Project Management (MPM)*
Application requirements *Prior education:* baccalaureate degree. *Other requirements:* college transcripts, an application fee of $75.
Completion requirements 45 credit hours are required.

▶ *Criminal Justice, Public Administration (MPA)*
In the fall of 1996 there were 96 students enrolled in this program. In 1995–96, 4 degrees were earned at a distance through this program.
Application requirements *Prior education:* baccalaureate degree. *Other requirements:* college transcripts, an application fee of $75.
Completion requirements 45–49 credits are required.

INDIVIDUAL COURSE SUBJECT AREAS

Undergraduate
Accounting; business; business administration and management; comparative literature; computer and information sciences; criminal justice; environmental science; health professions and related sciences; journalism; liberal arts, general studies, and humanities; marketing; mathematics; philosophy and religion; physical sciences; political science; protective services; social psychology; social sciences; sociology

Graduate
Business; business administration and management; computer and information sciences; criminal justice; curriculum and instruction; education; education administration; educational psychology; English as a second language (ESL); finance; health professions and related sciences; mental health services; protective services; social psychology; special education; student counseling; telecommunications

See full description on page 402.

CLACKAMAS COMMUNITY COLLEGE

Oregon City, Oregon

Instructional Media Services

Clackamas Community College, founded in 1966, is a district-supported two-year college. It is accredited by the Northwest Association of Schools and Colleges. It first offered distance learning courses in 1980. In 1996–97, it offered 10 courses at a distance. In the fall of 1996, there was a total of 100 students enrolled in distance learning courses.
Course delivery sites Courses are delivered to your home, your workplace.
Media Courses are delivered via television, videotapes, World Wide Web, e-mail, print. Students and teachers interact via mail, telephone, fax, e-mail. A computer is required for some courses.
Restrictions Programs are available to local area students only.
Services Distance learners have access to library services at a distance.
Credit-earning options Students may transfer credits from another institution or may earn credits through institutionally developed exams, portfolio assessment, military training, business training.
Typical costs Tuition of $34 per credit plus mandatory fees of $2 per credit for in-state residents. Tuition of $119 per credit plus mandatory fees of $2 per credit for out-of-state residents. Costs may vary by specific program of study, number of credits taken, course delivery options. Financial aid is available to distance learners enrolled full-time or part-time.
Registration Students may register by mail, phone.
Contact Cynthia R. Andrews, Director, Learning Resource Center, Clackamas Community College, 19600 South Molalla Avenue, Oregon City, OR 97045. *Telephone:* 503-657-6958, Ext. 2417. *Fax:* 503-655-5153. *E-mail:* cyndia@clackamas.cc.or.us.

INDIVIDUAL COURSE SUBJECT AREAS

Undergraduate
Area, ethnic, and cultural studies; business; business administration and management; European languages and literatures; health and physical education/fitness; history; psychology; sociology

CLARK COLLEGE

Vancouver, Washington

Clark College, founded in 1933, is a state-supported two-year college. It is accredited by the Northwest Association of Schools and Colleges. It first offered distance learning courses in 1982. In 1996–97, it offered 6 courses at a distance. In the fall of 1996, there was a total of 157 students enrolled in distance learning courses.
Course delivery sites Courses are delivered to your home.
Media Courses are delivered via television, videotapes, audiotapes, e-mail. Students and teachers interact via mail, telephone, e-mail, on-campus meetings. A computer is required for some courses.

Profiles: Clark College

Services Distance learners have access to library services, the campus computer network, e-mail services, academic advising, career placement assistance at a distance.
Credit-earning options Students may transfer credits from another institution or may earn credits through examinations.
Typical costs Tuition of $50.35 per credit for in-state residents. Tuition of $192.85 per credit for out-of-state residents. $20 telecourse fee. Financial aid is available to distance learners.
Contact Susan Wolff, Associate Dean of Instruction, Clark College, 1800 East McLoughlin Boulevard, Vancouver, WA 98663. *Telephone:* 360-992-2314. *Fax:* 360-992-2870. *E-mail:* swolff@clark.edu. *Web site:* http://clark.edu.

INDIVIDUAL COURSE SUBJECT AREAS

Undergraduate
Business; business administration and management; developmental and child psychology; film studies; health and physical education/fitness; psychology

CLARKSON COLLEGE

Omaha, Nebraska

Office of Distance Education

Clarkson College, founded in 1888, is an independent-religious comprehensive institution affiliated with the Episcopal Church. It is accredited by the North Central Association of Colleges and Schools. It first offered distance learning courses in 1986. In 1996–97, it offered 100 courses at a distance. In the fall of 1996, there was a total of 200 students enrolled in distance learning courses.
Course delivery sites Courses are delivered to your home.
Media Courses are delivered via videotapes, audiotapes, audioconferencing, computer software, print. Students and teachers interact via audioconferencing, mail, telephone, fax, e-mail. A computer is required for all courses.
Restrictions Courses are available to US students only.
Services Distance learners have access to library services, academic advising, career placement assistance at a distance.
Credit-earning options Students may transfer credits from another institution or may earn credits through standardized exams, institutionally developed exams, portfolio assessment, military training, business training.
Typical costs *Undergraduate:* Tuition of $272 per credit hour plus mandatory fees of $16 per credit hour. *Graduate:* Tuition of $314 per credit hour plus mandatory fees of $16 per credit hour. $200 per semester distance education fee. Financial aid is available to distance learners.
Registration Students may register by mail, fax, phone, e-mail.
Contact Heidi E. Ajrami, Coordinator of Distance Education, Clarkson College, 101 South 42nd Street, Omaha, NE 68131. *Telephone:* 402-552-3037. *Fax:* 402-552-6058. *E-mail:* ajrami@clrkcol.crhsnet.edu.

DEGREE & CERTIFICATE PROGRAMS

Baccalaureate Degrees

▶ *Business Administration (BS)*
In the fall of 1996 there was 1 student enrolled in this program.
Application requirements *Prior education:* none required. *Other requirements:* ACT or SAT, high school transcript, college transcripts, an essay or personal statement, letter(s) of recommendation, an application fee of $15.
Completion requirements 128 hours are required. 64 hours must be completed through the institution. *Maximum time for completion:* 10 years.
Program contact Jeff Beals, Director, Student Enrollment Services, Clarkson College, 101 South 42nd Street, Omaha, NE 68131. Phone: 402-552-2551. Fax: 402-552-6057.

▶ *Medical Imaging (BS)*
Application requirements *Prior education:* associate's degree or certification in Radiography. *Other requirements:* ACT or SAT, high school transcript, college transcripts, an essay or personal statement, letter(s) of recommendation, an application fee of $15.
Completion requirements 128 hours are required. 43 hours must be completed through the institution. This is a degree completion program. *Maximum time for completion:* seven years.
Program contact Jeff Beals, Director, Student Enrollment Services, Clarkson College, 101 South 42nd Street, Omaha, NE 68131. Phone: 402-552-2551. Fax: 402-552-6057.

▶ *Nursing (BSN)*
In the fall of 1996 there were 10 students enrolled in this program. In 1995–96, 5 degrees were earned at a distance through this program.
Application requirements *Prior education:* associate's degree or Diploma in Nursing. *Other requirements:* ACT or SAT, high school transcript, college transcripts, an essay or personal statement, letter(s) of recommendation, an application fee of $15, RN license.
Completion requirements 128 hours are required. 41 hours must be completed through the institution. This is a degree completion program. *Maximum time for completion:* 10 years.
On-campus requirements Three weeks for clinicals during the summer.
Program contact Jeff Beals, Director, Student Enrollment Services, Clarkson College, 101 South 42nd Street, Omaha, NE 68131. Phone: 402-552-2551. Fax: 402-552-6057.

Graduate Degrees

▶ *Health Services Management (MS)*
In the fall of 1996 there were 5 students enrolled in this program. In 1995–96, 2 degrees were earned at a distance through this program.
Application requirements *Prior education:* baccalaureate degree. *Other requirements:* high school transcript, college transcripts, an essay or personal statement, letter(s) of recommendation, an application fee of $15.
Completion requirements 36 hours are required. 27 hours must be completed through the institution. *Maximum time for completion:* seven years.
Program contact Jeff Beals, Director, Student Enrollment Services, Clarkson College, 101 South 42nd Street, Omaha, NE 68131. Phone: 402-552-2551. Fax: 402-552-6057.

▶ *Nursing (MSN)*
In the fall of 1996 there were 175 students enrolled in this program. In 1995–96, 15 degrees were earned at a distance through this program.
Application requirements *Prior education:* baccalaureate degree. *Other requirements:* high school transcript, college transcripts, an essay or personal statement, letter(s) of recommendation, an application fee of $15.
Completion requirements 36 hours are required. 27 hours must be completed through the institution. *Other requirements:* 45 hours for Nurse Practitioner degree, 36 hours of these have to be completed through Clarkson College. *Maximum time for completion:* seven years.
On-campus requirements One day to defend the thesis.
Program contact Jeff Beals, Director, Student Enrollment Services, Clarkson College, 101 South 42nd Street, Omaha, NE 68131. Phone: 402-552-2551. Fax: 402-552-6057.

Graduate certificates

▶ *Family Nurse Practitioner*
In the fall of 1996 there were 10 students enrolled in this program. In 1995–96, 5 certificates were earned at a distance through this program.

Application requirements *Prior education:* MSN. *Other requirements:* high school transcript, college transcripts, an essay or personal statement, letter(s) of recommendation, an application fee of $15.
Completion requirements 27 hours are required. 18 hours must be completed through the institution. *Maximum time for completion:* seven years.
Program contact Jeff Beals, Director, Student Enrollment Services, Clarkson College, 101 South 42nd Street, Omaha, NE 68131. Phone: 402-552-2551. Fax: 402-552-6057.

INDIVIDUAL COURSE SUBJECT AREAS

Undergraduate
Accounting; business administration and management; developmental and child psychology; economics; English composition; English language and literature; fine arts; health professions and related sciences; history; liberal arts, general studies, and humanities; mathematics; nursing; philosophy and religion; political science; social psychology; sociology

Graduate
Business administration and management; health professions and related sciences; hospitality services management; mathematics; nursing

See full description on page 404.

CLARK STATE COMMUNITY COLLEGE

Springfield, Ohio

Alternative Methods of Instructional Delivery

Clark State Community College, founded in 1962, is a state-supported two-year college. It is accredited by the North Central Association of Colleges and Schools. It first offered distance learning courses in 1996.
Course delivery sites Courses are delivered to your home.
Media Courses are delivered via television, videotapes, World Wide Web, e-mail. Students and teachers interact via mail, telephone, fax, e-mail. A computer is required for some courses.
Services Distance learners have access to library services, e-mail services, academic advising, tutoring, career placement assistance at a distance.
Credit-earning options Students may transfer credits from another institution or may earn credits through standardized exams, institutionally developed exams, portfolio assessment, military training.
Typical costs Tuition of $52 per credit hour for in-state residents. Tuition of $104 per credit hour for out-of-state residents. Financial aid is available to distance learners enrolled full-time or part-time.
Contact Jane Cape, Alternative Methods of Instructional Delivery Coordinator, Clark State Community College, PO Box 570, Springfield, OH 45501-0570. *Telephone:* 937-328-6038. *Fax:* 937-328-6077. *E-mail:* capej@clark.cc.oh.us. *Web site:* http://www.clark.cc.oh.us.

INDIVIDUAL COURSE SUBJECT AREAS

Undergraduate
Abnormal psychology; American (US) history; art history and criticism; comparative literature; creative writing; English composition; health professions and related sciences

CLATSOP COMMUNITY COLLEGE

Astoria, Oregon

Clatsop Community College, founded in 1958, is a county-supported two-year college. It is accredited by the Northwest Association of Schools and Colleges.
Course delivery sites Courses are delivered to your home.
Media Courses are delivered via television, videotapes, computer conferencing.
Credit-earning options Students may transfer credits from another institution or may earn credits through examinations, portfolio assessment. Financial aid is available to distance learners.
Contact Telecommunications Specialist, Clatsop Community College, 1680 Lexington, Astoria, OR 97103. *Telephone:* 503-325-2341. *Fax:* 503-325-5738.

INDIVIDUAL COURSE SUBJECT AREAS

Undergraduate
Business; economics; English composition; geography; history; home economics and family studies; psychology; sociology; theological studies

CLAYTON COLLEGE & STATE UNIVERSITY

Morrow, Georgia

Office of Distance Learning

Clayton College & State University, founded in 1969, is a state-supported four-year college. It is accredited by the Southern Association of Colleges and Schools. It first offered distance learning courses in 1995. In 1996–97, it offered 11 courses at a distance. In the fall of 1996, there was a total of 150 students enrolled in distance learning courses.
Course delivery sites Courses are delivered to your home, military bases, 3 off-campus centers in Atlanta, Conyers, Fayetteville.
Media Courses are delivered via television, videotapes, videoconferencing, audiotapes, World Wide Web. Students and teachers interact via videoconferencing, mail, telephone, e-mail. A computer is required for all courses. The institution provides assistance with acquiring computer equipment.
Restrictions Programs are available to local area students only.
Services Distance learners have access to library services, the campus computer network, e-mail services at a distance.
Credit-earning options Students may transfer credits from another institution or may earn credits through standardized exams, institutionally developed exams.
Typical costs Tuition of $656 per quarter plus mandatory fees of $200 per quarter for in-state residents. Tuition of $2143 per quarter plus mandatory fees of $200 per quarter for out-of-state residents. Students pay $20 per course in additional fees. *Noncredit courses:* $100 per course. Financial aid is available to distance learners enrolled full-time.
Contact Dr. C. Blaine Carpenter, Academic Director of Distance Learning, Clayton College & State University, 5900 North Lee Street, Morrow, GA 30260-0285. *Telephone:* 770-961-3634. *Fax:* 770-961-3630. *E-mail:* carpenter@gg.clayton.edu.

Profiles: Clayton College & State University

DEGREE & CERTIFICATE PROGRAMS

Associate Degrees
▶ *Integrative Studies (AA)*
Application requirements *Prior education:* high school diploma or equivalent. *Other requirements:* SAT or ACT, high school transcript, college transcripts, an application fee of $20.
Completion requirements 90 quarter hours are required.
On-campus requirements For purposes of testing and assessment.

INDIVIDUAL COURSE SUBJECT AREAS

Undergraduate
Algebra; American (US) history; art history and criticism; developmental and child psychology; English composition; ethics; political science; psychology; sociology

---

CLEARY COLLEGE

Ypsilanti, Michigan

Center for Distance Learning

Cleary College, founded in 1883, is an independent-nonprofit four-year college. It is accredited by the North Central Association of Colleges and Schools. It first offered distance learning courses in 1995. In 1996–97, it offered 73 courses at a distance. In the fall of 1996, there was a total of 104 students enrolled in distance learning courses.
Course delivery sites Courses are delivered to your home.
Media Courses are delivered via e-mail. Students and teachers interact via telephone, fax, e-mail. A computer is required for some courses.
Restrictions Students must have sophomore standing.
Services Distance learners have access to library services, e-mail services, tutoring at a distance.
Credit-earning options Students may transfer credits from another institution or may earn credits through examinations, portfolio assessment, military training, business training.
Typical costs Tuition of $156 per credit hour. Financial aid is available to distance learners enrolled full-time or part-time.
Registration Students may register by phone.
Contact Admission Office, Cleary College, 3750 Cleary Drive, Howell, MI 48843. *Telephone:* 517-548-3670. *Fax:* 517-548-2170.

INDIVIDUAL COURSE SUBJECT AREAS

Undergraduate
Administrative and secretarial services; business; business administration and management; computer and information sciences; human resources management; law and legal studies; liberal arts, general studies, and humanities

---

CLEVELAND STATE UNIVERSITY

Cleveland, Ohio

Instructional Media Services

Cleveland State University, founded in 1964, is a state-supported university. It is accredited by the North Central Association of Colleges and Schools. It first offered distance learning courses in 1994. In 1996–97, it offered 30 courses at a distance. In the fall of 1996, there was a total of 67 students enrolled in distance learning courses.
Course delivery sites Courses are delivered to your workplace, The Ohio State University (Columbus), The University of Akron (Akron), off-campus center(s) in Cleveland.
Media Courses are delivered via television, videotapes, videoconferencing, audiotapes, audioconferencing, computer software, e-mail, print. Students and teachers interact via videoconferencing, audioconferencing, mail, telephone, fax, e-mail. A computer is required for some courses. The institution provides assistance with acquiring computer equipment.
Services Distance learners have access to library services, the campus computer network, e-mail services, academic advising, tutoring, career placement assistance at a distance.
Credit-earning options Students may earn credits through institutionally developed exams.
Typical costs *Undergraduate:* Tuition of $97.10 per credit hour plus mandatory fees of $1.50 per credit hour for in-state residents. Tuition of $194.20 per credit hour plus mandatory fees of $1.50 per credit hour for out-of-state residents. *Graduate:* Tuition of $127.60 per credit hour plus mandatory fees of $3 per credit hour for in-state residents. Tuition of $255.20 per credit hour plus mandatory fees of $3 per credit hour for out-of-state residents. Costs may vary by specific program of study, number of credits taken. Financial aid is available to distance learners enrolled full-time.
Registration Students may register by mail, fax.
Contact Dr. J. Fred Gage, Vice Provost, Information Technology and Academic Innovation, Cleveland State University, 1860 East 22nd Street, Rhodes Towers 1209, Cleveland, OH 44115. *Telephone:* 216-687-3588. *Fax:* 216-687-9290. *E-mail:* j.f.gage@csuohio.edu.

DEGREE & CERTIFICATE PROGRAMS

Graduate Degrees
▶ *Social Work (MSW)*
In the fall of 1996 there were 33 students enrolled in this program. In 1995–96, 10 degrees were earned at a distance through this program.
Application requirements *Prior education:* baccalaureate degree. *Other requirements:* GRE (for applicants with a GPA under 2.75 or when degree is over 6 years old), college transcripts, an essay or personal statement, letter(s) of recommendation, an application fee.
Completion requirements 60 semester credits are required. 60 semester credits must be completed through the institution. *Other requirements:* field practicum. *Maximum time for completion:* two years.
Program contact Dr. Maggie Jackson, Chairperson, Cleveland State University, 1983 East 24 Street, Cleveland, OH 44115. Phone: 216-687-4560. Fax: 216-687-5590. E-mail: mag.jackson@csuohio.edu.

INDIVIDUAL COURSE SUBJECT AREAS

Undergraduate
Physical therapy

Graduate
Education; educational research; electrical engineering; industrial engineering; social work

---

CLOVIS COMMUNITY COLLEGE

Clovis, New Mexico

Clovis Community College, founded in 1971, is a state-supported two-year college. It is accredited by the North Central Association of Colleges and Schools. It first offered distance learning courses in 1990. In 1996–97, it offered 40 courses at a distance. In the fall of 1996, there was a total of 175 students enrolled in distance learning courses.

Course delivery sites Courses are delivered to 9 off-campus centers in Clayton, Fort Sumner, Grady, House, Logan, Mosquero, Roy, San Jon, Santa Rosa.
Media Courses are delivered via television. Students and teachers interact via videoconferencing, audioconferencing, mail, telephone, fax.
Restrictions Courses are available to regional area students only.
Services Distance learners have access to library services, academic advising at a distance.
Credit-earning options Students may transfer credits from another institution or may earn credits through standardized exams, institutionally developed exams.
Typical costs Tuition of $22 per credit hour plus mandatory fees of $4 per credit hour for in-state residents. Additional $8 added to the first credit. Costs may vary by number of credits taken. Financial aid is available to distance learners enrolled full-time or part-time.
Registration Students may register by mail.
Contact Ms. Kathy Cogdill, School Relations Coordinator, Clovis Community College, 417 Schepps Boulevard, Clovis, NM 88101-8381. *Telephone:* 505-769-4112. *Fax:* 505-769-4190. *E-mail:* cogdillk@clovis.cc.nm.us.

INDIVIDUAL COURSE SUBJECT AREAS

Undergraduate
Algebra; American (US) history; art history and criticism; biology; business administration and management; cognitive psychology; communications; computer and information sciences; criminal justice; developmental and child psychology; economics; English composition; English literature; foods and nutrition studies; geology; health and physical education/fitness; music; philosophy and religion; sociology; Spanish language and literature

COASTLINE COMMUNITY COLLEGE

Fountain Valley, California

Distance Learning Department

Coastline Community College, founded in 1976, is a state and locally supported two-year college. It is accredited by the Western Association of Schools and Colleges, Inc. It first offered distance learning courses in 1976. In 1996–97, it offered 48 courses at a distance. In the fall of 1996, there was a total of 3,900 students enrolled in distance learning courses.
Course delivery sites Courses are delivered to your home, your workplace, military bases, California State University (Long Beach), 3 off-campus centers in Dominguez Hills, Fountain Valley, Garden Grove.
Media Courses are delivered via television, videotapes, videoconferencing, audiotapes, computer software, e-mail, print. Students and teachers interact via videoconferencing, audioconferencing, mail, telephone, fax, e-mail, site visits. A computer is required for some courses.
Services Distance learners have access to library services, academic advising at a distance.
Credit-earning options Students may transfer credits from another institution or may earn credits through examinations.
Typical costs Tuition of $13 per unit plus mandatory fees of $7 per semester for in-state residents. Tuition of $127 per unit plus mandatory fees of $7 per semester for out-of-state residents. *Noncredit courses:* $13 per unit. Financial aid is available to distance learners.
Registration Students may register by mail, phone.
Contact Distance Learning Department/General Information Line, Coastline Community College, 11460 Warner Avenue, Fountain Valley, CA 92708. *Telephone:* 714-241-6216. *Fax:* 714-241-6287.

DEGREE & CERTIFICATE PROGRAMS

Associate Degrees
▶ *Accounting, Business, Fine/Applied Arts, Humanities (AA)*
In the fall of 1996 there were 3,900 students enrolled in this program.
Application requirements *Prior education:* high school diploma or equivalent. *Minimum age:* 18. *Other requirements:* SAT or ACT, high school transcript, college transcripts.
Completion requirements 60 units are required. 32 units must be completed through the institution.

INDIVIDUAL COURSE SUBJECT AREAS

Undergraduate
Area, ethnic, and cultural studies; astronomy and astrophysics; biological and life sciences; biology; business; business administration and management; chemistry; computer and information sciences; developmental and child psychology; English composition; English language and literature; European languages and literatures; geology; health and physical education/fitness; history; human resources management; law and legal studies; liberal arts, general studies, and humanities; mathematics; philosophy and religion; physical sciences; political science; psychology; social sciences; sociology

Noncredit
Area, ethnic, and cultural studies; astronomy and astrophysics; biological and life sciences; biology; business; business administration and management; chemistry; computer and information sciences; developmental and child psychology; English composition; English language and literature; European languages and literatures; geology; health and physical education/fitness; history; human resources management; law and legal studies; liberal arts, general studies, and humanities; mathematics; philosophy and religion; physical sciences; political science; psychology; social sciences; sociology

COFFEYVILLE COMMUNITY COLLEGE

Coffeyville, Kansas

Center for Economic and Community Development

Coffeyville Community College, founded in 1923, is a state and locally supported two-year college. It is accredited by the North Central Association of Colleges and Schools. It first offered distance learning courses in 1987. In 1996–97, it offered 2 courses at a distance. In the fall of 1996, there was a total of 25 students enrolled in distance learning courses.
Course delivery sites Courses are delivered to Fort Scott Community College (Fort Scott), area high schools.
Media Courses are delivered via videoconferencing. Students and teachers interact via videoconferencing. A computer is required for some courses.
Restrictions Programs are available to in-state students only.
Services Distance learners have access to academic advising at a distance.
Credit-earning options Students may transfer credits from another institution or may earn credits through military training, business training.
Typical costs Tuition of $26 per credit plus mandatory fees of $13 per credit for in-state residents. Tuition of $71 per credit plus mandatory fees of $13 per credit for out-of-state residents. *Noncredit courses:* $350 for 48 contact hours. Costs may vary by campus or location, course delivery options. Financial aid is available to distance learners enrolled full-time.
Registration Students may register by phone.
Contact Marlon Thornburg, Director of the Center for Economic and Community Development, Coffeyville Community College, 400 West

Profiles: Coffeyville Community College

11th Street, Coffeyville, KS 67337. *Telephone:* 316-251-7700, Ext. 2130. *Fax:* 316-252-7098. *E-mail:* marlont@raven.ccc.cc.ks.us.

INDIVIDUAL COURSE SUBJECT AREAS

Undergraduate
Health professions and related sciences

Noncredit
Health professions and related sciences

COLBY COMMUNITY COLLEGE

Colby, Kansas

Community Services

Colby Community College, founded in 1964, is a state and locally supported two-year college. It is accredited by the North Central Association of Colleges and Schools. It first offered distance learning courses in 1992. In 1996–97, it offered 23 courses at a distance. In the fall of 1996, there was a total of 160 students enrolled in distance learning courses.
Course delivery sites Courses are delivered to 17 locations around Kansas.
Media Courses are delivered via television, videotapes. Students and teachers interact via mail, telephone, fax.
Restrictions Courses are available to students in northwest Kansas only.
Services Distance learners have access to library services, the campus computer network, academic advising, tutoring, career placement assistance at a distance.
Credit-earning options Students may transfer credits from another institution or may earn credits through standardized exams, military training, business training.
Typical costs Tuition of $34 per credit hour plus mandatory fees of $5 per credit hour for in-state residents. Tuition of $67 per credit hour plus mandatory fees of $5 per credit hour for out-of-state residents. *Noncredit courses:* $25 per course. Costs may vary by campus or location, number of credits taken. Financial aid is available to distance learners enrolled full-time or part-time.
Registration Students may register by mail, phone.
Contact Joe Mildrexler, Dean of Community Services, Colby Community College, 1255 South Range, Colby, KS 67701. *Telephone:* 913-462-3984. *Fax:* 913-462-4699. *E-mail:* joe@katie.colby.cc.ks.us. *Web site:* http://www.colby.cc.ks.us.

INDIVIDUAL COURSE SUBJECT AREAS

Undergraduate
Accounting; administrative and secretarial services; agriculture; biological and life sciences; biology; business; computer and information sciences; creative writing; developmental and child psychology; economics; English as a second language (ESL); English composition; English language and literature; fine arts; health professions and related sciences; history; home economics and family studies; human resources management; liberal arts, general studies, and humanities; mathematics; nursing; physical sciences; political science; psychology; public administration and services; public health; social psychology; social sciences; social work; sociology

Noncredit
Nursing; public health

COLLEGE FOR FINANCIAL PLANNING

Denver, Colorado

College for Financial Planning is an independent-nonprofit graduate institution. It is accredited by the North Central Association of Colleges and Schools. It first offered distance learning courses in 1972. In 1996–97, it offered 27 courses at a distance.
Course delivery sites Courses are delivered to your home, your workplace, military bases.
Media Courses are delivered via audiotapes, computer software, World Wide Web, print. Students and teachers interact via mail, telephone, fax, e-mail. A computer is required for some courses.
Services Distance learners have access to e-mail services, academic advising, tutoring at a distance.
Credit-earning options Students may transfer credits from another institution or may earn credits through institutionally developed exams, business training.
Typical costs Tuition of $525 per course. Costs may vary by specific program of study.
Registration Students may register by mail, fax, phone, e-mail, World Wide Web.
Contact Student Service Center, College for Financial Planning, College for Financial Planning/National Endowment for Financial Education, 4695 South Monaco Street, Denver, CO 80237. *Telephone:* 303-220-4800. *Web site:* http://nefe.org.

DEGREE & CERTIFICATE PROGRAMS

Graduate Degrees
▶ *Personal Financial Planning (MS)*
In 1995–96, 300 degrees were earned at a distance through this program.
Application requirements *Prior education:* baccalaureate degree. *Other requirements:* college transcripts, an essay or personal statement, an application fee of $75.
Completion requirements 36 credit hours are required. *Maximum time for completion:* seven years.

INDIVIDUAL COURSE SUBJECT AREAS

Undergraduate
Accounting; finance; investments and securities

Graduate
Finance

COLLEGE MISERICORDIA

Dallas, Pennsylvania

College Misericordia, founded in 1924, is an independent-religious Roman Catholic comprehensive institution. It is accredited by the Middle States Association of Colleges and Schools. It first offered distance learning courses in 1994.
Course delivery sites Courses are delivered to other colleges.
Media Courses are delivered via videoconferencing.
Credit-earning options Students may transfer credits from another institution. Financial aid is available to distance learners.
Contact Dr. Associate Professor, College Misericordia, 301 Lake Street, Dallas, PA 18612. *Telephone:* 717-674-6436. *Fax:* 717-675-2441.

INDIVIDUAL COURSE SUBJECT AREAS

Undergraduate
Developmental and child psychology; fine arts; political science; sociology

Graduate
Special education; teacher education

Noncredit
Special education; teacher education

COLLEGE OF DUPAGE

Glen Ellyn, Illinois

Center for Independent Learning

College of DuPage, founded in 1967, is a state and locally supported two-year college. It is accredited by the North Central Association of Colleges and Schools. It first offered distance learning courses in 1980. In 1996–97, it offered 130 courses at a distance.
Course delivery sites Courses are delivered to your home, your workplace, Aurora University (Aurora), Benedictine University (Lisle), DePaul University (Chicago), DeVry Institute of Technology (Chicago), Elmhurst College (Elmhurst), Illinois Institute of Technology (Chicago), Illinois State University (Normal), Lewis University (Romeoville), Midwestern University (Downers Grove), Morton College (Cicero), The National College of Chiropractic (Lombard), National-Louis University (Evanston), North Central College (Naperville), Northeastern Illinois University (Chicago), Northern Illinois University (De Kalb), Robert Morris College (Chicago), Triton College (River Grove), University of Illinois at Chicago (Chicago), off-campus center(s) in Glendale Heights, Lombard, Naperville, Westmont.
Media Courses are delivered via television, videotapes, videoconferencing, audiotapes, radio broadcast, computer software, World Wide Web, print. Students and teachers interact via videoconferencing, mail, telephone, fax, e-mail.
Services Distance learners have access to e-mail services at a distance.
Credit-earning options Students may transfer credits from another institution or may earn credits through standardized exams, institutionally developed exams, portfolio assessment, military training.
Typical costs Tuition of $30 per quarter credit for local area residents. Tuition of $92 per quarter credit for in-state residents. Tuition of $129 per quarter credit for out-of-state residents. *Noncredit courses:* $55 per course. Costs may vary by number of credits taken. Financial aid is available to distance learners.
Registration Students may register by mail, fax, phone, World Wide Web.
Contact Ron Schiesz, Associate Dean, Alternative Learning Program, College of DuPage, Center for Independent Learning, 425 22nd Street, Glen Ellyn, IL 60137-6599. *Telephone:* 630-942-2130. *Fax:* 630-942-3749. *E-mail:* schiesz@cdnet.cod.edu. *Web site:* http://www.cod.edu/Academic/AcadProg/SelfLear.htm.

INDIVIDUAL COURSE SUBJECT AREAS

Undergraduate
Accounting; area, ethnic, and cultural studies; biological and life sciences; biology; business; business administration and management; chemistry; computer and information sciences; developmental and child psychology; economics; education; educational psychology; English as a second language (ESL); English composition; English language and literature; European languages and literatures; geology; history; liberal arts, general studies, and humanities; mathematics; music; philosophy and religion; physical sciences; physics; political science; psychology; social psychology; social sciences; sociology; teacher education

COLLEGE OF LAKE COUNTY

Grayslake, Illinois

Educational Technology

College of Lake County, founded in 1967, is a district-supported two-year college. It is accredited by the North Central Association of Colleges and Schools. It first offered distance learning courses in 1994. In 1996–97, it offered 30 courses at a distance. In the fall of 1996, there was a total of 150 students enrolled in distance learning courses.
Course delivery sites Courses are delivered to your home, other colleges.
Media Courses are delivered via television, videoconferencing. Students and teachers interact via videoconferencing.
Restrictions Programs are available to local area students only.
Services Distance learners have access to library services, tutoring at a distance.
Credit-earning options Students may transfer credits from another institution or may earn credits through examinations, military training.
Typical costs Tuition of $50 per credit. Financial aid is available to distance learners.
Registration Students may register by mail, phone.
Contact Tom Buchta, Dean, Learning Resource Center, College of Lake County, 19351 West Washington Street, Grayslake, IL 60030. *Telephone:* 847-223-6601. *Fax:* 847-223-7690. *E-mail:* tbuchta@clc.cc.il.us.

INDIVIDUAL COURSE SUBJECT AREAS

Undergraduate
Asian languages and literatures; business administration and management; English composition; English language and literature; European languages and literatures; geology; hospitality services management; liberal arts, general studies, and humanities; library and information studies; mathematics

Noncredit
English as a second language (ESL)

COLLEGE OF ST. FRANCIS

Joliet, Illinois

College of St. Francis, founded in 1920, is an independent-religious Roman Catholic comprehensive institution. It is accredited by the North Central Association of Colleges and Schools. It first offered distance learning courses in 1995. In 1996–97, it offered 3 courses at a distance. In the fall of 1996, there was a total of 60 students enrolled in distance learning courses.
Course delivery sites Courses are delivered to your home, your workplace, Olivet Nazarene University (Kankakee), Saint Xavier University (Chicago).
Media Courses are delivered via videoconferencing, World Wide Web, e-mail. Students and teachers interact via videoconferencing, fax, e-mail. A computer is required for some courses.
Restrictions Programs are available to in-state students only.
Services Distance learners have access to library services, e-mail services, academic advising at a distance.

Profiles: College of St. Francis

Credit-earning options Students may transfer credits from another institution or may earn credits through standardized exams, portfolio assessment, military training.
Typical costs *Undergraduate:* Tuition of $340 per hour. *Graduate:* Tuition of $272 per hour. Financial aid is available to distance learners enrolled full-time.
Registration Students may register by mail, fax, e-mail.
Contact Mr. Charles M. Beutel, Registrar, College of St. Francis, 500 North Wilcox Street, Joliet, IL 60431. *Telephone:* 815-740-3391. *Fax:* 815-740-4285. *E-mail:* regbeutel@vax.colsf.edu.

INDIVIDUAL COURSE SUBJECT AREAS

Undergraduate
Biology; French language and literature; history; Spanish language and literature; teacher education

Graduate
Business administration and management

COLLEGE OF ST. SCHOLASTICA

Duluth, Minnesota

Graduate Studies

College of St. Scholastica, founded in 1912, is an independent-religious comprehensive institution affiliated with the Roman Catholic Church. It is accredited by the North Central Association of Colleges and Schools. It first offered distance learning courses in 1986. In 1996–97, it offered 50 courses at a distance. In the fall of 1996, there was a total of 290 students enrolled in distance learning courses.
Course delivery sites Courses are delivered to your home.
Media Courses are delivered via television, videotapes, audiotapes, World Wide Web, print. Students and teachers interact via videoconferencing, mail, telephone, fax, e-mail.
Services Distance learners have access to library services, the campus computer network, e-mail services, academic advising at a distance.
Credit-earning options Students may transfer credits from another institution.
Typical costs *Undergraduate:* Tuition of $272 per quarter credit. *Graduate:* Tuition of $292 per quarter credit. Costs may vary by specific program of study. Financial aid is available to distance learners enrolled full-time or part-time.
Registration Students may register by mail.
Contact Admissions/Encore , College of St. Scholastica, 1200 Kenwood Avenue, Duluth, MN 55811. *Telephone:* 218-723-6046. *Fax:* 218-723-5991. *E-mail:* admiss@stf1.css.edu. *Web site:* http://www.css.edu/acad/grad/gradpage.html.

DEGREE & CERTIFICATE PROGRAMS

Graduate Degrees

▶ *Curriculum and Instruction (MEd)*
In the fall of 1996 there were 287 students enrolled in this program.
Application requirements *Prior education:* baccalaureate degree. *Other requirements:* two years of experience working in education.
Completion requirements 48 quarter credits are required. 40 quarter credits must be completed through the institution. *Maximum time for completion:* seven years.
On-campus requirements Overnight seminars at the beginning and end of the program.
Program contact Sr. Clare Marie Trettel, Assistant Professor, College of St. Scholastica, 1200 Kenwood Avenue, Duluth, MN 55811. Phone: 800-888-8796. Fax: 218-723-6709. E-mail: ctrettel@fac1.css.edu.

INDIVIDUAL COURSE SUBJECT AREAS

Undergraduate
Abnormal psychology; accounting; anthropology; biological and life sciences; business administration and management; communications; developmental and child psychology; English language and literature; French language and literature; history; international business; political science; psychology; sociology

Graduate
Abnormal psychology; accounting; anthropology; biological and life sciences; business administration and management; communications; curriculum and instruction; developmental and child psychology; English language and literature; French language and literature; history; instructional media; international business; political science; psychology; sociology; teacher education

COLLEGE OF SAN MATEO

San Mateo, California

Distance Learning Office

College of San Mateo, founded in 1922, is a state and locally supported two-year college. It is accredited by the Western Association of Schools and Colleges, Inc. It first offered distance learning courses in 1977. In 1996–97, it offered 73 courses at a distance. In the fall of 1996, there was a total of 900 students enrolled in distance learning courses.
Course delivery sites Courses are delivered to your home, your workplace, local correctional facilities.
Media Courses are delivered via television, videotapes, print. Students and teachers interact via mail, telephone, fax, e-mail. A computer is required for some courses.
Restrictions Programs are available to local area students only.
Services Distance learners have access to e-mail services at a distance.
Credit-earning options Students may transfer credits from another institution or may earn credits through examinations, military training.
Typical costs Tuition of $0 per unit plus mandatory fees of $13 per unit for in-state residents. Tuition of $113 per unit plus mandatory fees of $13 per unit for out-of-state residents. Costs may vary by number of credits taken. Financial aid is available to distance learners.
Registration Students may register by mail, phone.
Contact Martha Mills, Telecourse Coordinator, College of San Mateo, 1700 West Hillsdale Boulevard, San Mateo, CA 94402. *Telephone:* 415-574-6120. *Fax:* 415-574-6675. *E-mail:* marthamills@kcsm.pbs.org. *Web site:* http://www.kcsm.org.

INDIVIDUAL COURSE SUBJECT AREAS

Undergraduate
Anthropology; area, ethnic, and cultural studies; astronomy and astrophysics; business; business administration and management; chemistry; computer and information sciences; conservation and natural resources; European languages and literatures; fine arts; geology; health and physical education/fitness; history; philosophy and religion; political science; psychology; sociology

COLLEGE OF THE CANYONS

Santa Clarita, California

Learning Resources

College of the Canyons, founded in 1969, is a state and locally supported two-year college. It is accredited by the Western Association of Schools and Colleges, Inc. It first offered distance learning courses in 1975. In 1996–97, it offered 11 courses at a distance. In the fall of 1996, there was a total of 225 students enrolled in distance learning courses.
Course delivery sites Courses are delivered to your home.
Media Courses are delivered via television. Students and teachers interact via mail, telephone, e-mail.
Restrictions Programs are available to local area students only.
Services Distance learners have access to the campus computer network at a distance.
Credit-earning options Students may transfer credits from another institution or may earn credits through examinations, portfolio assessment, military training, business training.
Typical costs Tuition of $13 per unit for in-state residents. Tuition of $123 per unit for out-of-state residents. Costs may vary by number of credits taken. Financial aid is available to distance learners enrolled full-time or part-time.
Registration Students may register by mail, phone.
Contact Mr. Jan K. Keller, Assistant Dean, Learning Resources, College of the Canyons, 26544 Rockwell Canyon Road, Santa Clarita, CA 91355. *Telephone:* 805-259-7800, Ext. 3330. *Fax:* 805-253-1845. *E-mail:* keller_j@coc.cc.ca.us. *Web site:* http://www.coc.cc.ca.us.

INDIVIDUAL COURSE SUBJECT AREAS

Undergraduate
Area, ethnic, and cultural studies; astronomy and astrophysics; developmental and child psychology; economics; history; political science; sociology

COLLEGE OF THE MAINLAND

Texas City, Texas

College of the Mainland, founded in 1967, is a state and locally supported two-year college. It is accredited by the Southern Association of Colleges and Schools. It first offered distance learning courses in 1996.
Course delivery sites Courses are delivered to your home, other colleges.
Media Courses are delivered via television, videotapes. Students and teachers interact via telephone.
Restrictions Programs are available to in-state students only.
Credit-earning options Students may transfer credits from another institution or may earn credits through examinations, military training, business training.
Typical costs Tuition of $87.75 per course plus mandatory fees of $19 per course for local area residents. Tuition of $186 per course plus mandatory fees of $19 per course for in-state residents. Tuition of $280 per course plus mandatory fees of $19 per course for out-of-state residents. Financial aid is available to distance learners.
Contact Dean of Instruction's Office, College of the Mainland, 1200 Amburn Road, Texas City, TX 77591-2499. *Telephone:* 409-938-1211, Ext. 229.

INDIVIDUAL COURSE SUBJECT AREAS

Undergraduate
History; political science

COLLEGE OF THE SOUTHWEST

Hobbs, New Mexico

College of the Southwest, founded in 1962, is an independent-nonprofit comprehensive institution. It is accredited by the North Central Association of Colleges and Schools. It first offered distance learning courses in 1994.
Course delivery sites Courses are delivered to 1 off-campus center in Carlsbad.
Media Courses are delivered via television. Students and teachers interact via videoconferencing.
Restrictions Programs are available to local area students only.
Services Distance learners have access to library services at a distance.
Credit-earning options Students may transfer credits from another institution or may earn credits through examinations, portfolio assessment, military training.
Typical costs *Undergraduate:* Tuition of $143 per semester hour. *Graduate:* Tuition of $150 per semester hour. Costs may vary by campus or location. Financial aid is available to distance learners.
Contact Glenna Ohaver, Director of Educational Services, College of the Southwest, 6610 Lovington Highway, Hobbs, NM 88240. *Telephone:* 505-392-6561. *Fax:* 505-392-6006.

DEGREE & CERTIFICATE PROGRAMS

Graduate Degrees

▶ *Curriculum and Instruction, Educational Administration/ Counseling (MSE)*
Application requirements *Prior education:* baccalaureate degree. *Other requirements:* ACT or SAT, high school transcript, college transcripts, letter(s) of recommendation, an application fee of $25.
Completion requirements 36 semester hours are required. 27 semester hours must be completed through the institution.
On-campus requirements To take three education classes.

INDIVIDUAL COURSE SUBJECT AREAS

Undergraduate
Accounting; advertising; area, ethnic, and cultural studies; biology; botany; business; business administration and management; conservation and natural resources; creative writing; developmental and child psychology; economics; education administration; educational psychology; English as a second language (ESL); English composition; English language and literature; fine arts; health and physical education/fitness; history; human resources management; industrial psychology; liberal arts, general studies, and humanities; mathematics; philosophy and religion; political science; social psychology; sociology; special education; teacher education; zoology

Graduate
Education administration; educational psychology

Distance Learning Programs

Profiles: The College of West Virginia

THE COLLEGE OF WEST VIRGINIA

Beckley, West Virginia

School of Academic Enrichment and Lifelong Learning (SAELL)

The College of West Virginia, founded in 1933, is an independent-nonprofit four-year college. It is accredited by the North Central Association of Colleges and Schools. It first offered distance learning courses in 1992. In 1996–97, it offered 150 courses at a distance. In the fall of 1996, there was a total of 376 students enrolled in distance learning courses.

Course delivery sites Courses are delivered to your home, your workplace, military bases.
Media Courses are delivered via videotapes, audiotapes, computer software, e-mail, print. Students and teachers interact via mail, telephone, fax, e-mail. A computer is required for some courses.
Services Distance learners have access to library services, e-mail services, academic advising, tutoring, career placement assistance, enrollment at a distance.
Credit-earning options Students may transfer credits from another institution or may earn credits through standardized exams, institutionally developed exams, portfolio assessment, military training, business training.
Typical costs Tuition of $115 per credit hour plus mandatory fees of $25 per credit hour. *Noncredit courses:* $420 per course. Financial aid is available to distance learners enrolled full-time or part-time.
Registration Students may register by mail, fax, phone, e-mail.
Contact Karen Carter-Harvey, Student Outreach Coordinator, The College of West Virginia, PO Box AG, Beckley, WV 25802-2830. *Telephone:* 304-253-7351. *Fax:* 304-253-3485. *E-mail:* saell@cwv.edu. *Web site:* http://www.cwv.edu/saell/index.html.

DEGREE & CERTIFICATE PROGRAMS

Associate Degrees

▶ *Aviation Technology (AS)*
Application requirements *Minimum age:* 25. *Other requirements:* ACT, SAT, high school transcript, college transcripts, an application fee of $25, actual flight certification and/or licensing prior to enrolling, cover letter, resume.
Completion requirements 66 credit hours are required. 18 credit hours must be completed through the institution.

▶ *Banking and Finance (AS)*
Application requirements *Prior education:* high school diploma or equivalent. *Minimum age:* 25. *Other requirements:* ACT, SAT, high school transcript, college transcripts, an application fee of $25, cover letter, resume.
Completion requirements 65 credit hours are required. 18 credit hours must be completed through the institution.

▶ *Business Administration (AS)*
Application requirements *Prior education:* high school diploma or equivalent. *Minimum age:* 25. *Other requirements:* ACT, SAT, high school transcript, college transcripts, an application fee of $25, cover letter, resume.
Completion requirements 65 credit hours are required. 18 credit hours must be completed through the institution.

▶ *Criminal Justice (AS)*
Application requirements *Prior education:* high school diploma or equivalent. *Minimum age:* 25. *Other requirements:* ACT, SAT, high school transcript, college transcripts, an application fee of $25, cover letter, resume.
Completion requirements 68 credit hours are required. 18 credit hours must be completed through the institution.

▶ *Elementary Teacher Preparation (AA)*
Application requirements *Prior education:* high school diploma or equivalent. *Minimum age:* 25. *Other requirements:* ACT, SAT, high school transcript, college transcripts, an application fee of $25, cover letter, resume.
Completion requirements 66 credit hours are required. 18 credit hours must be completed through the institution.

▶ *Environmental Studies (AS)*
Application requirements *Prior education:* high school diploma or equivalent. *Minimum age:* 25. *Other requirements:* ACT, SAT, high school transcript, college transcripts, an application fee of $25, cover letter, resume.
Completion requirements 66 credit hours are required. 18 credit hours must be completed through the institution.

▶ *General Studies (AA, AS)*
Application requirements *Prior education:* high school diploma or equivalent. *Minimum age:* 25. *Other requirements:* ACT, SAT, high school transcript, college transcripts, an application fee of $25, cover letter, resume.
Completion requirements 65 credit hours are required. 18 credit hours must be completed through the institution.

▶ *Medical Assisting (AS)*
Application requirements *Prior education:* high school diploma or equivalent. *Minimum age:* 25. *Other requirements:* ACT, SAT, high school transcript, college transcripts, an application fee of $25, cover letter, resume.
Completion requirements 67 credit hours are required. 18 credit hours must be completed through the institution.

▶ *Paralegal Studies (AS)*
Application requirements *Prior education:* high school diploma or equivalent. *Minimum age:* 25. *Other requirements:* ACT, SAT, high school transcript, college transcripts, an application fee of $25, cover letter, resume.
Completion requirements 65 credit hours are required. 18 credit hours must be completed through the institution.

▶ *Secondary Teacher Preparation (AA)*
Application requirements *Prior education:* high school diploma or equivalent. *Minimum age:* 25. *Other requirements:* ACT, SAT, high school transcript, an application fee of $25, cover letter, resume.
Completion requirements 67 credit hours are required. 18 credit hours must be completed through the institution.

▶ *Secretarial Science (AS)*
Application requirements *Prior education:* high school diploma or equivalent. *Minimum age:* 25. *Other requirements:* ACT, SAT, high school transcript, college transcripts, an application fee of $25, cover letter, resume.
Completion requirements 68 credit hours are required. 18 credit hours must be completed through the institution.

▶ *Travel (AS)*
Application requirements *Prior education:* high school diploma or equivalent. *Minimum age:* 25. *Other requirements:* ACT, SAT, high school transcript, college transcripts, an application fee of $25, cover letter, resume.
Completion requirements 65 credit hours are required. 18 credit hours must be completed through the institution.

Baccalaureate Degrees

▶ *Business Administration (BS)*
Application requirements *Prior education:* high school diploma or equivalent. *Minimum age:* 25. *Other requirements:* ACT, SAT, high school transcript, college transcripts, an application fee of $25, cover letter, resume.

Completion requirements 128 credit hours are required. 18 credit hours must be completed through the institution.

▶ *Criminal Justice (BS)*

Application requirements *Prior education:* high school diploma or equivalent. *Minimum age:* 25. *Other requirements:* ACT, SAT, high school transcript, college transcripts, an application fee of $25, cover letter, resume.

Completion requirements 128 credit hours are required. 18 credit hours must be completed through the institution.

▶ *Health Care Management (BS)*

Application requirements *Prior education:* high school diploma or equivalent. *Minimum age:* 25. *Other requirements:* ACT, SAT, high school transcript, college transcripts, an application fee of $25, cover letter, resume.

Completion requirements 128 credit hours are required. 18 credit hours must be completed through the institution.

▶ *Interdisciplinary Studies (BA, BS)*

Application requirements *Prior education:* high school diploma or equivalent. *Minimum age:* 25. *Other requirements:* ACT, SAT, high school transcript, college transcripts, an application fee of $25, cover letter, resume.

Completion requirements 128 credit hours are required. 18 credit hours must be completed through the institution.

▶ *Nursing (BSN)*

Application requirements *Prior education:* associates degree or diploma in nursing. *Minimum age:* 25. *Other requirements:* ACT, SAT, college transcripts, an application fee of $25, RN license.

Completion requirements 23 credit hours prior to upper division nursing courses are required, then 14 total upper division nursing courses. 18 credit hours must be completed through the institution.

Undergraduate Certificates

▶ *Aviation Technology*

Application requirements *Prior education:* high school diploma or equivalent. *Minimum age:* 25. *Other requirements:* ACT, SAT, high school transcript, college transcripts, an application fee of $25, actual flight certification and/or licensing prior to enrolling, cover letter, resume.

Completion requirements 40 credit hours are required. 18 credit hours must be completed through the institution. *Other requirements:* this program is completed at a distance by licensed/certified pilots.

▶ *General Business Management*

Application requirements *Prior education:* high school diploma or equivalent. *Minimum age:* 25. *Other requirements:* ACT, SAT, high school transcript, college transcripts, an application fee of $25, cover letter, resume.

Completion requirements 33 credit hours are required. 18 credit hours must be completed through the institution.

▶ *Office Technology*

Application requirements *Prior education:* high school diploma or equivalent. *Minimum age:* 25. *Other requirements:* ACT, SAT, high school transcript, college transcripts, an application fee of $25, cover letter, resume.

Completion requirements 33 credit hours are required. 18 credit hours must be completed through the institution.

▶ *Travel and Tourism*

Application requirements *Prior education:* high school diploma or equivalent. *Minimum age:* 25. *Other requirements:* ACT, SAT, high school transcript, college transcripts, an application fee of $25, cover letter, resume.

Completion requirements 33 credit hours are required. 18 credit hours must be completed through the institution.

INDIVIDUAL COURSE SUBJECT AREAS

Undergraduate

Accounting; administrative and secretarial services; advertising; area, ethnic, and cultural studies; biological and life sciences; biology; business; business administration and management; chemistry; communications; computer and information sciences; conservation and natural resources; developmental and child psychology; economics; English composition; English language and literature; fine arts; health professions and related sciences; history; hospitality services management; human resources management; law and legal studies; liberal arts, general studies, and humanities; mathematics; microbiology; music; nursing; philosophy and religion; physical sciences; physics; political science; psychology; public administration and services; public health; social sciences; social work; sociology; teacher education

COLLIN COUNTY COMMUNITY COLLEGE

McKinney, Texas

Media Services Department

Collin County Community College, founded in 1985, is a state and locally supported two-year college. It is accredited by the Southern Association of Colleges and Schools. It first offered distance learning courses in 1987. In 1996–97, it offered 18 courses at a distance. In the fall of 1996, there was a total of 579 students enrolled in distance learning courses.

Course delivery sites Courses are delivered to your home.

Media Courses are delivered via television, videotapes. Students and teachers interact via mail, telephone, fax, e-mail.

Restrictions Students must be able to travel to campus.

Services Distance learners have access to library services, the campus computer network, academic advising, tutoring at a distance.

Credit-earning options Students may transfer credits from another institution or may earn credits through examinations.

Typical costs Tuition of $74 per course for local area residents. Tuition of $95 per course for in-state residents. Tuition of $230 per course for out-of-state residents. *Noncredit courses:* $80 per course. Costs may vary by number of credits taken. Financial aid is available to distance learners.

Registration Students may register by mail, fax, phone.

Contact Wendy Burton, Coordinator of Distance Learning, Collin County Community College, 2800 East Spring Creek Parkway, Plano, TX 75074. *Telephone:* 972-881-5828. *Fax:* 972-881-5911. *E-mail:* wburton@fs7host.ccccd.edu. *Web site:* http://www.ccccd.edu.

INDIVIDUAL COURSE SUBJECT AREAS

Undergraduate

Accounting; business administration and management; English composition; European languages and literatures; history; liberal arts, general studies, and humanities; mathematics; political science; social psychology; sociology

COLORADO ELECTRONIC COMMUNITY COLLEGE

Aurora, Colorado

Colorado Electronic Community College is a state-supported two-year college. It first offered distance learning courses in 1995. In 1996–97, it

Profiles: Colorado Electronic Community College

offered 20 courses at a distance. In the fall of 1996, there was a total of 200 students enrolled in distance learning courses.

Course delivery sites Courses are delivered to your home, your workplace, military bases.

Media Courses are delivered via television, videotapes, audiotapes, computer software, e-mail, print. Students and teachers interact via videoconferencing, audioconferencing, mail, telephone, fax, e-mail. A computer is required for some courses.

Services Distance learners have access to library services, e-mail services, academic advising, tutoring at a distance.

Credit-earning options Students may transfer credits from another institution or may earn credits through standardized exams, institutionally developed exams, portfolio assessment, military training, business training.

Typical costs Tuition of $120 per credit plus mandatory fees of $65 per course. Costs may vary by number of credits taken, course delivery options. Financial aid is available to distance learners enrolled full-time or part-time.

Registration Students may register by mail, fax, phone, e-mail, World Wide Web.

Contact Michael Rusk, Director of Student Services, Colorado Electronic Community College, 8880 East 10th Place, Aurora, CO 80010. *Telephone:* 303-340-5706. *Fax:* 303-340-5876. *E-mail:* sb_mike@cccs.cccoes.edu. *Web site:* http://www.cccoes.edu.

DEGREE & CERTIFICATE PROGRAMS

Associate Degrees
▶ *Liberal Arts (AA)*
In the fall of 1996 there were 200 students enrolled in this program.
Application requirements *Minimum age:* 16. *Other requirements:* ACT, SAT, CPT, ASSET, application form.
Completion requirements 60 credits are required. 15 credits must be completed through the institution.

INDIVIDUAL COURSE SUBJECT AREAS

Undergraduate
Algebra; anthropology; astronomy and astrophysics; computer and information sciences; developmental and child psychology; English composition; ethics; geography; geology; history of science and technology; mass media; music; psychology; sociology; statistics

See full description on page 406.

COLORADO MOUNTAIN COLLEGE DISTRICT

Glenwood Springs, Colorado

Colorado Mountain College District is a locally supported college system. It first offered distance learning courses in 1985. In 1996–97, it offered 62 courses at a distance. In the fall of 1996, there was a total of 702 students enrolled in distance learning courses.

Course delivery sites Courses are delivered to your home, 9 off-campus centers in Aspen, Breckenridge, Eagle, Glenwood Springs, Leadville, Rifle, Steamboat Springs, Vail.

Media Courses are delivered via videotapes, videoconferencing. Students and teachers interact via videoconferencing, mail, telephone, fax, e-mail.

Restrictions Programs are available to local area students only.

Services Distance learners have access to library services, the campus computer network, e-mail services, academic advising, tutoring, career placement assistance at a distance.

Credit-earning options Students may transfer credits from another institution or may earn credits through examinations, portfolio assessment, military training, business training.

Typical costs Tuition of $34 per credit for local area residents. Tuition of $63 per credit for in-state residents. Tuition of $200 per credit for out-of-state residents. Fees vary. Costs may vary by number of credits taken. Financial aid is available to distance learners enrolled full-time.

Registration Students may register by fax, phone.

Contact Ms. Teri Kinkade, Director of Pre-enrollment Services, Colorado Mountain College District, 831 Grand Avenue, Glenwood Springs, CO 81601. *Telephone:* 970-945-8691. *Fax:* 970-945-7279. *E-mail:* kinkade@coloradomtn.edu. *Web site:* http://www.coloradomtn.edu/services.html.

INDIVIDUAL COURSE SUBJECT AREAS

Undergraduate
Abnormal psychology; accounting; algebra; anthropology; archaeology; area, ethnic, and cultural studies; art history and criticism; biology; business administration and management; business communications; business law; calculus; chemistry; child care and development; creative writing; criminal justice; developmental and child psychology; drama and theater; economics; electronics; English as a second language (ESL); English composition; English language and literature; ethics; fine arts; foods and nutrition studies; geography; health and physical education/fitness; history; liberal arts, general studies, and humanities; marketing; mathematics; philosophy and religion; physics; political science; social psychology; sociology; Spanish language and literature; statistics; teacher education; visual and performing arts

COLORADO NORTHWESTERN COMMUNITY COLLEGE

Rangely, Colorado

Distance Learning Department

Colorado Northwestern Community College, founded in 1962, is a district-supported two-year college. It is accredited by the North Central Association of Colleges and Schools. It first offered distance learning courses in 1989. In 1996–97, it offered 29 courses at a distance. In the fall of 1996, there was a total of 69 students enrolled in distance learning courses.

Course delivery sites Courses are delivered to your home.

Media Courses are delivered via videotapes, audiotapes, audioconferencing, print. Students and teachers interact via audioconferencing, mail, telephone, fax.

Services Distance learners have access to academic advising at a distance.

Credit-earning options Students may transfer credits from another institution or may earn credits through examinations, portfolio assessment, military training.

Typical costs Tuition of $552 per semester plus mandatory fees of $35 per course for in-state residents. Tuition of $2095 per semester plus mandatory fees of $35 per course for out-of-state residents. Costs may vary by number of credits taken.

Registration Students may register by mail, phone.

Contact Brenna Kenney, Distance Learning, Colorado Northwestern Community College, 500 Kennedy Drive, Rangely, CO 81648. *Telephone:* 970-675-3273. *Fax:* 970-675-3291. *E-mail:* bkenney@sage.cncc.cc.co.us.

DEGREE & CERTIFICATE PROGRAMS

Associate Degrees

▶ Criminal Justice (AS)
In the fall of 1996 there were 6 students enrolled in this program.
Application requirements *Prior education:* high school diploma or equivalent. *Other requirements:* SAT or ACT, high school transcript, college transcripts, an essay or personal statement, letter(s) of recommendation, an application fee of $10.
Completion requirements 68 hours are required. 15 hours must be completed through the institution.
On-campus requirements For hands-on training.

INDIVIDUAL COURSE SUBJECT AREAS

Undergraduate
Accounting; algebra; American (US) history; anthropology; art history and criticism; astronomy and astrophysics; biology; criminology; developmental and child psychology; economics; educational psychology; English composition; English literature; geology; health professions and related sciences; physics; protective services; sociology; Spanish language and literature; special education; statistics; teacher education

COLORADO STATE UNIVERSITY

Fort Collins, Colorado

Division of Continuing and Distance Education

Colorado State University, founded in 1870, is a state-supported university. It is accredited by the North Central Association of Colleges and Schools. It first offered distance learning courses in 1967. In 1996–97, it offered 136 courses at a distance. In the fall of 1996, there was a total of 900 students enrolled in distance learning courses.
Course delivery sites Courses are delivered to your home, your workplace, military bases.
Media Courses are delivered via television, videotapes, videoconferencing, audiotapes, computer software, World Wide Web, print. Students and teachers interact via videoconferencing, mail, telephone, fax, e-mail. A computer is required for some courses.
Services Distance learners have access to library services, the campus computer network, e-mail services, academic advising at a distance.
Credit-earning options Students may transfer credits from another institution or may earn credits through examinations.
Typical costs *Undergraduate:* Tuition of $94 per credit hour for in-state residents. Tuition of $94 per credit hour for out-of-state residents. *Graduate:* Tuition of $312 per credit hour for in-state residents. Tuition of $350 per credit hour for out-of-state residents. Graduate home delivery courses are $364 credit hour. Costs may vary by course delivery options. Financial aid is available to distance learners.
Registration Students may register by mail, fax, phone.
Contact Administrative Assistant, Colorado State University, Division of Continuing and Distance Education, Spruce Hall, Fort Collins, CO 80523-1040. *Telephone:* 970-491-5288. *Fax:* 970-491-7885. *E-mail:* inquiries@vines.colostate.edu. *Web site:* http://www.colostate.edu/Depts/CE/.

DEGREE & CERTIFICATE PROGRAMS

Graduate Degrees

▶ Agricultural Education (MAg)
Application requirements *Prior education:* baccalaureate degree. *Other requirements:* GRE, college transcripts, an essay or personal statement, letter(s) of recommendation, an application fee of $30.
Completion requirements 30 credits are required. 24 credits must be completed through the institution. *Other requirements:* this program is designed primarily for those interested in the profession of Cooperative Extension.

▶ Business Administration (MBA)
In the fall of 1996 there were 300 students enrolled in this program. In 1995–96, 45 degrees were earned at a distance through this program.
Restrictions Program is available to US and Canadian students only.
Application requirements *Prior education:* baccalaureate degree. *Other requirements:* GMAT, college transcripts, an application fee of $30.
Completion requirements 33 credits are required. 24 credits must be completed through the institution.

▶ Chemical Engineering (MS)
In the fall of 1996 there were 20 students enrolled in this program. In 1995–96, 5 degrees were earned at a distance through this program.
Restrictions Program is available to US and Canadian students only.
Application requirements *Prior education:* baccalaureate degree. *Other requirements:* GRE, college transcripts, an application fee of $30.
Completion requirements 33 credits are required. 24 credits must be completed through the institution.

▶ Civil Engineering (MS)
In the fall of 1996 there were 25 students enrolled in this program. In 1995–96, 5 degrees were earned at a distance through this program.
Restrictions Program is available to US and Canadian students only.
Application requirements *Prior education:* baccalaureate degree. *Other requirements:* GRE, college transcripts, an application fee of $30.
Completion requirements 33 credits are required. 24 credits must be completed through the institution.

▶ Computer Science (MS)
In the fall of 1996 there were 40 students enrolled in this program. In 1995–96, 3 degrees were earned at a distance through this program.
Restrictions Program is available to US and Canadian students only.
Application requirements *Prior education:* baccalaureate degree. *Other requirements:* GRE, college transcripts, an application fee of $30.
Completion requirements 33 credits are required. 24 credits must be completed through the institution.

▶ Education (Human Resource Development) (MEd)
In the fall of 1996 there were 10 students enrolled in this program. In 1995–96, 2 degrees were earned at a distance through this program.
Restrictions Program is available to US and Canadian students only.
Application requirements *Prior education:* baccalaureate degree. *Other requirements:* GRE, college transcripts, an application fee of $30.
Completion requirements 42 credits are required. 24 credits must be completed through the institution.

▶ Electrical Engineering (MS)
In the fall of 1996 there were 25 students enrolled in this program. In 1995–96, 5 degrees were earned at a distance through this program.
Restrictions Program is available to US and Canadian students only.
Application requirements *Prior education:* baccalaureate degree. *Other requirements:* GRE, college transcripts, an application fee of $30.
Completion requirements 33 credits are required. 24 credits must be completed through the institution.

▶ Environmental Engineering (MS)
In the fall of 1996 there were 10 students enrolled in this program. In 1995–96, 2 degrees were earned at a distance through this program.
Restrictions Program is available to US and Canadian students only.
Application requirements *Prior education:* baccalaureate degree. *Other requirements:* GRE, college transcripts, an application fee of $30.
Completion requirements 42 credits are required. 24 credits must be completed through the institution.

▶ Industrial Engineering (MS)
In the fall of 1996 there were 10 students enrolled in this program. In 1995–96, 2 degrees were earned at a distance through this program.
Restrictions Program is available to US and Canadian students only.

Profiles: Colorado State University

Application requirements *Prior education:* baccalaureate degree. *Other requirements:* GRE, college transcripts, an application fee of $30.
Completion requirements 33 credits are required. 24 credits must be completed through the institution.

▶ *Management (MS)*
In the fall of 1996 there were 25 students enrolled in this program. In 1995–96, 5 degrees were earned at a distance through this program.
Restrictions Program is available to US and Canadian students only.
Application requirements *Prior education:* baccalaureate degree. *Other requirements:* GMAT, college transcripts, an application fee of $30.
Completion requirements 32 credits are required. 24 credits must be completed through the institution.

▶ *Mechanical Engineering (MS)*
In the fall of 1996 there were 25 students enrolled in this program. In 1995–96, 5 degrees were earned at a distance through this program.
Restrictions Program is available to US and Canadian students only.
Application requirements *Prior education:* baccalaureate degree. *Other requirements:* GRE, college transcripts, an application fee of $30.
Completion requirements 33 credits are required. 24 credits must be completed through the institution.

▶ *Statistics (MS)*
In the fall of 1996 there were 10 students enrolled in this program. In 1995–96, 2 degrees were earned at a distance through this program.
Restrictions Program is available to US and Canadian students only.
Application requirements *Prior education:* baccalaureate degree. *Other requirements:* GRE, college transcripts, an application fee of $30.
Completion requirements 33 credits are required. 24 credits must be completed through the institution.

▶ *Systems Engineering (MS)*
In the fall of 1996 there were 10 students enrolled in this program. In 1995–96, 2 degrees were earned at a distance through this program.
Restrictions Program is available to US and Canadian students only.
Application requirements *Prior education:* baccalaureate degree. *Other requirements:* GRE, college transcripts, an application fee of $30.
Completion requirements 33 credits are required. 24 credits must be completed through the institution.

Undergraduate Certificates

▶ *Gerontology*
In the fall of 1996 there were 5 students enrolled in this program.
Application requirements *Prior education:* some undergraduate course work. *Other requirements:* high school transcript, an essay or personal statement.
Completion requirements 20 credits are required. 11 credits must be completed through the institution.

INDIVIDUAL COURSE SUBJECT AREAS

Undergraduate
Abnormal psychology; agriculture; animal sciences; child care and development; cognitive psychology; conservation and natural resources; developmental and child psychology; economics; educational psychology; foods and nutrition studies; gerontology; history; home economics and family studies; individual and family development studies; philosophy and religion; plant sciences; psychology; sociology; zoology

Graduate
Accounting; agriculture; business; business administration and management; chemical engineering; civil engineering; computer and information sciences; conservation and natural resources; electrical engineering; engineering mechanics; engineering/industrial management; environmental engineering; finance; human resources management; industrial engineering; marketing; mathematics; mechanical engineering; teacher education

See full description on page 408.

COLUMBIA BASIN COLLEGE

Pasco, Washington

Columbia Basin College, founded in 1955, is a state-supported two-year college. It is accredited by the Northwest Association of Schools and Colleges. It first offered distance learning courses in 1985. In 1996–97, it offered 6 courses at a distance. In the fall of 1996, there was a total of 135 students enrolled in distance learning courses.
Course delivery sites Courses are delivered to your home.
Media Courses are delivered via videotapes, World Wide Web, e-mail, print. Students and teachers interact via mail, telephone, e-mail, in-person meetings. A computer is required for some courses.
Services Distance learners have access to library services, the campus computer network, e-mail services, academic advising, tutoring, career placement assistance, OnLine Writing Lab (OWL) at a distance.
Credit-earning options Students may transfer credits from another institution or may earn credits through examinations.
Typical costs Tuition of $1400 per year plus mandatory fees of $20 per quarter. Financial aid is available to distance learners.
Registration Students may register by mail, fax, phone, e-mail.
Contact Richard Cummins, Director of Information Technology Applications, Columbia Basin College, 2600 North 20th Avenue, Pasco, WA 99301. *Telephone:* 509-547-0511, Ext. 379. *Fax:* 509-546-0401. *E-mail:* rcummins@ctc.edu. *Web site:* http://www.ctc.edu/~cbcwww.

Special note
Columbia Basin College (CBC) has been offering distance education through telecourses since the mid-80s to serve the needs of time- and place-bound students. CBC now offers a variety of integrated delivery formats, including correspondence, video, Internet, and directed study courses.

CBC plans to offer an associate degree beginning in 1998. The requirements for degree completion will be the same as those for completing the on-ground degree, with the exception that students will be able, in most cases, to complete the degree without on-campus attendance. Successful degree students should be able to continue to any baccalaureate institution that accepts the associate transfer degree, including other virtual colleges.

The same instructors who teach on-ground classes teach the distance education classes. In addition to the formats listed above, some instructors may include material on the World Wide Web, PC diskettes, or CD-ROM. Students are expected to possess the computer and technology skills appropriate to the curriculum. Support services, such as a staffed Internet lab and VCR players in area libraries, are available for local students.

Access to distance learning instructors is provided through e-mail, telephone, and Internet conferencing. The Coordinator of Distance Education is also available for limited technical assistance and can make arrangements for course materials that need to be mailed or rented. Student services are provided by the counseling staff.

Potential students are encouraged to visit the virtual campus at http://www.ctc.edu/~cbcwww or to call the Coordinator of Distance Education at 509-547-0511 ext. 379.

INDIVIDUAL COURSE SUBJECT AREAS

Undergraduate
Abnormal psychology; accounting; algebra; anthropology; art history and criticism; creative writing; English composition; English language and literature; film studies; psychology; sociology; technical writing

COLUMBIA-GREENE COMMUNITY COLLEGE

Hudson, New York

Educational Technology Center

Columbia-Greene Community College, founded in 1969, is a state and locally supported two-year college. It is accredited by the Middle States Association of Colleges and Schools. It first offered distance learning courses in 1995. In 1996–97, it offered 6 courses at a distance. In the fall of 1996, there was a total of 41 students enrolled in distance learning courses.
Course delivery sites Courses are delivered to your home, local high schools.
Media Courses are delivered via television, videoconferencing, World Wide Web. Students and teachers interact via videoconferencing, mail, telephone, fax, e-mail. A computer is required for some courses.
Services Distance learners have access to the campus computer network at a distance.
Credit-earning options Students may transfer credits from another institution or may earn credits through examinations, portfolio assessment, military training, business training.
Typical costs Tuition of $1032 per semester plus mandatory fees of $63 per semester for in-state residents. Tuition of $2064 per semester plus mandatory fees of $63 per semester for out-of-state residents. Costs may vary by number of credits taken.
Registration Students may register by mail, phone.
Contact Patricia Hallenbeck, Admissions Office, Columbia-Greene Community College, 4400 Route 23, Hudson, NY 12534. *Telephone:* 518-828-4181, Ext. 5514. *Fax:* 518-828-8543. *Web site:* http://www.sunycgcc.edu.

INDIVIDUAL COURSE SUBJECT AREAS

Undergraduate
Art history and criticism; business administration and management; developmental and child psychology; mathematics; philosophy and religion; psychology; sociology

COLUMBIA INTERNATIONAL UNIVERSITY

Columbia, South Carolina

Columbia Extension

Columbia International University, founded in 1923, is an independent-religious nondenominational comprehensive institution. It is accredited by the Southern Association of Colleges and Schools. It first offered distance learning courses in 1978. In 1996–97, it offered 53 courses at a distance. In the fall of 1996, there was a total of 580 students enrolled in distance learning courses.
Course delivery sites Courses are delivered to your home.
Media Courses are delivered via videotapes, audiotapes, print. Students and teachers interact via mail, telephone, fax, e-mail.
Restrictions Students must agree with doctrinal standard.
Services Distance learners have access to library services, academic advising at a distance.
Credit-earning options Students may transfer credits from another institution.
Typical costs *Undergraduate:* Tuition of $95 per semester hour plus mandatory fees of $10 per course. *Graduate:* Tuition of $160 per semester hour plus mandatory fees of $10 per course. *Noncredit courses:* $120 per course.
Registration Students may register by mail, fax, phone.
Contact Associate Director of Admissions for Extension, Columbia International University, PO Box 3122, Columbia, SC 29230-3122. *Telephone:* 800-777-2227, Ext. 3043. *Fax:* 803-786-4209. *E-mail:* yesciu@ciu.edu. *Web site:* http://www.ciu.edu.

Special note

Columbia International University is a multidenominational Christian higher education institution dedicated to preparing world Christians to serve God with excellence that offers college and graduate-/seminary-level degree programs ranging from associate to Doctor of Ministry. All postsecondary programs emphasize spiritual formation, mastery of biblical content and interpretation skills, cultivation of a biblical world view, and ministry skills development. The University is accredited by the Commission on Colleges of the Southern Association of Colleges and Schools (1866 Southern Lane, Decatur, Georgia 30033) to award degrees at the associate, bachelor's, master's, first professional, and doctoral levels; the college is also accredited by the Accrediting Association of Bible Colleges and the seminary by the Association of Theological Schools.

The Columbia Extension Department, with 17 years experience, facilitates the distance education opportunities available through the college seminary. All 18 undergraduate and 35 graduate independent distance learning courses are available in audio and print format; some courses are also available in video (VHS) format. Residential study is required to earn a degree, though the graduate level 1-year (31 semester hours) Certificate in Biblical Studies may be earned entirely through distance education. Toll-free telephone, postal, and e-mail communication with the professor or faculty assistant facilitates the learning process. The on-line catalog and e-mail book request service provide excellent resource support.

Students can call 800-777-2227 and ask for either the college or seminary Admissions Department. They can also view information on the University and the college or seminary distance learning courses on the World Wide Web at http://www.ciu.edu.

DEGREE & CERTIFICATE PROGRAMS

Graduate certificates
▶ *Biblical Studies*
In the fall of 1996 there were 5 students enrolled in this program.
Application requirements *Prior education:* baccalaureate degree. *Other requirements:* college transcripts, letter(s) of recommendation, an application fee of $20, evidence of Christian conversion.
Completion requirements 31 semester hours are required. *Other requirements:* a spiritual formation component and a ministry development component, each requiring local mentoring.

INDIVIDUAL COURSE SUBJECT AREAS

Undergraduate
Theological studies

Graduate
Theological studies

Noncredit
Theological studies

Profiles: Columbia State Community College

COLUMBIA STATE COMMUNITY COLLEGE

Columbia, Tennessee

Columbia State Community College, founded in 1966, is a state-supported two-year college. It is accredited by the Southern Association of Colleges and Schools. It first offered distance learning courses in 1994. In 1996–97, it offered 27 courses at a distance. In the fall of 1996, there was a total of 938 students enrolled in distance learning courses.
Course delivery sites Courses are delivered to your home, your workplace, Middle Tennessee State University (Murfreesboro), 3 off-campus centers in Franklin, Lawrenceburg, Lewisburg.
Media Courses are delivered via videotapes, videoconferencing, audiotapes, computer software, print. Students and teachers interact via videoconferencing, mail, telephone, fax, e-mail. A computer is required for some courses.
Restrictions Programs are available to in-state students only.
Services Distance learners have access to library services, the campus computer network, e-mail services at a distance.
Credit-earning options Students may transfer credits from another institution or may earn credits through standardized exams, institutionally developed exams, military training.
Typical costs Tuition of $512 per semester plus mandatory fees of $20 per semester for in-state residents. Tuition of $2048 per semester plus mandatory fees of $20 per semester for out-of-state residents. Financial aid is available to distance learners.
Contact Vice President for Academic Services, Columbia State Community College, PO Box 1315, Columbia, TN 38402-1315. *Telephone:* 615-540-2517. *Fax:* 615-540-2535.

INDIVIDUAL COURSE SUBJECT AREAS

Undergraduate

Accounting; administrative and secretarial services; animal sciences; business; business administration and management; communications; criminal justice; developmental and child psychology; economics; English composition; health and physical education/fitness; liberal arts, general studies, and humanities; mathematics; nursing; philosophy and religion

COLUMBUS STATE COMMUNITY COLLEGE

Columbus, Ohio

Columbus State Community College, founded in 1963, is a state-supported two-year college. It is accredited by the North Central Association of Colleges and Schools. It first offered distance learning courses in 1980. In 1996–97, it offered 10 courses at a distance. In the fall of 1996, there was a total of 300 students enrolled in distance learning courses.
Course delivery sites Courses are delivered to your home, your workplace.
Media Courses are delivered via television, videotapes, audiotapes, World Wide Web, e-mail. Students and teachers interact via mail, telephone, fax, e-mail. A computer is required for some courses.
Services Distance learners have access to library services, the campus computer network, e-mail services at a distance.
Credit-earning options Students may transfer credits from another institution or may earn credits through portfolio assessment.
Typical costs Tuition of $59 per credit plus mandatory fees of $20 per course for in-state residents. Tuition of $130 per credit plus mandatory fees of $20 per course for out-of-state residents. Costs may vary by number of credits taken. Financial aid is available to distance learners enrolled full-time or part-time.
Registration Students may register by phone.
Contact Gregory Golden, Director, Educational Resources, Columbus State Community College, 550 East Spring Street, Columbus, OH 43215. *Telephone:* 614-227-2461. *Fax:* 614-227-2457. *E-mail:* ggolden@cscc.edu.

DEGREE & CERTIFICATE PROGRAMS

Associate Degrees
▶ *Business Management (AAS)*
Application requirements *Prior education:* high school diploma or equivalent. *Other requirements:* placement test, high school transcript.
Completion requirements 110 quarter hours are required. 35 hours must be completed through the institution.
On-campus requirements Requirements vary according to class.
Program contact Kathy Pullins, Instructor, Columbus State Community College, Columbus State Community College, 550 East Spring Street, Columbus, OH 43215. Phone: 614-227-2560. E-mail: kpullins@cscc.edu.

INDIVIDUAL COURSE SUBJECT AREAS

Undergraduate

Accounting; business administration and management; business communications; business law; computer and information sciences; economics; English composition; finance; French language and literature; marketing; mathematics; psychology; Spanish language and literature; technical writing

COLUMBUS STATE UNIVERSITY

Columbus, Georgia

Columbus State University, founded in 1958, is a state-supported comprehensive institution. It is accredited by the Southern Association of Colleges and Schools. It first offered distance learning courses in 1991. In 1996–97, it offered 28 courses at a distance. In the fall of 1996, there was a total of 304 students enrolled in distance learning courses.
Course delivery sites Courses are delivered to Georgia Southwestern State University (Americus), Flint River Technical School, University System of Georgia institutions.
Media Courses are delivered via videoconferencing. Students and teachers interact via videoconferencing, mail, telephone, fax, e-mail.
Restrictions Programs are available to in-state students only.
Services Distance learners have access to library services, the campus computer network, e-mail services, academic advising at a distance.
Credit-earning options Students may transfer credits from another institution or may earn credits through standardized exams, portfolio assessment.
Typical costs *Undergraduate:* Tuition of $301 per course for in-state residents. Tuition of $921 per course for out-of-state residents. *Graduate:* Tuition of $326 per course for in-state residents. Tuition of $1016 per course for out-of-state residents. *Noncredit courses:* $3–$50 per course. Costs may vary by number of credits taken. Financial aid is available to distance learners.
Registration Students may register by mail.
Contact Ms. Susan M. Simkowski, Distance Learning Coordinator, Columbus State University, Instructional Technology, Columbus, GA 31907. *Telephone:* 706-569-3455. *Fax:* 706-568-2459. *E-mail:* simkowski_susan@colstate.edu.

INDIVIDUAL COURSE SUBJECT AREAS

Undergraduate
Curriculum and instruction; English literature; gerontology; history of science and technology

Graduate
Counseling psychology; criminal justice; curriculum and instruction; education administration; educational psychology; English literature; school psychology; special education; teacher education

Noncredit
Real estate

COMMUNITY COLLEGE OF DENVER

Denver, Colorado

Division of Continuing Education

Community College of Denver, founded in 1970, is a state-supported two-year college. It is accredited by the North Central Association of Colleges and Schools. It first offered distance learning courses in 1986. In 1996–97, it offered 40 courses at a distance. In the fall of 1996, there was a total of 300 students enrolled in distance learning courses.
Course delivery sites Courses are delivered to your home, your workplace.
Media Courses are delivered via television, videotapes, audiotapes, computer software, World Wide Web, e-mail, print. Students and teachers interact via mail, telephone, fax, e-mail. A computer is required for some courses.
Restrictions Programs are available to in-state students only.
Services Distance learners have access to library services, the campus computer network, e-mail services, academic advising at a distance.
Typical costs Tuition of $162.90 per course plus mandatory fees of $18 per course for in-state residents. Tuition of $756.75 per course plus mandatory fees of $18 per course for out-of-state residents. Costs may vary by number of credits taken, course delivery options, term of enrollment. Financial aid is available to distance learners enrolled full-time or part-time.
Registration Students may register by mail, phone.
Contact Carolyn Counihan, Director of Non-Traditional Learning Program, Community College of Denver, 1391 North Speer Boulevard, Suite 200, Denver, CO 80209. *Telephone:* 303-620-4433, Ext. 322. *Fax:* 303-620-4942. *E-mail:* cd-carolyn@cccs.cccoes.edu/.

INDIVIDUAL COURSE SUBJECT AREAS

Undergraduate
English composition; history; psychology

COMMUNITY COLLEGE OF PHILADELPHIA

Philadelphia, Pennsylvania

Division of Community Services and Continuing Education

Community College of Philadelphia, founded in 1964, is a state and locally supported two-year college. It is accredited by the Middle States Association of Colleges and Schools. It first offered distance learning courses in 1981.
Course delivery sites Courses are delivered to your home, your workplace, military bases.
Media Courses are delivered via television, videotapes, audiotapes, computer software, World Wide Web, e-mail. Students and teachers interact via mail, telephone, fax, e-mail.
Services Distance learners have access to academic advising at a distance.
Credit-earning options Students may transfer credits from another institution or may earn credits through examinations, portfolio assessment, military training, business training.
Typical costs Tuition of $69 per credit hour plus mandatory fees of $20 per course. Financial aid is available to distance learners.
Contact Bradshaw P. Kinsey, Dean, Community College of Philadelphia, 1600 Callowhill Street, Community Service Annex, Second Floor, Philadelphia, PA 19130. *Telephone:* 215-751-8377. *Fax:* 215-751-8954.

INDIVIDUAL COURSE SUBJECT AREAS

Undergraduate
Business; business administration and management; chemistry; conservation and natural resources; developmental and child psychology; economics; European languages and literatures; history; human resources management; philosophy and religion; political science; sociology

COMMUNITY COLLEGE OF RHODE ISLAND

Warwick, Rhode Island

Off-Campus Credit Programs

Community College of Rhode Island, founded in 1964, is a state-supported two-year college. It is accredited by the New England Association of Schools and Colleges. It first offered distance learning courses in 1982. In 1996–97, it offered 63 courses at a distance. In the fall of 1996, there was a total of 820 students enrolled in distance learning courses.
Course delivery sites Courses are delivered to your home.
Media Courses are delivered via television, videotapes. Students and teachers interact via mail, telephone, e-mail, on-campus meetings.
Restrictions Students must be able to travel to campus.
Credit-earning options Students may transfer credits from another institution or may earn credits through standardized exams, institutionally developed exams, portfolio assessment, military training, business training.
Typical costs Tuition of $74 per credit plus mandatory fees of $4 per credit for in-state residents. Tuition of $220 per credit plus mandatory fees of $4 per credit for out-of-state residents. All students pay an additional $21 per semester fee. *Noncredit courses:* $220 per course. Financial aid is available to distance learners enrolled full-time or part-time.
Registration Students may register by mail, phone.
Contact Judeth A. Crowley, Dean, Community College of Rhode Island, 1762 Louisquisset Pike, Lincoln, RI 02865-4585. *Telephone:* 401-333-7126. *Fax:* 401-333-7113. *E-mail:* jcrowley@ccri.cc.ri.us.

INDIVIDUAL COURSE SUBJECT AREAS

Undergraduate
Biological and life sciences; business administration and management; Classical languages and literatures; developmental and child psychology; economics; English composition; English language and literature; health and physical education/fitness; history; law and legal studies; liberal arts, general studies, and humanities; mathematics; philosophy and religion; political science; psychology; sociology

Profiles: Community College of the Air Force

COMMUNITY COLLEGE OF THE AIR FORCE

Maxwell Air Force Base, Alabama

Technology Division

Community College of the Air Force, founded in 1972, is a federally supported two-year college. It is accredited by the Southern Association of Colleges and Schools. In 1996–97, it offered 20 courses at a distance. In the fall of 1996, there was a total of 5,000 students enrolled in distance learning courses.
Course delivery sites Courses are delivered to military bases.
Media Courses are delivered via television. Students and teachers interact via videoconferencing, telephone, fax. A computer is required for some courses.
Restrictions Courses are available to active duty Air Force, Air National Guard, and Air Force Reserve personnel only.
Credit-earning options Students may earn credits through standardized exams, military training, business training.
Typical costs Air Force covers cost of course.
Contact Gary Martyn, Director of College Outreach, Community College of the Air Force, 130 West Maxwell Boulevard, Maxwell AFB, AL 36112-6613. *Telephone:* 334-953-6684. *Fax:* 334-953-5231. *E-mail:* emartyn@ccaf.au.af.mil.

INDIVIDUAL COURSE SUBJECT AREAS

Undergraduate
Electronics; law and legal studies; philosophy and religion

COMMUNITY COLLEGE OF VERMONT

Waterbury, Vermont

Community College of Vermont, founded in 1970, is a state-supported two-year college. It is accredited by the New England Association of Schools and Colleges. It first offered distance learning courses in 1996. In 1996–97, it offered 25 courses at a distance. In the fall of 1996, there was a total of 50 students enrolled in distance learning courses.
Course delivery sites Courses are delivered to your home.
Media Courses are delivered via World Wide Web. Students and teachers interact via telephone, e-mail, World Wide Web. A computer is required for all courses.
Services Distance learners have access to library services, academic advising at a distance.
Credit-earning options Students may transfer credits from another institution or may earn credits through examinations, portfolio assessment, military training, business training.
Typical costs Tuition of $288 per course plus mandatory fees of $60 per course. Costs may vary by number of credits taken. Financial aid is available to distance learners enrolled full-time or part-time.
Registration Students may register by mail, fax, phone.
Contact John Christensen, Coordinator of Academic Services, Community College of Vermont, 38 Main Street, St. Johnsbury, VT 05819. *Telephone:* 802-748-6673. *Fax:* 802-748-5014.

INDIVIDUAL COURSE SUBJECT AREAS

Undergraduate
American (US) history; American literature; business law; cognitive psychology; computer and information sciences; English language and literature; ethics; Jewish studies; law and legal studies; political science; technical writing

CONCORDIA COLLEGE

Ann Arbor, Michigan

Concordia College, founded in 1963, is an independent-religious four-year college affiliated with the Lutheran Church–Missouri Synod. It is accredited by the North Central Association of Colleges and Schools. It first offered distance learning courses in 1996.
Course delivery sites Courses are delivered to other colleges.
Media Courses are delivered via videoconferencing. Students and teachers interact via videoconferencing, e-mail.
Services Distance learners have access to library services, academic advising, tutoring, career placement assistance at a distance.
Credit-earning options Students may transfer credits from another institution or may earn credits through examinations.
Typical costs Tuition of $300 per credit hour plus mandatory fees of $120 per semester. Financial aid is available to distance learners.
Contact Dr. Jonathan Laabs, Director of Teacher Education, Concordia College, 4090 Geddes Road, Ann Arbor, MI 48105. *Telephone:* 313-995-7392. *Fax:* 313-995-4610. *E-mail:* laabsjc@crf.cuis.edu.

INDIVIDUAL COURSE SUBJECT AREAS

Undergraduate
Education; English language and literature; Hebrew language and literature; teacher education

CONCORDIA UNIVERSITY

Irvine, California

Information Resources

Concordia University, founded in 1972, is an independent-religious comprehensive institution affiliated with the Lutheran Church–Missouri Synod. It is accredited by the Western Association of Schools and Colleges, Inc. It first offered distance learning courses in 1995. In 1996–97, it offered 4 courses at a distance. In the fall of 1996, there was a total of 24 students enrolled in distance learning courses.
Course delivery sites Courses are delivered to Concordia College (Seward, NE), Concordia College (Bronxville, NY), Concordia College (Ann Arbor, MI), Concordia College (Selma, AL), Concordia University (Portland, OR), Concordia University (St. Paul, MN), Concordia University (River Forest, IL), Concordia University at Austin (Austin, TX), Concordia University Wisconsin (Mequon, WI).
Media Courses are delivered via videoconferencing. Students and teachers interact via videoconferencing, mail, telephone, fax, e-mail.
Restrictions Courses are available to students enrolled at one of the ten Concordia University System campuses only.
Services Distance learners have access to library services, academic advising, career placement assistance at a distance.
Credit-earning options Students may transfer credits from another institution.

Typical costs *Undergraduate:* Tuition of $395 per credit. *Graduate:* Tuition of $275 per credit. Costs may vary by campus or location. Financial aid is available to distance learners.
Registration Students may register by mail.
Contact Hal H. Whelply, Jr., Vice President of Learning and Dean of Information Resources, Concordia University, 1530 Concordia, W, Irvine, CA 92612. *Telephone:* 714-854-8002, Ext. 275. *Fax:* 714-854-6854. *E-mail:* whelply@cui.edu. *Web site:* http://www.cui.edu.

INDIVIDUAL COURSE SUBJECT AREAS

Undergraduate
Accounting; astronomy and astrophysics; biological and life sciences; biology; business; business administration and management; chemistry; creative writing; developmental and child psychology; economics; education administration; educational psychology; English composition; English language and literature; fine arts; geology; health and physical education/fitness; history; liberal arts, general studies, and humanities; mathematics; music; philosophy and religion; physics; political science; social psychology; social sciences; social work; sociology; teacher education; theological studies

Graduate
Education administration; educational psychology; liberal arts, general studies, and humanities; philosophy and religion; teacher education; theological studies

CONCORDIA UNIVERSITY

River Forest, Illinois

College of Continuing Education

Concordia University, founded in 1864, is an independent-religious comprehensive institution affiliated with the Lutheran Church–Missouri Synod. It is accredited by the North Central Association of Colleges and Schools. It first offered distance learning courses in 1950. In 1996–97, it offered 40 courses at a distance. In the fall of 1996, there was a total of 400 students enrolled in distance learning courses.
Course delivery sites Courses are delivered to your home, Concordia College (Bronxville, NY), Concordia University at Austin (Austin, TX).
Media Courses are delivered via World Wide Web, e-mail, print, interactive television. Students and teachers interact via videoconferencing, mail, telephone, fax, e-mail. A computer is required for some courses.
Services Distance learners have access to library services, e-mail services at a distance.
Credit-earning options Students may earn credits through standardized exams.
Typical costs Tuition of $118 per quarter hour. Costs may vary by number of credits taken, course delivery options.
Registration Students may register by mail, fax.
Contact Dr. Elaine Sipe, Dean, College of Continuing Education, Concordia University, 7400 Augusta Street, River Forest, IL 60305. *Telephone:* 708-209-3262. *Fax:* 708-209-3176. *E-mail:* crfsipede@crf.cuis.edu.

INDIVIDUAL COURSE SUBJECT AREAS

Undergraduate
Algebra; American (US) history; developmental and child psychology; economics; English literature; religious studies; teacher education; theological studies

CONCORDIA UNIVERSITY AT AUSTIN

Austin, Texas

Center for Distance Education

Concordia University at Austin, founded in 1926, is an independent-religious four-year college affiliated with the Lutheran Church–Missouri Synod. It is accredited by the Southern Association of Colleges and Schools. It first offered distance learning courses in 1992. In 1996–97, it offered 32 courses at a distance. In the fall of 1996, there was a total of 130 students enrolled in distance learning courses.
Course delivery sites Courses are delivered to your home, your workplace, Concordia College (Seward, NE), Concordia College (Bronxville, NY), Concordia College (Ann Arbor, MI), Concordia University (St. Paul, MN), Concordia University (River Forest, IL), Concordia University (Portland, OR), Concordia University (Irvine, CA).
Media Courses are delivered via television, videotapes, videoconferencing. Students and teachers interact via videoconferencing, audioconferencing, mail, telephone, fax, e-mail.
Services Distance learners have access to library services, the campus computer network, e-mail services, academic advising at a distance.
Credit-earning options Students may transfer credits from another institution or may earn credits through standardized exams, portfolio assessment, military training, business training.
Typical costs Tuition of $885 per course plus mandatory fees of $25 per credit hour. *Noncredit courses:* $885 per course. Costs may vary by number of credits taken. Financial aid is available to distance learners enrolled full-time.
Registration Students may register by mail.
Contact Jay Krause, Dean of Enrollment, Concordia University at Austin, 3400 Interstate Highway 35, N, Austin, TX 78705. *Telephone:* 512-452-7661. *Fax:* 512-459-8517.

INDIVIDUAL COURSE SUBJECT AREAS

Undergraduate
Biology; business; business administration and management; communications; developmental and child psychology; English language and literature; fine arts; liberal arts, general studies, and humanities; mathematics; philosophy and religion; political science; psychology; theological studies

Noncredit
Biology; business; business administration and management; communications; developmental and child psychology; English language and literature; fine arts; liberal arts, general studies, and humanities; mathematics; philosophy and religion; political science; psychology; theological studies

CONCORDIA UNIVERSITY WISCONSIN

Mequon, Wisconsin

Continuing Education Division

Concordia University Wisconsin, founded in 1881, is an independent-religious comprehensive institution affiliated with the Lutheran Church–Missouri Synod. It is accredited by the North Central Association of Colleges and Schools. It first offered distance learning courses in 1992. In 1996–97, it offered 14 courses at a distance. In the fall of 1996, there was a total of 300 students enrolled in distance learning courses.
Course delivery sites Courses are delivered to your home.

Profiles: Concordia University Wisconsin

Media Courses are delivered via videotapes, audiotapes. Students and teachers interact via mail, telephone, fax, e-mail.
Services Distance learners have access to academic advising at a distance.
Credit-earning options Students may transfer credits from another institution.
Typical costs Tuition of $375 per course. Financial aid is available to distance learners enrolled full-time or part-time.
Registration Students may register by mail, fax, phone.
Contact Cheryl Carter, Continuing Education Director, Concordia University Wisconsin, 12800 North Lake Shore Drive, Mequon, WI 53097. *Telephone:* 414-243-4400. *Fax:* 414-243-4388. *E-mail:* ccarter@bach.cuw.edu.

INDIVIDUAL COURSE SUBJECT AREAS

Undergraduate
Area, ethnic, and cultural studies; chemistry; English composition; English language and literature; European languages and literatures; history; liberal arts, general studies, and humanities; philosophy and religion; social psychology

Graduate
Area, ethnic, and cultural studies; chemistry; English composition; English language and literature; European languages and literatures; history; liberal arts, general studies, and humanities; philosophy and religion; social psychology

CONNORS STATE COLLEGE

Warner, Oklahoma

Academics and Technology

Connors State College, founded in 1908, is a state-supported two-year college. It is accredited by the North Central Association of Colleges and Schools. It first offered distance learning courses in 1997.
Course delivery sites Courses are delivered to 1 off-campus center in Muskogee.
Media Courses are delivered via videoconferencing. Students and teachers interact via videoconferencing, mail, telephone.
Restrictions Programs are available to in-state students only.
Services Distance learners have access to library services at a distance.
Credit-earning options Students may transfer credits from another institution or may earn credits through institutionally developed exams.
Typical costs Tuition of $38.75 per hour for in-state residents. Tuition of $98.75 per hour for out-of-state residents. Costs may vary by number of credits taken. Financial aid is available to distance learners.
Registration Students may register by mail.
Contact Dr. Jo Lynn Autry Digranes, Vice President for Academics and Technology, Connors State College, RR 1, Box 1000, Warner, OK 74469. *Telephone:* 918-463-2931. *Fax:* 918-463-2233.

INDIVIDUAL COURSE SUBJECT AREAS

Undergraduate
Mathematics

CONTRA COSTA COLLEGE

San Pablo, California

Contra Costa College, founded in 1948, is a state and locally supported two-year college. It is accredited by the Western Association of Schools and Colleges, Inc. It first offered distance learning courses in 1991.
Course delivery sites Courses are delivered to your home, your workplace.
Media Courses are delivered via television, videotapes, videoconferencing.
Restrictions Programs are available to local area students only.
Credit-earning options Students may transfer credits from another institution. Financial aid is available to distance learners.
Contact Ron Weston, Professor, Contra Costa College, 2600 Mission Bell Drive, San Pablo, CA 94805. *Telephone:* 510-235-7800. *Fax:* 510-236-6768.

INDIVIDUAL COURSE SUBJECT AREAS

Undergraduate
Biology; business; health and physical education/fitness; philosophy and religion; psychology; sociology

COPIAH-LINCOLN COMMUNITY COLLEGE

Wesson, Mississippi

Copiah-Lincoln Community College, founded in 1928, is a state and locally supported two-year college. It is accredited by the Southern Association of Colleges and Schools. It first offered distance learning courses in 1995. In 1996–97, it offered 8 courses at a distance. In the fall of 1996, there was a total of 125 students enrolled in distance learning courses.
Course delivery sites Courses are delivered to your home, your workplace, Jackson State University (Jackson), Mississippi State University (Mississippi State), University of Mississippi Medical Center (Jackson), 21 off-campus centers in Crystal Springs, Magee, Mendenhall, Monticello.
Media Courses are delivered via television, videotapes, videoconferencing, print. Students and teachers interact via videoconferencing, mail, fax.
Restrictions Programs are available to in-state students only.
Services Distance learners have access to library services, e-mail services at a distance.
Credit-earning options Students may transfer credits from another institution or may earn credits through standardized exams, institutionally developed exams, portfolio assessment, military training, business training.
Typical costs *Undergraduate:* Tuition of $500 per semester for in-state residents. Tuition of $1100 per semester for out-of-state residents. *Graduate:* Tuition of $340 per course for in-state residents. Graduate, out-of-state tuition varies by course. *Noncredit courses:* $45 per course. Costs may vary by campus or location, number of credits taken, course delivery options. Financial aid is available to distance learners enrolled full-time.
Registration Students may register by mail, fax, phone.
Contact Ralph Frazier, Director, Admissions, Copiah-Lincoln Community College, PO Box 457, Wesson, MS 39191. *Telephone:* 601-643-8307. *Fax:* 601-643-8307.

INDIVIDUAL COURSE SUBJECT AREAS

Undergraduate
Classical languages and literatures; fire science; fire services administration; foods and nutrition studies; geography; health professions and related sciences; home economics and family studies; social sciences

Graduate
Health professions and related sciences; social psychology

Noncredit
Agriculture

CORNELL UNIVERSITY

Ithaca, New York

Cornell Office of Distance Learning

Cornell University, founded in 1865, is an independent-nonprofit university. It is accredited by the Middle States Association of Colleges and Schools.
Course delivery sites Courses are delivered to your home, your workplace, other colleges.
Media Courses are delivered via videoconferencing, computer software, World Wide Web, e-mail, print. Students and teachers interact via videoconferencing, e-mail. A computer is required for some courses.
Services Distance learners have access to academic advising, tutoring at a distance.
Typical costs Contact school for information.
Registration Students may register by phone.
Contact Cornell Distance Education Program, Cornell University, 247 Warren Hall, Ithaca, NY 14853. *Telephone:* 607-255-3028. *Fax:* 607-254-5122. *E-mail:* distance-ed@cornell.edu. *Web site:* http://www.ilr.cornell.edu/distlearn/dl.html.

DEGREE & CERTIFICATE PROGRAMS

Graduate Degrees
▶ *Industrial and Labor Relations (MILR)*
Restrictions Program is available to students in New York City only.
Program contact Amelia Ellsworth, Consultant, Cornell University, 169 Ives Hall, Ithaca, NY 14853. Phone: 607-255-3228. Fax: 607-255-7774. E-mail: ale1@cornell.edu.

INDIVIDUAL COURSE SUBJECT AREAS

Undergraduate
Accounting; business; hospitality services management

Graduate
Organizational behavior studies

Noncredit
Hospitality services management

CORNING COMMUNITY COLLEGE

Corning, New York

Open Learning Program

Corning Community College, founded in 1956, is a state and locally supported two-year college. It is accredited by the Middle States Association of Colleges and Schools. It first offered distance learning courses in 1996. In 1996–97, it offered 3 courses at a distance. In the fall of 1996, there was a total of 20 students enrolled in distance learning courses.
Course delivery sites Courses are delivered to 9 off-campus centers in Addison, Alfred Almond, Arkport, Aroca, BOCES-Coopers Center, BOCES-Wildwood, Canaseraga, Hammondsport, Prattsburgh.
Media Courses are delivered via television, videoconferencing. Students and teachers interact via videoconferencing, interactive television. A computer is required for some courses.
Restrictions Interactive video programs are available over a closed network only.
Services Distance learners have access to e-mail services, career placement assistance at a distance.
Credit-earning options Students may transfer credits from another institution or may earn credits through examinations, portfolio assessment, military training.
Typical costs Tuition of $100 per credit for in-state residents. Tuition of $300 per credit for out-of-state residents. Financial aid is available to distance learners.
Registration Students may register by phone.
Contact Office of Registration and Records, Corning Community College, 1 Academic Drive, Corning, NY 14830. *Telephone:* 607-962-9230.

INDIVIDUAL COURSE SUBJECT AREAS

Undergraduate
Accounting; business administration and management; Classical languages and literatures; English composition; English language and literature; health and physical education/fitness; journalism; liberal arts, general studies, and humanities; mathematics; psychology; social sciences

COSUMNES RIVER COLLEGE

Sacramento, California

Media Department

Cosumnes River College, founded in 1970, is a district-supported two-year college. It is accredited by the Western Association of Schools and Colleges, Inc. It first offered distance learning courses in 1991. In 1996–97, it offered 39 courses at a distance. In the fall of 1996, there was a total of 1,100 students enrolled in distance learning courses.
Course delivery sites Courses are delivered to your home, your workplace, American River College (Sacramento), 3 off-campus centers in Folsom, Placerville, Sacramento.
Media Courses are delivered via television. Students and teachers interact via mail, telephone, fax, e-mail.
Services Distance learners have access to e-mail services at a distance.
Credit-earning options Students may transfer credits from another institution or may earn credits through institutionally developed exams, portfolio assessment, business training.
Typical costs Tuition of $13 per unit for in-state residents. Tuition of $138 per unit for out-of-state residents. Costs may vary by number of credits taken. Financial aid is available to distance learners.

Distance Learning Programs

Profiles: Cosumnes River College

Registration Students may register by mail, phone.
Contact Suzan Harris, Supervisor, Cosumnes River College, 8401 Center Parkway, Sacramento, CA 95823. *Telephone:* 916-688-7289. *Fax:* 916-688-7476. *E-mail:* harriss@crc.losrios.cc.ca.us.

INDIVIDUAL COURSE SUBJECT AREAS

Undergraduate
Accounting; area, ethnic, and cultural studies; business; business administration and management; communications; conservation and natural resources; creative writing; developmental and child psychology; economics; English as a second language (ESL); English language and literature; fine arts; health and physical education/fitness; health professions and related sciences; history; home economics and family studies; journalism; liberal arts, general studies, and humanities; mathematics; philosophy and religion; physical sciences; radio and television broadcasting

COUNTY COLLEGE OF MORRIS

Randolph, New Jersey

Professional Programs and Distance Education

County College of Morris, founded in 1966, is a county-supported two-year college. It is accredited by the Middle States Association of Colleges and Schools. It first offered distance learning courses in 1979. In 1996–97, it offered 27 courses at a distance. In the fall of 1996, there was a total of 215 students enrolled in distance learning courses.
Course delivery sites Courses are delivered to your home.
Media Courses are delivered via television, audiotapes. Students and teachers interact via mail, telephone, fax, e-mail, on-campus meetings.
Restrictions Courses are available to US students only.
Services Distance learners have access to e-mail services at a distance.
Credit-earning options Students may transfer credits from another institution or may earn credits through standardized exams, institutionally developed exams.
Typical costs Tuition of $67 per credit plus mandatory fees of $10 per credit for local area residents. Tuition of $134 per credit plus mandatory fees of $10 per credit for in-state residents. Tuition of $184 per credit plus mandatory fees of $10 per credit for out-of-state residents. Telecourse students are also charged a telecourse fee of $25. Financial aid is available to distance learners enrolled full-time.
Registration Students may register by mail, fax, phone.
Contact Alane Sheaves, Coordinator of Distance Learning, County College of Morris, 214 Center Grove Road, Randolph, NJ 07869. *Telephone:* 201-328-5184. *Fax:* 201-328-5082. *E-mail:* asheaves@ccm.edu. *Web site:* http://www.ccm.edu.

DEGREE & CERTIFICATE PROGRAMS

Associate Degrees
▶ *Humanities (AA)*
Application requirements *Prior education:* high school diploma or equivalent. *Other requirements:* Basic Skills Test (for placement only), high school transcript, an application fee of $25.
Completion requirements 64 credits are required. 30 credits must be completed through the institution.
On-campus requirements Telecourse students must attend on-campus course orientations and tests.

INDIVIDUAL COURSE SUBJECT AREAS

Undergraduate
Business administration and management; chemistry; developmental and child psychology; economics; English composition; health and physical education/fitness; history; music; political science; sociology

COVENANT THEOLOGICAL SEMINARY

St. Louis, Missouri

External Studies Office

Covenant Theological Seminary, founded in 1956, is an independent-religious graduate institution. It is accredited by the North Central Association of Colleges and Schools. It first offered distance learning courses in 1988. In 1996–97, it offered 15 courses at a distance. In the fall of 1996, there was a total of 170 students enrolled in distance learning courses.
Course delivery sites Courses are delivered to your home, churches.
Media Courses are delivered via videotapes, audiotapes, print. Students and teachers interact via mail, telephone, fax, e-mail.
Restrictions Students must live further than 60 miles from main campus.
Services Distance learners have access to library services, e-mail services, academic advising, tutoring at a distance.
Credit-earning options Students may transfer credits from another institution or may earn credits through examinations.
Typical costs Tuition of $120 per credit. *Noncredit courses:* $105 per course. Costs may vary by course delivery options. Financial aid is available to distance learners.
Registration Students may register by mail, fax, phone, e-mail, World Wide Web.
Contact Kevin VandenBrink, Director of Seminary Extension Training, Covenant Theological Seminary, 12330 Conway Road, St. Louis, MO 63141. *Telephone:* 314-434-4044. *Fax:* 314-434-4819. *E-mail:* 75442.2757@compuserve.com. *Web site:* http://www.inlink.com/~covenant.

DEGREE & CERTIFICATE PROGRAMS

Graduate Degrees
▶ *Theology (MA)*
In the fall of 1996 there were 39 students enrolled in this program.
Restrictions Program is available to students in Nashville, Memphis, and Naperville (IL) only.
Application requirements *Prior education:* baccalaureate degree. *Other requirements:* college transcripts, an essay or personal statement, letter(s) of recommendation, an application fee of $25, testimony.
Completion requirements 30 credit hours are required. *Maximum time for completion:* nine years.

Graduate certificates
▶ *Theology*
In the fall of 1996 there were 37 students enrolled in this program.
Application requirements *Prior education:* undergraduate degree. *Other requirements:* college transcripts, an essay or personal statement, letter(s) of recommendation, an application fee of $25, testimony.

INDIVIDUAL COURSE SUBJECT AREAS

Graduate
Communications; liberal arts, general studies, and humanities; philosophy and religion; theological studies

Noncredit
Communications; liberal arts, general studies, and humanities; philosophy and religion; theological studies

CRAFTON HILLS COLLEGE

Yucaipa, California

Distance Education Office

Crafton Hills College, founded in 1972, is a state and locally supported two-year college. It is accredited by the Western Association of Schools and Colleges, Inc. In 1996–97, it offered 37 courses at a distance.
Course delivery sites Courses are delivered to your home.
Media Courses are delivered via television, e-mail. Students and teachers interact via mail, telephone, fax, e-mail. A computer is required for some courses.
Restrictions Students must be able to travel to campus.
Credit-earning options Students may transfer credits from another institution or may earn credits through standardized exams.
Typical costs Tuition of $13 per unit for in-state residents. Tuition of $118 per unit for out-of-state residents. Financial aid is available to distance learners.
Registration Students may register by mail, phone.
Contact Office of Distance Education and Off-Campus Program, Crafton Hills College, 701 South Mount Vernon Avenue, San Bernardino, CA 92410. *Telephone:* 909-888-6511, Ext. 1131. *Fax:* 909-825-3104.

INDIVIDUAL COURSE SUBJECT AREAS

Undergraduate
American (US) history; anthropology; biology; business; business administration and management; child care and development; ecology; economics; English literature; ethics; geography; geology; history; home economics and family studies; oceanography; political science; psychology; sociology

CUMBERLAND COUNTY COLLEGE

Vineland, New Jersey

Multimedia and Distance Learning Services

Cumberland County College, founded in 1963, is a state and locally supported two-year college. It is accredited by the Middle States Association of Colleges and Schools. It first offered distance learning courses in 1990. In 1996–97, it offered 20 courses at a distance.
Course delivery sites Courses are delivered to your home, your workplace, other colleges.
Media Courses are delivered via television, videoconferencing, World Wide Web. Students and teachers interact via videoconferencing, mail, telephone, fax, e-mail. A computer is required for some courses.
Services Distance learners have access to library services, e-mail services at a distance.
Credit-earning options Students may transfer credits from another institution or may earn credits through standardized exams.
Typical costs Tuition of $67.25 per credit plus mandatory fees of $25 per course for local area residents. Tuition of $134.50 per credit plus mandatory fees of $25 per course for in-state residents. Financial aid is available to distance learners enrolled full-time or part-time.
Contact Timothy Tirrell, Director, Cumberland County College, College Drive, Vineland, NJ 08360. *Telephone:* 609-691-8600, Ext. 302. *Fax:* 609-691-8813. *E-mail:* ttirrell@cccnj.net. *Web site:* http://www.cccnj.net.

DEGREE & CERTIFICATE PROGRAMS

Associate Degrees
▶*Liberal Arts (AA)*
Application requirements *Prior education:* high school diploma or equivalent. *Other requirements:* high school transcript.
Completion requirements 65 credits are required.
On-campus requirements Five on-campus meetings per course.

INDIVIDUAL COURSE SUBJECT AREAS

Undergraduate
Biology; business administration and management; creative writing; developmental and child psychology; economics; English composition; English language and literature; European languages and literatures; history; mathematics; philosophy and religion; social psychology; sociology

CUYAHOGA COMMUNITY COLLEGE, METROPOLITAN CAMPUS

Cleveland, Ohio

Distance Learning Center

Cuyahoga Community College, Metropolitan Campus, founded in 1963, is a state and locally supported two-year college. It is accredited by the North Central Association of Colleges and Schools. It first offered distance learning courses in 1973. In 1996–97, it offered 80 courses at a distance. In the fall of 1996, there was a total of 1,642 students enrolled in distance learning courses.
Course delivery sites Courses are delivered to your home, your workplace.
Media Courses are delivered via television, videotapes, videoconferencing, audiotapes, computer software, World Wide Web, print. Students and teachers interact via videoconferencing, mail, telephone, fax, e-mail. A computer is required for some courses.
Restrictions Students must be able to travel to campus.
Services Distance learners have access to library services, the campus computer network, e-mail services at a distance.
Credit-earning options Students may transfer credits from another institution.
Typical costs Tuition of $38.65 per credit for local area residents. Tuition of $51.35 per credit for in-state residents. Tuition of $102.45 per credit for out-of-state residents. *Noncredit courses:* $60 per course. Costs may vary by course delivery options. Financial aid is available to distance learners enrolled full-time or part-time.
Registration Students may register by mail, fax, phone.
Contact Cindy Potteiger, Assistant Coordinator, Distance Learning, Cuyahoga Community College, Metropolitan Campus, 2900 Community College Avenue, Cleveland, OH 44115. *Telephone:* 216-987-4257. *Fax:* 216-987-4101. *E-mail:* cindy.potteiger@tri-c.cc.oh.us.

DEGREE & CERTIFICATE PROGRAMS

Associate Degrees
▶*Liberal Arts (AA)*
Application requirements *Prior education:* high school diploma or equivalent. *Other requirements:* high school transcript, an application fee of $10.

Distance Learning Programs

Completion requirements 93 credits are required. 30 credits must be completed through the institution.
On-campus requirements For testing.

INDIVIDUAL COURSE SUBJECT AREAS

Undergraduate
Accounting; African-American studies; anthropology; archaeology; area, ethnic, and cultural studies; art history and criticism; Asian languages and literatures; business administration and management; calculus; computer and information sciences; creative writing; developmental and child psychology; economics; English composition; European languages and literatures; film studies; foods and nutrition studies; health and physical education/fitness; history; information sciences and systems; investments and securities; journalism; liberal arts, general studies, and humanities; library and information studies; marketing; mathematics; philosophy and religion; plant sciences; social psychology; sociology; women's studies

CUYAMACA COLLEGE

El Cajon, California

Telecourse Program

Cuyamaca College, founded in 1978, is a state-supported two-year college. It is accredited by the Western Association of Schools and Colleges, Inc. It first offered distance learning courses in 1985. In 1996–97, it offered 36 courses at a distance.
Course delivery sites Courses are delivered to your home.
Media Courses are delivered via television, videotapes. Students and teachers interact via telephone.
Restrictions Televised courses are available in San Diego County only.
Credit-earning options Students may earn credits through business training.
Typical costs Tuition of $13 per unit plus mandatory fees of $7 per semester for in-state residents. Tuition of $114 per unit plus mandatory fees of $7 per semester for out-of-state residents. Costs may vary by number of credits taken. Financial aid is available to distance learners.
Registration Students may register by phone.
Contact Sharron Hamlett, Administrative Secretary, Telecourse Program, Cuyamaca College, 900 Rancho San Diego Parkway, El Cajon, CA 92019-4304. *Telephone:* 619-660-4444. *Fax:* 619-670-3998. *E-mail:* sharron_hamlett@gcccd.cc.ca.us. *Web site:* http://michele.gcccd.cc.ca.us/cuyamaca/library/welcome.html.

INDIVIDUAL COURSE SUBJECT AREAS

Undergraduate
Astronomy and astrophysics; business administration and management; developmental and child psychology; economics; English language and literature; geology; history; liberal arts, general studies, and humanities; political science; sociology

DAKOTA STATE UNIVERSITY

Madison, South Dakota

Office of Distance Education

Dakota State University, founded in 1881, is a state-supported four-year college. It is accredited by the North Central Association of Colleges and Schools. It first offered distance learning courses in 1989. In 1996–97, it offered 15 courses at a distance. In the fall of 1996, there was a total of 76 students enrolled in distance learning courses.
Course delivery sites Courses are delivered to your home, your workplace, military bases.
Media Courses are delivered via computer software, World Wide Web, e-mail. Students and teachers interact via mail, telephone, fax, e-mail. A computer is required for all courses.
Services Distance learners have access to library services, the campus computer network, e-mail services at a distance.
Credit-earning options Students may transfer credits from another institution or may earn credits through examinations, portfolio assessment, military training, business training.
Typical costs *Undergraduate:* Tuition of $125 per credit for in-state residents. Tuition of $149.25 per credit for out-of-state residents. *Graduate:* Tuition of $153 per credit for in-state residents. Tuition of $174 per credit for out-of-state residents. Costs may vary by campus or location, number of credits taken.
Registration Students may register by mail, fax, phone, e-mail, World Wide Web.
Contact Deb Gearhart, Director of Distance Education, Dakota State University, 201A Karl E. Mundt Library, Madison, SD 57042-1799. *Telephone:* 800-641-4309. *Fax:* 605-256-5208. *E-mail:* gearhard@columbia.dsu.edu. *Web site:* http://www.courses.dsu.edu/disted/.

INDIVIDUAL COURSE SUBJECT AREAS

Undergraduate
Business administration and management; computer and information sciences; economics; English composition; music; teacher education

DALHOUSIE UNIVERSITY

Halifax, Nova Scotia, Canada

Dalhousie University, founded in 1818, is a province-supported university. It is provincially chartered.
Course delivery sites Courses are delivered to your home, your workplace, military bases, other colleges, off-campus center(s).
Media Courses are delivered via videotapes, videoconferencing, audiotapes, audioconferencing, computer software, World Wide Web, e-mail, print. Students and teachers interact via videoconferencing, audioconferencing, mail, telephone, fax, e-mail.
Typical costs Tuition of $630 per course plus mandatory fees of $100 per course. Costs may vary by specific program of study.
Contact Registrar's Office, Dalhousie University, Halifax, NS B3H 4H6, Canada. *Telephone:* 902-494-2450. *Fax:* 902-494-1630. *E-mail:* admissions@dal.ca.

INDIVIDUAL COURSE SUBJECT AREAS

Undergraduate
Anatomy; community health services; health services administration; nursing; physiology

Graduate
Anatomy; community health services; health services administration; nursing; physiology

DALLAS COUNTY COMMUNITY COLLEGE DISTRICT

Dallas, Texas

LeCroy Center for Educational Telecommunications

Dallas County Community College District is a locally supported college system. It first offered distance learning courses in 1972. In 1996–97, it offered 65 courses at a distance. In the fall of 1996, there was a total of 2,669 students enrolled in distance learning courses.
Course delivery sites Courses are delivered to your home, your workplace, military bases.
Media Courses are delivered via television, videotapes, audioconferencing, computer software, World Wide Web, e-mail, print. Students and teachers interact via videoconferencing, audioconferencing, mail, telephone, fax, e-mail. A computer is required for some courses.
Services Distance learners have access to e-mail services, academic advising, tutoring, career placement assistance at a distance.
Credit-earning options Students may transfer credits from another institution or may earn credits through examinations, portfolio assessment, military training, business training.
Typical costs Tuition of $54 per course plus mandatory fees of $25 per course for local area residents. Tuition of $110 per course plus mandatory fees of $25 per course for in-state residents. Tuition of $201 per course plus mandatory fees of $25 per course for out-of-state residents. Costs may vary by number of credits taken. Financial aid is available to distance learners.
Registration Students may register by mail, fax, phone, World Wide Web.
Contact Distance Learning Hotline, Dallas County Community College District, LeCroy Center, 9596 Walnut Street, Dallas, TX 75243. *Telephone:* 888-468-4268. *Fax:* 972-669-6409. *Web site:* http://ollie.dcccd.edu.

DEGREE & CERTIFICATE PROGRAMS

Associate Degrees
▶ *General Studies (AAS)*
Application requirements *Prior education:* high school diploma or equivalent. *Minimum age:* 18. *Other requirements:* high school transcript, college transcripts.
Completion requirements 61 credit hours are required.

INDIVIDUAL COURSE SUBJECT AREAS

Undergraduate
Accounting; algebra; astronomy and astrophysics; biology; business administration and management; business communications; computer programming; creative writing; developmental and child psychology; economics; English as a second language (ESL); English composition; European languages and literatures; foods and nutrition studies; health and physical education/fitness; history; liberal arts, general studies, and humanities; marketing; mathematics; philosophy and religion; political science; sociology
See full description on page 410.

DALLAS THEOLOGICAL SEMINARY

Dallas, Texas

External Studies Department

Dallas Theological Seminary, founded in 1924, is an independent-nonprofit graduate institution. It is accredited by the Southern Association of Colleges and Schools. It first offered distance learning courses in 1987. In 1996–97, it offered 29 courses at a distance. In the fall of 1996, there was a total of 14 students enrolled in distance learning courses.
Course delivery sites Courses are delivered to your home, Bryan College (Dayton, TN), 3 off-campus centers in Houston, San Antonio, Tampa (FL).
Media Courses are delivered via videoconferencing, audiotapes, print. Students and teachers interact via videoconferencing, mail, telephone, fax, e-mail.
Services Distance learners have access to library services, e-mail services, academic advising at a distance.
Credit-earning options Students may transfer credits from another institution or may earn credits through institutionally developed exams.
Typical costs Tuition of $220 per semester hour. *Noncredit courses:* $110 per hour. Financial aid is available to distance learners enrolled full-time or part-time.
Registration Students may register by mail, fax, phone, e-mail, World Wide Web.
Contact Ben Scott, Director of External Studies, Dallas Theological Seminary, 3909 Swiss Avenue, Dallas, TX 75204. *Telephone:* 214-841-3677. *Fax:* 214-841-3565. *E-mail:* external_studies@dts.edu.

INDIVIDUAL COURSE SUBJECT AREAS

Graduate
Philosophy and religion; theological studies

Noncredit
Philosophy and religion; theological studies

DANVILLE AREA COMMUNITY COLLEGE

Danville, Illinois

Distance Learning Department

Danville Area Community College, founded in 1946, is a state and locally supported two-year college. It is accredited by the North Central Association of Colleges and Schools.
Course delivery sites Courses are delivered to your home, your workplace, other colleges.
Media Courses are delivered via videoconferencing.
Restrictions Programs are available to in-state students only.
Services Distance learners have access to tutoring at a distance.
Credit-earning options Students may transfer credits from another institution or may earn credits through examinations, military training. Financial aid is available to distance learners.
Contact Coordinator of Audiovisual Services and Distance Learning, Danville Area Community College, 2000 East Main Street, Danville, IL 61832. *Telephone:* 217-443-8577. *Fax:* 217-443-3178.

Profiles: Danville Area Community College

INDIVIDUAL COURSE SUBJECT AREAS

Undergraduate
Accounting; English composition; human resources management; liberal arts, general studies, and humanities; mathematics; psychology; social sciences

DANVILLE COMMUNITY COLLEGE

Danville, Virginia

Learning Resource Center

Danville Community College, founded in 1967, is a state-supported two-year college. It is accredited by the Southern Association of Colleges and Schools. It first offered distance learning courses in 1990. In 1996–97, it offered 6 courses at a distance. In the fall of 1996, there was a total of 78 students enrolled in distance learning courses.
Course delivery sites Courses are delivered to your home, Virginia Community College System (Richmond), 1 off-campus center in South Boston.
Media Courses are delivered via videotapes, videoconferencing. Students and teachers interact via videoconferencing, mail, telephone, fax, e-mail. A computer is required for some courses.
Services Distance learners have access to library services, academic advising at a distance.
Credit-earning options Students may transfer credits from another institution or may earn credits through portfolio assessment.
Typical costs Tuition of $47.65 per credit hour plus mandatory fees of $5 per semester for in-state residents. Tuition of $157 per credit hour plus mandatory fees of $5 per semester for out-of-state residents. Financial aid is available to distance learners.
Contact Betty Jo Foster, Dean of Instruction, Danville Community College, 1008 South Main Street, Danville, VA 24541. *Telephone:* 804-797-8410. *Fax:* 804-797-8541. *E-mail:* dcfostb@vccscent.bitnet. *Web site:* http://www.dc.cc.va.us.

INDIVIDUAL COURSE SUBJECT AREAS

Undergraduate
Accounting; business; business administration and management; English composition; health and physical education/fitness; marketing; mathematics; music

DARTON COLLEGE

Albany, Georgia

Office of Distance Learning

Darton College, founded in 1965, is a state-supported two-year college. It is accredited by the Southern Association of Colleges and Schools. It first offered distance learning courses in 1993. In 1996–97, it offered 30 courses at a distance. In the fall of 1996, there was a total of 350 students enrolled in distance learning courses.
Course delivery sites Courses are delivered to your home, your workplace, military bases, Abraham Baldwin Agricultural College (Tifton), Middle Georgia College (Cochran), South Georgia College (Douglas), Waycross College (Waycross), 6 off-campus centers in Camilla, Leesburg, Sylvester.
Media Courses are delivered via television, videotapes, videoconferencing, World Wide Web, e-mail, print. Students and teachers interact via videoconferencing, audioconferencing, mail, telephone, fax, e-mail. A computer is required for some courses.
Restrictions Programs are available to in-state students only.
Services Distance learners have access to library services, the campus computer network, e-mail services, academic advising, tutoring, career placement assistance at a distance.
Credit-earning options Students may transfer credits from another institution or may earn credits through standardized exams.
Typical costs Tuition of $30 per quarter hour plus mandatory fees of $40 per quarter for in-state residents. Tuition of $81 per quarter hour plus mandatory fees of $40 per quarter for out-of-state residents. *Noncredit courses:* $79 per course. Costs may vary by number of credits taken. Financial aid is available to distance learners enrolled full-time or part-time.
Registration Students may register by phone.
Contact Chris Robbins, Coordinator, Distance Learning, Darton College, 2400 Gillionville Road, Albany, GA 31707. *Telephone:* 912-430-6732. *Fax:* 912-430-6698. *E-mail:* crobbins@cavalier.dartnet.peachnet.edu. *Web site:* http://www.dartnet.peachnet.edu.

INDIVIDUAL COURSE SUBJECT AREAS

Undergraduate
Asian languages and literatures; English composition; English language and literature; European languages and literatures; fine arts; health professions and related sciences; industrial engineering; mathematics; music; political science; visual and performing arts

Noncredit
Classical languages and literatures

DAVID N. MYERS COLLEGE

Cleveland, Ohio

COOL Program (College Options On-Line)

David N. Myers College, founded in 1848, is an independent-nonprofit four-year college. It is accredited by the North Central Association of Colleges and Schools. It first offered distance learning courses in 1995. In 1996–97, it offered 14 courses at a distance. In the fall of 1996, there was a total of 42 students enrolled in distance learning courses.
Course delivery sites Courses are delivered to your home.
Media Courses are delivered via computer software, World Wide Web, e-mail, print. Students and teachers interact via mail, telephone, e-mail, in-person meetings.
Services Distance learners have access to the campus computer network, e-mail services at a distance.
Credit-earning options Students may transfer credits from another institution or may earn credits through examinations, portfolio assessment, military training, business training.
Typical costs Tuition of $250 per semester hour plus mandatory fees of $8 per semester hour. Financial aid is available to distance learners.
Contact Tiffany Payton, Assistant Director Admissions, David N. Myers College, 112 Prospect Avenue, Cleveland, OH 44115. *Telephone:* 216-696-9000, Ext. 805. *Fax:* 216-696-6430. *E-mail:* admissions@dnmyers.edu. *Web site:* http://ellen.dnmyers.edu.

INDIVIDUAL COURSE SUBJECT AREAS

Undergraduate
Accounting; business; business administration and management; communications; English composition; English language and literature

DAWSON COMMUNITY COLLEGE

Glendive, Montana

Continuing and Extension Education Department

Dawson Community College, founded in 1940, is a state and locally supported two-year college. It is accredited by the Northwest Association of Schools and Colleges. It first offered distance learning courses in 1990. In 1996–97, it offered 32 courses at a distance. In the fall of 1996, there was a total of 133 students enrolled in distance learning courses.
Course delivery sites Courses are delivered to Miles Community College (Miles City), Montana State University–Billings (Billings), 11 off-campus centers in Baker, Circle, Ekalaka, Glendive, Lambert, Miles City, Plevna, Richey, Savage, Sidney, Terry.
Media Courses are delivered via interactive television. Students and teachers interact via videoconferencing, mail, telephone, fax, e-mail.
Restrictions Programs are available to in-state students only. Students must have access to ITV network.
Services Distance learners have access to library services, e-mail services, academic advising, tutoring, career placement assistance at a distance.
Credit-earning options Students may transfer credits from another institution or may earn credits through standardized exams, institutionally developed exams, portfolio assessment, military training, business training.
Typical costs Tuition of $30 per credit plus mandatory fees of $20 per credit for local area residents. Tuition of $51.50 per credit plus mandatory fees of $20 per credit for in-state residents. Tuition of $124.75 per credit plus mandatory fees of $20 per credit for out-of-state residents. Costs may vary by number of credits taken. Financial aid is available to distance learners.
Contact Diane Dohrman, Director, Instructional Support Services, Dawson Community College, 300 College Drive, Glendive, MT 59330. *Telephone:* 406-365-3396. *Fax:* 406-365-8132. *E-mail:* diane_d@dawson.cc.mt.us.

DEGREE & CERTIFICATE PROGRAMS

Associate Degrees

▶ *Business Management (AA, AS, AAS)*
Application requirements *Prior education:* high school diploma or equivalent. *Other requirements:* ASSET, high school transcript.
Completion requirements 60 credits are required. 12 credits must be completed through the institution. *Other requirements:* internship. *Maximum time for completion:* three-year rotation of course work.

▶ *Human Services (AAS)*
Application requirements *Prior education:* high school diploma or equivalent. *Other requirements:* ASSET, high school transcript.
Completion requirements 60 credits are required. *Other requirements:* internship. *Maximum time for completion:* three-year rotation of courses.

INDIVIDUAL COURSE SUBJECT AREAS

Undergraduate

Administrative and secretarial services; agriculture; biology; business; business administration and management; creative writing; developmental and child psychology; economics; English composition; English language and literature; fine arts; health and physical education/fitness; history; liberal arts, general studies, and humanities; mathematics; sociology; teacher education

Noncredit

Agriculture

DAYTONA BEACH COMMUNITY COLLEGE

Daytona Beach, Florida

Interactive Telecommunications Services

Daytona Beach Community College, founded in 1958, is a state-supported two-year college. It is accredited by the Southern Association of Colleges and Schools. It first offered distance learning courses in 1991.
Course delivery sites Courses are delivered to your home, your workplace.
Media Courses are delivered via television, videoconferencing.
Restrictions Programs are available to local area students only.
Services Distance learners have access to library services, academic advising, tutoring, career placement assistance at a distance.
Credit-earning options Students may transfer credits from another institution or may earn credits through examinations, portfolio assessment, military training. Financial aid is available to distance learners.
Contact Registration Supervisor, Daytona Beach Community College, 1200 West International Speedway Boulevard, Daytona Beach, FL 32114. *Telephone:* 904-254-3000, Ext. 3646.

DEGREE & CERTIFICATE PROGRAMS

Associate Degrees

▶ *Liberal Arts (AA)*
▶ *Science (AS)*

INDIVIDUAL COURSE SUBJECT AREAS

Undergraduate

Administrative and secretarial services; astronomy and astrophysics; biological and life sciences; business; business administration and management; chemistry; communications; computer and information sciences; developmental and child psychology; education; English composition; European languages and literatures; fine arts; geology; health and physical education/fitness; health professions and related sciences; hospitality services management; law and legal studies; liberal arts, general studies, and humanities; mathematics; nursing; physical sciences; radio and television broadcasting; social sciences; special education; teacher education; visual and performing arts

DE ANZA COLLEGE

Cupertino, California

Distance Learning Center

De Anza College, founded in 1967, is a state and locally supported two-year college. It is accredited by the Western Association of Schools and Colleges, Inc. It first offered distance learning courses in 1974. In 1996–97, it offered 75 courses at a distance. In the fall of 1996, there was a total of 1,600 students enrolled in distance learning courses.
Course delivery sites Courses are delivered to your home, your workplace.
Media Courses are delivered via television, videotapes, videoconferencing, audiotapes, computer software, World Wide Web, e-mail, print. Students and teachers interact via videoconferencing, mail, telephone, fax, e-mail, in-person meetings, computer conferencing. A computer is required for some courses.
Restrictions Programs are available to local area students only.

Profiles: De Anza College

Services Distance learners have access to library services, admissions, grades at a distance.
Credit-earning options Students may transfer credits from another institution or may earn credits through examinations.
Typical costs Tuition of $9 per unit plus mandatory fees of $36 per quarter for in-state residents. Costs may vary by number of credits taken. Financial aid is available to distance learners enrolled full-time or part-time.
Registration Students may register by mail, phone, World Wide Web.
Contact Distance Learning Center, De Anza College, 21250 Stevens Creek Boulevard, Cupertino, CA 95014. *Telephone:* 408-864-8969. *Fax:* 408-864-8245. *E-mail:* information@dadistance.fhda.edu. *Web site:* http://dadistance.fhda.edu.

DEGREE & CERTIFICATE PROGRAMS

Associate Degrees

▶ *Liberal Arts, General Studies (AA)*
Application requirements *Prior education:* high school diploma or equivalent. *Minimum age:* 18. *Other requirements:* high school transcript.
Completion requirements 90 quarters are required. 24 quarters must be completed through the institution. *Other requirements:* regular personal contact between instructor and students is required by California education code for distance learning.
On-campus requirements One course, orientation, exams.

Undergraduate Certificates

▶ *Business Administration*
Application requirements *Prior education:* high school diploma or equivalent. *Minimum age:* 18. *Other requirements:* high school transcript.
Completion requirements 27 quarters are required. 21 quarters must be completed through the institution. *Other requirements:* regular personal contact between instructor and students is required by California education code for distance learning.
On-campus requirements One course.

INDIVIDUAL COURSE SUBJECT AREAS

Undergraduate

Abnormal psychology; accounting; advertising; African-American studies; algebra; American (US) history; anthropology; area, ethnic, and cultural studies; biological and life sciences; biology; business; business administration and management; business law; computer and information sciences; conservation and natural resources; design; developmental and child psychology; economics; education; English composition; English language and literature; fine arts; foods and nutrition studies; French language and literature; health and physical education/fitness; health professions and related sciences; journalism; liberal arts, general studies, and humanities; marketing; mathematics; music; nursing; philosophy and religion; political science; psychology; religious studies; social psychology; social sciences; sociology; Spanish language and literature; special education; statistics; technical writing

DEKALB COLLEGE

Decatur, Georgia

DeKalb College, founded in 1964, is a state-supported two-year college. It is accredited by the Southern Association of Colleges and Schools. It first offered distance learning courses in 1981. In 1996–97, it offered 20 courses at a distance. In the fall of 1996, there was a total of 500 students enrolled in distance learning courses.

Course delivery sites Courses are delivered to your home, other colleges, 5 off-campus centers in Clarkston, Conyers, Decatur, Dunwoody, Lawrenceville.
Media Courses are delivered via television, videotapes, videoconferencing, computer software. Students and teachers interact via videoconferencing, mail, telephone.
Restrictions Courses are available to students in eastern metropolitan Atlanta and surrounding areas only.
Services Distance learners have access to library services, e-mail services at a distance.
Credit-earning options Students may transfer credits from another institution.
Typical costs Tuition of $26 per credit for in-state residents. Tuition of $87 per credit for out-of-state residents. Costs may vary by number of credits taken. Financial aid is available to distance learners enrolled full-time.
Registration Students may register by mail, fax, phone.
Contact Robert R. Clark, Distance Learning Coordinator, DeKalb College, 555 North Indian Creek Drive, Clarkston, GA 30021-2396. *Telephone:* 404-298-3953. *Fax:* 404-298-3955. *E-mail:* rclark@dekalb.dc.peachnet.edu.

INDIVIDUAL COURSE SUBJECT AREAS

Undergraduate

Developmental and child psychology; economics; European languages and literatures; health and physical education/fitness; health professions and related sciences; history; liberal arts, general studies, and humanities; political science; sign language; sociology

DELAWARE COUNTY COMMUNITY COLLEGE

Media, Pennsylvania

Delaware County Community College, founded in 1967, is a state and locally supported two-year college. It is accredited by the Middle States Association of Colleges and Schools.
Course delivery sites Courses are delivered to your home, off-campus center(s).
Media Courses are delivered via television, videotapes, audiotapes, audioconferencing, computer software, World Wide Web, e-mail, print. Students and teachers interact via mail, telephone, fax, e-mail.
Services Distance learners have access to academic advising at a distance.
Credit-earning options Students may transfer credits from another institution or may earn credits through examinations, portfolio assessment.
Typical costs Tuition of $60 per credit plus mandatory fees of $7 per credit for local area residents. Tuition of $123 per credit plus mandatory fees of $7 per credit for in-state residents. Tuition of $182 per credit plus mandatory fees of $7 per credit for out-of-state residents.
Contact Distance Learning Office, Delaware County Community College, Distance Learning Department, 901 South Media Line Road, Media, PA 19063-1094. *Telephone:* 610-359-5158. *E-mail:* tmurray@dcccnet.dccc.edu.

INDIVIDUAL COURSE SUBJECT AREAS

Undergraduate

Business; business administration and management; computer and information sciences; developmental and child psychology; economics; history; law and legal studies; liberal arts, general studies, and humanities; philosophy and religion; political science; psychology; social sciences; sociology

DELAWARE STATE UNIVERSITY

Dover, Delaware

Distance Learning Program

Delaware State University, founded in 1891, is a state-supported comprehensive institution. It is accredited by the Middle States Association of Colleges and Schools.
Course delivery sites Courses are delivered to military bases, other colleges.
Media Courses are delivered via television, videoconferencing, print, audiographics conferencing.
Restrictions Programs are available to in-state students only.
Credit-earning options Students may transfer credits from another institution or may earn credits through examinations, portfolio assessment, military training, business training. Financial aid is available to distance learners.
Contact Distance Learning Coordinator, Delaware State University, 1200 North DuPont Highway, Mass Communications Department, Dover, DE 19901. *Telephone:* 302-739-4855.

INDIVIDUAL COURSE SUBJECT AREAS

Undergraduate
Business administration and management; English composition; special education; teacher education

Graduate
Social work

DELAWARE TECHNICAL & COMMUNITY COLLEGE, JACK F. OWENS CAMPUS

Georgetown, Delaware

Delaware Technical & Community College, Jack F. Owens Campus, founded in 1967, is a state-supported two-year college. It is accredited by the Middle States Association of Colleges and Schools.
Course delivery sites Courses are delivered to your home, other colleges.
Media Courses are delivered via television, videotapes. Students and teachers interact via telephone, on-campus meetings.
Credit-earning options Students may transfer credits from another institution or may earn credits through examinations, military training.
Typical costs Costs vary. Contact school for information. Financial aid is available to distance learners.
Contact Student Services Office, Delaware Technical & Community College, Jack F. Owens Campus, PO Box 610, Route 18, Georgetown, DE 19947. *Telephone:* 302-856-5400.

INDIVIDUAL COURSE SUBJECT AREAS

Undergraduate
Business; business administration and management; chemistry; education; psychology; sociology; Spanish language and literature

DELAWARE TECHNICAL & COMMUNITY COLLEGE, STANTON/WILMINGTON CAMPUS

Newark, Delaware

Distance Learning Programs and Outreach

Delaware Technical & Community College, Stanton/Wilmington Campus, founded in 1968, is a state-supported two-year college. It is accredited by the Middle States Association of Colleges and Schools. It first offered distance learning courses in 1980. In 1996–97, it offered 22 courses at a distance. In the fall of 1996, there was a total of 401 students enrolled in distance learning courses.
Course delivery sites Courses are delivered to your home, your workplace.
Media Courses are delivered via television, videotapes, videoconferencing, e-mail, print. Students and teachers interact via videoconferencing, mail, telephone, fax, e-mail.
Services Distance learners have access to library services, the campus computer network, e-mail services, academic advising, tutoring, career placement assistance at a distance.
Credit-earning options Students may transfer credits from another institution or may earn credits through standardized exams, portfolio assessment, military training, business training.
Typical costs Tuition of $55 per credit hour plus mandatory fees of $17 per course for in-state residents. Tuition of $137.50 per credit hour plus mandatory fees of $17 per course for out-of-state residents. Costs may vary by number of credits taken. Financial aid is available to distance learners.
Registration Students may register by mail, fax, phone.
Contact Charles Poplos, Distance Learning Outreach Coordinator, Delaware Technical & Community College, Stanton/Wilmington Campus, 400 Stanton-Christiana Road, Newark, DE 19713. *Telephone:* 302-454-3192. *Fax:* 302-453-3025. *E-mail:* dlearn@hopi.dtcc.edu. *Web site:* http://www.dtcc.edu.

INDIVIDUAL COURSE SUBJECT AREAS

Undergraduate
Advertising; algebra; American literature; business administration and management; calculus; chemistry; developmental and child psychology; economics; English composition; English language and literature; health professions and related sciences; home economics and family studies; journalism; marketing; mathematics; political science; psychology; social psychology; sociology; statistics; technical writing

DELGADO COMMUNITY COLLEGE

New Orleans, Louisiana

Delgado Community College, founded in 1921, is a state-supported two-year college. It is accredited by the Southern Association of Colleges and Schools. It first offered distance learning courses in 1990. In 1996–97, it offered 8 courses at a distance. In the fall of 1996, there was a total of 500 students enrolled in distance learning courses.
Course delivery sites Courses are delivered to your home.
Media Courses are delivered via television, videotapes. Students and teachers interact via telephone, in-person meetings.
Restrictions Programs are available to local area students only.

Profiles: Delgado Community College

Services Distance learners have access to library services, e-mail services, academic advising, tutoring, career placement assistance at a distance.
Credit-earning options Students may transfer credits from another institution or may earn credits through standardized exams.
Typical costs Tuition of $225 per course plus mandatory fees of $40 per course for in-state residents. Tuition of $225 per course plus mandatory fees of $85 per course for out-of-state residents. *Noncredit courses:* $20–$280 per course. Costs may vary by number of credits taken, term of enrollment, status of residency. Financial aid is available to distance learners enrolled full-time or part-time.
Registration Students may register by phone.
Contact Dr. Margaret D. Montgomery, Dean of Community Campus, Delgado Community College, 615 City Park Avenue, New Orleans, LA 70119. *Telephone:* 504-483-4173. *Fax:* 504-483-4895. *E-mail:* mmontg@pop3.dcc.edu. *Web site:* http://www.dcc.edu/.

INDIVIDUAL COURSE SUBJECT AREAS

Undergraduate
Art history and criticism; business; business administration and management; business law; developmental and child psychology; ethics; European history; finance; psychology

DELTA COLLEGE

University Center, Michigan

Telelearning Network Services

Delta College, founded in 1961, is a district-supported two-year college. It is accredited by the North Central Association of Colleges and Schools. It first offered distance learning courses in 1982. In 1996–97, it offered 26 courses at a distance. In the fall of 1996, there was a total of 502 students enrolled in distance learning courses.
Course delivery sites Courses are delivered to your home, Kirtland Community College (Roscommon), Mid Michigan Community College (Harrison), 2 off-campus centers in Saginaw, prisons.
Media Courses are delivered via television, videotapes, videoconferencing, audiotapes, World Wide Web, e-mail, print. Students and teachers interact via videoconferencing, mail, telephone, fax, e-mail. A computer is required for some courses.
Services Distance learners have access to library services, e-mail services, academic advising, tutoring, career placement assistance at a distance.
Credit-earning options Students may transfer credits from another institution or may earn credits through examinations, portfolio assessment, military training, business training.
Typical costs Tuition of $56 per credit hour for local area residents. Tuition of $70 per credit hour for in-state residents. Tuition of $100 per credit hour for out-of-state residents. Financial aid is available to distance learners.
Registration Students may register by phone.
Contact Patti Davidson, Telelearning Coordinator/Developer, Delta College, 1961 Delta Road, University Center, MI 48710-0002. *Telephone:* 517-686-9088. *Fax:* 517-686-8736. *E-mail:* pldavids@alpha.delta.edu.

DEGREE & CERTIFICATE PROGRAMS

Associate Degrees
▶ *General Studies (AA)*
Application requirements *Prior education:* high school diploma or equivalent. *Other requirements:* high school transcript.
Completion requirements 62 credit hours are required.
On-campus requirements For tests, orientation sessions.

INDIVIDUAL COURSE SUBJECT AREAS

Undergraduate
Abnormal psychology; algebra; art history and criticism; biology; business administration and management; business law; chemistry; developmental and child psychology; economics; English composition; English literature; ethics; health and physical education/fitness; health professions and related sciences; history; liberal arts, general studies, and humanities; marketing; nursing; philosophy and religion; physiology; political science; sociology

DELTA STATE UNIVERSITY

Cleveland, Mississippi

Division of Continuing Education and Distance Learning

Delta State University, founded in 1925, is a state-supported comprehensive institution. It is accredited by the Southern Association of Colleges and Schools. It first offered distance learning courses in 1993. In 1996–97, it offered 3 courses at a distance. In the fall of 1996, there was a total of 20 students enrolled in distance learning courses.
Course delivery sites Courses are delivered to Coahoma Community College (Clarksdale).
Media Courses are delivered via television, videoconferencing. Students and teachers interact via videoconferencing, telephone.
Restrictions Programs are available to in-state students only.
Services Distance learners have access to library services, the campus computer network, e-mail services, academic advising, career placement assistance at a distance.
Credit-earning options Students may transfer credits from another institution or may earn credits through examinations.
Typical costs *Undergraduate:* Tuition of $83 per hour for in-state residents. Tuition of $191 per hour for out-of-state residents. *Graduate:* Tuition of $110 per hour for in-state residents. Tuition of $254 per hour for out-of-state residents. *Noncredit courses:* $50 per course. Costs may vary by number of credits taken, term of enrollment. Financial aid is available to distance learners.
Registration Students may register by mail, phone.
Contact Marjorie Taylor, Off-Campus Program Coordinator, Delta State University, Box C-1, Cleveland, MS 38733. *Telephone:* 601-846-4027. *Fax:* 601-846-4016. *E-mail:* mataylor@asu.deltast.edu.

INDIVIDUAL COURSE SUBJECT AREAS

Undergraduate
Business; education administration; English language and literature; library and information studies; nursing; social sciences; special education; teacher education

Graduate
Business; education administration; English language and literature; library and information studies; nursing; social sciences; special education; teacher education

DENVER CONSERVATIVE BAPTIST SEMINARY

Denver, Colorado

Denver Conservative Baptist Seminary, founded in 1950, is an independent-religious graduate institution. It is accredited by the North Central Association of Colleges and Schools. It first offered distance

learning courses in 1988. In 1996–97, it offered 8 courses at a distance. In the fall of 1996, there was a total of 20 students enrolled in distance learning courses.
Course delivery sites Courses are delivered to your home.
Media Courses are delivered via videotapes, audiotapes, print. Students and teachers interact via mail, telephone, e-mail.
Services Distance learners have access to library services, e-mail services, academic advising, tutoring, career placement assistance at a distance.
Credit-earning options Students may transfer credits from another institution or may earn credits through institutionally developed exams, portfolio assessment.
Typical costs Tuition of $175 per quarter hour plus mandatory fees of $95 per course. *Noncredit courses:* one-half of credit cost plus $95 fee.
Registration Students may register by mail, fax, phone.
Contact William W. Klein, Associate Dean, Denver Conservative Baptist Seminary, PO Box 10,000, Denver, CO 80250. *Telephone:* 303-761-2482, Ext. 241. *Fax:* 303-761-8060. *E-mail:* billk@densem.edu. *Web site:* http://www.gospelcom.net/densem/.

INDIVIDUAL COURSE SUBJECT AREAS

Graduate
Bible studies; counseling psychology; education administration; ethics; history; philosophy and religion; psychology; theological studies

Noncredit
Bible studies; counseling psychology; education administration; ethics; history; philosophy and religion; psychology; theological studies

DEPAUL UNIVERSITY

Chicago, Illinois

Office of Distance Learning

DePaul University, founded in 1898, is an independent-religious Roman Catholic university. It is accredited by the North Central Association of Colleges and Schools.
Course delivery sites Courses are delivered to your home, other colleges.
Media Courses are delivered via videotapes, videoconferencing, computer software, computer conferencing.
Restrictions Programs are available to local area students only.
Services Distance learners have access to library services at a distance.
Credit-earning options Students may transfer credits from another institution or may earn credits through examinations, portfolio assessment. Financial aid is available to distance learners.
Contact Office of Distance Learning, DePaul University, 23 East Jackson Boulevard, Chicago, IL 60604. *Telephone:* 312-362-6300. *Fax:* 312-362-6309.

DEGREE & CERTIFICATE PROGRAMS

Baccalaureate Degrees
▶*General Liberal Arts (BA)*
▶*Nursing (BSN)*
Application requirements RN license, 2.5 GPA.

Graduate Degrees
▶*Advanced Practice Nursing (MSN)*
Application requirements *Prior education:* baccalaureate degree. *Other requirements:* RN license.

Distance Learning Programs

Graduate certificates
▶*Case Management*

INDIVIDUAL COURSE SUBJECT AREAS

Undergraduate
Business; computer and information sciences

Graduate
Accounting; business; computer and information sciences

DES MOINES AREA COMMUNITY COLLEGE

Ankeny, Iowa

Distance Learning/Continuing Education

Des Moines Area Community College, founded in 1966, is a state and locally supported two-year college. It is accredited by the North Central Association of Colleges and Schools. It first offered distance learning courses in 1970.
Course delivery sites Courses are delivered to your home, other colleges.
Media Courses are delivered via television, videotapes, videoconferencing, audiotapes, audioconferencing, computer software, e-mail. Students and teachers interact via audioconferencing, mail, telephone, e-mail. A computer is required for some courses.
Services Distance learners have access to library services, e-mail services, academic advising, career placement assistance at a distance.
Credit-earning options Students may transfer credits from another institution or may earn credits through examinations.
Typical costs Tuition of $57.40 per credit hour plus mandatory fees of $30 per course for in-state residents. Tuition of $114.80 per credit hour plus mandatory fees of $30 per course for out-of-state residents. Financial aid is available to distance learners.
Registration Students may register by mail, fax, phone, World Wide Web.
Contact Jane Herrmann, Director, Distance Learning, Des Moines Area Community College, 2006 South Ankeny Boulevard, Ankeny, IA 50021. *Telephone:* 515-965-7130. *Fax:* 515-965-6002. *E-mail:* jmherrmann@dmacc.cc.ia.us.

INDIVIDUAL COURSE SUBJECT AREAS

Undergraduate
Accounting; administrative and secretarial services; area, ethnic, and cultural studies; biology; business administration and management; computer and information sciences; developmental and child psychology; economics; English composition; English language and literature; history; liberal arts, general studies, and humanities; mathematics; music; nursing; political science; psychology; sociology; teacher education

Noncredit
Health professions and related sciences; home economics and family studies

Profiles: Dodge City Community College

DODGE CITY COMMUNITY COLLEGE

Dodge City, Kansas

ITV

Dodge City Community College, founded in 1935, is a state and locally supported two-year college. It is accredited by the North Central Association of Colleges and Schools. It first offered distance learning courses in 1996.
Course delivery sites Courses are delivered to Fort Hays State University (Hays), Southwest Kansas high schools.
Media Courses are delivered via television, videotapes, videoconferencing, computer software. Students and teachers interact via videoconferencing.
Restrictions Courses are available through members of the A-Plus Network only.
Services Distance learners have access to academic advising, tutoring, career placement assistance at a distance.
Credit-earning options Students may transfer credits from another institution or may earn credits through examinations, portfolio assessment, military training, business training.
Typical costs Tuition of $114 per course plus mandatory fees of $5 per credit hour for in-state residents. Tuition of $160 per course plus mandatory fees of $5 per credit hour for out-of-state residents. Costs may vary by campus or location. Financial aid is available to distance learners.
Contact Sam Seybold, Assistant Dean of Instruction, Dodge City Community College, 2501 North 14th, Dodge City, KS 67801. *Telephone:* 316-227-9325. *Fax:* 316-227-9200.

INDIVIDUAL COURSE SUBJECT AREAS

Undergraduate

Agriculture; Classical languages and literatures; creative writing; English composition; English language and literature; European languages and literatures; home economics and family studies; liberal arts, general studies, and humanities; mathematics; physics; radio and television broadcasting; social work

DRAKE UNIVERSITY

Des Moines, Iowa

Drake University, founded in 1881, is an independent-nonprofit university. It is accredited by the North Central Association of Colleges and Schools. It first offered distance learning courses in 1991.
Course delivery sites Courses are delivered to your home, other colleges.
Media Courses are delivered via television, videotapes, videoconferencing, computer software, print, computer conferencing.
Restrictions Programs are available to in-state students only.
Services Distance learners have access to library services, academic advising at a distance.
Credit-earning options Students may transfer credits from another institution. Financial aid is available to distance learners.
Contact Director of Marketing, Drake University, School of Education, 3206 University, Des Moines, IA 50311. *Telephone:* 515-271-2183. *Fax:* 515-271-4812.

INDIVIDUAL COURSE SUBJECT AREAS

Graduate

Accounting; administrative and secretarial services; business; business administration and management; education; education administration; educational psychology; human resources management; special education; teacher education

DUKE UNIVERSITY

Durham, North Carolina

Executive MBA Programs

Duke University, founded in 1838, is an independent-religious university affiliated with the United Methodist Church. It is accredited by the Southern Association of Colleges and Schools. It first offered distance learning courses in 1996. In 1996–97, it offered 15 courses at a distance. In the fall of 1996, there was a total of 40 students enrolled in distance learning courses.
Course delivery sites Courses are delivered to your home, your workplace, sites in Hong Kong, Shanghai (China), Prague (Czech Republic), Salzburg (Austria), Durham (NC), Sao Paulo (Brazil), Buenos Aires (Argentina).
Media Courses are delivered via computer software, World Wide Web, e-mail, computer conferencing. Students and teachers interact via telephone, fax, e-mail, computer conferencing. A computer is required for all courses.
Restrictions Students must be managers with global responsibilities, 8 years work experience and English fluency.
Services Distance learners have access to library services, the campus computer network, e-mail services, academic advising, tutoring at a distance.
Typical costs Tuition of $75,000 per degree program. Financial aid is available to distance learners enrolled full-time.
Registration Students may register by phone.
Contact Sam Veraldi, Assistant Dean, Recruiting Admissions, Duke University, The Fuqua School of Business, Durham, NC 27708. *Telephone:* 919-660-7802. *Fax:* 919-660-8044. *E-mail:* veraldi@mail.duke.edu. *Web site:* http://www.fuqua.duke.edu.

DEGREE & CERTIFICATE PROGRAMS

Graduate Degrees

▶ *General Management (MBA)*
In the fall of 1996 there were 40 students enrolled in this program.
Application requirements *Prior education:* baccalaureate degree. *Other requirements:* TOEFL (for non-native English speakers), college transcripts, an essay or personal statement, letter(s) of recommendation, an application fee, work experience, global management responsibility, corporate support.
Completion requirements 45 credits are required.
On-campus requirements 11 weeks of residency during 19 month program. Sites in North Carolina, Europe, Asia and South America.

INDIVIDUAL COURSE SUBJECT AREAS

Graduate

Accounting; business; business administration and management; economics; finance; international business; marketing; organizational behavior studies; statistics

DUQUESNE UNIVERSITY

Pittsburgh, Pennsylvania

Division of Continuing Education

Duquesne University, founded in 1878, is an independent-religious Roman Catholic university. It is accredited by the Middle States Association of Colleges and Schools. It first offered distance learning courses in 1996. In 1996–97, it offered 50 courses at a distance. In the fall of 1996, there was a total of 5 students enrolled in distance learning courses.
Course delivery sites Courses are delivered to your home, your workplace.
Media Courses are delivered via videotapes, videoconferencing, e-mail. Students and teachers interact via telephone, fax, e-mail. A computer is required for some courses.
Services Distance learners have access to library services, the campus computer network, e-mail services, academic advising at a distance.
Credit-earning options Students may transfer credits from another institution or may earn credits through portfolio assessment, military training.
Typical costs *Undergraduate:* Tuition of $419 per credit hour plus mandatory fees of $35 per credit. *Graduate:* Tuition of $438 per credit hour plus mandatory fees of $35 per credit. Costs may vary by specific program of study.
Registration Students may register by mail, fax.
Contact Dr. Benjamin Hodes, Dean, Duquesne University, 210 Rockwell Hall, Pittsburgh, PA 15282. *Telephone:* 412-396-5632. *Fax:* 412-396-5072. *E-mail:* hodes@duq2.cc.duq.edu. *Web site:* http://www.duq.edu.

Special note
Duquesne University, a mid-sized private institution located in the heart of downtown Pittsburgh, Pennsylvania, is ranked among the leading Catholic universities in America. Duquesne enrolls nearly 10,000 students and serves more than 2,000 adult learners each year through a variety of evening and weekend degree, certificate, and professional development programs.

Duquesne has the unique advantage of being a leader in delivering high-quality interactive courses taught by faculty members who are experts in their fields. Programs are offered through a variety of distance learning technologies, including interactive compressed video and computer conferencing and more conventional technologies such as satellite uplinks and downlinks, instructional television and radio, audio conferencing, and print-based delivery.

A variety of interesting and unique course offerings are available through the following schools: McAnulty College and Graduate School of Liberal Arts; Graduate Center for Social and Public Policy; A.J. Palumbo School of Business Administration; Division of Continuing Education; School of Education; John G. Rangos Sr. School of Health Sciences; School of Law; School of Music; and the Bayer School of Natural and Environmental Sciences and School of Nursing. For more information, students should visit Duquesne's Web site at http://www.duq.edu.

INDIVIDUAL COURSE SUBJECT AREAS

Undergraduate
Anatomy; art history and criticism; business; educational psychology; environmental science; ethics; music; nursing; physiology

Graduate
Business; education; environmental science; law and legal studies; music; nursing; public policy analysis

Noncredit
Business

DUTCHESS COMMUNITY COLLEGE

Poughkeepsie, New York

Dutchess Community College, founded in 1957, is a state and locally supported two-year college. It is accredited by the Middle States Association of Colleges and Schools. It first offered distance learning courses in 1977.
Course delivery sites Courses are delivered to your home.
Media Courses are delivered via television, computer software, World Wide Web. Students and teachers interact via mail, telephone, e-mail.
Credit-earning options Students may transfer credits from another institution or may earn credits through examinations, portfolio assessment, military training.
Typical costs Tuition of $89 per credit for in-state residents. Tuition of $178 per credit for out-of-state residents. Financial aid is available to distance learners.
Contact Deborah Weibman, Registrar, Dutchess Community College, 53 Pendell Road, Poughkeepsie, NY 12601. *Telephone:* 914-431-8000, Ext. 1509.

INDIVIDUAL COURSE SUBJECT AREAS

Undergraduate
Accounting; business administration and management; Classical languages and literatures; developmental and child psychology; economics; English composition; English language and literature; geology; history; human resources management; journalism; liberal arts, general studies, and humanities; physical sciences; psychology

EAST CAROLINA UNIVERSITY

Greenville, North Carolina

Division of Continuing Studies

East Carolina University, founded in 1907, is a state-supported university. It is accredited by the Southern Association of Colleges and Schools.
Course delivery sites Courses are delivered to your home, your workplace, military bases, other colleges.
Media Courses are delivered via videoconferencing, audioconferencing, World Wide Web, e-mail, desktop interactive television. Students and teachers interact via telephone, fax, e-mail, Internet.
Restrictions Internet-based programs are available only in Manufacturing, Digital Communication Technology, and Safety.
Credit-earning options Students may transfer credits from another institution or may earn credits through examinations, portfolio assessment.
Typical costs Tuition of $345 per course. Costs may vary by course delivery options.
Contact James W. Byrd, Jr., Distance Learning Specialist, East Carolina University, Erwin Building, Greenville, NC 27858. *Telephone:* 800-398-9275. *Fax:* 919-328-4350. *E-mail:* byrdj@mail.ecu.edu. *Web site:* http://www.dcs.ecu.edu.

Profiles: East Carolina University

DEGREE & CERTIFICATE PROGRAMS

Baccalaureate Degrees

▶ *Industrial Technology (BS)*
Restrictions Students must have Internet service provider and e-mail service.
Application requirements *Prior education:* high school diploma or equivalent. *Other requirements:* SAT, high school transcript, college transcripts, an essay or personal statement, an application fee of $35.
Completion requirements 127 semester hours are required. 30 semester hours must be completed through the institution.

Graduate Degrees

▶ *Education (MEd)*
Restrictions This program is available to in-state students only.
Application requirements *Prior education:* baccalaureate degree. *Other requirements:* GRE, high school transcript, college transcripts, an essay or personal statement, letter(s) of recommendation, an application fee of $40.
Completion requirements 30 semester hours are required. 21 semester hours must be completed through the institution. *Maximum time for completion:* six years.

▶ *Industrial Technology (MS)*
Restrictions Students must have Internet service provider and e-mail service.
Application requirements *Prior education:* baccalaureate degree. *Other requirements:* MAT, high school transcript, college transcripts, an essay or personal statement, letter(s) of recommendation, an application fee of $40.
Completion requirements 30 semester hours are required. 21 semester hours must be completed through the institution. *Maximum time for completion:* six years.

INDIVIDUAL COURSE SUBJECT AREAS

Undergraduate
Computer and information sciences; engineering; engineering-related technologies; European history; fine arts; history; technical writing

Graduate
Biological and life sciences; computer and information sciences; education; engineering; engineering-related technologies; European history; fine arts; health professions and related sciences; history

Noncredit
Education

EAST CENTRAL COMMUNITY COLLEGE

Decatur, Mississippi

Adult and Continuing Education

East Central Community College, founded in 1928, is a state and locally supported two-year college. It is accredited by the Southern Association of Colleges and Schools. It first offered distance learning courses in 1993. In 1996–97, it offered 5 courses at a distance. In the fall of 1996, there was a total of 100 students enrolled in distance learning courses.
Course delivery sites Courses are delivered to your home.
Media Courses are delivered via television, videoconferencing. Students and teachers interact via videoconferencing, mail, telephone, fax, on-campus meetings.
Restrictions Students must be within television reception area or have access to a videoconferencing classroom.
Services Distance learners have access to library services at a distance.
Credit-earning options Students may transfer credits from another institution or may earn credits through examinations, military training.
Typical costs Tuition of $150 per course for in-state residents. *Noncredit courses:* $50 per credit hour. Costs may vary by number of credits taken. Financial aid is available to distance learners enrolled full-time or part-time.
Contact Raymond McMullan, Director of Admissions, Records and Research, East Central Community College, PO Box 129, Decatur, MS 39327. *Telephone:* 601-635-2111. *Fax:* 601-635-2150.

INDIVIDUAL COURSE SUBJECT AREAS

Undergraduate
Fine arts; fire science; history; sociology

EASTERN IDAHO TECHNICAL COLLEGE

Idaho Falls, Idaho

Distance Learning Center

Eastern Idaho Technical College, founded in 1970, is a state-supported two-year college. It is accredited by the Northwest Association of Schools and Colleges. It first offered distance learning courses in 1996. In 1996–97, it offered 50 courses at a distance. In the fall of 1996, there was a total of 300 students enrolled in distance learning courses.
Course delivery sites Courses are delivered to 8 off-campus centers in Arco, Ashton, Challis, Driggs, Mackay, Rexburg, Rigby, St. Anthony.
Media Courses are delivered via videoconferencing. Students and teachers interact via videoconferencing, mail, telephone, fax, e-mail.
Restrictions Students must be able to travel to receive site.
Services Distance learners have access to library services, academic advising, tutoring, career placement assistance at a distance.
Credit-earning options Students may transfer credits from another institution or may earn credits through examinations, military training.
Typical costs Tuition of $54 per credit. *Noncredit courses:* $50–$80 per course. Costs may vary by number of credits taken. Financial aid is available to distance learners.
Registration Students may register by mail, fax, phone, e-mail.
Contact Ryan Carsten, Manager, Eastern Idaho Technical College, 1600 South 2500 East, Idaho Falls, ID 83404. *Telephone:* 208-524-3000, Ext. 3380. *Fax:* 208-524-3007. *Web site:* http://www.eitc.edu.

INDIVIDUAL COURSE SUBJECT AREAS

Undergraduate
Accounting; adult education; astronomy and astrophysics; business administration and management; computer and information sciences; economics; English as a second language (ESL); English composition; English language and literature; European languages and literatures; history; human resources management; journalism; law and legal studies; liberal arts, general studies, and humanities; marketing; mathematics; nursing; physical sciences; political science; psychology; sociology; teacher education; visual and performing arts

Noncredit
Business

EASTERN ILLINOIS UNIVERSITY

Charleston, Illinois

School of Adult and Continuing Education

Eastern Illinois University, founded in 1895, is a state-supported comprehensive institution. It is accredited by the North Central Association of Colleges and Schools. It first offered distance learning courses in 1994. In 1996–97, it offered 10 courses at a distance. In the fall of 1996, there was a total of 100 students enrolled in distance learning courses.
Course delivery sites Courses are delivered to your home, your workplace, Danville Area Community College (Danville), Lake Land College (Mattoon), Parkland College (Champaign), Richland Community College (Decatur).
Media Courses are delivered via television, computer software, World Wide Web. Students and teachers interact via videoconferencing, mail, telephone, fax, e-mail.
Services Distance learners have access to library services, the campus computer network, e-mail services, academic advising, tutoring, career placement assistance at a distance.
Credit-earning options Students may transfer credits from another institution or may earn credits through standardized exams, institutionally developed exams, portfolio assessment, military training, business training.
Typical costs *Undergraduate:* Tuition of $1026 per semester plus mandatory fees of $426.55 per semester for in-state residents. Tuition of $3078 per semester plus mandatory fees of $426.55 per semester for out-of-state residents. *Graduate:* Tuition of $1083 per semester plus mandatory fees of $426.55 per semester for in-state residents. Tuition of $3249 per semester plus mandatory fees of $426.55 per semester for out-of-state residents. *Noncredit courses:* $150 per course. Costs may vary by course delivery options. Financial aid is available to distance learners enrolled part-time.
Registration Students may register by phone.
Contact Dr. Thomas Hawkins, Director of the Office of Off-Campus Programs, Eastern Illinois University, Blair Hall 206, Charleston, IL 61920. *Telephone:* 217-581-5114. *Fax:* 217-581-6697. *Web site:* http://www.eiu.edu/~adulted.

INDIVIDUAL COURSE SUBJECT AREAS

Undergraduate
Business administration and management; human resources management

Graduate
Business administration and management; human resources management; teacher education

Noncredit
Business administration and management

EASTERN KENTUCKY UNIVERSITY

Richmond, Kentucky

Division of Extended Programs

Eastern Kentucky University, founded in 1906, is a state-supported comprehensive institution. It is accredited by the Southern Association of Colleges and Schools. It first offered distance learning courses in 1941. In 1996–97, it offered 160 courses at a distance. In the fall of 1996, there was a total of 1,500 students enrolled in distance learning courses.
Course delivery sites Courses are delivered to your home, Morehead State University (Morehead), 3 off-campus centers in Corbin, Danville, Manchester, area high schools.
Media Courses are delivered via television, videotapes, videoconferencing, audiotapes, World Wide Web, print. Students and teachers interact via mail, telephone, e-mail. A computer is required for some courses.
Services Distance learners have access to library services, the campus computer network, e-mail services at a distance.
Credit-earning options Students may transfer credits from another institution or may earn credits through institutionally developed exams.
Typical costs *Undergraduate:* Tuition of $82 per credit for in-state residents. Tuition of $227 per credit for out-of-state residents. *Graduate:* Tuition of $120 per credit for in-state residents. Tuition of $333 per credit for out-of-state residents. Financial aid is available to distance learners enrolled full-time.
Registration Students may register by mail, phone.
Contact Kenneth R. Nelson, Director, Eastern Kentucky University, Box 27-A, Richmond, KY 40475. *Telephone:* 606-622-2001. *Fax:* 606-622-1177. *E-mail:* sosnelso@acs.eku.edu.

INDIVIDUAL COURSE SUBJECT AREAS

Undergraduate
Algebra; American (US) history; anthropology; biology; business administration and management; comparative literature; corrections; criminal justice; curriculum and instruction; economics; educational psychology; English composition; English literature; ethics; family and marriage counseling; foods and nutrition studies; geography; German language and literature; health and physical education/fitness; information sciences and systems; marketing; mass media; political science; psychology; radio and television broadcasting; real estate; religious studies; sign language; sociology; special education; teacher education

Graduate
Curriculum and instruction; education administration; educational psychology; library and information studies; nursing; student counseling

EASTERN MAINE TECHNICAL COLLEGE

Bangor, Maine

Eastern Maine Technical College, founded in 1966, is a state-supported two-year college. It is accredited by the New England Association of Schools and Colleges. It first offered distance learning courses in 1991.
Course delivery sites Courses are delivered to your home, your workplace, other colleges.
Media Courses are delivered via videoconferencing, print.
Restrictions Programs are available to in-state students only.
Services Distance learners have access to library services, academic advising, tutoring, career placement assistance at a distance.
Credit-earning options Students may transfer credits from another institution or may earn credits through examinations, portfolio assessment, military training, business training. Financial aid is available to distance learners.
Contact Beth Mahoney, Director, Eastern Maine Technical College, PO Box 560, East Millinocket, ME 04462. *Telephone:* 207-746-5741. *Fax:* 207-746-9389. *E-mail:* mahoney@maine.maine.edu.

Profiles: Eastern Maine Technical College

DEGREE & CERTIFICATE PROGRAMS

Undergraduate Certificates
▶ *Maine Guide Certificate*

INDIVIDUAL COURSE SUBJECT AREAS

Undergraduate
Conservation and natural resources

Noncredit
Public health

EASTERN MICHIGAN UNIVERSITY

Ypsilanti, Michigan

Distance Education

Eastern Michigan University, founded in 1849, is a state-supported comprehensive institution. It is accredited by the North Central Association of Colleges and Schools. In 1996–97, it offered 35 courses at a distance. In the fall of 1996, there was a total of 400 students enrolled in distance learning courses.

Course delivery sites Courses are delivered to your home, Northwestern Michigan College (Traverse City), Washtenaw Community College (Ann Arbor), 2 off-campus centers in Flint, Jackson.

Media Courses are delivered via television, videotapes, audiotapes, World Wide Web. Students and teachers interact via mail, telephone, fax, e-mail.

Services Distance learners have access to library services, e-mail services, academic advising at a distance.

Credit-earning options Students may transfer credits from another institution or may earn credits through standardized exams, institutionally developed exams, portfolio assessment, military training, business training.

Typical costs Tuition of $100 per credit hour. Students pay a $40 registration fee. Costs may vary by course delivery options. Financial aid is available to distance learners enrolled full-time.

Registration Students may register by mail, fax, phone.

Contact Michael McPhillips, Distance Education Coordinator, Eastern Michigan University, 327 Goodison Hall, Ypsilanti, MI 48197. *Telephone:* 313-487-1081. *Fax:* 313-487-6695. *E-mail:* distance.education@emich.edu.

INDIVIDUAL COURSE SUBJECT AREAS

Undergraduate
American (US) history; American literature; business communications; English composition; genetics; psychology; sociology

Graduate
Education administration; teacher education

EASTERN NEW MEXICO UNIVERSITY

Portales, New Mexico

Extended Learning

Eastern New Mexico University, founded in 1934, is a state-supported comprehensive institution. It is accredited by the North Central Association of Colleges and Schools. It first offered distance learning courses in 1957. In 1996–97, it offered 125 courses at a distance. In the fall of 1996, there was a total of 329 students enrolled in distance learning courses.

Course delivery sites Courses are delivered to military bases, Clovis Community College (Clovis), Eastern New Mexico University–Roswell (Roswell), New Mexico Junior College (Hobbs), 7 off-campus centers in Artesia, Dora, Elida, Floyd, Melrose, Portales, Ruidoso.

Media Courses are delivered via television, World Wide Web, e-mail. Students and teachers interact via audioconferencing, mail, telephone, fax, e-mail, computer conferencing.

Restrictions Courses are available to students in southeastern New Mexico only. Students must be degree seeking. Internet courses require English proficiency.

Services Distance learners have access to library services, the campus computer network, e-mail services, academic advising, tutoring, career placement assistance at a distance.

Typical costs *Undergraduate:* Tuition of $99.85 per credit. *Graduate:* Tuition of $107.85 per credit. *Noncredit courses:* $70 for continuing education units. Financial aid is available to distance learners enrolled full-time or part-time.

Registration Students may register by mail, fax, phone.

Contact Anthony B. Schroeder, Director of Extended Learning, Eastern New Mexico University, Station #9, Portales, NM 88130. *Telephone:* 505-562-2166. *Fax:* 505-562-2168. *E-mail:* a.schroeder@enmu.edu. *Web site:* http://www.enmu.edu/~schroeda/learn/home.html.

DEGREE & CERTIFICATE PROGRAMS

Baccalaureate Degrees

▶ *Business Administration (BBA)*

In the fall of 1996 there were 117 students enrolled in this program. In 1995–96, 21 degrees were earned at a distance through this program.

Application requirements *Prior education:* some undergraduate course work. *Other requirements:* ACT, high school transcript, college transcripts, an application fee of $15.

Completion requirements 128 credits are required. This is a degree completion program.

▶ *Nursing (BSN)*

In the fall of 1996 there were 75 students enrolled in this program. In 1995–96, 5 degrees were earned at a distance through this program.

Application requirements *Prior education:* active RN license, associates degree in nursing, and current certification. *Other requirements:* ACT, high school transcript, college transcripts, an essay or personal statement, letter(s) of recommendation, an application fee of $15, grade of C or better in prerequisite science courses, at least one year of working experience.

Completion requirements 128 credits are required. This is a degree completion program.

▶ *University Studies (BS)*

In the fall of 1996 there were 23 students enrolled in this program. In 1995–96, 4 degrees were earned at a distance through this program.

Application requirements *Prior education:* some undergraduate course work. *Minimum age:* 26. *Other requirements:* ACT, high school transcript, college transcripts, an application fee of $15.

Completion requirements 128 credits are required. 60 credits must be completed through the institution. This is a degree completion program.

Graduate Degrees

▶ *Business Administration (MBA)*

In the fall of 1996 there were 30 students enrolled in this program. In 1995–96, 1 degree was earned at a distance through this program.

Application requirements *Prior education:* baccalaureate degree. *Other requirements:* GMAT, college transcripts, letter(s) of recommendation, an application fee of $10.

Completion requirements 33 credits are required.

▶ *Special Education (MS)*
In the fall of 1996 there were 52 students enrolled in this program. In 1995–96, 2 degrees were earned at a distance through this program.
Application requirements *Prior education:* baccalaureate degree. *Other requirements:* college transcripts, letter(s) of recommendation, an application fee of $10, teaching experience and NM licensure preferred.
Completion requirements 30 credits are required. *Maximum time for completion:* six years.

INDIVIDUAL COURSE SUBJECT AREAS

Undergraduate
Accounting; area, ethnic, and cultural studies; business; computer and information sciences; education; English language and literature; history; mathematics; nursing; psychology; public administration and services; sociology

Graduate
Accounting; area, ethnic, and cultural studies; business; computer and information sciences; education; English language and literature; history; mathematics; nursing; psychology; public administration and services; sociology

EASTERN OKLAHOMA STATE COLLEGE

Wilburton, Oklahoma

Eastern Oklahoma State College, founded in 1908, is a state-supported two-year college. It is accredited by the North Central Association of Colleges and Schools. It first offered distance learning courses in 1992. In 1996–97, it offered 4 courses at a distance. In the fall of 1996, there was a total of 30 students enrolled in distance learning courses.
Course delivery sites Courses are delivered to 1 off-campus center in Idabel, high schools.
Media Courses are delivered via television, interactive television. Students and teachers interact via fax, interactive television.
Restrictions Programs are available to local area students only.
Services Distance learners have access to library services, the campus computer network, e-mail services at a distance.
Credit-earning options Students may transfer credits from another institution or may earn credits through examinations.
Typical costs Tuition of $38 per credit hour. Costs may vary by number of credits taken. Financial aid is available to distance learners.
Contact J. C. Hunt, Vice President of Academic Affairs, Eastern Oklahoma State College, 1301 West Main Street, Wilburton, OK 74578. *Telephone:* 918-465-2361, Ext. 210. *Fax:* 918-465-2431.

INDIVIDUAL COURSE SUBJECT AREAS

Undergraduate
Algebra; American (US) history; English composition; nursing; political science

EASTERN OREGON UNIVERSITY

La Grande, Oregon

Division of Extended Programs

Eastern Oregon University, founded in 1929, is a state-supported comprehensive institution. It is accredited by the Northwest Association of Schools and Colleges. It first offered distance learning courses in 1978. In 1996–97, it offered 300 courses at a distance. In the fall of 1996, there was a total of 800 students enrolled in distance learning courses.
Course delivery sites Courses are delivered to your home, your workplace, military bases, Blue Mountain Community College (Pendleton), Central Oregon Community College (Bend), Treasure Valley Community College (Ontario), 8 off-campus centers in Baker City, Bend, Burns, Enterprise, John Day, Ontario, Pendleton, Portland.
Media Courses are delivered via television, videotapes, videoconferencing, audiotapes, audioconferencing, computer software, World Wide Web, e-mail, print. Students and teachers interact via videoconferencing, audioconferencing, mail, telephone, e-mail. A computer is required for some courses.
Services Distance learners have access to library services, e-mail services, academic advising, career placement assistance at a distance.
Credit-earning options Students may transfer credits from another institution or may earn credits through standardized exams, institutionally developed exams, portfolio assessment, military training, business training.
Typical costs *Undergraduate:* Tuition of $80 per credit. *Graduate:* Tuition of $132 per credit. *Noncredit courses:* $25–$50 per course. Costs may vary by course delivery options. Financial aid is available to distance learners enrolled full-time or part-time.
Registration Students may register by mail, fax, phone, e-mail, World Wide Web.
Contact Joseph Hart, Director, Distance Learning, Eastern Oregon University, Zabel Hall, 1410 L Avenue, La Grande, OR 97850-2899. *Telephone:* 541-962-3614. *Fax:* 541-962-3627. *E-mail:* jhart@eosc.osshe.edu. *Web site:* http://www.eosc.osshe.edu/dep.

Special note
Established in 1927, Eastern is a member of the Oregon State System of Higher Education and accredited by the Northwest Association of Schools and Colleges. Eastern has been a leader in distance education for 19 years; the distance learning program is administered by the Division of Extended Programs (DEP).

The degrees offered at a distance include the office administration AS degree, the interdisciplinary liberal studies BA/BS, and the philosophy, politics, and economics BA/BS. In addition, Eastern offers a distance learning Master of Teacher Education degree within the state of Oregon. Eastern is a contact center for the Western Governors University, providing its students a wide range of distance learning choices for courses and programs.

Eastern does not charge additional out-of-state tuition for distance learning students who do not live in Oregon but currently restricts its out-of-country offerings to English-language instruction for students in North America (unless special arrangements can be made to offset the costs of postage, faxing, and proctoring).

Distance learning courses are offered using a variety of modalities to accommodate the requirements of each degree program; in 1997–98, Eastern offers 160 correspondence courses (usually enhanced by videotapes/audiotapes), 65 computer conferencing courses, 30 interactive satellite courses, 9–12 Web-based courses, and 25 regional weekend courses. Students should contact DEP for a full listing of courses and degree programs.

DEGREE & CERTIFICATE PROGRAMS

Associate Degrees
▶ *Office Administration (AS)*
In the fall of 1996 there were 20 students enrolled in this program. In 1995–96, 5 degrees were earned at a distance through this program.
Application requirements *Prior education:* high school diploma or equivalent. *Other requirements:* high school transcript, an application fee of $50.

Profiles: Eastern Oregon University

Completion requirements 96 quarter units are required.

Baccalaureate Degrees

▶ *Accounting, Business, Economics (BA, BS)*
Application requirements *Prior education:* high school diploma or equivalent. *Other requirements:* an application fee of $50.
Completion requirements 186 quarter units are required. 45 quarter units must be completed through the institution. This is a degree completion program.

▶ *Liberal Studies (BA, BS)*
In the fall of 1996 there were 630 students enrolled in this program. In 1995–96, 100 degrees were earned at a distance through this program.
Application requirements *Prior education:* high school diploma or equivalent. *Other requirements:* high school transcript, an application fee of $50.
Completion requirements 186 quarter units are required. 45 quarter units must be completed through the institution. This is a degree completion program.

▶ *Economics, Philosophy, Political Science (BA)*
Application requirements *Prior education:* high school diploma or equivalent. *Other requirements:* an application fee of $50.
Completion requirements 186 quarter units are required. 45 quarter units must be completed through the institution. This is a degree completion program.

INDIVIDUAL COURSE SUBJECT AREAS

Undergraduate
Accounting; administrative and secretarial services; agriculture; area, ethnic, and cultural studies; biological and life sciences; business; business administration and management; computer and information sciences; education; English language and literature; health and physical education/fitness; human resources management; journalism; liberal arts, general studies, and humanities; mathematics; nursing; philosophy and religion; physical sciences; psychology; social sciences; teacher education; visual and performing arts

Graduate
Education

EASTERN WASHINGTON UNIVERSITY

Cheney, Washington

Division of Continuing Education, Summer Session and Outreach

Eastern Washington University, founded in 1882, is a state-supported comprehensive institution. It is accredited by the Northwest Association of Schools and Colleges. It first offered distance learning courses in 1970. In 1996–97, it offered 57 courses at a distance. In the fall of 1996, there was a total of 80 students enrolled in distance learning courses.
Course delivery sites Courses are delivered to your home, your workplace, military bases, other colleges, 1 off-campus center in Spokane.
Media Courses are delivered via television, videotapes, print. Students and teachers interact via mail, telephone, fax, e-mail.
Services Distance learners have access to e-mail services, academic advising at a distance.
Credit-earning options Students may transfer credits from another institution or may earn credits through institutionally developed exams, portfolio assessment, military training, business training.
Typical costs *Undergraduate:* Tuition of $75 per quarter hour. *Graduate:* Tuition of $120 per quarter hour. Costs may vary by campus or location, specific program of study, course delivery options, credit option. Financial aid is available to distance learners enrolled full-time or part-time.
Registration Students may register by mail, fax, phone.
Contact Alice Dionne, Associate Vice Provost, Eastern Washington University, Spokane Center, MS 1, 705 West First, Spokane, WA 99204-0400. *Telephone:* 509-623-4355. *Fax:* 509-623-4354. *E-mail:* adionne@ewu.edu. *Web site:* http://www.ewu.edu/.

INDIVIDUAL COURSE SUBJECT AREAS

Undergraduate
Abnormal psychology; accounting; African-American studies; American (US) history; American literature; business; creative writing; education; health and physical education/fitness; history; human resources management; mathematics; philosophy and religion; political science; psychology; social psychology; teacher education; women's studies

EASTERN WYOMING COLLEGE

Torrington, Wyoming

Eastern Wyoming College, founded in 1948, is a state and locally supported two-year college. It is accredited by the North Central Association of Colleges and Schools. It first offered distance learning courses in 1990. In 1996–97, it offered 1 course at a distance. In the fall of 1996, there was a total of 15 students enrolled in distance learning courses.
Course delivery sites Courses are delivered to your home, 12 off-campus centers in Chugwater, Douglas, Glendo, Glenrock, Guernsey, Hulett, Lusk, Moorcroft, Newcastle, Sundance, Upton, Whesland.
Media Courses are delivered via television. Students and teachers interact via mail, in-person meetings.
Restrictions Courses are available to students in Ocean, Niobrara, Platte, Converse, Weston and Crook Counties only. Courses are available only to students in college service area.
Services Distance learners have access to library services, academic advising, career placement assistance at a distance.
Credit-earning options Students may transfer credits from another institution or may earn credits through examinations, military training.
Typical costs Tuition of $36 per credit hour plus mandatory fees of $12 per credit hour for local area residents. Tuition of $36 per credit hour plus mandatory fees of $5 per credit hour for in-state residents. *Noncredit courses:* $30 per course. Financial aid is available to distance learners enrolled full-time or part-time.
Contact Chuck Engbretson, Vice President, Eastern Wyoming College, 3200 West C Street, Torrington, WY 82240. *Telephone:* 307-532-8261. *Fax:* 307-532-8222. *E-mail:* cengbret@ewcl.ewc.whecu.edu.

INDIVIDUAL COURSE SUBJECT AREAS

Undergraduate
Area, ethnic, and cultural studies; business; business administration and management; economics; fine arts; history; human resources management; law and legal studies; liberal arts, general studies, and humanities; philosophy and religion; political science; psychology; sociology

EAST TENNESSEE STATE UNIVERSITY

Johnson City, Tennessee

Office of Distance Education

East Tennessee State University, founded in 1911, is a state-supported university. It is accredited by the Southern Association of Colleges and Schools. It first offered distance learning courses in 1991. In 1996–97, it offered 75 courses at a distance. In the fall of 1996, there was a total of 1,408 students enrolled in distance learning courses.
Course delivery sites Courses are delivered to Pellissippi State Technical Community College (Knoxville), 3 off-campus centers in Bristol, Greeneville, Kingsport.
Media Courses are delivered via television, videotapes, videoconferencing. Students and teachers interact via videoconferencing, telephone. A computer is required for some courses.
Restrictions Programs are available to in-state students only.
Services Distance learners have access to library services, academic advising, tutoring, career placement assistance at a distance.
Credit-earning options Students may transfer credits from another institution or may earn credits through examinations, portfolio assessment, military training.
Typical costs *Undergraduate:* Tuition of $79 per credit plus mandatory fees of $10 per credit for in-state residents. Tuition of $190 per credit for out-of-state residents. *Graduate:* Tuition of $119 per credit plus mandatory fees of $10 per credit for in-state residents. Tuition of $190 per credit for out-of-state residents. Costs may vary by number of credits taken. Financial aid is available to distance learners.
Registration Students may register by phone.
Contact Darcey Cuffman, Video Resource Coordinator, East Tennessee State University, Box 70427, Johnson City, TN 37614. *Telephone:* 423-439-6809. *Fax:* 423-439-7029. *E-mail:* cuffmando@access.etsu-tn.edu.

INDIVIDUAL COURSE SUBJECT AREAS

Undergraduate
Business administration and management; chemistry; developmental and child psychology; economics; educational psychology; English language and literature; geology; history; home economics and family studies; liberal arts, general studies, and humanities; mathematics; nursing; protective services; public health; special education

Graduate
Business administration and management; economics; educational psychology; teacher education

EDISON COMMUNITY COLLEGE

Fort Myers, Florida

Distance Learning

Edison Community College, founded in 1962, is a state and locally supported two-year college. It is accredited by the Southern Association of Colleges and Schools. It first offered distance learning courses in 1993. In 1996–97, it offered 25 courses at a distance. In the fall of 1996, there was a total of 1,000 students enrolled in distance learning courses.
Course delivery sites Courses are delivered to your home, Broward Community College (Fort Lauderdale), 2 off-campus centers in Naples, Punta Gorda.
Media Courses are delivered via television, videotapes, videoconferencing, e-mail. Students and teachers interact via telephone, fax, e-mail.
Restrictions Programs are available to local area students only.
Services Distance learners have access to library services, academic advising at a distance.
Credit-earning options Students may transfer credits from another institution or may earn credits through standardized exams.
Typical costs Tuition of $38.28 per credit hour for local area residents. Tuition of $142.38 per credit hour for in-state residents. *Noncredit courses:* $30 per course. Costs may vary by number of credits taken. Financial aid is available to distance learners.
Registration Students may register by phone.
Contact Ray Medhurst, Interim Director of Distance Learning, Edison Community College, PO Box 60210, Fort Myers, FL 33910. *Telephone:* 941-489-9455. *Fax:* 941-432-5227.

DEGREE & CERTIFICATE PROGRAMS

Associate Degrees
▶ *Liberal Arts (AA)*
In the fall of 1996 there were 1,000 students enrolled in this program.
Application requirements *Prior education:* high school diploma or equivalent. *Other requirements:* SAT, ACT, high school transcript.
Completion requirements 60 credits are required. Last 15 credits must be completed through the institution.

INDIVIDUAL COURSE SUBJECT AREAS

Undergraduate
Area, ethnic, and cultural studies; astronomy and astrophysics; business; business administration and management; chemistry; communications; developmental and child psychology; economics; educational psychology; English composition; English language and literature; European languages and literatures; geology; health and physical education/fitness; history; liberal arts, general studies, and humanities; mathematics; political science; psychology; sociology; statistics

EDISON STATE COMMUNITY COLLEGE

Piqua, Ohio

Edison State Community College, founded in 1973, is a state-supported two-year college. It is accredited by the North Central Association of Colleges and Schools. It first offered distance learning courses in 1987. In 1996–97, it offered 8 courses at a distance. In the fall of 1996, there was a total of 60 students enrolled in distance learning courses.
Course delivery sites Courses are delivered to your home, your workplace, military bases, 1 off-campus center in Greenville.
Media Courses are delivered via audiotapes, World Wide Web, e-mail. Students and teachers interact via mail, telephone, fax, e-mail. A computer is required for some courses.
Services Distance learners have access to library services, the campus computer network, e-mail services, academic advising at a distance.
Credit-earning options Students may transfer credits from another institution or may earn credits through standardized exams, institutionally developed exams, portfolio assessment, military training, business training.
Typical costs Tuition of $75.25 per quarter credit plus mandatory fees of $25 per course for in-state residents. Tuition of $140.50 per quarter credit plus mandatory fees of $25 per course for out-of-state residents. Costs may vary by number of credits taken. Financial aid is available to distance learners enrolled full-time or part-time.
Registration Students may register by mail, fax, phone, e-mail.

Profiles: Edison State Community College

Contact Admissions Office, Edison State Community College, 1973 Edison Drive, Piqua, OH 45350. *Telephone:* 937-778-8600. *Fax:* 937-778-1920. *E-mail:* info@edison.cc.oh.us.

INDIVIDUAL COURSE SUBJECT AREAS

Undergraduate
Art history and criticism; business; business administration and management; economics; English literature; marketing; psychology; sociology; technical writing

EDMONDS COMMUNITY COLLEGE

Lynnwood, Washington

Continuing Education

Edmonds Community College, founded in 1967, is a state and locally supported two-year college. It is accredited by the Northwest Association of Schools and Colleges. It first offered distance learning courses in 1995.
Course delivery sites Courses are delivered to your home.
Media Courses are delivered via television, computer software, computer conferencing.
Credit-earning options Students may transfer credits from another institution or may earn credits through examinations, military training, business training. Financial aid is available to distance learners.
Contact Associate Director, Continuing Education, Edmonds Community College, 20000 68th Avenue, West, Lynnwood, WA 98036. *Telephone:* 206-640-1361. *Fax:* 206-640-1496. *Web site:* http://web.edcc.ctc.edu/cce/edmonds.htm.

INDIVIDUAL COURSE SUBJECT AREAS

Undergraduate
Accounting; business administration and management; computer and information sciences; developmental and child psychology; liberal arts, general studies, and humanities

ELLSWORTH COMMUNITY COLLEGE

Iowa Falls, Iowa

Iowa Valley Continuing Education

Ellsworth Community College, founded in 1890, is a state and locally supported two-year college. It is accredited by the North Central Association of Colleges and Schools. It first offered distance learning courses in 1994. In 1996–97, it offered 7 courses at a distance. In the fall of 1996, there was a total of 76 students enrolled in distance learning courses.
Course delivery sites Courses are delivered to your workplace, other colleges.
Media Courses are delivered via videoconferencing. Students and teachers interact via videoconferencing, telephone.
Restrictions Programs are available to in-state students only. Students must come through a school system.
Services Distance learners have access to library services, academic advising, tutoring, career placement assistance at a distance.
Credit-earning options Students may transfer credits from another institution.
Typical costs Tuition of $66 per credit hour. Costs may vary by term of enrollment. Financial aid is available to distance learners.
Registration Students may register by mail.
Contact Paul Rusley, Registrar, Ellsworth Community College, 1100 College Avenue, Iowa Falls, IA 50126. *Telephone:* 515-648-4611. *Fax:* 515-648-3128.

INDIVIDUAL COURSE SUBJECT AREAS

Undergraduate
Agriculture; biological and life sciences; biology; chemistry; chemistry, organic; educational psychology; protective services; social psychology; sociology

Noncredit
Agriculture

EL PASO COMMUNITY COLLEGE

El Paso, Texas

El Paso Community College, founded in 1969, is a county-supported two-year college. It is accredited by the Southern Association of Colleges and Schools. It first offered distance learning courses in 1983. In 1996–97, it offered 40 courses at a distance. In the fall of 1996, there was a total of 1,000 students enrolled in distance learning courses.
Course delivery sites Courses are delivered to your home, your workplace, military bases, 4 off-campus centers in El Paso.
Media Courses are delivered via television, videoconferencing. Students and teachers interact via videoconferencing, audioconferencing, mail, telephone, fax, e-mail.
Restrictions Televised courses require students to be in the broadcast area. Videoconferencing is limited to a regional service area.
Services Distance learners have access to e-mail services at a distance.
Credit-earning options Students may transfer credits from another institution or may earn credits through standardized exams, institutionally developed exams, portfolio assessment.
Typical costs Tuition of $151 per course for in-state residents. Tuition of $236 per course for out-of-state residents. Lab fee for some courses. Costs may vary by number of credits taken. Financial aid is available to distance learners enrolled full-time.
Registration Students may register by mail, phone.
Contact Jenny Grion, Associate Vice President, Instructional Services, El Paso Community College, PO Box 20500, El Paso, TX 79998. *Telephone:* 913-594-2348. *Fax:* 913-594-2322. *E-mail:* jennyg@lagunaepcc.edu.

INDIVIDUAL COURSE SUBJECT AREAS

Undergraduate
Accounting; American (US) history; anthropology; business administration and management; economics; English as a second language (ESL); geology; marketing; political science; psychology; sociology; Spanish language and literature

Noncredit
Spanish language and literature

EMBRY-RIDDLE AERONAUTICAL UNIVERSITY, EXTENDED CAMPUS

Daytona Beach, Florida

Department of Independent Studies

Embry-Riddle Aeronautical University, Extended Campus, founded in 1970, is an independent-nonprofit comprehensive institution. It is parentally accredited by the Southern Association of Colleges and Schools. It first offered distance learning courses in 1980. In 1996–97, it offered 47 courses at a distance. In the fall of 1996, there was a total of 1,468 students enrolled in distance learning courses.

Course delivery sites Courses are delivered to your home, your workplace, military bases.

Media Courses are delivered via videotapes, audiotapes, print, Compuserve (graduate program only). Students and teachers interact via mail, telephone, fax, e-mail, Compuserve (graduate program only). A computer is required for some courses.

Services Distance learners have access to library services, academic advising, career placement assistance at a distance.

Credit-earning options Students may transfer credits from another institution or may earn credits through institutionally developed exams, portfolio assessment, military training.

Typical costs *Undergraduate:* Tuition of $130 per credit hour. *Graduate:* Tuition of $280 per credit hour. Computer disk is $20.

Registration Students may register by mail, fax, phone, e-mail.

Contact Thomas W. Pettit, Director, Department of Independent Studies, Embry-Riddle Aeronautical University, Extended Campus, 600 South Clyde Morris Boulevard, Daytona Beach, FL 32114-3900. *Telephone:* 904-226-6398. *Fax:* 904-226-7627. *E-mail:* pettitt@cts.db.erau.edu. *Web site:* http://www.erau.edu.

DEGREE & CERTIFICATE PROGRAMS

Associate Degrees

▶ *Aviation Business Administration (AS)*

In the fall of 1996 there were 110 students enrolled in this program. In 1995–96, 1 degree was earned at a distance through this program.

Application requirements *Prior education:* high school diploma or equivalent. *Other requirements:* high school transcript, college transcripts, an application fee of $30.

Completion requirements 63 semester hours are required. 15 credit hours must be completed through the institution.

Program contact John Holub, Application Processor, Embry-Riddle Aeronautical University, Extended Campus, 600 South Clyde Morris Boulevard, Daytona Beach, FL 32114-3900. Phone: 800-FLY-ERAU. Fax: 904-226-7627. E-mail: holubj@cts.db.erau.edu.

▶ *Professional Aeronautics (AS)*

In the fall of 1996 there were 400 students enrolled in this program. In 1995–96, 10 degrees were earned at a distance through this program.

Application requirements *Prior education:* high school diploma or equivalent. *Other requirements:* high school transcript, college transcripts, an application fee of $30.

Completion requirements 63 semester hours are required. 15 credit hours must be completed through the institution.

Program contact John Holub, Application Processor, Embry-Riddle Aeronautical University, Extended Campus, 600 South Clyde Morris Boulevard, Daytona Beach, FL 32114-3900. Phone: 800-FLY-ERAU. Fax: 904-226-7627. E-mail: holubj@cts.db.erau.edu.

Baccalaureate Degrees

▶ *Management of Technical Operations (BS)*

In the fall of 1996 there were 55 students enrolled in this program.

Application requirements *Prior education:* high school diploma or equivalent. *Other requirements:* high school transcript, college transcripts, an application fee of $30.

Completion requirements 126 semester hours are required. 30 credit hours must be completed through the institution.

Program contact John Holub, Application Processor, Embry-Riddle Aeronautical University, Extended Campus, 600 South Clyde Morris Boulevard, Daytona Beach, FL 32114-3900. Phone: 800-FLY-ERAU. Fax: 904-226-7627. E-mail: holubj@cts.db.erau.edu.

▶ *Professional Aeronautics (BS)*

In the fall of 1996 there were 935 students enrolled in this program. In 1995–96, 74 degrees were earned at a distance through this program.

Application requirements *Prior education:* high school diploma or equivalent. *Other requirements:* high school transcript, college transcripts, an application fee of $30.

Completion requirements 126 semester hours are required. 30 credit hours must be completed through the institution.

Program contact John Holub, Application Processor, Embry-Riddle Aeronautical University, Extended Campus, 600 South Clyde Morris Boulevard, Daytona Beach, FL 32114-3900. Phone: 800-FLY-ERAU. Fax: 904-226-7627. E-mail: holubj@cts.db.erau.edu.

Graduate Degrees

▶ *Aeronautical Science (MAS)*

In the fall of 1996 there were 309 students enrolled in this program. In 1995–96, 42 degrees were earned at a distance through this program.

Restrictions Students must be able to access CompuServe.

Application requirements *Prior education:* baccalaureate degree. *Other requirements:* college transcripts, an application fee of $30, 2.5 GPA.

Completion requirements 36 credit hours are required. 24 credit hours must be completed through the institution. *Maximum time for completion:* seven years.

INDIVIDUAL COURSE SUBJECT AREAS

Undergraduate

Accounting; business; business administration and management; business law; calculus; computer and information sciences; economics; English composition; English language and literature; finance; human resources management; marketing; mathematics; organizational behavior studies; physics; psychology; statistics; technical writing

Graduate

Business administration and management; computer and information sciences; labor relations/studies; management information systems

See full description on page 412.

EMPORIA STATE UNIVERSITY

Emporia, Kansas

Office of Continuing Education

Emporia State University, founded in 1863, is a state-supported comprehensive institution. It is accredited by the North Central Association of Colleges and Schools. It first offered distance learning courses in 1970. In 1996–97, it offered 31 courses at a distance. In the fall of 1996, there was a total of 252 students enrolled in distance learning courses.

Course delivery sites Courses are delivered to your home, your workplace.

Media Courses are delivered via television, videotapes, videoconferencing, audiotapes, computer software, World Wide Web, e-mail, print. Students

Profiles: Emporia State University

and teachers interact via videoconferencing, mail, telephone, fax, e-mail, computer conferencing. A computer is required for some courses.

Services Distance learners have access to academic advising, career placement assistance at a distance.

Credit-earning options Students may earn credits through institutionally developed exams.

Typical costs *Undergraduate:* Tuition of $72 per credit hour. *Graduate:* Tuition of $102 per credit hour. Some courses may require materials fee in addition to tuition. Financial aid is available to distance learners enrolled full-time.

Registration Students may register by mail, fax, phone.

Contact Office of Continuing Education, Emporia State University, 1200 Commercial Street, Emporia, KS 66801-5087. *Telephone:* 316-341-5385. *Fax:* 316-341-5744. *E-mail:* conted@esumail.emporia.edu. *Web site:* http://www.emporia.edu/s/www/conted/home.htm.

INDIVIDUAL COURSE SUBJECT AREAS

Undergraduate
Biological and life sciences; business; education; English language and literature; genetics; geology; health and physical education/fitness; library and information studies

Graduate
Biological and life sciences; business; education; English language and literature; genetics; geology; health and physical education/fitness; library and information studies

ESSEX COMMUNITY COLLEGE

Baltimore, Maryland

Essex Community College, founded in 1957, is a state and locally supported two-year college. It is accredited by the Middle States Association of Colleges and Schools. It first offered distance learning courses in 1972. In 1996–97, it offered 25 courses at a distance. In the fall of 1996, there was a total of 170 students enrolled in distance learning courses.

Course delivery sites Courses are delivered to your home, your workplace, military bases, Carroll Community College (Westminster), Catonsville Community College (Catonsville), Howard Community College (Columbia).

Media Courses are delivered via television, videoconferencing. Students and teachers interact via videoconferencing, mail, telephone, fax.

Restrictions Programs are available to in-state students only.

Credit-earning options Students may transfer credits from another institution or may earn credits through standardized exams, portfolio assessment, military training, business training.

Typical costs Tuition of $60 per credit plus mandatory fees of $35 per course for local area residents. Tuition of $106 per credit plus mandatory fees of $35 per course for in-state residents. Tuition of $166 per credit plus mandatory fees of $35 per course for out-of-state residents. *Noncredit courses:* $50–$200 per course. Costs may vary by number of credits taken. Financial aid is available to distance learners.

Registration Students may register by mail, fax, phone.

Contact Linda L. Brothers, Coordinator, Office for Extended Learning, Essex Community College, 7201 Rossville Boulevard, Baltimore, MD 21237. *Telephone:* 410-780-6715. *Fax:* 410-686-9564. *E-mail:* llb2@eccmain.essex.cc.md.us.

INDIVIDUAL COURSE SUBJECT AREAS

Undergraduate
Area, ethnic, and cultural studies; astronomy and astrophysics; business; business administration and management; communications; creative writing; English language and literature; English literature; European languages and literatures; French language and literature; geology; health and physical education/fitness; history; law and legal studies; liberal arts, general studies, and humanities; marketing; oceanography; philosophy and religion; political science; sociology; Spanish language and literature

EVERGREEN VALLEY COLLEGE

San Jose, California

Telecourse Program

Evergreen Valley College, founded in 1975, is a state and locally supported two-year college. It is accredited by the Western Association of Schools and Colleges, Inc. It first offered distance learning courses in 1981.

Course delivery sites Courses are delivered to your home.

Media Courses are delivered via television.

Restrictions Programs are available to in-state students only.

Credit-earning options Students may transfer credits from another institution or may earn credits through examinations, business training.

Typical costs Tuition of $13 per credit for in-state residents. Tuition of $126 per credit for out-of-state residents.

Contact Jan Tomisaka, Staff Assistant, Evergreen Valley College, 3095 Yerba Buena Road, San Jose, CA 95135-1598. *Telephone:* 408-270-6422. *Fax:* 408-239-0316. *E-mail:* jtomisak@unix.sjeccd.cc.ca.us. *Web site:* http://www.evc.edu.

INDIVIDUAL COURSE SUBJECT AREAS

Undergraduate
Accounting; astronomy and astrophysics; business administration and management; computer and information sciences; European languages and literatures; history; political science; social psychology; sociology

FAIRLEIGH DICKINSON UNIVERSITY, FLORHAM-MADISON CAMPUS

Madison, New Jersey

Fairleigh Dickinson University, Florham-Madison Campus, founded in 1942, is an independent-nonprofit comprehensive institution. It is accredited by the Middle States Association of Colleges and Schools. It first offered distance learning courses in 1990.

Course delivery sites Courses are delivered to your home.

Media Courses are delivered via videoconferencing.

Restrictions Programs are available to in-state students only.

Services Distance learners have access to library services at a distance. Financial aid is available to distance learners.

Contact Director, Teaching on Television Project, Fairleigh Dickinson University, Florham-Madison Campus, 2000 River Road, Teaneck, NJ 07666. *Telephone:* 201-692-2449. *Fax:* 201-692-2503.

INDIVIDUAL COURSE SUBJECT AREAS

Undergraduate
Business administration and management; communications; teacher education; visual and performing arts

FAIRLEIGH DICKINSON UNIVERSITY, TEANECK–HACKENSACK

Teaneck, New Jersey

Office of Educational Technology

Fairleigh Dickinson University, Teaneck–Hackensack, founded in 1942, is an independent-nonprofit comprehensive institution. It is accredited by the Middle States Association of Colleges and Schools. It first offered distance learning courses in 1990. In 1996–97, it offered 12 courses at a distance.
Course delivery sites Courses are delivered to your home, your workplace, Bloomfield College (Bloomfield), corporations, high schools.
Media Courses are delivered via videoconferencing, computer software, World Wide Web, e-mail, print. Students and teachers interact via videoconferencing, mail, telephone, fax, e-mail, World Wide Web. A computer is required for some courses.
Restrictions Availability varies by course, program, or delivery means.
Services Distance learners have access to library services, e-mail services, academic advising, career placement assistance at a distance.
Typical costs *Undergraduate:* Tuition of $409 per credit. *Graduate:* Tuition of $471 per credit. Non-standard tuition rates may apply to distance learning courses. Costs may vary by campus or location, specific program of study, number of credits taken, course delivery options. Financial aid is available to distance learners enrolled full-time.
Registration Students may register by mail, fax.
Contact Ellen Spaldo, Coordinator of Instructional Design/ITV, Fairleigh Dickinson University, Teaneck–Hackensack, 1000 River Road, H328A, Teaneck, NJ 07666. *Telephone:* 201-692-7155. *Fax:* 201-692-7273. *E-mail:* spaldo@fdu.edu. *Web site:* http://www.fdu.edu.

DEGREE & CERTIFICATE PROGRAMS

Graduate certificates

▶ *Information Systems*
In the fall of 1996 there were 15 students enrolled in this program.
Restrictions This program is available to in-state students only. Open to students at Eatontown, NJ extension.
Application requirements *Prior education:* baccalaureate degree. *Other requirements:* college transcripts, an application fee of $35.
Completion requirements 15 are required. 15 must be completed through the institution. *Maximum time for completion:* five years.
On-campus requirements For final exams in some courses.
Program contact Dr. Gil Steiner, Director, School of Computer Science & Information System, Fairleigh Dickinson University, Teaneck–Hackensack, 1000 River Road, Teaneck, NJ 07666. Phone: 201-692-6500. Fax: 201-692-2773. E-mail: steiner@alpha.fdu.edu.

INDIVIDUAL COURSE SUBJECT AREAS

Undergraduate
Drama and theater; logic; marketing

Graduate
Accounting; business; communications; European history; information sciences and systems; nursing; teacher education

FAYETTEVILLE TECHNICAL COMMUNITY COLLEGE

Fayetteville, North Carolina

Fayetteville Technical Community College, founded in 1961, is a state-supported two-year college. It is accredited by the Southern Association of Colleges and Schools. It first offered distance learning courses in 1980. In 1996–97, it offered 30 courses at a distance. In the fall of 1996, there was a total of 450 students enrolled in distance learning courses.
Course delivery sites Courses are delivered to your home, your workplace, military bases, other colleges.
Media Courses are delivered via television, World Wide Web, e-mail. Students and teachers interact via mail, telephone, fax, e-mail. A computer is required for some courses.
Services Distance learners have access to library services, academic advising, tutoring at a distance.
Credit-earning options Students may transfer credits from another institution or may earn credits through standardized exams, military training.
Typical costs Tuition of $20 per semester hour plus mandatory fees of $9.25 per semester for in-state residents. Tuition of $163 per semester hour plus mandatory fees of $9.25 per semester for out-of-state residents. *Noncredit courses:* $35 per course. Financial aid is available to distance learners enrolled full-time or part-time.
Registration Students may register by mail, fax, World Wide Web.
Contact Bobby J. Ervin, Dean of Business, Fayetteville Technical Community College, PO Box 35236, Fayetteville, NC 28303. *Telephone:* 910-678-8466. *Fax:* 910-678-8215. *E-mail:* bervin@atlas.faytech.cc.nc.us. *Web site:* http://www.faytech.cc.nc.us.

INDIVIDUAL COURSE SUBJECT AREAS

Undergraduate
Accounting; business; business administration and management; creative writing; economics; English composition; human resources management; social psychology; sociology

FIELDING INSTITUTE

Santa Barbara, California

Fielding Institute, founded in 1974, is an independent-nonprofit graduate institution. It is accredited by the Western Association of Schools and Colleges, Inc. It first offered distance learning courses in 1974.
Course delivery sites Courses are delivered to your home, your workplace, military bases.
Media Courses are delivered via audioconferencing, computer software, World Wide Web, e-mail, print. Students and teachers interact via audioconferencing, mail, telephone, fax, e-mail, computer conferencing. A computer is required for all courses.
Restrictions Students must be either degree seeking or in certificate programs.
Services Distance learners have access to library services, the campus computer network, e-mail services, academic advising, tutoring at a distance.
Credit-earning options Students may earn credits through portfolio assessment.

Distance Learning Programs

Profiles: Fielding Institute

Typical costs Tuition of $11,000 per year. Costs may vary by specific program of study. Financial aid is available to distance learners enrolled full-time.
Contact Sylvia Williams, Director, Enrollment Management Services, Fielding Institute, 2112 Santa Barbara Street, Santa Barbara, CA 93105. *Telephone:* 805-687-1099, Ext. 3116. *Fax:* 805-687-9793. *E-mail:* sawilliams@fielding.edu. *Web site:* http://www.fielding.edu.

Special note

The Fielding Institute provides graduate degree and certificate learning opportunities for midcareer professionals in clinical psychology, education, organization development, and other related fields of applied behavioral and social science. Fielding seeks as students creative adults who are committed to taking responsibility for their learning and integrating theory, research, and professional practice in all their endeavors.

Fielding's learning model recognizes the multiple commitments of adult students and places emphasis on their needs for flexibility of time and location for their studies. Collaborative learning, competence-based assessment, and multicultural and global awareness are also integral to the learning process.

In addition to an electronic network, which serves as a primary means of communication and an educational resource for the community, a wide range of services are provided to support student learning. These include library and research support, detailed study guides of the program curriculum, and various types of face-to-face learning opportunities.

DEGREE & CERTIFICATE PROGRAMS

Graduate Degrees

▶ *Clinical Psychology (PhD)*
In the fall of 1996 there were 489 students enrolled in this program. In 1995–96, 69 degrees were earned at a distance through this program.
Application requirements *Prior education:* graduate degree. *Other requirements:* college transcripts, an essay or personal statement, letter(s) of recommendation, an application fee of $75, interview.
Completion requirements 13 courses are required. 13 courses must be completed through the institution. *Other requirements:* comprehensive assessment; dissertation; 500 hours of practicum. *Maximum time for completion:* 10 years.
On-campus requirements Initial one-week orientation.

▶ *Educational Leadership and Change (EdD)*
In the fall of 1996 there were 20 students enrolled in this program.
Restrictions Students must be from a common environment (geographic or a school district).
Application requirements *Prior education:* baccalaureate degree. *Other requirements:* college transcripts, an essay or personal statement, letter(s) of recommendation, an application fee of $75, resume.
Completion requirements 8 courses are required. 8 courses must be completed through the institution. *Other requirements:* comprehensive examination; dissertation.
On-campus requirements One-week orientation.

▶ *Human and Organization Development (PhD)*
In the fall of 1996 there were 403 students enrolled in this program. In 1995–96, 110 degrees were earned at a distance through this program.
Application requirements *Prior education:* baccalaureate degree. *Other requirements:* college transcripts, an essay or personal statement, letter(s) of recommendation, an application fee of $75, resume, orientation with faculty member strongly recommended.
Completion requirements 8 courses are required. 8 courses must be completed through the institution. *Other requirements:* dissertation; comprehensive assessment.
On-campus requirements One-week orientation.

▶ *Organizational Design and Effectiveness (MA)*
Application requirements *Prior education:* baccalaureate degree. *Other requirements:* college transcripts, an essay or personal statement, letter(s) of recommendation, an application fee of $75, resume.
Completion requirements 52 units are required. 52 units must be completed through the institution. *Maximum time for completion:* 20 months.
On-campus requirements One-week orientation and semi-annual events.

Graduate certificates

▶ *Group Psychotherapy*
In the fall of 1996 there were 10 students enrolled in this program.
Restrictions Program is available to students in five states only. Students must be licensed psychologists, social workers, mental health counselors, psychiatrists, or marriage and family counselors.
Application requirements *Prior education:* graduate degree. *Other requirements:* college transcripts, letter(s) of recommendation, an application fee of $50, curriculum vitae, interview with faculty member.
Completion requirements 96 hours are required. 96 hours must be completed through the institution. *Other requirements:* supervision at a practicum site. *Maximum time for completion:* two years.
On-campus requirements Eight monthly cluster meetings/year for six hours each.

▶ *Neuropsychology*
In the fall of 1996 there were 79 students enrolled in this program.
Restrictions Students must be licensed or certified psychologists (counseling, academic, school) and must be able to form cluster work groups.
Application requirements *Prior education:* graduate degree. *Other requirements:* college transcripts, an essay or personal statement, letter(s) of recommendation, an application fee of $75.
Completion requirements 32 hours are required. 32 hours must be completed through the institution. *Other requirements:* final professional examination. *Maximum time for completion:* two years.
On-campus requirements Monthly practicum sessions where students meet for three hours in study groups.

FITCHBURG STATE COLLEGE

Fitchburg, Massachusetts

Division of Graduate and Continuing Education

Fitchburg State College, founded in 1894, is a state-supported comprehensive institution. It is accredited by the New England Association of Schools and Colleges. It first offered distance learning courses in 1989. In 1996–97, it offered 20 courses at a distance. In the fall of 1996, there was a total of 71 students enrolled in distance learning courses.
Course delivery sites Courses are delivered to your home, your workplace, one off-campus center in South Hampton, Bermuda.
Media Courses are delivered via television, computer software, Independent Computer Network. Students and teachers interact via mail, telephone, fax, e-mail. A computer is required for some courses.
Restrictions Availability varies by course, program, or delivery means.
Services Distance learners have access to library services, e-mail services, academic advising at a distance.
Credit-earning options Students may transfer credits from another institution or may earn credits through examinations, portfolio assessment, military training.
Typical costs *Undergraduate:* Tuition of $330 per course plus mandatory fees of $76 per course. *Graduate:* Tuition of $420 per course plus mandatory fees of $76 per course. Costs may vary by campus or location, specific program of study, number of credits taken, course

delivery options. Financial aid is available to distance learners enrolled full-time or part-time.
Registration Students may register by mail, fax, phone, e-mail, World Wide Web.
Contact Catherine Canney, Director of Continuing Education, Fitchburg State College, 160 Pearl Street, Fitchburg, MA 01420. *Telephone:* 508-665-3181. *Fax:* 508-665-3658. *E-mail:* dgce@fsc.edu.

DEGREE & CERTIFICATE PROGRAMS

Graduate Degrees

▶ *Business Administration (MBA)*
Restrictions Program is available to students in Bermuda only.
Application requirements *Prior education:* baccalaureate degree. *Other requirements:* GMAT, college transcripts, letter(s) of recommendation, an application fee of $10.
Completion requirements 54 semester hours are required. 24 semester hours must be completed through the institution. *Maximum time for completion:* six years.
Program contact Dr. Janette Purcell, Graduate Program Chair, MBA, Fitchburg State College, 160 Pearl Street, Fitchburg, MA 01420. Phone: 508-665-3567. Fax: 508-665-3550.

▶ *Elementary Education, Secondary Education (MEd)*
In the fall of 1996 there were 11 students enrolled in this program.
Restrictions Program is available to students in Bermuda only.
Application requirements *Prior education:* baccalaureate degree. *Other requirements:* GRE or GMAT, college transcripts, letter(s) of recommendation, an application fee of $10, teaching certificate.
Completion requirements 36 semester hours are required. 30 semester hours must be completed through the institution. *Maximum time for completion:* six years.
Program contact Dr. Ronald Colbert, Department Chair, Education, Fitchburg State College, 160 Pearl Street, Fitchburg, MA 01420. Phone: 508-665-3493. Fax: 508-665-3517.

INDIVIDUAL COURSE SUBJECT AREAS

Undergraduate
Biology; business administration and management; developmental and child psychology; economics; geology; history; liberal arts, general studies, and humanities; sociology

Graduate
Business administration and management; teacher education

FLATHEAD VALLEY COMMUNITY COLLEGE

Kalispell, Montana

Education Services

Flathead Valley Community College, founded in 1967, is a state and locally supported two-year college. It is accredited by the Northwest Association of Schools and Colleges. In 1996–97, it offered 3 courses at a distance. In the fall of 1996, there was a total of 42 students enrolled in distance learning courses.
Course delivery sites Courses are delivered to your home, your workplace.
Media Courses are delivered via television, audiotapes, World Wide Web. Students and teachers interact via telephone, on-campus meetings.
Services Distance learners have access to e-mail services at a distance.
Credit-earning options Students may transfer credits from another institution or may earn credits through examinations, portfolio assessment, military training, business training.

Typical costs Tuition of $38.25 per credit plus mandatory fees of $16.25 per credit for local area residents. Tuition of $62.50 per credit plus mandatory fees of $16.25 per credit for in-state residents. Tuition of $148.75 per credit plus mandatory fees of $16.25 per credit for out-of-state residents. Students pay an additional $15 per semester in mandatory fees. *Noncredit courses:* $64 per course. Costs may vary by number of credits taken. Financial aid is available to distance learners.
Registration Students may register by mail.
Contact Faith Hodges, Assistant Dean of Instruction, Flathead Valley Community College, 777 Grandview Drive, Kalispell, MT 59901. *Telephone:* 406-756-3812. *Fax:* 406-756-3815. *E-mail:* fhodges@mail.fvcc.cc.mt.us.

INDIVIDUAL COURSE SUBJECT AREAS

Undergraduate
Area, ethnic, and cultural studies; astronomy and astrophysics; English language and literature; geography

FLORENCE-DARLINGTON TECHNICAL COLLEGE

Florence, South Carolina

Learning Resources Division

Florence-Darlington Technical College, founded in 1963, is a state-supported two-year college. It is accredited by the Southern Association of Colleges and Schools. It first offered distance learning courses in 1985. In 1996–97, it offered 25 courses at a distance. In the fall of 1996, there was a total of 125 students enrolled in distance learning courses.
Course delivery sites Courses are delivered to your home, your workplace, Chesterfield-Marlboro Technical College (Cheraw), Denmark Technical College (Denmark), Orangeburg-Calhoun Technical College (Orangeburg), Technical College of the Lowcountry (Beaufort), Williamsburg Technical College (Kingstree), 2 off-campus centers in Hartsville, Lake City.
Media Courses are delivered via television, videotapes, videoconferencing, audiotapes, computer software, World Wide Web, print. Students and teachers interact via videoconferencing, audioconferencing, mail, telephone, fax, e-mail. A computer is required for some courses.
Services Distance learners have access to library services, academic advising, tutoring, career placement assistance at a distance.
Credit-earning options Students may transfer credits from another institution or may earn credits through institutionally developed exams.
Typical costs Tuition of $46 per credit for local area residents. Tuition of $52 per credit for in-state residents. Tuition of $62 per credit for out-of-state residents. Costs may vary by number of credits taken. Financial aid is available to distance learners enrolled full-time or part-time.
Registration Students may register by mail, fax, phone, e-mail, World Wide Web.
Contact Angela Jordan, Administration Specialist, Florence-Darlington Technical College, PO Box 100548, Florence, SC 29501. *Telephone:* 803-661-8133. *Fax:* 803-661-8217. *E-mail:* jordana@fdtc.flo.tec.sc.us.

INDIVIDUAL COURSE SUBJECT AREAS

Undergraduate
Business; business administration and management; developmental and child psychology; educational psychology; English composition; English language and literature; mathematics; psychology; sociology; teacher education

Profiles: Florida Atlantic University

FLORIDA ATLANTIC UNIVERSITY

Boca Raton, Florida

Open University

Florida Atlantic University, founded in 1961, is a state-supported university. It is accredited by the Southern Association of Colleges and Schools.
Course delivery sites Courses are delivered to your home, your workplace, military bases, other colleges.
Media Courses are delivered via television, videotapes, videoconferencing, computer software, World Wide Web, e-mail. Students and teachers interact via videoconferencing, audioconferencing, telephone, fax, e-mail.
Credit-earning options Students may transfer credits from another institution or may earn credits through examinations, portfolio assessment, military training, business training.
Typical costs *Undergraduate:* Tuition of $63 per hour for in-state residents. Tuition of $238 per hour for out-of-state residents. *Graduate:* Tuition of $119 per hour for in-state residents. Tuition of $389 per hour for out-of-state residents. Financial aid is available to distance learners.
Contact Open University, Florida Atlantic University, 777 Glades Road, Boca Raton, FL 33431. *Telephone:* 561-367-2465.

INDIVIDUAL COURSE SUBJECT AREAS

Graduate
Business; chemistry; computer and information sciences; education; engineering; health professions and related sciences; nursing

FLORIDA COMMUNITY COLLEGE AT JACKSONVILLE

Jacksonville, Florida

Open Campus

Florida Community College at Jacksonville, founded in 1963, is a state-supported two-year college. It is accredited by the Southern Association of Colleges and Schools.
Course delivery sites Courses are delivered to your home.
Media Courses are delivered via television, videotapes, computer conferencing.
Restrictions Programs are available to local area students only.
Credit-earning options Students may transfer credits from another institution or may earn credits through examinations, military training. Financial aid is available to distance learners.
Contact Telecourse Coordinator, Florida Community College at Jacksonville, 101 West State Street, Room A-1162, Jacksonville, FL 32202. *Telephone:* 904-633-8116. *Fax:* 904-633-8435. *Web site:* http://www.fccj.cc.fl.us.

INDIVIDUAL COURSE SUBJECT AREAS

Undergraduate
Accounting; administrative and secretarial services; biology; business; business administration and management; chemistry; computer and information sciences; developmental and child psychology; economics; English composition; English language and literature; European languages and literatures; geology; history; law and legal studies; liberal arts, general studies, and humanities; mathematics; philosophy and religion; political science; sociology

FLORIDA STATE UNIVERSITY

Tallahassee, Florida

Office of Interactive Distance Learning

Florida State University, founded in 1857, is a state-supported university. It is accredited by the Southern Association of Colleges and Schools. It first offered distance learning courses in 1987. In 1996–97, it offered 10 courses at a distance. In the fall of 1996, there was a total of 400 students enrolled in distance learning courses.
Course delivery sites Courses are delivered to your home, other colleges, 4 off-campus centers in Gainesville, Jacksonville, Orlando, Pensacola.
Media Courses are delivered via television, videoconferencing, computer software, World Wide Web, e-mail. Students and teachers interact via videoconferencing, mail, telephone, fax, e-mail. A computer is required for some courses.
Services Distance learners have access to library services, e-mail services, academic advising, tutoring, career placement assistance at a distance.
Credit-earning options Students may transfer credits from another institution or may earn credits through examinations.
Typical costs Contact university for details. Financial aid is available to distance learners.
Contact Owen F. Gaede, Acting Director and Professor, Florida State University, Learning Systems Institute, 4600C University Center, Tallahassee, FL 32306. *Telephone:* 904-644-1604. *Fax:* 904-644-5803. *E-mail:* dl@lsi.fsu.edu. *Web site:* http://www.idl.fsu.edu.

DEGREE & CERTIFICATE PROGRAMS

Graduate Degrees
▶*Information Studies (MS)*
Application requirements *Prior education:* baccalaureate degree. *Other requirements:* GRE, college transcripts.
Completion requirements 36 semester hours are required.
Program contact Beth Logan, Associate Dean, Florida State University, College of Information Studies, 101 Library Studies Building, Tallahassee, FL 32306. Phone: 904-644-8106.

INDIVIDUAL COURSE SUBJECT AREAS

Undergraduate
Biology; geography; history

Graduate
Chemical engineering; civil engineering; education administration; electrical engineering; industrial engineering; library and information studies; mechanical engineering; social work; teacher education

FLOYD COLLEGE

Rome, Georgia

Extended Learning

Floyd College, founded in 1970, is a state-supported two-year college. It is accredited by the Southern Association of Colleges and Schools. It first offered distance learning courses in 1977. In 1996–97, it offered 35 courses at a distance.
Course delivery sites Courses are delivered to your home, your workplace, other colleges, 3 off-campus centers in Acworth, Bremen, Cartersville, over 300 GSAMS Teleconferencing classroom sites.

Media Courses are delivered via television, videotapes, videoconferencing, computer software, World Wide Web, e-mail, print. Students and teachers interact via videoconferencing, audioconferencing, mail, telephone, fax, e-mail. A computer is required for some courses. The institution provides assistance with acquiring computer equipment.
Restrictions Programs are available to in-state students only.
Services Distance learners have access to library services, the campus computer network, e-mail services, academic advising, tutoring, career placement assistance at a distance.
Credit-earning options Students may transfer credits from another institution or may earn credits through standardized exams.
Typical costs Tuition of $32 per quarter hour for in-state residents. Tuition of $121 per quarter hour for out-of-state residents. Costs may vary by number of credits taken, course delivery options. Financial aid is available to distance learners enrolled full-time or part-time.
Registration Students may register by phone, World Wide Web.
Contact Carla Patterson, Director of Extended Learning, Floyd College, PO Box 1864, Rome, GA 30162. *Telephone:* 706-802-5300. *Fax:* 706-802-5997. *E-mail:* carla_patterson@heritage.fc.peachnet.edu.

INDIVIDUAL COURSE SUBJECT AREAS

Undergraduate
Algebra; American (US) history; American literature; anatomy; chemistry; comparative literature; developmental and child psychology; economics; English composition; English literature; European history; geology; health and physical education/fitness; nursing; physiology; political science; sign language; sociology

FORT HAYS STATE UNIVERSITY

Hays, Kansas

Office of Continuing Education

Fort Hays State University, founded in 1902, is a state-supported comprehensive institution. It is accredited by the North Central Association of Colleges and Schools. It first offered distance learning courses in 1987.
Course delivery sites Courses are delivered to your home, your workplace, other colleges.
Media Courses are delivered via television, videotapes, videoconferencing, audiotapes, audioconferencing, computer conferencing.
Restrictions Programs are available to in-state students only.
Services Distance learners have access to library services, academic advising at a distance.
Credit-earning options Students may transfer credits from another institution or may earn credits through examinations, military training. Financial aid is available to distance learners.
Contact Assistant Dean of Continuing Education, Fort Hays State University, 600 Park Street, Hays, KS 67601. *Telephone:* 913-628-4291. *Fax:* 913-628-4037.

DEGREE & CERTIFICATE PROGRAMS

Baccalaureate Degrees
▶ *Business Administration (BS)*
Program contact Dr. Robert Meier, Chair, Computer and Information Systems Department, Fort Hays State University, 600 Park Street, Hays, KS 67601.
▶ *Elementary Education (BS)*
Completion requirements *Other requirements:* students must have admission to teacher education program before enrolling in most upper division education and method courses.

▶ *General Studies (BGS)*
Program contact Dr. Louis J. Caplan, Professor, Fort Hays State University, 600 Park Street Hays, Hays, KS 67601. Phone: 913-628-5347.
▶ *Nursing (BS)*
Program contact Dianna Koerner, Instructor, Fort Hays State University, 600 Park Street, Hays, KS 67601.

Graduate Degrees
▶ *Education (MS)*

INDIVIDUAL COURSE SUBJECT AREAS

Undergraduate
Accounting; agriculture; area, ethnic, and cultural studies; biology; business administration and management; creative writing; developmental and child psychology; economics; education administration; educational psychology; English as a second language (ESL); English composition; English language and literature; geology; history; law and legal studies; library and information studies; mathematics; microbiology; nursing; political science; public health; social work; sociology; special education; teacher education

Graduate
Developmental and child psychology; education administration; educational psychology; English as a second language (ESL); English language and literature; library and information studies; mathematics; nursing; political science; public health; social work; sociology; special education; teacher education

Noncredit
Law and legal studies

FRANCISCAN UNIVERSITY OF STEUBENVILLE

Steubenville, Ohio

Distance Education

Franciscan University of Steubenville, founded in 1946, is an independent-religious Roman Catholic comprehensive institution. It is accredited by the North Central Association of Colleges and Schools. It first offered distance learning courses in 1995. In 1996–97, it offered 11 courses at a distance. In the fall of 1996, there was a total of 134 students enrolled in distance learning courses.
Course delivery sites Courses are delivered to your home.
Media Courses are delivered via audiotapes. Students and teachers interact via mail, telephone, fax, e-mail.
Services Distance learners have access to library services, e-mail services, academic advising, career placement assistance at a distance.
Credit-earning options Students may transfer credits from another institution.
Typical costs *Undergraduate:* Tuition of $400 per course. *Graduate:* Tuition of $400 per course. *Noncredit courses:* $150 per course.
Registration Students may register by mail, fax.
Contact Lorrie Campana, Administrative Clerk, Franciscan University of Steubenville, University Boulevard, Steubenville, OH 43952. *Telephone:* 614-283-6517. *Fax:* 614-284-7037. *E-mail:* lcampana@franuniv.edu. *Web site:* http://gabriel.franuniv.edu/distance.html.

INDIVIDUAL COURSE SUBJECT AREAS

Undergraduate
History; philosophy and religion; theological studies

Profiles: Franciscan University of Steubenville

Graduate
Theological studies

Noncredit
History; philosophy and religion; theological studies

FRANKLIN UNIVERSITY

Columbus, Ohio

Instructional Technology

Franklin University, founded in 1902, is an independent-nonprofit comprehensive institution. It is accredited by the North Central Association of Colleges and Schools. It first offered distance learning courses in 1996. In 1996–97, it offered 150 courses at a distance. In the fall of 1996, there was a total of 25 students enrolled in distance learning courses.

Course delivery sites Courses are delivered to your home, your workplace.
Media Courses are delivered via World Wide Web, e-mail, print. Students and teachers interact via mail, telephone, fax, e-mail. A computer is required for all courses.
Services Distance learners have access to library services at a distance.
Credit-earning options Students may transfer credits from another institution or may earn credits through examinations, portfolio assessment, military training.
Typical costs Tuition of $161 per credit hour. *Noncredit courses:* $161 per credit hour. Costs may vary by specific program of study. Financial aid is available to distance learners.
Contact Assistant Director of Student Services, Franklin University, 201 South Grant Avenue, Columbus, OH 43215. *Telephone:* 614-341-6256. *Fax:* 614-224-8027. *E-mail:* register@franklin.edu. *Web site:* http://www.franklin.edu.

DEGREE & CERTIFICATE PROGRAMS

Baccalaureate Degrees

▶ *Technical Administration (BS)*
Application requirements *Prior education:* associate degree. *Other requirements:* college transcripts, an application fee of $25.
Completion requirements 130 semester credits are required. 60 semester credits must be completed through the institution. This is a degree completion program.
Program contact Peter R. Giuliani, Assistant Dean, Instructional Technology, Franklin University, 201 South Grant Avenue, Columbus, OH 43215. Phone: 614-341-6266. Fax: 614-224-4025. E-mail: giuliani@franklin.edu.

INDIVIDUAL COURSE SUBJECT AREAS

Undergraduate
Business; computer and information sciences

Noncredit
Computer and information sciences

See full description on page 414.

FRONT RANGE COMMUNITY COLLEGE

Westminster, Colorado

Distance Learning Office

Front Range Community College, founded in 1968, is a state-supported two-year college. It is accredited by the North Central Association of Colleges and Schools. It first offered distance learning courses in 1986. In 1996–97, it offered 50 courses at a distance. In the fall of 1996, there was a total of 750 students enrolled in distance learning courses.

Course delivery sites Courses are delivered to your home, your workplace.
Media Courses are delivered via television, videoconferencing, audiotapes, audioconferencing, computer software, e-mail, print. Students and teachers interact via videoconferencing, audioconferencing, mail, telephone, fax, e-mail. A computer is required for some courses.
Services Distance learners have access to library services, academic advising at a distance.
Credit-earning options Students may transfer credits from another institution or may earn credits through standardized exams, portfolio assessment, military training, business training.
Typical costs Tuition of $54.60 per credit hour for in-state residents. Tuition of $253.50 per credit hour for out-of-state residents.
Registration Students may register by mail, phone.
Contact Gertrude Dathe, Distance Learning Secretary, Front Range Community College, 3645 West 112th Avenue, Westminster, CO 80030. *Telephone:* 303-404-5554. *Fax:* 303-466-1623. *E-mail:* gertrude@cccs.cccoes.edu. *Web site:* http://mosquito.frcc.cccoes.edu.

INDIVIDUAL COURSE SUBJECT AREAS

Undergraduate
Astronomy and astrophysics; biology; business administration and management; computer and information sciences; English composition; English language and literature; geology; history; liberal arts, general studies, and humanities; library and information studies; mathematics; philosophy and religion; political science; psychology; sociology; teacher education

FROSTBURG STATE UNIVERSITY

Frostburg, Maryland

Frostburg State University, founded in 1898, is a state-supported comprehensive institution. It is accredited by the Middle States Association of Colleges and Schools. It first offered distance learning courses in 1995. In 1996–97, it offered 10 courses at a distance. In the fall of 1996, there was a total of 114 students enrolled in distance learning courses.

Course delivery sites Courses are delivered to Garrett Community College (McHenry), 1 off-campus center in Hagerstown.
Media Courses are delivered via television, videotapes, videoconferencing, computer software, World Wide Web, e-mail. Students and teachers interact via videoconferencing, audioconferencing, mail, telephone, fax, e-mail.
Restrictions Programs are available to in-state students only.
Services Distance learners have access to library services, e-mail services, academic advising at a distance.
Credit-earning options Students may transfer credits from another institution or may earn credits through institutionally developed exams.
Typical costs *Undergraduate:* Tuition of $128 per credit hour plus mandatory fees of $31 per credit hour for in-state residents. Tuition of

$214 per credit hour plus mandatory fees of $31 per credit hour for out-of-state residents. *Graduate:* Tuition of $168 per credit hour plus mandatory fees of $31 per credit hour for in-state residents. Tuition of $195 per credit hour plus mandatory fees of $31 per credit hour for out-of-state residents. Costs may vary by campus or location. Financial aid is available to distance learners enrolled full-time or part-time.
Registration Students may register by mail, fax, phone.
Contact Dr. John Bowman, Associate Provost, Frostburg State University, Frostburg, MD 21532. *Telephone:* 301-687-4211. *E-mail:* d2pcbwm@fra00.fsu.umd.edu.

INDIVIDUAL COURSE SUBJECT AREAS

Undergraduate
Accounting; criminal justice; curriculum and instruction; political science; social psychology; social work

Graduate
Accounting; curriculum and instruction; social psychology; social work

FULLERTON COLLEGE

Fullerton, California

Distance Education–Media Production Center

Fullerton College, founded in 1913, is a state and locally supported two-year college. It is accredited by the Western Association of Schools and Colleges, Inc. It first offered distance learning courses in 1984. In 1996–97, it offered 9 courses at a distance. In the fall of 1996, there was a total of 610 students enrolled in distance learning courses.
Course delivery sites Courses are delivered to your home, your workplace, military bases, Cypress College (Cypress).
Media Courses are delivered via television, videotapes, World Wide Web. Students and teachers interact via telephone, fax.
Restrictions Programs are available to local area students only.
Services Distance learners have access to the campus computer network, e-mail services at a distance.
Credit-earning options Students may transfer credits from another institution.
Typical costs Tuition of $0 per unit plus mandatory fees of $13 per unit. Costs may vary by number of credits taken. Financial aid is available to distance learners enrolled full-time.
Registration Students may register by mail, phone.
Contact Jay Goldstein, Director, Distance Education, Fullerton College, 321 East Fullerton, Fullerton, CA 92632. *Telephone:* 714-992-7487. *Fax:* 714-879-3972. *E-mail:* goldsteinj@nocccd.cc.ca.us.

INDIVIDUAL COURSE SUBJECT AREAS

Undergraduate
American (US) history; business; developmental and child psychology; English as a second language (ESL); health and physical education/fitness; history; journalism; marketing; oceanography; political science; psychology; social sciences

GADSDEN STATE COMMUNITY COLLEGE

Gadsden, Alabama

Distance Learning

Gadsden State Community College, founded in 1985, is a state-supported two-year college. It is accredited by the Southern Association of Colleges and Schools. It first offered distance learning courses in 1978. In 1996–97, it offered 20 courses at a distance. In the fall of 1996, there was a total of 278 students enrolled in distance learning courses.
Course delivery sites Courses are delivered to your home, military bases, 2 off-campus centers in Anniston, Fort McClellan.
Media Courses are delivered via television, videotapes. Students and teachers interact via mail, telephone.
Restrictions Programs are available to local area students only.
Services Distance learners have access to library services, academic advising, tutoring, career placement assistance at a distance.
Credit-earning options Students may transfer credits from another institution or may earn credits through standardized exams, institutionally developed exams, business training.
Typical costs Tuition of $29 per hour for in-state residents. Tuition of $54 per hour for out-of-state residents. Costs may vary by number of credits taken. Financial aid is available to distance learners.
Registration Students may register by phone.
Contact Dr. David Tipton, Director of Distance Learning, Gadsden State Community College, PO Box 227, Gadsden, AL 35999. *Telephone:* 205-549-8331.

DEGREE & CERTIFICATE PROGRAMS

Associate Degrees
▶ *General Studies (AS)*
In the fall of 1996 there were 278 students enrolled in this program.
Application requirements *Prior education:* high school diploma or equivalent. *Other requirements:* high school transcript.
Completion requirements 49 quarter hours are required. 96 quarter hours must be completed through the institution.
On-campus requirements To pick up videocassettes and to take course exams.

▶ *General Studies (AA)*
In the fall of 1996 there were 278 students enrolled in this program.
Application requirements *Prior education:* high school diploma or equivalent. *Other requirements:* high school transcript.
Completion requirements 49 quarter hours are required. 96 quarter hours must be completed through the institution.
On-campus requirements To pick up videocassettes and to take course exams.

INDIVIDUAL COURSE SUBJECT AREAS

Undergraduate
Biology; communications; economics; English composition; English language and literature; fine arts; health and physical education/fitness; history; psychology; sociology

Profiles: Galveston College

GALVESTON COLLEGE

Galveston, Texas

Galveston College, founded in 1967, is a state and locally supported two-year college. It is accredited by the Southern Association of Colleges and Schools. It first offered distance learning courses in 1987.
Course delivery sites Courses are delivered to your home.
Media Courses are delivered via videotapes. Students and teachers interact via mail, telephone, fax.
Credit-earning options Students may transfer credits from another institution.
Typical costs Tuition of $115 per course for in-state residents. Tuition of $115 per course plus mandatory fees of $240 per semester for out-of-state residents. Financial aid is available to distance learners.
Contact Sid Young, Director of Distance Education, Galveston College, 4015 Avenue Q, Galveston, TX 77550. *Telephone:* 409-762-8286. *Fax:* 409-762-9367.

DEGREE & CERTIFICATE PROGRAMS

Associate Degrees
▶*Applied Sciences (AS)*

INDIVIDUAL COURSE SUBJECT AREAS

Undergraduate
Area, ethnic, and cultural studies; biology; developmental and child psychology; economics; English language and literature; history; liberal arts, general studies, and humanities; political science; sociology

GANNON UNIVERSITY

Erie, Pennsylvania

Office of Part-Time Studies

Gannon University, founded in 1925, is an independent-religious Roman Catholic comprehensive institution. It is accredited by the Middle States Association of Colleges and Schools.
Course delivery sites Courses are delivered to your home.
Media Courses are delivered via print. Students and teachers interact via mail, telephone, fax, e-mail.
Services Distance learners have access to library services, e-mail services, academic advising, tutoring, career placement assistance at a distance.
Credit-earning options Students may transfer credits from another institution or may earn credits through standardized exams, institutionally developed exams.
Typical costs *Undergraduate:* Tuition of $385 per credit. *Graduate:* Tuition of $420 per credit. Costs may vary by specific program of study. Financial aid is available to distance learners enrolled full-time or part-time.
Registration Students may register by mail, phone, e-mail.
Contact Jean Downing, Assistant Director, Part-Time Studies, Gannon University, University Square, Erie, PA 16541. *Telephone:* 814-871-5563. *Fax:* 814-871-5827. *E-mail:* openu@cluster.gannon.edu.

INDIVIDUAL COURSE SUBJECT AREAS

Undergraduate
Business administration and management; business communications; earth science; economics; English composition; history; marketing; music; philosophy and religion; psychology

GARDEN CITY COMMUNITY COLLEGE

Garden City, Kansas

Garden City Community College, founded in 1919, is a district-supported two-year college. It is accredited by the North Central Association of Colleges and Schools. It first offered distance learning courses in 1995.
Course delivery sites Courses are delivered to other colleges, 3 off-campus centers.
Media Courses are delivered via television, videoconferencing. Students and teachers interact via videoconferencing, mail, telephone, fax.
Restrictions Programs are available to local area students only.
Typical costs Tuition of $38 per credit hour for in-state residents. Tuition of $65 per credit hour for out-of-state residents.
Contact Office of Assistant Dean of Instruction, Garden City Community College, 801 Campus Drive, Garden City, KS 67846. *Telephone:* 316-276-9532. *Fax:* 316-276-9537.

INDIVIDUAL COURSE SUBJECT AREAS

Undergraduate
Education

GARLAND COUNTY COMMUNITY COLLEGE

Hot Springs, Arkansas

Distance Education

Garland County Community College, founded in 1973, is a state and locally supported two-year college. It is accredited by the North Central Association of Colleges and Schools. It first offered distance learning courses in 1985. In 1996–97, it offered 8 courses at a distance. In the fall of 1996, there was a total of 90 students enrolled in distance learning courses.
Course delivery sites Courses are delivered to your home.
Media Courses are delivered via television. Students and teachers interact via mail, telephone, fax, e-mail.
Restrictions Courses are available to students within television transmission area only.
Services Distance learners have access to library services, academic advising, tutoring, career placement assistance at a distance.
Credit-earning options Students may transfer credits from another institution or may earn credits through military training.
Typical costs Tuition of $37 per credit for local area residents. Tuition of $46 per credit for in-state residents. Tuition of $115 per credit for out-of-state residents. All students pay a $10 registration fee. *Noncredit courses:* $45 per credit hour. Costs may vary by number of credits taken. Financial aid is available to distance learners.
Contact Dr. Alan Hoffman, Dean of Instruction, Garland County Community College, 101 College Drive, Hot Springs, AR 71913. *Telephone:* 501-760-4222. *Fax:* 501-760-6896. *E-mail:* ahoffman@jill.gccc.cc.ar.us.

INDIVIDUAL COURSE SUBJECT AREAS

Undergraduate
Accounting; administrative and secretarial services; astronomy and astrophysics; biology; botany; business; business administration and management; chemistry; computer and information sciences; conservation and natural resources; creative writing; design; developmental and child psychology; economics; English composition; English language and literature; European languages and literatures; fine arts; geology; health and physical education/fitness; health professions and related sciences; history; journalism; liberal arts, general studies, and humanities; mathematics; microbiology; music; nursing; philosophy and religion; physics; political science; protective services; public health; sociology; teacher education; zoology

Noncredit
Hospitality services management; human resources management

GARRETT COMMUNITY COLLEGE

McHenry, Maryland

Garrett Communiversity

Garrett Community College, founded in 1966, is a state and locally supported two-year college. It is accredited by the Middle States Association of Colleges and Schools. It first offered distance learning courses in 1994.
Course delivery sites Courses are delivered to your home.
Media Courses are delivered via television, videotapes, videoconferencing, computer conferencing.
Services Distance learners have access to library services, academic advising, tutoring, career placement assistance at a distance.
Credit-earning options Students may transfer credits from another institution or may earn credits through examinations, portfolio assessment, military training, business training. Financial aid is available to distance learners.
Contact Dr. Assistant to the Dean of Academic Affairs, Garrett Community College, 687 Mosser Road, PO Box 151, McHenry, MD 21541. *Telephone:* 301-387-3043. *Fax:* 301-387-3055.

INDIVIDUAL COURSE SUBJECT AREAS

Undergraduate
Agriculture; business administration and management; English composition; mathematics

Noncredit
Agriculture; business administration and management; computer and information sciences; design; health professions and related sciences; mathematics; nursing; social work

GATEWAY TECHNICAL COLLEGE

Kenosha, Wisconsin

Gateway Technical College, founded in 1911, is a state and locally supported two-year college. It is accredited by the North Central Association of Colleges and Schools.
Course delivery sites Courses are delivered to your home, your workplace, other colleges.
Media Courses are delivered via television, videotapes. Students and teachers interact via mail, telephone, fax.
Restrictions Programs are available to local area students only.
Services Distance learners have access to library services, academic advising, career placement assistance at a distance.
Credit-earning options Students may transfer credits from another institution or may earn credits through examinations, portfolio assessment.
Typical costs Tuition of $54.20 per credit for in-state residents. Tuition of $373 per credit for out-of-state residents. Financial aid is available to distance learners.
Contact Student Services Office, Gateway Technical College, 3520 30th Avenue, Kenosha, WI 53144. *Telephone:* 414-656-6911.

INDIVIDUAL COURSE SUBJECT AREAS

Undergraduate
Accounting; area, ethnic, and cultural studies; business; business administration and management; economics; health professions and related sciences; hospitality services management; mathematics; nursing; psychology; sociology

GENESEE COMMUNITY COLLEGE

Batavia, New York

Learning Resources

Genesee Community College, founded in 1966, is a state and locally supported two-year college. It is accredited by the Middle States Association of Colleges and Schools. It first offered distance learning courses in 1988. In 1996–97, it offered 35 courses at a distance. In the fall of 1996, there was a total of 550 students enrolled in distance learning courses.
Course delivery sites Courses are delivered to your home, your workplace, 4 off-campus centers in Albion, Arcade, Lakeville, Warsaw.
Media Courses are delivered via television, videotapes, videoconferencing, audiotapes, audioconferencing, computer software, e-mail, print. Students and teachers interact via audioconferencing, mail, telephone, fax, e-mail. A computer is required for some courses.
Restrictions Programs are available to local area students only.
Services Distance learners have access to library services, the campus computer network, e-mail services, academic advising, tutoring at a distance.
Credit-earning options Students may transfer credits from another institution or may earn credits through examinations, military training.
Typical costs Tuition of $94 per credit hour. Financial aid is available to distance learners enrolled full-time or part-time.
Registration Students may register by mail.
Contact Robert G. Knipe, Associate Dean, Learning Resources, Genesee Community College, 1 College Road, Batavia, NY 14020-9704. *Telephone:* 716-343-0055, Ext. 6595. *Fax:* 716-343-0433. *E-mail:* knipe@sgccva.sunygenesee.cc.ny.us.

INDIVIDUAL COURSE SUBJECT AREAS

Undergraduate
Abnormal psychology; accounting; administrative and secretarial services; algebra; anthropology; area, ethnic, and cultural studies; art history and criticism; biology; business; business administration and management; computer and information sciences; creative writing; developmental and child psychology; economics; engineering-related technologies; English composition; English language and literature; environmental science; European history; film studies; gerontology; health and physical education/fitness; history; law and legal studies; liberal arts, general studies, and

Distance Learning Programs

humanities; marketing; mathematics; physics; political science; psychology; sociology; statistics; technical writing; women's studies

GEORGE C. WALLACE STATE COMMUNITY COLLEGE

Dothan, Alabama

George C. Wallace State Community College, founded in 1949, is a state-supported two-year college. It is accredited by the Southern Association of Colleges and Schools. It first offered distance learning courses in 1996.
Course delivery sites Courses are delivered to your home.
Media Courses are delivered via videotapes, print.
Restrictions Programs are available to local area students only. Financial aid is available to distance learners.
Contact Dr. Director of Distance Learning, George C. Wallace State Community College, Route 6, PO Box 62, Dothan, AL 36303-9234. *Telephone:* 334-983-3521. *Fax:* 334-983-3600.

INDIVIDUAL COURSE SUBJECT AREAS

Undergraduate
Biology; business; computer and information sciences; English language and literature; health and physical education/fitness; liberal arts, general studies, and humanities; mathematics; physical sciences; psychology; social sciences

THE GEORGE WASHINGTON UNIVERSITY

Washington, District of Columbia

The George Washington University, founded in 1821, is an independent-nonprofit university. It is accredited by the Middle States Association of Colleges and Schools.
Course delivery sites Courses are delivered to your home, your workplace, other colleges.
Media Courses are delivered via television, videotapes. Students and teachers interact via e-mail.
Services Distance learners have access to academic advising at a distance.
Credit-earning options Students may transfer credits from another institution.
Typical costs Tuition of $725 per course. Fees vary. Financial aid is available to distance learners enrolled full-time or part-time.
Contact Diane Atkinson, Executive Aide, The George Washington University, 2134 G Street, NW, Suite B-6, Washington, DC 20052. *Telephone:* 202-994-1701. *Fax:* 202-994-2145. *E-mail:* swaj@gwis2.circ.gwu.edu.

DEGREE & CERTIFICATE PROGRAMS

Graduate Degrees
▶ *Educational Technology Leadership (MA)*

INDIVIDUAL COURSE SUBJECT AREAS

Graduate
Education

GEORGIA INSTITUTE OF TECHNOLOGY

Atlanta, Georgia

Center for Distance Learning

Georgia Institute of Technology, founded in 1885, is a state-supported university. It is accredited by the Southern Association of Colleges and Schools. It first offered distance learning courses in 1977. In 1996–97, it offered 115 courses at a distance. In the fall of 1996, there was a total of 400 students enrolled in distance learning courses.
Course delivery sites Courses are delivered to your home, your workplace, military bases, other colleges.
Media Courses are delivered via television, videotapes, videoconferencing, World Wide Web. Students and teachers interact via videoconferencing, mail, telephone, fax, e-mail, World Wide Web. A computer is required for some courses.
Services Distance learners have access to library services, the campus computer network, e-mail services, academic advising, career placement assistance at a distance.
Credit-earning options Students may transfer credits from another institution or may earn credits through examinations.
Typical costs Tuition of $297 per quarter hour. Tuition given is for 1997-98. *Noncredit courses:* $297 per course.
Registration Students may register by mail, fax.
Contact Joe Boland, Director, Center for Distance Learning, Georgia Institute of Technology, Center for Distance Learning, Atlanta, GA 30332-0385. *Telephone:* 404-894-8572. *Fax:* 404-894-8924. *E-mail:* joe.boland@conted.gatech.edu. *Web site:* http://www.conted.gatech.edu/distance.

DEGREE & CERTIFICATE PROGRAMS

Graduate Degrees
▶ *Electrical Engineering (MS)*
In the fall of 1996 there were 101 students enrolled in this program. In 1995–96, 5 degrees were earned at a distance through this program.
Application requirements *Prior education:* baccalaureate degree. *Other requirements:* GRE, college transcripts, an essay or personal statement, letter(s) of recommendation, an application fee of $50.
Completion requirements 50 quarter hours are required. 41 quarter hours must be completed through the institution. *Maximum time for completion:* six years.
Program contact Dr. Dale C. Ray, Associate Chair and Professor, Georgia Institute of Technology, Electrical and Computer Engineering, Atlanta, GA 30332-0250. Phone: 404-894-2904. Fax: 404-894-4641. E-mail: dale.ray@ee.gatech.edu.

▶ *Environmental Engineering (MS)*
In the fall of 1996 there were 56 students enrolled in this program.
Application requirements *Prior education:* baccalaureate degree. *Other requirements:* GRE, college transcripts, an essay or personal statement, letter(s) of recommendation, an application fee of $50.
Completion requirements 50 quarter hours are required. 41 quarter hours must be completed through the institution. *Maximum time for completion:* six years.
Program contact Ms. Donna Brown, School Graduate Admissions Coordinator - Administrative Coordinator, Georgia Institute of Technology, School of Civil and Environmental Engineering, Atlanta, GA 30332-0512. Phone: 404-894-9725. Fax: 404-894-9724. E-mail: donna.brown@ce.gatech.edu.

▶ *Health Physics (MS)*
In the fall of 1996 there were 61 students enrolled in this program. In 1995–96, 3 degrees were earned at a distance through this program.

Application requirements *Prior education:* baccalaureate degree. *Other requirements:* GRE, college transcripts, an essay or personal statement, letter(s) of recommendation, an application fee of $50.
Completion requirements 45 quarter hours are required. 36 quarter hours must be completed through the institution. *Maximum time for completion:* six years.
Program contact Dr. William J. Wepfer, Director of Graduate Studies, Georgia Institute of Technology, School of Mechanical Engineering, Atlanta, GA 30332-0405. Phone: 404-894-3204. Fax: 404-894-8336. E-mail: bill.wepfer@me.gatech.edu.

▶ *Industrial and Systems Engineering (MS)*
In the fall of 1996 there were 16 students enrolled in this program. In 1995–96, 3 degrees were earned at a distance through this program.
Application requirements *Prior education:* baccalaureate degree. *Other requirements:* GRE, college transcripts, an essay or personal statement, letter(s) of recommendation, an application fee of $50.
Completion requirements 48 quarter hours are required. 39 quarter hours must be completed through the institution. *Maximum time for completion:* six years.
Program contact Ms. Pam Morrison, Administrative Coordinator, Georgia Institute of Technology, School of Industrial and Systems Engineering, Atlanta, GA 30332-0205. Phone: 404-894-4289. Fax: 404-894-2301. E-mail: pam.morrison@isye.gatech.edu.

▶ *Mechanical Engineering (MS)*
In the fall of 1996 there were 49 students enrolled in this program. In 1995–96, 2 degrees were earned at a distance through this program.
Application requirements *Prior education:* baccalaureate degree. *Other requirements:* GRE, college transcripts, an essay or personal statement, letter(s) of recommendation, an application fee of $50.
Completion requirements 45 quarter hours are required. 36 quarter hours must be completed through the institution. *Maximum time for completion:* six years.
Program contact Dr. William J. Wepfer, Director of Graduate Studies, Georgia Institute of Technology, School of Mechanical Engineering, Atlanta, GA 30332-0405. Phone: 404-894-3204. Fax: 404-894-8336. E-mail: bill.wepfer@me.gatech.edu.

Graduate certificates

▶ *Computer Integrated Manufacturing Systems*
In the fall of 1996 there was 1 student enrolled in this program.
Application requirements *Prior education:* Georgia Tech graduate degree. *Other requirements:* GRE, college transcripts, an essay or personal statement, letter(s) of recommendation, an application fee of $50.
Completion requirements 24 quarter hours are required. 15 quarter hours must be completed through the institution. *Maximum time for completion:* six years.
Program contact Ms. BettyJo Funk, Administrative Assistant, Georgia Institute of Technology, School of Industrial and Systems Engineering, Atlanta, GA 30332-0205. Phone: 404-894-5562. Fax: 404-894-0957. E-mail: jo.funk@marc.gatech.edu.

▶ *Testing and Evaluation*
In the fall of 1996 there were 5 students enrolled in this program. In 1995–96, 2 certificates were earned at a distance through this program.
Application requirements *Prior education:* baccalaureate degree. *Other requirements:* GRE, college transcripts, an essay or personal statement, letter(s) of recommendation, an application fee of $50.
Completion requirements 27 credit hours are required. 18 credit hours must be completed through the institution. *Maximum time for completion:* six years.
Program contact Lajauna Ennis, Administrative Assistant, Georgia Institute of Technology, School of Electrical and Computer Engineering, Atlanta, GA 30332-0250. Phone: 404-894-7584. Fax: 404-894-7583. E-mail: lajauna.ennis@ee.gatech.edu.

INDIVIDUAL COURSE SUBJECT AREAS

Graduate
Aerospace, aeronautical engineering; biology; civil engineering; electrical engineering; environmental engineering; industrial engineering; mathematics; mechanical engineering; physics

Noncredit
Aerospace, aeronautical engineering; biology; civil engineering; electrical engineering; environmental engineering; industrial engineering; mathematics; mechanical engineering; physics

See full description on page 416.

GEORGIA SOUTHERN UNIVERSITY

Statesboro, Georgia

Distance Learning Center

Georgia Southern University, founded in 1906, is a state-supported comprehensive institution. It is accredited by the Southern Association of Colleges and Schools. It first offered distance learning courses in 1992.
Course delivery sites Courses are delivered to other colleges.
Media Courses are delivered via videoconferencing.
Restrictions Programs are available to in-state students only.
Services Distance learners have access to library services at a distance.
Credit-earning options Students may transfer credits from another institution or may earn credits through examinations, military training. Financial aid is available to distance learners.
Contact Lynn Fail, Administrative Assistant, Georgia Southern University, LB 8018, Statesboro, GA 30460. *Telephone:* 912-681-0882. *Fax:* 912-871-1424. *E-mail:* lfail@gsums2.cc.gasou.edu.

INDIVIDUAL COURSE SUBJECT AREAS

Undergraduate
Accounting; astronomy and astrophysics; business; business administration and management; economics; education administration; engineering mechanics; English composition; European languages and literatures; geology; history; law and legal studies; mathematics; nursing; physics; political science; sociology; special education; teacher education

Graduate
Accounting; business; business administration and management; economics; education administration; geology; mathematics; nursing; political science; sociology; special education; teacher education

Noncredit
European languages and literatures; geology; history; home economics and family studies; mathematics

GLENDALE COMMUNITY COLLEGE

Glendale, California

Letters, Arts and Sciences

Glendale Community College, founded in 1927, is a state and locally supported two-year college. It is accredited by the Western Association of Schools and Colleges, Inc. It first offered distance learning courses in

Distance Learning Programs

Profiles: Glendale Community College

1980. In 1996–97, it offered 11 courses at a distance. In the fall of 1996, there was a total of 360 students enrolled in distance learning courses.
Course delivery sites Courses are delivered to your home.
Media Courses are delivered via television, videotapes, audiotapes, print. Students and teachers interact via mail, telephone, fax, e-mail.
Restrictions Programs are available to in-state students only.
Services Distance learners have access to e-mail services, counseling for personal problems at a distance.
Credit-earning options Students may transfer credits from another institution.
Typical costs Tuition of $13 per credit plus mandatory fees of $28 per semester for in-state residents. Tuition of $117 per credit plus mandatory fees of $28 per semester for out-of-state residents. Financial aid is available to distance learners enrolled full-time.
Registration Students may register by mail, phone.
Contact Dr. Veloris Lang, Dean, Letters, Arts and Sciences, Glendale Community College, 1500 North Verdugo Road, Glendale, CA 91208. *Telephone:* 818-240-1000, Ext. 5149. *Fax:* 818-551-5228. *E-mail:* vlang@glendale.cc.ca.us.

INDIVIDUAL COURSE SUBJECT AREAS

Undergraduate
Astronomy and astrophysics; biology; business; business administration and management; developmental and child psychology; economics; English language and literature; geology; health and physical education/fitness; history; liberal arts, general studies, and humanities; mathematics; political science; sociology

GLENVILLE STATE COLLEGE

Glenville, West Virginia

Glenville State College, founded in 1872, is a state-supported four-year college. It is accredited by the North Central Association of Colleges and Schools. It first offered distance learning courses in 1980. In 1996–97, it offered 3 courses at a distance. In the fall of 1996, there was a total of 40 students enrolled in distance learning courses.
Course delivery sites Courses are delivered to your home.
Media Courses are delivered via television. Students and teachers interact via telephone, e-mail.
Credit-earning options Students may transfer credits from another institution or may earn credits through standardized exams, institutionally developed exams, portfolio assessment.
Typical costs Tuition of $175 per semester plus mandatory fees of $716 per semester for in-state residents. Costs may vary by campus or location, number of credits taken. Financial aid is available to distance learners.
Contact Dr. Phillip Cottrill, Director of Enrollment Management, Glenville State College, 200 High Street, Glenville, WV 26351-1200. *Telephone:* 304-462-4117. *Fax:* 304-462-8619. *E-mail:* cottrill@wvngsc.wvnet.edu.

INDIVIDUAL COURSE SUBJECT AREAS

Undergraduate
Astronomy and astrophysics; business administration and management; economics

GMI ENGINEERING & MANAGEMENT INSTITUTE

Flint, Michigan

Graduate Studies Department

GMI Engineering & Management Institute, founded in 1919, is an independent-nonprofit comprehensive institution. It is accredited by the North Central Association of Colleges and Schools. It first offered distance learning courses in 1982.
Course delivery sites Courses are delivered to your workplace, other colleges.
Media Courses are delivered via videotapes. Students and teachers interact via mail, telephone, fax, e-mail. A computer is required for some courses.
Services Distance learners have access to library services, academic advising at a distance.
Credit-earning options Students may transfer credits from another institution or may earn credits through institutionally developed exams.
Typical costs Tuition of $1086 per course plus mandatory fees of $45 per course.
Registration Students may register by mail, fax, phone, e-mail.
Contact Betty Bedore, Coordinator of Publicity for the Graduate Department, GMI Engineering & Management Institute, 1700 West Third Street, Flint, MI 48504-4898. *Telephone:* 810-762-7494. *Fax:* 810-762-9935. *E-mail:* bbedore@nova.gmi.edu. *Web site:* http://www.gmi.edu/official/acad/grad.

DEGREE & CERTIFICATE PROGRAMS

Graduate Degrees
▶ *Engineering (MS)*
Restrictions Students must participate at companies/corporations where our programs are currently offered.
Application requirements *Prior education:* undergraduate degree in engineering. *Other requirements:* GRE, college transcripts, letter(s) of recommendation, application form, TOEFL (for international students).
Completion requirements 45 credits are required. 45 credits must be completed through the institution. *Maximum time for completion:* five years.

▶ *Manufacturing Management (MS)*
Restrictions Students must participate at companies/corporations where our programs have been established.
Application requirements *Prior education:* baccalaureate degree. *Other requirements:* GMAT, college transcripts, an essay or personal statement, letter(s) of recommendation, TOEFL (for international students).
Completion requirements 54 credits are required. 54 credits must be completed through the institution. *Maximum time for completion:* six years.

INDIVIDUAL COURSE SUBJECT AREAS

Graduate
Accounting; business administration and management; finance; human resources management; industrial engineering; international business; management information systems; marketing; mechanical engineering
See full description on page 418.

GORDON-CONWELL THEOLOGICAL SEMINARY

South Hamilton, Massachusetts

Independent Studies Program

Gordon-Conwell Theological Seminary, founded in 1884, is an independent-religious graduate institution. It is accredited by the New England Association of Schools and Colleges. It first offered distance learning courses in 1986. In 1996–97, it offered 26 courses at a distance. In the fall of 1996, there was a total of 243 students enrolled in distance learning courses.

Course delivery sites Courses are delivered to your home, Coalition for Christian Outreach (Pittsburgh, PA).
Media Courses are delivered via videotapes, audiotapes, World Wide Web, e-mail, print. Students and teachers interact via mail, telephone, fax, e-mail.
Services Distance learners have access to library services, e-mail services, academic advising at a distance.
Credit-earning options Students may transfer credits from another institution.
Typical costs Tuition of $450 per course. *Noncredit courses:* $87.95 per course. Costs may vary by campus or location, specific program of study.
Registration Students may register by mail, fax, phone.
Contact Tim Myrick, Admissions Director, Gordon-Conwell Theological Seminary, 130 Essex Street, South Hamilton, MA 01982. *Telephone:* 508-468-7111. *Fax:* 508-468-6691.

INDIVIDUAL COURSE SUBJECT AREAS

Graduate
Bible studies; developmental and child psychology; education administration; ethics; history; philosophy and religion; religious studies; theological studies

Noncredit
Bible studies; developmental and child psychology; education administration; ethics; history; philosophy and religion; religious studies; theological studies

GOUCHER COLLEGE

Baltimore, Maryland

Center for Graduate and Continuing Studies

Goucher College, founded in 1885, is an independent-nonprofit comprehensive institution. It is accredited by the Middle States Association of Colleges and Schools. It first offered distance learning courses in 1995. In 1996–97, it offered 18 courses at a distance. In the fall of 1996, there was a total of 30 students enrolled in distance learning courses.

Course delivery sites Courses are delivered to your home.
Media Courses are delivered via World Wide Web, e-mail, print. Students and teachers interact via mail, telephone, fax, e-mail.
Restrictions Courses are available to US and Canadian students only.
Services Distance learners have access to library services, the campus computer network, e-mail services, academic advising at a distance.
Credit-earning options Students may transfer credits from another institution.
Typical costs Master of Fine Arts is $4650 per semester. MA in Historic Preservation is $1350 per course. All students must pay a $50 application fee. Costs may vary by specific program of study. Financial aid is available to distance learners enrolled full-time or part-time.
Registration Students may register by mail, fax.
Contact Debbie Culbertson, Director, Center for Graduate and Continuing Studies, Goucher College, 1021 Dulaney Valley Road, Baltimore, MD 21204. *Telephone:* 410-337-6200. *Fax:* 410-337-6085. *E-mail:* center@goucher.edu. *Web site:* http://www.goucher.edu/announce/mahp.html.

Special note
Goucher College's distance learning graduate programs include the Master of Arts in historic preservation, the Master of Fine Arts in creative nonfiction, and the Master of Arts in arts administration. All 3 programs are limited-residency programs that offer a number of distinct advantages for many students. The programs provide great flexibility in time and place of learning. Students are able to undertake academically rigorous education without undue disruption to professional or family life. They usually establish their own pace of learning, sometimes taking only 1 course per semester. In addition, since time spent on campus is minimal, the cost of relocating to pursue an education or of maintaining 2 households is eliminated.

Limited-residency programs require students to be independent learners. Typically, this means that students must have clear goals for undertaking the program, such as obtaining knowledge to assist them in their current profession or a new one. Successful independent learners are also self-directed and able to communicate effectively orally and in writing. Independent learners also know how to manage their time. All 3 graduate programs require, as part of the admission process, an essay that addresses the applicant's ability to undertake successfully a limited-residency program and his or her goals.

DEGREE & CERTIFICATE PROGRAMS

Graduate Degrees

▶ *Creative Non-fiction (MFA)*
Application requirements *Prior education:* baccalaureate degree. *Other requirements:* college transcripts, an essay or personal statement, letter(s) of recommendation, an application fee of $50, minimum of two years paid or volunteer post-baccalaureate work experience, 25–35 pages (original work, published or unpublished).
Completion requirements 4 semesters are required. 4 semesters must be completed through the institution. *Other requirements:* an editorial/publishing internship, an original manuscript of publishable-quality/public reading. *Maximum time for completion:* five years.
On-campus requirements Three 2-week summer sessions.
Program contact Larry Bielawski, Program Director, Goucher College, Center for Graduate and Continuing Studies, 1021 Dulaney Valley Road, Baltimore, MD 21204. Phone: 410-337-6344. Fax: 410-337-6085. E-mail: center@goucher.edu.

▶ *Historic Preservation (MA)*
In the fall of 1996 there were 28 students enrolled in this program.
Application requirements *Prior education:* baccalaureate degree. *Other requirements:* college transcripts, an essay or personal statement, letter(s) of recommendation, an application fee of $50, minimum of two years paid or volunteer post-baccalaureate work experience.
Completion requirements 36 credits are required. 29 credits must be completed through the institution. *Maximum time for completion:* five years.
On-campus requirements Three 2-week summer sessions.
Program contact Richard Wagner, Program Director, Goucher College, Center for Graduate and Continuing Studies, 1021 Dulaney Valley

Profiles: Goucher College

Road, Baltimore, MD 21204. Phone: 410-337-6473. Fax: 410-337-6085. E-mail: rwagner@goucher.edu.
See full description on page 420.

GOVERNORS STATE UNIVERSITY

University Park, Illinois

Center for Extended Learning and Communications Services

Governors State University, founded in 1969, is a state-supported upper-level institution. It is accredited by the North Central Association of Colleges and Schools. It first offered distance learning courses in 1981. In 1996–97, it offered 52 courses at a distance. In the fall of 1996, there was a total of 1,221 students enrolled in distance learning courses.
Course delivery sites Courses are delivered to your home, your workplace.
Media Courses are delivered via television, videotapes, audiotapes, computer software, World Wide Web, e-mail, print. Students and teachers interact via audioconferencing, mail, telephone, fax, e-mail. A computer is required for some courses.
Restrictions Students must have 60 hours of lower/upper division credit (for BOG/BA students: 30 hours).
Services Distance learners have access to academic advising at a distance.
Credit-earning options Students may transfer credits from another institution or may earn credits through institutionally developed exams, portfolio assessment, military training.
Typical costs *Undergraduate:* Tuition of $291 per term. *Graduate:* Tuition of $306 per term. *Noncredit courses:* $306 per course. Financial aid is available to distance learners enrolled full-time or part-time.
Registration Students may register by mail, fax.
Contact Sally Petrilli, Director, Media-Based Instruction, Governors State University, University Parkway, University Park, IL 60466. Telephone: 708-534-4087. Fax: 708-534-8458. E-mail: s-petril@govst.edu. Web site: http://www.govst.edu.

DEGREE & CERTIFICATE PROGRAMS

Baccalaureate Degrees

▶*Liberal Arts (BA)*
In the fall of 1996 there were 379 students enrolled in this program. In 1995–96, 157 degrees were earned at a distance through this program.
Application requirements *Prior education:* 30 hours lower/upper division credit. *Other requirements:* Math and writing competency exams, Illinois Constitution exam, Federal constitution exam, college transcripts, 30 hours lower/upper division credit.
Completion requirements 120 hours are required. This is a degree completion program.
Program contact Dr. Glenn Shive, Director, BOG/BA Program, Governors State University, University Parkway, University Park, IL 60466. Phone: 708-534-3088. Fax: 708-534-1645. E-mail: g-shive@govst.edu.

INDIVIDUAL COURSE SUBJECT AREAS

Undergraduate

Anthropology; art history and criticism; biological and life sciences; business; business administration and management; communications; developmental and child psychology; economics; English composition; English language and literature; geography; history; liberal arts, general studies, and humanities; marketing; music; philosophy and religion; psychology; public health; social work; sociology; special education; teacher education

Graduate

Anthropology; art history and criticism; developmental and child psychology; English language and literature; history; liberal arts, general studies, and humanities; music; psychology; public health; social work; sociology; special education

GRACELAND COLLEGE

Lamoni, Iowa

Distance Learning

Graceland College, founded in 1895, is an independent-religious Reorganized Latter Day Saints comprehensive institution. It is accredited by the North Central Association of Colleges and Schools. It first offered distance learning courses in 1988. In 1996–97, it offered 30 courses at a distance.
Course delivery sites Courses are delivered to your home, American Institute of Business (Des Moines), Indian Hills Community College (Ottumwa), North Central Missouri College (Trenton, MO), Southwestern Community College (Creston).
Media Courses are delivered via videotapes, videoconferencing, print. Students and teachers interact via videoconferencing, mail, telephone, fax, e-mail, site visits. A computer is required for some courses.
Restrictions Students must have associate degree.
Services Distance learners have access to academic advising at a distance.
Credit-earning options Students may transfer credits from another institution or may earn credits through examinations, portfolio assessment, military training, business training.
Typical costs Tuition of $160 per semester hour for local area residents. Tuition of $336 per semester hour for out-of-state residents. *Noncredit courses:* $160 per semester hour. Costs may vary by campus or location, specific program of study, course delivery options, term of enrollment. Financial aid is available to distance learners.
Registration Students may register by mail, fax, phone, e-mail.
Contact Karen Robb, Office of Continuing Education and Distance Learning, Graceland College, 700 College Avenue, Lamoni, IA 50140. *Telephone:* 515-784-5309. *Fax:* 515-784-5405. *E-mail:* robb@graceland.edu.

INDIVIDUAL COURSE SUBJECT AREAS

Undergraduate

Accounting; biology; business administration and management; chemistry; computer and information sciences; developmental and child psychology; economics; English composition; English language and literature; fine arts; health and physical education/fitness; health professions and related sciences; history; liberal arts, general studies, and humanities; mathematics; microbiology; nursing; philosophy and religion; sociology

THE GRADUATE SCHOOL OF AMERICA

Minneapolis, Minnesota

The Graduate School of America is a proprietary graduate institution. It is a candidate for accreditation by the North Central Association of Colleges and Schools. It first offered distance learning courses in 1993.

In 1996–97, it offered 225 courses at a distance. In the fall of 1996, there was a total of 184 students enrolled in distance learning courses.
Course delivery sites Courses are delivered to your home, your workplace.
Media Courses are delivered via World Wide Web, e-mail, print. Students and teachers interact via mail, telephone, fax, e-mail, World Wide Web. A computer is required for some courses.
Services Distance learners have access to library services, e-mail services, academic advising, tutoring at a distance.
Credit-earning options Students may transfer credits from another institution.
Typical costs Tuition of $2445 per quarter. Costs may vary by specific program of study. Financial aid is available to distance learners enrolled full-time.
Registration Students may register by mail, fax, e-mail, World Wide Web.
Contact Tom Larson, Director of Admissions, The Graduate School of America, 330 Second Avenue South, Suite 550, Minneapolis, MN 55401. *Telephone:* 800-987-1133. *Fax:* 612-339-8022. *E-mail:* tgsainfo@aol.com. *Web site:* http://www.tgsa.edu.

DEGREE & CERTIFICATE PROGRAMS

Graduate Degrees

▶ *Education (PhD)*
In the fall of 1996 there were 12 students enrolled in this program.
Application requirements *Prior education:* graduate degree. *Other requirements:* college transcripts, an essay or personal statement, an application fee of $35, resume, application.
Completion requirements 120 quarter credits are required. *Maximum time for completion:* seven years.
On-campus requirements Two-week summer session, three-day seminar.

▶ *Education (MS)*
In the fall of 1996 there were 4 students enrolled in this program.
Application requirements *Prior education:* baccalaureate degree. *Other requirements:* college transcripts, an essay or personal statement, an application fee of $35, resume, application.
Completion requirements 48 quarter credits are required. *Maximum time for completion:* three years.
On-campus requirements Two-week summer session, three-day seminar.

▶ *Human Services (PhD)*
In the fall of 1996 there were 58 students enrolled in this program.
Application requirements *Prior education:* graduate degree. *Other requirements:* college transcripts, an essay or personal statement, an application fee of $35, resume, application.
Completion requirements 120 quarter credits are required. *Maximum time for completion:* seven years.
On-campus requirements Two-week summer session, three-day seminar.

▶ *Human Services (MS)*
In the fall of 1996 there were 16 students enrolled in this program.
Application requirements *Prior education:* baccalaureate degree. *Other requirements:* college transcripts, an essay or personal statement, an application fee of $35, resume, application.
Completion requirements 48 quarter credits are required. *Maximum time for completion:* three years.
On-campus requirements Two-week summer session, three-day seminar.

▶ *Interdisciplinary Studies (PhD)*
Application requirements *Prior education:* graduate degree. *Other requirements:* college transcripts, an essay or personal statement, an application fee of $35, resume, application.
Completion requirements 120 quarter credits are required. *Maximum time for completion:* seven years.
On-campus requirements Two-week summer session, three-day seminar.

▶ *Interdisciplinary Studies (MS)*
In the fall of 1996 there were 3 students enrolled in this program.
Application requirements *Prior education:* baccalaureate degree. *Other requirements:* college transcripts, an essay or personal statement, an application fee of $35, resume, application.
Completion requirements 48 quarter credits are required. *Maximum time for completion:* three years.
On-campus requirements Two-week summer session, three-day seminar.

▶ *Organization and Management (PhD)*
In the fall of 1996 there were 66 students enrolled in this program.
Application requirements *Prior education:* graduate degree. *Other requirements:* college transcripts, an essay or personal statement, an application fee of $35, resume, application.
Completion requirements 120 quarter credits are required. *Maximum time for completion:* seven years.
On-campus requirements Two-week summer session, three-day seminar.

▶ *Organization and Management (MS)*
In the fall of 1996 there were 6 students enrolled in this program.
Application requirements *Prior education:* baccalaureate degree. *Other requirements:* college transcripts, an essay or personal statement, an application fee of $35, resume, application.
Completion requirements 48 quarter credits are required. *Maximum time for completion:* three years.
On-campus requirements Two-week summer session, three-day seminar.

INDIVIDUAL COURSE SUBJECT AREAS

Graduate
Abnormal psychology; accounting; adult education; area, ethnic, and cultural studies; business; business administration and management; business communications; cognitive psychology; continuing education; counseling psychology; curriculum and instruction; developmental and child psychology; education; education administration; educational psychology; educational research; health professions and related sciences; human resources management; industrial psychology; international business; international relations; labor relations/studies; marketing; organizational behavior studies; philosophy and religion; political science; psychology; school psychology; social psychology; social work; sociology; special education; student counseling

GRAND CANYON UNIVERSITY

Phoenix, Arizona

College of Education

Grand Canyon University, founded in 1949, is an independent-religious Southern Baptist comprehensive institution. It is accredited by the North Central Association of Colleges and Schools. It first offered distance learning courses in 1990. In 1996–97, it offered 20 courses at a distance. In the fall of 1996, there was a total of 480 students enrolled in distance learning courses.
Course delivery sites Courses are delivered to your home.
Media Courses are delivered via videotapes, e-mail. Students and teachers interact via mail, telephone, fax, e-mail.
Restrictions Courses are available to students in Arizona and contiguous states only.
Services Distance learners have access to library services, e-mail services, academic advising, career placement assistance at a distance.
Credit-earning options Students may transfer credits from another institution.
Typical costs Tuition of $184 per semester hour plus mandatory fees of $65 per course.
Registration Students may register by mail, fax.
Contact Dr. Ron Graham, Director for Distance Learning, Grand Canyon University, College of Education, 3300 West Camelback Road,

Distance Learning Programs

Profiles: Grand Canyon University

Phoenix, AZ 85017. *Telephone:* 800-600-5019. *Fax:* 602-589-2447. *E-mail:* rgraham@grand-canyon.edu. *Web site:* http://www.grand-canyon.edu.

DEGREE & CERTIFICATE PROGRAMS

Graduate Degrees
▶ *Teaching (MAT)*
In the fall of 1996 there were 52 students enrolled in this program.
Restrictions Students must have access to a K-12 classroom for application of material presented in courses.
Application requirements *Prior education:* baccalaureate degree. *Other requirements:* college transcripts, an essay or personal statement, letter(s) of recommendation, an application fee of $50, teacher evaluation/teaching certificate.
Completion requirements 30 semester hours are required. *Other requirements:* professional portfolio required as part of the capstone project. *Maximum time for completion:* five years.

INDIVIDUAL COURSE SUBJECT AREAS

Graduate
Educational psychology; health and physical education/fitness; special education; teacher education

GRAND RAPIDS BAPTIST SEMINARY

Grand Rapids, Michigan

Grand Rapids Baptist Seminary is an independent-religious graduate institution. It is accredited by the North Central Association of Colleges and Schools. It first offered distance learning courses in 1969. In 1996–97, it offered 40 courses at a distance. In the fall of 1996, there was a total of 65 students enrolled in distance learning courses.
Course delivery sites Courses are delivered to your home.
Media Courses are delivered via audiotapes, print. Students and teachers interact via telephone, fax, e-mail.
Services Distance learners have access to e-mail services, academic advising, career placement assistance at a distance.
Credit-earning options Students may transfer credits from another institution or may earn credits through institutionally developed exams.
Typical costs Tuition of $233 per credit.
Registration Students may register by mail, fax.
Contact John F. VerBerkmoes, Director of Advancement, Grand Rapids Baptist Seminary, 1001 East Beltline, NE, Grand Rapids, MI 49505. *Telephone:* 616-222-1422. *Fax:* 616-222-1414. *E-mail:* j.verberkmoes@cornerstone.edu.

DEGREE & CERTIFICATE PROGRAMS

Graduate Degrees
▶ *Christian Education, Christian School Administration, Missions, Pastoral Studies (MRE)*
Restrictions Program is limited to those engaged in full-time ministry employment.
Application requirements *Prior education:* baccalaureate degree. *Other requirements:* college transcripts, an essay or personal statement, letter(s) of recommendation, an application fee of $25, 3 years of professional Ministry experience.
Completion requirements 32 credits are required. 20 credits must be completed through the institution. *Other requirements:* program culminates in a 3 semester credit Ministry Research Project which blends the academic task with professional activity/responsibility. *Maximum time for completion:* five years.

On-campus requirements Two-week summer sessions.

INDIVIDUAL COURSE SUBJECT AREAS

Graduate
Education administration; philosophy and religion; theological studies

GRAND RAPIDS COMMUNITY COLLEGE

Grand Rapids, Michigan

Distance Learning Committee

Grand Rapids Community College, founded in 1914, is a district-supported two-year college. It is accredited by the North Central Association of Colleges and Schools. It first offered distance learning courses in 1982. In 1996–97, it offered 19 courses at a distance. In the fall of 1996, there was a total of 275 students enrolled in distance learning courses.
Course delivery sites Courses are delivered to your workplace, 4 off-campus centers in Caledonia, Grandville, Holland, Rockford.
Media Courses are delivered via television, videotapes, videoconferencing, computer software, World Wide Web, print. Students and teachers interact via videoconferencing, mail, telephone, fax, e-mail.
Restrictions Students must be in cable television area for telecourses.
Services Distance learners have access to the campus computer network, e-mail services, academic advising at a distance.
Credit-earning options Students may transfer credits from another institution or may earn credits through examinations.
Typical costs Tuition of $54 per credit for local area residents. Tuition of $80 per credit for in-state residents. Tuition of $91 per credit for out-of-state residents. *Noncredit courses:* $125 per hour. Financial aid is available to distance learners enrolled full-time or part-time.
Registration Students may register by mail, fax, phone.
Contact Dr. Donald R. Boyer, Dean of School of Workforce Development, Grand Rapids Community College, 143 Bostwick, NE, Grand Rapids, MI 49503. *Telephone:* 616-771-3920. *Fax:* 616-771-4075. *E-mail:* dboyer@post.grcc.cc.mi.us.

INDIVIDUAL COURSE SUBJECT AREAS

Undergraduate
Anthropology; business; calculus; computer and information sciences; economics; engineering-related technologies; English composition; European languages and literatures; geography; history; philosophy and religion; political science; psychology; social psychology; social sciences; sociology; statistics; visual and performing arts

GRAND VALLEY STATE UNIVERSITY

Allendale, Michigan

Division of Continuing Education

Grand Valley State University, founded in 1960, is a state-supported comprehensive institution. It is accredited by the North Central Association of Colleges and Schools. It first offered distance learning courses in 1980.
Course delivery sites Courses are delivered to other colleges.
Media Courses are delivered via television, videotapes, videoconferencing, print, computer conferencing.
Restrictions Programs are available to in-state students only.

Credit-earning options Students may transfer credits from another institution or may earn credits through examinations, military training, business training. Financial aid is available to distance learners.
Contact Director of Distance Education, Grand Valley State University, Eberhard Center, 301 West Fulton, Grand Rapids, MI 49504. *Telephone:* 616-771-6617. *Fax:* 616-771-6642. *Web site:* http://www.gvsu.edu/acad/continue/index.htm.

INDIVIDUAL COURSE SUBJECT AREAS

Undergraduate
Accounting; area, ethnic, and cultural studies; Asian languages and literatures; business; business administration and management; economics; education administration; educational psychology; engineering/industrial management; history; hospitality services management; liberal arts, general studies, and humanities; mathematics; nursing; political science; protective services; public administration and services; social psychology; social work; sociology; special education; teacher education

Graduate
Accounting; area, ethnic, and cultural studies; business; business administration and management; economics; education administration; educational psychology; engineering/industrial management; history; hospitality services management; liberal arts, general studies, and humanities; mathematics; nursing; political science; protective services; public administration and services; social psychology; social work; sociology; special education; teacher education

GRAYSON COUNTY COLLEGE

Denison, Texas

Center for Distance Learning

Grayson County College, founded in 1964, is a state and locally supported two-year college. It is accredited by the Southern Association of Colleges and Schools. It first offered distance learning courses in 1990. In 1996–97, it offered 12 courses at a distance. In the fall of 1996, there was a total of 300 students enrolled in distance learning courses.
Course delivery sites Courses are delivered to your home.
Media Courses are delivered via television, World Wide Web. Students and teachers interact via mail, telephone, e-mail. A computer is required for some courses.
Services Distance learners have access to library services at a distance.
Credit-earning options Students may earn credits through institutionally developed exams.
Typical costs Tuition of $144 per course. $33 per hour for Internet courses. Costs may vary by specific program of study, number of credits taken, course delivery options. Financial aid is available to distance learners enrolled full-time or part-time.
Registration Students may register by mail, e-mail, World Wide Web.
Contact Gary F. Paikowski, Dean of Information Technology, Grayson County College, 6101 Grayson Road, Denison, TX 75020. *Telephone:* 903-463-8707. *Fax:* 903-465-4123. *E-mail:* paikowski@grayson.edu. *Web site:* http://www.grayson.edu/ecampus/ecampus.htm.

INDIVIDUAL COURSE SUBJECT AREAS

Undergraduate
Social sciences

GREAT BASIN COLLEGE

Elko, Nevada

Great Basin College, founded in 1967, is a state-supported two-year college. It is accredited by the Northwest Association of Schools and Colleges. It first offered distance learning courses in 1968. In 1996–97, it offered 50 courses at a distance. In the fall of 1996, there was a total of 500 students enrolled in distance learning courses.
Course delivery sites Courses are delivered to your home, your workplace, 4 off-campus centers in Battle Mountain, Ely, Eureka, Winnemucca.
Media Courses are delivered via videotapes, videoconferencing, audiotapes, e-mail, print. Students and teachers interact via videoconferencing, e-mail. A computer is required for some courses.
Services Distance learners have access to the campus computer network, e-mail services, tutoring at a distance.
Credit-earning options Students may transfer credits from another institution or may earn credits through institutionally developed exams, portfolio assessment, military training, business training.
Typical costs Tuition of $36.50 per quarter credit. Students taking interactive video courses who are out-of-state residents pay $52 per semester credit. Financial aid is available to distance learners enrolled full-time.
Registration Students may register by phone.
Contact Dr. Cliff Ferry, Assistant Vice President for Academic Affairs, Great Basin College, 1500 College Parkway, Elko, NV 89801. *Telephone:* 702-753-2213. *Fax:* 702-738-8771. *E-mail:* cferry@scs.unr.edu.

INDIVIDUAL COURSE SUBJECT AREAS

Undergraduate
Business; computer and information sciences; economics; English composition; protective services; social sciences; teacher education

GREENVILLE TECHNICAL COLLEGE

Greenville, South Carolina

Distance Learning

Greenville Technical College, founded in 1962, is a state-supported two-year college. It is accredited by the Southern Association of Colleges and Schools. It first offered distance learning courses in 1991. In 1996–97, it offered 45 courses at a distance. In the fall of 1996, there was a total of 1,400 students enrolled in distance learning courses.
Course delivery sites Courses are delivered to your home, your workplace, Anderson College (Anderson), 2 off-campus centers in Greer, Simpsonville, South Carolina State Technical Colleges.
Media Courses are delivered via television, videotapes, videoconferencing, World Wide Web. Students and teachers interact via videoconferencing, mail, telephone, fax, e-mail. A computer is required for some courses.
Services Distance learners have access to library services at a distance.
Credit-earning options Students may transfer credits from another institution or may earn credits through examinations, military training, business training.
Typical costs Tuition of $42 per credit hour plus mandatory fees of $15 per semester for local area residents. Tuition of $45 per credit hour plus mandatory fees of $15 per semester for in-state residents. Tuition of $67 per credit hour plus mandatory fees of $15 per semester for out-of-state residents. Costs may vary by number of credits taken. Financial aid is available to distance learners.

Distance Learning Programs

Profiles: Greenville Technical College

Contact John Walsh, Director of Distance Learning, Greenville Technical College, 506 South Pleasantbury Drive, Greenville, SC 29606. *Telephone:* 864-250-8098. *Fax:* 864-250-8085. *E-mail:* walshjpw@gvltec.edu.

DEGREE & CERTIFICATE PROGRAMS

Associate Degrees

▶ *Liberal Arts (AA)*
In the fall of 1996 there were 1,310 students enrolled in this program.
Application requirements *Prior education:* high school diploma or equivalent. *Other requirements:* ASSET or COMPASS, an application fee of $15.
Completion requirements 64 credit hours are required.
Program contact Martha Duncan, Weekend College - Secretary, Greenville Technical College, PO Box 5616, Greenville, SC 29606-5616. Phone: 864-250-8130.

INDIVIDUAL COURSE SUBJECT AREAS

Undergraduate
Accounting; art history and criticism; astronomy and astrophysics; biology; business administration and management; business law; computer and information sciences; developmental and child psychology; economics; English composition; English language and literature; history; liberal arts, general studies, and humanities; mathematics; philosophy and religion; protective services; social psychology; sociology; Spanish language and literature

GRIGGS UNIVERSITY

Silver Spring, Maryland

Griggs University, founded in 1990, is an independent-religious Seventh-day Adventist four-year college. It is accredited by the Distance Education and Training Council. It first offered distance learning courses in 1909. In 1996–97, it offered 105 courses at a distance. In the fall of 1996, there was a total of 375 students enrolled in distance learning courses.
Course delivery sites Courses are delivered to your home.
Media Courses are delivered via videotapes, audiotapes, e-mail, print. Students and teachers interact via mail, telephone, fax, e-mail.
Services Distance learners have access to library services, e-mail services, academic advising at a distance.
Credit-earning options Students may transfer credits from another institution or may earn credits through standardized exams, institutionally developed exams, portfolio assessment, military training, business training.
Typical costs Tuition of $150 per semester hour. Costs may vary by number of credits taken.
Registration Students may register by mail, fax.
Contact Dorothy M. Bascom, Director of Admissions/Registrar, Griggs University, PO Box 4437, Silver Spring, MD 20914-4437. *Telephone:* 301-680-6579. *Fax:* 301-680-6577. *E-mail:* 74617.3274@compuserve.com.

DEGREE & CERTIFICATE PROGRAMS

Associate Degrees

▶ *Personal Ministries (AA)*
Application requirements *Prior education:* high school diploma or equivalent. *Other requirements:* high school transcript, an essay or personal statement, an application fee of $50.

Completion requirements 60 semester hours are required. 30 semester hours must be completed through the institution.

Baccalaureate Degrees

▶ *Church Business Management, Religious Education (BS)*
Application requirements *Prior education:* high school diploma or equivalent. *Other requirements:* high school transcript, an essay or personal statement, an application fee of $50.
Completion requirements 120 semester hours are required. 30 semester hours must be completed through the institution.

▶ *Religion, Theological Studies (BA)*
Application requirements *Prior education:* high school diploma or equivalent. *Other requirements:* high school transcript, an essay or personal statement, an application fee of $50.
Completion requirements 120 semester hours are required. 30 semester hours must be completed through the institution.

INDIVIDUAL COURSE SUBJECT AREAS

Undergraduate
Biology; business; communications; education; English language and literature; European languages and literatures; fine arts; foods and nutrition studies; geography; mathematics; political science; psychology; sociology; theological studies

HAMPTON UNIVERSITY

Hampton, Virginia

College of Continuing Education

Hampton University, founded in 1868, is an independent-nonprofit comprehensive institution. It is accredited by the Southern Association of Colleges and Schools. It first offered distance learning courses in 1983. In 1996–97, it offered 25 courses at a distance. In the fall of 1996, there was a total of 20 students enrolled in distance learning courses.
Course delivery sites Courses are delivered to your home, your workplace.
Media Courses are delivered via videotapes, audiotapes, print. Students and teachers interact via videoconferencing, mail, telephone.
Services Distance learners have access to library services, the campus computer network, e-mail services, academic advising, tutoring, career placement assistance at a distance.
Credit-earning options Students may earn credits through examinations, portfolio assessment, military training, business training.
Typical costs *Undergraduate:* Tuition of $115 per credit hour. *Graduate:* Tuition of $125 per credit hour. All students pay $35 in application and registration fees. *Noncredit courses:* $25 per course. Financial aid is available to distance learners.
Registration Students may register by mail, fax, phone.
Contact Mrs. April M. Hart, Administrative Assistant to the Dean, Hampton University, College of Continuing Education, Hampton, VA 23668. *Telephone:* 804-727-5773. *Fax:* 804-727-5949.

DEGREE & CERTIFICATE PROGRAMS

Baccalaureate Degrees

▶ *Business Management (BS)*
In the fall of 1996 there were 20 students enrolled in this program.
Application requirements *Prior education:* high school diploma or equivalent. *Other requirements:* high school transcript.
Completion requirements 122 credits are required. 122 credits must be completed through the institution.

Program contact W. O. Lawton, Dean, Hampton University, College of Continuing Education, Hampton, VA 23668. Phone: 804-727-5773. Fax: 804-727-5949.

INDIVIDUAL COURSE SUBJECT AREAS

Undergraduate
Accounting; area, ethnic, and cultural studies; biological and life sciences; business; business administration and management; chemistry; computer and information sciences; economics; education; education administration; English as a second language (ESL); English composition; English language and literature; health and physical education/fitness; health professions and related sciences; history; hospitality services management; human resources management; law and legal studies; liberal arts, general studies, and humanities; mathematics; music; philosophy and religion; physical sciences; physics; political science; social psychology; social work; sociology; special education; teacher education

Graduate
Education; health professions and related sciences; music; nursing; special education; teacher education

Noncredit
Administrative and secretarial services; area, ethnic, and cultural studies; business; computer and information sciences; creative writing; English as a second language (ESL); health and physical education/fitness; human resources management

HARRISBURG AREA COMMUNITY COLLEGE

Harrisburg, Pennsylvania

Distance Education Office

Harrisburg Area Community College, founded in 1964, is a state and locally supported two-year college. It is accredited by the Middle States Association of Colleges and Schools. It first offered distance learning courses in 1987. In 1996–97, it offered 55 courses at a distance. In the fall of 1996, there was a total of 800 students enrolled in distance learning courses.
Course delivery sites Courses are delivered to your home.
Media Courses are delivered via videotapes, videoconferencing, print. Students and teachers interact via videoconferencing, mail, telephone, fax, e-mail.
Services Distance learners have access to library services, the campus computer network, e-mail services at a distance.
Credit-earning options Students may transfer credits from another institution or may earn credits through institutionally developed exams, portfolio assessment.
Typical costs Tuition of $60.75 per credit plus mandatory fees of $5 per credit for local area residents. Tuition of $121.50 per credit plus mandatory fees of $5 per credit for in-state residents. Tuition of $182.25 per credit plus mandatory fees of $5 per credit for out-of-state residents. *Noncredit courses:* $50 per course. Costs may vary by campus or location. Financial aid is available to distance learners enrolled full-time or part-time.
Registration Students may register by mail, fax, phone.
Contact Elaine Stoneroad, Distance Education Specialist, Harrisburg Area Community College, One HACC Drive, Harrisburg, PA 17110. *Telephone:* 717-780-2541. *Fax:* 717-236-0709. *Web site:* http://www.hacc.edu.

INDIVIDUAL COURSE SUBJECT AREAS

Undergraduate
Abnormal psychology; accounting; biology; business; business administration and management; chemistry; developmental and child psychology; earth science; economics; English composition; English language and literature; geography; geology; history; liberal arts, general studies, and humanities; mathematics; philosophy and religion; political science; public health; sociology

Noncredit
Health professions and related sciences

HAWKEYE COMMUNITY COLLEGE

Waterloo, Iowa

Department of Academic Telecommunications

Hawkeye Community College, founded in 1967, is a state and locally supported two-year college. It is accredited by the North Central Association of Colleges and Schools. It first offered distance learning courses in 1993. In 1996–97, it offered 27 courses at a distance. In the fall of 1996, there was a total of 160 students enrolled in distance learning courses.
Course delivery sites Courses are delivered to your home, your workplace, military bases, 15 off-campus centers in Allison, Cedar Falls, Independence, Waterloo, Waverly, community colleges in Iowa.
Media Courses are delivered via television, videotapes, videoconferencing. Students and teachers interact via videoconferencing, telephone, fax, e-mail.
Restrictions Programs are primarily available to in-state students.
Services Distance learners have access to library services, academic advising at a distance.
Credit-earning options Students may transfer credits from another institution or may earn credits through institutionally developed exams, portfolio assessment, military training.
Typical costs Tuition of $64 per credit hour plus mandatory fees of $8.50 per credit hour for in-state residents. Tuition of $128 per credit hour plus mandatory fees of $8.50 per credit hour for out-of-state residents. *Noncredit courses:* $85 per course. Financial aid is available to distance learners enrolled full-time or part-time.
Registration Students may register by mail, fax, phone, e-mail.
Contact Roger Rezabek, Director of Telecommunications, Hawkeye Community College, 1501 East Orange Road, Waterloo, IA 50704. *Telephone:* 319-296-4017. *Fax:* 319-296-4018. *E-mail:* rezaber8166@uni.edu. *Web site:* http://www.hawkeye.cc.ia.us.

DEGREE & CERTIFICATE PROGRAMS

Associate Degrees
▶**Arts and Sciences (AA, AS)**
In the fall of 1996 there were 150 students enrolled in this program.
Application requirements *Prior education:* high school diploma or equivalent. *Other requirements:* high school transcript, assessment tests.
Completion requirements 64 semester hours are required. 16 semester hours must be completed through the institution.
Program contact Delano Cox, Director, Arts and Sciences, Hawkeye Community College, 1501 East Orange Road, Waterloo, IA 50704. Phone: 319-296-2320. Fax: 319-296-2874.

Profiles: Hawkeye Community College

INDIVIDUAL COURSE SUBJECT AREAS

Undergraduate
Agriculture; biological and life sciences; business administration and management; education; English composition; liberal arts, general studies, and humanities; mathematics; psychology; social sciences

HERIOT-WATT UNIVERSITY

Edinburgh, United Kingdom

Edinburgh Business School

Heriot-Watt University, founded in 1966, is a university in the United Kingdom. It first offered distance learning courses in 1990. In 1996–97, it offered 14 courses at a distance. In the fall of 1996, there was a total of 8,000 students enrolled in distance learning courses.
Course delivery sites Courses are delivered to your home.
Media Courses are delivered via computer software, print. Students and teachers interact via mail, fax, e-mail.
Services Distance learners have access to library services, the campus computer network at a distance.
Credit-earning options Students may transfer credits from another institution.
Typical costs Tuition of $820 per course plus mandatory fees of $85 per course.
Registration Students may register by mail, fax, phone.
Contact Dr. John Bear, Director of North American Distributorship, Heriot-Watt University, 6921 Stockton Avenue, El Cerrito, CA 94530. *Telephone:* 888-534-2378. *Fax:* 510-528-3555. *E-mail:* heriotwatt@degree.net. *Web site:* http://www.ebs.hw.ac.uk.

DEGREE & CERTIFICATE PROGRAMS

Graduate Degrees
▶ *Business Administration (MBA)*
In the fall of 1996 there were 8,000 students enrolled in this program. In 1995–96, 400 degrees were earned at a distance through this program.
Application requirements *Prior education:* baccalaureate degree. *Other requirements:* college transcripts.
Completion requirements 9 courses are required. 7 courses must be completed through the institution. *Maximum time for completion:* seven years.

INDIVIDUAL COURSE SUBJECT AREAS

Graduate
Accounting; business; economics; finance; human resources management; international business; management information systems; marketing; mathematics; organizational behavior studies
See full description on page 422.

HIBBING COMMUNITY COLLEGE

Hibbing, Minnesota

Hibbing Community College, founded in 1916, is a state-supported two-year college. It is accredited by the North Central Association of Colleges and Schools.
Course delivery sites Courses are delivered to Itasca Community College (Grand Rapids), Rainy River Community College (International Falls), public schools in region.
Media Courses are delivered via television, videotapes, videoconferencing, audiotapes, audioconferencing, computer software, World Wide Web, e-mail, print. Students and teachers interact via videoconferencing, audioconferencing, mail, telephone, fax, e-mail.
Credit-earning options Students may transfer credits from another institution or may earn credits through examinations, military training.
Typical costs Tuition of $43 per credit for in-state residents. Tuition of $83 per credit for out-of-state residents. Costs may vary by cost of materials.
Contact Jane Harmon, Vice President for Academic Affairs, Hibbing Community College, 1515 East 25th Street, Hibbing, MN 55746-3300. *Telephone:* 218-262-7250. *Fax:* 218-262-7222. *E-mail:* harmonja@hib.tec.mn.us.

DEGREE & CERTIFICATE PROGRAMS

Associate Degrees
▶ *Call Center Sales Specialist (AAS)*
Application requirements *Prior education:* high school diploma or equivalent. *Other requirements:* proof of graduation.
Completion requirements 96 credits are required. 48 credits must be completed through the institution.
Program contact Colleen Swanson, Director of Call Center Sales Specialist Program, Hibbing Community College, 1515 East 25th Street, Hibbing, MN 55746-3300. Phone: 218-262-7275. E-mail: colleen.s@tc-instruct-hibbing.ins.tec.mn.us.

INDIVIDUAL COURSE SUBJECT AREAS

Undergraduate
Anthropology; astronomy and astrophysics; business; chemistry; engineering; English language and literature; geology; liberal arts, general studies, and humanities; philosophy and religion; physics; political science; psychology; social sciences; sociology; visual and performing arts

HIGHLAND COMMUNITY COLLEGE

Freeport, Illinois

Highland Community College, founded in 1962, is a state and locally supported two-year college. It is accredited by the North Central Association of Colleges and Schools. It first offered distance learning courses in 1994.
Course delivery sites Courses are delivered to other colleges.
Media Courses are delivered via television, videotapes, videoconferencing, audiotapes, print.
Restrictions Programs are available to in-state students only.
Services Distance learners have access to library services, academic advising, tutoring, career placement assistance at a distance.
Credit-earning options Students may transfer credits from another institution or may earn credits through examinations. Financial aid is available to distance learners.
Contact Dean of Learning Resources, Highland Community College, 2998 West Pearl City Road, Freeport, IL 61032-9341. *Telephone:* 815-235-6121. *Fax:* 815-235-1366.

INDIVIDUAL COURSE SUBJECT AREAS

Undergraduate
Music; sociology

HILLSBOROUGH COMMUNITY COLLEGE

Tampa, Florida

Distance Learning Office of Open College

Hillsborough Community College, founded in 1968, is a state-supported two-year college. It is accredited by the Southern Association of Colleges and Schools. It first offered distance learning courses in 1971. In 1996–97, it offered 22 courses at a distance. In the fall of 1996, there was a total of 600 students enrolled in distance learning courses.
Course delivery sites Courses are delivered to your home, your workplace, military bases.
Media Courses are delivered via television, videotapes, audioconferencing, computer software, World Wide Web, e-mail, print. Students and teachers interact via audioconferencing, mail, telephone, fax, e-mail.
Services Distance learners have access to library services, academic advising, tutoring, career placement assistance at a distance.
Credit-earning options Students may transfer credits from another institution or may earn credits through standardized exams, institutionally developed exams.
Typical costs Tuition of $37.47 per credit for in-state residents. Tuition of $139.58 per credit for out-of-state residents. Financial aid is available to distance learners.
Registration Students may register by phone.
Contact Michael Comins, Coordinator, Distance Learning, Hillsborough Community College, 10414 East Columbus Drive, BACA 207-E, Tampa, FL 33619. *Telephone:* 813-253-7961. *Fax:* 813-253-7868. *E-mail:* cominsm@mail.firn.edu. *Web site:* http://www.hcc.cc.fl.us.

INDIVIDUAL COURSE SUBJECT AREAS

Undergraduate
Astronomy and astrophysics; biology; business; business administration and management; chemistry; computer and information sciences; developmental and child psychology; economics; geology; health and physical education/fitness; history; liberal arts, general studies, and humanities; marketing; mathematics; political science; psychology; sociology

HOCKING COLLEGE

Nelsonville, Ohio

Hocking College, founded in 1968, is a state-supported two-year college. It is accredited by the North Central Association of Colleges and Schools. It first offered distance learning courses in 1995. In 1996–97, it offered 20 courses at a distance. In the fall of 1996, there was a total of 76 students enrolled in distance learning courses.
Course delivery sites Courses are delivered to 1 off-campus center in New Lexington.
Media Courses are delivered via videoconferencing. Students and teachers interact via videoconferencing, telephone, fax.
Restrictions Programs are available to local area students only.
Services Distance learners have access to library services, academic advising, tutoring at a distance.
Credit-earning options Students may transfer credits from another institution or may earn credits through institutionally developed exams, portfolio assessment, military training, business training.
Typical costs Tuition of $58 per credit. Costs may vary by number of credits taken. Financial aid is available to distance learners.
Contact Elaine Dabelko, Director of Instructional Services, Hocking College, 3301 Hocking Parkway, Nelsonville, OH 45764. *Telephone:* 614-753-3591, Ext. 2272. *Fax:* 614-753-4097. *E-mail:* dabelko_e@ccmgate.hocking.cc.oh.us.

INDIVIDUAL COURSE SUBJECT AREAS

Undergraduate
Anatomy; business; business administration and management; corrections; foods and nutrition studies; health professions and related sciences; marketing; mathematics; nursing; psychology; public administration and services; real estate; social work

HOLY NAMES COLLEGE

Oakland, California

Nursing Department

Holy Names College, founded in 1868, is an independent-religious Roman Catholic comprehensive institution. It is accredited by the Western Association of Schools and Colleges, Inc. It first offered distance learning courses in 1995. In 1996–97, it offered 6 courses at a distance. In the fall of 1996, there was a total of 96 students enrolled in distance learning courses.
Course delivery sites Courses are delivered to your workplace, 8 off-campus centers in Hayward, Martinez, Oakland, Sacramento, San Francisco, Santa Cruz, Walnut Creek.
Media Courses are delivered via videoconferencing, computer software, e-mail, print, interactive television. Students and teachers interact via videoconferencing, mail, telephone, fax, e-mail. A computer is required for some courses.
Restrictions Programs are available to in-state students only. Currently all students are Kaiser employees.
Services Distance learners have access to library services, e-mail services, academic advising, tutoring at a distance.
Credit-earning options Students may transfer credits from another institution or may earn credits through standardized exams, institutionally developed exams, military training, business training.
Typical costs Tuition of $200 per unit. Financial aid is available to distance learners.
Registration Students may register by mail, fax.
Contact Arlene Sargent, Chair, Nursing, Holy Names College, 3500 Mountain Boulevard, Oakland, CA 94619. *Telephone:* 510-436-1024. *Fax:* 510-436-1376. *E-mail:* sargent@academ.hnc.edu.

DEGREE & CERTIFICATE PROGRAMS

Baccalaureate Degrees
▶*Nursing Science (BSN)*
In the fall of 1996 there were 96 students enrolled in this program.
Restrictions Program is available to students in northern California only.
Application requirements *Prior education:* RN license, diploma or associate's degree in nursing. *Other requirements:* NLN exams, high school transcript, college transcripts, an essay or personal statement, letter(s) of recommendation, an application fee of $35.
Completion requirements 120 units are required. 45 units must be completed through the institution. This is a degree completion program.
On-campus requirements For orientation.

Profiles: Houston Community College System

HOUSTON COMMUNITY COLLEGE SYSTEM

Houston, Texas

Distance Education Department

Houston Community College System, founded in 1971, is a state and locally supported two-year college. It is accredited by the Southern Association of Colleges and Schools.
Course delivery sites Courses are delivered to your home, your workplace.
Media Courses are delivered via television, videotapes, audiotapes, computer software, World Wide Web, e-mail, print, computer conferencing. Students and teachers interact via mail, telephone, fax, e-mail.
Credit-earning options Students may transfer credits from another institution or may earn credits through examinations.
Typical costs Tuition of $101 per course plus mandatory fees of $24 per course for local area residents. Tuition of $158 per course plus mandatory fees of $24 per course for in-state residents. Tuition of $360 per course plus mandatory fees of $24 per course for out-of-state residents. Costs may vary by number of credits taken. Financial aid is available to distance learners.
Contact Distance Education Department, Houston Community College System, 4310 Dunlavy, Houston, TX 77006. *Telephone:* 713-718-5275.

INDIVIDUAL COURSE SUBJECT AREAS

Undergraduate

Accounting; architecture; business; business administration and management; computer and information sciences; developmental and child psychology; engineering; English composition; English language and literature; history; law and legal studies; liberal arts, general studies, and humanities; marketing; photography; psychology; real estate; social sciences; sociology; Spanish language and literature

HOWARD COMMUNITY COLLEGE

Columbia, Maryland

Learning Centers Division

Howard Community College, founded in 1966, is a state and locally supported two-year college. It is accredited by the Middle States Association of Colleges and Schools. It first offered distance learning courses in 1995. In 1996–97, it offered 60 courses at a distance. In the fall of 1996, there was a total of 175 students enrolled in distance learning courses.
Course delivery sites Courses are delivered to your home, University of Baltimore (Baltimore).
Media Courses are delivered via television, World Wide Web, interactive television. Students and teachers interact via telephone, e-mail, computer conferencing. A computer is required for some courses.
Services Distance learners have access to library services, the campus computer network, e-mail services, tutoring at a distance.
Credit-earning options Students may transfer credits from another institution or may earn credits through standardized exams, institutionally developed exams, portfolio assessment, military training.
Typical costs Tuition of $76 per credit for local area residents. Tuition of $123 per credit for in-state residents. Tuition of $175 per credit for out-of-state residents. Costs may vary by number of credits taken, country of residence. Financial aid is available to distance learners enrolled full-time or part-time.
Registration Students may register by phone, e-mail.
Contact Barbara Greenfeld, Director of Admissions, Howard Community College, 10901 Little Patuxent Parkway, Columbia, MD 21044. *Telephone:* 410-992-4856. *Fax:* 410-715-2426. *E-mail:* bgreenfeld@ccm.howardcc.edu. *Web site:* http://www.howardcc.edu.

DEGREE & CERTIFICATE PROGRAMS

Associate Degrees

▶ *General Studies (AA)*
Application requirements *Prior education:* high school diploma or equivalent. *Other requirements:* high school transcript, college transcripts, an application fee of $15, English placement test.
Completion requirements 60 quarter credits are required. 15 semester credits must be completed through the institution.
Program contact John Hawkins, Director of Lifelong Learning and Professional Education, Howard Community College, 10901 Little Patuxent Parkway, Columbia, MD 21044. Phone: 410-772-4974. Fax: 410-772-4986. E-mail: jhawkins@ccm.howardcc.edu.

INDIVIDUAL COURSE SUBJECT AREAS

Undergraduate

Accounting; architecture; area, ethnic, and cultural studies; biological and life sciences; computer and information sciences; engineering; engineering-related technologies; English composition; English language and literature; European languages and literatures; health professions and related sciences; human resources management; law and legal studies; liberal arts, general studies, and humanities; mathematics; psychology; social sciences

Noncredit

Business

HUDSON VALLEY COMMUNITY COLLEGE

Troy, New York

Office of Continuing Education

Hudson Valley Community College, founded in 1953, is a state and locally supported two-year college. It is accredited by the Middle States Association of Colleges and Schools. It first offered distance learning courses in 1992. In 1996–97, it offered 6 courses at a distance. In the fall of 1996, there was a total of 60 students enrolled in distance learning courses.
Course delivery sites Courses are delivered to your home, 3 off-campus centers in Albany, Malta, Troy.
Media Courses are delivered via television, videoconferencing, computer software, World Wide Web, e-mail, print. Students and teachers interact via videoconferencing, mail, telephone, fax, e-mail. A computer is required for some courses.
Restrictions Programs are available to local area students only.
Services Distance learners have access to library services at a distance.
Credit-earning options Students may transfer credits from another institution or may earn credits through examinations, portfolio assessment.
Typical costs Tuition of $90 per semester hour plus mandatory fees of $50 per semester for in-state residents. Tuition of $208 per semester hour plus mandatory fees of $50 per semester for out-of-state residents. *Noncredit courses:* $330 per course. Costs may vary by number of credits taken, course delivery options. Financial aid is available to distance learners.

Registration Students may register by mail, phone, e-mail, World Wide Web.
Contact Office of Continuing Education, Hudson Valley Community College, Vandenburgh Avenue, Troy, NY 12180. *Telephone:* 518-270-7338. *Web site:* http://www.hvcc.edu.

INDIVIDUAL COURSE SUBJECT AREAS

Undergraduate
Child care and development; creative writing; economics; English composition; labor relations/studies; mathematics; psychology; sociology; telecommunications

IDAHO STATE UNIVERSITY

Pocatello, Idaho

Distance Learning Center

Idaho State University, founded in 1901, is a state-supported university. It is accredited by the Northwest Association of Schools and Colleges. It first offered distance learning courses in 1988.
Course delivery sites Courses are delivered to your home, your workplace, other colleges.
Media Courses are delivered via television, videotapes, videoconferencing.
Restrictions Programs are available to in-state students only.
Credit-earning options Students may transfer credits from another institution or may earn credits through examinations, portfolio assessment, military training.
Contact Registrar, Idaho State University, PO Box 8196, Pocatello, ID 83209. *Telephone:* 208-236-2661. *Web site:* http://www.isu.edu.

INDIVIDUAL COURSE SUBJECT AREAS

Undergraduate
Accounting; administrative and secretarial services; area, ethnic, and cultural studies; biological and life sciences; biology; botany; business; business administration and management; chemical engineering; chemistry; computer and information sciences; creative writing; developmental and child psychology; economics; education administration; educational psychology; electrical engineering; engineering mechanics; English as a second language (ESL); English composition; environmental engineering; geology; health and physical education/fitness; health professions and related sciences; history; home economics and family studies; hospitality services management; human resources management; industrial engineering; liberal arts, general studies, and humanities; library and information studies; mathematics; mechanical engineering; microbiology; nursing; physical sciences; physics; political science; public health; social psychology; social work; sociology; special education; teacher education; zoology

Graduate
Accounting; administrative and secretarial services; area, ethnic, and cultural studies; biological and life sciences; biology; botany; business; business administration and management; chemical engineering; chemistry; computer and information sciences; creative writing; developmental and child psychology; economics; education administration; educational psychology; electrical engineering; engineering mechanics; English as a second language (ESL); English composition; environmental engineering; geology; health and physical education/fitness; health professions and related sciences; history; home economics and family studies; hospitality services management; human resources management; industrial engineering; liberal arts, general studies, and humanities; library and information studies; mathematics; mechanical engineering; microbiology; nursing; physical sciences; physics; political science; public health; social psychology; social work; sociology; special education; teacher education; zoology

ILLINOIS CENTRAL COLLEGE

East Peoria, Illinois

Instructional Technology Department

Illinois Central College, founded in 1967, is a state and locally supported two-year college. It is accredited by the North Central Association of Colleges and Schools.
Course delivery sites Courses are delivered to your home, your workplace, other colleges.
Media Courses are delivered via television, videotapes, videoconferencing, print.
Restrictions Programs are available to local area students only.
Credit-earning options Students may transfer credits from another institution or may earn credits through examinations, military training. Financial aid is available to distance learners.
Contact Director, Enrollment Management, Illinois Central College, One College Drive, East Peoria, IL 61635. *Telephone:* 309-694-5354. *Fax:* 309-694-5450.

INDIVIDUAL COURSE SUBJECT AREAS

Undergraduate
Accounting; advertising; biology; business administration and management; creative writing; developmental and child psychology; economics; English composition; English language and literature; health professions and related sciences; human resources management; mathematics; nursing; political science; sociology

ILLINOIS EASTERN COMMUNITY COLLEGES, OLNEY CENTRAL COLLEGE

Olney, Illinois

Illinois Eastern Community Colleges, Olney Central College, founded in 1962, is a state and locally supported two-year college. It is accredited by the North Central Association of Colleges and Schools. It first offered distance learning courses in 1994.
Course delivery sites Courses are delivered to your home, your workplace, other colleges.
Media Courses are delivered via television, videotapes, videoconferencing.
Restrictions Programs are available to in-state students only.
Services Distance learners have access to academic advising, tutoring, career placement assistance at a distance.
Credit-earning options Students may transfer credits from another institution or may earn credits through examinations, portfolio assessment, military training, business training. Financial aid is available to distance learners.
Contact Dean of Instruction, Illinois Eastern Community Colleges, Olney Central College, 305 North West Street, Olney, IL 62450. *Telephone:* 618-395-7777. *Fax:* 618-395-5212.

Profiles: Illinois Eastern Community Colleges, Olney Central College

INDIVIDUAL COURSE SUBJECT AREAS

Undergraduate

Accounting; administrative and secretarial services; business; business administration and management; creative writing; design; developmental and child psychology; economics; education administration; educational psychology; English composition; English language and literature; European languages and literatures; history; hospitality services management; human resources management; law and legal studies; liberal arts, general studies, and humanities; mathematics; nursing; political science; social psychology; special education; teacher education

ILLINOIS INSTITUTE OF TECHNOLOGY

Chicago, Illinois

Distance Learning Technologies

Illinois Institute of Technology, founded in 1890, is an independent-nonprofit university. It is accredited by the North Central Association of Colleges and Schools. It first offered distance learning courses in 1976. In 1996–97, it offered 200 courses at a distance. In the fall of 1996, there was a total of 550 students enrolled in distance learning courses.
Course delivery sites Courses are delivered to your home, your workplace, Finch University of Health Sciences/The Chicago Medical School (North Chicago), Oakton Community College (Des Plaines), William Rainey Harper College (Palatine).
Media Courses are delivered via television, videotapes, videoconferencing, World Wide Web. Students and teachers interact via videoconferencing, telephone, fax, e-mail. A computer is required for some courses.
Services Distance learners have access to library services, the campus computer network, e-mail services, academic advising at a distance.
Credit-earning options Students may transfer credits from another institution.
Typical costs *Undergraduate:* Tuition of $495 per credit. *Graduate:* Tuition of $545 per credit. Costs may vary by number of credits taken, course delivery options. Financial aid is available to distance learners enrolled full-time or part-time.
Registration Students may register by mail, fax.
Contact Holli Pryor-Harris, Director, Client Services, Illinois Institute of Technology, IITV, 10 West 31st Street, 226 SB, Chicago, IL 60616. Telephone: 312-567-3167. Fax: 312-567-5913. E-mail: ia_pryor@vax1.ais.iit.edu. Web site: http://www.dlt.iit.edu.

DEGREE & CERTIFICATE PROGRAMS

Graduate Degrees

▶ *Chemical Engineering, Chemistry, Computer Science, Electrical Engineering, Environmental Engineering, Mechanical and Aerospace Engineering (MS)*
In the fall of 1996 there were 233 students enrolled in this program. In 1995–96, 28 degrees were earned at a distance through this program.
Restrictions This program is available to local area students only.
Application requirements *Prior education:* baccalaureate degree. *Other requirements:* GRE, college transcripts, an essay or personal statement, letter(s) of recommendation, an application fee of $30.
Completion requirements 32 semester hours are required. 26 semester hours must be completed through the institution. *Maximum time for completion:* six years.
On-campus requirements Students may be required to come to campus for examinations and presentations.

▶ *Chemical Engineering (MCE)*
In the fall of 1996 there were 4 students enrolled in this program.
Restrictions This program is available to local area students only.
Application requirements *Prior education:* baccalaureate degree. *Other requirements:* GRE, college transcripts, an essay or personal statement, letter(s) of recommendation, an application fee of $30.
Completion requirements 32 semester hours are required. 26 semester hours must be completed through the institution. *Maximum time for completion:* six years.
On-campus requirements Students may be required to come to campus for examinations and presentations.

▶ *Chemistry (MChem)*
In the fall of 1996 there were 29 students enrolled in this program.
Application requirements *Prior education:* baccalaureate degree. *Other requirements:* GRE, college transcripts, an essay or personal statement, letter(s) of recommendation, an application fee of $30.
Completion requirements 32 semester hours are required. 26 semester hours must be completed through the institution. *Maximum time for completion:* six years.

▶ *Mechanical and Aerospace Engineering (MMAE)*
In the fall of 1996 there were 6 students enrolled in this program.
Restrictions This program is available to local area students only.
Application requirements *Prior education:* baccalaureate degree. *Other requirements:* GRE, college transcripts, an essay or personal statement, letter(s) of recommendation, an application fee of $30.
Completion requirements 32 semester hours are required. 26 semester hours must be completed through the institution. *Maximum time for completion:* six years.
On-campus requirements Students may be required to come to campus for examinations and presentations.

Graduate certificates

▶ *Computer Networking and Telecommunications, Computer Science, Electrical and Computer Engineering, Intelligent Information Systems, Software Engineering, Wireless Communications*
In the fall of 1996 there were 3 students enrolled in this program.
Restrictions This program is available to local area students only.
Application requirements *Prior education:* baccalaureate degree. *Other requirements:* college transcripts, an application fee of $30.
Completion requirements 15 semester hours are required. 15 semester hours must be completed through the institution. *Maximum time for completion:* five years.
On-campus requirements Students may be required to come to campus for examinations and presentations.

INDIVIDUAL COURSE SUBJECT AREAS

Undergraduate

Aerospace, aeronautical engineering; biological and life sciences; computer and information sciences; electrical engineering; engineering; engineering mechanics; mathematics; mechanical engineering; physics

Graduate

Aerospace, aeronautical engineering; biological and life sciences; chemical engineering; chemistry; computer and information sciences; electrical engineering; engineering; environmental engineering; industrial engineering; mathematics; mechanical engineering

ILLINOIS VALLEY COMMUNITY COLLEGE

Oglesby, Illinois

Learning Resources

Illinois Valley Community College, founded in 1924, is a district-supported two-year college. It is accredited by the North Central Association of Colleges and Schools. It first offered distance learning courses in 1984. In 1996–97, it offered 10 courses at a distance. In the fall of 1996, there was a total of 264 students enrolled in distance learning courses.

Course delivery sites Courses are delivered to your home, your workplace, Bradley University (Peoria), Illinois Central College (East Peoria), University of Illinois at Springfield (Springfield), 7 off-campus centers in La Salle, Mendota, Ottawa, Peru, Princeton, Seneca, Streator, Bloomington Junior College.

Media Courses are delivered via videotapes, videoconferencing, computer software, print. Students and teachers interact via videoconferencing, mail, telephone, fax.

Services Distance learners have access to the campus computer network, academic advising at a distance.

Credit-earning options Students may transfer credits from another institution or may earn credits through standardized exams, institutionally developed exams, portfolio assessment, military training.

Typical costs Tuition of $37 per credit hour plus mandatory fees of $1.50 per credit hour for local area residents. Tuition of $136 per credit hour plus mandatory fees of $1.50 per credit hour for in-state residents. Tuition of $179 per credit hour plus mandatory fees of $1.50 per credit hour for out-of-state residents. *Noncredit courses:* $40–$50 per course. Financial aid is available to distance learners.

Registration Students may register by mail, fax, phone.

Contact Robert Marshall, Director of Admissions, Illinois Valley Community College, 815 Orlando Smith Avenue, Oglesby, IL 61348. *Telephone:* 815-224-2720. *Fax:* 815-224-3303. *E-mail:* marshall@rs6000.ivcc.edu.

INDIVIDUAL COURSE SUBJECT AREAS

Undergraduate
Accounting; administrative and secretarial services; advertising; area, ethnic, and cultural studies; astronomy and astrophysics; biological and life sciences; business; business administration and management; computer and information sciences; developmental and child psychology; economics; English language and literature; geography; geology; health and physical education/fitness; history; home economics and family studies; liberal arts, general studies, and humanities; political science; social psychology; sociology

INDIANA HIGHER EDUCATION TELECOMMUNICATION SYSTEM

Bloomington, Indiana

Indiana Partnership for Statewide Education

Indiana Higher Education Telecommunication System is a statewide university consortium. It first offered distance learning courses in 1992.

Media Courses are delivered via television, videotapes, videoconferencing, World Wide Web, e-mail, print. Students and teachers interact via videoconferencing, mail, e-mail.

Typical costs Costs vary. Contact member institutions for details.

Contact ICN Student Services Center, Indiana Higher Education Telecommunication System, 2805 East Tenth Street, Bloomington, IN 47408. *Telephone:* 800-426-8899. *Fax:* 812-855-9380. *Web site:* http://www.icn.org.

See full description on page 424.

INDIANA STATE UNIVERSITY

Terre Haute, Indiana

Continuing Education/Instructional Services

Indiana State University, founded in 1865, is a state-supported university. It is accredited by the North Central Association of Colleges and Schools. It first offered distance learning courses in 1969. In 1996–97, it offered 44 courses at a distance. In the fall of 1996, there was a total of 517 students enrolled in distance learning courses.

Course delivery sites Courses are delivered to your workplace, military bases, Ivy Tech State College System (Indianapolis), University of Southern Indiana (Evansville), Vincennes University (Vincennes), 300 sites at locations throughout Indiana.

Media Courses are delivered via television, videotapes, videoconferencing, World Wide Web, print. Students and teachers interact via videoconferencing, mail, telephone, fax, e-mail.

Restrictions Programs are available to in-state students only.

Services Distance learners have access to library services, the campus computer network, academic advising, career placement assistance at a distance.

Credit-earning options Students may transfer credits from another institution.

Typical costs *Undergraduate:* Tuition of $110 per credit hour. *Graduate:* Tuition of $132 per credit hour. Financial aid is available to distance learners.

Registration Students may register by mail.

Contact Keith B. Hawkins, Director of Distance Education, Indiana State University, Reeve Hall, 312, Terre Haute, IN 47809. *Telephone:* 812-237-3181. *Fax:* 812-237-3495. *E-mail:* tvshawk@ruby.indstate.edu. *Web site:* http://web.indstate.edu/mtr/disted.

DEGREE & CERTIFICATE PROGRAMS

Baccalaureate Degrees

▶ *Human Resource Development (BS)*

In the fall of 1996 there were 27 students enrolled in this program. In 1995–96, 1 degree was earned at a distance through this program.

Application requirements *Prior education:* high school diploma or equivalent. *Other requirements:* SAT, high school transcript, an application fee of $20.

Completion requirements 126 hours are required.

On-campus requirements Students must attend one Saturday class per semester.

Program contact Dr. Anthony Gilberti, Chairperson, Indiana State University, Department of Industrial Technology Education, Terre Haute, IN 47809. Phone: 812-237-2342. Fax: 812-237-4479. E-mail: tchgil@ruby.indstate.edu.

Graduate Degrees

▶ *Human Resource Development (MS)*

In the fall of 1996 there were 82 students enrolled in this program. In 1995–96, 31 degrees were earned at a distance through this program.

Application requirements *Prior education:* baccalaureate degree. *Other requirements:* college transcripts, an application fee of $20, 2.5 or higher undergraduate grade point average.

Completion requirements 33–36 credit hours are required. *Maximum time for completion:* five years from date of admission.

On-campus requirements Students must attend one Saturday class per semester.

Program contact Dr. Anthony Gilberti, Chairperson, Indiana State University, Department of Industrial Technology Education, Terre Haute, IN 47809. Phone: 812-237-2342. Fax: 812-237-4479. E-mail: tchgil@ruby.indstate.edu.

Profiles: Indiana State University

▶ *Occupational Safety Management (MS)*
In the fall of 1996 there were 72 students enrolled in this program.
Application requirements *Prior education:* baccalaureate degree. *Other requirements:* college transcripts, an essay or personal statement, letter(s) of recommendation, an application fee of $20.
Completion requirements 32 hours are required. *Maximum time for completion:* five years.
On-campus requirements Classroom sessions are held once or twice per semester.
Program contact Dr. Portia Plummer, Chairperson, Indiana State University, Department of Health and Safety, Terre Haute, IN 47809. Phone: 812-237-3071. Fax: 812-237-4338. E-mail: hsplumm@scifac.indstate.edu.

Graduate certificates

▶ *Educational Administration*
In the fall of 1996 there were 49 students enrolled in this program.
Application requirements *Prior education:* baccalaureate degree. *Other requirements:* college transcripts, an essay or personal statement, letter(s) of recommendation, an application fee of $20, must have a valid teacher's license.
Completion requirements 45 hours are required. 12 hours must be completed through the institution.
On-campus requirements Students must attend three class sessions on the Indiana State campus for each course.
Program contact Dr. Rebecca Libler, Office of Educational Leadership, Indiana State University, School of Education (ELAF) Administration, Terre Haute, IN 47809. Phone: 812-237-2900. E-mail: ealibir@befac.indstate.edu.

INDIVIDUAL COURSE SUBJECT AREAS

Undergraduate
Biology; business administration and management; human resources management

Graduate
Education administration; nursing; public health

INDIANA UNIVERSITY SYSTEM

Bloomington, Indiana

School of Continuing Studies

Indiana University System is a state-supported university system. It first offered distance learning courses in 1912. In 1996–97, it offered 405 courses at a distance. In the fall of 1996, there was a total of 7,619 students enrolled in distance learning courses.
Course delivery sites Courses are delivered to your home, your workplace, military bases, 300 satellite locations around the US.
Media Courses are delivered via television, videotapes, videoconferencing, audiotapes, computer software, World Wide Web, e-mail, print. Students and teachers interact via videoconferencing, audioconferencing, mail, telephone, fax, e-mail, World Wide Web. A computer is required for some courses.
Services Distance learners have access to library services, the campus computer network, e-mail services, academic advising at a distance.
Credit-earning options Students may transfer credits from another institution or may earn credits through examinations, portfolio assessment, military training, business training.
Typical costs *Undergraduate:* Tuition of $103 per credit. *Graduate:* Tuition of $140 per credit. *Noncredit courses:* $150 per course. Costs may vary by campus or location, specific program of study. Financial aid is available to distance learners.
Registration Students may register by mail, fax, phone, e-mail, World Wide Web.
Contact Michael Yoakam, Director, Office of Distance Learning, School of Continuing Studies, Indiana University System, Owen Hall, Room 205, Bloomington, IN 47405. *Telephone:* 812-855-8995. *Fax:* 812-855-8997. *E-mail:* myoakam@indiana.edu. *Web site:* http://www.indiana.edu/~scs/dl.html.

DEGREE & CERTIFICATE PROGRAMS

Associate Degrees

▶ *General Studies (AGS)*
In the fall of 1996 there were 1,374 students enrolled in this program. In 1995–96, 54 degrees were earned at a distance through this program.
Restrictions Students who have earned a similar Associate or Bachelor's degree will not be admitted to the Associate of General Studies degree..
Application requirements *Prior education:* high school diploma or equivalent. *Other requirements:* high school transcript, college transcripts, an application fee of $30.
Completion requirements 60 semester hours are required. 15 semester hours must be completed through the institution.
Program contact Lawrence J. Keller, Director, Division of Extended Studies, Indiana University System, Owen Hall 001, Bloomington, IN 47405. Phone: 800-334-1011. Fax: 812-855-8680. E-mail: bulletin@indiana.edu.

▶ *Labor Studies (ASLS)*
In the fall of 1996 there were 47 students enrolled in this program.
Application requirements *Prior education:* high school diploma or equivalent. *Other requirements:* high school transcript, college transcripts, an essay or personal statement.
Completion requirements 60 credit hours are required. 12 credit hours must be completed through the institution.
Program contact Peter Seybold, Director, Division of Labor Studies, Indiana University System, Poplars 628, Bloomington, IN 47405-3085. Phone: 812-855-9082. Fax: 812-855-1563. E-mail: pseybold@indiana.edu.

Baccalaureate Degrees

▶ *General Studies (BGS)*
In the fall of 1996 there were 2,254 students enrolled in this program. In 1995–96, 87 degrees were earned at a distance through this program.
Restrictions Students who have earned a similar Bachelor's degree will not be admitted to the Bachelor of General Studies degree..
Application requirements *Prior education:* high school diploma or equivalent. *Other requirements:* high school transcript, college transcripts, an application fee of $30.
Completion requirements 120 semester hours are required. 30 semester hours must be completed through the institution.
Program contact Lawrence J. Keller, Director, Division of Extended Studies, Indiana University System, Owen Hall 001, Bloomington, IN 47405. Phone: 800-334-1011. Fax: 812-855-8680. E-mail: bulletin@indiana.edu.

▶ *Labor Studies (BSLS)*
In the fall of 1996 there were 47 students enrolled in this program.
Application requirements *Prior education:* high school diploma or equivalent. *Other requirements:* high school transcript, college transcripts.
Completion requirements 120 credit hours are required. 24 credit hours must be completed through the institution.
Program contact Peter Seybold, Director, Division of Labor Studies, Indiana University System, Poplars 628, Bloomington, IN 47405-3085. Phone: 812-855-9082. Fax: 812-855-1563. E-mail: pseybold@indiana.edu.

Graduate Degrees

▶ *Adult Education (MS)*
In the fall of 1996 there were 75 students enrolled in this program.

Application requirements *Prior education:* baccalaureate degree. *Other requirements:* college transcripts.
Completion requirements 36 semester hours are required. *Maximum time for completion:* six years.
Program contact Dr. Travis Shipp, Department Chair, Indiana University System, 620 Union Drive, Room 503, Indianapolis, IN 46202. Phone: 317-274-6823. Fax: 317-278-2280. E-mail: tshipp@indyvax.iupui.edu.

▶ *Language and Literacy Education (MSE)*
Application requirements *Prior education:* baccalaureate degree. *Other requirements:* GRE, college transcripts, an essay or personal statement, letter(s) of recommendation, an application fee of $40.
Completion requirements 36 credits are required. 27 credits must be completed through the institution.
Program contact Dr. Larry Mikulecky, Chair of Language Education, Indiana University System, School of Education 3038, Bloomington, IN 47405. Phone: 812-856-8277. Fax: 812-856-8440. E-mail: mikuleck@indiana.edu.

▶ *Nursing (MS)*
In the fall of 1996 there were 300 students enrolled in this program. In 1995–96, 290 degrees were earned at a distance through this program.
Restrictions Courses are only broadcast in the state of Indiana.
Application requirements *Prior education:* BSN from NLN accredited nursing program plus RN licensure or, for the mobility option, nursing diploma or ASN from NLN accredited program plus RN licensure. *Other requirements:* GRE, college transcripts, letter(s) of recommendation.
Completion requirements 42 credit hours are required. 33 credit hours must be completed through the institution.
On-campus requirements Students may be required to attend an IU campus to complete elective and clinical requirements.

▶ *Therapeutic Recreation (MS)*
In the fall of 1996 there were 20 students enrolled in this program. In 1995–96, 3 degrees were earned at a distance through this program.
Restrictions Program is available to students in Indiana, Cincinnati, Ohio, Oregon and Maryland only.
Application requirements *Prior education:* baccalaureate degree. *Other requirements:* GRE, college transcripts, an essay or personal statement, letter(s) of recommendation, an application fee of $40.
Completion requirements 35 semester credits are required. 30 semester credits must be completed through the institution. *Maximum time for completion:* seven years.
Program contact David Austin, Professor, Indiana University System, Indiana University, HPER 133, Bloomington, IN 47405. Phone: 812-855-3086. Fax: 812-855-3998. E-mail: daustin@indiana.edu.

Undergraduate Certificates

▶ *Distance Learning*
In the fall of 1996 there were 76 students enrolled in this program. In 1995–96, 70 certificates were earned at a distance through this program.
Application requirements *Prior education:* none required. *Other requirements:* an application fee of $225.
Completion requirements 1 course is required.

▶ *Labor Studies*
In the fall of 1996 there were 47 students enrolled in this program.
Application requirements *Prior education:* high school diploma or equivalent. *Other requirements:* high school transcript, college transcripts, an essay or personal statement.
Completion requirements 30 credit hours are required.
Program contact Peter Seybold, Director, Division of Labor Studies, Indiana University System, Poplars 628, Bloomington, IN 47405-3085. Phone: 812-855-9082. Fax: 812-855-1563. E-mail: pseybold@indiana.edu.

Graduate certificates

▶ *Library Services*
Restrictions This program is available to in-state students only.

Application requirements *Prior education:* baccalaureate degree. *Other requirements:* college transcripts.
Completion requirements *Maximum time for completion:* five years.
Program contact Mary E. Krutulis, Assistant Dean, Indiana University System, School of Library and Information Science, 10th and Jordan, Library 012, Bloomington, IN 47405-1801. Phone: 812-855-2018. Fax: 812-855-6166. E-mail: krutulis@indiana.edu.

INDIVIDUAL COURSE SUBJECT AREAS

Undergraduate
Accounting; African-American studies; American studies; anthropology; area, ethnic, and cultural studies; astronomy and astrophysics; biology; business; business administration and management; Classical languages and literatures; communications; computer and information sciences; conservation and natural resources; creative writing; developmental and child psychology; economics; English composition; English language and literature; European languages and literatures; fine arts; geology; health and physical education/fitness; health professions and related sciences; history; hospitality services management; human resources management; journalism; labor relations/studies; liberal arts, general studies, and humanities; mathematics; music; nursing; philosophy and religion; physics; political science; protective services; public health; radio and television broadcasting; social psychology; sociology; teacher education; women's studies

Graduate
Adult education; area, ethnic, and cultural studies; education administration; fine arts; health and physical education/fitness; health professions and related sciences; journalism; library and information studies; nursing; teacher education; telecommunications

INDIANA WESLEYAN UNIVERSITY

Marion, Indiana

Indiana Wesleyan University, founded in 1920, is an independent-religious Wesleyan comprehensive institution. It is accredited by the North Central Association of Colleges and Schools. It first offered distance learning courses in 1992. In 1996–97, it offered 11 courses at a distance. In the fall of 1996, there was a total of 5,348 students enrolled in distance learning courses.
Course delivery sites Courses are delivered to your home, your workplace.
Media Courses are delivered via videotapes, World Wide Web. Students and teachers interact via mail, fax, e-mail, computer conferencing. A computer is required for some courses.
Restrictions Video courses are offered only to licensed teachers.
Services Distance learners have access to library services, academic advising at a distance.
Credit-earning options Students may transfer credits from another institution or may earn credits through standardized exams, portfolio assessment, military training, business training.
Typical costs *Undergraduate:* Tuition of $160 per credit hour. *Graduate:* Tuition of $345 per credit hour. Financial aid is available to distance learners enrolled full-time.
Registration Students may register by mail, fax.
Contact Bonnie Briggs, Graduate Education Coordinator, Indiana Wesleyan University, 4406 South Harmon Street, Marion, IN 46953. *Telephone:* 765-677-2360.

Profiles: Indiana Wesleyan University

DEGREE & CERTIFICATE PROGRAMS

Graduate Degrees

▶ *Business Administration (MBA)*
Application requirements *Prior education:* baccalaureate degree. *Other requirements:* college transcripts, an essay or personal statement, letter(s) of recommendation, an application fee, 3 years work experience (full-time), 2.5 GPA, 2 letters of recommendation.
Completion requirements 46 credit hours are required. All course work must be completed through the institution.
On-campus requirements Two courses require two intensive weekends on campus.
Program contact Beth Dickerson, Student Enrollment Manager, Indiana Wesleyan University, 4406 South Harmon Street, Marion, IN 46953. Phone: 765-677-2860. Fax: 765-677-2380. E-mail: bdickers@indwes.edu.

INDIVIDUAL COURSE SUBJECT AREAS

Undergraduate
Bible studies; information sciences and systems; liberal arts, general studies, and humanities

Graduate
Teacher education

INSTITUTE OF TRANSPERSONAL PSYCHOLOGY

Palo Alto, California

Global Program

Institute of Transpersonal Psychology, founded in 1975, is an independent-nonprofit graduate institution. It is a candidate for accreditation by the Western Association of Schools and Colleges, Inc. It first offered distance learning courses in 1985. In 1996–97, it offered 30 courses at a distance. In the fall of 1996, there was a total of 120 students enrolled in distance learning courses.
Course delivery sites Courses are delivered to your home.
Media Courses are delivered via World Wide Web, e-mail, print. Students and teachers interact via mail, telephone, fax, e-mail. A computer is required for some courses.
Services Distance learners have access to library services, e-mail services, academic advising, tutoring at a distance.
Credit-earning options Students may transfer credits from another institution.
Typical costs Tuition of $774 per course. *Noncredit courses:* $475 per course. Financial aid is available to distance learners enrolled full-time.
Registration Students may register by mail, fax, phone, e-mail.
Contact Rita Kaufman, Admissions, Institute of Transpersonal Psychology, 744 San Antonio Road, Palo Alto, CA 94303. *Telephone:* 415-493-4430. *Fax:* 415-493-6835. *E-mail:* itpinfo@netcom.com. *Web site:* http://www.tmn.com/itp/index.html.

DEGREE & CERTIFICATE PROGRAMS

Graduate Degrees

▶ *Transpersonal Psychology (MTP)*
Application requirements *Prior education:* baccalaureate degree. *Other requirements:* college transcripts, an essay or personal statement, letter(s) of recommendation, an application fee of $50.
Completion requirements 54 units are required. 45 units must be completed through the institution. *Other requirements:* thesis. *Maximum time for completion:* 27 months.
On-campus requirements For seminar.

▶ *Transpersonal Studies (MA)*
Application requirements *Prior education:* baccalaureate degree. *Other requirements:* college transcripts, an essay or personal statement, letter(s) of recommendation, an application fee of $50.
Completion requirements 48 units are required. 42 units must be completed through the institution. *Other requirements:* application project.
On-campus requirements For seminar.

Undergraduate Certificates

▶ *Creative Expression*
Application requirements *Prior education:* high school diploma or equivalent. *Other requirements:* college transcripts, an essay or personal statement, letter(s) of recommendation, an application fee of $55.
Completion requirements 27 units are required. 27 units must be completed through the institution. *Other requirements:* creative expression portfolio. *Maximum time for completion:* one year.
On-campus requirements For seminar.

▶ *Spiritual Psychology*
Application requirements *Prior education:* high school diploma or equivalent. *Other requirements:* college transcripts, an essay or personal statement, letter(s) of recommendation, an application fee of $55.
Completion requirements 27 units are required. 27 units must be completed through the institution. *Maximum time for completion:* one year.
On-campus requirements For seminar.

▶ *Wellness-Body Mind Consciousness*
Application requirements *Prior education:* high school diploma or equivalent. *Other requirements:* high school transcript, an essay or personal statement, letter(s) of recommendation, an application fee of $50.
Completion requirements 27 units are required. 27 units must be completed through the institution. *Maximum time for completion:* one year.
On-campus requirements For seminar.

▶ *Women's Spiritual Development*
Application requirements *Prior education:* high school diploma or equivalent. *Other requirements:* college transcripts, an essay or personal statement, letter(s) of recommendation, an application fee of $50.
Completion requirements 27 units are required. 27 units must be completed through the institution. *Maximum time for completion:* one year.
On-campus requirements For seminar.

Graduate certificates

▶ *Transpersonal Studies*
In the fall of 1996 there were 120 students enrolled in this program. In 1995–96, 50 certificates were earned at a distance through this program.
Application requirements *Prior education:* baccalaureate degree. *Other requirements:* college transcripts, an essay or personal statement, letter(s) of recommendation, an application fee of $55.
Completion requirements 27 units are required. *Maximum time for completion:* one year.
On-campus requirements For seminar.

INDIVIDUAL COURSE SUBJECT AREAS

Graduate
Philosophy and religion; psychology

Noncredit
Philosophy and religion; psychology

INTERNATIONAL BIBLE COLLEGE

Florence, Alabama

Distance Learning

International Bible College, founded in 1971, is an independent-religious four-year college affiliated with the Church of Christ. It is accredited by the Accrediting Association of Bible Colleges. It first offered distance learning courses in 1992. In 1996–97, it offered 35 courses at a distance. In the fall of 1996, there was a total of 37 students enrolled in distance learning courses.

Course delivery sites Courses are delivered to your home.
Media Courses are delivered via videotapes. Students and teachers interact via telephone.
Restrictions Students must be able to travel to campus.
Services Distance learners have access to library services, academic advising, career placement assistance at a distance.
Credit-earning options Students may transfer credits from another institution or may earn credits through institutionally developed exams.
Typical costs Tuition of $149 per course. *Noncredit courses:* $92.50 per course. Financial aid is available to distance learners.
Registration Students may register by mail, phone.
Contact Admissions Office, International Bible College, PO Box IBC, Florence, AL 35630. *Telephone:* 800-367-3565. *Fax:* 205-760-0981.

DEGREE & CERTIFICATE PROGRAMS

Baccalaureate Degrees
▶ *Bible, Theology (BA)*
In the fall of 1996 there were 37 students enrolled in this program.
Application requirements *Prior education:* high school diploma or equivalent. *Other requirements:* high school transcript, college transcripts, letter(s) of recommendation.
Completion requirements 128 semester hours are required. 32 semester hours must be completed through the institution. This is a degree completion program.
On-campus requirements 14 hours offered in short term two-week courses in summer.
Program contact Jim Collins, Director of Admission Services, International Bible College, PO Box IBC, Florence, AL 35630. Phone: 800-367-3565. E-mail: jdcollinsadm@juno.comm.

INDIVIDUAL COURSE SUBJECT AREAS

Undergraduate
Classical languages and literatures; history; liberal arts, general studies, and humanities; philosophy and religion; psychology; theological studies

INTERNATIONAL UNIVERSITY

Englewood, Colorado

International University is an independent-nonprofit upper-level institution. It is a candidate for accreditation by the North Central Association of Colleges and Schools. It first offered distance learning courses in 1995. In 1996–97, it offered 32 courses at a distance. In the fall of 1996, there was a total of 99 students enrolled in distance learning courses.

Course delivery sites Courses are delivered to your home, your workplace, military bases, any location with Internet access.
Media Courses are delivered via television, videotapes, World Wide Web, e-mail. Students and teachers interact via telephone, fax, e-mail. A computer is required for all courses.
Services Distance learners have access to the campus computer network, e-mail services, academic advising at a distance.
Typical costs *Undergraduate:* Tuition of $600 per course plus mandatory fees of $25 per course. *Graduate:* Tuition of $700 per course plus mandatory fees of $25 per course. Students also pay a $35 processing fee and a $75 application fee. *Noncredit courses:* $600–$700 per course.
Registration Students may register by mail, fax, phone, e-mail, World Wide Web.
Contact Ms. Joy Aden, Manager, Enrollment and Student Services, International University, PO Box 6512, Englewood, CO 80155-6512. *Telephone:* 303-705-3153. *Fax:* 303-784-8547. *E-mail:* jaden@international.edu. *Web site:* http://www.international.edu.

Special note
International University offers 8-week intensive courses that combine the theoretical and the experiential, have articulated and well-planned outcomes, are collaborative in structure, are highly interactive and, most of all, focus on the motivated adult learner.

International University classes are offered over the Internet and Web and may be taken from any location and, within a focused academic structure, at the learner's convenience. Electronic mail permits constant and easy communication among the learners and faculty in these small classes.

The use of accessible technology that permits International University to operate also gives learners mastery of skills needed everywhere in the modern world.

DEGREE & CERTIFICATE PROGRAMS

Baccalaureate Degrees
▶ *Business Communication (BA)*
Application requirements *Prior education:* associate degree. *Other requirements:* college transcripts, an essay or personal statement, an application fee of $75, one writing sample.
Completion requirements 120 credits are required. 30 credits must be completed through the institution. *Maximum time for completion:* seven years.

Graduate Degrees
▶ *Business Communication (MA)*
Application requirements *Prior education:* baccalaureate degree. *Other requirements:* college transcripts, an application fee of $75.
Completion requirements 35 credits are required. 26 credits must be completed through the institution. *Maximum time for completion:* seven years.

INDIVIDUAL COURSE SUBJECT AREAS

Undergraduate
Business communications

Graduate
Business communications

Profiles: Iowa State University of Science and Technology

IOWA STATE UNIVERSITY OF SCIENCE AND TECHNOLOGY

Ames, Iowa

Extended and Continuing Education

Iowa State University of Science and Technology, founded in 1858, is a state-supported university. It is accredited by the North Central Association of Colleges and Schools. In 1996–97, it offered 65 courses at a distance. In the fall of 1996, there was a total of 215 students enrolled in distance learning courses.

Course delivery sites Courses are delivered to your home, your workplace, military bases, Iowa Area Community Colleges System (West Des Moines).

Media Courses are delivered via videotapes, videoconferencing, World Wide Web. Students and teachers interact via videoconferencing, mail, telephone, fax, e-mail. A computer is required for some courses.

Services Distance learners have access to library services, the campus computer network, e-mail services, academic advising, career placement assistance at a distance.

Credit-earning options Students may transfer credits from another institution or may earn credits through standardized exams.

Typical costs *Undergraduate:* Tuition of $107 per credit. *Graduate:* Tuition of $170 per credit. Costs may vary by course delivery options. Financial aid is available to distance learners enrolled full-time or part-time.

Registration Students may register by mail, fax, phone.

Contact Joyce Hanson, Secretary, Iowa State University of Science and Technology, 102 Scheman, Ames, IA 50011-1112. *Telephone:* 515-294-0013. *Fax:* 515-294-6146. *E-mail:* x1joyce@exnet.iastate.edu. *Web site:* http://www.exnet.iastate.edu/pages/ece/.

DEGREE & CERTIFICATE PROGRAMS

Baccalaureate Degrees

▶ *Professional Agriculture (BS)*

In the fall of 1996 there were 45 students enrolled in this program.
Application requirements *Prior education:* some undergraduate course work. *Other requirements:* college transcripts, an application fee of $20.
Completion requirements 128 credits are required. 32 credits must be completed through the institution. This is a degree completion program.
Program contact Helen Olson, PROAG Advisor, Iowa State University of Science and Technology, 206B Curtiss Hall, Ames, IA 50011. Phone: 515-294-1438. Fax: 515-294-0530. E-mail: holson@iastate.edu.

Graduate Degrees

▶ *Agriculture (MS)*

Application requirements *Prior education:* baccalaureate degree. *Other requirements:* ISU English exam, college transcripts, letter(s) of recommendation, an application fee of $20.
Completion requirements 32 credits are required. 22 credits must be completed through the institution.

▶ *Family and Consumer Sciences (MS)*

In the fall of 1996 there were 12 students enrolled in this program.
Restrictions This program is available to in-state students only.
Application requirements *Prior education:* baccalaureate degree. *Other requirements:* GRE, college transcripts, an essay or personal statement, letter(s) of recommendation, an application fee of $20, upper half of college class, TOEFL (for international students).
Completion requirements 36 credits are required. 22 credits must be completed through the institution. *Other requirements:* ISU English exam; written and oral final exam for non-thesis degree program. *Maximum time for completion:* five years.

Program contact Ceci Johnson, Administrative Specialist, Iowa State University of Science and Technology, 126 MacKay Hall, Ames, IA 50011. Phone: 515-294-0211. Fax: 515-294-9449. E-mail: cecijohn@iastate.edu.

▶ *School Mathematics (MS)*

In the fall of 1996 there were 35 students enrolled in this program.
Restrictions This program is available to in-state students only.
Application requirements *Prior education:* baccalaureate degree. *Other requirements:* ISU English exam, college transcripts, an essay or personal statement, letter(s) of recommendation, an application fee of $20, upper half of college graduating class.
Completion requirements 36 credits are required. 22 credits must be completed through the institution. *Other requirements:* 2-hour oral exam over course work and creative component. *Maximum time for completion:* five years.
Program contact Elgin Johnston, Professor, Iowa State University of Science and Technology, 400 Carver Hall, Ames, IA 50011. Phone: 515-294-7294. Fax: 515-294-5454. E-mail: ehjohnst@iastate.edu.

▶ *Systems Engineering (ME)*

In the fall of 1996 there were 10 students enrolled in this program.
Restrictions Program is available to US students only.
Application requirements *Prior education:* baccalaureate degree. *Other requirements:* college transcripts, an essay or personal statement, letter(s) of recommendation, an application fee of $20.
Completion requirements 30 credits are required. 22 credits must be completed through the institution. *Other requirements:* creative component or project. *Maximum time for completion:* five years.
On-campus requirements For defense of creative component or thesis.
Program contact Edwin Jones, Jr., Professor, Iowa State University of Science and Technology, 240 Engineering Annex, Ames, IA 50011-2077. Phone: 515-294-7470. Fax: 515-294-6184. E-mail: n2ecj@iastate.edu.

Graduate certificates

▶ *Public Management*

Restrictions This program is available to in-state students only.
Application requirements *Prior education:* baccalaureate degree. *Other requirements:* GRE, college transcripts, an essay or personal statement, letter(s) of recommendation, an application fee of $20, 3.0 GPA.
Completion requirements 15 credits are required.
Program contact Dianne Rahm, Director, Iowa State University of Science and Technology, 515 Ross Hall, Ames, IA 50011. Phone: 515-294-0586. E-mail: drahm@iastate.edu.

▶ *School Superintendent License*

Restrictions This program is available to in-state students only.
Application requirements *Prior education:* graduate degree. *Other requirements:* principal's certificate.
Completion requirements 30 credits are required.
Program contact Bill Poston, Associate Professor, Iowa State University of Science and Technology, N225 Lagomarcino, Ames, IA 50011. Phone: 515-294-9468. E-mail: wkposton@iastate.edu.

INDIVIDUAL COURSE SUBJECT AREAS

Undergraduate

Agricultural economics; agriculture; animal sciences; area, ethnic, and cultural studies; biochemistry; biology; business administration and management; computer and information sciences; electrical engineering; genetics; liberal arts, general studies, and humanities; marketing; mathematics; meteorology; microbiology; political science; public administration and services; Spanish language and literature; zoology

Graduate

Adult education; aerospace, aeronautical engineering; agricultural economics; agriculture; animal sciences; biochemistry; business administration and management; chemical engineering; child care and development; civil engineering; computer and information sciences; curriculum and instruction; education administration; electrical engineering; engineering mechanics; engineering/industrial management; genetics; home economics and family studies; individual and family development studies; industrial engineering; marketing; mathematics; mechanical engineering; meteorology; microbiology; political science; public administration and services; teacher education

Noncredit
Civil engineering

IOWA WESLEYAN COLLEGE

Mount Pleasant, Iowa

Office of Continuing Education

Iowa Wesleyan College, founded in 1842, is an independent-religious United Methodist four-year college. It is accredited by the North Central Association of Colleges and Schools.
Course delivery sites Courses are delivered to your home, your workplace, other colleges.
Media Courses are delivered via television, Iowa Communications Network. Students and teachers interact via mail, telephone, fax, Iowa Communications Network.
Restrictions Programs are available to in-state students only.
Services Distance learners have access to library services, academic advising at a distance.
Credit-earning options Students may transfer credits from another institution or may earn credits through examinations, portfolio assessment, military training.
Typical costs *Undergraduate:* Tuition of $180 per credit hour. *Graduate:* Tuition of $180 per credit hour. Financial aid is available to distance learners.
Contact David C. File, Director of Continuing Education, Iowa Wesleyan College, Assistant Vice President of Non-Traditional Programming, 601 North Main Street, Mount Pleasant, IA 52641-1398. *Telephone:* 319-385-6247. *Fax:* 319-385-6296.

INDIVIDUAL COURSE SUBJECT AREAS

Undergraduate
Business administration and management; fine arts; health and physical education/fitness; mathematics; psychology; sociology

IOWA WESTERN COMMUNITY COLLEGE

Council Bluffs, Iowa

Iowa Western Community College, founded in 1966, is a district-supported two-year college. It is accredited by the North Central Association of Colleges and Schools. It first offered distance learning courses in 1983. In 1996–97, it offered 20 courses at a distance. In the fall of 1996, there was a total of 120 students enrolled in distance learning courses.
Course delivery sites Courses are delivered to your home, your workplace, 4 off-campus centers in Atlantic, Clarinda, Harlan, Shenandoah.
Media Courses are delivered via television, videotapes, Iowa Communications Network. Students and teachers interact via mail, telephone, fax, e-mail, Iowa Communications Network.
Restrictions Courses are available to students in the state of Iowa or within the midwest only.
Services Distance learners have access to academic advising, career placement assistance at a distance.
Credit-earning options Students may transfer credits from another institution or may earn credits through standardized exams, institutionally developed exams, portfolio assessment, military training.
Typical costs Tuition of $65 per semester hour plus mandatory fees of $7 per semester hour for in-state residents. Tuition of $96.50 per semester hour plus mandatory fees of $7 per semester hour for out-of-state residents. Tuition given is for 1997-98. Financial aid is available to distance learners.
Registration Students may register by mail, phone.
Contact Dr. Bob Franzese, Dean, School of Arts and Sciences, Iowa Western Community College, 2700 College Road, Box 4-C, Council Bluffs, IA 51502. *Telephone:* 712-325-3257. *Fax:* 712-325-3717. *E-mail:* bfranzes@iwcc.cc.ia.us.

DEGREE & CERTIFICATE PROGRAMS

Associate Degrees
▶ *General Studies (AA)*
Application requirements *Prior education:* high school diploma or equivalent. *Other requirements:* ASSET, high school transcript, college transcripts.
Completion requirements 62 semester hours are required. 20 semester hours must be completed through the institution.
On-campus requirements Students may need to meet with individual instructors from time to time.

INDIVIDUAL COURSE SUBJECT AREAS

Undergraduate
Accounting; biology; chemistry; English language and literature; fine arts; geology; history; law and legal studies; liberal arts, general studies, and humanities; mathematics; microbiology; nursing; philosophy and religion; political science; public health; social work; sociology

ISIM UNIVERSITY

Denver, Colorado

ISIM University, founded in 1987, is an independent-nonprofit graduate institution. It is accredited by the Distance Education and Training Council. It first offered distance learning courses in 1992. In 1996–97, it offered 22 courses at a distance. In the fall of 1996, there was a total of 100 students enrolled in distance learning courses.
Course delivery sites Courses are delivered to your home, your workplace, military bases.
Media Courses are delivered via computer software, World Wide Web, e-mail, print. Students and teachers interact via mail, telephone, fax, e-mail. A computer is required for some courses.
Services Distance learners have access to e-mail services, academic advising at a distance.
Credit-earning options Students may transfer credits from another institution or may earn credits through examinations, portfolio assessment, military training, business training.
Typical costs Tuition of $375 per unit. Costs may vary by number of credits taken.
Registration Students may register by mail, fax, e-mail.
Contact Kevin Rendos, Account Manager, ISIM University, 501 South Cherry Street, Suite #350, Denver, CO 80222. *Telephone:* 303-333-4224. *Fax:* 303-336-1175. *E-mail:* admissions@isimu.edu. *Web site:* http://www.isimu.edu.

Profiles: ISIM University

DEGREE & CERTIFICATE PROGRAMS

Graduate Degrees

▶ *Business Administration (MBA)*
In the fall of 1996 there were 50 students enrolled in this program. In 1995–96, 1 degree was earned at a distance through this program.
Application requirements *Prior education:* undergraduate degree. *Other requirements:* college transcripts, letter(s) of recommendation, an application fee of $50, resume, goals statement.
Completion requirements 36 units are required.

▶ *Information Management (MS)*
In the fall of 1996 there were 50 students enrolled in this program. In 1995–96, 5 degrees were earned at a distance through this program.
Application requirements *Prior education:* undergraduate degree. *Other requirements:* college transcripts, letter(s) of recommendation, an application fee of $50, resume, goals statement.
Completion requirements 36 units are required.

INDIVIDUAL COURSE SUBJECT AREAS

Graduate

Accounting; business; business administration and management; computer and information sciences; human resources management

See full description on page 426.

IVY TECH STATE COLLEGE–NORTHCENTRAL

South Bend, Indiana

Instructional Technology

Ivy Tech State College–Northcentral, founded in 1968, is a state-supported two-year college. It is accredited by the North Central Association of Colleges and Schools. It first offered distance learning courses in 1989. In the fall of 1996, there was a total of 410 students enrolled in distance learning courses.
Course delivery sites Courses are delivered to your home, your workplace, Indiana State University (Terre Haute).
Media Courses are delivered via television, videotapes, videoconferencing. Students and teachers interact via audioconferencing, mail, telephone, fax, e-mail. A computer is required for some courses.
Restrictions Programs are available to in-state students only.
Services Distance learners have access to library services, the campus computer network, e-mail services, academic advising at a distance.
Credit-earning options Students may transfer credits from another institution or may earn credits through institutionally developed exams, portfolio assessment, military training.
Typical costs Tuition of $62.50 per credit hour. Financial aid is available to distance learners enrolled full-time.
Registration Students may register by phone.
Contact Elaine Bennington, Instructional Technologist, Ivy Tech State College–Northcentral, 1534 West Sample Street, South Bend, IN 46619. *Telephone:* 219-289-7001, Ext. 334. *Fax:* 219-236-7178. *E-mail:* ebenning@ivy.tec.in.us.

DEGREE & CERTIFICATE PROGRAMS

Undergraduate Certificates

▶ *Paralegal*
In the fall of 1996 there were 25 students enrolled in this program.
Application requirements *Prior education:* high school diploma or equivalent. *Other requirements:* ASSET, SAT, high school transcript.
Completion requirements 30 credits are required. *Other requirements:* students are required to attend labs and externships near receiving sites.
On-campus requirements One day.

▶ *Pharmacy Technician*
In the fall of 1996 there were 16 students enrolled in this program. In 1995–96, 10 certificates were earned at a distance through this program.
Application requirements *Prior education:* high school diploma or equivalent. *Other requirements:* ASSET, SAT, high school transcript.
Completion requirements 30 credits are required. *Other requirements:* students are required to attend labs and externships near receiving sites. *Maximum time for completion:* 4–5 semesters.
On-campus requirements One day.

INDIVIDUAL COURSE SUBJECT AREAS

Undergraduate

Administrative and secretarial services; advertising; biology; business administration and management; economics; engineering-related technologies; English composition; health professions and related sciences; law and legal studies; nursing; psychology; sociology

IVY TECH STATE COLLEGE–WABASH VALLEY

Terre Haute, Indiana

Ivy Tech State College–Wabash Valley, founded in 1966, is a state-supported two-year college. It is accredited by the North Central Association of Colleges and Schools. It first offered distance learning courses in 1996. In 1996–97, it offered 40 courses at a distance. In the fall of 1996, there was a total of 30 students enrolled in distance learning courses.
Course delivery sites Courses are delivered to your home, other colleges, any location with Internet access.
Media Courses are delivered via videoconferencing, World Wide Web, e-mail. Students and teachers interact via videoconferencing, e-mail, Internet. A computer is required for some courses.
Services Distance learners have access to library services, academic advising, tutoring at a distance.
Credit-earning options Students may transfer credits from another institution or may earn credits through examinations, portfolio assessment, military training, business training.
Typical costs Tuition of $62.50 per credit. Costs may vary by course delivery options. Financial aid is available to distance learners.
Registration Students may register by mail, e-mail, World Wide Web.
Contact Norma Cottrell, Director of Instruction, Ivy Tech State College–Wabash Valley, 7999 US Highway 41, S, Terre Haute, IN 47802. *Telephone:* 812-299-1121. *Fax:* 812-299-5723. *E-mail:* ncottrel@ivy.tec.in.us.

DEGREE & CERTIFICATE PROGRAMS

Associate Degrees

▶ *Accounting (AAS)*
Application requirements *Prior education:* high school diploma or equivalent. *Other requirements:* ASSET, SAT, ACT, high school transcript.
Completion requirements 60 credits are required.
Program contact Ron Deisher, Program Chair, Ivy Tech State College–Wabash Valley, 7999 US Highway 41, S, Terre Haute, IN 47802. E-mail: rdeisher@ivy.tec.in.us.

▶ *Business Management–Hospitality (AS)*
Application requirements *Prior education:* high school diploma or equivalent. *Other requirements:* ASSET, SAT, ACT, high school transcript.
Completion requirements 60 credits are required.

Program contact Janet Trout, Program Chair, Ivy Tech State College–Wabash Valley, 7999 US Highway 41, S, Terre Haute, IN 47802. E-mail: jtrout@ivy.tec.in.us.

▶ *Drafting/Design Technology (AAS)*
Application requirements *Prior education:* high school diploma or equivalent. *Other requirements:* ASSET, SAT, ACT, high school transcript.
Completion requirements 60 credits are required.
Program contact Mike Stolfe, Program Chair, Ivy Tech State College–Wabash Valley, 7999 US Highway 41, S, Terre Haute, IN 47802. E-mail: mstolfe@ivy.tec.in.us.

▶ *Manufacturing Technology (AAS)*
Application requirements *Prior education:* high school diploma or equivalent. *Other requirements:* ASSET, SAT, ACT, high school transcript.
Completion requirements 60 credits are required.
Program contact Don Arney, Instructional Affair Chair, Faculty and Curriculum Development, Ivy Tech State College–Wabash Valley, 7999 US Highway 41, S, Terre Haute, IN 47802. Phone: 812-299-1121. Fax: 812-299-5723. E-mail: darney@ivy.tec.in.us.

INDIVIDUAL COURSE SUBJECT AREAS

Undergraduate
Accounting; administrative and secretarial services; business; business administration and management; computer and information sciences; design; economics; English composition; hospitality services management; liberal arts, general studies, and humanities; mathematics; physics; social psychology; sociology

JACKSON COMMUNITY COLLEGE

Jackson, Michigan

Jackson Community College, founded in 1928, is a county-supported two-year college. It is accredited by the North Central Association of Colleges and Schools.
Course delivery sites Courses are delivered to your workplace, other colleges.
Media Courses are delivered via television, videotapes, videoconferencing.
Restrictions Programs are available to in-state students only.
Services Distance learners have access to library services at a distance.
Credit-earning options Students may transfer credits from another institution or may earn credits through examinations. Financial aid is available to distance learners.
Contact Media and Distance Learning Director, Jackson Community College, 2111 Emmons Road, Jackson, MI 49201. *Telephone:* 517-787-0800, Ext. 365. *Fax:* 517-787-1623.

DEGREE & CERTIFICATE PROGRAMS

Graduate Degrees
▶ *Business Administration (MBA)*
▶ *Nursing (MSN)*
Program contact Victoria Daulton, Regional Coordinator, Jackson Community College, 2111 Emmons Road, Jackson, MI 49201. Phone: 517-787-7265. Fax: 517-789-1633. E-mail: ced_moffett@online.emich.edu.

▶ *Quality (MA)*
Program contact Victoria Daulton, Regional Coordinator, Jackson Community College, 2111 Emmons Road, Jackson, MI 49201. Phone: 517-787-7265. Fax: 517-789-1633. E-mail: ced_moffett@online.emich.edu.

INDIVIDUAL COURSE SUBJECT AREAS

Undergraduate
Advertising; business; business administration and management; educational psychology; health professions and related sciences

Graduate
Business administration and management

JACKSONVILLE STATE UNIVERSITY

Jacksonville, Alabama

Jacksonville State University, founded in 1883, is a state-supported comprehensive institution. It is accredited by the Southern Association of Colleges and Schools. It first offered distance learning courses in 1994. In 1996–97, it offered 20 courses at a distance. In the fall of 1996, there was a total of 525 students enrolled in distance learning courses.
Course delivery sites Courses are delivered to your home, 1 off-campus center in Gadsden.
Media Courses are delivered via videotapes, videoconferencing, World Wide Web. Students and teachers interact via videoconferencing, mail, telephone, e-mail. A computer is required for some courses.
Restrictions Programs are available to local area students only.
Services Distance learners have access to library services, the campus computer network, e-mail services at a distance.
Credit-earning options Students may transfer credits from another institution or may earn credits through institutionally developed exams, portfolio assessment, military training.
Typical costs Contact school for information. Financial aid is available to distance learners enrolled full-time or part-time.
Registration Students may register by phone, World Wide Web.
Contact Dr. Franklin L. King, Director, Instructional Services Unit, Jacksonville State University, 700 Pelham Road, N, Jacksonville, AL 36265. *Telephone:* 205-782-5616. *Fax:* 205-782-5169. *E-mail:* fking@jsucc.jsu.edu. *Web site:* http://jsucc.jsu.edu/depart/distance.

DEGREE & CERTIFICATE PROGRAMS

Associate Degrees
▶ *General Studies (AA)*
In the fall of 1996 there were 215 students enrolled in this program.
Restrictions Students must be US citizens and have been a legal Alabama resident for 1 year.
Application requirements *Prior education:* high school diploma or equivalent. *Other requirements:* ACT or SAT, high school transcript.
Completion requirements 64 credit hours are required. *Other requirements:* this program is offered jointly with Gadsden State Community College.
On-campus requirements Limited number of on-campus meetings.

INDIVIDUAL COURSE SUBJECT AREAS

Undergraduate
Anthropology; business administration and management; computer and information sciences; developmental and child psychology; English language and literature; geology; health and physical education/fitness; history; mathematics; political science; sociology; special education

Graduate
Education administration; educational psychology; teacher education

Profiles: Jamestown Community College

JAMESTOWN COMMUNITY COLLEGE

Jamestown, New York

Distance Education

Jamestown Community College, founded in 1950, is a state and locally supported two-year college. It is accredited by the Middle States Association of Colleges and Schools. It first offered distance learning courses in 1995. In 1996–97, it offered 13 courses at a distance. In the fall of 1996, there was a total of 145 students enrolled in distance learning courses.
Course delivery sites Courses are delivered to your home, 2 off-campus centers in Dunkirk, Olean, area high schools.
Media Courses are delivered via videoconferencing. Students and teachers interact via videoconferencing, mail, telephone, fax, e-mail.
Services Distance learners have access to library services, the campus computer network, e-mail services at a distance.
Typical costs Tuition of $88 per credit hour for in-state residents. Tuition of $154 per credit hour for out-of-state residents. *Noncredit courses:* $40 per course. Costs may vary by number of credits taken. Financial aid is available to distance learners enrolled full-time or part-time.
Registration Students may register by mail.
Contact Admissions Office, Jamestown Community College, 525 Falconer Street, Jamestown, NY 14702-0020. *Telephone:* 716-665-5220, Ext. 239. *Fax:* 716-664-9592. *Web site:* http://143.67.10.37.

INDIVIDUAL COURSE SUBJECT AREAS

Undergraduate

Accounting; astronomy and astrophysics; business administration and management; chemistry; computer and information sciences; fine arts; human resources management; music; philosophy and religion; sociology

JEFFERSON COLLEGE

Hillsboro, Missouri

Learning Resources

Jefferson College, founded in 1963, is a state and locally supported two-year college. It is accredited by the North Central Association of Colleges and Schools. It first offered distance learning courses in 1984. In 1996–97, it offered 16 courses at a distance. In the fall of 1996, there was a total of 326 students enrolled in distance learning courses.
Course delivery sites Courses are delivered to your home.
Media Courses are delivered via television, videotapes. Students and teachers interact via mail, telephone, in-person meetings.
Restrictions Courses are available to students in Missouri and Illinois only.
Services Distance learners have access to library services, academic advising at a distance.
Credit-earning options Students may transfer credits from another institution or may earn credits through standardized exams, institutionally developed exams.
Typical costs Tuition of $40 per credit plus mandatory fees of $3 per credit for local area residents. Tuition of $52 per credit plus mandatory fees of $3 per credit for in-state residents. Tuition of $61 per credit plus mandatory fees of $3 per credit for out-of-state residents. Students pay an additional $40 telecourse fee. Costs may vary by course delivery options. Financial aid is available to distance learners enrolled full-time or part-time.
Registration Students may register by mail, fax, phone.
Contact Linda Bigelow, Director - Learning Resources, Jefferson College, 1000 Viking Drive, Hillsboro, MO 63050-2441. *Telephone:* 314-797-3000, Ext. 162. *Fax:* 314-797-3954. *E-mail:* lbigelow@gateway.jeffco.edu.

INDIVIDUAL COURSE SUBJECT AREAS

Undergraduate

Algebra; American (US) history; biology; business; economics; English composition; English language and literature; French language and literature; health and physical education/fitness; psychology; sociology; Spanish language and literature

JEFFERSON COMMUNITY COLLEGE

Watertown, New York

Division of Continuing Education

Jefferson Community College, founded in 1961, is a state and locally supported two-year college. It is accredited by the Middle States Association of Colleges and Schools. It first offered distance learning courses in 1995. In 1996–97, it offered 4 courses at a distance. In the fall of 1996, there was a total of 20 students enrolled in distance learning courses.
Course delivery sites Courses are delivered to your home.
Media Courses are delivered via television. Students and teachers interact via mail, telephone, in-person meetings.
Restrictions Programs are available to local area students only.
Services Distance learners have access to library services, academic advising, tutoring at a distance.
Credit-earning options Students may transfer credits from another institution or may earn credits through standardized exams, military training.
Typical costs Tuition of $84 per credit hour. Costs may vary by number of credits taken. Financial aid is available to distance learners.
Registration Students may register by mail.
Contact Barry Jennison, Associate Dean for Continuing Education, Jefferson Community College, Coffeen Street, Watertown, NY 13601. *Telephone:* 315-786-2238. *Fax:* 315-786-2391.

INDIVIDUAL COURSE SUBJECT AREAS

Undergraduate

European history; political science; psychology; sociology

JEFFERSON DAVIS COMMUNITY COLLEGE

Brewton, Alabama

Jefferson Davis Community College, founded in 1965, is a state-supported two-year college. It is accredited by the Southern Association of Colleges and Schools. It first offered distance learning courses in 1994. In 1996–97, it offered 4 courses at a distance. In the fall of 1996, there was a total of 104 students enrolled in distance learning courses.
Course delivery sites Courses are delivered to 2 off-campus centers in Atmore, Brewton.
Media Courses are delivered via videoconferencing. Students and teachers interact via videoconferencing.

Restrictions Programs are available to local area students only.
Services Distance learners have access to library services, academic advising, tutoring, career placement assistance at a distance.
Credit-earning options Students may transfer credits from another institution or may earn credits through military training.
Typical costs Tuition of $25 per credit hour plus mandatory fees of $10 per credit hour for in-state residents. Tuition of $50 per credit hour plus mandatory fees of $10 per credit hour for out-of-state residents. Costs may vary by number of credits taken. Financial aid is available to distance learners enrolled full-time or part-time.
Contact Kathleen V. Hall, Director of Special Programs, Jefferson Davis Community College, PO Box 1119, Atmore, AL 36504. *Telephone:* 334-368-7631. *Fax:* 334-368-8211.

INDIVIDUAL COURSE SUBJECT AREAS

Undergraduate
Accounting; administrative and secretarial services; business; economics; history; law and legal studies; political science; psychology; statistics

JEFFERSON STATE COMMUNITY COLLEGE

Birmingham, Alabama

Special Studies

Jefferson State Community College, founded in 1965, is a state-supported two-year college. It is accredited by the Southern Association of Colleges and Schools. It first offered distance learning courses in 1978.
Course delivery sites Courses are delivered to your home.
Media Courses are delivered via television, videoconferencing, World Wide Web, e-mail, print. Students and teachers interact via videoconferencing, mail, telephone, fax, e-mail.
Services Distance learners have access to library services, academic advising at a distance.
Credit-earning options Students may transfer credits from another institution or may earn credits through examinations, military training.
Typical costs Tuition of $25 per quarter hour plus mandatory fees of $9 per quarter hour for in-state residents. Tuition of $50 per quarter hour plus mandatory fees of $9 per quarter hour for out-of-state residents. Costs may vary by number of credits taken. Financial aid is available to distance learners.
Contact Charles S. Cobb, Jr., Director, Media Services, Jefferson State Community College, 2601 Carson Road, Birmingham, AL 35215. *Telephone:* 205-856-6057. *Fax:* 205-853-0340.

INDIVIDUAL COURSE SUBJECT AREAS

Undergraduate
Area, ethnic, and cultural studies; business administration and management; health and physical education/fitness; history; liberal arts, general studies, and humanities; political science; psychology; sociology; visual and performing arts

JOHN A. LOGAN COLLEGE

Carterville, Illinois

Learning Resources

John A. Logan College, founded in 1967, is a state and locally supported two-year college. It is accredited by the North Central Association of Colleges and Schools. It first offered distance learning courses in 1979. In 1996–97, it offered 37 courses at a distance. In the fall of 1996, there was a total of 500 students enrolled in distance learning courses.
Course delivery sites Courses are delivered to your home, your workplace, other colleges.
Media Courses are delivered via videotapes, videoconferencing, print. Students and teachers interact via videoconferencing, telephone, fax, e-mail.
Restrictions Programs are available to in-state students only.
Services Distance learners have access to library services at a distance.
Credit-earning options Students may transfer credits from another institution or may earn credits through examinations, military training.
Typical costs Tuition of $32 per credit hour. Financial aid is available to distance learners.
Contact Thomas L. Bell, Director, Media Services and Telecommunications, John A. Logan College, Route 2, Carterville, IL 62918. *Telephone:* 618-985-3741, Ext. 270. *Fax:* 618-985-3899. *E-mail:* tombell@jal.cc.il.us. *Web site:* http://www.jal.cc.il.us.

INDIVIDUAL COURSE SUBJECT AREAS

Undergraduate
Accounting; business administration and management; developmental and child psychology; electrical engineering; English language and literature; health professions and related sciences; history; journalism; social psychology

JOHN C. CALHOUN STATE COMMUNITY COLLEGE

Decatur, Alabama

Telecourse Program

John C. Calhoun State Community College, founded in 1965, is a state-supported two-year college. It is accredited by the Southern Association of Colleges and Schools. It first offered distance learning courses in 1992. In 1996–97, it offered 35 courses at a distance. In the fall of 1996, there was a total of 1,000 students enrolled in distance learning courses.
Course delivery sites Courses are delivered to your home, military bases, 1 off-campus center in Huntsville.
Media Courses are delivered via videotapes, audiotapes, computer software. Students and teachers interact via mail, telephone, fax, e-mail. A computer is required for some courses.
Restrictions Programs are primarily available to in-district students.
Services Distance learners have access to library services, e-mail services at a distance.
Credit-earning options Students may transfer credits from another institution or may earn credits through standardized exams, military training.

Profiles: John C. Calhoun State Community College

Typical costs Tuition of $145 per course for local area residents. Tuition of $265 per course for in-state residents. Financial aid is available to distance learners.
Registration Students may register by mail, phone.
Contact Dr. Chris Hamilton, Director of Special Projects, John C. Calhoun State Community College, PO Box 2216, Decatur, AL 35609-2216. *Telephone:* 205-306-2620. *Fax:* 205-306-2507. *E-mail:* cth@calhoun.cc.al.us.

INDIVIDUAL COURSE SUBJECT AREAS

Undergraduate
Area, ethnic, and cultural studies; business; business administration and management; computer and information sciences; design; English composition; English language and literature; European languages and literatures; fine arts; health and physical education/fitness; history; human resources management; law and legal studies; mathematics; music; psychology; social sciences; sociology; statistics; visual and performing arts

JOHNS HOPKINS UNIVERSITY

Baltimore, Maryland

Johns Hopkins University, founded in 1876, is an independent-nonprofit university. It is accredited by the Middle States Association of Colleges and Schools. It first offered distance learning courses in 1995. In 1996–97, it offered 18 courses at a distance. In the fall of 1996, there was a total of 380 students enrolled in distance learning courses.
Course delivery sites Courses are delivered to other colleges.
Media Courses are delivered via television, videotapes, videoconferencing, audiotapes, audioconferencing, computer software, World Wide Web. Students and teachers interact via videoconferencing, audioconferencing, e-mail. A computer is required for some courses.
Services Distance learners have access to library services, the campus computer network, e-mail services at a distance.
Credit-earning options Students may earn credits through examinations.
Typical costs *Undergraduate:* Tuition of $695 per credit. *Graduate:* Tuition of $695 per credit. Financial aid is available to distance learners enrolled full-time.
Registration Students may register by mail.
Contact Robert Lawrence, Associate Dean, Professional Education, Johns Hopkins University, School of Hygiene and Public Health, 3400 North Charles Street, Baltimore, MD 21218. *Telephone:* 410-614-4590. *Fax:* 410-955-8126. *E-mail:* rlawrence@phnet.sph.jhu.edu.

DEGREE & CERTIFICATE PROGRAMS

Graduate certificates
▶ *Public Health*
Application requirements *Prior education:* baccalaureate degree. *Other requirements:* college transcripts, an application fee.
Completion requirements 35 credits are required. 35 credits must be completed through the institution. *Maximum time for completion:* one year.
On-campus requirements Two-week on-campus blocks.

JOHNSON BIBLE COLLEGE

Knoxville, Tennessee

Distance Learning Office

Johnson Bible College, founded in 1893, is an independent-religious comprehensive institution affiliated with the Christian Churches and Churches of Christ. It is accredited by the Southern Association of Colleges and Schools. It first offered distance learning courses in 1988. In 1996–97, it offered 16 courses at a distance. In the fall of 1996, there was a total of 50 students enrolled in distance learning courses.
Course delivery sites Courses are delivered to your home.
Media Courses are delivered via videotapes, print. Students and teachers interact via mail, telephone, fax, e-mail.
Services Distance learners have access to library services, academic advising at a distance.
Credit-earning options Students may transfer credits from another institution.
Typical costs Tuition of $125 per credit hour.
Registration Students may register by mail.
Contact John C. Ketchen, Director of Distance Learning, Johnson Bible College, Box 777031, Knoxville, TN 37998. *Telephone:* 423-579-2254. *Fax:* 423-579-2285. *E-mail:* jketchen@ashley.jbc.edu.

DEGREE & CERTIFICATE PROGRAMS

Graduate Degrees
▶ *New Testament (MA)*
In the fall of 1996 there were 50 students enrolled in this program. In 1995–96, 5 degrees were earned at a distance through this program.
Application requirements *Prior education:* baccalaureate degree. *Other requirements:* GRE, college transcripts, an essay or personal statement, letter(s) of recommendation, an application fee of $15.
Completion requirements 30 credit hours are required. 21 credit hours must be completed through the institution. *Maximum time for completion:* six years.
On-campus requirements Five days.

INDIVIDUAL COURSE SUBJECT AREAS

Graduate
Theological studies

JOHNSON COUNTY COMMUNITY COLLEGE

Overland Park, Kansas

Johnson County Community College, founded in 1967, is a state and locally supported two-year college. It is accredited by the North Central Association of Colleges and Schools. It first offered distance learning courses in 1975. In 1996–97, it offered 55 courses at a distance. In the fall of 1996, there was a total of 900 students enrolled in distance learning courses.
Course delivery sites Courses are delivered to your home.
Media Courses are delivered via television, videotapes, videoconferencing, World Wide Web, e-mail, print. Students and teachers interact via videoconferencing, mail, telephone, fax, e-mail. A computer is required for some courses.
Services Distance learners have access to library services, e-mail services at a distance.

Credit-earning options Students may transfer credits from another institution or may earn credits through standardized exams, institutionally developed exams, portfolio assessment, military training.
Typical costs Tuition of $46 per credit hour for local area residents. Tuition of $122 per credit hour for in-state residents. Tuition of $122 per credit hour for out-of-state residents. Financial aid is available to distance learners enrolled full-time.
Registration Students may register by phone, World Wide Web.
Contact Mel Cunningham, Assistant Dean, Educational Media Center, Johnson County Community College, 12345 College Boulevard, Overland Park, KS 66210-1289. *Telephone:* 913-469-8500, Ext. 3288. *Fax:* 913-469-4417. *E-mail:* mcunning@johnco.cc.ks.us.

INDIVIDUAL COURSE SUBJECT AREAS

Undergraduate
Accounting; American (US) history; biology; business; chemistry; computer and information sciences; economics; English composition; environmental science; geology; health and physical education/fitness; liberal arts, general studies, and humanities; marketing; oceanography; philosophy and religion; psychology; sociology

JOHN WOOD COMMUNITY COLLEGE

Quincy, Illinois

John Wood Community College, founded in 1974, is a district-supported two-year college. It is accredited by the North Central Association of Colleges and Schools. It first offered distance learning courses in 1987. In 1996–97, it offered 40 courses at a distance. In the fall of 1996, there was a total of 200 students enrolled in distance learning courses.
Course delivery sites Courses are delivered to other colleges, 2 off-campus centers in Mount Sterling, Pittsfield.
Media Courses are delivered via videotapes, videoconferencing, audiotapes. Students and teachers interact via videoconferencing, telephone, fax, e-mail.
Services Distance learners have access to library services, academic advising, tutoring, career placement assistance at a distance.
Credit-earning options Students may transfer credits from another institution or may earn credits through examinations, portfolio assessment, military training.
Typical costs Tuition of $51 per credit hour. *Noncredit courses:* $20 per course. Financial aid is available to distance learners enrolled full-time or part-time.
Registration Students may register by mail, phone.
Contact Mark McNett, Admissions, John Wood Community College, 150 South 48th Street, Quincy, IL 62301. *Telephone:* 217-224-6500. *Fax:* 217-224-4339. *E-mail:* mcnett@jwcc.edu.

INDIVIDUAL COURSE SUBJECT AREAS

Undergraduate
Astronomy and astrophysics; biological and life sciences; business administration and management; economics; European languages and literatures; industrial psychology; liberal arts, general studies, and humanities; mathematics; political science; social psychology; social sciences; teacher education

JOLIET JUNIOR COLLEGE

Joliet, Illinois

Distance Education Office

Joliet Junior College, founded in 1901, is a state and locally supported two-year college. It is accredited by the North Central Association of Colleges and Schools. It first offered distance learning courses in 1988. In 1996–97, it offered 35 courses at a distance. In the fall of 1996, there was a total of 227 students enrolled in distance learning courses.
Course delivery sites Courses are delivered to your home, your workplace, College of St. Francis (Joliet), Governors State University (University Park), Kankakee Community College (Kankakee), Lewis University (Romeoville), Moraine Valley Community College (Palos Hills), Olivet Nazarene University (Kankakee), Prairie State College (Chicago Heights), Saint Xavier University (Chicago), South Suburban College (South Holland), 3 off-campus centers in Coal City, Morris, Romeoville.
Media Courses are delivered via videotapes, videoconferencing. Students and teachers interact via videoconferencing, mail, telephone, fax, e-mail.
Services Distance learners have access to library services, e-mail services at a distance.
Credit-earning options Students may transfer credits from another institution or may earn credits through standardized exams, institutionally developed exams, portfolio assessment.
Typical costs Tuition of $143 per course. Costs may vary by campus or location, number of credits taken. Financial aid is available to distance learners enrolled full-time or part-time.
Registration Students may register by phone.
Contact Dr. Robert E. Sterling, Director of Distance Education, Joliet Junior College, 1215 Houbolt Road, Joliet, IL 60431. *Telephone:* 815-773-6613. *Fax:* 815-725-0422. *E-mail:* rsterlin@jjc.cc.il.us.

INDIVIDUAL COURSE SUBJECT AREAS

Undergraduate
Agriculture; biology; business; communications; German language and literature; history; hospitality services management; liberal arts, general studies, and humanities; marketing; mathematics; music; political science; psychology; real estate; social sciences; sociology; Spanish language and literature

J. SARGEANT REYNOLDS COMMUNITY COLLEGE

Richmond, Virginia

Division of Instructional Technologies and Distance Education

J. Sargeant Reynolds Community College, founded in 1972, is a state-supported two-year college. It is accredited by the Southern Association of Colleges and Schools. It first offered distance learning courses in 1982.
Course delivery sites Courses are delivered to your home, other colleges, high schools.
Media Courses are delivered via television, videotapes, videoconferencing, audioconferencing, computer software, World Wide Web, e-mail, print, audiographics conferencing. Students and teachers interact via videoconferencing, audioconferencing, mail, telephone, fax, e-mail, audiographics conferencing.

Profiles: J. Sargeant Reynolds Community College

Services Distance learners have access to library services, academic advising, tutoring, career placement assistance at a distance.
Credit-earning options Students may transfer credits from another institution or may earn credits through examinations.
Typical costs Tuition of $49 per semester credit plus mandatory fees of $2.40 per credit for in-state residents. Tuition of $158.40 per semester credit plus mandatory fees of $2.40 per credit for out-of-state residents. Financial aid is available to distance learners.
Contact Mark S. Raby, Director of Instructional Technologies and Distance Education, J. Sargeant Reynolds Community College, PO Box 85622, Richmond, VA 23285-5622. *Telephone:* 804-371-3612. *Fax:* 804-371-3414. *E-mail:* srrabym@jsr.cc.va.us. *Web site:* http://www.jsr.cc.va.us/cpd/cpd_09.htm.

DEGREE & CERTIFICATE PROGRAMS

Associate Degrees

▶ *Opticianry, Respiratory Therapy (AAS)*
Restrictions This program is available to in-state students only.
Application requirements *Prior education:* high school diploma or equivalent. *Minimum age:* 18. *Other requirements:* high school transcript, college transcripts, letter(s) of recommendation, general education classes.
Completion requirements 71 credits are required. *Maximum time for completion:* two years.
On-campus requirements For clinicals.
Program contact Don O'Donohue, Program Head, J. Sargeant Reynolds Community College, PO Box 85622, Richmond, VA 23285. Phone: 804-786-3009. E-mail: srodond@jsr.cc.va.us.

INDIVIDUAL COURSE SUBJECT AREAS

Undergraduate

Abnormal psychology; accounting; business; business administration and management; calculus; chemistry; computer and information sciences; creative writing; developmental and child psychology; economics; engineering-related technologies; English composition; English language and literature; European languages and literatures; health professions and related sciences; history; liberal arts, general studies, and humanities; mathematics; nursing; political science; protective services; sociology

JUDSON COLLEGE

Marion, Alabama

External Degree Program

Judson College, founded in 1838, is an independent-religious Baptist four-year college. It is accredited by the Southern Association of Colleges and Schools. It first offered distance learning courses in 1976. In 1996–97, it offered 30 courses at a distance. In the fall of 1996, there was a total of 65 students enrolled in distance learning courses.
Course delivery sites Courses are delivered to your home.
Media Courses are delivered via print. Students and teachers interact via mail, telephone, fax, e-mail. A computer is required for some courses.
Restrictions Students must be able to travel to campus. No international students may enroll.
Services Distance learners have access to academic advising at a distance.
Credit-earning options Students may transfer credits from another institution or may earn credits through standardized exams, institutionally developed exams, portfolio assessment, military training, business training.
Typical costs Tuition of $194 per semester hour. Financial aid is available to distance learners.
Registration Students may register by mail, fax.
Contact Dr. N. Christine Henson, Director of External Studies, Judson College, PO Box 120, Marion, AL 36756. *Telephone:* 800-447-9472, Ext. 123. *Fax:* 334-683-5147. *E-mail:* admissions@future.judson.edu.

DEGREE & CERTIFICATE PROGRAMS

Baccalaureate Degrees

▶ *Business (BA, BS)*
Application requirements *Prior education:* high school diploma or equivalent. *Minimum age:* 22. *Other requirements:* high school transcript, college transcripts, an essay or personal statement, an application fee of $40.
Completion requirements 128 credits are required. 32 must be completed through the institution. *Other requirements:* 36 semester hours plus a minor in another discipline.
On-campus requirements One day.

▶ *Criminal Justice (BA, BS)*
In the fall of 1996 there were 65 students enrolled in this program. In 1995–96, 3 degrees were earned at a distance through this program.
Application requirements *Prior education:* high school diploma or equivalent. *Minimum age:* 22. *Other requirements:* high school transcript, college transcripts, an essay or personal statement, an application fee of $40.
Completion requirements 128 credits are required. 32 must be completed through the institution. *Other requirements:* 33 semester hours plus a minor in another discipline.
On-campus requirements One day.

▶ *English (BA)*
In the fall of 1996 there were 65 students enrolled in this program. In 1995–96, 3 degrees were earned at a distance through this program.
Application requirements *Prior education:* high school diploma or equivalent. *Minimum age:* 22. *Other requirements:* high school transcript, college transcripts, an essay or personal statement, an application fee of $40.
Completion requirements 128 credits are required. 32 must be completed through the institution. *Other requirements:* 36 semester hours for major, plus a minor in another discipline.
On-campus requirements One day.

▶ *History (BA)*
In the fall of 1996 there were 65 students enrolled in this program. In 1995–96, 3 degrees were earned at a distance through this program.
Application requirements *Prior education:* high school diploma or equivalent. *Minimum age:* 22. *Other requirements:* high school transcript, college transcripts, an essay or personal statement, an application fee of $40.
Completion requirements 128 credits are required. 32 must be completed through the institution. *Other requirements:* 30 semester hours for major, plus a minor in another discipline.
On-campus requirements One day.

▶ *Ministry Studies (BA, BMin)*
In the fall of 1996 there were 63 students enrolled in this program. In 1995–96, 5 degrees were earned at a distance through this program.
Restrictions Students must be jointly enrolled in the Seminary Extension program of the six Southern Baptist Seminaries.
Application requirements *Prior education:* high school diploma or equivalent. *Minimum age:* 22. *Other requirements:* high school transcript, college transcripts, an essay or personal statement, an application fee of $40.
Completion requirements 128 credits are required. 20 must be completed through the institution. *Other requirements:* 36 semester hours in ministry studies, plus a minor in another discipline. For a Bachelor of Ministry degree, the minor must be Ministry Skills Studies.
On-campus requirements One day.

▶ *Music (BA)*
In the fall of 1996 there were 65 students enrolled in this program. In 1995–96, 3 degrees were earned at a distance through this program.
Application requirements *Prior education:* high school diploma or equivalent. *Minimum age:* 22. *Other requirements:* high school transcript, college transcripts, an essay or personal statement, an application fee of $40.
Completion requirements 128 credits are required. 32 must be completed through the institution.
On-campus requirements One day.

▶ *Psychology (BA, BS)*
In the fall of 1996 there were 65 students enrolled in this program. In 1995–96, 3 degrees were earned at a distance through this program.
Application requirements *Prior education:* high school diploma or equivalent. *Minimum age:* 22. *Other requirements:* high school transcript, college transcripts, an essay or personal statement, an application fee of $40.
Completion requirements 128 credits are required. 32 must be completed through the institution. *Other requirements:* 30 semester hours for major, plus a minor in another discipline.
On-campus requirements One day.

▶ *Religious Studies (BA)*
In the fall of 1996 there were 65 students enrolled in this program. In 1995–96, 3 degrees were earned at a distance through this program.
Application requirements *Prior education:* high school diploma or equivalent. *Minimum age:* 22. *Other requirements:* high school transcript, college transcripts, an application fee of $40.
Completion requirements 128 credits are required. 32 must be completed through the institution. *Other requirements:* 30 semester hours for major, plus a minor in another discipline.
On-campus requirements One day.

▶ *Technical Communications/Journalism (BA)*
Application requirements *Prior education:* high school diploma or equivalent. *Minimum age:* 22. *Other requirements:* high school transcript, college transcripts, an essay or personal statement, an application fee of $40.
Completion requirements 128 credits are required. 32 must be completed through the institution.
On-campus requirements One day.

INDIVIDUAL COURSE SUBJECT AREAS

Undergraduate
Biochemistry; biology; business; computer and information sciences; creative writing; educational psychology; English composition; English language and literature; fine arts; history; journalism; music; philosophy and religion; political science; psychology; sociology; technical writing; theological studies; women's studies

JUNIATA COLLEGE

Huntingdon, Pennsylvania

Juniata College, founded in 1876, is an independent-nonprofit four-year college. It is accredited by the Middle States Association of Colleges and Schools. It first offered distance learning courses in 1995.
Course delivery sites Courses are delivered to 26 members of CAPE (Council for Agile Pennsylvania Education).
Media Courses are delivered via videoconferencing. Students and teachers interact via videoconferencing, mail, telephone, fax, e-mail.
Restrictions Courses are available to students at other participating colleges only.

Services Distance learners have access to library services, academic advising, tutoring, career placement assistance at a distance.
Credit-earning options Students may transfer credits from another institution or may earn credits through examinations.
Typical costs Tuition of $16,980 per year. Financial aid is available to distance learners.
Contact David Hawsey, Dean of Enrollment, Juniata College, 1700 Moore Street, Huntingdon, PA 16652. *Telephone:* 814-641-3425. *Fax:* 814-641-3100.

INDIVIDUAL COURSE SUBJECT AREAS

Undergraduate
European languages and literatures; political science

KANKAKEE COMMUNITY COLLEGE

Kankakee, Illinois

Office of Instruction and Workforce Development

Kankakee Community College, founded in 1966, is a state and locally supported two-year college. It is accredited by the North Central Association of Colleges and Schools. It first offered distance learning courses in 1995. In 1996–97, it offered 4 courses at a distance. In the fall of 1996, there was a total of 30 students enrolled in distance learning courses.
Course delivery sites Courses are delivered to Joliet Junior College (Joliet), Prairie State College (Chicago Heights), South Suburban College (South Holland), 3 off-campus centers in Clifton, Herscher, Watseka.
Media Courses are delivered via videotapes, videoconferencing. Students and teachers interact via videoconferencing, telephone, fax, in-person meetings.
Services Distance learners have access to academic advising at a distance.
Credit-earning options Students may transfer credits from another institution or may earn credits through examinations, military training.
Typical costs Tuition of $35.50 per semester hour plus mandatory fees of $2.50 per semester hour. *Noncredit courses:* $60 per course. Financial aid is available to distance learners enrolled full-time or part-time.
Registration Students may register by phone.
Contact Sam Hill, Vice President for Instruction and Workforce Development, Kankakee Community College, PO Box 888, River Road, Kankakee, IL 60901. *Telephone:* 815-933-0207. *Fax:* 815-933-0217.

INDIVIDUAL COURSE SUBJECT AREAS

Undergraduate
Biology; business administration and management; criminal justice; English language and literature; mathematics; psychology

KANSAS STATE UNIVERSITY

Manhattan, Kansas

Division of Continuing Education, Academic Services

Kansas State University, founded in 1863, is a state-supported university. It is accredited by the North Central Association of Colleges and Schools. It first offered distance learning courses in 1919. In 1996–97, it offered 142 courses at a distance. In the fall of 1996, there was a total of 701 students enrolled in distance learning courses.
Course delivery sites Courses are delivered to your home, your workplace, military bases, other colleges.

Profiles: Kansas State University

Media Courses are delivered via videotapes, videoconferencing, audiotapes, audioconferencing, computer software, World Wide Web, e-mail, print. Students and teachers interact via videoconferencing, audioconferencing, mail, telephone, fax, e-mail. A computer is required for some courses.
Services Distance learners have access to library services, the campus computer network, e-mail services, academic advising, career placement assistance at a distance.
Credit-earning options Students may transfer credits from another institution or may earn credits through standardized exams, institutionally developed exams, portfolio assessment, military training.
Typical costs *Undergraduate:* Tuition of $85 per semester hour plus mandatory fees of $6 per course. *Graduate:* Tuition of $125 per semester hour plus mandatory fees of $6 per course. *Noncredit courses:* $85 semester hour, plus fees of $6.50 per course. Costs may vary by course delivery options. Financial aid is available to distance learners enrolled full-time or part-time.
Registration Students may register by mail, fax, phone, World Wide Web.
Contact Academic Services, Kansas State University, Division of Continuing Education, 131 College Court, Manhattan, KS 66506. *Telephone:* 800-622-2KSU. *Fax:* 913-532-5637. *E-mail:* academic/services@dce.ksu.edu. *Web site:* http://www.dce.ksu.edu.

DEGREE & CERTIFICATE PROGRAMS

Baccalaureate Degrees

▶*Animal Science and Industry (BS)*
In the fall of 1996 there were 40 students enrolled in this program. In 1995–96, 2 degrees were earned at a distance through this program.
Restrictions Program is available to US students only.
Application requirements *Prior education:* associate degree. *Other requirements:* college transcripts, an application fee of $25, 2.0 GPA.
Completion requirements 127 semester hours are required. 30 semester hours must be completed through the institution. This is a degree completion program. *Other requirements:* 20 of the last 30 hours earned must be KSU hours.

▶*Interdisciplinary Social Sciences (BS)*
In the fall of 1996 there were 160 students enrolled in this program. In 1995–96, 12 degrees were earned at a distance through this program.
Restrictions Program is available to US students only.
Application requirements *Prior education:* associate degree. *Other requirements:* college transcripts, an application fee of $25, 2.0 GPA.
Completion requirements 120 semester hours are required. 30 semester hours must be completed through the institution. This is a degree completion program. *Other requirements:* 20 of the last 30 hours earned must be KSU hours.

Graduate Degrees

▶*Chemical Engineering (MS)*
In the fall of 1996 there were 5 students enrolled in this program.
Application requirements *Prior education:* in chemical engineering from an ABET accredited institution or equivalent background. *Other requirements:* SAT or ACT, high school transcript, college transcripts, an application fee.
Completion requirements 30 semester hours are required. 24 semester hours must be completed through the institution.
Program contact John Matthews, Department of Chemical Engineering, Kansas State University, Durland Hall, Manhattan, KS 66506-5102. Phone: 913-532-4315. Fax: 913-532-7372. E-mail: jmatt@cheme.ksu.edu.

▶*Civil Engineering (MS)*
In the fall of 1996 there were 15 students enrolled in this program.
Application requirements *Prior education:* baccalaureate degree in civil engineering from an ABET accredited institution or equivalent background. *Other requirements:* SAT or ACT, high school transcript, college transcripts, an application fee.
Completion requirements 30 semester hours are required. 24 semester hours must be completed through the institution.
Program contact Stu Swartz, Department of Electrical and Computer Engineering, Kansas State University, 261 Durland Hall, Manhattan, KS 66506-5105. Phone: 913-532-5862. Fax: 913-532-7717.

▶*Electrical Engineering (MS)*
In the fall of 1996 there were 17 students enrolled in this program.
Application requirements *Prior education:* baccalaureate degree in electrical or computer engineering, physics, mathematics, computer science, or related field background. *Other requirements:* SAT or ACT, high school transcript, college transcripts, an application fee.
Completion requirements 30 semester hours are required. 24 semester hours must be completed through the institution.
Program contact Anil Pahwa, Department of Electrical and Computer Engineering, Kansas State University, 261 Durland Hall, Manhattan, KS 66506-5105. Phone: 913-532-4654. Fax: 913-532-1188. E-mail: pahwa@eece.ksu.edu.

▶*Industrial and Manufacturing Systems Engineering (MS)*
In the fall of 1996 there were 24 students enrolled in this program.
Application requirements *Prior education:* baccalaureate degree in engineering, applied math, or applied science. *Other requirements:* SAT or ACT, high school transcript, college transcripts, an application fee.
Completion requirements 36 semester hours are required. 30 semester hours must be completed through the institution.
Program contact Brad Kramer, Department of Industrial and Manufacturing Systems Engineering, Kansas State University, 261 Durland Hall, Manhattan, KS 66506-5105. Phone: 913-532-5606. Fax: 913-532-7810. E-mail: bradleyk@taylor.ie.ksu.edu.

▶*Software Engineering (MS)*
In the fall of 1996 there were 46 students enrolled in this program.
Application requirements *Prior education:* baccalaureate degree in computer science, computer engineering, a mathematical science or related engineering or science degree. *Other requirements:* SAT or ACT, high school transcript, college transcripts, an application fee.
Completion requirements 33 semester hours are required. 27 semester hours must be completed through the institution.
Program contact Angie Taylor, Graduate Admissions Secretary, Kansas State University, 234 Nichols Hall, Computing and Information Services Department, Manhattan, KS 66506. Phone: 913-532-6350. Fax: 913-532-7353. E-mail: cns@ksu.edu.

Undergraduate Certificates

▶*Food Science*
In 1995–96, 20 certificates were earned at a distance through this program.
Application requirements *Prior education:* none required. *Other requirements:* SAT or ACT, high school transcript, college transcripts, an application fee.
Completion requirements 20 semester hours are required. 15 must be completed through the institution.
Program contact Linda Henderson, Interim Coordinator, Kansas State University, Division of Continuing Education, 221 College Court Building, Manhattan, KS 66506. Phone: 913-532-5686. Fax: 913-532-5637. E-mail: Distance@dce.ksu.edu.

INDIVIDUAL COURSE SUBJECT AREAS

Undergraduate

Abnormal psychology; agriculture; algebra; American (US) history; American studies; animal sciences; area, ethnic, and cultural studies; business administration and management; calculus; chemistry; community health services; conservation and natural resources; developmental and child psychology; English language and literature; film studies; foods and nutrition studies; geology; history; home economics and family studies; horticulture; international relations; labor relations/studies; Latin American studies; liberal arts, general studies, and humanities; mathematics; Medieval/Renaissance studies; music; plant sciences; political science; social psychology; sociology; statistics; women's studies

Graduate
Agriculture; animal sciences; area, ethnic, and cultural studies; business administration and management; chemical engineering; civil engineering; community health services; computer and information sciences; conservation and natural resources; educational psychology; electrical engineering; engineering/industrial management; foods and nutrition studies; home economics and family studies; industrial engineering; information sciences and systems; statistics; women's studies

Noncredit
Abnormal psychology; agriculture; American (US) history; American studies; animal sciences; area, ethnic, and cultural studies; business administration and management; chemical engineering; civil engineering; community health services; computer and information sciences; conservation and natural resources; developmental and child psychology; electrical engineering; engineering/industrial management; English language and literature; foods and nutrition studies; history; home economics and family studies; horticulture; industrial engineering; labor relations/studies; Latin American studies; liberal arts, general studies, and humanities; mathematics; Medieval/Renaissance studies; music; social psychology; sociology; statistics; women's studies

KASKASKIA COLLEGE

Centralia, Illinois

Kaskaskia College, founded in 1966, is a state and locally supported two-year college. It is accredited by the North Central Association of Colleges and Schools. It first offered distance learning courses in 1993. In 1996–97, it offered 19 courses at a distance. In the fall of 1996, there was a total of 212 students enrolled in distance learning courses.
Course delivery sites Courses are delivered to your workplace, Lewis and Clark Community College (Godfrey), Southern Illinois University at Edwardsville (Edwardsville), 2 off-campus centers in Nashville, Vandalia.
Media Courses are delivered via television, videotapes, videoconferencing, audiotapes. Students and teachers interact via videoconferencing, mail, telephone, fax.
Services Distance learners have access to academic advising, career placement assistance at a distance.
Credit-earning options Students may transfer credits from another institution or may earn credits through examinations, military training, business training.
Typical costs Tuition of $36 per credit hour for local area residents. Tuition of $87 per credit hour for in-state residents. Tuition of $166 per credit hour for out-of-state residents. Costs may vary by number of credits taken.
Registration Students may register by mail, phone.
Contact Jan Ripperda, Admissions Office, Kaskaskia College, 27210 College Road, Centralia, IL 62801. *Telephone:* 618-532-1981. *Fax:* 618-532-1135.

INDIVIDUAL COURSE SUBJECT AREAS

Undergraduate
Agriculture; area, ethnic, and cultural studies; developmental and child psychology; economics; educational psychology; English as a second language (ESL); English language and literature; fine arts; geology; history; liberal arts, general studies, and humanities; library and information studies; mathematics; music; philosophy and religion; political science; sociology

Graduate
Teacher education

Noncredit
Agriculture; area, ethnic, and cultural studies

KELLOGG COMMUNITY COLLEGE

Battle Creek, Michigan

Learning Resources/Distance Learning

Kellogg Community College, founded in 1956, is a state and locally supported two-year college. It is accredited by the North Central Association of Colleges and Schools. It first offered distance learning courses in 1990. In 1996–97, it offered 24 courses at a distance. In the fall of 1996, there was a total of 441 students enrolled in distance learning courses.
Course delivery sites Courses are delivered to your home, your workplace, 2 off-campus centers in Coldwater, Hastings.
Media Courses are delivered via television, videotapes, videoconferencing, World Wide Web, e-mail. Students and teachers interact via videoconferencing, mail, telephone, fax, e-mail.
Services Distance learners have access to library services, the campus computer network, e-mail services, academic advising, tutoring, career placement assistance at a distance.
Credit-earning options Students may transfer credits from another institution or may earn credits through standardized exams, institutionally developed exams, portfolio assessment, military training, business training.
Typical costs Tuition of $44 per credit hour plus mandatory fees of $4 per credit hour for local area residents. Tuition of $73.80 per credit hour plus mandatory fees of $4 per credit hour for in-state residents. Tuition of $115.95 per credit hour plus mandatory fees of $4 per credit hour for out-of-state residents. Special rate for nearby Indiana residents is available. Financial aid is available to distance learners enrolled full-time or part-time.
Registration Students may register by mail, fax, phone.
Contact Frances M. Marz, Assistant Director of Learning Resources and Distance Learning, Kellogg Community College, 450 North Avenue, Battle Creek, MI 49017. *Telephone:* 616-965-3931, Ext. 2248. *Fax:* 616-965-4133. *E-mail:* marzf@mlc.lib.mi.us. *Web site:* http://www.kellogg.cc.mi.us.

INDIVIDUAL COURSE SUBJECT AREAS

Undergraduate
Accounting; area, ethnic, and cultural studies; biology; business; business administration and management; communications; creative writing; economics; English composition; history; law and legal studies; liberal arts, general studies, and humanities; mathematics; political science; psychology; social sciences; sociology; Spanish language and literature

KENNESAW STATE UNIVERSITY

Kennesaw, Georgia

Kennesaw State University, founded in 1963, is a state-supported comprehensive institution. It is accredited by the Southern Association of Colleges and Schools. It first offered distance learning courses in 1995.
Course delivery sites Courses are delivered to your home.
Media Courses are delivered via videoconferencing.
Restrictions Programs are available to in-state students only.

Distance Learning Programs 133

Profiles: Kennesaw State University

Services Distance learners have access to library services at a distance.
Credit-earning options Students may earn credits through examinations.
Contact Admissions Office, Kennesaw State University, 1000 Chastain Road, Kennesaw, GA 30144. *Telephone:* 770-423-6300.

INDIVIDUAL COURSE SUBJECT AREAS

Undergraduate
Asian languages and literatures; history

KINGWOOD COLLEGE

Kingwood, Texas

Kingwood College, founded in 1984, is a state and locally supported two-year college. It is accredited by the Southern Association of Colleges and Schools. It first offered distance learning courses in 1990. In 1996–97, it offered 22 courses at a distance. In the fall of 1996, there was a total of 480 students enrolled in distance learning courses.
Course delivery sites Courses are delivered to your home.
Media Courses are delivered via television, videotapes, computer software, World Wide Web, e-mail, print. Students and teachers interact via mail, telephone, fax, e-mail. A computer is required for some courses.
Restrictions Telecourses are available to local area students only.
Services Distance learners have access to library services, the campus computer network, e-mail services, academic advising, tutoring, career placement assistance at a distance.
Credit-earning options Students may transfer credits from another institution or may earn credits through institutionally developed exams.
Typical costs Tuition of $22 per credit hour plus mandatory fees of $4 per credit hour for local area residents. Tuition of $57 per credit hour plus mandatory fees of $4 per credit hour for in-state residents. Tuition of $67 per credit hour plus mandatory fees of $4 per credit hour for out-of-state residents. Costs may vary by number of credits taken. Financial aid is available to distance learners enrolled full-time or part-time.
Registration Students may register by mail, fax, phone.
Contact Dr. Rose Austin, Dean for Educational Resources, Kingwood College, 2000 Kingwood Drive, Kingwood, TX 77339. *Telephone:* 281-359-1674. *Fax:* 281-359-0438. *E-mail:* raustin@mail.nhmccd.cc.tx.us.

INDIVIDUAL COURSE SUBJECT AREAS

Undergraduate
Accounting; administrative and secretarial services; American (US) history; computer programming; database management; drama and theater; economics; English composition; health and physical education/fitness; information sciences and systems; political science; psychology; Spanish language and literature

LABETTE COMMUNITY COLLEGE

Parsons, Kansas

Labette Community College, founded in 1923, is a state and locally supported two-year college. It is accredited by the North Central Association of Colleges and Schools. It first offered distance learning courses in 1992. In 1996–97, it offered 188 courses at a distance. In the fall of 1996, there was a total of 184 students enrolled in distance learning courses.
Course delivery sites Courses are delivered to your home, 3 off-campus centers in Columbus, Riverton, Weir.
Media Courses are delivered via television, videotapes. Students and teachers interact via videoconferencing, telephone, in-person meetings.
Services Distance learners have access to library services at a distance.
Credit-earning options Students may earn credits through examinations.
Typical costs Tuition of $81 per course plus mandatory fees of $30 per course. Financial aid is available to distance learners enrolled full-time or part-time.
Registration Students may register by mail, fax, phone.
Contact Dale Aikins, Director, Media Services, Labette Community College, 200 South 14th Street, Parsons, KS 67357. *Telephone:* 316-421-6700. *Fax:* 316-421-4481.

INDIVIDUAL COURSE SUBJECT AREAS

Undergraduate
English language and literature; history; psychology; social sciences; visual and performing arts

LACKAWANNA JUNIOR COLLEGE

Scranton, Pennsylvania

Distance Learning Center

Lackawanna Junior College, founded in 1894, is an independent-nonprofit two-year college. It is accredited by the Middle States Association of Colleges and Schools. It first offered distance learning courses in 1994. In 1996–97, it offered 9 courses at a distance. In the fall of 1996, there was a total of 50 students enrolled in distance learning courses.
Course delivery sites Courses are delivered to 3 off-campus centers in Hazleton, Honesdale, Towanda.
Media Courses are delivered via videoconferencing. Students and teachers interact via videoconferencing, mail, telephone, fax.
Restrictions Programs are available to in-state students only.
Services Distance learners have access to the campus computer network, academic advising, tutoring, career placement assistance at a distance.
Credit-earning options Students may transfer credits from another institution or may earn credits through standardized exams, institutionally developed exams, military training.
Typical costs Tuition of $220 per credit. $50 lab fee for some courses. *Noncredit courses:* $175 per course. Financial aid is available to distance learners enrolled full-time.
Contact Griffith R. Lewis, Chief, Distance Learning Operations, Lackawanna Junior College, 501 Vine Street, Scranton, PA 18509. *Telephone:* 717-961-7840. *Fax:* 717-961-7858. *E-mail:* grifflew@aol.com. *Web site:* http://members.aol.com/grifflew/ljc/dlc.html.

INDIVIDUAL COURSE SUBJECT AREAS

Undergraduate
Business administration and management; economics; English composition; history; liberal arts, general studies, and humanities; mathematics; philosophy and religion; psychology; sociology

Noncredit
English composition; mathematics

LAFAYETTE COLLEGE

Easton, Pennsylvania

Lafayette College, founded in 1826, is an independent-religious four-year college affiliated with the Presbyterian Church (U.S.A.). It is accredited by the Middle States Association of Colleges and Schools. It first offered distance learning courses in 1995. In 1996–97, it offered 6 courses at a distance. In the fall of 1996, there was a total of 100 students enrolled in distance learning courses.

Course delivery sites Courses are delivered to Lehigh University (Bethlehem), Allentown College, Vesalius College (Belgium).
Media Courses are delivered via videoconferencing, World Wide Web, e-mail. Students and teachers interact via videoconferencing, e-mail.
Restrictions Courses are only for students enrolled full-time at Lafayette or in schools with course-sharing agreements.
Services Distance learners have access to library services, the campus computer network, e-mail services at a distance.
Typical costs Contact school for information. Financial aid is available to distance learners enrolled full-time.
Contact Lawrence L. Malinconico, Jr., Special Assistant to Provost, Lafayette College, Van Wickle Hall, Easton, PA 18042. *Telephone:* 610-250-5193. *Fax:* 610-252-3904. *E-mail:* malincol@lafayette.edu.

INDIVIDUAL COURSE SUBJECT AREAS

Undergraduate

Anthropology; engineering; French language and literature; political science; sociology; theological studies

LAKEHEAD UNIVERSITY

Thunder Bay, Ontario, Canada

Distance Education

Lakehead University, founded in 1965, is a province-supported comprehensive institution. It is provincially chartered. It first offered distance learning courses in 1987. In 1996–97, it offered 32 courses at a distance.

Course delivery sites Courses are delivered to your home, your workplace, off-campus centers in western Ontario.
Media Courses are delivered via television, videotapes, videoconferencing, audiotapes, audioconferencing, computer software, e-mail, print. Students and teachers interact via videoconferencing, audioconferencing, mail, telephone, fax, e-mail. A computer is required for some courses.
Services Distance learners have access to library services at a distance.
Credit-earning options Students may transfer credits from another institution or may earn credits through institutionally developed exams.
Typical costs *Undergraduate:* Tuition of $322.50 per credit. *Graduate:* Tuition of $884 per credit. Costs may vary by specific program of study. Financial aid is available to distance learners enrolled full-time or part-time.
Registration Students may register by mail, fax, phone, e-mail.
Contact Leslie Malcolm, Distance Education, Lakehead University, 955 Oliver Road, Thunder Bay, ON P7B 5S1, Canada. *Telephone:* 807-343-8210. *Fax:* 807-343-8008. *E-mail:* leslie.malcolm@lakeheadu.ca. *Web site:* http://www.lakeheadu.ca/~disedwww.

DEGREE & CERTIFICATE PROGRAMS

Baccalaureate Degrees

▶ *General Studies (BA)*
Application requirements *Prior education:* high school diploma or equivalent. *Other requirements:* high school transcript, college transcripts.
Completion requirements 15 full credit courses are required. 10 full credit courses must be completed through the institution.

▶ *Nursing (BSN)*
Application requirements *Prior education:* Nursing diploma. *Other requirements:* college transcripts, CPR, BCLS, RN license.
Completion requirements 13 full credit courses are required. *Maximum time for completion:* eight years.
Program contact Dr. Lorne McDougall, Director, School of Nursing, Lakehead University, Distance Education, 955 Oliver Road, Thunder Bay, ON P7B 5S1, Canada. Phone: 807-343-8115. Fax: 807-343-8246. E-mail: lorne.mcdougall@lakeheadu.ca.

Graduate Degrees

▶ *Forestry (Master of Forestry)*
Application requirements *Prior education:* baccalaureate degree. *Other requirements:* an application fee, honors degree in forestry (HBA and HBsc in geography, geology, etc. are considered).
Completion requirements 5 full-credit courses and 1 non-full-credit course are required.
On-campus requirements Four-month term.
Program contact Dr. David Euler, Distance Education, Lakehead University, 955 Oliver Road, Thunder Bay, ON P7B 5S1, Canada. Phone: 807-343-8623. Fax: 807-343-8116. E-mail: david.euler@lakeheadu.ca.

Undergraduate Certificates

▶ *Environmental Assessment*
In the fall of 1996 there were 75 students enrolled in this program. In 1995–96, 23 certificates were earned at a distance through this program.
Application requirements *Prior education:* high school diploma or equivalent. *Other requirements:* high school transcript.
Completion requirements 5 half course equivalents are required. All course work must be completed through the institution.
Program contact Dr. Harun Rasid, Coordinator for Environmental Assessment Certificate, Lakehead University, Distance Education, 955 Oliver Road, Thunder Bay, ON P7B 5S1, Canada. Phone: 807-343-8472. Fax: 807-343-8008. E-mail: harun.rasid@lakeheadu.ca.

INDIVIDUAL COURSE SUBJECT AREAS

Undergraduate

Biology; chemistry; developmental and child psychology; economics; history; liberal arts, general studies, and humanities; mathematics; microbiology; nursing; philosophy and religion; political science; sociology; teacher education

Graduate

Education administration; forestry; special education

LAKE LAND COLLEGE

Mattoon, Illinois

Continuing Education Department

Lake Land College, founded in 1966, is a state and locally supported two-year college. It is accredited by the North Central Association of Colleges and Schools. It first offered distance learning courses in 1994.

Profiles: Lake Land College

In 1996–97, it offered 75 courses at a distance. In the fall of 1996, there was a total of 330 students enrolled in distance learning courses.
Course delivery sites Courses are delivered to 9 off-campus centers in Arthur, Charleston, Effingham, Martinsville, Mattoon, Pana, Paris, Shelbyville, Stew-Stras.
Media Courses are delivered via television. Students and teachers interact via telephone.
Restrictions Programs are available to in-state students only.
Services Distance learners have access to library services, the campus computer network, e-mail services, academic advising, tutoring, career placement assistance at a distance.
Credit-earning options Students may transfer credits from another institution or may earn credits through standardized exams, institutionally developed exams, portfolio assessment, military training.
Typical costs Tuition of $39 per credit hour plus mandatory fees of $8.50 per credit hour for in-state residents. Tuition of $207.96 per credit hour plus mandatory fees of $8.50 per credit hour for out-of-state residents. *Noncredit courses:* $3 per hour of class. Financial aid is available to distance learners enrolled full-time or part-time.
Registration Students may register by mail, phone.
Contact Cheryl Yount, Associate Dean of Continuing Education, Lake Land College, 5001 Lake Land Boulevard, Mattoon, IL 61938. *Telephone:* 217-234-5450. *Fax:* 217-234-5400. *E-mail:* cyount@lakeland.cc.il.us.

INDIVIDUAL COURSE SUBJECT AREAS

Undergraduate
Algebra; American (US) history; business law; criminal justice; economics; ethics; health and physical education/fitness; history; logic; psychology; sociology; statistics; substance abuse counseling

Noncredit
Astronomy and astrophysics

LAKELAND COMMUNITY COLLEGE

Kirtland, Ohio

Instructional Technology

Lakeland Community College, founded in 1967, is a state and locally supported two-year college. It is accredited by the North Central Association of Colleges and Schools. It first offered distance learning courses in 1980. In 1996–97, it offered 15 courses at a distance. In the fall of 1996, there was a total of 65 students enrolled in distance learning courses.
Course delivery sites Courses are delivered to your home, your workplace.
Media Courses are delivered via television. Students and teachers interact via mail, telephone, fax, e-mail, on-campus meetings.
Restrictions Programs are available to local area students only.
Services Distance learners have access to library services, academic advising, tutoring at a distance.
Credit-earning options Students may transfer credits from another institution or may earn credits through examinations, portfolio assessment, military training.
Typical costs Tuition of $41.70 per credit hour plus mandatory fees of $20 per course for local area residents. Tuition of $51.15 per credit hour plus mandatory fees of $20 per course for in-state residents. Tuition of $109.15 per credit hour plus mandatory fees of $20 per course for out-of-state residents. *Noncredit courses:* $40 per course. Costs may vary by number of credits taken. Financial aid is available to distance learners enrolled full-time or part-time.
Registration Students may register by mail, fax, phone.
Contact William Ryan, Director of Instructional Technology, Lakeland Community College, 7700 Clocktower Drive, Kirtland, OH 44094-5198. *Telephone:* 216-953-7127. *Fax:* 216-953-9710. *E-mail:* wjryan@lakeland.cc.oh.us.

INDIVIDUAL COURSE SUBJECT AREAS

Undergraduate
Business administration and management; economics; health and physical education/fitness; political science; sociology

LAKE MICHIGAN COLLEGE

Benton Harbor, Michigan

Information Technologies

Lake Michigan College, founded in 1946, is a district-supported two-year college. It is accredited by the North Central Association of Colleges and Schools. It first offered distance learning courses in 1988. In 1996–97, it offered 15 courses at a distance.
Course delivery sites Courses are delivered to your home.
Media Courses are delivered via television, videotapes. Students and teachers interact via videoconferencing, mail, telephone, fax.
Services Distance learners have access to library services at a distance.
Credit-earning options Students may transfer credits from another institution or may earn credits through standardized exams, portfolio assessment, military training.
Typical costs Tuition of $45 per credit hour plus mandatory fees of $6 per credit hour for local area residents. Tuition of $55 per credit hour plus mandatory fees of $6 per credit hour for in-state residents. Tuition of $65 per credit hour plus mandatory fees of $6 per credit hour for out-of-state residents. Financial aid is available to distance learners enrolled full-time or part-time.
Registration Students may register by mail, fax.
Contact Michael J. Vidmar, Registrar, Lake Michigan College, 2755 East Napier Avenue, Benton Harbor, MI 49022. *Telephone:* 616-927-8614. *Fax:* 616-927-6874.

INDIVIDUAL COURSE SUBJECT AREAS

Undergraduate
Accounting; business; business administration and management; English language and literature; history; law and legal studies; mathematics; political science; psychology; social sciences; sociology

LAKESHORE TECHNICAL COLLEGE

Cleveland, Wisconsin

Lakeshore Technical College, founded in 1967, is a state and locally supported two-year college. It is accredited by the North Central Association of Colleges and Schools. It first offered distance learning courses in 1985.
Course delivery sites Courses are delivered to your home, your workplace, other colleges.
Media Courses are delivered via television, videotapes, videoconferencing, print.
Restrictions Programs are available to in-state students only.
Services Distance learners have access to academic advising at a distance.

Credit-earning options Students may transfer credits from another institution or may earn credits through examinations, portfolio assessment. Financial aid is available to distance learners.
Contact Student Services, Lakeshore Technical College, 1290 North Avenue, Cleveland, WI 53015. *Telephone:* 414-458-4183. *Fax:* 414-693-3561.

DEGREE & CERTIFICATE PROGRAMS

Undergraduate Certificates
▶ *Certified Nursing Assistant*
▶ *Paramedic*

INDIVIDUAL COURSE SUBJECT AREAS

Undergraduate
Business; business administration and management; communications; computer and information sciences; educational psychology; engineering; English composition; English language and literature; health professions and related sciences; home economics and family studies; law and legal studies; liberal arts, general studies, and humanities; mathematics; political science; psychology; social sciences; sociology

LAKE-SUMTER COMMUNITY COLLEGE

Leesburg, Florida

Television Studio

Lake-Sumter Community College, founded in 1962, is a state and locally supported two-year college. It is accredited by the Southern Association of Colleges and Schools. It first offered distance learning courses in 1986. In 1996–97, it offered 6 courses at a distance. In the fall of 1996, there was a total of 50 students enrolled in distance learning courses.
Course delivery sites Courses are delivered to your home, your workplace, 1 off-campus center in Sumterville.
Media Courses are delivered via television, videotapes. Students and teachers interact via telephone, fax, e-mail.
Restrictions Courses are available to students in Lake County and Sumtner County only.
Services Distance learners have access to e-mail services at a distance.
Credit-earning options Students may transfer credits from another institution or may earn credits through examinations.
Typical costs Tuition of $38.90 per credit hour for in-state residents. Tuition of $144.95 per credit hour for out-of-state residents. *Noncredit courses:* $25 per course. Financial aid is available to distance learners.
Contact Mr. Terry Longordo, Manager, Television and Distance Learning, Lake-Sumter Community College, 9501 Highway 441, Leesburg, FL 34788. *Telephone:* 352-365-3566. *Fax:* 352-365-3501. *E-mail:* longordt@lscc.cc.fl.us. *Web site:* http://www.lscc.cc.fl.us.

INDIVIDUAL COURSE SUBJECT AREAS

Undergraduate
American (US) history; biological and life sciences; business; business administration and management; business law; geology; health and physical education/fitness; political science

Profiles: Lake Superior State University

LAKE SUPERIOR STATE UNIVERSITY

Sault Sainte Marie, Michigan

Community Services and Development

Lake Superior State University, founded in 1946, is a state-supported comprehensive institution. It is accredited by the North Central Association of Colleges and Schools. It first offered distance learning courses in 1988. In 1996–97, it offered 20 courses at a distance. In the fall of 1996, there was a total of 228 students enrolled in distance learning courses.
Course delivery sites Courses are delivered to Alpena Community College (Alpena), Bay de Noc Community College (Escanaba), North Central Michigan College (Petoskey), Northwestern Michigan College (Traverse City).
Media Courses are delivered via videotapes, videoconferencing, print. Students and teachers interact via videoconferencing, mail, telephone, fax, e-mail.
Restrictions Students must be able to travel to receive site.
Services Distance learners have access to library services, academic advising, career placement assistance at a distance.
Credit-earning options Students may transfer credits from another institution or may earn credits through standardized exams, military training.
Typical costs *Undergraduate:* Tuition of $153 per credit hour plus mandatory fees of $50 per semester for in-state residents. Tuition of $301 per credit hour plus mandatory fees of $50 per semester for out-of-state residents. *Graduate:* Tuition of $170 per credit hour plus mandatory fees of $50 per semester for in-state residents. Tuition of $170 per credit hour plus mandatory fees of $50 per semester for out-of-state residents. *Noncredit courses:* $79 per course. Financial aid is available to distance learners enrolled full-time or part-time.
Registration Students may register by mail, fax, phone.
Contact Susan K. Camp, Director of Continuing Education, Lake Superior State University, 844 North Campus Court, Sault Sainte Marie, MI 49783. *Telephone:* 906-635-2554. *Fax:* 906-635-2762. *E-mail:* scamp@lakers.lssu.edu. *Web site:* http://www.lssu.edu.

Special note

Lake Superior State University is located in the beautiful and rugged eastern Upper Peninsula of the state of Michigan. Distance education at Lake State consists of interactive television courses and degree programs that are currently available at four community colleges in northern Michigan in the cities of Alpena, Escanaba, Petoskey, and Traverse City.

A variety of degrees are available at these sites, including bachelor's degrees in accounting, business administration, criminal justice, and engineering management as well as BSN nursing completion. Two graduate degrees are also available: a Master of Business Administration and a Master of Public Administration. Each of these degrees can be completed entirely at the distant sites.

LSSU is in the process of developing other courses for alternative delivery. These include courses on-line to be available on the World Wide Web, as well as self-contained asynchronous courses available on CD-ROM and video tape, with student/teacher interaction available over the Web. For more information, students should contact LSSU on the World Wide Web at http://www.lakers.issu.edu or phone 906-635-2802 or 888-800-LSSU ext. 2802.

For information on LSSU courses and degrees available at distant sites, students should contact the University's Regional Site Directors: Alpena, Michigan: Kelly Smith (telephone: 517-356-9021 ext. 302; e-mail smithk@ns.alpena.cc.mi.us); Escanaba, Michigan:

Distance Learning Programs

Profiles: Lake Superior State University

Beth Beaudoin Noreus (telephone: 906-786-5802 ext. 261; e-mail: noreusb@baydenoc.cc.mi.us); Petoskey and Traverse City, Michigan: Rebecca Scheelk (telephone: 616-348-6623; e-mail: rscheelk@lakers.lssu.edu).

DEGREE & CERTIFICATE PROGRAMS

Baccalaureate Degrees
▶ *Accounting, Business Administration, Criminal Justice, Engineering Management, Nursing (BS)*
In the fall of 1996 there were 228 students enrolled in this program. In 1995–96, 60 degrees were earned at a distance through this program.
Application requirements *Prior education:* associate degree. *Other requirements:* ACT or SAT, high school transcript, college transcripts.
Completion requirements 120 semester hours are required. 32 semester hours must be completed through the institution. This is a degree completion program. *Other requirements:* 50% of department-required 300/400 level courses must be from Lake Superior University.
Program contact Bruce Johnson, Director of Admissions, Lake Superior State University, 650 West Easterday, Sault Sainte Marie, MI 49783. Phone: 906-635-2231. E-mail: bjohnson@lakers.lssu.edu.

Graduate Degrees
▶ *Business Administration (MBA)*
▶ *Public Administration (MPA)*

INDIVIDUAL COURSE SUBJECT AREAS

Undergraduate
Accounting; business; engineering/industrial management; nursing; protective services

Graduate
Business administration and management

LAMAR UNIVERSITY

Beaumont, Texas

Center for Adult Studies

Lamar University, founded in 1923, is a state-supported university. It is accredited by the Southern Association of Colleges and Schools. It first offered distance learning courses in 1994. In 1996–97, it offered 30 courses at a distance. In the fall of 1996, there was a total of 500 students enrolled in distance learning courses.
Course delivery sites Courses are delivered to your home, Lamar University–Orange (Orange), 4 off-campus centers in Buna, Jasper, Silsbee, Vidor.
Media Courses are delivered via television, videotapes, videoconferencing. Students and teachers interact via videoconferencing, mail, telephone, fax, e-mail.
Restrictions Programs are available to local area students only.
Services Distance learners have access to library services, e-mail services, academic advising, tutoring at a distance.
Credit-earning options Students may transfer credits from another institution or may earn credits through standardized exams, institutionally developed exams, portfolio assessment, military training, business training.
Typical costs *Undergraduate:* Tuition of $120 per course plus mandatory fees of $128 per course for in-state residents. Tuition of $738 per course plus mandatory fees of $140 per course for out-of-state residents. *Graduate:* Tuition of $120 per course plus mandatory fees of $128 per course for in-state residents. Tuition of $738 per course plus mandatory fees of $140 per course for out-of-state residents. *Noncredit courses:* $100 per course. Costs may vary by number of credits taken. Financial aid is available to distance learners enrolled full-time or part-time.
Registration Students may register by mail, phone.
Contact Janice Trammell, Director, Center for Adult Studies, Lamar University, PO Box 10008, Beaumont, TX 77710. *Telephone:* 409-880-8209. *Fax:* 409-880-8683. *E-mail:* trammjd@lub002.lamar.edu. *Web site:* http://hal.lamar.edu/~psce.

INDIVIDUAL COURSE SUBJECT AREAS

Undergraduate
Business; communications; economics; education administration; educational psychology; English composition; English language and literature; fine arts; history; home economics and family studies; liberal arts, general studies, and humanities; political science; psychology; sociology; special education; teacher education

Graduate
Education administration; educational psychology; home economics and family studies; special education; teacher education

LANE COMMUNITY COLLEGE

Eugene, Oregon

Distance Learning Department

Lane Community College, founded in 1964, is a state and locally supported two-year college. It is accredited by the Northwest Association of Schools and Colleges. It first offered distance learning courses in 1979. In 1996–97, it offered 30 courses at a distance. In the fall of 1996, there was a total of 850 students enrolled in distance learning courses.
Course delivery sites Courses are delivered to your home, your workplace, 3 off-campus centers in Cottage Grove, Eugene, Florence.
Media Courses are delivered via television, videotapes, World Wide Web, e-mail. Students and teachers interact via mail, telephone, fax, e-mail. A computer is required for some courses.
Services Distance learners have access to library services, academic advising at a distance.
Credit-earning options Students may transfer credits from another institution.
Typical costs Tuition of $34 per credit. Costs may vary by number of credits taken. Financial aid is available to distance learners.
Registration Students may register by phone.
Contact Cynde Leathers, Distance Learning Coordinator, Lane Community College, 4000 East 30th Avenue, Eugene, OR 97405. *Telephone:* 541-726-2260. *Fax:* 541-744-3974. *E-mail:* leathersc@lanecc.edu. *Web site:* http://www.lanecc.edu.

DEGREE & CERTIFICATE PROGRAMS

Associate Degrees
▶ *Oregon Transfer Degree (AA)*
In the fall of 1996 there were 850 students enrolled in this program.
Application requirements *Minimum age:* 18.
Completion requirements 90 credits are required.

INDIVIDUAL COURSE SUBJECT AREAS

Undergraduate
Abnormal psychology; algebra; anthropology; archaeology; art history and criticism; Asian studies; business; chemistry; child care and development; computer and information sciences; earth science; English composi-

tion; film studies; foods and nutrition studies; geography; health and physical education/fitness; oceanography; photography; sociology; women's studies

LANEY COLLEGE

Oakland, California

Laney College, founded in 1953, is a state and locally supported two-year college. It is accredited by the Western Association of Schools and Colleges, Inc.
Course delivery sites Courses are delivered to your home.
Media Courses are delivered via television, videotapes, computer software, print, computer conferencing.
Restrictions Programs are available to local area students only. Financial aid is available to distance learners.
Contact Dean of Instruction, Laney College, 900 Fallon Street, Oakland, CA 94607. *Telephone:* 510-748-2301.

INDIVIDUAL COURSE SUBJECT AREAS

Undergraduate
Biology; business; business administration and management; computer and information sciences; developmental and child psychology; economics; European languages and literatures; health and physical education/fitness; history; liberal arts, general studies, and humanities; political science; psychology; social psychology; sociology

LANSING COMMUNITY COLLEGE

Lansing, Michigan

Lansing Community College, founded in 1957, is a state and locally supported two-year college. It is accredited by the North Central Association of Colleges and Schools. It first offered distance learning courses in 1979. In 1996–97, it offered 30 courses at a distance. In the fall of 1996, there was a total of 280 students enrolled in distance learning courses.
Course delivery sites Courses are delivered to your home, your workplace.
Media Courses are delivered via television, videotapes, computer software, World Wide Web, e-mail, print. Students and teachers interact via mail, telephone, fax, e-mail, computer conferencing. A computer is required for some courses.
Services Distance learners have access to library services, the campus computer network, e-mail services, academic advising, tutoring, career placement assistance at a distance.
Credit-earning options Students may transfer credits from another institution or may earn credits through examinations, portfolio assessment, military training, business training.
Typical costs Tuition of $47 per semester credit for local area residents. Tuition of $76 per semester credit for in-state residents. Tuition of $105 per semester credit for out-of-state residents. $20 registration fee. Financial aid is available to distance learners enrolled full-time or part-time.
Registration Students may register by mail, fax, phone.
Contact Ms. Jean Morciglio, Director, Extension and Community Education, Lansing Community College, PO Box 40010, Lansing, MI 48901. *Telephone:* 517-483-1860. *Fax:* 517-483-9750. *E-mail:* jm1860@lois.lansing.cc.mi.us.

DEGREE & CERTIFICATE PROGRAMS

Associate Degrees
▶ *Business (AD)*
Restrictions Students must have personal computer with Internet service provider.
Application requirements *Prior education:* high school diploma or equivalent.
Completion requirements 60 semester hours are required. 20 semester hours must be completed through the institution.
Program contact Kirby M. Milton, Virtual College Coordinator, Lansing Community College, Mail Code 8270, PO Box 40010, Lansing, MI 48901. Phone: 517-483-1703. E-mail: km@luis.lansing.cc.mi.us.

INDIVIDUAL COURSE SUBJECT AREAS

Undergraduate
Accounting; algebra; biology; business administration and management; computer and information sciences; earth science; economics; English composition; gerontology; home economics and family studies; philosophy and religion; physics; political science; social psychology; sociology

LARAMIE COUNTY COMMUNITY COLLEGE

Cheyenne, Wyoming

Community Outreach

Laramie County Community College, founded in 1968, is a county-supported two-year college. It is accredited by the North Central Association of Colleges and Schools. It first offered distance learning courses in 1981. In 1996–97, it offered 32 courses at a distance. In the fall of 1996, there was a total of 366 students enrolled in distance learning courses.
Course delivery sites Courses are delivered to your home, your workplace, military bases, 1 off-campus center in Laramie.
Media Courses are delivered via videotapes, videoconferencing, World Wide Web. Students and teachers interact via videoconferencing, mail, telephone, fax, e-mail. A computer is required for some courses.
Services Distance learners have access to library services at a distance.
Credit-earning options Students may transfer credits from another institution or may earn credits through examinations, military training.
Typical costs Tuition of $447 per semester plus mandatory fees of $84 per semester for in-state residents. Tuition of $1341 per semester plus mandatory fees of $84 per semester for out-of-state residents. Costs may vary by number of credits taken, course delivery options. Financial aid is available to distance learners enrolled full-time or part-time.
Registration Students may register by mail, phone.
Contact Craig E. Anderson, Associate Dean, Community Outreach Division, Laramie County Community College, 1400 East College Drive, Cheyenne, WY 82007. *Telephone:* 307-778-1174. *Fax:* 307-778-1344. *E-mail:* anderson@mail.lcc.whecn.edu.

INDIVIDUAL COURSE SUBJECT AREAS

Undergraduate
American (US) history; astronomy and astrophysics; business; business administration and management; calculus; comparative literature; computer and information sciences; creative writing; criminal justice; curriculum and instruction; developmental and child psychology; economics; English composition; ethics; geography; human resources management; international business; liberal arts, general studies, and humanities; organizational behavior studies; political science; psychology; sociology; statistics; women's studies; zoology

Profiles: Lassen College

LASSEN COLLEGE

Susanville, California

Office of Distance Learning

Lassen College, founded in 1925, is a state and locally supported two-year college. It is accredited by the Western Association of Schools and Colleges, Inc. It first offered distance learning courses in 1992. In 1996–97, it offered 35 courses at a distance. In the fall of 1996, there was a total of 475 students enrolled in distance learning courses.
Course delivery sites Courses are delivered to your home, military bases, 6 off-campus centers in Alturas, Bieber, Coleville, Downieville, Herlong, Westwood, prisons.
Media Courses are delivered via television, videotapes, computer software, asynchronous computer conferencing. Students and teachers interact via mail, telephone, fax, e-mail, in-person meetings. A computer is required for some courses. The institution provides assistance with acquiring computer equipment.
Services Distance learners have access to library services, academic advising at a distance.
Credit-earning options Students may transfer credits from another institution or may earn credits through portfolio assessment, military training, business training.
Typical costs Tuition of $13 per unit. Financial aid is available to distance learners enrolled full-time or part-time.
Registration Students may register by mail.
Contact Kay Carranza, Administrative Assistant, Office of Distance Learning, Lassen College, PO Box 3000, Highway 139, Susanville, CA 96130. *Telephone:* 916-257-6181, Ext. 8955. *Fax:* 916-251-8889. *E-mail:* kcarranza@lassen.cc.ca.us.

INDIVIDUAL COURSE SUBJECT AREAS

Undergraduate

Accounting; area, ethnic, and cultural studies; business; economics; education; English composition; fine arts; history; human resources management; law and legal studies; liberal arts, general studies, and humanities; mathematics; philosophy and religion; political science; psychology; sociology; statistics; theological studies; visual and performing arts

LAURENTIAN UNIVERSITY

Sudbury, Ontario, Canada

Centre for Continuing Education

Laurentian University, founded in 1960, is a province-supported comprehensive institution. It is provincially chartered. It first offered distance learning courses in 1972. In 1996–97, it offered 56 courses at a distance.
Course delivery sites Courses are delivered to your home, other colleges.
Media Courses are delivered via television, videotapes, videoconferencing, audiotapes, audioconferencing, computer software, print. Students and teachers interact via audioconferencing, mail, telephone, fax, e-mail. A computer is required for some courses.
Services Distance learners have access to library services, e-mail services, academic advising at a distance.
Credit-earning options Students may transfer credits from another institution or may earn credits through institutionally developed exams, portfolio assessment, military training, business training.
Typical costs *Undergraduate:* Tuition of $646 per course. *Graduate:* Tuition of $461 per course. *Noncredit courses:* $430 per 3-credit course. Costs may vary by specific program of study, number of credits taken. Financial aid is available to distance learners enrolled full-time or part-time.
Registration Students may register by mail, fax.
Contact Ruby Gervais, Program Manager, Laurentian University, Ramsey Lake Road, Sudbury, ON P3E 2C6, Canada. *Telephone:* 705-675-4819. *Fax:* 705-675-4897. *E-mail:* rgervais@nickel.laurentian.ca. *Web site:* http://www.laurentian.ca.

DEGREE & CERTIFICATE PROGRAMS

Baccalaureate Degrees

▶ *Folklore (BA)*

▶ *Liberal Science (BS)*
Program contact Ian Robb, Vice Dean of Science, Laurentian University, Ramsey Lake Road, Sudbury, ON P3E 2C6, Canada. Phone: 705-675-1151, Ext. 2230. Fax: 705-673-6532. E-mail: nirobb@nickel.laurentian.ca.

▶ *Native Studies (BA)*

▶ *Nursing (BSN)*
Program contact Sandy Bullock, Clinical and Administrative Supervisor, Laurentian University, Ramsey Lake Road, Sudbury, ON P3E 2C6, Canada. Phone: 705-673-6589. Fax: 705-675-4861. E-mail: sbullock@nickel.laurentian.ca.

▶ *Psychology (BA)*

▶ *Religious Studies (BA)*

▶ *Social Work (BS)*
Program contact Jean Marc Belanger, Service Social, Laurentian University, Ramsey Lake Road, Sudbury, ON P3E 2C6, Canada. Phone: 705-675-1151, Ext. 5061. Fax: 705-675-4817. E-mail: belanger@nickel.laurentinn.

▶ *Social Work (Native Human Services) (BSW)*
Program contact Sheila Hardy, Coordinator, Laurentian University, Native Human Services Department, Sudbury, ON P3E 2C6, Canada. Phone: 705-675-1151, Ext. 5063. Fax: 705-673-4912. E-mail: shardy@nickel.laurentian.ca.

▶ *Sociology (BA)*

Graduate Degrees

▶ *Business Administration (MBA)*
Program contact Dr. Ozhand Ganjavi, Graduate Coordinator, Laurentian University, School of Commerce, Sudbury, ON P3E 2C6, Canada. Phone: 705-675-1151, Ext. 2138. Fax: 705-673-6518. E-mail: oganjavi@nickel.laurentian.ca.

▶ *Humanities (MA)*
Program contact Dr. Laurence Steven, Program Director, Laurentian University, Department of English, Sudbury, ON P3E 2C6, Canada. Phone: 705-675-1151, Ext. 4353. Fax: 705-675-4887. E-mail: lsteven@nickel.laurentian.ca.

INDIVIDUAL COURSE SUBJECT AREAS

Undergraduate

Accounting; astronomy and astrophysics; biology; business; business administration and management; chemistry; computer and information sciences; creative writing; developmental and child psychology; economics; educational psychology; English composition; environmental engineering; geology; history; human resources management; law and legal studies; mathematics; music; nursing; philosophy and religion; physics; political science; social psychology; social sciences; social work; sociology

Graduate
Accounting; advertising; business; business administration and management; human resources management

Noncredit
Business administration and management

LAWSON STATE COMMUNITY COLLEGE

Birmingham, Alabama

Lawson State Community College, founded in 1965, is a state-supported two-year college. It is accredited by the Southern Association of Colleges and Schools. It first offered distance learning courses in 1995.
Course delivery sites Courses are delivered to your home, your workplace, other colleges, prisons.
Media Courses are delivered via videoconferencing.
Restrictions Programs are available to local area students only.
Credit-earning options Students may transfer credits from another institution or may earn credits through examinations, portfolio assessment, military training, business training. Financial aid is available to distance learners.
Contact Admissions Office, Lawson State Community College, 3060 Wilson Road, SW, Birmingham, AL 35221. *Telephone:* 205-925-2515.

INDIVIDUAL COURSE SUBJECT AREAS

Undergraduate
Accounting; biology; business administration and management; developmental and child psychology; educational psychology; history; industrial psychology; political science; radio and television broadcasting; social psychology; social work; sociology

LEE COLLEGE

Baytown, Texas

Lee College, founded in 1934, is a district-supported two-year college. It is accredited by the Southern Association of Colleges and Schools. It first offered distance learning courses in 1987. In 1996–97, it offered 12 courses at a distance. In the fall of 1996, there was a total of 96 students enrolled in distance learning courses.
Course delivery sites Courses are delivered to your home.
Media Courses are delivered via television, videotapes, audiotapes. Students and teachers interact via mail, telephone, fax, e-mail, Internet.
Restrictions Programs are available to in-state students only.
Services Distance learners have access to library services, e-mail services, academic advising, tutoring, career placement assistance at a distance.
Credit-earning options Students may transfer credits from another institution or may earn credits through standardized exams, institutionally developed exams, military training.
Typical costs Tuition of $14 per semester hour plus mandatory fees of $73 per semester for local area residents. Tuition of $14 per semester hour plus mandatory fees of $82 per semester for in-state residents. Distance education fee: $20 per course. Out-of-district fee is $14 per semester hour. Costs may vary by campus or location, number of credits taken. Financial aid is available to distance learners enrolled full-time or part-time.
Registration Students may register by phone.
Contact Donnetta Suchon, Academic Dean, Lee College, PO Box 818, Baytown, TX 77522-0818. *Telephone:* 281-425-6444. *Fax:* 281-425-6826. *E-mail:* dsuchon@lee.edu.

INDIVIDUAL COURSE SUBJECT AREAS

Undergraduate
Accounting; American (US) history; biology; business; business administration and management; computer and information sciences; economics; English composition; European languages and literatures; history; information sciences and systems; political science; psychology; sociology; Spanish language and literature

LEHIGH CARBON COMMUNITY COLLEGE

Schnecksville, Pennsylvania

Office of Distance Learning

Lehigh Carbon Community College, founded in 1967, is a state and locally supported two-year college. It is accredited by the Middle States Association of Colleges and Schools. It first offered distance learning courses in 1991. In 1996–97, it offered 27 courses at a distance. In the fall of 1996, there was a total of 186 students enrolled in distance learning courses.
Course delivery sites Courses are delivered to your home, Northampton County Area Community College (Bethlehem), 2 off-campus centers in Allentown, Nesquehoning.
Media Courses are delivered via television, videotapes, videoconferencing. Students and teachers interact via videoconferencing, mail, telephone, fax, e-mail.
Restrictions Programs are primarily available to in-district students.
Services Distance learners have access to academic advising at a distance.
Credit-earning options Students may transfer credits from another institution or may earn credits through examinations, portfolio assessment, military training.
Typical costs Tuition of $189 per course plus mandatory fees of $45 per course for local area residents. Tuition of $378 per course plus mandatory fees of $45 per course for in-state residents. Tuition of $567 per course plus mandatory fees of $45 per course for out-of-state residents. Financial aid is available to distance learners enrolled full-time or part-time.
Registration Students may register by mail, fax, phone.
Contact David Voros, Director, Library Services and Distance Learning, Lehigh Carbon Community College, 4525 Education Park Drive, Schnecksville, PA 18078. *Telephone:* 610-799-1196. *Fax:* 610-799-1159. *E-mail:* dsv1@lex.lccc.edu. *Web site:* http://www.lccc.edu.

INDIVIDUAL COURSE SUBJECT AREAS

Undergraduate
Accounting; American (US) history; art history and criticism; business administration and management; business law; communications; economics; English composition; geography; gerontology; health and physical education/fitness; history; home economics and family studies; journalism; law and legal studies; liberal arts, general studies, and humanities; marketing; mathematics; political science; psychology; sociology; statistics; visual and performing arts

Profiles: Lehigh University

LEHIGH UNIVERSITY

Bethlehem, Pennsylvania

Office of Distance Learning

Lehigh University, founded in 1865, is an independent-nonprofit university. It is accredited by the Middle States Association of Colleges and Schools. It first offered distance learning courses in 1992. In 1996–97, it offered 40 courses at a distance. In the fall of 1996, there was a total of 275 students enrolled in distance learning courses.
Course delivery sites Courses are delivered to your workplace.
Media Courses are delivered via television, videoconferencing. Students and teachers interact via videoconferencing, mail, telephone, fax, e-mail, computer conferencing. A computer is required for some courses.
Services Distance learners have access to library services, the campus computer network, e-mail services, academic advising at a distance.
Credit-earning options Students may transfer credits from another institution or may earn credits through institutionally developed exams.
Typical costs Tuition of $555 per credit hour. *Noncredit courses:* $555 per course.
Registration Students may register by mail, fax.
Contact Peg Kercsmar, Manager, Distance Education, Lehigh University, 205 Johnson Hall, 36 University Drive, Bethlehem, PA 18015. *Telephone:* 610-758-5794. *Fax:* 610-758-6269. *E-mail:* mak5@lehigh.edu. *Web site:* http://www.lehigh.edu/~indis/indis.html.

Special note

Lehigh University's Lehigh Educational Satellite Network (LESN) carries live, on-campus classes to students at corporate sites, enabling them to pursue graduate and continuing education while at work. Companies use LESN to offer their employees the opportunity to earn master's degrees in chemistry, chemical engineering, molecular biology, quality engineering, and business administration (MBA); noncredit options and short courses are also available. Additional programs under consideration for satellite delivery include civil/structural engineering (scheduled for spring 1998), polymer science, mechanical engineering, and environmental engineering.

Lehigh's distance education is highly interactive, with emphasis on the relationship of the distance student to individual faculty members and the University as a whole. During class, distance students interact with the instructor and other students via phone, fax, or interactive computer. Outside of class, students communicate with instructors by phone, fax, or e-mail. Students also have access to Lehigh's computer, library, and student chat rooms. Since distance students are expected to complete the same requirements as on-campus students, they receive the same degree.

Students express high satisfaction with Lehigh's distance education programs, particularly its convenience and quality of instruction and Lehigh's responsiveness to distance students. Since Lehigh began offering distance education in 1992, LESN has grown to serve more than 250 students at 25 corporate sites of major companies, including 3M, Air Products, Allied Signal, BetzDearborn Laboratories, Buckman Laboratories, Cytec Industries, Dupont Merck, Exxon Chemical, Mack Trucks, Merck, Rhone Poulenc Rorer, Rohm & Haas, SmithKline Beecham, TVA, and Zeneca Pharmaceuticals.

DEGREE & CERTIFICATE PROGRAMS

Graduate Degrees

▶ *Business Administration (MBA)*
In the fall of 1996 there were 86 students enrolled in this program.
Application requirements *Prior education:* baccalaureate degree. *Other requirements:* GMAT, college transcripts, an essay or personal statement, letter(s) of recommendation, an application fee of $30.
Completion requirements 30 credits are required. All but 6 credits of course work must be completed through the institution. *Maximum time for completion:* six years.
On-campus requirements Two courses require on-campus segment (one or two Saturdays).

▶ *Chemical Engineering (MS)*
In the fall of 1996 there were 27 students enrolled in this program. In 1995–96, 2 degrees were earned at a distance through this program.
Application requirements *Prior education:* baccalaureate degree. *Other requirements:* college transcripts, an essay or personal statement, letter(s) of recommendation, an application fee of $30.
Completion requirements 30 credits are required. All but 6 credits of course work must be completed through the institution. *Maximum time for completion:* six years.

▶ *Chemistry (MS)*
In the fall of 1996 there were 105 students enrolled in this program. In 1995–96, 7 degrees were earned at a distance through this program.
Application requirements *Prior education:* baccalaureate degree. *Other requirements:* college transcripts, letter(s) of recommendation, an application fee of $30.
Completion requirements 30 credits are required. All but 6 credits of course work must be completed through the institution. *Other requirements:* some concentrations require research project and thesis. *Maximum time for completion:* six years.

▶ *Molecular Biology (MS)*
In the fall of 1996 there were 26 students enrolled in this program.
Application requirements *Prior education:* baccalaureate degree. *Other requirements:* college transcripts, an essay or personal statement, letter(s) of recommendation, an application fee of $30.
Completion requirements 30 credits are required. All but 6 credits of course work must be completed through the institution. *Maximum time for completion:* six years.

▶ *Quality Engineering (MS)*
In the fall of 1996 there were 24 students enrolled in this program.
Application requirements *Prior education:* bachelor's degree in engineering or science. *Other requirements:* college transcripts, letter(s) of recommendation, an application fee of $30.
Completion requirements 30 credits are required. All but 6 credits of course work must be completed through the institution. *Maximum time for completion:* six years.

INDIVIDUAL COURSE SUBJECT AREAS

Graduate
Biology; business; chemical engineering; chemistry; engineering-related technologies

Noncredit
Biology; business; chemical engineering; chemistry; engineering-related technologies

LESLEY COLLEGE

Cambridge, Massachusetts

Lesley College, founded in 1909, is an independent-nonprofit comprehensive institution. It is accredited by the New England Association of Schools and Colleges. It first offered distance learning courses in 1996. In 1996–97, it offered 10 courses at a distance. In the fall of 1996, there was a total of 50 students enrolled in distance learning courses.

Course delivery sites Courses are delivered to your home, your workplace.
Media Courses are delivered via videotapes, videoconferencing, audioconferencing, computer software, World Wide Web, e-mail, print, CD-ROM. Students and teachers interact via audioconferencing, mail, telephone, fax, e-mail. A computer is required for some courses.
Restrictions Some courses may be limited to degree students only.
Services Distance learners have access to library services, the campus computer network, e-mail services, academic advising at a distance.
Credit-earning options Students may transfer credits from another institution.
Typical costs Tuition of $280 per credit. Financial aid is available to distance learners.
Registration Students may register by mail.
Contact Dr. Jean Moon, Director, Lesley College, Center for Mathematics, Science and Technology, 29 Everett Street, Cambridge, MA 02138. *Telephone:* 617-349-8960. *Fax:* 617-349-8169. *E-mail:* jmoon@mail.lesley.edu.

DEGREE & CERTIFICATE PROGRAMS

Graduate Degrees

▶ *Individualized Specializations (MEd)*
Application requirements *Prior education:* baccalaureate degree. *Other requirements:* college transcripts, an essay or personal statement, letter(s) of recommendation, an application fee of $45, self-designed program of study.
Completion requirements 36 credits are required. *Maximum time for completion:* seven years.
Program contact Judi Sapaugh, Program Advisor, Lesley College, 29 Everett Street, Cambridge, MA 02138. Phone: 617-349-8454. E-mail: jsapaugh@mail.lesley.edu.

▶ *Individualized Specializations (MA)*
Application requirements *Prior education:* baccalaureate degree. *Other requirements:* college transcripts, an essay or personal statement, letter(s) of recommendation, an application fee of $45, self-designed program of study.
Completion requirements 36 credits are required. *Maximum time for completion:* seven years.
Program contact Judi Sapaugh, Program Advisor, Lesley College, 29 Everett Street, Cambridge, MA 02138. Phone: 617-349-8454. E-mail: jsapaugh@mail.lesley.edu.

▶ *Technology in Education (MEd)*
Application requirements *Prior education:* baccalaureate degree. *Other requirements:* college transcripts, an essay or personal statement, letter(s) of recommendation, an application fee of $45.
Completion requirements 33 credits are required. *Maximum time for completion:* seven years.
Program contact Maureen Brown-Yoder, Associate Professor, Lesley College, 29 Everett Street, Cambridge, MA 02138. E-mail: myoder@mail.lesley.edu.

Graduate certificates

▶ *Individualized Specializations*
Application requirements *Prior education:* baccalaureate degree. *Other requirements:* college transcripts, an essay or personal statement, letter(s) of recommendation, an application fee of $45, self-designed program of study.
Completion requirements 36 credits are required. *Maximum time for completion:* seven years.
Program contact Judi Sapaugh, Program Advisor, Lesley College, 29 Everett Street, Cambridge, MA 02138. Phone: 617-349-8454. E-mail: jsapaugh@mail.lesley.edu.

INDIVIDUAL COURSE SUBJECT AREAS

Graduate
Business administration and management; curriculum and instruction

LIBERTY UNIVERSITY

Lynchburg, Virginia

External Degree Program

Liberty University, founded in 1971, is an independent-religious nondenominational comprehensive institution. It is accredited by the Southern Association of Colleges and Schools. It first offered distance learning courses in 1985. In 1996–97, it offered 146 courses at a distance. In the fall of 1996, there was a total of 2,110 students enrolled in distance learning courses.
Course delivery sites Courses are delivered to your home, your workplace, military bases, other colleges.
Media Courses are delivered via videotapes. Students and teachers interact via mail, telephone, fax, e-mail. A computer is required for some courses.
Services Distance learners have access to library services, the campus computer network, e-mail services, academic advising, tutoring, career placement assistance at a distance.
Credit-earning options Students may transfer credits from another institution or may earn credits through standardized exams, institutionally developed exams, portfolio assessment, military training, business training.
Typical costs *Undergraduate:* Tuition of $180 per credit. *Graduate:* Tuition of $195 per credit. Financial aid is available to distance learners enrolled full-time or part-time.
Registration Students may register by mail, phone.
Contact Mr. Shaun Redgate, Liberty University, 1971 University Boulevard, Lynchburg, VA 24502. *Telephone:* 800-424-9595. *Fax:* 804-628-7977. *E-mail:* webmaster@liberty.edu. *Web site:* http://www.liberty.edu.

DEGREE & CERTIFICATE PROGRAMS

Baccalaureate Degrees

▶ *Business, General Studies, Interdisciplinary Studies, Psychology, Religion (BS)*
In the fall of 1996 there were 1,341 students enrolled in this program.
Application requirements *Prior education:* high school diploma or equivalent. *Minimum age:* 25. *Other requirements:* SAT or ACT, high school transcript, an application fee of $35.
Completion requirements 120 semester hours are required. 12 semester hours must be completed through the institution.
Program contact Mr. Jay Spencer, Dean, Liberty University, 1971 University Boulevard, Lynchburg, VA 24502. Phone: 800-424-9595. Fax: 800-628-7977.

Graduate Degrees

▶ *Counseling (MA)*
In the fall of 1996 there were 379 students enrolled in this program. In 1995–96, 49 degrees were earned at a distance through this program.
Application requirements *Prior education:* baccalaureate degree. *Minimum age:* 25. *Other requirements:* college transcripts, an application fee of $35, 3.0 GPA, minimum 6 hours undergraduate semester hours in psychology, counseling, sociology, 3 hours of statistics.
Completion requirements 36–48 semester hours are required. 9 semester hours must be completed through the institution.

Profiles: Liberty University

Program contact Mr. Jay Spencer, Dean, Liberty University, 1971 University Boulevard, Lynchburg, VA 24502. Phone: 800-424-9595. Fax: 800-628-7977.

▶ *Religion (MDiv)*
In the fall of 1996 there were 50 students enrolled in this program. In 1995–96, 3 degrees were earned at a distance through this program.
Application requirements *Prior education:* baccalaureate degree. *Minimum age:* 25. *Other requirements:* college transcripts, an application fee of $35.
Completion requirements 90 semester hours are required. 14 semester hours must be completed through the institution.
Program contact Mr. Jay Spencer, Dean, Liberty University, 1971 University Boulevard, Lynchburg, VA 24502. Phone: 800-424-9595. Fax: 800-628-7977.

▶ *Religion (MAR)*
In the fall of 1996 there were 310 students enrolled in this program. In 1995–96, 19 degrees were earned at a distance through this program.
Application requirements *Prior education:* baccalaureate degree. *Minimum age:* 25. *Other requirements:* college transcripts, an application fee of $35, 2.0 GPA.
Completion requirements 45 semester hours are required. 6 semester hours must be completed through the institution.
Program contact Mr. Jay Spencer, Dean, Liberty University, 1971 University Boulevard, Lynchburg, VA 24502. Phone: 800-424-9595. Fax: 800-628-7977.

INDIVIDUAL COURSE SUBJECT AREAS

Undergraduate
Accounting; business administration and management; liberal arts, general studies, and humanities; marketing; psychology; religious studies

Graduate
Counseling psychology; philosophy and religion; religious studies

LIFE BIBLE COLLEGE

San Dimas, California

School of Correspondence Studies

LIFE Bible College, founded in 1925, is an independent-religious four-year college affiliated with the International Church of the Foursquare Gospel. It is accredited by the Accrediting Association of Bible Colleges. It first offered distance learning courses in 1927. In 1996–97, it offered 20 courses at a distance. In the fall of 1996, there was a total of 1,000 students enrolled in distance learning courses.
Course delivery sites Courses are delivered to your home, other colleges.
Media Courses are delivered via print. Students and teachers interact via mail, telephone, fax, e-mail.
Services Distance learners have access to library services, the campus computer network, e-mail services, academic advising, career placement assistance at a distance.
Credit-earning options Students may transfer credits from another institution or may earn credits through standardized exams, institutionally developed exams, portfolio assessment.
Typical costs Tuition of $50 per credit plus mandatory fees of $20 per course. Costs may vary by number of credits taken, cost of materials. Financial aid is available to distance learners enrolled full-time.
Registration Students may register by mail, phone.
Contact Rhonda Bollig, Director, LIFE Bible College, 1100 Covina Boulevard, San Dimas, CA 91773. *Telephone:* 909-599-5433. *Fax:* 909-599-6690. *E-mail:* correspo@lifebible.edu. *Web site:* http://www.lifebible.edu.

DEGREE & CERTIFICATE PROGRAMS

Associate Degrees
▶ *Biblical Studies (AA)*
In the fall of 1996 there were 30 students enrolled in this program. In 1995–96, 1 degree was earned at a distance through this program.
Restrictions Statement of Christian faith is required.
Application requirements *Prior education:* high school diploma or equivalent. *Other requirements:* high school transcript, college transcripts, an essay or personal statement, an application fee.
Completion requirements 64 credits are required. 32 credits must be completed through the institution.

INDIVIDUAL COURSE SUBJECT AREAS

Undergraduate
Bible studies; Classical languages and literatures; communications; ethics; history; physical sciences; religious studies

LINCOLN CHRISTIAN COLLEGE

Lincoln, Illinois

Video Correspondence Department

Lincoln Christian College, founded in 1944, is an independent-religious four-year college affiliated with the Christian Churches and Churches of Christ. It is accredited by the North Central Association of Colleges and Schools. It first offered distance learning courses in 1993. In 1996–97, it offered 26 courses at a distance. In the fall of 1996, there was a total of 80 students enrolled in distance learning courses.
Course delivery sites Courses are delivered to your home.
Media Courses are delivered via videotapes. Students and teachers interact via mail, telephone, fax, e-mail.
Services Distance learners have access to library services, academic advising, tutoring at a distance.
Credit-earning options Students may transfer credits from another institution or may earn credits through military training.
Typical costs *Undergraduate:* Tuition of $170 per credit hour. *Graduate:* Tuition of $170 per credit hour. *Noncredit courses:* $50 per course. Financial aid is available to distance learners enrolled full-time.
Registration Students may register by mail, fax.
Contact Tom Sowers, Director, Video Correspondence, Lincoln Christian College, 100 Campus View Drive, Lincoln, IL 62656. *Telephone:* 217-732-3168. *Fax:* 217-732-1821. *E-mail:* lccs-video@prairienet.org. *Web site:* http://www.prairienet.org/lccs.

DEGREE & CERTIFICATE PROGRAMS

Undergraduate Certificates
▶ *Theological Studies*
Application requirements *Prior education:* high school diploma or equivalent. *Other requirements:* high school transcript, letter(s) of recommendation.
Completion requirements 30 semester credits are required. 12 semester credits must be completed through the institution.
Program contact Alan Kline, Registrar, Lincoln Christian College, 100 Campus View Drive, Lincoln, IL 62656. Phone: 217-732-3168. Fax: 217-732-5914. E-mail: awkline@prairienet.org.

INDIVIDUAL COURSE SUBJECT AREAS

Undergraduate
Adult education; Greek language and literature; Hebrew language and literature; management information systems; theological studies

Graduate
Counseling psychology; Greek language and literature; Hebrew language and literature; theological studies

Noncredit
Adult education; counseling psychology; Greek language and literature; Hebrew language and literature; management information systems; theological studies

LINCOLN LAND COMMUNITY COLLEGE

Springfield, Illinois

Learning Resource Center

Lincoln Land Community College, founded in 1967, is a district-supported two-year college. It is accredited by the North Central Association of Colleges and Schools. It first offered distance learning courses in 1980. In 1996–97, it offered 12 courses at a distance. In the fall of 1996, there was a total of 500 students enrolled in distance learning courses.
Course delivery sites Courses are delivered to your home, 5 off-campus centers in Hillsboro, Jacksonville, Litchfield, Petersburg, Taylorville.
Media Courses are delivered via television, videotapes, videoconferencing, computer software, World Wide Web, e-mail. Students and teachers interact via mail, telephone, fax, e-mail. A computer is required for some courses.
Restrictions Programs are available to in-state students only. Courses are available in school service region only.
Services Distance learners have access to library services, e-mail services, academic advising at a distance.
Credit-earning options Students may earn credits through institutionally developed exams.
Typical costs Tuition of $39 per credit hour for local area residents. Tuition of $105.97 per credit hour for in-state residents. Tuition of $170.64 per credit hour for out-of-state residents. Financial aid is available to distance learners enrolled part-time.
Registration Students may register by mail.
Contact Dr. James W. Jackson, Director, Learning Resource Center, Lincoln Land Community College, Shepherd Road, Springfield, IL 62704. Telephone: 217-786-2427. Fax: 217-786-2251. E-mail: jjackson@cabin.llcc.cc.il.us. Web site: http://www.llcc.cc.il.us/.

INDIVIDUAL COURSE SUBJECT AREAS

Undergraduate
Advertising; business; economics; English language and literature; history; psychology; public health; sociology

LOMA LINDA UNIVERSITY

Loma Linda, California

Loma Linda University, founded in 1905, is an independent-religious Seventh-day Adventist university. It is accredited by the Western Association of Schools and Colleges, Inc. It first offered distance learning courses in 1996. In 1996–97, it offered 6 courses at a distance. In the fall of 1996, there was a total of 20 students enrolled in distance learning courses.
Course delivery sites Courses are delivered to your workplace, Atlantic Union College (South Lancaster, MA), 1 off-campus center in Glendale.
Media Courses are delivered via videotapes, videoconferencing, World Wide Web, e-mail, print, interactive television. Students and teachers interact via videoconferencing, mail, telephone, fax, e-mail.
Services Distance learners have access to library services, academic advising, tutoring, career placement assistance at a distance.
Credit-earning options Students may transfer credits from another institution or may earn credits through examinations.
Typical costs Tuition of $315 per unit. Costs may vary by campus or location, specific program of study, number of credits taken. Financial aid is available to distance learners enrolled full-time.
Registration Students may register by mail, fax, phone.
Contact Office of the President, Loma Linda University, Magan Hall, Room 110, Loma Linda, CA 92350. Telephone: 909-824-4542. Fax: 909-478-4242. E-mail: president@llu.edu.

DEGREE & CERTIFICATE PROGRAMS

Baccalaureate Degrees

▶ *Health Information Administration (BS)*
In the fall of 1996 there were 27 students enrolled in this program.
Application requirements *Prior education:* associate degree. *Other requirements:* registry exam for accredited record technician, high school transcript, college transcripts, an essay or personal statement, letter(s) of recommendation, an application fee of $50.
Completion requirements 192 units are required. 50 units must be completed through the institution. This is a degree completion program. *Maximum time for completion:* four years.
Program contact Susan Heisler, RRA, Recruitment Coordinator, Loma Linda University, 1905 Nichol Hall, Loma Linda, CA 92350. Phone: 909-824-4976. Fax: 909-824-4291. E-mail: sheisler@ccmail.llu.edu.

▶ *Public Health (BSPH)*
Application requirements *Prior education:* some undergraduate course work. *Other requirements:* college transcripts, an essay or personal statement, letter(s) of recommendation, an application fee of $25.
Completion requirements 192 units are required. 50 units must be completed through the institution. This is a degree completion program.
Program contact Dr. Patricia Johnston, Associate Dean, Loma Linda University, 1709 Nichol Hall, School of Public Health, Loma Linda, CA 92350. Phone: 909-478-8621. Fax: 909-824-4087.

INDIVIDUAL COURSE SUBJECT AREAS

Undergraduate
Biological and life sciences; health professions and related sciences; social work

LONG BEACH CITY COLLEGE

Long Beach, California

Long Beach City College, founded in 1927, is a state-supported two-year college. It is accredited by the Western Association of Schools and Colleges, Inc. In 1996–97, it offered 9 courses at a distance. In the fall of 1996, there was a total of 587 students enrolled in distance learning courses.
Course delivery sites Courses are delivered to your home.
Media Courses are delivered via television, videotapes. Students and teachers interact via on-campus meetings.

Profiles: Long Beach City College

Restrictions Programs are available to local area students only.
Credit-earning options Students may transfer credits from another institution or may earn credits through institutionally developed exams, military training.
Typical costs Tuition of $15 per unit for in-state residents. Tuition of $127 per unit for out-of-state residents. Undergraduate students outside the country pay $132 per unit. Financial aid is available to distance learners enrolled full-time or part-time.
Registration Students may register by phone.
Contact Clifford Uejio, Interim Dean, Long Beach City College, 4901 East Carson Street, Long Beach, CA 90808. *Telephone:* 562-938-4177. *Fax:* 562-938-4057. *E-mail:* cuejio@lbcc.cc.ca.us.

INDIVIDUAL COURSE SUBJECT AREAS

Undergraduate

Anthropology; astronomy and astrophysics; biological and life sciences; biology; business; business administration and management; English composition; history; home economics and family studies; physical sciences; political science; psychology; social sciences; sociology

LONGVIEW COMMUNITY COLLEGE

Lee's Summit, Missouri

Program for Adult College Education (PACE)

Longview Community College, founded in 1969, is a state and locally supported two-year college. It is accredited by the North Central Association of Colleges and Schools. It first offered distance learning courses in 1992. In 1996–97, it offered 15 courses at a distance. In the fall of 1996, there was a total of 500 students enrolled in distance learning courses.
Course delivery sites Courses are delivered to your home, your workplace, 5 off-campus centers in Blue Springs, Independence, Kansas City.
Media Courses are delivered via television. Students and teachers interact via mail, telephone, fax. A computer is required for some courses.
Restrictions Programs are available to local area students only.
Services Distance learners have access to library services, the campus computer network, academic advising at a distance.
Credit-earning options Students may transfer credits from another institution or may earn credits through standardized exams.
Typical costs Tuition of $55 per credit hour. Financial aid is available to distance learners enrolled full-time or part-time.
Registration Students may register by mail, fax, phone.
Contact Tamara Miller, PACE Outreach Coordinator, Longview Community College, 500 Southwest Longview Road, Lee's Summit, MO 64081. *Telephone:* 816-672-2369. *Fax:* 816-672-2426.

DEGREE & CERTIFICATE PROGRAMS

Associate Degrees
▶ *General Studies (AA)*
In the fall of 1996 there were 500 students enrolled in this program. In 1995–96, 100 degrees were earned at a distance through this program.
Application requirements *Prior education:* high school diploma or equivalent.
Completion requirements 62 credits are required. 15 credits must be completed through the institution.
On-campus requirements For some testing.

INDIVIDUAL COURSE SUBJECT AREAS

Undergraduate

Accounting; biology; business; business administration and management; computer and information sciences; economics; English composition; English language and literature; history; law and legal studies; liberal arts, general studies, and humanities; mathematics; nursing; philosophy and religion; physical sciences; psychology; social work; sociology; teacher education

LORAIN COUNTY COMMUNITY COLLEGE

Elyria, Ohio

Instructional Television

Lorain County Community College, founded in 1963, is a state and locally supported two-year college. It is accredited by the North Central Association of Colleges and Schools. It first offered distance learning courses in 1990.
Course delivery sites Courses are delivered to your home, your workplace.
Media Courses are delivered via television, videotapes, videoconferencing, audioconferencing, print.
Restrictions Programs are available to local area students only.
Credit-earning options Students may transfer credits from another institution or may earn credits through examinations, portfolio assessment, military training, business training. Financial aid is available to distance learners.
Contact Lee Kias, Director, Lorain County Community College, 1005 North Abbe Road, Elyria, OH 44035. *Telephone:* 800-995-5222. *Fax:* 216-365-6519.

INDIVIDUAL COURSE SUBJECT AREAS

Undergraduate

Accounting; Asian languages and literatures; business administration and management; creative writing; English as a second language (ESL); English composition; English language and literature; history; liberal arts, general studies, and humanities; mathematics; music; philosophy and religion; physics; psychology; social psychology; sociology; teacher education

LORD FAIRFAX COMMUNITY COLLEGE

Middletown, Virginia

Lord Fairfax Community College, founded in 1969, is a state-supported two-year college. It is accredited by the Southern Association of Colleges and Schools. It first offered distance learning courses in 1995. In 1996–97, it offered 14 courses at a distance. In the fall of 1996, there was a total of 200 students enrolled in distance learning courses.
Course delivery sites Courses are delivered to Virginia Community College System (Richmond), 5 off-campus centers in Berryville, Mount Jackson, Strasburg, Woodstock.
Media Courses are delivered via television, videotapes, print. Students and teachers interact via mail, telephone, fax, e-mail.
Restrictions Programs are available to in-state students only.
Services Distance learners have access to library services, academic advising, tutoring, career placement assistance at a distance.

Typical costs Tuition of $46.65 per credit plus mandatory fees of $14 per semester for local area residents. Tuition of $156 per credit plus mandatory fees of $14 per semester for out-of-state residents. Financial aid is available to distance learners.
Registration Students may register by mail, phone.
Contact Dr. Ron Ludwick, Director of Continuing Education, Lord Fairfax Community College, PO Box 47, Middletown, VA 22645. *Telephone:* 540-869-1120. *Fax:* 540-869-6424.

INDIVIDUAL COURSE SUBJECT AREAS

Undergraduate
Biological and life sciences; communications; English composition; history; psychology; sociology

LOS ANGELES COMMUNITY COLLEGE DISTRICT

Los Angeles, California

Instructional Television

Los Angeles Community College District is a locally supported college system. It first offered distance learning courses in 1964. In 1996–97, it offered 28 courses at a distance. In the fall of 1996, there was a total of 1,832 students enrolled in distance learning courses.
Course delivery sites Courses are delivered to your home, your workplace.
Media Courses are delivered via television, videotapes. Students and teachers interact via mail, telephone, fax, e-mail.
Services Distance learners have access to e-mail services at a distance.
Credit-earning options Students may earn credits through institutionally developed exams.
Typical costs Tuition of $13 per credit plus mandatory fees of $7.50 per semester for in-state residents. Tuition of $125 per credit plus mandatory fees of $7.50 per semester for out-of-state residents. Costs may vary by number of credits taken. Financial aid is available to distance learners enrolled full-time or part-time.
Registration Students may register by mail, fax, phone.
Contact Instructional Television, Los Angeles Community College District, 855 North Vermont Avenue, Los Angeles, CA 90029. *Telephone:* 213-953-4488. *Fax:* 213-666-4042. *Web site:* http://www.lacc.cc.ca.us

Special note
Instructional Television has provided distance learning opportunities in southern California for more than 30 years; the program is now the largest telecourse program in the area. The program currently offers more than 15 courses each semester that meet the general education requirements for the associate and bachelor's degrees. Courses include anthropology, astronomy, English, geology, history, humanities, management, political science, psychology, and sociology. Although the majority of students reside in the Los Angeles Basin, assistance is available to anyone who owns a television set and a VCR.

Students are supported by an innovative combination of nationally produced videos, faculty letters, materials mailed throughout the semester, telephone contacts by faculty members, and e-mail. Faculty members, who can be reached by telephone, e-mail, and fax, maintain extended office hours each week and contact each student personally throughout the term. In addition, faculty members conduct seminars on local campuses to provide enhanced instruction for students who are able to attend them. Textbooks and study guides are available by mail; video components may be rented for a minimal fee and can be shipped by UPS.

Requirements and expectations for distance education courses are equivalent to those of regular college courses in terms of quantity and quality of material and rigor of assignments. All courses are 3 units of transferable college credit.

INDIVIDUAL COURSE SUBJECT AREAS

Undergraduate
American (US) history; anthropology; astronomy and astrophysics; business administration and management; developmental and child psychology; economics; English language and literature; geology; history; home economics and family studies; law and legal studies; liberal arts, general studies, and humanities; oceanography; political science; social psychology; sociology

LOS ANGELES PIERCE COLLEGE

Woodland Hills, California

Los Angeles Pierce College, founded in 1947, is a state and locally supported two-year college. It is accredited by the Western Association of Schools and Colleges, Inc. It first offered distance learning courses in 1997.
Course delivery sites Courses are delivered to California Polytechnic State University, San Luis Obispo (San Luis Obispo), California State Polytechnic University, Pomona (Pomona).
Media Courses are delivered via television, videoconferencing. Students and teachers interact via videoconferencing.
Restrictions Programs are available to local area students only.
Services Distance learners have access to academic advising at a distance.
Credit-earning options Students may transfer credits from another institution or may earn credits through examinations.
Typical costs Tuition of $13 per unit for in-state residents. Tuition of $128 per unit for out-of-state residents. Costs may vary by campus or location, number of credits taken.
Registration Students may register by phone.
Contact Carlos Martinez, Dean, Academic Affairs, Los Angeles Pierce College, 6201 Winnetka Avenue, Woodland Hills, CA 91371. *Telephone:* 818-719-6444. *Fax:* 818-710-9844. *E-mail:* martinc@laccd.cc.ca.us.

INDIVIDUAL COURSE SUBJECT AREAS

Undergraduate
Animal sciences; conservation and natural resources

LOUISIANA COLLEGE

Pineville, Louisiana

LC Online

Louisiana College, founded in 1906, is an independent-religious Southern Baptist four-year college. It is accredited by the Southern Association of Colleges and Schools. It first offered distance learning courses in 1995. In 1996–97, it offered 30 courses at a distance.
Course delivery sites Courses are delivered to your home, your workplace, military bases.

Profiles: Louisiana College

Media Courses are delivered via World Wide Web, e-mail, Internet. Students and teachers interact via e-mail, computer conferencing. A computer is required for all courses.
Services Distance learners have access to library services, academic advising, tutoring, career placement assistance at a distance.
Credit-earning options Students may transfer credits from another institution or may earn credits through examinations.
Typical costs Tuition of $197 per credit hour plus mandatory fees of $23.50 per semester. Costs may vary by number of credits taken. Financial aid is available to distance learners enrolled full-time.
Registration Students may register by World Wide Web.
Contact Rosanne Osborne, Director, LC Online, Louisiana College, Box 606, 1140 College Drive, Pineville, LA 71359. *Telephone:* 318-487-7211. *Fax:* 318-487-7310. *E-mail:* osborne@andria.lacollege.edu. *Web site:* http://lconline.lacollege.edu.

DEGREE & CERTIFICATE PROGRAMS

Baccalaureate Degrees
▶ *General Studies (BGS)*
Application requirements *Prior education:* high school diploma or equivalent. *Other requirements:* high school transcript, college transcripts, must be out of high school for 2 years.
Completion requirements 127 hours are required. 30 hours must be completed through the institution.

INDIVIDUAL COURSE SUBJECT AREAS

Undergraduate
Creative writing; education; English composition; English language and literature; history; journalism; philosophy and religion; sociology; theological studies

---

LOUISIANA STATE UNIVERSITY AND AGRICULTURAL AND MECHANICAL COLLEGE

Baton Rouge, Louisiana

Louisiana State University and Agricultural and Mechanical College, founded in 1860, is a state-supported university. It is accredited by the Southern Association of Colleges and Schools. It first offered distance learning courses in 1984.
Course delivery sites Courses are delivered to your home.
Media Courses are delivered via television, videotapes, videoconferencing, computer software, print, audiographics conferencing, computer conferencing.
Restrictions Programs are available to in-state students only.
Services Distance learners have access to library services, academic advising, career placement assistance at a distance.
Credit-earning options Students may transfer credits from another institution or may earn credits through examinations.
Contact Director, Distance Learning, Louisiana State University and Agricultural and Mechanical College, 118 Himes Hall, Baton Rouge, LA 70810. *Telephone:* 504-388-1135. *Fax:* 504-388-5789. *Web site:* http://himes133-1.disd.lsu.edu/index.html.

INDIVIDUAL COURSE SUBJECT AREAS

Undergraduate
Business administration and management; communications; history; home economics and family studies; political science; psychology; sociology

Graduate
Agriculture; business administration and management; home economics and family studies; library and information studies; teacher education

---

LOUISIANA STATE UNIVERSITY AT EUNICE

Eunice, Louisiana

Continuing Education

Louisiana State University at Eunice, founded in 1967, is a state-supported two-year college. It is accredited by the Southern Association of Colleges and Schools. It first offered distance learning courses in 1996. In 1996–97, it offered 20 courses at a distance. In the fall of 1996, there was a total of 100 students enrolled in distance learning courses.
Course delivery sites Courses are delivered to your home, your workplace, Louisiana State University and Agricultural and Mechanical College (Baton Rouge), Louisiana State University at Alexandria (Alexandria), Louisiana State University Medical Center (New Orleans).
Media Courses are delivered via television, videoconferencing. Students and teachers interact via videoconferencing, mail, telephone, fax, e-mail.
Restrictions Programs are available to in-state students only.
Services Distance learners have access to library services, the campus computer network, e-mail services, academic advising, financial aid services at a distance.
Credit-earning options Students may transfer credits from another institution or may earn credits through standardized exams, institutionally developed exams, military training.
Typical costs Tuition of $44 per hour. *Noncredit courses:* $50 per course. Costs may vary by number of credits taken. Financial aid is available to distance learners enrolled full-time or part-time.
Registration Students may register by mail, fax, e-mail.
Contact Monty Sullivan, Director, Continuing Education, Louisiana State University at Eunice, PO Box 1129, Eunice, LA 70535-1129. *Telephone:* 318-457-7311, Ext. 390. *Fax:* 318-546-6620. *E-mail:* msulliva@lsue.edu.

INDIVIDUAL COURSE SUBJECT AREAS

Undergraduate
Adult education; animal sciences; European languages and literatures; fire science; French language and literature; health professions and related sciences; horticulture; physical sciences; physics; psychology; sociology

Graduate
Adult education; library and information studies; special education

---

LOUISIANA STATE UNIVERSITY IN SHREVEPORT

Shreveport, Louisiana

Division of Continuing Education and Public Service

Louisiana State University in Shreveport, founded in 1965, is a state-supported comprehensive institution. It is accredited by the Southern Association of Colleges and Schools. It first offered distance learning courses in 1995.
Course delivery sites Courses are delivered to other colleges.
Media Courses are delivered via television, videoconferencing, audiographics conferencing, computer conferencing.

Profiles: Lycoming College

Credit-earning options Students may transfer credits from another institution or may earn credits through examinations, military training. Financial aid is available to distance learners.
Contact Dr. Dean, Continuing Education and Public Service, Louisiana State University in Shreveport, 1 University Place, Bronson Hall, Shreveport, LA 71115. *Telephone:* 318-797-5306. *Fax:* 318-797-5395.

INDIVIDUAL COURSE SUBJECT AREAS

Undergraduate
Business administration and management; conservation and natural resources; education; education administration; history; library and information studies; political science; special education; teacher education; zoology

Graduate
Business administration and management; conservation and natural resources; education; education administration; history; library and information studies; political science; special education; teacher education; zoology

Noncredit
Political science

LOYOLA UNIVERSITY NEW ORLEANS

New Orleans, Louisiana

Off-Campus Learning Program

Loyola University New Orleans, founded in 1912, is an independent-religious Roman Catholic (Jesuit) comprehensive institution. It is accredited by the Southern Association of Colleges and Schools. It first offered distance learning courses in 1990.
Course delivery sites Courses are delivered to your workplace.
Media Courses are delivered via videotapes. Students and teachers interact via mail, telephone, fax, e-mail.
Restrictions Programs are available to in-state students only.
Services Distance learners have access to library services, academic advising, tutoring, career placement assistance at a distance.
Credit-earning options Students may transfer credits from another institution or may earn credits through examinations, portfolio assessment, military training, business training.
Typical costs Tuition of $190 per credit. Costs may vary by number of credits taken. Financial aid is available to distance learners enrolled full-time or part-time.
Registration Students may register by phone.
Contact Kristel Scheuermann, Coordinator, Off-Campus Learning Program, Loyola University New Orleans, Box 14, 6363 Saint Charles Avenue, New Orleans, LA 70118. *Telephone:* 504-865-3250. *Fax:* 504-865-3883. *E-mail:* scheuer@beta.loyno.edu.

DEGREE & CERTIFICATE PROGRAMS

Baccalaureate Degrees
▶ *Nursing (BSN)*
Application requirements *Prior education:* RN license. *Other requirements:* Louisiana RN license.
Completion requirements 129 hours are required. 32 hours must be completed through the institution. This is a degree completion program.
On-campus requirements One course is required to be completed on a campus; however, satellite campuses are available.

Distance Learning Programs

INDIVIDUAL COURSE SUBJECT AREAS

Undergraduate
English composition; fine arts; liberal arts, general studies, and humanities; music; nursing; sociology; statistics; theological studies

LUZERNE COUNTY COMMUNITY COLLEGE

Nanticoke, Pennsylvania

Telecollege

Luzerne County Community College, founded in 1966, is a county-supported two-year college. It is accredited by the Middle States Association of Colleges and Schools. It first offered distance learning courses in 1981.
Course delivery sites Courses are delivered to your home, your workplace, correctional facility.
Media Courses are delivered via television, videotapes, print.
Credit-earning options Students may transfer credits from another institution or may earn credits through examinations, portfolio assessment, military training, business training. Financial aid is available to distance learners.
Contact Director, Non-Traditional Learning Services, Luzerne County Community College, 1333 South Prospect Street, Nanticoke, PA 18634. *Telephone:* 717-740-0423. *Fax:* 717-735-6130.

DEGREE & CERTIFICATE PROGRAMS

Associate Degrees
▶ *General Studies (AS)*

INDIVIDUAL COURSE SUBJECT AREAS

Undergraduate
Advertising; astronomy and astrophysics; business administration and management; conservation and natural resources; developmental and child psychology; economics; English composition; English language and literature; European languages and literatures; fine arts; geology; health and physical education/fitness; history; home economics and family studies; journalism; law and legal studies; mathematics; philosophy and religion; political science; sociology

LYCOMING COLLEGE

Williamsport, Pennsylvania

Lycoming College, founded in 1812, is an independent-religious United Methodist four-year college. It is accredited by the Middle States Association of Colleges and Schools. It first offered distance learning courses in 1996. In 1996–97, it offered 1 course at a distance. In the fall of 1996, there was a total of 10 students enrolled in distance learning courses.
Course delivery sites Courses are delivered to your home, your workplace, military bases, Juniata College (Huntingdon).
Media Courses are delivered via videotapes, videoconferencing, World Wide Web, e-mail, print. Students and teachers interact via videoconferencing, mail, telephone, fax, e-mail.
Services Distance learners have access to library services, academic advising at a distance.
Credit-earning options Students may earn credits through institutionally developed exams.

149

Profiles: Lycoming College

Typical costs Tuition of $2006 per course. Financial aid is available to distance learners.
Registration Students may register by mail, fax.
Contact Dr. John F. Piper, Jr., Dean of the College, Lycoming College, 700 College Place, Williamsport, PA 17701. *Telephone:* 717-321-4038. *Fax:* 717-321-4106. *E-mail:* piper@lycoming.edu. *Web site:* http://www.lycoming.edu/dept/av/vc.htm.

INDIVIDUAL COURSE SUBJECT AREAS

Undergraduate
Accounting; area, ethnic, and cultural studies; astronomy and astrophysics; business; business administration and management; Classical languages and literatures; creative writing; developmental and child psychology; economics; educational psychology; English composition; English language and literature; European languages and literatures; fine arts; history; industrial psychology; liberal arts, general studies, and humanities; mathematics; music; philosophy and religion; political science; social psychology; sociology; teacher education

MADISON AREA TECHNICAL COLLEGE

Madison, Wisconsin

Instructional Media/Distance Education Department

Madison Area Technical College, founded in 1911, is a district-supported two-year college. It is accredited by the North Central Association of Colleges and Schools. It first offered distance learning courses in 1994. In 1996–97, it offered 35 courses at a distance. In the fall of 1996, there was a total of 200 students enrolled in distance learning courses.
Course delivery sites Courses are delivered to your workplace, 17 off-campus centers in Mauston, Pardeeville, Spring Green, Sun Prairie.
Media Courses are delivered via videotapes, videoconferencing. Students and teachers interact via videoconferencing, mail, fax.
Restrictions Students must be able to travel to campus.
Credit-earning options Students may transfer credits from another institution or may earn credits through standardized exams, portfolio assessment, military training, business training.
Typical costs *Undergraduate:* Tuition of $54 per credit plus mandatory fees of $3.50 per credit for in-state residents. Tuition of $373 per credit plus mandatory fees of $3.50 per credit for out-of-state residents. *Graduate:* Tuition of $71.55 per credit plus mandatory fees of $3.50 per credit for in-state residents. Tuition of $175.15 per credit plus mandatory fees of $3.50 per credit for out-of-state residents. Financial aid is available to distance learners enrolled full-time or part-time.
Registration Students may register by mail, phone.
Contact Paul Meske, Instructional Media/Distance Education Specialist, Madison Area Technical College, 3550 Anderson Street, Madison, WI 53704. *Telephone:* 608-246-6050. *Fax:* 608-246-6287. *E-mail:* meske@madison.tec.wi.us. *Web site:* http://www.madison.tec.wi.us.

DEGREE & CERTIFICATE PROGRAMS

Undergraduate Certificates
▶ *Quality Management*
Application requirements *Prior education:* high school diploma or equivalent. *Other requirements:* high school transcript, an application fee.
Completion requirements 12 credits are required. 12 credits must be completed through the institution.
Program contact Mr. Warren Hillmer, Associate Dean, Marketing Department, Madison Area Technical College, 3550 Anderson Street, Madison, WI 53704. Phone: 608-246-6550. Fax: 608-246-6948.

INDIVIDUAL COURSE SUBJECT AREAS

Undergraduate
Accounting; algebra; American (US) history; American literature; business; business administration and management; business law; economics; English composition; English language and literature; English literature; European languages and literatures; home economics and family studies; liberal arts, general studies, and humanities; nursing; psychology; sociology; Spanish language and literature; statistics

Noncredit
Business administration and management

MADONNA UNIVERSITY

Livonia, Michigan

College of Continuing and Professional Studies

Madonna University, founded in 1947, is an independent-religious Roman Catholic comprehensive institution. It is accredited by the North Central Association of Colleges and Schools. It first offered distance learning courses in 1983. In 1996–97, it offered 12 courses at a distance. In the fall of 1996, there was a total of 50 students enrolled in distance learning courses.
Course delivery sites Courses are delivered to your home, your workplace, Schoolcraft College (Livonia), 1 off-campus center in Gaylord.
Media Courses are delivered via television, videotapes, videoconferencing, audiotapes, audioconferencing, computer software, World Wide Web, e-mail, print. Students and teachers interact via videoconferencing, audioconferencing, mail, telephone, fax, e-mail. A computer is required for some courses.
Restrictions Some courses are available to in-state students only.
Services Distance learners have access to library services, the campus computer network, e-mail services, academic advising, tutoring, career placement assistance at a distance.
Credit-earning options Students may transfer credits from another institution or may earn credits through standardized exams, institutionally developed exams, portfolio assessment, military training, business training.
Typical costs *Undergraduate:* Tuition of $198 per semester hour plus mandatory fees of $50 per semester. *Graduate:* Tuition of $248 per semester hour plus mandatory fees of $50 per semester. *Noncredit courses:* $100 per continuing education unit. Costs may vary by specific program of study, number of credits taken. Financial aid is available to distance learners enrolled full-time or part-time.
Registration Students may register by mail, fax, phone, e-mail.
Contact Dr. James Novak, Dean, College of Continuing and Professional Studies, Madonna University, 36600 Schoolcraft, Livonia, MI 48150-1173. *Telephone:* 313-432-5731. *Fax:* 313-432-5364. *E-mail:* novak@smtp.munet.edu. *Web site:* http://www.munet.edu.

DEGREE & CERTIFICATE PROGRAMS

Baccalaureate Degrees
▶ *Social Work (BSW)*
Restrictions This program is available to in-state students only.
Application requirements *Prior education:* some undergraduate course work. *Other requirements:* SAT or ACT, high school transcript, an essay or personal statement, general education courses.
Completion requirements 120 semester hours are required. This is a degree completion program. *Maximum time for completion:* two-and-a-half years.

Graduate Degrees

▶ *Medical and Dental Practice Administration (MSBA)*
Application requirements *Prior education:* graduate degree. *Other requirements:* TOEFL, college transcripts, 2 years in private practice, completion of residency, state licensure evidence.
Completion requirements 30 semester hours are required. *Maximum time for completion:* 20 months.
On-campus requirements Five weekends.

INDIVIDUAL COURSE SUBJECT AREAS

Undergraduate
Business administration and management; marketing; social sciences

Graduate
Business; business administration and management

MAHARISHI UNIVERSITY OF MANAGEMENT

Fairfield, Iowa

Department of Distance Education

Maharishi University of Management, founded in 1971, is an independent-nonprofit university. It is accredited by the North Central Association of Colleges and Schools. It first offered distance learning courses in 1995. In 1996–97, it offered 45 courses at a distance. In the fall of 1996, there was a total of 300 students enrolled in distance learning courses.
Course delivery sites Courses are delivered to sites in New Delhi, Bangalore, Chennai, Hydelabau, Lucknow (India).
Media Courses are delivered via videotapes. Students and teachers interact via telephone, fax, e-mail.
Services Distance learners have access to library services, the campus computer network, e-mail services, academic advising, tutoring, career placement assistance at a distance.
Credit-earning options Students may earn credits through institutionally developed exams.
Typical costs Tuition of $75 per credit. Financial aid is available to distance learners enrolled full-time.
Contact Michael Matzkin, Coordinator, Maharishi University of Management, Department of Distance Education, Fairfield, IA 52557. *Telephone:* 515-472-1128. *Fax:* 515-472-1128. *E-mail:* distance@mum.edu. *Web site:* http://www.mum.edu.

DEGREE & CERTIFICATE PROGRAMS

Graduate Degrees

▶ *Business Administration (MBA)*
In the fall of 1996 there were 300 students enrolled in this program.
Application requirements *Prior education:* undergraduate degree. *Other requirements:* TOEFL, entrance examination, high school transcript, college transcripts, an essay or personal statement, letter(s) of recommendation, an application fee of $10.
Completion requirements 88 credits are required.
Program contact Mr. Pyarelal Kadalbaju, National Registrar, Maharishi University of Management, 55 Golf Links, New Delhi, 110 003, India. Phone: 911-14624563. Fax: 911-14619603. E-mail: maharis.mimgmt@axcess.net.in.

MANATEE COMMUNITY COLLEGE

Bradenton, Florida

Manatee Community College, founded in 1957, is a state-supported two-year college. It is accredited by the Southern Association of Colleges and Schools. It first offered distance learning courses in 1990.
Course delivery sites Courses are delivered to your home, high schools.
Media Courses are delivered via television, videotapes, computer software, e-mail, print. Students and teachers interact via audioconferencing, mail, telephone, fax, e-mail.
Restrictions Programs are available to local area students only.
Credit-earning options Students may transfer credits from another institution or may earn credits through standardized exams, institutionally developed exams, portfolio assessment.
Typical costs Tuition of $112 per course for in-state residents. Tuition of $411 per course for out-of-state residents. Financial aid is available to distance learners enrolled full-time or part-time.
Registration Students may register by phone.
Contact Dr. Nancy Hoover, Provost and Dean of Educational Services, Manatee Community College, 8000 South Tamiami Trail, Venice, FL 34293. *Telephone:* 941-493-3504. *Fax:* 941-493-3504, Ext. 2150. *E-mail:* hoovern@fob.sc.mcc.cc.fl.us.

INDIVIDUAL COURSE SUBJECT AREAS

Undergraduate
Algebra; biology; business administration and management; computer and information sciences; design; English composition; history; liberal arts, general studies, and humanities; marketing; psychology; religious studies; statistics

MANCHESTER COMMUNITY-TECHNICAL COLLEGE

Manchester, Connecticut

Manchester Community-Technical College, founded in 1963, is a state-supported two-year college. It is accredited by the New England Association of Schools and Colleges. It first offered distance learning courses in 1989. In 1996–97, it offered 14 courses at a distance. In the fall of 1996, there was a total of 125 students enrolled in distance learning courses.
Course delivery sites Courses are delivered to your home, your workplace.
Media Courses are delivered via television, World Wide Web. Students and teachers interact via mail, telephone, fax, e-mail. A computer is required for some courses.
Services Distance learners have access to library services at a distance.
Credit-earning options Students may transfer credits from another institution or may earn credits through standardized exams, institutionally developed exams, military training.
Typical costs Tuition of $65 per credit for in-state residents. Tuition of $195 per credit for out-of-state residents. *Noncredit courses:* $231 per course. Financial aid is available to distance learners.
Registration Students may register by fax.
Contact Diane Goldsmith, Director of Transition and Women's Program, Manchester Community-Technical College, MS# 1B, PO Box 1046, Manchester, CT 06045-1046. *Telephone:* 860-647-6056. *Fax:* 860-647-6238. *E-mail:* ma-goldsmith@commnet.edu.

Profiles: Manchester Community-Technical College

INDIVIDUAL COURSE SUBJECT AREAS

Undergraduate
Criminology; English composition; English literature; geography; Japanese language and literature; occupational therapy

MARSHALL UNIVERSITY

Huntington, West Virginia

Adult and Extended Education

Marshall University, founded in 1837, is a state-supported comprehensive institution. It is accredited by the North Central Association of Colleges and Schools. It first offered distance learning courses in 1986. In 1996–97, it offered 49 courses at a distance. In the fall of 1996, there was a total of 743 students enrolled in distance learning courses.

Course delivery sites Courses are delivered to other colleges, 3 off-campus centers in Capitol Center, Mid-Ohio Valley Center, Southern Mountain Center, public libraries, hospitals, vocational technical centers, high schools.

Media Courses are delivered via television, videoconferencing, World Wide Web. Students and teachers interact via videoconferencing, audioconferencing, telephone, fax, e-mail. A computer is required for some courses.

Restrictions Programs are available to in-state students only.

Services Distance learners have access to library services at a distance.

Credit-earning options Students may transfer credits from another institution or may earn credits through institutionally developed exams, portfolio assessment.

Typical costs *Undergraduate:* Tuition of $91.25 per hour for in-state residents. Tuition of $253 per hour for out-of-state residents. *Graduate:* Tuition of $128.75 per hour for in-state residents. Tuition of $369.50 per hour for out-of-state residents. Costs may vary by specific program of study, number of credits taken. Financial aid is available to distance learners.

Registration Students may register by mail, phone, World Wide Web.

Contact Gail H. Sheets, Program Manager, Marshall University, 400 Hal Greer Boulevard, Huntington, WV 25755-2140. *Telephone:* 304-696-2970. *Fax:* 304-696-2973. *E-mail:* sheets@marshall.edu. *Web site:* http://www.marshall.edu/aee/.

INDIVIDUAL COURSE SUBJECT AREAS

Undergraduate
Accounting; administrative and secretarial services; anthropology; area, ethnic, and cultural studies; business; business administration and management; criminology; developmental and child psychology; economics; education administration; educational psychology; fine arts; geography; geology; health professions and related sciences; history; home economics and family studies; journalism; law and legal studies; liberal arts, general studies, and humanities; marketing; nursing; philosophy and religion; social work; sociology; special education; teacher education

Graduate
Area, ethnic, and cultural studies; business; business administration and management; education administration; educational psychology; history; liberal arts, general studies, and humanities; nursing; social work; sociology; special education; teacher education

MARYGROVE COLLEGE

Detroit, Michigan

Master in the Art of Teaching Program

Marygrove College, founded in 1905, is an independent-religious Roman Catholic comprehensive institution. It is accredited by the North Central Association of Colleges and Schools. It first offered distance learning courses in 1989. In 1996–97, it offered 10 courses at a distance. In the fall of 1996, there was a total of 1,230 students enrolled in distance learning courses.

Course delivery sites Courses are delivered to your home.

Media Courses are delivered via videotapes. Students and teachers interact via mail, telephone, fax.

Restrictions Courses are available to students in Pennsylvania, Ohio, New Jersey, and Michigan only. Students must have baccalaureate degree, be in education, and have access to a classroom on a regular basis.

Services Distance learners have access to library services, academic advising at a distance.

Credit-earning options Students may transfer credits from another institution or may earn credits through portfolio assessment.

Typical costs Tuition of $205 per credit hour plus mandatory fees of $75 per course. Students also pay a $15 registration fee.

Registration Students may register by mail, fax, phone.

Contact Dr. Sharon R. Lockett, Director, Master in the Art of Teaching Program, Marygrove College, 8425 West McNichols Road, Detroit, MI 48221. *Telephone:* 313-862-8000, Ext. 450. *Fax:* 800-284-7054.

Special note

Marygrove College, located in Detroit, is an accredited college (North Central Association of Colleges and Schools) with more than 2,000 graduate and undergraduate students. The College has an established reputation for teacher preparation and has been distinguished by the National Council for Accreditation of Teacher Education.

Marygrove's distance learning Master in the Art of Teaching (MAT) degree program is available to all K–12 educators who desire to become better teachers. The program uses an innovative, student-centered learning model that allows the learner to participate at his or her own convenience.

A few of the features of this noteworthy, video-based MAT program include learning the latest practical classroom strategies applicable to today's children from nationally known experts; seeing master teachers model the practical strategies in actual classrooms with real students; regular contact by phone, e-mail, fax, or optional in-person visits with Marygrove's faculty mentors (mentors are available for feedback, consultation, advice, and guidance as students progress through the program); and working collaboratively with a peer study team.

Marygrove College is approved by the North Central Association to offer the MAT degree program in Ohio, Michigan, New Jersey, and Pennsylvania. The entire program can be completed in 5 semesters and is designed for working teachers seeking career advancement. For more information on the MAT program, call 800-604-6088 (toll-free) and ask for Maureen.

DEGREE & CERTIFICATE PROGRAMS

Graduate Degrees
▶ *Teacher Education (MAT)*
Application requirements *Prior education:* baccalaureate degree. *Other requirements:* high school transcript, college transcripts, an essay or personal statement, an application fee of $50, teaching certificate or letters of recommendation.
Completion requirements 30 credit hours are required. *Other requirements:* student must be in a study group of 3–8 other students. *Maximum time for completion:* five years.

INDIVIDUAL COURSE SUBJECT AREAS

Graduate
Teacher education

MARYWOOD UNIVERSITY

Scranton, Pennsylvania

Office of Distance Education

Marywood University, founded in 1915, is an independent-religious Roman Catholic comprehensive institution. It is accredited by the Middle States Association of Colleges and Schools. It first offered distance learning courses in 1975. In 1996–97, it offered 60 courses at a distance. In the fall of 1996, there was a total of 150 students enrolled in distance learning courses.
Course delivery sites Courses are delivered to your home, your workplace, military bases, other colleges.
Media Courses are delivered via videoconferencing, World Wide Web, e-mail, print. Students and teachers interact via videoconferencing, mail, telephone, fax, e-mail. A computer is required for some courses.
Services Distance learners have access to library services, e-mail services, academic advising at a distance.
Credit-earning options Students may transfer credits from another institution or may earn credits through standardized exams, portfolio assessment, military training, business training.
Typical costs *Undergraduate:* Tuition of $251 per credit. *Graduate:* Tuition of $424 per credit. Registration fee for 1 course is $50; for 2 or more courses, $90. Costs may vary by specific program of study, number of credits taken. Financial aid is available to distance learners enrolled full-time or part-time.
Registration Students may register by mail, fax.
Contact Peggi Munkittrick, Director of Distance Education, Marywood University, 2300 Adams Avenue, Scranton, PA 18509. *Telephone:* 717-348-6235. *Fax:* 717-961-4751. *E-mail:* pmunk@ac.marywood.edu. *Web site:* http://www.marywood.edu.

DEGREE & CERTIFICATE PROGRAMS

Baccalaureate Degrees
▶ *Accounting, Business Administration (BS)*
In the fall of 1996 there were 90 students enrolled in this program. In 1995–96, 4 degrees were earned at a distance through this program.
Restrictions Students must be 21 and live 25 miles or more from campus.
Application requirements *Prior education:* high school diploma or equivalent. *Minimum age:* 21. *Other requirements:* high school transcript, college transcripts, an essay or personal statement, an application fee of $40.
Completion requirements 126 credits are required. 12 credits must be completed through the institution.
On-campus requirements Four weeks.

Undergraduate Certificates
▶ *Comprehensive Business Skills, Office Administration, Professional Communications*
In the fall of 1996 there were 10 students enrolled in this program.
Application requirements *Prior education:* high school diploma or equivalent. *Minimum age:* 21. *Other requirements:* high school transcript, college transcripts, an essay or personal statement, must reside 25 miles or more from campus.
Completion requirements 24–48 credits are required.

Graduate certificates
▶ *Instructional Technology Specialist*
In the fall of 1996 there were 15 students enrolled in this program. In 1995–96, 1 certificate was earned at a distance through this program.
Application requirements *Prior education:* baccalaureate degree. *Other requirements:* GRE or MAT, college transcripts, an essay or personal statement, letter(s) of recommendation.
Completion requirements 24 credits are required.
Program contact Sr. Patt Walsh, Director of Media Services, Marywood University, 2300 Adams Avenue, Scranton, PA 18509. Phone: 717-348-6271. Fax: 717-961-4769. E-mail: spw@ac.marywood.edu.

INDIVIDUAL COURSE SUBJECT AREAS

Undergraduate
Accounting; advertising; algebra; American literature; art history and criticism; business administration and management; business communications; business law; communications; earth science; English composition; English language and literature; ethics; finance; French language and literature; health and physical education/fitness; human resources management; international business; management information systems; marketing; philosophy and religion; religious studies; sociology; Spanish language and literature; statistics

Graduate
Advertising; communications; instructional media
See full description on page 428.

MASSACHUSETTS INSTITUTE OF TECHNOLOGY

Cambridge, Massachusetts

Center for Advanced Educational Services (CAES)

Massachusetts Institute of Technology, founded in 1861, is an independent-nonprofit university. It is accredited by the New England Association of Schools and Colleges. It first offered distance learning courses in 1996.
Course delivery sites Courses are delivered to your home, your workplace, military bases, other colleges, San Ignacio de Loyola University (Lima, Peru), Universidad Gabriela Mistral (Santiago, Chile).
Media Courses are delivered via television, videotapes, videoconferencing, computer software, World Wide Web, e-mail, print. Students and teachers interact via videoconferencing, mail, telephone, fax, e-mail. A computer is required for some courses.
Services Distance learners have access to library services, the campus computer network, academic advising, tutoring at a distance.
Credit-earning options Students may earn credits through examinations.

Profiles: Massachusetts Institute of Technology

Typical costs Tuition of $4600 per course. $50,000 for System Design and Management degree program. *Noncredit courses:* $2500 per course. Costs may vary by course delivery options.
Registration Students may register by mail, fax, phone, e-mail, World Wide Web.
Contact Kris Kipp, Marketing Manager, CAES, Massachusetts Institute of Technology, 77 Massachusetts Avenue, Room 9-234, Cambridge, MA 02139. *Telephone:* 617-253-2836. *Fax:* 617-253-8301. *E-mail:* kipp@mit.edu. *Web site:* http://www-caes.mit.edu.

DEGREE & CERTIFICATE PROGRAMS

Graduate Degrees

▶ *Engineering and Management (MS)*
In the fall of 1996 there were 42 students enrolled in this program.
Restrictions Students must have company sponsorship.
Application requirements *Prior education:* baccalaureate degree. *Other requirements:* GRE or GMAT, college transcripts, an essay or personal statement, letter(s) of recommendation, an application fee of $50, SDM application form.
Completion requirements *Maximum time for completion:* three years.
On-campus requirements Students must be on-campus the first January, and then for one semester during the duration of the program.
Program contact Margee Best, Corporate Liaison, Massachusetts Institute of Technology, Building 20B-040, 77 Massachusetts Avenue, Cambridge, MA 02139-4307. Phone: 617-253-3799. Fax: 617-258-5229. E-mail: sdm@mit.edu.

INDIVIDUAL COURSE SUBJECT AREAS

Graduate
Business administration and management

Noncredit
Business; engineering-related technologies; engineering/industrial management; industrial engineering

See full descriptions on pages 430 and 432.

MAYLAND COMMUNITY COLLEGE

Spruce Pine, North Carolina

Learning Resources Center

Mayland Community College, founded in 1971, is a state and locally supported two-year college. It is accredited by the Southern Association of Colleges and Schools. It first offered distance learning courses in 1990.
Course delivery sites Courses are delivered to your home.
Media Courses are delivered via videotapes. Students and teachers interact via mail, telephone, fax, e-mail.
Services Distance learners have access to e-mail services, academic advising, career placement assistance at a distance.
Credit-earning options Students may earn credits through examinations.
Typical costs Tuition of $13.25 per hour plus mandatory fees of $28 per year for in-state residents. Tuition of $107.50 per hour plus mandatory fees of $28 per year for out-of-state residents. Financial aid is available to distance learners.
Contact Vice President of Academic Affairs, Mayland Community College, Box 547, Spruce Pine, NC 28777. *Telephone:* 704-765-7351. *Fax:* 704-765-0728.

INDIVIDUAL COURSE SUBJECT AREAS

Undergraduate
Business; business administration and management

MCCOOK COMMUNITY COLLEGE

McCook, Nebraska

McCook Community College, founded in 1926, is a state and locally supported two-year college. It is accredited by the North Central Association of Colleges and Schools. It first offered distance learning courses in 1996.
Media Courses are delivered via videoconferencing.
Restrictions Programs are available to local area students only.
Credit-earning options Students may transfer credits from another institution or may earn credits through examinations, portfolio assessment, military training. Financial aid is available to distance learners.
Contact Distance Learning Coordinator, McCook Community College, 1205 East Third Street, McCook, NE 69001. *Telephone:* 308-345-6303. *Fax:* 308-345-3305.

INDIVIDUAL COURSE SUBJECT AREAS

Undergraduate
Accounting; business administration and management; economics; English composition; history; mathematics; political science; psychology; sociology

---

MCDOWELL TECHNICAL COMMUNITY COLLEGE

Marion, North Carolina

McDowell Technical Community College, founded in 1964, is a state-supported two-year college. It is accredited by the Southern Association of Colleges and Schools. It first offered distance learning courses in 1992. In 1996–97, it offered 18 courses at a distance. In the fall of 1996, there was a total of 50 students enrolled in distance learning courses.
Course delivery sites Courses are delivered to your home.
Media Courses are delivered via television, videotapes, videoconferencing. Students and teachers interact via mail, telephone.
Restrictions Programs are available to local area students only.
Services Distance learners have access to library services, academic advising, tutoring, career placement assistance at a distance.
Credit-earning options Students may transfer credits from another institution or may earn credits through examinations.
Typical costs Tuition of $13.25 per quarter hour. Financial aid is available to distance learners.
Contact Donald G. Ford, Director of Evening Programs and Telecourse Coordinator, McDowell Technical Community College, Route 1, Box 170, Marion, NC 28752. *Telephone:* 704-652-6021. *Fax:* 704-652-1014.

INDIVIDUAL COURSE SUBJECT AREAS

Undergraduate
Abnormal psychology; business; business administration and management; finance; history; social psychology; sociology

Distance Learning Programs

MCGRAW-HILL WORLD UNIVERSITY

Washington, District of Columbia

McGraw-Hill World University, founded in 1996, is a proprietary two-year college. It is accredited by the Distance Education and Training Council. It first offered distance learning courses in 1997. In 1996–97, it offered 70 courses at a distance.
Course delivery sites Courses are delivered to your home, your workplace, military bases.
Media Courses are delivered via audiotapes, computer software, World Wide Web, e-mail, print. Students and teachers interact via mail, telephone, fax, e-mail. A computer is required for all courses. The institution provides assistance with acquiring computer equipment.
Services Distance learners have access to the campus computer network, e-mail services, academic advising, tutoring at a distance.
Credit-earning options Students may transfer credits from another institution or may earn credits through business training.
Typical costs Tuition of $199 per course. *Noncredit courses:* $295 per course. Costs may vary by campus or location, term of enrollment, country of residence.
Registration Students may register by mail, fax, phone, World Wide Web.
Contact Donna Corrao, Curriculum Counselor, McGraw-Hill World University, 4401 Connecticut Avenue, NW, Washington, DC 20008. *Telephone:* 202-274-9288. *Fax:* 202-244-2047. *E-mail:* info@mhcec.com. *Web site:* http://www.mhwu.edu.

DEGREE & CERTIFICATE PROGRAMS

Associate Degrees
▶ *Accounting, Business Management (AAS)*
Application requirements *Prior education:* high school diploma or equivalent. *Other requirements:* high school transcript, college transcripts.
Completion requirements 60 credits are required. 30 credits must be completed through the institution.

Undergraduate Certificates
▶ *Interactive Web Page Design, Internet Basics, Web Page Design, Windows NT*
Application requirements *Prior education:* high school diploma or equivalent. *Minimum age:* 18.
Completion requirements *Maximum time for completion:* nine months (plus three-month extension on request).
Program contact Marc Jean-Michel, Information and Guidance Specialist, McGraw-Hill World University, 4401 Connecticut Avenue, NW, Washington, DC 20008. Phone: 202-244-9792. Fax: 202-244-2047. E-mail: info@mhcec.com.

Graduate certificates
▶ *Accounting and Auditing, Advisory Services, Taxation*
In the fall of 1996 there were 2,240 students enrolled in this program. In 1995–96, 900 certificates were earned at a distance through this program.
Application requirements Contact school; courses are intended for certified public accountants.
Completion requirements *Maximum time for completion:* one year.
Program contact Marilyn Judd, CPE Sales Representative, McGraw-Hill World University, 4401 Connecticut Avenue, NW, Washington, DC 20008. Phone: 202-274-9280. Fax: 202-237-7574. E-mail: info@mhcec.com.

Distance Learning Programs

Profiles: The McGregor School of Antioch University

INDIVIDUAL COURSE SUBJECT AREAS

Undergraduate
Accounting; business administration and management

Noncredit
Computer and information sciences; design; management information systems

THE MCGREGOR SCHOOL OF ANTIOCH UNIVERSITY

Yellow Springs, Ohio

The McGregor School of Antioch University, founded in 1988, is an independent-nonprofit upper-level institution. It is accredited by the North Central Association of Colleges and Schools. It first offered distance learning courses in 1988. In the fall of 1996, there was a total of 448 students enrolled in distance learning courses.
Course delivery sites Courses are delivered to your home, your workplace, military bases, other colleges.
Media Students and teachers interact via mail, telephone, fax, e-mail.
Services Distance learners have access to e-mail services, academic advising at a distance.
Credit-earning options Students may transfer credits from another institution or may earn credits through examinations, portfolio assessment, military training, business training.
Typical costs $1488–2100 per quarter. Costs may vary by specific program of study. Financial aid is available to distance learners enrolled part-time.
Registration Students may register by mail.
Contact Admissions Office, The McGregor School of Antioch University, 800 Livermore Street, Yellow Springs, OH 45387. *Telephone:* 937-767-6325. *Fax:* 937-767-6461. *E-mail:* admiss@mcgregor.antioch.edu.

DEGREE & CERTIFICATE PROGRAMS

Graduate Degrees
▶ *Conflict Resolution (MA)*
Application requirements *Prior education:* baccalaureate degree. *Minimum age:* 21. *Other requirements:* college transcripts, an essay or personal statement, letter(s) of recommendation, an application fee of $35, professional/work experience in a relevant field.
Completion requirements 60 quarter credits are required. *Other requirements:* students work with advisers to design teaching method. *Maximum time for completion:* five years.
On-campus requirements Two 3-week sessions.

▶ *Individualized Studies (MA)*
In the fall of 1996 there were 448 students enrolled in this program. In 1995–96, 106 degrees were earned at a distance through this program.
Application requirements *Prior education:* baccalaureate degree. *Minimum age:* 21. *Other requirements:* college transcripts, an essay or personal statement, letter(s) of recommendation, an application fee of $35, professional/work experience in a relevant field.
Completion requirements 60 quarter credits are required. *Other requirements:* students work with advisors to design teaching method. *Maximum time for completion:* five years.
On-campus requirements Two 1-week sessions.

Profiles: The McGregor School of Antioch University

▶ Intercultural Relations (MA)
Application requirements *Minimum age:* 21. *Other requirements:* college transcripts, an essay or personal statement, letter(s) of recommendation, an application fee of $35, professional/work experience in a relevant field.
Completion requirements 60 quarter credits are required. *Other requirements:* students work with advisors to design teaching method. *Maximum time for completion:* five years.
On-campus requirements Two 1-week sessions and two 2-week sessions.

INDIVIDUAL COURSE SUBJECT AREAS

Graduate
Advertising; agriculture; area, ethnic, and cultural studies; Asian languages and literatures; business; business administration and management; Classical languages and literatures; conservation and natural resources; creative writing; design; developmental and child psychology; economics; education administration; educational psychology; English as a second language (ESL); English composition; English language and literature; European languages and literatures; fine arts; history; home economics and family studies; human resources management; industrial psychology; journalism; liberal arts, general studies, and humanities; Middle Eastern languages and literatures; music; philosophy and religion; political science; psychology; public administration and services; radio and television broadcasting; social psychology; social sciences; social work; sociology; special education; teacher education; theological studies; visual and performing arts

See full description on page 378.

MEDICAL COLLEGE OF GEORGIA

Augusta, Georgia

Medical College of Georgia, founded in 1828, is a state-supported university. It is accredited by the Southern Association of Colleges and Schools.
Course delivery sites Courses are delivered to other colleges.
Media Courses are delivered via videoconferencing, e-mail, satellite. Students and teachers interact via videoconferencing, telephone, fax, e-mail.
Restrictions Programs are available to in-state students only.
Services Distance learners have access to library services, the campus computer network, e-mail services at a distance.
Typical costs Contact college for information.
Contact Elizabeth Griffin, Director of Academic Admissions, Medical College of Georgia, AA170, Augusta, GA 30912. *Telephone:* 706-721-2725. *Fax:* 706-721-0186. *E-mail:* underadm@mail.mcg.edu. *Web site:* http://www.mcg.edu.

INDIVIDUAL COURSE SUBJECT AREAS

Undergraduate
Nursing

Graduate
Health professions and related sciences; physical therapy

MEDICAL UNIVERSITY OF SOUTH CAROLINA

Charleston, South Carolina

Distance Education

Medical University of South Carolina, founded in 1824, is a state-supported upper-level institution. It is accredited by the Southern Association of Colleges and Schools. In 1996–97, it offered 30 courses at a distance.
Course delivery sites Courses are delivered to your home, your workplace, military bases, hospitals, health agencies.
Media Courses are delivered via television, videotapes, videoconferencing, audiotapes, computer software, World Wide Web, e-mail, print. Students and teachers interact via videoconferencing, mail, telephone, fax, e-mail. A computer is required for some courses.
Restrictions Some courses are only offered in certain areas in the state.
Services Distance learners have access to library services, the campus computer network, e-mail services, academic advising, tutoring, career placement assistance at a distance.
Credit-earning options Students may transfer credits from another institution or may earn credits through examinations, military training.
Typical costs Costs may vary greatly. Contact the university for details. Financial aid is available to distance learners.
Registration Students may register by mail, phone.
Contact Office of Enrollment Services, Medical University of South Carolina, 171 Ashley Avenue, Charleston, SC 29425. *Telephone:* 803-792-5396. *Fax:* 803-792-3764.

DEGREE & CERTIFICATE PROGRAMS

Baccalaureate Degrees
▶ Health Science (BHS)
On-campus requirements Some meetings may be required at the Charleston campus.
Program contact Rich Hernandez, Program Director, Medical University of South Carolina, 171 Ashley Avenue, Charleston, SC 29425. Phone: 803-792-9265.

INDIVIDUAL COURSE SUBJECT AREAS

Undergraduate
Health professions and related sciences; nursing

Graduate
Health professions and related sciences; nursing

MEMORIAL UNIVERSITY OF NEWFOUNDLAND

St. John's, Newfoundland, Canada

School of Continuing Education

Memorial University of Newfoundland, founded in 1925, is a province-supported university. It is provincially chartered. It first offered distance learning courses in 1969. In 1996–97, it offered 154 courses at a distance. In the fall of 1996, there was a total of 1,788 students enrolled in distance learning courses.
Course delivery sites Courses are delivered to public health offices, hospitals, schools in the K–12 system, community campuses of the province's regional college system.

Media Courses are delivered via videotapes, audiotapes, audioconferencing, computer software, World Wide Web, e-mail, print. Students and teachers interact via mail, telephone, fax, e-mail. A computer is required for some courses.
Restrictions Students taking teleconference courses must have access to the provincial teleconferencing network.
Services Distance learners have access to library services, the campus computer network, e-mail services, academic advising, customer representation/advocacy at a distance.
Credit-earning options Students may transfer credits from another institution or may earn credits through institutionally developed exams, challenge for credit (in very limited circumstances).
Typical costs Canadian residents pay Can$105 per credit hour. Non-Canadian students pay Can$210 per credit hour. *Noncredit courses:* Can$155. Costs may vary by campus or location, specific program of study, number of credits taken, course delivery options, term of enrollment.
Registration Students may register by phone.
Contact V. Edison, Customer Service Representative, Memorial University of Newfoundland, School of Continuing Education, St. John's, NF A1B 3X8, Canada. *Telephone:* 709-737-8700. *Fax:* 709-737-7941. *E-mail:* cstudies@morgan.ucs.mun.ca. *Web site:* http://www.det.mun.ca/cs.

DEGREE & CERTIFICATE PROGRAMS

Undergraduate Certificates

▶*Business Administration*
Application requirements At least two years of full-time work experience or equivalent.
Completion requirements 10 courses are required. 9 credit hours must be completed through the institution.
Program contact Diana R. Deacon, Program Developer, Memorial University of Newfoundland, Division of Continuing Education, St. John's, NF A1B 3X8, Canada. Phone: 709-737-3068. Fax: 709-737-8486. E-mail: ddeacon@morgan.ucs.mun.ca.

▶*Criminology*
Completion requirements 9 courses are required. 9 credit hours must be completed through the institution.
Program contact Diana R. Deacon, Program Developer, Memorial University of Newfoundland, Division of Continuing Education, St. John's, NF A1B 3X8, Canada. Phone: 709-737-3068. Fax: 709-737-8486. E-mail: ddeacon@morgan.ucs.mun.ca.

▶*Library Studies*
Completion requirements 6 courses are required. 9 credit hours must be completed through the institution.
Program contact Diana R. Deacon, Program Developer, Memorial University of Newfoundland, Division of Continuing Education, St. John's, NF A1B 3X8, Canada. Phone: 709-737-3068. Fax: 709-737-8486. E-mail: ddeacon@morgan.ucs.mun.ca.

▶*Municipal Administration*
Restrictions Program tends to be specific to local administrative structures. May not have application in other municipalities.
Completion requirements 8 courses are required. 9 credit hours must be completed through the institution.
Program contact Diana R. Deacon, Program Developer, Memorial University of Newfoundland, Division of Continuing Education, St. John's, NF A1B 3X8, Canada. Phone: 709-737-3068. Fax: 709-737-8486. E-mail: ddeacon@morgan.ucs.mun.ca.

▶*Newfoundland Studies*
Completion requirements 8 courses are required. 9 credit hours must be completed through the institution.
Program contact Diana R. Deacon, Program Developer, Memorial University of Newfoundland, Division of Continuing Education, St. John's, NF A1B 3X8, Canada. Phone: 709-737-3068. Fax: 709-737-8486. E-mail: ddeacon@morgan.ucs.mun.ca.

▶*Public Administration*
Completion requirements 10 courses are required. 9 credit hours must be completed through the institution.
Program contact Diana R. Deacon, Program Developer, Memorial University of Newfoundland, Division of Continuing Education, St. John's, NF A1B 3X8, Canada. Phone: 709-737-3068. Fax: 709-737-8486. E-mail: ddeacon@morgan.ucs.mun.ca.

INDIVIDUAL COURSE SUBJECT AREAS

Undergraduate
Accounting; administrative and secretarial services; area, ethnic, and cultural studies; biological and life sciences; biology; business; business administration and management; computer and information sciences; conservation and natural resources; developmental and child psychology; economics; education; education administration; educational psychology; English composition; English language and literature; history; human resources management; industrial psychology; law and legal studies; liberal arts, general studies, and humanities; library and information studies; mathematics; nursing; philosophy and religion; political science; psychology; public administration and services; social psychology; social sciences; social work; sociology; special education; teacher education; women's studies

Graduate
Education

Noncredit
European languages and literatures; law and legal studies; library and information studies; mathematics; protective services; public administration and services

MENDOCINO COLLEGE

Ukiah, California

Distance Education

Mendocino College, founded in 1973, is a state and locally supported two-year college. It is accredited by the Western Association of Schools and Colleges, Inc. It first offered distance learning courses in 1980. In 1996–97, it offered 20 courses at a distance. In the fall of 1996, there was a total of 350 students enrolled in distance learning courses.
Course delivery sites Courses are delivered to your home, 2 off-campus centers in Lakeport, Willits.
Media Courses are delivered via television, videotapes, videoconferencing, audiotapes. Students and teachers interact via videoconferencing, telephone, on-campus meetings.
Services Distance learners have access to academic advising at a distance.
Credit-earning options Students may transfer credits from another institution or may earn credits through institutionally developed exams.
Typical costs Tuition of $13 per unit plus mandatory fees of $11 per semester for in-state residents. Tuition of $142 per unit plus mandatory fees of $11 per semester for out-of-state residents. Financial aid is available to distance learners.
Contact Christie Taylor, Director, Admissions and Records, Mendocino College, 1000 Hensley Creek Road, Ukiah, CA 95482. *Telephone:* 707-468-3100. *Fax:* 707-468-3120.

INDIVIDUAL COURSE SUBJECT AREAS

Undergraduate
Administrative and secretarial services; area, ethnic, and cultural studies; astronomy and astrophysics; business; business administration and management; developmental and child psychology; English language

Profiles: Mendocino College

and literature; history; liberal arts, general studies, and humanities; philosophy and religion; political science; psychology; social sciences; sociology

MERCY COLLEGE

Dobbs Ferry, New York

MerLIN

Mercy College, founded in 1951, is an independent-nonprofit comprehensive institution. It is accredited by the Middle States Association of Colleges and Schools. It first offered distance learning courses in 1992. In 1996–97, it offered 60 courses at a distance. In the fall of 1996, there was a total of 447 students enrolled in distance learning courses.
Course delivery sites Courses are delivered to your home.
Media Courses are delivered via World Wide Web, e-mail, print. Students and teachers interact via e-mail. A computer is required for all courses.
Services Distance learners have access to library services, the campus computer network, e-mail services, academic advising, tutoring, career placement assistance at a distance.
Credit-earning options Students may transfer credits from another institution or may earn credits through examinations, portfolio assessment, military training, business training.
Typical costs Tuition of $285 per credit. Costs may vary by number of credits taken. Financial aid is available to distance learners.
Registration Students may register by mail, fax, phone, World Wide Web.
Contact Christine Greenberg, Admissions Coordinator, Mercy College, 555 Broadway, Dobbs Ferry, NY 10522. *Telephone:* 800-MERCY-NY. *Fax:* 914-674-7382. *E-mail:* admission@merlin.mercynet.edu. *Web site:* http://merlin.mercynet.edu.

Special note

Mercy College offers 4 degree programs and a number of courses through MerLIN, the Mercy College Long-Distance Instructional Network. This on-line interactive environment allows learners and instructors to exchange ideas through forums and e-mail. Students may connect to the MerLIN system through the Internet or through direct dial-up via modem. Mercy College has offered distance learning courses since 1992.

Bachelor of Science degrees are offered in international business and computer information science. A Bachelor of Arts degree is offered in psychology. Mercy also offers a two-year associate degree in liberal studies through MerLIN. Students also have access to many support services, including the library, advising, registration, and financial aid.

The learner-centered course delivery system is best suited for those who are self-disciplined and can work independently of the traditional school environment. The programs and courses offered through MerLIN reflect Mercy College's mission statement: Mercy College encourages self-discovery, and personal and social responsibility in a supportive learning environment in which students are challenged to live a life enhanced by the spirit of inquiry.

For more information about Mercy College, call 800-MERCY-NY (toll-free) or visit the College's Web site (http://www.Mercynet.edu). For more information regarding MerLIN, contact the Director of Distance Learning at 914-674-7527, send e-mail (merlin@merlin.mercynet.edu), or visit the MerLIN Web site (http://merlin.mercynet.edu).

DEGREE & CERTIFICATE PROGRAMS

Associate Degrees

▶ *Liberal Arts and Sciences (AA, AS)*
Application requirements *Prior education:* high school diploma or equivalent. *Other requirements:* high school transcript, college transcripts, an application fee of $35.
Completion requirements 60 semester hours are required. 30 semester hours must be completed through the institution.

Baccalaureate Degrees

▶ *Business Administration, Computer Science (BS)*
Application requirements *Prior education:* high school diploma or equivalent. *Other requirements:* high school transcript, college transcripts, an application fee of $35.
Completion requirements 120 semester hours are required. 30 semester hours must be completed through the institution.

▶ *Psychology (BA, BS)*
Application requirements *Prior education:* high school diploma or equivalent. *Other requirements:* high school transcript, college transcripts, an application fee of $35.
Completion requirements 120 semester hours are required. 30 semester hours must be completed through the institution.

INDIVIDUAL COURSE SUBJECT AREAS

Undergraduate

Abnormal psychology; accounting; algebra; American (US) history; art history and criticism; biology; business; business administration and management; business communications; business law; communications; comparative literature; computer and information sciences; criminal justice; developmental and child psychology; economics; English composition; English literature; environmental science; European history; finance; history; human resources management; international business; international relations; law and legal studies; liberal arts, general studies, and humanities; logic; management information systems; marketing; mathematics; music; organizational behavior studies; philosophy and religion; political science; psychology; religious studies; social psychology; sociology; statistics

MERIDIAN COMMUNITY COLLEGE

Meridian, Mississippi

Media Center

Meridian Community College, founded in 1937, is a state and locally supported two-year college. It is accredited by the Southern Association of Colleges and Schools. It first offered distance learning courses in 1994. In 1996–97, it offered 4 courses at a distance. In the fall of 1996, there was a total of 47 students enrolled in distance learning courses.
Course delivery sites Courses are delivered to your home, all community colleges in the state.
Media Courses are delivered via television, videotapes, videoconferencing, World Wide Web, interactive television. Students and teachers interact via mail, telephone, fax, e-mail, interactive television.
Services Distance learners have access to the campus computer network, e-mail services, academic advising at a distance.
Credit-earning options Students may transfer credits from another institution or may earn credits through institutionally developed exams.
Typical costs Tuition of $480 per semester for in-state residents. Tuition of $1000 per semester for out-of-state residents. $1200 for international students. Costs may vary by specific program of study, number of credits taken. Financial aid is available to distance learners enrolled full-time or part-time.

Registration Students may register by mail, fax, phone, e-mail, World Wide Web.
Contact Ray Denton, Director, Meridian Community College, 910 Highway 19 North, Meridian, MS 39307. *Telephone:* 601-484-8785. *Fax:* 601-484-8824.

INDIVIDUAL COURSE SUBJECT AREAS

Undergraduate
Anatomy; fire science; physiology

MESA STATE COLLEGE

Grand Junction, Colorado

Continuing Education Center

Mesa State College, founded in 1925, is a state-supported four-year college. It is accredited by the North Central Association of Colleges and Schools. It first offered distance learning courses in 1996. In 1996–97, it offered 3 courses at a distance. In the fall of 1996, there was a total of 6 students enrolled in distance learning courses.
Course delivery sites Courses are delivered to other colleges, 1 off-campus center in Montrose.
Media Courses are delivered via videoconferencing. Students and teachers interact via videoconferencing.
Restrictions Students must be able to travel to Montrose site.
Services Distance learners have access to library services, the campus computer network, academic advising at a distance.
Credit-earning options Students may transfer credits from another institution or may earn credits through standardized exams.
Typical costs Costs may vary by number of credits taken. Financial aid is available to distance learners enrolled full-time.
Registration Students may register by mail, fax, phone.
Contact Velda Bailey, Director, Continuing Education Center, Mesa State College, PO Box 2647, Grand Junction, CO 81502-2647. *Telephone:* 970-248-1732. *Fax:* 970-248-1923. *E-mail:* vbailey@mesa5.mesa.colorado.edu. *Web site:* http://www.mesastate.edu.

INDIVIDUAL COURSE SUBJECT AREAS

Undergraduate
Business; English literature; finance; nursing; organizational behavior studies

METROPOLITAN COMMUNITY COLLEGE

Omaha, Nebraska

Student and Instructional Services

Metropolitan Community College, founded in 1974, is a state and locally supported two-year college. It is accredited by the North Central Association of Colleges and Schools. It first offered distance learning courses in 1985. In 1996–97, it offered 55 courses at a distance. In the fall of 1996, there was a total of 1,300 students enrolled in distance learning courses.
Course delivery sites Courses are delivered to your home, other colleges.
Media Courses are delivered via television, videotapes, audiotapes, computer software, e-mail, print. Students and teachers interact via mail, telephone, fax, e-mail. A computer is required for some courses.
Services Distance learners have access to library services, e-mail services, academic advising, career placement assistance at a distance.
Credit-earning options Students may transfer credits from another institution or may earn credits through examinations, portfolio assessment, military training, business training.
Typical costs Tuition of $25.50 per credit plus mandatory fees of $2 per credit for local area residents. Tuition of $31.88 per credit plus mandatory fees of $2 per credit for in-state residents. Financial aid is available to distance learners enrolled full-time or part-time.
Registration Students may register by phone.
Contact Jim Grotrian, Director of Enrollment Management, Metropolitan Community College, PO Box 3777, Omaha, NE 68103. *Telephone:* 402-457-2419. *Fax:* 402-457-2564. *E-mail:* jgrotrian@metropo.mccneb.edu.

DEGREE & CERTIFICATE PROGRAMS

Associate Degrees

▶ *Liberal Arts (AA)*
In the fall of 1996 there were 1,300 students enrolled in this program.
Application requirements *Prior education:* none required. *Minimum age:* 18.

▶ *Professional Studies (AA)*
In the fall of 1996 there were 1,300 students enrolled in this program.
Application requirements *Prior education:* none required. *Minimum age:* 18.

INDIVIDUAL COURSE SUBJECT AREAS

Undergraduate
Accounting; art history and criticism; biology; business administration and management; English composition; film studies; finance; French language and literature; liberal arts, general studies, and humanities; mathematics; music; philosophy and religion; physical sciences; political science; psychology; sociology; Spanish language and literature

METROPOLITAN COMMUNITY COLLEGE

East St. Louis, Illinois

Distance Learning

Metropolitan Community College, founded in 1996, is a county-supported two-year college. It is accredited by the North Central Association of Colleges and Schools. It first offered distance learning courses in 1995. In 1996–97, it offered 27 courses at a distance. In the fall of 1996, there was a total of 187 students enrolled in distance learning courses.
Course delivery sites Courses are delivered to your home, your workplace, military bases.
Media Courses are delivered via television, videotapes, videoconferencing, print, interactive television. Students and teachers interact via mail, telephone, fax.
Services Distance learners have access to library services, academic advising, tutoring at a distance.
Credit-earning options Students may transfer credits from another institution or may earn credits through institutionally developed exams, portfolio assessment, military training.
Typical costs Tuition of $40 per credit hour plus mandatory fees of $50 per semester for local area residents. Tuition of $97 per credit hour plus mandatory fees of $50 per semester for in-state residents. Tuition of $145 per credit hour plus mandatory fees of $50 per semester for out-of-state residents. Financial aid is available to distance learners enrolled full-time or part-time.

Distance Learning Programs

Profiles: Metropolitan Community College

Registration Students may register by mail, phone.
Contact W. J. Van Grunsven, Director, Distance Learning, Metropolitan Community College, Governor James R. Thompson Boulevard, East St. Louis, IL 62201. *Telephone:* 618-482-2020, Ext. 314. *Fax:* 618-482-2034.

DEGREE & CERTIFICATE PROGRAMS

Associate Degrees

▶*African-American Studies (AA)*
Application requirements *Prior education:* high school diploma or equivalent. *Other requirements:* high school transcript.
Completion requirements 63 credit hours are required.

▶*Addiction Counseling, Child Care Services, Family, Social and Community Development (AAS)*
Application requirements *Prior education:* high school diploma or equivalent. *Other requirements:* high school transcript.
Completion requirements 63 credit hours are required.

▶*Education, Government, History, Liberal Arts, Political Science, Psychology, Religious Studies, Sociology (AA)*
Application requirements *Prior education:* high school diploma or equivalent. *Other requirements:* high school transcript.
Completion requirements 63 credit hours are required.

Undergraduate Certificates

▶*Addiction Counseling*
Application requirements *Prior education:* high school diploma or equivalent. *Other requirements:* high school transcript.
Completion requirements 63 credit hours are required.

INDIVIDUAL COURSE SUBJECT AREAS

Undergraduate

African-American studies; area, ethnic, and cultural studies; biology; business; business administration and management; chemistry; computer and information sciences; creative writing; developmental and child psychology; economics; education; English language and literature; fine arts; geology; health professions and related sciences; history; home economics and family studies; journalism; liberal arts, general studies, and humanities; mathematics; philosophy and religion; political science; psychology; radio and television broadcasting; religious studies; sociology; special education; teacher education

METROPOLITAN STATE COLLEGE OF DENVER

Denver, Colorado

Extended Education

Metropolitan State College of Denver, founded in 1963, is a state-supported four-year college. It is accredited by the North Central Association of Colleges and Schools. It first offered distance learning courses in 1990. In 1996–97, it offered 74 courses at a distance. In the fall of 1996, there was a total of 434 students enrolled in distance learning courses.
Course delivery sites Courses are delivered to your home, 2 off-campus centers in Englewood, Northglenn.
Media Courses are delivered via television, videotapes, videoconferencing, audiotapes, audioconferencing, World Wide Web, e-mail, print. Students and teachers interact via videoconferencing, audioconferencing, mail, telephone, fax, e-mail. A computer is required for some courses.
Services Distance learners have access to library services, the campus computer network, e-mail services, academic advising at a distance.

Credit-earning options Students may transfer credits from another institution or may earn credits through examinations, portfolio assessment, military training.
Typical costs Tuition of $204 per course plus mandatory fees of $93 per course for in-state residents. Tuition of $804 per course plus mandatory fees of $93 per course for out-of-state residents. Costs may vary by campus or location, number of credits taken. Financial aid is available to distance learners enrolled full-time or part-time.
Registration Students may register by mail, fax, phone.
Contact Claudia Romans, Coordinator for Academic Support Services and Extended Education, Metropolitan State College of Denver, 11990 Grant Street #102, Northglenn, CO 80233. *Telephone:* 303-450-5111. *Fax:* 303-450-9973. *E-mail:* romansc@mscd.edu. *Web site:* http://www.mscd.edu/~options.

INDIVIDUAL COURSE SUBJECT AREAS

Undergraduate

Accounting; American (US) history; area, ethnic, and cultural studies; biological and life sciences; chemistry; communications; computer and information sciences; computer programming; criminal justice; developmental and child psychology; economics; education; English composition; European history; geology; history; marketing; mathematics; protective services; Spanish language and literature; statistics; surveying; teacher education; women's studies

METROPOLITAN STATE UNIVERSITY

St. Paul, Minnesota

Metropolitan State University, founded in 1971, is a state-supported comprehensive institution. It is accredited by the North Central Association of Colleges and Schools. It first offered distance learning courses in 1994. In 1996–97, it offered 15 courses at a distance. In the fall of 1996, there was a total of 93 students enrolled in distance learning courses.
Course delivery sites Courses are delivered to your home, your workplace.
Media Courses are delivered via television, videoconferencing. Students and teachers interact via videoconferencing, mail, telephone, fax. A computer is required for some courses.
Restrictions Programs are available to in-state students only.
Services Distance learners have access to library services, academic advising at a distance.
Credit-earning options Students may transfer credits from another institution or may earn credits through standardized exams, portfolio assessment, military training, business training.
Typical costs *Undergraduate:* Tuition of $2561 per year plus mandatory fees of $107 per year for in-state residents. Tuition of $6093 per year plus mandatory fees of $107 per year for out-of-state residents. *Graduate:* Tuition of $2972 per year plus mandatory fees of $80 per year for in-state residents. Tuition of $4707 per year plus mandatory fees of $80 per year for out-of-state residents. *Noncredit courses:* $218 per course. Financial aid is available to distance learners enrolled full-time or part-time.
Registration Students may register by mail.
Contact Leah S. Harvey, Vice President for Academic Affairs, Metropolitan State University, 700 East Seventh Street, St. Paul, MN 55106-5000. *Telephone:* 612-772-7721. *Fax:* 612-772-7669. *E-mail:* leah_harvey@metro2.metro.msus.edu.

INDIVIDUAL COURSE SUBJECT AREAS

Undergraduate
Communications; economics; educational psychology; engineering-related technologies; finance; French language and literature; human resources management; marketing; mass media

Graduate
Marketing; nursing

MICHIGAN STATE UNIVERSITY

East Lansing, Michigan

Office of Off-Campus and Evening Programs

Michigan State University, founded in 1855, is a state-supported university. It is accredited by the North Central Association of Colleges and Schools. In 1996–97, it offered 60 courses at a distance. In the fall of 1996, there was a total of 1,265 students enrolled in distance learning courses.

Course delivery sites Courses are delivered to your home, your workplace, Northwestern Michigan College (Traverse City), 6 off-campus centers in Birmingham, Grand Rapids, Kalamazoo, Marquette, Midland, Traverse City.

Media Courses are delivered via television, videotapes, videoconferencing, World Wide Web. Students and teachers interact via videoconferencing, mail, telephone, fax, e-mail. A computer is required for some courses.

Services Distance learners have access to library services, the campus computer network, e-mail services, academic advising, career placement assistance at a distance.

Credit-earning options Students may transfer credits from another institution.

Typical costs *Undergraduate:* Tuition of $145 per semester hour plus mandatory fees of $234 per semester for in-state residents. Tuition of $378 per semester hour plus mandatory fees of $234 per semester for out-of-state residents. *Graduate:* Tuition of $210 per semester hour for in-state residents. Tuition of $424 per semester hour for out-of-state residents. *Noncredit courses:* $40 per clock hour. Costs may vary by specific program of study, course delivery options. Financial aid is available to distance learners enrolled full-time.

Registration Students may register by mail, fax, phone, World Wide Web.

Contact Dr. Michael Spurgin, Director, Michigan State University, 51 Kellogg Center, East Lansing, MI 48824. *Telephone:* 517-353-0791. *Fax:* 517-432-1327. *E-mail:* spurginm@msu.edu. *Web site:* http://www.msu.edu/unit/outreach.

DEGREE & CERTIFICATE PROGRAMS

Baccalaureate Degrees

▶ *Nursing (BSN)*
In the fall of 1996 there were 25 students enrolled in this program. In 1995–96, 18 degrees were earned at a distance through this program.
Restrictions Students must be able to commute to one of two sites.
Application requirements *Prior education:* diploma or associates degree in Nursing. *Other requirements:* NLN Mobility Profile II, college transcripts, an application fee of $30, RN license, prerequisite courses must be completed with a 2.5 GPA overall and a 2.2 GPA in the sciences.
Completion requirements 120 semester credits are required. 30 semester credits must be completed through the institution. This is a degree completion program.

Program contact Dr. Joan Predko, Director of Nursing Outreach, Michigan State University, A212 Life Sciences Building, East Lansing, MI 48824. Phone: 517-432-1185. Fax: 517-353-9553. E-mail: predko@msu.edu.

Graduate Degrees

▶ *Computer Science (MS)*
In the fall of 1996 there were 3 students enrolled in this program.
Application requirements *Prior education:* degree in computer science or closely related area. *Other requirements:* college transcripts, an application fee of $30.
Completion requirements 30 semester credits are required. 21 must be completed through the institution. *Maximum time for completion:* five years.
Program contact Dr. John Forsyth, Professor, Michigan State University, Department of Computer Science, East Lansing, MI 48824. Phone: 517-355-1646. Fax: 517-353-7782. E-mail: forsyth@cps.msu.edu.

▶ *Criminal Justice (MS)*
In the fall of 1996 there were 12 students enrolled in this program.
Restrictions Program is available to students at Birmingham and Grand Rapids, MI sites only.
Application requirements *Prior education:* baccalaureate degree. *Other requirements:* GRE, MAT, college transcripts, an essay or personal statement, letter(s) of recommendation, an application fee of $30.
Completion requirements 30 semester credits are required. 21 semester credits must be completed through the institution. *Maximum time for completion:* six years.
Program contact Dr. Merry Morash, Director, School of Criminal Justice, Michigan State University, 560 Baker Hall, East Lansing, MI 48824. Phone: 517-355-2192. Fax: 517-432-1787. E-mail: 16491dam@msu.edu.

▶ *Electrical Engineering (MS)*
In the fall of 1996 there were 6 students enrolled in this program. In 1995–96, 1 degree was earned at a distance through this program.
Application requirements *Prior education:* degree in electrical engineering or closely related area. *Other requirements:* college transcripts, an application fee of $30.
Completion requirements 30 semester credits are required. 21 must be completed through the institution. *Maximum time for completion:* five years.
Program contact Dr. John Forsyth, Professor, Michigan State University, Department of Computer Science, East Lansing, MI 48824. Phone: 517-355-1646. Fax: 517-353-7782. E-mail: forsyth@cps.msu.edu.

▶ *Mechanical Engineering (MS)*
In the fall of 1996 there were 17 students enrolled in this program.
Application requirements *Prior education:* degree in mechanical engineering or a related area. *Other requirements:* college transcripts, an application fee of $30.
Completion requirements 30 semester credits are required. 21 must be completed through the institution. *Maximum time for completion:* five years.
Program contact Dr. John Forsyth, Professor, Michigan State University, Department of Computer Science, East Lansing, MI 48824. Phone: 517-355-1646. Fax: 517-353-7782. E-mail: forsyth@cps.msu.edu.

▶ *Nursing (MSN)*
In the fall of 1996 there were 63 students enrolled in this program. In 1995–96, 25 degrees were earned at a distance through this program.
Restrictions Students must be able to commute to one of three sites.
Application requirements *Prior education:* baccalaureate degree and RN license. *Other requirements:* GRE, college transcripts, an essay or personal statement, letter(s) of recommendation, an application fee of $30, 3.0 GPA for last two years of baccalaureate program, at least one year of clinical experience, general statistics course.
Completion requirements 30 credits must be completed through the institution. *Other requirements:* comprehensive exam; thesis or scholarly project. *Maximum time for completion:* six years.

Profiles: Michigan State University

Program contact Dr. Joan Predko, Director of Nursing Outreach, Michigan State University, A212 Life Sciences Building, East Lansing, MI 48824. Phone: 517-432-1185. Fax: 517-353-9553. E-mail: predko@msu.edu.

▶ *Social Work (MSW)*

In the fall of 1996 there were 78 students enrolled in this program.
Restrictions Students must be within driving distance of a CODEC site in Michigan.
Application requirements *Prior education:* baccalaureate degree. *Other requirements:* college transcripts, an essay or personal statement, letter(s) of recommendation, an application fee of $30, 3.0 GPA, liberal arts background.
Completion requirements 42 credits must be completed through the institution. *Maximum time for completion:* six years.
On-campus requirements An annual weekend seminar on campus, generally held in September.
Program contact Dr. Paul Freddolino, Coordinator of Distance Education, Michigan State University, School of Social Work, Baker Hall, East Lansing, MI 48824. Phone: 517-432-3723. Fax: 517-353-3038. E-mail: paul.freddolino@ssc.msu.edu.

▶ *Telecommunications (MA)*

In the fall of 1996 there were 21 students enrolled in this program. In 1995–96, 4 degrees were earned at a distance through this program.
Restrictions Program is available to students at specific sites in Michigan only.
Application requirements *Prior education:* baccalaureate degree. *Other requirements:* GRE, college transcripts, an essay or personal statement, letter(s) of recommendation, an application fee of $30.
Completion requirements 30 credits are required. 21 credits must be completed through the institution. *Other requirements:* comprehensive examination. *Maximum time for completion:* five years.
Program contact Gilbert A. Williams, Associate Professor, Michigan State University, 425 Communications Arts and Sciences Building, Department of Telecommunications, East Lansing, MI 48824-1212. Phone: 517-353-9151. Fax: 517-355-1292. E-mail: 21998gaw@msu.edu.

INDIVIDUAL COURSE SUBJECT AREAS

Undergraduate
Accounting; agriculture; computer and information sciences

Graduate
Adult education; advertising; chemical engineering; communications; computer and information sciences; curriculum and instruction; database management; education administration; electrical engineering; home economics and family studies; information sciences and systems; instructional media; mechanical engineering; social work; student counseling; teacher education; telecommunications

See full description on page 434.

MICHIGAN TECHNOLOGICAL UNIVERSITY

Houghton, Michigan

Extended University Programs

Michigan Technological University, founded in 1885, is a state-supported university. It is accredited by the North Central Association of Colleges and Schools. It first offered distance learning courses in 1984. In 1996–97, it offered 23 courses at a distance. In the fall of 1996, there was a total of 56 students enrolled in distance learning courses.

Course delivery sites Courses are delivered to your workplace, military bases, 11 off-campus centers in Bloomfield Hills, Dexter, Flint, Howell, Lansing, Milford, Mount Clemens, Plymouth, Rochester Hills, Warren, Ypsilanti.
Media Courses are delivered via videotapes, videoconferencing, e-mail, print. Students and teachers interact via videoconferencing, mail, telephone, fax, e-mail, site visits. A computer is required for some courses.
Services Distance learners have access to library services, the campus computer network, e-mail services, academic advising, career placement assistance, learning centers at a distance.
Credit-earning options Students may transfer credits from another institution or may earn credits through institutionally developed exams, portfolio assessment.
Typical costs Costs vary. Contact school for information. Financial aid is available to distance learners enrolled part-time.
Registration Students may register by mail, fax.
Contact James Schultz, Distance Education Specialist, Michigan Technological University, 1400 Townsend Drive, Houghton, MI 49931. *Telephone:* 906-487-3170. *Fax:* 906-487-2463. *E-mail:* jschultz@mtu.edu. *Web site:* http://www.admin.mtu.edu/eup.

DEGREE & CERTIFICATE PROGRAMS

Baccalaureate Degrees

▶ *Engineering (BS)*

In the fall of 1996 there were 42 students enrolled in this program.
Restrictions Students must be in proximity to laboratories.
Application requirements *Prior education:* some undergraduate course work. *Other requirements:* college transcripts, an application fee of $30.
Completion requirements 196 quarter credits are required. 45 quarter credits must be completed through the institution. This is a degree completion program.

▶ *Surveying (BS)*

In the fall of 1996 there were 17 students enrolled in this program. In 1995–96, 1 degree was earned at a distance through this program.
Application requirements *Prior education:* high school diploma or equivalent. *Other requirements:* high school transcript, college transcripts, an application fee of $30.
Completion requirements 202 quarter credits are required. 45 quarter credits must be completed through the institution. This is a degree completion program.

Graduate Degrees

▶ *Mechanical Engineering (PhD)*

In the fall of 1996 there were 3 students enrolled in this program.
Restrictions Students must be sponsored by a corporation or business.
Application requirements *Prior education:* graduate degree. *Other requirements:* college transcripts, an essay or personal statement, letter(s) of recommendation, an application fee of $30 ($35 for international students).
Completion requirements 30 quarter credits of course work, continuing enrollment, 6 credits/quarter to include course work and research credit. 3 credits of course work or research per quarter must be completed through the institution. *Maximum time for completion:* eight years.
On-campus requirements Two weeks each for qualifying, comprehensive, and final doctoral dissertation defense examinations.
Program contact Dr. William W. Predebon, Associate Chair and Professor, Director of Graduate Studies, Michigan Technological University, Department of ME-EM, 1400 Townsend Drive, Houghton, MI 49931. Phone: 906-487-2551. Fax: 906-487-2822. E-mail: wwpredeb@mtu.edu.

INDIVIDUAL COURSE SUBJECT AREAS

Undergraduate
Business; business administration and management; civil engineering; electrical engineering; engineering mechanics; engineering-related technologies; geology; mechanical engineering; surveying

Graduate
Environmental engineering

Noncredit
Business; business administration and management; civil engineering; electrical engineering; engineering mechanics; engineering-related technologies; geology; mechanical engineering; surveying

MIDDLE GEORGIA COLLEGE

Cochran, Georgia

Office of Continuing Education

Middle Georgia College, founded in 1884, is a state-supported two-year college. It is accredited by the Southern Association of Colleges and Schools.
Course delivery sites Courses are delivered to your home, 6 off-campus centers.
Media Courses are delivered via videoconferencing. Students and teachers interact via mail, telephone, fax, e-mail.
Restrictions Programs are available to in-state students only.
Credit-earning options Students may transfer credits from another institution.
Typical costs Tuition of $145 per course. Financial aid is available to distance learners.
Contact Office of Admissions, Middle Georgia College, 1100 Second Street, SE, Cochran, GA 31014. *Telephone:* 912-934-3031. *Fax:* 912-934-3049.

INDIVIDUAL COURSE SUBJECT AREAS

Undergraduate
Biology; English composition; English language and literature; European languages and literatures; mathematics

MIDDLE TENNESSEE STATE UNIVERSITY

Murfreesboro, Tennessee

Division of Continuing Studies

Middle Tennessee State University, founded in 1911, is a state-supported university. It is accredited by the Southern Association of Colleges and Schools. It first offered distance learning courses in 1994. In 1996–97, it offered 19 courses at a distance. In the fall of 1996, there was a total of 285 students enrolled in distance learning courses.
Course delivery sites Courses are delivered to your home, your workplace, Columbia State Community College (Columbia), Motlow State Community College (Tullahoma), 1 off-campus center in Spring Hill.
Media Courses are delivered via television, videoconferencing, audiotapes, World Wide Web, print. Students and teachers interact via videoconferencing, mail, telephone, fax, e-mail. A computer is required for some courses.
Services Distance learners have access to library services, e-mail services, academic advising at a distance.
Credit-earning options Students may transfer credits from another institution or may earn credits through standardized exams, portfolio assessment, military training.
Typical costs *Undergraduate:* Tuition of $72 per credit plus mandatory fees of $40 per semester for in-state residents. Tuition of $244 per credit plus mandatory fees of $40 per semester for out-of-state residents. *Graduate:* Tuition of $107 per credit plus mandatory fees of $40 per semester for in-state residents. Tuition of $279 per credit plus mandatory fees of $40 per semester for out-of-state residents. Costs may vary by number of credits taken. Financial aid is available to distance learners.
Registration Students may register by mail, phone, World Wide Web.
Contact James Thomas, Director of Special Academic Programs, Middle Tennessee State University, Division of Continuing Studies, 1301 East Main Street, Cope 113, Murfreesboro, TN 37132. *Telephone:* 615-898-5611. *Fax:* 615-904-8108. *E-mail:* jthomas@al.mtsu.edu. *Web site:* http://www.mtsu.edu/~contstud.

Special note

Middle Tennessee State University (MTSU) now offers accredited classes through a variety of technologies for students who may not be able to come to the campus.

Compressed video courses are instructed at one site and simultaneously sent to distant sites. Students and instructors can see one another on television monitors and talk to one another using microphones. Telecourses are offered via cable television or videotape. Students consult with instructors during telephone office hours or through e-mail. Students can view course segments on the MTSU cable channel or the local PBS affiliate or at the McWherter Learning Resources Center at MTSU. Students are required to attend an orientation, a midterm exam, and a final exam on campus.

Correspondence courses involve individual instruction of a student by an instructor. Typically, students study at home. Interaction between correspondence course faculty members and students consists of written assignments, testing, and assistance via such media as print/written word, telephone, fax, and e-mail. After registration, students receive a packet in the mail from the correspondence course coordinator that contains information about assignments and directions for completing and submitting them.

On-line courses are taught primarily over the Internet through e-mail, newsgroups, distribution lists, and the World Wide Web. Students must attend at least one proctored exam and bring a photo ID. All other assignments and quizzes are available through the Internet.

These various distance learning programs are closing the gap between students and the campus.

INDIVIDUAL COURSE SUBJECT AREAS

Undergraduate
Accounting; business; business administration and management; economics; education administration; English language and literature; health and physical education/fitness; law and legal studies; liberal arts, general studies, and humanities; mathematics; special education; teacher education

Graduate
Business; business administration and management; special education

Noncredit
Human resources management

Distance Learning Programs

Profiles: Midland College

MIDLAND COLLEGE

Midland, Texas

Distance Learning Program

Midland College, founded in 1969, is a state and locally supported two-year college. It is accredited by the Southern Association of Colleges and Schools. It first offered distance learning courses in 1996. In 1996–97, it offered 20 courses at a distance. In the fall of 1996, there was a total of 100 students enrolled in distance learning courses.
Course delivery sites Courses are delivered to your home, your workplace, military bases, Howard College (Big Spring), Odessa College (Odessa), The University of Texas of the Permian Basin (Odessa), 3 off-campus centers in Fort Stockton, Iraan, Ozona.
Media Courses are delivered via videoconferencing, computer software, e-mail. Students and teachers interact via videoconferencing, mail, telephone, fax, e-mail.
Services Distance learners have access to library services, the campus computer network, e-mail services, academic advising, tutoring, career placement assistance at a distance.
Credit-earning options Students may transfer credits from another institution or may earn credits through institutionally developed exams, portfolio assessment, military training, business training.
Typical costs Tuition of $327 per semester for local area residents. Tuition of $351 per semester for in-state residents. Tuition of $423 per semester for out-of-state residents. Costs may vary by campus or location, number of credits taken. Financial aid is available to distance learners enrolled full-time or part-time.
Registration Students may register by mail, fax, phone.
Contact William G. Morris, Director, Midland College, 3600 North Garfield, Midland, TX 79705. *Telephone:* 915-685-4507. *Fax:* 915-685-4769. *E-mail:* wmorris@midland.cc.tx.us.

INDIVIDUAL COURSE SUBJECT AREAS

Undergraduate
Accounting; administrative and secretarial services; algebra; American (US) history; business; business administration and management; business communications; calculus; computer and information sciences; computer programming; database management; developmental and child psychology; history; information sciences and systems; mathematics; political science; psychology; social psychology; statistics

MID-PLAINS COMMUNITY COLLEGE

North Platte, Nebraska

Mid-Plains Community College, founded in 1965, is a district-supported two-year college. It is accredited by the North Central Association of Colleges and Schools. It first offered distance learning courses in 1994.
Course delivery sites Courses are delivered to other colleges, off-campus center(s).
Media Courses are delivered via television, videotapes, print. Students and teachers interact via mail, telephone, fax, e-mail.
Services Distance learners have access to academic advising, career placement assistance at a distance.
Credit-earning options Students may transfer credits from another institution or may earn credits through examinations.
Typical costs Tuition of $32 per credit hour for in-state residents. Tuition of $36.50 per credit hour for out-of-state residents. Financial aid is available to distance learners.
Contact Janis Ridnour, Dean of Academic Instruction, Mid-Plains Community College, 601 West State Farm Road, North Platte, NE 69101. *Telephone:* 308-532-8980. *Fax:* 308-532-8590. *E-mail:* jmridnou@ziggy.mpcc.cc.ne.us.

INDIVIDUAL COURSE SUBJECT AREAS

Undergraduate
Business; English composition; history; mathematics; sociology

MID-STATE TECHNICAL COLLEGE

Wisconsin Rapids, Wisconsin

General Education and Academic Support Services

Mid-State Technical College, founded in 1917, is a state and locally supported two-year college. It is accredited by the North Central Association of Colleges and Schools. It first offered distance learning courses in 1996. In 1996–97, it offered 45 courses at a distance.
Course delivery sites Courses are delivered to other colleges.
Media Courses are delivered via videotapes, videoconferencing. Students and teachers interact via videoconferencing, mail, telephone, fax. A computer is required for some courses.
Restrictions Courses are available to members of our fiber-optics network only.
Services Distance learners have access to academic advising at a distance.
Credit-earning options Students may earn credits through standardized exams, institutionally developed exams.
Typical costs *Noncredit courses:* $16–$25 per course. Costs may vary by number of credits taken. Financial aid is available to distance learners.
Contact William Lindroth, Dean, General Education, Mid-State Technical College, 500 32nd Street, N, Wisconsin Rapids, WI 54494. *Telephone:* 715-422-5460. *Fax:* 715-422-5466.

INDIVIDUAL COURSE SUBJECT AREAS

Undergraduate
Administrative and secretarial services; business; conservation and natural resources; economics; health professions and related sciences; home economics and family studies; law and legal studies; mathematics; psychology; sociology; technical writing

MIDWESTERN STATE UNIVERSITY

Wichita Falls, Texas

Midwestern State University, founded in 1922, is a state-supported comprehensive institution. It is accredited by the Southern Association of Colleges and Schools. It first offered distance learning courses in 1987. In 1996–97, it offered 8 courses at a distance. In the fall of 1996, there was a total of 250 students enrolled in distance learning courses.
Course delivery sites Courses are delivered to your home, your workplace, The Texas A&M University System (College Station), The University of Texas at Arlington (Arlington), Vernon Regional Junior College (Vernon).
Media Courses are delivered via television, videotapes, videoconferencing, audioconferencing, print. Students and teachers interact via videoconferencing, audioconferencing, mail, telephone, fax, e-mail.
Restrictions Programs are available to in-state students only.

Services Distance learners have access to library services, the campus computer network, e-mail services, academic advising, tutoring, career placement assistance at a distance.
Credit-earning options Students may transfer credits from another institution or may earn credits through standardized exams, institutionally developed exams, portfolio assessment.
Typical costs *Undergraduate:* Tuition of $32 per credit hour plus mandatory fees of $892 per year for in-state residents. Tuition of $246 per credit hour plus mandatory fees of $892 per year for out-of-state residents. *Graduate:* Tuition of $42 per credit hour plus mandatory fees of $892 per year for in-state residents. Tuition of $256 per credit hour plus mandatory fees of $892 per year for out-of-state residents. *Noncredit courses:* $32 per course. Costs may vary by number of credits taken. Financial aid is available to distance learners enrolled full-time or part-time.
Registration Students may register by mail, phone.
Contact Mrs. Barbara Merkle, Director of School Relations, Midwestern State University, 3410 Taft Boulevard, Wichita Falls, TX 76308. *Telephone:* 940-397-4334. *Fax:* 940-397-4042. *E-mail:* school.relations@nexus.mwsu.edu.

INDIVIDUAL COURSE SUBJECT AREAS

Undergraduate
Business administration and management; developmental and child psychology; economics; English language and literature; finance; health professions and related sciences; history; marketing; nursing; political science; social sciences; sociology

Graduate
Business administration and management; business law; chemistry; educational psychology; finance; health professions and related sciences; marketing; mathematics; physics; teacher education

MILWAUKEE AREA TECHNICAL COLLEGE

Milwaukee, Wisconsin

Instructional Design Division–College of the Air Department

Milwaukee Area Technical College, founded in 1912, is a district-supported two-year college. It is accredited by the North Central Association of Colleges and Schools. In 1996–97, it offered 70 courses at a distance. In the fall of 1996, there was a total of 3,000 students enrolled in distance learning courses.
Course delivery sites Courses are delivered to your home, your workplace.
Media Courses are delivered via television, videotapes, videoconferencing, audioconferencing, World Wide Web, e-mail, print. Students and teachers interact via videoconferencing, audioconferencing, mail, telephone, fax, e-mail.
Services Distance learners have access to library services at a distance.
Credit-earning options Students may transfer credits from another institution or may earn credits through examinations.
Typical costs Tuition of $224.50 per course. Financial aid is available to distance learners.
Contact John Lewinski, Coordinator, College of the Air, Milwaukee Area Technical College, 700 West State Street, Milwaukee, WI 53233. *Telephone:* 414-297-6889. *Fax:* 414-297-6329. *Web site:* http://www.milwaukee.tec.wi.us.

DEGREE & CERTIFICATE PROGRAMS

Associate Degrees
▶*Liberal Arts (AA)*
Application requirements *Prior education:* high school diploma or equivalent. *Minimum age:* 18. *Other requirements:* high school transcript, college transcripts, an application fee of $15.
Completion requirements 64 credits are required.
On-campus requirements Exams must be taken on campus or at receive site.
Program contact Mr. Pablo Cardona, Director of Admissions, Milwaukee Area Technical College, 700 West State Street, Milwaukee, WI 53233. Phone: 414-297-7001.

INDIVIDUAL COURSE SUBJECT AREAS

Undergraduate
Accounting; area, ethnic, and cultural studies; astronomy and astrophysics; business; business administration and management; chemistry; communications; computer and information sciences; developmental and child psychology; economics; English as a second language (ESL); English composition; English language and literature; European languages and literatures; geology; health and physical education/fitness; history; human resources management; law and legal studies; liberal arts, general studies, and humanities; mathematics; political science; social psychology; sociology

MILWAUKEE SCHOOL OF ENGINEERING

Milwaukee, Wisconsin

University Media Services

Milwaukee School of Engineering, founded in 1903, is an independent-nonprofit comprehensive institution. It is accredited by the North Central Association of Colleges and Schools. It first offered distance learning courses in 1989. In 1996–97, it offered 10 courses at a distance. In the fall of 1996, there was a total of 25 students enrolled in distance learning courses.
Course delivery sites Courses are delivered to your home, your workplace.
Media Courses are delivered via videotapes, audioconferencing, World Wide Web, e-mail. Students and teachers interact via audioconferencing, mail, telephone, fax, e-mail. A computer is required for some courses.
Restrictions Enrollment for credit is restricted to in-state students only.
Services Distance learners have access to library services, the campus computer network, e-mail services at a distance.
Credit-earning options Students may transfer credits from another institution.
Typical costs *Undergraduate:* Tuition of $280 per credit. *Graduate:* Tuition of $340 per credit. *Noncredit courses:* $695 per course. Financial aid is available to distance learners enrolled part-time.
Registration Students may register by mail, fax.
Contact Cheryl Donnelly, Director of Continuing Education, Milwaukee School of Engineering, Continuing Education Department, 1025 North Broadway, Milwaukee, WI 53202-3109. *Telephone:* 414-277-7155. *Fax:* 414-277-7475. *E-mail:* donnelly@admin.msoe.edu. *Web site:* http://www.msoe.edu/dist_ed/dist_ed_home.html.

INDIVIDUAL COURSE SUBJECT AREAS

Graduate
Accounting; business administration and management; business communications; finance; international business; marketing; organizational behavior studies

Profiles: Milwaukee School of Engineering

Noncredit
Accounting; business administration and management; business communications; finance; international business; marketing; organizational behavior studies

MINNESOTA WEST COMMUNITY AND TECHNICAL COLLEGE–WORTHINGTON CAMPUS

Worthington, Minnesota

Minnesota West Community and Technical College–Worthington Campus, founded in 1936, is a state-supported two-year college. It is accredited by the North Central Association of Colleges and Schools. It first offered distance learning courses in 1988. In 1996–97, it offered 28 courses at a distance. In the fall of 1996, there was a total of 203 students enrolled in distance learning courses.
Course delivery sites Courses are delivered to your home, area high schools throughout southwestern Minnesota, schools within the Minnesota West Community-Technical College System.
Media Courses are delivered via television, e-mail. Students and teachers interact via mail, telephone, fax, e-mail, interactive television. A computer is required for some courses.
Restrictions Programs are available to local area students only.
Services Distance learners have access to library services, the campus computer network, e-mail services, academic advising at a distance.
Credit-earning options Students may transfer credits from another institution or may earn credits through standardized exams, portfolio assessment, military training.
Typical costs Tuition of $46 per quarter hour for in-state residents. Tuition of $87.63 per quarter hour for out-of-state residents. Financial aid is available to distance learners.
Registration Students may register by mail, fax, phone, e-mail, World Wide Web.
Contact Dale R. Carlson, Executive Vice President of Instruction, Minnesota West Community and Technical College–Worthington Campus, 1450 Collegeway, Worthington, MN 56187-3099. *Telephone:* 507-372-3408. *Fax:* 507-372-5801. *E-mail:* d.carlson@wr.cc.mn.us.

DEGREE & CERTIFICATE PROGRAMS

Associate Degrees
▶ *Liberal Arts (AA)*
Application requirements *Prior education:* high school diploma or equivalent. *Other requirements:* ACT, high school transcript, an application fee of $20, computer placement exams.
Completion requirements 96 quarter hours are required. 30 quarter hours must be completed through the institution.

INDIVIDUAL COURSE SUBJECT AREAS

Undergraduate
Area, ethnic, and cultural studies; biology; chemistry; computer and information sciences; conservation and natural resources; developmental and child psychology; economics; English composition; English language and literature; European languages and literatures; fine arts; health and physical education/fitness; history; liberal arts, general studies, and humanities; mathematics; music; philosophy and religion; physics; political science; psychology; sociology; visual and performing arts

MINOT STATE UNIVERSITY

Minot, North Dakota

Continuing Education

Minot State University, founded in 1913, is a state-supported comprehensive institution. It is accredited by the North Central Association of Colleges and Schools. It first offered distance learning courses in 1991. In 1996–97, it offered 52 courses at a distance. In the fall of 1996, there was a total of 303 students enrolled in distance learning courses.
Course delivery sites Courses are delivered to your home, your workplace, military bases, Bismarck State College (Bismarck).
Media Courses are delivered via television, World Wide Web, e-mail, print. Students and teachers interact via mail, telephone, fax, e-mail, interactive television. A computer is required for some courses.
Services Distance learners have access to library services, the campus computer network, e-mail services, academic advising, tutoring, career placement assistance, bookstore at a distance.
Credit-earning options Students may transfer credits from another institution or may earn credits through examinations.
Typical costs *Undergraduate:* Tuition of $95 per semester hour. *Graduate:* Tuition of $108 per semester hour. Costs may vary by course delivery options. Financial aid is available to distance learners enrolled full-time or part-time.
Registration Students may register by mail, fax, phone, e-mail, World Wide Web.
Contact Teresa Loftesnes, Director of Continuing Education, Minot State University, 500 University Avenue West, Minot, ND 58707. *Telephone:* 701-858-3062. *Fax:* 701-858-4343. *E-mail:* loftesne@warp6.cs.misu.nodak.edu. *Web site:* http://www.misu.nodak.edu/conted/.

INDIVIDUAL COURSE SUBJECT AREAS

Undergraduate
Accounting; advertising; area, ethnic, and cultural studies; business; business administration and management; creative writing; English composition; English language and literature; history; human resources management; mathematics; philosophy and religion; sociology

Graduate
Teacher education

MIRACOSTA COLLEGE

Oceanside, California

MiraCosta College, founded in 1934, is a state-supported two-year college. It is accredited by the Western Association of Schools and Colleges, Inc.
Course delivery sites Courses are delivered to your home.
Media Courses are delivered via television, videotapes, audioconferencing, print, computer conferencing.
Restrictions Programs are available to local area students only.
Services Distance learners have access to library services at a distance.
Credit-earning options Students may transfer credits from another institution or may earn credits through examinations. Financial aid is available to distance learners.
Contact Julie Romaine, Administrative Secretary, MiraCosta College, 1 Barnard Drive, Oceanside, CA 92056. *Telephone:* 619-757-2121, Ext. 261. *Fax:* 619-721-8671. *E-mail:* jromaine@miracosta.cc.ca.us.

INDIVIDUAL COURSE SUBJECT AREAS

Undergraduate
Anthropology; business administration and management; developmental and child psychology; economics; English as a second language (ESL); English language and literature; geology; liberal arts, general studies, and humanities; music; social psychology; sociology

Noncredit
English as a second language (ESL)

MISSISSIPPI DELTA COMMUNITY COLLEGE

Moorhead, Mississippi

Mississippi Delta Community College, founded in 1926, is a district-supported two-year college. It is accredited by the Southern Association of Colleges and Schools. It first offered distance learning courses in 1994. In 1996–97, it offered 3 courses at a distance. In the fall of 1996, there was a total of 30 students enrolled in distance learning courses.
Course delivery sites Courses are delivered to your home, 15 community colleges in Mississippi.
Media Courses are delivered via television, videoconferencing. Students and teachers interact via videoconferencing.
Restrictions Programs are available to local area students only.
Services Distance learners have access to library services, academic advising, tutoring, career placement assistance at a distance.
Credit-earning options Students may transfer credits from another institution.
Typical costs Tuition of $450 per semester for in-state residents. Tuition of $1050 per semester for out-of-state residents. Part-time tuition: $50 per hour. Costs may vary by number of credits taken. Financial aid is available to distance learners enrolled full-time or part-time.
Contact Larry Bailey, Dean of Academic Affairs, Mississippi Delta Community College, PO Box 668, Moorhead, MS 38761. *Telephone:* 601-246-6318. *Fax:* 601-246-6321.

INDIVIDUAL COURSE SUBJECT AREAS

Undergraduate
Educational psychology; French language and literature; geography; health professions and related sciences; social work

Noncredit
Creative writing; education administration; English language and literature; teacher education

MISSISSIPPI STATE UNIVERSITY

Mississippi State, Mississippi

Division of Continuing Education

Mississippi State University, founded in 1878, is a state-supported university. It is accredited by the Southern Association of Colleges and Schools. It first offered distance learning courses in 1989. In 1996–97, it offered 30 courses at a distance. In the fall of 1996, there was a total of 750 students enrolled in distance learning courses.
Course delivery sites Courses are delivered to your home, other colleges, Statewide Interactive Video Network sites including the Community College Network and the ETV Interactive Network (K-12 sites).
Media Courses are delivered via videotapes, videoconferencing, audioconferencing, World Wide Web, print. Students and teachers interact via videoconferencing, audioconferencing, mail, telephone, fax, e-mail.
Services Distance learners have access to library services, the campus computer network, e-mail services, academic advising at a distance.
Credit-earning options Students may transfer credits from another institution.
Typical costs *Undergraduate:* Tuition of $74 per hour. *Graduate:* Tuition of $111 per hour. Costs may vary by number of credits taken. Financial aid is available to distance learners.
Registration Students may register by mail, fax, phone, e-mail.
Contact Dr. Kathleen C. Olivieri, Distance Learning Coordinator, Mississippi State University, PO Box 5247, Mississippi State, MS 39762. *Telephone:* 601-325-2639. *Fax:* 601-325-8578. *E-mail:* kolivieri@ce.msstate.edu. *Web site:* http://www.msstate.edu/Dept/CED.

DEGREE & CERTIFICATE PROGRAMS

Graduate Degrees

▶ *Chemical Engineering, Civil Engineering, Electrical Engineering, Industrial Engineering, Mechanical Engineering (PhD)*
In the fall of 1996 there were 11 students enrolled in this program. In 1995–96, 2 degrees were earned at a distance through this program.
Application requirements *Prior education:* graduate degree. *Other requirements:* college transcripts, an essay or personal statement, letter(s) of recommendation, an application fee of $25.
Completion requirements *Maximum time for completion:* eight years.
On-campus requirements One semester residency requirement.
Program contact Rusty Foster, Coordinator of Services, Mississippi State University, PO Box 9544, Mississippi State, MS 39762-9544. Phone: 601-325-3825. Fax: 601-325-8573. E-mail: rgf@demsstate.edu.

▶ *Chemical Engineering, Civil Engineering, Electrical Engineering, Industrial Engineering, Mechanical Engineering (MS)*
In the fall of 1996 there were 74 students enrolled in this program. In 1995–96, 10 degrees were earned at a distance through this program.
Application requirements *Prior education:* baccalaureate degree. *Other requirements:* college transcripts, an essay or personal statement, letter(s) of recommendation, an application fee of $25.
Completion requirements 30 semester hours are required. *Maximum time for completion:* six years.
On-campus requirements Once for oral exam.
Program contact Rusty Foster, Coordinator of Services, Mississippi State University, PO Box 9544, Mississippi State, MS 39762-9544. Phone: 601-325-3825. Fax: 601-325-8573. E-mail: rgf@demsstate.edu.

▶ *Counselor Education (MS)*
In the fall of 1996 there were 20 students enrolled in this program.
Restrictions This program is available to in-state students only.
Application requirements *Prior education:* baccalaureate degree. *Other requirements:* college transcripts, an essay or personal statement, letter(s) of recommendation.
Completion requirements 48 credit hours are required. 36 credit hours must be completed through the institution. *Maximum time for completion:* six years.
On-campus requirements Some classes are offered on-campus in the summer.

▶ *Systems Management (MS)*
Restrictions This program is available to in-state students only.
Application requirements *Prior education:* baccalaureate degree. *Other requirements:* GMAT, college transcripts, an essay or personal statement, letter(s) of recommendation.
Completion requirements 36 semester hours are required. 36 semester hours must be completed through the institution. *Maximum time for completion:* six years.

Profiles: Mississippi State University

Undergraduate Certificates
▶ *Broadcast Meteorology*
Application requirements *Prior education:* high school diploma or equivalent. *Other requirements:* high school transcript, college transcripts.
Completion requirements 39 semester hours are required.
On-campus requirements Capstone experience is held on campus for the last class.

INDIVIDUAL COURSE SUBJECT AREAS

Undergraduate
Meteorology; philosophy and religion

Graduate
Aerospace, aeronautical engineering; agriculture; business administration and management; chemical engineering; civil engineering; computer and information sciences; educational psychology; electrical engineering; engineering; engineering mechanics; engineering/industrial management; environmental engineering; home economics and family studies; industrial engineering; mathematics; mechanical engineering; meteorology

MISSISSIPPI UNIVERSITY FOR WOMEN

Columbus, Mississippi

Continuing Education

Mississippi University for Women, founded in 1884, is a state-supported comprehensive institution. It is accredited by the Southern Association of Colleges and Schools. It first offered distance learning courses in 1994.
Course delivery sites Courses are delivered to your home.
Media Courses are delivered via computer software, computer conferencing.
Services Distance learners have access to library services, tutoring at a distance.
Credit-earning options Students may transfer credits from another institution or may earn credits through examinations. Financial aid is available to distance learners.
Contact Coordinator, RN/BSN, Mississippi University for Women, 655 Eason Boulevard, Tupelo, MS 38834. *Telephone:* 601-844-0284. *Fax:* 601-842-6883.

DEGREE & CERTIFICATE PROGRAMS

Baccalaureate Degrees
▶ *Nursing (BSN)*
Application requirements 2.5 GPA.

INDIVIDUAL COURSE SUBJECT AREAS

Undergraduate
Nursing

MISSOURI SOUTHERN STATE COLLEGE

Joplin, Missouri

Continuing Education

Missouri Southern State College, founded in 1937, is a state-supported four-year college. It is accredited by the North Central Association of Colleges and Schools.
Course delivery sites Courses are delivered to your home, your workplace, vo-tech centers.
Media Courses are delivered via television, videotapes, videoconferencing, computer software, World Wide Web, e-mail. Students and teachers interact via videoconferencing, audioconferencing, mail, telephone, fax, e-mail.
Restrictions Programs are available to in-state students only.
Services Distance learners have access to library services, tutoring at a distance.
Credit-earning options Students may transfer credits from another institution or may earn credits through examinations, portfolio assessment, military training.
Typical costs Tuition of $70 per semester hour plus mandatory fees of $40 per semester for in-state residents. Tuition of $140 per semester hour plus mandatory fees of $40 per semester for out-of-state residents. Financial aid is available to distance learners.
Contact Jerry Williams, Director, Missouri Southern State College, 3950 East Newman Road, Joplin, MO 64801. *Telephone:* 417-625-9384. *Fax:* 417-625-3024. *E-mail:* williams@vm.mssc.edu.

INDIVIDUAL COURSE SUBJECT AREAS

Undergraduate
Accounting; biological and life sciences; biology; botany; business; business administration and management; communications; computer and information sciences; developmental and child psychology; economics; English language and literature; fine arts; geology; health professions and related sciences; history; home economics and family studies; human resources management; law and legal studies; mass media; nursing; physical sciences; political science; psychology; public administration and services; radio and television broadcasting; social psychology; social sciences; sociology; visual and performing arts

MISSOURI WESTERN STATE COLLEGE

St. Joseph, Missouri

Division of Continuing Education

Missouri Western State College, founded in 1915, is a state-supported four-year college. It is accredited by the North Central Association of Colleges and Schools. It first offered distance learning courses in 1987. In the fall of 1996, there was a total of 150 students enrolled in distance learning courses.
Course delivery sites Courses are delivered to your home, your workplace, military bases, high schools.
Media Courses are delivered via television, videotapes, videoconferencing, computer software, World Wide Web, e-mail. Students and teachers interact via videoconferencing, mail, telephone, fax, e-mail. A computer is required for some courses.
Restrictions Video-based courses are available to regional students only.
Services Distance learners have access to library services, the campus computer network, e-mail services, academic advising at a distance.
Credit-earning options Students may transfer credits from another institution or may earn credits through standardized exams, institutionally developed exams, military training.
Typical costs Tuition of $88 per credit plus mandatory fees of $12 per credit. Costs may vary by campus or location, specific program of study. Financial aid is available to distance learners enrolled full-time or part-time.
Registration Students may register by mail, fax.
Contact Dr. Edwin L. Gorsky, Dean of Continuing Education and Special Programs, Missouri Western State College, 4525 Downs Drive,

MC 105, St. Joseph, MO 64507. *Telephone:* 816-271-4100. *Fax:* 816-271-5922. *E-mail:* gorsky@griffon.mwsc.edu.

Special note
Missouri Western has been active in brokering distance education to the northwest Missouri region since 1991 through videocommunications links with the University of Missouri–Kansas City (UMKC). Missouri Western receives courses from UMKC and other partners in the University of Missouri Interactive Video Network. Some courses are received via a 1-way, 3-channel point-to-point microwave link. Others are facilitated by a dedicated CODEC to the Network. In addition, Missouri Western operates 2 desktop video units capable of T1, ISDN, frame relay, and Ethernet connectivity.
MWSC serves 16 business, industry, and health-care sites by a 4-channel ITFS system and 33,000 homes by cable television. To date, more than 100 graduate and undergraduate courses have been facilitated.
MWSC is currently partnering with the St. Joseph School District and other outlying school districts via cable television, ITFS, analog 2-way video, and desktop video. For 1997–98, in addition to live courses brokered via links with UMKC, MWSC is producing 3 live classes and airing 3 telecourses; all 6 classes meet general education requirements at Missouri Western. Missouri Western has also participated in a Web-based class and plans in the coming year to produce its first class over the Internet.

INDIVIDUAL COURSE SUBJECT AREAS

Undergraduate
Biology; chemistry; comparative literature; computer programming; developmental and child psychology; English as a second language (ESL); fire science; physics; protective services

Graduate
Agriculture; education administration; electrical engineering; engineering/industrial management; nursing; physics

MODESTO JUNIOR COLLEGE

Modesto, California

College Services

Modesto Junior College, founded in 1921, is a state and locally supported two-year college. It is accredited by the Western Association of Schools and Colleges, Inc. In 1996–97, it offered 19 courses at a distance. In the fall of 1996, there was a total of 1,852 students enrolled in distance learning courses.
Course delivery sites Courses are delivered to your home.
Media Courses are delivered via television, e-mail. Students and teachers interact via mail, telephone, fax, e-mail.
Restrictions Televised courses are available in the local area only only.
Services Distance learners have access to library services, the campus computer network, e-mail services, academic advising, tutoring, career placement assistance at a distance.
Credit-earning options Students may transfer credits from another institution.
Typical costs Tuition of $13 per credit plus mandatory fees of $10 per semester for local area residents. Tuition of $114 per credit plus mandatory fees of $10 per semester for out-of-state residents. *Noncredit courses:* $13 per unit. Costs may vary by number of credits taken. Financial aid is available to distance learners enrolled full-time or part-time.

Registration Students may register by phone.
Contact Admissions Office, Modesto Junior College, 435 College Avenue, Modesto, CA 95350. *Telephone:* 209-575-6013.

INDIVIDUAL COURSE SUBJECT AREAS

Undergraduate
Accounting; African-American studies; agriculture; area, ethnic, and cultural studies; astronomy and astrophysics; business administration and management; chemistry; geology; health and physical education/fitness; health professions and related sciences; history; home economics and family studies; mathematics; political science; psychology; sociology

MOHAWK VALLEY COMMUNITY COLLEGE

Utica, New York

Division of Corporate and Customized Training

Mohawk Valley Community College, founded in 1946, is a state and locally supported two-year college. It is accredited by the Middle States Association of Colleges and Schools. It first offered distance learning courses in 1991. In 1996–97, it offered 10 courses at a distance. In the fall of 1996, there was a total of 90 students enrolled in distance learning courses.
Course delivery sites Courses are delivered to your home, 8 off-campus centers in Clinton, New Hartford, Oriskany, Sauquoit, Utica, Waterville, Westmoreland.
Media Courses are delivered via videoconferencing, e-mail. Students and teachers interact via videoconferencing, e-mail. A computer is required for some courses.
Services Distance learners have access to library services, the campus computer network, e-mail services, academic advising, tutoring, career placement assistance at a distance.
Credit-earning options Students may earn credits through examinations.
Typical costs Tuition of $1250 per semester for local area residents. Tuition of $2500 per semester for in-state residents. Tuition of $2500 per semester for out-of-state residents. *Noncredit courses:* $25 per course. Financial aid is available to distance learners enrolled full-time or part-time.
Registration Students may register by mail, phone.
Contact Admissions Office, Mohawk Valley Community College, Academic Building, 1101 Sherman Drive, Utica, NY 13501-5394. *Telephone:* 315-792-5354. *Fax:* 315-792-5666.

INDIVIDUAL COURSE SUBJECT AREAS

Undergraduate
Accounting; business administration and management; developmental and child psychology; educational psychology; English language and literature; Medieval/Renaissance studies; special education; teacher education

MONTANA STATE UNIVERSITY–BOZEMAN

Bozeman, Montana

The Burns Telecommunications Center/Extended Studies

Montana State University–Bozeman, founded in 1893, is a state-supported university. It is accredited by the Northwest Association of Schools and Colleges.

Profiles: Montana State University–Bozeman

Course delivery sites Courses are delivered to your home, your workplace, military bases, other colleges.
Media Courses are delivered via television, videotapes, videoconferencing, audioconferencing, computer software, print, computer conferencing.
Services Distance learners have access to library services, academic advising at a distance.
Credit-earning options Students may transfer credits from another institution or may earn credits through examinations, military training, business training. Financial aid is available to distance learners.
Contact Distance Learning Specialist, Montana State University–Bozeman, 204 Culbertson Hall, Bozeman, MT 59715. *Telephone:* 406-994-6550. *Fax:* 406-994-6546.

DEGREE & CERTIFICATE PROGRAMS

Graduate Degrees
▶ *Science Education (MS)*

INDIVIDUAL COURSE SUBJECT AREAS

Undergraduate
Computer and information sciences; English language and literature

Graduate
Chemistry; civil engineering; geology; health and physical education/fitness; mathematics; mechanical engineering; nursing; physics; social psychology; teacher education

Noncredit
Electrical engineering

MONTANA TECH OF THE UNIVERSITY OF MONTANA

Butte, Montana

Office of Extended Studies

Montana Tech of The University of Montana, founded in 1895, is a state-supported comprehensive institution. It is accredited by the Northwest Association of Schools and Colleges. It first offered distance learning courses in 1996. In 1996–97, it offered 7 courses at a distance. In the fall of 1996, there was a total of 22 students enrolled in distance learning courses.
Course delivery sites Courses are delivered to your home.
Media Courses are delivered via e-mail, print. Students and teachers interact via mail, telephone, fax, e-mail. A computer is required for some courses.
Services Distance learners have access to library services, academic advising at a distance.
Credit-earning options Students may transfer credits from another institution or may earn credits through standardized exams, military training.
Typical costs Tuition of $750 per course. *Noncredit courses:* $175 per course. Costs may vary by specific program of study. Financial aid is available to distance learners.
Registration Students may register by mail, fax.
Contact Karl Burgher, Director of Extended Studies, Montana Tech of The University of Montana, 1300 West Park Street, Butte, MT 59701-8997. *Telephone:* 406-496-4410. *Fax:* 406-496-4116. *E-mail:* kburgher@po1.mtech.edu. *Web site:* http://www.mtech.edu.

INDIVIDUAL COURSE SUBJECT AREAS

Undergraduate
Business; English language and literature; health professions and related sciences

MONTGOMERY COLLEGE–ROCKVILLE CAMPUS

Rockville, Maryland

Distance Learning Programs

Montgomery College–Rockville Campus, founded in 1965, is a state and locally supported two-year college. It is accredited by the Middle States Association of Colleges and Schools.
Course delivery sites Courses are delivered to your home, your workplace, other colleges.
Media Courses are delivered via television, videoconferencing, computer conferencing.
Credit-earning options Students may transfer credits from another institution or may earn credits through examinations, military training, business training. Financial aid is available to distance learners.
Contact Acting Program Director, Montgomery College–Rockville Campus, 7200 Takoma Avenue, Takoma Park, MD 20912. *Telephone:* 301-587-9216. *Fax:* 301-650-1550.

INDIVIDUAL COURSE SUBJECT AREAS

Undergraduate
Area, ethnic, and cultural studies; astronomy and astrophysics; biological and life sciences; business; business administration and management; chemistry; computer and information sciences; economics; English composition; English language and literature; European languages and literatures; health and physical education/fitness; history; human resources management; law and legal studies; liberal arts, general studies, and humanities; mathematics; philosophy and religion; political science; psychology; sociology

Noncredit
English as a second language (ESL)

MONTGOMERY COUNTY COMMUNITY COLLEGE

Blue Bell, Pennsylvania

Montgomery County Community College, founded in 1964, is a county-supported two-year college. It is accredited by the Middle States Association of Colleges and Schools. It first offered distance learning courses in 1992. In 1996–97, it offered 20 courses at a distance. In the fall of 1996, there was a total of 300 students enrolled in distance learning courses.
Course delivery sites Courses are delivered to your home, your workplace.
Media Courses are delivered via television, videotapes, videoconferencing, computer software. Students and teachers interact via mail, telephone, fax, e-mail. A computer is required for some courses.
Restrictions Courses are available to US students only.
Services Distance learners have access to library services, the campus computer network, e-mail services, academic advising at a distance.

Credit-earning options Students may transfer credits from another institution or may earn credits through standardized exams, portfolio assessment.
Typical costs Tuition of $64 per credit plus mandatory fees of $2 per credit for local area residents. Tuition of $128 per credit plus mandatory fees of $2 per credit for in-state residents. Tuition of $192 per credit plus mandatory fees of $2 per credit for out-of-state residents. Financial aid is available to distance learners enrolled full-time or part-time.
Registration Students may register by mail, fax, phone.
Contact Dr. Brad Gottfried, Dean of Academic Affairs, Montgomery County Community College, 340 DeKalb Pike, PO Box 400, Blue Bell, PA 19422-0796. *Telephone:* 215-641-6430. *Fax:* 215-619-7161. *E-mail:* bgottfri@admin.mc3.edu. *Web site:* http://www.mc3.edu.

INDIVIDUAL COURSE SUBJECT AREAS

Undergraduate
Accounting; business administration and management; developmental and child psychology; economics; English composition; health and physical education/fitness; history; liberal arts, general studies, and humanities; psychology; social psychology; social sciences; sociology

MOODY BIBLE INSTITUTE

Chicago, Illinois

Moody Bible Institute External Studies Division

Moody Bible Institute, founded in 1886, is an independent-religious nondenominational comprehensive institution. It is accredited by the North Central Association of Colleges and Schools. It first offered distance learning courses in 1901. In 1996–97, it offered 27 courses at a distance.
Course delivery sites Courses are delivered to your home.
Media Courses are delivered via print. Students and teachers interact via mail, telephone.
Restrictions Students must be believers in Christ.
Services Distance learners have access to academic advising at a distance.
Credit-earning options Students may transfer credits from another institution or may earn credits through examinations.
Typical costs Tuition of $100 per semester hour. *Noncredit courses:* $19 per course.
Registration Students may register by mail, fax, phone.
Contact Neil Storms, Customer Services Supervisor, Moody Bible Institute, 820 North LaSalle Boulevard, Chicago, IL 60610. *Telephone:* 312-329-8019. *Fax:* 312-329-2081. *Web site:* http://www.moody.edu.

DEGREE & CERTIFICATE PROGRAMS

Associate Degrees
▶ *Biblical Studies (ABS)*
Application requirements *Prior education:* high school diploma or equivalent. *Other requirements:* high school transcript, an essay or personal statement, letter(s) of recommendation.
Completion requirements 25 semester hours must be completed through the institution.
Program contact Brian Talbot, External Studies Admissions and Records Coordinator, Moody Bible Institute, 820 North LaSalle Boulevard, Chicago, IL 60610. Phone: 312-329-2090. Fax: 312-329-2081.

INDIVIDUAL COURSE SUBJECT AREAS

Undergraduate
Classical languages and literatures; educational psychology; history; philosophy and religion; theological studies

Noncredit
Theological studies

MORAINE VALLEY COMMUNITY COLLEGE

Palos Hills, Illinois

Academic Services and Learning Technologies

Moraine Valley Community College, founded in 1967, is a state and locally supported two-year college. It is accredited by the North Central Association of Colleges and Schools. It first offered distance learning courses in 1976. In 1996–97, it offered 32 courses at a distance. In the fall of 1996, there was a total of 500 students enrolled in distance learning courses.
Course delivery sites Courses are delivered to Joliet Junior College (Joliet), Prairie State College (Chicago Heights), South Suburban College (South Holland), 3 off-campus centers in Evergreen Park, Oak Lawn, Tinley Park.
Media Courses are delivered via videotapes, videoconferencing, print. Students and teachers interact via videoconferencing, mail, telephone, fax.
Restrictions Students must have ISDN-compatible equipment.
Services Distance learners have access to library services, academic advising, tutoring, career placement assistance at a distance.
Credit-earning options Students may transfer credits from another institution or may earn credits through standardized exams, institutionally developed exams, portfolio assessment.
Typical costs Tuition of $42 per credit hour for local area residents. Tuition of $169 per credit hour for in-state residents. Tuition of $192 per credit hour for out-of-state residents. Mandatory fees vary according to class. Costs may vary by number of credits taken. Financial aid is available to distance learners enrolled full-time or part-time.
Registration Students may register by mail, phone.
Contact Diane Grund, Dean, Academic Services and Learning Technologies, Moraine Valley Community College, 10900 South 88th Avenue, Palos Hills, IL 60465. *Telephone:* 708-974-5290. *Fax:* 708-974-1184. *E-mail:* grund@moraine.cc.il.us.

INDIVIDUAL COURSE SUBJECT AREAS

Undergraduate
Abnormal psychology; astronomy and astrophysics; business; business law; design; developmental and child psychology; economics; engineering; English language and literature; film studies; French language and literature; geography; health professions and related sciences; history; horticulture; law and legal studies; philosophy and religion; physics; psychology; sociology

MOREHEAD STATE UNIVERSITY

Morehead, Kentucky

Office of Distance Learning

Morehead State University, founded in 1922, is a state-supported comprehensive institution. It is accredited by the Southern Association of Colleges and Schools. It first offered distance learning courses in 1995. In 1996–97, it offered 49 courses at a distance. In the fall of 1996, there was a total of 622 students enrolled in distance learning courses.

Distance Learning Programs

Profiles: Morehead State University

Course delivery sites Courses are delivered to your home, your workplace, Eastern Kentucky University (Richmond), Northern Kentucky University (Highland Heights), 3 off-campus centers in Ashland, Jackson, West Liberty, eleven high schools and middle schools in the region.
Media Courses are delivered via videotapes, videoconferencing, audiotapes, computer software, World Wide Web, e-mail, print. Students and teachers interact via videoconferencing, mail, telephone, fax, e-mail. A computer is required for some courses.
Services Distance learners have access to library services, the campus computer network, e-mail services, academic advising, tutoring, career placement assistance at a distance.
Credit-earning options Students may transfer credits from another institution or may earn credits through examinations, portfolio assessment.
Typical costs *Undergraduate:* Tuition of $88 per credit. *Graduate:* Tuition of $127 per credit. Costs may vary by specific program of study, number of credits taken, term of enrollment. Financial aid is available to distance learners.
Registration Students may register by mail, fax, phone, e-mail, World Wide Web.
Contact Dr. Autumn Grubb, Director, Distance Learning, Morehead State University, UPO 940, Morehead, KY 40351. *Telephone:* 606-783-2579. *Fax:* 606-783-5052.

DEGREE & CERTIFICATE PROGRAMS

Baccalaureate Degrees
▶ *Business Administration (BBA)*
In the fall of 1996 there were 99 students enrolled in this program.
Application requirements *Prior education:* high school diploma or equivalent. *Other requirements:* ACT, high school transcript, college transcripts.
Completion requirements 128 credits are required. 32 credits must be completed through the institution.
Program contact Green Miller, Chair, Accounting and Economics, Morehead State University, 222 Combs Building, Morehead, KY 40351. Phone: 606-783-2152. Fax: 606-783-5025. E-mail: g.miller@morehead-st.edu.

Graduate Degrees
▶ *Business Administration (MBA)*
In the fall of 1996 there were 203 students enrolled in this program.
Application requirements *Prior education:* baccalaureate degree. *Other requirements:* GMAT, college transcripts.
Completion requirements 50 credits are required. 30 credits must be completed through the institution.
Program contact John Alcorn, Coordinator, MBA Program, Morehead State University, 218 Combs Building, Morehead, KY 40351. Phone: 606-783-2795. Fax: 606-783-5025. E-mail: j.alcorn@morehead-st.edu.

INDIVIDUAL COURSE SUBJECT AREAS

Undergraduate
Accounting; administrative and secretarial services; area, ethnic, and cultural studies; business; business administration and management; education; education administration; English composition; English language and literature; health and physical education/fitness; home economics and family studies; mathematics; nursing; public health; special education; teacher education

Graduate
Accounting; administrative and secretarial services; business; business administration and management; education; education administration; English composition; nursing; public health; special education; teacher education

MORGAN COMMUNITY COLLEGE

Fort Morgan, Colorado

Extended Studies/Telecommunications

Morgan Community College, founded in 1967, is a state-supported two-year college. It is accredited by the North Central Association of Colleges and Schools. It first offered distance learning courses in 1985.
Course delivery sites Courses are delivered to your home, other colleges.
Media Courses are delivered via television, videoconferencing, audiographics conferencing.
Restrictions Programs are available to in-state students only.
Services Distance learners have access to library services, academic advising, tutoring, career placement assistance at a distance.
Credit-earning options Students may transfer credits from another institution or may earn credits through examinations, military training, business training. Financial aid is available to distance learners.
Contact Division Chair, Arts and Sciences, Morgan Community College, 17800 County Road 20, Fort Morgan, CO 80701. *Telephone:* 970-867-3081. *Fax:* 970-867-6608.

DEGREE & CERTIFICATE PROGRAMS

Associate Degrees
▶ *Liberal Arts and Sciences (AA, AS)*

INDIVIDUAL COURSE SUBJECT AREAS

Undergraduate
Astronomy and astrophysics; biology; chemistry; Classical languages and literatures; developmental and child psychology; economics; English composition; English language and literature; health and physical education/fitness; history; liberal arts, general studies, and humanities; mathematics; philosophy and religion; political science; social psychology; sociology

Noncredit
Astronomy and astrophysics; biology; chemistry; Classical languages and literatures; developmental and child psychology; economics; English composition; English language and literature; health and physical education/fitness; history; liberal arts, general studies, and humanities; mathematics; philosophy and religion; political science; social psychology; sociology

MORRIS BROWN COLLEGE

Atlanta, Georgia

Distance Learning Center

Morris Brown College, founded in 1881, is an independent-religious four-year college affiliated with the African Methodist Episcopal Church. It is accredited by the Southern Association of Colleges and Schools. It first offered distance learning courses in 1993.
Course delivery sites Courses are delivered to your workplace.
Media Courses are delivered via videotapes, videoconferencing, print, computer conferencing.
Restrictions Programs are available to in-state students only.
Credit-earning options Students may transfer credits from another institution or may earn credits through portfolio assessment, military training.

Contact Dr. Robert B. Lee, Director, Morris Brown College, 643 Martin Luther King, Jr. Drive, NW, Atlanta, GA 30314. *Telephone:* 404-220-0268. *Fax:* 404-220-0051.

INDIVIDUAL COURSE SUBJECT AREAS

Undergraduate
Developmental and child psychology; educational psychology; liberal arts, general studies, and humanities; music; teacher education

MOUNTAIN VIEW COLLEGE

Dallas, Texas

Mountain View College, founded in 1970, is a county-supported two-year college. It is accredited by the Southern Association of Colleges and Schools.
Course delivery sites Courses are delivered to your home.
Media Courses are delivered via television, videotapes, computer software, computer conferencing.
Restrictions Programs are available to local area students only.
Credit-earning options Students may transfer credits from another institution or may earn credits through examinations, portfolio assessment, military training. Financial aid is available to distance learners.
Contact Registrar/Director of Admission, Mountain View College, 4849 West Illinois Avenue, Dallas, TX 75211. *Telephone:* 214-860-8600. *Fax:* 214-860-8570.

DEGREE & CERTIFICATE PROGRAMS

Associate Degrees
▶ *Arts and Science (AA)*

INDIVIDUAL COURSE SUBJECT AREAS

Undergraduate
Accounting; business administration and management; economics; English composition; English language and literature; health professions and related sciences; history; mathematics; political science

MOUNT SAINT VINCENT UNIVERSITY

Halifax, Nova Scotia, Canada

Distance University Education via Technology (DUET)

Mount Saint Vincent University, founded in 1873, is a province-supported comprehensive institution. It is provincially chartered. It first offered distance learning courses in 1980. In 1996–97, it offered 50 courses at a distance. In the fall of 1996, there was a total of 500 students enrolled in distance learning courses.
Course delivery sites Courses are delivered to your home, your workplace, 15 community colleges in Nova Scotia.
Media Courses are delivered via television, videotapes, videoconferencing, audioconferencing, computer software, print. Students and teachers interact via audioconferencing, mail, telephone, fax, e-mail. A computer is required for some courses.
Services Distance learners have access to library services, the campus computer network, e-mail services, academic advising, tutoring at a distance.
Credit-earning options Students may transfer credits from another institution or may earn credits through examinations, portfolio assessment.
Typical costs *Undergraduate:* Tuition of $405.50 per course. *Graduate:* Tuition of $837 per course. *Noncredit courses:* $60–$200 per course. Financial aid is available to distance learners enrolled full-time or part-time.
Registration Students may register by mail, fax, phone, e-mail, World Wide Web.
Contact Mary Hart-Baker, DUET Secretary, Mount Saint Vincent University, 166 Bedford Highway, Halifax, NS B3M 2J6, Canada. *Telephone:* 902-457-6437. *Fax:* 902-445-3960. *E-mail:* mhbaker@msvu1.msvu.ca. *Web site:* http://www.msvu.ca.

DEGREE & CERTIFICATE PROGRAMS

Baccalaureate Degrees
▶ *Business Administration (BBA)*
In the fall of 1996 there were 100 students enrolled in this program.
Application requirements *Prior education:* high school diploma or equivalent. *Other requirements:* high school transcript, an application fee of $30.
Completion requirements 20 credits are required. 10 credits must be completed through the institution. This is a degree completion program.
Program contact Carolyn Nobes, Open Learning Program Coordinator, Mount Saint Vincent University, Halifax, NS B3M 2J6, Canada. Phone: 902-457-6511. Fax: 902-457-2618. E-mail: Carolyn.Nobes@msvu.ca.

▶ *Tourism and Hospitality Management (BTHM)*
In the fall of 1996 there were 24 students enrolled in this program.
Application requirements *Prior education:* high school diploma or equivalent. *Other requirements:* high school transcript, an essay or personal statement, letter(s) of recommendation, an application fee of $30.
Completion requirements 20 credits are required. 10 credits must be completed through the institution. This is a degree completion program.
Program contact Carolyn Nobes, Open Learning Program Coordinator, Mount Saint Vincent University, Halifax, NS B3M 2J6, Canada. Phone: 902-457-6511. Fax: 902-457-2618. E-mail: Carolyn.Nobes@msvu.ca.

Graduate Degrees
▶ *Education (MEd)*
In the fall of 1996 there were 100 students enrolled in this program.
Restrictions Program enrollment is limited.
Application requirements *Prior education:* undergraduate degree. *Other requirements:* an essay or personal statement, letter(s) of recommendation, an application fee of $40.
Completion requirements 6 credits are required. *Other requirements:* practicum; thesis.
Program contact Carolyn Nobes, Open Learning Program Coordinator, Mount Saint Vincent University, Halifax, NS B3M 2J6, Canada. Phone: 902-457-6511. Fax: 902-457-2618. E-mail: Carolyn.Nobes@msvu.ca.

Undergraduate Certificates
▶ *Business Administration*
In the fall of 1996 there were 200 students enrolled in this program.
Application requirements *Prior education:* high school diploma or equivalent. *Other requirements:* high school transcript.
Completion requirements 6 credits are required.
Program contact Chris Beckett, Coordinator, Distance University Education, Mount Saint Vincent University, 166 Bedford Highway, Halifax, NS B3M 2J6, Canada. Phone: 902-457-6388. Fax: 902-445-3960. E-mail: chris.beckett@msvu.ca.

▶ *French*
In the fall of 1996 there were 6 students enrolled in this program.
Application requirements *Prior education:* some undergraduate course work. *Other requirements:* competency test.
Completion requirements 3 credits are required.

Profiles: Mount Saint Vincent University

▶ *Gerontology*
In the fall of 1996 there were 250 students enrolled in this program.
Application requirements *Prior education:* high school diploma or equivalent. *Other requirements:* high school transcript, an application fee of $30.
Completion requirements 6 credits are required.

INDIVIDUAL COURSE SUBJECT AREAS

Undergraduate
Accounting; administrative and secretarial services; advertising; business; business administration and management; economics; English language and literature; European languages and literatures; history; home economics and family studies; hospitality services management; human resources management; liberal arts, general studies, and humanities; mathematics; philosophy and religion; psychology; social sciences; sociology; teacher education; theological studies

Graduate
Teacher education

Noncredit
Theological studies

MT. SAN ANTONIO COLLEGE

Walnut, California

Distance Learning

Mt. San Antonio College, founded in 1946, is a district-supported two-year college. It is accredited by the Western Association of Schools and Colleges, Inc. It first offered distance learning courses in 1993. In 1996–97, it offered 10 courses at a distance. In the fall of 1996, there was a total of 280 students enrolled in distance learning courses.
Course delivery sites Courses are delivered to your home.
Media Courses are delivered via television, videotapes, audiotapes, computer software, World Wide Web, e-mail, print. Students and teachers interact via mail, telephone, fax, e-mail. A computer is required for some courses.
Services Distance learners have access to library services, the campus computer network, e-mail services, academic advising at a distance.
Credit-earning options Students may transfer credits from another institution or may earn credits through institutionally developed exams, military training.
Typical costs Tuition of $13 per unit for in-state residents. Tuition of $114 per unit for out-of-state residents. *Noncredit courses:* $13 per unit. Financial aid is available to distance learners enrolled full-time or part-time.
Registration Students may register by mail, fax, phone.
Contact Kerry C. Stern, Dean, Learning Resources, Mt. San Antonio College, 1100 North Grand Avenue, Walnut, CA 91789. *Telephone:* 909-594-5611, Ext. 5658. *Fax:* 909-468-3992. *E-mail:* kstern@ibm.mtsac.edu. *Web site:* http://ibm.mtsac.edu:80/distance.

INDIVIDUAL COURSE SUBJECT AREAS

Undergraduate
Area, ethnic, and cultural studies; astronomy and astrophysics; business administration and management; home economics and family studies; hospitality services management; psychology; sociology

MOUNT WACHUSETT COMMUNITY COLLEGE

Gardner, Massachusetts

Mount Wachusett Community College, founded in 1963, is a state-supported two-year college. It is accredited by the New England Association of Schools and Colleges. It first offered distance learning courses in 1994. In the fall of 1996, there was a total of 75 students enrolled in distance learning courses.
Course delivery sites Courses are delivered to your home, 1 off-campus center in Leominster.
Media Courses are delivered via television, videotapes, computer software, World Wide Web. Students and teachers interact via mail, telephone, fax, e-mail. A computer is required for some courses.
Services Distance learners have access to academic advising, tutoring, career placement assistance at a distance.
Credit-earning options Students may transfer credits from another institution or may earn credits through standardized exams, institutionally developed exams, portfolio assessment.
Typical costs Tuition of $97 per credit plus mandatory fees of $50 per semester. *Noncredit courses:* $305 per course. Costs may vary by course delivery options. Financial aid is available to distance learners enrolled full-time or part-time.
Registration Students may register by mail, fax, phone.
Contact Stuart Shuman, Associate Dean of Continuing Education, Mount Wachusett Community College, Gardner, MA 01440. *Telephone:* 508-632-6600, Ext. 309. *Fax:* 508-632-6155. *E-mail:* s_shuman@mwcc.mass.edu.

INDIVIDUAL COURSE SUBJECT AREAS

Undergraduate
American (US) history; anthropology; foods and nutrition studies; gerontology; mathematics; psychology; sociology

MURRAY STATE UNIVERSITY

Murray, Kentucky

Continuing Education

Murray State University, founded in 1922, is a state-supported comprehensive institution. It is accredited by the Southern Association of Colleges and Schools.
Course delivery sites Courses are delivered to your home, your workplace, military bases, other colleges.
Media Courses are delivered via television, videotapes, videoconferencing, computer software, World Wide Web, e-mail, print. Students and teachers interact via videoconferencing, audioconferencing, mail, telephone, fax, e-mail.
Restrictions Programs are available to in-state students only.
Typical costs Tuition of $77 per credit plus mandatory fees of $20 per semester for in-state residents. Tuition of $113 per credit plus mandatory fees of $20 per semester for out-of-state residents.
Contact John Yates, Dean, Murray State University, PO Box 9, Murray, KY 42071-0009. *Telephone:* 800-669-7654. *Fax:* 502-762-3593.

INDIVIDUAL COURSE SUBJECT AREAS

Undergraduate
Social sciences

NASSAU COMMUNITY COLLEGE

Garden City, New York

College of the Air

Nassau Community College, founded in 1959, is a state and locally supported two-year college. It is accredited by the Middle States Association of Colleges and Schools. It first offered distance learning courses in 1991.
Course delivery sites Courses are delivered to your home.
Media Courses are delivered via television, videotapes, audiotapes, radio broadcast, print. Students and teachers interact via mail, telephone.
Restrictions Courses are available to regional area students only.
Services Distance learners have access to library services, academic advising at a distance.
Credit-earning options Students may transfer credits from another institution or may earn credits through examinations, portfolio assessment.
Typical costs Tuition of $84 per credit.
Contact Arthur L. Friedman, Coordinator, Nassau Community College, One Education Drive, Garden City, NY 11530-6793. *Telephone:* 516-572-7883. *Fax:* 516-572-7503.

INDIVIDUAL COURSE SUBJECT AREAS

Undergraduate

Area, ethnic, and cultural studies; Asian languages and literatures; business; business administration and management; communications; developmental and child psychology; economics; English language and literature; European languages and literatures; fine arts; health and physical education/fitness; history; law and legal studies; liberal arts, general studies, and humanities; mathematics; music; psychology; sociology

Noncredit

Mathematics

NATIONAL TECHNOLOGICAL UNIVERSITY

Fort Collins, Colorado

National Technological University

National Technological University is an independent-nonprofit graduate institution. It is accredited by the North Central Association of Colleges and Schools. It first offered distance learning courses in 1984. In 1996–97, it offered 500 courses at a distance. In the fall of 1996, there was a total of 1,700 students enrolled in distance learning courses.
Course delivery sites Courses are delivered to your home, your workplace, military bases, other colleges, 20–30 off-campus centers.
Media Courses are delivered via television. Students and teachers interact via videoconferencing, audioconferencing, mail, telephone, fax, e-mail. A computer is required for some courses.
Restrictions Students must be employed at a subscribing NTU company or near a community site.
Services Distance learners have access to academic advising at a distance.
Credit-earning options Students may transfer credits from another institution.
Typical costs Tuition of $263 per credit plus mandatory fees of $322 per credit. *Noncredit courses:* $100–$1000 per course. Costs may vary by number of credits taken, term of enrollment, originating university from which the course comes.
Registration Students may register by mail, fax, World Wide Web.

Contact Jeanne Breiner, Director of Admissions and Records, National Technological University, 700 Centre Avenue, Fort Collins, CO 80526. *Telephone:* 970-495-6408. *Fax:* 970-495-0601. *E-mail:* jeanne@mail.ntu.edu. *Web site:* http://www.ntu.edu.

DEGREE & CERTIFICATE PROGRAMS

Graduate Degrees

▶ *Chemical Engineering (MS)*
In the fall of 1996 there were 11 students enrolled in this program.
Application requirements *Prior education:* baccalaureate degree. *Other requirements:* college transcripts, an application fee of $50.
Completion requirements 33 credit hours are required. 18 credit hours must be completed through the institution. *Maximum time for completion:* seven years.

▶ *Computer Engineering (MS)*
In the fall of 1996 there were 116 students enrolled in this program. In 1995–96, 29 degrees were earned at a distance through this program.
Application requirements *Prior education:* baccalaureate degree. *Other requirements:* college transcripts, an application fee of $50.
Completion requirements 30 credit hours are required. 18 credit hours must be completed through the institution. *Maximum time for completion:* seven years.
Program contact Joan Schoonveld, Admissions Officer, National Technological University, 700 Centre Avenue, Fort Collins, CO 80526. Phone: 970-495-6403. Fax: 970-498-0601. E-mail: joan@mail.ntu.edu.

▶ *Computer Science (MS)*
In the fall of 1996 there were 119 students enrolled in this program. In 1995–96, 20 degrees were earned at a distance through this program.
Application requirements *Prior education:* baccalaureate degree. *Other requirements:* college transcripts, an application fee of $50.
Completion requirements 30 credit hours are required. 18 credit hours must be completed through the institution. *Maximum time for completion:* seven years.
Program contact Joan Schoonveld, Admissions Officer, National Technological University, 700 Centre Avenue, Fort Collins, CO 80526. Phone: 970-495-6403. Fax: 970-498-0601. E-mail: joan@mail.ntu.edu.

▶ *Electrical Engineering (MS)*
In the fall of 1996 there were 241 students enrolled in this program. In 1995–96, 23 degrees were earned at a distance through this program.
Application requirements *Prior education:* baccalaureate degree. *Other requirements:* college transcripts, an application fee of $50.
Completion requirements 33 credit hours are required. 18 credit hours must be completed through the institution. *Maximum time for completion:* seven years.
Program contact Joan Schoonveld, Admissions Officer, National Technological University, 700 Centre Avenue, Fort Collins, CO 80526. Phone: 970-495-6403. Fax: 970-498-0601. E-mail: joan@mail.ntu.edu.

▶ *Engineering Management (MS)*
In the fall of 1996 there were 98 students enrolled in this program. In 1995–96, 21 degrees were earned at a distance through this program.
Application requirements *Prior education:* baccalaureate degree. *Other requirements:* college transcripts, an application fee of $50.
Completion requirements 33 credit hours are required. 18 credit hours must be completed through the institution. *Maximum time for completion:* seven years.
Program contact Joan Schoonveld, Admissions Officer, National Technological University, 700 Centre Avenue, Fort Collins, CO 80526. Phone: 970-495-6403. Fax: 970-498-0601. E-mail: joan@mail.ntu.edu.

▶ *Hazardous Waste Management (MS)*
In the fall of 1996 there were 32 students enrolled in this program. In 1995–96, 15 degrees were earned at a distance through this program.
Application requirements *Prior education:* baccalaureate degree. *Other requirements:* college transcripts, an application fee of $50.

Profiles: National Technological University

Completion requirements 33 credit hours are required. 18 credit hours must be completed through the institution. *Maximum time for completion:* seven years.

Program contact Joan Schoonveld, Admissions Officer, National Technological University, 700 Centre Avenue, Fort Collins, CO 80526. Phone: 970-495-6403. Fax: 970-498-0601. E-mail: joan@mail.ntu.edu.

▶ *Health Physics (MS)*

In the fall of 1996 there were 8 students enrolled in this program. In 1995–96, 3 degrees were earned at a distance through this program.

Application requirements *Prior education:* baccalaureate degree. *Other requirements:* college transcripts, an application fee of $50.

Completion requirements 32 credit hours are required. 18 credit hours must be completed through the institution. *Maximum time for completion:* seven years.

Program contact Joan Schoonveld, Admissions Officer, National Technological University, 700 Centre Avenue, Fort Collins, CO 80526. Phone: 970-495-6403. Fax: 970-498-0601. E-mail: joan@mail.ntu.edu.

▶ *Management of Technology (MS)*

In the fall of 1996 there were 45 students enrolled in this program. In 1995–96, 20 degrees were earned at a distance through this program.

Application requirements *Prior education:* baccalaureate degree. *Other requirements:* college transcripts, an application fee of $50, 2 years work experience in an engineering environment.

Completion requirements 36 credit hours are required. 36 credit hours must be completed through the institution. *Maximum time for completion:* seven years.

On-campus requirements Four 1-week residencies in different locations.

Program contact Ms. Tina Kellogg, Academic Assistant, National Technological University, 700 Centre Avenue, Fort Collins, CO 80526. Phone: 970-495-6430. Fax: 970-498-0601. E-mail: tina@mail.ntu.edu.

▶ *Manufacturing Systems Engineering (MS)*

In the fall of 1996 there were 28 students enrolled in this program. In 1995–96, 5 degrees were earned at a distance through this program.

Application requirements *Prior education:* baccalaureate degree. *Other requirements:* college transcripts, an application fee of $50.

Completion requirements 33 credit hours are required. 18 credit hours must be completed through the institution. *Maximum time for completion:* seven years.

Program contact Joan Schoonveld, Admissions Officer, National Technological University, 700 Centre Avenue, Fort Collins, CO 80526. Phone: 970-495-6403. Fax: 970-498-0601. E-mail: joan@mail.ntu.edu.

▶ *Material Sciences and Engineering (MS)*

In the fall of 1996 there were 23 students enrolled in this program. In 1995–96, 3 degrees were earned at a distance through this program.

Application requirements *Prior education:* baccalaureate degree. *Other requirements:* college transcripts, an application fee of $50.

Completion requirements 33 credit hours are required. 18 credit hours must be completed through the institution. *Maximum time for completion:* seven years.

Program contact Joan Schoonveld, Admissions Officer, National Technological University, 700 Centre Avenue, Fort Collins, CO 80526. Phone: 970-495-6403. Fax: 970-498-0601. E-mail: joan@mail.ntu.edu.

▶ *Software Engineering (MS)*

In the fall of 1996 there were 65 students enrolled in this program. In 1995–96, 12 degrees were earned at a distance through this program.

Application requirements *Prior education:* baccalaureate degree. *Other requirements:* college transcripts, an application fee of $50.

Completion requirements 33 credit hours are required. 18 credit hours must be completed through the institution. *Maximum time for completion:* seven years.

Program contact Joan Schoonveld, Admissions Officer, National Technological University, 700 Centre Avenue, Fort Collins, CO 80526. Phone: 970-495-6403. Fax: 970-498-0601. E-mail: joan@mail.ntu.edu.

▶ *Transportation Systems Engineering (MS)*

Application requirements *Prior education:* baccalaureate degree. *Other requirements:* college transcripts, an application fee of $50.

Completion requirements 33 credit hours are required. 18 credit hours must be completed through the institution. *Maximum time for completion:* seven years.

Program contact Joan Schoonveld, Admissions Officer, National Technological University, 700 Centre Avenue, Fort Collins, CO 80526. Phone: 970-495-6403. Fax: 970-498-0601. E-mail: joan@mail.ntu.edu.

Graduate certificates

▶ *Chemical Engineering*

Application requirements *Prior education:* baccalaureate degree.

Completion requirements 12 credit hours are required. 9 credit hours must be completed through the institution. *Maximum time for completion:* seven years.

▶ *Computer Engineering*

In 1995–96, 1 certificate was earned at a distance through this program.

Application requirements *Prior education:* baccalaureate degree.

Completion requirements 12 credit hours are required. 12 credit hours must be completed through the institution. *Maximum time for completion:* seven years.

▶ *Computer Sciences*

Application requirements *Prior education:* baccalaureate degree.

Completion requirements 12 credit hours are required. 12 credit hours must be completed through the institution. *Maximum time for completion:* seven years.

▶ *Electrical Engineering*

In 1995–96, 2 certificates were earned at a distance through this program.

Application requirements *Prior education:* baccalaureate degree.

Completion requirements 12 credit hours are required. 12 credit hours must be completed through the institution. *Maximum time for completion:* seven years.

▶ *Engineering Management*

In 1995–96, 10 certificates were earned at a distance through this program.

Application requirements *Prior education:* baccalaureate degree.

Completion requirements 12 credit hours are required. 12 credit hours must be completed through the institution. *Maximum time for completion:* seven years.

▶ *Hazardous Waste Management*

In 1995–96, 18 certificates were earned at a distance through this program.

Application requirements *Prior education:* baccalaureate degree.

Completion requirements 12 credit hours are required. 12 credit hours must be completed through the institution. *Maximum time for completion:* seven years.

▶ *Health Physics*

Application requirements *Prior education:* baccalaureate degree.

Completion requirements 12 credit hours are required. 12 credit hours must be completed through the institution. *Maximum time for completion:* 7 years.

▶ *Manufacturing Systems Engineering*

In 1995–96, 2 certificates were earned at a distance through this program.

Application requirements *Prior education:* baccalaureate degree.

Completion requirements 12 credit hours are required. 12 credit hours must be completed through the institution. *Maximum time for completion:* seven years.

▶ *Material Sciences and Engineering*

Application requirements *Prior education:* baccalaureate degree.

Completion requirements 12 credit hours are required. 12 credit hours must be completed through the institution. *Maximum time for completion:* seven years.

▶ *Software Engineering*
In 1995–96, 6 certificates were earned at a distance through this program.
Application requirements *Prior education:* baccalaureate degree.
Completion requirements 12 credit hours are required. 12 credit hours must be completed through the institution. *Maximum time for completion:* seven years.

▶ *Technical Japanese*
In 1995–96, 3 certificates were earned at a distance through this program.
Application requirements *Prior education:* baccalaureate degree.
Completion requirements 12 credit hours are required. 12 credit hours must be completed through the institution. *Maximum time for completion:* seven years.

▶ *Transportation Systems Engineering*
Application requirements *Prior education:* baccalaureate degree.
Completion requirements 12 credit hours are required. 12 credit hours must be completed through the institution. *Maximum time for completion:* seven years.

INDIVIDUAL COURSE SUBJECT AREAS

Graduate
Accounting; aerospace, aeronautical engineering; chemical engineering; chemistry; civil engineering; computer and information sciences; computer programming; database management; economics; electrical engineering; engineering mechanics; engineering-related technologies; engineering/industrial management; environmental engineering; industrial engineering; Japanese language and literature; mathematics; mechanical engineering; physics; telecommunications

Noncredit
Aerospace, aeronautical engineering; business; business administration and management; chemical engineering; chemistry; civil engineering; computer and information sciences; computer programming; database management; economics; electrical engineering; engineering mechanics; engineering-related technologies; engineering/industrial management; environmental engineering; human resources management; industrial engineering; Japanese language and literature; management information systems; mathematics; mechanical engineering; physics; telecommunications

NATIONAL UNIVERSITY

La Jolla, California

Extended Studies Institute

National University, founded in 1971, is an independent-nonprofit comprehensive institution. It is accredited by the Western Association of Schools and Colleges, Inc. It first offered distance learning courses in 1994. In 1996–97, it offered 10 courses at a distance.
Course delivery sites Courses are delivered to your home, your workplace, military bases, other colleges.
Media Courses are delivered via videotapes, videoconferencing, audioconferencing, computer software, World Wide Web, e-mail, print. Students and teachers interact via mail, telephone, fax, e-mail. A computer is required for all courses.
Services Distance learners have access to library services, the campus computer network, e-mail services, academic advising at a distance.
Credit-earning options Students may transfer credits from another institution.
Typical costs Tuition of $200 per unit. *Noncredit courses:* $200 per unit. Financial aid is available to distance learners.
Registration Students may register by mail, fax, phone, e-mail, World Wide Web.

Contact Pamela Montroy, Academic Advisor, National University, 11255 North Torrey Pines Road, La Jolla, CA 92037. *Telephone:* 619-642-8212. *Fax:* 619-642-8709. *E-mail:* pmontroy@nunir.nu.edu. *Web site:* http://www.nu.edu.

DEGREE & CERTIFICATE PROGRAMS

Graduate Degrees

▶ *Business Administration (GMBA)*
Application requirements *Prior education:* baccalaureate degree. *Other requirements:* TOEFL (if English is second language), college transcripts, an essay or personal statement, an application fee of $60 ($100 for international students), 2.5 GPA.
Completion requirements 60 units are required. 45 units must be completed through the institution.
On-campus requirements For final 3 courses.

INDIVIDUAL COURSE SUBJECT AREAS

Undergraduate
Business

Graduate
Business

See full description on page 436.

NEW HAMPSHIRE COLLEGE

Manchester, New Hampshire

Distance Education Program

New Hampshire College, founded in 1932, is an independent-nonprofit comprehensive institution. It is accredited by the New England Association of Schools and Colleges. It first offered distance learning courses in 1996. In 1996–97, it offered 50 courses at a distance. In the fall of 1996, there was a total of 97 students enrolled in distance learning courses.
Course delivery sites Courses are delivered to your home, your workplace, military bases.
Media Courses are delivered via computer software, World Wide Web, e-mail, print. Students and teachers interact via mail, telephone, fax, e-mail. A computer is required for all courses.
Services Distance learners have access to library services, e-mail services, academic advising at a distance.
Credit-earning options Students may transfer credits from another institution or may earn credits through standardized exams, institutionally developed exams, portfolio assessment, military training, business training.
Typical costs *Undergraduate:* Tuition of $447 per course. *Graduate:* Tuition of $840 per course. Financial aid is available to distance learners enrolled full-time or part-time.
Registration Students may register by mail, fax, phone, e-mail, World Wide Web.
Contact Dr. J. Lee Williams, Jr., Director of Distance Education, New Hampshire College, 2500 North River Road, Manchester, NH 03106. *Telephone:* 603-668-2211, Ext. 2270. *Fax:* 603-645-9665. *E-mail:* leewil@nhc.edu. *Web site:* http://www.dist-ed.nhc.edu.

Profiles: New Hampshire College

DEGREE & CERTIFICATE PROGRAMS

Undergraduate Certificates

▶ *Accounting*
In the fall of 1996 there were 4 students enrolled in this program.
Application requirements *Prior education:* high school diploma or equivalent. *Other requirements:* SAT, ACT, high school transcript, college transcripts, an essay or personal statement, letter(s) of recommendation.
Completion requirements 24 credits are required. 12 credits must be completed through the institution.

▶ *Computer Information Systems, Human Resources Management*
In the fall of 1996 there were 10 students enrolled in this program.
Application requirements *Prior education:* high school diploma or equivalent. *Other requirements:* ACT or SAT, high school transcript, college transcripts, an essay or personal statement, letter(s) of recommendation.
Completion requirements 18 credits are required. 12 credits must be completed through the institution.

INDIVIDUAL COURSE SUBJECT AREAS

Undergraduate
Abnormal psychology; accounting; advertising; business; business administration and management; business law; computer and information sciences; computer programming; creative writing; developmental and child psychology; economics; English composition; English language and literature; English literature; finance; history; human resources management; international business; liberal arts, general studies, and humanities; marketing; mathematics; organizational behavior studies; philosophy and religion; political science; psychology; sociology; statistics

Graduate
Computer and information sciences; marketing; organizational behavior studies

See full description on page 438.

NEW JERSEY INSTITUTE OF TECHNOLOGY

Newark, New Jersey

Continuing Professional Education

New Jersey Institute of Technology, founded in 1881, is a state-supported university. It is accredited by the Middle States Association of Colleges and Schools. It first offered distance learning courses in 1985. In 1996–97, it offered 120 courses at a distance. In the fall of 1996, there was a total of 700 students enrolled in distance learning courses.
Course delivery sites Courses are delivered to your home, your workplace, military bases, other colleges.
Media Courses are delivered via television, videotapes, videoconferencing, audioconferencing, World Wide Web, e-mail, print, CD-ROM. Students and teachers interact via videoconferencing, mail, telephone, fax, e-mail. A computer is required for all courses.
Services Distance learners have access to library services, the campus computer network, e-mail services, academic advising, tutoring, career placement assistance at a distance.
Credit-earning options Students may transfer credits from another institution or may earn credits through examinations.
Typical costs *Undergraduate:* Tuition of $516 per course plus mandatory fees of $136 per course for in-state residents. Tuition of $1071 per course plus mandatory fees of $136 per course for out-of-state residents. *Graduate:* Tuition of $978 per course plus mandatory fees of $136 per course for in-state residents. Tuition of $1353 per course plus mandatory fees of $136 per course for out-of-state residents. $105 for application and registration fees. Financial aid is available to distance learners.
Registration Students may register by mail, fax, World Wide Web.
Contact Traci Moore, Secretarial Assistant, New Jersey Institute of Technology, University Heights, Newark, NJ 07102. *Telephone:* 201-596-3177. *Fax:* 201-596-3203. *E-mail:* dl@njit.edu. *Web site:* http://www.njit.edu/dl.

DEGREE & CERTIFICATE PROGRAMS

Baccalaureate Degrees

▶ *Computer Science (BS)*
Restrictions Students must have access to a PC and modem.
Application requirements *Prior education:* high school diploma or equivalent. *Other requirements:* high school transcript, an application fee of $35.
Completion requirements 134 credits are required.

▶ *Information Systems (BA)*
Restrictions Students must have access to a PC and modem.
Application requirements *Prior education:* high school diploma or equivalent. *Other requirements:* SAT, ACT, high school transcript, an application fee of $35.
Completion requirements 125 credits are required.

Graduate Degrees

▶ *Engineering Management (MS)*
Restrictions Students must have access to a PC and modem.
Application requirements *Prior education:* undergraduate degree in engineering, the sciences, or closely-related area. *Other requirements:* letter(s) of recommendation, an application fee, 2.8 GPA.
Completion requirements 30 credits are required. 21 credits must be completed through the institution. *Maximum time for completion:* 10 years.

▶ *Information Systems (MS)*
Restrictions Students must have access to a PC and modem.
Application requirements *Prior education:* baccalaureate degree from an accredited program in computer science, mathematics or equivalent knowledge base with 3.0 GPA. *Other requirements:* college transcripts, letter(s) of recommendation, an application fee.
Completion requirements 36 credits are required. 27 credits must be completed through the institution. *Maximum time for completion:* 10 years.

Graduate certificates

▶ *Programming Environment Tools*
Restrictions Students must have access to a PC and modem.
Application requirements *Prior education:* undergraduate degree. *Other requirements:* an application fee of $35, C language programming background.
Completion requirements 12 credits are required. 9 credits must be completed through the institution. *Maximum time for completion:* three years.

▶ *Project Management*
Restrictions Students must have access to a PC and modem.
Application requirements *Prior education:* undergraduate degree. *Other requirements:* an application fee of $35.
Completion requirements 12 credits are required. 9 credits must be completed through the institution. *Maximum time for completion:* three years.

▶ *Telecommunications Networking*
Restrictions Students must have access to a PC and modem.
Application requirements *Prior education:* undergraduate degree. *Other requirements:* an application fee of $35.

Completion requirements 12 credits are required. 9 credits must be completed through the institution. *Maximum time for completion:* three years.

INDIVIDUAL COURSE SUBJECT AREAS

Undergraduate
Business administration and management; chemistry; computer and information sciences; conservation and natural resources; economics; electrical engineering; engineering-related technologies; English language and literature; human resources management; liberal arts, general studies, and humanities; mathematics; physics; social psychology

Graduate
Business; business administration and management; chemical engineering; civil engineering; computer and information sciences; conservation and natural resources; economics; electrical engineering; engineering/industrial management; environmental engineering; health professions and related sciences; human resources management; industrial engineering; journalism; law and legal studies; library and information studies

See full description on page 440.

NEW MEXICO JUNIOR COLLEGE

Hobbs, New Mexico

Continuing Education

New Mexico Junior College, founded in 1965, is a state and locally supported two-year college. It is accredited by the North Central Association of Colleges and Schools. It first offered distance learning courses in 1994.
Course delivery sites Courses are delivered to your home.
Media Courses are delivered via television, videoconferencing, print.
Restrictions Programs are available to local area students only.
Credit-earning options Students may transfer credits from another institution or may earn credits through examinations. Financial aid is available to distance learners.
Contact Director, Continuing Education, New Mexico Junior College, 5317 Lovington Highway, Hobbs, NM 88240. *Telephone:* 505-392-5544. *Fax:* 505-392-2527.

INDIVIDUAL COURSE SUBJECT AREAS

Undergraduate
Accounting; business; business administration and management; developmental and child psychology; education administration; educational psychology; English composition; English language and literature; European languages and literatures; fine arts; liberal arts, general studies, and humanities; mathematics; social psychology; sociology; special education; teacher education

NEW MEXICO STATE UNIVERSITY

Las Cruces, New Mexico

Office of Distance Education

New Mexico State University, founded in 1888, is a state-supported university. It is accredited by the North Central Association of Colleges and Schools. It first offered distance learning courses in 1989. In 1996–97, it offered 27 courses at a distance. In the fall of 1996, there was a total of 500 students enrolled in distance learning courses.
Course delivery sites Courses are delivered to your workplace, military bases, New Mexico State University–Alamogordo (Alamogordo), New Mexico State University–Carlsbad (Carlsbad), San Juan College (Farmington).
Media Courses are delivered via television, videotapes, videoconferencing. Students and teachers interact via videoconferencing, telephone, fax, e-mail. A computer is required for some courses.
Restrictions Students must be able to receive satellite transmission.
Services Distance learners have access to the campus computer network, e-mail services, academic advising at a distance.
Credit-earning options Students may transfer credits from another institution or may earn credits through examinations, military training.
Typical costs *Undergraduate:* Tuition of $125 per credit. *Graduate:* Tuition of $125 per credit. Financial aid is available to distance learners.
Registration Students may register by mail, fax, phone, e-mail.
Contact Lynford L. Ames, Director of Distance Education, New Mexico State University, Box 3WEC, Las Cruces, NM 88003. *Telephone:* 505-646-5837. *Fax:* 505-646-2044. *E-mail:* lames@nmsu.edu.

DEGREE & CERTIFICATE PROGRAMS

Baccalaureate Degrees
▶ *General Business (BBA)*
In the fall of 1996 there were 40 students enrolled in this program.
Restrictions This program is available to local area students only.
Application requirements *Prior education:* some undergraduate course work. *Other requirements:* ACT, high school transcript, college transcripts, an application fee of $15.
Completion requirements 50 credits are required. 30 credits must be completed through the institution.

Graduate Degrees
▶ *Education (MS)*
In the fall of 1996 there were 157 students enrolled in this program.
Restrictions This program is available to in-state students only.
Application requirements *Prior education:* baccalaureate degree. *Other requirements:* MAT, college transcripts, an application fee of $15.
Completion requirements 32 credits are required. 24 credits must be completed through the institution. *Maximum time for completion:* seven years.

▶ *Engineering (MS)*
Application requirements *Prior education:* baccalaureate degree. *Other requirements:* GRE, college transcripts, an application fee of $15.
Completion requirements 32 credits are required. 24 credits must be completed through the institution. *Maximum time for completion:* seven years.

INDIVIDUAL COURSE SUBJECT AREAS

Undergraduate
Accounting; business; business administration and management; human resources management

Graduate
Accounting; business; business administration and management; chemical engineering; civil engineering; education administration; electrical engineering; engineering/industrial management; environmental engineering; human resources management; industrial engineering; public health; special education; teacher education

Profiles: New River Community College

NEW RIVER COMMUNITY COLLEGE

Dublin, Virginia

Distance Education and Learning Resources

New River Community College, founded in 1969, is a state-supported two-year college. It is accredited by the Southern Association of Colleges and Schools. It first offered distance learning courses in 1980. In 1996–97, it offered 56 courses at a distance. In the fall of 1996, there was a total of 802 students enrolled in distance learning courses.
Course delivery sites Courses are delivered to your home, your workplace, other colleges, 1 off-campus center in Christiansburg.
Media Courses are delivered via television, videotapes, videoconferencing, audiotapes, audioconferencing, computer software, World Wide Web, e-mail, print. Students and teachers interact via videoconferencing, audioconferencing, mail, telephone, fax, e-mail. A computer is required for some courses.
Services Distance learners have access to library services, academic advising, tutoring, career placement assistance at a distance.
Credit-earning options Students may transfer credits from another institution or may earn credits through examinations.
Typical costs Tuition of $46.65 per credit hour plus mandatory fees of $4 per credit hour for in-state residents. Tuition of $156 per credit hour plus mandatory fees of $4 per credit hour for out-of-state residents. Financial aid is available to distance learners enrolled full-time or part-time.
Registration Students may register by mail, fax, phone.
Contact Bridget Franklin, Coordinator, Distance Learning and Instructional Television, New River Community College, PO Box 1127, Dublin, VA 24084. *Telephone:* 540-674-3614. *Fax:* 540-674-3626. *E-mail:* nrfranb@nr.cc.va.us.

DEGREE & CERTIFICATE PROGRAMS

Associate Degrees

▶ *Education (AAS)*

Application requirements *Prior education:* high school diploma or equivalent. *Other requirements:* high school transcript, application, math and English placement test.
Completion requirements 62 credit hours are required. 25% of course work must be completed through the institution.

▶ *General Studies (AAS)*

Application requirements *Prior education:* high school diploma or equivalent. *Other requirements:* high school transcript, application, math and English placement test.
Completion requirements 62 credit hours are required. 16 credit hours must be completed through the institution.

INDIVIDUAL COURSE SUBJECT AREAS

Undergraduate

Abnormal psychology; accounting; administrative and secretarial services; American (US) history; American literature; biology; business; business administration and management; business law; computer and information sciences; developmental and child psychology; economics; educational psychology; English composition; English language and literature; English literature; finance; foods and nutrition studies; geology; health and physical education/fitness; history; information sciences and systems; library and information studies; marketing; mathematics; music; organizational behavior studies; psychology; sign language; social psychology; sociology; statistics

NEW SCHOOL FOR SOCIAL RESEARCH

New York, New York

Distance Learning Program

New School for Social Research, founded in 1919, is an independent-nonprofit university. It is accredited by the Middle States Association of Colleges and Schools. It first offered distance learning courses in 1994. In 1996–97, it offered 300 courses at a distance. In the fall of 1996, there was a total of 245 students enrolled in distance learning courses.
Course delivery sites Courses are delivered to your home, your workplace, military bases, other colleges.
Media Courses are delivered via World Wide Web. Students and teachers interact via mail, telephone, fax, e-mail. A computer is required for all courses.
Services Distance learners have access to library services, academic advising, tutoring at a distance.
Credit-earning options Students may transfer credits from another institution or may earn credits through portfolio assessment.
Typical costs *Undergraduate:* Tuition of $540 per credit plus mandatory fees of $40 per semester. *Graduate:* Tuition of $582 per credit plus mandatory fees of $95 per semester. *Noncredit courses:* $340–$450 per course. Costs may vary by specific program of study, number of credits taken. Financial aid is available to distance learners.
Registration Students may register by mail, fax, phone, e-mail, World Wide Web.
Contact Vitha Sehwani, Admissions Coordinator, New School for Social Research, 66 West 12th Street, New York, NY 10011. *Telephone:* 212-229-5630. *Fax:* 212-989-3887. *E-mail:* admissions@dialnsa.edu. *Web site:* http://dialnsa.edu.

DEGREE & CERTIFICATE PROGRAMS

Baccalaureate Degrees

▶ *Liberal Arts (BA)*

Application requirements *Prior education:* 60 transferable undergraduate credits. *Other requirements:* college transcripts, an essay or personal statement, an application fee of $30.
Completion requirements 120 credits are required. 30 credits must be completed through the institution. This is a degree completion program.

INDIVIDUAL COURSE SUBJECT AREAS

Undergraduate

Accounting; area, ethnic, and cultural studies; Asian languages and literatures; astronomy and astrophysics; business; business administration and management; Classical languages and literatures; communications; computer and information sciences; creative writing; design; developmental and child psychology; economics; English as a second language (ESL); English composition; English language and literature; European languages and literatures; fine arts; geology; health and physical education/fitness; history; human resources management; industrial psychology; journalism; liberal arts, general studies, and humanities; mathematics; Middle Eastern languages and literatures; music; philosophy and religion; physics; political science; social psychology; social sciences; sociology; teacher education

Graduate

Communications; creative writing; teacher education

Noncredit

Accounting; area, ethnic, and cultural studies; Asian languages and literatures; astronomy and astrophysics; business; business administration and management; Classical languages and literatures; communications; computer and information sciences; creative writing; design;

developmental and child psychology; economics; English as a second language (ESL); English composition; English language and literature; European languages and literatures; fine arts; geology; health and physical education/fitness; history; human resources management; industrial psychology; journalism; liberal arts, general studies, and humanities; mathematics; Middle Eastern languages and literatures; music; philosophy and religion; physics; political science; social psychology; social sciences; sociology; teacher education

See full description on page 442.

NEW YORK INSTITUTE OF TECHNOLOGY

Old Westbury, New York

On-Line Campus

New York Institute of Technology, founded in 1955, is an independent-nonprofit comprehensive institution. It is accredited by the Middle States Association of Colleges and Schools. It first offered distance learning courses in 1985. In 1996–97, it offered 200 courses at a distance. In the fall of 1996, there was a total of 500 students enrolled in distance learning courses.

Course delivery sites Courses are delivered to your home, your workplace, military bases.

Media Courses are delivered via videoconferencing, audioconferencing, World Wide Web, e-mail. Students and teachers interact via videoconferencing, audioconferencing, e-mail, World Wide Web. A computer is required for all courses.

Services Distance learners have access to library services, academic advising, tutoring, career placement assistance, admissions at a distance.

Credit-earning options Students may transfer credits from another institution or may earn credits through standardized exams, portfolio assessment, military training, business training.

Typical costs *Undergraduate:* Tuition of $245 per credit. *Graduate:* Tuition of $390 per credit. *Noncredit courses:* $100 per hour. Financial aid is available to distance learners enrolled full-time.

Registration Students may register by mail, fax, phone, e-mail, World Wide Web.

Contact Patricia Fenn, Director, Admissions and Recruitment, New York Institute of Technology, On-Line Campus, PO Box 9029, Central Islip, NY 11722-9029. *Telephone:* 800-222-NYIT. *Fax:* 516-348-1107. *E-mail:* pfenn@acl.nyit.edu. *Web site:* http://www.nyit.edu/olc.

DEGREE & CERTIFICATE PROGRAMS

Baccalaureate Degrees

▶ *Business (BS)*
Application requirements *Prior education:* high school diploma or equivalent. *Other requirements:* high school transcript, college transcripts, an application fee of $40, foreign students need transcript evaluation.
Completion requirements 120 credits are required. 30 credits must be completed through the institution.
Program contact J. C. Spender, Dean, New York Institute of Technology, PO Box 9029, Central Islip, NY 11722-9029. Phone: 800-222-NYIT. Fax: 516-348-3399.

▶ *Hospitality Management (BPS)*
Application requirements *Prior education:* high school diploma or equivalent. *Other requirements:* high school transcript, college transcripts, an application fee of $40, foreign students need transcript evaluation.
Completion requirements 120 credits are required. 30 must be completed through the institution.
Program contact James Turley, Chair, New York Institute of Technology, On-Line Campus, PO Box 9029, Central Islip, NY 11722-9029. Phone: 800-222-NYIT. Fax: 516-348-1107.

▶ *Interdisciplinary Studies (BS)*
Application requirements *Prior education:* high school diploma or equivalent. *Other requirements:* high school transcript, college transcripts, an application fee of $40, foreign students need transcript evaluations.
Completion requirements 120 credits are required. 30 credits must be completed through the institution.
Program contact Dr. Luis Navia, Dean, New York Institute of Technology, On - Line Campus, PO Box 9029, Central Islip, NY 11722-9029. Phone: 800-222-NYIT. Fax: 516-348-1107.

▶ *Community Mental Health, Criminology, Psychology, Sociology (BS)*
Application requirements *Prior education:* high school diploma or equivalent. *Other requirements:* high school transcript, an application fee of $40, foreign students need transcript evaluations.
Completion requirements 128 credits are required. 30 credits must be completed through the institution.
Program contact Dr. Robert Goldblatt, Chair, New York Institute of Technology, On-Line Campus, PO Box 9029, Central Islip, NY 11722-9029. Phone: 800-222-NYIT. Fax: 516-348-1107.

▶ *Telecommunications Management (BS)*
Application requirements *Prior education:* high school diploma or equivalent. *Other requirements:* high school transcript, college transcripts, an application fee of $40, foreign students need transcript evaluation.
Completion requirements 120 credits are required. 30 credits must be completed through the institution.
Program contact Dr. Ed Nelson, Chair, New York Institute of Technology, On-Line Campus, PO Box 9029, Central Islip, NY 11722-9029. Phone: 800-222-NYIT. Fax: 516-348-1107.

Graduate Degrees

▶ *Business (MBA)*
Application requirements *Prior education:* baccalaureate degree. *Other requirements:* GMAT, high school transcript, college transcripts, letter(s) of recommendation, an application fee of $50, foreign students need transcript evaluation.
Completion requirements 36 credits are required. 30 credits must be completed through the institution.
Program contact Dr. William Lawrence, Director - MBA, New York Institute of Technology, Box 9029, Central Islip, NY 11722-9029. Phone: 800-222-NYIT. Fax: 516-348-1107.

INDIVIDUAL COURSE SUBJECT AREAS

Undergraduate
Accounting; anthropology; business; business administration and management; communications; criminal justice; criminology; economics; English composition; English language and literature; history; hospitality services management; human resources management; liberal arts, general studies, and humanities; philosophy and religion; political science; psychology; public administration and services; social psychology; social work; sociology; statistics; technical writing; telecommunications

Graduate
Business administration and management; instructional media

Noncredit
Technical writing

See full description on page 444.

Profiles: New York University

NEW YORK UNIVERSITY

New York, New York

The Virtual College–School of Continuing Education

New York University, founded in 1831, is an independent-nonprofit university. It is accredited by the Middle States Association of Colleges and Schools. It first offered distance learning courses in 1992. In 1996–97, it offered 6 courses at a distance. In the fall of 1996, there was a total of 40 students enrolled in distance learning courses.
Course delivery sites Courses are delivered to your home.
Media Courses are delivered via computer software, World Wide Web, e-mail, interactive television. Students and teachers interact via telephone, e-mail, computer conferencing. A computer is required for all courses.
Services Distance learners have access to library services, the campus computer network, e-mail services, academic advising, tutoring, career placement assistance at a distance.
Credit-earning options Students may transfer credits from another institution.
Typical costs Tuition of $575 per credit. *Noncredit courses:* $830 per course. Financial aid is available to distance learners.
Registration Students may register by phone, World Wide Web.
Contact Christina Camus, Administrative Aide, New York University, 48 Cooper Square, Room 104, New York, NY 10003. *Telephone:* 212-998-9112. *Fax:* 212-995-3550. *Web site:* http://www.sce.nyu.edu/virtual/index.html.

DEGREE & CERTIFICATE PROGRAMS

Graduate Degrees

▶*Management (MS)*
Restrictions Students must have ISDN digital phone service at home.
Application requirements *Prior education:* baccalaureate degree. *Other requirements:* GMAT, college transcripts, an essay or personal statement, letter(s) of recommendation, an application fee of $50.
Completion requirements 36 credits are required. 24 credits must be completed through the institution. *Maximum time for completion:* four years.

Graduate certificates

▶*Information Technology*
In the fall of 1996 there were 40 students enrolled in this program. In 1995–96, 18 certificates were earned at a distance through this program.
Restrictions Students must have ISDN digital phone service at home.
Application requirements *Prior education:* baccalaureate degree. *Other requirements:* college transcripts, an essay or personal statement, an application fee of $20.
Completion requirements 16 credits are required. 16 credits must be completed through the institution. *Maximum time for completion:* two years.

INDIVIDUAL COURSE SUBJECT AREAS

Graduate
Business; computer and information sciences; management information systems
See full description on page 446.

NICHOLLS STATE UNIVERSITY

Thibodaux, Louisiana

Division of Continuing Education

Nicholls State University, founded in 1948, is a state-supported comprehensive institution. It is accredited by the Southern Association of Colleges and Schools. In 1996–97, it offered 20 courses at a distance. In the fall of 1996, there was a total of 130 students enrolled in distance learning courses.
Course delivery sites Courses are delivered to your home.
Media Courses are delivered via television, videotapes, World Wide Web. Students and teachers interact via mail, telephone, fax, e-mail. A computer is required for some courses.
Restrictions Telecourses require 5 class meetings on campus.
Services Distance learners have access to library services, academic advising, tutoring at a distance.
Credit-earning options Students may transfer credits from another institution or may earn credits through standardized exams, institutionally developed exams, military training.
Typical costs *Undergraduate:* Tuition of $1008.15 per semester for in-state residents. Tuition of $2309.15 per semester for out-of-state residents. *Graduate:* Tuition of $1008.15 per semester for in-state residents. Tuition of $2304.15 per semester for out-of-state residents. Costs may vary by specific program of study. Financial aid is available to distance learners enrolled full-time or part-time.
Registration Students may register by mail, fax.
Contact Dr. Janet E. Worthington, Director of Continuing Education, Nicholls State University, PO Box 2011, Thibodaux, LA 70310-2011. *Telephone:* 504-448-4131. *Fax:* 504-449-7027. *E-mail:* cone-jew@nich-nsunet.nich.edu.

INDIVIDUAL COURSE SUBJECT AREAS

Undergraduate
Business administration and management; gerontology; health and physical education/fitness; history; nursing; political science; sociology; visual and performing arts

Graduate
Special education

NORMANDALE COMMUNITY COLLEGE

Bloomington, Minnesota

Telecommunications and Media Services

Normandale Community College, founded in 1968, is a state-supported two-year college. It is accredited by the North Central Association of Colleges and Schools. It first offered distance learning courses in 1981. In 1996–97, it offered 8 courses at a distance. In the fall of 1996, there was a total of 68 students enrolled in distance learning courses.
Course delivery sites Courses are delivered to your home.
Media Courses are delivered via television. Students and teachers interact via telephone, fax, e-mail.
Restrictions Programs are available to local area students only.
Credit-earning options Students may transfer credits from another institution or may earn credits through standardized exams, portfolio assessment, military training.

Profiles: North Arkansas College

Typical costs Tuition of $48 per credit plus mandatory fees of $25 per course for in-state residents. Tuition of $91.85 per credit plus mandatory fees of $25 per course for out-of-state residents. $20 one-time enrollment fee. Costs may vary by number of credits taken. Financial aid is available to distance learners enrolled full-time or part-time.
Registration Students may register by mail.
Contact James H. Chaffee, Associate Dean of Academic Affairs, Normandale Community College, 9700 France Avenue, S, Bloomington, MN 55431. *Telephone:* 612-832-6319. *Fax:* 612-832-6571. *E-mail:* j.chaffee@nr.cc.mn.us.

INDIVIDUAL COURSE SUBJECT AREAS

Undergraduate
Biology; business administration and management; economics; English composition; health and physical education/fitness; liberal arts, general studies, and humanities

NORTHAMPTON COUNTY AREA COMMUNITY COLLEGE

Bethlehem, Pennsylvania

College-at-Home Program

Northampton County Area Community College, founded in 1967, is a state and locally supported two-year college. It is accredited by the Middle States Association of Colleges and Schools. It first offered distance learning courses in 1974. In 1996–97, it offered 61 courses at a distance. In the fall of 1996, there was a total of 409 students enrolled in distance learning courses.
Course delivery sites Courses are delivered to your home, Lehigh Carbon Community College (Schnecksville).
Media Courses are delivered via television, videotapes, videoconferencing, audiotapes, computer software, print. Students and teachers interact via videoconferencing, mail, telephone, fax, e-mail. A computer is required for some courses.
Restrictions Courses are available to in-state and bordering-state students only.
Services Distance learners have access to library services, academic advising, tutoring at a distance.
Credit-earning options Students may transfer credits from another institution or may earn credits through standardized exams, institutionally developed exams.
Typical costs Tuition of $73 per credit for local area residents. Tuition of $152 per credit for in-state residents. Tuition of $231 per credit for out-of-state residents. All students pay a $25 application fee. Costs may vary by number of credits taken. Financial aid is available to distance learners.
Registration Students may register by mail, fax, phone.
Contact Admissions Office, Northampton County Area Community College, 3835 Green Pond Road, Bethlehem, PA 18017. *Telephone:* 610-861-5500. *Fax:* 610-861-5373. *E-mail:* www.nrhm.cc.pa.us *Web site:* http://www.nrhm.cc.pa.us.

DEGREE & CERTIFICATE PROGRAMS

Associate Degrees
▶ *Business Administration (AA)*
In the fall of 1996 there were 15 students enrolled in this program.
Application requirements *Prior education:* high school diploma or equivalent. *Other requirements:* high school transcript, college transcripts, an application fee of $25.
Completion requirements 60 credits are required. 9 credits must be completed through the institution.

Undergraduate Certificates
▶ *Home-based Early Childhood Education (Specialized diploma)*
In the fall of 1996 there were 10 students enrolled in this program. In 1995–96, 2 certificates were earned at a distance through this program.
Application requirements *Prior education:* high school diploma or equivalent. *Other requirements:* high school transcript, an application fee of $25.
Completion requirements 5 credits are required. All course work must be completed through the institution.

▶ *Library Technical Assistant (Specialized diploma)*
In the fall of 1996 there were 35 students enrolled in this program. In 1995–96, 10 certificates were earned at a distance through this program.
Application requirements *Prior education:* high school diploma or equivalent. *Other requirements:* high school transcript, an application fee of $25.
Completion requirements 15 credits are required. 9 credits must be completed through the institution.

INDIVIDUAL COURSE SUBJECT AREAS

Undergraduate
Business administration and management; education; liberal arts, general studies, and humanities; library and information studies; social sciences

NORTH ARKANSAS COLLEGE

Harrison, Arkansas

North Arkansas College, founded in 1974, is a state and locally supported two-year college. It is accredited by the North Central Association of Colleges and Schools. It first offered distance learning courses in 1988.
Course delivery sites Courses are delivered to your home, Arkansas State University (State University), 9 off-campus centers in Bergman, Berryville, Green Forest, Harrison, Lydhill, Marshall, Omaha, Valley Springs, Yellville.
Media Courses are delivered via television, videoconferencing. Students and teachers interact via videoconferencing, mail, fax, e-mail.
Restrictions Programs are available to in-state students only.
Credit-earning options Students may transfer credits from another institution or may earn credits through examinations, military training, business training.
Typical costs Tuition of $36 per credit hour for in-state residents. Tuition of $91 per credit hour for out-of-state residents. *Noncredit courses:* $25 per course. Financial aid is available to distance learners.
Contact Dr. Gordon E. Watts, Vice President of Instruction, North Arkansas College, 1515 Pioneer Drive, Harrison, AR 72601. *Telephone:* 870-743-3000. *Fax:* 870-743-3577. *E-mail:* gwatts@northark.cc.ar.us.

INDIVIDUAL COURSE SUBJECT AREAS

Undergraduate
Fine arts; history; liberal arts, general studies, and humanities; political science

Profiles: North Carolina State University

NORTH CAROLINA STATE UNIVERSITY

Raleigh, North Carolina

Office of Instructional Telecommunications

North Carolina State University, founded in 1887, is a state-supported university. It is accredited by the Southern Association of Colleges and Schools. It first offered distance learning courses in 1976. In 1996–97, it offered 230 courses at a distance. In the fall of 1996, there was a total of 600 students enrolled in distance learning courses.

Course delivery sites Courses are delivered to your home, your workplace, military bases.

Media Courses are delivered via television, videotapes, computer software. Students and teachers interact via mail, telephone, fax, e-mail. A computer is required for some courses.

Services Distance learners have access to library services, the campus computer network, e-mail services, academic advising at a distance.

Credit-earning options Students may earn credits through examinations.

Typical costs *Undergraduate:* Tuition of $395 per course for in-state residents. Tuition of $495 per course for out-of-state residents. *Graduate:* Tuition of $525 per course for in-state residents. Tuition of $625 per course for out-of-state residents. Costs may vary by specific program of study, course delivery options. Financial aid is available to distance learners enrolled full-time or part-time.

Registration Students may register by mail, fax, phone.

Contact Thomas L. Russell, Director, Instructional Telecommunications, North Carolina State University, Campus Box 7401, Raleigh, NC 27695-7401. *Telephone:* 919-515-7730. *Fax:* 919-515-5778. *E-mail:* tom_russell@ncsu.edu. *Web site:* http://www2.ncsu.edu/ncsu/cont_ed/out_ex.

DEGREE & CERTIFICATE PROGRAMS

Graduate Degrees

▶ *Engineering (ME)*

Application requirements *Prior education:* baccalaureate degree. *Other requirements:* college transcripts.

Completion requirements 36 hours are required. *Maximum time for completion:* six years.

▶ *Textiles (MT)*

Application requirements *Prior education:* baccalaureate degree. *Other requirements:* college transcripts.

Completion requirements 36 hours are required. *Maximum time for completion:* six years.

On-campus requirements For final comprehensive oral exam.

Graduate certificates

▶ *Textile Manufacturing*

Application requirements *Prior education:* baccalaureate degree. *Other requirements:* college transcripts.

Completion requirements 15 hours are required.

▶ *Training and Development*

Application requirements *Prior education:* baccalaureate degree. *Other requirements:* college transcripts.

Completion requirements 15 hours are required.

INDIVIDUAL COURSE SUBJECT AREAS

Undergraduate

Accounting; agriculture; area, ethnic, and cultural studies; biological and life sciences; biology; botany; business; chemistry; Classical languages and literatures; communications; computer and information sciences; creative writing; economics; English as a second language (ESL); English composition; English language and literature; European languages and literatures; health and physical education/fitness; history; liberal arts, general studies, and humanities; mathematics; microbiology; music; philosophy and religion; physical sciences; physics; political science; psychology; radio and television broadcasting; social sciences; sociology; visual and performing arts

Graduate

Aerospace, aeronautical engineering; chemical engineering; civil engineering; developmental and child psychology; education; education administration; educational psychology; electrical engineering; engineering; engineering mechanics; engineering-related technologies; engineering/industrial management; environmental engineering; human resources management; industrial engineering; mechanical engineering; political science; public administration and services; teacher education

See full description on page 448.

NORTH CENTRAL BIBLE COLLEGE

Minneapolis, Minnesota

Carlson Institute of Church Leadership

North Central Bible College, founded in 1930, is an independent-religious four-year college affiliated with the Assemblies of God. It is accredited by the North Central Association of Colleges and Schools. It first offered distance learning courses in 1991. In 1996–97, it offered 71 courses at a distance. In the fall of 1996, there was a total of 378 students enrolled in distance learning courses.

Course delivery sites Courses are delivered to your home, churches.

Media Courses are delivered via videotapes, print. Students and teachers interact via mail, telephone, fax, e-mail.

Restrictions Courses are available to US and Canadian students only.

Services Distance learners have access to library services, academic advising, career placement assistance at a distance.

Credit-earning options Students may transfer credits from another institution or may earn credits through examinations, portfolio assessment.

Typical costs Tuition of $79 per credit. Students pay a $10 enrollment fee. *Noncredit courses:* $87 per course. Costs may vary by number of credits taken.

Registration Students may register by mail, fax, phone.

Contact Carlson Institute of Church Leadership, North Central Bible College, 910 Elliot Avenue South, Minneapolis, MN 55404. *Telephone:* 800-446-1176. *Fax:* 612-343-4435. *E-mail:* carlinst@ncbc.edu. *Web site:* http://www.ncbc.edu.

DEGREE & CERTIFICATE PROGRAMS

Associate Degrees

▶ *Christian Education (AA)*

Application requirements *Prior education:* high school diploma or equivalent. *Other requirements:* high school transcript.

Completion requirements 65 credits are required. 27 credits must be completed through the institution.

▶ *Theology (AA)*

In the fall of 1996 there were 2 students enrolled in this program.

Application requirements *Prior education:* high school diploma or equivalent. *Other requirements:* high school transcript.

Completion requirements 65 credits are required. 27 credits must be completed through the institution.

Baccalaureate Degrees

▶ *Christian Education (BA, BS)*
In the fall of 1996 there were 27 students enrolled in this program.
Application requirements *Prior education:* high school diploma or equivalent. *Other requirements:* high school transcript, an application fee of $30.
Completion requirements 130 credits are required. 27 credits must be completed through the institution.

▶ *Christian Studies (BA, BS)*
In the fall of 1996 there were 80 students enrolled in this program.
Application requirements *Prior education:* high school diploma or equivalent. *Other requirements:* high school transcript.
Completion requirements 128 credits are required. 27 credits must be completed through the institution.

▶ *Church Ministries (BA, BS)*
In the fall of 1996 there were 63 students enrolled in this program.
Application requirements *Prior education:* high school diploma or equivalent. *Other requirements:* high school transcript, an application fee of $30.
Completion requirements 130 credits are required. 27 credits must be completed through the institution.

Undergraduate Certificates

▶ *Bible*
Application requirements *Prior education:* high school diploma or equivalent. *Other requirements:* high school transcript.
Completion requirements 31 credits are required. 27 credits must be completed through the institution.

▶ *Christian Education*
Application requirements *Prior education:* high school diploma or equivalent. *Other requirements:* high school transcript.
Completion requirements 98 credits are required. 27 credits must be completed through the institution.

▶ *Church Ministries*
Application requirements *Prior education:* high school diploma or equivalent. *Other requirements:* high school transcript.
Completion requirements 98 credits are required. 27 credits must be completed through the institution.

INDIVIDUAL COURSE SUBJECT AREAS

Undergraduate
Bible studies; business administration and management; Classical languages and literatures; education administration; educational psychology; English composition; English language and literature; ethics; health and physical education/fitness; Hebrew language and literature; history; journalism; liberal arts, general studies, and humanities; mathematics; music; philosophy and religion; physical sciences; psychology; religious studies; sociology; teacher education; theological studies

Noncredit
Bible studies; business administration and management; Classical languages and literatures; education administration; educational psychology; English composition; English language and literature; ethics; health and physical education/fitness; Hebrew language and literature; history; journalism; liberal arts, general studies, and humanities; mathematics; music; philosophy and religion; physical sciences; psychology; religious studies; sociology; teacher education; theological studies

NORTHCENTRAL TECHNICAL COLLEGE

Wausau, Wisconsin

Alternative Delivery Systems

Northcentral Technical College, founded in 1912, is a district-supported two-year college. It is accredited by the North Central Association of Colleges and Schools. It first offered distance learning courses in 1986. In 1996–97, it offered 110 courses at a distance. In the fall of 1996, there was a total of 330 students enrolled in distance learning courses.
Course delivery sites Courses are delivered to your home, your workplace, Chippewa Valley Technical College (Eau Claire), Fox Valley Technical College (Appleton), Nicolet Area Technical College (Rhinelander), Western Wisconsin Technical College (La Crosse), 15 off-campus centers in Abbotsford, Antigo, Athens, Edgar, Granton, Keshena, Loyal, Medford, Merrill, Mosinee, Phillips, Spencer, Spencer, Stratford, Wittenberg.
Media Courses are delivered via television, videotapes, videoconferencing, World Wide Web, e-mail. Students and teachers interact via videoconferencing, audioconferencing, mail, telephone, fax, e-mail, interactive television. A computer is required for some courses.
Services Distance learners have access to library services, the campus computer network, academic advising, career placement assistance at a distance.
Credit-earning options Students may transfer credits from another institution or may earn credits through examinations, portfolio assessment, military training, business training.
Typical costs Tuition of $51.20 per credit plus mandatory fees of $3.50 per course. *Noncredit courses:* $2.60 per 2 hours of instruction. Financial aid is available to distance learners enrolled full-time or part-time.
Registration Students may register by mail, phone.
Contact Barbara Cummings, Team Leader, Instructional Resources, Northcentral Technical College, 1000 Campus Drive, Wausau, WI 54401-1899. *Telephone:* 715-675-3331, Ext. 4056. *Fax:* 715-675-9776. *E-mail:* cummings@northcentral.tec.wi.us. *Web site:* http://www.northcentral.tec.wi.us.

DEGREE & CERTIFICATE PROGRAMS

Associate Degrees

▶ *Dental Hygiene (AAS)*
In the fall of 1996 there were 118 students enrolled in this program. In 1995–96, 25 degrees were earned at a distance through this program.
Application requirements *Prior education:* high school diploma or equivalent. *Other requirements:* Allied Health Aptitude Test, high school transcript, college transcripts.
Completion requirements 72 credits are required. 24 credits must be completed through the institution.
On-campus requirements Two visits to the NTC Dental Hygiene Clinic.
Program contact Helen Larson, Dental Hygiene Counselor, Northcentral Technical College, 1000 Campus Drive, Wausau, WI 54401. Phone: 715-675-3331, Ext. 4003. Fax: 715-675-9776.

▶ *Educational Interpreter Technician (AA)*
In the fall of 1996 there were 70 students enrolled in this program.
Application requirements *Prior education:* high school diploma or equivalent. *Other requirements:* Accuplacer or equivalent, high school transcript, college transcripts, an application fee of $25.
Completion requirements 68 credits are required.
On-campus requirements Interpreting classes that use labs.
Program contact Maggie Holt, Instructor, Educational Interpreter Technician Program, Northcentral Technical College, 1000 Campus Drive, Wausau, WI 54401. Phone: 715-675-3331, Ext. 4093. Fax: 715-675-9776. E-mail: holt@northcentral.tec.wi.us.

Profiles: Northcentral Technical College

▶ *Nursing (AAS)*
In the fall of 1996 there were 110 students enrolled in this program.
Restrictions Program is available to students in a ten-county region only.
Application requirements *Prior education:* high school diploma or equivalent. *Other requirements:* Registered Nurse Entry Exam (RNEE).
Completion requirements 70 semester credits are required. 24 semester credits must be completed through the institution.
On-campus requirements For skills labs, some lectures, clinicals throughout the district.
Program contact Ellen Kafka, Educational Administrator, Northcentral Technical College, 1000 Campus Drive, Wausau, WI 54401. Phone: 715-675-3331, Ext. 4502. Fax: 715-675-9776. E-mail: kafka@northcentral.tec.wi.us.

▶ *Supervisory Management (ASM)*
In the fall of 1996 there were 22 students enrolled in this program. In 1995–96, 16 degrees were earned at a distance through this program.
Application requirements *Prior education:* high school diploma or equivalent. *Other requirements:* ASSET, high school transcript.
Completion requirements 68 credits are required. *Maximum time for completion:* seven years.
Program contact Charles Kennedy, Instructor, Northcentral Technical College, 1000 Campus Drive, Wausau, WI 54401. Phone: 715-675-3331, Ext. 4364. Fax: 715-675-4707.

INDIVIDUAL COURSE SUBJECT AREAS

Undergraduate
Accounting; administrative and secretarial services; agriculture; business; chemistry; developmental and child psychology; economics; education; health professions and related sciences; home economics and family studies; human resources management; industrial engineering; mathematics; nursing; protective services; social psychology; sociology

NORTH CENTRAL TECHNICAL COLLEGE

Mansfield, Ohio

North Central Technical College, founded in 1961, is a state-supported two-year college. It is accredited by the North Central Association of Colleges and Schools. It first offered distance learning courses in 1994. In 1996–97, it offered 8 courses at a distance. In the fall of 1996, there was a total of 200 students enrolled in distance learning courses.
Course delivery sites Courses are delivered to your home.
Media Courses are delivered via videotapes. Students and teachers interact via mail, telephone.
Restrictions Programs are available to local area students only. Students on probation may not participate.
Services Distance learners have access to library services at a distance.
Credit-earning options Students may transfer credits from another institution or may earn credits through examinations, portfolio assessment, military training, business training.
Typical costs Tuition of $56 per credit hour. One-time $35 application fee. Financial aid is available to distance learners.
Registration Students may register by mail.
Contact Daniel Kraska, Distance Learning Coordinator, North Central Technical College, Kenwood Circle, Mansfield, OH 44901. *Telephone:* 419-755-4800. *Fax:* 419-755-4750.

INDIVIDUAL COURSE SUBJECT AREAS

Undergraduate
Business; business administration and management; health professions and related sciences; human resources management; liberal arts, general studies, and humanities

NORTH CENTRAL TEXAS COLLEGE

Gainesville, Texas

North Central Texas College, founded in 1924, is a county-supported two-year college. It is accredited by the Southern Association of Colleges and Schools. It first offered distance learning courses in 1992. In 1996–97, it offered 7 courses at a distance. In the fall of 1996, there was a total of 200 students enrolled in distance learning courses.
Course delivery sites Courses are delivered to your home, your workplace.
Media Courses are delivered via television. Students and teachers interact via mail, telephone, fax, e-mail.
Restrictions Programs are available to local area students only.
Services Distance learners have access to library services, e-mail services, academic advising, tutoring, career placement assistance at a distance.
Credit-earning options Students may transfer credits from another institution or may earn credits through examinations, military training.
Typical costs Tuition of $18 per hour plus mandatory fees of $58 per course for in-state residents. Tuition of $28 per hour plus mandatory fees of $83 per course for out-of-state residents. Financial aid is available to distance learners enrolled full-time or part-time.
Contact Dr. Eddie C. Hadlock, Dean of Arts and Sciences, North Central Texas College, 1525 West California, Gainesville, TX 76240. *Telephone:* 817-668-4234. *Fax:* 817-668-4258. *E-mail:* ehadlock@nctc.cc.tx.us.

INDIVIDUAL COURSE SUBJECT AREAS

Undergraduate
Economics; history; political science; psychology; sociology

NORTH DAKOTA STATE COLLEGE OF SCIENCE

Wahpeton, North Dakota

North Dakota State College of Science, founded in 1903, is a state-supported two-year college. It is accredited by the North Central Association of Colleges and Schools. It first offered distance learning courses in 1968.
Course delivery sites Courses are delivered to your workplace, military bases, other colleges.
Media Courses are delivered via television, videoconferencing. Students and teachers interact via mail, telephone, fax, e-mail.
Services Distance learners have access to library services, academic advising, career placement assistance at a distance.
Credit-earning options Students may transfer credits from another institution or may earn credits through examinations.
Typical costs Tuition of $72.95 per credit for in-state residents. Tuition of $180.95 per credit for out-of-state residents. Tuition reciprocity agreement with Minnesota, South Dakota, and Montana. Financial aid is available to distance learners.

Contact Steve Krohn, Coordinator, North Dakota State College of Science, 800 North 6th Street, Wahpeton, ND 58076-0002. *Telephone:* 701-671-2626. *Fax:* 701-671-2674. *E-mail:* krohn@plains.nodak.edu.

DEGREE & CERTIFICATE PROGRAMS

Associate Degrees
▶ *Practical Nursing (AS)*
Application requirements ACT, older than average students take pre-admissions test (PSB).
Program contact Marlys Baumann, Department Chair, North Dakota State College of Science, Horton Hall, 800 North 6th Street, Wahpeton, ND 58076-0002. Phone: 701-671-2968. Fax: 701-671-2529. E-mail: mabauman@plains.nodak.edu.

INDIVIDUAL COURSE SUBJECT AREAS

Undergraduate
Biological and life sciences; chemistry; developmental and child psychology; English composition; foods and nutrition studies; liberal arts, general studies, and humanities; microbiology; nursing; philosophy and religion; sociology

NORTH DAKOTA STATE UNIVERSITY

Fargo, North Dakota

North Dakota State University, founded in 1890, is a state-supported university. It is accredited by the North Central Association of Colleges and Schools. It first offered distance learning courses in 1974.
Course delivery sites Courses are delivered to your home, North Dakota University System (Bismarck).
Media Courses are delivered via videotapes, videoconferencing, audiotapes, computer software, World Wide Web, e-mail, print. Students and teachers interact via videoconferencing, audioconferencing, mail, telephone, fax, e-mail. A computer is required for some courses.
Services Distance learners have access to library services, the campus computer network, e-mail services, career placement assistance at a distance.
Credit-earning options Students may transfer credits from another institution or may earn credits through standardized exams, institutionally developed exams, military training, business training.
Typical costs *Undergraduate:* Tuition of $87.92 per credit plus mandatory fees of $12.50 per credit for in-state residents. Tuition of $258 per credit plus mandatory fees of $12.50 per credit for out-of-state residents. *Graduate:* Tuition of $96.67 per credit plus mandatory fees of $12.50 per credit for in-state residents. Tuition of $258 per credit plus mandatory fees of $12.50 per credit for out-of-state residents. Costs may vary by campus or location, specific program of study, number of credits taken, course delivery options. Financial aid is available to distance learners enrolled full-time or part-time.
Registration Students may register by phone, e-mail, World Wide Web.
Contact Richard Chenoweth, Special Assistant to the Vice President for Academic Affairs, North Dakota State University, PO Box 5014, Fargo, ND 58105-5014. *Telephone:* 701-231-9654. *Fax:* 701-231-1013. *E-mail:* rchenowe@prairie.nodak.edu.

DEGREE & CERTIFICATE PROGRAMS

Graduate Degrees
▶ *Business Administration (MBA)*
In the fall of 1996 there were 12 students enrolled in this program.

Restrictions Students must be able to travel to the distance learning site.
Application requirements *Prior education:* baccalaureate degree. *Other requirements:* GMAT, college transcripts, an essay or personal statement, letter(s) of recommendation, an application fee of $25.
Completion requirements 30 credits are required. 21 credits must be completed through the institution. *Maximum time for completion:* seven years.
▶ *Transportation Program (MS)*
In the fall of 1996 there were 19 students enrolled in this program. In 1995–96, 7 degrees were earned at a distance through this program.
Application requirements *Prior education:* baccalaureate degree. *Other requirements:* GRE, college transcripts, letter(s) of recommendation, an application fee of $25.
Completion requirements 30 credits are required. 24 credits must be completed through the institution. *Maximum time for completion:* seven years.
On-campus requirements To defend thesis.
Program contact Denver Tolliver, Research Scientist, North Dakota State University, Room 430, IACC, Fargo, ND 58105. Phone: 701-231-7190. Fax: 701-231-1945. E-mail: tolliver@badlands.nodak.edu.

INDIVIDUAL COURSE SUBJECT AREAS

Undergraduate
Home economics and family studies

Graduate
Agriculture; business administration and management; civil engineering; education; education administration; home economics and family studies

NORTHEAST COMMUNITY COLLEGE

Norfolk, Nebraska

Division of Continuing Education and Distance Learning

Northeast Community College, founded in 1973, is a state and locally supported two-year college. It is accredited by the North Central Association of Colleges and Schools. In 1996–97, it offered 30 courses at a distance. In the fall of 1996, there was a total of 120 students enrolled in distance learning courses.
Course delivery sites Courses are delivered to your home, your workplace, 32 centers in Nebraska.
Media Courses are delivered via videotapes, videoconferencing. Students and teachers interact via videoconferencing, mail, telephone, fax, e-mail.
Services Distance learners have access to library services, academic advising, career placement assistance at a distance.
Credit-earning options Students may transfer credits from another institution or may earn credits through standardized exams.
Typical costs Tuition of $36 per credit hour plus mandatory fees of $3.50 per credit hour for in-state residents. Tuition of $45 per credit hour plus mandatory fees of $3.50 per credit hour for out-of-state residents. *Noncredit courses:* $1.75 per contact hour. Costs may vary by campus or location. Financial aid is available to distance learners enrolled part-time.
Registration Students may register by mail, fax, phone.
Contact Mary Honke, Division Chair, Northeast Community College, PO Box 469, Norfolk, NE 68701. *Telephone:* 402-644-0469. *Fax:* 402-644-0650. *E-mail:* maryh@alpha.necc.cc.ne.us.

Profiles: Northeast Community College

DEGREE & CERTIFICATE PROGRAMS

Associate Degrees

▶ *Business (AA)*
In the fall of 1996 there were 12 students enrolled in this program.
Application requirements *Prior education:* high school diploma or equivalent. *Other requirements:* ACT or SAT, high school transcript, college transcripts, must be high school graduate or have GED.
Completion requirements 61 credit hours are required.
Program contact Roger Feuerbacher, Division Chair - Business Division, Northeast Community College, PO Box 469, Norfolk, NE 68701. Phone: 402-644-0439. Fax: 402-644-0650.

INDIVIDUAL COURSE SUBJECT AREAS

Undergraduate

Accounting; administrative and secretarial services; agriculture; astronomy and astrophysics; biological and life sciences; business administration and management; chemistry; computer and information sciences; creative writing; developmental and child psychology; economics; English as a second language (ESL); English composition; English language and literature; geology; health and physical education/fitness; history; home economics and family studies; nursing; physical sciences; physics; political science; protective services; public administration and services; radio and television broadcasting; social psychology; sociology; teacher education; visual and performing arts

NORTHEASTERN UNIVERSITY

Boston, Massachusetts

Network Northeastern

Northeastern University, founded in 1898, is an independent-nonprofit university. It is accredited by the New England Association of Schools and Colleges. It first offered distance learning courses in 1983. In 1996–97, it offered 200 courses at a distance. In the fall of 1996, there was a total of 2,000 students enrolled in distance learning courses.
Course delivery sites Courses are delivered to your workplace, military bases, other colleges, 2 off-campus centers in Burlington, Dedham.
Media Courses are delivered via television, videotapes. Students and teachers interact via mail, telephone, fax, e-mail. A computer is required for some courses.
Restrictions Generally, students must be at a participating corporation.
Services Distance learners have access to academic advising, career placement assistance at a distance.
Credit-earning options Students may transfer credits from another institution.
Typical costs *Undergraduate:* Tuition of $760 per course. *Graduate:* Tuition of $1660 per course. *Noncredit courses:* $350 per person, $2800 per group. Costs may vary by specific program of study. Financial aid is available to distance learners.
Registration Students may register by mail, fax, phone, e-mail, World Wide Web.
Contact Mary Perkins, Assistant Director, Northeastern University, 360 Huntington Avenue, 328 CP, Boston, MA 02115. *Telephone:* 617-373-5620. *Fax:* 617-373-5625. *E-mail:* perkins@lynx.neu.edu. *Web site:* http://www.neu.edu/network-nu.

DEGREE & CERTIFICATE PROGRAMS

Graduate Degrees

▶ *Electrical and Computer Engineering (MSEE)*
Application requirements *Prior education:* baccalaureate degree. *Other requirements:* college transcripts, an essay or personal statement, letter(s) of recommendation.
Completion requirements 11 courses are required. 8 courses must be completed through the institution. *Maximum time for completion:* seven years.

▶ *Information Systems (MSIS)*
Application requirements *Prior education:* baccalaureate degree. *Other requirements:* college transcripts, an essay or personal statement, letter(s) of recommendation, an application fee of $55.
Completion requirements 11 courses are required. 8 courses must be completed through the institution. *Maximum time for completion:* seven years.

Undergraduate Certificates

▶ *C++/Unix Programming*
Application requirements *Prior education:* high school diploma or equivalent.
Completion requirements 9 courses are required. 9 courses must be completed through the institution.

INDIVIDUAL COURSE SUBJECT AREAS

Undergraduate
Algebra; calculus; engineering-related technologies

Graduate
Computer and information sciences; electrical engineering; engineering/industrial management; industrial engineering; mechanical engineering

Noncredit
Accounting

NORTHEAST LOUISIANA UNIVERSITY

Monroe, Louisiana

Northeast Louisiana University, founded in 1931, is a state-supported comprehensive institution. It is accredited by the Southern Association of Colleges and Schools.
Course delivery sites Courses are delivered to your home, your workplace, military bases, other colleges.
Media Courses are delivered via television, World Wide Web. Students and teachers interact via mail, telephone, fax, e-mail.
Restrictions Programs are available to in-state students only.
Credit-earning options Students may transfer credits from another institution or may earn credits through examinations, military training, business training.
Typical costs Tuition of $534 per course plus mandatory fees of $40 per course for in-state residents. Tuition of $1134.25 per course plus mandatory fees of $40 per course for out-of-state residents.
Contact Continuing Education, Northeast Louisiana University, 700 University Avenue, Monroe, LA 71209-0001. *Telephone:* 318-342-1031. *Fax:* 318-342-1049. *E-mail:* ceupshaw@alpha.nlu.edu.

DEGREE & CERTIFICATE PROGRAMS

Associate Degrees
▶ *General Studies (AA)*

INDIVIDUAL COURSE SUBJECT AREAS

Undergraduate
Area, ethnic, and cultural studies; biology; business; business administration and management; chemistry; computer and information sciences; developmental and child psychology; educational psychology; English language and literature; geology; health and physical education/fitness; history; human resources management; liberal arts, general studies, and humanities; philosophy and religion; physics; social psychology; social work; sociology; special education; teacher education; theological studies

Graduate
Biology; developmental and child psychology; educational psychology; social psychology; special education; teacher education

NORTHEAST WISCONSIN TECHNICAL COLLEGE

Green Bay, Wisconsin

Media Services

Northeast Wisconsin Technical College, founded in 1913, is a state and locally supported two-year college. It is accredited by the North Central Association of Colleges and Schools.
Course delivery sites Courses are delivered to your home, your workplace, 14 off-campus centers.
Media Courses are delivered via television, videotapes, videoconferencing. Students and teachers interact via videoconferencing, mail, telephone, fax.
Services Distance learners have access to library services, academic advising, career placement assistance at a distance.
Credit-earning options Students may transfer credits from another institution or may earn credits through examinations, portfolio assessment, military training, business training.
Typical costs Tuition of $57.12 per credit. Financial aid is available to distance learners.
Contact Sherry Olive, TCA Aide, Northeast Wisconsin Technical College, 2740 West Mason, Green Bay, WI 54307. *Telephone:* 414-498-5571. *Fax:* 414-498-5490.

INDIVIDUAL COURSE SUBJECT AREAS

Undergraduate
Advertising; agriculture; business; business administration and management; child care and development; cognitive psychology; communications; economics; educational psychology; English language and literature; foods and nutrition studies; health professions and related sciences; hospitality services management; international business; law and legal studies; marketing; mathematics; protective services; psychology; real estate; sociology

NORTHERN ARIZONA UNIVERSITY

Flagstaff, Arizona

NAU Net

Northern Arizona University, founded in 1899, is a state-supported university. It is accredited by the North Central Association of Colleges and Schools.
Course delivery sites Courses are delivered to other colleges.
Media Courses are delivered via videoconferencing, audiographics conferencing.
Credit-earning options Students may transfer credits from another institution or may earn credits through examinations.
Contact Continuing Education, Northern Arizona University, PO Box 04117, Flagstaff, AZ 86011. *Telephone:* 520-523-4212. *Fax:* 520-523-1169.

DEGREE & CERTIFICATE PROGRAMS

Baccalaureate Degrees
▶ *Business Administration (BS)*
▶ *Elementary Education (BS)*
▶ *Hotel and Restaurant Management (BS)*
▶ *Liberal Studies (BA)*
▶ *Special Education (BS)*

Graduate Degrees
▶ *Counseling/Human Relations (MEd)*
▶ *Educational Leadership (MEd)*
▶ *Elementary Education (MEd)*
▶ *Special Education (MEd)*

INDIVIDUAL COURSE SUBJECT AREAS

Undergraduate
Accounting; advertising; area, ethnic, and cultural studies; biological and life sciences; business; business administration and management; creative writing; design; developmental and child psychology; education administration; educational psychology; English language and literature; environmental engineering; history; journalism; law and legal studies; liberal arts, general studies, and humanities; mathematics; music; nursing; philosophy and religion; political science; public health; radio and television broadcasting; social psychology; social work; sociology; teacher education

Graduate
Education administration; educational psychology; teacher education

NORTHERN ESSEX COMMUNITY COLLEGE

Haverhill, Massachusetts

Northern Essex Community College, founded in 1960, is a state-supported two-year college. It is accredited by the New England Association of Schools and Colleges. It first offered distance learning courses in 1979. In 1996–97, it offered 7 courses at a distance.
Course delivery sites Courses are delivered to your home.

Distance Learning Programs

Profiles: Northern Essex Community College

Media Courses are delivered via television. Students and teachers interact via mail, telephone, fax, e-mail, in-person meetings.
Restrictions Courses are available to students in southern New Hampshire only.
Services Distance learners have access to the campus computer network, e-mail services, academic advising at a distance.
Credit-earning options Students may transfer credits from another institution or may earn credits through standardized exams, institutionally developed exams, portfolio assessment, military training, business training.
Typical costs Tuition of $85 per credit for in-state residents. Tuition of $103 per credit for out-of-state residents. *Noncredit courses:* $30 per hour. Costs may vary by number of credits taken. Financial aid is available to distance learners.
Registration Students may register by mail, phone.
Contact Mary Prunty, Associate Dean of Academic Services, Northern Essex Community College, 100 Elliott Way, Haverhill, MA 01830. *Telephone:* 508-374-5805. *Fax:* 508-374-3775.

INDIVIDUAL COURSE SUBJECT AREAS

Undergraduate
Biological and life sciences; business; English language and literature; liberal arts, general studies, and humanities; psychology; social sciences

NORTHERN ILLINOIS UNIVERSITY

De Kalb, Illinois

Division of Continuing Education

Northern Illinois University, founded in 1895, is a state-supported university. It is accredited by the North Central Association of Colleges and Schools. It first offered distance learning courses in 1995. In 1996–97, it offered 22 courses at a distance. In the fall of 1996, there was a total of 210 students enrolled in distance learning courses.
Course delivery sites Courses are delivered to military bases, College of DuPage (Glen Ellyn), 4 off-campus centers in Hoffman Estates, Moline, Oak Brook, Rockford.
Media Courses are delivered via television. Students and teachers interact via videoconferencing, mail, telephone, e-mail.
Restrictions Programs are available to in-state students only.
Services Distance learners have access to library services, the campus computer network, e-mail services, academic advising at a distance.
Credit-earning options Students may earn credits through institutionally developed exams.
Typical costs *Undergraduate:* Tuition of $94.85 per hour plus mandatory fees of $34 per hour for in-state residents. Tuition of $284.55 per hour plus mandatory fees of $34 per hour for out-of-state residents. *Graduate:* Tuition of $95.90 per hour plus mandatory fees of $34.14 per hour for in-state residents. Tuition of $287.70 per hour plus mandatory fees of $34.14 per hour for out-of-state residents. Costs may vary by course delivery options. Financial aid is available to distance learners enrolled full-time or part-time.
Registration Students may register by phone.
Contact Gail Crawford, Distance Education Coordinator, Northern Illinois University, Division of Continuing Education, DeKalb, IL 60115-2860. *Telephone:* 815-753-6931. *Fax:* 815-753-6900. *E-mail:* gcrawford@niu.edu. *Web site:* http://www.niu.edu/acad/dce/.

INDIVIDUAL COURSE SUBJECT AREAS

Graduate
Adult education; business administration and management; continuing education; curriculum and instruction; finance; geology; human resources management; instructional media; management information systems; marketing; nursing; physical therapy; public policy analysis; Russian language and literature

NORTHERN KENTUCKY UNIVERSITY

Highland Heights, Kentucky

Credit Continuing Education and Distance Learning

Northern Kentucky University, founded in 1968, is a state-supported comprehensive institution. It is accredited by the Southern Association of Colleges and Schools. It first offered distance learning courses in 1983. In 1996–97, it offered 26 courses at a distance. In the fall of 1996, there was a total of 305 students enrolled in distance learning courses.
Course delivery sites Courses are delivered to your home, other colleges, K-12 sites.
Media Courses are delivered via television, videoconferencing, World Wide Web. Students and teachers interact via videoconferencing, mail, telephone, fax, e-mail. A computer is required for some courses.
Restrictions Students must be able to travel to campus or receive site.
Services Distance learners have access to the campus computer network, e-mail services at a distance.
Credit-earning options Students may transfer credits from another institution or may earn credits through standardized exams, portfolio assessment, military training.
Typical costs *Undergraduate:* Tuition of $89 per credit hour for in-state residents. Tuition of $231 per credit hour for out-of-state residents. *Graduate:* Tuition of $120 per credit hour for in-state residents. Tuition of $333 per credit hour for out-of-state residents. Full-time undergraduate in-state: $1010 per semester, out-of-state: $2750 per semester. Full-time graduate in-state: $1100 per semester, out-of-state: $3020 per semester. Costs may vary by number of credits taken. Financial aid is available to distance learners.
Contact Barbara Hedges, Interim Director, Credit Continuing Education and Distance Learning, Northern Kentucky University, AC 115, Highland Heights, KY 41099-5700. *Telephone:* 606-572-5601. *Fax:* 606-572-5566. *Web site:* http://www.nku.edu/~dist_learn.

INDIVIDUAL COURSE SUBJECT AREAS

Undergraduate
Business administration and management; developmental and child psychology; health and physical education/fitness; history; journalism; liberal arts, general studies, and humanities; political science; public administration and services; sociology; special education; teacher education

Graduate
Business administration and management; economics; political science; public administration and services; teacher education

NORTHERN OKLAHOMA COLLEGE

Tonkawa, Oklahoma

Northern Oklahoma College, founded in 1901, is a state-supported two-year college. It is accredited by the North Central Association of Colleges and Schools. It first offered distance learning courses in 1994. In 1996–97, it offered 36 courses at a distance. In the fall of 1996, there was a total of 986 students enrolled in distance learning courses.

Course delivery sites Courses are delivered to Northeastern Oklahoma Agricultural and Mechanical College (Miami), 1 off-campus center in Enid.
Media Courses are delivered via videoconferencing, audioconferencing, computer software. Students and teachers interact via videoconferencing, audioconferencing.
Services Distance learners have access to library services, academic advising, tutoring, career placement assistance at a distance.
Credit-earning options Students may transfer credits from another institution or may earn credits through examinations, military training.
Typical costs Costs may vary. Contact college for information. Financial aid is available to distance learners.
Contact Wanda F. Webb, Registrar, Northern Oklahoma College, 1220 East Grand Avenue, PO Box 310, Tonkawa, OK 74653-0310. *Telephone:* 405-628-6221. *Fax:* 405-628-6209.

INDIVIDUAL COURSE SUBJECT AREAS

Undergraduate

Accounting; biological and life sciences; business administration and management; creative writing; economics; English composition; English language and literature; geography; history; mathematics; nursing; physical sciences; political science; psychology; sociology

NORTHERN STATE UNIVERSITY

Aberdeen, South Dakota

Continuing Education

Northern State University, founded in 1901, is a state-supported comprehensive institution. It is accredited by the North Central Association of Colleges and Schools.
Course delivery sites Courses are delivered to your home, your workplace, other colleges.
Media Courses are delivered via videotapes, videoconferencing, print. Financial aid is available to distance learners.
Contact Continuing Education, Northern State University, 1200 South Jay Street, Aberdeen, SD 57401. *Telephone:* 605-626-2568. *Fax:* 605-626-2542.

INDIVIDUAL COURSE SUBJECT AREAS

Undergraduate

Biology; business administration and management; educational psychology; history; music; political science; public health; sociology

NORTHERN VIRGINIA COMMUNITY COLLEGE

Annandale, Virginia

Extended Learning Institute

Northern Virginia Community College, founded in 1965, is a state-supported two-year college. It is accredited by the Southern Association of Colleges and Schools. It first offered distance learning courses in 1975. In 1996–97, it offered 98 courses at a distance. In the fall of 1996, there was a total of 2,928 students enrolled in distance learning courses.
Course delivery sites Courses are delivered to your home, your workplace, military bases, Dabney S. Lancaster Community College (Clifton Forge), Lord Fairfax Community College (Middletown), Piedmont Virginia Community College (Charlottesville).
Media Courses are delivered via television, videotapes, audiotapes, computer software, print, computer conferencing. Students and teachers interact via mail, telephone, fax, e-mail, computer conferencing. A computer is required for some courses.
Restrictions Courses are available to US students only.
Services Distance learners have access to library services, academic advising, tutoring at a distance.
Credit-earning options Students may transfer credits from another institution or may earn credits through examinations, portfolio assessment, military training, business training.
Typical costs Tuition of $48 per credit for in-state residents. Tuition of $157.35 per credit for out-of-state residents. Financial aid is available to distance learners enrolled full-time or part-time.
Registration Students may register by mail, fax, phone.
Contact Admissions and Records, Northern Virginia Community College, Extended Learning Institute, 8333 Little River Turnpike, Annandale, VA 22003-3796. *Telephone:* 703-323-3368. *Fax:* 703-323-3392. *E-mail:* nvtownj@eli.nv.cc.va.us. *Web site:* http://eli.nv.cc.va.us.

DEGREE & CERTIFICATE PROGRAMS

Associate Degrees

▶ *Business Administration (AS)*
In 1995–96, 245 degrees were earned at a distance through this program.
Application requirements *Prior education:* high school diploma or equivalent. *Other requirements:* high school transcript, GED or test into school.
Completion requirements 62 credit hours are required. 25% of course work must be completed through the institution.
On-campus requirements Some on-campus meetings required for science labs, physical education.

▶ *Engineering (AS)*
In the fall of 1996 there were 780 students enrolled in this program. In 1995–96, 20 degrees were earned at a distance through this program.
Application requirements *Prior education:* high school diploma or equivalent. *Other requirements:* high school transcript, GED or test into college.
Completion requirements 63 credits are required. 25% of course work must be completed through the institution.
On-campus requirements For lab science, physical education, and speech.

▶ *General Studies (AS)*
In 1995–96, 701 degrees were earned at a distance through this program.
Application requirements *Prior education:* high school diploma or equivalent. *Other requirements:* high school transcript, GED or test into school to show benefit of college education.
Completion requirements 60 credit hours are required. 15 credit hours must be completed through the institution.
On-campus requirements For speech, physical education.

INDIVIDUAL COURSE SUBJECT AREAS

Undergraduate

Accounting; administrative and secretarial services; advertising; algebra; American (US) history; American literature; art history and criticism; biology; business; business administration and management; business law; calculus; chemistry; comparative literature; computer and information sciences; creative writing; criminal justice; criminology; developmental and child psychology; economics; engineering; English composition; English language and literature; English literature; ethics; European languages and literatures; film studies; finance; fine arts; geography; health professions and related sciences; history; instructional media; liberal arts, general studies, and humanities; logic; management information systems; marketing; mathematics; mechanical engineering; philosophy

Profiles: Northern Virginia Community College

and religion; physics; political science; psychology; sociology; Spanish language and literature; technical writing

NORTH GEORGIA COLLEGE & STATE UNIVERSITY

Dahlonega, Georgia

Office of Distance Education

North Georgia College & State University, founded in 1873, is a state-supported comprehensive institution. It is accredited by the Southern Association of Colleges and Schools. It first offered distance learning courses in 1995. In 1996–97, it offered 8 courses at a distance. In the fall of 1996, there was a total of 75 students enrolled in distance learning courses.
Course delivery sites Courses are delivered to your home, other colleges, GSAMS sites in Georgia.
Media Courses are delivered via videotapes, videoconferencing, e-mail, print. Students and teachers interact via videoconferencing, mail, telephone, fax, e-mail.
Restrictions Courses are available to students in northeast Georgia only.
Services Distance learners have access to library services, the campus computer network, e-mail services, academic advising, tutoring at a distance.
Credit-earning options Students may transfer credits from another institution or may earn credits through institutionally developed exams.
Typical costs *Undergraduate:* Tuition of $498 per quarter plus mandatory fees of $111 per term for in-state residents. Tuition of $1640 per quarter for out-of-state residents. *Graduate:* Tuition of $617 per quarter plus mandatory fees of $111 per term for in-state residents. Tuition of $1987 per quarter for out-of-state residents. Costs may vary by specific program of study, number of credits taken. Financial aid is available to distance learners.
Registration Students may register by mail.
Contact Thomas Moseley, Distance Learning Coordinator, North Georgia College & State University, Room 329, Education Building, Dahlonega, GA 30597-1001. *Telephone:* 706-864-1844. *Fax:* 706-864-1886. *E-mail:* temoseley@nugget.ngc.peachnet.edu.

INDIVIDUAL COURSE SUBJECT AREAS

Undergraduate
Biological and life sciences; education administration; educational psychology; nursing; special education; teacher education

Graduate
Biological and life sciences; education administration; educational psychology; educational research; special education

NORTH HARRIS COLLEGE

Houston, Texas

North Harris College, founded in 1972, is a state and locally supported two-year college. It is accredited by the Southern Association of Colleges and Schools. It first offered distance learning courses in 1993. In 1996–97, it offered 97 courses at a distance. In the fall of 1996, there was a total of 2,500 students enrolled in distance learning courses.
Course delivery sites Courses are delivered to your home, 3 off-campus centers in Conroe, Houston, Tomball.
Media Courses are delivered via television, videotapes, videoconferencing, audiotapes, computer software, World Wide Web, e-mail, print. Students and teachers interact via videoconferencing, audioconferencing, telephone, fax, e-mail. A computer is required for some courses.
Restrictions Programs are available to local area students only.
Services Distance learners have access to the campus computer network, e-mail services at a distance.
Credit-earning options Students may transfer credits from another institution or may earn credits through examinations.
Typical costs Tuition of $41 per credit hour for local area residents. Tuition of $76 per credit hour for in-state residents. Tuition of $216 per credit hour for out-of-state residents. $16 registration fee. *Noncredit courses:* $50 per course. Costs may vary by number of credits taken. Financial aid is available to distance learners.
Registration Students may register by phone.
Contact Cliff B. Blackerby, Training Manager, North Harris College, 3200 College Park Drive, Conroe, TX 77384. *Telephone:* 409-273-7416. *Fax:* 409-273-7433. *E-mail:* cliff@nhmccd.edu.

INDIVIDUAL COURSE SUBJECT AREAS

Undergraduate
Accounting; administrative and secretarial services; biology; business administration and management; communications; computer and information sciences; developmental and child psychology; economics; English composition; English language and literature; European languages and literatures; health and physical education/fitness; history; journalism; liberal arts, general studies, and humanities; mathematics; political science; social psychology; sociology

NORTH HENNEPIN COMMUNITY COLLEGE

Minneapolis, Minnesota

North Hennepin Community College, founded in 1966, is a state-supported two-year college. It is accredited by the North Central Association of Colleges and Schools. It first offered distance learning courses in 1996.
Course delivery sites Courses are delivered to other colleges.
Media Courses are delivered via television, videotapes, World Wide Web. Students and teachers interact via videoconferencing, telephone, fax, e-mail.
Services Distance learners have access to library services at a distance.
Typical costs Tuition of $47.82 per credit for in-state residents. Tuition of $92.47 per credit for out-of-state residents. Costs may vary by course delivery options. Financial aid is available to distance learners.
Contact Office of the Registrar, North Hennepin Community College, 7411 85th Avenue, Brooklyn Park, MN 55445. *Telephone:* 612-424-0719.

INDIVIDUAL COURSE SUBJECT AREAS

Undergraduate
Business administration and management; education administration; engineering; engineering-related technologies; geology

NORTH IOWA AREA COMMUNITY COLLEGE

Mason City, Iowa

North Iowa Area Community College, founded in 1918, is a state and locally supported two-year college. It is accredited by the North Central

Association of Colleges and Schools. It first offered distance learning courses in 1993. In 1996–97, it offered 10 courses at a distance. In the fall of 1996, there was a total of 150 students enrolled in distance learning courses.
Course delivery sites Courses are delivered to your home, your workplace, Kirkwood Community College (Cedar Rapids), 11 off-campus centers in Charles City, Forest City, Garner, Greene, Hampton, Lake Mills, Latimer, Northwood, Osage, Sheffield, St. Ansgar.
Media Courses are delivered via television, videotapes, videoconferencing, e-mail. Students and teachers interact via videoconferencing, mail, telephone, fax, e-mail.
Restrictions Programs are available to in-state students only.
Services Distance learners have access to library services at a distance.
Credit-earning options Students may transfer credits from another institution or may earn credits through examinations, portfolio assessment, military training.
Typical costs Tuition of $55.40 per credit plus mandatory fees of $6.65 per credit for in-state residents. Tuition of $83.10 per credit plus mandatory fees of $6.65 per credit for out-of-state residents. All students pay an additional fee of $6.80 per course. *Noncredit courses:* $50 per course. Costs may vary by number of credits taken. Financial aid is available to distance learners enrolled full-time or part-time.
Registration Students may register by mail.
Contact Don Kamps, Evening Dean, North Iowa Area Community College, 500 College Drive, Mason City, IA 50401. *Telephone:* 515-422-4326. *Fax:* 515-423-1711. *E-mail:* kampsdon@niacc.cc.ia.us.

INDIVIDUAL COURSE SUBJECT AREAS

Undergraduate
Business; communications; developmental and child psychology; economics; history; law and legal studies; mathematics; music; philosophy and religion; political science; sociology

NORTH SEATTLE COMMUNITY COLLEGE

Seattle, Washington

Distance Learning Office/Continuing Education

North Seattle Community College, founded in 1970, is a state-supported two-year college. It is accredited by the Northwest Association of Schools and Colleges. It first offered distance learning courses in 1994. In 1996–97, it offered 25 courses at a distance. In the fall of 1996, there was a total of 200 students enrolled in distance learning courses.
Course delivery sites Courses are delivered to your home, your workplace, Olympic College (Bremerton), 6 off-campus centers, Seattle public schools and public libraries.
Media Courses are delivered via television, videotapes, videoconferencing, audiotapes, computer software, World Wide Web, e-mail, print. Students and teachers interact via mail, telephone, fax, e-mail. A computer is required for some courses.
Services Distance learners have access to library services, e-mail services, free Internet training at a distance.
Credit-earning options Students may transfer credits from another institution or may earn credits through institutionally developed exams.
Typical costs Tuition of $43 per credit for in-state residents. Tuition of $182.95 per credit for out-of-state residents. *Noncredit courses:* $200 per course. Costs may vary by number of credits taken, course delivery options. Financial aid is available to distance learners enrolled full-time.
Registration Students may register by mail, phone, World Wide Web.
Contact Parker Lindner, Video Telecommunications and Distance Learning Specialist, North Seattle Community College, 9600 College Way

North, Seattle, WA 98103. *Telephone:* 206-527-3619. *Fax:* 206-527-3729. *E-mail:* bparker@seaccd.sccd.ctc.edu.

INDIVIDUAL COURSE SUBJECT AREAS

Undergraduate
Accounting; area, ethnic, and cultural studies; Asian languages and literatures; astronomy and astrophysics; business; business administration and management; chemistry; computer programming; economics; European languages and literatures; geology; health and physical education/fitness; liberal arts, general studies, and humanities; psychology; real estate

NORTH SHORE COMMUNITY COLLEGE

Danvers, Massachusetts

Distance Learning

North Shore Community College, founded in 1965, is a state-supported two-year college. It is accredited by the New England Association of Schools and Colleges. It first offered distance learning courses in 1986.
Course delivery sites Courses are delivered to your home.
Media Courses are delivered via television, videotapes, audiotapes, print. Students and teachers interact via telephone, e-mail, in-person meetings.
Restrictions Students must be able to travel to campus.
Credit-earning options Students may transfer credits from another institution or may earn credits through examinations, military training, business training.
Typical costs Tuition of $250 per course. Financial aid is available to distance learners.
Contact Liz Frutiger, Assistant to the Coordinator, North Shore Community College, 1 Ferncroft Road, Danvers, MA 01923. *Telephone:* 508-762-4000, Ext. 6682. *Fax:* 617-477-2140.

INDIVIDUAL COURSE SUBJECT AREAS

Undergraduate
Area, ethnic, and cultural studies; business administration and management; chemistry; communications; developmental and child psychology; English language and literature; European languages and literatures; fine arts; health and physical education/fitness; history; music; philosophy and religion; political science; social psychology; social sciences; sociology; visual and performing arts

NORTHWEST ARKANSAS COMMUNITY COLLEGE

Bentonville, Arkansas

NorthWest Arkansas Community College, founded in 1989, is a state and locally supported two-year college. It is accredited by the North Central Association of Colleges and Schools. It first offered distance learning courses in 1997. In 1996–97, it offered 2 courses at a distance.
Course delivery sites Courses are delivered to University of Arkansas (Fayetteville).
Media Courses are delivered via videoconferencing. Students and teachers interact via videoconferencing, e-mail.
Restrictions Programs are available to in-state students only.
Services Distance learners have access to e-mail services at a distance.

Profiles: NorthWest Arkansas Community College

Credit-earning options Students may transfer credits from another institution or may earn credits through standardized exams, institutionally developed exams, military training, business training.
Typical costs Tuition of $37 per credit hour plus mandatory fees of $1 per credit hour for local area residents. Tuition of $74 per credit hour plus mandatory fees of $1 per credit hour for in-state residents. Tuition of $95 per credit hour plus mandatory fees of $1 per credit hour for out-of-state residents. Financial aid is available to distance learners enrolled full-time or part-time.
Registration Students may register by mail.
Contact Dr. Karen Hodges, Dean of Instruction, NorthWest Arkansas Community College, One College Drive, Bentonville, AR 72712. *Telephone:* 501-619-4144. *Fax:* 501-619-4117. *E-mail:* khodges@eagle.nwacc.cc.ar.us. *Web site:* http://www.nwacc.cc.ar.us/disted/nwaccde.htm.

INDIVIDUAL COURSE SUBJECT AREAS

Noncredit
Algebra; business

NORTHWESTERN COLLEGE

St. Paul, Minnesota

Center for Distance Education

Northwestern College, founded in 1902, is an independent-religious nondenominational four-year college. It is accredited by the North Central Association of Colleges and Schools. It first offered distance learning courses in 1994. In 1996–97, it offered 8 courses at a distance. In the fall of 1996, there was a total of 30 students enrolled in distance learning courses.
Course delivery sites Courses are delivered to your home.
Media Courses are delivered via videotapes, audiotapes, World Wide Web, print. Students and teachers interact via mail, telephone, fax, e-mail.
Services Distance learners have access to library services, academic advising, career placement assistance at a distance.
Credit-earning options Students may transfer credits from another institution or may earn credits through standardized exams, institutionally developed exams, portfolio assessment, military training.
Typical costs Tuition of $110 per credit plus mandatory fees of $50 per course. *Noncredit courses:* $100 per course. Financial aid is available to distance learners enrolled full-time or part-time.
Registration Students may register by mail, fax, phone.
Contact Betty Piper, Student Relations Coordinator, Northwestern College, Center for Distance Education, 3003 Snelling Avenue North, St. Paul, MN 55113. *Telephone:* 612-631-5494. *Fax:* 612-631-5133. *E-mail:* td1@nwc.edu. *Web site:* http://www.nwc.edu/disted/.

DEGREE & CERTIFICATE PROGRAMS

Baccalaureate Degrees
▶*Intercultural Ministries (BA)*
In the fall of 1996 there were 30 students enrolled in this program.
Application requirements *Prior education:* some undergraduate course work. *Other requirements:* college transcripts, an essay or personal statement, letter(s) of recommendation, an application fee of $50, high school diploma or GED, 2 years undergraduate course work.
Completion requirements 180 quarter credits are required. 72 quarter credits must be completed through the institution. This is a degree completion program.

INDIVIDUAL COURSE SUBJECT AREAS

Undergraduate
Astronomy and astrophysics; history; psychology; theological studies

NORTHWESTERN COLLEGE

Lima, Ohio

Division of Distance Learning

Northwestern College, founded in 1920, is an independent-nonprofit two-year college. It is accredited by the North Central Association of Colleges and Schools. It first offered distance learning courses in 1993. In 1996–97, it offered 45 courses at a distance. In the fall of 1996, there was a total of 110 students enrolled in distance learning courses.
Course delivery sites Courses are delivered to your home.
Media Courses are delivered via World Wide Web, e-mail, print. Students and teachers interact via mail, telephone, fax, e-mail.
Restrictions Students must be working adults over age 22.
Services Distance learners have access to e-mail services, academic advising, career placement assistance at a distance.
Credit-earning options Students may transfer credits from another institution or may earn credits through institutionally developed exams, portfolio assessment, military training, business training.
Typical costs Tuition of $125 per credit. Costs may vary by number of credits taken. Financial aid is available to distance learners enrolled full-time or part-time.
Registration Students may register by mail, fax, phone, e-mail, World Wide Web.
Contact Rick Morrison, Admissions, Northwestern College, 1441 North Cable Road, Lima, OH 45805. *Telephone:* 419-227-3141. *Fax:* 419-229-6926. *E-mail:* info@nc.edu. *Web site:* http://www.nc.edu.

DEGREE & CERTIFICATE PROGRAMS

Associate Degrees
▶*Automotive Management (AAB)*
Application requirements *Prior education:* high school diploma or equivalent. *Minimum age:* 22. *Other requirements:* high school transcript, an application fee of $50, personal or telephone interview.
Completion requirements 108 credit hours are required. 53 credit hours must be completed through the institution.

▶*Business Administration (AAB)*
In the fall of 1996 there were 81 students enrolled in this program. In 1995–96, 21 degrees were earned at a distance through this program.
Application requirements *Prior education:* high school diploma or equivalent. *Minimum age:* 22. *Other requirements:* high school transcript, an application fee of $50, personal or telephone interview.
Completion requirements 108 credit hours are required. 53 credit hours must be completed through the institution.

▶*Marketing (AAB)*
In the fall of 1996 there were 18 students enrolled in this program. In 1995–96, 7 degrees were earned at a distance through this program.
Application requirements *Prior education:* high school diploma or equivalent. *Minimum age:* 22. *Other requirements:* high school transcript, an application fee of $50, personal or telephone interview.
Completion requirements 108 credit hours are required. 53 credit hours must be completed through the institution.

INDIVIDUAL COURSE SUBJECT AREAS

Undergraduate

Accounting; administrative and secretarial services; advertising; algebra; American (US) history; business; business administration and management; business law; computer and information sciences; creative writing; economics; English composition; English language and literature; ethics; history; human resources management; international business; liberal arts, general studies, and humanities; marketing; mathematics; physical sciences; political science; social psychology; sociology; statistics

NORTHWESTERN MICHIGAN COLLEGE

Traverse City, Michigan

Distance Education Services

Northwestern Michigan College, founded in 1951, is a state and locally supported two-year college. It is accredited by the North Central Association of Colleges and Schools. It first offered distance learning courses in 1982. In 1996–97, it offered 17 courses at a distance. In the fall of 1996, there was a total of 280 students enrolled in distance learning courses.
Course delivery sites Courses are delivered to your home, 1 off-campus center in Cadillac.
Media Courses are delivered via television, videoconferencing. Students and teachers interact via videoconferencing, audioconferencing, mail, telephone, fax, e-mail.
Restrictions Programs are available to in-state students only.
Services Distance learners have access to library services, the campus computer network, e-mail services, academic advising, career placement assistance at a distance.
Credit-earning options Students may transfer credits from another institution or may earn credits through standardized exams, institutionally developed exams, portfolio assessment.
Typical costs Tuition of $50.50 per contact hour plus mandatory fees of $2.75 per contact hour for local area residents. Tuition of $83.50 per contact hour plus mandatory fees of $2.75 per contact hour for in-state residents. Tuition of $93.75 per contact hour plus mandatory fees of $2.75 per contact hour for out-of-state residents. Financial aid is available to distance learners enrolled full-time or part-time.
Registration Students may register by phone.
Contact Ronda Edwards, Director, Media Services, Northwestern Michigan College, 1701 East Front Street, Traverse City, MI 49686. *Telephone:* 616-922-1075. *Fax:* 616-922-1080. *E-mail:* redwards@nmc.edu. *Web site:* http://www.nmc.edu.

INDIVIDUAL COURSE SUBJECT AREAS

Undergraduate

Accounting; American (US) history; anthropology; biology; business; business administration and management; calculus; child care and development; computer and information sciences; creative writing; developmental and child psychology; English composition; English language and literature; European history; European languages and literatures; health professions and related sciences; history; Japanese language and literature; law and legal studies; liberal arts, general studies, and humanities; nursing; political science; psychology; social work; sociology

NORTHWESTERN STATE UNIVERSITY OF LOUISIANA

Natchitoches, Louisiana

Northwestern State University of Louisiana, founded in 1884, is a state-supported comprehensive institution. It is accredited by the Southern Association of Colleges and Schools. It first offered distance learning courses in 1990. In 1996–97, it offered 40 courses at a distance. In the fall of 1996, there was a total of 400 students enrolled in distance learning courses.
Course delivery sites Courses are delivered to your home, your workplace, military bases, 6 off-campus centers in Alexandria, Bunkie, Ferriday, Leesville/Ft. Polk, Shreveport, Winnfield.
Media Courses are delivered via television, videotapes, videoconferencing, computer software, World Wide Web, e-mail, print. Students and teachers interact via videoconferencing, mail, telephone, fax, e-mail. A computer is required for some courses.
Restrictions Programs are primarily available to in-state students.
Services Distance learners have access to library services, the campus computer network, e-mail services, academic advising at a distance.
Credit-earning options Students may transfer credits from another institution or may earn credits through examinations, portfolio assessment, military training.
Typical costs *Undergraduate:* Tuition of $321.25 per course plus mandatory fees of $52.75 per semester. *Graduate:* Tuition of $321.25 per course plus mandatory fees of $73.50 per semester. Mandatory fees given are for full-time students. Costs may vary by campus or location, number of credits taken. Financial aid is available to distance learners.
Registration Students may register by mail, fax, e-mail.
Contact Yvonne Richardson, Coordinator of Courses for Credit, Northwestern State University of Louisiana, Natchitoches, LA 71497. *Telephone:* 318-357-5222. *Fax:* 318-357-6125. *E-mail:* yvonne@alpha.nsula.edu. *Web site:* http://www.nsula.edu.

INDIVIDUAL COURSE SUBJECT AREAS

Undergraduate

Biology; botany; chemistry; computer and information sciences; developmental and child psychology; education administration; educational psychology; English composition; English language and literature; fine arts; health and physical education/fitness; history; home economics and family studies; hospitality services management; law and legal studies; liberal arts, general studies, and humanities; library and information studies; mathematics; microbiology; nursing; philosophy and religion; protective services; social psychology; social work; sociology; special education; teacher education

Graduate

Education administration; educational psychology; nursing; special education; teacher education

Noncredit

Advertising; area, ethnic, and cultural studies; business; business administration and management; computer and information sciences; creative writing; design; health and physical education/fitness; health professions and related sciences; home economics and family studies; law and legal studies; music; nursing; special education; teacher education

Profiles: Northwest Iowa Community College

NORTHWEST IOWA COMMUNITY COLLEGE

Sheldon, Iowa

ICN Office

Northwest Iowa Community College, founded in 1966, is a state-supported two-year college. It is accredited by the North Central Association of Colleges and Schools. It first offered distance learning courses in 1994. In 1996–97, it offered 20 courses at a distance. In the fall of 1996, there was a total of 400 students enrolled in distance learning courses.
Course delivery sites Courses are delivered to your home, your workplace, military bases, other colleges.
Media Courses are delivered via videoconferencing. Students and teachers interact via videoconferencing, mail, telephone, fax, e-mail.
Restrictions Programs are available to local area students only.
Services Distance learners have access to library services, e-mail services, academic advising, career placement assistance at a distance.
Credit-earning options Students may earn credits through examinations.
Typical costs Tuition of $52 per credit. Financial aid is available to distance learners.
Registration Students may register by mail, fax, phone, e-mail.
Contact Colette Scott, Iowa Communications Network Coordinator, Northwest Iowa Community College, 603 West Park Street, Sheldon, IA 51247. *Telephone:* 712-324-5061. *Fax:* 712-324-4136. *E-mail:* cscott@nwicc.cc.ia.us. *Web site:* http://www.nwicc.cc.ia.us.

INDIVIDUAL COURSE SUBJECT AREAS

Undergraduate
Agriculture; American (US) history; creative writing; developmental and child psychology; education administration; educational psychology; English composition; English language and literature; European history; European languages and literatures; liberal arts, general studies, and humanities; mathematics; philosophy and religion; social psychology; sociology; special education; teacher education

Graduate
Agriculture

Noncredit
Agriculture; health professions and related sciences; nursing; public health

NORTHWOOD UNIVERSITY

Midland, Michigan

Northwood University, founded in 1959, is an independent-nonprofit comprehensive institution. It is accredited by the North Central Association of Colleges and Schools.
Course delivery sites Courses are delivered to your home, your workplace, military bases, other colleges, over 30 off-campus sites.
Media Courses are delivered via television, videotapes, audiotapes, World Wide Web, e-mail, print. Students and teachers interact via mail, telephone, fax, e-mail.
Typical costs Tuition of $220 per credit hour. Costs may vary by campus or location, specific program of study, number of credits taken, course delivery options, term of enrollment.
Contact Carl F. Vander Woude, Provost of University College, Northwood University, 3225 Cook Road, Midland, MI 48640-2398. *Telephone:* 517-837-4455. *Fax:* 517-837-4457.

DEGREE & CERTIFICATE PROGRAMS

Baccalaureate Degrees
▶ *Management (BBA)*
Application requirements *Prior education:* high school diploma or equivalent. *Other requirements:* high school transcript, college transcripts, an essay or personal statement, an application fee of $15, a combination of undergraduate and/or professional experience preferred.
Completion requirements 180 quarter hours are required. 36 quarter hours must be completed through the institution.
On-campus requirements Two- to three-day seminar, two-hour written/oral comprehensive exam.

INDIVIDUAL COURSE SUBJECT AREAS

Undergraduate
Business administration and management

NOVA SOUTHEASTERN UNIVERSITY

Fort Lauderdale, Florida

Nova Southeastern University, founded in 1964, is an independent-nonprofit university. It is accredited by the Southern Association of Colleges and Schools. It first offered distance learning courses in 1984. In 1996–97, it offered 120 courses at a distance. In the fall of 1996, there was a total of 700 students enrolled in distance learning courses.
Course delivery sites Courses are delivered to your home, any location with Internet access.
Media Courses are delivered via computer software, World Wide Web, e-mail, custom-designed computer-based system. Students and teachers interact via mail, telephone, fax, e-mail, World Wide Web. A computer is required for all courses.
Services Distance learners have access to library services, the campus computer network, e-mail services, academic advising, career placement assistance at a distance.
Credit-earning options Students may transfer credits from another institution or may earn credits through examinations.
Typical costs Tuition of $345 per credit hour. Costs may vary by specific program of study. Financial aid is available to distance learners enrolled full-time or part-time.
Registration Students may register by mail.
Contact Rose Lemos, Program Representative, Nova Southeastern University, School of Computer and Information Sciences, 3100 Southwest 9th Avenue, Fort Lauderdale, FL 33315. *Telephone:* 800-986-2247, Ext. 2000. *Fax:* 954-262-3872. *E-mail:* scisinfo@scis.nova.edu.

DEGREE & CERTIFICATE PROGRAMS

Graduate Degrees
▶ *Computer Information Systems (MS)*
In the fall of 1996 there were 49 students enrolled in this program. In 1995–96, 25 degrees were earned at a distance through this program.
Application requirements *Prior education:* baccalaureate degree. *Other requirements:* college transcripts, an essay or personal statement, letter(s) of recommendation, an application fee of $50, 2.5 GPA with a minimum of 3.0 in major, GRE or portfolio.
Completion requirements 36 credits are required. 30 credits must be completed through the institution. *Maximum time for completion:* five years.

▶ *Computer Science (MS)*
In the fall of 1996 there were 3 students enrolled in this program.

Application requirements *Prior education:* baccalaureate degree. *Other requirements:* college transcripts, an essay or personal statement, letter(s) of recommendation, an application fee of $50, 2.5 GPA with a minimum of 3.0 in major, GRE or portfolio.
Completion requirements 36 credits are required. 30 credits must be completed through the institution. *Maximum time for completion:* five years.

▶ *Computing Technology in Education (MS)*
In the fall of 1996 there were 78 students enrolled in this program. In 1995–96, 23 degrees were earned at a distance through this program.
Application requirements *Prior education:* baccalaureate degree. *Other requirements:* college transcripts, an essay or personal statement, letter(s) of recommendation, an application fee of $50, 2.5 GPA with a minimum of 3.0 in major, GRE or portfolio.
Completion requirements 36 credits are required. 30 credits must be completed through the institution. *Maximum time for completion:* five years.

▶ *Computing Technology in Education (PhD/EdD)*
In 1995–96, 10 degrees were earned at a distance through this program.
Application requirements *Prior education:* graduate degree. *Other requirements:* college transcripts, an essay or personal statement, letter(s) of recommendation, an application fee of $50, 3.25 GPA, GRE or portfolio.
Completion requirements 64 credits are required. Two consecutive terms must be completed through the institution. *Maximum time for completion:* seven years.
On-campus requirements Four extended weekends per year or two weeks per year for classes.

▶ *Information Science (PhD)*
In 1995–96, 3 degrees were earned at a distance through this program.
Application requirements *Prior education:* graduate degree. *Other requirements:* college transcripts, an essay or personal statement, letter(s) of recommendation, an application fee of $50, 3.25 GPA, GRE or portfolio.
Completion requirements 64 credits are required. Two consecutive terms must be completed through the institution. *Maximum time for completion:* seven years.
On-campus requirements Four extended weekends per year or two weeks per year for classes.

▶ *Information Systems (PhD)*
In 1995–96, 9 degrees were earned at a distance through this program.
Application requirements *Prior education:* graduate degree. *Other requirements:* college transcripts, an essay or personal statement, letter(s) of recommendation, an application fee of $50, 3.25 GPA, GRE or portfolio.
Completion requirements 64 credits are required. Two consecutive terms must be completed through the institution. *Maximum time for completion:* seven years.
On-campus requirements Four extended weekends per year or two weeks per year for classes.

▶ *Management Information Systems (MS)*
In the fall of 1996 there were 46 students enrolled in this program. In 1995–96, 15 degrees were earned at a distance through this program.
Application requirements *Prior education:* baccalaureate degree. *Other requirements:* college transcripts, an essay or personal statement, letter(s) of recommendation, an application fee of $50, 2.5 GPA with a minimum of 3.0 in major, GRE or portfolio.
Completion requirements 36 credits are required. 30 credits must be completed through the institution. *Maximum time for completion:* five years.

INDIVIDUAL COURSE SUBJECT AREAS

Graduate
Computer and information sciences
See full description on page 450.

NRI SCHOOLS

Washington, District of Columbia

McGraw-Hill Continuing Education Center

NRI Schools is a proprietary two-year college. It is accredited by the Distance Education and Training Council. It first offered distance learning courses in 1914. In 1996–97, it offered 35 courses at a distance. In the fall of 1996, there was a total of 55,000 students enrolled in distance learning courses.
Course delivery sites Courses are delivered to your home, your workplace, military bases.
Media Courses are delivered via videotapes, audiotapes, computer software, World Wide Web, e-mail, print. Students and teachers interact via mail, telephone, fax, e-mail. A computer is required for some courses.
Restrictions Courses are available to US and Canadian students only.
Services Distance learners have access to the campus computer network, e-mail services, academic advising, tutoring at a distance.
Typical costs Costs vary. Contact school for information.
Registration Students may register by mail, fax, phone.
Contact Marc Jean-Michel, Information and Guidance Specialist, NRI Schools, 4401 Connecticut Avenue, NW, Washington, DC 20008. *Telephone:* 202-244-9792. *Fax:* 202-244-2047. *E-mail:* info@mhec.com. *Web site:* http://www.mhcec.com.

INDIVIDUAL COURSE SUBJECT AREAS

Noncredit
Accounting; administrative and secretarial services; computer programming; creative writing; electronics; information sciences and systems; mechanical engineering
See full description on page 452.

OAKLAND COMMUNITY COLLEGE

Bloomfield Hills, Michigan

Oakland Community College, founded in 1964, is a state and locally supported two-year college. It is accredited by the North Central Association of Colleges and Schools. In 1996–97, it offered 5 courses at a distance. In the fall of 1996, there was a total of 108 students enrolled in distance learning courses.
Course delivery sites Courses are delivered to your home, your workplace.
Media Courses are delivered via television, videotapes, World Wide Web. Students and teachers interact via mail, telephone, e-mail. A computer is required for some courses.
Credit-earning options Students may transfer credits from another institution.
Typical costs Tuition of $46 per credit plus mandatory fees of $35 per semester for local area residents. Tuition of $78 per credit plus mandatory fees of $35 per semester for in-state residents. Tuition of $109 per credit plus mandatory fees of $35 per semester for out-of-state residents. Costs may vary by number of credits taken. Financial aid is available to distance learners.
Registration Students may register by phone.
Contact Admissions Office, Oakland Community College, 27055 Orchard Lake Road, Farmington Hills, MI 48334. *Telephone:* 810-471-7628.

Profiles: Oakland Community College

INDIVIDUAL COURSE SUBJECT AREAS

Undergraduate
English language and literature; history; political science; psychology; social sciences

OAKLAND UNIVERSITY

Rochester, Michigan

Oakland University, founded in 1957, is a state-supported university. It is accredited by the North Central Association of Colleges and Schools. It first offered distance learning courses in 1995.
Course delivery sites Courses are delivered to your workplace, Northwestern Michigan College (Traverse City), 1 off-campus center in Birmingham.
Media Courses are delivered via television, videotapes, computer software, print. Students and teachers interact via mail, telephone, fax, e-mail.
Services Distance learners have access to library services at a distance.
Credit-earning options Students may transfer credits from another institution or may earn credits through examinations.
Typical costs *Undergraduate:* Tuition of $118.50 per credit for in-state residents. Tuition of $342 per credit for out-of-state residents. *Graduate:* Tuition of $200.25 per credit for in-state residents. Tuition of $443.50 per credit for out-of-state residents. Financial aid is available to distance learners.
Registration Students may register by phone.
Contact Susan Awbrey, Assistant Vice President for Academic Affairs, Oakland University, Wilson Hall, Rochester, MI 48309. *Telephone:* 810-370-2190. *Fax:* 810-370-4475. *E-mail:* awbrey@oakland.edu.

DEGREE & CERTIFICATE PROGRAMS

Baccalaureate Degrees
▶ *General Studies (BS)*
Application requirements *Prior education:* high school diploma or equivalent. *Other requirements:* high school transcript, college transcripts, an essay or personal statement, an application fee of $25.
Completion requirements 124 semester credits are required. 32 semester credits must be completed through the institution. *Maximum time for completion:* six years.
Program contact Carole Crum, Director of Academic Services and General Studies, Oakland University, Rochester, MI 48309-4401. Phone: 810-370-3229. E-mail: ccrum@oakland.edu.

INDIVIDUAL COURSE SUBJECT AREAS

Undergraduate
Asian languages and literatures; business; communications; European languages and literatures; history; music; social sciences; sociology

OAKTON COMMUNITY COLLEGE

Des Plaines, Illinois

Library and Media Services

Oakton Community College, founded in 1969, is a district-supported two-year college. It is accredited by the North Central Association of Colleges and Schools. It first offered distance learning courses in 1975. In 1996–97, it offered 120 courses at a distance. In the fall of 1996, there was a total of 850 students enrolled in distance learning courses.
Course delivery sites Courses are delivered to your home, College of Lake County (Grayslake), William Rainey Harper College (Palatine), North Suburban Higher Education Network, two public libraries in Illinois.
Media Courses are delivered via television, videotapes, videoconferencing, audiotapes, CD-ROM. Students and teachers interact via videoconferencing, mail, telephone, fax, e-mail. A computer is required for some courses.
Restrictions Programs are available to local area students only. Students must be able to come to campus.
Services Distance learners have access to library services, e-mail services, academic advising at a distance.
Credit-earning options Students may transfer credits from another institution or may earn credits through standardized exams, institutionally developed exams.
Typical costs Tuition of $37 per semester hour plus mandatory fees of $50 per semester for local area residents. Tuition of $128 per semester hour plus mandatory fees of $50 per semester for in-state residents. Tuition of $153 per semester hour plus mandatory fees of $50 per semester for out-of-state residents. Costs may vary by number of credits taken. Financial aid is available to distance learners enrolled full-time or part-time.
Registration Students may register by mail, phone.
Contact Gary Newhouse, Director of Library and Media Services, Oakton Community College, 1600 East Golf Road, Des Plaines, IL 60016. *Telephone:* 847-635-1640. *Fax:* 847-635-1987. *E-mail:* garyn@oakton.edu. *Web site:* http://www.oakton.edu.

INDIVIDUAL COURSE SUBJECT AREAS

Undergraduate
Accounting; anthropology; area, ethnic, and cultural studies; Asian languages and literatures; astronomy and astrophysics; business administration and management; business law; computer and information sciences; developmental and child psychology; English composition; English language and literature; European languages and literatures; health and physical education/fitness; history; hospitality services management; Latin American studies; liberal arts, general studies, and humanities; marketing; mass media; mechanical engineering; physical sciences; physics; political science; psychology; radio and television broadcasting; sociology; Spanish language and literature

ODESSA COLLEGE

Odessa, Texas

Division of Distance Education

Odessa College, founded in 1946, is a state and locally supported two-year college. It is accredited by the Southern Association of Colleges and Schools. It first offered distance learning courses in 1986. In 1996–97, it offered 77 courses at a distance. In the fall of 1996, there was a total of 1,700 students enrolled in distance learning courses.
Course delivery sites Courses are delivered to your home, Howard College (Big Spring), Midland College (Midland), The University of Texas of the Permian Basin (Odessa), 1 off-campus center in Provo.
Media Courses are delivered via television, videotapes, videoconferencing, World Wide Web, e-mail, computer conferencing. Students and teachers interact via videoconferencing, mail, telephone, fax, e-mail. A computer is required for some courses.
Services Distance learners have access to library services, academic advising, career placement assistance at a distance.

Credit-earning options Students may transfer credits from another institution or may earn credits through examinations, military training.
Typical costs Tuition of $42 per course plus mandatory fees of $58 per course for local area residents. Tuition of $57 per course plus mandatory fees of $58 per course for in-state residents. Tuition of $310 per course plus mandatory fees of $58 per course for out-of-state residents. Costs may vary by specific program of study, number of credits taken. Financial aid is available to distance learners.
Contact Dr. Mary Koeninger, Dean of Arts, Humanities, and Distance Education, Odessa College, 201 West University, Odessa, TX 79764. *Telephone:* 915-335-6412. *E-mail:* mkoeninger@odessa.edu.

INDIVIDUAL COURSE SUBJECT AREAS

Undergraduate
Biology; business administration and management; communications; developmental and child psychology; economics; English composition; English language and literature; geology; history; law and legal studies; mathematics; nursing; political science; social psychology; sociology

THE OHIO STATE UNIVERSITY

Columbus, Ohio

The Ohio State University, founded in 1870, is a state-supported university. It is accredited by the North Central Association of Colleges and Schools.
Course delivery sites Courses are delivered to your home, your workplace, military bases, The Ohio State University at Lima (Lima), The Ohio State University at Marion (Marion), Ohio State University–Mansfield Campus (Mansfield), Ohio State University–Newark Campus (Newark).
Media Courses are delivered via television, videotapes, videoconferencing, World Wide Web. Students and teachers interact via videoconferencing, mail, telephone, fax, e-mail. A computer is required for some courses.
Typical costs *Undergraduate:* Tuition of $482 per course for in-state residents. Tuition of $1436 per course for out-of-state residents. *Graduate:* Tuition of $495 per course for in-state residents. Tuition of $1284 per course for out-of-state residents. Costs may vary by specific program of study, number of credits taken, course delivery options.
Registration Students may register by mail, fax, phone, e-mail, World Wide Web.
Contact Office of Continuing Education, The Ohio State University, 1050 Carmack Road, Room 152, Mount Hall, Columbus, OH 43210. *Telephone:* 614-292-8860. *Fax:* 614-292-0492.

INDIVIDUAL COURSE SUBJECT AREAS

Undergraduate
African-American studies; area, ethnic, and cultural studies; communications; home economics and family studies; mathematics; political science; Russian language and literature

Graduate
African-American studies; education; engineering; home economics and family studies; mathematics; political science

OHIO STATE UNIVERSITY–MANSFIELD CAMPUS

Mansfield, Ohio

Ohio State University–Mansfield Campus, founded in 1958, is a state-supported four-year college. It is accredited by the North Central Association of Colleges and Schools. It first offered distance learning courses in 1995. In 1996–97, it offered 3 courses at a distance. In the fall of 1996, there was a total of 5 students enrolled in distance learning courses.
Course delivery sites Courses are delivered to your home, The Ohio State University (Columbus).
Media Courses are delivered via videotapes, videoconferencing, e-mail. Students and teachers interact via videoconferencing, mail, telephone, fax, e-mail.
Restrictions Students must have access to broadcast signal.
Services Distance learners have access to library services, the campus computer network, e-mail services, academic advising, tutoring, career placement assistance at a distance.
Credit-earning options Students may transfer credits from another institution or may earn credits through institutionally developed exams.
Typical costs Tuition of $465 per course for in-state residents. Tuition of $954 per course for out-of-state residents. *Noncredit courses:* $150 per course. Costs may vary by number of credits taken. Financial aid is available to distance learners enrolled full-time.
Registration Students may register by mail, phone.
Contact Frederick C. Dahlstrand, Associate Dean, Ohio State University–Mansfield Campus, 1680 University Drive, Mansfield, OH 44906. *Telephone:* 419-755-4222. *Fax:* 419-755-4241. *E-mail:* dahlstrand.1@osu.edu.

INDIVIDUAL COURSE SUBJECT AREAS

Undergraduate
Area, ethnic, and cultural studies; mathematics; political science

OHIO UNIVERSITY

Athens, Ohio

Independent Study

Ohio University, founded in 1804, is a state-supported university. It is accredited by the North Central Association of Colleges and Schools. It first offered distance learning courses in 1924. In 1996–97, it offered 300 courses at a distance. In the fall of 1996, there was a total of 3,450 students enrolled in distance learning courses.
Course delivery sites Courses are delivered to your home.
Media Courses are delivered via videotapes, audiotapes, World Wide Web, print. Students and teachers interact via mail, fax, e-mail. A computer is required for some courses.
Services Distance learners have access to academic advising at a distance.
Credit-earning options Students may transfer credits from another institution or may earn credits through institutionally developed exams, portfolio assessment, military training, business training.
Typical costs Tuition of $60 per credit plus mandatory fees of $15 per course. Costs may vary by number of credits taken.
Registration Students may register by mail, fax.
Contact Independent Study, Ohio University, 302 Tupper Hall, Athens, OH 45701. *Telephone:* 800-444-2910. *Fax:* 614-593-2901. *E-mail:*

Profiles: Ohio University

indstudy@ouvaxa.cats.ohiou.edu. *Web site:* http://www.cats.ohiou.edu/~indstu/index.htm.

DEGREE & CERTIFICATE PROGRAMS

Associate Degrees

▶ *Arts and Humanities (AA)*
In 1995–96, 30 degrees were earned at a distance through this program.
Application requirements *Prior education:* high school diploma or equivalent. *Other requirements:* high school transcript, college transcripts, an application fee of $100.
Completion requirements 96–105 quarter hours are required. 30 quarter hours must be completed through the institution.

▶ *Business Management Technology (AAB)*
In 1995–96, 30 degrees were earned at a distance through this program.
Application requirements *Prior education:* high school diploma or equivalent. *Other requirements:* high school transcript, college transcripts, an application fee of $100.
Completion requirements 96–105 quarter hours are required. 30 quarter hours must be completed through the institution.

▶ *Individualized Studies (AIS)*
In 1995–96, 30 degrees were earned at a distance through this program.
Application requirements *Prior education:* high school diploma or equivalent. *Other requirements:* high school transcript, college transcripts, an application fee of $100.
Completion requirements 96–105 quarter hours are required. 30 quarter hours must be completed through the institution.

▶ *Natural Science (AS)*
In 1995–96, 30 degrees were earned at a distance through this program.
Application requirements *Prior education:* high school diploma or equivalent. *Other requirements:* high school transcript, college transcripts, an application fee of $100.
Completion requirements 96–105 quarter hours are required. 30 quarter hours must be completed through the institution.

▶ *Social Sciences (AA)*
In 1995–96, 30 degrees were earned at a distance through this program.
Application requirements *Prior education:* high school diploma or equivalent. *Other requirements:* high school transcript, college transcripts, an application fee of $100.
Completion requirements 96–105 quarter hours are required. 30 quarter hours must be completed through the institution.

Baccalaureate Degrees

▶ *Specialized Studies (BS)*
In 1995–96, 30 degrees were earned at a distance through this program.
Application requirements *Prior education:* high school diploma or equivalent. *Other requirements:* high school transcript, college transcripts, an application fee of $100.
Completion requirements 192 quarter hours are required. 48 quarter hours must be completed through the institution.

INDIVIDUAL COURSE SUBJECT AREAS

Undergraduate
Accounting; astronomy and astrophysics; biology; botany; business; business administration and management; chemistry; Classical languages and literatures; creative writing; developmental and child psychology; economics; educational psychology; engineering-related technologies; English composition; English language and literature; European languages and literatures; health and physical education/fitness; health professions and related sciences; history; home economics and family studies; journalism; liberal arts, general studies, and humanities; mathematics; music; philosophy and religion; physics; political science; protective services; social psychology; sociology

See full description on page 454.

OHIO UNIVERSITY–EASTERN

St. Clairsville, Ohio

Media Center

Ohio University–Eastern, founded in 1957, is a state-supported four-year college. It is accredited by the North Central Association of Colleges and Schools. It first offered distance learning courses in 1985. In 1996–97, it offered 20 courses at a distance. In the fall of 1996, there was a total of 200 students enrolled in distance learning courses.
Course delivery sites Courses are delivered to your home, other colleges.
Media Courses are delivered via television, videotapes, videoconferencing, audiotapes, radio broadcast, computer software, World Wide Web, e-mail, print. Students and teachers interact via videoconferencing, mail, telephone, fax, e-mail. A computer is required for some courses.
Services Distance learners have access to library services, the campus computer network, e-mail services, academic advising, career placement assistance at a distance.
Credit-earning options Students may transfer credits from another institution or may earn credits through examinations, portfolio assessment.
Typical costs Tuition of $91 per credit hour for in-state residents. Tuition of $170 per credit hour for out-of-state residents. *Noncredit courses:* $364 for 4 credit hours. Costs may vary by campus or location, number of credits taken. Financial aid is available to distance learners.
Registration Students may register by mail, fax, phone.
Contact Jay Morris, Director of Media, Ohio University–Eastern, 45425 National Road, St. Clairsville, OH 43950. *Telephone:* 614-695-1720, Ext. 272. *Fax:* 614-695-7078. *E-mail:* jmorris1@ohiou.edu.

INDIVIDUAL COURSE SUBJECT AREAS

Undergraduate
Asian languages and literatures; astronomy and astrophysics; biology; developmental and child psychology; history; journalism; mathematics; political science; public health; sociology; zoology

OHIO UNIVERSITY–SOUTHERN CAMPUS

Ironton, Ohio

Higher Education Microwave Services (HEMS)

Ohio University–Southern Campus, founded in 1956, is a state-supported primarily two-year college. It is accredited by the North Central Association of Colleges and Schools. It first offered distance learning courses in 1983. In 1996–97, it offered 75 courses at a distance. In the fall of 1996, there was a total of 715 students enrolled in distance learning courses.
Course delivery sites Courses are delivered to your home, your workplace, University of Toledo (Toledo), 5 off-campus centers in Chillicothe, Ironton, Lancaster, St. Clairsville, Zanesville.
Media Courses are delivered via television, World Wide Web. Students and teachers interact via videoconferencing, telephone, fax, e-mail.
Services Distance learners have access to library services, the campus computer network, e-mail services, academic advising, tutoring, career placement assistance at a distance.
Credit-earning options Students may transfer credits from another institution or may earn credits through standardized exams, institutionally developed exams, portfolio assessment, military training, business training.

Typical costs *Undergraduate:* Tuition of $4326 per year for in-state residents. Tuition of $9090 per year for out-of-state residents. *Graduate:* Tuition of $1630 per quarter for in-state residents. Tuition of $3128 per quarter for out-of-state residents. Financial aid is available to distance learners enrolled full-time or part-time.
Registration Students may register by mail, phone.
Contact Eric Cunningham, Assistant Dean, Ohio University–Southern Campus, 1804 Liberty Avenue, Ironton, OH 45638. *Telephone:* 614-533-4608. *Fax:* 614-533-4632. *E-mail:* cunningham@ouvaxa.cats.ohiou.edu. *Web site:* http://www.tcom.ohiou.edu/hems/.

DEGREE & CERTIFICATE PROGRAMS

Graduate Degrees
▶ *Business (MBA)*
On-campus requirements Long weekends and two week long sessions.
Program contact John Stinson, Director, Ohio University–Southern Campus, Copeland Hall, Athens, OH 45701. Phone: 614-593-2073. Fax: 614-593-9342.

INDIVIDUAL COURSE SUBJECT AREAS

Undergraduate
Accounting; business; business administration and management; chemical engineering; Classical languages and literatures; economics; education administration; educational psychology; English language and literature; European languages and literatures; history; human resources management; journalism; law and legal studies; liberal arts, general studies, and humanities; mathematics; nursing; special education; teacher education

Graduate
Business administration and management

Noncredit
Engineering/industrial management; environmental engineering

OHLONE COLLEGE

Fremont, California

Learning Resources and Technology

Ohlone College, founded in 1967, is a state and locally supported two-year college. It is accredited by the Western Association of Schools and Colleges, Inc. In 1996–97, it offered 8 courses at a distance. In the fall of 1996, there was a total of 200 students enrolled in distance learning courses.
Course delivery sites Courses are delivered to your home, your workplace, military bases, 1 off-campus center in Newark.
Media Courses are delivered via television, videotapes, audiotapes, radio broadcast, e-mail, print. Students and teachers interact via mail, telephone, fax, e-mail.
Restrictions Programs are available to local area students only.
Services Distance learners have access to e-mail services, academic advising, career placement assistance at a distance.
Credit-earning options Students may transfer credits from another institution or may earn credits through institutionally developed exams.
Typical costs Tuition of $13 per unit. *Noncredit courses:* $50–$100 per course.
Registration Students may register by mail, fax, phone.
Contact Michael Gros, Dean of Fine, Performing, and Language Arts, Ohlone College, 43600 Mission Boulevard, Fremont, CA 94539-5884. *Telephone:* 510-659-6216. *Fax:* 510-659-6188. *E-mail:* mgros@ohlone.cc.ca.us. *Web site:* http://www.ohlone.cc.ca.us.

INDIVIDUAL COURSE SUBJECT AREAS

Undergraduate
Anthropology; astronomy and astrophysics; business administration and management; European languages and literatures; health and physical education/fitness

OKLAHOMA CITY COMMUNITY COLLEGE

Oklahoma City, Oklahoma

Distance Education

Oklahoma City Community College, founded in 1969, is a state-supported two-year college. It is accredited by the North Central Association of Colleges and Schools. It first offered distance learning courses in 1971. In 1996–97, it offered 70 courses at a distance. In the fall of 1996, there was a total of 940 students enrolled in distance learning courses.
Course delivery sites Courses are delivered to your home, vocational centers, high schools.
Media Courses are delivered via television, videotapes, videoconferencing, audiotapes. Students and teachers interact via videoconferencing, mail, telephone, fax, e-mail.
Restrictions Programs are available to local area students only.
Services Distance learners have access to library services at a distance.
Credit-earning options Students may transfer credits from another institution or may earn credits through standardized exams, institutionally developed exams.
Typical costs Tuition of $28 per credit hour plus mandatory fees of $20.10 per credit hour for in-state residents. Tuition of $28 per credit hour plus mandatory fees of $80.10 per credit hour for out-of-state residents. Costs may vary by number of credits taken, course delivery options. Financial aid is available to distance learners enrolled full-time.
Registration Students may register by mail, fax, phone.
Contact Glenda Prince, Coordinator for Distance Education, Oklahoma City Community College, 7777 South May Avenue, Oklahoma City, OK 73159. *Telephone:* 405-682-7574. *Fax:* 405-682-7559. *E-mail:* gprince@okc.cc.ok.us.

DEGREE & CERTIFICATE PROGRAMS

Associate Degrees
▶ *Diversified Studies (AS)*
Application requirements *Prior education:* high school diploma or equivalent. *Other requirements:* SAT, ACT, high school transcript, college transcripts, an application fee of $25.
Completion requirements 60 credits are required.
On-campus requirements For orientation, testing if applicable, review sessions.

INDIVIDUAL COURSE SUBJECT AREAS

Undergraduate
Astronomy and astrophysics; biological and life sciences; biology; business; business administration and management; developmental and child psychology; economics; English as a second language (ESL); English composition; English language and literature; geology; history; liberal arts, general studies, and humanities; mathematics; philosophy and religion; physical sciences; physics; political science; psychology; social sciences; sociology; visual and performing arts

Profiles: Oklahoma State University

OKLAHOMA STATE UNIVERSITY

Stillwater, Oklahoma

Distance Learning

Oklahoma State University, founded in 1890, is a state-supported university. It is accredited by the North Central Association of Colleges and Schools.

Course delivery sites Courses are delivered to your home, your workplace, military bases, Oklahoma State University, Oklahoma City (Oklahoma City), Southwestern Oklahoma State University (Weatherford), 2 off-campus centers in Ardmore, Idabel.

Media Courses are delivered via television, videotapes, videoconferencing, audiotapes, audioconferencing, computer software, World Wide Web, e-mail, print. Students and teachers interact via videoconferencing, audioconferencing, mail, telephone, fax, e-mail. A computer is required for some courses.

Services Distance learners have access to library services, the campus computer network, e-mail services, academic advising, tutoring, career placement assistance at a distance.

Credit-earning options Students may transfer credits from another institution or may earn credits through standardized exams, institutionally developed exams, military training, business training.

Typical costs Contact sponsor for specific course costs. Financial aid is available to distance learners enrolled full-time or part-time.

Registration Students may register by mail, fax, phone, e-mail, World Wide Web.

Contact Sharon Nivens, Associate Director, University Extension, Oklahoma State University, 107 CITD Building, Stillwater, OK 74078. *Telephone:* 405-744-6606. *Fax:* 405-744-7923. *E-mail:* xtra@okway.okstate.edu.

DEGREE & CERTIFICATE PROGRAMS

Graduate Degrees

▶ *Agricultural Education (MAg)*
Application requirements *Prior education:* baccalaureate degree. *Other requirements:* college transcripts, letter(s) of recommendation, an application fee of $25.
Completion requirements 36 semester hours are required. 27 semester hours must be completed through the institution. *Maximum time for completion:* six years.
Program contact James P. Key, Professor, Oklahoma State University, 451 AG Hall, Stillwater, OK 74078. Phone: 405-744-8136. Fax: 405-744-5176. E-mail: agedjpk@okway.okstate.edu.

▶ *Business Administration (MBA)*
In the fall of 1996 there were 55 students enrolled in this program. In 1995–96, 10 degrees were earned at a distance through this program.
Application requirements *Prior education:* baccalaureate degree. *Other requirements:* GMAT, college transcripts, an essay or personal statement, letter(s) of recommendation, an application fee of $25.
Completion requirements 48 credit hours are required. 33 credit hours must be completed through the institution. *Maximum time for completion:* five years.
Program contact Alexa Bargmann, Program Coordinator, Oklahoma State University, Business Extension, 215 College of Business Administration, Stillwater, OK 74078-0555. Phone: 405-744-5208. Fax: 405-744-6143. E-mail: alexa@okway.okstate.edu.

▶ *Chemical Engineering (MS)*
In the fall of 1996 there were 2 students enrolled in this program. In 1995–96, 3 degrees were earned at a distance through this program.
Restrictions This program is available to in-state students only. Students must have access to a compressed video classroom site.
Application requirements *Prior education:* Chemical engineering degree from an accredited institution. *Other requirements:* college transcripts, letter(s) of recommendation, an application fee of $25.
Completion requirements 32 semester credits are required. 21 semester credits must be completed through the institution. *Maximum time for completion:* four years after filing plan of study.
Program contact Laura Gann, Credit Programs Coordinator, Oklahoma State University, Engineering Extension, 512 Engineering North, Stillwater, OK 74078-0532. Phone: 405-744-5146. Fax: 405-744-5033. E-mail: laugann@okway.okstate.edu.

▶ *Computer Science (MS)*
In the fall of 1996 there were 8 students enrolled in this program.
Restrictions Students must have access to a compressed video classroom site.
Application requirements *Prior education:* baccalaureate degree. *Other requirements:* college transcripts, an application fee of $25.
Completion requirements 30 semester credits are required. 21 semester credits must be completed through the institution.
On-campus requirements For defense of thesis.
Program contact Nancy Sherman, Program Coordinator, Oklahoma State University, Arts and Science Extension, 205 Life Science East, Stillwater, OK 74078-3017. Phone: 405-744-8459. Fax: 405-744-6992. E-mail: nancys@okway.okstate.edu.

▶ *Electrical Engineering (MS)*
In the fall of 1996 there were 55 students enrolled in this program. In 1995–96, 9 degrees were earned at a distance through this program.
Restrictions This program is available to in-state students only. Students must have access to a compressed video classroom site.
Application requirements *Prior education:* Bachelor of Science in Electrical Engineering. *Other requirements:* college transcripts, letter(s) of recommendation, an application fee of $25.
Completion requirements 32 semester credits are required. 21 semester credits must be completed through the institution. *Maximum time for completion:* four years after filing plan of study.
Program contact Laura Gann, Credit Programs Coordinator, Oklahoma State University, Engineering Extension, 512 Engineering North, Stillwater, OK 74078-0532. Phone: 405-744-5146. Fax: 405-744-5033. E-mail: laugann@okway.okstate.edu.

▶ *Mechanical Engineering (MS)*
In the fall of 1996 there were 26 students enrolled in this program. In 1995–96, 4 degrees were earned at a distance through this program.
Restrictions This program is available to in-state students only. Students must have access to a compressed video classroom site.
Application requirements College transcripts, letter(s) of recommendation, an application fee of $25.
Completion requirements 35 semester credits are required. 21 semester credits must be completed through the institution. *Maximum time for completion:* four years after filing plan of study.
Program contact Laura Gann, Credit Programs Coordinator, Oklahoma State University, Engineering Extension, 512 Engineering North, Stillwater, OK 74078-0532. Phone: 405-744-5146. Fax: 405-744-5033. E-mail: laugann@okway.okstate.edu.

▶ *Telecommunication Management (MS)*
In the fall of 1996 there were 40 students enrolled in this program. In 1995–96, 5 degrees were earned at a distance through this program.
Restrictions This program is available to in-state students only.
Application requirements *Prior education:* baccalaureate degree. *Other requirements:* GRE or GMAT, high school transcript, college transcripts, an essay or personal statement, letter(s) of recommendation, an application fee of $25.
Completion requirements 35 semester credits are required. 27 semester credits must be completed through the institution. *Maximum time for completion:* five years.
On-campus requirements Four days on campus for telecommunication lab.

Program contact Peter Rosen, Program Coordinator, Oklahoma State University, Business Extension, 215 College of Business Administration, Stillwater, OK 74078-4014. Phone: 405-744-5208. Fax: 405-744-6143. E-mail: peter.rosen@okway.okstate.edu.

Graduate certificates

▶ *Educational Administration*

In the fall of 1996 there were 40 students enrolled in this program.
Restrictions Students must have access to a compressed video classroom site.
Application requirements *Prior education:* graduate degree. *Other requirements:* college transcripts, letter(s) of recommendation.
Completion requirements 39 semester hours are required. 30 semester hours must be completed through the institution. *Maximum time for completion:* six years.
On-campus requirements Six Saturdays per semester.
Program contact Martin Burlingame, Department Head, Oklahoma State University, Department of Educational Administration and Higher Education, 322 Willard, Stillwater, OK 74078. Phone: 405-744-7244. Fax: 405-744-7713. E-mail: mburled@okway.okstate.edu.

INDIVIDUAL COURSE SUBJECT AREAS

Undergraduate

Accounting; agricultural economics; agriculture; algebra; American (US) history; animal sciences; area, ethnic, and cultural studies; business administration and management; business communications; business law; calculus; chemical engineering; computer and information sciences; computer programming; creative writing; developmental and child psychology; economics; educational psychology; electronics; engineering-related technologies; English composition; European languages and literatures; finance; fire science; French language and literature; geography; geology; German language and literature; health and physical education/fitness; history; home economics and family studies; journalism; law and legal studies; liberal arts, general studies, and humanities; management information systems; marketing; mathematics; meteorology; organizational behavior studies; philosophy and religion; political science; psychology; sociology; Spanish language and literature; statistics; teacher education; technical writing; visual and performing arts

Graduate

Agriculture; business; chemical engineering; communications; education administration; electrical engineering; environmental engineering; health professions and related sciences; industrial engineering; mechanical engineering; radio and television broadcasting

Noncredit

Community health services; continuing education; real estate

OLD DOMINION UNIVERSITY

Norfolk, Virginia

Office of Distance Learning and Extended Education

Old Dominion University, founded in 1930, is a state-supported university. It is accredited by the Southern Association of Colleges and Schools. It first offered distance learning courses in 1987. In 1996–97, it offered 150 courses at a distance. In the fall of 1996, there was a total of 2,112 students enrolled in distance learning courses.
Course delivery sites Courses are delivered to your workplace, military bases, Blue Ridge Community College (Weyers Cave), Central Virginia Community College (Lynchburg), Dabney S. Lancaster Community College (Clifton Forge), Danville Community College (Danville), Eastern Shore Community College (Melfa), Germanna Community College (Locust Grove), John Tyler Community College (Chester), J. Sargeant Reynolds Community College (Richmond), Lord Fairfax Community College (Middletown), Mountain Empire Community College (Big Stone Gap), New River Community College (Dublin), Northern Virginia Community College (Annandale), Patrick Henry Community College (Martinsville), Paul D. Camp Community College (Franklin), Piedmont Virginia Community College (Charlottesville), Rappahannock Community College (Glenns), Southside Virginia Community College (Alberta), Southwest Virginia Community College (Richlands), Thomas Nelson Community College (Hampton), Tidewater Community College (Portsmouth), Virginia Highlands Community College (Abingdon), Virginia Western Community College (Roanoke), Wytheville Community College (Wytheville), 3 off-campus centers in Hampton, Portsmouth, Virginia Beach, state library.
Media Courses are delivered via videoconferencing, computer software. Students and teachers interact via videoconferencing, mail, telephone, fax, e-mail. A computer is required for some courses.
Restrictions Teletechnet has primarily in-state sites; some programs available at sites in Indiana.
Services Distance learners have access to library services, the campus computer network, e-mail services, academic advising, tutoring, career placement assistance at a distance.
Credit-earning options Students may transfer credits from another institution or may earn credits through standardized exams, military training.
Typical costs *Undergraduate:* Tuition of $121 per credit hour plus mandatory fees of $10 per semester for in-state residents. Tuition of $230 per credit hour plus mandatory fees of $10 per semester for out-of-state residents. *Graduate:* Tuition of $162 per credit hour plus mandatory fees of $10 per semester for in-state residents. Tuition of $288 per credit hour plus mandatory fees of $10 per semester for out-of-state residents. Costs may vary by campus or location. Financial aid is available to distance learners enrolled full-time or part-time.
Registration Students may register by phone.
Contact Dr. Jeanie Kline, Associate Director of Distance Learning, Old Dominion University, Education Building, Room 145, Norfolk, VA 23529. *Telephone:* 757-683-3163. *Fax:* 757-683-5492. *E-mail:* jpkl00f@eagle.cc.odu.edu.

DEGREE & CERTIFICATE PROGRAMS

Baccalaureate Degrees

▶ *Business Administration (BS)*

In the fall of 1996 there were 80 students enrolled in this program. In 1995–96, 2 degrees were earned at a distance through this program.
Application requirements *Prior education:* some undergraduate course work. *Other requirements:* college transcripts, an application fee of $30.
Completion requirements 120 semester hours are required. 30 semester hours must be completed through the institution. *Other requirements:* Exit Examination of Writing Proficiency is a university requirement.
Program contact Sandra Waters, Director of Undergraduate Advisory Services, Old Dominion University, College of Business and Public Administration, Norfolk, VA 23508. Phone: 757-683-5777. Fax: 757-683-4076. E-mail: smw@economy.bpa.odu.edu.

▶ *Civil Engineering Technology (BSET)*

In the fall of 1996 there were 50 students enrolled in this program.
Application requirements *Prior education:* some undergraduate course work. *Other requirements:* college transcripts, an application fee of $30.
Completion requirements 131 credits are required. 30 must be completed through the institution. This is a degree completion program. *Other requirements:* Exit Examination of Writing Proficiency is a university requirement.
Program contact Richard K. Keplar, CET Program Director, Old Dominion University, Kaufman Hall, Room 129D, Norfolk, VA 23529. Phone: 757-683-3782. Fax: 757-683-5655. E-mail: rkkl00f@etfs.0l.kdh.odu.edu.

Profiles: Old Dominion University

▶ Criminal Justice (BA, BS)
In the fall of 1996 there were 70 students enrolled in this program. In 1995–96, 1 degree was earned at a distance through this program.
Application requirements *Prior education:* associate degree. *Other requirements:* college transcripts, an application fee of $30.
Completion requirements 120 credit hours are required. 45 credit hours must be completed through the institution. *Other requirements:* Exit Examination of Writing Proficiency is a university requirement.
Program contact Dr. Garland White, Department Chair, Old Dominion University, BAL Building, Room 730, Norfolk, VA 23529. Phone: 757-683-3791. Fax: 757-683-3241. E-mail: gfw200f@hamlet.bal.odu.edu.

▶ Electrical Engineering Technology (BS)
In the fall of 1996 there were 123 students enrolled in this program. In 1995–96, 10 degrees were earned at a distance through this program.
Application requirements *Prior education:* associate degree. *Other requirements:* college transcripts, an application fee of $30.
Completion requirements 124 semester hours are required. 30 semester hours must be completed through the institution. *Other requirements:* Exit Examination of Writing Proficiency is a university requirement.
On-campus requirements Laboratory courses are offered only on-campus and at a limited number of off-campus sites in Virginia.
Program contact John Hackworth, Program Director, Old Dominion University, Kaufman Hall, Room 211D, Norfolk, VA 23529. Phone: 757-683-3775. Fax: 757-683-5655. E-mail: jrhloof@etfs01.kdh.odu.edu.

▶ Elementary/Middle School Math and Science Education (BS)
In the fall of 1996 there were 33 students enrolled in this program.
Application requirements *Prior education:* high school diploma or equivalent. *Other requirements:* college transcripts, an application fee of $30.
Completion requirements 120 credit hours are required. 30 credit hours must be completed through the institution. *Other requirements:* Exit Examination of Writing Proficiency is a university requirement. Students must complete the 30-credit-hour master's degree in education in order to be certified to teach.
Program contact Nola Nicholson, Academic Advisor, Old Dominion University, BAL Building, Room 430, Norfolk, VA 23529. Phone: 757-683-4044. Fax: 757-683-3241. E-mail: nhnl00f@hamlet.bal.odu.edu.

▶ Health Sciences (BS)
In the fall of 1996 there were 114 students enrolled in this program. In 1995–96, 8 degrees were earned at a distance through this program.
Application requirements *Prior education:* associate degree in a health related area, a license or certification to practice in a health-related area. *Other requirements:* college transcripts, an application fee of $30, certification or licensure as a health professional.
Completion requirements 120 semester hours are required. 30 semester hours must be completed through the institution. This is a degree completion program. *Other requirements:* Exit Examination of Writing Proficiency is a university requirement. A minor in either management or human services counseling is required.
Program contact Sandra Breeden, Assistant to the Dean, Old Dominion University, College of Health Sciences, Norfolk, VA 23529. Phone: 757-683-5137. Fax: 757-683-5674. E-mail: slbloof@cranium.hs.odu.edu.

▶ Human Services Counseling (BS)
In the fall of 1996 there were 188 students enrolled in this program. In 1995–96, 4 degrees were earned at a distance through this program.
Application requirements *Prior education:* some undergraduate course work. *Other requirements:* college transcripts, an application fee of $30.
Completion requirements 120 hours are required. 30 hours must be completed through the institution. This is a degree completion program. *Other requirements:* Exit Examination of Writing Proficiency is a university requirement. A one-semester, unpaid internship is required after all other major course work is completed.
Program contact Pam Edmonds, Associate Director for Degree Programs, Old Dominion University, Room 152, Education Building, Norfolk, VA 23529. Phone: 757-683-3348. Fax: 757-683-5406. E-mail: pjel00f@eagle.cc.odv.edu.

▶ Mechanical Engineering Technology (BS)
In the fall of 1996 there were 67 students enrolled in this program. In 1995–96, 9 degrees were earned at a distance through this program.
Restrictions This program is available to in-state students only.
Application requirements *Prior education:* associate degree. *Other requirements:* high school transcript, college transcripts, an application fee of $30.
Completion requirements 124 semester hours are required. 30 semester hours must be completed through the institution. This is a degree completion program. *Other requirements:* Exit Examination of Writing Proficiency is a university requirement.
On-campus requirements Laboratories are currently offered on campus in summer during weekends. In the future, labs may be offered at various sites by a mobile lab.
Program contact Alok Verma, Program Director, Old Dominion University, Kaufman Hall, Room 214, Norfolk, VA 23529. Phone: 757-683-3765. Fax: 757-683-5655. E-mail: akv100f@etfs01.kdh.odu.edu.

▶ Nursing (BSN)
In the fall of 1996 there were 296 students enrolled in this program. In 1995–96, 58 degrees were earned at a distance through this program.
Application requirements *Prior education:* nursing education leading to RN license. *Other requirements:* college transcripts, an application fee of $30, RN license.
Completion requirements 120 semester hours are required. 30 semester hours must be completed through the institution. This is a degree completion program. *Other requirements:* Exit Examination of Writing Proficiency is a university requirement.
Program contact Dr. Rob Curry, Coordinator for Corporate Sites/Advisor, Old Dominion University, Technology Building, Room 346, Norfolk, VA 23529. Phone: 757-683-5246. Fax: 757-683-5253. E-mail: rfc100u@giraffe.tech.odu.edu.

▶ Occupational and Technical Studies (BS)
Application requirements *Prior education:* associate degree. *Other requirements:* college transcripts, an application fee of $30.
Completion requirements 120 semester credits are required. 30 semester credits must be completed through the institution. *Maximum time for completion:* six years.
Program contact Dr. John Ritz, Professor and Chair, Old Dominion University, Occupational and Technical Studies, Norfolk, VA 23529. Phone: 757-683-4305. Fax: 757-683-5227. E-mail: jmrloof@giraffe.tech.odu.edu.

▶ Professional Communications (BS)
In the fall of 1996 there were 48 students enrolled in this program.
Application requirements *Prior education:* high school diploma or equivalent. *Other requirements:* college transcripts, an application fee of $30.
Completion requirements 120 hours are required. 30 hours must be completed through the institution. This is a degree completion program. *Other requirements:* Exit Examination of Writing Proficiency is a university requirement.
Program contact Dr. Brenda Neuman Lewis, Director, Old Dominion University, BAL Building, Room 430, Norfolk, VA 23529. Phone: 757-683-4044. Fax: 757-683-3241. E-mail: bnlloof@hamlet.bal.odu.

Graduate Degrees
▶ Business Administration (MBA)
In the fall of 1996 there were 15 students enrolled in this program.

Application requirements *Prior education:* baccalaureate degree. *Other requirements:* GMAT, college transcripts, an essay or personal statement, letter(s) of recommendation, an application fee of $30.
Completion requirements 49 semester hours are required. 18 credits must be completed through the institution. *Maximum time for completion:* six years.
Program contact Jean Turpin, MBA Program Manager, Old Dominion University, MBA Program Office, Norfolk, VA 23529. Phone: 757-683-3585. Fax: 757-683-5750. E-mail: jht100u@economy.bpa.odu.edu.

▶ *Engineering Management (MEM)*
In the fall of 1996 there were 25 students enrolled in this program. In 1995–96, 10 degrees were earned at a distance through this program.
Application requirements *Prior education:* undergraduate degree in engineering or applied science. *Other requirements:* GRE, college transcripts, an essay or personal statement, letter(s) of recommendation, an application fee of $30.
Completion requirements 36 semester credits are required. 18 semester credits must be completed through the institution. *Maximum time for completion:* six years.
On-campus requirements During four semester visits students take the capstone project course.
Program contact Gerri Dutton, Program Support Technician, Old Dominion University, Room 105, Engineering Management, Norfolk, VA 23529-0248. Phone: 757-683-5541. Fax: 757-683-5640.

▶ *Environmental Engineering (ME)*
In the fall of 1996 there were 7 students enrolled in this program.
Restrictions This program is available to local area students only.
Application requirements *Prior education:* baccalaureate degree. *Other requirements:* GRE, college transcripts, an essay or personal statement, letter(s) of recommendation, an application fee of $30.
Completion requirements 30 hours are required. 18 hours must be completed through the institution. *Maximum time for completion:* six years.
On-campus requirements For comprehensive examination.
Program contact Dr. A. Akan, Graduate Program Director, Old Dominion University, Room 135, Kaufman Hall, Norfolk, VA 23529. Phone: 757-683-3753. Fax: 757-683-5354. E-mail: aoal00f@triton.kdh.odu.edu.

▶ *Family Nurse Practitioner (MSN)*
In the fall of 1996 there were 45 students enrolled in this program. In 1995–96, 5 degrees were earned at a distance through this program.
Restrictions This program is available to in-state students only.
Application requirements *Prior education:* baccalaureate degree. *Other requirements:* GRE or MAT, RN license, completion of undergraduate course in statistics, physical assessment course.
Completion requirements 45 credits are required. 36 credits must be completed through the institution. *Maximum time for completion:* five years.
On-campus requirements For comprehensive exam.
Program contact Angela Martin, Lecturer, Old Dominion University, School of Nursing, Norfolk, VA 23529. Phone: 757-683-5234. Fax: 757-683-5253. E-mail: acml00f@giraffe.tech.odv.edu.

▶ *Middle School Education–Math and Science Concentration (MS)*
In the fall of 1996 there were 7 students enrolled in this program.
Application requirements *Prior education:* baccalaureate degree. *Other requirements:* college transcripts, an application fee of $30.
Completion requirements 30 semester hours are required. 18 semester hours must be completed through the institution. *Other requirements:* this is a five-year program consisting of a Bachelor of Science, Interdisciplinary Studies and Master of Science, Elementary/Middle Education. *Maximum time for completion:* six years.
Program contact Dr. Jane Hager, Associate Dean, Old Dominion University, Room 122, Education Building, Norfolk, VA 23529. Phone: 757-683-3777. Fax: 757-683-5406. E-mail: jmhl00f@eagle.cc.odv.edu.

▶ *Special Education (MS)*
In the fall of 1996 there were 83 students enrolled in this program.
Application requirements *Prior education:* baccalaureate degree. *Other requirements:* GRE, college transcripts, an essay or personal statement, an application fee of $30.
Completion requirements 30 credit hours are required. 24 credit hours must be completed through the institution. *Maximum time for completion:* six years.
Program contact Cheryl S. Baker, Graduate Program Director, Old Dominion University, Child Study Center, Norfolk, VA 23529. Phone: 757-683-3226. Fax: 757-683-5406. E-mail: csb100f@eagle.cc.odu.edu.

INDIVIDUAL COURSE SUBJECT AREAS

Undergraduate
Business; business administration and management; communications; computer and information sciences; engineering-related technologies; English language and literature; health professions and related sciences; history; human resources management; industrial psychology; journalism; mathematics; music; nursing; political science; public health; social psychology; sociology

Graduate
Aerospace, aeronautical engineering; civil engineering; computer and information sciences; education; electrical engineering; environmental engineering; mechanical engineering; nursing; special education; teacher education

See full description on page 456.

ORAL ROBERTS UNIVERSITY

Tulsa, Oklahoma

School of Lifelong Education

Oral Roberts University, founded in 1963, is an independent-religious interdenominational university. It is accredited by the North Central Association of Colleges and Schools. It first offered distance learning courses in 1975. In 1996–97, it offered 146 courses at a distance. In the fall of 1996, there was a total of 400 students enrolled in distance learning courses.
Course delivery sites Courses are delivered to your home.
Media Courses are delivered via television, videotapes, audiotapes, computer software, World Wide Web, print. Students and teachers interact via mail, telephone, fax, e-mail. A computer is required for some courses.
Services Distance learners have access to library services, e-mail services, academic advising, career placement assistance at a distance.
Credit-earning options Students may transfer credits from another institution or may earn credits through standardized exams, institutionally developed exams, portfolio assessment, military training, business training.
Typical costs *Undergraduate:* Tuition of $105 per credit hour plus mandatory fees of $5 per course. *Graduate:* Tuition of $135 per credit hour plus mandatory fees of $5 per course. Financial aid is available to distance learners enrolled full-time or part-time.
Registration Students may register by mail, fax, phone, e-mail.
Contact Joshua T. Fischer, Director of Correspondence Studies, Oral Roberts University, 7777 South Lewis Avenue, Tulsa, OK 74171. *Telephone:* 918-495-6238. *Fax:* 918-495-7965. *E-mail:* slle@oru.edu. *Web site:* http://oru.edu/slle/.

Profiles: Oral Roberts University

DEGREE & CERTIFICATE PROGRAMS

Baccalaureate Degrees
▶ *Business Administration, Christian Care and Counseling, Church Ministries, Elementary Christian School Teaching, Liberal Studies (BS)*
In the fall of 1996 there were 400 students enrolled in this program. In 1995–96, 4 degrees were earned at a distance through this program.
Application requirements *Prior education:* high school diploma or equivalent. *Minimum age:* 22. *Other requirements:* high school transcript, college transcripts, an essay or personal statement, letter(s) of recommendation, an application fee of $35.
Completion requirements 129 semester hours are required. 30 semester hours must be completed through the institution.

Undergraduate Certificates
▶ *Theology*
In the fall of 1996 there were 56 students enrolled in this program.
Application requirements *Prior education:* none required.
Completion requirements 12 courses are required. 12 courses must be completed through the institution. *Other requirements:* each course has a one-year time limit.
Program contact Cheryl Wade, Senior Coordinator of Enrollment, Oral Roberts University, 7777 South Lewis Avenue, Tulsa, OK 74171. Phone: 918-495-6238. Fax: 918-495-7965. E-mail: cwade@oru.edu.

INDIVIDUAL COURSE SUBJECT AREAS

Undergraduate
Business; counseling psychology; education; theological studies

Graduate
Curriculum and instruction; education administration; English as a second language (ESL); special education; teacher education

Noncredit
Bible studies

OREGON HEALTH SCIENCES UNIVERSITY

Portland, Oregon

School of Nursing

Oregon Health Sciences University, founded in 1974, is a state-related upper-level institution. It is accredited by the Northwest Association of Schools and Colleges. It first offered distance learning courses in 1992. In the fall of 1996, there was a total of 150 students enrolled in distance learning courses.
Course delivery sites Courses are delivered to other colleges, off-campus center(s).
Media Courses are delivered via television, videotapes, print, computer conferencing. Students and teachers interact via mail, telephone, e-mail, computer conferencing. A computer is required for some courses.
Restrictions Programs are available to in-state students only. Program is for registered nurses or nursing students.
Services Distance learners have access to library services, the campus computer network, e-mail services, academic advising, tutoring at a distance.
Credit-earning options Students may transfer credits from another institution or may earn credits through standardized exams, institutionally developed exams, portfolio assessment.
Typical costs Costs vary among programs and campuses. Contact university for details. Financial aid is available to distance learners enrolled full-time or part-time.
Registration Students may register by mail.
Contact Mary McFarland, Associate Dean, Portland Campus, Oregon Health Sciences University, 3181 Southwest Sam Jackson Park Road, Portland, OR 97201. *Telephone:* 503-494-3658. *Fax:* 503-494-4350. *E-mail:* mcfarlnm@ohsu.edu.

INDIVIDUAL COURSE SUBJECT AREAS

Undergraduate
Nursing

Graduate
Nursing

OREGON STATE UNIVERSITY

Corvallis, Oregon

Extended Education

Oregon State University, founded in 1868, is a state-supported university. It is accredited by the Northwest Association of Schools and Colleges.
Course delivery sites Courses are delivered to your home, your workplace, other colleges.
Media Courses are delivered via television, videoconferencing, print, computer conferencing.
Services Distance learners have access to library services, academic advising, tutoring at a distance.
Credit-earning options Students may transfer credits from another institution. Financial aid is available to distance learners.
Contact Director, Communication Media Center, Oregon State University, Kidder Hall 109, Communication Media Center, Corvallis, OR 97331-4604. *Telephone:* 541-737-2121. *Fax:* 541-737-2159. *Web site:* http://www.orst.edu.

DEGREE & CERTIFICATE PROGRAMS

Baccalaureate Degrees
▶ *Liberal Studies (BS)*
Restrictions Program is available to students in six Oregon communities only.
Completion requirements 45 hours must be completed through the institution.
Program contact Gary Tiedeman, Liberal Studies Degree Program, Oregon State University, College of Liberal Arts, Corvallis, OR 97331. Phone: 541-737-0628. Fax: 541-737-2434.

INDIVIDUAL COURSE SUBJECT AREAS

Undergraduate
Computer and information sciences; conservation and natural resources; developmental and child psychology; English language and literature; history; home economics and family studies; liberal arts, general studies, and humanities; mathematics; philosophy and religion; political science; social psychology; sociology; theological studies

Graduate
Civil engineering; computer and information sciences; education administration; electrical engineering; environmental engineering; industrial engineering; mechanical engineering; teacher education

OTTAWA UNIVERSITY

Ottawa, Kansas

Ottawa University, founded in 1865, is an independent-religious American Baptist comprehensive institution. It is accredited by the North Central Association of Colleges and Schools. It first offered distance learning courses in 1976. In 1996–97, it offered 20 courses at a distance. In the fall of 1996, there was a total of 100 students enrolled in distance learning courses.
Course delivery sites Courses are delivered to your home.
Media Courses are delivered via videotapes, computer software, e-mail, print. Students and teachers interact via mail, telephone, fax, e-mail. A computer is required for some courses.
Restrictions Students must be able to travel to campus.
Services Distance learners have access to e-mail services, academic advising at a distance.
Credit-earning options Students may transfer credits from another institution or may earn credits through standardized exams, portfolio assessment, military training, business training.
Typical costs *Undergraduate:* Tuition of $172 per hour. *Graduate:* Tuition of $243 per hour. Costs may vary by number of credits taken.
Contact David Leiter, Admissions, Ottawa University, 10865 Grandview, Overland Park, KS 66210. *Telephone:* 913-451-1431. *Fax:* 913-451-0806. *E-mail:* ottawainfo@aol.com. *Web site:* http://www.ott.edu/~oukc/main.html.

DEGREE & CERTIFICATE PROGRAMS

Baccalaureate Degrees

▶ *Management of Health Services (BA)*
In the fall of 1996 there were 70 students enrolled in this program. In 1995–96, 50 degrees were earned at a distance through this program.
Application requirements *Prior education:* some undergraduate course work. *Other requirements:* college transcripts, an essay or personal statement, an application fee of $50.
Completion requirements 128 quarter credits are required. 28 quarter credits must be completed through the institution. This is a degree completion program.
On-campus requirements In Kansas City or other various locations for 3 weekends yearly.

Graduate Degrees

▶ *Human Resources (MA)*
In the fall of 1996 there were 30 students enrolled in this program. In 1995–96, 10 degrees were earned at a distance through this program.
Application requirements *Prior education:* baccalaureate degree. *Other requirements:* college transcripts, an essay or personal statement, letter(s) of recommendation, an application fee of $50.
Completion requirements 36 semester hours are required. 27 semester hours must be completed through the institution. *Maximum time for completion:* two years.
On-campus requirements Three weekends per year in Kansas City.

INDIVIDUAL COURSE SUBJECT AREAS

Undergraduate
Health services administration

Graduate
Human resources management

OUR LADY OF THE LAKE UNIVERSITY OF SAN ANTONIO

San Antonio, Texas

Our Lady of the Lake University of San Antonio, founded in 1895, is an independent-religious Roman Catholic comprehensive institution. It is accredited by the Southern Association of Colleges and Schools. It first offered distance learning courses in 1996. In 1996–97, it offered 2 courses at a distance. In the fall of 1996, there was a total of 20 students enrolled in distance learning courses.
Course delivery sites Courses are delivered to your home.
Media Courses are delivered via computer software, World Wide Web, e-mail, print. Students and teachers interact via telephone, fax, e-mail. A computer is required for some courses.
Services Distance learners have access to library services, academic advising at a distance.
Credit-earning options Students may transfer credits from another institution or may earn credits through standardized exams, portfolio assessment, military training.
Typical costs *Undergraduate:* Tuition of $310 per credit hour. *Graduate:* Tuition of $333 per credit hour. *Noncredit courses:* $310 per credit hour for undergraduates, $333 per credit hour for graduates. Financial aid is available to distance learners.
Registration Students may register by mail, phone.
Contact Dr. Madeleine Pepin, Department of Philosophy, Our Lady of the Lake University of San Antonio, 411 Southwest 24th Street, San Antonio, TX 78207-4689. *Telephone:* 210-434-6711. *Fax:* 210-436-0824. *E-mail:* pepin@lake.ollusa.edu.

INDIVIDUAL COURSE SUBJECT AREAS

Graduate
Health professions and related sciences

OWENS COMMUNITY COLLEGE

Toledo, Ohio

Center for Development and Training

Owens Community College, founded in 1966, is a state-supported two-year college. It is accredited by the North Central Association of Colleges and Schools. It first offered distance learning courses in 1993. In 1996–97, it offered 46 courses at a distance. In the fall of 1996, there was a total of 850 students enrolled in distance learning courses.
Course delivery sites Courses are delivered to your home, your workplace.
Media Courses are delivered via television, videotapes, videoconferencing, audiotapes. Students and teachers interact via videoconferencing, mail, telephone, fax, e-mail.
Services Distance learners have access to library services, academic advising, tutoring, career placement assistance at a distance.
Credit-earning options Students may transfer credits from another institution or may earn credits through examinations, portfolio assessment, military training, business training.
Typical costs Costs may vary by number of credits taken. Financial aid is available to distance learners.
Registration Students may register by mail, fax, phone.
Contact Nancy Stolla, Director, Distance Learning, Owens Community College, PO Box 10000, Toledo, OH 43699. *Telephone:* 419-

Profiles: Owens Community College

661-7244. *Fax:* 419-661-7662. *E-mail:* nstolla@owens.cc.oh.us. *Web site:* http://www.owens.cc.oh.us/CDT.

DEGREE & CERTIFICATE PROGRAMS

Undergraduate Certificates
▶*Supervision*
In the fall of 1996 there were 135 students enrolled in this program. In 1995–96, 70 certificates were earned at a distance through this program. **Application requirements** *Prior education:* high school diploma or equivalent. *Other requirements:* ASSET under some circumstances, high school transcript, college transcripts, $10 registration fee.
Completion requirements 6–12 credits are required. 6–12 credits must be completed through the institution.

INDIVIDUAL COURSE SUBJECT AREAS

Undergraduate
Accounting; American (US) history; American literature; business; business administration and management; business law; computer and information sciences; conservation and natural resources; criminal justice; developmental and child psychology; English composition; environmental engineering; environmental science; European languages and literatures; fire science; health and physical education/fitness; industrial psychology; liberal arts, general studies, and humanities; marketing; mathematics; organizational behavior studies; psychology; sociology; statistics

PACIFIC OAKS COLLEGE

Pasadena, California

Distance Learning

Pacific Oaks College, founded in 1945, is an independent-nonprofit upper-level institution. It is accredited by the Western Association of Schools and Colleges, Inc. It first offered distance learning courses in 1996. In 1996–97, it offered 15 courses at a distance. In the fall of 1996, there was a total of 50 students enrolled in distance learning courses.
Course delivery sites Courses are delivered to your home.
Media Courses are delivered via e-mail. Students and teachers interact via e-mail. A computer is required for all courses. The institution provides assistance with acquiring computer equipment.
Services Distance learners have access to library services, e-mail services, academic advising at a distance.
Credit-earning options Students may transfer credits from another institution or may earn credits through standardized exams, portfolio assessment.
Typical costs *Undergraduate:* Tuition of $455 per unit plus mandatory fees of $30 per semester. *Graduate:* Tuition of $455 per unit plus mandatory fees of $30 per semester. Financial aid is available to distance learners enrolled full-time or part-time.
Registration Students may register by mail, fax.
Contact Admissions Office, Pacific Oaks College, 5 Westmoreland Place, Pasadena, CA 91103. *Telephone:* 800-684-0900. *Fax:* 818-577-6144. *E-mail:* pacoaks@earthlink.net. *Web site:* http://www.pacoaks.org.

INDIVIDUAL COURSE SUBJECT AREAS

Undergraduate
Education

Graduate
Education

PALO ALTO COLLEGE

San Antonio, Texas

Extended Services

Palo Alto College, founded in 1987, is a state and locally supported two-year college. It is accredited by the Southern Association of Colleges and Schools.
Course delivery sites Courses are delivered to your home, your workplace, other colleges.
Media Courses are delivered via television, videoconferencing, computer software, World Wide Web, e-mail, print. Students and teachers interact via mail, telephone, fax, e-mail.
Restrictions Courses are available to students in an 8-county region only only.
Credit-earning options Students may transfer credits from another institution or may earn credits through examinations.
Typical costs Tuition of $367 per credit for local area residents. Tuition of $631 per credit for in-state residents. Tuition of $1183 per credit for out-of-state residents. Costs may vary by number of credits taken. Financial aid is available to distance learners.
Contact Ginny Stowitts, Assistant Professor, Palo Alto College, 1400 West Villaret, San Antonio, TX 78239. *Telephone:* 210-921-5022. *Fax:* 210-921-5115.

INDIVIDUAL COURSE SUBJECT AREAS

Undergraduate
Biology; business administration and management; economics; history; information sciences and systems; liberal arts, general studies, and humanities; political science

PALOMAR COLLEGE

San Marcos, California

Educational Television

Palomar College, founded in 1946, is a state and locally supported two-year college. It is accredited by the Western Association of Schools and Colleges, Inc. It first offered distance learning courses in 1978. In 1996–97, it offered 25 courses at a distance. In the fall of 1996, there was a total of 892 students enrolled in distance learning courses.
Course delivery sites Courses are delivered to your home, military bases, 2 off-campus centers in Escondido, Poway.
Media Courses are delivered via television, videotapes, print. Students and teachers interact via mail, telephone, fax, e-mail, in-person meetings.
Restrictions Courses are available to students in San Diego County only.
Services Distance learners have access to library services, academic advising, career placement assistance at a distance.
Credit-earning options Students may transfer credits from another institution or may earn credits through standardized exams, institutionally developed exams.
Typical costs Tuition of $13 per credit plus mandatory fees of $9 per semester for in-state residents. Tuition of $130 per credit plus mandatory fees of $9 per semester for out-of-state residents. *Noncredit courses:* $9 per semester. Costs may vary by status of residency. Financial aid is available to distance learners enrolled full-time or part-time.
Registration Students may register by mail, phone.

Profiles: Pennsylvania State University University Park Campus

Contact Educational Television, Palomar College, 1140 West Mission Road, San Marcos, CA 92069. *Telephone:* 760-744-1150, Ext. 2431. *Fax:* 760-744-1150, Ext. 2430.

INDIVIDUAL COURSE SUBJECT AREAS

Undergraduate

Abnormal psychology; accounting; anthropology; area, ethnic, and cultural studies; biology; business; business administration and management; business law; developmental and child psychology; finance; home economics and family studies; law and legal studies; liberal arts, general studies, and humanities; music; psychology; real estate; sign language; sociology; Spanish language and literature; visual and performing arts

PARK COLLEGE

Parkville, Missouri

School for Extended Learning

Park College, founded in 1875, is an independent-religious comprehensive institution affiliated with the Reorganized Church of Jesus Christ of Latter Day Saints. It is accredited by the North Central Association of Colleges and Schools. It first offered distance learning courses in 1996. In 1996–97, it offered 27 courses at a distance. In the fall of 1996, there was a total of 26 students enrolled in distance learning courses.
Course delivery sites Courses are delivered to your home, your workplace, military bases.
Media Courses are delivered via videoconferencing, audioconferencing, World Wide Web. Students and teachers interact via videoconferencing, audioconferencing, e-mail, Internet. A computer is required for some courses.
Restrictions For on-line courses, students must have access to the Internet.
Services Distance learners have access to library services, e-mail services at a distance.
Credit-earning options Students may transfer credits from another institution or may earn credits through standardized exams, military training.
Typical costs Tuition of $107 per semester hour. Financial aid is available to distance learners enrolled full-time.
Registration Students may register by mail, fax, e-mail, World Wide Web.
Contact Cathy Beatty, Administrator, Park College, 8700 Northwest River Park Drive, Parkville, MO 64152. *Telephone:* 800-492-2538. *Fax:* 816-522-6051. *E-mail:* cbeatty@allten.net. *Web site:* http://www.park.edu.

INDIVIDUAL COURSE SUBJECT AREAS

Undergraduate

American (US) history; biology; business administration and management; chemistry; computer programming; creative writing; criminal justice; ethics; finance; health services administration; social psychology; statistics; technical writing

PARKLAND COLLEGE

Champaign, Illinois

Distance Education

Parkland College, founded in 1967, is a district-supported two-year college. It is accredited by the North Central Association of Colleges and Schools. It first offered distance learning courses in 1988. In 1996–97, it offered 25 courses at a distance. In the fall of 1996, there was a total of 652 students enrolled in distance learning courses.
Course delivery sites Courses are delivered to your home, 3 off-campus centers in Le Roy, Rantoul, Tuscola.
Media Courses are delivered via television, videotapes, videoconferencing, computer software, World Wide Web, e-mail, print. Students and teachers interact via videoconferencing, mail, telephone, fax, e-mail. A computer is required for some courses.
Services Distance learners have access to the campus computer network, e-mail services at a distance.
Credit-earning options Students may transfer credits from another institution.
Typical costs Tuition of $47 per credit for local area residents. Tuition of $87 per credit for in-state residents. Tuition of $208 per credit for out-of-state residents. Internet course out-of-state cost: $248. Costs may vary by number of credits taken, course delivery options. Financial aid is available to distance learners enrolled full-time or part-time.
Registration Students may register by mail, fax, phone.
Contact Haiti Eastin, Program Coordinator, Parkland College, 2400 West Bradley Avenue, Champaign, IL 61821. *Telephone:* 217-373-3893. *Fax:* 217-353-2241. *E-mail:* heastin@parkland.cc.il.us.

INDIVIDUAL COURSE SUBJECT AREAS

Undergraduate

Area, ethnic, and cultural studies; biological and life sciences; business; business administration and management; communications; developmental and child psychology; economics; history; law and legal studies; mathematics; philosophy and religion; political science; psychology; sociology; theological studies

PENNSYLVANIA STATE UNIVERSITY UNIVERSITY PARK CAMPUS

University Park, Pennsylvania

Department of Distance Education

Pennsylvania State University University Park Campus, founded in 1855, is a state-related university. It is accredited by the Middle States Association of Colleges and Schools. It first offered distance learning courses in 1892. In 1996–97, it offered 450 courses at a distance. In the fall of 1996, there was a total of 12,500 students enrolled in distance learning courses.
Course delivery sites Courses are delivered to your home, your workplace, military bases.
Media Courses are delivered via television, videotapes, videoconferencing, audiotapes, audioconferencing, computer software, World Wide Web, e-mail, print. Students and teachers interact via videoconferencing, audioconferencing, mail, telephone, fax, e-mail. A computer is required for some courses.
Services Distance learners have access to academic advising, career placement assistance at a distance.

Distance Learning Programs

Profiles: Pennsylvania State University University Park Campus

Credit-earning options Students may transfer credits from another institution or may earn credits through examinations, portfolio assessment.
Typical costs Tuition of $115 per credit plus mandatory fees of $28 per course. *Noncredit courses:* $150 per course. Costs may vary by campus or location, specific program of study, number of credits taken, course delivery options.
Registration Students may register by mail, fax, phone, e-mail, World Wide Web.
Contact Bruce Heasley, Associate Director, Distance Education, Pennsylvania State University University Park Campus, 207 Mitchell Building, University Park, PA 16802. *Telephone:* 800-252-3592. *Fax:* 814-865-3290. *E-mail:* psude@cde.psu.edu. *Web site:* http://www.cde.psu.edu/de.

DEGREE & CERTIFICATE PROGRAMS

Associate Degrees

▶ *Business Administration (AA)*
In the fall of 1996 there were 150 students enrolled in this program. In 1995–96, 4 degrees were earned at a distance through this program.
Application requirements *Prior education:* high school diploma or equivalent. *Other requirements:* ACT or SAT, high school transcript, college transcripts, an application fee of $40.
Completion requirements 68 semester credit hours are required. 18 semester credit hours must be completed through the institution.

▶ *Dietetic Food Systems Management (AA)*
In the fall of 1996 there were 215 students enrolled in this program. In 1995–96, 16 degrees were earned at a distance through this program.
Application requirements *Prior education:* high school diploma or equivalent. *Other requirements:* ACT or SAT, high school transcript, college transcripts, an application fee of $40.
Completion requirements 60 semester credit hours are required. 18 semester credit hours must be completed through the institution.

▶ *Human Development and Family Studies (AA)*
In the fall of 1996 there were 3 students enrolled in this program.
Application requirements *Prior education:* high school diploma or equivalent. *Other requirements:* ACT or SAT, high school transcript, college transcripts, an application fee of $40.
Completion requirements 60 semester credit hours are required. 18 semester credit hours must be completed through the institution.

▶ *Liberal Arts and Sciences (AA)*
In the fall of 1996 there were 400 students enrolled in this program. In 1995–96, 5 degrees were earned at a distance through this program.
Application requirements *Prior education:* high school diploma or equivalent. *Other requirements:* ACT or SAT, high school transcript, college transcripts, an application fee of $40.
Completion requirements 60 semester credit hours are required. 18 semester credit hours must be completed through the institution.

▶ *Sociology (AA)*
In the fall of 1996 there were 2 students enrolled in this program.
Application requirements *Prior education:* high school diploma or equivalent. *Other requirements:* ACT or SAT, high school transcript, college transcripts, an application fee of $40.
Completion requirements 60 semester credit hours are required. 18 semester credit hours must be completed through the institution.

Graduate Degrees

▶ *Acoustical Engineering (MS)*
In the fall of 1996 there were 31 students enrolled in this program. In 1995–96, 4 degrees were earned at a distance through this program.
Restrictions Students must have access to videoconferencing equipment.
Application requirements *Prior education:* bachelor's degree in engineering or related technical discipline. *Other requirements:* GRE, college transcripts, an essay or personal statement, letter(s) of recommendation, evaluation of relevant work experience.
Completion requirements 30 semester credit hours are required. 20 semester credit hours must be completed through the institution.

On-campus requirements Two courses during a two-week summer session.

▶ *Elementary Education (MS)*
In the fall of 1996 there were 31 students enrolled in this program.
Application requirements *Prior education:* BS or BA in elementary education or BA with specialized professional courses. *Other requirements:* GRE, college transcripts, an essay or personal statement, letter(s) of recommendation.
Completion requirements 30 semester credit hours are required. *Maximum time for completion:* three years.

Undergraduate Certificates

▶ *Administration of Justice*
In the fall of 1996 there were 13 students enrolled in this program.
Application requirements *Prior education:* high school diploma or equivalent. *Other requirements:* application.
Completion requirements 21 semester credits are required.

▶ *Adult Development of Aging Services*
In the fall of 1996 there were 5 students enrolled in this program.
Application requirements *Prior education:* high school diploma or equivalent. *Other requirements:* application.
Completion requirements 30 semester credits are required.

▶ *Advanced Business Management*
In the fall of 1996 there were 3 students enrolled in this program.
Application requirements *Prior education:* high school diploma or equivalent. *Other requirements:* application.
Completion requirements 32 semester credits are required.

▶ *Business Logistics*
In the fall of 1996 there were 3 students enrolled in this program.
Application requirements *Prior education:* high school diploma or equivalent. *Other requirements:* application.
Completion requirements 12 semester credits are required.

▶ *Business Management*
In the fall of 1996 there were 13 students enrolled in this program.
Application requirements *Prior education:* high school diploma or equivalent. *Other requirements:* application.
Completion requirements 20 semester credits are required.

▶ *Children, Youth and Family Services*
In the fall of 1996 there were 4 students enrolled in this program.
Application requirements *Prior education:* high school diploma or equivalent. *Other requirements:* application.
Completion requirements 30 semester credits are required.

▶ *Dietary Manager*
In the fall of 1996 there were 152 students enrolled in this program.
Application requirements *Prior education:* high school diploma or equivalent. *Other requirements:* application.
Completion requirements 15 semester credits are required.

▶ *Dietetics and Aging*
In the fall of 1996 there were 10 students enrolled in this program.
Application requirements *Prior education:* high school diploma or equivalent. *Other requirements:* application.
Completion requirements 21 semester credit hours are required.

▶ *General Business*
In the fall of 1996 there were 2 students enrolled in this program.
Application requirements *Prior education:* high school diploma or equivalent. *Other requirements:* application.
Completion requirements 20 semester credit hours are required.

▶ *Human Resources*
In the fall of 1996 there were 11 students enrolled in this program.
Application requirements *Prior education:* high school diploma or equivalent. *Other requirements:* application.
Completion requirements 18 semester credits are required.

▶ *Marketing Management*
Application requirements *Prior education:* high school diploma or equivalent. *Other requirements:* application.
Completion requirements 19 semester credits are required.

▶ *Nursing Management*
In the fall of 1996 there were 15 students enrolled in this program.
Application requirements *Prior education:* high school diploma or equivalent. *Other requirements:* application.
Completion requirements 12 semester credits are required.

▶ *Paralegal Certificate Program*
In the fall of 1996 there were 14 students enrolled in this program.
Application requirements *Prior education:* high school diploma or equivalent. *Other requirements:* application.
Completion requirements 8 noncredit courses are required.

▶ *Purchasing Management*
In the fall of 1996 there were 2 students enrolled in this program.
Application requirements *Prior education:* high school diploma or equivalent. *Other requirements:* application.
Completion requirements 12 semester credits are required.

▶ *Retail Management*
In the fall of 1996 there were 8 students enrolled in this program.
Application requirements *Prior education:* high school diploma or equivalent. *Other requirements:* application.
Completion requirements 31 semester credits are required.

▶ *Retail Management*
In the fall of 1996 there were 10 students enrolled in this program.
Application requirements *Prior education:* high school diploma or equivalent. *Other requirements:* application.
Completion requirements 18 semester credits are required.

▶ *Small Business Management*
In the fall of 1996 there were 3 students enrolled in this program.
Application requirements *Prior education:* high school diploma or equivalent. *Other requirements:* application.
Completion requirements 26 semester credits are required.

▶ *Writing Social Commentary*
In the fall of 1996 there was 1 student enrolled in this program.
Application requirements *Prior education:* high school diploma or equivalent. *Other requirements:* application.
Completion requirements 21 semester credit hours are required.

INDIVIDUAL COURSE SUBJECT AREAS

Undergraduate
Accounting; agriculture; architecture; area, ethnic, and cultural studies; biological and life sciences; biology; business; business administration and management; chemistry; civil engineering; creative writing; design; developmental and child psychology; economics; education administration; educational psychology; engineering; engineering mechanics; English composition; English language and literature; European languages and literatures; health and physical education/fitness; health professions and related sciences; history; home economics and family studies; human resources management; liberal arts, general studies, and humanities; mathematics; music; nursing; philosophy and religion; physical sciences; physics; political science; protective services; psychology; social psychology; social work; sociology; visual and performing arts

Graduate
Business; education administration; engineering; nursing; teacher education

Noncredit
Agriculture; business; civil engineering; engineering; engineering-related technologies; English composition; health professions and related sciences; law and legal studies; public health

---

Profiles: Penn Valley Community College

PENN VALLEY COMMUNITY COLLEGE

Kansas City, Missouri

Distance Education and Media

Penn Valley Community College, founded in 1969, is a state and locally supported two-year college. It is accredited by the North Central Association of Colleges and Schools. It first offered distance learning courses in 1993. In 1996–97, it offered 40 courses at a distance. In the fall of 1996, there was a total of 736 students enrolled in distance learning courses.
Course delivery sites Courses are delivered to your home, your workplace, Longview Community College (Lee's Summit), Maple Woods Community College (Kansas City), 1 off-campus center in Kansas City.
Media Courses are delivered via television, World Wide Web. Students and teachers interact via mail, telephone, fax, e-mail. A computer is required for some courses.
Restrictions Programs are available to local area students only.
Services Distance learners have access to library services, e-mail services, academic advising, tutoring at a distance.
Credit-earning options Students may transfer credits from another institution.
Typical costs Tuition of $47 per credit hour plus mandatory fees of $10 per credit hour for local area residents. Tuition of $79 per credit hour plus mandatory fees of $10 per credit hour for in-state residents. Tuition of $112 per credit hour plus mandatory fees of $10 per credit hour for out-of-state residents. Costs may vary by specific program of study. Financial aid is available to distance learners enrolled full-time.
Registration Students may register by phone.
Contact Charles Gosselin, Associate Dean of Instructional Technology, Penn Valley Community College, 3201 Southwest Traffic Way, Kansas City, MO 64111-2764. *Telephone:* 816-759-4489. *Fax:* 816-759-4367. *E-mail:* gosselin@pennvalley.cc.mo.us. *Web site:* http://www.kcmetro.cc.mo.us

DEGREE & CERTIFICATE PROGRAMS

Associate Degrees
▶ *Liberal Arts (AA)*
In the fall of 1996 there were 272 students enrolled in this program.
Application requirements *Prior education:* high school diploma or equivalent. *Other requirements:* high school transcript.
Completion requirements 62 credit hours are required. 15 credit hours must be completed through the institution.
On-campus requirements Requirements vary based on course, instructor, testing mode, and requirements for conferences.
Program contact Sarah Hopkins, Director of Pace Program, Penn Valley Community College, 500 Southwest Longview Road, Lee's Summit, MO 64081-2015. Phone: 816-672-2218. E-mail: hopkins@longview.cc.mo.us

INDIVIDUAL COURSE SUBJECT AREAS

Undergraduate
Accounting; African-American studies; biology; business; cell biology; chemistry; child care and development; developmental and child psychology; economics; engineering; English composition; European languages and literatures; family and marriage counseling; fire science; fire services administration; history; individual and family development studies; Latin American studies; liberal arts, general studies, and humanities; nursing; physical sciences; physics; teacher education

Profiles: Pensacola Junior College

PENSACOLA JUNIOR COLLEGE

Pensacola, Florida

Distance Learning Department

Pensacola Junior College, founded in 1948, is a state-supported two-year college. It is accredited by the Southern Association of Colleges and Schools. It first offered distance learning courses in 1977. In 1996–97, it offered 30 courses at a distance. In the fall of 1996, there was a total of 780 students enrolled in distance learning courses.
Course delivery sites Courses are delivered to your home.
Media Courses are delivered via television. Students and teachers interact via mail, telephone, e-mail.
Services Distance learners have access to library services, academic advising, tutoring, career placement assistance at a distance.
Credit-earning options Students may transfer credits from another institution or may earn credits through examinations, portfolio assessment, military training, business training.
Typical costs Tuition of $120.60 per course plus mandatory fees of $20 per course for in-state residents. Tuition of $432.60 per course plus mandatory fees of $20 per course for out-of-state residents. Financial aid is available to distance learners enrolled full-time or part-time.
Registration Students may register by mail.
Contact Katherine E. Schultz, Director, Distance Learning, Pensacola Junior College, 1000 College Boulevard, Pensacola, FL 32504-8998. *Telephone:* 904-484-1238. *Fax:* 904-484-1255. *E-mail:* kschultz@pjc.cc.fl.us. *Web site:* http://www.pjc.cc.fl.us.

INDIVIDUAL COURSE SUBJECT AREAS

Undergraduate

Astronomy and astrophysics; business; business administration and management; developmental and child psychology; economics; geology; history; home economics and family studies; liberal arts, general studies, and humanities; mathematics; social psychology; sociology

PEOPLES COLLEGE

Kissimmee, Florida

Peoples College, founded in 1985, is a proprietary two-year college. It is accredited by the Distance Education and Training Council. It first offered distance learning courses in 1978. In 1996–97, it offered 2 courses at a distance. In the fall of 1996, there was a total of 25 students enrolled in distance learning courses.
Course delivery sites Courses are delivered to your home, military bases.
Media Courses are delivered via print. Students and teachers interact via mail, telephone, fax, e-mail.
Services Distance learners have access to library services, e-mail services, academic advising, tutoring at a distance.
Credit-earning options Students may transfer credits from another institution.
Typical costs Tuition of $1995 per course.
Registration Students may register by mail.
Contact Admissions Department, Peoples College, 233 Academy Drive, Kissimmee, FL 34742. *Telephone:* 407-847-4444. *Fax:* 407-847-8793. *E-mail:* peoples@gdi.net.

DEGREE & CERTIFICATE PROGRAMS

Associate Degrees
▶ *Travel and Tourism (AAS)*
Restrictions Program requires student to have professional travel experience or a diploma from an accredited travel school.
Application requirements *Prior education:* some undergraduate course work. *Other requirements:* high school transcript, college transcripts, an application fee of $150.
Completion requirements 92 credit hours are required. 78.5 credit hours must be completed through the institution. *Maximum time for completion:* two years.

INDIVIDUAL COURSE SUBJECT AREAS

Undergraduate
Hospitality services management

PHILLIPS COMMUNITY COLLEGE OF THE UNIVERSITY OF ARKANSAS

Helena, Arkansas

Phillips Community College of the University of Arkansas, founded in 1965, is a state and locally supported two-year college. It is accredited by the North Central Association of Colleges and Schools. It first offered distance learning courses in 1995.
Course delivery sites Courses are delivered to your home.
Media Courses are delivered via television, videotapes, videoconferencing, print.
Restrictions Programs are available to in-state students only.
Credit-earning options Students may transfer credits from another institution or may earn credits through examinations. Financial aid is available to distance learners.
Contact Assistant Registrar, Phillips Community College of the University of Arkansas, PO Box 785, Helena, AR 72342. *Telephone:* 501-338-6474. *Fax:* 501-338-7542.

INDIVIDUAL COURSE SUBJECT AREAS

Undergraduate
Accounting; business administration and management; English as a second language (ESL); history; mathematics; political science; social psychology

PIEDMONT COLLEGE

Demorest, Georgia

Piedmont College, founded in 1897, is an independent-religious comprehensive institution affiliated with the Congregational Christian Church. It is accredited by the Southern Association of Colleges and Schools. It first offered distance learning courses in 1994. In 1996–97, it offered 14 courses at a distance. In the fall of 1996, there was a total of 58 students enrolled in distance learning courses.
Course delivery sites Courses are delivered to your home, 1 off-campus center in Athens, local high schools.
Media Courses are delivered via videoconferencing, computer software, World Wide Web, e-mail. Students and teachers interact via videoconferencing, telephone, e-mail. A computer is required for some courses.

Services Distance learners have access to the campus computer network, e-mail services, academic advising, career placement assistance at a distance.
Credit-earning options Students may transfer credits from another institution or may earn credits through standardized exams, portfolio assessment, military training, business training.
Typical costs *Undergraduate:* Tuition of $265 per semester hour. *Graduate:* Tuition of $150 per semester hour. Financial aid is available to distance learners enrolled full-time.
Registration Students may register by mail, fax, phone, e-mail.
Contact James L. Clement, Director of Admissions, Piedmont College, PO Box 10, Demorest, GA 30535. *Telephone:* 706-776-0103. *Fax:* 706-776-2811. *E-mail:* jem.clement@gateway.piedmont.edu.

INDIVIDUAL COURSE SUBJECT AREAS

Undergraduate
Asian languages and literatures; communications; English composition; European languages and literatures; history; mathematics; sociology

PIERCE COLLEGE

Lakewood, Washington

Developmental Education

Pierce College, founded in 1967, is a state-supported two-year college. It is accredited by the Northwest Association of Schools and Colleges. It first offered distance learning courses in 1982. In 1996–97, it offered 26 courses at a distance. In the fall of 1996, there was a total of 150 students enrolled in distance learning courses.
Course delivery sites Courses are delivered to your home.
Media Courses are delivered via television, videotapes, audiotapes, e-mail, print. Students and teachers interact via mail, telephone, fax, e-mail. A computer is required for some courses.
Services Distance learners have access to academic advising at a distance.
Credit-earning options Students may transfer credits from another institution.
Typical costs Tuition of $258.50 per course. *Noncredit courses:* $258.50 per course. Costs may vary by number of credits taken. Financial aid is available to distance learners.
Registration Students may register by mail, phone.
Contact Shawna Martens, Program Assistant, Pierce College, 9401 Farwest Drive, SW, Lakewood, WA 98499-6299. *Telephone:* 253-964-6244. *Fax:* 253-964-6299. *E-mail:* smartens@pierce.ctc.edu.

DEGREE & CERTIFICATE PROGRAMS

Associate Degrees
▶ *General Studies (AAS)*
In the fall of 1996 there were 150 students enrolled in this program.
Application requirements *Prior education:* high school diploma or equivalent. *Other requirements:* Assessment College Placement.
Completion requirements 90 credits are required.

INDIVIDUAL COURSE SUBJECT AREAS

Undergraduate
Abnormal psychology; anthropology; biology; developmental and child psychology; earth science; economics; English composition; English language and literature; English literature; French language and literature; geology; health and physical education/fitness; psychology

Distance Learning Programs

PIKES PEAK COMMUNITY COLLEGE

Colorado Springs, Colorado

Learning Technologies

Pikes Peak Community College, founded in 1968, is a state-supported two-year college. It is accredited by the North Central Association of Colleges and Schools. It first offered distance learning courses in 1978.
Course delivery sites Courses are delivered to your home, your workplace, military bases, community colleges in Colorado.
Media Courses are delivered via television, videotapes, videoconferencing, World Wide Web, print. Students and teachers interact via videoconferencing, mail, telephone, fax, e-mail.
Services Distance learners have access to library services, academic advising at a distance.
Credit-earning options Students may transfer credits from another institution or may earn credits through examinations, portfolio assessment, military training, business training.
Typical costs Tuition of $54.30 per credit hour plus mandatory fees of $35 per course for in-state residents. Tuition of $252.25 per credit hour plus mandatory fees of $35 per course for out-of-state residents. Financial aid is available to distance learners.
Contact Fay Cover, Director of Learning Technologies, Pikes Peak Community College, 5675 South Academy Boulevard, Colorado Springs, CO 80906-5498. *Telephone:* 719-540-7397.

INDIVIDUAL COURSE SUBJECT AREAS

Undergraduate
Accounting; administrative and secretarial services; business; business administration and management; chemistry; communications; computer and information sciences; conservation and natural resources; geology; history; hospitality services management; human resources management; library and information studies; mathematics; philosophy and religion; radio and television broadcasting; social psychology; sociology

Noncredit
Accounting; administrative and secretarial services; business; business administration and management; chemistry; communications; computer and information sciences; conservation and natural resources; geology; history; hospitality services management; human resources management; library and information studies; mathematics; philosophy and religion; radio and television broadcasting; social psychology; sociology

PIMA COMMUNITY COLLEGE

Tucson, Arizona

Telecommunications and Production Service

Pima Community College, founded in 1966, is a state-supported two-year college. It is accredited by the North Central Association of Colleges and Schools. It first offered distance learning courses in 1975.
Course delivery sites Courses are delivered to your home, your workplace, military bases, other colleges.
Media Courses are delivered via television, videotapes, videoconferencing, computer software, print, computer conferencing.
Restrictions Programs are available to local area students only.
Services Distance learners have access to library services, academic advising, tutoring, career placement assistance at a distance.

Profiles: Pima Community College

Credit-earning options Students may transfer credits from another institution or may earn credits through examinations, military training, business training. Financial aid is available to distance learners.
Contact Director, Telecommunications/Production Service, Pima Community College, 1901 North Stone Avenue, Tucson, AZ 85709-5080. *Telephone:* 520-884-6410. *Fax:* 520-884-6542. *Web site:* http://community.cc.pima.edu.

INDIVIDUAL COURSE SUBJECT AREAS

Undergraduate
Area, ethnic, and cultural studies; business administration and management; computer and information sciences; education; English composition; English language and literature; European languages and literatures; history; home economics and family studies; liberal arts, general studies, and humanities; physical sciences; psychology; public health; sociology

PINE TECHNICAL COLLEGE

Pine City, Minnesota

Pine Technical College, founded in 1965, is a state-supported two-year college. It is accredited by the North Central Association of Colleges and Schools. It first offered distance learning courses in 1985. In 1996–97, it offered 90 courses at a distance.
Course delivery sites Courses are delivered to your home, your workplace, military bases, St. Cloud Technical College (St. Cloud).
Media Courses are delivered via audiotapes, e-mail, print. Students and teachers interact via mail, telephone, fax, e-mail. A computer is required for all courses.
Services Distance learners have access to library services, career placement assistance at a distance.
Credit-earning options Students may earn credits through institutionally developed exams.
Typical costs Tuition of $48 per credit plus mandatory fees of $4.70 per credit for in-state residents. Tuition of $96 per credit for out-of-state residents. Costs may vary by campus or location.
Registration Students may register by mail, phone.
Contact Jay Hutchins, Admissions, Pine Technical College, Pine Technical College, 1000 Fourth Street, Pine City, MN 55063. *Telephone:* 320-629-6764. *Web site:* http://www.ptc.tec.mn.us/.

INDIVIDUAL COURSE SUBJECT AREAS

Undergraduate
Accounting; criminal justice; nursing; public health

PITT COMMUNITY COLLEGE

Greenville, North Carolina

North Carolina Information Highway

Pitt Community College, founded in 1961, is a state and locally supported two-year college. It is accredited by the Southern Association of Colleges and Schools. It first offered distance learning courses in 1995. In 1996–97, it offered 25 courses at a distance. In the fall of 1996, there was a total of 95 students enrolled in distance learning courses.
Course delivery sites Courses are delivered to your home, your workplace, military bases, Brunswick Community College (Supply), Elizabeth City State University (Elizabeth City), Fayetteville State University (Fayetteville).
Media Courses are delivered via television, videotapes, videoconferencing, computer software, World Wide Web, e-mail, print. Students and teachers interact via videoconferencing, mail, fax, e-mail. A computer is required for some courses.
Restrictions Courses are available to US students only.
Services Distance learners have access to library services at a distance.
Credit-earning options Students may earn credits through standardized exams, institutionally developed exams, portfolio assessment.
Typical costs Tuition of $20 per credit for in-state residents. Tuition of $163 per credit for out-of-state residents. *Noncredit courses:* $35–$100 per course. Financial aid is available to distance learners.
Registration Students may register by mail, fax, phone, e-mail.
Contact Dan Bain, Distance Education Facilitator, Pitt Community College, PO Drawer 7007, Highway 11, South, Greenville, NC 27835-7007. *Telephone:* 919-321-4348. *Fax:* 919-321-4404. *E-mail:* dbain@pcc.pitt.cc.nc.us. *Web site:* http://sphynx.pitt.cc.nc.us:8080/home.htm.

DEGREE & CERTIFICATE PROGRAMS

Associate Degrees

▶ *Health Information Technology (AAS)*
Restrictions This program is available to in-state students only.
Application requirements *Prior education:* high school diploma or equivalent. *Other requirements:* Pitt Community College health sciences entrance exam, high school transcript.
Completion requirements 76 credits are required.
Program contact Kay Gooding, Chairperson, Department of Health Information Technology, Pitt Community College, PO Drawer 7007, Highway 11, South, Greenville, NC 27835-7007. Phone: 919-321-4361.

▶ *Nuclear Medicine (AAS)*
Restrictions This program is available to in-state students only.
Application requirements *Prior education:* some undergraduate course work. *Other requirements:* Pitt Community College health sciences entrance exam, high school transcript.
Completion requirements 75 credits are required. *Other requirements:* clinical affiliation with approved hospital.
On-campus requirements For orientation; some testing.
Program contact Bill Clark, Chairperson, Department of Radiological Sciences, Pitt Community College, PO Drawer 7007, Highway 11, South, Greenville, NC 27835-7007. Phone: 919-321-4465.

▶ *Radiation Therapy (AAS)*
Restrictions This program is available to in-state students only.
Application requirements *Prior education:* some undergraduate course work. *Other requirements:* Pitt Community College health sciences entrance exam, high school transcript.
Completion requirements 76 credits are required.
Program contact Bill Clark, Chairperson, Department of Radiological Sciences, Pitt Community College, PO Drawer 7007, Highway 11, South, Greenville, NC 27835-7007. Phone: 919-321-4465.

▶ *Sonography (Radiological Technology) (AAS)*
Restrictions This program is available to in-state students only.
Application requirements *Prior education:* some undergraduate course work. *Other requirements:* Pitt Community College health sciences entrance exam, high school transcript.
Completion requirements 70 credits are required.
Program contact Bill Clark, Chairperson, Department of Radiological Sciences, Pitt Community College, PO Drawer 7007, Highway 11, South, Greenville, NC 27835-7007. Phone: 919-321-4465.

INDIVIDUAL COURSE SUBJECT AREAS

Undergraduate
African-American studies; business; business administration and management; computer and information sciences; computer programming; economics; health professions and related sciences; nursing

Noncredit
African-American studies; business; business administration and management; computer and information sciences; computer programming; continuing education; economics

POLYTECHNIC UNIVERSITY, BROOKLYN CAMPUS

Brooklyn, New York

Institute For Distance Learning

Polytechnic University, Brooklyn Campus, founded in 1854, is an independent-nonprofit university. It is accredited by the Middle States Association of Colleges and Schools. It first offered distance learning courses in 1985.
Course delivery sites Courses are delivered to your home, your workplace, military bases, other colleges.
Media Courses are delivered via computer software, computer conferencing.
Services Distance learners have access to library services, academic advising, tutoring, career placement assistance at a distance.
Credit-earning options Students may transfer credits from another institution. Financial aid is available to distance learners.
Contact Office of Admissions, Continuing Professional Education, Polytechnic University, Brooklyn Campus, Six Metrotech Center, Brooklyn, NY 11201-2990. *Telephone:* 718-260-3200. *Web site:* http://www.poly.edu.

INDIVIDUAL COURSE SUBJECT AREAS

Graduate
Advertising; design; economics; history; journalism; liberal arts, general studies, and humanities; philosophy and religion; political science; sociology

Noncredit
Advertising; business; business administration and management; computer and information sciences; design; economics; engineering/industrial management; English as a second language (ESL); history; journalism; liberal arts, general studies, and humanities; political science; sociology

POLYTECHNIC UNIVERSITY, WESTCHESTER GRADUATE CENTER

Hawthorne, New York

Lifelong Learning

Polytechnic University, Westchester Graduate Center is an independent-nonprofit graduate institution. It is accredited by the Middle States Association of Colleges and Schools.
Course delivery sites Courses are delivered to your home, your workplace.
Media Courses are delivered via television, videoconferencing, World Wide Web. Students and teachers interact via telephone, e-mail, Internet, World Wide Web. A computer is required for some courses.
Services Distance learners have access to library services, the campus computer network, e-mail services, academic advising, tutoring, career placement assistance at a distance.
Credit-earning options Students may earn credits through institutionally developed exams.
Typical costs Tuition of $645 per unit. *Noncredit courses:* $500 per course. Costs may vary by campus or location, specific program of study, course delivery options. Financial aid is available to distance learners.
Registration Students may register by mail, fax, phone, e-mail, World Wide Web.
Contact LaVerne Clark, Director of Executive Degree Programs, Polytechnic University, Westchester Graduate Center, 36 Saw Mill River Road, Hawthorne, NY 10532. *Telephone:* 914-323-2002. *Fax:* 914-323-2010. *E-mail:* laverne@west.poly.edu. *Web site:* http://www.poly.edu.

INDIVIDUAL COURSE SUBJECT AREAS

Graduate
Biology; computer and information sciences; computer programming; electrical engineering; industrial engineering; technical writing

PORTLAND COMMUNITY COLLEGE

Portland, Oregon

Distance Learning Department

Portland Community College, founded in 1961, is a state and locally supported two-year college. It is accredited by the Northwest Association of Schools and Colleges. It first offered distance learning courses in 1981.
Course delivery sites Courses are delivered to your home, your workplace, other colleges.
Media Courses are delivered via television, videotapes, videoconferencing, World Wide Web, e-mail. Students and teachers interact via mail, telephone, fax, e-mail.
Services Distance learners have access to library services at a distance.
Credit-earning options Students may transfer credits from another institution or may earn credits through examinations, portfolio assessment, military training, business training.
Typical costs Tuition of $35 per credit for in-state residents. Tuition of $125 per credit for out-of-state residents. Financial aid is available to distance learners.
Contact Loraine Schmitt, Credit Distance Learning Coordinator, Portland Community College, PO Box 19000, Portland, OR 97280. *Telephone:* 503-977-4481. *Fax:* 503-977-4858. *E-mail:* lschmitt@pcc.edu. *Web site:* http://www.pcc.edu/distlrn.

DEGREE & CERTIFICATE PROGRAMS

Associate Degrees
▶ *General Studies (AA)*

Undergraduate Certificates
▶ *Medical Assistant*

INDIVIDUAL COURSE SUBJECT AREAS

Undergraduate
Accounting; astronomy and astrophysics; biology; business; business administration and management; chemistry; computer and information sciences; creative writing; developmental and child psychology; economics; English composition; English language and literature; fine arts; health and physical education/fitness; history; law and legal studies; liberal arts, general studies, and humanities; mathematics; music; philosophy and religion; political science; psychology; sociology

Profiles: Portland Community College

Noncredit
Administrative and secretarial services; business administration and management; health professions and related sciences; human resources management

PORTLAND STATE UNIVERSITY

Portland, Oregon

School of Extended Studies

Portland State University, founded in 1946, is a state-supported university. It is accredited by the Northwest Association of Schools and Colleges. It first offered distance learning courses in 1907. In 1996–97, it offered 150 courses at a distance. In the fall of 1996, there was a total of 3,500 students enrolled in distance learning courses.
Course delivery sites Courses are delivered to your home, your workplace, military bases, other colleges.
Media Courses are delivered via television, videotapes, videoconferencing, audiotapes, computer software, World Wide Web, e-mail, print. Students and teachers interact via videoconferencing, mail, telephone, fax, e-mail.
Services Distance learners have access to library services, the campus computer network, e-mail services at a distance.
Credit-earning options Students may transfer credits from another institution or may earn credits through institutionally developed exams, business training.
Typical costs Tuition of $69 per quarter credit. $15 registration fee. *Noncredit courses:* $100 per course. Costs may vary by specific program of study, number of credits taken, course delivery options. Financial aid is available to distance learners enrolled full-time.
Registration Students may register by mail, fax, phone, e-mail, World Wide Web.
Contact Office of Independent Study, Portland State University, 1633 Southwest Park Avenue, Portland, OR 97207. *Telephone:* 503-725-4865. *Web site:* http://extended.portals.org.

DEGREE & CERTIFICATE PROGRAMS

Graduate Degrees

▶ *Business Administration (MBA)*
Restrictions This program is available to in-state students only.
Application requirements *Prior education:* baccalaureate degree. *Other requirements:* college transcripts, an essay or personal statement, an application fee.
On-campus requirements For periodic visits; orientation.
Program contact Katherine Novy, Director of Experimental Programs, Portland State University, School of Business Administration, 1633 Southwest Park Avenue, Portland, OR 97207. Phone: 503-725-4823.

▶ *Social Work (MSW)*
Restrictions This program is available to in-state students only.
Application requirements *Prior education:* baccalaureate degree. *Other requirements:* college transcripts, an essay or personal statement, an application fee.
On-campus requirements For periodic visits; orientation.
Program contact Katherine Novy, Director of Experimental Programs, Portland State University, School of Business Administration, 1633 Southwest Park Avenue, Portland, OR 97207. Phone: 503-725-4823.

INDIVIDUAL COURSE SUBJECT AREAS

Undergraduate
Accounting; algebra; anthropology; area, ethnic, and cultural studies; Asian languages and literatures; biology; business; business administration and management; calculus; Classical languages and literatures; computer and information sciences; creative writing; developmental and child psychology; economics; education administration; educational psychology; engineering-related technologies; engineering/industrial management; English as a second language (ESL); English composition; English language and literature; European languages and literatures; fine arts; geography; geology; history; human resources management; liberal arts, general studies, and humanities; mathematics; Middle Eastern languages and literatures; music; philosophy and religion; social psychology; social work; sociology; special education; statistics; teacher education

Graduate
Business administration and management; computer and information sciences; education administration; educational psychology; engineering-related technologies; engineering/industrial management; human resources management; social work; special education; teacher education

Noncredit
Earth science

PRAIRIE STATE COLLEGE

Chicago Heights, Illinois

Learning Resources Center

Prairie State College, founded in 1958, is a state and locally supported two-year college. It is accredited by the North Central Association of Colleges and Schools. It first offered distance learning courses in 1981. In 1996–97, it offered 39 courses at a distance. In the fall of 1996, there was a total of 215 students enrolled in distance learning courses.
Course delivery sites Courses are delivered to your home, other colleges, off-campus center(s), high schools.
Media Courses are delivered via television, videotapes, videoconferencing. Students and teachers interact via videoconferencing, mail, fax.
Services Distance learners have access to library services at a distance.
Credit-earning options Students may transfer credits from another institution or may earn credits through standardized exams, portfolio assessment, military training.
Typical costs Tuition of $51 per credit hour plus mandatory fees of $3 per credit hour for local area residents. Tuition of $141 per credit hour plus mandatory fees of $3 per credit hour for in-state residents. Tuition of $174 per credit hour plus mandatory fees of $3 per credit hour for out-of-state residents. *Noncredit courses:* $100–$150 per course. Financial aid is available to distance learners.
Registration Students may register by mail, fax, phone.
Contact Carol Cleator, Director of Admissions, Prairie State College, 202 South Halsted Street, Chicago Heights, IL 60411. *Telephone:* 708-709-3552. *Fax:* 708-755-2587.

INDIVIDUAL COURSE SUBJECT AREAS

Undergraduate
Business administration and management; design; economics; English composition; English language and literature; health professions and related sciences; history; mathematics; political science; psychology; sociology

PRATT COMMUNITY COLLEGE AND AREA VOCATIONAL SCHOOL

Pratt, Kansas

Pratt Community College and Area Vocational School, founded in 1938, is a district-supported two-year college. It is accredited by the North Central Association of Colleges and Schools. It first offered distance learning courses in 1995. In 1996–97, it offered 35 courses at a distance.
Course delivery sites Courses are delivered to your home, Emporia State University (Emporia), Fort Hays State University (Hays), Kansas Newman College (Wichita), Kansas State University (Manhattan), 5 off-campus centers in Chaparral, Coldwater, Greensburg, Haviland.
Media Courses are delivered via television, videotapes, videoconferencing. Students and teachers interact via mail, telephone, fax, interactive television.
Services Distance learners have access to library services, e-mail services, academic advising, tutoring, career placement assistance at a distance.
Credit-earning options Students may transfer credits from another institution or may earn credits through standardized exams, portfolio assessment, military training, business training.
Typical costs Tuition of $39 per credit hour. Financial aid is available to distance learners enrolled full-time.
Registration Students may register by mail, fax, phone, e-mail.
Contact Lisa Kolm, Admissions Office, Pratt Community College and Area Vocational School, 348 Northeast State Route 61, Pratt, KS 67124-8317. *Telephone:* 316-672-5641.

INDIVIDUAL COURSE SUBJECT AREAS

Undergraduate

Accounting; adult education; agricultural economics; agriculture; algebra; American (US) history; American literature; bible studies; biological and life sciences; biology; business; business administration and management; chemistry, inorganic; community services; computer and information sciences; continuing education; creative writing; criminal justice; developmental and child psychology; education; English composition; English language and literature; English literature; geography; geology; health and physical education/fitness; history; marketing; mathematics; nursing; philosophy and religion; physical sciences; psychology; sign language; Spanish language and literature; student counseling; substance abuse counseling; teacher education

Graduate

Community services; criminal justice; nursing; student counseling; teacher education

PRINCE GEORGE'S COMMUNITY COLLEGE

Largo, Maryland

Telecommunications and Weekend Programs

Prince George's Community College, founded in 1958, is a county-supported two-year college. It is accredited by the Middle States Association of Colleges and Schools. It first offered distance learning courses in 1976.
Course delivery sites Courses are delivered to your home, your workplace.
Media Courses are delivered via television, videoconferencing, World Wide Web. Students and teachers interact via telephone.
Credit-earning options Students may transfer credits from another institution or may earn credits through examinations, portfolio assessment.
Typical costs Tuition of $69 per credit for local area residents. Tuition of $132 per credit for in-state residents. Tuition of $213 per credit for out-of-state residents. Fees vary. Financial aid is available to distance learners.
Contact Linda Bruce, Program Supervisor, Prince George's Community College, 301 Largo Road, K211A, Largo, MD 20772. *Telephone:* 301-322-0792. *Fax:* 301-386-7502. *E-mail:* lb1@pgstumail.pg.cc.md.us.

DEGREE & CERTIFICATE PROGRAMS

Associate Degrees
▶ *Business Management (AA)*
▶ *General Studies (AA)*

Undergraduate Certificates
▶ *General Management*

INDIVIDUAL COURSE SUBJECT AREAS

Undergraduate

Accounting; area, ethnic, and cultural studies; astronomy and astrophysics; biology; business administration and management; computer and information sciences; developmental and child psychology; economics; English composition; English language and literature; geology; health and physical education/fitness; history; human resources management; liberal arts, general studies, and humanities; marketing; mathematics; philosophy and religion; political science; social psychology; sociology

Noncredit

Business; business administration and management; computer and information sciences; developmental and child psychology; economics; English composition; English language and literature; health and physical education/fitness; history; marketing; mathematics; philosophy and religion; political science; social psychology; sociology

PUEBLO COMMUNITY COLLEGE

Pueblo, Colorado

Pueblo Community College, founded in 1933, is a state-supported two-year college. It is accredited by the North Central Association of Colleges and Schools.
Course delivery sites Courses are delivered to your home, military bases.
Media Courses are delivered via television, videotapes, videoconferencing. Students and teachers interact via telephone.
Restrictions Courses are available to students within television transmission area only.
Services Distance learners have access to library services, academic advising, tutoring at a distance.
Credit-earning options Students may transfer credits from another institution or may earn credits through portfolio assessment, military training, business training.
Typical costs Tuition of $72.55 per credit for in-state residents. Tuition of $262 per credit for out-of-state residents. Financial aid is available to distance learners.
Contact Distance Learning Office, Pueblo Community College, 900 West Orman Avenue, Pueblo, CO 81004-1499. *Telephone:* 719-549-3343. *Fax:* 719-549-3453. *E-mail:* weber@pcc.ccoes.edu.

Profiles: Pueblo Community College

INDIVIDUAL COURSE SUBJECT AREAS

Undergraduate
Accounting; astronomy and astrophysics; biological and life sciences; business administration and management; chemistry; computer and information sciences; economics; English composition; English language and literature; European languages and literatures; foods and nutrition studies; geology; journalism; law and legal studies; mathematics; psychology; sociology; visual and performing arts

PURDUE UNIVERSITY

West Lafayette, Indiana

Distance and Media-Based Programs

Purdue University, founded in 1869, is a state-supported university. It is accredited by the North Central Association of Colleges and Schools. It first offered distance learning courses in 1965.
Course delivery sites Courses are delivered to your home, your workplace, other colleges within Indiana.
Media Courses are delivered via television, videoconferencing, radio broadcast, audioconferencing, computer software, print.
Services Distance learners have access to academic advising, career placement assistance at a distance.
Typical costs Costs vary. Contact school for information.
Contact Jenny Towler, Manager, Purdue University, 116 Stewart Center, West Lafayette, IN 47907-1586. *Telephone:* 800-359-2968. *Fax:* 765-494-0567. *E-mail:* jltowler@cea.purdue.edu.

DEGREE & CERTIFICATE PROGRAMS

Graduate Degrees

▶ *Electrical Engineering (MS)*
Program contact Dr. Leah H. Jamieson, Professor of Electrical Engineering, Purdue University, 1285 Electrical Engineering Building, West Lafayette, IN 47907-1288. Phone: 765-494-3653.

▶ *Executive Level Management (EMS)*
On-campus requirements Six 2-week sessions.
Program contact Martin Rapisardia, Director of Krannert Executive Masters, Purdue University, 1310 Krannert Center, West Lafayette, IN 47907. Phone: 765-494-7700. E-mail: rapisarm@mgmt.purdue.edu.

▶ *Industrial Engineering (MS)*
Program contact Dr. James W. Barany, Professor of Industrial Engineering, Purdue University, Grissom Hall, School of Industrial Engineering, West Lafayette, IN 47907. Phone: 765-494-5406.

▶ *Mechanical Engineering (MSME)*
Program contact Dr. Satish Ramadhyani, Professor of Mechanical Engineering, Purdue University, 1288 Mechanical Engineering Building, West Lafayette, IN 47907-1288. Phone: 765-494-5701.

INDIVIDUAL COURSE SUBJECT AREAS

Undergraduate
Health professions and related sciences; hospitality services management

Graduate
Business administration and management; engineering

Noncredit
Agriculture

QUINCY COLLEGE

Quincy, Massachusetts

Continuing Education

Quincy College, founded in 1958, is a city-supported two-year college. It is accredited by the New England Association of Schools and Colleges. It first offered distance learning courses in 1995.
Course delivery sites Courses are delivered to your home.
Media Courses are delivered via television, print.
Services Distance learners have access to academic advising, career placement assistance at a distance.
Credit-earning options Students may transfer credits from another institution or may earn credits through examinations, portfolio assessment, military training, business training. Financial aid is available to distance learners.
Contact Dean of Continuing Education, Quincy College, 34 Coddington Street, Quincy, MA 02169. *Telephone:* 617-984-1655. *Fax:* 617-984-1794.

INDIVIDUAL COURSE SUBJECT AREAS

Undergraduate
Area, ethnic, and cultural studies; biological and life sciences; biology; business; business administration and management; communications; developmental and child psychology; journalism; liberal arts, general studies, and humanities; philosophy and religion; psychology; social psychology; social sciences; sociology

REDLANDS COMMUNITY COLLEGE

El Reno, Oklahoma

Redlands Community College, founded in 1938, is a state-supported two-year college. It is accredited by the North Central Association of Colleges and Schools. It first offered distance learning courses in 1985. In 1996–97, it offered 17 courses at a distance. In the fall of 1996, there was a total of 305 students enrolled in distance learning courses.
Course delivery sites Courses are delivered to your home, your workplace.
Media Courses are delivered via television, videotapes, videoconferencing, computer software, print. Students and teachers interact via videoconferencing, mail, telephone, fax, e-mail. A computer is required for some courses.
Restrictions Telecourses are available to local area students only. Interactive television courses are available at participating sites only.
Services Distance learners have access to library services, e-mail services, academic advising at a distance.
Credit-earning options Students may transfer credits from another institution or may earn credits through standardized exams, institutionally developed exams, portfolio assessment, military training, business training.
Typical costs Tuition of $28 per credit plus mandatory fees of $22.75 per credit for in-state residents. Tuition of $28 per credit plus mandatory fees of $102.75 per credit for out-of-state residents. Costs may vary by course delivery options. Financial aid is available to distance learners.
Registration Students may register by mail, phone, World Wide Web.
Contact Tricia Hobson, Director of Admissions, Redlands Community College, 1300 South Country Club Road, El Reno, OK 73036-5304. *Telephone:* 405-262-2552. *Fax:* 405-422-1200. *Web site:* http://www.redlands.cc.ok.us.

INDIVIDUAL COURSE SUBJECT AREAS

Undergraduate
Biological and life sciences; business; business administration and management; creative writing; developmental and child psychology; economics; English composition; English language and literature; health and physical education/fitness; health professions and related sciences; history; home economics and family studies; law and legal studies; liberal arts, general studies, and humanities; mathematics; physical sciences; political science; sociology

Noncredit
Biological and life sciences; computer and information sciences; health professions and related sciences; protective services

RED ROCKS COMMUNITY COLLEGE

Lakewood, Colorado

Learning and Resource Center

Red Rocks Community College, founded in 1969, is a state-supported two-year college. It is accredited by the North Central Association of Colleges and Schools. It first offered distance learning courses in 1980. In 1996–97, it offered 55 courses at a distance.
Course delivery sites Courses are delivered to your home, your workplace, other colleges.
Media Courses are delivered via television, videoconferencing, computer software, e-mail, print. Students and teachers interact via videoconferencing, mail, telephone, fax, e-mail. A computer is required for some courses.
Services Distance learners have access to library services, academic advising, tutoring at a distance.
Credit-earning options Students may transfer credits from another institution or may earn credits through examinations, portfolio assessment, military training, business training.
Typical costs Tuition of $165 per course plus mandatory fees of $35 per course. Costs may vary by course delivery options. Financial aid is available to distance learners.
Contact Diane Hegeman, Assistant to the Vice President, Red Rocks Community College, 13300 West 6th Avenue, Box 37, Littleton, CO 80228-1255. *Telephone:* 303-914-6704. *Fax:* 303-914-6721. *E-mail:* diane@rrcc.cccoes.edu.

INDIVIDUAL COURSE SUBJECT AREAS

Undergraduate
Accounting; art history and criticism; biological and life sciences; business; business administration and management; communications; computer and information sciences; developmental and child psychology; economics; education; English as a second language (ESL); English composition; English language and literature; geography; geology; health and physical education/fitness; health professions and related sciences; history; liberal arts, general studies, and humanities; mathematics; music; philosophy and religion; political science; protective services; psychology; social psychology; social sciences; sociology; teacher education

REFORMED THEOLOGICAL SEMINARY

Maitland, Florida

External Education Department

Reformed Theological Seminary is an independent-religious graduate institution. It is accredited by the Association of Theological Schools in the United States and Canada. It first offered distance learning courses in 1991.
Course delivery sites Courses are delivered to your home, 4 off-campus centers in Atlanta (GA), Lawrence (KS), Memphis (TN), Washington (DC).
Media Courses are delivered via audiotapes. Students and teachers interact via mail.
Services Distance learners have access to library services, academic advising at a distance.
Credit-earning options Students may transfer credits from another institution.
Typical costs Tuition of $200 per credit hour. *Noncredit courses:* $80 per course.
Registration Students may register by mail.
Contact Lyn Perez, Vice President, Reformed Theological Seminary, 1015 Maitland Center Commons, Maitland, FL 32751. *Telephone:* 407-875-8388. *Fax:* 407-875-0879. *E-mail:* 74403.2474@compuserve.com. *Web site:* http://www.rts.edu.

DEGREE & CERTIFICATE PROGRAMS

Graduate certificates

▶ *Biblical Studies*
In the fall of 1996 there were 4 students enrolled in this program. In 1995–96, 1 certificate was earned at a distance through this program.
Application requirements *Prior education:* baccalaureate degree. *Other requirements:* college transcripts, letter(s) of recommendation, an application fee of $20.
Completion requirements 32 hours are required. 32 hours must be completed through the institution.

▶ *Church History*
Application requirements *Prior education:* baccalaureate degree. *Other requirements:* college transcripts, letter(s) of recommendation, an application fee of $20.
Completion requirements 32 hours are required. 32 hours must be completed through the institution.

▶ *Missions*
Application requirements *Prior education:* baccalaureate degree. *Other requirements:* college transcripts, letter(s) of recommendation, an application fee of $20.
Completion requirements 32 hours are required. 32 hours must be completed through the institution.

▶ *Theological Studies*
In the fall of 1996 there were 11 students enrolled in this program. In 1995–96, 1 certificate was earned at a distance through this program.
Application requirements *Prior education:* baccalaureate degree. *Other requirements:* college transcripts, letter(s) of recommendation, an application fee of $20.
Completion requirements 32 hours are required. 30 hours must be completed through the institution.

INDIVIDUAL COURSE SUBJECT AREAS

Graduate
Theological studies

Profiles: Reformed Theological Seminary

Noncredit
Theological studies

REGENT UNIVERSITY

Virginia Beach, Virginia

Regent University, founded in 1977, is an independent-nonprofit graduate institution. It is accredited by the Southern Association of Colleges and Schools. It first offered distance learning courses in 1991. In 1996–97, it offered 24 courses at a distance. In the fall of 1996, there was a total of 125 students enrolled in distance learning courses.
Course delivery sites Courses are delivered to your home, your workplace, military bases.
Media Courses are delivered via videotapes, audiotapes, World Wide Web, e-mail, print. Students and teachers interact via telephone, e-mail. A computer is required for all courses.
Services Distance learners have access to library services, academic advising, tutoring, career placement assistance at a distance.
Credit-earning options Students may transfer credits from another institution or may earn credits through military training.
Typical costs Tuition of $315 per credit. Financial aid is available to distance learners.
Registration Students may register by World Wide Web.
Contact Mike Cray, Enrollment Manager - School of Business, Regent University, 1000 Regent University Drive, Virginia Beach, VA 23464. Telephone: 804-579-4096. Fax: 804-579-4369. E-mail: michcra@beacon.regent.edu.

DEGREE & CERTIFICATE PROGRAMS

Graduate Degrees
▶ *Business Administration (MBA)*
In the fall of 1996 there were 120 students enrolled in this program. In 1995–96, 30 degrees were earned at a distance through this program.
Application requirements *Prior education:* baccalaureate degree. *Other requirements:* college transcripts, letter(s) of recommendation, an application fee of $45.
Completion requirements 39 credits are required. *Maximum time for completion:* five years.
On-campus requirements Two 1-week sessions.

INDIVIDUAL COURSE SUBJECT AREAS

Graduate
Accounting; business; business administration and management; human resources management

REGIS UNIVERSITY

Denver, Colorado

School for Professional Studies–Distance Learning

Regis University, founded in 1877, is an independent-religious Roman Catholic (Jesuit) comprehensive institution. It is accredited by the North Central Association of Colleges and Schools. It first offered distance learning courses in 1992. In 1996–97, it offered 42 courses at a distance. In the fall of 1996, there was a total of 640 students enrolled in distance learning courses.
Course delivery sites Courses are delivered to your home, your workplace, military bases, other colleges.
Media Courses are delivered via television, videotapes, audiotapes, computer software, World Wide Web, e-mail, print. Students and teachers interact via mail, telephone, fax, e-mail. A computer is required for some courses.
Services Distance learners have access to library services, academic advising at a distance.
Credit-earning options Students may transfer credits from another institution or may earn credits through standardized exams, institutionally developed exams, portfolio assessment, military training, business training.
Typical costs Tuition of $203 per credit hour for in-state residents. Tuition of $194 per credit hour for out-of-state residents. Graduate tuition ranges from $250 to $335 per credit hour depending on program. Fees vary. Costs may vary by campus or location, specific program of study. Financial aid is available to distance learners.
Registration Students may register by mail, fax, phone, e-mail, World Wide Web.
Contact J. Stephen Jacobs, Assistant Dean, Regis University, 3333 Regis Boulevard, Englewood, CO 80111. Telephone: 303-458-3560. Fax: 303-694-5532. E-mail: spsdean@regis.edu. Web site: http://www.regis.edu.

DEGREE & CERTIFICATE PROGRAMS

Baccalaureate Degrees
▶ *Business Administration (BS)*
In the fall of 1996 there were 640 students enrolled in this program.
Application requirements *Prior education:* some undergraduate course work. *Other requirements:* college transcripts, an essay or personal statement, letter(s) of recommendation, an application fee of $75, 3 years work experience.
Completion requirements 128 credit hours are required. 30 credit hours must be completed through the institution. This is a degree completion program. *Maximum time for completion:* seven years.
Program contact Greg Grauberger, Program Representative, Regis University, 7600 East Orchard Road, Suite 100N, Englewood, CO 80111. Phone: 303-458-4919. Fax: 303-694-1554.

Graduate Degrees
▶ *Business Administration (EMBA)*
Application requirements *Prior education:* baccalaureate degree. *Other requirements:* GMAT (waiver is available under some conditions), college transcripts, an essay or personal statement, letter(s) of recommendation, an application fee of $75, 2 years work experience required.
Completion requirements 30 credit hours are required. 6 credit hours must be completed through the institution. *Maximum time for completion:* six years.
Program contact Erin Zimmer, Program Coordinator, Graduate Distance Learning, Regis University, 7600 East Orchard Road, Suite 100N, Englewood, CO 80111. Phone: 800-388-2366, Ext. 5448. Fax: 303-694-1554.

INDIVIDUAL COURSE SUBJECT AREAS

Undergraduate
Accounting; administrative and secretarial services; business; business administration and management; computer and information sciences; economics; human resources management; liberal arts, general studies, and humanities; philosophy and religion; sociology

Graduate
Ethics; finance; health professions and related sciences; international business; marketing

REND LAKE COLLEGE

Ina, Illinois

Learning Resource Center

Rend Lake College, founded in 1967, is a state-supported two-year college. It is accredited by the North Central Association of Colleges and Schools. It first offered distance learning courses in 1995. In 1996–97, it offered 14 courses at a distance. In the fall of 1996, there was a total of 45 students enrolled in distance learning courses.
Course delivery sites Courses are delivered to your home, 5 off-campus centers in Benton, McLeansboro, Mt. Vernon, Pinckneyville, Sesser.
Media Courses are delivered via videotapes, videoconferencing, print. Students and teachers interact via videoconferencing, telephone, fax.
Services Distance learners have access to academic advising, career placement assistance at a distance.
Credit-earning options Students may transfer credits from another institution or may earn credits through examinations.
Typical costs Tuition of $35 per credit hour for local area residents. Tuition of $87.86 per credit hour for in-state residents. Tuition of $87.86 per credit hour for out-of-state residents. *Noncredit courses:* $30 per course. Financial aid is available to distance learners.
Registration Students may register by mail, fax.
Contact Walt Montgomery, Alternative and Optional Education Program Director, Rend Lake College, 468 North Ken Gray Parkway, Ina, IL 62846. *Telephone:* 618-437-5321, Ext. 366. *Fax:* 618-437-5677. *E-mail:* montgomery@rlc.cc.il.us. *Web site:* http://www.rlc.cc.il.us.

INDIVIDUAL COURSE SUBJECT AREAS

Undergraduate
Agriculture; botany; computer and information sciences; English language and literature; fine arts; journalism; microbiology; zoology

Graduate
Accounting; business; business administration and management; human resources management

RENSSELAER POLYTECHNIC INSTITUTE

Troy, New York

The Office for Continuing and Distance Education

Rensselaer Polytechnic Institute, founded in 1824, is an independent-nonprofit university. It is accredited by the Middle States Association of Colleges and Schools. It first offered distance learning courses in 1987. In 1996–97, it offered 20 courses at a distance. In the fall of 1996, there was a total of 900 students enrolled in distance learning courses.
Course delivery sites Courses are delivered to your home, your workplace, military bases, other colleges.
Media Courses are delivered via television, videotapes, videoconferencing, computer software, World Wide Web, e-mail, print. Students and teachers interact via videoconferencing, mail, telephone, fax, e-mail. A computer is required for some courses.
Restrictions Students must be members of corporate partnerships.
Services Distance learners have access to library services, the campus computer network, e-mail services, academic advising, career placement assistance at a distance.
Credit-earning options Students may transfer credits from another institution.

Profiles: The Richard Stockton College of New Jersey

Typical costs Tuition of $570 per credit hour. Students pay a $35 application fee and a $25 transcript fee. *Noncredit courses:* $500 per course. Costs may vary by number of credits taken.
Registration Students may register by mail, fax, phone, e-mail.
Contact Coordinator of Student Services, Rensselaer Polytechnic Institute, CII, Suite 4011, Troy, NY 12180. *Telephone:* 518-276-7787. *Fax:* 518-276-8026. *Web site:* http://rsvp.rpi.edu/.

DEGREE & CERTIFICATE PROGRAMS

Graduate Degrees

▶ *Computer Science, Engineering Science, Industrial and Management Engineering, Management of Technology, Manufacturing Systems Engineering, Mechanical Engineering, Microelectronics Manufacturing, Service Systems, Technical Communications (MS)*
Application requirements *Prior education:* baccalaureate degree. *Other requirements:* college transcripts, an application fee of $35.
Completion requirements 30 credit hours are required. 6 credit hours must be completed through the institution.

▶ *Management and Technology (MS, MBA)*
Application requirements *Prior education:* baccalaureate degree. *Other requirements:* college transcripts, letter(s) of recommendation, an application fee of $35.
Completion requirements 30 credit hours are required. 6 credit hours must be completed through the institution.

Graduate certificates

▶ *Information Science, Management and Technology, Manufacturing Systems Engineering, Mechanical Engineering, Microelectronics Manufacturing, Reliability, Service Systems, Technical Communications*
Application requirements *Prior education:* baccalaureate degree. *Other requirements:* college transcripts, letter(s) of recommendation, an application fee of $35.
Completion requirements 30 credit hours are required. 6 credit hours must be completed through the institution.

INDIVIDUAL COURSE SUBJECT AREAS

Graduate
Accounting; business administration and management; communications; computer and information sciences; electrical engineering; engineering/industrial management; human resources management; industrial engineering; mechanical engineering

Noncredit
Accounting; communications; computer and information sciences

See full description on page 458.

THE RICHARD STOCKTON COLLEGE OF NEW JERSEY

Pomona, New Jersey

Office of Distance Education

The Richard Stockton College of New Jersey, founded in 1971, is a state-supported comprehensive institution. It is accredited by the Middle States Association of Colleges and Schools. It first offered distance

Profiles: The Richard Stockton College of New Jersey

learning courses in 1996. In 1996–97, it offered 39 courses at a distance. In the fall of 1996, there was a total of 300 students enrolled in distance learning courses.

Course delivery sites Courses are delivered to your home, your workplace, Cumberland County College (Vineland), Ocean County College (Toms River), 1 off-campus center.

Media Courses are delivered via television, videotapes, videoconferencing, World Wide Web. Students and teachers interact via videoconferencing, mail, telephone, fax, e-mail. A computer is required for some courses.

Restrictions Testing is, for the most part, completed on-campus.

Services Distance learners have access to library services, the campus computer network, e-mail services at a distance.

Credit-earning options Students may transfer credits from another institution.

Typical costs Tuition of $328 per course plus mandatory fees of $156 per course for in-state residents. Tuition of $528 per course plus mandatory fees of $156 per course for out-of-state residents. Financial aid is available to distance learners.

Registration Students may register by mail, fax.

Contact Carol Ferguson, Coordinator of Distance Education, The Richard Stockton College of New Jersey, Office of General Studies, Jim Leeds Road, Pomona, NJ 08240. *Telephone:* 609-652-4580. *Fax:* 609-652-4958. *E-mail:* fergusoc@pollux.stockton.edu. *Web site:* http://loki.stockton.edu/~fergusoc/dist.html.

INDIVIDUAL COURSE SUBJECT AREAS

Undergraduate
Area, ethnic, and cultural studies; Asian languages and literatures; business; business administration and management; conservation and natural resources; English composition; English language and literature; European languages and literatures; fine arts; geology; health professions and related sciences; liberal arts, general studies, and humanities; mathematics; physical sciences; psychology; social sciences; sociology; visual and performing arts

Noncredit
Area, ethnic, and cultural studies; Asian languages and literatures; business; computer and information sciences; education; English as a second language (ESL); English language and literature; European languages and literatures; home economics and family studies; liberal arts, general studies, and humanities; philosophy and religion; teacher education

RICHLAND COMMUNITY COLLEGE

Decatur, Illinois

Lifelong Learning Division

Richland Community College, founded in 1971, is a district-supported two-year college. It is accredited by the North Central Association of Colleges and Schools. It first offered distance learning courses in 1994. In 1996–97, it offered 14 courses at a distance. In the fall of 1996, there was a total of 85 students enrolled in distance learning courses.

Course delivery sites Courses are delivered to Danville Area Community College (Danville), Lake Land College (Mattoon), Parkland College (Champaign), 5 off-campus centers in Clinton, Illiopolis, Macon, Mount Zion, Moweaqua.

Media Courses are delivered via television, videoconferencing, audioconferencing. Students and teachers interact via videoconferencing, audioconferencing.

Services Distance learners have access to library services, academic advising at a distance.

Credit-earning options Students may transfer credits from another institution or may earn credits through examinations, portfolio assessment.

Typical costs Tuition of $39.50 per credit for in-state residents. Tuition of $156.56 per credit for out-of-state residents. *Noncredit courses:* $25–$65 per course. Costs may vary by number of credits taken. Financial aid is available to distance learners.

Registration Students may register by mail, fax, phone, e-mail, World Wide Web.

Contact Cathy Sebok, Extension Coordinator, Richland Community College, One College Park, Decatur, IL 62521. *Telephone:* 217-875-7200, Ext. 269. *Fax:* 217-875-6964. *E-mail:* csebok@richland.cc.il.us.

INDIVIDUAL COURSE SUBJECT AREAS

Undergraduate
Accounting; algebra; art history and criticism; creative writing; developmental and child psychology; economics; English composition; English language and literature; European history; history; liberal arts, general studies, and humanities; social psychology; sociology

Noncredit
European languages and literatures

RIO SALADO COLLEGE

Tempe, Arizona

Rio Salado College, founded in 1978, is a state and locally supported two-year college. It is accredited by the North Central Association of Colleges and Schools. It first offered distance learning courses in 1979. In 1996–97, it offered 132 courses at a distance.

Course delivery sites Courses are delivered to your home, your workplace, military bases, 3 off-campus centers in Glendale, Mesa, Phoenix.

Media Courses are delivered via television, videotapes, videoconferencing, audiotapes, audioconferencing, computer software, World Wide Web, e-mail, print. Students and teachers interact via audioconferencing, mail, telephone, fax, e-mail, in-person meetings. A computer is required for some courses.

Services Distance learners have access to library services, the campus computer network, e-mail services, academic advising, career placement assistance at a distance.

Credit-earning options Students may earn credits through standardized exams, institutionally developed exams, military training, business training, DANTES.

Typical costs Tuition of $37 per credit hour plus mandatory fees of $5 per semester for local area residents. Tuition of $62 per credit hour plus mandatory fees of $5 per semester for in-state residents. Tuition of $62 per credit hour plus mandatory fees of $5 per semester for out-of-state residents. Financial aid is available to distance learners enrolled part-time.

Registration Students may register by mail, fax, phone, World Wide Web.

Contact Student Services, Rio Salado College, 2323 West 14th Street, Tempe, AZ 85281. *Telephone:* 602-717-8540. *Web site:* http://www.rio.maricopa.edu.

Special note

With Rio's Flex Start schedule, students have the opportunity to enroll in and begin classes 26 times throughout the year. With few exceptions, classes begin every other week.

In most cases, students have 13 weeks to complete the course. They may work ahead and complete the course in less time than required. A course calendar provides the specific dates for submitting assignments and taking exams.

Credit classes offered through Flex Start include academic subjects such as accounting, business, English, math, computers, and Spanish. Several hundred course sections in 29 different subjects are now offered every other week through Flex Start.
Delivery modes include print-based, mixed media (audiocassette and/or videocassette, teleconference, computer), and Internet.
As with all distance learning classes, in-person testing is required for the midterm and final exams. For out-of-country or out-of-state students, the College will work with a proctor for the in-person testing.
More information is available by visiting Rio's Web site at http://www.rio.maricopa.edu/ or by calling the College's Student Services Department at 602-517-8540.

DEGREE & CERTIFICATE PROGRAMS

Associate Degrees
▶ *General Studies (AA)*
Application requirements *Prior education:* none required.
Completion requirements 60 credit hours are required.

INDIVIDUAL COURSE SUBJECT AREAS

Undergraduate
Accounting; anthropology; astronomy and astrophysics; biology; business; business administration and management; chemistry; communications; computer and information sciences; counseling psychology; drama and theater; economics; education; English language and literature; foods and nutrition studies; geography; geology; health professions and related sciences; history; home economics and family studies; liberal arts, general studies, and humanities; mathematics; philosophy and religion; political science; psychology; sociology; Spanish language and literature

See full description on page 460.

RIVERLAND COMMUNITY COLLEGE

Austin, Minnesota

Riverland Community College, founded in 1940, is a state-supported two-year college. It is accredited by the North Central Association of Colleges and Schools. It first offered distance learning courses in 1978. In 1996–97, it offered 26 courses at a distance. In the fall of 1996, there was a total of 210 students enrolled in distance learning courses.
Course delivery sites Courses are delivered to Rochester Community and Technical College (Rochester), 5 off-campus centers in Albert Lea, Cleveland, Owatonna, St. Clair, St. Peter.
Media Courses are delivered via television, videotapes, audiotapes. Students and teachers interact via videoconferencing, mail, telephone, fax, e-mail.
Restrictions Programs are available to local area students only.
Services Distance learners have access to library services, e-mail services, limited testing and advising at a distance.
Credit-earning options Students may transfer credits from another institution or may earn credits through examinations.
Typical costs Tuition of $41.60 per credit plus mandatory fees of $3.25 per credit for in-state residents. Tuition of $83.20 per credit plus mandatory fees of $3.25 per credit for out-of-state residents. Financial aid is available to distance learners.
Registration Students may register by mail, fax, phone.
Contact Carolyn Meier, ITV Coordinator, Riverland Community College, 1600 8th Avenue, NW, Austin, MN 55912. *Telephone:* 507-433-0534. *Fax:* 507-433-0515. *E-mail:* meierca@au.cc.mn.us.

INDIVIDUAL COURSE SUBJECT AREAS

Undergraduate
American (US) history; developmental and child psychology; English composition; European languages and literatures; home economics and family studies; information sciences and systems; social psychology; sociology

Noncredit
Business administration and management; law and legal studies

RIVERSIDE COMMUNITY COLLEGE

Riverside, California

Instructional Television

Riverside Community College, founded in 1916, is a state and locally supported two-year college. It is accredited by the Western Association of Schools and Colleges, Inc.
Course delivery sites Courses are delivered to your home.
Media Courses are delivered via television, videotapes, videoconferencing, audiotapes, print.
Restrictions Programs are available to local area students only.
Credit-earning options Students may transfer credits from another institution. Financial aid is available to distance learners.
Contact Telecourse Coordinator, Riverside Community College, 4800 Magnolia Avenue, Riverside, CA 92506. *Telephone:* 909-222-8309. *Fax:* 909-222-8036.

INDIVIDUAL COURSE SUBJECT AREAS

Undergraduate
Astronomy and astrophysics; business administration and management; Classical languages and literatures; economics; history; home economics and family studies; law and legal studies; mathematics; political science; social psychology; sociology; teacher education

ROCHESTER INSTITUTE OF TECHNOLOGY

Rochester, New York

Educational Technology Center

Rochester Institute of Technology, founded in 1829, is an independent-nonprofit comprehensive institution. It is accredited by the Middle States Association of Colleges and Schools. It first offered distance learning courses in 1980. In 1996–97, it offered 140 courses at a distance. In the fall of 1996, there was a total of 900 students enrolled in distance learning courses.
Course delivery sites Courses are delivered to your home, your workplace, Broome Community College (Binghamton), Cayuga County Community College (Auburn), Corning Community College (Corning), Delaware Technical & Community College, Terry Campus (Dover, DE), Jamestown Community College (Jamestown), Onondaga Community College (Syracuse), Tompkins Cortland Community College (Dryden), corporate contract sites.

Profiles: Rochester Institute of Technology

Media Courses are delivered via television, videotapes, videoconferencing, audiotapes, audioconferencing, computer software, World Wide Web, e-mail, print. Students and teachers interact via videoconferencing, audioconferencing, mail, telephone, fax, e-mail. A computer is required for all courses.

Services Distance learners have access to library services, the campus computer network, e-mail services, academic advising, career placement assistance at a distance.

Credit-earning options Students may transfer credits from another institution or may earn credits through examinations, portfolio assessment, military training, business training.

Typical costs *Undergraduate:* Tuition of $231 per credit hour. *Graduate:* Tuition of $253 per credit hour. Financial aid is available to distance learners.

Registration Students may register by mail, fax, phone, e-mail, World Wide Web.

Contact Distance Learning, Rochester Institute of Technology, 91 Lomb Memorial Drive, Rochester, NY 14623. *Telephone:* 800-CALL-RIT. *Fax:* 716-475-5077. *E-mail:* disted@rit.edu. *Web site:* http://www.rit.edu.

DEGREE & CERTIFICATE PROGRAMS

Baccalaureate Degrees

▶*Applied Arts and Science (BS)*
Application requirements *Prior education:* some undergraduate course work. *Other requirements:* high school transcript, college transcripts, an essay or personal statement, an application fee of $40.
Completion requirements 180 credit hours are required. 45 credit hours must be completed through the institution.
Program contact Joyce D'Ortenzio, Advisor, Rochester Institute of Technology, Center for Multidisciplinary Studies, 31 Lomb Memorial Drive, Rochester, NY 14623. Phone: 800-CALL-RIT. Fax: 716-475-6292. E-mail: jmdcad@rit.edu.

▶*Electrical/Mechanical Engineering Technology (BS)*
Restrictions Program is available to students at sites around the United States only. Students must be located near one of our community colleges or corporate extension sites.
Application requirements *Prior education:* associate degree. *Other requirements:* high school transcript, college transcripts, an essay or personal statement, an application fee of $40.
Completion requirements 193 credit hours are required. 45 credit hours must be completed through the institution.
Program contact James Scudder, Program Director/Advisor, Rochester Institute of Technology, RIT Engineering Technology, 78 Lomb Memorial Drive, Rochester, NY 14623. Phone: 716-475-2055. Fax: 716-475-5077. E-mail: jfsite@rit.edu.

▶*Environmental Management (BS)*
Application requirements *Prior education:* high school diploma or equivalent. *Other requirements:* high school transcript, college transcripts, an essay or personal statement, an application fee of $40.
Completion requirements 191 credits are required. 45 credits must be completed through the institution.
Program contact John Morelli, Program Chair, Rochester Institute of Technology, Center for Multidisciplinary Studies, 31 Lomb Memorial Drive, Rochester, NY 14623. Phone: 800-CALL-RIT. Fax: 716-475-5077. E-mail: ljrcad@rit.edu.

Graduate Degrees

▶*Health Systems Administration (MS)*
Application requirements *Prior education:* baccalaureate degree. *Other requirements:* college transcripts, an essay or personal statement, letter(s) of recommendation, an application fee of $40.
Completion requirements 57 credit hours are required. 36 credit hours must be completed through the institution. *Maximum time for completion:* 21 months.
On-campus requirements Three 1-week sessions.

Program contact William Wallence, Program Chair, Rochester Institute of Technology, Multidisciplinary Studies, 2162 Eastman Building, 31 Lomb Memorial Drive, Rochester, NY 14623. Phone: 800-CALL-RIT. Fax: 716-475-5077. E-mail: wwwcad@rit.edu.

▶*Information Technology (MS)*
Application requirements *Prior education:* baccalaureate degree. *Other requirements:* high school transcript, college transcripts, an essay or personal statement, letter(s) of recommendation, an application fee of $40.
Completion requirements 48 credit hours are required. 36 credit hours must be completed through the institution.
Program contact Rayno Niemi, Program Coordinator, Rochester Institute of Technology, Department of Information Technology, 99 Lomb Memorial Drive, Rochester, NY 14623. Phone: 800-CALL-RIT. Fax: 716-475-5077. E-mail: rdn@cs.rit.edu.

▶*Software Development and Management (MS)*
Application requirements *Prior education:* baccalaureate degree. *Other requirements:* high school transcript, college transcripts, an essay or personal statement, letter(s) of recommendation, an application fee of $40.
Completion requirements 48 credit hours are required. 36 credit hours must be completed through the institution.
Program contact Rayno Niemi, Program Coordinator, Rochester Institute of Technology, Department of Information Technology, 99 Lomb Memorial Drive, Rochester, NY 14623. Phone: 800-CALL-RIT. Fax: 716-475-5077. E-mail: rdn@cs.rit.edu.

Undergraduate Certificates

▶*Basic Quality Management*
Application requirements *Prior education:* high school diploma or equivalent. *Other requirements:* high school transcript, college transcripts, an essay or personal statement, an application fee of $40.
Completion requirements 12 credits are required. 12 credits must be completed through the institution.
Program contact Daniel Smialek, Program Chair, Rochester Institute of Technology, Center for Multidisciplinary Studies, 31 Lomb Memorial Drive, Rochester, NY 14623. Phone: 800-CALL-RIT. Fax: 716-475-5077.

▶*Data Communications*
Application requirements *Prior education:* high school diploma or equivalent. *Other requirements:* high school transcript, an essay or personal statement, an application fee of $40.
Completion requirements 12 credit hours are required. 12 credit hours must be completed through the institution.
Program contact Mark Indelicato, Program Chair, Rochester Institute of Technology, Telecommunications Engineering Technology, 78 Lomb Memorial Drive, Rochester, NY 14623. Phone: 800-CALL-RIT. Fax: 716-475-5077. E-mail: mjiiee@rit.edu.

▶*Emergency Management*
Application requirements *Prior education:* high school diploma or equivalent. *Other requirements:* high school transcript, an essay or personal statement, an application fee of $40.
Completion requirements 20 credit hours are required. 20 credit hours must be completed through the institution.
Program contact Linda Rummel, Program Chair, Rochester Institute of Technology, Center for Multidisciplinary Studies, 31 Lomb Memorial Drive, Rochester, NY 14623. Phone: 800-CALL-RIT. Fax: 716-475-5077.

▶*Environmental Management and Technology*
Application requirements *Prior education:* some undergraduate course work. *Other requirements:* high school transcript, college transcripts, an essay or personal statement, an application fee of $40.
Completion requirements 24 credits are required. 24 credits must be completed through the institution.

Program contact John Morelli, Program Chair, Rochester Institute of Technology, Center for Multidisciplinary Studies, 31 Lomb Memorial Drive, Rochester, NY 14623. Phone: 800-CALL-RIT. Fax: 716-475-5077. E-mail: ljrcad@rit.edu.

▶ *Environmental Management Science*
Application requirements *Prior education:* some undergraduate course work. *Other requirements:* high school transcript, college transcripts, an essay or personal statement, an application fee of $40.
Completion requirements 12 credits are required. 12 credits must be completed through the institution.
Program contact John Morelli, Program Chair, Rochester Institute of Technology, Center for Multidisciplinary Studies, 31 Lomb Memorial Drive, Rochester, NY 14623. Phone: 800-CALL-RIT. Fax: 716-475-5077. E-mail: ljrcad@rit.edu.

▶ *Health Systems Administration*
Application requirements *Prior education:* high school diploma or equivalent. *Other requirements:* high school transcript, an essay or personal statement, an application fee of $40.
Completion requirements 24 credit hours are required. 24 credit hours must be completed through the institution.
Program contact William Wallence, Program Chair, Rochester Institute of Technology, Multidisciplinary Studies, 2162 Eastman Building, 31 Lomb Memorial Drive, Rochester, NY 14623. Phone: 800-CALL-RIT. Fax: 716-475-5077. E-mail: wwwcad@rit.edu.

▶ *Telecommunications Network Management*
Application requirements *Prior education:* high school diploma or equivalent. *Other requirements:* high school transcript, an essay or personal statement, letter(s) of recommendation, an application fee of $40, courses from data communications and voice communications.
Completion requirements 16 credit hours are required. 16 credit hours must be completed through the institution.
Program contact Mark Indelicato, Program Chair, Rochester Institute of Technology, Telecommunications Engineering Technology, 78 Lomb Memorial Drive, Rochester, NY 14623. Phone: 800-CALL-RIT. Fax: 716-475-5077. E-mail: mjiiee@rit.edu.

▶ *Voice Communications*
Application requirements *Prior education:* high school diploma or equivalent. *Other requirements:* high school transcript, an essay or personal statement, an application fee of $40.
Completion requirements 12 credit hours are required. 12 credit hours must be completed through the institution.
Program contact Mark Indelicato, Program Chair, Rochester Institute of Technology, Telecommunications Engineering Technology, 78 Lomb Memorial Drive, Rochester, NY 14623. Phone: 800-CALL-RIT. Fax: 716-475-5077. E-mail: mjiiee@rit.edu.

Graduate certificates

▶ *Integrated Health Systems, Health Systems Finance*
Application requirements *Prior education:* baccalaureate degree. *Other requirements:* college transcripts, an essay or personal statement, letter(s) of recommendation, an application fee of $40.
Completion requirements 16 credit hours are required. 16 credit hours must be completed through the institution.
Program contact William Wallence, Program Chair, Rochester Institute of Technology, Multidisciplinary Studies, 2162 Eastman Building, 31 Lomb Memorial Drive, Rochester, NY 14623. Phone: 800-CALL-RIT. Fax: 716-475-5077. E-mail: wwwcad@rit.edu.

▶ *Statistical Quality*
Application requirements *Prior education:* baccalaureate degree. *Other requirements:* college transcripts, an essay or personal statement, letter(s) of recommendation, an application fee of $40.
Completion requirements 18 credit hours are required. 18 credit hours must be completed through the institution.
Program contact Patrick McNenny, Program Coordinator, Rochester Institute of Technology, Lomb Memorial Drive, 2532 Carey, Rochester, NY 14623. Phone: 800-CALL-RIT. Fax: 716-475-5077. E-mail: pjm2207@rit.edu.

INDIVIDUAL COURSE SUBJECT AREAS

Undergraduate
Accounting; area, ethnic, and cultural studies; business; business administration and management; chemistry; communications; computer and information sciences; conservation and natural resources; economics; electrical engineering; engineering; engineering mechanics; engineering-related technologies; engineering/industrial management; English composition; English language and literature; environmental science; geology; health and physical education/fitness; health professions and related sciences; history; information sciences and systems; liberal arts, general studies, and humanities; mathematics; mechanical engineering; philosophy and religion; physical sciences; political science; psychology; public health; social sciences; sociology; telecommunications

Graduate
Computer and information sciences; health professions and related sciences; information sciences and systems; public health; telecommunications

See full description on page 462.

ROCKLAND COMMUNITY COLLEGE

Suffern, New York

Telecourse and Distance Learning Department

Rockland Community College, founded in 1959, is a state and locally supported two-year college. It is accredited by the Middle States Association of Colleges and Schools. It first offered distance learning courses in 1985. In 1996–97, it offered 50 courses at a distance. In the fall of 1996, there was a total of 1,000 students enrolled in distance learning courses.

Course delivery sites Courses are delivered to your home, military bases, county prison.
Media Courses are delivered via television, videotapes, e-mail, print. Students and teachers interact via mail, telephone, e-mail.
Restrictions ESL students may not register.
Services Distance learners have access to academic advising, tutoring, career placement assistance at a distance.
Credit-earning options Students may transfer credits from another institution or may earn credits through standardized exams, institutionally developed exams.
Typical costs Tuition of $94.50 per credit plus mandatory fees of $20 per course for in-state residents. Tuition of $184.50 per credit plus mandatory fees of $20 per course for out-of-state residents. Financial aid is available to distance learners enrolled full-time or part-time.
Registration Students may register by mail, phone.
Contact Lynne Koplik, Telecourse/Distance Learning Supervisor, Rockland Community College, 145 College Road, Room 4104, Suffern, NY 10901. *Telephone:* 914-574-4780. *Fax:* 914-356-5811.

DEGREE & CERTIFICATE PROGRAMS

Associate Degrees

▶ *Liberal Arts and Sciences (AA)*
In the fall of 1996 there were 1,000 students enrolled in this program.
Application requirements *Prior education:* none required. *Other requirements:* an application fee of $25, English and math placement exams.
Completion requirements 63 credits are required.

Profiles: Rockland Community College

INDIVIDUAL COURSE SUBJECT AREAS

Undergraduate

Abnormal psychology; accounting; area, ethnic, and cultural studies; art history and criticism; astronomy and astrophysics; botany; business; business administration and management; computer and information sciences; developmental and child psychology; economics; English composition; English language and literature; fine arts; geography; health and physical education/fitness; history; liberal arts, general studies, and humanities; mathematics; nursing; philosophy and religion; political science; sociology

ROGERS UNIVERSITY

Claremore, Oklahoma

Rogers University, founded in 1909, is a state-supported two-year college. It is accredited by the North Central Association of Colleges and Schools. It first offered distance learning courses in 1989. In 1996–97, it offered 44 courses at a distance. In the fall of 1996, there was a total of 1,068 students enrolled in distance learning courses.
Course delivery sites Courses are delivered to your home, your workplace, military bases, Oklahoma State University (Stillwater), University of Oklahoma (Norman), 2 off-campus centers in Bartlesville, Pryor, any location with Internet access.
Media Courses are delivered via television, videotapes, World Wide Web, e-mail. Students and teachers interact via mail, telephone, fax, e-mail. A computer is required for some courses.
Restrictions Courses are only for high school concurrent enrollment.
Services Distance learners have access to library services, the campus computer network, e-mail services, academic advising, tutoring, career placement assistance, administrative services at a distance.
Credit-earning options Students may transfer credits from another institution or may earn credits through examinations, military training.
Typical costs Tuition of $29.50 per credit hour plus mandatory fees of $15 per course. On-line courses, in-state: $265 per course without video component, $315 with video. Out-of-state: $445 without a video component and $495 with video. All on-line students pay $40 on-line course fee per course. Financial aid is available to distance learners enrolled full-time or part-time.
Registration Students may register by mail, phone, e-mail, World Wide Web.
Contact Mary Sirkel, Distance Learning Counselor, Rogers University, 1701 West Will Rogers, Claremore, OK 74017. *Telephone:* 918-343-7548. *Fax:* 918-343-7546. *E-mail:* msirkel@rogersu.edu. *Web site:* http://www.rogersu.edu.

DEGREE & CERTIFICATE PROGRAMS

Associate Degrees

▶ *Business Administration (AA)*
In the fall of 1996 there were 208 students enrolled in this program.
Application requirements *Prior education:* high school diploma or equivalent. *Other requirements:* ACT, high school transcript, college transcripts.
Completion requirements 60–62 semester hours are required. Last 12 hours of program must be completed through the institution.

▶ *Computer Science (AA)*
In the fall of 1996 there were 109 students enrolled in this program. In 1995–96, 1 degree was earned at a distance through this program.
Application requirements *Prior education:* high school diploma or equivalent. *Other requirements:* ACT, high school transcript, college transcripts.

Completion requirements 60 semester hours are required. Last 12 hours of program must be completed through the institution.

▶ *Humanities (AA)*
Application requirements *Prior education:* high school diploma or equivalent. *Other requirements:* ACT, high school transcript, college transcripts.
Completion requirements 60 semester hours are required.

▶ *Liberal Arts (AA)*
In the fall of 1996 there were 43 students enrolled in this program.
Application requirements *Prior education:* high school diploma or equivalent. *Other requirements:* ACT, high school transcript, college transcripts.
Completion requirements 60 semester hours are required. Last 12 hours of program must be completed through the institution.

INDIVIDUAL COURSE SUBJECT AREAS

Undergraduate

Accounting; agriculture; astronomy and astrophysics; biological and life sciences; biology; business; business administration and management; Classical languages and literatures; computer and information sciences; creative writing; developmental and child psychology; economics; English composition; history; liberal arts, general studies, and humanities; mathematics; nursing; physical sciences; political science; psychology; radio and television broadcasting; sociology

See full description on page 464.

ROGER WILLIAMS UNIVERSITY

Bristol, Rhode Island

Open Program

Roger Williams University, founded in 1956, is an independent-nonprofit comprehensive institution. It is accredited by the New England Association of Schools and Colleges. It first offered distance learning courses in 1974. In 1996–97, it offered 125 courses at a distance. In the fall of 1996, there was a total of 70 students enrolled in distance learning courses.
Course delivery sites Courses are delivered to your home, military bases.
Media Courses are delivered via videotapes, audiotapes, computer software, World Wide Web, e-mail, print. Students and teachers interact via mail, telephone, fax, e-mail. A computer is required for some courses.
Services Distance learners have access to library services, the campus computer network, e-mail services, academic advising, career placement assistance at a distance.
Credit-earning options Students may transfer credits from another institution or may earn credits through standardized exams, portfolio assessment, military training, business training.
Typical costs Tuition varies by the type of course. Financial aid is available to distance learners enrolled full-time or part-time.
Registration Students may register by mail, fax, phone, e-mail.
Contact Mary Dionisopoulos, Administrative Assistant, Roger Williams University, 1 Old Ferry Road, Bristol, RI 02809. *Telephone:* 401-254-3530. *Fax:* 401-254-3560. *E-mail:* jws@alpha.rwu.edu.

DEGREE & CERTIFICATE PROGRAMS

Baccalaureate Degrees

▶ *Administration of Justice (BS)*
In the fall of 1996 there were 25 students enrolled in this program. In 1995–96, 6 degrees were earned at a distance through this program.
Application requirements *Prior education:* associate degree. *Other requirements:* college transcripts.
Completion requirements 120 credits are required. 30 credits must be completed through the institution.
Program contact John P. Shanley, Professor, Roger Williams University, Open Program, One Old Ferry Road, Bristol, RI 02809. Phone: 401-254-3354. Fax: 401-254-3560. E-mail: jps2@alpha.rwu.edu.

▶ *Business Management (BS)*
In the fall of 1996 there were 4 students enrolled in this program. In 1995–96, 3 degrees were earned at a distance through this program.
Application requirements *Prior education:* some undergraduate course work. *Other requirements:* high school transcript.
Completion requirements 120 credits are required. 30 credits must be completed through the institution.
Program contact Thomas Carroll, Department Coordinator, Roger Williams University, Open Program, One Old Ferry Road, Bristol, RI 02809. Phone: 401-254-3037. Fax: 401-254-3560. E-mail: tjc@alph.rwu.edu.

▶ *Industrial Technology (BS)*
In the fall of 1996 there were 15 students enrolled in this program. In 1995–96, 6 degrees were earned at a distance through this program.
Application requirements *Prior education:* some undergraduate course work. *Other requirements:* high school transcript.
Completion requirements 120 credits are required. 30 credits must be completed through the institution.
Program contact Louis M. Swiczewicz, Department Coordinator for Engineering and Technology, Roger Williams University, Open Program, One Old Ferry Road, Bristol, RI 02809. Phone: 401-254-3231. Fax: 401-254-3560. E-mail: lms@alpha.rwu.edu.

▶ *Public Administration (BS)*
In the fall of 1996 there were 24 students enrolled in this program. In 1995–96, 6 degrees were earned at a distance through this program.
Application requirements *Prior education:* some undergraduate course work. *Other requirements:* high school transcript.
Completion requirements 120 credits are required. 30 credits must be completed through the institution.

INDIVIDUAL COURSE SUBJECT AREAS

Undergraduate
Accounting; anthropology; biology; business administration and management; business law; communications; computer and information sciences; criminology; engineering-related technologies; engineering/industrial management; English language and literature; history of science and technology; human resources management; insurance; investments and securities; logic; marketing; political science; protective services; public administration and services; sociology

ROOSEVELT UNIVERSITY

Chicago, Illinois

External Studies Program

Roosevelt University, founded in 1945, is an independent-nonprofit comprehensive institution. It is accredited by the North Central Association of Colleges and Schools. It first offered distance learning courses in 1974. In 1996–97, it offered 70 courses at a distance. In the fall of 1996, there was a total of 354 students enrolled in distance learning courses.
Course delivery sites Courses are delivered to your home.
Media Courses are delivered via print. Students and teachers interact via mail, telephone, e-mail. A computer is required for some courses.
Services Distance learners have access to library services, academic advising at a distance.
Credit-earning options Students may transfer credits from another institution.
Typical costs Tuition of $341 per credit. Students pay $70 in technology and general fees, and a $25 admissions fee. Financial aid is available to distance learners enrolled full-time or part-time.
Registration Students may register by mail.
Contact Admissions Office, Roosevelt University, 430 South Michigan, Chicago, IL 60605. Telephone: 312-341-3515. Fax: 312-341-3523. E-mail: dessim@admrs6k.roosevelt.edu. Web site: http://www.roosevelt.edu/distance-learning.

INDIVIDUAL COURSE SUBJECT AREAS

Undergraduate
Accounting; American (US) history; business; business administration and management; business communications; business information and data processing services; business law; computer and information sciences; computer programming; database management; economics; English composition; finance; geography; history; hospitality services management; physical sciences; social psychology; social sciences

ROSEMONT COLLEGE

Rosemont, Pennsylvania

Graduate Studies in Technology in Education

Rosemont College, founded in 1921, is an independent-religious Roman Catholic comprehensive institution. It is accredited by the Middle States Association of Colleges and Schools. It first offered distance learning courses in 1996. In 1996–97, it offered 10 courses at a distance. In the fall of 1996, there was a total of 50 students enrolled in distance learning courses.
Course delivery sites Courses are delivered to your home.
Media Courses are delivered via World Wide Web. Students and teachers interact via e-mail, Internet. A computer is required for all courses.
Services Distance learners have access to academic advising, career placement assistance at a distance.
Credit-earning options Students may transfer credits from another institution.
Typical costs Tuition of $325 per credit. Financial aid is available to distance learners.
Registration Students may register by mail, fax, e-mail, World Wide Web.
Contact Stan Rostkowski, Enrollment Coordinator, Rosemont College, 1400 Montgomery Avenue, Rosemont, PA 19010. Telephone: 610-527-0200, Ext. 2187. Fax: 610-526-2964. E-mail: roscolgrad@rosemont.edu. Web site: http://techined.rosemont.edu/cste/info.html.

DEGREE & CERTIFICATE PROGRAMS

Graduate certificates
▶ *Technology in Education*
In the fall of 1996 there were 67 students enrolled in this program. In 1995–96, 18 certificates were earned at a distance through this program.
Restrictions Assessment is required before registration.

Profiles: Rosemont College

Application requirements *Prior education:* baccalaureate degree. *Other requirements:* GRE or MAT, college transcripts, an essay or personal statement, letter(s) of recommendation, an application fee of $50.
Completion requirements 18 credits are required. 18 credits must be completed through the institution.

INDIVIDUAL COURSE SUBJECT AREAS

Graduate
Education; education administration; educational psychology; teacher education

ROSE STATE COLLEGE

Midwest City, Oklahoma

Rose State College, founded in 1968, is a state and locally supported two-year college. It is accredited by the North Central Association of Colleges and Schools. It first offered distance learning courses in 1972. In 1996–97, it offered 50 courses at a distance. In the fall of 1996, there was a total of 450 students enrolled in distance learning courses.
Course delivery sites Courses are delivered to your home, your workplace, military bases, other colleges.
Media Courses are delivered via television, videotapes, videoconferencing. Students and teachers interact via videoconferencing, mail, telephone, fax, e-mail.
Restrictions Courses are available to students in eastern Oklahoma County only.
Services Distance learners have access to the campus computer network at a distance.
Credit-earning options Students may transfer credits from another institution or may earn credits through examinations, military training.
Typical costs Tuition of $28 per credit hour for in-state residents. Tuition of $88 per credit hour for out-of-state residents. Students pay a $6 telecourse fee. Costs may vary by course delivery options. Financial aid is available to distance learners.
Registration Students may register by mail, phone.
Contact James F. Beavers, III, Director, Learning Resources Center, Rose State College, 6420 Southeast 15th Street, Midwest City, OK 73110. *Telephone:* 405-733-7322. *Fax:* 405-736-0260. *E-mail:* jfbeavers@ms.rose.cc.ok.us.

DEGREE & CERTIFICATE PROGRAMS

Associate Degrees
▶ *Library Technical Assistant (AA)*
Restrictions This program is available to in-state students only.
Application requirements *Prior education:* high school diploma or equivalent. *Other requirements:* ACT.
Completion requirements 62 credit hours are required. 12 credit hours must be completed through the institution.
Program contact Kay Britton, Professor, Rose State College, 6420 Southeast 15th Street, Midwest City, OK 73110. Phone: 405-733-7512.

Undergraduate Certificates
▶ *Library Technical Assistant*
Program contact Kay Britton, Professor, Rose State College, 6420 Southeast 15th Street, Midwest City, OK 73110. Phone: 405-733-7512.

INDIVIDUAL COURSE SUBJECT AREAS

Undergraduate
Business; business administration and management; developmental and child psychology; economics; English composition; English language and literature; European languages and literatures; geology; health and physical education/fitness; history; home economics and family studies; liberal arts, general studies, and humanities; library and information studies; mathematics; physical sciences; political science; psychology; social psychology; social sciences; sociology

RUTGERS, THE STATE UNIVERSITY OF NEW JERSEY, NEWARK

Newark, New Jersey

Office of Vice President for Continuous Education and Outreach

Rutgers, The State University of New Jersey, Newark, founded in 1892, is a state-supported university. It is accredited by the Middle States Association of Colleges and Schools. It first offered distance learning courses in 1995. In 1996–97, it offered 17 courses at a distance. In the fall of 1996, there was a total of 350 students enrolled in distance learning courses.
Course delivery sites Courses are delivered to your workplace, military bases, Atlantic Community College (Mays Landing), County College of Morris (Randolph), Sussex County Community College (Newton), 4 off-campus centers in Bloomfield, Denville, Edison, Mays Landing.
Media Courses are delivered via television, videoconferencing, audioconferencing, computer software, World Wide Web, e-mail, print. Students and teachers interact via videoconferencing, audioconferencing, mail, telephone, fax, e-mail. A computer is required for some courses.
Services Distance learners have access to library services, the campus computer network, e-mail services, academic advising, tutoring, career placement assistance at a distance.
Credit-earning options Students may transfer credits from another institution or may earn credits through examinations, portfolio assessment.
Typical costs Contact school for information. Financial aid is available to distance learners enrolled full-time.
Registration Students may register by mail, fax, phone.
Contact Dr. Charline S. Russo, Director of Continuing Education and Summer Sessions, Rutgers, The State University of New Jersey, Newark, 249 University–Blumenthal 208, Newark, NJ 07102. *Telephone:* 973-648-5760. *Fax:* 973-648-1587. *E-mail:* csrusso@andromeda.rutgers.edu. *Web site:* http://www.rutgers.edu.

DEGREE & CERTIFICATE PROGRAMS

Baccalaureate Degrees
▶ *Business Administration (BS)*
Restrictions Students must be able to attend classes at Newark, Newton, Randolph, NJ sites.
Application requirements *Prior education:* some undergraduate course work. *Other requirements:* high school transcript, college transcripts.
Completion requirements 64 credits are required. 29–60 credits must be completed through the institution. This is a degree completion program.

INDIVIDUAL COURSE SUBJECT AREAS

Undergraduate
Advertising; biology; business administration and management; calculus; chemistry; Chinese language and literature; criminal justice; education

administration; German language and literature; history; human resources management; law and legal studies; liberal arts, general studies, and humanities; nursing; organizational behavior studies; religious studies; social work; teacher education

Graduate
Adult education; business administration and management; continuing education; education administration; human resources management; instructional media; nursing; organizational behavior studies; teacher education

Noncredit
Adult education; biology; business administration and management; continuing education; education administration; human resources management; instructional media; law and legal studies; liberal arts, general studies, and humanities; nursing; organizational behavior studies; religious studies; social work; teacher education

RYERSON POLYTECHNIC UNIVERSITY

Toronto, Ontario, Canada

Continuing Education Division

Ryerson Polytechnic University, founded in 1948, is a province-supported four-year college. It is provincially chartered. It first offered distance learning courses in 1970.
Course delivery sites Courses are delivered to your home, your workplace.
Media Courses are delivered via audiotapes, World Wide Web, print. Students and teachers interact via mail, telephone, fax, e-mail, in-person meetings. A computer is required for some courses.
Services Distance learners have access to library services, e-mail services, academic advising, tutoring at a distance.
Credit-earning options Students may transfer credits from another institution or may earn credits through institutionally developed exams.
Typical costs Tuition of $413.90 per semester for in-state residents. *Noncredit courses:* $399 per course. Costs may vary by number of credits taken, citizenship or immigration visa status.
Registration Students may register by mail, fax, phone.
Contact Lorraine Wilson, Program Director, Continuing Education, Ryerson Polytechnic University, 350 Victoria Street, Toronto, ON M5B 2K3, Canada. *Telephone:* 416-979-5000, Ext. 6667. *Fax:* 416-979-5277. *E-mail:* lwilson@acs.ryerson.ca. *Web site:* http://www.ryerson.ca/ce/.

DEGREE & CERTIFICATE PROGRAMS

Undergraduate Certificates

▶ *Canadian Studies, Gerontology*
In the fall of 1996 there were 500 students enrolled in this program.
Application requirements *Prior education:* high school diploma or equivalent.
Completion requirements 8 courses are required. *Maximum time for completion:* four years.

▶ *Fundraising Management*
Application requirements *Prior education:* high school diploma or equivalent. *Other requirements:* experience in the non-profit sector is recommended.
Completion requirements 8 courses are required.
Program contact Martha Ireland, Program Assistant, Ryerson Polytechnic University, 350 Victoria Street, Toronto, ON M5B 2K3, Canada. Phone: 416-979-5183. Fax: 416-979-5277. E-mail: mireland@acs.ryerson.ca.

▶ *Non-profit Sector Management*
Application requirements *Prior education:* high school diploma or equivalent. *Other requirements:* experience in the non-profit sector is recommended.
Completion requirements 6 courses are required.
Program contact Martha Ireland, Program Assistant, Ryerson Polytechnic University, 350 Victoria Street, Toronto, ON M5B 2K3, Canada. Phone: 416-979-5183. Fax: 416-979-5277. E-mail: mireland@acs.ryerson.ca.

▶ *Occupational Health and Safety*
In the fall of 1996 there were 320 students enrolled in this program.
Application requirements *Prior education:* high school diploma or equivalent.
Completion requirements 8 courses are required. 4 courses must be completed through the institution. *Maximum time for completion:* five years.

▶ *Public Administration*
In the fall of 1996 there were 360 students enrolled in this program.
Application requirements *Prior education:* high school diploma or equivalent. *Other requirements:* high school transcript.
Completion requirements 8 courses are required. *Maximum time for completion:* five years.
Program contact Gloria DaBreo, Acting Program Assistant, Ryerson Polytechnic University, Continuing Education Division, 350 Victoria Street, Room A-100, Toronto, ON M5B 2K3, Canada. Phone: 416-979-5311. Fax: 416-979-5277. E-mail: gdabreo@acs.ryerson.ca.

INDIVIDUAL COURSE SUBJECT AREAS

Undergraduate
Business administration and management; Canadian studies; communications; economics; English language and literature; environmental health; gerontology; history; home economics and family studies; human resources management; liberal arts, general studies, and humanities; political science; psychology; public administration and services; sociology

Noncredit
Business administration and management; human resources management

SACRAMENTO CITY COLLEGE

Sacramento, California

Courses by Television

Sacramento City College, founded in 1916, is a state and locally supported two-year college. It is accredited by the Western Association of Schools and Colleges, Inc. It first offered distance learning courses in 1986. In 1996–97, it offered 19 courses at a distance. In the fall of 1996, there was a total of 725 students enrolled in distance learning courses.
Course delivery sites Courses are delivered to your home, your workplace.
Media Courses are delivered via television, videotapes. Students and teachers interact via mail, telephone, fax, e-mail, on-campus meetings.
Credit-earning options Students may transfer credits from another institution.
Typical costs Tuition of $0 per credit plus mandatory fees of $13 per unit for in-state residents. Tuition of $125 per unit plus mandatory fees of $13 per unit for out-of-state residents. International fee of $10 per unit. Financial aid is available to distance learners enrolled full-time or part-time.
Registration Students may register by mail, phone.
Contact Andrea Valdez, Coordinator of Distance Education, Sacramento City College, 3835 Freeport Boulevard, P-25, Sacramento, CA 95822.

Profiles: Sacramento City College

Telephone: 916-558-2636. *Fax:* 916-558-2636. *E-mail:* valdez@wserver.scc.losrios.cc.ca.us.

INDIVIDUAL COURSE SUBJECT AREAS

Undergraduate
Area, ethnic, and cultural studies; business; business administration and management; English language and literature; European languages and literatures; gerontology; health and physical education/fitness; philosophy and religion; psychology; sociology

ST. CLOUD TECHNICAL COLLEGE

St. Cloud, Minnesota

Central Minnesota Distance Learning Network

St. Cloud Technical College, founded in 1948, is a state-supported two-year college. It is accredited by the North Central Association of Colleges and Schools. It first offered distance learning courses in 1988. In 1996–97, it offered 300 courses at a distance. In the fall of 1996, there was a total of 2,000 students enrolled in distance learning courses.
Course delivery sites Courses are delivered to your home, other colleges, 60 off-campus centers.
Media Courses are delivered via videotapes, videoconferencing, audiotapes, audioconferencing, computer software, World Wide Web, e-mail, print. Students and teachers interact via videoconferencing, audioconferencing, mail, telephone, fax, e-mail.
Restrictions Programs are available to in-state students only.
Services Distance learners have access to library services, the campus computer network, e-mail services, academic advising, tutoring, career placement assistance at a distance.
Credit-earning options Students may transfer credits from another institution or may earn credits through examinations.
Typical costs *Undergraduate:* Tuition of $63 per credit for in-state residents. *Graduate:* Tuition of $76 per credit for in-state residents. Undergraduate classes for the 2-year program are $53 per credit. *Noncredit courses:* $10 per course. Costs may vary by campus or location. Financial aid is available to distance learners enrolled full-time or part-time.
Registration Students may register by mail, fax, phone.
Contact Jim Decker, Interim Executive Director, St. Cloud Technical College, 1540 Northway Drive, St. Cloud, MN 56303. *Telephone:* 320-654-5045. *Fax:* 320-654-5958. *E-mail:* jed@cloud.tec.mn.us.

DEGREE & CERTIFICATE PROGRAMS

Associate Degrees
▶ *Accounting (AA)*
▶ *Legal Secretary (AA)*
▶ *Practical Nursing (AA)*
Application requirements Asset test.
On-campus requirements For clinicals.

INDIVIDUAL COURSE SUBJECT AREAS

Undergraduate
Accounting; administrative and secretarial services; area, ethnic, and cultural studies; Asian languages and literatures; economics; English composition; European languages and literatures; human resources management; mathematics; nursing; social work; sociology

Graduate
Education administration; special education; teacher education

SAINT FRANCIS COLLEGE

Loretto, Pennsylvania

Saint Francis College, founded in 1847, is an independent-religious Roman Catholic comprehensive institution. It is accredited by the Middle States Association of Colleges and Schools. It first offered distance learning courses in 1994. In 1996–97, it offered 10 courses at a distance. In the fall of 1996, there was a total of 24 students enrolled in distance learning courses.
Course delivery sites Courses are delivered to your workplace, military bases.
Media Courses are delivered via videotapes, videoconferencing, computer software, e-mail, print. Students and teachers interact via videoconferencing, mail, telephone, fax, e-mail.
Services Distance learners have access to library services, the campus computer network, e-mail services, academic advising, tutoring, career placement assistance at a distance.
Credit-earning options Students may transfer credits from another institution or may earn credits through standardized exams, military training, business training.
Typical costs Tuition of $430 per credit hour plus mandatory fees of $39 per semester. Costs may vary by number of credits taken. Financial aid is available to distance learners enrolled full-time or part-time.
Registration Students may register by mail, fax, phone, e-mail.
Contact Dr. William Duryea, Director, MMS Program, Saint Francis College, Sullivan Hall, Loretto, PA 15940. *Telephone:* 814-472-3130. *Fax:* 814-472-3137.

DEGREE & CERTIFICATE PROGRAMS

Graduate Degrees
▶ *Health Science (Physician Assistant) (MMS)*
In the fall of 1996 there were 32 students enrolled in this program.
Application requirements *Prior education:* certified physician assistant (PA). *Other requirements:* Physician Assistant certifying exam (NCCPA), college transcripts, an essay or personal statement, letter(s) of recommendation, an application fee of $50.
Completion requirements 30 semester credits are required. 20 credits must be completed through the institution. *Maximum time for completion:* five years.

SAINT FRANCIS COLLEGE

Fort Wayne, Indiana

Saint Francis College, founded in 1890, is an independent-religious Roman Catholic comprehensive institution. It is accredited by the North Central Association of Colleges and Schools. It first offered distance learning courses in 1994. In 1996–97, it offered 15 courses at a distance. In the fall of 1996, there was a total of 30 students enrolled in distance learning courses.
Course delivery sites Courses are delivered to your workplace.
Media Courses are delivered via videoconferencing. Students and teachers interact via videoconferencing, telephone.
Restrictions Programs are available to in-state students only.
Credit-earning options Students may transfer credits from another institution or may earn credits through portfolio assessment.
Typical costs *Undergraduate:* Tuition of $5155 per semester plus mandatory fees of $200 per semester. *Graduate:* Tuition of $335 per credit

hour plus mandatory fees of $35 per semester. Costs may vary by number of credits taken.
Contact Office of Graduate Studies, Saint Francis College, 2701 Spring Street, Fort Wayne, IN 46808. *Telephone:* 800-729-4732. *Fax:* 219-434-3194.

DEGREE & CERTIFICATE PROGRAMS

Graduate Degrees
▶ *Nursing (MSN)*
In the fall of 1996 there were 30 students enrolled in this program.
Application requirements *Prior education:* BS in nursing. *Other requirements:* college transcripts.
Completion requirements 44 semester hours are required. 30 semester hours must be completed through the institution. *Maximum time for completion:* five years.

INDIVIDUAL COURSE SUBJECT AREAS

Graduate
Nursing

ST. JOHNS RIVER COMMUNITY COLLEGE

Palatka, Florida

Continuing Education

St. Johns River Community College, founded in 1958, is a state-supported two-year college. It is accredited by the Southern Association of Colleges and Schools. It first offered distance learning courses in 1996. In 1996–97, it offered 27 courses at a distance. In the fall of 1996, there was a total of 131 students enrolled in distance learning courses.
Course delivery sites Courses are delivered to your home, your workplace.
Media Courses are delivered via television, computer software. Students and teachers interact via mail, telephone, fax, e-mail. A computer is required for some courses.
Restrictions Courses are available to in-district students only.
Services Distance learners have access to library services, academic advising, career placement assistance at a distance.
Credit-earning options Students may transfer credits from another institution or may earn credits through examinations, military training.
Typical costs Tuition of $36.35 per credit hour for in-state residents. Tuition of $136.43 per credit hour for out-of-state residents. Financial aid is available to distance learners.
Contact Dr. John T. Skelton, Coordinator, Continuing Education, St. Johns River Community College, 5001 St. Johns Avenue, Palatka, FL 32177. *Telephone:* 904-312-4211. *Fax:* 904-312-4292. *Web site:* http://www.firn.edu/sjcc.

INDIVIDUAL COURSE SUBJECT AREAS

Undergraduate
Astronomy and astrophysics; business; business administration and management; communications; computer and information sciences; developmental and child psychology; economics; English composition; English language and literature; history; human resources management; liberal arts, general studies, and humanities; mathematics; political science; sociology

SAINT JOSEPH'S COLLEGE

Standish, Maine

Distance Education Program

Saint Joseph's College, founded in 1912, is an independent-religious comprehensive institution affiliated with the Roman Catholic Church. It is accredited by the New England Association of Schools and Colleges. It first offered distance learning courses in 1976. In 1996–97, it offered 185 courses at a distance. In the fall of 1996, there was a total of 4,000 students enrolled in distance learning courses.
Course delivery sites Courses are delivered to your home.
Media Courses are delivered via videotapes, audiotapes, computer software, World Wide Web, e-mail. Students and teachers interact via mail, telephone, fax, e-mail. A computer is required for some courses.
Services Distance learners have access to library services, academic advising, tutoring at a distance.
Credit-earning options Students may transfer credits from another institution or may earn credits through standardized exams, portfolio assessment, military training.
Typical costs *Undergraduate:* Tuition of $175 per credit. *Graduate:* Tuition of $215 per credit. Financial aid is available to distance learners.
Registration Students may register by mail, phone.
Contact Admissions Office, Saint Joseph's College, Department 840, 278 Whites Bridge Road, Standish, ME 04084-5263. *Telephone:* 800-752-4723. *Fax:* 207-892-7480. *E-mail:* gcarro@sjcme.edu. *Web site:* http://www.sjcme.edu.

DEGREE & CERTIFICATE PROGRAMS

Associate Degrees
▶ *Management (ASM)*
In the fall of 1996 there were 64 students enrolled in this program. In 1995–96, 1 degree was earned at a distance through this program.
Application requirements *Prior education:* high school diploma or equivalent. *Other requirements:* high school transcript, college transcripts, an essay or personal statement, an application fee of $50.
Completion requirements 66 semester hours are required. 25 semester hours must be completed through the institution.
On-campus requirements One 2-week residency.

Baccalaureate Degrees
▶ *American Studies, Christian Tradition, Women's Studies (BLS)*
In the fall of 1996 there were 22 students enrolled in this program.
Application requirements *Prior education:* high school diploma or equivalent. *Other requirements:* high school transcript, college transcripts, an essay or personal statement, an application fee of $50.
Completion requirements 128 semester hours are required. 40 semester hours must be completed through the institution.
On-campus requirements One 2-week summer residency.

▶ *Business Administration, Health Care Administration, Long-Term Care Administration (BS)*
In the fall of 1996 there were 1,090 students enrolled in this program. In 1995–96, 44 degrees were earned at a distance through this program.
Application requirements *Prior education:* high school diploma or equivalent. *Other requirements:* high school transcript, college transcripts, an essay or personal statement, an application fee of $50.
Completion requirements 128 semester hours are required. 40 semester hours must be completed through the institution.
On-campus requirements One 2-week summer residency.

▶ *Nursing (BS)*
In 1995–96, 6 degrees were earned at a distance through this program.

Profiles: Saint Joseph's College

Restrictions Students must be able to attend weekly clinicals in southern Maine.
Application requirements *Prior education:* RN track: diploma or Associates degree in Nursing. LPN track: some undergraduate course work. *Other requirements:* college transcripts, an essay or personal statement, letter(s) of recommendation, an application fee of $50, interview.
Completion requirements 129 semester hours are required. 32–45 semester hours must be completed through the institution. This is a degree completion program. *Maximum time for completion:* seven years.
On-campus requirements One-week residency, two-week residency, and weekly clinicals for LPN track.

▶ *Professional Arts (BSPA)*
In the fall of 1996 there were 1,200 students enrolled in this program. In 1995–96, 154 degrees were earned at a distance through this program.
Application requirements *Prior education:* some undergraduate course work. *Other requirements:* high school transcript, college transcripts, an essay or personal statement, an application fee of $50, proof of licensure or certification in a health profession.
Completion requirements 128 semester hours are required. 40 semester hours must be completed through the institution. This is a degree completion program.
On-campus requirements One 2-week summer residency.

▶ *Radiological Science (BSRS)*
In the fall of 1996 there were 133 students enrolled in this program. In 1995–96, 5 degrees were earned at a distance through this program.
Application requirements *Prior education:* must be a graduate of an accredited radiological science program and have passed National Registry Exam and be in good standing with a national certifying body. *Other requirements:* college transcripts, an essay or personal statement, an application fee.
Completion requirements 128 semester hours are required. 40 semester hours must be completed through the institution. This is a degree completion program.
On-campus requirements One 2-week summer residency.

▶ *Respiratory Care (BSRC)*
In the fall of 1996 there were 8 students enrolled in this program.
Application requirements *Prior education:* must be a graduate of an AMA-accredited respiratory therapy program, must have passed NBRC registry exam, and be in good standing with the NBRC. *Other requirements:* college transcripts, an essay or personal statement, an application fee of $50.
Completion requirements 128 semester hours are required. 40 semester hours must be completed through the institution.
On-campus requirements One 2-week summer residency.

Graduate Degrees
▶ *Health Services Administration (MHSA)*
In the fall of 1996 there were 1,306 students enrolled in this program. In 1995–96, 42 degrees were earned at a distance through this program.
Application requirements *Prior education:* baccalaureate degree. *Other requirements:* college transcripts, an essay or personal statement, letter(s) of recommendation, an application fee of $50, 3 years substantive experience in the field.
Completion requirements 48 semester hours are required. 42 semester hours must be completed through the institution. *Maximum time for completion:* 10 years.
On-campus requirements Two 2-week summer residencies.

▶ *Nursing (MS)*
Application requirements *Prior education:* baccalaureate degree. *Other requirements:* GRE or GMAT, college transcripts, an essay or personal statement, letter(s) of recommendation, an application fee of $50, prerequisite courses in statistics or research, interview, 3.0 GPA, evidence of 2 years full-time nursing experience.
Completion requirements 42 semester hours are required. 36 semester hours must be completed through the institution. *Maximum time for completion:* seven years.

On-campus requirements Two-week residency.

Undergraduate Certificates
▶ *American Studies, Business Administration, Christian Tradition, Health Care Management, Long-Term Care Administration, Women's Studies*
In the fall of 1996 there were 3 students enrolled in this program.
Application requirements *Prior education:* high school diploma or equivalent. *Other requirements:* high school transcript, an application fee of $25.
Completion requirements 18 semester hours are required. 12 semester hours must be completed through the institution.
On-campus requirements Two weeks.

▶ *Professional Studies*
In the fall of 1996 there were 4 students enrolled in this program.
Application requirements *Prior education:* high school diploma or equivalent. *Other requirements:* high school transcript, an application fee of $25.
Completion requirements 18 semester hours are required. 12 semester hours must be completed through the institution. *Other requirements:* this is a self-designed certificate program.
On-campus requirements Two weeks.

Graduate certificates
▶ *Health Care Finance*
In the fall of 1996 there were 7 students enrolled in this program.
Application requirements *Prior education:* baccalaureate degree. *Other requirements:* college transcripts, an application fee of $25.
Completion requirements 18 semester hours are required. 12 semester hours must be completed through the institution.

▶ *Medical and Dental Administration*
Restrictions Students must be physicians or dentists.
Application requirements *Prior education:* graduate degree. *Other requirements:* an application fee of $25.
Completion requirements 18 semester hours are required. 12 semester hours must be completed through the institution.

INDIVIDUAL COURSE SUBJECT AREAS

Undergraduate
Accounting; business; business administration and management; developmental and child psychology; economics; education administration; educational psychology; English composition; English language and literature; fine arts; health professions and related sciences; history; human resources management; industrial psychology; law and legal studies; liberal arts, general studies, and humanities; mathematics; music; nursing; philosophy and religion; public health; social psychology; sociology

Graduate
Health professions and related sciences; human resources management; law and legal studies; nursing
See full description on page 466.

ST. LOUIS COMMUNITY COLLEGE

St. Louis, Missouri

Telelearning Services

St. Louis Community College, founded in 1962, is a district-supported two-year college. It is accredited by the North Central Association of Colleges and Schools. It first offered distance learning courses in 1980.

In 1996–97, it offered 66 courses at a distance. In the fall of 1996, there was a total of 2,032 students enrolled in distance learning courses.

Course delivery sites Courses are delivered to your home, your workplace, 1 off-campus center in Rolla.

Media Courses are delivered via television, videotapes, videoconferencing, audiotapes, audioconferencing, computer software, World Wide Web, e-mail, print. Students and teachers interact via videoconferencing, audioconferencing, mail, telephone, fax, e-mail. A computer is required for some courses.

Restrictions Courses are available to students in Missouri and Illinois only.

Services Distance learners have access to library services, the campus computer network, e-mail services, academic advising, tutoring, career placement assistance at a distance.

Credit-earning options Students may transfer credits from another institution or may earn credits through standardized exams, institutionally developed exams, military training, business training.

Typical costs Tuition of $42 per credit plus mandatory fees of $20 per course for local area residents. Tuition of $53 per credit plus mandatory fees of $20 per course for in-state residents. Tuition of $67 per credit plus mandatory fees of $20 per course for out-of-state residents. Financial aid is available to distance learners enrolled full-time or part-time.

Registration Students may register by mail.

Contact Philip D. Hanson, Manager, Continuing Education Programs-Telecourses, St. Louis Community College, 5600 Oakland Avenue, St. Louis, MO 63110. *Telephone:* 314-644-9212. *Fax:* 314-644-9752. *E-mail:* phanson@fpmail.stlcc.cc.mo.us. *Web site:* http://www.stlcc.cc.mo.us.

Special note

For more than 17 years, St. Louis Community College has been offering college credit courses at a distance through telecourses by way of over the air broadcast on PBS station KETC/Channel 9, the Higher Education Channel (HEC-TV) on local cable television, and campus audiocassette/videocassette checkout. The telecourse program serves more than 5,500 students annually, allowing them access to education that may not have been possible otherwise. St. Louis Community College offers nearly 50 telecourses each academic year in topics ranging from anthropology to sociology and is consistently ranked in the top 10 nationwide in both telecourse offerings and enrollments.

St. Louis Community College is a member of the Missouri-Illinois Telecourse Cooperative (MITCO). A network of 10 higher education institutions located in and around the St. Louis metropolitan region, MITCO is committed to providing comprehensive and cost-effective distance learning programs for the students they serve. MITCO has consistently ranked among the top 10 consortiums nationwide in total annual enrollments. Since 1980, MITCO has served more than 100,000 distance learners, and currently offers more than 50 telecourses.

In addition to telecourses, St. Louis Community College provides students, faculty, staff, and the community with capabilities for interactive classes, meetings, and satellite conferences over distance. Technologies utilized include interactive video (compressed and full motion), satellite uplinks and downlinks, instructional television fixed service (ITFS), microwave and cable interconnect links, and on-line instruction via the Internet.

For more information on distance learning opportunities at St. Louis Community College, students should call Phil Hanson, Telecourse Manager (telephone: 314-644-9212; fax: 314-644-9752; e-mail: phanson@fpmail.stlcc.cc.mo.us).

INDIVIDUAL COURSE SUBJECT AREAS

Undergraduate
Accounting; administrative and secretarial services; American (US) history; anthropology; archaeology; art history and criticism; biology; business; business administration and management; computer and information sciences; developmental and child psychology; earth science; economics; English as a second language (ESL); English composition; European languages and literatures; fine arts; fire services administration; health and physical education/fitness; health professions and related sciences; investments and securities; liberal arts, general studies, and humanities; marketing; mathematics; occupational therapy; physical therapy; physics; physiology; political science; psychology; social sciences; sociology; substance abuse counseling; visual and performing arts

Noncredit
Fire services administration

SAINT MARY-OF-THE-WOODS COLLEGE

Saint Mary-of-the-Woods, Indiana

Women's External Degree Program

Saint Mary-of-the-Woods College, founded in 1840, is an independent-religious Roman Catholic comprehensive institution. It is accredited by the North Central Association of Colleges and Schools. It first offered distance learning courses in 1973. In 1996–97, it offered 250 courses at a distance. In the fall of 1996, there was a total of 1,050 students enrolled in distance learning courses.

Course delivery sites Courses are delivered to your home.

Media Courses are delivered via videotapes, audiotapes, computer software, e-mail, print. Students and teachers interact via mail, telephone, fax, e-mail, in-person meetings. A computer is required for some courses.

Restrictions Students must reside within 200 miles of the college.

Services Distance learners have access to library services, academic advising, career placement assistance at a distance.

Credit-earning options Students may transfer credits from another institution or may earn credits through standardized exams, portfolio assessment, military training, business training.

Typical costs *Undergraduate:* Tuition of $240 per semester hour. *Graduate:* Tuition of $265 per semester hour. Financial aid is available to distance learners enrolled full-time or part-time.

Contact Gwen Hagemeyer, WED Admissions Director, Saint Mary-of-the-Woods College, Saint Mary-of-the-Woods, IN 47876. *Telephone:* 812-535-5107. *Fax:* 812-535-5186. *E-mail:* wedadms@woods.smwc.edu.

DEGREE & CERTIFICATE PROGRAMS

Associate Degrees

▶ *Early Childhood Education, General Business, Gerontology, Humanities, Paralegal Studies (AA, AS)*
In the fall of 1996 there were 47 students enrolled in this program. In 1995–96, 7 degrees were earned at a distance through this program.

Restrictions Students must live within 200 miles of campus for student teaching and fieldwork supervision.

Application requirements *Prior education:* high school diploma or equivalent. *Other requirements:* high school transcript, college transcripts, an essay or personal statement, letter(s) of recommendation, an application fee of $30.

Completion requirements 65 semester hours are required. 30 semester hours must be completed through the institution. *Maximum time for completion:* six years.

Profiles: Saint Mary-of-the-Woods College

On-campus requirements Two-day orientation/registration, half-day per semester.

Baccalaureate Degrees

▶ *Accounting, Business Administration, Computer Information Systems, Gerontology, Human Resource Management, Human Services, Marketing, Paralegal Studies, Psychology (BS)*

In the fall of 1996 there were 820 students enrolled in this program. In 1995–96, 43 degrees were earned at a distance through this program.

Application requirements *Prior education:* high school diploma or equivalent. *Other requirements:* high school transcript, college transcripts, an essay or personal statement, letter(s) of recommendation, an application fee of $30.

Completion requirements 125 semester hours are required. 30 semester hours must be completed through the institution. *Maximum time for completion:* 12 years.

On-campus requirements Two-day orientation/registration, half-day per semester.

▶ *Early Childhood Education, Elementary Education, Kindergarten–Primary Education, Special Education (BS)*

Restrictions Students must live within 200 miles of campus for student teaching and fieldwork supervision.

Application requirements *Prior education:* high school diploma or equivalent. *Other requirements:* high school transcript, college transcripts, an essay or personal statement, letter(s) of recommendation, an application fee of $30.

Completion requirements 125 semester hours are required. 30 semester hours must be completed through the institution. *Maximum time for completion:* 12 years.

On-campus requirements Two-day orientation/registration, half-day per semester.

▶ *English, Humanities, Journalism, Mathematics, Theology (BA)*

In the fall of 1996 there were 92 students enrolled in this program. In 1995–96, 21 degrees were earned at a distance through this program.

Application requirements *Prior education:* high school diploma or equivalent. *Other requirements:* high school transcript, college transcripts, an essay or personal statement, letter(s) of recommendation, an application fee of $30.

Completion requirements 125 semester hours are required. 30 semester hours must be completed through the institution. *Maximum time for completion:* 12 years.

On-campus requirements Two-day orientation/registration, half-day per semester.

Graduate Degrees

▶ *Earth Literacy (MA)*

Application requirements *Prior education:* baccalaureate degree. *Other requirements:* college transcripts, an essay or personal statement, letter(s) of recommendation, an application fee.

Completion requirements 36 credits are required. 30 credits must be completed through the institution. *Maximum time for completion:* seven years.

On-campus requirements Five-day residency for each of six required 4-credit courses.

Program contact Mary Lou Dolan, CSJ, Director, MA Program in Earth Literacy, Saint Mary-of-the-Woods College, Saint Mary-of-the-Woods, IN 47876. Phone: 812-535-5160. Fax: 812-535-5228. E-mail: mldolan@woods.smwc.edu.

▶ *Pastoral Theology (MA)*

In the fall of 1996 there were 64 students enrolled in this program. In 1995–96, 14 degrees were earned at a distance through this program.

Application requirements *Prior education:* baccalaureate degree. *Other requirements:* college transcripts, an essay or personal statement, letter(s) of recommendation, an application fee of $30.

Completion requirements 36 semester hours are required. 21 semester hours must be completed through the institution. *Maximum time for completion:* seven years.

On-campus requirements One weekend on campus, three times a year, one week in the summer, twice during the program.

Program contact Ruth Eileen Dwyer, SP, MAPT Director, Saint Mary-of-the-Woods College, Saint Mary-of-the-Woods, IN 47876. Phone: 812-535-5170. Fax: 812-535-4613. E-mail: rdwyer@woods.smwc.edu.

Undergraduate Certificates

▶ *Gerontology, Microcomputers, Paralegal Studies, Pastoral Theology, Theology*

In the fall of 1996 there were 22 students enrolled in this program. In 1995–96, 5 certificates were earned at a distance through this program.

Application requirements *Prior education:* high school diploma or equivalent. *Other requirements:* high school transcript, college transcripts, an essay or personal statement, letter(s) of recommendation, an application fee of $30.

Completion requirements 16–36 semester hours are required. 12–30 semester hours must be completed through the institution. *Maximum time for completion:* four years.

On-campus requirements Two-day orientation/registration, half-day per semester.

See full description on page 468.

ST. PETERSBURG JUNIOR COLLEGE

St. Petersburg, Florida

St. Petersburg Junior College, founded in 1927, is a state and locally supported two-year college. It is accredited by the Southern Association of Colleges and Schools.

Course delivery sites Courses are delivered to your home, your workplace, military bases, 1 off-campus center.

Media Courses are delivered via television, videotapes, audiotapes, audioconferencing, computer software, World Wide Web, e-mail, print. Students and teachers interact via audioconferencing, mail, telephone, fax, e-mail.

Services Distance learners have access to library services, tutoring at a distance.

Credit-earning options Students may transfer credits from another institution or may earn credits through institutionally developed exams.

Typical costs Tuition of $40 per credit hour for in-state residents. Tuition of $143 per credit hour for out-of-state residents. Financial aid is available to distance learners.

Contact Bonny Peters, Telecourse Coordinator, St. Petersburg Junior College, Seminole Recreation Center, PO Box 13489, St. Petersburg, FL 33733. *Telephone:* 813-341-6563. *Fax:* 813-341-6543. *E-mail:* petersb@mail.spjc.cc.fl.us.

DEGREE & CERTIFICATE PROGRAMS

Associate Degrees

▶ *Veterinary Technology (AS)*

Completion requirements 73 credit hours are required. 51 must be completed through the institution. *Maximum time for completion:* three years.

On-campus requirements For clinical exams.

Program contact Guy Hancock, Director of Veterinary Technology, St. Petersburg Junior College, Health Education Center, PO Box 13489, St. Petersburg, FL 33733. Phone: 813-341-3653. E-mail: hancockg@mail.spjc.cc.fl.us.

INDIVIDUAL COURSE SUBJECT AREAS

Undergraduate
Accounting; astronomy and astrophysics; biology; business; business administration and management; computer and information sciences; creative writing; developmental and child psychology; economics; English composition; European languages and literatures; geology; health and physical education/fitness; history; journalism; law and legal studies; liberal arts, general studies, and humanities; mathematics; political science; social psychology; sociology

SAINT PETER'S COLLEGE

Jersey City, New Jersey

Institute for the Advancement of Urban Education

Saint Peter's College, founded in 1872, is an independent-religious Roman Catholic (Jesuit) comprehensive institution. It is accredited by the Middle States Association of Colleges and Schools. It first offered distance learning courses in 1992. In 1996–97, it offered 8 courses at a distance. In the fall of 1996, there was a total of 70 students enrolled in distance learning courses.
Course delivery sites Courses are delivered to your home, your workplace, high schools.
Media Courses are delivered via television, videotapes, videoconferencing. Students and teachers interact via videoconferencing, audioconferencing, telephone.
Restrictions Programs are available to in-state students only. Undergraduate courses are limited to high school students. Graduate students may only take a limited number of courses.
Services Distance learners have access to library services, the campus computer network, e-mail services, academic advising at a distance.
Credit-earning options Students may earn credits through institutionally developed exams, portfolio assessment.
Typical costs *Undergraduate:* Tuition of $401 per course. *Graduate:* Tuition of $375 per course. Costs may vary by specific program of study, course delivery options. Financial aid is available to distance learners enrolled full-time.
Registration Students may register by mail, fax, phone, e-mail.
Contact Dr. David S. Surrey, Director, Saint Peter's College, 2641 Kennedy Boulevard, Jersey City, NJ 07306-5997. *Telephone:* 201-915-9329. *Fax:* 201-435-3662. *E-mail:* surrey_d@spcvxa.spc.edu.

INDIVIDUAL COURSE SUBJECT AREAS

Undergraduate
American (US) history; comparative literature

Graduate
Business administration and management; business communications; curriculum and instruction; education administration; teacher education

ST. THOMAS AQUINAS COLLEGE

Sparkill, New York

Office of Continuing Education

St. Thomas Aquinas College, founded in 1952, is an independent-nonprofit comprehensive institution. It is accredited by the Middle States Association of Colleges and Schools. It first offered distance learning courses in 1996. In 1996–97, it offered 4 courses at a distance. In the fall of 1996, there was a total of 25 students enrolled in distance learning courses.
Course delivery sites Courses are delivered to your home.
Media Courses are delivered via World Wide Web, e-mail. Students and teachers interact via mail, e-mail. A computer is required for all courses.
Services Distance learners have access to e-mail services, academic advising, tutoring, career placement assistance at a distance.
Typical costs Tuition of $395 per course. *Noncredit courses:* $395 per course.
Registration Students may register by mail, fax, phone, e-mail.
Contact William B. Grogan, Director, Continuing Education, St. Thomas Aquinas College, St. Thomas Aquinas College, Sparkill, NY 10976. *Telephone:* 914-398-4207. *Fax:* 914-398-4224.

INDIVIDUAL COURSE SUBJECT AREAS

Noncredit
Psychology; technical writing

SALT LAKE COMMUNITY COLLEGE

Salt Lake City, Utah

Division of Continuing Education

Salt Lake Community College, founded in 1948, is a state-supported two-year college. It is accredited by the Northwest Association of Schools and Colleges. It first offered distance learning courses in 1991. In 1996–97, it offered 27 courses at a distance. In the fall of 1996, there was a total of 674 students enrolled in distance learning courses.
Course delivery sites Courses are delivered to your home, your workplace, other colleges, 2 off-campus centers in Salt Lake City.
Media Courses are delivered via television, videotapes, audioconferencing, computer software, World Wide Web, e-mail, print. Students and teachers interact via audioconferencing, mail, telephone, fax, e-mail. A computer is required for some courses. The institution provides assistance with acquiring computer equipment.
Services Distance learners have access to library services, the campus computer network, e-mail services, tutoring at a distance.
Credit-earning options Students may transfer credits from another institution or may earn credits through examinations, military training.
Typical costs Tuition of $81 per credit hour for in-state residents. Tuition of $199 per credit hour for out-of-state residents. Costs may vary by number of credits taken. Financial aid is available to distance learners.
Registration Students may register by mail, phone, World Wide Web.
Contact Shanna Schaefermeyer, Director of Distance Learning, Salt Lake Community College, 4600 South Redwood Road, Salt Lake City, UT 84130. *Telephone:* 801-957-4064. *Fax:* 801-957-4890. *E-mail:* schaefsh@slcc.edu. *Web site:* http://www.slcc.edu.

INDIVIDUAL COURSE SUBJECT AREAS

Undergraduate
Accounting; astronomy and astrophysics; biology; business; business administration and management; chemistry; computer and information sciences; economics; English composition; environmental science; European languages and literatures; history; liberal arts, general studies, and humanities; library and information studies; mathematics; physics; sociology; telecommunications

Noncredit
Education

Profiles: Salve Regina University

SALVE REGINA UNIVERSITY

Newport, Rhode Island

Extension Study

Salve Regina University, founded in 1934, is an independent-religious Roman Catholic comprehensive institution. It is accredited by the New England Association of Schools and Colleges. It first offered distance learning courses in 1985. In 1996–97, it offered 60 courses at a distance. In the fall of 1996, there was a total of 285 students enrolled in distance learning courses.

Course delivery sites Courses are delivered to your home, 1 off-campus center in Providence.

Media Courses are delivered via videotapes, e-mail, print. Students and teachers interact via mail, telephone, fax, e-mail. A computer is required for some courses.

Services Distance learners have access to library services, e-mail services, academic advising, career placement assistance at a distance.

Credit-earning options Students may transfer credits from another institution or may earn credits through standardized exams, institutionally developed exams, military training, business training.

Typical costs *Undergraduate:* Tuition of $150 per credit for in-state residents. Tuition of $175 per credit for out-of-state residents. *Graduate:* Tuition of $900 per course for in-state residents. Tuition of $900 per course for out-of-state residents. Graduate students pay application, commitment, and graduation fees totaling $285. Undergraduates pay $125 in application and commitment fees. Financial aid is available to distance learners enrolled full-time or part-time.

Registration Students may register by mail, fax, phone, e-mail, World Wide Web.

Contact Sr. Leona Misto, Director, Extension Study, Salve Regina University, 100 Ochre Point Avenue, Newport, RI 02840. *Telephone:* 800-637-0002. *Fax:* 401-849-0702. *E-mail:* mistol@salve.edu. *Web site:* http://www.salve.edu.

DEGREE & CERTIFICATE PROGRAMS

Baccalaureate Degrees

▶ *Business (BS)*

Application requirements *Prior education:* high school diploma or equivalent. *Other requirements:* high school transcript, an essay or personal statement, letter(s) of recommendation, an application fee of $25.
Completion requirements 120 credits are required. 60 credits must be completed through the institution. This is a degree completion program. *Maximum time for completion:* five years.
On-campus requirements Five days.

▶ *Liberal Studies (BA)*

Application requirements *Prior education:* high school diploma or equivalent. *Other requirements:* high school transcript, an essay or personal statement, letter(s) of recommendation, an application fee of $25.
Completion requirements 120 credits are required. 60 credits must be completed through the institution. This is a degree completion program. *Maximum time for completion:* five years.
On-campus requirements Five days.

▶ *Nursing (BS)*

Application requirements *Prior education:* high school diploma or equivalent. *Other requirements:* high school transcript, an essay or personal statement, letter(s) of recommendation, an application fee of $25.
Completion requirements 120 credits are required. 60 credits must be completed through the institution. This is a degree completion program. *Maximum time for completion:* five years.
On-campus requirements Five days.

Graduate Degrees

▶ *Human Development (MA)*

In the fall of 1996 there were 6 students enrolled in this program.
Application requirements *Prior education:* baccalaureate degree. *Other requirements:* GRE, MAT, GMAT, college transcripts, an essay or personal statement, letter(s) of recommendation, an application fee of $35.
Completion requirements 36 credits are required. 15 credits must be completed through the institution. *Maximum time for completion:* five years.
On-campus requirements Five days.

▶ *International Relations (MA)*

In the fall of 1996 there were 65 students enrolled in this program. In 1995–96, 12 degrees were earned at a distance through this program.
Application requirements *Prior education:* baccalaureate degree. *Other requirements:* GRE, GMAT, MAT, college transcripts, an essay or personal statement, letter(s) of recommendation, an application fee of $35.
Completion requirements 36 credits are required. 15 credits must be completed through the institution. *Maximum time for completion:* five years.
On-campus requirements Five days.

▶ *Management (MS)*

In the fall of 1996 there were 79 students enrolled in this program. In 1995–96, 15 degrees were earned at a distance through this program.
Application requirements *Prior education:* baccalaureate degree. *Other requirements:* GRE, MAT, GMAT, college transcripts, an essay or personal statement, letter(s) of recommendation, an application fee of $35.
Completion requirements 36 credits are required. 15 credits must be completed through the institution. *Maximum time for completion:* five years.
On-campus requirements Five days.

Undergraduate Certificates

▶ *Management*

In the fall of 1996 there were 2 students enrolled in this program.
Application requirements *Prior education:* high school diploma or equivalent. *Other requirements:* high school transcript, an essay or personal statement, letter(s) of recommendation, an application fee of $25.
Completion requirements 15 credits are required. 12 credits must be completed through the institution. *Maximum time for completion:* five years.

▶ *Management/Correctional Administration*

In the fall of 1996 there was 1 student enrolled in this program.
Application requirements *Prior education:* high school diploma or equivalent. *Other requirements:* high school transcript, an essay or personal statement, letter(s) of recommendation, an application fee of $25.
Completion requirements 15 credits are required. 12 credits must be completed through the institution. *Maximum time for completion:* five years.

INDIVIDUAL COURSE SUBJECT AREAS

Undergraduate

American (US) history; American literature; art history and criticism; business; business administration and management; business law; community health services; comparative literature; English language and literature; ethics; finance; gerontology; human resources management; international business; labor relations/studies; liberal arts, general studies, and humanities; marketing; music; nursing; organizational behavior studies; philosophy and religion; protective services; psychology; religious studies; social psychology

Graduate

Accounting; business; business administration and management; business law; cognitive psychology; computer and information sciences; database management; developmental and child psychology; economics; English language and literature; ethics; finance; human resources management; international business; international relations; labor relations/studies; Latin American studies; liberal arts, general studies, and humanities; management information systems; marketing; organizational behavior studies; philosophy and religion; political science; protective services; social psychology

Noncredit
Accounting; American (US) history; American literature; art history and criticism; business; business administration and management; business law; cognitive psychology; community health services; comparative literature; computer and information sciences; database management; developmental and child psychology; economics; English language and literature; ethics; finance; gerontology; human resources management; international business; international relations; labor relations/studies; Latin American studies; liberal arts, general studies, and humanities; management information systems; marketing; music; nursing; organizational behavior studies; philosophy and religion; political science; protective services; psychology; religious studies; social psychology

SAN ANTONIO COLLEGE

San Antonio, Texas

Distance Education

San Antonio College, founded in 1925, is a state and locally supported two-year college. It is accredited by the Southern Association of Colleges and Schools.
Course delivery sites Courses are delivered to your home, military bases, off-campus center(s).
Media Courses are delivered via television, videoconferencing, World Wide Web. Students and teachers interact via telephone, fax, e-mail, in-person meetings.
Restrictions Programs are available to in-state students only.
Credit-earning options Students may transfer credits from another institution or may earn credits through examinations.
Typical costs Contact school for information.
Contact Helen Torres, Director of Distance Education, San Antonio College, 1300 San Pedro Avenue, San Antonio, TX 78212. *Telephone:* 210-733-2045. *Fax:* 210-733-2725. *E-mail:* hhinojos@accd.edu.

INDIVIDUAL COURSE SUBJECT AREAS

Undergraduate
Developmental and child psychology; English composition; European languages and literatures; history; microbiology; nursing; sociology

SAN BERNARDINO VALLEY COLLEGE

San Bernardino, California

San Bernardino Valley College, founded in 1926, is a state and locally supported two-year college. It is accredited by the Western Association of Schools and Colleges, Inc. It first offered distance learning courses in 1973. In 1996–97, it offered 60 courses at a distance.
Course delivery sites Courses are delivered to your home.
Media Courses are delivered via television, computer software, e-mail. Students and teachers interact via mail, telephone, fax, e-mail. A computer is required for some courses.
Restrictions Students must be able to travel to campus.
Credit-earning options Students may transfer credits from another institution or may earn credits through standardized exams.
Typical costs Tuition of $13 per unit for in-state residents. Tuition of $118 per unit for out-of-state residents. Financial aid is available to distance learners.
Registration Students may register by mail, phone.
Contact Office of Distance Education and Off-Campus Programs, San Bernardino Valley College, 701 South Mount Vernon Avenue, San Bernardino, CA 92410. *Telephone:* 909-888-6511, Ext. 1131. *Fax:* 909-825-3104.

INDIVIDUAL COURSE SUBJECT AREAS

Undergraduate
American (US) history; anthropology; astronomy and astrophysics; biological and life sciences; business; business administration and management; child care and development; conservation and natural resources; ecology; economics; English as a second language (ESL); English language and literature; English literature; ethics; film studies; geography; geology; health and physical education/fitness; history; home economics and family studies; liberal arts, general studies, and humanities; oceanography; philosophy and religion; photography; physical sciences; physics; political science; psychology; radio and television broadcasting; religious studies; social sciences; sociology

SANDHILLS COMMUNITY COLLEGE

Pinehurst, North Carolina

Sandhills Community College, founded in 1963, is a state and locally supported two-year college. It is accredited by the Southern Association of Colleges and Schools.
Course delivery sites Courses are delivered to your home, your workplace, military bases.
Media Courses are delivered via television, videotapes, audiotapes, computer software, World Wide Web, e-mail. Students and teachers interact via telephone, e-mail.
Credit-earning options Students may transfer credits from another institution or may earn credits through examinations, portfolio assessment, military training, business training.
Typical costs Tuition of $20 per semester hour plus mandatory fees of $14 per semester hour for in-state residents. Tuition of $163 per semester hour plus mandatory fees of $14 per semester hour for out-of-state residents. Financial aid is available to distance learners.
Contact Director of Admission, Sandhills Community College, 2200 Airport Road, Pinehurst, NC 28374. *Telephone:* 910-692-6185.

INDIVIDUAL COURSE SUBJECT AREAS

Undergraduate
Business administration and management; computer and information sciences; developmental and child psychology; English composition; history; sociology

SAN DIEGO CITY COLLEGE

San Diego, California

Office of Distance Education

San Diego City College, founded in 1914, is a state and locally supported two-year college. It is accredited by the Western Association of Schools and Colleges, Inc. It first offered distance learning courses in

Distance Learning Programs

Profiles: San Diego City College

1994. In 1996–97, it offered 16 courses at a distance. In the fall of 1996, there was a total of 669 students enrolled in distance learning courses.

Course delivery sites Courses are delivered to your home, your workplace, military bases.
Media Courses are delivered via television, videotapes, videoconferencing. Students and teachers interact via videoconferencing, telephone, e-mail.
Restrictions Students must be able to travel to campus.
Typical costs Tuition of $13 per unit for in-state residents. Tuition of $110 per unit for out-of-state residents. Students pay a $10 health fee. *Noncredit courses:* $13 per unit plus $10 health fee and $17 parking fee. Costs may vary by number of credits taken. Financial aid is available to distance learners enrolled full-time or part-time.
Registration Students may register by mail, phone.
Contact Curtis J. McCarty, Faculty Coordinator, Distance Education, San Diego City College, 1313 12th Avenue, San Diego, CA 92101-4787. *Telephone:* 619-230-2534. *Fax:* 619-230-2063. *E-mail:* cmccarty@sdccd.cc.ca.us.

INDIVIDUAL COURSE SUBJECT AREAS

Undergraduate
Anthropology; astronomy and astrophysics; business; business administration and management; business law; Classical languages and literatures; computer and information sciences; economics; geography; geology; health professions and related sciences; history; home economics and family studies; liberal arts, general studies, and humanities; political science; psychology

SAN DIEGO STATE UNIVERSITY

San Diego, California

College of Extended Studies

San Diego State University, founded in 1897, is a state-supported university. It is accredited by the Western Association of Schools and Colleges, Inc. It first offered distance learning courses in 1984. In 1996–97, it offered 19 courses at a distance. In the fall of 1996, there was a total of 220 students enrolled in distance learning courses.

Course delivery sites Courses are delivered to your home, your workplace.
Media Courses are delivered via television, videotapes, videoconferencing, computer software, World Wide Web, e-mail. Students and teachers interact via mail, telephone, fax, e-mail. A computer is required for some courses.
Restrictions Availability varies by course, program, or delivery means.
Services Distance learners have access to library services at a distance.
Credit-earning options Students may earn credits through institutionally developed exams.
Typical costs *Undergraduate:* Tuition of $120 per credit. *Graduate:* Tuition of $120 per credit. *Noncredit courses:* $120 per credit. Costs may vary by specific program of study, number of credits taken, course delivery options, term of enrollment.
Registration Students may register by mail, fax, phone.
Contact Larry Cobb, Assistant Dean, San Diego State University, College of Extended Studies, 5250 Campanile Drive, San Diego, CA 92182-1919. *Telephone:* 619-594-4704. *Fax:* 619-594-7080. *E-mail:* lcobb@mail.sdsu.edu. *Web site:* http://rohan.sdsu.edu/dept/extstd/extstudies.html.

INDIVIDUAL COURSE SUBJECT AREAS

Undergraduate
Computer and information sciences; education administration; music; teacher education

Graduate
Education administration; teacher education

Noncredit
Human resources management; international business; labor relations/studies; marketing; organizational behavior studies

SAN JOAQUIN DELTA COLLEGE

Stockton, California

Instructional Development

San Joaquin Delta College, founded in 1935, is a district-supported two-year college. It is accredited by the Western Association of Schools and Colleges, Inc. It first offered distance learning courses in 1976. In 1996–97, it offered 12 courses at a distance. In the fall of 1996, there was a total of 333 students enrolled in distance learning courses.

Course delivery sites Courses are delivered to your home, 4 off-campus centers in Jackson, Manteca, San Andreas, Tracy.
Media Courses are delivered via television, videotapes. Students and teachers interact via telephone, e-mail, on-campus meetings.
Services Distance learners have access to library services at a distance.
Credit-earning options Students may transfer credits from another institution or may earn credits through institutionally developed exams.
Typical costs Tuition of $0 per credit plus mandatory fees of $13 per unit for local area residents. Tuition of $0 per credit plus mandatory fees of $13 per unit for in-state residents. Tuition of $114 per unit plus mandatory fees of $13 per unit for out-of-state residents. Costs may vary by number of credits taken. Financial aid is available to distance learners enrolled full-time or part-time.
Registration Students may register by phone.
Contact Kathryn Campbell, Dean for Instructional Development, San Joaquin Delta College, 5151 Pacific, Stockton, CA 95207. *Telephone:* 209-954-5039. *Fax:* 209-954-5600. *E-mail:* campbell@sjdccd.cc.ca.us.

INDIVIDUAL COURSE SUBJECT AREAS

Undergraduate
Accounting; business administration and management; health professions and related sciences; home economics and family studies; mathematics

SAN JOSE STATE UNIVERSITY

San Jose, California

Television Education Network

San Jose State University, founded in 1857, is a state-supported comprehensive institution. It is accredited by the Western Association of Schools and Colleges, Inc. It first offered distance learning courses in 1985. In 1996–97, it offered 83 courses at a distance. In the fall of 1996, there was a total of 300 students enrolled in distance learning courses.

Course delivery sites Courses are delivered to your workplace, Cabrillo College (Aptos), Gavilan College (Gilroy), Monterey Peninsula College (Monterey), California State University–Monterey Bay, Ohlone College–Newark, 30 business and industry sites in the Silicon Valley.
Media Courses are delivered via television, videotapes, videoconferencing, computer software, World Wide Web, e-mail. Students and teachers interact via videoconferencing, mail, telephone, fax, e-mail. A computer is required for some courses.
Restrictions Credit courses are limited to the broadcast area.
Services Distance learners have access to library services, the campus computer network, e-mail services, academic advising at a distance.
Credit-earning options Students may transfer credits from another institution.
Typical costs Tuition varies based on which fees are applicable. Contact school for information. Financial aid is available to distance learners enrolled full-time.
Registration Students may register by mail, fax, phone.
Contact Betty C. Benson, Director, Television Education Network, San Jose State University, One Washington Square, San Jose, CA 95192-0169. *Telephone:* 408-924-2636. *Fax:* 408-924-1881. *E-mail:* bcbenson@sjsuvm1.sjsu.edu. *Web site:* http://conted.sjsu.edu.

DEGREE & CERTIFICATE PROGRAMS

Graduate Degrees

▶ *Electrical Engineering (MSEE)*
Application requirements *Prior education:* baccalaureate degree. *Other requirements:* GMAT, college transcripts, letter(s) of recommendation, an application fee of $65.
Completion requirements 30 units are required. *Maximum time for completion:* 6–8 semesters.
Program contact Dr. Belle Wei, Graduate Coordinator, San Jose State University, One Washington Square, San Jose, CA 95192-0084. Phone: 408-924-3950. Fax: 408-924-3925. E-mail: bwei@email.sjsu.edu.

Undergraduate Certificates

▶ *ISO 9000*
In the fall of 1996 there were 77 students enrolled in this program. In 1995–96, 75 certificates were earned at a distance through this program.
Application requirements *Prior education:* some undergraduate course work.
Completion requirements 4 continuing education units are required. 4 continuing education units must be completed through the institution.

▶ *Quality Design and Manufacturing*
In the fall of 1996 there were 131 students enrolled in this program.
Application requirements *Prior education:* some undergraduate course work.
Completion requirements 6 continuing education units are required.

▶ *Total Quality Management*
In the fall of 1996 there were 43 students enrolled in this program. In 1995–96, 40 certificates were earned at a distance through this program.
Application requirements *Prior education:* some undergraduate course work.
Completion requirements 12 continuing education units are required.

INDIVIDUAL COURSE SUBJECT AREAS

Undergraduate
Accounting; Asian languages and literatures; business administration and management; continuing education; developmental and child psychology; ethics; geography; geology; liberal arts, general studies, and humanities; nursing; philosophy and religion; political science; sociology; special education; teacher education

Graduate
Electrical engineering; library and information studies; special education; teacher education

Noncredit
Industrial engineering

SAN JUAN COLLEGE

Farmington, New Mexico

Distance Education

San Juan College, founded in 1958, is a county-supported two-year college. It is accredited by the North Central Association of Colleges and Schools. In the fall of 1996, there was a total of 372 students enrolled in distance learning courses.
Course delivery sites Courses are delivered to your home, your workplace, 6 off-campus centers in Aztec, Bloomfield, Kirtland, high schools in Aztec, Bloomfield, Kirtland, and Farmington.
Media Courses are delivered via television, videotapes, videoconferencing, World Wide Web. Students and teachers interact via videoconferencing, mail, telephone, fax, e-mail.
Services Distance learners have access to library services, academic advising, tutoring, career placement assistance at a distance.
Credit-earning options Students may transfer credits from another institution or may earn credits through institutionally developed exams, portfolio assessment, military training.
Typical costs Tuition of $15 per credit hour for in-state residents. Tuition of $25 per credit hour for out-of-state residents. Financial aid is available to distance learners enrolled full-time or part-time.
Registration Students may register by phone.
Contact Gary Golden, Vice President of Student Services, San Juan College, 4601 College Boulevard, Farmington, NM 87402. *Telephone:* 505-599-0335. *Fax:* 505-599-0385. *Web site:* http://sjc.cc.nm.us.

INDIVIDUAL COURSE SUBJECT AREAS

Undergraduate
Algebra; American literature; business; marketing; mathematics; music; nursing; psychology; social sciences

SANTA FE COMMUNITY COLLEGE

Santa Fe, New Mexico

External Programs

Santa Fe Community College, founded in 1983, is a state and locally supported two-year college. It is accredited by the North Central Association of Colleges and Schools. It first offered distance learning courses in 1986.
Course delivery sites Courses are delivered to your home.
Media Courses are delivered via television, videotapes, videoconferencing, computer software, print.
Restrictions Programs are available to local area students only.
Credit-earning options Students may transfer credits from another institution or may earn credits through examinations. Financial aid is available to distance learners.
Contact Flex Lab Coordinator, Santa Fe Community College, PO Box 4187, Santa Fe, NM 87502. *Telephone:* 505-438-1647. *Fax:* 505-438-1237.

INDIVIDUAL COURSE SUBJECT AREAS

Undergraduate
Accounting; business; Classical languages and literatures; computer and information sciences; English composition; mathematics; nursing; sociology; visual and performing arts

Profiles: Santa Rosa Junior College

SANTA ROSA JUNIOR COLLEGE

Santa Rosa, California

Santa Rosa Junior College, founded in 1918, is a state and locally supported two-year college. It is accredited by the Western Association of Schools and Colleges, Inc. It first offered distance learning courses in 1989. In 1996–97, it offered 12 courses at a distance. In the fall of 1996, there was a total of 400 students enrolled in distance learning courses.
Course delivery sites Courses are delivered to your home, your workplace, 2 off-campus centers in Petaluma, Two Rock.
Media Courses are delivered via television, videotapes, World Wide Web, e-mail. Students and teachers interact via mail, telephone, fax, e-mail. A computer is required for some courses.
Services Distance learners have access to library services, the campus computer network, e-mail services, academic advising at a distance.
Credit-earning options Students may transfer credits from another institution.
Typical costs Tuition of $13 per unit plus mandatory fees of $10 per semester for in-state residents. Tuition of $119 per unit plus mandatory fees of $10 per semester for out-of-state residents. Costs may vary by number of credits taken. Financial aid is available to distance learners enrolled full-time or part-time.
Registration Students may register by mail, fax, phone, World Wide Web.
Contact Steve Olson, Dean of Instruction, Santa Rosa Junior College, 1501 Mendocino Avenue, Santa Rosa, CA 95401. *Telephone:* 707-527-4441. *Fax:* 707-527-4816. *E-mail:* steve_olson@garfield.santarosa.edu. *Web site:* http://www.santarosa.edu.

INDIVIDUAL COURSE SUBJECT AREAS

Undergraduate
Accounting; administrative and secretarial services; anthropology; archaeology; business; business administration and management; communications; computer and information sciences; European languages and literatures; foods and nutrition studies; law and legal studies; marketing; philosophy and religion; social psychology; sociology

SAUK VALLEY COMMUNITY COLLEGE

Dixon, Illinois

Sauk Valley Community College, founded in 1965, is a district-supported two-year college. It is accredited by the North Central Association of Colleges and Schools. It first offered distance learning courses in 1993. In 1996–97, it offered 7 courses at a distance. In the fall of 1996, there was a total of 27 students enrolled in distance learning courses.
Course delivery sites Courses are delivered to Carl Sandburg College (Galesburg), John Wood Community College (Quincy).
Media Courses are delivered via television, computer software. Students and teachers interact via videoconferencing, mail, telephone, fax, e-mail.
Restrictions Courses are available through members of Western Illinois Education Consortium only.
Services Distance learners have access to e-mail services at a distance.
Credit-earning options Students may transfer credits from another institution or may earn credits through examinations, portfolio assessment, military training, business training.
Typical costs Tuition of $43 per credit hour. Financial aid is available to distance learners enrolled full-time or part-time.
Registration Students may register by mail, phone.
Contact Zollie W. Hall, Dean of Business, Technology, and Natural Science, Sauk Valley Community College, 173 Illinois Route 2, Dixon, IL 61021. *Telephone:* 815-288-5511, Ext. 356. *Fax:* 815-288-5958. *E-mail:* hallz@hpuxl.svcc.cc.il.us.

DEGREE & CERTIFICATE PROGRAMS

Associate Degrees
▶ *Criminal Justice (AAS)*
Application requirements *Prior education:* high school diploma or equivalent. *Minimum age:* 21. *Other requirements:* high school transcript, college transcripts.
Completion requirements 64 credits are required. 16 credits must be completed through the institution. *Maximum time for completion:* 10 years.
Program contact Steve Ullrick, Director of Admissions, Sauk Valley Community College, 173 Illinois Route 2, Dixon, IL 61021. Phone: 815-288-5111, Ext. 310. Fax: 815-288-5958.

INDIVIDUAL COURSE SUBJECT AREAS

Undergraduate
Accounting; American (US) history; biology; criminal justice; English composition; psychology; sociology; visual and performing arts

SAVANNAH STATE UNIVERSITY

Savannah, Georgia

Distance Learning Center

Savannah State University, founded in 1890, is a state-supported four-year college. It is accredited by the Southern Association of Colleges and Schools.
Course delivery sites Courses are delivered to your home, off-campus center(s).
Media Courses are delivered via videotapes, videoconferencing, computer software. Students and teachers interact via videoconferencing, audioconferencing, telephone, fax, e-mail.
Restrictions Programs are available to in-state students only.
Typical costs Contact school for information. Financial aid is available to distance learners.
Contact James D. Scott, Instructional Technology Support Specialist, Savannah State University, Savannah State College Library, PO Box 20394, Savannah, GA 31404. *Telephone:* 912-353-5131. *Fax:* 912-353-3297.

INDIVIDUAL COURSE SUBJECT AREAS

Undergraduate
Education; teacher education

SCHOOLCRAFT COLLEGE

Livonia, Michigan

Distance Learning Office

Schoolcraft College, founded in 1961, is a district-supported two-year college. It is accredited by the North Central Association of Colleges and Schools. It first offered distance learning courses in 1982.
Course delivery sites Courses are delivered to your home.

Media Courses are delivered via television, videotapes, audiotapes, print.
Restrictions Programs are available to local area students only.
Credit-earning options Students may transfer credits from another institution or may earn credits through examinations, portfolio assessment, military training, business training. Financial aid is available to distance learners.
Contact Coordinator, Distance Learning, Schoolcraft College, 18600 Haggerts Road, Livonia, MI 48152. *Telephone:* 313-462-4532. *Fax:* 313-462-4495.

INDIVIDUAL COURSE SUBJECT AREAS

Undergraduate
Area, ethnic, and cultural studies; business; business administration and management; computer and information sciences; developmental and child psychology; economics; English composition; English language and literature; history; liberal arts, general studies, and humanities; mathematics; philosophy and religion; political science; psychology; social sciences; sociology

SCOTT COMMUNITY COLLEGE

Bettendorf, Iowa

Scott Community College, founded in 1966, is a state and locally supported two-year college. It is accredited by the North Central Association of Colleges and Schools.
Course delivery sites Courses are delivered to your home, military bases, other colleges.
Media Courses are delivered via videoconferencing, audiographics conferencing.
Credit-earning options Students may transfer credits from another institution or may earn credits through examinations, portfolio assessment, military training, business training.
Contact Admissions Office, Scott Community College, 500 Belmont Road, Bettendorf, IA 52722-6804. *Telephone:* 319-359-7531, Ext. 254. *Fax:* 319-359-0306.

DEGREE & CERTIFICATE PROGRAMS

Associate Degrees
▶ *Hazardous Materials Technology (AAS)*
▶ *Industrial Health and Safety (AAS)*
▶ *Liberal Arts (AA)*

Undergraduate Certificates
▶ *Hazardous Materials Technology*

INDIVIDUAL COURSE SUBJECT AREAS

Undergraduate
Biological and life sciences; business; business administration and management; chemistry; conservation and natural resources; economics; engineering-related technologies; English composition; English language and literature; environmental engineering; fine arts; geology; health and physical education/fitness; history; industrial engineering; liberal arts, general studies, and humanities; mathematics; music; philosophy and religion; physical sciences; political science; psychology; sociology

SCOTTSDALE COMMUNITY COLLEGE

Scottsdale, Arizona

Scottsdale Community College, founded in 1969, is a state and locally supported two-year college. It is accredited by the North Central Association of Colleges and Schools. It first offered distance learning courses in 1994. In 1996–97, it offered 7 courses at a distance. In the fall of 1996, there was a total of 150 students enrolled in distance learning courses.
Course delivery sites Courses are delivered to your home.
Media Courses are delivered via television, World Wide Web. Students and teachers interact via mail, telephone, fax, e-mail. A computer is required for some courses.
Restrictions Programs are available to in-state students only.
Services Distance learners have access to library services, the campus computer network, e-mail services, academic advising, career placement assistance at a distance.
Credit-earning options Students may transfer credits from another institution or may earn credits through institutionally developed exams, portfolio assessment, military training.
Typical costs Tuition of $37 per credit hour for in-state residents. Tuition of $163 per credit hour for out-of-state residents. *Noncredit courses:* $111 per course. Financial aid is available to distance learners enrolled full-time.
Registration Students may register by mail, fax.
Contact John Fitzpatric, Video-Dean, Scottsdale Community College, 9000 East Chaparral, Scottsdale, AZ 85250. *Telephone:* 602-423-6656. *Fax:* 602-423-6066. *E-mail:* fitzpatric@sc.maricopa.edu.

INDIVIDUAL COURSE SUBJECT AREAS

Undergraduate
Business; computer and information sciences; creative writing; music

SEABURY-WESTERN THEOLOGICAL SEMINARY

Evanston, Illinois

Seabury-Western Theological Seminary, founded in 1933, is an independent-religious graduate institution. It is accredited by the North Central Association of Colleges and Schools. It first offered distance learning courses in 1995. In 1996–97, it offered 1 course at a distance.
Course delivery sites Courses are delivered to your home.
Media Courses are delivered via World Wide Web, e-mail. Students and teachers interact via e-mail, computer conferencing. A computer is required for all courses.
Typical costs Tuition of $1150 per course. *Noncredit courses:* $350 per course. Costs may vary by specific program of study.
Contact Rev. Meredith Woods Potter, Director of Academic Affairs, Seabury-Western Theological Seminary, 2122 Sheridan Road, Evanston, IL 60201. *Telephone:* 847-328-9300. *Fax:* 847-328-9624. *E-mail:* swts@nwu.edu. *Web site:* http://www.swts.nwu.edu.

INDIVIDUAL COURSE SUBJECT AREAS

Graduate
Theological studies

Noncredit
Theological studies

Profiles: Seattle Central Community College

SEATTLE CENTRAL COMMUNITY COLLEGE

Seattle, Washington

Center for Educational Telecommunications

Seattle Central Community College, founded in 1966, is a state-supported two-year college. It is accredited by the Northwest Association of Schools and Colleges. It first offered distance learning courses in 1990. In 1996–97, it offered 50 courses at a distance. In the fall of 1996, there was a total of 180 students enrolled in distance learning courses.
Course delivery sites Courses are delivered to your home, your workplace, military bases.
Media Courses are delivered via television, videotapes, audiotapes, e-mail, print. Students and teachers interact via mail, telephone, fax, e-mail.
Services Distance learners have access to e-mail services, academic advising at a distance.
Credit-earning options Students may transfer credits from another institution or may earn credits through standardized exams, portfolio assessment, work experience.
Typical costs Tuition of $229.75 per course plus mandatory fees of $55 per course for in-state residents. Tuition of $370 per course plus mandatory fees of $50 per course for out-of-state residents. Costs may vary by number of credits taken, course delivery options. Financial aid is available to distance learners enrolled full-time.
Registration Students may register by mail, fax, phone, e-mail, World Wide Web.
Contact Josie Corsilles, Program Assistant, Seattle Central Community College, 1701 Broadway, BE 144, Seattle, WA 98122-2400. *Telephone:* 800-510-1724. *Fax:* 206-287-5562. *E-mail:* jcorsi@seaccc.sccd.ctc.edu. *Web site:* http://seaccd.sccd.ctc.edu/central/virtcoll/index.html.

DEGREE & CERTIFICATE PROGRAMS

Associate Degrees

▶ *Liberal Arts (AA)*
In the fall of 1996 there were 180 students enrolled in this program.
Application requirements *Prior education:* high school diploma or equivalent. *Minimum age:* 16. *Other requirements:* ASSET, high school transcript, college transcripts.
Completion requirements 90 quarter credits are required. 30 quarter credits must be completed through the institution.

Undergraduate Certificates

▶ *English as a Second Language*
In the fall of 1996 there were 200 students enrolled in this program. In 1995–96, 10 certificates were earned at a distance through this program.
Restrictions This program is available to in-state students only.
Application requirements *Prior education:* high school diploma or equivalent. *Minimum age:* 16. *Other requirements:* ASSET, high school transcript.
Completion requirements 24 quarter credits are required.
On-campus requirements Three weeks in the summer must be on campus.

INDIVIDUAL COURSE SUBJECT AREAS

Undergraduate

Abnormal psychology; accounting; algebra; American literature; American studies; anthropology; Asian studies; astronomy and astrophysics; biology; business administration and management; chemistry; child care and development; developmental and child psychology; economics; English as a second language (ESL); English composition; English language and literature; English literature; environmental science; ethics; film studies; foods and nutrition studies; geography; journalism; logic; mass media; Medieval/Renaissance studies; music; oceanography; political science; sociology; Spanish language and literature; statistics; women's studies

SEATTLE PACIFIC UNIVERSITY

Seattle, Washington

Division of Continuing Studies

Seattle Pacific University, founded in 1891, is an independent-religious Free Methodist comprehensive institution. It is accredited by the Northwest Association of Schools and Colleges. It first offered distance learning courses in 1984. In 1996–97, it offered 50 courses at a distance. In the fall of 1996, there was a total of 1,047 students enrolled in distance learning courses.
Course delivery sites Courses are delivered to your home.
Media Courses are delivered via videotapes, audiotapes, computer software, World Wide Web, print. Students and teachers interact via mail, telephone, e-mail. A computer is required for some courses.
Services Distance learners have access to library services, the campus computer network, e-mail services, academic advising at a distance.
Typical costs *Undergraduate:* Tuition of $95 per quarter credit. *Graduate:* Tuition of $60 per quarter credit. Course materials cost varies by course. Costs may vary by number of credits taken, course delivery options.
Registration Students may register by mail, fax, phone.
Contact Distance Learning Office, Seattle Pacific University, 3307 Third Avenue, W, Seattle, WA 98119. *Telephone:* 800-648-7898. *Fax:* 206-281-2662. *Web site:* http://www.spu.edu/dcs/.

INDIVIDUAL COURSE SUBJECT AREAS

Undergraduate

American (US) history; bible studies; biology; comparative literature; developmental and child psychology; English language and literature; history; philosophy and religion; political science

Graduate

American (US) history; continuing education; education; history; special education; teacher education

SEMINOLE STATE COLLEGE

Seminole, Oklahoma

Seminole State College, founded in 1931, is a state-supported two-year college. It is accredited by the North Central Association of Colleges and Schools. It first offered distance learning courses in 1995.
Media Courses are delivered via videoconferencing.
Restrictions Programs are available to local area students only.
Credit-earning options Students may transfer credits from another institution or may earn credits through examinations, military training. Financial aid is available to distance learners.
Contact Vice President for Academic Affairs, Seminole State College, PO Box 351, Seminole, OK 74818-0351. *Telephone:* 405-382-9203. *Fax:* 405-382-3122.

INDIVIDUAL COURSE SUBJECT AREAS

Undergraduate
Mathematics; sociology

SETON HALL UNIVERSITY

South Orange, New Jersey

College of Education and Human Services

Seton Hall University, founded in 1856, is an independent-religious Roman Catholic university. It is accredited by the Middle States Association of Colleges and Schools. It first offered distance learning courses in 1995.
Course delivery sites Courses are delivered to your home.
Media Courses are delivered via videoconferencing, print, computer conferencing.
Restrictions Programs are available to in-state students only.
Contact Associate Dean, Seton Hall University, 400 South Orange Avenue, South Orange, NJ 07079. *Telephone:* 201-761-9668. *Fax:* 201-761-7642.

INDIVIDUAL COURSE SUBJECT AREAS

Graduate
Education administration; special education; teacher education

SHAWNEE COMMUNITY COLLEGE

Ullin, Illinois

Learning Resources

Shawnee Community College, founded in 1967, is a state and locally supported two-year college. It is accredited by the North Central Association of Colleges and Schools. It first offered distance learning courses in 1994. In 1996–97, it offered 21 courses at a distance. In the fall of 1996, there was a total of 351 students enrolled in distance learning courses.
Course delivery sites Courses are delivered to your home, your workplace, other colleges, 5 off-campus centers in Anna, Cairo, Goreville, Metropolis, Vienna.
Media Courses are delivered via videotapes, videoconferencing. Students and teachers interact via videoconferencing, mail, telephone, fax, e-mail.
Restrictions Interactive video courses are available to in-state students only. Telecourses are available to students in Illinois, Kentucky and Missouri only.
Services Distance learners have access to library services at a distance.
Credit-earning options Students may transfer credits from another institution or may earn credits through examinations.
Typical costs Tuition of $33.75 per credit hour. Financial aid is available to distance learners.
Contact Andrea Witthoft, Distance Learning Technician, Shawnee Community College, 8364 Shawnee College Road, Ullin, IL 62992. *Telephone:* 618-634-2242. *Fax:* 618-634-9028. *E-mail:* andreaw@shawnee.cc.il.us. *Web site:* http://www.shawnee.cc.il.us/index2.htm.

Distance Learning Programs

INDIVIDUAL COURSE SUBJECT AREAS

Undergraduate
Biology; computer and information sciences; developmental and child psychology; engineering/industrial management; English composition; English language and literature; geology; health professions and related sciences; liberal arts, general studies, and humanities; mathematics; nursing; zoology

SHELBY STATE COMMUNITY COLLEGE

Memphis, Tennessee

Distance Learning Department

Shelby State Community College, founded in 1970, is a state-supported two-year college. It is accredited by the Southern Association of Colleges and Schools. It first offered distance learning courses in 1981. In 1996–97, it offered 50 courses at a distance. In the fall of 1996, there was a total of 550 students enrolled in distance learning courses.
Course delivery sites Courses are delivered to your home, your workplace, 4 off-campus centers in Fayette County, Memphis, Millington, North Memphis.
Media Courses are delivered via television, videotapes, videoconferencing, audiotapes, e-mail. Students and teachers interact via mail, telephone, fax, e-mail.
Services Distance learners have access to library services, e-mail services, academic advising at a distance.
Credit-earning options Students may transfer credits from another institution or may earn credits through standardized exams, institutionally developed exams, military training.
Typical costs Tuition of $512 per semester plus mandatory fees of $13 per semester for in-state residents. Tuition of $2048 per semester plus mandatory fees of $13 per semester for out-of-state residents. Costs may vary by number of credits taken. Financial aid is available to distance learners enrolled full-time or part-time.
Registration Students may register by phone.
Contact Jane B. Sipes, Director of Distance Learning, Shelby State Community College, PO Box 40568, Memphis, TN 38174-0568. *Telephone:* 901-544-5335. *Fax:* 901-544-5714. *E-mail:* sisipes@sscc.cc.tn.us. *Web site:* http://www.sscc.cc.tn.us.

INDIVIDUAL COURSE SUBJECT AREAS

Undergraduate
Business; business administration and management; developmental and child psychology; economics; English composition; fine arts; health and physical education/fitness; history; liberal arts, general studies, and humanities; mathematics; music; political science; psychology; sociology; special education

SHENANDOAH UNIVERSITY

Winchester, Virginia

Division of Continuing Education

Shenandoah University, founded in 1875, is an independent-religious United Methodist comprehensive institution. It is accredited by the Southern Association of Colleges and Schools. It first offered distance learning courses in 1988. In 1996–97, it offered 12 courses at a distance.

Profiles: Shenandoah University

In the fall of 1996, there was a total of 1,027 students enrolled in distance learning courses.
Course delivery sites Courses are delivered to your home, your workplace.
Media Courses are delivered via television, videoconferencing, e-mail. Students and teachers interact via mail, telephone, e-mail. A computer is required for some courses.
Services Distance learners have access to e-mail services at a distance.
Credit-earning options Students may transfer credits from another institution or may earn credits through examinations.
Typical costs *Undergraduate:* Tuition of $340 per course. *Graduate:* Tuition of $390 per course. $50 material fee. Costs may vary by specific program of study.
Registration Students may register by mail.
Contact Ralph E. Lewis, Director, Continuing Education, Shenandoah University, 1460 University Drive, Winchester, VA 22601. *Telephone:* 540-665-4643. *Fax:* 540-665-3496. *E-mail:* rlewis@su.edu.

INDIVIDUAL COURSE SUBJECT AREAS

Graduate
Aerospace, aeronautical engineering; chemical engineering; civil engineering; electrical engineering; engineering mechanics; engineering/industrial management; environmental engineering; industrial engineering; mathematics; mechanical engineering; teacher education

SIERRA COLLEGE

Rocklin, California

Distance Learning Department

Sierra College, founded in 1936, is a state-supported two-year college. It is accredited by the Western Association of Schools and Colleges, Inc. It first offered distance learning courses in 1986. In 1996–97, it offered 14 courses at a distance. In the fall of 1996, there was a total of 525 students enrolled in distance learning courses.
Course delivery sites Courses are delivered to your home, your workplace, 2 off-campus centers in Grass Valley, Nevada City.
Media Courses are delivered via television. Students and teachers interact via mail, telephone, fax, e-mail.
Restrictions Programs are available to local area students only.
Services Distance learners have access to library services, the campus computer network, e-mail services, academic advising at a distance.
Credit-earning options Students may earn credits through institutionally developed exams.
Typical costs Tuition of $13 per unit for in-state residents. Tuition of $125 per unit for out-of-state residents. Financial aid is available to distance learners enrolled full-time or part-time.
Registration Students may register by mail, phone.
Contact Suzanne Davenport, Multi-Media Specialist, Sierra College, 5000 Rocklin Road, Rocklin, CA 95677. *Telephone:* 916-789-2638. *Fax:* 916-789-2632. *E-mail:* davenport_su@email.sierra.cc.ca.us.

INDIVIDUAL COURSE SUBJECT AREAS

Undergraduate
Business administration and management; developmental and child psychology; English composition; English language and literature; fine arts; history; liberal arts, general studies, and humanities; mathematics; political science; social psychology; sociology

SIMPSON COLLEGE

Indianola, Iowa

Division of Adult Learning

Simpson College, founded in 1860, is an independent-religious United Methodist four-year college. It is accredited by the North Central Association of Colleges and Schools. It first offered distance learning courses in 1996. In 1996–97, it offered 3 courses at a distance. In the fall of 1996, there was a total of 25 students enrolled in distance learning courses.
Course delivery sites Courses are delivered to your home.
Media Courses are delivered via World Wide Web, e-mail. Students and teachers interact via mail, telephone, fax, e-mail. A computer is required for all courses.
Services Distance learners have access to library services, the campus computer network, academic advising, tutoring at a distance.
Credit-earning options Students may transfer credits from another institution or may earn credits through standardized exams, portfolio assessment, military training.
Typical costs Tuition of $175 per credit. Financial aid is available to distance learners enrolled full-time or part-time.
Registration Students may register by mail, fax, phone, e-mail.
Contact Walter Pearson, Director, Simpson College, 701 North C Street, Indianola, IA 50125. *Telephone:* 515-961-1615. *Fax:* 515-961-1498. *E-mail:* pearsonw@storm.simpson.edu. *Web site:* http://www.simpson.edu/dal/dal.html.

INDIVIDUAL COURSE SUBJECT AREAS

Undergraduate
Business administration and management; communications

SINCLAIR COMMUNITY COLLEGE

Dayton, Ohio

Distance Learning Division

Sinclair Community College, founded in 1887, is a state and locally supported two-year college. It is accredited by the North Central Association of Colleges and Schools. It first offered distance learning courses in 1979. In 1996–97, it offered 75 courses at a distance. In the fall of 1996, there was a total of 1,800 students enrolled in distance learning courses.
Course delivery sites Courses are delivered to your home, your workplace, military bases, 12 off-campus centers in Dayton.
Media Courses are delivered via television, videotapes, videoconferencing, audiotapes, World Wide Web, print. Students and teachers interact via videoconferencing, mail, telephone, fax, e-mail. A computer is required for some courses.
Restrictions Programs are available to in-state students only.
Services Distance learners have access to e-mail services, academic advising at a distance.
Credit-earning options Students may transfer credits from another institution or may earn credits through standardized exams, institutionally developed exams, portfolio assessment, military training, business training.
Typical costs Tuition of $31 per credit hour for local area residents. Tuition of $49 per credit hour for in-state residents. Tuition of $80 per credit hour for out-of-state residents. Financial aid is available to distance learners.

Registration Students may register by mail, fax, phone.
Contact Peggy Falkenstein, Dean, Distance Learning, Sinclair Community College, 444 West Third Street, Dayton, OH 45402. *Telephone:* 937-449-6144. *Fax:* 937-226-2891. *E-mail:* Pfalkens@Sinclair.edu. *Web site:* http://www.sinclair.edu/sec/.

DEGREE & CERTIFICATE PROGRAMS

Associate Degrees

▶ *Business Technology (AS)*
Restrictions Televised courses are available to in-state students only.
Application requirements *Prior education:* high school diploma or equivalent. *Other requirements:* COMPASS, ASSET, an application fee of $10.
Completion requirements 98 quarter hours are required. 30 quarter hours must be completed through the institution.

▶ *Liberal Arts (AA)*
Restrictions Televised courses are available to in-state students only.
Application requirements *Prior education:* high school diploma or equivalent. *Other requirements:* COMPASS, ASSET, an application fee of $10.
Completion requirements 94 quarter hours are required. 30 quarter hours must be completed through the institution.

INDIVIDUAL COURSE SUBJECT AREAS

Undergraduate

Abnormal psychology; accounting; American (US) history; anthropology; area, ethnic, and cultural studies; art history and criticism; astronomy and astrophysics; business; business administration and management; business communications; business law; chemistry; communications; computer and information sciences; creative writing; developmental and child psychology; economics; engineering-related technologies; English composition; English literature; film studies; fine arts; geology; history; law and legal studies; liberal arts, general studies, and humanities; marketing; mathematics; music; organizational behavior studies; philosophy and religion; physics; psychology; social sciences; sociology; Spanish language and literature

SKAGIT VALLEY COLLEGE

Mount Vernon, Washington

Distance Education

Skagit Valley College, founded in 1926, is a state-supported two-year college. It is accredited by the Northwest Association of Schools and Colleges. It first offered distance learning courses in 1978. In 1996–97, it offered 50 courses at a distance. In the fall of 1996, there was a total of 750 students enrolled in distance learning courses.
Course delivery sites Courses are delivered to your home, your workplace, military bases, 15 off-campus centers in Anacortes, Burlington, Clinton, Concrete, Coupeville, Friday Harbor, LaConner, Lopez Island, Mount Vernon, Oak Harbor, Orcas, Sedrow Woolley, Skagit Valley, Stanwood, Whilbey Island.
Media Courses are delivered via videotapes, videoconferencing, audiotapes, computer software, World Wide Web, e-mail, print. Students and teachers interact via videoconferencing, mail, telephone, fax, e-mail. A computer is required for some courses. The institution provides assistance with acquiring computer equipment.
Services Distance learners have access to library services, the campus computer network, e-mail services, academic advising at a distance.

Credit-earning options Students may transfer credits from another institution or may earn credits through institutionally developed exams, military training, business training.
Typical costs Tuition of $46 per credit for in-state residents. Tuition of $183.70 per credit for out-of-state residents. $25 per telecourse Internet and SVC Network fee. Costs may vary by course delivery options. Financial aid is available to distance learners enrolled full-time.
Contact Jill Shinn, Program Assistant, Skagit Valley College, 2405 East College Way, Mount Vernon, WA 98273. *Telephone:* 360-428-1268. *Fax:* 360-428-1078. *E-mail:* jshinn@ctc.ctc.edu.

DEGREE & CERTIFICATE PROGRAMS

Associate Degrees

▶ *General Studies (AA)*
In the fall of 1996 there were 750 students enrolled in this program. In 1995–96, 40 degrees were earned at a distance through this program.
Application requirements *Prior education:* high school diploma or equivalent. *Other requirements:* ASSET, high school transcript.
Completion requirements 90 hours are required. 25 quarter credits must be completed through the institution.
On-campus requirements Two seminars per quarter.

INDIVIDUAL COURSE SUBJECT AREAS

Undergraduate

Astronomy and astrophysics; business administration and management; chemistry; computer and information sciences; creative writing; developmental and child psychology; economics; English composition; English language and literature; geology; health and physical education/fitness; history; liberal arts, general studies, and humanities; mathematics; Middle Eastern languages and literatures; philosophy and religion; political science; social psychology; sociology

SKIDMORE COLLEGE

Saratoga Springs, New York

University Without Walls

Skidmore College, founded in 1903, is an independent-nonprofit comprehensive institution. It is accredited by the Middle States Association of Colleges and Schools. It first offered distance learning courses in 1971. In the fall of 1996, there was a total of 250 students enrolled in distance learning courses.
Course delivery sites Courses are delivered to your home.
Media Courses are delivered via World Wide Web, e-mail, print. Students and teachers interact via mail, telephone, fax, e-mail, World Wide Web. A computer is required for some courses.
Services Distance learners have access to academic advising at a distance.
Credit-earning options Students may transfer credits from another institution or may earn credits through examinations, portfolio assessment, military training, business training.
Typical costs Tuition of $400 per course plus mandatory fees of $2400 per year. Costs may vary by number of credits taken. Financial aid is available to distance learners.
Registration Students may register by mail, fax, e-mail, World Wide Web.
Contact Cornel Reinhart, Director, Skidmore College, University Without Walls, Saratoga Springs, NY 12866. *Telephone:* 518-581-7400, Ext. 2295. *Fax:* 518-581-7422. *E-mail:* uww@skidmore.edu. *Web site:* http://www.skidmore.edu.

Profiles: Skidmore College

DEGREE & CERTIFICATE PROGRAMS

Baccalaureate Degrees

▶*Individualized Studies (BA, BS)*
In the fall of 1996 there were 270 students enrolled in this program.
Application requirements *Prior education:* high school diploma or equivalent. *Other requirements:* high school transcript, college transcripts, an essay or personal statement, letter(s) of recommendation, an application fee of $30, on-campus admissions interview.
Completion requirements 120 credits are required. 6 credit final project must be completed through the institution.
On-campus requirements For admissions interview, pre-advising session, degree plan approval.

INDIVIDUAL COURSE SUBJECT AREAS

Undergraduate

Accounting; area, ethnic, and cultural studies; biology; botany; business; business administration and management; Classical languages and literatures; communications; computer and information sciences; creative writing; developmental and child psychology; economics; education; English composition; English language and literature; European languages and literatures; history; human resources management; liberal arts, general studies, and humanities; mathematics; microbiology; philosophy and religion; physical sciences; political science; psychology; public administration and services; social sciences; social work; sociology; visual and performing arts; zoology

See full description on page 470.

SOUTHEAST ARKANSAS TECHNICAL COLLEGE

Pine Bluff, Arkansas

Southeast Arkansas Technical College, founded in 1991, is a state-supported two-year college. It is a candidate for accreditation by the North Central Association of Colleges and Schools. It first offered distance learning courses in 1995. In 1996–97, it offered 6 courses at a distance. In the fall of 1996, there was a total of 125 students enrolled in distance learning courses.
Course delivery sites Courses are delivered to your home.
Media Courses are delivered via television, videotapes. Students and teachers interact via mail, telephone, fax, e-mail.
Services Distance learners have access to e-mail services, academic advising, tutoring, career placement assistance at a distance.
Credit-earning options Students may transfer credits from another institution or may earn credits through institutionally developed exams, portfolio assessment, military training, business training.
Typical costs Tuition of $30 per credit hour plus mandatory fees of $20 per course for in-state residents. Tuition of $60 per credit hour plus mandatory fees of $20 per course for out-of-state residents. $450 is maximum tuition for in-state students, $900 is maximum tuition for out-of-state students. *Noncredit courses:* $40 per course. Costs may vary by number of credits taken, course delivery options. Financial aid is available to distance learners enrolled full-time.
Registration Students may register by mail.
Contact Brenda Scruggs, Interim Dean of Instruction, Southeast Arkansas Technical College, 1900 South Hazel Street, Pine Bluff, AR 71603. *Telephone:* 501-543-5962. *Fax:* 501-543-5927. *E-mail:* bscruggs@stc.seark.tec.ar.us.

INDIVIDUAL COURSE SUBJECT AREAS

Undergraduate

Fine arts; geography; health and physical education/fitness; history; political science; psychology; sociology

SOUTHEAST COMMUNITY COLLEGE, BEATRICE CAMPUS

Beatrice, Nebraska

Southeast Community College, Beatrice Campus, founded in 1976, is a district-supported two-year college. It is accredited by the North Central Association of Colleges and Schools. It first offered distance learning courses in 1996.
Course delivery sites Courses are delivered to other colleges.
Media Courses are delivered via television, videoconferencing.
Restrictions Programs are available to in-state students only.
Credit-earning options Students may transfer credits from another institution. Financial aid is available to distance learners.
Contact Distance Learning Coordinator, Southeast Community College, Beatrice Campus, Route 2, Box 35A, Beatrice, NE 68310. *Telephone:* 402-228-3468, Ext. 321. *Fax:* 402-223-2121.

INDIVIDUAL COURSE SUBJECT AREAS

Undergraduate

Accounting; education administration; English composition; European languages and literatures; health professions and related sciences; nursing; social psychology; special education; teacher education

SOUTHEAST COMMUNITY COLLEGE, LINCOLN CAMPUS

Lincoln, Nebraska

Continuing Education

Southeast Community College, Lincoln Campus, founded in 1973, is a district-supported two-year college. It is accredited by the North Central Association of Colleges and Schools. It first offered distance learning courses in 1994. In 1996–97, it offered 15 courses at a distance. In the fall of 1996, there was a total of 250 students enrolled in distance learning courses.
Course delivery sites Courses are delivered to your home, your workplace, 24 off-campus centers.
Media Courses are delivered via television. Students and teachers interact via telephone, in-person meetings.
Services Distance learners have access to library services, academic advising, career placement assistance at a distance.
Credit-earning options Students may transfer credits from another institution or may earn credits through institutionally developed exams, military training.
Typical costs Tuition of $27.50 per quarter credit. *Noncredit courses:* $2–$5 per contact hour. Costs may vary by campus or location. Financial aid is available to distance learners enrolled part-time.
Registration Students may register by mail, fax.
Contact Randy Hiatt, Director of Distance Education, Southeast Community College, Lincoln Campus, 8800 "O" Street, Lincoln, NE 68520. *Telephone:* 402-437-2705. *Fax:* 402-437-2704.

DEGREE & CERTIFICATE PROGRAMS

Associate Degrees

▶ *General Studies (AA/AAS)*
In the fall of 1996 there were 20 students enrolled in this program.
Application requirements *Prior education:* none required. *Other requirements:* high school transcript, college transcripts.
Completion requirements 90 quarter credits are required.
On-campus requirements For testing, lab.

INDIVIDUAL COURSE SUBJECT AREAS

Undergraduate
Accounting; American (US) history; area, ethnic, and cultural studies; business administration and management; communications; economics; English composition; English language and literature; ethics; European history; foods and nutrition studies; geology; mathematics; psychology; sociology; Spanish language and literature

SOUTHEASTERN COMMUNITY COLLEGE, NORTH CAMPUS

West Burlington, Iowa

Southeastern Community College, North Campus, founded in 1968, is a state and locally supported two-year college. It is accredited by the North Central Association of Colleges and Schools. It first offered distance learning courses in 1982. In 1996–97, it offered 5 courses at a distance. In the fall of 1996, there was a total of 50 students enrolled in distance learning courses.
Course delivery sites Courses are delivered to your home, Southeastern Community College, South Campus (Keokuk).
Media Courses are delivered via television, videotapes, print. Students and teachers interact via mail, telephone, fax.
Restrictions Programs are primarily available to in-state students.
Services Distance learners have access to academic advising at a distance.
Credit-earning options Students may transfer credits from another institution or may earn credits through standardized exams.
Typical costs Tuition of $57 per credit hour for in-state residents. Tuition of $85.50 per credit hour for out-of-state residents. Financial aid is available to distance learners.
Registration Students may register by mail, phone.
Contact Admissions Office, Southeastern Community College, North Campus, PO Drawer F, West Burlington, IA 52655. *Telephone:* 319-752-2731. *Fax:* 319-752-4957.

INDIVIDUAL COURSE SUBJECT AREAS

Undergraduate
Astronomy and astrophysics; biology; business administration and management; developmental and child psychology; European languages and literatures; human resources management; liberal arts, general studies, and humanities; mathematics; physics; political science; social work

Noncredit
Business; business administration and management

SOUTHEASTERN LOUISIANA UNIVERSITY

Hammond, Louisiana

Continuing Education

Southeastern Louisiana University, founded in 1925, is a state-supported comprehensive institution. It is accredited by the Southern Association of Colleges and Schools. It first offered distance learning courses in 1982. In 1996–97, it offered 10 courses at a distance. In the fall of 1996, there was a total of 150 students enrolled in distance learning courses.
Course delivery sites Courses are delivered to your home, Grambling State University (Grambling), Louisiana State University and Agricultural and Mechanical College (Baton Rouge), Louisiana State University in Shreveport (Shreveport), Louisiana Tech University (Ruston), McNeese State University (Lake Charles), Nicholls State University (Thibodaux), Northeast Louisiana University (Monroe), Northwestern State University of Louisiana (Natchitoches), Southern University and Agricultural and Mechanical College (Baton Rouge).
Media Courses are delivered via television, videotapes, videoconferencing. Students and teachers interact via videoconferencing, mail, telephone, fax, e-mail.
Restrictions Programs are available to in-state students only.
Services Distance learners have access to library services, the campus computer network, e-mail services, academic advising at a distance.
Credit-earning options Students may transfer credits from another institution or may earn credits through examinations.
Typical costs *Undergraduate:* Tuition of $272.25 per credit for in-state residents. Tuition of $272.25 per credit for out-of-state residents. *Graduate:* Tuition of $272.25 per credit for in-state residents. Tuition of $272.25 per credit for out-of-state residents. Out-of-state fees must be paid when the student enrolls in 4 or more credit hours at approximately $136 per credit hour. Costs may vary by number of credits taken. Financial aid is available to distance learners.
Registration Students may register by phone.
Contact Dr. Gerald Guidroz, Dean, Continuing Education, Southeastern Louisiana University, SLUN 858, Hammond, LA 70402. *Telephone:* 504-549-2301. *Fax:* 504-549-5078. *E-mail:* gguidroz@selu.edu. *Web site:* http://www.selu.edu.

INDIVIDUAL COURSE SUBJECT AREAS

Undergraduate
Business administration and management; developmental and child psychology; English as a second language (ESL); English language and literature; finance; health and physical education/fitness; history; nursing; psychology; sociology; special education

Graduate
English as a second language (ESL); special education

SOUTHEAST MISSOURI STATE UNIVERSITY

Cape Girardeau, Missouri

Extended Learning

Southeast Missouri State University, founded in 1873, is a state-supported comprehensive institution. It is accredited by the North Central Association of Colleges and Schools. It first offered distance

Profiles: Southeast Missouri State University

learning courses in 1995. In 1996–97, it offered 13 courses at a distance. In the fall of 1996, there was a total of 53 students enrolled in distance learning courses.

Course delivery sites Courses are delivered to Mineral Area College (Park Hills), Three Rivers Community-Technical College (Norwich, CT), 2 off-campus centers in Malden, Sikeston.
Media Courses are delivered via videoconferencing. Students and teachers interact via videoconferencing, mail, telephone, fax, e-mail.
Restrictions Programs are available to local area students only.
Services Distance learners have access to library services, e-mail services, academic advising at a distance.
Credit-earning options Students may transfer credits from another institution or may earn credits through standardized exams, military training.
Typical costs *Undergraduate:* Tuition of $90.30 per semester hour for in-state residents. Tuition of $167.30 per semester hour for out-of-state residents. *Graduate:* Tuition of $96.30 per semester hour for in-state residents. Tuition of $178.30 per semester hour for out-of-state residents. Costs may vary by number of credits taken. Financial aid is available to distance learners enrolled full-time or part-time.
Registration Students may register by mail, phone, e-mail.
Contact Dr. Stephen S. Chapman, Director, Extended Learning, Southeast Missouri State University, 1 University Plaza, Cape Girardeau, MO 63701. *Telephone:* 573-651-2189. *Fax:* 573-651-2001.

INDIVIDUAL COURSE SUBJECT AREAS

Undergraduate
Business; business administration and management; communications; developmental and child psychology; education; mathematics; philosophy and religion; psychology; social psychology

Graduate
Education administration; mathematics

SOUTHERN ARKANSAS UNIVERSITY TECH

Camden, Arkansas

Business and Industry Productivity Center

Southern Arkansas University Tech, founded in 1968, is a state-supported two-year college. It is accredited by the North Central Association of Colleges and Schools. It first offered distance learning courses in 1995. In 1996–97, it offered 5 courses at a distance. In the fall of 1996, there was a total of 42 students enrolled in distance learning courses.
Course delivery sites Courses are delivered to 2 off-campus centers in Camden, Lonoke.
Media Courses are delivered via videoconferencing. Students and teachers interact via videoconferencing. A computer is required for some courses.
Restrictions Programs are available to local area students only.
Credit-earning options Students may transfer credits from another institution or may earn credits through examinations, portfolio assessment, military training, business training.
Typical costs Tuition of $45 per credit.
Contact Sheila C. Self, Business and Industry Coordinator, Southern Arkansas University Tech, SAU Tech Station, Camden, AR 71701. *Telephone:* 870-574-4495. *Fax:* 870-574-4520. *E-mail:* sself@sautech.edu.

INDIVIDUAL COURSE SUBJECT AREAS

Undergraduate
Administrative and secretarial services; algebra; business administration and management; computer and information sciences; history

SOUTHERN CHRISTIAN UNIVERSITY

Montgomery, Alabama

Extended Learning Program

Southern Christian University is an independent-religious comprehensive institution affiliated with the Church of Christ. It is accredited by the Southern Association of Colleges and Schools. It first offered distance learning courses in 1993. In 1996–97, it offered 148 courses at a distance. In the fall of 1996, there was a total of 110 students enrolled in distance learning courses.
Course delivery sites Courses are delivered to your home.
Media Courses are delivered via videotapes, World Wide Web. Students and teachers interact via mail, telephone, fax, e-mail. A computer is required for some courses.
Restrictions Courses are available to US and Canadian students only.
Services Distance learners have access to library services, e-mail services, academic advising, career placement assistance at a distance.
Credit-earning options Students may transfer credits from another institution or may earn credits through military training.
Typical costs *Undergraduate:* Tuition of $137 per quarter hour plus mandatory fees of $55 per quarter hour. *Graduate:* Tuition of $137 per quarter hour plus mandatory fees of $55 per quarter hour. *Noncredit courses:* $150 per course. Financial aid is available to distance learners.
Registration Students may register by mail, phone, e-mail, World Wide Web.
Contact Mac Adkins, Director of Admissions, Southern Christian University, 1200 Taylor Road, Montgomery, AL 36117-3553. *Telephone:* 800-351-4040. *Fax:* 334-271-0002. *E-mail:* scuniversity@mindspring.com. *Web site:* http://www.southernchristian.edu.

DEGREE & CERTIFICATE PROGRAMS

Baccalaureate Degrees
▶ *Biological Studies (BA, BS)*
In 1995–96, 7 degrees were earned at a distance through this program.
Application requirements *Prior education:* some undergraduate course work. *Other requirements:* high school transcript, college transcripts, letter(s) of recommendation, an application fee of $35.
Completion requirements 192 quarter hours are required. 48 quarter hours must be completed through the institution. *Maximum time for completion:* seven years.

Graduate Degrees
▶ *Counseling (MS)*
In 1995–96, 8 degrees were earned at a distance through this program.
Application requirements *Prior education:* baccalaureate degree. *Other requirements:* MAT or GRE, college transcripts, letter(s) of recommendation, an application fee of $35.
Completion requirements 50 quarter hours are required. *Maximum time for completion:* four years.

▶ *Divinity (MDiv)*
In 1995–96, 3 degrees were earned at a distance through this program.
Application requirements *Prior education:* baccalaureate degree. *Other requirements:* MAT or GRE, college transcripts, letter(s) of recommendation, an application fee of $35.

Completion requirements 120 quarter hours are required. *Maximum time for completion:* seven years.
▶ *Ministry (MA)*
Application requirements *Prior education:* baccalaureate degree. *Other requirements:* MAT or GRE, college transcripts, letter(s) of recommendation, an application fee of $35.
Completion requirements 54 quarter hours are required. *Maximum time for completion:* four years.

INDIVIDUAL COURSE SUBJECT AREAS

Undergraduate
Philosophy and religion; theological studies

Graduate
Counseling psychology; philosophy and religion; theological studies

Noncredit
Philosophy and religion; theological studies

SOUTHERN ILLINOIS UNIVERSITY AT CARBONDALE

Carbondale, Illinois

Library Affairs

Southern Illinois University at Carbondale, founded in 1869, is a state-supported university. It is accredited by the North Central Association of Colleges and Schools. It first offered distance learning courses in 1995. In 1996–97, it offered 9 courses at a distance. In the fall of 1996, there was a total of 16 students enrolled in distance learning courses.
Course delivery sites Courses are delivered to your workplace, Belleville Area College (Belleville), John A. Logan College (Carterville), Kaskaskia College (Centralia), Lewis and Clark Community College (Godfrey), Metropolitan Community College (East St. Louis), Rend Lake College (Ina), Shawnee Community College (Ullin), Southeastern Illinois College (Harrisburg), Southern Illinois University at Edwardsville (Edwardsville), Wabash College (Crawfordsville, IN), high schools, hospitals.
Media Courses are delivered via videoconferencing. Students and teachers interact via videoconferencing, mail, telephone, fax, e-mail, World Wide Web.
Restrictions Courses are available to students in the bottom third of Illinois only.
Services Distance learners have access to library services, the campus computer network, e-mail services, academic advising, tutoring, career placement assistance at a distance.
Credit-earning options Students may transfer credits from another institution or may earn credits through standardized exams, institutionally developed exams, portfolio assessment, military training, business training.
Typical costs *Undergraduate:* Tuition of $45 per semester credit. *Graduate:* Tuition of $85 per semester credit. Financial aid is available to distance learners enrolled full-time or part-time.
Registration Students may register by mail, fax.
Contact Heidi Greer, Distance Learning Coordinator, Southern Illinois University at Carbondale, Morris Library, Carbondale, IL 62901-6632. *Telephone:* 618-453-1018. *Fax:* 618-453-3010. *E-mail:* hgreer@lib.siu.edu. *Web site:* http://www.lib.siu.edu/dlearn.

DEGREE & CERTIFICATE PROGRAMS

Baccalaureate Degrees
▶ *Electrical Engineering (BS)*
In the fall of 1996 there were 5 students enrolled in this program.

Application requirements *Prior education:* high school diploma or equivalent. *Other requirements:* ACT, high school transcript, college transcripts.
Completion requirements 128 credit hours are required. 90 credit hours must be completed through the institution.
On-campus requirements Some courses require three full-day visits on-campus for lab work. This time is flexible.
Program contact Darcy Murphy, Advisor, Southern Illinois University at Carbondale, Engineering Advisement, Carbondale, IL 62901-6603. Phone: 618-453-1638. Fax: 618-453-4235. E-mail: darcy@engr.siu.edu.

INDIVIDUAL COURSE SUBJECT AREAS

Undergraduate
Accounting; administrative and secretarial services; agricultural economics; electrical engineering; law and legal studies; telecommunications

Graduate
Instructional media; social psychology; sociology

SOUTHERN ILLINOIS UNIVERSITY AT EDWARDSVILLE

Edwardsville, Illinois

Office of Continuing Education

Southern Illinois University at Edwardsville, founded in 1957, is a state-supported comprehensive institution. It is accredited by the North Central Association of Colleges and Schools. It first offered distance learning courses in 1994. In 1996–97, it offered 30 courses at a distance. In the fall of 1996, there was a total of 64 students enrolled in distance learning courses.
Course delivery sites Courses are delivered to Belleville Area College (Belleville), Kaskaskia College (Centralia), Rend Lake College (Ina), Shawnee Community College (Ullin), off-campus center(s) in East St. Louis, Effingham.
Media Courses are delivered via videoconferencing, audioconferencing. Students and teachers interact via videoconferencing, mail, telephone, fax, e-mail. A computer is required for some courses.
Restrictions Courses are available to regional area students only.
Services Distance learners have access to library services, e-mail services, academic advising, tutoring, career placement assistance at a distance.
Credit-earning options Students may transfer credits from another institution or may earn credits through standardized exams.
Typical costs *Undergraduate:* Tuition of $84.15 per credit hour plus mandatory fees of $72 per course for in-state residents. Tuition of $252.45 per credit hour plus mandatory fees of $72 per course for out-of-state residents. *Graduate:* Tuition of $90.15 per credit hour plus mandatory fees of $72 per course for in-state residents. Tuition of $270.45 per credit hour plus mandatory fees of $72 per course for out-of-state residents. Costs may vary by number of credits taken. Financial aid is available to distance learners enrolled full-time or part-time.
Registration Students may register by mail, fax, phone, e-mail.
Contact Christa Oxford, Director, Admission and Records, Southern Illinois University at Edwardsville, Campus Box 1047, Edwardsville, IL 62026-1047. *Telephone:* 618-692-2080. *Fax:* 618-692-2081. *E-mail:* coxford@siue.edu. *Web site:* http://www.siue.edu.

Profiles: Southern Illinois University at Edwardsville

DEGREE & CERTIFICATE PROGRAMS

Baccalaureate Degrees

▶ *Nursing (BSN)*

In the fall of 1996 there were 55 students enrolled in this program. In 1995–96, 14 degrees were earned at a distance through this program.
Application requirements *Prior education:* RN license, associate's degree in nursing. *Other requirements:* NLN exams, high school transcript, college transcripts.
Completion requirements 124 semester hours are required. 76 semester hours must be completed through the institution. This is a degree completion program.
Program contact Karen Montgomery, School of Nursing, Southern Illinois University at Edwardsville, Campus Box 1066, Edwardsville, IL 62026-1066. Phone: 618-692-3904. Fax: 618-692-3854. E-mail: kmontgo@siue.edu.

Graduate Degrees

▶ *Business Administration (MBA)*

In the fall of 1996 there were 9 students enrolled in this program.
Application requirements *Prior education:* baccalaureate degree. *Other requirements:* GMAT, college transcripts, an application fee of $25.
Completion requirements 30 semester hours are required. 30 semester hours must be completed through the institution. *Maximum time for completion:* seven years.
Program contact Loretta Dieckman, Coordinator, Off-Campus MBA Program, Southern Illinois University at Edwardsville, Campus Box 1035, Edwardsville, IL 62026-1035. Phone: 618-692-2922. Fax: 618-692-3979. E-mail: ldiekm@siue.edu.

INDIVIDUAL COURSE SUBJECT AREAS

Graduate
Education

SOUTHERN METHODIST UNIVERSITY

Dallas, Texas

School of Engineering and Applied Science–Distance Learning

Southern Methodist University, founded in 1911, is an independent-religious university affiliated with the United Methodist Church. It is accredited by the Southern Association of Colleges and Schools. It first offered distance learning courses in 1962. In 1996–97, it offered 180 courses at a distance. In the fall of 1996, there was a total of 700 students enrolled in distance learning courses.
Course delivery sites Courses are delivered to your home, your workplace, military bases.
Media Courses are delivered via television, videotapes, videoconferencing. Students and teachers interact via mail, telephone, fax, e-mail.
Services Distance learners have access to library services, academic advising, career placement assistance at a distance.
Credit-earning options Students may transfer credits from another institution.
Typical costs Tuition of $600 per credit hour. Costs may vary by number of credits taken. Financial aid is available to distance learners enrolled full-time or part-time.
Registration Students may register by mail, fax.
Contact Mike Kirkpatrick, Director, Distance Education, Southern Methodist University, School of Engineering and Applied Science, PO Box 750335, Dallas, TX 75275-0335. *Telephone:* 214-768-1452. *Fax:* 214-768-3778. *E-mail:* rmk@seas.smu.edu. *Web site:* http://www.seas.smu.edu.

DEGREE & CERTIFICATE PROGRAMS

Graduate Degrees

▶ *Engineering Management (MS)*

In the fall of 1996 there were 37 students enrolled in this program. In 1995–96, 8 degrees were earned at a distance through this program.
Application requirements *Prior education:* baccalaureate degree. *Other requirements:* college transcripts, an essay or personal statement, an application fee of $25.
Completion requirements 30 credit hours are required. 24 credit hours must be completed through the institution. *Maximum time for completion:* seven years.

▶ *Hazardous and Waste Materials Management (MS)*

In the fall of 1996 there were 83 students enrolled in this program. In 1995–96, 17 degrees were earned at a distance through this program.
Application requirements *Prior education:* baccalaureate degree. *Other requirements:* college transcripts, an essay or personal statement, an application fee of $25.
Completion requirements 36 credit hours are required. 30 credit hours must be completed through the institution. *Maximum time for completion:* seven years.

▶ *Manufacturing Systems Management (MS)*

In the fall of 1996 there were 25 students enrolled in this program. In 1995–96, 2 degrees were earned at a distance through this program.
Application requirements *Prior education:* baccalaureate degree. *Other requirements:* college transcripts, an essay or personal statement, an application fee of $25.
Completion requirements 30 credit hours are required. 24 credit hours must be completed through the institution. *Maximum time for completion:* seven years.

▶ *Software Engineering (MS)*

In the fall of 1996 there were 139 students enrolled in this program. In 1995–96, 5 degrees were earned at a distance through this program.
Application requirements *Prior education:* baccalaureate degree. *Other requirements:* college transcripts, an essay or personal statement, an application fee of $25.
Completion requirements 30 credit hours are required. 24 credit hours must be completed through the institution. *Maximum time for completion:* seven years.

▶ *Systems Engineering (MS)*

In the fall of 1996 there were 30 students enrolled in this program.
Application requirements *Prior education:* baccalaureate degree. *Other requirements:* college transcripts, an essay or personal statement, an application fee of $25.
Completion requirements 30 credit hours are required. 24 credit hours must be completed through the institution. *Maximum time for completion:* seven years.

▶ *Telecommunications (MS)*

In the fall of 1996 there were 385 students enrolled in this program. In 1995–96, 39 degrees were earned at a distance through this program.
Application requirements *Prior education:* baccalaureate degree. *Other requirements:* college transcripts, an essay or personal statement, an application fee of $25.
Completion requirements 30 credit hours are required. 24 credit hours must be completed through the institution. *Maximum time for completion:* seven years.

INDIVIDUAL COURSE SUBJECT AREAS

Graduate
Communications; electrical engineering; engineering; engineering-related technologies; engineering/industrial management; environmental engineering; mechanical engineering; radio and television broadcasting

See full description on page 472.

SOUTHERN OREGON UNIVERSITY

Ashland, Oregon

Extended Campus Programs

Southern Oregon University, founded in 1926, is a state-supported comprehensive institution. It is accredited by the Northwest Association of Schools and Colleges. It first offered distance learning courses in 1992. In 1996–97, it offered 25 courses at a distance. In the fall of 1996, there was a total of 150 students enrolled in distance learning courses.

Course delivery sites Courses are delivered to your home, your workplace, Oregon Institute of Technology (Klamath Falls), Rogue Community College (Grants Pass), Southwestern Oregon Community College (Coos Bay), Umpqua Community College (Roseburg), off-campus center(s) in Gold Beach, Lakeview.
Media Courses are delivered via television, videotapes, computer software, e-mail, print. Students and teachers interact via videoconferencing, mail, telephone, fax, e-mail. A computer is required for some courses.
Restrictions Courses are available to regional area students only.
Services Distance learners have access to library services, the campus computer network, e-mail services, academic advising, career placement assistance, bookstore at a distance.
Credit-earning options Students may transfer credits from another institution or may earn credits through examinations, portfolio assessment.
Typical costs *Undergraduate:* Tuition of $270 per course. *Graduate:* Tuition of $429 per course. Costs may vary by number of credits taken, term of enrollment. Financial aid is available to distance learners enrolled full-time or part-time.
Registration Students may register by mail, fax, phone, e-mail.
Contact Pat Trowbridge, Director, Regional Academic Programs, Southern Oregon University, 1250 Siskiyou Boulevard, Ashland, OR 97520. *Telephone:* 541-552-6902. *Fax:* 541-552-6047. *E-mail:* trowbridge@sou.edu. *Web site:* http://www.sou.edu.

DEGREE & CERTIFICATE PROGRAMS

Baccalaureate Degrees

▶ *Business Administration (BS)*
Restrictions This program is available to local area students only. Program is designed for working adults who have completed equivalent of SOU general education requirements and are qualified for admission to SOU.
Application requirements *Prior education:* some undergraduate course work. *Other requirements:* college transcripts, application to SOU and School of Business.
Completion requirements 180 credit hours are required.
Program contact Barbara Scott, Associate Director, Extended Campus Programs, Southern Oregon University, 1250 Siskiyou Boulevard, Ashland, OR 97520. Phone: 541-552-6517. Fax: 541-552-6047. E-mail: scott@sou.edu.

Graduate Degrees

▶ *Secondary Education (MS)*
Restrictions Only available to students with access to Oregon Ed Net.
Application requirements *Prior education:* Baccalaureate in Teacher Education. *Other requirements:* college transcripts.
Completion requirements 45 credits are required. *Other requirements:* 45 credit hours: 21 hours from professional care, 15 hours secondary subject area or elementary area of certification, and 9 hours of electives. *Maximum time for completion:* seven years.
On-campus requirements Summer session.

▶ *Early Childhood Education, Special Education (MS)*
Restrictions Only available to students with access to Oregon Ed Net.
Application requirements *Prior education:* Baccalaureate in Teacher Education. *Other requirements:* college transcripts.
Completion requirements 45 credits are required. *Other requirements:* 45 credit hours: 21 hours from professional care, 15 hours secondary subject area or elementary area of concentration, and 9 hours of electives. *Maximum time for completion:* seven years.
On-campus requirements Summer session.

Graduate certificates

▶ *Early Childhood Education (License)*
Restrictions Only available to students with access to Oregon Ed Net.
Application requirements *Prior education:* Baccalaureate in Teacher Education. *Other requirements:* college transcripts.
Completion requirements 21 credit hours are required. *Maximum time for completion:* seven years.
On-campus requirements Summer session.

▶ *Special Education (License)*
Restrictions Only available to students with access to Oregon Ed Net.
Application requirements *Prior education:* BS/BA in Teacher Education. *Other requirements:* college transcripts.
Completion requirements 21 credit hours are required. *Maximum time for completion:* three years.
On-campus requirements Summer session.

INDIVIDUAL COURSE SUBJECT AREAS

Undergraduate
Criminology; education; environmental science

Graduate
Education; special education; teacher education

SOUTHERN POLYTECHNIC STATE UNIVERSITY

Marietta, Georgia

Southern Polytechnic State University, founded in 1948, is a state-supported comprehensive institution. It is accredited by the Southern Association of Colleges and Schools. It first offered distance learning courses in 1995.
Course delivery sites Courses are delivered to your home, your workplace, other colleges, off-campus center(s).
Media Courses are delivered via videoconferencing, World Wide Web. Students and teachers interact via videoconferencing, mail, telephone, fax, e-mail. A computer is required for some courses.
Services Distance learners have access to library services, the campus computer network, e-mail services, academic advising, career placement assistance at a distance.
Credit-earning options Students may transfer credits from another institution or may earn credits through standardized exams, military training, business training.
Typical costs *Undergraduate:* Tuition of $44 per credit hour for in-state residents. Tuition of $108 per credit hour for out-of-state residents. *Graduate:* Tuition of $47 per credit hour for in-state residents. Tuition

Profiles: Southern Polytechnic State University

of $114 per credit hour for out-of-state residents. *Noncredit courses:* $150 per day. Costs may vary by number of credits taken. Financial aid is available to distance learners enrolled full-time or part-time.
Registration Students may register by mail, phone.
Contact Dawn Ramsey, OIS/OCE Director, Southern Polytechnic State University, 1100 South Marietta Parkway, Marietta, GA 30060. *Telephone:* 770-528-5531. *Fax:* 770-528-7490. *E-mail:* dramsey@spsu.edu. *Web site:* http://www2.spsu.edu/ois/ois.htm.

DEGREE & CERTIFICATE PROGRAMS

Baccalaureate Degrees

▶ *Industrial Distribution (BS)*
In the fall of 1996 there were 20 students enrolled in this program.
Restrictions Students must have access to GSAMS site.
Application requirements *Prior education:* some undergraduate course work. *Other requirements:* high school transcript, college transcripts.
Completion requirements 199 credits are required. This is a degree completion program.
Program contact James McKee, Program Director, Southern Polytechnic State University, 1100 South Marietta Parkway, Marietta, GA 30060. Phone: 770-528-7317. Fax: 770-528-4990. E-mail: jmckee@spsu.edu.

Graduate Degrees

▶ *Computer Science (MS)*
In the fall of 1996 there were 5 students enrolled in this program.
Restrictions Students must have access to GSAMS site.
Application requirements *Prior education:* baccalaureate degree. *Other requirements:* GRE or GMAT, college transcripts, an application fee.
Completion requirements 60 hours are required. 45 hours must be completed through the institution.
Program contact Michael Murphy, Department Chair, Computer Science, Southern Polytechnic State University, 1100 South Marietta Parkway, Marietta, GA 30060. Phone: 770-528-7406. Fax: 770-528-5511. E-mail: mmurphy@spsu.edu.

▶ *Electrical Engineering Technology (MS)*
Application requirements *Prior education:* baccalaureate degree. *Other requirements:* GRE, college transcripts, letter(s) of recommendation.
Completion requirements 36 hours are required. *Other requirements:* all students must successfully complete a research paper. *Maximum time for completion:* five years.
Program contact Prof. Kim Davis, Director of Graduate Studies, Southern Polytechnic State University, 1100 South Marietta Parkway, Marietta, GA 30060. Phone: 770-528-7246. Fax: 770-528-7285. E-mail: kdavis@spsu.edu.

▶ *Quality Assurance (MS)*
Application requirements *Prior education:* baccalaureate degree. *Other requirements:* GRE or GMAT, college transcripts.
Completion requirements 60 credits are required. 2 symposiums must be completed through the institution.
On-campus requirements Two 2-day, on-campus symposiums.
Program contact Lawrence Aft, MSQA Coordinator, Southern Polytechnic State University, 1100 South Marietta Parkway, Marietta, GA 30060. Phone: 770-528-7242. Fax: 770-528-4991. E-mail: daft0@spsu.edu.

INDIVIDUAL COURSE SUBJECT AREAS

Undergraduate
Civil engineering; industrial engineering

Graduate
Computer and information sciences; computer programming; electrical engineering; industrial engineering; information sciences and systems

SOUTHERN UTAH UNIVERSITY

Cedar City, Utah

Telelearning

Southern Utah University, founded in 1897, is a state-supported comprehensive institution. It is accredited by the Northwest Association of Schools and Colleges. It first offered distance learning courses in 1993. In 1996–97, it offered 23 courses at a distance. In the fall of 1996, there was a total of 300 students enrolled in distance learning courses.
Course delivery sites Courses are delivered to Dixie College (St. George), 80 off-campus centers.
Media Courses are delivered via videoconferencing, World Wide Web, e-mail, print. Students and teachers interact via videoconferencing, mail, telephone, fax, e-mail. A computer is required for some courses.
Restrictions Televised courses are available to in-state students only.
Services Distance learners have access to library services, e-mail services, academic advising, career placement assistance at a distance.
Credit-earning options Students may transfer credits from another institution or may earn credits through institutionally developed exams.
Typical costs *Undergraduate:* Tuition of $161 per course. *Graduate:* Tuition of $178 per course. Costs may vary by number of credits taken. Financial aid is available to distance learners enrolled full-time.
Registration Students may register by mail, fax, phone, World Wide Web.
Contact Mr. William O'Neill, Director of Grants and Telelearning, Southern Utah University, 351 West Center Street, Cedar City, UT 84720-2498. *Telephone:* 801-865-8175. *Fax:* 801-865-8152. *E-mail:* oneill@suu.edu.

DEGREE & CERTIFICATE PROGRAMS

Baccalaureate Degrees

▶ *Business Administration (BA)*
In the fall of 1996 there were 50 students enrolled in this program.
Restrictions This program is available to in-state students only.
Application requirements College transcripts, 2.3 GPA, completion of 85 quarter hours.
Completion requirements 181 quarter credits are required. This is a degree completion program.
Program contact Dr. John Groesbeck, Chair, Department of Business, Southern Utah University, 351 West Center Street, Cedar City, UT 84720. Phone: 801-865-7784. E-mail: groesbeck@suu.edu.

INDIVIDUAL COURSE SUBJECT AREAS

Undergraduate
Administrative and secretarial services; business; computer and information sciences; education administration; English composition; English language and literature; fine arts; history; human resources management; liberal arts, general studies, and humanities; library and information studies; music; political science; teacher education

Graduate
Teacher education

SOUTHERN VERMONT COLLEGE

Bennington, Vermont

Southern Vermont College, founded in 1926, is an independent-nonprofit four-year college. It is accredited by the New England Association of Schools and Colleges. It first offered distance learning courses in 1996. In the fall of 1996, there was a total of 10 students enrolled in distance learning courses.
Course delivery sites Courses are delivered to your home.
Media Courses are delivered via television, videotapes, audiotapes, computer software, e-mail, print. Students and teachers interact via audioconferencing, mail, telephone, fax, e-mail. A computer is required for some courses.
Restrictions Courses are available to US students only.
Services Distance learners have access to the campus computer network, e-mail services, academic advising, career placement assistance at a distance.
Credit-earning options Students may transfer credits from another institution or may earn credits through standardized exams, institutionally developed exams, portfolio assessment, military training, business training.
Typical costs Tuition of $353 per credit. Costs may vary by term of enrollment. Financial aid is available to distance learners enrolled full-time or part-time.
Registration Students may register by mail, fax, phone, e-mail.
Contact Mary Van Arsdale, Director of Admissions, Southern Vermont College, Bennington, VT 05201. *Telephone:* 800-378-2782. *Fax:* 802-447-4695. *E-mail:* admis@svc.edu. *Web site:* http://www.svc.edu.

INDIVIDUAL COURSE SUBJECT AREAS

Undergraduate

Accounting; creative writing; information sciences and systems; nursing

SOUTHERN WEST VIRGINIA COMMUNITY AND TECHNICAL COLLEGE

Mount Gay, West Virginia

Southern West Virginia Community and Technical College, founded in 1971, is a state-supported two-year college. It is accredited by the North Central Association of Colleges and Schools.
Course delivery sites Courses are delivered to other colleges, off-campus center(s).
Media Courses are delivered via television, videoconferencing. Students and teachers interact via videoconferencing, audioconferencing, mail, telephone, fax, e-mail.
Restrictions Programs are available to local area students only.
Typical costs Tuition of $43 per credit hour for in-state residents. Tuition of $121 per credit hour for out-of-state residents.
Contact Vice President for Academic Affairs, Southern West Virginia Community and Technical College, PO Box 2900, Mount Gay, WV 25637. *Telephone:* 304-792-7098, Ext. 116.

INDIVIDUAL COURSE SUBJECT AREAS

Undergraduate

Art history and criticism; business; business administration and management; computer and information sciences; criminology; economics; English language and literature; marketing; mathematics; nursing; political science; psychology; sociology

SOUTH FLORIDA COMMUNITY COLLEGE

Avon Park, Florida

South Florida Community College, founded in 1965, is a state-supported two-year college. It is accredited by the Southern Association of Colleges and Schools. It first offered distance learning courses in 1985.
Course delivery sites Courses are delivered to your home.
Media Courses are delivered via videotapes. Students and teachers interact via videoconferencing, audioconferencing, mail, telephone, fax, e-mail.
Services Distance learners have access to academic advising at a distance.
Credit-earning options Students may transfer credits from another institution or may earn credits through examinations, portfolio assessment.
Typical costs Tuition of $116.25 per course plus mandatory fees of $20 per course for in-state residents. Tuition of $413.97 per course plus mandatory fees of $20 per course for out-of-state residents. Financial aid is available to distance learners.
Contact Dr. Robert Fitzgerald, Dean, Arts and Sciences, South Florida Community College, 600 West College Drive, Avon Park, FL 33825. *Telephone:* 941-453-6661.

INDIVIDUAL COURSE SUBJECT AREAS

Undergraduate

Astronomy and astrophysics; biology; business administration and management; chemistry; developmental and child psychology; economics; English language and literature; geography; geology; history; law and legal studies; physical sciences; political science; sociology

SOUTH PUGET SOUND COMMUNITY COLLEGE

Olympia, Washington

South Puget Sound Community College, founded in 1970, is a state-supported two-year college. It is accredited by the Northwest Association of Schools and Colleges. It first offered distance learning courses in 1983. In 1996–97, it offered 3 courses at a distance. In the fall of 1996, there was a total of 60 students enrolled in distance learning courses.
Course delivery sites Courses are delivered to your home, your workplace.
Media Courses are delivered via television, videotapes, videoconferencing. Students and teachers interact via mail, telephone, e-mail.
Services Distance learners have access to library services, academic advising, tutoring, career placement assistance at a distance.
Credit-earning options Students may transfer credits from another institution or may earn credits through examinations, portfolio assessment, military training, business training.
Typical costs Tuition of $48 per credit plus mandatory fees of $40 per course. Financial aid is available to distance learners enrolled full-time or part-time.
Registration Students may register by phone, World Wide Web.
Contact Russell Rose, Director, Library and Media Center, South Puget Sound Community College, 2011 Mottman Road, Southwest, Olympia, WA 98512. *Telephone:* 360-754-7711, Ext. 258. *Fax:* 360-664-0780. *E-mail:* rrose@spscc.ctc.edu.

Profiles: South Puget Sound Community College

INDIVIDUAL COURSE SUBJECT AREAS

Undergraduate
Anthropology; astronomy and astrophysics; history; mathematics

SOUTHWESTERN ADVENTIST UNIVERSITY

Keene, Texas

Adult Degree Program

Southwestern Adventist University, founded in 1894, is an independent-religious Seventh-day Adventist comprehensive institution. It is accredited by the Southern Association of Colleges and Schools. It first offered distance learning courses in 1978. In 1996–97, it offered 250 courses at a distance. In the fall of 1996, there was a total of 220 students enrolled in distance learning courses.
Course delivery sites Courses are delivered to your home.
Media Courses are delivered via videotapes. Students and teachers interact via mail, telephone, fax, e-mail.
Services Distance learners have access to library services, the campus computer network, academic advising at a distance.
Credit-earning options Students may transfer credits from another institution or may earn credits through standardized exams, institutionally developed exams, portfolio assessment, military training, business training.
Typical costs Tuition of $280 per hour. $100 one-time seminar fee. Financial aid is available to distance learners enrolled full-time or part-time.
Registration Students may register by mail, fax, World Wide Web.
Contact Dr. Larry Philbeck, Director, Adult Degree Program, Southwestern Adventist University, PO Box 567, Keene, TX 76059. *Telephone:* 888-732-7928. *Fax:* 817-556-4742. *E-mail:* adpsec@swau.edu. *Web site:* http://www.swau.edu.

DEGREE & CERTIFICATE PROGRAMS

Associate Degrees

▶ *Computer Information Systems, Office Systems Administration (AS)*

Application requirements *Prior education:* high school diploma or equivalent. *Minimum age:* 22. *Other requirements:* high school transcript, college transcripts.
Completion requirements 64 hours are required. 32 hours must be completed through the institution.
On-campus requirements Six days.

Baccalaureate Degrees

▶ *Business Administration (BA)*

Application requirements *Prior education:* high school diploma or equivalent. *Other requirements:* high school transcript, college transcripts.
Completion requirements 128 hours are required. 32 hours must be completed through the institution.
On-campus requirements Six days.

▶ *Computer Information Systems, History, Journalism, Mathematics (BA, BS)*

In the fall of 1996 there were 13 students enrolled in this program. In 1995–96, 1 degree was earned at a distance through this program.
Application requirements *Prior education:* high school diploma or equivalent. *Minimum age:* 22. *Other requirements:* high school transcript, college transcripts.
Completion requirements 128 hours are required. 32 hours must be completed through the institution.
On-campus requirements Six days.

▶ *Broadcasting, Business Management, Computer Science, Corporate Communications, Elementary Education, Office Administration, Office Information Systems, Psychology, Social Sciences (BS)*

In the fall of 1996 there were 162 students enrolled in this program. In 1995–96, 38 degrees were earned at a distance through this program.
Application requirements *Prior education:* high school diploma or equivalent. *Minimum age:* 22. *Other requirements:* high school transcript, college transcripts.
Completion requirements 128 hours are required. 32 hours must be completed through the institution.
On-campus requirements Six days.

▶ *English, International Affairs, Religion, Social Sciences, Theology (BA)*

In the fall of 1996 there were 33 students enrolled in this program. In 1995–96, 8 degrees were earned at a distance through this program.
Application requirements *Prior education:* high school diploma or equivalent. *Minimum age:* 22. *Other requirements:* high school transcript, college transcripts.
Completion requirements 128 hours are required. 32 hours must be completed through the institution.
On-campus requirements Six days.

SOUTHWESTERN ASSEMBLIES OF GOD UNIVERSITY

Waxahachie, Texas

School of Distance Education

Southwestern Assemblies of God University, founded in 1927, is an independent-religious four-year college affiliated with the Assemblies of God. It is accredited by the Southern Association of Colleges and Schools. It first offered distance learning courses in 1983. In 1996–97, it offered 150 courses at a distance. In the fall of 1996, there was a total of 297 students enrolled in distance learning courses.
Course delivery sites Courses are delivered to your home.
Media Courses are delivered via videotapes, audioconferencing, e-mail, print. Students and teachers interact via mail, telephone, fax, e-mail. A computer is required for all courses.
Services Distance learners have access to library services, the campus computer network, e-mail services, academic advising, career placement assistance at a distance.
Credit-earning options Students may transfer credits from another institution or may earn credits through standardized exams, institutionally developed exams, portfolio assessment, military training, business training.
Typical costs Tuition of $149.50 per credit. Financial aid is available to distance learners enrolled full-time or part-time.
Registration Students may register by mail, fax, phone, e-mail.
Contact Steve Tiger, Enrollment Counselor, Southwestern Assemblies of God University, 1200 Sycamore Street, Waxahachie, TX 75165-2342. *Telephone:* 214-937-4010. *Fax:* 214-923-0488. *E-mail:* stiger@sagu.edu.

DEGREE & CERTIFICATE PROGRAMS

Baccalaureate Degrees

▶ *Business (BA, BS)*

In the fall of 1996 there were 29 students enrolled in this program. In 1995–96, 7 degrees were earned at a distance through this program.
Restrictions All students are required to adhere to the Christian faith.
Application requirements *Prior education:* high school diploma or equivalent. *Minimum age:* 23. *Other requirements:* high school transcript,

college transcripts, an essay or personal statement, letter(s) of recommendation, an application fee of $35.
Completion requirements 126 quarter credits are required. 30 quarter credits must be completed through the institution.
On-campus requirements For opening sessions.

▶ *Church Ministries (BA, BS)*
In the fall of 1996 there were 178 students enrolled in this program. In 1995–96, 42 degrees were earned at a distance through this program.
Restrictions All students are required to adhere to the Christian faith.
Application requirements *Prior education:* high school diploma or equivalent. *Minimum age:* 23. *Other requirements:* ACT or SAT, high school transcript, college transcripts, an essay or personal statement, letter(s) of recommendation, an application fee of $35.
Completion requirements 126 quarter credits are required. 30 quarter credits must be completed through the institution.
On-campus requirements Students must attend opening sessions in person.

▶ *Professional Studies (BA, BS)*
In the fall of 1996 there were 51 students enrolled in this program. In 1995–96, 8 degrees were earned at a distance through this program.
Restrictions All students are required to adhere to the Christian faith.
Application requirements *Prior education:* high school diploma or equivalent. *Minimum age:* 23. *Other requirements:* ACT or SAT, high school transcript, college transcripts, an essay or personal statement, letter(s) of recommendation, an application fee of $35.
Completion requirements 126 semester hours are required. 30 credits must be completed through the institution.
On-campus requirements For opening sessions.

INDIVIDUAL COURSE SUBJECT AREAS

Undergraduate
Accounting; area, ethnic, and cultural studies; biological and life sciences; biology; business; business administration and management; communications; computer and information sciences; creative writing; developmental and child psychology; education; educational psychology; English composition; English language and literature; fine arts; health and physical education/fitness; history; human resources management; mathematics; music; philosophy and religion; physical sciences; psychology; social psychology; social sciences; sociology; teacher education; theological studies

SOUTHWESTERN BAPTIST THEOLOGICAL SEMINARY

Fort Worth, Texas

Department of Continuing Education

Southwestern Baptist Theological Seminary, founded in 1908, is an independent-religious graduate institution. It is accredited by the Southern Association of Colleges and Schools. It first offered distance learning courses in 1993. In 1996–97, it offered 7 courses at a distance. In the fall of 1996, there was a total of 40 students enrolled in distance learning courses.
Course delivery sites Courses are delivered to your home, 2 off-campus centers in San Antonio, Shawnee (OK).
Media Courses are delivered via compressed video. Students and teachers interact via videoconferencing, mail, telephone, fax, e-mail.
Restrictions Courses are available to US students only.
Services Distance learners have access to library services, the campus computer network, e-mail services, academic advising at a distance.
Credit-earning options Students may transfer credits from another institution or may earn credits through examinations, portfolio assessment.
Typical costs *Undergraduate:* Tuition of $100 per semester hour plus mandatory fees of $50 per semester. *Graduate:* Tuition of $100 per semester hour plus mandatory fees of $50 per semester. *Noncredit courses:* $125 per course. Costs may vary by term of enrollment. Financial aid is available to distance learners enrolled full-time or part-time.
Registration Students may register by mail, phone.
Contact J. David Fite, Director of Continuing Education/Off Campus Programs, Southwestern Baptist Theological Seminary, PO Box 22207, Fort Worth, TX 76122. *Telephone:* 817-923-1921, Ext. 2440. *Fax:* 817-921-8753. *E-mail:* jdf@swbts.swbts.edu.

INDIVIDUAL COURSE SUBJECT AREAS

Undergraduate
Philosophy and religion; theological studies

Graduate
Philosophy and religion; theological studies

Noncredit
Philosophy and religion; theological studies

SOUTHWESTERN MICHIGAN COLLEGE

Dowagiac, Michigan

Southwestern Michigan College, founded in 1964, is a state and locally supported two-year college. It is accredited by the North Central Association of Colleges and Schools. It first offered distance learning courses in 1991. In 1996–97, it offered 14 courses at a distance. In the fall of 1996, there was a total of 110 students enrolled in distance learning courses.
Course delivery sites Courses are delivered to your home, 1 off-campus center in Lawrence.
Media Courses are delivered via television, videotapes, videoconferencing. Students and teachers interact via videoconferencing, mail, telephone, fax, e-mail.
Restrictions Programs are available to local area students only.
Services Distance learners have access to library services, the campus computer network, e-mail services at a distance.
Credit-earning options Students may transfer credits from another institution or may earn credits through standardized exams, institutionally developed exams, military training.
Typical costs Tuition of $45 per credit plus mandatory fees of $9 per credit for local area residents. Tuition of $57 per credit plus mandatory fees of $9 per credit for in-state residents. Tuition of $69 per credit plus mandatory fees of $9 per credit for out-of-state residents. Financial aid is available to distance learners enrolled full-time or part-time.
Registration Students may register by mail, phone.
Contact Student Services Office, Southwestern Michigan College, 58900 Cherry Grove Road, Dowagiac, MI 49047. *Telephone:* 616-782-5113. *Fax:* 616-782-8414.

INDIVIDUAL COURSE SUBJECT AREAS

Undergraduate
Business; business administration and management; communications; education; European languages and literatures; film studies; health and physical education/fitness; health professions and related sciences; liberal arts, general studies, and humanities; mathematics; political science; psychology; social psychology; social sciences; sociology

Profiles: Southwestern Oklahoma State University

SOUTHWESTERN OKLAHOMA STATE UNIVERSITY

Weatherford, Oklahoma

Tele-Learning

Southwestern Oklahoma State University, founded in 1901, is a state-supported comprehensive institution. It is accredited by the North Central Association of Colleges and Schools. It first offered distance learning courses in 1981. In 1996–97, it offered 41 courses at a distance. In the fall of 1996, there was a total of 296 students enrolled in distance learning courses.

Course delivery sites Courses are delivered to your home, your workplace, military bases, Southwestern Oklahoma State University at Sayre (Sayre), University of Science and Arts of Oklahoma (Chickasha), Western Oklahoma State College (Altus), off-campus center(s) in Cheyenne, Fort Cobb, Woodward.

Media Courses are delivered via television, videotapes, videoconferencing, computer software, e-mail. Students and teachers interact via videoconferencing, mail, telephone, fax, e-mail.

Restrictions Programs are available to local area students only.

Services Distance learners have access to library services, e-mail services, academic advising, tutoring, career placement assistance at a distance.

Credit-earning options Students may transfer credits from another institution or may earn credits through standardized exams, institutionally developed exams, military training, business training.

Typical costs *Undergraduate:* Tuition of $47 per credit hour for in-state residents. Tuition of $135 per credit hour for out-of-state residents. *Graduate:* Tuition of $57 per credit hour for in-state residents. Tuition of $145 per credit hour for out-of-state residents. Financial aid is available to distance learners.

Registration Students may register by mail, fax, phone.

Contact Registrar's Office, Southwestern Oklahoma State University, 100 Campus Drive, Weatherford, OK 73096. *Telephone:* 405-774-3777.

DEGREE & CERTIFICATE PROGRAMS

Graduate Degrees

▶ *Business Administration (MBA)*

Application requirements *Prior education:* baccalaureate degree. *Other requirements:* GMAT, an essay or personal statement, letter(s) of recommendation, an application fee of $15, minimum GPA, interview.

Completion requirements 33 semester hours are required. 24 semester hours must be completed through the institution. *Maximum time for completion:* six years.

On-campus requirements For comprehensive exam, oral exam.

▶ *Education (MEd)*

In the fall of 1996 there were 40 students enrolled in this program. In 1995–96, 1 degree was earned at a distance through this program.

Restrictions This program is available to in-state students only.

Application requirements *Prior education:* baccalaureate degree. *Other requirements:* GRE, college transcripts, letter(s) of recommendation, an application fee of $15, 2.5 GPA.

Completion requirements 34 semester credits are required. 24 quarter credits must be completed through the institution. *Other requirements:* comprehensive exam. *Maximum time for completion:* six years.

INDIVIDUAL COURSE SUBJECT AREAS

Undergraduate

Business; business administration and management; chemistry; computer and information sciences; developmental and child psychology; economics; English composition; English language and literature; geology; health professions and related sciences; history; liberal arts, general studies, and humanities; mathematics; nursing; philosophy and religion; political science; social work; sociology

Graduate

Business; business administration and management; education administration; teacher education

SOUTHWEST MISSOURI STATE UNIVERSITY

Springfield, Missouri

College of Continuing Education and the Extended University

Southwest Missouri State University, founded in 1905, is a state-supported comprehensive institution. It is accredited by the North Central Association of Colleges and Schools. It first offered distance learning courses in 1974. In 1996–97, it offered 60 courses at a distance. In the fall of 1996, there was a total of 609 students enrolled in distance learning courses.

Course delivery sites Courses are delivered to your home, Missouri Southern State College (Joplin), Southwest Missouri State University–West Plains (West Plains), 2 off-campus centers in Lebanon, Nevada.

Media Courses are delivered via television, videotapes, videoconferencing, audiotapes, audioconferencing, World Wide Web. Students and teachers interact via videoconferencing, audioconferencing, mail, telephone, e-mail. A computer is required for some courses.

Services Distance learners have access to library services, the campus computer network, e-mail services, academic advising at a distance.

Credit-earning options Students may transfer credits from another institution or may earn credits through standardized exams, institutionally developed exams, military training, business training.

Typical costs *Undergraduate:* Tuition of $93 per credit. *Graduate:* Tuition of $105 per credit. Students pay $60 in mandatory fees. *Noncredit courses:* $75–$135 per course. Costs may vary by specific program of study, number of credits taken. Financial aid is available to distance learners.

Registration Students may register by mail, fax.

Contact Diana Garland, Associate Director, Academic Outreach, Southwest Missouri State University, 901 South National, Springfield, MO 65804. *Telephone:* 417-836-4128. *Fax:* 417-836-6016. *E-mail:* dkg988f@wpgate.smsu.edu. *Web site:* http://ce.smsu.edu.

DEGREE & CERTIFICATE PROGRAMS

Graduate Degrees

▶ *Computer Information Systems (MS)*

Restrictions Program enrollment is limited.

Application requirements *Prior education:* baccalaureate degree. *Other requirements:* GMAT, three years of professional information systems work experience.

Completion requirements 36 credit hours are required.

On-campus requirements Four seven-and-a-half-day sessions.

Program contact Dr. Jerry Chin, Department Head, CIS - Computer Information Systems, Southwest Missouri State University, 901 South National, Springfield, MO 65804. Phone: 417-836-4131. Fax: 417-836-6907.

INDIVIDUAL COURSE SUBJECT AREAS

Undergraduate

Accounting; American (US) history; anthropology; biology; chemistry; child care and development; Classical languages and literatures; communications; design; economics; English language and literature; European languages and literatures; film studies; foods and nutrition studies; French language and literature; individual and family development studies; music; nursing; political science; psychology; Spanish language and literature

Graduate
Agriculture; computer and information sciences; curriculum and instruction; education administration; marketing; teacher education

SOUTHWEST STATE UNIVERSITY

Marshall, Minnesota

Continuing Education

Southwest State University, founded in 1963, is a state-supported comprehensive institution. It is accredited by the North Central Association of Colleges and Schools. It first offered distance learning courses in 1968. In 1996–97, it offered 35 courses at a distance. In the fall of 1996, there was a total of 2,600 students enrolled in distance learning courses.
Course delivery sites Courses are delivered to your home, your workplace, Central Lakes College (Brainerd), Ridgewater College (Willmar), St. Paul Technical College (St. Paul), 43 off-campus sites in Minnesota and South Dakota.
Media Courses are delivered via television, videotapes, videoconferencing, computer software, World Wide Web. Students and teachers interact via videoconferencing, mail, telephone, fax, e-mail. A computer is required for some courses.
Services Distance learners have access to library services, e-mail services, academic advising, tutoring, career placement assistance at a distance.
Credit-earning options Students may transfer credits from another institution or may earn credits through examinations, portfolio assessment, military training.
Typical costs *Undergraduate:* Tuition of $1170 per year. *Graduate:* Tuition of $720 per year. Mandatory fees for on campus students. Costs may vary by campus or location. Financial aid is available to distance learners.
Registration Students may register by mail, phone.
Contact Office of Continuing Education, Southwest State University, North Highway 23, Marshall, MN 56258. *Telephone:* 507-537-6251. *Fax:* 507-537-6200.

DEGREE & CERTIFICATE PROGRAMS

Baccalaureate Degrees
▶ *Business Administration, Education (BA)*
In 1995–96, 45 degrees were earned at a distance through this program.
Application requirements *Prior education:* high school diploma or equivalent. *Other requirements:* high school transcript, college transcripts.
Completion requirements 124 credits are required. 24 credits must be completed through the institution. This is a degree completion program.
Program contact John M. Bowden, Dean, Southwest State University, North Highway 23, Marshall, MN 56258. Phone: 507-537-6108. Fax: 507-537-6200.

INDIVIDUAL COURSE SUBJECT AREAS

Undergraduate
Accounting; administrative and secretarial services; advertising; area, ethnic, and cultural studies; biological and life sciences; biology; botany; business administration and management; chemistry; communications; computer and information sciences; creative writing; design; developmental and child psychology; economics; education; education administration; English composition; English language and literature; European languages and literatures; fine arts; health and physical education/fitness; history; hospitality services management; human resources management; industrial psychology; liberal arts, general studies, and humanities; mathematics; music; philosophy and religion; physical sciences; political science; psychology; public administration and services; radio and television broadcasting; social psychology; social sciences; social work; sociology; teacher education; visual and performing arts; zoology

Graduate
Business administration and management; teacher education

SOUTHWEST TEXAS STATE UNIVERSITY

San Marcos, Texas

Correspondence and Extension Studies

Southwest Texas State University, founded in 1899, is a state-supported comprehensive institution. It is accredited by the Southern Association of Colleges and Schools. It first offered distance learning courses in 1953. In 1996–97, it offered 60 courses at a distance. In the fall of 1996, there was a total of 2,000 students enrolled in distance learning courses.
Course delivery sites Courses are delivered to your home, your workplace, military bases.
Media Courses are delivered via videotapes, print. Students and teachers interact via mail, telephone, fax, e-mail.
Services Distance learners have access to e-mail services at a distance.
Typical costs Tuition of $57 per unit. Costs may vary by number of credits taken.
Registration Students may register by mail, fax, phone.
Contact James P. Andrews, Director, Southwest Texas State University, 105 Medina Hall, 601 University Drive, San Marcos, TX 78666. *Telephone:* 512-245-2322. *Fax:* 512-245-8934. *E-mail:* ja09@a1.swt.edu. *Web site:* http://www.ideal.swt.edu/correspondence.

Special note
Southwest Texas State University is a state-supported university, and is accredited by the Southern Association of College and Schools. Distance learning courses were first offered in 1953. Currently the distance learning program at SWT is delivered via print-based instruction with some courses containing audiotapes, CD-ROM, and videotapes. In 1996 SWT offered its first Internet-delivered course.

Distance learning courses are available to students worldwide. The print-based format allows students who do not have access to technologies such as e-mail and the Internet, to take many courses that may otherwise be inaccessible because of technology. Courses are primarily print-based though some include additional media such as videotapes, audiotapes, and CD-ROM. Distance learners have access to assistance in acquiring necessary distance learning equipment, library services, and academic counseling/advising.

Undergraduate courses typically cost $171 per course ($57 per credit hour). For students outside the U.S. add $50 per course for overseas postage.

Students may apply directly to the Office of Correspondence & Extension Studies. For more information, students should contact Debra Perkins, Administrative Assistant, Southwest Texas State University, Office of Correspondence & Extension Studies, 105 Medina Hall, 601 University Drive San Marcos, TX 78666-4616. Telephone: 512-245-2322; fax: 512-245-8934; e-mail: DP01@A1.swt.edu.

Profiles: Southwest Texas State University

INDIVIDUAL COURSE SUBJECT AREAS

Undergraduate
Abnormal psychology; agricultural economics; agriculture; algebra; American (US) history; calculus; computer and information sciences; criminology; developmental and child psychology; English language and literature; European history; foods and nutrition studies; geography; health services administration; home economics and family studies; industrial psychology; instructional media; logic; mathematics; political science; psychology; social psychology; sociology; visual and performing arts

SOUTHWEST VIRGINIA COMMUNITY COLLEGE

Richlands, Virginia

Audiovisual and Distance Education Services

Southwest Virginia Community College, founded in 1968, is a state-supported two-year college. It is accredited by the Southern Association of Colleges and Schools. It first offered distance learning courses in 1991. In 1996–97, it offered 32 courses at a distance. In the fall of 1996, there was a total of 625 students enrolled in distance learning courses.
Course delivery sites Courses are delivered to your home, your workplace, Virginia Community College System (Richmond), area high schools.
Media Courses are delivered via videotapes, videoconferencing, audiotapes, computer software, World Wide Web, print. Students and teachers interact via mail, telephone, fax, e-mail. A computer is required for some courses.
Services Distance learners have access to library services, the campus computer network, e-mail services, academic advising, tutoring, career placement assistance at a distance.
Credit-earning options Students may transfer credits from another institution or may earn credits through institutionally developed exams, portfolio assessment, military training.
Typical costs Tuition of $48.65 per credit for in-state residents. Tuition of $158 per credit for out-of-state residents. Costs may vary by number of credits taken. Financial aid is available to distance learners enrolled full-time or part-time.
Registration Students may register by mail, fax, phone.
Contact Sylvia Dye, Program Support Technician, Southwest Virginia Community College, PO Box SVCC, Richlands, VA 24641. *Telephone:* 540-964-7279. *Fax:* 540-964-7581. *E-mail:* sylvia-dye@sw.cc.va.us.

INDIVIDUAL COURSE SUBJECT AREAS

Undergraduate
Accounting; aerospace, aeronautical engineering; business; business administration and management; chemical engineering; civil engineering; creative writing; developmental and child psychology; economics; education administration; educational psychology; electrical engineering; engineering mechanics; engineering-related technologies; engineering/industrial management; environmental engineering; European languages and literatures; health professions and related sciences; history; industrial engineering; law and legal studies; liberal arts, general studies, and humanities; library and information studies; mathematics; mechanical engineering; nursing; philosophy and religion; social psychology; sociology; special education; teacher education

SPERTUS INSTITUTE OF JEWISH STUDIES

Chicago, Illinois

Spertus Institute of Jewish Studies, founded in 1925, is an independent-nonprofit graduate institution. It is accredited by the North Central Association of Colleges and Schools. It first offered distance learning courses in 1995. In 1996–97, it offered 20 courses at a distance. In the fall of 1996, there was a total of 140 students enrolled in distance learning courses.
Course delivery sites Courses are delivered to your home.
Media Courses are delivered via videotapes, audiotapes, print. Students and teachers interact via mail, telephone, fax, e-mail.
Services Distance learners have access to library services, e-mail services, academic advising at a distance.
Credit-earning options Students may transfer credits from another institution or may earn credits through institutionally developed exams.
Typical costs Tuition of $495 per course plus mandatory fees of $25 per course. Costs may vary by specific program of study, number of credits taken. Financial aid is available to distance learners enrolled full-time or part-time.
Registration Students may register by mail, fax, phone, e-mail.
Contact Lisa Burnstein, Office of the Registrar, Spertus Institute of Jewish Studies, 618 South Michigan Avenue, Chicago, IL 60605. *Telephone:* 312-922-1769. *Fax:* 312-922-6406. *E-mail:* college@spertus.edu.

Special note
Accredited by the North Central Association of Colleges and Schools, Spertus currently offers 2 degree programs on a distance learning basis: the Master of Science in Jewish Studies (MSJS) and the Doctor of Jewish Studies (DJS).

The MSJS is designed for students with an accredited undergraduate degree and a desire to enrich their Jewish education or to acquire a professional credential in Jewish education or Jewish communal service. Courses are delivered in a variety of ways, including "distance learning packages," intensive seminars, and independent study. The program progresses at the learner's individual rate. Distance learners are encouraged to spend a minimum of 6 days per year at Spertus' Chicago campus for intensive course work. Fifty quarter hours are required for the degree. Tuition is currently $195 per quarter hour. Scholarships, in the form of partial tuition remission, are available.

The DJS is designed for in-service Jewish clergy, educators, and communal service workers interested in and committed to building upon and enhancing previously acquired Judaica knowledge and professional skills and who desire to make a "cutting-edge" contribution to their respective fields. Admission to the DJS program is highly selective. Eighteen courses are required for the degree: 7 reading courses, 7 intensive seminars, and 4 courses toward the completion of a Project Demonstrating Excellence. Tuition for the program is currently $200 per quarter hour.

For more information, contact the Office of the Registrar at 312-322-1769. Fax: 312-922-6406. E-mail: college@spertus.edu.

DEGREE & CERTIFICATE PROGRAMS

Graduate Degrees
▶*Jewish Studies (DJS)*
In the fall of 1996 there were 25 students enrolled in this program.

Application requirements *Prior education:* MA in Jewish studies and/or Rabbinical Ordination. *Other requirements:* college transcripts, an essay or personal statement, letter(s) of recommendation, an application fee of $75.
Completion requirements 54 quarter hours are required. 48 quarter hours must be completed through the institution. *Maximum time for completion:* seven years.
On-campus requirements Five days per year.
▶ *Jewish Studies (MSJS)*
In the fall of 1996 there were 100 students enrolled in this program.
Application requirements *Prior education:* baccalaureate degree. *Other requirements:* college transcripts, an essay or personal statement, letter(s) of recommendation, an application fee of $50.
Completion requirements 45–50 quarter hours are required. 45 quarter hours must be completed through the institution. *Maximum time for completion:* five years.
On-campus requirements Six days per year.

INDIVIDUAL COURSE SUBJECT AREAS

Graduate
Area, ethnic, and cultural studies; Jewish studies

STANFORD UNIVERSITY

Stanford, California

Stanford Center for Professional Development

Stanford University, founded in 1891, is an independent-nonprofit university. It is accredited by the Western Association of Schools and Colleges, Inc. It first offered distance learning courses in 1969.
Course delivery sites Courses are delivered to your workplace.
Media Courses are delivered via television, videotapes, videoconferencing, print, computer conferencing.
Credit-earning options Students may transfer credits from another institution.
Contact Associate Marketing Manager, Stanford University, 401 Durand Building, Stanford, CA 94305-4036. *Telephone:* 415-725-6963. *Fax:* 415-725-2868. *Web site:* http://www-scpd.stanford.edu/scpd.

DEGREE & CERTIFICATE PROGRAMS

Graduate Degrees
▶ *Aerospace/Astronautical Engineering (MS)*
▶ *Computer Science (MS)*
▶ *Electrical Engineering (MS)*
▶ *Engineering Economics Systems (MS)*
▶ *Industrial Engineering (MS)*
▶ *Mechanical Engineering (MS)*

INDIVIDUAL COURSE SUBJECT AREAS

Graduate
Aerospace, aeronautical engineering; electrical engineering; engineering/industrial management; industrial engineering; mechanical engineering

Noncredit
Aerospace, aeronautical engineering; electrical engineering; engineering/industrial management; industrial engineering; mechanical engineering

STANLY COMMUNITY COLLEGE

Albemarle, North Carolina

Stanly Community College, founded in 1971, is a state-supported two-year college. It is accredited by the Southern Association of Colleges and Schools. It first offered distance learning courses in 1990.
Course delivery sites Courses are delivered to your home.
Media Courses are delivered via television. Students and teachers interact via mail, telephone, fax, e-mail.
Credit-earning options Students may transfer credits from another institution or may earn credits through examinations.
Typical costs Tuition of $13.25 per credit plus mandatory fees of $0.50 per credit for in-state residents. Tuition of $107.50 per credit plus mandatory fees of $0.50 per credit for out-of-state residents. Financial aid is available to distance learners.
Contact Miriam L. Runyon, Director of Instructional Services, Stanly Community College, 141 College Drive, Albemarle, NC 28001. *Telephone:* 704-982-0121, Ext. 256. *Fax:* 704-982-0819.

INDIVIDUAL COURSE SUBJECT AREAS

Undergraduate
Business administration and management; developmental and child psychology; history; liberal arts, general studies, and humanities; social psychology

STATE TECHNICAL INSTITUTE AT MEMPHIS

Memphis, Tennessee

Corporate Center

State Technical Institute at Memphis, founded in 1967, is a state-supported two-year college. It is accredited by the Southern Association of Colleges and Schools. It first offered distance learning courses in 1991. In 1996–97, it offered 23 courses at a distance. In the fall of 1996, there was a total of 553 students enrolled in distance learning courses.
Course delivery sites Courses are delivered to your home, your workplace, Jackson State Community College (Jackson).
Media Courses are delivered via television, videotapes, videoconferencing, audiotapes. Students and teachers interact via videoconferencing, mail, telephone, fax, e-mail.
Services Distance learners have access to the campus computer network, e-mail services, academic advising, tutoring, career placement assistance at a distance.
Credit-earning options Students may transfer credits from another institution or may earn credits through examinations.
Typical costs Tuition of $45 per credit hour plus mandatory fees of $12 per credit for in-state residents. Tuition of $179 per credit hour plus mandatory fees of $12 per credit for out-of-state residents. Costs may vary by number of credits taken. Financial aid is available to distance learners.
Registration Students may register by mail, fax.
Contact Cynthia Thompson, Assistant Director, State Technical Institute at Memphis, 5983 Macon Cove, Memphis, TN 38134. *Telephone:* 901-383-4612. *Fax:* 901-383-4519. *E-mail:* cthompson@stim.tec.tn.us.

Profiles: State Technical Institute at Memphis

INDIVIDUAL COURSE SUBJECT AREAS

Undergraduate
Accounting; algebra; American (US) history; anthropology; business; business administration and management; business communications; business law; economics; English composition; ethics; film studies; geography; human resources management; marketing; political science; psychology; sociology; Spanish language and literature

STATE UNIVERSITY OF NEW YORK AT BINGHAMTON

Binghamton, New York

State University of New York at Binghamton, founded in 1946, is a state-supported university. It is accredited by the Middle States Association of Colleges and Schools. It first offered distance learning courses in 1989. In 1996–97, it offered 10 courses at a distance. In the fall of 1996, there was a total of 50 students enrolled in distance learning courses.
Course delivery sites Courses are delivered to your home, State University of New York College at Cortland (Cortland), State University of New York College of Environmental Science and Forestry (Syracuse), University at Albany, State University of New York (Albany).
Media Courses are delivered via videotapes, videoconferencing. Students and teachers interact via videoconferencing.
Services Distance learners have access to library services, e-mail services, academic advising, career placement assistance at a distance.
Credit-earning options Students may transfer credits from another institution or may earn credits through institutionally developed exams, military training.
Typical costs Costs vary by number of credits taken. Contact university for details. Financial aid is available to distance learners.
Registration Students may register by mail, World Wide Web.
Contact Geof Gould, Director of Admissions, State University of New York at Binghamton, Vestal Parkway, Binghamton, NY 13902. *Telephone:* 607-777-2171.

DEGREE & CERTIFICATE PROGRAMS

Graduate Degrees
▶*Education and Human Development (MASS)*
In the fall of 1996 there were 30 students enrolled in this program.
Application requirements *Prior education:* baccalaureate degree. *Other requirements:* college transcripts, an application fee of $50.
Completion requirements 48 credits are required.
Program contact Theodore Rector, Associate Dean, State University of New York at Binghamton, Binghamton, NY 13902. Phone: 607-777-2631. E-mail: trector@binghamton.edu.

INDIVIDUAL COURSE SUBJECT AREAS

Undergraduate
Biology; conservation and natural resources; English language and literature; Middle Eastern languages and literatures

Graduate
Education; electrical engineering; industrial engineering; mechanical engineering; nursing; social work

STATE UNIVERSITY OF NEW YORK AT BUFFALO

Buffalo, New York

State University of New York at Buffalo, founded in 1846, is a state-supported university. It is accredited by the Middle States Association of Colleges and Schools. It first offered distance learning courses in 1994.
Course delivery sites Courses are delivered to your home, your workplace, military bases, other colleges.
Media Courses are delivered via videotapes, videoconferencing, audioconferencing, print, computer conferencing.
Restrictions Programs are available to in-state students only.
Services Distance learners have access to library services, academic advising at a distance.
Credit-earning options Students may transfer credits from another institution or may earn credits through examinations, portfolio assessment. Financial aid is available to distance learners.
Contact Dr. Chairman, Distance Learning Committee, State University of New York at Buffalo, Emergency Medicine, ECMC, 100 High Street, Buffalo, NY 14203. *Telephone:* 716-898-4430.

DEGREE & CERTIFICATE PROGRAMS

Graduate Degrees
▶*Electrical and Computer Engineering–Controls, Communications and Software (MS, ME)*
▶*Electrical and Computer Engineering–Microelectronics (MS, ME)*
▶*Family, Women's Health, and Pediatric Nurse Practitioner Program (MS)*
▶*Industrial Engineering–Manufacturing and Production Engineering (ME)*
▶*Mechanical and Aerospace Engineering–Computer-Aided Design (MS)*

Graduate certificates
▶*Electrical and Computer Engineering–Controls, Communications and Software*
▶*Electrical and Computer Engineering–Microelectronics*
▶*Mechanical and Aerospace Engineering–Computer-Aided Design*

INDIVIDUAL COURSE SUBJECT AREAS

Graduate
Aerospace, aeronautical engineering; civil engineering; education; education administration; electrical engineering; engineering mechanics; engineering/industrial management; environmental engineering; industrial engineering; mechanical engineering; nursing; teacher education

Noncredit
Education; education administration; special education; teacher education

STATE UNIVERSITY OF NEW YORK AT FARMINGDALE

Farmingdale, New York

State University of New York at Farmingdale, founded in 1912, is a state-supported primarily two-year college. It is accredited by the Middle States Association of Colleges and Schools. It first offered distance learning courses in 1989.
Course delivery sites Courses are delivered to your home, your workplace.
Media Courses are delivered via television, videoconferencing, computer software, e-mail, print. Students and teachers interact via mail, telephone, fax, e-mail.
Typical costs Tuition of $128 per credit plus mandatory fees of $11.10 per credit for in-state residents. Tuition of $346 per credit plus mandatory fees of $11.10 per credit for out-of-state residents.
Contact Admissions Office, State University of New York at Farmingdale, Memorial Hall, Farmingdale, NY 11735. *Telephone:* 516-420-2200. *Fax:* 516-420-2633.

INDIVIDUAL COURSE SUBJECT AREAS

Undergraduate
Business; engineering-related technologies; physics

STATE UNIVERSITY OF NEW YORK AT NEW PALTZ

New Paltz, New York

Center for Continuing and Professional Education

State University of New York at New Paltz, founded in 1828, is a state-supported comprehensive institution. It is accredited by the Middle States Association of Colleges and Schools. It first offered distance learning courses in 1995. In 1996–97, it offered 25 courses at a distance. In the fall of 1996, there was a total of 99 students enrolled in distance learning courses.
Course delivery sites Courses are delivered to your home, your workplace, military bases, Orange County Community College (Middletown).
Media Courses are delivered via videoconferencing, World Wide Web, e-mail. Students and teachers interact via videoconferencing, e-mail, Internet. A computer is required for some courses.
Services Distance learners have access to library services, the campus computer network, e-mail services at a distance.
Credit-earning options Students may transfer credits from another institution or may earn credits through standardized exams, portfolio assessment, military training, business training.
Typical costs *Undergraduate:* Tuition of $177 per credit for in-state residents. Tuition of $386 per credit for out-of-state residents. *Graduate:* Tuition of $253 per credit for in-state residents. Tuition of $391 per credit for out-of-state residents. Costs may vary by number of credits taken. Financial aid is available to distance learners enrolled full-time or part-time.
Registration Students may register by mail, fax, phone.
Contact Jean Whitlow, Extension Program Coordinator, State University of New York at New Paltz, 75 South Manheim Boulevard, Grimm House, New Paltz, NY 12561-2499. *Telephone:* 914-257-2904. *Fax:* 914-257-2899. *E-mail:* edl@newpaltz.edu. *Web site:* http://www.newpaltz.edu.

INDIVIDUAL COURSE SUBJECT AREAS

Undergraduate
Art history and criticism; communications; philosophy and religion; psychology; sociology

Graduate
Business; education administration

STATE UNIVERSITY OF NEW YORK AT OSWEGO

Oswego, New York

Office of Distance Learning

State University of New York at Oswego, founded in 1861, is a state-supported comprehensive institution. It is accredited by the Middle States Association of Colleges and Schools. It first offered distance learning courses in 1995. In 1996–97, it offered 12 courses at a distance. In the fall of 1996, there was a total of 85 students enrolled in distance learning courses.
Course delivery sites Courses are delivered to your home, your workplace, military bases, Jefferson Community College (Watertown), State University of New York College of Technology at Canton (Canton), University at Albany, State University of New York (Albany).
Media Courses are delivered via television, videotapes, videoconferencing, computer software, World Wide Web, e-mail. Students and teachers interact via videoconferencing, mail, telephone, fax, e-mail. A computer is required for some courses.
Restrictions Cable television and video conference courses are available to regional students only.
Services Distance learners have access to the campus computer network, e-mail services, academic advising, tutoring at a distance.
Credit-earning options Students may transfer credits from another institution or may earn credits through standardized exams, institutionally developed exams.
Typical costs *Undergraduate:* Tuition of $137 per credit hour plus mandatory fees of $4.17 per credit hour. *Graduate:* Tuition of $213 per credit hour plus mandatory fees of $4.17 per credit hour. Costs may vary by number of credits taken. Financial aid is available to distance learners enrolled full-time.
Registration Students may register by mail, fax, phone, e-mail.
Contact Dr. Michael S. Ameigh, Assistant Provost for Distance Learning, State University of New York at Oswego, 35A Lanigan Hall, Oswego, NY 13126. *Telephone:* 315-341-4041. *Fax:* 315-341-3195. *E-mail:* ameigh@oswego.edu.

INDIVIDUAL COURSE SUBJECT AREAS

Undergraduate
Cognitive psychology; computer programming; economics; European history; geology; mass media; radio and television broadcasting; Russian language and literature; statistics; teacher education

Graduate
Abnormal psychology; education administration

STATE UNIVERSITY OF NEW YORK COLLEGE AT PLATTSBURGH

Plattsburgh, New York

Faculty of Professional Studies

State University of New York College at Plattsburgh, founded in 1889, is a state-supported comprehensive institution. It is accredited by the Middle States Association of Colleges and Schools. It first offered distance learning courses in 1992. In 1996–97, it offered 10 courses at a distance. In the fall of 1996, there was a total of 191 students enrolled in distance learning courses.
Course delivery sites Courses are delivered to Adirondack Community College (Queensbury), Fulton-Montgomery Community College (Johnstown), Jefferson Community College (Watertown), North Country Community College (Saranac Lake), State University of New York College at Potsdam (Potsdam).
Media Courses are delivered via videoconferencing, e-mail. Students and teachers interact via videoconferencing, e-mail. A computer is required for some courses.
Restrictions Programs are available to in-state students only.
Services Distance learners have access to library services, academic advising at a distance.
Credit-earning options Students may transfer credits from another institution or may earn credits through standardized exams.
Typical costs *Undergraduate:* Tuition of $137 per credit hour plus mandatory fees of $8.85 per credit hour for in-state residents. Tuition of $346 per credit hour plus mandatory fees of $8.85 per credit hour for out-of-state residents. *Graduate:* Tuition of $213 per credit hour plus mandatory fees of $8.85 per credit hour for in-state residents. Tuition of $351 per credit hour plus mandatory fees of $8.85 per credit hour for out-of-state residents. Costs may vary by number of credits taken. Financial aid is available to distance learners.
Registration Students may register by mail.
Contact Mrs. Cheryl Marshall, Coordinator, Distance Learning Office, State University of New York College at Plattsburgh, 101 Broad Street, Sibley Hall 418A, Plattsburgh, NY 12901. *Telephone:* 518-564-4234. *Fax:* 518-564-4069. *E-mail:* marshaca@splava.cc.plattsburgh.edu. *Web site:* http://www.plattsburgh.edu.

DEGREE & CERTIFICATE PROGRAMS

Baccalaureate Degrees
▶*Nursing (BS)*
In the fall of 1996 there were 191 students enrolled in this program. In 1995–96, 30 degrees were earned at a distance through this program.
Application requirements *Prior education:* diploma or associate degree in nursing and RN license. *Other requirements:* college transcripts, an application fee of $30, graduation from a Diploma School of Nursing.
Completion requirements 120 credit hours are required. 36 credit hours must be completed through the institution. This is a degree completion program.

INDIVIDUAL COURSE SUBJECT AREAS

Undergraduate
Nursing

Graduate
Education administration

STATE UNIVERSITY OF NEW YORK COLLEGE OF ENVIRONMENTAL SCIENCE AND FORESTRY

Syracuse, New York

Office of Continuing Education

State University of New York College of Environmental Science and Forestry, founded in 1911, is a state-supported university. It is accredited by the Middle States Association of Colleges and Schools. It first offered distance learning courses in 1996. In 1996–97, it offered 3 courses at a distance. In the fall of 1996, there was a total of 10 students enrolled in distance learning courses.
Course delivery sites Courses are delivered to your home, your workplace, State University of New York at Binghamton (Binghamton), State University of New York College at Cortland (Cortland), State University of New York Health Science Center at Syracuse (Syracuse).
Media Courses are delivered via television, videotapes, computer software, World Wide Web, e-mail, print, CD-ROM. Students and teachers interact via mail, telephone, fax, e-mail. A computer is required for some courses.
Restrictions Students must have network accessibility.
Services Distance learners have access to the campus computer network, e-mail services, academic advising, tutoring, career placement assistance at a distance.
Credit-earning options Students may transfer credits from another institution or may earn credits through examinations, military training.
Typical costs *Undergraduate:* Tuition of $137 per credit plus mandatory fees of $30 per semester for in-state residents. Tuition of $346 per credit plus mandatory fees of $30 per semester for out-of-state residents. *Graduate:* Tuition of $213 per credit plus mandatory fees of $85 per year for in-state residents. Tuition of $351 per credit plus mandatory fees of $85 per year for out-of-state residents. *Noncredit courses:* $35 per course. Costs may vary by number of credits taken. Financial aid is available to distance learners enrolled full-time.
Registration Students may register by mail, fax, phone.
Contact Robert C. Koepper, Dean of Nonresident Programs, State University of New York College of Environmental Science and Forestry, 1 Forestry Drive, Syracuse, NY 13201. *Telephone:* 315-470-6891. *Fax:* 315-470-6890. *E-mail:* rkoepper@mailbox.syr.edu. *Web site:* http://www.esf.edu.

INDIVIDUAL COURSE SUBJECT AREAS

Undergraduate
Biology; ecology; environmental engineering

Graduate
Civil engineering; engineering mechanics; engineering-related technologies; environmental engineering

STATE UNIVERSITY OF NEW YORK EMPIRE STATE COLLEGE

Saratoga Springs, New York

Center for Distance Learning

State University of New York Empire State College, founded in 1971, is a state-supported comprehensive institution. It is accredited by the

Middle States Association of Colleges and Schools. It first offered distance learning courses in 1982. In 1996–97, it offered 196 courses at a distance. In the fall of 1996, there was a total of 1,400 students enrolled in distance learning courses.
Course delivery sites Courses are delivered to your home, your workplace, military bases.
Media Courses are delivered via videotapes, audiotapes, computer software, World Wide Web, e-mail, print. Students and teachers interact via mail, telephone, fax, e-mail, computer conferencing. A computer is required for some courses.
Services Distance learners have access to library services, the campus computer network, e-mail services, academic advising, tutoring at a distance.
Credit-earning options Students may transfer credits from another institution or may earn credits through standardized exams, portfolio assessment, military training, business training.
Typical costs *Undergraduate:* Tuition of $113 per credit plus mandatory fees of $0.85 per credit. *Graduate:* Tuition of $216.35 per credit plus mandatory fees of $2.50 per credit. Costs may vary by number of credits taken. Financial aid is available to distance learners enrolled full-time or part-time.
Registration Students may register by mail, fax, phone, e-mail.
Contact Stephanie Thomas, Marketing Assistant, State University of New York Empire State College, Center for Distance Learning, 2 Union Avenue, Saratoga Springs, NY 12866. *Telephone:* 518-587-2100, Ext. 300. *Fax:* 518-587-2660. *E-mail:* cdl@sescva.esc.edu.

DEGREE & CERTIFICATE PROGRAMS

Associate Degrees

▶ *Business, Management and Economics, Community and Human Services, Interdisciplinary Studies (AA)*
Application requirements *Prior education:* high school diploma or equivalent. *Other requirements:* an essay or personal statement, an application fee of $50.
Completion requirements 64 credits are required. 24 credits must be completed through the institution.

▶ *Business, Management and Economics, Community and Human Services, Interdisciplinary Studies (AS)*
Application requirements *Prior education:* high school diploma or equivalent. *Other requirements:* an essay or personal statement, an application fee of $50.
Completion requirements 64 credits are required. 24 credits must be completed through the institution.

Baccalaureate Degrees

▶ *Business, Management and Economics, Community and Human Services (BPS)*
Application requirements *Prior education:* high school diploma or equivalent. *Other requirements:* an essay or personal statement, an application fee of $50.
Completion requirements 128 credits are required. 32 credits must be completed through the institution.

▶ *Business, Management and Economics, Community and Human Services, Interdisciplinary Studies (BS)*
Application requirements *Prior education:* high school diploma or equivalent. *Other requirements:* an essay or personal statement, an application fee of $50.
Completion requirements 128 credits are required. 32 credits must be completed through the institution.

▶ *Business, Management and Economics, Community and Human Services, Interdisciplinary Studies (BA)*
Application requirements *Prior education:* high school diploma or equivalent. *Other requirements:* an essay or personal statement, an application fee of $50.
Completion requirements 128 credits are required. 32 credits must be completed through the institution.

INDIVIDUAL COURSE SUBJECT AREAS

Undergraduate
Abnormal psychology; accounting; administrative and secretarial services; algebra; American (US) history; area, ethnic, and cultural studies; biology; business; business administration and management; business communications; business law; calculus; child care and development; communications; community health services; computer and information sciences; counseling psychology; criminal justice; economics; English composition; English language and literature; finance; fire services administration; health professions and related sciences; history; home economics and family studies; human resources management; individual and family development studies; information sciences and systems; international business; labor relations/studies; liberal arts, general studies, and humanities; management information systems; mathematics; organizational behavior studies; philosophy and religion; political science; public administration and services; religious studies; social psychology; social sciences; sociology; statistics; telecommunications

See full description on page 474.

STATE UNIVERSITY OF WEST GEORGIA

Carrollton, Georgia

Special Programs

State University of West Georgia, founded in 1933, is a state-supported comprehensive institution. It is accredited by the Southern Association of Colleges and Schools. It first offered distance learning courses in 1995. In 1996–97, it offered 35 courses at a distance. In the fall of 1996, there was a total of 1,153 students enrolled in distance learning courses.
Course delivery sites Courses are delivered to Dalton College (Dalton), Floyd College (Rome), 1 off-campus center in Newnan, schools throughout Georgia.
Media Courses are delivered via videoconferencing, World Wide Web. Students and teachers interact via videoconferencing, mail, telephone, fax, e-mail. A computer is required for some courses.
Restrictions Most courses are limited to in-state students only.
Services Distance learners have access to library services, the campus computer network, e-mail services, career placement assistance at a distance.
Credit-earning options Students may transfer credits from another institution or may earn credits through standardized exams, institutionally developed exams.
Typical costs *Undergraduate:* Tuition of $663 per quarter for in-state residents. Tuition of $1956 per quarter for out-of-state residents. *Graduate:* Tuition of $689 per quarter for in-state residents. Tuition of $2047 per quarter for out-of-state residents. Costs may vary by number of credits taken. Financial aid is available to distance learners enrolled full-time or part-time.
Registration Students may register by mail, phone.
Contact Melanie Hill, Distance Learning Program Coordinator, State University of West Georgia, Sanford Hall, Carrollton, GA 30118. *Telephone:* 770-836-4647. *Fax:* 770-830-2244. *E-mail:* mhill@westga.edu. *Web site:* http://www.westga.edu.

Profiles: State University of West Georgia

INDIVIDUAL COURSE SUBJECT AREAS

Undergraduate
Accounting; administrative and secretarial services; algebra; American (US) history; American literature; art history and criticism; business administration and management; business law; calculus; computer and information sciences; creative writing; drama and theater; economics; education; education administration; educational psychology; English as a second language (ESL); English composition; English language and literature; English literature; European history; history; management information systems; marketing; mass media; mathematics; music; nursing; philosophy and religion; political science; psychology; public administration and services; real estate; social sciences; sociology; special education; student counseling; teacher education

Graduate
Accounting; American (US) history; American literature; business administration and management; education; education administration; educational psychology; educational research; English language and literature; English literature; European history; history; instructional media; psychology; public administration and services; real estate; special education; teacher education

STEPHENS COLLEGE

Columbia, Missouri

School of Continuing Education

Stephens College, founded in 1833, is an independent-nonprofit four-year college. It is accredited by the North Central Association of Colleges and Schools. It first offered distance learning courses in 1971. In 1996–97, it offered 100 courses at a distance. In the fall of 1996, there was a total of 300 students enrolled in distance learning courses.
Course delivery sites Courses are delivered to your home.
Media Courses are delivered via World Wide Web, print. Students and teachers interact via mail, telephone, e-mail. A computer is required for some courses.
Services Distance learners have access to e-mail services, academic advising at a distance.
Credit-earning options Students may transfer credits from another institution or may earn credits through standardized exams, portfolio assessment, military training, business training.
Typical costs Tuition of $650 per semester hour. *Noncredit courses:* $650 per course.
Registration Students may register by mail.
Contact Mariea Caruthers, Academic Services Coordinator, Stephens College, Campus Box 2083, 1200 East Broadway, Columbia, MO 65215. *Telephone:* 800-388-7579. *Fax:* 573-876-7248. *E-mail:* mc_stu@wc.stephens.edu.

DEGREE & CERTIFICATE PROGRAMS

Baccalaureate Degrees
▶ *Business, English, Language and Rhetoric, Philosophy, Psychology (BA)*
Application requirements *Prior education:* high school diploma or equivalent. *Minimum age:* 23. *Other requirements:* high school transcript, college transcripts, TOEFL (if English is not first language).
Completion requirements 120 semester hours are required. 36 semester hours must be completed through the institution.
On-campus requirements Short format seminar: two 3-day weekends or 7 days.

▶ *Health Care (BA)*
Application requirements *Prior education:* RN license.
Completion requirements 60 semester hours are required.
On-campus requirements Short format seminar: two 3-day weekends or 7 days.

▶ *Health Information Management (BS)*
Application requirements *Prior education:* high school diploma or equivalent. *Minimum age:* 23. *Other requirements:* high school transcript, college transcripts, TOEFL (if English is not first language).
Completion requirements 120 semester hours are required. 36 semester hours must be completed through the institution.
On-campus requirements Short format seminar: two 3-day weekends or 7 days.

▶ *Health Science (BA)*
Application requirements *Prior education:* associate degree in an allied health area.
Completion requirements 60 semester hours are required.
On-campus requirements Short format seminar: two 3-day weekends or 7 days.

Graduate Degrees
▶ *Business Administration, Clinical Information Systems Management, Entrepreneurship Management (MBA)*
Application requirements *Prior education:* baccalaureate degree. *Other requirements:* GMAT, TOEFL, college transcripts, letter(s) of recommendation, 3.0 GPA, personal interview.
Completion requirements 60 semester hours are required.
Program contact Dr. Joan Rines, Interim Director of Graduate Program, Stephens College, 1200 East Broadway, Campus Box 2083, Columbia, MO 65215. Phone: 800-388-7579. Fax: 573-876-7248.

▶ *Inclusion Counseling (MEd)*
Application requirements *Prior education:* baccalaureate degree. *Other requirements:* GRE, TOEFL, college transcripts, an essay or personal statement, letter(s) of recommendation, personal interview.
Completion requirements 24 semester hours are required.
On-campus requirements Summer meetings.
Program contact Dr. Joan Rines, Interim Director of Graduate Program, Stephens College, 1200 East Broadway, Campus Box 2083, Columbia, MO 65215. Phone: 800-388-7579. Fax: 573-876-7248.

Graduate certificates
▶ *Health Information Management*
Application requirements *Prior education:* baccalaureate degree. *Other requirements:* high school transcript, college transcripts.

INDIVIDUAL COURSE SUBJECT AREAS

Undergraduate
Accounting; American literature; anatomy; business administration and management; business law; chemistry; creative writing; earth science; economics; education; English literature; ethics; finance; Hebrew language and literature; history; human resources management; information sciences and systems; Japanese language and literature; Latin American studies; logic; marketing; organizational behavior studies; physiology; psychology; religious studies; statistics; teacher education

See full description on page 476.

STEVENS INSTITUTE OF TECHNOLOGY

Hoboken, New Jersey

The Graduate School

Stevens Institute of Technology, founded in 1870, is an independent-nonprofit university. It is accredited by the Middle States Association of Colleges and Schools. It first offered distance learning courses in 1993. In 1996–97, it offered 10 courses at a distance. In the fall of 1996, there was a total of 40 students enrolled in distance learning courses.
Course delivery sites Courses are delivered to your home, your workplace, County College of Morris (Randolph).
Media Courses are delivered via television, videoconferencing, computer software, World Wide Web, e-mail, print. Students and teachers interact via videoconferencing, mail, telephone, fax, e-mail. A computer is required for some courses.
Restrictions Students must be employees of participating companies.
Services Distance learners have access to library services, the campus computer network, e-mail services, academic advising at a distance.
Credit-earning options Students may transfer credits from another institution or may earn credits through institutionally developed exams, business training.
Typical costs Tuition of $625 per credit plus mandatory fees of $75 per semester. *Noncredit courses:* $300 per course. Costs may vary by course delivery options. Financial aid is available to distance learners enrolled full-time or part-time.
Registration Students may register by mail, fax, e-mail.
Contact Joseph J. Moeller, Jr., Vice President, Stevens Institute of Technology, Castle Point on Hudson, Hoboken, NJ 07030. *Telephone:* 201-216-5229. *Fax:* 201-216-8044. *E-mail:* jmoeller@stevens-tech.edu. *Web site:* http://attila.stevens-tech.edu/gradschool.

DEGREE & CERTIFICATE PROGRAMS

Graduate Degrees

▶ *Computer Science (MS)*
In the fall of 1996 there were 10 students enrolled in this program.
Application requirements *Prior education:* baccalaureate degree. *Other requirements:* college transcripts, letter(s) of recommendation, an application fee of $40, 3.0 GPA.
Completion requirements 30 semester credits are required. 20 semester credits must be completed through the institution.

▶ *Human Factors (MS)*
In the fall of 1996 there were 12 students enrolled in this program.
Application requirements *Prior education:* baccalaureate degree. *Other requirements:* high school transcript, letter(s) of recommendation, an application fee of $40, 3.0 GPA.
Completion requirements 30 semester credits are required. 20 semester credits must be completed through the institution.

▶ *Management (MS)*
In the fall of 1996 there were 10 students enrolled in this program.
Application requirements *Prior education:* baccalaureate degree. *Other requirements:* college transcripts, letter(s) of recommendation, an application fee of $40, 3.0 GPA.
Completion requirements 30 semester credits are required. 20 semester credits must be completed through the institution.

Graduate certificates

▶ *Concurrent Engineering*
Application requirements *Prior education:* baccalaureate degree. *Other requirements:* high school transcript, letter(s) of recommendation, an application fee of $40, 3.0 GPA.
Completion requirements 10 semester credits are required. 7.5 semester credits must be completed through the institution.

▶ *Telecommunications Management*
In the fall of 1996 there were 12 students enrolled in this program.
Application requirements *Prior education:* baccalaureate degree. *Other requirements:* college transcripts, letter(s) of recommendation, an application fee of $40, 3.0 GPA.
Completion requirements 10 semester credits are required. 7.5 semester credits must be completed through the institution.

INDIVIDUAL COURSE SUBJECT AREAS

Graduate
Business administration and management; computer and information sciences; engineering; industrial psychology

Noncredit
Electronics

STRAYER COLLEGE

Washington, District of Columbia

Student Distance Learning Program

Strayer College, founded in 1892, is a proprietary comprehensive institution. It is accredited by the Middle States Association of Colleges and Schools. It first offered distance learning courses in 1996. In 1996–97, it offered 10 courses at a distance. In the fall of 1996, there was a total of 98 students enrolled in distance learning courses.
Course delivery sites Courses are delivered to your home, your workplace, military bases.
Media Courses are delivered via computer software, World Wide Web, e-mail, Internet. Students and teachers interact via e-mail, computer conferencing. A computer is required for all courses.
Restrictions Courses are available to students in Maryland, Virginia, and Washington, DC only. Students must be proficient in the use of the Internet. A prerequisite Internet usage course is offered.
Credit-earning options Students may transfer credits from another institution or may earn credits through standardized exams, institutionally developed exams, portfolio assessment, military training, business training.
Typical costs Tuition of $240 per quarter credit. Costs may vary by number of credits taken. Financial aid is available to distance learners enrolled full-time or part-time.
Registration Students may register by phone.
Contact Pamela Bell, Campus Coordinator, Strayer College, Distance Learning Center, 8382-F Terminal Road, Lorton, VA 22079. *Telephone:* 703-339-1850. *Web site:* http://www.strayer.edu.

INDIVIDUAL COURSE SUBJECT AREAS

Graduate
Accounting; business administration and management; business law; computer and information sciences

SUFFOLK COUNTY COMMUNITY COLLEGE–AMMERMAN CAMPUS

Selden, New York

Corporate and Extended Learning

Suffolk County Community College–Ammerman Campus, founded in 1962, is a state and locally supported two-year college. It is accredited by the Middle States Association of Colleges and Schools. It first offered distance learning courses in 1989. In 1996–97, it offered 40 courses at a distance. In the fall of 1996, there was a total of 337 students enrolled in distance learning courses.
Course delivery sites Courses are delivered to your home, your workplace.
Media Courses are delivered via television, videotapes. Students and teachers interact via telephone, e-mail.
Credit-earning options Students may transfer credits from another institution or may earn credits through business training.
Typical costs Tuition of $90 per credit hour plus mandatory fees of $40 per course.
Registration Students may register by phone.
Contact John Barham, Provost, Corporate and Extended Learning, Suffolk County Community College–Ammerman Campus, 533 College Road, Selden, NY 11784. *Telephone:* 516-451-4399. *Fax:* 516-451-4808. *E-mail:* barhamj@sunysuffolk.edu.

INDIVIDUAL COURSE SUBJECT AREAS

Undergraduate
Accounting; area, ethnic, and cultural studies; astronomy and astrophysics; biological and life sciences; biology; business; business administration and management; communications; creative writing; developmental and child psychology; economics; English composition; English language and literature; fine arts; health and physical education/fitness; history; liberal arts, general studies, and humanities; mathematics; music; philosophy and religion; physical sciences; political science; psychology; sociology; visual and performing arts

Noncredit
Home economics and family studies

SUL ROSS STATE UNIVERSITY

Alpine, Texas

School of Arts and Sciences

Sul Ross State University, founded in 1920, is a state-supported comprehensive institution. It is accredited by the Southern Association of Colleges and Schools. It first offered distance learning courses in 1995. In 1996–97, it offered 13 courses at a distance. In the fall of 1996, there was a total of 84 students enrolled in distance learning courses.
Course delivery sites Courses are delivered to public high schools in Iraan and Presidio.
Media Courses are delivered via videoconferencing. Students and teachers interact via videoconferencing, mail, telephone, fax, e-mail.
Restrictions Courses are available to students in Alpine, Presidio, and Iraan only.
Services Distance learners have access to library services, the campus computer network, e-mail services, academic advising at a distance.
Credit-earning options Students may earn credits through standardized exams.
Typical costs *Undergraduate:* Tuition of $120 per course plus mandatory fees of $96 per course for in-state residents. Tuition of $738 per course plus mandatory fees of $96 per course for out-of-state residents. *Graduate:* Tuition of $120 per course plus mandatory fees of $96 per course for in-state residents. Tuition of $738 per course plus mandatory fees of $96 per course for out-of-state residents. Costs may vary by number of credits taken. Financial aid is available to distance learners enrolled full-time or part-time.
Contact Dr. Bruce Glasrud, Dean, Sul Ross State University, School of Arts and Sciences, Alpine, TX 79832. *Telephone:* 915-837-8368. *Fax:* 915-837-8028. *E-mail:* bglasrud@sul-ross-1.sulross.edu.

INDIVIDUAL COURSE SUBJECT AREAS

Undergraduate
American (US) history; art history and criticism; communications; computer and information sciences; English composition; English literature; environmental science; mathematics; psychology; sociology

SUSSEX COUNTY COMMUNITY COLLEGE

Newton, New Jersey

Sussex County Community College, founded in 1981, is a state and locally supported two-year college. It is accredited by the Middle States Association of Colleges and Schools. It first offered distance learning courses in 1990. In 1996–97, it offered 8 courses at a distance. In the fall of 1996, there was a total of 50 students enrolled in distance learning courses.
Course delivery sites Courses are delivered to your home, other colleges.
Media Courses are delivered via television, videotapes. Students and teachers interact via videoconferencing.
Restrictions Programs are available to local area students only.
Credit-earning options Students may transfer credits from another institution or may earn credits through examinations, portfolio assessment, military training, business training.
Typical costs Tuition of $68 per credit plus mandatory fees of $9 per credit for local area residents. Tuition of $136 per credit plus mandatory fees of $9 per credit for in-state residents. Tuition of $204 per credit plus mandatory fees of $9 per credit for out-of-state residents. $15 admission charge (one time fee). Technology fee of $15–$45 per semester.
Contact Sue Rafter, Director, Counseling Center, Sussex County Community College, 1 College Hill, Newton, NJ 07860. *Telephone:* 201-300-2205.

INDIVIDUAL COURSE SUBJECT AREAS

Undergraduate
Astronomy and astrophysics; business administration and management; history; social psychology

SYRACUSE UNIVERSITY

Syracuse, New York

Division of Continuing Education

Syracuse University, founded in 1870, is an independent-nonprofit university. It is accredited by the Middle States Association of Colleges and Schools. It first offered distance learning courses in 1966.

Course delivery sites Courses are delivered to your home.

Media Courses are delivered via audiotapes, computer software, World Wide Web, e-mail, print. Students and teachers interact via mail, telephone, fax, e-mail, in-person meetings. A computer is required for some courses.

Services Distance learners have access to library services, the campus computer network, e-mail services, academic advising, career placement assistance at a distance.

Credit-earning options Students may transfer credits from another institution or may earn credits through standardized exams, portfolio assessment, military training, business training.

Typical costs *Undergraduate:* Tuition of $320 per credit. *Graduate:* Tuition of $529 per credit. Costs may vary by number of credits taken. Financial aid is available to distance learners enrolled full-time or part-time.

Registration Students may register by mail.

Contact Roberta S. Jones, Director, Independent Study Degree Programs, Syracuse University, 301 Reid Hall, 610 East Fayette Street, Syracuse, NY 13244-6020. *Telephone:* 800-442-0501. *Fax:* 315-443-4174. *E-mail:* suisdp@uc.syr.edu. *Web site:* http://cwis.syr.edu.

DEGREE & CERTIFICATE PROGRAMS

Associate Degrees

▶ *Liberal Arts (AA)*

Application requirements *Prior education:* high school diploma or equivalent. *Other requirements:* high school transcript, college transcripts, an essay or personal statement, letter(s) of recommendation, an application fee of $40.

Completion requirements 60 credits are required. 30 credits must be completed through the institution.

On-campus requirements 1–3 weeks.

Baccalaureate Degrees

▶ *Liberal Studies (BA)*

Application requirements *Prior education:* high school diploma or equivalent. *Other requirements:* high school transcript, college transcripts, an essay or personal statement, letter(s) of recommendation, an application fee of $40.

Completion requirements 120 credits are required. 30 credits must be completed through the institution.

On-campus requirements 1–3 weeks.

Graduate Degrees

▶ *Advertising Design (MA)*

Restrictions Program is for mid-career students only.

Application requirements *Prior education:* baccalaureate degree. *Other requirements:* college transcripts, an essay or personal statement, letter(s) of recommendation, an application fee of $40, portfolio.

Completion requirements 30 credits are required. 30 credits must be completed through the institution. *Maximum time for completion:* seven years.

On-campus requirements Two weeks.

▶ *Business Administration (MBA)*

Application requirements *Prior education:* baccalaureate degree. *Other requirements:* GMAT, college transcripts, an essay or personal statement, letter(s) of recommendation, an application fee of $40, 2–3 years of work experience.

Completion requirements 54 credits are required. 30 credits must be completed through the institution. *Maximum time for completion:* seven years.

On-campus requirements 1–3 weeks.

▶ *Communications Management (MS)*

Application requirements *Prior education:* baccalaureate degree. *Other requirements:* GRE or GMAT, college transcripts, an essay or personal statement, letter(s) of recommendation, an application fee of $40, portfolio, 5 years relevant professional experience.

Completion requirements 36 credits are required. 30 credits must be completed through the institution. *Maximum time for completion:* seven years.

On-campus requirements 1–3 weeks per semester.

▶ *Illustration (MA)*

Restrictions Program is for mid-career students only.

Application requirements *Prior education:* baccalaureate degree. *Other requirements:* college transcripts, an essay or personal statement, letter(s) of recommendation, an application fee of $40, portfolio.

Completion requirements 30 credits are required. 30 credits must be completed through the institution. *Maximum time for completion:* seven years.

On-campus requirements Two weeks for three consecutive summers, short contact periods during the year in other locations.

▶ *Information Resource Management (MS)*

Application requirements *Prior education:* baccalaureate degree. *Other requirements:* GRE, TOEFL (for international students), college transcripts, an essay or personal statement, letter(s) of recommendation, an application fee of $40, basic computer and Internet skills, access to the Internet and World Wide Web, a minimum 486 computer (pentium preferred), 14.4 baud or higher modem, and fax machine.

Completion requirements 42 credits are required. 30 credits must be completed through the institution. *Maximum time for completion:* seven years.

On-campus requirements 1–3 weeks per year.

▶ *Library Science (MLS)*

Application requirements *Prior education:* baccalaureate degree. *Other requirements:* GRE, TOEFL (for international students), college transcripts, an essay or personal statement, letter(s) of recommendation, an application fee of $40, basic computer and Internet skills, access to the Internet and World Wide Web, a minimum 486 computer (pentium preferred), 14.4 baud or higher modem, and fax machine.

Completion requirements 36 credits are required. 30 credits must be completed through the institution. *Maximum time for completion:* seven years.

On-campus requirements 1–4 weeks per year.

▶ *Nursing (MS)*

Restrictions Program is for working professionals only.

Application requirements *Prior education:* baccalaureate degree. *Other requirements:* GRE, college transcripts, an essay or personal statement, letter(s) of recommendation, an application fee of $40.

Completion requirements 45 credits are required. 39 credits must be completed through the institution. *Maximum time for completion:* seven years.

On-campus requirements 1–3 weeks.

▶ *Social Sciences (MSS)*

Application requirements *Prior education:* baccalaureate degree. *Other requirements:* college transcripts, an essay or personal statement, letter(s) of recommendation, an application fee of $40.

Completion requirements 30 credits are required. 30 credits must be completed through the institution. *Maximum time for completion:* seven years.

On-campus requirements Two weeks per year.

▶ *Telecommunications and Network Management (MS)*

Application requirements *Prior education:* baccalaureate degree. *Other requirements:* GRE, TOEFL (for international students), college transcripts, an essay or personal statement, letter(s) of recommendation, an application fee of $40, basic computer and Internet skills, access to the Internet and World Wide Web, a minimum 486 computer (pentium preferred), 14.4 baud or higher modem, fax machine, 3 years of experience or sufficient relevant course work.

Completion requirements 42 credits are required. 30 credits must be completed through the institution. *Maximum time for completion:* seven years.

On-campus requirements 1–3 weeks per year.

Profiles: Syracuse University

INDIVIDUAL COURSE SUBJECT AREAS

Undergraduate
Accounting; anthropology; area, ethnic, and cultural studies; biology; business; business administration and management; business communications; calculus; comparative literature; developmental and child psychology; earth science; economics; English composition; English language and literature; ethics; fine arts; foods and nutrition studies; genetics; geology; history; hospitality services management; international relations; liberal arts, general studies, and humanities; logic; mathematics; philosophy and religion; physics; political science; social psychology; sociology; statistics

Graduate
Anthropology; history; international relations; political science; social sciences

See full description on page 478.

TACOMA COMMUNITY COLLEGE

Tacoma, Washington

Sciences Division

Tacoma Community College, founded in 1965, is a state-supported two-year college. It is accredited by the Northwest Association of Schools and Colleges. It first offered distance learning courses in 1980. In 1996–97, it offered 13 courses at a distance. In the fall of 1996, there was a total of 117 students enrolled in distance learning courses.
Course delivery sites Courses are delivered to your home, 2 off-campus centers in Gig Harbor, Tacoma.
Media Courses are delivered via television, videotapes. Students and teachers interact via mail, telephone, e-mail.
Services Distance learners have access to the campus computer network, e-mail services at a distance.
Credit-earning options Students may transfer credits from another institution or may earn credits through standardized exams, institutionally developed exams, military training.
Typical costs Tuition of $233.65 per course plus mandatory fees of $20 per course for in-state residents. Tuition of $918.65 per course plus mandatory fees of $20 per course for out-of-state residents. *Noncredit courses:* $22 to $85. Costs may vary by number of credits taken. Financial aid is available to distance learners.
Registration Students may register by mail, fax, phone.
Contact Ivonna McCabe, Associate Dean for Sciences, Tacoma Community College, 6501 South 19th Street, Tacoma, WA 98466. *Telephone:* 253-566-5059. *Fax:* 253-566-5202. *E-mail:* imccabe@tcc.tacoma.ctc.edu.

INDIVIDUAL COURSE SUBJECT AREAS

Undergraduate
Abnormal psychology; anthropology; biology; English language and literature; European languages and literatures; geography; geology; history; liberal arts, general studies, and humanities; philosophy and religion; psychology; social psychology; sociology

TALLAHASSEE COMMUNITY COLLEGE

Tallahassee, Florida

Extended Studies Division

Tallahassee Community College, founded in 1966, is a state and locally supported two-year college. It is accredited by the Southern Association of Colleges and Schools. It first offered distance learning courses in 1985.
Course delivery sites Courses are delivered to your home, your workplace.
Media Courses are delivered via television, videotapes, radio broadcast, computer software, print, computer conferencing.
Restrictions Programs are available to local area students only.
Credit-earning options Students may transfer credits from another institution or may earn credits through examinations. Financial aid is available to distance learners.
Contact Coordinator, Extended Studies, Tallahassee Community College, 444 Appleyard Drive, Tallahassee, FL 32304. *Telephone:* 904-922-8168. *Fax:* 904-921-4489.

DEGREE & CERTIFICATE PROGRAMS

Associate Degrees
▶ *General Studies (AA)*
On-campus requirements For exams.

INDIVIDUAL COURSE SUBJECT AREAS

Undergraduate
Accounting; advertising; area, ethnic, and cultural studies; biological and life sciences; biology; business; business administration and management; chemistry; communications; computer and information sciences; creative writing; developmental and child psychology; English composition; English language and literature; geography; geology; history; law and legal studies; liberal arts, general studies, and humanities; mathematics; philosophy and religion; physical sciences; political science; public health; social psychology; social sciences; sociology

TARLETON STATE UNIVERSITY

Stephenville, Texas

Center for Instructional Technology and Distance Learning

Tarleton State University, founded in 1899, is a state-supported comprehensive institution. It is accredited by the Southern Association of Colleges and Schools. It first offered distance learning courses in 1992. In 1996–97, it offered 14 courses at a distance. In the fall of 1996, there was a total of 183 students enrolled in distance learning courses.
Course delivery sites Courses are delivered to military bases, The Texas A&M University System (College Station), Weatherford College (Weatherford), 1 off-campus center in Fort Hood, Trans Texas Video Network.
Media Courses are delivered via videoconferencing, computer software, World Wide Web, e-mail, print. Students and teachers interact via videoconferencing, mail, telephone, fax, e-mail.
Services Distance learners have access to library services, e-mail services, academic advising, tutoring, career placement assistance at a distance.

Credit-earning options Students may transfer credits from another institution or may earn credits through examinations, portfolio assessment, military training, business training.
Typical costs *Undergraduate:* Tuition of $200 per course. *Graduate:* Tuition of $250 per course. Costs may vary by campus or location, number of credits taken. Financial aid is available to distance learners enrolled full-time.
Registration Students may register by phone.
Contact Dr. LaVelle Mills, Director, Center for Instructional Technology and Distance Learning, Tarleton State University, Box T-0810, Stephenville, TX 76402. *Telephone:* 817-968-9060. *Fax:* 817-968-9540. *E-mail:* mills@tarleton.edu.

INDIVIDUAL COURSE SUBJECT AREAS

Undergraduate
Business; business administration and management; computer programming; mathematics; nursing; physics

Graduate
Business administration and management; computer programming; curriculum and instruction; educational psychology; marketing

TARRANT COUNTY JUNIOR COLLEGE

Fort Worth, Texas

Center for Distance Learning

Tarrant County Junior College, founded in 1967, is a county-supported two-year college. It is accredited by the Southern Association of Colleges and Schools. It first offered distance learning courses in 1973. In 1996–97, it offered 50 courses at a distance. In the fall of 1996, there was a total of 4,000 students enrolled in distance learning courses.
Course delivery sites Courses are delivered to your home, your workplace, military bases, prisons.
Media Courses are delivered via television, videotapes, audiotapes, computer software, computer conferencing. Students and teachers interact via telephone, computer conferencing. A computer is required for some courses.
Credit-earning options Students may transfer credits from another institution or may earn credits through standardized exams, institutionally developed exams, military training.
Typical costs Tuition of $22 per semester hour plus mandatory fees of $8 per semester hour for local area residents. Tuition of $42 per semester hour plus mandatory fees of $10 per semester hour for in-state residents. Tuition of $140 per semester hour for out-of-state residents. Costs may vary by number of credits taken. Financial aid is available to distance learners enrolled full-time or part-time.
Registration Students may register by phone.
Contact Kevin Eason, Assistant Director of Distance Learning, Tarrant County Junior College, 5301 Campus Drive, Fort Worth, TX 76119. *Telephone:* 817-515-4430. *Fax:* 817-515-4400.

DEGREE & CERTIFICATE PROGRAMS

Associate Degrees
▶ *General Studies (AA)*
In the fall of 1996 there were 4,000 students enrolled in this program.
Application requirements *Prior education:* high school diploma or equivalent. *Other requirements:* high school transcript, college transcripts, an application fee of $10.
Completion requirements 64 semester hours are required. 25% of course work must be completed through the institution.

On-campus requirements For orientations; some courses have seminars and testing.

INDIVIDUAL COURSE SUBJECT AREAS

Undergraduate
Astronomy and astrophysics; biological and life sciences; biology; business; business administration and management; computer and information sciences; creative writing; developmental and child psychology; economics; engineering mechanics; English composition; English language and literature; fine arts; geology; health and physical education/fitness; history; home economics and family studies; liberal arts, general studies, and humanities; mathematics; mechanical engineering; music; philosophy and religion; physical sciences; political science; social psychology; sociology

TAYLOR UNIVERSITY, FORT WAYNE CAMPUS

Fort Wayne, Indiana

Institute of Correspondence Studies

Taylor University, Fort Wayne Campus, founded in 1992, is an independent-religious interdenominational four-year college. It is accredited by the North Central Association of Colleges and Schools. It first offered distance learning courses in 1938. In 1996–97, it offered 75 courses at a distance. In the fall of 1996, there was a total of 1,865 students enrolled in distance learning courses.
Course delivery sites Courses are delivered to your home.
Media Courses are delivered via print. Students and teachers interact via mail, telephone, e-mail. A computer is required for some courses.
Services Distance learners have access to e-mail services at a distance.
Typical costs Tuition of $75 per credit plus mandatory fees of $27 per course. Discounts are available for Christian workers, inmates.
Registration Students may register by mail, fax, phone, e-mail, World Wide Web.
Contact Mary Ann Grate, Taylor University, Fort Wayne Campus, Institute of Correspondence Studies, 1025 West Rudisill Boulevard, Fort Wayne, IN 46807-2197. *Telephone:* 219-456-2111, Ext. 32225. *Fax:* 219-456-2119. *E-mail:* icstudies@tayloru.edu. *Web site:* http://www.tayloru.edu/~ics.

DEGREE & CERTIFICATE PROGRAMS

Undergraduate Certificates
▶ *Christian Workers*
In the fall of 1996 there were 5 students enrolled in this program.
Application requirements *Prior education:* none required.
Completion requirements 18 credit hours are required. 18 credits must be completed through the institution.

▶ *Justice and Ministry*
In the fall of 1996 there were 5 students enrolled in this program.
Application requirements *Prior education:* none required.
Completion requirements 18 credit hours are required. 18 credits must be completed through the institution.
On-campus requirements Two 2-week summer sessions.

INDIVIDUAL COURSE SUBJECT AREAS

Undergraduate
Abnormal psychology; American (US) history; American literature; anthropology; bible studies; biology; communications; computer and information sciences; counseling psychology; criminal justice; educational psychology; English language and literature; fine arts; geography; Greek

Profiles: Taylor University, Fort Wayne Campus

language and literature; Hebrew language and literature; history; journalism; logic; mathematics; music; philosophy and religion; physical sciences; psychology; religious studies; social sciences; theological studies

TECHNICAL COLLEGE OF THE LOWCOUNTRY

Beaufort, South Carolina

Technical College of the Lowcountry, founded in 1972, is a state-supported two-year college. It is accredited by the Southern Association of Colleges and Schools. It first offered distance learning courses in 1996. In 1996–97, it offered 40 courses at a distance. In the fall of 1996, there was a total of 234 students enrolled in distance learning courses.

Course delivery sites Courses are delivered to 2 off-campus centers in Hilton Head Island, Varnville, public schools, technical colleges in South Carolina.

Media Courses are delivered via television, videotapes, compressed video. Students and teachers interact via mail, telephone, fax.

Restrictions Students must have access to video network to take teleclasses.

Services Distance learners have access to library services, academic advising, tutoring, career placement assistance at a distance.

Credit-earning options Students may transfer credits from another institution or may earn credits through examinations, portfolio assessment, military training.

Typical costs Tuition of $42 per credit hour for in-state residents. Tuition of $63 per credit hour for out-of-state residents. Costs may vary by number of credits taken. Financial aid is available to distance learners enrolled full-time or part-time.

Registration Students may register by mail.

Contact Fred Seitz, Director, Curriculum Development, Technical College of the Lowcountry, 921 South Ribaut Road, PO Box 1288, Beaufort, SC 29901. *Telephone:* 803-525-8204. *Fax:* 803-525-8330. *E-mail:* fseitz@tcl.tec.sc.us.

INDIVIDUAL COURSE SUBJECT AREAS

Undergraduate

Administrative and secretarial services; business administration and management; English composition; English language and literature; environmental science; history; law and legal studies; liberal arts, general studies, and humanities; mathematics; political science; protective services; psychology

TEMPLE BAPTIST SEMINARY

Chattanooga, Tennessee

External Studies

Temple Baptist Seminary is an independent-religious graduate institution. It is accredited by the Accrediting Association of Bible Colleges. It first offered distance learning courses in 1993. In 1996–97, it offered 40 courses at a distance. In the fall of 1996, there was a total of 40 students enrolled in distance learning courses.

Course delivery sites Courses are delivered to your home.

Media Courses are delivered via videotapes, audiotapes, print. Students and teachers interact via mail, telephone, fax, e-mail.

Services Distance learners have access to academic advising, tutoring, career placement assistance at a distance.

Credit-earning options Students may transfer credits from another institution or may earn credits through institutionally developed exams, portfolio assessment.

Typical costs Tuition of $135 per semester hour plus mandatory fees of $25 per course. Audio tapes, $70.00; video tapes, $120.00.. *Noncredit courses:* $50 personal enrichment fee and $70 audio tapes - $120. There is no registration (matriculation fee for personal enrichment). Costs may vary by number of credits taken, course delivery options.

Registration Students may register by mail, fax.

Contact Paulette M. Trachian, Secretary, Temple Baptist Seminary, 1815 Union Avenue, Chattanooga, TN 37404. *Telephone:* 423-493-4221. *Fax:* 423-493-4471.

DEGREE & CERTIFICATE PROGRAMS

Graduate Degrees

▶ *Biblical Studies (MABS)*

In the fall of 1996 there were 5 students enrolled in this program.

Restrictions Students must agree with doctrinal statement.

Application requirements *Prior education:* baccalaureate degree. *Other requirements:* college transcripts, an essay or personal statement, letter(s) of recommendation, an application fee of $25.

Completion requirements 64 semester hours are required.

Program contact Barkev S. Trachian, President, Temple Baptist Seminary, 1815 Union Avenue, Chattanooga, TN 37404. Phone: 423-493-4221. Fax: 423-493-4471.

▶ *Church Ministries (MMin)*

In the fall of 1996 there were 15 students enrolled in this program. In 1995–96, 2 degrees were earned at a distance through this program.

Restrictions Students must agree with doctrinal statement.

Application requirements *Prior education:* baccalaureate degree. *Other requirements:* college transcripts, an essay or personal statement, letter(s) of recommendation, an application fee of $25.

Completion requirements 32 semester hours are required.

Program contact Barkev S. Trachian, President, Temple Baptist Seminary, 1815 Union Avenue, Chattanooga, TN 37404. Phone: 423-493-4221. Fax: 423-493-4471.

▶ *Ministry (DMin)*

In the fall of 1996 there were 10 students enrolled in this program. In 1995–96, 1 degree was earned at a distance through this program.

Restrictions Students must agree with doctrinal statement.

Application requirements *Prior education:* Masters in Divinity or its equivalent. *Other requirements:* college transcripts, an essay or personal statement, letter(s) of recommendation, an application fee of $35, currently active in the ministry, 3.0 GPA or evidence of superior ability.

Completion requirements 30 semester hours are required. *Other requirements:* written examination, doctoral project. *Maximum time for completion:* six years.

Program contact Barkev S. Trachian, President, Temple Baptist Seminary, 1815 Union Avenue, Chattanooga, TN 37404. Phone: 423-493-4221. Fax: 423-493-4471.

▶ *Religious Education (MRE)*

In the fall of 1996 there was 1 student enrolled in this program.

Restrictions Students must agree with doctrinal statement.

Application requirements *Prior education:* baccalaureate degree. *Other requirements:* college transcripts, an essay or personal statement, letter(s) of recommendation, an application fee of $25.

Completion requirements 64 semester hours are required.

Program contact Barkev S. Trachian, President, Temple Baptist Seminary, 1815 Union Avenue, Chattanooga, TN 37404. Phone: 423-493-4221. Fax: 423-493-4471.

Undergraduate Certificates

▶ *Biblical Studies*

In the fall of 1996 there were 2 students enrolled in this program.

Restrictions Students must agree with doctrinal statement.

Application requirements *Prior education:* some undergraduate course work. *Minimum age:* 30. *Other requirements:* college transcripts, an essay or personal statement, letter(s) of recommendation, an application fee of $25, 2 years of ministry experience.
Completion requirements 24 semester hours are required.
Program contact Barkev S. Trachian, President, Temple Baptist Seminary, 1815 Union Avenue, Chattanooga, TN 37404. Phone: 423-493-4221. Fax: 423-493-4471.

INDIVIDUAL COURSE SUBJECT AREAS

Graduate
Bible studies; counseling psychology; philosophy and religion; religious studies; teacher education; theological studies

Noncredit
Bible studies; counseling psychology; philosophy and religion; religious studies; teacher education; theological studies

TENNESSEE STATE UNIVERSITY

Nashville, Tennessee

Center for Extended Education and Public Service

Tennessee State University, founded in 1912, is a state-supported comprehensive institution. It is accredited by the Southern Association of Colleges and Schools. It first offered distance learning courses in 1996. In 1996–97, it offered 8 courses at a distance. In the fall of 1996, there was a total of 85 students enrolled in distance learning courses.
Course delivery sites Courses are delivered to Austin Peay State University (Clarksville), University of Tennessee at Chattanooga (Chattanooga), Volunteer State Community College (Gallatin).
Media Courses are delivered via videoconferencing. Students and teachers interact via videoconferencing, mail, telephone, fax, e-mail.
Restrictions Compressed video courses are available only at specific sites.
Services Distance learners have access to library services, e-mail services, academic advising at a distance.
Credit-earning options Students may transfer credits from another institution or may earn credits through examinations, military training.
Typical costs *Undergraduate:* Tuition of $91 per hour for in-state residents. Tuition of $281 per hour for out-of-state residents. *Graduate:* Tuition of $131 per hour for in-state residents. Tuition of $321 per hour for out-of-state residents. Costs may vary by credit option. Financial aid is available to distance learners.
Registration Students may register by mail, phone.
Contact Dr. Ken Looney, Dean, Tennessee State University, 330 Tenth Avenue, N, Nashville, TN 37203. *Telephone:* 615-963-7004. *Fax:* 615-963-7007. *E-mail:* klooney@picard.tnstate.edu.

INDIVIDUAL COURSE SUBJECT AREAS

Undergraduate
Nursing

Graduate
Accounting; business administration and management; civil engineering; education administration; English as a second language (ESL); English language and literature; environmental engineering; hospitality services management; human resources management; mathematics; mechanical engineering; nursing; political science; public policy analysis; teacher education

Noncredit
Business administration and management; English as a second language (ESL); environmental engineering; hospitality services management; human resources management; nursing

TENNESSEE TECHNOLOGICAL UNIVERSITY

Cookeville, Tennessee

Extended Education

Tennessee Technological University, founded in 1915, is a state-supported university. It is accredited by the Southern Association of Colleges and Schools. It first offered distance learning courses in 1985. In 1996–97, it offered 7 courses at a distance. In the fall of 1996, there was a total of 52 students enrolled in distance learning courses.
Course delivery sites Courses are delivered to your home, Austin Peay State University (Clarksville), 9 off-campus centers in Byrdstown, Celina, Clarkrange, Gainesboro, Jamestown, Livingston, Red Boiling Springs.
Media Courses are delivered via television, videoconferencing. Students and teachers interact via videoconferencing, mail, telephone, fax, e-mail.
Restrictions Programs are available to in-state students only.
Services Distance learners have access to library services, the campus computer network, e-mail services, academic advising, career placement assistance at a distance.
Credit-earning options Students may transfer credits from another institution or may earn credits through standardized exams.
Typical costs *Undergraduate:* Tuition of $945 per semester plus mandatory fees of $15 per semester for in-state residents. Tuition of $2168 per semester plus mandatory fees of $15 per semester for out-of-state residents. *Graduate:* Tuition of $1238 per semester plus mandatory fees of $15 per semester for in-state residents. Tuition of $2168 per semester plus mandatory fees of $15 per semester for out-of-state residents. Costs may vary by number of credits taken. Financial aid is available to distance learners enrolled full-time or part-time.
Registration Students may register by mail, fax, phone.
Contact Susan A. Elkins, Director, Extended Education, Tennessee Technological University, Box 5073, Cookeville, TN 38505. *Telephone:* 615-372-3394. *Fax:* 615-372-3499. *E-mail:* sae9444@tntech.edu. *Web site:* http://www.tntech.edu/www/acad/extend/.

INDIVIDUAL COURSE SUBJECT AREAS

Undergraduate
Accounting; English language and literature; philosophy and religion; sociology; teacher education

Graduate
Accounting; education administration; educational psychology; English language and literature; teacher education

Noncredit
Public health

TENNESSEE TEMPLE UNIVERSITY

Chattanooga, Tennessee

School of External Studies

Tennessee Temple University, founded in 1946, is an independent-religious Baptist comprehensive institution. It is accredited by the Accredit-

Profiles: Tennessee Temple University

ing Association of Bible Colleges. It first offered distance learning courses in 1988. In 1996–97, it offered 72 courses at a distance. In the fall of 1996, there was a total of 300 students enrolled in distance learning courses.
Course delivery sites Courses are delivered to your home, your workplace.
Media Courses are delivered via videotapes, audiotapes, print. Students and teachers interact via mail, telephone, fax. A computer is required for some courses.
Services Distance learners have access to academic advising, tutoring at a distance.
Credit-earning options Students may transfer credits from another institution or may earn credits through examinations.
Typical costs Tuition of $75 per credit hour. Students pay $100-$125 per course in fees. *Noncredit courses:* $250 for a 2-hour course, $325 for a 3-hour course. Costs may vary by term of enrollment. Financial aid is available to distance learners enrolled full-time.
Registration Students may register by mail, fax, phone.
Contact Dr. John E. Waters, Director of External Studies, Tennessee Temple University, 1815 Union Avenue, Chattanooga, TN 37404. *Telephone:* 423-493-4288. *Fax:* 423-493-4497.

DEGREE & CERTIFICATE PROGRAMS

Associate Degrees
▶ *Biblical Studies (AA)*
In the fall of 1996 there were 15 students enrolled in this program.
Restrictions Statement of Faith in Christ and when and how that experience happened required.
Application requirements *Prior education:* high school diploma or equivalent. *Other requirements:* high school transcript, college transcripts, an essay or personal statement, letter(s) of recommendation, an application fee of $25.
Completion requirements 65 credits are required. *Maximum time for completion:* eight years.

Baccalaureate Degrees
▶ *Biblical Studies (BS)*
In the fall of 1996 there were 30 students enrolled in this program.
Restrictions Statement of faith in Jesus Christ as personal savior.
Application requirements *Prior education:* high school diploma or equivalent. *Other requirements:* high school transcript, college transcripts, an essay or personal statement, letter(s) of recommendation, an application fee of $25.
Completion requirements 128 credits are required. *Maximum time for completion:* 12 years.

INDIVIDUAL COURSE SUBJECT AREAS

Undergraduate
Biology; creative writing; developmental and child psychology; economics; educational psychology; English composition; English language and literature; family and marriage counseling; history; home economics and family studies; liberal arts, general studies, and humanities; mathematics; Middle Eastern languages and literatures; philosophy and religion; political science; psychology; social sciences; sociology; theological studies

TERRA STATE COMMUNITY COLLEGE

Fremont, Ohio

Educational Catalyst Center

Terra State Community College, founded in 1968, is a state-supported two-year college. It is accredited by the North Central Association of Colleges and Schools. It first offered distance learning courses in 1996. In 1996–97, it offered 3 courses at a distance. In the fall of 1996, there was a total of 20 students enrolled in distance learning courses.
Course delivery sites Courses are delivered to your home, your workplace.
Media Courses are delivered via videotapes, audiotapes, computer software, print. Students and teachers interact via mail, telephone, e-mail, in-person meetings. A computer is required for some courses.
Services Distance learners have access to library services, e-mail services at a distance.
Credit-earning options Students may transfer credits from another institution or may earn credits through institutionally developed exams.
Typical costs Tuition of $59 per credit plus mandatory fees of $10 per credit hour for local area residents. Tuition of $116 per credit plus mandatory fees of $10 per credit hour for out-of-state residents. *Noncredit courses:* $11.25 per hour of training. Costs may vary by number of credits taken. Financial aid is available to distance learners enrolled full-time or part-time.
Registration Students may register by mail, fax, phone.
Contact Theresa L. Eishen, Coordinator, Terra State Community College, 2830 Napoleon Road, Fremont, OH 43420-9670. *Telephone:* 419-334-8400, Ext. 321. *Fax:* 419-334-3667. *E-mail:* teishen@terra.cc.oh.us. *Web site:* http://www.terra.cc.oh.us/.

INDIVIDUAL COURSE SUBJECT AREAS

Undergraduate
Business; engineering; mathematics

TEXAS A&M UNIVERSITY–COMMERCE

Commerce, Texas

Northeast Texas Education Partnership

Texas A&M University–Commerce, founded in 1889, is a state-supported university. It is accredited by the Southern Association of Colleges and Schools. It first offered distance learning courses in 1993. In 1996–97, it offered 30 courses at a distance. In the fall of 1996, there was a total of 268 students enrolled in distance learning courses.
Course delivery sites Courses are delivered to Grayson County College (Denison), Northeast Texas Community College (Mount Pleasant), Paris Junior College (Paris), 11 off-campus centers in Alba-Golden, Cumby, Gilmer, Gladewater, Greenville, Harmony, Mount Vernon, Quitnan, Rains, Winnsboro, Yantis.
Media Courses are delivered via videotapes, videoconferencing, World Wide Web, e-mail, print. Students and teachers interact via videoconferencing, audioconferencing, mail, telephone, fax, e-mail. A computer is required for some courses.
Restrictions Courses are available to students in northeastern Texas only.
Services Distance learners have access to library services, e-mail services, academic advising at a distance.
Credit-earning options Students may earn credits through standardized exams.
Typical costs *Undergraduate:* Tuition of $300 per course for in-state residents. Tuition of $900 per course for out-of-state residents. *Graduate:* Tuition of $350 per course for in-state residents. Tuition of $960 per course for out-of-state residents. Costs may vary by number of credits taken. Financial aid is available to distance learners.
Registration Students may register by phone, World Wide Web.
Contact Mary W. Hendrix, Director, Texas A&M University–Commerce, East Texas Station, Commerce, TX 75429. *Telephone:* 903-886-5992. *Fax:* 903-886-5991. *E-mail:* mary_hendrix@etsu.edu.

INDIVIDUAL COURSE SUBJECT AREAS

Undergraduate
Creative writing; developmental and child psychology; economics; education; education administration; educational psychology; English composition; history; journalism; library and information studies; political science; radio and television broadcasting; social work; sociology; special education; teacher education

Graduate
Business; education administration; educational psychology; human resources management; library and information studies; radio and television broadcasting; special education; teacher education

Noncredit
Education administration; educational psychology; health professions and related sciences; library and information studies; nursing; public health; special education; teacher education

TEXAS A&M UNIVERSITY–CORPUS CHRISTI

Corpus Christi, Texas

Texas A&M University–Corpus Christi, founded in 1947, is a state-supported comprehensive institution. It is accredited by the Southern Association of Colleges and Schools. It first offered distance learning courses in 1989. In 1996–97, it offered 30 courses at a distance. In the fall of 1996, there was a total of 300 students enrolled in distance learning courses.
Course delivery sites Courses are delivered to Texas A&M International University (Laredo), Victoria College (Victoria), 1 off-campus center in Temple.
Media Courses are delivered via videoconferencing. Students and teachers interact via videoconferencing.
Restrictions Programs are available to in-state students only.
Services Distance learners have access to library services, academic advising, tutoring, career placement assistance at a distance.
Credit-earning options Students may transfer credits from another institution or may earn credits through examinations, portfolio assessment, military training, business training.
Typical costs *Undergraduate:* Tuition of $1028 per year plus mandatory fees of $1312 per year for in-state residents. Tuition of $7440 per year plus mandatory fees of $1312 per year for out-of-state residents. *Graduate:* Tuition of $1028 per year plus mandatory fees of $1312 per year for in-state residents. Tuition of $7440 per year plus mandatory fees of $1312 per year for out-of-state residents. Costs may vary by number of credits taken. Financial aid is available to distance learners enrolled full-time or part-time.
Registration Students may register by phone.
Contact Margaret M. Dechant, Director of Admissions, Texas A&M University–Corpus Christi, 6300 Ocean Drive, Corpus Christi, TX 78412-5503. *Telephone:* 512-994-2624. *Fax:* 512-994-5887.

DEGREE & CERTIFICATE PROGRAMS

Graduate Degrees
▶ *Nursing Administration (MSN)*

INDIVIDUAL COURSE SUBJECT AREAS

Undergraduate
Health professions and related sciences

Graduate
Nursing

TEXAS TECH UNIVERSITY

Lubbock, Texas

Texas Tech University, founded in 1923, is a state-supported university. It is accredited by the Southern Association of Colleges and Schools. It first offered distance learning courses in 1927. In 1996–97, it offered 125 courses at a distance. In the fall of 1996, there was a total of 2,000 students enrolled in distance learning courses.
Course delivery sites Courses are delivered to your home, your workplace, military bases, Amarillo College (Amarillo), South Plains College (Levelland), Texas State Technical College (Sweetwater), University of Houston (Houston), The University of Texas at Tyler (Tyler), West Texas A&M University (Canyon).
Media Courses are delivered via videotapes, videoconferencing, audiotapes, computer software, World Wide Web, e-mail, print, asynchronous computer conferencing. Students and teachers interact via videoconferencing, audioconferencing, mail, telephone, fax, e-mail. A computer is required for some courses.
Services Distance learners have access to library services, the campus computer network, e-mail services, academic advising, bookstore at a distance.
Credit-earning options Students may transfer credits from another institution or may earn credits through standardized exams.
Typical costs Contact university for details. Financial aid is available to distance learners enrolled full-time or part-time.
Registration Students may register by mail, fax, phone, e-mail, World Wide Web.
Contact LaNelle Ethridge, Distance Learning College Advisor, Extended Learning, Texas Tech University, MS 2191, Lubbock, TX 79409-2191. *Telephone:* 806-742-2352, Ext. 249. *Fax:* 806-742-2318. *E-mail:* ethridge@ttdcel.coed.ttu.edu.

DEGREE & CERTIFICATE PROGRAMS

Graduate Degrees
▶ *Engineering (MS)*
In the fall of 1996 there were 23 students enrolled in this program. In 1995–96, 2 degrees were earned at a distance through this program.
Application requirements *Prior education:* baccalaureate degree in engineering. *Other requirements:* GRE, college transcripts, an application fee of $25.
Completion requirements 36 hours are required. 18 hours must be completed through the institution. *Other requirements:* final comprehensive exam. *Maximum time for completion:* nine years.
Program contact Brent Guinn, Director of Distance Learning, College of Engineering, Texas Tech University, MS 3103, Texas Tech University, Lubbock, TX 79409-3103. Phone: 806-742-3451. Fax: 806-742-3493. E-mail: bguinn@coe.ttu.edu.

INDIVIDUAL COURSE SUBJECT AREAS

Undergraduate
Accounting; agricultural economics; agriculture; algebra; American (US) history; American literature; anthropology; archaeology; biology; botany; business administration and management; business law; calculus; computer and information sciences; conservation and natural resources; creative writing; developmental and child psychology; economics; educational psychology; engineering; engineering/industrial management; English composition; English language and literature; English literature; ethics; European history; finance; foods and nutrition studies; health and physical education/fitness; health services administration; history; home economics and family studies; hospitality services management; individual and family development studies; information sciences and systems;

Profiles: Texas Tech University

instructional media; journalism; Latin American studies; liberal arts, general studies, and humanities; marketing; mathematics; music; philosophy and religion; plant sciences; political science; public relations; radio and television broadcasting; social psychology; sociology; Spanish language and literature; teacher education; technical writing; telecommunications; zoology

Graduate
Archaeology; chemical engineering; civil engineering; computer programming; curriculum and instruction; database management; education; education administration; educational psychology; educational research; electrical engineering; engineering; English as a second language (ESL); home economics and family studies; industrial engineering; instructional media; special education

Noncredit
Agricultural economics; algebra; American (US) history; American literature; anthropology; architecture; business; business law; calculus; engineering; English literature; ethics; European history; finance; foods and nutrition studies; health services administration; hospitality services management; individual and family development studies; information sciences and systems; instructional media; Latin American studies; law and legal studies; marketing; plant sciences; public relations; real estate; Spanish language and literature; teacher education; technical writing; telecommunications

See full description on page 480.

TEXAS WESLEYAN UNIVERSITY

Fort Worth, Texas

Distance Learning Master of Education Degree Program

Texas Wesleyan University, founded in 1890, is an independent-religious United Methodist comprehensive institution. It is accredited by the Southern Association of Colleges and Schools. It first offered distance learning courses in 1996. In 1996–97, it offered 14 courses at a distance. In the fall of 1996, there was a total of 70 students enrolled in distance learning courses.
Course delivery sites Courses are delivered to your home, your workplace.
Media Courses are delivered via videotapes, audiotapes, audioconferencing, e-mail, print. Students and teachers interact via audioconferencing, mail, telephone, fax, e-mail.
Services Distance learners have access to library services, e-mail services, academic advising, tutoring, career placement assistance at a distance.
Credit-earning options Students may transfer credits from another institution.
Typical costs Tuition of $239 per credit hour. Financial aid is available to distance learners enrolled full-time or part-time.
Registration Students may register by mail, fax, phone, e-mail.
Contact Dr. Joy Edwards, Program Director, Texas Wesleyan University, 1201 Wesleyan Street, Fort Worth, TX 76105-1536. *Telephone:* 800-604-6088. *Fax:* 817-531-4204. *E-mail:* joyedwards@aol.com. *Web site:* http://info@txwesleyan.edu.

DEGREE & CERTIFICATE PROGRAMS

Graduate Degrees
▶ *Education (MEd)*
In the fall of 1996 there were 70 students enrolled in this program.
Application requirements *Prior education:* baccalaureate degree. *Other requirements:* college transcripts, an application fee of $40, must have one year of classroom teaching experience and be currently under contract.

Completion requirements 36 credits are required.

TEXAS WOMAN'S UNIVERSITY

Denton, Texas

Texas Woman's University, founded in 1901, is a state-supported university. It is accredited by the Southern Association of Colleges and Schools. It first offered distance learning courses in 1994.
Course delivery sites Courses are delivered to other colleges.
Media Courses are delivered via videoconferencing, audioconferencing, computer software, print, computer conferencing.
Services Distance learners have access to library services, academic advising, tutoring, career placement assistance at a distance.
Credit-earning options Students may transfer credits from another institution.
Typical costs *Undergraduate:* Tuition of $254.37 per course for in-state residents. Tuition of $892.37 per course for out-of-state residents. *Graduate:* Tuition of $310.37 per course for in-state residents. Tuition of $952.37 per course for out-of-state residents. Costs may vary by number of credits taken. Financial aid is available to distance learners.
Contact Leslie M. Thompson, Associate Vice President/Dean of Graduate School, Texas Woman's University, PO Box 425649, Denton, TX 76204. *Telephone:* 940-898-3415. *Fax:* 940-898-3412. *E-mail:* a_thompson@twu.edu.

DEGREE & CERTIFICATE PROGRAMS

Graduate Degrees
▶ *Library Science (MLS)*
Program contact Dr. Keith Swigger, Dean, Texas Woman's University, School of Library and Information Studies, Denton, TX 76204. Phone: 940-898-2602. Fax: 940-898-2611. E-mail: f_swigger@twu.edu.
▶ *Speech-Language Pathology (MS)*
Program contact Dr. Al White, Chair, Texas Woman's University, Department of Communication Sciences, Denton, TX 76204. Phone: 940-898-2025. Fax: 940-898-2070.

INDIVIDUAL COURSE SUBJECT AREAS

Graduate
Health professions and related sciences; library and information studies

THOMAS COLLEGE

Waterville, Maine

Graduate and Continuing Education

Thomas College, founded in 1894, is an independent-nonprofit comprehensive institution. It is accredited by the New England Association of Schools and Colleges. It first offered distance learning courses in 1997. In 1996–97, it offered 4 courses at a distance.
Course delivery sites Courses are delivered to your home, your workplace.
Media Courses are delivered via computer software, World Wide Web, e-mail. Students and teachers interact via e-mail, World Wide Web. A computer is required for all courses.
Services Distance learners have access to library services, the campus computer network, e-mail services, academic advising, tutoring, career placement assistance at a distance.

Typical costs Tuition of $1275 per course.
Registration Students may register by mail, fax, phone, e-mail, World Wide Web.
Contact Mr. Robert Whitcomb, Associate Vice President for Graduate and Continuing Education, Thomas College, 180 West River Road, Waterville, ME 04901. *Telephone:* 207-873-0771, Ext. 102. *Fax:* 207-877-0114. *E-mail:* whitcomb@thomas.edu. *Web site:* http://www.thomas.edu.

INDIVIDUAL COURSE SUBJECT AREAS

Undergraduate
Business administration and management; computer programming; database management; earth science; information sciences and systems

Graduate
Business administration and management; information sciences and systems

THOMAS EDISON STATE COLLEGE

Trenton, New Jersey

DIAL–Distance and Independent Adult Learning

Thomas Edison State College, founded in 1972, is a state-supported comprehensive institution. It is accredited by the Middle States Association of Colleges and Schools. It first offered distance learning courses in 1972. In 1996–97, it offered 116 courses at a distance. In the fall of 1996, there was a total of 1,915 students enrolled in distance learning courses.

Course delivery sites Courses are delivered to your home, your workplace, military bases.
Media Courses are delivered via videotapes, audiotapes, computer software, World Wide Web, e-mail, print. Students and teachers interact via mail, telephone, fax, e-mail. A computer is required for some courses.
Services Distance learners have access to the campus computer network, e-mail services, academic advising at a distance.
Credit-earning options Students may transfer credits from another institution or may earn credits through standardized exams, institutionally developed exams, portfolio assessment, military training, business training.
Typical costs *Undergraduate:* Tuition of $56 per credit hour plus mandatory fees of $14 per semester for in-state residents. Tuition of $84 per credit hour plus mandatory fees of $14 per semester for out-of-state residents. *Graduate:* Tuition of $289 per credit hour plus mandatory fees of $14 per semester for in-state residents. Tuition of $289 per credit hour plus mandatory fees of $14 per semester for out-of-state residents. Financial aid is available to distance learners.
Registration Students may register by mail, fax, phone, e-mail, World Wide Web.
Contact Janice Toliver, Director of Admissions, Thomas Edison State College, Office of Admissions, 101 West State Street, Trenton, NJ 08608. *Telephone:* 609-984-1150. *Fax:* 609-984-8447. *E-mail:* info@tesc.edu. *Web site:* http://www.tesc.edu.

DEGREE & CERTIFICATE PROGRAMS

Associate Degrees

▶ *Applied Science and Technology (ASAST)*
In the fall of 1996 there were 802 students enrolled in this program. In 1995–96, 93 degrees were earned at a distance through this program.
Application requirements *Prior education:* high school diploma or equivalent. *Minimum age:* 21. *Other requirements:* college transcripts, an application fee of $75, experience in the major area of study.
Completion requirements 60 semester hours are required.

▶ *Liberal Arts (AA)*
In the fall of 1996 there were 623 students enrolled in this program. In 1995–96, 63 degrees were earned at a distance through this program.
Application requirements *Prior education:* high school diploma or equivalent. *Minimum age:* 21. *Other requirements:* an application fee of $75.
Completion requirements 60 semester hours are required.

▶ *Management (AS)*
In the fall of 1996 there were 657 students enrolled in this program. In 1995–96, 32 degrees were earned at a distance through this program.
Application requirements *Prior education:* high school diploma or equivalent. *Minimum age:* 21. *Other requirements:* college transcripts, an application fee of $75.
Completion requirements 60 semester hours are required.

▶ *Natural Sciences and Mathematics (ASNSM)*
In the fall of 1996 there were 68 students enrolled in this program. In 1995–96, 2 degrees were earned at a distance through this program.
Application requirements *Prior education:* high school diploma or equivalent. *Minimum age:* 21. *Other requirements:* college transcripts, an application fee of $75.
Completion requirements 60 semester hours are required.

▶ *Public and Social Services (ASPSS)*
In the fall of 1996 there were 229 students enrolled in this program. In 1995–96, 10 degrees were earned at a distance through this program.
Application requirements *Prior education:* high school diploma or equivalent. *Minimum age:* 21. *Other requirements:* college transcripts, an application fee of $75, experience in the major area of study.
Completion requirements 60 semester hours are required.

▶ *Radiological Technology (AASRT)*
In the fall of 1996 there were 14 students enrolled in this program. In 1995–96, 1 degree was earned at a distance through this program.
Restrictions Students must be either New Jersey Licensing Board based Certified X-Ray Technologists, or American Registry of Radiological Technologists (Radiographer).
Application requirements *Prior education:* high school diploma or equivalent. *Minimum age:* 21. *Other requirements:* college transcripts, an application fee of $75, x-ray license/registry.
Completion requirements 60 semester hours are required.

Baccalaureate Degrees

▶ *Applied Science and Technology (BSAST)*
In the fall of 1996 there were 2,340 students enrolled in this program. In 1995–96, 241 degrees were earned at a distance through this program.
Application requirements *Prior education:* high school diploma or equivalent. *Minimum age:* 21. *Other requirements:* college transcripts, an application fee of $75, experience in the major area of study.
Completion requirements 120 semester hours are required. This is a degree completion program.

▶ *Business Administration (BSBA)*
In the fall of 1996 there were 2,103 students enrolled in this program. In 1995–96, 130 degrees were earned at a distance through this program.
Application requirements *Prior education:* high school diploma or equivalent. *Minimum age:* 21. *Other requirements:* college transcripts, an application fee of $75.
Completion requirements 120 semester hours are required. This is a degree completion program.

▶ *Human Services (BS)*
In the fall of 1996 there were 787 students enrolled in this program. In 1995–96, 48 degrees were earned at a distance through this program.
Application requirements *Prior education:* high school diploma or equivalent. *Minimum age:* 21. *Other requirements:* college transcripts, an application fee of $75, experience in major field.
Completion requirements 120 semester hours are required. This is a degree completion program.

Profiles: Thomas Edison State College

▶ *Liberal Arts (BA)*
In the fall of 1996 there were 2,551 students enrolled in this program. In 1995–96, 330 degrees were earned at a distance through this program.
Application requirements *Prior education:* high school diploma or equivalent. *Minimum age:* 21. *Other requirements:* college transcripts, an application fee of $75.
Completion requirements 120 semester hours are required. This is a degree completion program.

▶ *Nursing (BSN)*
In the fall of 1996 there were 347 students enrolled in this program. In 1995–96, 18 degrees were earned at a distance through this program.
Restrictions This program is available to in-state students only.
Application requirements *Prior education:* high school diploma or equivalent. *Minimum age:* 21. *Other requirements:* college transcripts, an application fee of $75, RN license.
Completion requirements 120 semester hours are required. This is a degree completion program.

Graduate Degrees

▶ *Management (MS)*
In the fall of 1996 there were 28 students enrolled in this program.
Restrictions Students must have computer, web browser.
Application requirements *Prior education:* baccalaureate degree. *Other requirements:* college transcripts, an essay or personal statement, letter(s) of recommendation, an application fee of $75.
Completion requirements 36 semester hours are required. 30 must be completed through the institution.
On-campus requirements Two weekends.

INDIVIDUAL COURSE SUBJECT AREAS

Undergraduate
Accounting; African-American studies; algebra; American (US) history; anthropology; archaeology; art history and criticism; Asian studies; astronomy and astrophysics; biology; business; business communications; business law; chemistry; chemistry, organic; computer and information sciences; creative writing; developmental and child psychology; earth science; economics; electronics; engineering mechanics; English composition; English language and literature; environmental science; ethics; European history; European languages and literatures; family and marriage counseling; film studies; finance; geography; geology; gerontology; history; journalism; liberal arts, general studies, and humanities; marketing; mathematics; Medieval/Renaissance studies; organizational behavior studies; philosophy and religion; photography; physics; religious studies; social psychology; sociology; Spanish language and literature; women's studies

See full description on page 482.

THOMAS NELSON COMMUNITY COLLEGE

Hampton, Virginia

Thomas Nelson Community College, founded in 1968, is a state-supported two-year college. It is accredited by the Southern Association of Colleges and Schools. It first offered distance learning courses in 1983. In 1996–97, it offered 11 courses at a distance. In the fall of 1996, there was a total of 150 students enrolled in distance learning courses.
Course delivery sites Courses are delivered to your home.
Media Courses are delivered via television, videotapes, computer software. Students and teachers interact via mail, telephone, fax, in-person meetings.
Restrictions Programs are available to local area students only.
Services Distance learners have access to tutoring at a distance.
Credit-earning options Students may transfer credits from another institution or may earn credits through examinations, military training, business training.
Typical costs Tuition of $46.65 per credit plus mandatory fees of $1 per credit for in-state residents. Tuition of $156 per credit plus mandatory fees of $1 per credit for out-of-state residents. Costs may vary by number of credits taken, term of enrollment. Financial aid is available to distance learners.
Contact Wayne E. Christian, Enrollment Services Coordinator, Thomas Nelson Community College, PO Box 9407, Center for Business and Community Services, Hampton, VA 23670. *Telephone:* 757-825-2936. *Fax:* 757-825-3552.

INDIVIDUAL COURSE SUBJECT AREAS

Undergraduate
History; mathematics; public health; social psychology; sociology

TIDEWATER COMMUNITY COLLEGE

Portsmouth, Virginia

Tidewater Community College, founded in 1968, is a state-supported two-year college. It is accredited by the Southern Association of Colleges and Schools. It first offered distance learning courses in 1975.
Course delivery sites Courses are delivered to your home, other colleges.
Media Courses are delivered via television, videotapes, videoconferencing, computer conferencing.
Restrictions Programs are available to in-state students only.
Services Distance learners have access to library services, academic advising, tutoring, career placement assistance at a distance.
Credit-earning options Students may transfer credits from another institution or may earn credits through examinations, portfolio assessment, military training. Financial aid is available to distance learners.
Contact Associate Dean for Curriculum Services, Tidewater Community College, 7000 College Drive, Portsmouth, VA 23703. *Telephone:* 804-484-2121. *Fax:* 804-483-5153.

INDIVIDUAL COURSE SUBJECT AREAS

Undergraduate
Accounting; astronomy and astrophysics; business; business administration and management; economics; English composition; geology; health professions and related sciences; history; liberal arts, general studies, and humanities; physics; political science; psychology; sociology

TOWSON UNIVERSITY

Towson, Maryland

Towson University, founded in 1866, is a state-supported comprehensive institution. It is accredited by the Middle States Association of Colleges and Schools. It first offered distance learning courses in 1995. In 1996–97, it offered 7 courses at a distance. In the fall of 1996, there was a total of 100 students enrolled in distance learning courses.
Course delivery sites Courses are delivered to your home, Frostburg State University (Frostburg), local high schools.
Media Courses are delivered via television, videoconferencing, e-mail, print. Students and teachers interact via videoconferencing, telephone, fax, e-mail.

Restrictions Availability varies by course, program, or delivery means.
Services Distance learners have access to library services, the campus computer network, e-mail services, academic advising at a distance.
Credit-earning options Students may transfer credits from another institution.
Typical costs *Undergraduate:* Tuition of $134 per credit plus mandatory fees of $35 per credit for in-state residents. Tuition of $300 per credit plus mandatory fees of $35 per credit for out-of-state residents. *Graduate:* Tuition of $174 per credit plus mandatory fees of $36 per credit for in-state residents. Tuition of $340 per credit plus mandatory fees of $36 per credit for out-of-state residents. Costs may vary by number of credits taken. Financial aid is available to distance learners enrolled full-time or part-time.
Registration Students may register by mail, phone.
Contact M. Frances Chiarnello, Coordinator, Extended Learning, Towson University, AD 343, 7800 York Road, Towson, MD 21252-0001. *Telephone:* 410-830-3534. *E-mail:* frances@towson.edu.

INDIVIDUAL COURSE SUBJECT AREAS

Undergraduate
Occupational therapy; psychology; sociology; teacher education

Graduate
Occupational therapy; teacher education

TREASURE VALLEY COMMUNITY COLLEGE

Ontario, Oregon

Division of Extended Learning

Treasure Valley Community College, founded in 1962, is a state and locally supported two-year college. It is accredited by the Northwest Association of Schools and Colleges. It first offered distance learning courses in 1985. In 1996–97, it offered 34 courses at a distance. In the fall of 1996, there was a total of 186 students enrolled in distance learning courses.
Course delivery sites Courses are delivered to your home, Blue Mountain Community College (Pendleton), 4 off-campus centers in Burns, Lakeview, Nyssa, Vale.
Media Courses are delivered via television, videotapes, audiotapes, print. Students and teachers interact via audioconferencing, mail, telephone, fax, e-mail.
Services Distance learners have access to library services, e-mail services, academic advising at a distance.
Credit-earning options Students may transfer credits from another institution or may earn credits through examinations, military training, business training.
Typical costs Tuition of $35 per credit plus mandatory fees of $25 per course for local area residents. Tuition of $35 per credit plus mandatory fees of $55 per course for in-state residents. Tuition of $52 per credit plus mandatory fees of $55 per course for out-of-state residents. Costs may vary by campus or location, number of credits taken, course delivery options. Financial aid is available to distance learners enrolled full-time or part-time.
Registration Students may register by mail, fax, phone.
Contact Mike Woodhead, Director, Continuing and Distance Education, Treasure Valley Community College, 650 College Boulevard, Ontario, OR 97914. *Telephone:* 541-889-6493. *Fax:* 541-881-2743. *E-mail:* woodhead@mailman.tvcc.cc.or.us.

INDIVIDUAL COURSE SUBJECT AREAS

Undergraduate
Agriculture; area, ethnic, and cultural studies; business; business administration and management; business law; chemistry; criminal justice; criminology; English composition; geology; history; law and legal studies; mathematics; physics; plant sciences; psychology; sociology; Spanish language and literature

TRINIDAD STATE JUNIOR COLLEGE

Trinidad, Colorado

Telecommunications and Distance Learning

Trinidad State Junior College, founded in 1925, is a state-supported two-year college. It is accredited by the North Central Association of Colleges and Schools.
Course delivery sites Courses are delivered to your home, your workplace, other colleges.
Media Courses are delivered via videotapes, videoconferencing, audioconferencing, computer software, print, audiographics conferencing, computer conferencing.
Services Distance learners have access to library services, academic advising, tutoring, career placement assistance at a distance.
Credit-earning options Students may transfer credits from another institution or may earn credits through examinations, portfolio assessment, business training. Financial aid is available to distance learners.
Contact Director of Technology, Trinidad State Junior College, Campus Box 312, 600 Prospect, Trinidad, CO 81082. *Telephone:* 719-846-5688.

INDIVIDUAL COURSE SUBJECT AREAS

Undergraduate
Biology; business; computer and information sciences; economics; European languages and literatures; mathematics; nursing; psychology

TRINITY COLLEGE OF VERMONT

Burlington, Vermont

Trinity College of Vermont, founded in 1925, is an independent-religious Roman Catholic comprehensive institution. It is accredited by the New England Association of Schools and Colleges. It first offered distance learning courses in 1995. In 1996–97, it offered 1 course at a distance. In the fall of 1996, there was a total of 6 students enrolled in distance learning courses.
Course delivery sites Courses are delivered to your home.
Media Courses are delivered via World Wide Web. Students and teachers interact via mail, telephone, fax, e-mail. A computer is required for all courses.
Services Distance learners have access to library services, academic advising, tutoring at a distance.
Typical costs Tuition of $404 per credit plus mandatory fees of $12 per credit. *Noncredit courses:* $149 per credit. Financial aid is available to distance learners.
Registration Students may register by mail, e-mail, World Wide Web.
Contact Joe DeLuca, Associate Professor, Trinity College of Vermont, Business and Economics Department, 208 Colchester Avenue, Burlington, VT 05401. *Telephone:* 802-658-0337. *Fax:* 802-658-5446. *E-mail:* jdeluca@charity.trinityvt.edu.

Profiles: Trinity College of Vermont

INDIVIDUAL COURSE SUBJECT AREAS

Undergraduate
Accounting

Noncredit
Accounting

TRINITY INTERNATIONAL UNIVERSITY

Deerfield, Illinois

Division of Open Studies

Trinity International University, founded in 1897, is an independent-religious university affiliated with the Evangelical Free Church of America. It is accredited by the North Central Association of Colleges and Schools. It first offered distance learning courses in 1979.
Course delivery sites Courses are delivered to your home.
Media Courses are delivered via videotapes, audiotapes, print.
Services Distance learners have access to library services, academic advising at a distance.
Contact Division of Open Studies, Trinity International University, 2065 Half Day Road, Deerfield, IL 60015. *Telephone:* 800-417-9199.

DEGREE & CERTIFICATE PROGRAMS

Graduate Degrees
▶ *Religion (MAR)*

Undergraduate Certificates
▶ *Biblical Studies*

INDIVIDUAL COURSE SUBJECT AREAS

Graduate
Theological studies

TRITON COLLEGE

River Grove, Illinois

Triton College, founded in 1964, is a state-supported two-year college. It is accredited by the North Central Association of Colleges and Schools. It first offered distance learning courses in 1979. In 1996–97, it offered 60 courses at a distance. In the fall of 1996, there was a total of 700 students enrolled in distance learning courses.
Course delivery sites Courses are delivered to your home, your workplace, College of DuPage (Glen Ellyn), Morton College (Cicero), Northeastern Illinois University (Chicago).
Media Courses are delivered via television, videotapes, videoconferencing, World Wide Web. Students and teachers interact via videoconferencing, telephone, e-mail. A computer is required for some courses.
Restrictions Telecourses, ITFS courses and videotape courses are available to local students only. Interactive television courses are available to in-state students only.
Services Distance learners have access to library services, e-mail services, career placement assistance at a distance.
Credit-earning options Students may transfer credits from another institution or may earn credits through examinations, portfolio assessment, military training.
Typical costs Tuition of $43 per credit hour plus mandatory fees of $3.50 per credit hour for local area residents. Tuition of $132.15 per credit hour plus mandatory fees of $3.50 per credit hour for in-state residents. Tuition of $195.86 per credit hour plus mandatory fees of $3.50 per credit hour for out-of-state residents. *Noncredit courses:* $50 per course. Costs may vary by course delivery options. Financial aid is available to distance learners enrolled full-time or part-time.
Registration Students may register by mail, phone.
Contact Gail Fuller, Director of Admissions and Records, Triton College, 2000 Fifth Avenue, River Grove, IL 60171. *Telephone:* 708-456-0300, Ext. 3397. *Fax:* 708-583-3121.

INDIVIDUAL COURSE SUBJECT AREAS

Undergraduate
Anthropology; business administration and management; business law; developmental and child psychology; economics; electronics; English composition; English language and literature; fine arts; health and physical education/fitness; history; mathematics; music; political science; psychology; real estate; sociology; statistics

TROY STATE UNIVERSITY

Troy, Alabama

Office of Information and Technology

Troy State University, founded in 1887, is a state-supported comprehensive institution. It is accredited by the Southern Association of Colleges and Schools. It first offered distance learning courses in 1993. In 1996–97, it offered 16 courses at a distance. In the fall of 1996, there was a total of 185 students enrolled in distance learning courses.
Course delivery sites Courses are delivered to your home, military bases, Troy State University Dothan (Dothan), Troy State University Montgomery (Montgomery).
Media Courses are delivered via television, videotapes, videoconferencing, print. Students and teachers interact via videoconferencing, mail, telephone, fax, e-mail.
Restrictions Students must be able to travel to receive site.
Services Distance learners have access to library services, e-mail services at a distance.
Credit-earning options Students may transfer credits from another institution or may earn credits through institutionally developed exams.
Typical costs *Undergraduate:* Tuition of $52.50 per credit hour plus mandatory fees of $6.50 per credit hour for in-state residents. Tuition of $105 per credit hour plus mandatory fees of $6.50 per credit hour for out-of-state residents. *Graduate:* Tuition of $50 per credit hour plus mandatory fees of $6.50 per credit hour for in-state residents. Tuition of $100 per credit hour plus mandatory fees of $6.50 per credit hour for out-of-state residents. Costs may vary by campus or location, specific program of study, number of credits taken. Financial aid is available to distance learners enrolled full-time or part-time.
Contact Suzanne Stokes, Coordinator of Distance Education, Troy State University, Wallace Hall, Troy, AL 36082. *Telephone:* 334-670-3787. *Fax:* 334-670-3934. *E-mail:* sstokes@trojan.troyst.edu. *Web site:* http://www.troyst.edu.

INDIVIDUAL COURSE SUBJECT AREAS

Undergraduate
Astronomy and astrophysics; foods and nutrition studies; nursing; physics

Graduate
Astronomy and astrophysics; nursing

TROY STATE UNIVERSITY DOTHAN

Dothan, Alabama

Division of Special Programs

Troy State University Dothan, founded in 1961, is a state-supported comprehensive institution. It is accredited by the Southern Association of Colleges and Schools. It first offered distance learning courses in 1991.
Course delivery sites Courses are delivered to your home, your workplace, military bases, other colleges.
Media Courses are delivered via television, videotapes, videoconferencing, audioconferencing, print.
Restrictions Programs are available to local area students only.
Credit-earning options Students may transfer credits from another institution or may earn credits through military training, business training. Financial aid is available to distance learners.
Contact Assistant Director for Distance Education, Troy State University Dothan, PO Box 8368, Dothan, AL 36304. *Telephone:* 334-983-6556, Ext. 326. *Fax:* 334-983-6322.

INDIVIDUAL COURSE SUBJECT AREAS

Undergraduate
Business; business administration and management; economics; English composition; geology; health and physical education/fitness; history; political science; psychology; sociology

TROY STATE UNIVERSITY–FLORIDA REGION

Fort Walton Beach, Florida

Distance Learning Center

Troy State University–Florida Region is a state-supported comprehensive institution. It is accredited by the Southern Association of Colleges and Schools. It first offered distance learning courses in 1992. In 1996–97, it offered 18 courses at a distance.
Course delivery sites Courses are delivered to your home, your workplace.
Media Courses are delivered via videotapes, audiotapes, World Wide Web. Students and teachers interact via telephone, fax, e-mail, computer conferencing. A computer is required for all courses.
Services Distance learners have access to library services, academic advising, tutoring, career placement assistance, bookstore at a distance.
Credit-earning options Students may transfer credits from another institution or may earn credits through standardized exams, military training, DANTES.
Typical costs *Undergraduate:* Tuition of $75 per quarter hour. *Graduate:* Tuition of $115 per quarter hour.
Registration Students may register by mail, fax, World Wide Web.
Contact Joann Wheeler, Distance Learning Coordinator, Troy State University–Florida Region, 81 Beal Parkway, SE, Fort Walton Beach, FL 32548. *Telephone:* 850-244-7414. *Fax:* 850-244-2384. *E-mail:* jkwheelr@tsufl.edu. *Web site:* http://www.tsufl.edu.

Special note
The Florida Region of Troy State University is the largest extension campus of the Troy State University system, which includes more than 60 sites around the world. From a beginning of 100 enrollments in 1973, the Florida Region has grown to almost 20,000 enrollments yearly and currently offers 11 undergraduate degrees and 6 graduate degrees. Troy State University is accredited by the Southern Association of Colleges and Schools to award associate, bachelor's, and master's degrees.

A very popular program in the Florida Region is distance learning. The program provides optimum flexibility for learners who may have commitments and/or are unable to attend classes in a traditional college environment. Technologically enhanced instruction allows distant learners to feel more a part of an academic community that is current, exciting, and accessible. Classes are delivered using a variety of methods, including audiotapes, videotapes, e-mail, computer-mediated conversations, peer interaction, and faculty conferences.

INDIVIDUAL COURSE SUBJECT AREAS

Undergraduate
Business administration and management; criminal justice; economics; European history; international relations; political science

Graduate
Business; European history; international relations; organizational behavior studies; public administration and services

TROY STATE UNIVERSITY MONTGOMERY

Montgomery, Alabama

External Degree Program

Troy State University Montgomery, founded in 1957, is a state-supported comprehensive institution. It is accredited by the Southern Association of Colleges and Schools. It first offered distance learning courses in 1987. In 1996–97, it offered 100 courses at a distance. In the fall of 1996, there was a total of 750 students enrolled in distance learning courses.
Course delivery sites Courses are delivered to your home, your workplace, military bases, other colleges.
Media Courses are delivered via television, World Wide Web, e-mail, print. Students and teachers interact via mail, telephone, fax, e-mail.
Services Distance learners have access to library services, academic advising, tutoring at a distance.
Credit-earning options Students may transfer credits from another institution or may earn credits through standardized exams, portfolio assessment, military training, DANTES.
Typical costs Tuition of $50 per quarter hour for in-state residents. Tuition of $70 per quarter hour for out-of-state residents. Costs may vary by number of credits taken, course delivery options.
Registration Students may register by mail, fax, phone, e-mail.
Contact Dr. James Macey, Director, Troy State University Montgomery, PO Drawer 4419, Montgomery, AL 36103. *Telephone:* 334-241-9553. *Fax:* 334-241-7320. *E-mail:* jmacey@tsum.edu. *Web site:* http://www.tsum.edu/edp.

DEGREE & CERTIFICATE PROGRAMS

Associate Degrees
▶ *General Education (AS)*
Application requirements *Prior education:* high school diploma or equivalent. *Other requirements:* high school transcript, college transcripts, an essay or personal statement, letter(s) of recommendation, an application fee of $65.

Profiles: Troy State University Montgomery

Completion requirements 95 quarter hours are required. 50 quarter hours must be completed through the institution.
On-campus requirements For defense of senior project, one day at the end of the program.

Baccalaureate Degrees

▶ *Professional Studies (BS)*
Application requirements *Prior education:* high school diploma or equivalent. *Other requirements:* high school transcript, college transcripts, an essay or personal statement, letter(s) of recommendation, an application fee of $65.
Completion requirements 192 quarter hours are required. 50 quarter hours must be completed through the institution.
On-campus requirements For defense of senior project, one day at the end of the program.

▶ *Professional Studies (BA)*
Application requirements *Prior education:* high school diploma or equivalent. *Other requirements:* high school transcript, college transcripts, an essay or personal statement, letter(s) of recommendation, an application fee of $65.
Completion requirements 192 quarter hours are required. 50 quarter hours must be completed through the institution.
On-campus requirements For defense of senior project, one day at the end of the program.

INDIVIDUAL COURSE SUBJECT AREAS

Undergraduate

Accounting; astronomy and astrophysics; biological and life sciences; biology; business; business administration and management; chemistry; child care and development; developmental and child psychology; economics; English composition; English language and literature; European languages and literatures; history; human resources management; liberal arts, general studies, and humanities; mathematics; philosophy and religion; political science; psychology; social sciences; sociology; Spanish language and literature

TULSA COMMUNITY COLLEGE

Tulsa, Oklahoma

Distance Learning Office

Tulsa Community College, founded in 1968, is a state-supported two-year college. It is accredited by the North Central Association of Colleges and Schools. It first offered distance learning courses in 1979. In 1996–97, it offered 25 courses at a distance. In the fall of 1996, there was a total of 700 students enrolled in distance learning courses.
Course delivery sites Courses are delivered to your home, your workplace.
Media Courses are delivered via print. Students and teachers interact via mail, telephone. A computer is required for some courses.
Services Distance learners have access to library services, academic advising, tutoring, career placement assistance at a distance.
Credit-earning options Students may transfer credits from another institution or may earn credits through examinations, military training.
Typical costs Tuition of $39.50 per credit hour for in-state residents. Tuition of $102 per credit hour for out-of-state residents. Financial aid is available to distance learners enrolled full-time or part-time.
Registration Students may register by phone.
Contact Randy Dominguez, Director of Distance Learning, Tulsa Community College, 909 South Boston, Tulsa, OK 74119. *Telephone:* 918-595-7144. *Fax:* 918-595-7306. *E-mail:* rdoming@tulsajc.tulsa.cc.ok.us.

DEGREE & CERTIFICATE PROGRAMS

Associate Degrees

▶ *Liberal Arts (AA)*
In the fall of 1996 there were 700 students enrolled in this program.
Application requirements *Prior education:* high school diploma or equivalent. *Other requirements:* ACT, high school transcript, an application fee of $15.
Completion requirements 61 credits are required.
On-campus requirements For orientation.

INDIVIDUAL COURSE SUBJECT AREAS

Undergraduate

Accounting; area, ethnic, and cultural studies; astronomy and astrophysics; business; business administration and management; computer and information sciences; conservation and natural resources; developmental and child psychology; economics; English composition; English language and literature; European languages and literatures; geology; liberal arts, general studies, and humanities; mathematics; political science; social psychology; sociology

TYLER JUNIOR COLLEGE

Tyler, Texas

Learning Resources

Tyler Junior College, founded in 1926, is a state and locally supported two-year college. It is accredited by the Southern Association of Colleges and Schools. It first offered distance learning courses in 1969. In 1996–97, it offered 21 courses at a distance. In the fall of 1996, there was a total of 1,122 students enrolled in distance learning courses.
Course delivery sites Courses are delivered to your home, your workplace, Tyler Independent School District, Van Independent School District, Grand Saline Independent School District.
Media Courses are delivered via television, videotapes, videoconferencing, audiotapes, computer software, World Wide Web. Students and teachers interact via videoconferencing, mail, telephone, fax, e-mail. A computer is required for some courses.
Restrictions Students must attend on-campus orientation and take exams on campus or at an approved testing center.
Services Distance learners have access to library services, e-mail services, academic advising, tutoring, career placement assistance at a distance.
Credit-earning options Students may transfer credits from another institution or may earn credits through examinations.
Typical costs Tuition of $45 per course plus mandatory fees of $38 per course for local area residents. Tuition of $45 per course plus mandatory fees of $88 per course for in-state residents. Tuition of $100 per course plus mandatory fees of $88 per course for out-of-state residents. *Noncredit courses:* $150 per course. Costs may vary by number of credits taken. Financial aid is available to distance learners.
Registration Students may register by phone.
Contact Jana Chauncy, Recruiter, Tyler Junior College, PO Box 9020, Tyler, TX 75211. *Telephone:* 903-510-2396. *Fax:* 903-510-2634. *Web site:* http://www.tyler.cc.tx.us.

INDIVIDUAL COURSE SUBJECT AREAS

Undergraduate

Algebra; biology; business; business administration and management; chemistry; computer and information sciences; English composition; English language and literature; environmental science; European languages and literatures; history; journalism; liberal arts, general studies, and humanities; political science; psychology; sociology; Spanish language and literature

ULSTER COUNTY COMMUNITY COLLEGE

Stone Ridge, New York

Ulster County Community College, founded in 1961, is a state and locally supported two-year college. It is accredited by the Middle States Association of Colleges and Schools. It first offered distance learning courses in 1983. In 1996–97, it offered 3 courses at a distance. In the fall of 1996, there was a total of 30 students enrolled in distance learning courses.
Course delivery sites Courses are delivered to your home, your workplace, military bases, 1 off-campus center in Kingston.
Media Courses are delivered via videotapes, computer software, World Wide Web, e-mail, print. Students and teachers interact via e-mail, computer conferencing. A computer is required for some courses.
Services Distance learners have access to e-mail services, academic advising at a distance.
Credit-earning options Students may transfer credits from another institution or may earn credits through examinations, portfolio assessment, military training, business training.
Typical costs Tuition of $87 per unit for in-state residents. Tuition of $174 per unit for out-of-state residents. All students pay $15 in fees. Costs may vary by specific program of study, number of credits taken, course delivery options. Financial aid is available to distance learners enrolled full-time or part-time.
Registration Students may register by mail, fax, phone, e-mail.
Contact Ms. Mary Cotton-Miller, Associate Dean of Student Development, Ulster County Community College, Cottekill Road, Stone Ridge, NY 12484. *Telephone:* 914-687-5075. *Fax:* 914-687-5126.

INDIVIDUAL COURSE SUBJECT AREAS

Undergraduate
Biological and life sciences; library and information studies; mathematics

UMPQUA COMMUNITY COLLEGE

Roseburg, Oregon

Media Services Department

Umpqua Community College, founded in 1964, is a state and locally supported two-year college. It is accredited by the Northwest Association of Schools and Colleges. It first offered distance learning courses in 1980. In 1996–97, it offered 7 courses at a distance. In the fall of 1996, there was a total of 20 students enrolled in distance learning courses.
Course delivery sites Courses are delivered to your home, your workplace.
Media Courses are delivered via television, videotapes, print. Students and teachers interact via mail, telephone, e-mail, in-person meetings.
Restrictions Courses are available to US students only.
Services Distance learners have access to library services at a distance.
Credit-earning options Students may transfer credits from another institution or may earn credits through examinations, military training, business training.
Typical costs Tuition of $34 per credit plus mandatory fees of $10 per course for in-state residents. Tuition of $100 per credit plus mandatory fees of $10 per course for out-of-state residents. Financial aid is available to distance learners.
Registration Students may register by mail.
Contact Christopher Bingham, Director of Media Services, Umpqua Community College, 1140 College Road, Roseburg, OR 97470. *Telephone:* 541-440-4717. *Fax:* 541-440-4665. *E-mail:* binghac@umpqua.cc.or.us.

INDIVIDUAL COURSE SUBJECT AREAS

Undergraduate
Astronomy and astrophysics; biological and life sciences; business administration and management; English language and literature; geology; liberal arts, general studies, and humanities; music; sociology

THE UNION INSTITUTE

Cincinnati, Ohio

The Union Institute, founded in 1964, is an independent-nonprofit university. It is accredited by the North Central Association of Colleges and Schools. It first offered distance learning courses in 1969. In the fall of 1996, there was a total of 1,286 students enrolled in distance learning courses.
Course delivery sites Courses are delivered to your home, your workplace.
Media Courses are delivered via audioconferencing, World Wide Web, e-mail, print. Students and teachers interact via mail, telephone, fax, e-mail. A computer is required for some courses.
Services Distance learners have access to library services, the campus computer network, e-mail services, academic advising, admissions counseling at a distance.
Credit-earning options Students may transfer credits from another institution or may earn credits through standardized exams, institutionally developed exams, portfolio assessment, military training, business training, agency articulation agreements.
Typical costs *Undergraduate:* Tuition of $242 per semester credit. *Graduate:* Tuition of $4090 per semester. Costs may vary by number of credits taken. Financial aid is available to distance learners enrolled full-time.
Registration Students may register by mail, fax.
Contact Dr. Timothy Mott, Dean, College of Undergraduate Studies, The Union Institute, 440 East McMillan Street, Cincinnati, OH 45206. *Telephone:* 800-486-3116. *Fax:* 513-861-9026. *E-mail:* tmott@tui.edu.

DEGREE & CERTIFICATE PROGRAMS

Baccalaureate Degrees
▶ *Liberal Arts and Sciences (BA, BS)*
In the fall of 1996 there were 37 students enrolled in this program. In 1995–96, 8 degrees were earned at a distance through this program.
Restrictions Students must have access to computer with modem.
Application requirements *Prior education:* high school diploma or equivalent. *Other requirements:* high school transcript, college transcripts, an essay or personal statement, letter(s) of recommendation, an application fee of $50, ability to use PC.
Completion requirements 128 semester credits are required. 32 semester credits must be completed through the institution.
On-campus requirements One weekend per semester.

Graduate Degrees
▶ *Clinical Psychology, Interdisciplinary Studies (PhD)*
In the fall of 1996 there were 1,249 students enrolled in this program. In 1995–96, 263 degrees were earned at a distance through this program.
Application requirements *Prior education:* graduate degree. *Other requirements:* college transcripts, an essay or personal statement, letter(s) of recommendation, an application fee of $50.

Distance Learning Programs

Profiles: The Union Institute

Completion requirements All course work must be completed through the institution. *Other requirements:* this is not a credit-hour-based program.
On-campus requirements One 10-day seminar, 3 five-day seminars.
Program contact Michael J. Robertson, Associate Registrar, The Union Institute, 440 East McMillan Street, Cincinnati, OH 45206. Phone: 800-486-3116. Fax: 513-861-0779. E-mail: mrobertson@tui.edu.

INDIVIDUAL COURSE SUBJECT AREAS

Undergraduate
Area, ethnic, and cultural studies; biological and life sciences; business; business administration and management; communications; computer and information sciences; creative writing; developmental and child psychology; economics; education; education administration; English composition; English language and literature; health professions and related sciences; history; human resources management; industrial psychology; liberal arts, general studies, and humanities; mathematics; philosophy and religion; physical sciences; political science; protective services; psychology; public administration and services; social psychology; social sciences; social work; sociology; visual and performing arts

See full description on page 484.

UNITED STATES SPORTS ACADEMY

Daphne, Alabama

Continuing Education and Distance Learning

United States Sports Academy, founded in 1972, is an independent-nonprofit graduate institution. It is accredited by the Southern Association of Colleges and Schools. It first offered distance learning courses in 1993. In 1996–97, it offered 46 courses at a distance.
Course delivery sites Courses are delivered to your home.
Media Courses are delivered via audiotapes, World Wide Web, e-mail, print. Students and teachers interact via mail, telephone, fax, e-mail.
Services Distance learners have access to library services, academic advising, tutoring, career placement assistance at a distance.
Credit-earning options Students may transfer credits from another institution.
Typical costs Tuition of $300 per semester hour. *Noncredit courses:* $100 per course. Financial aid is available to distance learners.
Registration Students may register by mail, fax, phone, e-mail, World Wide Web.
Contact Admissions Office, United States Sports Academy, One Academy Drive, Daphne, AL 36526. *Telephone:* 800-223-2668. *Fax:* 334-621-2527. *E-mail:* Academy@ussa-sport.ussa.edu. *Web site:* http://www.sport.ussa.edu.

Special note
The United States Sports Academy provides traditional and innovative professional development opportunities in higher education that are sport-specific for students with diverse needs through a variety of programs dedicated to the betterment of sport throughout the world.
Distance learning allows students to take classes independently from the campus environment. Courses are instructed by an Academy faculty member who is responsible for facilitating the learning experience during the structured offering of distance learning. Faculty members maintain regular contact with students via telephone, fax, e-mail, and/or surface mail.

The Academy offers a Master of Sport Science degree with 4 majors: sport management, sport fitness management, sport coaching, and sports medicine. A number of dual majors are also available. The entire sport management and sport fitness management programs are available via distance learning. The sport coaching program requires 1 laboratory course, and sports medicine requires 3 laboratory courses that are typically taken on the Daphne, Alabama, campus. Students can take the laboratory courses at a predetermined laboratory facility that is approved by the Academy. Courses are available through the mail and can be accessed via the World Wide Web. In addition, select courses have audiotapes available to provide supplemental information.

It is possible to complete the degree within a year, although students may take up to 3 years to complete the program. Academy graduates are found in all areas of sport in the United States and worldwide.

DEGREE & CERTIFICATE PROGRAMS

Graduate Degrees
▶ *Sport Science in Fitness Management (MSS)*
Application requirements *Prior education:* baccalaureate degree. *Other requirements:* GRE, MAT, college transcripts, letter(s) of recommendation.
Completion requirements 33 semester hours are required. 27 semester hours must be completed through the institution. *Maximum time for completion:* three years.
On-campus requirements To take comprehensive exams.

INDIVIDUAL COURSE SUBJECT AREAS

Graduate
Business; business administration and management; education administration; health and physical education/fitness; health professions and related sciences; human resources management; journalism; law and legal studies; public administration and services; social psychology

Noncredit
Business; business administration and management; education administration; health and physical education/fitness; health professions and related sciences; human resources management; journalism; law and legal studies; public administration and services; social psychology

UNIVERSITÈ LAVAL

Sainte-Foy, Québec, Canada

Direction générale de la formation continue

Université Laval, founded in 1852, is an independent-nonprofit university. It is provincially chartered. It first offered distance learning courses in 1984. In 1996–97, it offered 51 courses at a distance. In the fall of 1996, there was a total of 4,200 students enrolled in distance learning courses.
Course delivery sites Courses are delivered to your home, your workplace.
Media Courses are delivered via television, videotapes, audiotapes, computer software, World Wide Web, print, CD-ROM. Students and teachers interact via videoconferencing, mail, telephone, fax, e-mail. A computer is required for some courses.
Restrictions Students must have French language fluency.
Services Distance learners have access to e-mail services, academic advising, tutoring at a distance.

Credit-earning options Students may transfer credits from another institution or may earn credits through institutionally developed exams, portfolio assessment.
Typical costs Tuition of $55.60 per credit plus mandatory fees of $5.75 per credit. Costs given in Canadian dollars. Costs may vary by number of credits taken.
Registration Students may register by mail, fax, phone, e-mail, World Wide Web.
Contact Suzanne Allaire, Coordonnatrice de l'Enseignement a distance, Universitè Laval, 5733 Pavillon Casault, Cité Universitaire, Québec, PQ G1K 7P4, Canada. *Telephone:* 418-656-2131, Ext. 8829. *Fax:* 418-656-3876. *E-mail:* suzanne.allaire@dgfc.ulaval.ca. *Web site:* http://www.ulaval.ca/dgfc.

DEGREE & CERTIFICATE PROGRAMS

Undergraduate Certificates

▶*Administration*
In the fall of 1996 there were 36 students enrolled in this program.
Application requirements *Prior education:* Quebec DEC (Diplôme d'ètudes collègiales) or equivalent. *Other requirements:* college transcripts, an application fee of Can$30, two years relevant experience.
Completion requirements 10 courses are required.
On-campus requirements For final exams.

▶*Computer Science*
In the fall of 1996 there were 49 students enrolled in this program.
Application requirements *Prior education:* Quebec DEC (Diplôme d'ètudes collègiales) or equivalent. *Other requirements:* college transcripts, an application fee of Can$30.
Completion requirements 10 courses are required.
On-campus requirements For final exams.

▶*Food Safety*
In the fall of 1996 there were 110 students enrolled in this program.
Application requirements *Prior education:* Quebec DEC (Diplôme d'ètudes collègiales) or equivalent. *Other requirements:* college transcripts, an application fee of Can$30, three years experience in the food science field.
Completion requirements 10 courses are required.
On-campus requirements For final exams.

▶*Personal Financial Planning*
In the fall of 1996 there were 844 students enrolled in this program.
Application requirements *Prior education:* Quebec DEC (Diplôme d'ètudes collègiales) or equivalent. *Other requirements:* college transcripts, an application fee of Can$30, two years relevant experience.
Completion requirements 11 courses are required.
On-campus requirements For final exams.

INDIVIDUAL COURSE SUBJECT AREAS

Undergraduate
Accounting; adult education; advertising; anthropology; business administration and management; business law; Canadian studies; cell biology; cognitive psychology; communications; computer and information sciences; computer programming; database management; economics; education administration; film studies; finance; foods and nutrition studies; French language and literature; geography; geology; German language and literature; gerontology; health services administration; human resources management; journalism; marketing; microbiology; philosophy and religion; psychology; public health; real estate; sociology; theological studies

THE UNIVERSITY OF AKRON

Akron, Ohio

Information Services

The University of Akron, founded in 1870, is a state-supported university. It is accredited by the North Central Association of Colleges and Schools. It first offered distance learning courses in 1994.
Course delivery sites Courses are delivered to other colleges, off-campus center(s).
Media Courses are delivered via videoconferencing, computer software, World Wide Web. Students and teachers interact via videoconferencing, telephone, e-mail.
Typical costs *Undergraduate:* Tuition of $135 per credit for in-state residents. Tuition of $186.30 per credit for out-of-state residents. *Graduate:* Tuition of $164.15 per credit for in-state residents. Tuition of $301.95 per credit for out-of-state residents.
Contact Dr. Larry Bradley, Distance Learning Coordinator, The University of Akron, Buchtel Hall 52, Akron, OH 44325. *Telephone:* 330-972-7421.

INDIVIDUAL COURSE SUBJECT AREAS

Undergraduate
Business administration and management; communications; English composition; history

Graduate
Business administration and management; education; engineering; social work

THE UNIVERSITY OF ALABAMA

Tuscaloosa, Alabama

College of Continuing Studies

The University of Alabama, founded in 1831, is a state-supported university. It is accredited by the Southern Association of Colleges and Schools. It first offered distance learning courses in 1991. In 1996–97, it offered 150 courses at a distance. In the fall of 1996, there was a total of 1,500 students enrolled in distance learning courses.
Course delivery sites Courses are delivered to your home, your workplace, military bases, other colleges, 3 off-campus centers in Dothan, Gadsden, Selma.
Media Courses are delivered via videotapes, videoconferencing, World Wide Web, e-mail, print. Students and teachers interact via videoconferencing, mail, telephone, fax, e-mail.
Services Distance learners have access to library services, the campus computer network, e-mail services, academic advising at a distance.
Credit-earning options Students may transfer credits from another institution.
Typical costs Tuition of $150 per semester hour plus mandatory fees of $25 per semester. Costs may vary by course delivery options. Financial aid is available to distance learners enrolled full-time or part-time.
Registration Students may register by mail, fax, phone, e-mail.
Contact Carroll Tingle, Director, Distance Education, The University of Alabama, Box 870388, Tuscaloosa, AL 35487-0388. *Telephone:* 205-348-9278. *Fax:* 205-348-0249. *E-mail:* ctingle@ccs.ua.edu. *Web site:* http://ua1vm.ua.edu/~cstudies/ccs.html.

Profiles: The University of Alabama

DEGREE & CERTIFICATE PROGRAMS

Graduate Degrees

▶ *Aerospace Engineering (MSAE)*

In the fall of 1996 there were 15 students enrolled in this program.

Application requirements *Prior education:* baccalaureate degree. *Other requirements:* GRE or GMAT, college transcripts, an essay or personal statement, letter(s) of recommendation, an application fee of $25, graduate school application.

Completion requirements 33 semester hours are required. 2 semesters must be completed through the institution. *Maximum time for completion:* six years.

Program contact Dr. John Jackson, Head, Department of Aerospace Engineering, The University of Alabama, Box 870280, Tuscaloosa, AL 35487-0280. Phone: 205-348-7300. Fax: 205-348-2094. E-mail: johnjackson@coe.eng.ua.edu.

▶ *Civil Engineering (MSCE)*

In the fall of 1996 there were 25 students enrolled in this program.

Application requirements *Prior education:* baccalaureate degree. *Other requirements:* GRE or GMAT, college transcripts, an essay or personal statement, letter(s) of recommendation, an application fee of $25, graduate school application.

Completion requirements 33 semester hours are required. 2 semesters must be completed through the institution. *Maximum time for completion:* six years.

Program contact Dr. Dan Turner, Head, Civil and Environmental Engineering, The University of Alabama, Box 870205, Tuscaloosa, AL 35487-0205. Phone: 205-348-6550. Fax: 205-348-0783. E-mail: dturner@coe.eng.ua.edu.

▶ *Electrical Engineering (MSEE)*

In the fall of 1996 there were 5 students enrolled in this program.

Application requirements *Prior education:* baccalaureate degree. *Other requirements:* GRE or GMAT, college transcripts, an essay or personal statement, letter(s) of recommendation, an application fee of $25, graduate school application.

Completion requirements 32 credit hours are required. *Maximum time for completion:* six years.

Program contact Dr. Russell Pimmel, Head, Department of Electrical Engineering, The University of Alabama, Box 870286, Tuscaloosa, AL 35487-0286. Phone: 205-348-1753. Fax: 205-348-6959. E-mail: rpimmel@ua1vm.ua.edu.

▶ *Engineering (MS)*

In the fall of 1996 there were 5 students enrolled in this program.

Application requirements *Prior education:* baccalaureate degree. *Other requirements:* GRE or GMAT, college transcripts, an essay or personal statement, letter(s) of recommendation, an application fee of $25, graduate school application.

Completion requirements 33 semester hours are required. 2 semesters must be completed through the institution. *Maximum time for completion:* six years.

Program contact Dr. Verle N. Schrodt, Associate Dean, College of Engineering, The University of Alabama, Box 870200, Tuscaloosa, AL 35487-0200. Phone: 205-348-6431. Fax: 205-348-8573. E-mail: vschrodt@ualvm.ua.edu.

▶ *Engineering Management (MSE)*

Application requirements *Prior education:* baccalaureate degree. *Other requirements:* GRE or GMAT, college transcripts, an essay or personal statement, letter(s) of recommendation, an application fee of $25, graduate school application.

Completion requirements 33 semester hours are required. 2 semesters must be completed through the institution. *Maximum time for completion:* six years.

Program contact Dr. Robert G. Batson, Head, Industrial Engineering, The University of Alabama, Box 870288, Tuscaloosa, AL 35487-0288. Phone: 205-348-1609. Fax: 205-348-8573. E-mail: rbatson@coe.eng.ua.edu.

▶ *Environmental Engineering (MS)*

In the fall of 1996 there were 20 students enrolled in this program.

Application requirements *Prior education:* baccalaureate degree. *Other requirements:* GRE or GMAT, college transcripts, an essay or personal statement, letter(s) of recommendation, an application fee of $25, graduate school application.

Completion requirements 33 semester hours are required. 2 semesters must be completed through the institution. *Maximum time for completion:* six years.

Program contact Dr. Dan Turner, Head, Civil and Environmental Engineering, The University of Alabama, Box 870205, Tuscaloosa, AL 35487-0205. Phone: 205-348-6550. Fax: 205-348-0783. E-mail: dturner@coe.eng.ua.edu.

▶ *Mechanical Engineering (MSME)*

In the fall of 1996 there were 10 students enrolled in this program.

Application requirements *Prior education:* baccalaureate degree. *Other requirements:* GRE or GMAT, college transcripts, an essay or personal statement, letter(s) of recommendation, an application fee of $25, graduate school application.

Completion requirements 33 semester hours are required. 2 semesters must be completed through the institution. *Maximum time for completion:* six years.

Program contact Dr. Stuart R. Bell, Head, Department of Mechanical Engineering, The University of Alabama, Box 870276, Tuscaloosa, AL 35487-0276. Phone: 205-348-1644. Fax: 205-348-6419. E-mail: sbell@coe.eng.ua.edu.

INDIVIDUAL COURSE SUBJECT AREAS

Undergraduate

Business; business administration and management; computer and information sciences; history; home economics and family studies; liberal arts, general studies, and humanities; mathematics; mechanical engineering; nursing

Graduate

Accounting; advertising; aerospace, aeronautical engineering; business administration and management; chemical engineering; civil engineering; computer and information sciences; education administration; electrical engineering; engineering mechanics; environmental engineering; health and physical education/fitness; health professions and related sciences; history; human resources management; industrial engineering; law and legal studies; liberal arts, general studies, and humanities; library and information studies; mathematics

See full description on page 486.

THE UNIVERSITY OF ALABAMA AT BIRMINGHAM

Birmingham, Alabama

UAB Options

The University of Alabama at Birmingham, founded in 1969, is a state-supported university. It is accredited by the Southern Association of Colleges and Schools. It first offered distance learning courses in

1991. In 1996–97, it offered 27 courses at a distance. In the fall of 1996, there was a total of 240 students enrolled in distance learning courses.
Course delivery sites Courses are delivered to Auburn University (Auburn University), UAB Walker College (Jasper), The University of Alabama (Tuscaloosa), The University of Alabama in Huntsville (Huntsville), 2 off-campus centers in Eufaula, Gadsden.
Media Courses are delivered via videoconferencing, e-mail, print. Students and teachers interact via videoconferencing, mail, fax, e-mail.
Restrictions Students must be able to travel to receive site.
Services Distance learners have access to library services, the campus computer network, e-mail services at a distance.
Credit-earning options Students may transfer credits from another institution or may earn credits through standardized exams, portfolio assessment, military training, business training.
Typical costs *Undergraduate:* Tuition of $80 per credit hour plus mandatory fees of $6 per credit hour for in-state residents. Tuition of $160 per credit hour plus mandatory fees of $6 per credit hour for out-of-state residents. *Graduate:* Tuition of $91 per credit hour plus mandatory fees of $6 per credit hour for in-state residents. Tuition of $182 per credit hour plus mandatory fees of $6 per credit hour for out-of-state residents. All students pay an additional $40 per term in fees. *Noncredit courses:* $80 per course. Costs may vary by campus or location, number of credits taken. Financial aid is available to distance learners enrolled full-time or part-time.
Registration Students may register by phone.
Contact Brenda Dill, Coordinator, The University of Alabama at Birmingham, 924 19th Street South, UAB Station, Birmingham, AL 35294. *Telephone:* 205-934-3295. *Fax:* 205-934-8251. *E-mail:* bdi@cec.conteduc.uab.edu. *Web site:* http://www.uab.edu/conted.

INDIVIDUAL COURSE SUBJECT AREAS

Undergraduate
Educational psychology; special education

Graduate
Adult education; advertising; chemistry; computer and information sciences; criminal justice; educational psychology; electrical engineering; engineering; health professions and related sciences; journalism; library and information studies; mathematics; nursing; psychology

THE UNIVERSITY OF ALABAMA IN HUNTSVILLE

Huntsville, Alabama

Engineering Management Distance Learning Programs

The University of Alabama in Huntsville, founded in 1950, is a state-supported university. It is accredited by the Southern Association of Colleges and Schools. It first offered distance learning courses in 1992. In 1996–97, it offered 25 courses at a distance. In the fall of 1996, there was a total of 150 students enrolled in distance learning courses.
Course delivery sites Courses are delivered to your home, your workplace, military bases, Gadsden State Community College (Gadsden).
Media Courses are delivered via videotapes, videoconferencing. Students and teachers interact via videoconferencing, audioconferencing, mail, telephone, fax, e-mail. A computer is required for some courses. The institution provides assistance with acquiring computer equipment.
Services Distance learners have access to library services, e-mail services, academic advising at a distance.
Credit-earning options Students may transfer credits from another institution.

Typical costs Tuition of $550 per course for local area residents. Tuition of $585 per course for in-state residents. Graduate, out-of-state cost is $630–$895 per course. International students: $995 per course. *Noncredit courses:* $295 per course. Costs may vary by campus or location. Financial aid is available to distance learners enrolled full-time.
Registration Students may register by mail, fax, phone, e-mail.
Contact Dottie Luke, Staff Assistant, The University of Alabama in Huntsville, Engineering Management, EB 120, Huntsville, AL 35899. *Telephone:* 205-890-6976. *Fax:* 205-890-6608. *E-mail:* luke@ebs330.eb.uah.edu.

DEGREE & CERTIFICATE PROGRAMS

Graduate Degrees
▶ *Engineering Management (MSE)*
In the fall of 1996 there were 185 students enrolled in this program. In 1995–96, 10 degrees were earned at a distance through this program.
Application requirements *Prior education:* undergraduate degree in engineering. *Other requirements:* GRE, high school transcript, college transcripts, an essay or personal statement, an application fee of $20, 2 years experience in engineering position with a US-based firm.
Completion requirements 36 hours are required. 24 hours must be completed through the institution. *Maximum time for completion:* six years.
On-campus requirements For oral exam at end of program of study (includes presentation of final project).
Program contact Dr. Dawn R. Utley, Assistant Professor, The University of Alabama in Huntsville, Engineering Management, EB 119, Huntsville, AL 35899. Phone: 205-890-6075. Fax: 205-890-6608. E-mail: utley@ebs330.eb.uah.edu.

▶ *Environmental Engineering (MSE)*
Application requirements *Prior education:* baccalaureate degree in civil engineering. *Other requirements:* GRE, high school transcript, college transcripts, an essay or personal statement, letter(s) of recommendation, an application fee of $20.
Completion requirements 24 hours are required. 18 hours must be completed through the institution. *Maximum time for completion:* six years.
On-campus requirements For oral exit exam and defense of thesis.
Program contact Dr. Kathleen Leonard, Associate Professor, Civil and Environmental Engineering, The University of Alabama in Huntsville, 301 Sparkman Drive, Huntsville, AL 35899. Phone: 205-890-6423. E-mail: leonard@ebs330.eb.uah.edu.

▶ *Industrial and Systems Engineering (MSE)*
Application requirements *Prior education:* undergraduate degree in engineering. *Other requirements:* GRE, high school transcript, college transcripts, an essay or personal statement, an application fee of $20.
Completion requirements 24 hours are required. 18 hours must be completed through the institution. *Maximum time for completion:* six years.
On-campus requirements For oral exit exam and defense of thesis.
Program contact Dr. Dawn R. Utley, Assistant Professor, The University of Alabama in Huntsville, Engineering Management, EB 119, Huntsville, AL 35899. Phone: 205-890-6075. Fax: 205-890-6608. E-mail: utley@ebs330.eb.uah.edu.

INDIVIDUAL COURSE SUBJECT AREAS

Graduate
Accounting; business; business administration and management; civil engineering; conservation and natural resources; economics; education administration; engineering-related technologies; engineering/industrial management; environmental engineering; human resources management; industrial engineering; law and legal studies

Profiles: The University of Alabama in Huntsville

Noncredit
Calculus; statistics
See full description on page 488.

UNIVERSITY OF ALASKA ANCHORAGE

Anchorage, Alaska

Distance Education Services

University of Alaska Anchorage, founded in 1954, is a state-supported comprehensive institution. It is accredited by the Northwest Association of Schools and Colleges.
Course delivery sites Courses are delivered to your home, your workplace, military bases, other colleges.
Media Courses are delivered via television, videotapes, videoconferencing, audiotapes, audioconferencing, computer software, World Wide Web, e-mail, print. Students and teachers interact via videoconferencing, audioconferencing, mail, telephone, fax, e-mail.
Restrictions Programs are available to in-state students only.
Credit-earning options Students may transfer credits from another institution.
Typical costs *Undergraduate:* Tuition of $71 per credit plus mandatory fees of $38 per course for in-state residents. *Graduate:* Tuition of $158 per credit plus mandatory fees of $38 per course for in-state residents.
Contact Distance Education Services, University of Alaska Anchorage, 3211 Providence Drive, Anchorage, AK 99508-8060. *Telephone:* 907-786-4488. *Fax:* 907-786-1027.

DEGREE & CERTIFICATE PROGRAMS

Associate Degrees
▶ *Liberal Arts (AA)*
Completion requirements 60 credits are required. 15 credits must be completed through the institution.

INDIVIDUAL COURSE SUBJECT AREAS

Undergraduate
Accounting; Asian languages and literatures; biology; business administration and management; creative writing; developmental and child psychology; economics; English composition; European languages and literatures; health and physical education/fitness; history; liberal arts, general studies, and humanities; mass media; mathematics; philosophy and religion; political science; sociology; special education

Graduate
History; special education

UNIVERSITY OF ALASKA FAIRBANKS

Fairbanks, Alaska

Center for Distance Education and Independent Learning

University of Alaska Fairbanks, founded in 1917, is a state-supported university. It is accredited by the Northwest Association of Schools and Colleges. It first offered distance learning courses in 1970. In 1996–97, it offered 200 courses at a distance. In the fall of 1996, there was a total of 2,527 students enrolled in distance learning courses.

Course delivery sites Courses are delivered to your home, 20 off-campus centers in Anchorage, Barrow, Bethel, Dillingham, Fort Yukon, Galena, Homer, Juneau, Kenai, Ketchikan, Kodiak, Kotzebue, McGrath, Nenana, Nome, Palmer, Sitka, Tok, Unalaska, Valdez.
Media Courses are delivered via videotapes, audiotapes, audioconferencing, computer software, World Wide Web, e-mail, print. Students and teachers interact via audioconferencing, mail, telephone, fax, e-mail. A computer is required for some courses.
Restrictions Availability varies by course, program, or delivery means.
Services Distance learners have access to library services, e-mail services, academic advising, tutoring, career placement assistance at a distance.
Credit-earning options Students may transfer credits from another institution or may earn credits through standardized exams, institutionally developed exams, portfolio assessment, military training, business training.
Typical costs *Undergraduate:* Tuition of $71 per credit plus mandatory fees of $20 per course. *Graduate:* Tuition of $153 per credit plus mandatory fees of $20 per course. Undergraduate tuition for 300- and 400-level courses is $79 per credit. Financial aid is available to distance learners enrolled full-time or part-time.
Registration Students may register by mail, fax, phone, e-mail, World Wide Web.
Contact James Stricks, Director, Center for Distance Education, University of Alaska Fairbanks, PO Box 756700, Fairbanks, AK 99775. *Telephone:* 907-474-5353. *Fax:* 907-474-5402. *E-mail:* sycde@orca.alaska.edu. *Web site:* http://uafcde.uaflrb.alaska.edu.

DEGREE & CERTIFICATE PROGRAMS

Associate Degrees
▶ *Community Health (AAS)*
Restrictions This program is available to in-state students only.
Application requirements *Prior education:* high school diploma or equivalent. *Other requirements:* SAT or ACT, high school transcript, college transcripts, an application fee of $35.
Completion requirements 60 credits are required. 15 credits must be completed through the institution.
On-campus requirements Four basic training sessions at training centers.

▶ *Early Childhood Development (AAS)*
Restrictions This program is available to local area students only.
Application requirements *Prior education:* high school diploma or equivalent. *Other requirements:* SAT or ACT, high school transcript, college transcripts, an application fee of $35.
Completion requirements 60 credits are required. 15 credits must be completed through the institution.

▶ *General Studies (AA)*
Restrictions This program is available to local area students only.
Application requirements *Prior education:* high school diploma or equivalent. *Other requirements:* SAT or ACT, high school transcript, college transcripts, an application fee of $35.
Completion requirements 60 credits are required. 15 credits must be completed through the institution.

▶ *Human Services Technology (AAS)*
Restrictions Program is open to UAF Rural students only.
Application requirements *Prior education:* high school diploma or equivalent. *Other requirements:* SAT or ACT, high school transcript, college transcripts, an application fee of $35.
Completion requirements 60 credits are required. 15 credits must be completed through the institution.

Baccalaureate Degrees
▶ *Rural Development (BA)*
Restrictions This program is available to in-state students only.
Application requirements *Prior education:* high school diploma or equivalent. *Other requirements:* SAT or ACT, high school transcript, college transcripts, an application fee of $35.

Completion requirements 120 credits are required. 30 credits must be completed through the institution.

▶ *Social Work (BA)*

Restrictions This program is available to local area students only.
Application requirements *Prior education:* high school diploma or equivalent. *Other requirements:* SAT or ACT, high school transcript, college transcripts, an application fee of $35.
Completion requirements 120 credits are required. 30 credits must be completed through the institution.

Undergraduate Certificates

▶ *Community Health*

Restrictions This program is available to in-state students only.
Application requirements *Prior education:* high school diploma or equivalent. *Other requirements:* SAT or ACT, high school transcript, college transcripts, an application fee of $35.
Completion requirements 34 credits are required.
On-campus requirements Four basic training sessions at training centers.

▶ *Early Childhood Development*

Restrictions This program is available to local area students only.
Application requirements *Prior education:* high school diploma or equivalent. *Other requirements:* SAT or ACT, high school transcript, college transcripts, an application fee of $35.
Completion requirements 30 credits are required.

INDIVIDUAL COURSE SUBJECT AREAS

Undergraduate

Abnormal psychology; accounting; administrative and secretarial services; advertising; algebra; anthropology; area, ethnic, and cultural studies; art history and criticism; biological and life sciences; biology; business; business administration and management; calculus; chemistry; child care and development; Classical languages and literatures; communications; computer and information sciences; conservation and natural resources; creative writing; developmental and child psychology; economics; education; education administration; educational psychology; English composition; English language and literature; film studies; geography; geology; health and physical education/fitness; history; hospitality services management; human resources management; journalism; liberal arts, general studies, and humanities; library and information studies; mathematics; music; philosophy and religion; physical sciences; physics; political science; psychology; public administration and services; radio and television broadcasting; real estate; social psychology; social sciences; social work; sociology; special education; statistics; teacher education

Graduate

Computer and information sciences; education administration; educational psychology; special education; teacher education

See full description on page 490.

UNIVERSITY OF ALASKA SOUTHEAST

Juneau, Alaska

University of Alaska Southeast, founded in 1972, is a state-supported comprehensive institution. It is accredited by the Northwest Association of Schools and Colleges. It first offered distance learning courses in 1986.
Course delivery sites Courses are delivered to your home, military bases, other colleges.
Media Courses are delivered via television, videotapes, audiotapes, audioconferencing, computer software, World Wide Web, e-mail, print.

Students and teachers interact via audioconferencing, mail, telephone, fax, e-mail. A computer is required for some courses.
Services Distance learners have access to library services, academic advising at a distance.
Credit-earning options Students may transfer credits from another institution or may earn credits through standardized exams, institutionally developed exams, military training.
Typical costs *Undergraduate:* Tuition of $71 per credit for local area residents. Tuition of $79 per credit for in-state residents. Tuition of $229 per credit for out-of-state residents. *Graduate:* Tuition of $158 per credit for local area residents. Tuition of $308 per credit for in-state residents. Costs may vary by campus or location, specific program of study, number of credits taken, course delivery options. Financial aid is available to distance learners enrolled full-time or part-time.
Registration Students may register by mail, fax, phone.
Contact Shirley Grubb, Assistant to the Dean, University of Alaska Southeast, 11120 Glacier Highway, Juneau, AK 99801. *Telephone:* 907-465-6353. *Fax:* 907-465-6383. *E-mail:* jnsdg@acad1.alaska.edu.

DEGREE & CERTIFICATE PROGRAMS

Baccalaureate Degrees

▶ *Business Administration (BBA)*

Restrictions This program is available to in-state students only. Students must be at a University of Alaska rural campus site or an authorized military base..
Application requirements *Prior education:* associate degree. *Other requirements:* high school transcript, college transcripts, an application fee of $35.
Completion requirements 120 semester hours are required. 30 semester hours must be completed through the institution.

Graduate Degrees

▶ *Educational Leadership (MEd)*

Restrictions This program is available to in-state students only.
Application requirements *Prior education:* Bachelor's of Education degree or an Alaskan teaching certificate. *Other requirements:* college transcripts, an essay or personal statement, letter(s) of recommendation.
Completion requirements 36 semester hours are required. 12 semester hours must be completed through the institution. *Maximum time for completion:* seven years.
Program contact Dr. Lawrence Lee Oldaker, Professor of Education, University of Alaska Southeast, 11120 Glacier Highway, Juneau, AK 99801. Phone: 907-465-6416. Fax: 907-465-6406. E-mail: jfllo@acad1.alaska.edu.

▶ *Public Administration (MPA)*

Restrictions This program is available to in-state students only. Program is for military personnel or military dependents only.
Application requirements *Prior education:* baccalaureate degree. *Other requirements:* GRE or GMAT, college transcripts, an essay or personal statement, letter(s) of recommendation, an application fee of $35, located at authorized military site: Eielson AFB, Fort Greely, Fort Wainwright.
Completion requirements 36 semester hours are required. 12 semester hours must be completed through the institution. *Maximum time for completion:* seven years.

INDIVIDUAL COURSE SUBJECT AREAS

Undergraduate

Biology; business administration and management; business law; curriculum and instruction; finance; human resources management; international business; management information systems; marketing; organizational behavior studies; teacher education

Graduate

Continuing education; curriculum and instruction; education administration; public administration and services; public policy analysis

Profiles: University of Alaska Southeast

Noncredit
Continuing education

UNIVERSITY OF ALASKA SOUTHEAST, SITKA CAMPUS

Sitka, Alaska

University of Alaska Southeast, Sitka Campus, founded in 1962, is a state-supported two-year college. It is accredited by the Northwest Association of Schools and Colleges. It first offered distance learning courses in 1986. In 1996–97, it offered 50 courses at a distance. In the fall of 1996, there was a total of 900 students enrolled in distance learning courses.

Course delivery sites Courses are delivered to your home, your workplace, military bases, other colleges.
Media Courses are delivered via television, videotapes, audiotapes, radio broadcast, audioconferencing, computer software, World Wide Web, e-mail, print. Students and teachers interact via audioconferencing, mail, telephone, fax, e-mail. A computer is required for some courses.
Restrictions Programs are primarily available to in-state students.
Services Distance learners have access to library services, academic advising at a distance.
Credit-earning options Students may transfer credits from another institution or may earn credits through examinations, military training.
Typical costs *Undergraduate:* Tuition of $71 per credit plus mandatory fees of $40 per course. *Graduate:* Tuition of $153 per credit plus mandatory fees of $40 per course. *Noncredit courses:* $35 per course. Costs may vary by number of credits taken. Financial aid is available to distance learners.
Contact Denise Blankenship, Coordinator, Distance Education, University of Alaska Southeast, Sitka Campus, 1332 Seward Avenue, Sitka, AK 99835. *Telephone:* 907-747-6653. *Fax:* 907-747-3552. *E-mail:* tndmb@acad1.alaska.edu.

DEGREE & CERTIFICATE PROGRAMS

Associate Degrees

▶ *Business Information Systems (AAS)*
Restrictions This program is available to in-state students only.
Application requirements *Prior education:* high school diploma or equivalent. *Other requirements:* high school transcript, letter(s) of recommendation, an application fee of $35.
Completion requirements 60 credits are required.

▶ *Early Childhood Education (AAS)*
Restrictions This program is available to in-state students only.
Application requirements *Prior education:* high school diploma or equivalent. *Other requirements:* high school transcript, letter(s) of recommendation, an application fee of $35.
Completion requirements 62 credits are required.

▶ *General Studies (AA)*
Restrictions This program is available to in-state students only.
Application requirements *Prior education:* high school diploma or equivalent. *Other requirements:* high school transcript, college transcripts, an application fee of $35.
Completion requirements 60 credits are required. 34 credits must be completed through the institution.

▶ *Health Information Management (AAS)*
Restrictions Program is available to students in Alaska, Hawaii, Wyoming, New Mexico only.
Application requirements *Prior education:* high school diploma or equivalent. *Other requirements:* high school transcript, letter(s) of recommendation, an application fee of $35.
Completion requirements 60 credits are required.

▶ *Human Services Technology (AAS)*
Restrictions This program is available to in-state students only.
Application requirements *Prior education:* high school diploma or equivalent. *Other requirements:* high school transcript, an essay or personal statement, letter(s) of recommendation, an application fee of $35.
Completion requirements 60 credits are required.

Undergraduate Certificates

▶ *Elementary Education*
Restrictions This program is available to in-state students only.
Application requirements High school transcript, college transcripts, letter(s) of recommendation, an application fee of $35.

INDIVIDUAL COURSE SUBJECT AREAS

Undergraduate
Accounting; administrative and secretarial services; area, ethnic, and cultural studies; biological and life sciences; biology; business; business administration and management; chemistry; communications; computer and information sciences; creative writing; developmental and child psychology; education; English composition; English language and literature; geology; health professions and related sciences; history; journalism; law and legal studies; liberal arts, general studies, and humanities; mathematics; philosophy and religion; physical sciences; psychology; social psychology; social sciences; sociology; teacher education

UNIVERSITY OF ALBERTA

Edmonton, Alberta, Canada

Academic Technologies for Learning

University of Alberta, founded in 1906, is a province-supported university. It is provincially chartered. It first offered distance learning courses in 1970. In 1996–97, it offered 6 courses at a distance. In the fall of 1996, there was a total of 250 students enrolled in distance learning courses.
Course delivery sites Courses are delivered to your home, your workplace, The University of Calgary (Calgary), Red Deer College (Red Deer, AB), Keyand College (Fort McMurray, AB).
Media Courses are delivered via videoconferencing, audioconferencing, World Wide Web, e-mail. Students and teachers interact via telephone, e-mail. A computer is required for some courses.
Restrictions Videoconferencing is limited to specific sites.
Services Distance learners have access to library services, the campus computer network, e-mail services, academic advising, tutoring at a distance.
Credit-earning options Students may transfer credits from another institution or may earn credits through institutionally developed exams.
Typical costs Contact university for details. Financial aid is available to distance learners enrolled full-time or part-time.
Registration Students may register by mail, phone.
Contact Mr. Lloyd Carswell, Director, University of Alberta, 4-107A Education, N, Edmonton, AB T6G 2T4, Canada. *Telephone:* 403-492-3411. *Fax:* 403-492-3764. *E-mail:* lloyd.carswell@ualberta.ca. *Web site:* http://www.atl.ualberta.ca.

INDIVIDUAL COURSE SUBJECT AREAS

Undergraduate
Biology; chemical engineering; computer and information sciences; economics; education administration; electrical engineering; history; liberal arts, general studies, and humanities; political science

Graduate
Adult education; nursing

Noncredit
Human resources management

UNIVERSITY OF ARIZONA

Tucson, Arizona

Extended University, Distance Learning Program

University of Arizona, founded in 1885, is a state-supported university. It is accredited by the North Central Association of Colleges and Schools. It first offered distance learning courses in 1972. In 1996–97, it offered 63 courses at a distance. In the fall of 1996, there was a total of 450 students enrolled in distance learning courses.
Course delivery sites Courses are delivered to your home, your workplace, military bases, National Technological University (Fort Collins, CO).
Media Courses are delivered via television, videotapes, computer software, World Wide Web, e-mail, print, asynchronous computer conferencing. Students and teachers interact via mail, telephone, fax, e-mail. A computer is required for some courses.
Restrictions Availability varies by course, program, or delivery means.
Services Distance learners have access to library services, the campus computer network, e-mail services, academic advising at a distance.
Credit-earning options Students may transfer credits from another institution.
Typical costs Contact school for information.
Registration Students may register by mail, fax, phone, e-mail.
Contact Mary Staugaard, Program Coordinator, Distance Learning Program, University of Arizona, Extended University, University Services Building, 888 North Euclid Avenue, PO Box 210158, Room 301P, Tucson, AZ 85721-0158. *Telephone:* 520-626-2073. *Fax:* 520-621-3269. *E-mail:* staugaar@u.arizona.edu. *Web site:* http://w3.arizona.edu/~uaextend/dist.

Special note
The technology explosion has revolutionized the college campus and the way people look at education. With distance learning, higher education can be delivered to students' doorsteps.

The University of Arizona is committed to distance learning. If the student can't come to the campus, the campus can be brought to the student. The University is reaching out—to the country and beyond.

Courses are taught by top faculty members and incorporate the latest research and technological developments.

Students can choose the distance learning course and format that best meets their needs:

The University offers classes on videotape and via satellite hookup in a wide range of engineering fields. Students can work toward a technical degree or complete a professional certificate program in aerospace and mechanical engineering, electrical and computer engineering, optical sciences, reliability engineering, or systems and industrial engineering.

The University's on-line master's degree in information resources and library science is Internet-based. A new Web-based course, Dialogs on Consciousness, allows students to engage in electronic dialogue with leaders in the field. Other Internet-based courses may be added in the months ahead. Students should visit the University's Web site at http://w3.arizona.edu/~~uaextend/dist.

To find out how to earn university credit at a distance, students should call 520-626-2079 or e-mail villafar@ccit.arizona.edu for details.

DEGREE & CERTIFICATE PROGRAMS

Graduate certificates
▶ *Reliability and Quality Engineering*
In the fall of 1996 there were 20 students enrolled in this program. In 1995–96, 5 certificates were earned at a distance through this program.
Application requirements *Prior education:* BS in engineering, mathematics, or physics. *Other requirements:* one undergraduate level course in probability and statistics.
Completion requirements 15 units for certificate are required. *Other requirements:* units earned in the certificate program may apply to the Master's degree.

INDIVIDUAL COURSE SUBJECT AREAS

Undergraduate
Agriculture; area, ethnic, and cultural studies

Graduate
Aerospace, aeronautical engineering; civil engineering; electrical engineering; engineering mechanics; engineering/industrial management; industrial engineering; library and information studies; mechanical engineering; public health

Noncredit
Mathematics

UNIVERSITY OF ARKANSAS

Fayetteville, Arkansas

Division for Continuing Education

University of Arkansas, founded in 1871, is a state-supported university. It is accredited by the North Central Association of Colleges and Schools.
Course delivery sites Courses are delivered to your home, your workplace, other colleges.
Media Courses are delivered via videotapes, videoconferencing, computer software, print, computer conferencing.
Services Distance learners have access to library services, academic advising, career placement assistance at a distance.
Credit-earning options Students may transfer credits from another institution.
Contact Office of Credit Studies, University of Arkansas, #2 University Center, Fayetteville, AR 72701. *Telephone:* 501-575-3648. *Fax:* 501-575-7232.

INDIVIDUAL COURSE SUBJECT AREAS

Undergraduate
Business administration and management; education

UNIVERSITY OF ARKANSAS AT LITTLE ROCK

Little Rock, Arkansas

Department of Computing Services

University of Arkansas at Little Rock, founded in 1927, is a state-supported university. It is accredited by the North Central Association of Colleges and Schools. It first offered distance learning courses in 1994. In 1996–97, it offered 16 courses at a distance. In the fall of 1996, there was a total of 108 students enrolled in distance learning courses.

Course delivery sites Courses are delivered to Pulaski Technical College (North Little Rock), Southern Arkansas University–Magnolia (Magnolia), University of Arkansas at Monticello (Monticello), Westark Community College (Fort Smith), area health education centers.
Media Courses are delivered via videoconferencing. Students and teachers interact via mail, telephone, fax, e-mail.
Restrictions Courses are available to US students only.
Services Distance learners have access to library services, academic advising, tutoring, career placement assistance at a distance.
Credit-earning options Students may transfer credits from another institution.
Typical costs *Undergraduate:* Tuition of $94.25 per semester hour for in-state residents. Tuition of $243 per semester hour for out-of-state residents. *Graduate:* Tuition of $130 per semester hour for in-state residents. Tuition of $278 per semester hour for out-of-state residents. 10% technology fee at off-campus sites. Costs may vary by campus or location, specific program of study, number of credits taken, course delivery options. Financial aid is available to distance learners.
Registration Students may register by mail, phone.
Contact Sonja Sanderson, Coordinator, Off Campus Programs, University of Arkansas at Little Rock, 2801 South University Avenue, Little Rock, AR 72204. *Telephone:* 501-569-3117. *E-mail:* sksanderson@ualr.edu.

DEGREE & CERTIFICATE PROGRAMS

Graduate Degrees

▶ *Business Administration (MBA)*
Application requirements *Prior education:* baccalaureate degree. *Other requirements:* GMAT.
Completion requirements 30 semester hours are required.
Program contact Tammy Lawrence, Director of Student Services, University of Arkansas at Little Rock, College of Business Administration - UALR, 2801 South University Avenue, Little Rock, AR 72204. Phone: 501-569-3356. Fax: 501-569-8898. E-mail: talawrence@ualr.edu.

INDIVIDUAL COURSE SUBJECT AREAS

Undergraduate
Adult education; creative writing; criminal justice; developmental and child psychology; education administration; English as a second language (ESL); English composition; English language and literature; fire science; history; marketing; occupational therapy; social psychology; teacher education; technical writing

Noncredit
Social work

UNIVERSITY OF BALTIMORE

Baltimore, Maryland

University of Baltimore, founded in 1925, is a state-supported upper-level institution. It is accredited by the Middle States Association of Colleges and Schools. It first offered distance learning courses in 1994. In 1996–97, it offered 20 courses at a distance. In the fall of 1996, there was a total of 50 students enrolled in distance learning courses.
Course delivery sites Courses are delivered to Catonsville Community College (Catonsville), Essex Community College (Baltimore), Howard Community College (Columbia), off-campus center(s) in Aberdeen, Baltimore, Hunt Valley.
Media Courses are delivered via television, World Wide Web. Students and teachers interact via videoconferencing, mail, fax, e-mail. A computer is required for some courses.
Services Distance learners have access to library services, academic advising, tutoring, career placement assistance at a distance.
Credit-earning options Students may transfer credits from another institution or may earn credits through examinations.
Typical costs Contact school for fee information. Financial aid is available to distance learners.
Registration Students may register by mail, phone.
Contact Janenne Corcoran, Associate Director, University of Baltimore, 1420 North Charles Street, Baltimore, MD 21201. *Telephone:* 410-837-4806. *Fax:* 410-837-4820. *E-mail:* jcorcoran@ubmail.ubalt.edu.

INDIVIDUAL COURSE SUBJECT AREAS

Undergraduate
Area, ethnic, and cultural studies; communications; criminology; history; political science; psychology

Graduate
Accounting; business; business administration and management; computer and information sciences; counseling psychology; public administration and services

UNIVERSITY OF BRIDGEPORT

Bridgeport, Connecticut

Office of Distance Learning

University of Bridgeport, founded in 1927, is an independent-nonprofit comprehensive institution. It is provisionally accredited by the New England Association of Schools and Colleges. It first offered distance learning courses in 1997.
Course delivery sites Courses are delivered to your home, your workplace, military bases.
Media Courses are delivered via audiotapes, computer software, World Wide Web, e-mail, print. Students and teachers interact via mail, telephone, e-mail. A computer is required for all courses.
Services Distance learners have access to library services, the campus computer network, e-mail services, academic advising, tutoring, career placement assistance at a distance.
Typical costs Tuition of $300 per credit plus mandatory fees of $25 per semester. Costs may vary by specific program of study, number of credits taken. Financial aid is available to distance learners enrolled full-time.
Registration Students may register by mail, fax, phone, e-mail, World Wide Web.

Contact Michael J. Giampaoli, Coordinator for Distance Education, University of Bridgeport, 126 Park Avenue, Bridgeport, CT 06601. *Telephone:* 203-576-4851. *Fax:* 203-576-4672. *E-mail:* gmichael@cse.bridgeport.edu.

DEGREE & CERTIFICATE PROGRAMS

Graduate Degrees
▶ *Human Nutrition (MS)*
Application requirements *Prior education:* baccalaureate degree. *Other requirements:* college transcripts, an essay or personal statement, letter(s) of recommendation, an application fee of $40.
Completion requirements 31 are required. *Maximum time for completion:* five years.
On-campus requirements For comprehensive exam.
See full description on page 492.

UNIVERSITY OF BRITISH COLUMBIA

Vancouver, British Columbia, Canada

Distance Education and Technology

University of British Columbia, founded in 1915, is a province-supported university. It is provincially chartered. It first offered distance learning courses in 1949. In 1996–97, it offered 105 courses at a distance. In the fall of 1996, there was a total of 4,000 students enrolled in distance learning courses.
Course delivery sites Courses are delivered to your home, your workplace, Open Learning Agency (Burnaby), off-campus center(s).
Media Courses are delivered via television, videotapes, videoconferencing, audiotapes, audioconferencing, computer software, World Wide Web, e-mail, print. Students and teachers interact via videoconferencing, audioconferencing, mail, telephone, fax, e-mail. A computer is required for some courses.
Services Distance learners have access to library services, the campus computer network, e-mail services, academic advising, tutoring at a distance.
Credit-earning options Students may earn credits through institutionally developed exams, portfolio assessment.
Typical costs Contact registrar's office for current costs. Financial aid is available to distance learners enrolled full-time or part-time.
Registration Students may register by mail, fax, phone, e-mail, World Wide Web.
Contact Heather Francis, Coordinator of Distance Education Marketing and External Relations, University of British Columbia, 2329 West Mall, Room 1170, University Services Building, Vancouver, BC V6T 1Z4, Canada. *Telephone:* 604-822-8889. *Fax:* 604-822-8636. *E-mail:* heather.francis@ubc.ca. *Web site:* http://www.cstudies.ubc.ca/disted/.

Special note
The Distance Education & Technology (DE&T) division of Continuing Studies develops and delivers programs, courses, and learning materials for individual and institutional clients who require cost-effective, quality education delivered in flexible formats. Established as the Department of University Extensions at UBC in 1949, the division continues to collaborate with twelve UBC faculties plus Continuing Studies program areas to produce distance education services and courses to serve local, national, and international clients.

UBC currently offers 105 courses via distance technology, including print-based materials, audio, video, CD-ROM, and World Wide Web and other Internet services. In addition, DE&T at UBC is now developing approximately 23 new courses annually, many with an on-line component. DE&T's inventory consists of degree-credit, non-credit, certificate, and diploma courses and programs. For a complete list of courses and projects, please visit the Web site at http://www.cstudies.ubc.ca/disted/ or call 604-822-6565 or 800-754-1811 (toll-free) for a printed catalogue and registration requirements.

Students interested in DE&T's consultation services, course development, training, research, or technological expertise should visit the director's Web site at http://bates.cstudies.ubc.ca or call 604-822-1573. Dr. Tony Bates, Director of DE&T, is a founding member of the British Open University, has authored 5 books on distance education, and has consulted for UNESCO, the World Bank, and other institutions in more than 30 countries. Along with a staff of 19 people, Dr. Bates has initiated several partnership franchises with organizations offering distance education around the world.

INDIVIDUAL COURSE SUBJECT AREAS

Undergraduate
Agriculture; astronomy and astrophysics; computer and information sciences; education; English language and literature; film studies; forestry; French language and literature; German language and literature; history; music; nursing; oceanography; philosophy and religion; psychology

Graduate
Education

THE UNIVERSITY OF CALGARY

Calgary, Alberta, Canada

Centre For Distance Learning and Innovative Technologies

The University of Calgary, founded in 1945, is a province-supported university. It is provincially chartered. It first offered distance learning courses in 1977. In 1996–97, it offered 70 courses at a distance. In the fall of 1996, there was a total of 400 students enrolled in distance learning courses.
Course delivery sites Courses are delivered to your home, your workplace, other colleges, 95 off-campus centers.
Media Courses are delivered via television, videoconferencing, audioconferencing, computer software, World Wide Web, e-mail. Students and teachers interact via videoconferencing, audioconferencing, mail, telephone, fax, e-mail. A computer is required for some courses.
Restrictions Availability varies by course, program, or delivery means.
Services Distance learners have access to library services, the campus computer network, academic advising, tutoring, career placement assistance at a distance.
Credit-earning options Students may transfer credits from another institution or may earn credits through institutionally developed exams.
Typical costs *Undergraduate:* Tuition of $344 per course plus mandatory fees of $26 per course. *Graduate:* Tuition of $419 per course plus mandatory fees of $59 per course. *Noncredit courses:* $200 per course. Costs may vary by specific program of study, number of credits taken, country of residence. Financial aid is available to distance learners enrolled full-time or part-time.
Registration Students may register by mail, fax, phone.
Contact Irena Kirek, Director, The University of Calgary, 2500 University Drive, NW, Calgary, AB T2N 1N4, Canada. *Telephone:* 403-220-7346.

Profiles: The University of Calgary

Fax: 403-777-1959. *E-mail:* ikirek@acs.ucalgary.ca. *Web site:* http://www.ucalgary.ca/UofC/departments/CDLIT/.

DEGREE & CERTIFICATE PROGRAMS

Baccalaureate Degrees

▶ *Community Rehabilitation (BCR)*
In the fall of 1996 there were 60 students enrolled in this program.
Restrictions This program is available to in-state students only.
Application requirements *Prior education:* associate degree. *Other requirements:* high school transcript, college transcripts.
Completion requirements 12 courses are required. 6 courses must be completed through the institution. *Maximum time for completion:* six years.

▶ *Nursing (BN)*
Application requirements *Prior education:* RN license. *Other requirements:* RN license.
Completion requirements 10 courses are required. *Maximum time for completion:* six years.

Graduate Degrees

▶ *Adult, Community and Higher Education (MEd)*
In the fall of 1996 there were 26 students enrolled in this program.
Restrictions This program is available to in-state students only.
Application requirements *Prior education:* baccalaureate degree. *Other requirements:* college transcripts, an essay or personal statement, letter(s) of recommendation, an application fee of $60, $2000 program fee.
Completion requirements 12 courses are required. 8 courses must be completed through the institution. *Maximum time for completion:* six years.
On-campus requirements Two weeks Summer Institute.

▶ *Continuing Education (MCE)*
In the fall of 1996 there were 45 students enrolled in this program.
Application requirements *Prior education:* baccalaureate degree. *Other requirements:* college transcripts, an essay or personal statement, letter(s) of recommendation, an application fee of $60, $6000 program fee, 3.0 GPA.
Completion requirements 10 courses are required. *Maximum time for completion:* six years.
On-campus requirements Three weeks.

▶ *Educational Leadership, Educational Technology, English as a Second Language, Teaching and Learning (MEd)*
Restrictions This program is available to in-state students only.
Application requirements *Prior education:* baccalaureate degree. *Other requirements:* college transcripts, an essay or personal statement, letter(s) of recommendation, an application fee of $60, $10,500 program fee.
Completion requirements 10 courses are required. 8 courses must be completed through the institution. *Maximum time for completion:* six years.

Undergraduate Certificates

▶ *Teacher Assistant*
In the fall of 1996 there were 80 students enrolled in this program.
Restrictions This program is available to in-state students only.
Application requirements *Prior education:* high school diploma or equivalent. *Other requirements:* high school transcript, an application fee of $35.
Completion requirements 9 courses are required. 9 courses must be completed through the institution.

INDIVIDUAL COURSE SUBJECT AREAS

Undergraduate
Biology; chemistry; civil engineering; creative writing; economics; education; education administration; electrical engineering; English composition; history; liberal arts, general studies, and humanities; nursing; philosophy and religion; physics; political science; sociology; special education; teacher education

Graduate
Chemistry; computer and information sciences; continuing education; education; education administration; electrical engineering; special education; teacher education

Noncredit
Conservation and natural resources; education; law and legal studies

UNIVERSITY OF CALIFORNIA, DAVIS

Davis, California

University of California, Davis, founded in 1905, is a state-supported university. It is accredited by the Western Association of Schools and Colleges, Inc. It first offered distance learning courses in 1987. In 1996–97, it offered 9 courses at a distance. In the fall of 1996, there was a total of 350 students enrolled in distance learning courses.
Course delivery sites Courses are delivered to your home, your workplace, 2 off-campus centers in Livermore, Sacramento.
Media Courses are delivered via television, videotapes, videoconferencing, computer software, World Wide Web, e-mail, print. Students and teachers interact via videoconferencing, mail, telephone, fax, e-mail. A computer is required for some courses.
Services Distance learners have access to e-mail services, academic advising, tutoring at a distance.
Credit-earning options Students may earn credits through institutionally developed exams.
Typical costs $200–$600 per course depending on program of study. *Noncredit courses:* $200–$600 per course. Costs may vary by specific program of study, course delivery options, credit option.
Registration Students may register by mail, fax, phone, e-mail, World Wide Web.
Contact Pat Aguilera, Administrative Assistant, University of California, Davis, University Extension, 1333 Research Park Drive, Davis, CA 95616. *Telephone:* 916-757-8663. *Fax:* 916-754-5015. *E-mail:* paguilera@unexmail.ucdavis.edu. *Web site:* http://universityextension.ucdavis.edu.

INDIVIDUAL COURSE SUBJECT AREAS

Undergraduate
Biological and life sciences; business administration and management; computer and information sciences; computer programming; database management; environmental science; home economics and family studies

UNIVERSITY OF CALIFORNIA EXTENSION

Berkeley, California

Center for Media and Independent Learning

University of California Extension is a state-related university extension. It first offered distance learning courses in 1913. In 1996–97, it offered 150 courses at a distance. In the fall of 1996, there was a total of 3,000 students enrolled in distance learning courses.
Course delivery sites Courses are delivered to your home, your workplace, military bases.
Media Courses are delivered via audiotapes, computer software, World Wide Web, print. Students and teachers interact via mail, telephone, fax,

e-mail, computer conferencing via America Online. A computer is required for some courses.
Restrictions Students must be able to understand courses taught in English.
Credit-earning options Students may earn credits through institutionally developed exams.
Typical costs Tuition of $395 per course. *Noncredit courses:* $350 per course. Costs may vary by specific program of study, number of credits taken.
Registration Students may register by mail, fax, phone, e-mail, World Wide Web.
Contact Student Services, University of California Extension, Center for Media and Independent Learning, 2000 Center Street, Suite 400, Berkeley, CA 94704. *Telephone:* 510-642-4124. *Fax:* 510-643-9271. *E-mail:* cmil@violet.berkeley.edu. *Web site:* http://www-cmil.unex.berkeley.edu.

DEGREE & CERTIFICATE PROGRAMS

Undergraduate Certificates
▶ *Computer Information Systems*
Application requirements An application fee of $60.
Completion requirements 6 courses are required. 6 courses must be completed through the institution. *Maximum time for completion:* four years.

Graduate certificates
▶ *Hazardous Materials Management*
In the fall of 1996 there were 64 students enrolled in this program.
Restrictions Students must have an account with America Online.
Application requirements *Prior education:* bachelor's degree or at least two years experience in the hazardous materials field. *Other requirements:* an application fee of $60.
Completion requirements 9 courses are required. 6 courses must be completed through the institution. *Maximum time for completion:* four years.

INDIVIDUAL COURSE SUBJECT AREAS

Undergraduate
Accounting; administrative and secretarial services; area, ethnic, and cultural studies; Asian languages and literatures; astronomy and astrophysics; biological and life sciences; biology; botany; business; business administration and management; chemistry; civil engineering; communications; computer and information sciences; conservation and natural resources; creative writing; design; developmental and child psychology; economics; electrical engineering; engineering; English composition; English language and literature; European languages and literatures; film studies; fine arts; geology; health professions and related sciences; history; human resources management; liberal arts, general studies, and humanities; mathematics; philosophy and religion; physical sciences; political science; psychology; public health; social psychology; social sciences; sociology

Noncredit
Creative writing; English composition; English language and literature; health professions and related sciences
See full description on page 494.

UNIVERSITY OF CALIFORNIA, SANTA BARBARA

Santa Barbara, California

Off-Campus Studies
University of California, Santa Barbara, founded in 1909, is a state-supported university. It is accredited by the Western Association of Schools and Colleges, Inc. It first offered distance learning courses in 1973. In 1996–97, it offered 40 courses at a distance. In the fall of 1996, there was a total of 100 students enrolled in distance learning courses.
Course delivery sites Courses are delivered to your home, your workplace, 1 off-campus center in Ventura.
Media Courses are delivered via television, videotapes, videoconferencing. Students and teachers interact via videoconferencing, mail, telephone, fax, e-mail. A computer is required for some courses.
Restrictions Programs are available to local area students only.
Services Distance learners have access to library services, the campus computer network, e-mail services, academic advising, career placement assistance at a distance.
Credit-earning options Students may transfer credits from another institution.
Typical costs *Undergraduate:* Tuition of $1459.65 per quarter for in-state residents. Tuition of $4026.65 per quarter for out-of-state residents. *Graduate:* Tuition of $1703.85 per quarter for in-state residents. Tuition of $4270.85 per quarter for out-of-state residents. Financial aid is available to distance learners.
Registration Students may register by mail, phone.
Contact Howard Adamson, Manager of Off Campus Studies, University of California, Santa Barbara, Off Campus Studies Department, Santa Barbara, CA 93106. *Telephone:* 805-893-8841. *Fax:* 805-893-8719. *E-mail:* hadamson@xlrn.ucsb.edu. *Web site:* http://www.xlrn.ucsb.edu.

DEGREE & CERTIFICATE PROGRAMS

Graduate Degrees
▶ *Computer Science (MS)*
In the fall of 1996 there were 25 students enrolled in this program. In 1995–96, 5 degrees were earned at a distance through this program.
Application requirements *Prior education:* undergraduate degree. *Other requirements:* GRE, college transcripts, letter(s) of recommendation.
On-campus requirements For final exams.
Program contact Marco Dominguez Lerma, Student Affairs Officer, University of California, Santa Barbara, Off Campus Studies Department, Santa Barbara, CA 93106. Phone: 805-893-4056. Fax: 805-893-4943. E-mail: mdominguez@xlrn.ucsb.edu.

▶ *Electrical and Computer Engineering (MS)*
In the fall of 1996 there were 25 students enrolled in this program. In 1995–96, 3 degrees were earned at a distance through this program.
Application requirements *Prior education:* baccalaureate degree. *Other requirements:* GRE, college transcripts, an essay or personal statement, letter(s) of recommendation, an application fee of $50.
Completion requirements 36 quarters are required. 30 must be completed through the institution.
On-campus requirements For final exams.
Program contact Marco Dominguez Lerma, Student Affairs Officer, University of California, Santa Barbara, Off Campus Studies Department, Santa Barbara, CA 93106. Phone: 805-893-4056. Fax: 805-893-4943. E-mail: mdominguez@xlrn.ucsb.edu.

Profiles: University of California, Santa Barbara

INDIVIDUAL COURSE SUBJECT AREAS

Undergraduate
Area, ethnic, and cultural studies; creative writing; developmental and child psychology; educational psychology; English composition; English language and literature; fine arts; history; liberal arts, general studies, and humanities; music; philosophy and religion; political science; sociology

Graduate
Computer and information sciences; electrical engineering

Noncredit
Accounting; business; business administration and management; communications; computer and information sciences; creative writing; developmental and child psychology; electrical engineering; English as a second language (ESL); English composition; English language and literature; fine arts; history; human resources management; industrial psychology; law and legal studies; liberal arts, general studies, and humanities; music; philosophy and religion; political science; social psychology; sociology

UNIVERSITY OF CALIFORNIA, SANTA CRUZ

Santa Cruz, California

Media Services

University of California, Santa Cruz, founded in 1965, is a state-supported university. It is accredited by the Western Association of Schools and Colleges, Inc. It first offered distance learning courses in 1995.
Course delivery sites Courses are delivered to other colleges.
Media Courses are delivered via videoconferencing.
Restrictions Programs are available to in-state students only.
Services Distance learners have access to library services, academic advising, tutoring, career placement assistance at a distance. Financial aid is available to distance learners.
Contact Videoconferencing and Distance Education Coordinator, University of California, Santa Cruz, 113 Communications Building, Santa Cruz, CA 95064. *Telephone:* 408-459-5790. *Fax:* 408-459-3953. *Web site:* http://media.ucsc.edu.

INDIVIDUAL COURSE SUBJECT AREAS

Undergraduate
Computer and information sciences; economics; history; liberal arts, general studies, and humanities; political science

Graduate
Computer and information sciences; economics; history; liberal arts, general studies, and humanities; political science

UNIVERSITY OF CENTRAL OKLAHOMA

Edmond, Oklahoma

Continuing Education

University of Central Oklahoma, founded in 1890, is a state-supported comprehensive institution. It is accredited by the North Central Association of Colleges and Schools.
Course delivery sites Courses are delivered to your workplace, other colleges, off-campus center(s).
Media Courses are delivered via television, videotapes, videoconferencing, computer software, World Wide Web, e-mail, print. Students and teachers interact via videoconferencing, mail, telephone, fax, e-mail.
Restrictions Programs are available to in-state students only.
Services Distance learners have access to library services, academic advising, career placement assistance at a distance.
Credit-earning options Students may transfer credits from another institution.
Typical costs *Undergraduate:* Tuition of $57.20 per credit hour for in-state residents. Tuition of $130.70 per credit hour for out-of-state residents. *Graduate:* Tuition of $72.20 per credit hour for in-state residents. Tuition of $167.20 per credit hour for out-of-state residents. Costs may vary by course level. Financial aid is available to distance learners.
Contact Continuing Education, University of Central Oklahoma, 100 North University Drive, Edmond, OK 73034. *Telephone:* 405-341-2980, Ext. 2413. *Fax:* 405-330-3803.

INDIVIDUAL COURSE SUBJECT AREAS

Undergraduate
Education; education administration; European languages and literatures; law and legal studies; visual and performing arts

Graduate
Education; education administration; law and legal studies; visual and performing arts

THE UNIVERSITY OF CHARLESTON

Charleston, West Virginia

Off-Campus Programs

The University of Charleston, founded in 1888, is an independent-nonprofit comprehensive institution. It is accredited by the North Central Association of Colleges and Schools. It first offered distance learning courses in 1982. In 1996–97, it offered 4 courses at a distance. In the fall of 1996, there was a total of 30 students enrolled in distance learning courses.
Course delivery sites Courses are delivered to your home, your workplace, military bases.
Media Courses are delivered via computer software, e-mail, print. Students and teachers interact via mail, telephone, fax, e-mail.
Services Distance learners have access to library services, the campus computer network at a distance.
Credit-earning options Students may transfer credits from another institution or may earn credits through standardized exams, institutionally developed exams, portfolio assessment, military training, business training.
Registration Students may register by mail, fax, phone.
Contact James Hoyer, Director of Off-Campus Programs, The University of Charleston, 2300 Mac Corkle Avenue, SE, Charleston, WV 25304. *Telephone:* 304-357-4814. *Fax:* 304-357-4715. *E-mail:* jhoyer@citynet.net. *Web site:* http://uchaswv.edu.

INDIVIDUAL COURSE SUBJECT AREAS

Undergraduate
Business; computer and information sciences; English language and literature

Noncredit
Business; computer and information sciences; English language and literature

UNIVERSITY OF CINCINNATI

Cincinnati, Ohio

College of Evening and Continuing Education (CECE)

University of Cincinnati, founded in 1819, is a state-supported university. It is accredited by the North Central Association of Colleges and Schools. It first offered distance learning courses in 1976. In 1996–97, it offered 55 courses at a distance. In the fall of 1996, there was a total of 575 students enrolled in distance learning courses.

Course delivery sites Courses are delivered to your home, 4 off-campus centers in Adams, Goshen, Grant Counties, Warren.
Media Courses are delivered via television, videotapes, videoconferencing, World Wide Web, e-mail, print. Students and teachers interact via videoconferencing, audioconferencing, mail, telephone, fax, e-mail. A computer is required for some courses.
Services Distance learners have access to library services, the campus computer network, e-mail services at a distance.
Credit-earning options Students may transfer credits from another institution or may earn credits through standardized exams, portfolio assessment.
Typical costs *Undergraduate:* Tuition of $115 per credit for in-state residents. Tuition of $290 per credit for out-of-state residents. *Graduate:* Tuition of $182 per credit for in-state residents. Tuition of $347 per credit for out-of-state residents. *Noncredit courses:* $69–$125 per course. Costs may vary by campus or location, specific program of study, number of credits taken. Financial aid is available to distance learners.
Registration Students may register by mail, fax, phone.
Contact Melody Clark, Director, Special Projects, University of Cincinnati, College of Evening and Continued Education, PO Box 210019, Cincinnati, OH 45221-0019. *Telephone:* 513-556-9154. *Fax:* 513-556-6380. *E-mail:* melody.clark@uc.edu. *Web site:* http://www.uc.edu/www/cece.

DEGREE & CERTIFICATE PROGRAMS

Associate Degrees

▶ *Fire Science Administration (AAS)*
Application requirements *Prior education:* high school diploma or equivalent. *Other requirements:* high school transcript, college transcripts, an application fee of $30, at least 5 years work experience.
Completion requirements 92 quarter credits are required.
Program contact Patrick Reynolds, Director, University of Cincinnati, 2220 Victory Parkway, Cincinnati, OH 45206. Phone: 513-556-6583. Fax: 513-556-4856. E-mail: ptreynolds@aol.com.

Baccalaureate Degrees

▶ *Fire Science Administration (BS)*
Application requirements *Prior education:* high school diploma or equivalent. *Other requirements:* high school transcript, college transcripts, an application fee of $30, at least 5 years work experience.
Completion requirements 186 quarter credits are required.
Program contact Patrick Reynolds, Director, University of Cincinnati, 2220 Victory Parkway, Cincinnati, OH 45206. Phone: 513-556-6583. Fax: 513-556-4856. E-mail: ptreynolds@aol.com.

▶ *Nursing (BSN)*
Restrictions This program is available to in-state students only.
Application requirements *Prior education:* associate degree. *Other requirements:* high school transcript, college transcripts, an essay or personal statement, letter(s) of recommendation, an application fee of $30.
Completion requirements 185 quarter credits are required. 45 quarter credits must be completed through the institution.
Program contact LaVern Sutton, Director of the Office of Student Affairs, University of Cincinnati, College of Nursing and Health, PO Box 210038, Cincinnati, OH 45221-0038. Phone: 513-558-0206. Fax: 513-558-7523. E-mail: lavern.sutton@uc.edu.

Graduate Degrees

▶ *Nursing (MSN)*
Restrictions This program is available to in-state students only.
Application requirements *Prior education:* baccalaureate degree. *Other requirements:* GRE, high school transcript, college transcripts, an essay or personal statement, letter(s) of recommendation, an application fee of $30.
Completion requirements 227 quarter credits are required. *Maximum time for completion:* seven years.
Program contact LaVern Sutton, Director of the Office of Student Affairs, University of Cincinnati, College of Nursing and Health, PO Box 210038, Cincinnati, OH 45221-0038. Phone: 513-558-0206. Fax: 513-558-7523. E-mail: lavern.sutton@uc.edu.

INDIVIDUAL COURSE SUBJECT AREAS

Undergraduate
Business; business administration and management; criminal justice; economics; ethics; fire science; history; logic; nursing; sociology

Graduate
Nursing

UNIVERSITY OF CINCINNATI RAYMOND WALTERS COLLEGE

Cincinnati, Ohio

Outreach and Continuing Education

University of Cincinnati Raymond Walters College, founded in 1967, is a state-supported two-year college. It is accredited by the North Central Association of Colleges and Schools. It first offered distance learning courses in 1995. In 1996–97, it offered 14 courses at a distance. In the fall of 1996, there was a total of 54 students enrolled in distance learning courses.

Course delivery sites Courses are delivered to your workplace.
Media Courses are delivered via computer software. Students and teachers interact via mail, telephone, fax, e-mail, computer conferencing. A computer is required for some courses.
Restrictions Programs are available to local area students only.
Services Distance learners have access to library services, the campus computer network, e-mail services at a distance.
Credit-earning options Students may transfer credits from another institution or may earn credits through examinations, military training, business training.
Typical costs *Undergraduate:* Tuition of $96 per credit for in-state residents. Tuition of $243 per credit for out-of-state residents. *Graduate:* Tuition of $182 per credit for in-state residents. Tuition of $347 per credit for out-of-state residents. $10 tape package. *Noncredit courses:* $288 per course. Costs may vary by campus or location, specific program of study, number of credits taken. Financial aid is available to distance learners enrolled full-time or part-time.
Registration Students may register by mail, phone.
Contact Dr. Susan Kemper, Assistant Dean, University of Cincinnati Raymond Walters College, 9555 Plainfield Road, Cincinnati, OH 45236-1096. *Telephone:* 513-745-5776. *Fax:* 513-745-8315. *E-mail:* susan.kemper@uc.edu.

Profiles: University of Cincinnati Raymond Walters College

INDIVIDUAL COURSE SUBJECT AREAS

Undergraduate
Biological and life sciences; business; communications; English composition; English language and literature; health professions and related sciences; human resources management; sociology

UNIVERSITY OF COLORADO AT BOULDER

Boulder, Colorado

Center for Advanced Training in Engineering and Computer Science (CATECS)

University of Colorado at Boulder, founded in 1876, is a state-supported university. It is accredited by the North Central Association of Colleges and Schools. It first offered distance learning courses in 1983. In 1996–97, it offered 129 courses at a distance. In the fall of 1996, there was a total of 500 students enrolled in distance learning courses.

Course delivery sites Courses are delivered to your home, your workplace, military bases, other colleges, 1 off-campus center in Littleton.
Media Courses are delivered via television, videotapes, videoconferencing. Students and teachers interact via videoconferencing, mail, telephone, fax, e-mail. A computer is required for some courses.
Services Distance learners have access to the campus computer network, e-mail services, academic advising at a distance.
Credit-earning options Students may transfer credits from another institution.
Typical costs Tuition of $996 per course. *Noncredit courses:* $996 per course. Costs may vary by number of credits taken, special mailing needs, special thesis/project options. Financial aid is available to distance learners.
Registration Students may register by mail, fax.
Contact Vincent P. Micucci, Director, CATECS, University of Colorado at Boulder, Campus Box 435, Boulder, CO 80309. *Telephone:* 303-492-6048. *Fax:* 303-492-5987. *E-mail:* micucciv@spot.colorado.edu. *Web site:* http://www.colorado.edu/CATECS.

DEGREE & CERTIFICATE PROGRAMS

Graduate Degrees

▶ *Aerospace Engineering (ME, MS)*
Application requirements *Prior education:* undergraduate degree in engineering or science. *Other requirements:* GRE, college transcripts, letter(s) of recommendation, an application fee of $40, 3.0 GPA.
Completion requirements 30 credit hours are required. 21 credit hours must be completed through the institution. *Maximum time for completion:* six years for ME, four years for MS.
On-campus requirements For defense of final project for ME candidates.
Program contact Mark Balas, Graduate Committee, University of Colorado at Boulder, Aerospace Department, CB 429, Boulder, CO 80309. Phone: 303-492-3177.

▶ *Computer Science (ME)*
Application requirements *Prior education:* baccalaureate degree. *Other requirements:* college transcripts, letter(s) of recommendation, an application fee of $40, 3.0 GPA.
Completion requirements 30 credit hours are required. 21 credit hours must be completed through the institution. *Maximum time for completion:* six years.
On-campus requirements To defend final project.
Program contact Hal Gabow, Graduate Director, University of Colorado at Boulder, Computer Science Department CB 430, Boulder, CO 80309. Phone: 303-492-6862. E-mail: hal@cs.colorado.edu.

▶ *Electrical/Computer Engineering (ME, MS)*
Application requirements *Prior education:* undergraduate degree in engineering with a GPA of at least 3.0. *Other requirements:* GRE, college transcripts, letter(s) of recommendation, an application fee of $40.
Completion requirements 30 credit hours are required. 21 credit hours must be completed through the institution. *Maximum time for completion:* six years for ME, four years for MS.
On-campus requirements To defend thesis or project if student's program includes either.
Program contact Thomas Cathey, Graduate Director, University of Colorado at Boulder, Electrical Engineering Department CB 425, Boulder, CO 80309. Phone: 303-492-1888. E-mail: cathey@colorado.edu.

▶ *Engineering Management (ME)*
Application requirements *Prior education:* undergraduate degree in engineering, science, or math with a GPA of at least 3.0. *Other requirements:* GRE, college transcripts, an essay or personal statement, letter(s) of recommendation, an application fee of $40, 2 years of professional work experience.
Completion requirements 30 credit hours are required. 21 credit hours must be completed through the institution. *Maximum time for completion:* six years.
On-campus requirements To defend final project.
Program contact William Daughton, Program Director, University of Colorado at Boulder, Engineering Management Program, CB 435, Boulder, CO 80309. Phone: 303-492-2570. E-mail: daughton@spot.colorado.edu.

▶ *Telecommunications (ME, MS)*
Application requirements *Prior education:* baccalaureate degree. *Other requirements:* GRE and/or GMAT (for applicants with a GPA under 3.0), college transcripts, letter(s) of recommendation, an application fee of $40.
Completion requirements 30 credit hours for ME, 32 credit hours for MS are required. All but 9 credit hours of course work must be completed through the institution. *Maximum time for completion:* six years for ME, four years for MS.
On-campus requirements To defend thesis/project if student chooses thesis/project option.
Program contact Gerald Mitchell, Graduate Director, University of Colorado at Boulder, Telecom Program, CB 530, Boulder, CO 80309. Phone: 303-492-3761. E-mail: gerald.mitchell@colorado.edu.

INDIVIDUAL COURSE SUBJECT AREAS

Graduate
Aerospace, aeronautical engineering; civil engineering; computer and information sciences; electrical engineering; engineering-related technologies; engineering/industrial management; environmental engineering; mechanical engineering; telecommunications

Noncredit
Aerospace, aeronautical engineering; civil engineering; computer and information sciences; electrical engineering; engineering-related technologies; engineering/industrial management; environmental engineering; mechanical engineering; telecommunications

UNIVERSITY OF COLORADO AT COLORADO SPRINGS

Colorado Springs, Colorado

CU-NET

University of Colorado at Colorado Springs, founded in 1965, is a state-supported comprehensive institution. It is accredited by the North Central Association of Colleges and Schools.
Course delivery sites Courses are delivered to your home, your workplace, military bases, other colleges.
Media Courses are delivered via television, videotapes. Students and teachers interact via mail, telephone, fax.
Restrictions Programs other than certificate and MBA limited to local broadcast area.
Credit-earning options Students may transfer credits from another institution.
Typical costs *Undergraduate:* Tuition of $99 per credit. *Graduate:* Tuition of $350 per course. MBA program: $750 per course.
Contact Mind Extension University, University of Colorado at Colorado Springs, 9697 East Mineral Avenue, Englewood, CO 80112. *Telephone:* 800-777-MIND.

DEGREE & CERTIFICATE PROGRAMS

Graduate Degrees
▶ *Business/Public Administration (MBA/MPA)*
Application requirements *Prior education:* baccalaureate degree. *Other requirements:* GMAT, TOEFL, college transcripts, letter(s) of recommendation, an application fee of $65, resume.
Completion requirements 36 credits are required. 30 credits must be completed through the institution. *Maximum time for completion:* five years.

Undergraduate Certificates
▶ *Early Reading Instruction*
Application requirements *Prior education:* baccalaureate degree.
Completion requirements 8 credit hours are required. 8 credit hours must be completed through the institution.

INDIVIDUAL COURSE SUBJECT AREAS

Undergraduate
Business administration and management; geology; liberal arts, general studies, and humanities

Graduate
Business administration and management; geology; liberal arts, general studies, and humanities

UNIVERSITY OF DALLAS

Irving, Texas

Center for Distance Education

University of Dallas, founded in 1955, is an independent-religious Roman Catholic university. It is accredited by the Southern Association of Colleges and Schools. It first offered distance learning courses in 1970. In 1996–97, it offered 21 courses at a distance. In the fall of 1996, there was a total of 250 students enrolled in distance learning courses.
Course delivery sites Courses are delivered to your workplace, military bases.
Media Courses are delivered via television, videotapes, videoconferencing, computer software, World Wide Web, e-mail, print. Students and teachers interact via videoconferencing, telephone, fax, e-mail. A computer is required for some courses.
Services Distance learners have access to academic advising, tutoring at a distance.
Credit-earning options Students may transfer credits from another institution or may earn credits through institutionally developed exams.
Typical costs Tuition of $1101 per course. Costs may vary by campus or location. Financial aid is available to distance learners enrolled full-time or part-time.
Registration Students may register by mail, fax, phone, e-mail.
Contact Roxanne Del Rio, Director of Admissions, University of Dallas, 1845 East Northgate Drive, Irving, TX 75062. *Telephone:* 800-UDAL-MBA. *Fax:* 214-721-4009. *E-mail:* rdelrio@gsm.udallas.edu. *Web site:* http://gsm.udallas.edu.

Special note
The University of Dallas Graduate School of Management offers its MBA in various modes of distance learning. The Health Services Management MBA utilizes satellite video broadcasting as a primary means of delivery to students from coast to coast. In this program, students may complete their entire MBA at their home sites. The Telecommunications Management Graduate Certificate Program is offered using video-conferencing systems in cooperation with various corporations for their employees' graduate education.
The University of Dallas will soon offer distance learning courses using the Internet. Students using an Internet Browser will be able to complete an entire course using this medium. Plans include offering a Telecommunications Management Certificate Program on the Internet as well as selected courses in other disciplines, including MIS and the MBA core.
The University of Dallas is working in partnership with corporate clients to develop mutually beneficial graduate-level, credit-bearing distance learning programs. The University is actively seeking other such alliances. For those interested in exploring relationships, please contact the University of Dallas, Graduate School of Management Distance Learning Program Director.

DEGREE & CERTIFICATE PROGRAMS

Graduate Degrees
▶ *Health Services Management (MBA)*
In the fall of 1996 there were 180 students enrolled in this program. In 1995–96, 35 degrees were earned at a distance through this program.
Application requirements *Prior education:* baccalaureate degree. *Other requirements:* college transcripts, letter(s) of recommendation.
Completion requirements 49 credit hours are required. 36 credit hours must be completed through the institution. *Maximum time for completion:* five years.

INDIVIDUAL COURSE SUBJECT AREAS

Graduate
Accounting; business; business administration and management; finance; health professions and related sciences; human resources management; insurance; marketing; organizational behavior studies; telecommunications

Profiles: University of Dayton

UNIVERSITY OF DAYTON

Dayton, Ohio

Continuing Education

University of Dayton, founded in 1850, is an independent-religious Roman Catholic university. It is accredited by the North Central Association of Colleges and Schools.
Course delivery sites Courses are delivered to your home.
Media Courses are delivered via television, videotapes, videoconferencing, print. Students and teachers interact via mail, telephone, fax, e-mail.
Restrictions Students must be able to travel to campus.
Credit-earning options Students may earn credits through examinations.
Typical costs Contact school for information.
Contact Office of Continuing Education, University of Dayton, 300 College Park, Dayton, OH 45469-1611. *Telephone:* 937-229-2347. *Fax:* 937-229-4666.

INDIVIDUAL COURSE SUBJECT AREAS

Undergraduate
Engineering; philosophy and religion

Noncredit
Philosophy and religion

UNIVERSITY OF DELAWARE

Newark, Delaware

Division of Continuing and Distance Education

University of Delaware, founded in 1743, is a state-related university. It is accredited by the Middle States Association of Colleges and Schools. It first offered distance learning courses in 1988. In 1996–97, it offered 180 courses at a distance. In the fall of 1996, there was a total of 652 students enrolled in distance learning courses.
Course delivery sites Courses are delivered to your home, your workplace, military bases, Atlantic Community College (Mays Landing, NJ), Northampton County Area Community College (Bethlehem, PA).
Media Courses are delivered via videotapes, videoconferencing, print. Students and teachers interact via videoconferencing, mail, telephone, fax, e-mail. A computer is required for some courses.
Restrictions Courses are available to US students only.
Services Distance learners have access to library services, the campus computer network, e-mail services, academic advising, career placement assistance at a distance.
Credit-earning options Students may transfer credits from another institution or may earn credits through institutionally developed exams.
Typical costs *Undergraduate:* Tuition of $172 per credit plus mandatory fees of $90 per course for in-state residents. Tuition of $490 per credit plus mandatory fees of $90 per course for out-of-state residents. *Graduate:* Tuition of $229 per credit plus mandatory fees of $90 per course for in-state residents. Tuition of $653 per credit plus mandatory fees of $90 per course for out-of-state residents. Work site instruction fee: undergraduate: $199 per credit; graduate: $559 per credit. *Noncredit courses:* $29.95 rental fee for nursing topics, $3900 for a full 36 hours of engineering courses. Costs may vary by number of credits taken. Financial aid is available to distance learners enrolled full-time or part-time.
Registration Students may register by mail, fax, phone.

Contact Mary Pritchard, Manager, Focus/Distance Learning, University of Delaware, John M. Clayton Hall, Newark, DE 19716. *Telephone:* 302-831-6442. *Fax:* 302-831-3292. *E-mail:* mary.pritchard@mvs.udel.edu. *Web site:* http://www.udel.edu.

DEGREE & CERTIFICATE PROGRAMS

Baccalaureate Degrees

▶ *Human Resources (BS)*
In the fall of 1996 there were 30 students enrolled in this program.
Application requirements High school transcript, college transcripts, an application fee of $40, 2.5 GPA in previous college work.
Completion requirements 120 semester credits are required. 30 semester credits must be completed through the institution.
On-campus requirements Two 10-day campus institutes.

▶ *Nursing (BS)*
In the fall of 1996 there were 440 students enrolled in this program. In 1995–96, 7 degrees were earned at a distance through this program.
Application requirements *Prior education:* nursing diploma and current license. *Other requirements:* high school transcript, college transcripts, an application fee of $40, RN license.
Completion requirements 125 semester credits are required. Last 30 credits (including 3 on-campus weekend courses) must be completed through the institution. This is a degree completion program. *Maximum time for completion:* five years after beginning first nursing course.
On-campus requirements Three weekends.
Program contact Dr. Madeline Lambrecht, Director, Division of Special Programs, University of Delaware, College of Nursing, Newark, DE 19716. Phone: 302-831-4549. Fax: 302-831-4550. E-mail: dsp@mvs.udel.edu.

INDIVIDUAL COURSE SUBJECT AREAS

Undergraduate
Agriculture; algebra; American (US) history; area, ethnic, and cultural studies; biology; business administration and management; calculus; chemical engineering; chemistry; child care and development; Classical languages and literatures; developmental and child psychology; economics; educational psychology; electrical engineering; engineering-related technologies; English composition; English language and literature; ethics; foods and nutrition studies; home economics and family studies; hospitality services management; human resources management; individual and family development studies; instructional media; liberal arts, general studies, and humanities; marketing; mathematics; mechanical engineering; microbiology; nursing; organizational behavior studies; philosophy and religion; political science; religious studies; sociology; teacher education

Graduate
Aerospace, aeronautical engineering; biology; chemical engineering; civil engineering; education administration; educational psychology; electrical engineering; engineering mechanics; environmental engineering; instructional media; mechanical engineering; nursing; political science; teacher education

Noncredit
Chemical engineering; electrical engineering; engineering mechanics; English composition; environmental engineering; fine arts; microbiology; nursing; protective services

See full description on page 496.

UNIVERSITY OF GEORGIA

Athens, Georgia

Georgia Center for Continuing Education

University of Georgia, founded in 1785, is a state-supported university. It is accredited by the Southern Association of Colleges and Schools. It first offered distance learning courses in 1985. In 1996–97, it offered 163 courses at a distance. In the fall of 1996, there was a total of 4,497 students enrolled in distance learning courses.
Course delivery sites Courses are delivered to your home, your workplace.
Media Courses are delivered via videotapes, computer software, World Wide Web, e-mail, print. Students and teachers interact via mail, telephone, fax, e-mail.
Services Distance learners have access to library services, e-mail services at a distance.
Credit-earning options Students may earn credits through institutionally developed exams.
Typical costs Tuition of $59 per quarter hour. *Noncredit courses:* $172–$499 per course.
Registration Students may register by mail, fax, phone, World Wide Web.
Contact Dr. Edward G. Simpson, Jr., Associate Vice President for Public Service and Outreach, University of Georgia, Georgia Center for Continuing Education, Athens, GA 30602-3603. *Telephone:* 706-542-3451. *Fax:* 706-542-1991. *E-mail:* simpsone@gactr.uga.edu. *Web site:* http://www.gactr.uga.edu.

DEGREE & CERTIFICATE PROGRAMS

Undergraduate Certificates
▶ *Turfgrass Management*
In the fall of 1996 there were 900 students enrolled in this program. In 1995–96, 122 certificates were earned at a distance through this program.
Application requirements *Prior education:* none required.
Completion requirements 120 hours are required. *Maximum time for completion:* one year.
Program contact Jackie Chastain, Student Representative, University of Georgia, Georgia Center for Continuing Education, Room 164, Athens, GA 30602-3603. Phone: 706-542-1756. Fax: 706-542-7537. E-mail: chastainj@gactr.uga.edu.

INDIVIDUAL COURSE SUBJECT AREAS

Undergraduate
Accounting; administrative and secretarial services; advertising; agriculture; area, ethnic, and cultural studies; biological and life sciences; biology; business; business administration and management; Classical languages and literatures; communications; conservation and natural resources; developmental and child psychology; economics; education; educational psychology; English composition; English language and literature; European languages and literatures; fine arts; geology; health and physical education/fitness; health professions and related sciences; history; home economics and family studies; human resources management; journalism; law and legal studies; liberal arts, general studies, and humanities; mathematics; philosophy and religion; political science; psychology; public health; social psychology; sociology; teacher education; theological studies; visual and performing arts

Noncredit
Area, ethnic, and cultural studies; business administration and management; developmental and child psychology; health professions and related sciences; veterinary science
See full description on page 498.

UNIVERSITY OF GREAT FALLS

Great Falls, Montana

University of Great Falls, founded in 1932, is an independent-religious Roman Catholic comprehensive institution. It is accredited by the Northwest Association of Schools and Colleges.
Course delivery sites Courses are delivered to your home, other colleges.
Media Courses are delivered via television, videotapes, videoconferencing, audioconferencing, print.
Credit-earning options Students may transfer credits from another institution or may earn credits through examinations, portfolio assessment.
Contact Telecommunications Office, University of Great Falls, 1301 20th Street, South, Great Falls, MT 59405. *Telephone:* 406-791-5321. *Fax:* 406-791-5394.

DEGREE & CERTIFICATE PROGRAMS

Associate Degrees
▶ *Business Administration (AA, AS)*
▶ *Chemical Dependency Counseling (AA, AS)*
▶ *Criminal Justice (AA, AS)*
▶ *Human Services (AA, AS)*
▶ *Microcomputer Management (AA, AS)*
▶ *Paralegal Studies (AA, AS)*

Baccalaureate Degrees
▶ *Business Administration (BA, BS)*
On-campus requirements One weekend.
▶ *Computer Science (BA, BS)*
▶ *Counseling Psychology (BA, BS)*
On-campus requirements One weekend class.
▶ *Criminal Justice (BA, BS)*
▶ *Health Care Administration (BA, BS)*
▶ *Human Services (BA, BS)*
▶ *Microcomputer Management (BA, BS)*
▶ *Paralegal (BA, BS)*
▶ *Religious Studies (BA, BS)*
▶ *Sociology (BA, BS)*

INDIVIDUAL COURSE SUBJECT AREAS

Undergraduate
Accounting; area, ethnic, and cultural studies; astronomy and astrophysics; biological and life sciences; biology; botany; business; business administration and management; chemistry; communications; computer and information sciences; creative writing; developmental and child psychology; economics; education; education administration; educational psychology; English as a second language (ESL); English composition; English language and literature; geology; health and physical education/fitness; health professions and related sciences; history; law and legal

Profiles: University of Great Falls

studies; liberal arts, general studies, and humanities; mathematics; philosophy and religion; physical sciences; physics; political science; protective services; psychology; public administration and services; social psychology; social sciences; social work; sociology; special education; teacher education; theological studies; visual and performing arts

UNIVERSITY OF GUELPH

Guelph, Ontario, Canada

Office of Open Learning–Distance Education

University of Guelph, founded in 1964, is a province-supported university. It is provincially chartered. It first offered distance learning courses in 1984.
Course delivery sites Courses are delivered to your home, your workplace.
Media Courses are delivered via videotapes, audiotapes, computer software, World Wide Web, e-mail, print. Students and teachers interact via audioconferencing, mail, telephone, fax, e-mail.
Services Distance learners have access to library services, academic advising, tutoring, career placement assistance at a distance.
Credit-earning options Students may transfer credits from another institution or may earn credits through examinations, business training.
Typical costs Tuition of $372 per course. Cost given in Canadian dollars. *Noncredit courses:* $372 per course. Financial aid is available to distance learners.
Contact Carol Partland, Distance Education Program Manager, University of Guelph, 153 Johnston Hall, Guelph, ON N1G 2W1, Canada. *Telephone:* 519-824-4120, Ext. 6050. *Fax:* 519-824-1112. *E-mail:* cpartlan@openlrng.uoguelph.ca.

DEGREE & CERTIFICATE PROGRAMS

Undergraduate Certificates
▶ *Food Science*
Application requirements Introductory chemistry and microbiology.
Completion requirements 5 courses are required. 5 courses must be completed through the institution.

INDIVIDUAL COURSE SUBJECT AREAS

Undergraduate
Agriculture; chemistry; Classical languages and literatures; conservation and natural resources; developmental and child psychology; economics; English composition; English language and literature; French language and literature; geology; history; home economics and family studies; industrial psychology; microbiology; music; physics; political science; public administration and services; social psychology

Noncredit
Agriculture; mathematics

UNIVERSITY OF HAWAII–LEEWARD COMMUNITY COLLEGE

Pearl City, Hawaii

University of Hawaii–Leeward Community College, founded in 1968, is a state-supported two-year college. It is accredited by the Western Association of Schools and Colleges, Inc. It first offered distance learning courses in 1990.
Course delivery sites Courses are delivered to your home, other colleges, education centers.
Media Courses are delivered via television, videotapes, videoconferencing, World Wide Web, e-mail. Students and teachers interact via videoconferencing, audioconferencing, mail, telephone, fax, e-mail.
Services Distance learners have access to academic advising, career placement assistance at a distance.
Credit-earning options Students may transfer credits from another institution or may earn credits through examinations.
Typical costs Tuition of $21 per credit hour for in-state residents. Tuition of $129 per credit hour plus mandatory fees of $25 per semester for out-of-state residents. Financial aid is available to distance learners.
Contact Irwin I. Yamamoto, Distance Learning Specialist, University of Hawaii–Leeward Community College, Educational Media Center, 96-045 Ala Ike, Pearl City, HI 96782. *Telephone:* 808-455-0272. *Fax:* 808-455-0473. *E-mail:* iyamamot@hawaii.edu.

INDIVIDUAL COURSE SUBJECT AREAS

Undergraduate
Administrative and secretarial services; agriculture; Asian languages and literatures; astronomy and astrophysics; botany; chemistry; geology; health and physical education/fitness; history; liberal arts, general studies, and humanities; mathematics; music; philosophy and religion; radio and television broadcasting

UNIVERSITY OF HAWAII–MAUI COMMUNITY COLLEGE

Kahului, Hawaii

University of Hawaii–Maui Community College, founded in 1967, is a state-supported two-year college. It is accredited by the Western Association of Schools and Colleges, Inc. It first offered distance learning courses in 1970. In 1996–97, it offered 93 courses at a distance. In the fall of 1996, there was a total of 275 students enrolled in distance learning courses.
Course delivery sites Courses are delivered to your home, your workplace, military bases, 3 off-campus centers in Hana, Kaunakakai, Lanai City.
Media Courses are delivered via television, computer software. Students and teachers interact via videoconferencing, audioconferencing, mail, telephone, fax, e-mail, site visits.
Services Distance learners have access to library services, the campus computer network, e-mail services, academic advising at a distance.
Credit-earning options Students may transfer credits from another institution.
Typical costs Tuition of $32 per credit for in-state residents. Tuition of $213 per credit for out-of-state residents. *Noncredit courses:* $30 per session. Costs may vary by number of credits taken. Financial aid is available to distance learners enrolled full-time or part-time.
Contact Alvin Tagomori, Dean of Students, University of Hawaii–Maui Community College, 310 Kaahumanu Avenue, Kahului, HI 96732. *Telephone:* 808-242-1268. *Fax:* 808-242-9618. *E-mail:* alvin.tagomori@mccada.mauicc.hawaii.edu.

DEGREE & CERTIFICATE PROGRAMS

Associate Degrees

▶ *Administration of Justice (AAS)*
Application requirements *Prior education:* high school diploma or equivalent. *Minimum age:* 18. *Other requirements:* an application fee of $25.
On-campus requirements For exams, orientation.
Program contact Steve Kameda, Registrar, University of Hawaii–Maui Community College, 310 Kaahumanu Avenue, Kahului, HI 96732. Phone: 808-984-3267.

▶ *Liberal Arts (AA)*
Application requirements *Prior education:* high school diploma or equivalent. *Minimum age:* 18. *Other requirements:* an application fee of $25.
Completion requirements 60 credits are required. 12 credits must be completed through the institution.
On-campus requirements For exams, orientation.
Program contact Steve Kameda, Registrar, University of Hawaii–Maui Community College, 310 Kaahumanu Avenue, Kahului, HI 96732. Phone: 808-984-3267.

Undergraduate Certificates

▶ *Administration of Justice, Business*
Application requirements *Prior education:* high school diploma or equivalent. *Minimum age:* 18. *Other requirements:* an application fee of $25.
Completion requirements 12 credits must be completed through the institution.
On-campus requirements For exams, orientation.
Program contact Steve Kameda, Registrar, University of Hawaii–Maui Community College, 310 Kaahumanu Avenue, Kahului, HI 96732. Phone: 808-984-3267.

INDIVIDUAL COURSE SUBJECT AREAS

Undergraduate
Accounting; administrative and secretarial services; agriculture; area, ethnic, and cultural studies; astronomy and astrophysics; biological and life sciences; biology; business; business administration and management; communications; computer and information sciences; design; developmental and child psychology; education; English composition; English language and literature; health and physical education/fitness; history; hospitality services management; human resources management; liberal arts, general studies, and humanities; mathematics; music; nursing; philosophy and religion; protective services; psychology; public administration and services; social psychology; social sciences; social work; sociology; teacher education; visual and performing arts

Noncredit
Computer and information sciences

UNIVERSITY OF HOUSTON

Houston, Texas

Division of Distance and Continuing Education

University of Houston, founded in 1927, is a state-supported university. It is accredited by the Southern Association of Colleges and Schools. It first offered distance learning courses in 1984. In 1996–97, it offered 75 courses at a distance. In the fall of 1996, there was a total of 1,800 students enrolled in distance learning courses.

Course delivery sites Courses are delivered to your home, your workplace, Alvin Community College (Alvin), Galveston College (Galveston), North Harris College (Houston), San Jacinto College–South Campus (Houston), Wharton County Junior College (Wharton), 4 off-campus centers in Conroe, Houston, Katy, Sugar Land, NASA, COMPAQ Computer Corporation, Texas Instruments.
Media Courses are delivered via television, videotapes, videoconferencing, World Wide Web, e-mail, print. Students and teachers interact via mail, telephone, fax, e-mail. A computer is required for some courses.
Services Distance learners have access to library services, the campus computer network, e-mail services, academic advising, tutoring, career placement assistance at a distance.
Credit-earning options Students may transfer credits from another institution or may earn credits through standardized exams, institutionally developed exams.
Typical costs *Undergraduate:* Tuition of $342.50 per course plus mandatory fees of $50 per semester for in-state residents. Tuition of $960.50 per course plus mandatory fees of $50 per semester for out-of-state residents. *Graduate:* Tuition of $390.50 per course plus mandatory fees of $50 per semester for in-state residents. Tuition of $960.50 per course plus mandatory fees of $50 per semester for out-of-state residents. *Noncredit courses:* $35–$500 per course. Costs may vary by specific program of study, number of credits taken, course delivery options, term of enrollment. Financial aid is available to distance learners enrolled full-time or part-time.
Registration Students may register by phone.
Contact Pam Williford, Distance Education Advisor, University of Houston, 4242 South Mason Road, Katy, TX 77450. *Telephone:* 281-395-2800. *Fax:* 281-395-2629. *E-mail:* deadvisor@uh.edu.

DEGREE & CERTIFICATE PROGRAMS

Baccalaureate Degrees

▶ *Computer Drafting Design (BST)*
In the fall of 1996 there were 10 students enrolled in this program.
Application requirements *Prior education:* high school diploma or equivalent. *Other requirements:* SAT or ACT, TOEFL (for international students), TASP, high school transcript, college transcripts, an application fee of $30 ($75 for international students), undergraduate application.
Completion requirements 132 credit hours are required. 30 credit hours must be completed through the institution. *Other requirements:* up to 66 hours may be transferred from a community college. Students must also pass the Writing Proficiency Exam.
On-campus requirements Half-day orientation, faculty meetings, exams.

▶ *Computer Engineering Technology (BST)*
In the fall of 1996 there were 10 students enrolled in this program.
Application requirements *Prior education:* high school diploma or equivalent. *Other requirements:* SAT or ACT, TOEFL (for international students), TASP, high school transcript, college transcripts, an application fee of $30 ($75 for international students), undergraduate application.
Completion requirements 132 credit hours are required. 30 credit hours must be completed through the institution. *Other requirements:* up to 66 hours may be transferred from a community college. Students must also pass the Writing Proficiency Exam.
On-campus requirements Half-day orientation, faculty meetings, exams.

▶ *English (BA)*
Application requirements *Prior education:* high school diploma or equivalent. *Other requirements:* SAT or ACT, TOEFL (for international students), TASP, high school transcript, college transcripts, an application fee of $30 ($75 for international students), undergraduate application.
Completion requirements 122 credit hours are required. 30 credit hours must be completed through the institution. *Other requirements:* up to 66 hours may be transferred from a community college. Students must also pass the Writing Proficiency Exam.
On-campus requirements Half-day orientation, faculty meetings, exams.

Profiles: University of Houston

▶ *Hotel and Restaurant Management (BS)*
In the fall of 1996 there were 20 students enrolled in this program.
Application requirements SAT or ACT, TOEFL (for international students), TASP, high school transcript, college transcripts, an application fee of $30 ($75 for international students), undergraduate application.
Completion requirements 132 credit hours are required. 30 credit hours must be completed through the institution. *Other requirements:* up to 66 hours may be transferred from a community college. Students must also pass the Writing Proficiency Exam.
On-campus requirements Half-day orientation, faculty meetings, exams.

▶ *Industrial Supervision (BST)*
In the fall of 1996 there were 12 students enrolled in this program.
Application requirements *Prior education:* high school diploma or equivalent. *Other requirements:* SAT or ACT, TOEFL (for international students), TASP, high school transcript, college transcripts, an application fee of $30 ($75 for international students), undergraduate application.
Completion requirements 125 credit hours are required. 30 credit hours must be completed through the institution. *Other requirements:* up to 66 hours may be transferred from a community college. Students must also pass the Writing Proficiency Exam.
On-campus requirements Half-day orientation, faculty meetings, exams.

▶ *Psychology (BA, BS)*
In the fall of 1996 there were 125 students enrolled in this program.
Application requirements *Prior education:* high school diploma or equivalent. *Other requirements:* SAT or ACT, TOEFL (for international students), TASP, high school transcript, college transcripts, an application fee of $30 ($75 for international students), undergraduate application.
Completion requirements 126 credit hours are required. 30 credit hours must be completed through the institution. *Other requirements:* up to 66 hours may be transferred from a community college. Students must also pass the Writing Proficiency Exam.
On-campus requirements Half-day orientation, faculty meetings, exams.

Graduate Degrees

▶ *Computer Science (MS)*
Restrictions This program is available to local area students only.
Application requirements *Prior education:* baccalaureate degree. *Other requirements:* GRE, TOEFL (for international students), college transcripts, letter(s) of recommendation, an application fee of $75 (for international students), official diploma or degree certificate, graduate application.
Completion requirements 36 credit hours are required. 21 credit hours must be completed through the institution. *Other requirements:* 6 hours Master's thesis. *Maximum time for completion:* five years.
On-campus requirements Half-day orientation, faculty meetings, exams.
Program contact Ernst L. Leiss, Director of Graduate Studies, University of Houston, Department of Computer Science, Houston, TX 77204-3475. Phone: 713-743-3350. Fax: 713-743-3335. E-mail: gradinfo@cs.uh.edu.

▶ *Electrical Engineering (MEE)*
In the fall of 1996 there were 20 students enrolled in this program.
Restrictions This program is available to local area students only.
Application requirements *Prior education:* BSEE or equivalent from an accredited institution. *Other requirements:* GRE, TOEFL (for international students), college transcripts, an essay or personal statement, letter(s) of recommendation, an application fee of $75 (for international students), graduate application, description of extracurricular activities, 3.0 GPA.
Completion requirements 36 credit hours are required. 27 credit hours must be completed through the institution. *Maximum time for completion:* five years.
On-campus requirements Half-day orientation, faculty meetings, exams, labs.
Program contact Dr. Charles Dalton, College of Engineering, University of Houston, 4800 Calhoun, Houston, TX 77204-4793. Phone: 713-743-4403. Fax: 713-743-4214.

▶ *Engineering Management (MIE)*
In the fall of 1996 there were 20 students enrolled in this program.
Restrictions This program is available to local area students only.
Application requirements *Prior education:* baccalaureate degree. *Other requirements:* GRE, TOEFL (for international students), college transcripts, letter(s) of recommendation, an application fee of $25 ($75 additional for international students), graduate application.
Completion requirements 36 credit hours are required. 27 credit hours must be completed through the institution. *Maximum time for completion:* five years.
On-campus requirements Half-day orientation, faculty meetings, exams.
Program contact Don Deal, College of Engineering, University of Houston, 4800 Calhoun, Houston, TX 77204-4812. Phone: 713-743-4191. Fax: 713-743-4190. E-mail: ddeal@uh.edu.

▶ *Hospitality Management (MHM)*
In the fall of 1996 there were 10 students enrolled in this program.
Application requirements GRE or GMAT (TOEFL for international students), college transcripts, an essay or personal statement, letter(s) of recommendation, an application fee of $25 ($75 additional for international students), current resume, graduate application.
Completion requirements 42 credit hours are required. 27 credit hours must be completed through the institution. *Maximum time for completion:* five years.
On-campus requirements Half-day orientation, faculty meetings, exams.
Program contact Lillian Binns, Graduate Advisor, University of Houston, Hilton College of Hotel and Restaurant Management, Houston, TX 77204-3902. Phone: 713-743-2457. Fax: 713-743-2498. E-mail: mhmhrm@uh.edu.

▶ *Training and Development (MSOT)*
In the fall of 1996 there were 35 students enrolled in this program.
Restrictions This program is available to in-state students only.
Application requirements *Prior education:* baccalaureate degree. *Other requirements:* GMAT, GRE or MAT, TOEFL (for international students), college transcripts, an essay or personal statement, letter(s) of recommendation, an application fee of $35 (additional $75 for international students), graduate application.
Completion requirements 36 credit hours are required. 21–27 credit hours must be completed through the institution. *Maximum time for completion:* five years.
On-campus requirements Half-day orientation, faculty meetings, exams.
Program contact Sue Schroeder, Graduate Advisor, University of Houston, College of Technology, Houston, TX 77204-2161. Phone: 713-743-4098. Fax: 713-743-4032.

INDIVIDUAL COURSE SUBJECT AREAS

Undergraduate
American literature; anthropology; communications; computer and information sciences; creative writing; developmental and child psychology; educational psychology; engineering-related technologies; English language and literature; European languages and literatures; film studies; geology; German language and literature; history; hospitality services management; journalism; liberal arts, general studies, and humanities; mathematics; political science; psychology; public health; social psychology; sociology; Spanish language and literature; visual and performing arts

Graduate
Accounting; business; business administration and management; computer and information sciences; curriculum and instruction; economics; education; education administration; educational psychology; electrical engineering; English as a second language (ESL); European languages and literatures; hospitality services management; industrial engineering; international business; social work; Spanish language and literature

See full description on page 500.

UNIVERSITY OF HOUSTON–CLEAR LAKE

Houston, Texas

University of Houston–Clear Lake, founded in 1974, is a state-supported upper-level institution. It is accredited by the Southern Association of Colleges and Schools. It first offered distance learning courses in 1995. In 1996–97, it offered 24 courses at a distance. In the fall of 1996, there was a total of 60 students enrolled in distance learning courses.
Course delivery sites Courses are delivered to your workplace, other colleges, 2 off-campus centers in Austin, Fort Bend.
Media Courses are delivered via videoconferencing, audioconferencing, computer software, World Wide Web, e-mail. Students and teachers interact via videoconferencing, telephone, fax, e-mail.
Services Distance learners have access to library services, e-mail services, academic advising, tutoring at a distance.
Credit-earning options Students may transfer credits from another institution.
Typical costs *Undergraduate:* Tuition of $36 per credit hour plus mandatory fees of $78.50 per credit hour for in-state residents. *Graduate:* Tuition of $68 per credit hour plus mandatory fees of $78.50 per credit hour for in-state residents. Costs may vary by number of credits taken. Financial aid is available to distance learners.
Registration Students may register by mail, phone, World Wide Web.
Contact Darella Banks, Executive Director of Enrollment Services, University of Houston–Clear Lake, 2700 Bay Area Boulevard, Houston, TX 77058. *Telephone:* 281-283-2520. *Fax:* 281-283-2530. *E-mail:* banks@cl4.uh.edu.

DEGREE & CERTIFICATE PROGRAMS

Graduate Degrees

▶ *Software Engineering (MS)*
Restrictions Program is available to students in Austin and Fort Bend county only. In Austin, the program is for IBM employees only.
Application requirements *Prior education:* baccalaureate degree.
Completion requirements 36 credit hours are required.
Program contact Dr. Glen Houston, Division Chair, University of Houston–Clear Lake, 2700 Bay Area Boulevard, Houston, TX 77058. Phone: 281-283-3860. Fax: 281-283-3870. E-mail: se@cl.uh.edu.

INDIVIDUAL COURSE SUBJECT AREAS

Undergraduate
English composition

Graduate
Abnormal psychology; computer and information sciences; instructional media

UNIVERSITY OF IDAHO

Moscow, Idaho

Engineering Outreach

University of Idaho, founded in 1889, is a state-supported university. It is accredited by the Northwest Association of Schools and Colleges. It first offered distance learning courses in 1976. In 1996–97, it offered 120 courses at a distance. In the fall of 1996, there was a total of 400 students enrolled in distance learning courses.
Course delivery sites Courses are delivered to your home, 3 off-campus centers in Boise, Coeur d'Alene, Idaho Falls.
Media Courses are delivered via videotapes, videoconferencing, World Wide Web, e-mail, print. Students and teachers interact via videoconferencing, mail, telephone, fax, e-mail. A computer is required for some courses.
Services Distance learners have access to library services, the campus computer network, academic advising, tutoring, career placement assistance at a distance.
Credit-earning options Students may transfer credits from another institution or may earn credits through institutionally developed exams.
Typical costs *Undergraduate:* Tuition of $299 per credit. *Graduate:* Tuition of $326 per credit. Costs may vary by number of credits taken. Financial aid is available to distance learners enrolled full-time.
Registration Students may register by mail, fax, phone, e-mail, World Wide Web.
Contact Barry Willis, Director, University of Idaho, Engineering Outreach, Moscow, ID 83844-1014. *Telephone:* 800-824-2889. *Fax:* 208-885-6165. *E-mail:* outreach@uidaho.edu. *Web site:* http://www.uidaho.edu/evo.

DEGREE & CERTIFICATE PROGRAMS

Graduate Degrees

▶ *Agricultural Engineering (MEngr, MS)*
In the fall of 1996 there were 5 students enrolled in this program.
Application requirements *Prior education:* baccalaureate degree. *Other requirements:* college transcripts, an essay or personal statement, letter(s) of recommendation, an application fee of $35.
Completion requirements 33 credits are required. *Maximum time for completion:* eight years.
On-campus requirements Two days on campus at the end of the program to write a comprehensive exam or defend thesis.

▶ *Civil Engineering (MEngr, MS)*
In the fall of 1996 there were 55 students enrolled in this program. In 1995–96, 2 degrees were earned at a distance through this program.
Application requirements *Prior education:* baccalaureate degree. *Other requirements:* college transcripts, an essay or personal statement, an application fee of $35.
Completion requirements 33 credits are required. 21 credits must be completed through the institution. *Maximum time for completion:* eight years.
On-campus requirements Two days on campus at the end of the program to write a comprehensive exam or defend thesis.

▶ *Computer Engineering (MEngr, MS)*
In the fall of 1996 there were 35 students enrolled in this program. In 1995–96, 1 degree was earned at a distance through this program.
Application requirements *Prior education:* baccalaureate degree. *Other requirements:* college transcripts, an application fee of $35.
Completion requirements 33 credits are required. 21 credits must be completed through the institution. *Maximum time for completion:* eight years.
On-campus requirements Two days on campus at the end of the program to write a comprehensive exam or defend thesis.

▶ *Computer Science (MS)*
In the fall of 1996 there were 45 students enrolled in this program. In 1995–96, 3 degrees were earned at a distance through this program.
Application requirements *Prior education:* baccalaureate degree. *Other requirements:* GRE, college transcripts, an essay or personal statement, letter(s) of recommendation, an application fee of $35.
Completion requirements 33 credits are required. 21 credits must be completed through the institution.
On-campus requirements Two days on campus at the end of the program to write a comprehensive exam or defend thesis.

Profiles: University of Idaho

▶ *Electrical Engineering (MEngr, MS)*
In the fall of 1996 there were 80 students enrolled in this program. In 1995–96, 3 degrees were earned at a distance through this program.
Application requirements *Prior education:* baccalaureate degree. *Other requirements:* college transcripts, an application fee of $35.
Completion requirements 33 credits are required. 21 credits must be completed through the institution. *Maximum time for completion:* eight years.
On-campus requirements Two days on campus at the end of the program to write a comprehensive exam or defend thesis.

▶ *Engineering Management (ME)*
In the fall of 1996 there were 5 students enrolled in this program.
Application requirements *Prior education:* baccalaureate degree. *Other requirements:* college transcripts, an essay or personal statement, letter(s) of recommendation, an application fee of $35.
Completion requirements 33 credits are required. 21 credits must be completed through the institution. *Maximum time for completion:* eight years.
On-campus requirements Two days on campus at the end of the program to write a comprehensive exam or defend thesis.

▶ *Geological Engineering (MEngr, MS)*
In the fall of 1996 there were 8 students enrolled in this program.
Application requirements *Prior education:* baccalaureate degree. *Other requirements:* college transcripts, an essay or personal statement, letter(s) of recommendation.
Completion requirements 30 credits are required. 21 credits must be completed through the institution. *Maximum time for completion:* eight years.
On-campus requirements Two days on campus at the end of the program to write a comprehensive exam or defend thesis.

▶ *Mechanical Engineering (ME)*
In the fall of 1996 there were 80 students enrolled in this program. In 1995–96, 2 degrees were earned at a distance through this program.
Application requirements *Prior education:* baccalaureate degree. *Other requirements:* GRE, college transcripts, an application fee of $35.
Completion requirements 33 credits are required. 21 credits must be completed through the institution. *Maximum time for completion:* eight years.
On-campus requirements Two days on campus at the end of the program to write a comprehensive exam or defend thesis.

▶ *Metallurgical Engineering (MS)*
▶ *Mining Engineering (MS)*
Application requirements *Prior education:* baccalaureate degree. *Other requirements:* GRE, college transcripts, an application fee of $35.
Completion requirements 33 credits are required. 21 credits must be completed through the institution. *Maximum time for completion:* eight years.
On-campus requirements Two days on campus at the end of the program to write a comprehensive exam or defend thesis.

▶ *Psychology (MS)*
In the fall of 1996 there were 45 students enrolled in this program. In 1995–96, 2 degrees were earned at a distance through this program.
Application requirements *Prior education:* baccalaureate degree. *Other requirements:* GRE, college transcripts, an essay or personal statement, letter(s) of recommendation, an application fee of $35.
Completion requirements 33 credits are required. 21 credits must be completed through the institution. *Maximum time for completion:* eight years.
On-campus requirements Two days on campus at the end of the program to write a comprehensive exam or defend thesis.

▶ *Teaching Mathematics (MAT)*
In the fall of 1996 there were 10 students enrolled in this program.
Application requirements *Prior education:* baccalaureate degree. *Other requirements:* college transcripts, an application fee of $35.
Completion requirements 33 credits are required. 21 credits must be completed through the institution. *Maximum time for completion:* eight years.
On-campus requirements Two days on campus at the end of the program to write a comprehensive exam or defend thesis.

INDIVIDUAL COURSE SUBJECT AREAS

Undergraduate
Agriculture; chemical engineering; civil engineering; computer and information sciences; education; electrical engineering; engineering; engineering/industrial management; geology; mathematics; mechanical engineering; psychology; statistics; teacher education

Graduate
Agriculture; chemical engineering; civil engineering; computer and information sciences; education; electrical engineering; engineering; engineering/industrial management; geology; mathematics; mechanical engineering; psychology; teacher education

See full description on page 502.

UNIVERSITY OF ILLINOIS AT SPRINGFIELD

Springfield, Illinois

Media Services

University of Illinois at Springfield, founded in 1969, is a state-supported upper-level institution. It is accredited by the North Central Association of Colleges and Schools. It first offered distance learning courses in 1984. In 1996–97, it offered 6 courses at a distance. In the fall of 1996, there was a total of 160 students enrolled in distance learning courses.
Course delivery sites Courses are delivered to your home, Millikin University (Decatur), University of Illinois at Chicago (Chicago), University of Illinois at Urbana–Champaign (Champaign), off-campus center(s) in Oak Brook, Oglesby, Peoria.
Media Courses are delivered via television, videotapes, videoconferencing, computer software, World Wide Web, e-mail. Students and teachers interact via videoconferencing, telephone, e-mail. A computer is required for some courses.
Restrictions Programs are available to in-state students only.
Services Distance learners have access to library services, the campus computer network, e-mail services, career placement assistance at a distance.
Credit-earning options Students may transfer credits from another institution.
Typical costs *Undergraduate:* Tuition of $85 per credit hour for in-state residents. Tuition of $255 per credit hour for out-of-state residents. *Graduate:* Tuition of $88 per credit hour for in-state residents. Tuition of $264 per credit hour for out-of-state residents. All students pay $78 in fees. Costs may vary by number of credits taken. Financial aid is available to distance learners enrolled full-time or part-time.
Registration Students may register by phone.
Contact Larry P. Dale, Director, Media Services and Instructional Design, University of Illinois at Springfield, Library 180, Springfield, IL 62794-9243. *Telephone:* 217-786-6550. *Fax:* 217-786-6287. *E-mail:* dale.larry@uis.edu.

INDIVIDUAL COURSE SUBJECT AREAS

Undergraduate
Accounting; computer and information sciences; mathematics; nursing; teacher education

Graduate

Accounting; business administration and management; computer and information sciences; management information systems; teacher education

UNIVERSITY OF ILLINOIS AT URBANA–CHAMPAIGN

Champaign, Illinois

Extramural Programs and Guided Individual Study

University of Illinois at Urbana–Champaign, founded in 1867, is a state-supported university. It is accredited by the North Central Association of Colleges and Schools. It first offered distance learning courses in 1925. In 1996–97, it offered 175 courses at a distance. In the fall of 1996, there was a total of 2,500 students enrolled in distance learning courses.

Course delivery sites Courses are delivered to your home, your workplace, off-campus center(s).

Media Courses are delivered via videotapes, videoconferencing, audiotapes, audioconferencing, World Wide Web, e-mail, print, satellite, audiographics conferencing. Students and teachers interact via videoconferencing, audioconferencing, mail, telephone, fax, e-mail, audiographics conferencing, World Wide Web. A computer is required for some courses.

Restrictions Availability varies by course, program, or delivery means.

Services Distance learners have access to library services, the campus computer network, e-mail services, academic advising, career placement assistance at a distance.

Credit-earning options Students may transfer credits from another institution.

Typical costs Contact school for information.

Registration Students may register by mail, fax.

Contact Morris J. Sammons, Assistant Head for Client Services-Extramural Programs/Guided Individual Study, University of Illinois at Urbana–Champaign, 302 East John Street, Suite 1405, Champaign, IL 61820. *Telephone:* 217-333-1320. *Fax:* 217-244-8481. *E-mail:* morriss@cecredit.extramural.uiuc.edu. *Web site:* http://www.extramural.uiuc.edu.

DEGREE & CERTIFICATE PROGRAMS

Graduate Degrees

▶ *Electrical Engineering (MS)*

Restrictions Cohort of 5 students required at each site.

Application requirements *Prior education:* baccalaureate degree. *Other requirements:* GRE, college transcripts, letter(s) of recommendation, an application fee of $40.

Completion requirements 8 units and a thesis are required. 7 units must be completed through the institution. *Maximum time for completion:* five years.

Program contact Dr. Ken Gustin, Program Director, University of Illinois at Urbana–Champaign, 302 East John Street, Suite 1405, Champaign, IL 61820. Phone: 217-333-9806. Fax: 217-244-8481. E-mail: gustin@uiuc.edu.

▶ *General Engineering (MS)*

Restrictions Cohort of 5 students required at each site.

Application requirements *Prior education:* baccalaureate degree. *Other requirements:* college transcripts, letter(s) of recommendation, an application fee of $40.

Completion requirements 8 units are required with thesis, 9 units without. 7 units must be completed through the institution. *Maximum time for completion:* five years.

Program contact Dr. Ken Gustin, Program Director, University of Illinois at Urbana–Champaign, 302 East John Street, Suite 1405, Champaign, IL 61820. Phone: 217-333-9806. Fax: 217-244-8481. E-mail: gustin@uiuc.edu.

▶ *Library and Information Science (MS)*

In the fall of 1996 there were 31 students enrolled in this program.

Application requirements *Prior education:* baccalaureate degree. *Other requirements:* GRE, TOEFL (for international students), college transcripts, an essay or personal statement, letter(s) of recommendation, an application fee of $40 ($50 for international students), TOEFL (for international students).

Completion requirements 40 semester hours are required. 36 semester hours must be completed through the institution. *Maximum time for completion:* five years.

On-campus requirements Two summer weeks, one weekend per semester per course.

Program contact Linda C. Smith, Associate Dean, University of Illinois at Urbana–Champaign, Graduate School of Library and Information Science, 501 East Daniel Street, Champaign, IL 61820-6211. Phone: 800-982-0914. Fax: 217-244-3302. E-mail: leep@alexia.lis.uiuc.edu.

▶ *Mechanical Engineering (MS)*

Restrictions Cohort of 5 students required at each site.

Application requirements *Prior education:* baccalaureate degree. *Other requirements:* college transcripts, letter(s) of recommendation, an application fee of $40.

Completion requirements 8 units with thesis are required, 9 units without. 7 units must be completed through the institution. *Maximum time for completion:* five years.

Program contact Dr. Ken Gustin, Program Director, University of Illinois at Urbana–Champaign, 302 East John Street, Suite 1405, Champaign, IL 61820. Phone: 217-333-9806. Fax: 217-244-8481. E-mail: gustin@uiuc.edu.

▶ *Theoretical and Applied Mechanics (MS)*

Restrictions Cohort of 5 students required at each site.

Application requirements *Prior education:* baccalaureate degree. *Other requirements:* college transcripts, letter(s) of recommendation, an application fee of $40.

Completion requirements 8 units with thesis are required, 9 units without. 7 units must be completed through the institution. *Maximum time for completion:* five years.

Program contact Dr. Ken Gustin, Program Director, University of Illinois at Urbana–Champaign, 302 East John Street, Suite 1405, Champaign, IL 61820. Phone: 217-333-9806. Fax: 217-244-8481. E-mail: gustin@uiuc.edu.

INDIVIDUAL COURSE SUBJECT AREAS

Undergraduate

Abnormal psychology; accounting; advertising; agricultural economics; American (US) history; American literature; anthropology; business administration and management; business communications; cognitive psychology; community health services; developmental and child psychology; economics; educational psychology; electrical engineering; engineering mechanics; English composition; English literature; European history; French language and literature; geography; German language and literature; health services administration; industrial psychology; international relations; Latin language and literature; marketing; mathematics; mechanical engineering; political science; public health; social psychology; sociology; Spanish language and literature; technical writing

Graduate

Electrical engineering; engineering mechanics; library and information studies; mechanical engineering

See full description on page 504.

Profiles: The University of Iowa

THE UNIVERSITY OF IOWA

Iowa City, Iowa

Center for Credit Programs

The University of Iowa, founded in 1847, is a state-supported university. It is accredited by the North Central Association of Colleges and Schools. It first offered distance learning courses in 1916. In 1996–97, it offered 200 courses at a distance.

Course delivery sites Courses are delivered to your home, your workplace, Iowa Communications Network (ICN) sites.

Media Courses are delivered via television, videotapes, audiotapes, computer software, World Wide Web, e-mail, print. Students and teachers interact via mail, telephone, fax, e-mail. A computer is required for some courses. The institution provides assistance with acquiring computer equipment.

Restrictions Interactive video programs are available to in-state students only.

Services Distance learners have access to library services, the campus computer network, e-mail services, academic advising at a distance.

Credit-earning options Students may transfer credits from another institution or may earn credits through standardized exams.

Typical costs *Undergraduate:* Tuition of $107 per semester hour. *Graduate:* Tuition of $170 per semester hour. All print-based courses are $77 per semester hour, with $15 per course in mandatory fees. Costs may vary by specific program of study, course delivery options. Financial aid is available to distance learners.

Registration Students may register by mail, fax, phone, e-mail, World Wide Web.

Contact Pat Vunderink, Promotions Coordinator, Credit Programs, The University of Iowa, 116 International Center, Iowa City, IA 52242. *Telephone:* 319-335-2038. *Fax:* 319-335-2740. *E-mail:* pat_vunderink@uiowa.edu. *Web site:* http://www.uiowa.edu/~ccp/.

DEGREE & CERTIFICATE PROGRAMS

Baccalaureate Degrees

▶ *Liberal Arts (BLS)*

Restrictions Program is available to US students only.

Application requirements *Prior education:* associate degree. *Other requirements:* high school transcript, college transcripts, an application fee of $20.

Completion requirements 124 semester hours are required. 32 semester hours must be completed through the institution. This is a degree completion program.

Program contact Elizabeth Hill, Coordinator, Student Services, The University of Iowa, 116 International Center, Iowa City, IA 52242. Phone: 319-335-2035. Fax: 319-335-2740. E-mail: elizabeth-hill@uiowa.edu.

INDIVIDUAL COURSE SUBJECT AREAS

Undergraduate

African-American studies; algebra; American (US) history; American studies; anthropology; archaeology; Asian studies; astronomy and astrophysics; business; calculus; criminology; earth science; economics; education; English language and literature; environmental health; European history; French language and literature; geography; geology; German language and literature; gerontology; journalism; Latin language and literature; nursing; political science; psychology; religious studies; social work; sociology; Spanish language and literature; statistics; visual and performing arts; women's studies

Graduate

African-American studies; algebra; American (US) history; anthropology; archaeology; Asian studies; astronomy and astrophysics; business; calculus; computer and information sciences; criminology; earth science; economics; education; engineering; English language and literature; environmental health; European history; geography; geology; gerontology; journalism; nursing; political science; psychology; religious studies; social work; sociology; statistics; visual and performing arts; women's studies

UNIVERSITY OF KANSAS

Lawrence, Kansas

Academic Outreach Programs

University of Kansas, founded in 1866, is a state-supported university. It is accredited by the North Central Association of Colleges and Schools. It first offered distance learning courses in 1891. In 1996–97, it offered 142 courses at a distance. In the fall of 1996, there was a total of 2,300 students enrolled in distance learning courses.

Course delivery sites Courses are delivered to your home, your workplace, other colleges.

Media Courses are delivered via videotapes, audiotapes, World Wide Web, e-mail, print. Students and teachers interact via mail, telephone, e-mail. A computer is required for some courses.

Services Distance learners have access to library services, e-mail services, academic advising at a distance.

Typical costs *Undergraduate:* Tuition of $88 per credit plus mandatory fees of $45 per course. *Graduate:* Tuition of $129 per credit plus mandatory fees of $45 per course. Costs may vary by specific program of study, number of credits taken, course delivery options, term of enrollment. Financial aid is available to distance learners enrolled full-time.

Registration Students may register by mail, fax, e-mail, World Wide Web.

Contact Sandra Hick, Registrar/Advisor, Independent Study, University of Kansas, Continuing Education, Annex A, Lawrence, KS 66045-2606. *Telephone:* 913-864-4440. *Fax:* 913-864-7895. *E-mail:* ssh@falcon.cc.ukans.edu.

INDIVIDUAL COURSE SUBJECT AREAS

Undergraduate

Area, ethnic, and cultural studies; biology; business administration and management; Classical languages and literatures; conservation and natural resources; creative writing; developmental and child psychology; economics; education administration; educational psychology; English composition; English language and literature; European languages and literatures; geology; health and physical education/fitness; history; home economics and family studies; journalism; liberal arts, general studies, and humanities; mathematics; music; philosophy and religion; political science; public administration and services; public health; radio and television broadcasting; social psychology; social work; sociology; special education; teacher education; theological studies

Graduate

Area, ethnic, and cultural studies; developmental and child psychology; education administration; health and physical education/fitness; history; liberal arts, general studies, and humanities; public health; special education; teacher education

Noncredit

Area, ethnic, and cultural studies; biology; business administration and management; Classical languages and literatures; conservation and natural resources; creative writing; developmental and child psychology; economics; education administration; educational psychology; English composition; English language and literature; European languages and literatures; geology; health and physical education/fitness; history; home economics and family studies; journalism; liberal arts, general studies, and humanities; mathematics; music; philosophy and religion; political science; public administration and services; public health; radio and television broadcasting; social psychology; social work; sociology; special education; teacher education; theological studies

UNIVERSITY OF KENTUCKY

Lexington, Kentucky

Distance Learning Programs

University of Kentucky, founded in 1865, is a state-supported university. It is accredited by the Southern Association of Colleges and Schools. It first offered distance learning courses in 1974. In 1996–97, it offered 168 courses at a distance. In the fall of 1996, there was a total of 756 students enrolled in distance learning courses.
Course delivery sites Courses are delivered to your home, your workplace, other colleges.
Media Courses are delivered via television, videotapes, videoconferencing, print. Students and teachers interact via videoconferencing, audioconferencing, mail, telephone, fax, e-mail.
Restrictions Availability varies by course, program, or delivery means.
Services Distance learners have access to library services, e-mail services, academic advising at a distance.
Credit-earning options Students may transfer credits from another institution.
Typical costs *Undergraduate:* Tuition of $98 per credit hour for in-state residents. Tuition of $293 per credit hour for out-of-state residents. *Graduate:* Tuition of $144 per credit hour for in-state residents. Tuition of $430 per credit hour for out-of-state residents. Costs may vary by specific program of study, number of credits taken.
Registration Students may register by mail, fax, phone.
Contact Distance Learning Programs, University of Kentucky, 4 Frazee Hall, Lexington, KY 40506-0032. *Telephone:* 606-257-3377. *Fax:* 606-257-5171. *E-mail:* bairdc@pop.uky.edu.

DEGREE & CERTIFICATE PROGRAMS

Baccalaureate Degrees

▶ *Clinical Laboratory Sciences (BHS)*
In the fall of 1996 there were 14 students enrolled in this program. In 1995–96, 2 degrees were earned at a distance through this program.
Application requirements *Prior education:* associate's degree or equivalent. *Other requirements:* high school transcript, college transcripts, an essay or personal statement, letter(s) of recommendation, an application fee of $20, voluntary work experience in health care, 2.5 GPA.
Completion requirements 120 credit hours are required. 36 credit hours must be completed through the institution. This is a degree completion program. *Other requirements:* clinical rotations are required, usually arranged within one hour driving time.
Program contact Donna Brown-Lubinksi, Director of Student Services, University of Kentucky, Center for Rural Health, 100 Airport Gardens Road, Suite 10, Hazard, KY 41701. Phone: 606-439-3557. Fax: 606-436-8833. E-mail: dlbrowl@pop.uky.edu.

▶ *Physician Assistant Studies (BHS)*
In the fall of 1996 there were 8 students enrolled in this program.
Restrictions This program is available to in-state students only. Admission to the program is highly competitive.
Application requirements *Prior education:* some undergraduate course work. *Other requirements:* Allied Health Professions Admission Test, high school transcript, college transcripts, an essay or personal statement, letter(s) of recommendation, an application fee of $20, voluntary work experience in health care.
Completion requirements 150 credit hours are required. 36 credit hours must be completed through the institution. This is a degree completion program. *Other requirements:* clinical rotations are required, usually arranged within one hour driving time.
Program contact Susan Maxey, Director of Student Services, University of Kentucky, UPO Box 715, Reed Hall 225, Morehead, KY 40351-1689. Phone: 606-783-2636. Fax: 606-783-5063. E-mail: maxey@pop.uky.edu.

Graduate Degrees

▶ *Educational Administration and Supervision (EdD)*
In the fall of 1996 there were 50 students enrolled in this program. In 1995–96, 10 degrees were earned at a distance through this program.
Restrictions This program is available to in-state students only. Positions in cohorts are limited.
Application requirements *Prior education:* graduate degree. *Other requirements:* GRE, college transcripts, an essay or personal statement, letter(s) of recommendation, an application fee of $30, admission is competitive; space is limited.
Completion requirements 60 semester hours are required. 60 semester hours must be completed through the institution. *Other requirements:* qualifying examination, dissertation. *Maximum time for completion:* five years after passage of qualifying examination.
Program contact Dr. Susan J. Scollay, Director of Graduate Studies, University of Kentucky, 111B Dickey Hall, Lexington, KY 40506-0017. Phone: 606-257-7834. Fax: 606-257-1015. E-mail: scollay@pop.uky.edu.

▶ *Educational Policy Studies and Evaluation (EdD)*
Restrictions This program is available to local area students only.
Application requirements *Prior education:* Master's degree or 30 graduate credit hours. *Other requirements:* GRE, college transcripts, an essay or personal statement, letter(s) of recommendation, an application fee of $30.
Completion requirements 43 credit hours are required. 18-24 credit hours must be completed through the institution. *Other requirements:* qualifying examinations, dissertation. *Maximum time for completion:* five years following successful completion of qualifying exams.
Program contact Dr. Beth L. Goldstein, Director of Graduate Studies, University of Kentucky, Educational Policy Studies and Evaluation, 131 Taylor Education Building, Lexington, KY 40506-0001. Phone: 606-257-2705. Fax: 606-257-4243. E-mail: cdpbethg@ukcc.uky.edu.

▶ *Engineering (ME)*
Restrictions This program is available to in-state students only.
Application requirements *Prior education:* baccalaureate degree. *Other requirements:* GRE, college transcripts, an application fee of $30.
Completion requirements 30 credits are required. 21 credits must be completed through the institution. *Other requirements:* at least one half of credits must be at 600–700 level. *Maximum time for completion:* seven years.
On-campus requirements For final examination.
Program contact Dr. G. T. Lineberry, Assistant to the Dean for Extended Campus Programs, University of Kentucky, 230 MMRB, Lexington, KY 40506-0107. Phone: 606-257-2833. Fax: 606-323-1962. E-mail: gtli@engr.uky.edu.

▶ *Mining Engineering (MME)*
In the fall of 1996 there were 8 students enrolled in this program. In 1995–96, 2 degrees were earned at a distance through this program.
Restrictions Program is available to students in North America only.
Application requirements *Prior education:* baccalaureate degree. *Other requirements:* GRE, college transcripts, an application fee of $30.

Profiles: University of Kentucky

Completion requirements 30 credits are required. 21 credits must be completed through the institution. *Other requirements:* one major report, one minor report; minimum of one half of hours must be at 600/700 level. *Maximum time for completion:* seven years.
On-campus requirements For final examination and selected laboratories.
Program contact Professor Joseph W. Leonard, Professor of Mining Engineering, University of Kentucky, 230 MMRB, Lexington, KY 40506-0107. Phone: 606-257-8026. Fax: 606-323-1962. E-mail: jleonard@engr.uky.edu.

▶ *Nursing (MSN)*
In the fall of 1996 there were 47 students enrolled in this program. In 1995–96, 10 degrees were earned at a distance through this program.
Application requirements *Prior education:* associate degree in Nursing (RN/MSN) or bachelor's degree in nursing. *Other requirements:* GRE, college transcripts, an essay or personal statement, an application fee of $30, references, faculty interview, Kentucky Nursing license.
Completion requirements 33–53 semester credits are required. 33 must be completed through the institution. *Maximum time for completion:* eight years.
On-campus requirements For diagnostic laboratory course work requiring two full days of study for practitioner track students.
Program contact Donna Brown-Lubinksi, Director of Student Services, University of Kentucky, Center for Rural Health, 100 Airport Gardens Road, Suite 10, Hazard, KY 41701. Phone: 606-439-3557. Fax: 606-436-8833. E-mail: dlbrowl@pop.uky.edu.

▶ *Nursing (MSN)*
In the fall of 1996 there were 9 students enrolled in this program.
Application requirements *Prior education:* Bachelor of Science in Nursing. *Other requirements:* GRE, college transcripts, an essay or personal statement, an application fee of $30, references, faculty interview, Kentucky Nursing license, one year post-Baccalaureate nursing experience.
Completion requirements 51–52 semester hours are required. 33 semester hours must be completed through the institution. *Maximum time for completion:* eight years.
On-campus requirements For diagnostic laboratory course work requiring two full days of study.
Program contact Susan Maxey, Director of Student Services, University of Kentucky, UPO Box 715, Reed Hall 225, Morehead, KY 40351-1689. Phone: 606-783-2636. Fax: 606-783-5063. E-mail: maxey@pop.uky.edu.

▶ *Physical Therapy (BHS/MSPT)*
In the fall of 1996 there were 32 students enrolled in this program. In 1995–96, 16 degrees were earned at a distance through this program.
Restrictions This program is available to in-state students only. Admission to the program is highly competitive.
Application requirements *Prior education:* some undergraduate course work. *Other requirements:* GRE, college transcripts, an essay or personal statement, letter(s) of recommendation, an application fee of $20, voluntary work experience in health care.
Completion requirements 190 credit hours are required. 36 credit hours must be completed through the institution. This is a degree completion program. *Other requirements:* baccalaureate and master's degrees are awarded concurrently. Clinical rotations are required, usually arranged within one hour driving time.
Program contact Donna Brown-Lubinksi, Director of Student Services, University of Kentucky, Center for Rural Health, 100 Airport Gardens Road, Suite 10, Hazard, KY 41701. Phone: 606-439-3557. Fax: 606-436-8833. E-mail: dlbrowl@pop.uky.edu.

▶ *Special Education (MS)*
Restrictions This program is available to in-state students only.
Application requirements *Prior education:* baccalaureate degree. *Other requirements:* GRE, college transcripts, an essay or personal statement, letter(s) of recommendation.
Completion requirements 36 hours are required. 27 hours must be completed through the institution. *Maximum time for completion:* eight years.
On-campus requirements Requirements vary according to class.
Program contact Jennifer Grisham-Brown, Assistant Professor, University of Kentucky, Taylor Education Building, Lexington, KY 40506-0001. Phone: 606-257-7909. Fax: 606-257-1325. E-mail: jgleat00@pop.uky.edu.

INDIVIDUAL COURSE SUBJECT AREAS

Undergraduate
Agriculture; architecture; health professions and related sciences; mathematics; nursing

Graduate
Agriculture; communications; computer and information sciences; education administration; educational psychology; engineering; home economics and family studies; library and information studies; mathematics; nursing; social work; special education

UNIVERSITY OF KENTUCKY, ASHLAND COMMUNITY COLLEGE

Ashland, Kentucky

University of Kentucky, Ashland Community College, founded in 1937, is a state-supported two-year college. It is accredited by the Southern Association of Colleges and Schools. It first offered distance learning courses in 1980. In 1996–97, it offered 10 courses at a distance. In the fall of 1996, there was a total of 20 students enrolled in distance learning courses.
Course delivery sites Courses are delivered to your home, your workplace, other colleges, 3 off-campus centers in Grayson, Greenup, Louisa.
Media Courses are delivered via television. Students and teachers interact via mail, telephone, fax, e-mail. A computer is required for some courses.
Restrictions Programs are available to in-state students only.
Services Distance learners have access to library services, the campus computer network, e-mail services at a distance.
Credit-earning options Students may transfer credits from another institution or may earn credits through standardized exams, institutionally developed exams.
Typical costs Tuition of $42 per credit hour plus mandatory fees of $4 per credit hour for in-state residents. Tuition of $125 per credit hour plus mandatory fees of $4 per credit hour for out-of-state residents. *Noncredit courses:* $138 per course. Costs may vary by number of credits taken. Financial aid is available to distance learners enrolled full-time or part-time.
Contact Dr. Carol Greene, Director of Library Services, University of Kentucky, Ashland Community College, 1400 College Drive, Ashland, KY 41101. *Telephone:* 606-329-2999, Ext. 581. *Fax:* 606-324-8124. *E-mail:* cgreene@ashcc.uky.edu.

DEGREE & CERTIFICATE PROGRAMS

Associate Degrees
▶ *General Education (AA)*
In the fall of 1996 there were 3 students enrolled in this program.
Application requirements *Prior education:* high school diploma or equivalent. *Other requirements:* high school transcript.
Completion requirements 60 hours are required. 24 hours must be completed through the institution.
On-campus requirements Requirements vary.

INDIVIDUAL COURSE SUBJECT AREAS

Undergraduate
Business; English language and literature; history; protective services; psychology; social sciences

UNIVERSITY OF KENTUCKY, ELIZABETHTOWN COMMUNITY COLLEGE

Elizabethtown, Kentucky

University of Kentucky, Elizabethtown Community College, founded in 1964, is a state-supported two-year college. It is accredited by the Southern Association of Colleges and Schools. It first offered distance learning courses in 1985. In 1996–97, it offered 12 courses at a distance. In the fall of 1996, there was a total of 250 students enrolled in distance learning courses.
Course delivery sites Courses are delivered to your home, military bases, other colleges throughout Kentucky.
Media Courses are delivered via television, videotapes, videoconferencing. Students and teachers interact via videoconferencing, mail, telephone.
Services Distance learners have access to library services, academic advising at a distance.
Credit-earning options Students may transfer credits from another institution or may earn credits through examinations, military training.
Typical costs Tuition of $43 per credit hour plus mandatory fees of $4 per credit hour. Costs may vary by number of credits taken. Financial aid is available to distance learners.
Contact Sharon Spratt, Dean of Student Affairs, University of Kentucky, Elizabethtown Community College, 600 College Street Road, Elizabethtown, KY 42701-3081. *Telephone:* 502-769-2371. *E-mail:* sspratt@pop.uky.edu.

INDIVIDUAL COURSE SUBJECT AREAS

Undergraduate
Asian languages and literatures; business administration and management; economics; English language and literature; German language and literature; history; home economics and family studies; human resources management; industrial engineering; law and legal studies; liberal arts, general studies, and humanities; physics; psychology; social psychology; sociology; Spanish language and literature

UNIVERSITY OF KENTUCKY, HAZARD COMMUNITY COLLEGE

Hazard, Kentucky

University of Kentucky, Hazard Community College, founded in 1968, is a state-supported two-year college. It is accredited by the Southern Association of Colleges and Schools.
Course delivery sites Courses are delivered to your home.
Media Courses are delivered via television. Students and teachers interact via videoconferencing, telephone.
Restrictions Programs are available to in-state students only.
Services Distance learners have access to academic advising at a distance.
Typical costs Tuition of $43 per credit hour plus mandatory fees of $4 per credit hour. Financial aid is available to distance learners.
Contact Julia B. Mitchell, Assistant Dean, Community Development, University of Kentucky, Hazard Community College, 601 Main Street, Hazard, KY 41701. *Telephone:* 606-439-5856. *Fax:* 606-439-1808.

INDIVIDUAL COURSE SUBJECT AREAS

Undergraduate
Business administration and management; history

UNIVERSITY OF KENTUCKY, HENDERSON COMMUNITY COLLEGE

Henderson, Kentucky

University of Kentucky, Henderson Community College, founded in 1963, is a state-supported two-year college. It is accredited by the Southern Association of Colleges and Schools. It first offered distance learning courses in 1985. In 1996–97, it offered 5 courses at a distance. In the fall of 1996, there was a total of 30 students enrolled in distance learning courses.
Course delivery sites Courses are delivered to your home, community colleges in Kentucky.
Media Courses are delivered via television. Students and teachers interact via videoconferencing, fax.
Restrictions Programs are available to in-state students only.
Services Distance learners have access to library services, the campus computer network, e-mail services, academic advising, career placement assistance at a distance.
Credit-earning options Students may transfer credits from another institution or may earn credits through standardized exams, institutionally developed exams, military training.
Typical costs Tuition of $43 per credit hour plus mandatory fees of $4 per credit hour for in-state residents. Tuition of $128 per credit hour plus mandatory fees of $4 per credit hour for out-of-state residents. Costs may vary by number of credits taken. Financial aid is available to distance learners enrolled full-time or part-time.
Contact Patty Mitchell, Dean of Student Affairs, University of Kentucky, Henderson Community College, 2660 South Green Street, Henderson, KY 42420. *Telephone:* 502-827-1867. *Fax:* 502-826-8391. *E-mail:* mitchellp@www.hence.uky.edu.

INDIVIDUAL COURSE SUBJECT AREAS

Undergraduate
Anthropology; biology; business administration and management; developmental and child psychology; history; law and legal studies; sociology

UNIVERSITY OF KENTUCKY, MADISONVILLE COMMUNITY COLLEGE

Madisonville, Kentucky

University of Kentucky, Madisonville Community College, founded in 1968, is a state-supported two-year college. It is accredited by the Southern Association of Colleges and Schools.
Course delivery sites Courses are delivered to your home.
Media Courses are delivered via television, videotapes. Students and teachers interact via videoconferencing, mail, telephone, fax, e-mail.
Restrictions Students must be able to travel to campus.

Distance Learning Programs

Profiles: University of Kentucky, Madisonville Community College

Typical costs Tuition of $42 per credit hour plus mandatory fees of $4 per credit hour for in-state residents. Tuition of $126 per credit hour plus mandatory fees of $4 per credit hour for out-of-state residents. Financial aid is available to distance learners.
Registration Students may register by mail.
Contact Cherry Berges, Director of Library Services, University of Kentucky, Madisonville Community College, 2000 College Drive, Madisonville, KY 42431. *Telephone:* 502-821-2250, Ext. 2251. *Fax:* 502-825-8553. *E-mail:* madclber@ukcc.uky.edu.

INDIVIDUAL COURSE SUBJECT AREAS

Undergraduate

Biology; business administration and management; creative writing; economics; English language and literature; history; liberal arts, general studies, and humanities; political science; psychology; sociology

UNIVERSITY OF LEICESTER

Leicester, United Kingdom

The Centre for Labour Market Studies

University of Leicester is a university in the United Kingdom. It first offered distance learning courses in 1991. In 1996–97, it offered 4 courses at a distance. In the fall of 1996, there was a total of 600 students enrolled in distance learning courses.
Course delivery sites Courses are delivered to your home.
Media Courses are delivered via videotapes, print. Students and teachers interact via mail, telephone, fax, e-mail.
Services Distance learners have access to library services, the campus computer network, academic advising, tutoring at a distance.
Typical costs Tuition of $2400 per semester.
Registration Students may register by mail.
Contact Student Services, University of Leicester, Leicester Masters in Training and Human Resources Management, 6921 Stockton Avenue, El Cerrito, CA 94530. *Telephone:* 888-534-2378. *Fax:* 510-528-3555. *E-mail:* leicester@degree.net. *Web site:* http://www.clms.le.ac.uk.

DEGREE & CERTIFICATE PROGRAMS

Graduate Degrees

▶ *Training, Human Resource Management (MS)*
In the fall of 1996 there were 600 students enrolled in this program. In 1995–96, 160 degrees were earned at a distance through this program.
Application requirements *Prior education:* baccalaureate degree. *Other requirements:* college transcripts, an essay or personal statement, letter(s) of recommendation, at least 3 years relevant experience.
Completion requirements 4 modules plus thesis are required. All course work must be completed through the institution. *Other requirements:* after four semesters (total of 18 months) of course work, a thesis must be completed. *Maximum time for completion:* four years.

UNIVERSITY OF LOUISVILLE

Louisville, Kentucky

Department of Special Education

University of Louisville, founded in 1798, is a state-supported university. It is accredited by the Southern Association of Colleges and Schools. It first offered distance learning courses in 1992. In 1996–97, it offered 16 courses at a distance. In the fall of 1996, there was a total of 400 students enrolled in distance learning courses.
Course delivery sites Courses are delivered to your home, your workplace, military bases, The University of Alabama (Tuscaloosa, AL), school districts, libraries, cable stations.
Media Courses are delivered via television, videotapes, videoconferencing, computer software, World Wide Web, e-mail, print. Students and teachers interact via videoconferencing, audioconferencing, mail, telephone, fax, e-mail, World Wide Web. A computer is required for all courses.
Restrictions Courses are available to students in the continental US only.
Services Distance learners have access to library services, the campus computer network, e-mail services, academic advising, tutoring, bookstore at a distance.
Credit-earning options Students may transfer credits from another institution or may earn credits through institutionally developed exams, portfolio assessment.
Typical costs Tuition of $166 per credit for in-state residents. Tuition of $459.50 per credit for out-of-state residents. Costs may vary by number of credits taken. Financial aid is available to distance learners enrolled full-time or part-time.
Registration Students may register by mail, fax, phone, e-mail, World Wide Web.
Contact Denzil Edge, Director, Distance Education, University of Louisville, School of Education, Louisville, KY 40292. *Telephone:* 502-852-6421. *Fax:* 502-852-1419. *E-mail:* d0edge0l@ulkyum.louisville.edu. *Web site:* http://www.louisville.edu/edu/edsp/distance/.

Special note
University of Louisville, Department of Special Education, located in Louisville, Kentucky, is an accredited college (National Council for Accreditation of Teacher Education) and now offers a master's degree in Teacher Preparation Program in Visual Impairment through a variety of technologies.

Based on the need for teacher preparation in the area of visual impairment, the Department of Special Education has created a new delivery system that combines summer institutes and distance education courses. Teachers seeking certification in the area of visual impairment have the opportunity to attend a summer institute conducted at the Kentucky School for the Blind in collaboration with the University of Louisville and to participate in courses during the fall and spring using interactive television through satellite links, electronic communication via e-mail, the World Wide Web, listserv connections, interactive distance education library support systems, and video series.

This program is available to students nationally and internationally. Students seeking certification in the area of visual impairment must hold a base certification in the area of elementary, middle, or secondary education prior to enrollment. Students interested in the area of visual impairment as an elective area of study must also meet the graduate school requirements for enrollment.

The Department of Special Education also offers distance education courses in autism, learning disabilities, technology, involving parents, and classroom management. In the fall of 1998, the department will be adding a new Master of Education degree program in technology and assistive technology. For more information on any of these programs or course schedules, call Darlene Hurd at 502-852-6421 or 502-852-0565.

DEGREE & CERTIFICATE PROGRAMS

Graduate Degrees
▶ *Social Work (PhD)*
Restrictions This program is available to in-state students only.

Application requirements *Prior education:* Masters degree in social work. *Other requirements:* GRE, college transcripts, an essay or personal statement, letter(s) of recommendation, an application fee of $25.
Completion requirements 90 credits are required. 60 credits must be completed through the institution. *Maximum time for completion:* five years.
On-campus requirements For orientation.

▶ *Visual Impairment (MEd)*
Application requirements *Prior education:* baccalaureate degree. *Other requirements:* GRE, college transcripts, an essay or personal statement, letter(s) of recommendation, an application fee of $25, certification in elementary, middle or secondary education.
Completion requirements 33 course hours are required. 27 course hours must be completed through the institution.
On-campus requirements For orientation.

INDIVIDUAL COURSE SUBJECT AREAS

Graduate
Social work; special education

UNIVERSITY OF MAINE

Orono, Maine

Continuing Education Division

University of Maine, founded in 1865, is a state-supported university. It is accredited by the New England Association of Schools and Colleges. It first offered distance learning courses in 1989. In 1996–97, it offered 45 courses at a distance. In the fall of 1996, there was a total of 900 students enrolled in distance learning courses.
Course delivery sites Courses are delivered to your home, your workplace, 10 off-campus centers, high schools, other University of Maine campuses.
Media Courses are delivered via television, videotapes, videoconferencing, audioconferencing, computer software, World Wide Web, e-mail. Students and teachers interact via videoconferencing, audioconferencing, mail, telephone, fax, e-mail. A computer is required for some courses.
Services Distance learners have access to library services, the campus computer network, e-mail services, academic advising, tutoring, career placement assistance at a distance.
Credit-earning options Students may transfer credits from another institution or may earn credits through examinations, portfolio assessment, military training, business training.
Typical costs *Undergraduate:* Tuition of $119 per credit. *Graduate:* Tuition of $179 per credit. *Noncredit courses:* $85–$180 per course. Financial aid is available to distance learners.
Registration Students may register by mail, fax, phone, e-mail, World Wide Web.
Contact James F. Toner, Associate Director, Continuing Education Division and Summer Session, University of Maine, 5713 Chadbourne Hall, Orono, ME 04469-5713. *Telephone:* 207-581-3142. *Fax:* 207-581-3141. *E-mail:* jtoner@maine.maine.edu. *Web site:* http://www.ume.maine.edu/.

DEGREE & CERTIFICATE PROGRAMS

Baccalaureate Degrees
▶ *University Studies (BUS)*
Application requirements *Prior education:* some undergraduate course work. *Other requirements:* high school transcript, college transcripts, an essay or personal statement, letter(s) of recommendation, an application fee of $25.

Completion requirements 120 credit hours are required. 60 credit hours must be completed through the institution.

INDIVIDUAL COURSE SUBJECT AREAS

Undergraduate
Area, ethnic, and cultural studies; civil engineering; developmental and child psychology; electrical engineering; English language and literature; European languages and literatures; health professions and related sciences; history; home economics and family studies; law and legal studies; liberal arts, general studies, and humanities; mathematics; mechanical engineering; music; nursing; philosophy and religion; political science; social psychology; sociology; special education; teacher education

Graduate
Area, ethnic, and cultural studies; civil engineering; education administration; electrical engineering; English language and literature; liberal arts, general studies, and humanities; mechanical engineering; special education; teacher education

Noncredit
Electrical engineering

UNIVERSITY OF MAINE AT AUGUSTA

Augusta, Maine

Education Network of Maine

University of Maine at Augusta, founded in 1965, is a state-supported primarily two-year college. It is accredited by the New England Association of Schools and Colleges. It first offered distance learning courses in 1990. In 1996–97, it offered 60 courses at a distance. In the fall of 1996, there was a total of 2,020 students enrolled in distance learning courses.
Course delivery sites Courses are delivered to your home, your workplace, University of Maine System (Bangor), 8 off-campus centers in Bath-Brunswick, East Millinocket, Ellsworth, Lewiston, Rumford, Saco, Sanford, Thomaston.
Media Courses are delivered via television, videotapes, audioconferencing, computer software, World Wide Web. Students and teachers interact via audioconferencing, telephone, e-mail.
Restrictions Programs are available to in-state students only.
Services Distance learners have access to library services, the campus computer network, e-mail services, academic advising at a distance.
Credit-earning options Students may transfer credits from another institution or may earn credits through standardized exams, portfolio assessment, military training.
Typical costs Tuition of $100 per credit plus mandatory fees of $10 per credit for in-state residents. Tuition of $220 per credit plus mandatory fees of $10 per credit for out-of-state residents. Costs may vary by number of credits taken. Financial aid is available to distance learners.
Registration Students may register by mail, fax, phone.
Contact Enrollment Services, University of Maine at Augusta, 46 University Drive, Augusta, ME 04330. *Telephone:* 207-621-3185. *Fax:* 207-621-3116. *E-mail:* umaar@maine.maine.edu.

DEGREE & CERTIFICATE PROGRAMS

Associate Degrees
▶ *Business Administration (AS)*
Application requirements *Prior education:* high school diploma or equivalent. *Other requirements:* high school transcript, college transcripts, an application fee of $25.

Profiles: University of Maine at Augusta

Completion requirements 60 credits are required. 15 credits must be completed through the institution.

▶ *General Studies (AS)*
Application requirements *Prior education:* high school diploma or equivalent. *Other requirements:* high school transcript, college transcripts, an application fee of $25.
Completion requirements 60 credits are required. 15 credits must be completed through the institution.

▶ *Liberal Arts (AA)*
Application requirements *Prior education:* high school diploma or equivalent. *Other requirements:* high school transcript, college transcripts, an application fee of $25.
Completion requirements 60 credits are required. 15 credits must be completed through the institution.

▶ *Library and Information Technology (AS)*
Application requirements *Prior education:* high school diploma or equivalent. *Other requirements:* high school transcript, college transcripts, an application fee of $25.
Completion requirements 60 credits are required. 15 credits must be completed through the institution.

▶ *Social Services (AA)*
Application requirements *Prior education:* high school diploma or equivalent. *Other requirements:* high school transcript, college transcripts, an application fee of $25.
Completion requirements 60 credits are required. 15 credits must be completed through the institution.

INDIVIDUAL COURSE SUBJECT AREAS

Undergraduate
Accounting; architecture; business; business administration and management; communications; developmental and child psychology; economics; English composition; English language and literature; European languages and literatures; fine arts; geology; history; human resources management; liberal arts, general studies, and humanities; mathematics; music; nursing; political science; psychology; social psychology; social sciences; sociology

UNIVERSITY OF MAINE AT FARMINGTON

Farmington, Maine

University of Maine at Farmington, founded in 1863, is a state-supported four-year college. It is accredited by the New England Association of Schools and Colleges. It first offered distance learning courses in 1989. In 1996–97, it offered 4 courses at a distance. In the fall of 1996, there was a total of 31 students enrolled in distance learning courses.
Course delivery sites Courses are delivered to University of Maine System (Bangor).
Media Courses are delivered via television. Students and teachers interact via audioconferencing, telephone.
Services Distance learners have access to library services, e-mail services, academic advising at a distance.
Credit-earning options Students may transfer credits from another institution or may earn credits through standardized exams, institutionally developed exams, military training.
Typical costs Tuition of $102 per credit for in-state residents. Tuition of $249 per credit for out-of-state residents. Costs may vary by number of credits taken. Financial aid is available to distance learners enrolled full-time or part-time.
Registration Students may register by phone.

Contact Hazel Doak, Registrar, University of Maine at Farmington, 86 Main Street, Farmington, ME 04938. *Telephone:* 207-778-7240. *Fax:* 207-778-7247. *E-mail:* hazel@maine.maine.edu.

INDIVIDUAL COURSE SUBJECT AREAS

Undergraduate
Education; special education

UNIVERSITY OF MAINE AT FORT KENT

Fort Kent, Maine

ITV

University of Maine at Fort Kent, founded in 1878, is a state-supported four-year college. It is accredited by the New England Association of Schools and Colleges.
Course delivery sites Courses are delivered to your home, your workplace, other colleges.
Media Courses are delivered via television, videotapes, World Wide Web, e-mail. Students and teachers interact via videoconferencing, audioconferencing, mail, telephone, fax, e-mail.
Services Distance learners have access to library services, academic advising, tutoring, career placement assistance at a distance.
Credit-earning options Students may transfer credits from another institution or may earn credits through examinations, portfolio assessment, military training.
Typical costs *Undergraduate:* Tuition of $94 per credit hour plus mandatory fees of $8 per credit hour for in-state residents. *Graduate:* Tuition of $179 per credit hour plus mandatory fees of $8 per credit hour for in-state residents. Costs may vary by campus or location. Financial aid is available to distance learners.
Contact Elizabeth Pinette, Director of Distance Learning, University of Maine at Fort Kent, 25 Pleasant Street, Fort Kent, ME 04743-1292. *Telephone:* 207-834-7562. *Fax:* 207-834-3335. *E-mail:* pinette@maine.maine.edu.

INDIVIDUAL COURSE SUBJECT AREAS

Undergraduate
Accounting; architecture; area, ethnic, and cultural studies; business; business administration and management; civil engineering; computer and information sciences; developmental and child psychology; economics; education administration; educational psychology; English composition; English language and literature; European languages and literatures; fine arts; geology; history; law and legal studies; liberal arts, general studies, and humanities; library and information studies; mathematics; music; nursing; philosophy and religion; political science; social psychology; sociology; special education; teacher education

Graduate
Area, ethnic, and cultural studies; civil engineering; education administration; library and information studies; nursing; special education; teacher education

Noncredit
Hospitality services management; human resources management

UNIVERSITY OF MAINE AT MACHIAS

Machias, Maine

University of Maine at Machias, founded in 1909, is a state-supported four-year college. It is accredited by the New England Association of Schools and Colleges. It first offered distance learning courses in 1996. In 1996–97, it offered 9 courses at a distance. In the fall of 1996, there was a total of 100 students enrolled in distance learning courses.
Course delivery sites Courses are delivered to your home, your workplace, military bases, 10 off-campus centers in Bath-Brunswick, Calais, East Millinocket, Ellsworth, Fort Kent, Houlton, Rumford-Mexico, Saco, Sanford, Thomaston.
Media Courses are delivered via television, World Wide Web. Students and teachers interact via mail, telephone, fax, e-mail, computer conferencing. A computer is required for some courses.
Restrictions Programs are available to in-state students only. Students must have an Associates Degree or 60 transferable credits.
Services Distance learners have access to library services, the campus computer network, e-mail services, academic advising at a distance.
Credit-earning options Students may transfer credits from another institution.
Typical costs Tuition of $94 per credit hour plus mandatory fees of $3 per credit hour for in-state residents. Tuition of $229 per credit hour plus mandatory fees of $3 per credit hour for out-of-state residents. ITV courses have an additional $5 per credit hour handling fee.. Financial aid is available to distance learners enrolled full-time or part-time.
Registration Students may register by mail, fax, phone.
Contact Dr. James Lehman, Associate Professor of Psychology, University of Maine at Machias, 9 O'Brien Avenue, Machias, ME 04654-1397. *Telephone:* 207-255-1336. *Fax:* 207-255-4864. *E-mail:* jlehman@acad.umm.maine.edu.

DEGREE & CERTIFICATE PROGRAMS

Baccalaureate Degrees
▶ *Behavioral Sciences (BA)*
In the fall of 1996 there were 50 students enrolled in this program.
Application requirements *Prior education:* associates degree or 60 credits. *Other requirements:* college transcripts, an essay or personal statement, an application fee of $25.
Completion requirements 120 credit hours are required. 30 credit hours must be completed through the institution. This is a degree completion program.

INDIVIDUAL COURSE SUBJECT AREAS

Undergraduate
Economics; English language and literature; physical sciences; social sciences

UNIVERSITY OF MARY

Bismarck, North Dakota

College for Professional Studies

University of Mary, founded in 1959, is an independent-religious Roman Catholic comprehensive institution. It is accredited by the North Central Association of Colleges and Schools. It first offered distance learning courses in 1982.
Course delivery sites Courses are delivered to your home, your workplace, military bases, 1 off-campus center in Fargo.
Media Courses are delivered via videotapes, e-mail, print. Students and teachers interact via audioconferencing, mail, telephone, fax, e-mail.
Typical costs *Undergraduate:* Tuition of $240 per credit. *Graduate:* Tuition of $255 per credit.
Contact Larry Brown, Dean, University of Mary, 7500 University Drive, Bismarck, ND 58504. *Telephone:* 701-255-7500. *Fax:* 701-255-7687.

DEGREE & CERTIFICATE PROGRAMS

Baccalaureate Degrees
▶ *Organizational Leadership (BS)*
Restrictions Students must have access to campus in Fargo, ND.
Application requirements *Prior education:* some undergraduate course work. *Other requirements:* high school transcript, college transcripts, an application fee of $25.
Completion requirements 128 credit hours are required. 37 credits must be completed through the institution. This is a degree completion program.
On-campus requirements Two 1-day seminars.

Graduate Degrees
▶ *Management (MIM)*
Restrictions Students must have access to campus in Fargo, ND.
Application requirements *Prior education:* baccalaureate degree. *Other requirements:* college transcripts, an essay or personal statement, an application fee of $15.
Completion requirements 30–39 credits are required. 21 credits must be completed through the institution. *Maximum time for completion:* seven years.

INDIVIDUAL COURSE SUBJECT AREAS

Undergraduate
Business; business administration and management; chemistry; communications; community health services; computer and information sciences; economics; education; environmental science; geography; health and physical education/fitness; health services administration; history; international relations; law and legal studies; mathematics; music; nursing; philosophy and religion; photography; political science; psychology; social work; sociology; theological studies

Graduate
Business; business administration and management; communications; community health services; computer and information sciences; economics; education; health services administration; international relations; law and legal studies; mathematics; nursing; philosophy and religion; psychology

UNIVERSITY OF MARYLAND, BALTIMORE

Baltimore, Maryland

School of Nursing Office of Learning Technologies

University of Maryland, Baltimore, founded in 1807, is a state-supported graduate institution. It is accredited by the Middle States Association of Colleges and Schools. It first offered distance learning courses in 1992. In 1996–97, it offered 5 courses at a distance.
Course delivery sites Courses are delivered to your home, Frostburg State University (Frostburg), 3 off-campus centers in Easton, Hereford, Shady Grove.

Profiles: University of Maryland, Baltimore

Media Courses are delivered via television, World Wide Web, e-mail, print. Students and teachers interact via videoconferencing, telephone, fax, e-mail, site visits. A computer is required for some courses.
Services Distance learners have access to library services, e-mail services, academic advising, tutoring, career placement assistance at a distance.
Credit-earning options Students may transfer credits from another institution or may earn credits through standardized exams.
Typical costs Costs may vary. Contact university for information. Financial aid is available to distance learners.
Contact Dr. Patricia Sokolove, Associate Vice President for Student Affairs, University of Maryland, Baltimore, 621 West Lombard Street, Baltimore, MD 21201. *Telephone:* 410-706-7117.

INDIVIDUAL COURSE SUBJECT AREAS

Undergraduate
Nursing

Graduate
Nursing; social work

UNIVERSITY OF MARYLAND, BALTIMORE COUNTY

Baltimore, Maryland

University of Maryland, Baltimore County, founded in 1963, is a state-supported university. It is accredited by the Middle States Association of Colleges and Schools. It first offered distance learning courses in 1990. In 1996–97, it offered 3 courses at a distance.
Course delivery sites Courses are delivered to your workplace, military bases, 11 University of Maryland system colleges.
Media Courses are delivered via television, videotapes, videoconferencing, audioconferencing, World Wide Web. Students and teachers interact via videoconferencing, audioconferencing, mail, telephone, fax, e-mail.
Restrictions Programs are available to in-state students only. Courses are for UM students only.
Services Distance learners have access to library services, e-mail services, academic advising at a distance.
Credit-earning options Students may transfer credits from another institution.
Typical costs *Undergraduate:* Tuition of $148 per credit plus mandatory fees of $40 per semester for in-state residents. Tuition of $330 per credit plus mandatory fees of $40 per semester for out-of-state residents. *Graduate:* Tuition of $231 per credit plus mandatory fees of $40 per semester for in-state residents. Tuition of $416 per credit plus mandatory fees of $40 per semester for out-of-state residents. Financial aid is available to distance learners.
Registration Students may register by phone.
Contact Kathleen Stitely, Program Coordinator, University of Maryland, Baltimore County, 100 Hilltop Circle, Baltimore, MD 21050. *Telephone:* 410-455-2797. *Fax:* 410-455-1115. *E-mail:* connect@umbc.edu.

INDIVIDUAL COURSE SUBJECT AREAS

Undergraduate
Electrical engineering; health professions and related sciences; physics

Graduate
Electrical engineering; physics

UNIVERSITY OF MARYLAND, COLLEGE PARK

College Park, Maryland

University of Maryland, College Park, founded in 1856, is a state-supported university. It is accredited by the Middle States Association of Colleges and Schools.
Course delivery sites Courses are delivered to your workplace, military bases, other colleges, off-campus center(s).
Media Courses are delivered via television, videoconferencing. Students and teachers interact via mail, telephone, fax, e-mail.
Credit-earning options Students may transfer credits from another institution or may earn credits through examinations, portfolio assessment, military training.
Typical costs Tuition of $510 per course for in-state residents. Tuition of $1287 per course for out-of-state residents. Costs may vary by campus or location.
Contact Dr. Arnold E. Seigel, Director of Educational Television, University of Maryland, College Park, 2104 Engineering Building, College Park, MD 20742. *Telephone:* 301-405-4910.

DEGREE & CERTIFICATE PROGRAMS

Graduate Degrees
▶ *Computer Engineering, Electrical Engineering, Mechanical Engineering, Reliability Engineering, Systems Engineering* (MS)
Completion requirements 30 are required. *Maximum time for completion:* five years.

INDIVIDUAL COURSE SUBJECT AREAS

Undergraduate
Business; communications; computer and information sciences; education; engineering; liberal arts, general studies, and humanities; physical sciences; social sciences

Graduate
Engineering

UNIVERSITY OF MARYLAND UNIVERSITY COLLEGE

College Park, Maryland

Open Learning

University of Maryland University College, founded in 1947, is a state-supported comprehensive institution. It is accredited by the Middle States Association of Colleges and Schools. It first offered distance learning courses in 1972. In 1996–97, it offered 594 courses at a distance. In the fall of 1996, there was a total of 3,334 students enrolled in distance learning courses.
Course delivery sites Courses are delivered to your home, your workplace, military bases, National Universities Degree Consortium, 17 sites in Maryland, Virginia and Washington, DC.
Media Courses are delivered via television, videotapes, videoconferencing, computer software, World Wide Web, print. Students and teachers interact via videoconferencing, mail, telephone, fax, e-mail, computer conferencing. A computer is required for some courses.

Services Distance learners have access to library services, the campus computer network, e-mail services, academic advising, tutoring, career placement assistance at a distance.
Credit-earning options Students may transfer credits from another institution or may earn credits through examinations, portfolio assessment, military training, business training.
Typical costs *Undergraduate:* Tuition of $181 per credit for in-state residents. Tuition of $209 per credit for out-of-state residents. *Graduate:* Tuition of $273 per credit for in-state residents. Tuition of $353 per credit for out-of-state residents. Costs may vary by course delivery options. Financial aid is available to distance learners enrolled full-time or part-time.
Registration Students may register by mail, fax, phone, e-mail, World Wide Web.
Contact Enrollment Team, Undergraduate Student Services, University of Maryland University College, University Boulevard at Adelphi Road, College Park, MD 20742-1636. *Telephone:* 800-283-6832, Ext. 7265. *Fax:* 301-985-7364. *E-mail:* distance@nova.umuc.edu. *Web site:* http://www.umuc.edu/distance/bdaad.html.

DEGREE & CERTIFICATE PROGRAMS

Baccalaureate Degrees

▶ *Behavioral and Social Sciences, Communications Studies, Computer and Information Science, Fire Science, Humanities, Management, Paralegal Studies, Technology Management (BA, BS)*
In the fall of 1996 there were 999 students enrolled in this program. In 1995–96, 64 degrees were earned at a distance through this program.
Restrictions Program is available to US and Canadian students only.
Application requirements *Prior education:* high school diploma or equivalent. *Other requirements:* high school transcript, college transcripts, an application fee of $25.
Completion requirements 120 semester hours are required. 30 semester hours must be completed through the institution. This is a degree completion program.

Graduate Degrees

▶ *Computer Systems Management, Technology Management (MS)*
In the fall of 1996 there were 5 students enrolled in this program.
Restrictions Students must have a Windows-based computer, Internet access, printer.
Application requirements *Prior education:* baccalaureate degree. *Other requirements:* college transcripts, an essay or personal statement, an application fee of $50, 3.0 GPA in last 60 hours of undergraduate program.
Completion requirements 36 semester hours are required. 30 semester hours must be completed through the institution. *Maximum time for completion:* seven years.
Program contact Donna Grube, UMUC Graduate School of Technology, University of Maryland University College, University Boulevard at Adelphi Road, College Park, MD 20741-0869. Phone: 301-985-4617. Fax: 301-985-4611. E-mail: gradschool@info.umuc.edu.

▶ *General Administration (MGA)*
In the fall of 1996 there were 14 students enrolled in this program.
Restrictions Students must have a Windows-based computer, Internet access, printer.
Application requirements *Prior education:* baccalaureate degree. *Other requirements:* college transcripts, an essay or personal statement, an application fee of $50, 2.5 GPA.
Completion requirements 36 semester hours are required. 30 semester hours must be completed through the institution. *Maximum time for completion:* seven years.
Program contact Donna Grube, UMUC Graduate School of Technology, University of Maryland University College, University Boulevard at Adelphi Road, College Park, MD 20741-0869. Phone: 301-985-4617. Fax: 301-985-4611. E-mail: gradschool@info.umuc.edu.

INDIVIDUAL COURSE SUBJECT AREAS

Undergraduate
Accounting; biology; business; business administration and management; communications; computer and information sciences; criminal justice; economics; English composition; English language and literature; fire science; French language and literature; history; human resources management; journalism; law and legal studies; liberal arts, general studies, and humanities; management information systems; mathematics; microbiology; physics; political science; psychology; sociology; Spanish language and literature

Graduate
Business administration and management; computer and information sciences; engineering/industrial management; information sciences and systems; international business; management information systems; telecommunications

See full description on page 506.

UNIVERSITY OF MASSACHUSETTS AMHERST

Amherst, Massachusetts

Video Instructional Program

University of Massachusetts Amherst, founded in 1863, is a state-supported university. It is accredited by the New England Association of Schools and Colleges. It first offered distance learning courses in 1974. In 1996–97, it offered 65 courses at a distance. In the fall of 1996, there was a total of 186 students enrolled in distance learning courses.
Course delivery sites Courses are delivered to your home, your workplace, military bases.
Media Courses are delivered via television, videotapes, videoconferencing, World Wide Web. Students and teachers interact via videoconferencing, mail, telephone, fax, e-mail. A computer is required for some courses.
Services Distance learners have access to library services, the campus computer network, e-mail services, academic advising at a distance.
Credit-earning options Students may transfer credits from another institution.
Typical costs Tuition of $1225 per semester plus mandatory fees of $20 per semester. International students pay $1425 per semester and the $20 per semester registration fee. *Noncredit courses:* $1225 per course. Financial aid is available to distance learners.
Registration Students may register by mail, fax, World Wide Web.
Contact Mary L. McCulloch, Marketing Coordinator, Video Instructional Program, University of Massachusetts Amherst, College of Engineering, 113 Marcus Hall, Amherst, MA 01003-5115. *Telephone:* 413-545-0063. *Fax:* 413-545-1227. *E-mail:* vip@vip.ecs.umass.edu. *Web site:* http://www.ecs.umass.edu/vip.

DEGREE & CERTIFICATE PROGRAMS

Graduate Degrees

▶ *Computer Science (MS)*
Application requirements *Prior education:* baccalaureate degree. *Other requirements:* GRE, 2.75 GPA, TOEFL (for international students).
Completion requirements 10 courses are required. *Maximum time for completion:* four years.

Profiles: University of Massachusetts Amherst

▶ *Electrical and Computer Engineering (MS)*
In the fall of 1996 there were 32 students enrolled in this program. In 1995–96, 17 degrees were earned at a distance through this program.
Application requirements *Prior education:* baccalaureate degree. *Other requirements:* GRE, 2.75 GPA, TOEFL (for international students).
Completion requirements 11 courses are required. *Other requirements:* this program is available with an emphasis in either Computer Systems Engineering or Communications and Control Systems or Microwave Electronics. Optional thesis. *Maximum time for completion:* four years.

▶ *Engineering Management (MS)*
In the fall of 1996 there were 42 students enrolled in this program. In 1995–96, 20 degrees were earned at a distance through this program.
Application requirements *Prior education:* baccalaureate degree. *Other requirements:* GRE, 2.75 GPA, TOEFL (for international students).
Completion requirements 12 courses are required. *Maximum time for completion:* four years.

INDIVIDUAL COURSE SUBJECT AREAS

Undergraduate
Computer and information sciences; electrical engineering; mathematics

Graduate
Chemical engineering; computer and information sciences; electrical engineering; engineering/industrial management; environmental engineering; industrial engineering; mathematics; mechanical engineering

Noncredit
Chemical engineering; computer and information sciences; electrical engineering; engineering-related technologies; engineering/industrial management; environmental engineering; industrial engineering; mathematics; mechanical engineering

UNIVERSITY OF MASSACHUSETTS BOSTON

Boston, Massachusetts

MUSE, Distance Learning Program

University of Massachusetts Boston, founded in 1964, is a state-supported university. It is accredited by the New England Association of Schools and Colleges. It first offered distance learning courses in 1994. In 1996–97, it offered 5 courses at a distance. In the fall of 1996, there was a total of 55 students enrolled in distance learning courses.
Course delivery sites Courses are delivered to University of Massachusetts System (Boston), Boston public schools.
Media Courses are delivered via television, videoconferencing, World Wide Web. Students and teachers interact via videoconferencing, audioconferencing, telephone, e-mail. A computer is required for some courses.
Restrictions Programs are available to in-state students only.
Services Distance learners have access to the campus computer network, e-mail services, academic advising, tutoring at a distance.
Credit-earning options Students may earn credits through examinations.
Typical costs *Undergraduate:* Tuition of $135 per credit for in-state residents. *Graduate:* Tuition of $150 per credit for in-state residents. $20 registration fee. Costs may vary by specific program of study, number of credits taken, course delivery options.
Registration Students may register by mail, phone, e-mail.
Contact Donald D. Babcock, Senior Associate Vice Chancellor, University of Massachusetts Boston, 100 Morrissey Boulevard, Boston, MA 02125. *Telephone:* 617-287-5400. *Fax:* 617-287-5110. *E-mail:* babcock@umbcky.cc.umb.edu.

INDIVIDUAL COURSE SUBJECT AREAS

Undergraduate
Business administration and management; electrical engineering; English composition; mathematics

Graduate
Curriculum and instruction
See full description on page 508.

UNIVERSITY OF MASSACHUSETTS DARTMOUTH

North Dartmouth, Massachusetts

Internet Development

University of Massachusetts Dartmouth, founded in 1895, is a state-supported comprehensive institution. It is accredited by the New England Association of Schools and Colleges. It first offered distance learning courses in 1995. In 1996–97, it offered 18 courses at a distance. In the fall of 1996, there was a total of 150 students enrolled in distance learning courses.
Course delivery sites Courses are delivered to your home, your workplace, military bases, any location with Internet access.
Media Courses are delivered via World Wide Web, e-mail, print. Students and teachers interact via mail, telephone, e-mail. A computer is required for all courses.
Typical costs *Undergraduate:* Tuition of $408 per credit. *Graduate:* Tuition of $483 per credit. *Noncredit courses:* $135 per course. Costs may vary by number of credits taken. Financial aid is available to distance learners.
Registration Students may register by mail, fax, phone, e-mail, World Wide Web.
Contact Greg Stone, Director, Internet Development, University of Massachusetts Dartmouth, 1346 Drift Road, Westport, MA 02790. *Telephone:* 508-636-4291. *E-mail:* gstone@umassd.edu. *Web site:* http://www.umassd.edu.

INDIVIDUAL COURSE SUBJECT AREAS

Undergraduate
Astronomy and astrophysics; chemistry; finance; Jewish studies; physics

Graduate
Technical writing

Noncredit
Marketing; telecommunications

UNIVERSITY OF MASSACHUSETTS LOWELL

Lowell, Massachusetts

Division of Continuing Education

University of Massachusetts Lowell, founded in 1894, is a state-supported university. It is accredited by the New England Association of Schools and Colleges. It first offered distance learning courses in 1995. In 1996–97, it offered 20 courses at a distance. In the fall of 1996, there was a total of 206 students enrolled in distance learning courses.

Course delivery sites Courses are delivered to your home, your workplace, Bunker Hill Community College (Boston), 20 off-campus centers.
Media Courses are delivered via television, World Wide Web, networked transmission. Students and teachers interact via telephone, fax, e-mail. A computer is required for some courses.
Services Distance learners have access to library services, academic advising at a distance.
Credit-earning options Students may transfer credits from another institution or may earn credits through examinations, military training, business training.
Typical costs $400–$600 per course. Financial aid is available to distance learners.
Contact Katherine Galaitsis, Coordinator, Special Programs, University of Massachusetts Lowell, College of Continuing Education, One University Avenue, Lowell, MA 01854-2881. *Telephone:* 508-934-2446. *Fax:* 508-934-3008. *E-mail:* galaitsik@woods.uml.edu. *Web site:* http://www.uml.edu/DCE.

Special note
The University of Massachusetts Lowell is part of the Massachusetts Consortium for Distance Education (MASSCODE), which includes Bunker Hill Community College, Middlesex Community College, North Shore Community College, Northern Essex Community College, and the Massachusetts Corporation for Educational Telecommunications (MCET). MASSCODE's goal is to share resources and increase course offerings throughout the state's higher education community. All the participating institutions are connected via a full-motion multichannel fiber-optic video network connecting each campus distance learning classroom. The network allows for both point-to-point and multipoint transmissions.

DEGREE & CERTIFICATE PROGRAMS

Undergraduate Certificates
▶ *Plastics Engineering Technology*
In the fall of 1996 there were 200 students enrolled in this program.

INDIVIDUAL COURSE SUBJECT AREAS

Undergraduate
Business administration and management; chemistry; civil engineering; computer and information sciences; developmental and child psychology; education; engineering-related technologies; English composition; geography; health professions and related sciences; journalism; liberal arts, general studies, and humanities; mathematics; nursing; philosophy and religion; sociology

THE UNIVERSITY OF MEMPHIS

Memphis, Tennessee

Extended Programs

The University of Memphis, founded in 1912, is a state-supported university. It is accredited by the Southern Association of Colleges and Schools. It first offered distance learning courses in 1985. In 1996–97, it offered 25 courses at a distance. In the fall of 1996, there was a total of 450 students enrolled in distance learning courses.
Course delivery sites Courses are delivered to your home, your workplace, military bases, Dyersburg State Community College (Dyersburg), Jackson State Community College (Jackson), 1 off-campus center in Jackson.
Media Courses are delivered via television, videotapes, videoconferencing, World Wide Web, e-mail. Students and teachers interact via mail, telephone, fax, e-mail. A computer is required for some courses.
Restrictions Some classes are geographically restricted.
Services Distance learners have access to library services, the campus computer network, e-mail services, academic advising at a distance.
Credit-earning options Students may transfer credits from another institution or may earn credits through standardized exams, portfolio assessment, military training.
Typical costs *Undergraduate:* Tuition of $105 per credit hour plus mandatory fees of $34 per semester for in-state residents. Tuition of $306 per credit hour plus mandatory fees of $34 per semester for out-of-state residents. *Graduate:* Tuition of $142 per credit hour plus mandatory fees of $34 per semester for in-state residents. Tuition of $343 per credit hour plus mandatory fees of $34 per semester for out-of-state residents. Costs may vary by number of credits taken. Financial aid is available to distance learners enrolled full-time.
Registration Students may register by mail, phone.
Contact Sam Brackstone, Director, Extended Programs, The University of Memphis, Administration 382, Memphis, TN 38152. *Telephone:* 901-678-2991. *Fax:* 901-678-4049. *E-mail:* sbrackstone@cc.memphis.edu. *Web site:* http://www.extended.memphis.edu.

DEGREE & CERTIFICATE PROGRAMS

Graduate Degrees
▶ *Journalism (MA)*
In the fall of 1996 there were 25 students enrolled in this program.
Application requirements *Prior education:* baccalaureate degree. *Other requirements:* GRE, college transcripts, an application fee of $25.
Completion requirements 30–36 hours are required. 24–30 hours must be completed through the institution. *Other requirements:* 30 hour track requires thesis and oral composition, 33 hour track requires a professional project and compositions, 36 hour track requires compositions and classwork. *Maximum time for completion:* six years.
Program contact Dan Lattimore, Department Chair, The University of Memphis, Journalism Department, University of Memphis, Memphis, TN 38152. Phone: 901-678-2401.

INDIVIDUAL COURSE SUBJECT AREAS

Undergraduate
Area, ethnic, and cultural studies; business; business administration and management; economics; education administration; educational psychology; engineering-related technologies; English composition; English language and literature; health and physical education/fitness; history; liberal arts, general studies, and humanities; nursing; philosophy and religion; sociology; special education; teacher education

Graduate
Business; business administration and management; education administration; educational psychology; English composition; English language and literature; journalism; special education; teacher education

UNIVERSITY OF MICHIGAN

Ann Arbor, Michigan

Office of Academic Outreach

University of Michigan, founded in 1817, is a state-supported university. It is accredited by the North Central Association of Colleges and Schools. It first offered distance learning courses in 1969. In 1996–97, it offered 50 courses at a distance. In the fall of 1996, there was a total of 750 students enrolled in distance learning courses.

Profiles: University of Michigan

Course delivery sites Courses are delivered to your home, your workplace.
Media Courses are delivered via videotapes, videoconferencing, audiotapes, World Wide Web, e-mail, print. Students and teachers interact via videoconferencing, mail, telephone, fax, e-mail. A computer is required for some courses.
Restrictions Some courses require employer's sponsorship.
Services Distance learners have access to library services, the campus computer network, e-mail services, academic advising, tutoring at a distance.
Typical costs *Undergraduate:* Tuition of $300 per credit hour plus mandatory fees of $275 per semester for in-state residents. Tuition of $800 per credit hour plus mandatory fees of $275 per semester for out-of-state residents. *Graduate:* Tuition of $700 per credit hour plus mandatory fees of $275 per semester for in-state residents. Tuition of $1100 per credit hour plus mandatory fees of $275 per semester for out-of-state residents. Costs may vary by specific program of study.
Registration Students may register by mail, fax.
Contact Glenda Radine, Interim Director, Extension Services, University of Michigan, Office of Academic Outreach, 837 Greene Street, Ann Arbor, MI 48104-3297. *Telephone:* 313-764-5300. *Fax:* 313-936-7736. *E-mail:* ao-courses@umich.edu. *Web site:* http://www.outreach.umich.edu/.

DEGREE & CERTIFICATE PROGRAMS

Graduate Degrees
▶ *Automotive Engineering (ME)*
In the fall of 1996 there were 145 students enrolled in this program.
Restrictions Students must have corporate sponsorship. Minimum of 4 students/class.
Application requirements *Prior education:* baccalaureate degree. *Other requirements:* GRE, college transcripts, an essay or personal statement, letter(s) of recommendation, an application fee of $55, 2 years college engineering math, undergraduate courses in 3 areas (Power and Propulsion, Dynamics and Controls, Aerodynamic and Structural Mechanical Electronics), 2 years or equivalent industrial experience.
Completion requirements 30 credits are required. 24 credits must be completed through the institution. *Other requirements:* Automotive Engineering Seminar and Project. *Maximum time for completion:* five years.
Program contact Kathy M. Friedrichs, Manager, Off-Campus Education Program, Center for Professional Development, University of Michigan, 273 Chrysler Center, Ann Arbor, MI 49109-2092. Phone: 313-647-7173. Fax: 313-647-7196. E-mail: kamf@engin.umich.edu.

▶ *Manufacturing Engineering (ME)*
In the fall of 1996 there were 145 students enrolled in this program.
Restrictions Students must have corporate sponsorship. Minimum of 4 students/class.
Application requirements *Prior education:* baccalaureate degree. *Other requirements:* GRE, college transcripts, an essay or personal statement, letter(s) of recommendation, an application fee of $55, 2 years college engineering math, 2 years or equivalent industrial experience, GRE highly recommended.
Completion requirements 30 semester hours are required. 24 credits must be completed through the institution. *Other requirements:* Manufacturing Seminar Series and work teams on project related to industry. *Maximum time for completion:* five years.
Program contact Kathy M. Friedrichs, Manager, Off-Campus Education Program, Center for Professional Development, University of Michigan, 273 Chrysler Center, Ann Arbor, MI 49109-2092. Phone: 313-647-7173. Fax: 313-647-7196. E-mail: kamf@engin.umich.edu.

INDIVIDUAL COURSE SUBJECT AREAS

Undergraduate
American literature; area, ethnic, and cultural studies; Asian studies; calculus; conservation and natural resources; nursing; psychology; women's studies

Graduate
Engineering; French language and literature; German language and literature

UNIVERSITY OF MINNESOTA, TWIN CITIES CAMPUS

Minneapolis, Minnesota

Independent and Distance Learning

University of Minnesota, Twin Cities Campus, founded in 1851, is a state-supported university. It is accredited by the North Central Association of Colleges and Schools. It first offered distance learning courses in 1909. In 1996–97, it offered 340 courses at a distance. In the fall of 1996, there was a total of 4,000 students enrolled in distance learning courses.
Course delivery sites Courses are delivered to your home.
Media Courses are delivered via videotapes, audiotapes, computer software, World Wide Web, print. Students and teachers interact via mail, e-mail, computer conferencing. A computer is required for some courses.
Services Distance learners have access to e-mail services, academic advising at a distance.
Credit-earning options Students may transfer credits from another institution or may earn credits through institutionally developed exams.
Typical costs *Undergraduate:* Tuition of $95 per quarter credit. *Graduate:* Tuition of $127.50 per quarter credit. *Noncredit courses:* $95 per equivalent of quarter credit. Costs may vary by specific program of study, course level. Financial aid is available to distance learners enrolled full-time.
Registration Students may register by mail, fax, phone, e-mail, World Wide Web.
Contact Receptionist, Independent and Distance Learning, University of Minnesota, Twin Cities Campus, 45 Wesbrook Hall, 77 Pleasant Street, SE, Minneapolis, MN 55455. *Telephone:* 612-624-0000. *Fax:* 612-626-7900. *E-mail:* indstudy@maroon.tc.umn.edu. *Web site:* http://www.cee.umn.edu/dis.

DEGREE & CERTIFICATE PROGRAMS

Undergraduate Certificates
▶ *Liberal Arts*
In 1995–96, 1 certificate was earned at a distance through this program.
Application requirements *Prior education:* some undergraduate course work. *Other requirements:* high school transcript, college transcripts, an application fee of $20.
Completion requirements 45 quarter credits are required. 12 quarter credits must be completed through the institution.

▶ *Science and Quantitative Methods*
Application requirements *Prior education:* some undergraduate course work. *Other requirements:* high school transcript, college transcripts, an application fee of $20, student proposal with a specific course plan.
Completion requirements 45 quarter credits are required. 12 quarter credits must be completed through the institution.

INDIVIDUAL COURSE SUBJECT AREAS

Undergraduate

Accounting; anthropology; architecture; area, ethnic, and cultural studies; Asian languages and literatures; astronomy and astrophysics; biological and life sciences; biology; business; business administration and management; chemistry; Classical languages and literatures; computer and information sciences; conservation and natural resources; creative writing; design; developmental and child psychology; economics; education administration; educational psychology; engineering; English composition; European languages and literatures; fine arts; foods and nutrition studies; geography; geology; history; home economics and family studies; industrial psychology; journalism; law and legal studies; liberal arts, general studies, and humanities; mathematics; microbiology; music; nursing; philosophy and religion; physics; political science; public health; social psychology; social work; sociology; statistics; teacher education; theological studies; visual and performing arts

Noncredit

Biology; business; business administration and management; English composition; English language and literature; European languages and literatures; mathematics; physics; psychology; social sciences

See full description on page 510.

UNIVERSITY OF MISSISSIPPI

University, Mississippi

Office of Distance Learning

University of Mississippi, founded in 1844, is a state-supported university. It is accredited by the Southern Association of Colleges and Schools. It first offered distance learning courses in 1995. In 1996–97, it offered 18 courses at a distance. In the fall of 1996, there was a total of 283 students enrolled in distance learning courses.
Course delivery sites Courses are delivered to 3 off-campus centers in Jackson, Southaven, Tupelo.
Media Courses are delivered via videoconferencing. Students and teachers interact via videoconferencing, fax.
Services Distance learners have access to library services, the campus computer network, e-mail services, academic advising at a distance.
Credit-earning options Students may transfer credits from another institution.
Typical costs *Undergraduate:* Tuition of $83 per credit hour for in-state residents. Tuition of $201 per credit hour for out-of-state residents. *Graduate:* Tuition of $111 per credit hour for in-state residents. Tuition of $268 per credit hour for out-of-state residents. Costs may vary by campus or location. Financial aid is available to distance learners enrolled full-time.
Registration Students may register by mail.
Contact Office of Distance Learning, University of Mississippi, Center for Public Service and Continuing Studies, University, MS 38677-0879. *Telephone:* 601-232-7282. *Fax:* 601-232-5138. *E-mail:* cstudies@olemiss.edu. *Web site:* http://sunset.backbone.olemiss.edu/depts/continuing_studies.

INDIVIDUAL COURSE SUBJECT AREAS

Undergraduate

Business; business administration and management; education; education administration; ethics; finance; marketing; real estate; special education

Graduate

Business; business administration and management; education; education administration; ethics; finance; marketing; real estate; special education

UNIVERSITY OF MISSOURI–COLUMBIA

Columbia, Missouri

Center for Independent Study

University of Missouri–Columbia, founded in 1839, is a state-supported university. It is accredited by the North Central Association of Colleges and Schools. It first offered distance learning courses in 1911. In 1996–97, it offered 184 courses at a distance.
Course delivery sites Courses are delivered to your home, military bases.
Media Courses are delivered via videotapes, audiotapes, print. Students and teachers interact via mail.
Restrictions Students must have good command of English language.
Services Distance learners have access to academic advising at a distance.
Typical costs *Undergraduate:* Tuition of $121 per credit hour. *Graduate:* Tuition of $158.20 per credit hour. *Noncredit courses:* $80 per course. Costs may vary by number of credits taken, course delivery options.
Registration Students may register by mail, fax, phone.
Contact Ellen L. Wyllie, Instructional Services Advisor, University of Missouri–Columbia, 136 Clark Hall, Columbia, MO 65211. *Telephone:* 800-858-6413. *Fax:* 573-882-6808. *E-mail:* wylliee@ext.missouri.edu. *Web site:* http://indepstudy.ext.missouri.edu.

INDIVIDUAL COURSE SUBJECT AREAS

Undergraduate

Abnormal psychology; accounting; advertising; African-American studies; agriculture; animal sciences; anthropology; area, ethnic, and cultural studies; astronomy and astrophysics; biological and life sciences; biology; business; business administration and management; business law; Classical languages and literatures; computer and information sciences; corrections; creative writing; criminal justice; curriculum and instruction; developmental and child psychology; earth science; economics; education; educational psychology; engineering; engineering mechanics; engineering/industrial management; English composition; English language and literature; ethics; European languages and literatures; finance; French language and literature; genetics; geography; geology; German language and literature; health and physical education/fitness; health professions and related sciences; health services administration; history; history of science and technology; home economics and family studies; horticulture; industrial psychology; law and legal studies; liberal arts, general studies, and humanities; logic; marketing; mass media; mathematics; meteorology; music; philosophy and religion; physical sciences; physics; political science; protective services; psychology; Russian language and literature; social psychology; social work; sociology; Spanish language and literature; statistics; technical writing; theological studies; visual and performing arts; women's studies

Graduate

Adult education; advertising; agriculture; animal sciences; astronomy and astrophysics; biological and life sciences; business; business administration and management; Classical languages and literatures; criminal justice; curriculum and instruction; economics; education; education administration; educational psychology; engineering/industrial management; English language and literature; geology; health professions and related sciences; history; home economics and family studies; human resources management; journalism; law and legal studies; library and information studies;

Profiles: University of Missouri–Columbia

marketing; mathematics; organizational behavior studies; physics; plant sciences; political science; protective services; psychology; social work; sociology; special education; teacher education

Noncredit
Fire services administration; health professions and related sciences; nursing; political science; protective services; public administration and services; theological studies

See full description on page 512.

UNIVERSITY OF MISSOURI–KANSAS CITY

Kansas City, Missouri

Interactive Video Network

University of Missouri–Kansas City, founded in 1929, is a state-supported university. It is accredited by the North Central Association of Colleges and Schools.
Course delivery sites Courses are delivered to your home, your workplace, other colleges.
Media Courses are delivered via television, videotapes, videoconferencing, computer software, print, computer conferencing.
Services Distance learners have access to library services, academic advising, tutoring at a distance.
Credit-earning options Students may transfer credits from another institution or may earn credits through examinations, military training.
Contact Interactive Video Network, University of Missouri–Kansas City, 5100 Rockhill Road, Kansas City, MO 64110-2499. *Telephone:* 816-235-1096. *Fax:* 816-235-1170.

DEGREE & CERTIFICATE PROGRAMS

Associate Degrees
▶ *Liberal Arts (AA)*
On-campus requirements Two weeks.

Graduate Degrees
▶ *Electrical Engineering with Power Emphasis (MS)*
On-campus requirements Two weeks.
▶ *Engineering Management (MS)*
Application requirements *Prior education:* degree in engineering.
On-campus requirements Two weeks.
▶ *Nursing (MSN)*
On-campus requirements Two weeks.
▶ *Software Engineering (MS)*
On-campus requirements Two weeks.

INDIVIDUAL COURSE SUBJECT AREAS

Undergraduate
Accounting; computer and information sciences; creative writing; economics; English composition; English language and literature; history; home economics and family studies; liberal arts, general studies, and humanities; mathematics; philosophy and religion; physics; social psychology; social work; sociology

Graduate
Business; chemical engineering; civil engineering; computer and information sciences; electrical engineering; engineering/industrial management; English composition; human resources management; industrial engineering; mechanical engineering; nursing; sociology

See full description on page 514.

UNIVERSITY OF MISSOURI–ST. LOUIS

St. Louis, Missouri

Video Instructional Program

University of Missouri–St. Louis, founded in 1963, is a state-supported university. It is accredited by the North Central Association of Colleges and Schools.
Course delivery sites Courses are delivered to your home, other colleges.
Media Courses are delivered via television, videotapes, videoconferencing, computer conferencing.
Services Distance learners have access to library services, academic advising, tutoring, career placement assistance at a distance.
Contact Linda Lockhart, Administrative Secretary, University of Missouri–St. Louis, 113 Lucas Hall, 8001 Natural Bridge Road, St. Louis, MO 63121. *Telephone:* 314-516-6171. *Fax:* 314-516-5294. *E-mail:* sllockh@wmslvma.umsl.edu. *Web site:* http://www.umsl.edu/services/itc/itc.htm.

INDIVIDUAL COURSE SUBJECT AREAS

Undergraduate
Area, ethnic, and cultural studies; developmental and child psychology; education administration; fine arts; history; philosophy and religion; radio and television broadcasting; teacher education

THE UNIVERSITY OF MONTANA–MISSOULA

Missoula, Montana

Extended Studies

The University of Montana–Missoula, founded in 1893, is a state-supported university. It is accredited by the Northwest Association of Schools and Colleges. It first offered distance learning courses in 1989. In 1996–97, it offered 55 courses at a distance. In the fall of 1996, there was a total of 2,500 students enrolled in distance learning courses.
Course delivery sites Courses are delivered to your home, your workplace, military bases, College of Technology of The University of Montana–Missoula (Missoula), Flathead Valley Community College (Kalispell), Montana Tech of The University of Montana (Butte), 5 off-campus centers in Billings, Butte, Great Falls, Helena, Kalispell.
Media Courses are delivered via videoconferencing, computer software, World Wide Web, e-mail, print. Students and teachers interact via videoconferencing, mail, telephone, fax, e-mail. A computer is required for all courses.
Services Distance learners have access to library services, the campus computer network, e-mail services, academic advising at a distance.
Credit-earning options Students may transfer credits from another institution or may earn credits through institutionally developed exams.
Typical costs *Undergraduate:* Tuition of $175 per semester credit. *Graduate:* Tuition of $250 per semester credit. Costs may vary by specific program of study. Financial aid is available to distance learners enrolled full-time.
Registration Students may register by mail, fax, phone, e-mail, World Wide Web.
Contact Dorothy Deschamps, Registrar, The University of Montana–Missoula, Missoula, MT 59812-0002. *Telephone:* 406-243-4626. *Fax:* 406-243-2047. *Web site:* http://www.umt.edu/ccesp/.

DEGREE & CERTIFICATE PROGRAMS

Graduate Degrees

▶ *Business Administration (MBA)*
Restrictions This program is available to in-state students only.
Application requirements *Prior education:* baccalaureate degree. *Other requirements:* GMAT, college transcripts, an essay or personal statement, letter(s) of recommendation, an application fee of $40.
Completion requirements 32 semester credits are required. 21 semester credits must be completed through the institution. *Maximum time for completion:* six years.
On-campus requirements Once a semester.

▶ *Education (EdD)*
Restrictions This program is available to local area students only. Compressed weekend module set-up required.
Application requirements *Prior education:* master's degree in education. *Other requirements:* GRE, college transcripts, an essay or personal statement, letter(s) of recommendation, an application fee of $40.
Completion requirements 53 semester credits are required. 44 semester credits must be completed through the institution. *Maximum time for completion:* four years.
On-campus requirements Four weekends per semester or 45 hours per 3 credit course.

▶ *Education (MEd)*
Restrictions This program is available to in-state students only.
Application requirements *Prior education:* baccalaureate degree in education. *Other requirements:* GRE, college transcripts, an essay or personal statement, letter(s) of recommendation, an application fee of $40.
Completion requirements 36 semester credits are required. 36 semester credits must be completed through the institution. *Maximum time for completion:* two-and-a-half years.
On-campus requirements Once a semester.

▶ *Pharmacy (PharmD)*
Application requirements *Prior education:* baccalaureate degree. *Other requirements:* college transcripts, letter(s) of recommendation, an application fee of $40.
Completion requirements 53 semester credits are required. 44 semester credits must be completed through the institution.
On-campus requirements Three-day orientation to program.

INDIVIDUAL COURSE SUBJECT AREAS

Undergraduate
Gerontology

Graduate
Business; business administration and management; computer and information sciences; education administration; English as a second language (ESL); gerontology; health professions and related sciences; human resources management; political science; teacher education

UNIVERSITY OF NEBRASKA AT KEARNEY

Kearney, Nebraska

Division of Continuing Education

University of Nebraska at Kearney, founded in 1903, is a state-supported comprehensive institution. It is accredited by the North Central Association of Colleges and Schools. It first offered distance learning courses in 1986. In 1996–97, it offered 13 courses at a distance. In the fall of 1996, there was a total of 188 students enrolled in distance learning courses.

Course delivery sites Courses are delivered to your home, workplace, Central Community College–Platte Campus (Columbus), Mid-Plains Community College (North Platte), 1 off-campus center in Grand Island.
Media Courses are delivered via television, videotapes, videoconferencing, audiotapes, audioconferencing, World Wide Web, e-mail, print. Students and teachers interact via videoconferencing, audioconferencing, mail, telephone, fax, e-mail. A computer is required for some courses.
Restrictions Programs are available to in-state students only.
Services Distance learners have access to library services, the campus computer network, e-mail services, academic advising, tutoring, career placement assistance at a distance.
Credit-earning options Students may transfer credits from another institution or may earn credits through examinations.
Typical costs *Undergraduate:* Tuition of $60 per credit plus mandatory fees of $5.50 per credit for local area residents. Tuition of $66 per credit plus mandatory fees of $5.50 per credit for in-state residents. Tuition of $113 per credit plus mandatory fees of $5.50 per credit for out-of-state residents. *Graduate:* Tuition of $80 per credit plus mandatory fees of $5.50 per credit for in-state residents. Tuition of $142 per credit plus mandatory fees of $5.50 per credit for out-of-state residents. Financial aid is available to distance learners enrolled full-time or part-time.
Registration Students may register by phone.
Contact Gloria Vavricka, Coordinator of Continuing Education, University of Nebraska at Kearney, Education Center Building, Kearney, NE 68849-4220. *Telephone:* 308-865-8390. *Fax:* 308-865-8090. *E-mail:* vavrickag@platte.unk.edu.

INDIVIDUAL COURSE SUBJECT AREAS

Undergraduate
Accounting; administrative and secretarial services; advertising; biology; botany; business; business administration and management; computer and information sciences; creative writing; developmental and child psychology; economics; educational psychology; English composition; English language and literature; European languages and literatures; health professions and related sciences; history; home economics and family studies; human resources management; journalism; liberal arts, general studies, and humanities; mathematics; microbiology; nursing; philosophy and religion; political science; public health; social psychology; social work; sociology; special education; teacher education; zoology

Graduate
Advertising; business; business administration and management; computer and information sciences; education administration; educational psychology; human resources management; special education; teacher education

UNIVERSITY OF NEBRASKA–LINCOLN

Lincoln, Nebraska

Division of Continuing Studies

University of Nebraska–Lincoln, founded in 1869, is a state-supported university. It is accredited by the North Central Association of Colleges and Schools. It first offered distance learning courses in 1909. In 1996–97, it offered 139 courses at a distance. In the fall of 1996, there was a total of 1,268 students enrolled in distance learning courses.
Course delivery sites Courses are delivered to your home, your workplace, military bases, Central Community College–Grand Island Campus (Grand Island), Central Community College–Hastings Campus (Hastings), Chadron State College (Chadron), Mid-Plains Community College (North Platte), Northeast Community College (Norfolk), Pennsylvania State University University Park Campus (University Park,

Profiles: University of Nebraska–Lincoln

PA), Peru State College (Peru), Southeast Community College, Beatrice Campus (Beatrice), University of Colorado at Boulder (Boulder, CO), University of Nebraska at Kearney (Kearney), University of South Dakota (Vermillion, SD), University of Southern California (Los Angeles, CA), Wayne State College (Wayne), 4 off-campus centers in Grand Island, Norfolk, North Platte, Scottsbluff, Co-op Extension Centers, Educational Service Units, job training centers, schools, correctional institutions.

Media Courses are delivered via television, videotapes, videoconferencing, audiotapes, audioconferencing, computer software, World Wide Web, e-mail, print. Students and teachers interact via videoconferencing, audioconferencing, mail, telephone, fax, e-mail, in-person meetings. A computer is required for some courses.

Services Distance learners have access to library services, the campus computer network, e-mail services, academic advising at a distance.

Credit-earning options Students may transfer credits from another institution.

Typical costs *Undergraduate:* Tuition of $85 per credit hour. *Graduate:* Tuition of $99.50 per credit hour. *Noncredit courses:* $67–$255 per course. Costs may vary by campus or location, specific program of study, number of credits taken, course delivery options. Financial aid is available to distance learners enrolled full-time.

Registration Students may register by mail, fax, phone, e-mail, World Wide Web.

Contact Marie A. Barber, Assistant Director, University of Nebraska–Lincoln, 332 C Nebraska Center for Continued Education, Department of Distance Education, Lincoln, NE 68588-9800. Telephone: 402-472-4354. Fax: 402-472-4317. E-mail: mbarber@unlinfo.unl.edu. Web site: http://www.unl.edu:80/conted/.

DEGREE & CERTIFICATE PROGRAMS

Graduate Degrees

▶ *Administration, Curriculum, and Instruction (EdD)*
In the fall of 1996 there were 44 students enrolled in this program.
Restrictions Students must have access to appropriate receive site equipment.
Application requirements *Prior education:* graduate degree. *Other requirements:* GRE, college transcripts, an essay or personal statement, letter(s) of recommendation, an application fee of $25.
Completion requirements 96 credits are required. 27 credits must be completed through the institution. *Maximum time for completion:* eight years.
On-campus requirements Five-week session, two years in a row.
Program contact Luise Berner, Department of Educational Administration, University of Nebraska–Lincoln, 1204 Seaton Hall, Lincoln, NE 68588-0638. Phone: 402-472-3726.

▶ *Business Administration (MBA)*
In the fall of 1996 there were 8 students enrolled in this program. In 1995–96, 1 degree was earned at a distance through this program.
Restrictions Students must have access to appropriate receive site equipment.
Application requirements *Prior education:* baccalaureate degree. *Other requirements:* GMAT, college transcripts, an essay or personal statement, letter(s) of recommendation, an application fee of $25.
Completion requirements 48 credit hours are required. 24 credit hours must be completed through the institution. *Maximum time for completion:* six years.

▶ *Educational Leadership in Higher Education (EdD)*
Application requirements *Prior education:* graduate degree. *Other requirements:* GRE, college transcripts, an essay or personal statement, letter(s) of recommendation, an application fee of $25.
Completion requirements 96 credits are required. 27 credits must be completed through the institution. *Maximum time for completion:* eight years.
On-campus requirements Five-week session.

Program contact Dr. Al Seagren, Director, Center for Study of Higher and Postsecondary Education, University of Nebraska–Lincoln, 1210 Seaton Hall, Lincoln, NE 68588-0638. Phone: 402-472-3726.

▶ *Human Resources and Family Sciences (MS)*
In the fall of 1996 there were 118 students enrolled in this program.
Application requirements *Prior education:* baccalaureate degree. *Other requirements:* GRE, college transcripts, an essay or personal statement, letter(s) of recommendation, an application fee of $25, major in home economics.
Completion requirements 36 credits are required. 18 credits must be completed through the institution. *Maximum time for completion:* six years.
Program contact Dr. Joan Laughlin, Associate Dean, University of Nebraska–Lincoln, Human Resources and Family Sciences, 105 Home Economics Building, Lincoln, NE 68588-0800. Phone: 800-755-7765.

▶ *Industrial and Management Systems Engineering (MS)*
In the fall of 1996 there were 20 students enrolled in this program. In 1995–96, 1 degree was earned at a distance through this program.
Restrictions Students must have access to appropriate receive site equipment.
Application requirements *Prior education:* baccalaureate degree. *Other requirements:* college transcripts, an essay or personal statement, letter(s) of recommendation, an application fee of $25.
Completion requirements 36 credit hours are required. 18 credit hours must be completed through the institution. *Other requirements:* this program is available with a specialization in Engineering Management. *Maximum time for completion:* six years.
Program contact Dr. Ram Bishu, Graduate Committee Chair, University of Nebraska–Lincoln, 182 NH, Lincoln, NE 68588-0518. Phone: 402-472-3495.

▶ *Journalism (MA)*
In the fall of 1996 there were 12 students enrolled in this program.
Restrictions Students must have access to appropriate receive site equipment.
Application requirements *Prior education:* baccalaureate degree. *Other requirements:* college transcripts, an essay or personal statement, letter(s) of recommendation, an application fee of $25, journalism major, professional experience.
Completion requirements 36 credit hours are required. 18 credit hours must be completed through the institution. *Maximum time for completion:* six years.
Program contact Dr. Will Norton, Dean, University of Nebraska–Lincoln, 206 Avery Hall, Lincoln, NE 68588-0127. Phone: 402-472-8279.

▶ *Manufacturing Systems Engineering (MS)*
In the fall of 1996 there were 20 students enrolled in this program.
Restrictions Students must have access to appropriate receive site equipment.
Application requirements *Prior education:* baccalaureate degree. *Other requirements:* college transcripts, an essay or personal statement, letter(s) of recommendation, an application fee of $25.
Completion requirements 36 credit hours are required. 18 credit hours must be completed through the institution. *Maximum time for completion:* six years.
Program contact Dr. Kamlakar Rajurkar, Graduate Committee Chair, University of Nebraska–Lincoln, 175 NH, Lincoln, NE 68588-0518. Phone: 402-472-3495.

▶ *Curriculum and Instruction, Educational Administration, Special Education and Communication Disorders, Vocational and Adult Education (MA)*
In the fall of 1996 there were 20 students enrolled in this program.
Application requirements *Prior education:* baccalaureate degree. *Other requirements:* MAT, college transcripts, an essay or personal statement, letter(s) of recommendation, an application fee of $25.

Completion requirements 36 credits are required. 18 credits must be completed through the institution. *Maximum time for completion:* six years.
Program contact Dr. Birdie Holder, Professor, University of Nebraska–Lincoln, 132 Mabel Lee, Lincoln, NE 68588-0515. E-mail: bholder@unlinfo.unl.edu.

INDIVIDUAL COURSE SUBJECT AREAS

Undergraduate
Accounting; administrative and secretarial services; agriculture; algebra; American (US) history; American literature; American studies; area, ethnic, and cultural studies; art history and criticism; Asian studies; biological and life sciences; biology; business; business administration and management; calculus; chemistry; civil engineering; Classical languages and literatures; communications; conservation and natural resources; curriculum and instruction; design; developmental and child psychology; ecology; economics; education; educational psychology; engineering; English composition; English language and literature; English literature; European history; European languages and literatures; finance; foods and nutrition studies; geography; geology; health and physical education/fitness; history; home economics and family studies; horticulture; human resources management; insurance; international business; international relations; journalism; Latin American studies; liberal arts, general studies, and humanities; logic; marketing; mathematics; Medieval/Renaissance studies; music; nursing; organizational behavior studies; philosophy and religion; physical sciences; physics; political science; psychology; public administration and services; radio and television broadcasting; real estate; religious studies; social psychology; social sciences; sociology; Spanish language and literature; statistics; teacher education; technical writing; visual and performing arts

Graduate
Accounting; administrative and secretarial services; business administration and management; civil engineering; computer and information sciences; education administration; educational psychology; electrical engineering; engineering mechanics; engineering/industrial management; home economics and family studies; hospitality services management; human resources management; industrial engineering; international business; international relations; mechanical engineering; teacher education

Noncredit
Agriculture; conservation and natural resources; engineering/industrial management; industrial engineering

UNIVERSITY OF NEVADA, LAS VEGAS

Las Vegas, Nevada

Distance Education

University of Nevada, Las Vegas, founded in 1957, is a state-supported university. It is accredited by the Northwest Association of Schools and Colleges. It first offered distance learning courses in 1986. In 1996–97, it offered 25 courses at a distance. In the fall of 1996, there was a total of 150 students enrolled in distance learning courses.
Course delivery sites Courses are delivered to your home, your workplace, military bases, other colleges.
Media Courses are delivered via television, videotapes, videoconferencing, e-mail. Students and teachers interact via videoconferencing, audioconferencing, mail, telephone, fax, e-mail. A computer is required for some courses.
Restrictions Compressed video courses are available to in-state students only.
Services Distance learners have access to library services, academic advising, tutoring, career placement assistance at a distance.
Credit-earning options Students may transfer credits from another institution or may earn credits through examinations, military training.
Typical costs *Undergraduate:* Tuition of $66.50 per credit plus mandatory fees of $3 per semester for in-state residents. Tuition of $130.50 per credit plus mandatory fees of $3 per semester for out-of-state residents. *Graduate:* Tuition of $90 per credit plus mandatory fees of $11 per semester for in-state residents. Tuition of $166 per credit plus mandatory fees of $11 per semester for out-of-state residents. Costs may vary by number of credits taken. Financial aid is available to distance learners enrolled full-time.
Registration Students may register by mail, fax, phone, e-mail.
Contact Distance Education Coordinator, University of Nevada, Las Vegas, PO Box 451038, Las Vegas, NV 89154-1038. *Telephone:* 702-895-0334. *Fax:* 702-895-3850. *E-mail:* distanceed@ccmail.nevada.edu.

INDIVIDUAL COURSE SUBJECT AREAS

Undergraduate
Area, ethnic, and cultural studies; business; computer and information sciences; conservation and natural resources; developmental and child psychology; education administration; English as a second language (ESL); English composition; European languages and literatures; geology; hospitality services management; liberal arts, general studies, and humanities; library and information studies; mathematics; nursing; sociology; special education; teacher education

Graduate
Geology; library and information studies

UNIVERSITY OF NEVADA, RENO

Reno, Nevada

University of Nevada, Reno, founded in 1874, is a state-supported university. It is accredited by the Northwest Association of Schools and Colleges.
Course delivery sites Courses are delivered to your home, your workplace, military bases, other colleges.
Media Courses are delivered via television, videoconferencing, radio broadcast, audioconferencing, computer software, print, audiographics conferencing, computer conferencing.
Credit-earning options Students may transfer credits from another institution or may earn credits through examinations, business training.
Contact Continuing Education, University of Nevada, Reno, Reno, NV 89557. *Telephone:* 702-784-4046. *Fax:* 702-784-4801.

DEGREE & CERTIFICATE PROGRAMS

Baccalaureate Degrees
▶ *General Studies (BA)*

Graduate Degrees
▶ *Business Administration (MBA)*
▶ *Learning and Literacy (MA)*

Undergraduate Certificates
▶ *Teacher Education*

INDIVIDUAL COURSE SUBJECT AREAS

Undergraduate
Accounting; astronomy and astrophysics; business; business administration and management; computer and information sciences; education

University of Nevada, Reno

...tion; educational psychology; electrical engineering; English ...on; environmental engineering; journalism; liberal arts, general st... nd humanities; library and information studies; mathematics; mechanical engineering; physics; political science; psychology; special education; teacher education

Graduate
Accounting; business; business administration and management; computer and information sciences; education administration; educational psychology; electrical engineering; environmental engineering; mechanical engineering; nursing; special education; teacher education

Noncredit
Agriculture; health professions and related sciences; nursing

UNIVERSITY OF NEW BRUNSWICK

Fredericton, New Brunswick, Canada

Department of Extension and Summer Session

University of New Brunswick, founded in 1785, is a province-supported university. It is provincially chartered. It first offered distance learning courses in 1970.
Course delivery sites Courses are delivered to your home, other colleges.
Media Courses are delivered via videotapes, videoconferencing, audiotapes, audioconferencing, print, audiographics conferencing.
Restrictions Programs are available to in-state students only.
Services Distance learners have access to library services at a distance.
Credit-earning options Students may transfer credits from another institution or may earn credits through examinations, portfolio assessment. Financial aid is available to distance learners.
Contact Program Director, Distance Education and Off-Campus Service, University of New Brunswick, PO Box 4400, Fredericton, NB E3B 5A3, Canada. *Telephone:* 506-453-4854. *Fax:* 506-453-3572. *Web site:* http://www.unb.ca/web/coned/de/de.html.

DEGREE & CERTIFICATE PROGRAMS

Baccalaureate Degrees
▶ *Nursing (BN)*
Application requirements *Prior education:* diploma in nursing. *Other requirements:* 1000 hours of practice experience.
Program contact Judith MacIntosh, Assistant Dean, BN/RN, University of New Brunswick, Faculty of Nursing, MacLaggan Hall, Room 118, Fredericton, NB E3B 5A3, Canada. Phone: 506-453-4642. Fax: 506-453-4503. E-mail: macintsh@unb.ca.

Graduate Degrees
▶ *Nursing (MN)*
Application requirements *Prior education:* BN degree.
Program contact Judith Wuest, Director, Graduate Studies, University of New Brunswick, Faculty of Nursing, MacLagganHall, Room 204, Fredericton, NB E3B 5A3, Canada. Fax: 506-453-4519. E-mail: wuest@unb.ca.

INDIVIDUAL COURSE SUBJECT AREAS

Undergraduate
Accounting; biology; business; business administration and management; computer and information sciences; education administration; educational psychology; history; human resources management; microbiology; nursing; sociology; special education; teacher education

Graduate
Education administration; educational psychology; nursing; special education; teacher education

UNIVERSITY OF NEW ENGLAND

Biddeford, Maine

Master of Science in Education Program

University of New England, founded in 1953, is an independent-nonprofit comprehensive institution. It is accredited by the New England Association of Schools and Colleges. It first offered distance learning courses in 1991. In 1996–97, it offered 10 courses at a distance. In the fall of 1996, there was a total of 300 students enrolled in distance learning courses.
Course delivery sites Courses are delivered to your home, your workplace.
Media Courses are delivered via videotapes. Students and teachers interact via mail, telephone, fax, e-mail.
Restrictions Courses are available to students in New York and New England only. Students must be classroom teachers or have access to classroom. Students must work with study team or study partners.
Services Distance learners have access to library services, academic advising, career placement assistance at a distance.
Credit-earning options Students may transfer credits from another institution.
Typical costs Tuition of $235 per credit plus mandatory fees of $60 per course. Financial aid is available to distance learners enrolled full-time or part-time.
Registration Students may register by mail, fax, phone.
Contact John E. Brandt, Director, Master of Science in Education Program, University of New England, 11 Hills Beach Road, Biddeford, ME 04005. *Telephone:* 207-283-0171, Ext. 2426. *Fax:* 207-286-9492. *E-mail:* msed@mailbox.une.edu. *Web site:* http://www.une.edu/CPCS/msedhm.html.

DEGREE & CERTIFICATE PROGRAMS

Graduate Degrees
▶ *Education (MSE)*
In the fall of 1996 there were 225 students enrolled in this program.
Restrictions Students must be employed as teachers and have 1 year teaching experience.
Application requirements *Prior education:* baccalaureate degree. *Other requirements:* college transcripts, an essay or personal statement, letter(s) of recommendation, an application fee of $40.
Completion requirements 33 credits are required.
On-campus requirements Three-credit summer residency.

INDIVIDUAL COURSE SUBJECT AREAS

Graduate
Teacher education

UNIVERSITY OF NEW HAMPSHIRE

Durham, New Hampshire

Interactive Instructional Television Center

University of New Hampshire, founded in 1866, is a state-supported university. It is accredited by the New England Association of Schools and Colleges. It first offered distance learning courses in 1980.
Course delivery sites Courses are delivered to 4 off-campus centers in Conway, Lebanon, Manchester, Portsmouth.
Media Courses are delivered via television, videotapes, videoconferencing, audioconferencing, print. Students and teachers interact via videoconferencing, audioconferencing, mail, telephone, fax, e-mail.
Services Distance learners have access to library services, academic advising at a distance.
Credit-earning options Students may transfer credits from another institution or may earn credits through examinations.
Typical costs *Undergraduate:* Tuition of $154 per credit plus mandatory fees of $15 per semester for in-state residents. Tuition of $170 per credit plus mandatory fees of $15 per semester for out-of-state residents. *Graduate:* Tuition of $179 per credit plus mandatory fees of $15 per semester for in-state residents. Tuition of $197 per credit plus mandatory fees of $15 per semester for out-of-state residents. *Noncredit courses:* $125 per 8 clock hours. Costs may vary by number of credits taken.
Registration Students may register by mail, phone.
Contact William F. Murphy, Dean, Division of Continuing Education, University of New Hampshire, 6 Garrison Avenue, Durham, NH 03824. *Telephone:* 603-862-1938. *Fax:* 603-862-1113. *E-mail:* wfm@christa.unh.edu.

DEGREE & CERTIFICATE PROGRAMS

Graduate Degrees

▶ *Communication Disorders (MST)*
Restrictions Program is for clinicians already working in the field who are required by federal mandate to receive a masters degree in Communication Disorders..
Application requirements *Prior education:* baccalaureate degree. *Other requirements:* experience as a school speech and hearing specialist.
Program contact Stephen Calculator, Professor, Communication Disorders, University of New Hampshire, Durham, NH 03824. Phone: 603-862-3836. Fax: 603-862-3108. E-mail: stephenc@christa.unh.edu.

INDIVIDUAL COURSE SUBJECT AREAS

Undergraduate
Business administration and management; engineering; liberal arts, general studies, and humanities; nursing; physical sciences; social sciences

Graduate
Health professions and related sciences; nursing

Noncredit
Business; health professions and related sciences; public health; teacher education

UNIVERSITY OF NEW ORLEANS

New Orleans, Louisiana

UNO Metropolitan College

University of New Orleans, founded in 1958, is a state-supported university. It is accredited by the Southern Association of Colleges and Schools. It first offered distance learning courses in 1985. In 1996–97, it offered 20 courses at a distance. In the fall of 1996, there was a total of 250 students enrolled in distance learning courses.
Course delivery sites Courses are delivered to your home, your workplace, military bases, other colleges, all Louisiana state colleges.
Media Courses are delivered via television, videotapes, videoconferencing. Students and teachers interact via videoconferencing, mail, telephone, fax, e-mail.
Services Distance learners have access to academic advising at a distance.
Credit-earning options Students may transfer credits from another institution or may earn credits through standardized exams.
Typical costs *Undergraduate:* Tuition of $418 per credit hour for in-state residents. Tuition of $948 per credit hour for out-of-state residents. *Graduate:* Tuition of $418 per credit hour for in-state residents. Tuition of $948 per credit hour for out-of-state residents. Costs may vary by campus or location, number of credits taken. Financial aid is available to distance learners.
Registration Students may register by phone.
Contact Carl E. Drichta, Associate Dean and Director, University of New Orleans, Metropolitan College, New Orleans, LA 70148. *Telephone:* 504-286-7100. *Fax:* 504-286-7317. *E-mail:* cedmc@uno.edu.

INDIVIDUAL COURSE SUBJECT AREAS

Undergraduate
English language and literature; geology; history; liberal arts, general studies, and humanities; political science; public administration and services; real estate; special education; teacher education

Graduate
Library and information studies; public administration and services; special education; teacher education

THE UNIVERSITY OF NORTH CAROLINA AT CHAPEL HILL

Chapel Hill, North Carolina

Division of Continuing Education

The University of North Carolina at Chapel Hill, founded in 1789, is a state-supported university. It is accredited by the Southern Association of Colleges and Schools. It first offered distance learning courses in 1913. In 1996–97, it offered 150 courses at a distance. In the fall of 1996, there was a total of 2,500 students enrolled in distance learning courses.
Course delivery sites Courses are delivered to your home, your workplace.
Media Courses are delivered via World Wide Web, print. Students and teachers interact via mail, telephone, fax, e-mail. A computer is required for some courses.
Services Distance learners have access to academic advising at a distance.
Credit-earning options Students may transfer credits from another institution or may earn credits through institutionally developed exams.

es: The University of North Carolina at Chapel Hill

al costs Tuition of $375 per course. Costs may vary by specific program of study, number of credits taken, course delivery options.
Registration Students may register by mail, fax.
Contact Student Services and Advising, The University of North Carolina at Chapel Hill, CB# 1020, The Friday Center, Chapel Hill, NC 27599-1020. *Telephone:* 919-962-1134. *Fax:* 919-962-5549. *E-mail:* stuserv.ce@mhs.unc.edu. *Web site:* http://www.unc.edu/depts/fri_cntr.

INDIVIDUAL COURSE SUBJECT AREAS

Undergraduate
Accounting; African-American studies; algebra; American (US) history; American literature; American studies; animal sciences; art history and criticism; astronomy and astrophysics; biology; business communications; calculus; chemistry; communications; computer and information sciences; creative writing; economics; education; English as a second language (ESL); English composition; English literature; environmental science; ethics; European history; foods and nutrition studies; French language and literature; geography; geology; health services administration; Latin language and literature; library and information studies; logic; mathematics; music; nursing; philosophy and religion; physics; political science; psychology; public administration and services; religious studies; Russian language and literature; sociology; Spanish language and literature; statistics

UNIVERSITY OF NORTH CAROLINA AT CHARLOTTE

Charlotte, North Carolina

Continuing Education, Extension and Summer Programs

University of North Carolina at Charlotte, founded in 1946, is a state-supported university. It is accredited by the Southern Association of Colleges and Schools. It first offered distance learning courses in 1985. In 1996–97, it offered 15 courses at a distance. In the fall of 1996, there was a total of 20 students enrolled in distance learning courses.
Course delivery sites Courses are delivered to your home, your workplace, other colleges, 1 off-campus center in Charlotte.
Media Courses are delivered via television, videoconferencing. Students and teachers interact via videoconferencing, audioconferencing, mail, telephone, fax, e-mail. A computer is required for some courses.
Services Distance learners have access to library services, the campus computer network, e-mail services, academic advising, tutoring, career placement assistance at a distance.
Credit-earning options Students may transfer credits from another institution or may earn credits through standardized exams, institutionally developed exams.
Typical costs *Undergraduate:* Tuition of $511.50 per semester plus mandatory fees of $347.50 per semester for in-state residents. Tuition of $4436 per semester plus mandatory fees of $347.50 per semester for out-of-state residents. *Graduate:* Tuition of $511.50 per semester plus mandatory fees of $347.50 per semester for in-state residents. Tuition of $4436 per semester plus mandatory fees of $347.50 per semester for out-of-state residents. Undergraduate cost given is for 12 hours or more, graduate cost is for 9 hours or more. *Noncredit courses:* $20 per hour of instruction. Costs may vary by number of credits taken. Financial aid is available to distance learners enrolled full-time or part-time.
Registration Students may register by mail, fax, phone.
Contact Dr. Connie Martin, Director, University of North Carolina at Charlotte, 9201 University City Boulevard, Charlotte, NC 28223. *Telephone:* 704-547-4449. *Fax:* 704-547-3158. *E-mail:* comartin@email.uncc.edu. *Web site:* http://www.uncc.edu/conteduc.

DEGREE & CERTIFICATE PROGRAMS

Baccalaureate Degrees
▶ *Engineering Technology (BS)*
Restrictions This program is available to in-state students only. Students participate in video classes at one of three North Carolina Community Colleges.
Application requirements *Prior education:* associate degree. *Other requirements:* high school transcript, college transcripts, an application fee of $35.
Completion requirements 124 semester credits are required. 54 must be completed through the institution. This is a degree completion program. *Maximum time for completion:* four years.
On-campus requirements Four Saturdays each of four summers.

Graduate Degrees
▶ *Special Education (MEd)*
Restrictions This program is available to in-state students only. Students participate in video classes at one of three North Carolina Community Colleges.
Application requirements *Prior education:* baccalaureate degree. *Other requirements:* GRE or MAT, college transcripts, an application fee of $35, "A" level teaching license.
Completion requirements 39 semester hours are required. 39 must be completed through the institution. *Maximum time for completion:* two years plus an additional Fall semester.
On-campus requirements Two summers.

INDIVIDUAL COURSE SUBJECT AREAS

Undergraduate
Engineering; engineering-related technologies
Graduate
Nursing; special education

UNIVERSITY OF NORTH CAROLINA AT GREENSBORO

Greensboro, North Carolina

Office of Continuing Education and Summer Session

University of North Carolina at Greensboro, founded in 1891, is a state-supported university. It is accredited by the Southern Association of Colleges and Schools. It first offered distance learning courses in 1972. In 1996–97, it offered 153 courses at a distance. In the fall of 1996, there was a total of 847 students enrolled in distance learning courses.
Course delivery sites Courses are delivered to your workplace, Alamance Community College (Graham), University of North Carolina at Asheville (Asheville).
Media Courses are delivered via videoconferencing, print. Students and teachers interact via videoconferencing, mail, telephone, fax, e-mail. A computer is required for some courses.
Restrictions Courses are available to regional area students only.
Services Distance learners have access to academic advising at a distance.
Credit-earning options Students may transfer credits from another institution or may earn credits through standardized exams.
Typical costs Contact school for information. Financial aid is available to distance learners.
Registration Students may register by mail, fax, phone.
Contact William H. Taylor, Assistant Director, Continuing Education, University of North Carolina at Greensboro, 209 Forney Building,

Greensboro, NC 27412-5001. *Telephone:* 910-334-5414. *Fax:* 910-334-5628. *Web site:* http://www.uncg.edu/cex/dli.

INDIVIDUAL COURSE SUBJECT AREAS

Undergraduate
Liberal arts, general studies, and humanities; nursing

Graduate
Liberal arts, general studies, and humanities; library and information studies; nursing

UNIVERSITY OF NORTH DAKOTA

Grand Forks, North Dakota

Division of Continuing Education

University of North Dakota, founded in 1883, is a state-supported university. It is accredited by the North Central Association of Colleges and Schools. It first offered distance learning courses in 1910. In 1996–97, it offered 650 courses at a distance.
Course delivery sites Courses are delivered to your home, other colleges, 1 off-campus center in Bismarck.
Media Courses are delivered via videotapes, videoconferencing, audioconferencing, World Wide Web, e-mail, print. Students and teachers interact via videoconferencing, audioconferencing, mail, telephone, fax, e-mail. A computer is required for some courses.
Restrictions Courses and programs may be available only at select sites.
Services Distance learners have access to library services, e-mail services, academic advising at a distance.
Credit-earning options Students may transfer credits from another institution or may earn credits through portfolio assessment.
Typical costs *Undergraduate:* Tuition of $1264 per credit for in-state residents. Tuition of $3026 per credit for out-of-state residents. *Graduate:* Tuition of $1369 per credit for in-state residents. Tuition of $1949 per credit for out-of-state residents. *Noncredit courses:* auditing a credit course is 50% of regular tuition; other noncredit courses vary by program. Costs may vary by campus or location, specific program of study, number of credits taken, course delivery options. Financial aid is available to distance learners enrolled full-time or part-time.
Registration Students may register by mail, fax, phone, e-mail, World Wide Web.
Contact Kim Pastir, IVN Program Assistant, University of North Dakota, Division of Continuing Education, Box 9021, Grand Forks, ND 58202-9021. Telephone: 701-777-3633. Fax: 701-777-4282. E-mail: kimberley_pastir@mail.und.nodak.edu. Web site: http://www.und.nodak.edu.

DEGREE & CERTIFICATE PROGRAMS

Baccalaureate Degrees

▶ *Business Administration (BBA)*
Restrictions Program is available to students in Grand Forks, Devils Lake and Williston only.
Application requirements *Prior education:* some undergraduate course work. *Other requirements:* college transcripts, an application fee, 2.5 GPA.
Completion requirements 125 semester credit hours are required. 30 semester credit hours must be completed through the institution. This is a degree completion program.

▶ *Chemical Engineering, Electrical Engineering, Mechanical Engineering (BS)*
In the fall of 1996 there were 65 students enrolled in this program.
Restrictions Program is available to US and Canadian students only. Students must be working for a company that is a member of the corporate engineering degree program consortium.
Application requirements *Prior education:* some undergraduate course work. *Other requirements:* an application fee of $25, company must be a member of the corporate engineering degree program consortium.
Completion requirements 136 semester credit hours are required. 30 semester credit hours must be completed through the institution. This is a degree completion program.
On-campus requirements Summer labs, or labs held at times other than summer.
Program contact Lynette Krenelka, CEDP Coordinator, University of North Dakota, Division of Continuing Education, Box 9021, Grand Forks, ND 58202-9021. Phone: 800-342-8230. Fax: 701-777-4282. E-mail: lynette_krenelka@mail.und.nodak.edu.

Graduate Degrees

▶ *Business Administration (MBA)*
In 1995–96, 10 degrees were earned at a distance through this program.
Restrictions Program is available to students in Grand Forks, Bismarck, and Dickinson only.
Application requirements *Prior education:* some graduate course work. *Other requirements:* GMAT, college transcripts, an essay or personal statement, letter(s) of recommendation, an application fee of $20, 2.75 GPA.
Completion requirements 32 semester credit hours are required. 24 semester credit hours must be completed through the institution. *Maximum time for completion:* seven years.

▶ *Educational Leadership (MEd)*
In the fall of 1996 there were 20 students enrolled in this program.
Restrictions Program is available to students in Grand Forks, Fargo, Bismarck, and Williston only. Program enrolls a maximum of 20 students.
Application requirements *Prior education:* baccalaureate degree. *Other requirements:* college transcripts, an essay or personal statement, letter(s) of recommendation, an application fee of $20, 2.85 GPA.
Completion requirements 36 semester hours are required. 28 semester hours must be completed through the institution. *Other requirements:* written and oral comprehensive exam, demonstration of portfolio, and 120 hours of field experience. *Maximum time for completion:* seven years.

▶ *Public Administration (MPA)*
In 1995–96, 8 degrees were earned at a distance through this program.
Restrictions Program is available to students in Grand Forks and Bismarck only.
Application requirements *Prior education:* baccalaureate degree. *Other requirements:* GMAT or GRE, college transcripts, an essay or personal statement, letter(s) of recommendation, 2.75 GPA.
Completion requirements 32 semester hours are required. 24 semester hours must be completed through the institution. *Other requirements:* comprehensive exam. *Maximum time for completion:* seven years.

▶ *Rural Health Nursing (MS)*
In the fall of 1996 there were 69 students enrolled in this program. In 1995–96, 16 degrees were earned at a distance through this program.
Restrictions This program is available to in-state students only.
Application requirements *Prior education:* baccalaureate degree. *Other requirements:* college transcripts, an essay or personal statement, letter(s) of recommendation, an application fee, 3.0 GPA for the last 2 years of baccalaureate study.
Completion requirements 37 semester credits are required. *Maximum time for completion:* seven years.
On-campus requirements Students are required to visit the campus once per semester.

▶ *Space Studies (MS)*
In the fall of 1996 there were 88 students enrolled in this program.
Restrictions Students must have a computer, modem/telephone, TV/VCR and an Internet account with access to World Wide Web.

Profiles: University of North Dakota

Application requirements *Prior education:* baccalaureate degree. *Other requirements:* college transcripts, an essay or personal statement, letter(s) of recommendation, an application fee of $20, course in statistics or calculus or computer programming and a course in social science and a course in science, 2.75 GPA.
Completion requirements 32 semester hours are required. 32 semester hours must be completed through the institution. *Maximum time for completion:* seven years.
On-campus requirements Seven-day capstone course/experience.

INDIVIDUAL COURSE SUBJECT AREAS

Undergraduate
Accounting; biological and life sciences; biology; business; business administration and management; chemical engineering; civil engineering; electrical engineering; engineering mechanics; English as a second language (ESL); industrial psychology; liberal arts, general studies, and humanities; mathematics; mechanical engineering; music; nursing; philosophy and religion; physical sciences; physics; political science; psychology; public administration and services; social sciences; social work; visual and performing arts

Graduate
Business administration and management; education administration; health professions and related sciences; nursing; physical sciences; political science; public administration and services; social work; special education; teacher education

Noncredit
Public health

UNIVERSITY OF NORTHERN COLORADO

Greeley, Colorado

College of Continuing Education

University of Northern Colorado, founded in 1890, is a state-supported university. It is accredited by the North Central Association of Colleges and Schools. It first offered distance learning courses in 1906. In 1996–97, it offered 70 courses at a distance. In the fall of 1996, there was a total of 300 students enrolled in distance learning courses.
Course delivery sites Courses are delivered to your home, your workplace, military bases, Fort Lewis College (Durango), Northeastern Junior College (Sterling), 5 off-campus centers in Colorado Springs, Denver, Durango, Grand Junction, Pueblo.
Media Courses are delivered via television, videotapes, videoconferencing, audiotapes, audioconferencing, computer software, World Wide Web, e-mail, print. Students and teachers interact via videoconferencing, audioconferencing, mail, telephone, fax, e-mail, site visits. A computer is required for some courses.
Restrictions Programs are available to in-state students only.
Services Distance learners have access to library services, academic advising at a distance.
Credit-earning options Students may transfer credits from another institution or may earn credits through standardized exams.
Typical costs Contact school for information. Financial aid is available to distance learners.
Registration Students may register by mail, fax, phone, e-mail, World Wide Web.
Contact Student Service Manager, University of Northern Colorado, College of Continuing Education, Greeley, CO 80634. *Telephone:* 970-351-2944. *Fax:* 970-351-2519. *E-mail:* askus@cce.univnorthco.edu. *Web site:* http://community.univnorthco.edu/cce/index.html.

DEGREE & CERTIFICATE PROGRAMS

Graduate Degrees

▶*Communication Disorders and Speech Language Pathology (MA)*
In the fall of 1996 there were 20 students enrolled in this program.
Restrictions In-state now, occasional out-of-state; may broaden with next cohort, fall 1999. Students must be employed in a school district.
Application requirements *Prior education:* undergraduate degree in speech language pathology. *Other requirements:* GRE, college transcripts, an essay or personal statement, letter(s) of recommendation, an application fee of $30.
Completion requirements 54 semester hours are required. 30 semester hours must be completed through the institution. *Maximum time for completion:* five years.
On-campus requirements One weekend a year.
Program contact Sharal Darling, Associate Director of Program Development, University of Northern Colorado, College of Continuing Education, Greeley, CO 80639. Phone: 970-351-1938. Fax: 970-351-2519. E-mail: sdarling@cce.univnorthco.edu.

Graduate certificates

▶*Dietetics*
In the fall of 1996 there were 21 students enrolled in this program.
Application requirements *Prior education:* baccalaureate degree. *Other requirements:* GRE, college transcripts, an essay or personal statement, letter(s) of recommendation, an application fee of $50, 2.7 GPA, GRE, proposed practice sites and rotation schedule.
Completion requirements 4 graduate semester credits are required. *Maximum time for completion:* one year.
On-campus requirements Two weeks at beginning of program.
Program contact Naomi M. Benell, Program Director, University of Northern Colorado, Gunter 2400, Greeley, CO 80639. Phone: 970-351-1769. Fax: 970-351-1489. E-mail: nmbenel@bentley.univnorthco.edu.

▶*Elementary or Secondary TESOL (Endorsement)*
Restrictions Students must be Colorado licensed or certified teachers, be familiar with a second language, and have an e-mail address.
Application requirements *Prior education:* baccalaureate degree. *Other requirements:* college transcripts, an application fee of $35, letter from the building principal that verifies current assignment teaching linguistically diverse students, and letter of achievement of how they acquired a second language familiarity.
Completion requirements 18 semester hours are required. *Maximum time for completion:* five years.
Program contact Ann Steele, Associate Director, Program Development, University of Northern Colorado, College of Continuing Education, Greeley, CO 80639. Phone: 970-351-1935. Fax: 970-351-2519. E-mail: esteele@cce.univnorthco.edu.

INDIVIDUAL COURSE SUBJECT AREAS

Undergraduate
Biology; community health services; economics; foods and nutrition studies; geography; gerontology; health professions and related sciences; mathematics; nursing; special education

Graduate
Law and legal studies; teacher education

UNIVERSITY OF NORTHERN IOWA

Cedar Falls, Iowa

Division of Continuing Education

University of Northern Iowa, founded in 1876, is a state-supported comprehensive institution. It is accredited by the North Central Association of Colleges and Schools. It first offered distance learning courses in 1920. In 1996–97, it offered 70 courses at a distance. In the fall of 1996, there was a total of 1,000 students enrolled in distance learning courses.
Course delivery sites Courses are delivered to your home.
Media Courses are delivered via World Wide Web, print. Students and teachers interact via videoconferencing, mail, telephone, fax, e-mail. A computer is required for some courses.
Restrictions Courses offered via the fiber optics network are available to in-state students only.
Services Distance learners have access to library services, academic advising at a distance.
Credit-earning options Students may transfer credits from another institution or may earn credits through standardized exams.
Typical costs *Undergraduate:* Tuition of $107 per credit hour. *Graduate:* Tuition of $170 per credit hour. All correspondence courses are $80 per credit hour, with $13 per course in fees. Costs may vary by course delivery options.
Registration Students may register by mail, fax, World Wide Web.
Contact Kent Johnson, Coordinator, Credit Programs, University of Northern Iowa, 124 SHC, Cedar Falls, IA 50614-0223. *Telephone:* 319-273-5970. *Fax:* 319-273-2872. *E-mail:* kent.johnson@uni.edu. *Web site:* http://www.uni.edu/contined/gcs.

DEGREE & CERTIFICATE PROGRAMS

Baccalaureate Degrees
▶ *Liberal Studies (BLS)*
In the fall of 1996 there were 122 students enrolled in this program. In 1995–96, 10 degrees were earned at a distance through this program.
Restrictions This program is available to in-state students only.
Application requirements *Prior education:* some undergraduate course work. *Other requirements:* 2.0 GPA.
Completion requirements 124 quarter credits are required. 32 semester credits must be completed through the institution. This is a degree completion program.
Program contact Nancy Bramhall, Administrator of Individual Studies Program, University of Northern Iowa, H15, Cedar Falls, IA 50614-0285. Phone: 800-772-1746. Fax: 319-273-7107. E-mail: nancy.bramhall@uni.edu.

INDIVIDUAL COURSE SUBJECT AREAS

Undergraduate
Accounting; area, ethnic, and cultural studies; business administration and management; communications; criminology; developmental and child psychology; economics; education; educational psychology; English language and literature; health and physical education/fitness; health professions and related sciences; history; home economics and family studies; international relations; liberal arts, general studies, and humanities; mathematics; music; philosophy and religion; political science; psychology; public health; social psychology; social sciences; social work; sociology; teacher education

Graduate
Area, ethnic, and cultural studies; communications; criminology; developmental and child psychology; education; educational psychology; English language and literature; history; mathematics; philosophy and religion; social work; sociology; teacher education

UNIVERSITY OF NORTH FLORIDA

Jacksonville, Florida

Division of Continuing Education and Extension

University of North Florida, founded in 1965, is a state-supported comprehensive institution. It is accredited by the Southern Association of Colleges and Schools. It first offered distance learning courses in 1983. In 1996–97, it offered 3 courses at a distance. In the fall of 1996, there was a total of 35 students enrolled in distance learning courses.
Course delivery sites Courses are delivered to your home, your workplace, military bases.
Media Courses are delivered via television, videotapes. Students and teachers interact via mail, telephone, fax, e-mail. A computer is required for some courses.
Restrictions Programs are available to local area students only.
Services Distance learners have access to library services, career placement assistance at a distance.
Credit-earning options Students may transfer credits from another institution or may earn credits through examinations.
Typical costs *Undergraduate:* Tuition of $58.26 per semester hour for in-state residents. Tuition of $221.67 per semester hour for out-of-state residents. *Graduate:* Tuition of $110.18 per semester hour for in-state residents. Tuition of $363.20 per semester hour for out-of-state residents. Financial aid is available to distance learners.
Registration Students may register by phone.
Contact Dr. Marcelle C. Lovett, Dean, University of North Florida, 4567 St. Johns Bluff Road, S, Jacksonville, FL 32224. *Telephone:* 904-620-2690. *Fax:* 904-620-2973. *E-mail:* mlovett@unf.edu.

INDIVIDUAL COURSE SUBJECT AREAS

Undergraduate
Health services administration; nursing

Graduate
Civil engineering; computer and information sciences; electrical engineering; engineering/industrial management; environmental engineering; industrial engineering; mechanical engineering

UNIVERSITY OF NORTH TEXAS HEALTH SCIENCE CENTER AT FORT WORTH

Fort Worth, Texas

Graduate School of Biomedical Sciences

University of North Texas Health Science Center at Fort Worth, founded in 1966, is a state-supported graduate institution. It is accredited by the Southern Association of Colleges and Schools. It first offered distance learning courses in 1995. In 1996–97, it offered 2 courses at a distance. In the fall of 1996, there was a total of 30 students enrolled in distance learning courses.
Course delivery sites Courses are delivered to University of North Texas (Denton).
Media Courses are delivered via videoconferencing. Students and teachers interact via videoconferencing.
Restrictions Programs are available to local area students only.

Profiles: University of North Texas Health Science Center at Fort Worth

Services Distance learners have access to library services, the campus computer network, e-mail services, academic advising at a distance.
Credit-earning options Students may transfer credits from another institution.
Typical costs Tuition of $38 per credit plus mandatory fees of $207 per semester for in-state residents. Tuition of $246 per credit plus mandatory fees of $207 per semester for out-of-state residents. *Noncredit courses:* $152 per course. Costs may vary by campus or location, number of credits taken. Financial aid is available to distance learners enrolled full-time or part-time.
Registration Students may register by mail.
Contact Carla J. Lee, Assistant to the Dean, University of North Texas Health Science Center at Fort Worth, 3500 Camp Bowie Boulevard, Fort Worth, TX 76107-2699. *Telephone:* 817-735-2560. *Fax:* 817-735-0243. *E-mail:* clee@hsc.unt.edu.

INDIVIDUAL COURSE SUBJECT AREAS

Graduate
Biology; public health

UNIVERSITY OF NOTRE DAME

Notre Dame, Indiana

Executive Programs

University of Notre Dame, founded in 1842, is an independent-religious Roman Catholic university. It is accredited by the North Central Association of Colleges and Schools. It first offered distance learning courses in 1995. In 1996–97, it offered 17 courses at a distance. In the fall of 1996, there was a total of 46 students enrolled in distance learning courses.
Course delivery sites Courses are delivered to your workplace.
Media Courses are delivered via videoconferencing. Students and teachers interact via videoconferencing, audioconferencing, mail, telephone, fax, e-mail.
Services Distance learners have access to library services, the campus computer network, e-mail services, academic advising, tutoring, career placement assistance at a distance.
Credit-earning options Students may transfer credits from another institution.
Typical costs Tuition of $11,188 per semester. Financial aid is available to distance learners enrolled full-time.
Registration Students may register by mail, fax, phone, e-mail.
Contact Barry Van Dyck, Associate Director, University of Notre Dame, 126 College of Business Administration, Notre Dame, IN 46556. *Telephone:* 219-631-5285. *Fax:* 219-631-6783. *E-mail:* barry.vandyck.1@nd.edu. *Web site:* http://www.nd.edu/~execprog.

DEGREE & CERTIFICATE PROGRAMS

Graduate Degrees
▶ *Business Administration (MBA)*
In the fall of 1996 there were 16 students enrolled in this program.
Application requirements *Prior education:* baccalaureate degree. *Other requirements:* college transcripts, an essay or personal statement, an application fee of $50, minimum of 5 years management experience.
Completion requirements 48 credits are required. 48 credits must be completed through the institution. *Maximum time for completion:* two years.
On-campus requirements One week in August, two days in January.

Program contact Arnie Ludwig, Assistant Dean, University of Notre Dame, 126 College of Business Administration, Notre Dame, IN 46556. Phone: 219-631-5285. Fax: 219-631-6783. E-mail: arnold.f.ludwig.1@nd.edu.

Undergraduate Certificates
▶ *Executive Management*
In the fall of 1996 there were 30 students enrolled in this program. In 1995–96, 1 certificate was earned at a distance through this program.
Application requirements *Prior education:* none required. *Other requirements:* an application fee.
Completion requirements 2 semesters are required. 2 semesters must be completed through the institution. *Maximum time for completion:* two semesters.

INDIVIDUAL COURSE SUBJECT AREAS

Noncredit
Accounting; business; business administration and management; finance; marketing

UNIVERSITY OF OKLAHOMA

Norman, Oklahoma

Independent Study and Distance Education

University of Oklahoma, founded in 1890, is a state-supported university. It is accredited by the North Central Association of Colleges and Schools. It first offered distance learning courses in 1913.
Course delivery sites Courses are delivered to your home, your workplace, military bases, other colleges.
Media Courses are delivered via television, videoconferencing, audiotapes, print.
Services Distance learners have access to academic advising at a distance.
Credit-earning options Students may transfer credits from another institution or may earn credits through examinations.
Contact Receptionist, University of Oklahoma, Independent Study and Distance Education, 1600 South Jenkins Avenue, Room 101, Norman, OK 73072-6507. *Telephone:* 800-942-5702. *Fax:* 405-325-7687.

INDIVIDUAL COURSE SUBJECT AREAS

Undergraduate
Accounting; advertising; area, ethnic, and cultural studies; Asian languages and literatures; astronomy and astrophysics; business administration and management; chemistry; Classical languages and literatures; developmental and child psychology; economics; engineering; English composition; English language and literature; European languages and literatures; fine arts; geology; health and physical education/fitness; history; human resources management; industrial psychology; journalism; law and legal studies; liberal arts, general studies, and humanities; library and information studies; mathematics; music; philosophy and religion; political science; social psychology; sociology; special education

Graduate
Aerospace, aeronautical engineering; civil engineering; computer and information sciences; conservation and natural resources; electrical engineering; engineering/industrial management; industrial engineering; library and information studies

Noncredit
Creative writing; European languages and literatures; journalism; mathematics; visual and performing arts

UNIVERSITY OF PENNSYLVANIA

Philadelphia, Pennsylvania

University of Pennsylvania, founded in 1740, is an independent-nonprofit university. It is accredited by the Middle States Association of Colleges and Schools. It first offered distance learning courses in 1994.
Course delivery sites Courses are delivered to your home, other colleges.
Media Courses are delivered via videotapes, videoconferencing, print, computer conferencing.
Services Distance learners have access to library services, academic advising at a distance.
Credit-earning options Students may transfer credits from another institution.
Typical costs Contact school for information. Financial aid is available to distance learners.
Contact Sr. Teresita Hinnegan, Director, Nurse-Midwifery Distance Learning Program, University of Pennsylvania, 420 Guardian Drive, Philadelphia, PA 19104-6096. *Telephone:* 215-898-1169. *Fax:* 215-573-7291. *E-mail:* hinnegan@pobox.upenn.edu.

DEGREE & CERTIFICATE PROGRAMS

Graduate Degrees
▶*Nurse Midwifery (MSN)*
Restrictions This program is available to in-state students only.
Application requirements *Prior education:* BSN. *Other requirements:* GRE, 3.0 GPA, personal interview.

INDIVIDUAL COURSE SUBJECT AREAS

Undergraduate
Classical languages and literatures; English language and literature; nursing

Graduate
Nursing; telecommunications

Noncredit
Archaeology; business administration and management; Classical languages and literatures; English composition; English language and literature; ethics

UNIVERSITY OF PHOENIX

Phoenix, Arizona

On-Line Campus

University of Phoenix, founded in 1976, is a proprietary comprehensive institution. It is accredited by the North Central Association of Colleges and Schools. It first offered distance learning courses in 1989.
Course delivery sites Courses are delivered to your home, your workplace, military bases.
Media Courses are delivered via computer conferencing. Students and teachers interact via computer conferencing.
Services Distance learners have access to library services, academic advising at a distance.
Credit-earning options Students may transfer credits from another institution or may earn credits through examinations, portfolio assessment, business training.
Typical costs *Undergraduate:* Tuition of $325 per credit hour. *Graduate:* Tuition of $425 per credit hour.

Contact Enrollment Department, University of Phoenix, Street, Suite 110, San Francisco, CA 94105. *Telephone:* 80 *Fax:* 415-541-7832. *Web site:* http://www.uophx.edu/online.

DEGREE & CERTIFICATE PROGRAMS

Baccalaureate Degrees
▶*Business and Administration (BS)*
Completion requirements 120 credit hours are required.
▶*Business and Information Systems (BS)*
Completion requirements 120 credit hours are required.
▶*Business and Management (BS)*
Completion requirements 120 credit hours are required.

Graduate Degrees
▶*Business Administration (MBA)*
Completion requirements 51 credit hours are required.
▶*Computer Information Systems (MBA)*
Completion requirements 45 credit hours are required.
▶*Global Management (MBA)*
Completion requirements 41 credit hours are required.
▶*Organizational Management (MA)*
Completion requirements 41 credit hours are required.
▶*Technology Management (MBA)*
Completion requirements 51 credit hours are required.

INDIVIDUAL COURSE SUBJECT AREAS

Undergraduate
Accounting; business; business administration and management; communications; computer and information sciences; human resources management; mathematics

Graduate
Accounting; business; business administration and management; communications; computer and information sciences; economics; human resources management

UNIVERSITY OF PITTSBURGH

Pittsburgh, Pennsylvania

Center for Instructional Development and Distance Education

University of Pittsburgh, founded in 1787, is a state-related university. It is accredited by the Middle States Association of Colleges and Schools. It first offered distance learning courses in 1972. In 1996–97, it offered 150 courses at a distance. In the fall of 1996, there was a total of 1,000 students enrolled in distance learning courses.
Course delivery sites Courses are delivered to your home, University of Pittsburgh at Bradford (Bradford), University of Pittsburgh at Johnstown (Johnstown), 4 off-campus centers in Bradford, Greensburg, Johnstown, Titusville.
Media Courses are delivered via videotapes, videoconferencing, World Wide Web, print. Students and teachers interact via videoconferencing, mail, telephone, fax, e-mail, on-campus meetings.
Restrictions Availability varies by course, program, or delivery means.
Services Distance learners have access to library services, the campus computer network, e-mail services, academic advising, career placement assistance at a distance.
Credit-earning options Students may transfer credits from another institution or may earn credits through standardized exams.

Profiles: University of Pittsburgh

Typical costs Tuition of $189 per credit for in-state residents. Tuition of $403 per credit for out-of-state residents. Full-time students pay $216 in fees. Costs may vary by specific program of study, number of credits taken. Financial aid is available to distance learners enrolled full-time or part-time.
Registration Students may register by mail.
Contact Andrea Abt, University of Pittsburgh, 3808 Forbes Avenue, Pittsburgh, PA 15260. *Telephone:* 412-624-7206. *Fax:* 412-624-7213. *E-mail:* aabtt@pitt.edu.

DEGREE & CERTIFICATE PROGRAMS

Graduate Degrees

▶ *Business Administration (MBA)*
In the fall of 1996 there were 55 students enrolled in this program. In 1995–96, 41 degrees were earned at a distance through this program.
Application requirements *Prior education:* baccalaureate degree. *Other requirements:* college transcripts, an essay or personal statement, letter(s) of recommendation, application form, GMAT.
Completion requirements 51 credits are required. 42 credits must be completed through the institution. *Other requirements:* students must participate in International Study trip during their second year in the program. *Maximum time for completion:* six years.
On-campus requirements 13 weeks in-residence classes, one to two weeks at a time over a 21 month period.
Program contact Sharon L. Hixson, Assistant Director, Executive and Flex MBA Programs, University of Pittsburgh, Center for Executive Education, 301 Mervis Hall, Pittsburgh, PA 15260. Phone: 412-648-1606. Fax: 412-624-1039.

▶ *Elementary Education (MEd)*
Application requirements *Prior education:* baccalaureate degree. *Other requirements:* college transcripts, an essay or personal statement, letter(s) of recommendation, an application fee of $30, teacher certification.
Completion requirements 39 credit hours are required. 33 credit hours must be completed through the institution. *Maximum time for completion:* five years.
Program contact Dr. Rita Bean, Professor, University of Pittsburgh, 5T23 FQ, Pittsburgh, PA 15260. Phone: 412-648-1774. Fax: 412-648-1825. E-mail: bean@fs2.sched.pitt.edu.

INDIVIDUAL COURSE SUBJECT AREAS

Undergraduate
Economics; history; psychology

Graduate
Business administration and management; nursing; teacher education

UNIVERSITY OF PITTSBURGH AT BRADFORD

Bradford, Pennsylvania

Continuing Education Department

University of Pittsburgh at Bradford, founded in 1963, is a state-related four-year college. It is accredited by the Middle States Association of Colleges and Schools. It first offered distance learning courses in 1995. In 1996–97, it offered 5 courses at a distance. In the fall of 1996, there was a total of 10 students enrolled in distance learning courses.
Course delivery sites Courses are delivered to your workplace, 1 off-campus center in St. Marys.
Media Courses are delivered via television, videoconferencing. Students and teachers interact via mail, telephone, fax, e-mail.
Restrictions Programs are available to local area students only.

Services Distance learners have access to library services, e-mail services, academic advising, career placement assistance at a distance.
Credit-earning options Students may transfer credits from another institution or may earn credits through standardized exams, institutionally developed exams.
Typical costs Tuition of $189 per semester hour for in-state residents. Tuition of $403 per semester hour for out-of-state residents. *Noncredit courses:* $170 for 16 hours of training. Costs may vary by specific program of study, number of credits taken. Financial aid is available to distance learners enrolled full-time or part-time.
Registration Students may register by mail, fax, phone.
Contact Greg Longacre, Director of Continuing Education, Regional Programs, and Distance Learning, University of Pittsburgh at Bradford, 300 Campus Drive, Bradford, PA 16701. *Telephone:* 814-362-0911. *Fax:* 814-362-0914. *E-mail:* gal2+@pitt.edu.

INDIVIDUAL COURSE SUBJECT AREAS

Undergraduate
Business administration and management; education; mathematics

Noncredit
Communications

UNIVERSITY OF ST. THOMAS

St. Paul, Minnesota

University of St. Thomas, founded in 1885, is an independent-religious Roman Catholic university. It is accredited by the North Central Association of Colleges and Schools. It first offered distance learning courses in 1994. In 1996–97, it offered 9 courses at a distance. In the fall of 1996, there was a total of 55 students enrolled in distance learning courses.
Course delivery sites Courses are delivered to other colleges, 2 off-campus centers in Chaska, Owatonna.
Media Courses are delivered via videoconferencing, e-mail. Students and teachers interact via videoconferencing, telephone, fax, e-mail.
Services Distance learners have access to library services at a distance.
Credit-earning options Students may transfer credits from another institution or may earn credits through institutionally developed exams.
Typical costs *Undergraduate:* Tuition of $1005 per semester. *Graduate:* Tuition of $1100 per semester. Costs may vary by specific program of study.
Registration Students may register by mail, phone.
Contact Robert Rehn, Director, University of St. Thomas, 2115 Summit Avenue, St. Paul, MN 55105. *Telephone:* 612-962-6800. *Fax:* 612-962-6816. *E-mail:* rarehn@stthomas.edu. *Web site:* http://www.iss.stthomas.edu.

INDIVIDUAL COURSE SUBJECT AREAS

Graduate
Accounting; business; business administration and management; computer and information sciences; engineering; law and legal studies; social work

Noncredit
Computer and information sciences

UNIVERSITY OF SARASOTA

Sarasota, Florida

Student Services

University of Sarasota, founded in 1974, is an independent-nonprofit graduate institution. It is accredited by the Southern Association of Colleges and Schools. It first offered distance learning courses in 1993. In 1996–97, it offered 85 courses at a distance. In the fall of 1996, there was a total of 850 students enrolled in distance learning courses.

Course delivery sites Courses are delivered to your home, your workplace.

Media Courses are delivered via audioconferencing, World Wide Web, e-mail, print. Students and teachers interact via audioconferencing, mail, telephone, fax, e-mail. A computer is required for some courses.

Services Distance learners have access to library services, e-mail services, academic advising, tutoring, career placement assistance at a distance.

Credit-earning options Students may transfer credits from another institution.

Typical costs Tuition of $336 per semester hour. Costs may vary by specific program of study.

Registration Students may register by mail, fax, phone, e-mail.

Contact Doug Waldo, Director of Student Services, University of Sarasota, 5250 17th Street, Sarasota, FL 34235. *Telephone:* 800-331-5995. *Fax:* 941-379-9464. *E-mail:* univsar@compuserve.com. *Web site:* http://www.sarasota-online.com/university/graduate.html.

Special note

The University of Sarasota has gained national and international distinction by offering high-quality traditional graduate education to midcareer professionals through flexible scheduling and innovative delivery. Students meet degree requirements by completing a mixture of intensive in-residence courses and one-to-one distance learning tutorials with full-time faculty members. Available degree programs include Ed D in educational leadership; Ed D in curriculum and instruction; Ed D in counseling psychology; Ed D in human services administration; DBA; MA in guidance counseling; MA in mental health counseling; and MA in human services administration.

At least half of the courses must be taken in residence in Sarasota, Florida, during weeklong intensive sessions that are scheduled during traditional school breaks (winter, spring, and summer). When not on campus, students work on tutorials at home, submitting assignments to their faculty mentors.

Admission criteria includes official transcripts from all undergraduate and graduate schools attended (showing a GPA of at least 3.0), 3 professional letters of recommendation, an admissions application with $50 fee, and a personal goal statement (including computer literacy). The Admissions Committee meets each month to review all complete admissions files so students may begin their studies throughout the year.

The University of Sarasota is accredited by the Commission on Colleges of the Southern Association of Colleges and Schools (1866 Southern Lane, Decatur, Georgia 30033-4097; telephone: 404-679-4501) to award master's and doctoral degrees. The University's accreditation was recently reaffirmed through 2005.

Interested applicants may call 800-331-5995 for a graduate catalog.

DEGREE & CERTIFICATE PROGRAMS

Graduate Degrees

▶ *Counseling Psychology, Curriculum and Instruction, Educational Leadership, Human Services Administration (EdD)*

▶ *Guidance Counseling, Human Services Administration, Mental Health Counseling (MA)*

INDIVIDUAL COURSE SUBJECT AREAS

Graduate

Business; business administration and management; education administration; educational psychology; health professions and related sciences; human resources management; psychology; special education

---

UNIVERSITY OF SASKATCHEWAN

Saskatoon, Saskatchewan, Canada

Extension Credit Studies

University of Saskatchewan, founded in 1907, is a province-supported university. It is provincially chartered. It first offered distance learning courses in 1920. In 1996–97, it offered 90 courses at a distance. In the fall of 1996, there was a total of 1,150 students enrolled in distance learning courses.

Course delivery sites Courses are delivered to your home, your workplace, 56 off-campus centers, Vancouver Community College (Vancouver, BC).

Media Courses are delivered via television, videotapes, audiotapes, computer software, print. Students and teachers interact via videoconferencing, audioconferencing, mail, telephone, fax, e-mail. A computer is required for some courses.

Services Distance learners have access to library services, the campus computer network, e-mail services, academic advising, tutoring at a distance.

Credit-earning options Students may transfer credits from another institution or may earn credits through institutionally developed exams, portfolio assessment.

Typical costs Tuition of $89 per credit. Cost given in Canadian dollars. Financial aid is available to distance learners.

Registration Students may register by mail, phone.

Contact Parminder Soor, Secretary, University of Saskatchewan, Room 326, Kirk Hall, 117 Science Place, Saskatoon, SK S7N 5C8, Canada. *Telephone:* 306-966-5563. *Fax:* 306-966-5590. *E-mail:* extcred@usask.ca. *Web site:* http://www.extension.usask.ca.

DEGREE & CERTIFICATE PROGRAMS

Undergraduate Certificates

▶ *Adult and Continuing Education*

In the fall of 1996 there were 85 students enrolled in this program. In 1995–96, 20 certificates were earned at a distance through this program.

Application requirements *Prior education:* high school diploma or equivalent. *Other requirements:* high school transcript, an application fee of $50.

Completion requirements 250 hours are required. 200 hours must be completed through the institution. *Maximum time for completion:* five years.

▶ *Agriculture*

In the fall of 1996 there were 165 students enrolled in this program. In 1995–96, 26 certificates were earned at a distance through this program.

Profiles: University of Saskatchewan

Restrictions Program is available to students in the province only.
Application requirements *Prior education:* high school diploma or equivalent. *Minimum age:* 17. *Other requirements:* high school transcript, an application fee of $35.
Completion requirements 7 courses are required.

▶ *English as a Second Language*

In the fall of 1996 there were 250 students enrolled in this program. In 1995–96, 35 certificates were earned at a distance through this program.
Application requirements *Prior education:* high school diploma or equivalent. *Other requirements:* high school transcript, college transcripts, an essay or personal statement, $50.00 admission fee, TOEFL (if English not first language).
Completion requirements 6 courses are required. 3 courses must be completed through the institution.

▶ *Prairie Horticulture*

In the fall of 1996 there were 150 students enrolled in this program.
Application requirements *Prior education:* high school diploma or equivalent. *Minimum age:* 17. *Other requirements:* high school transcript, an application fee of $35.
Completion requirements 8 courses are required.

INDIVIDUAL COURSE SUBJECT AREAS

Undergraduate

Biology; business; computer and information sciences; economics; English language and literature; European languages and literatures; geology; history; liberal arts, general studies, and humanities; mathematics; microbiology; music; nursing; philosophy and religion; psychology; teacher education

UNIVERSITY OF SOUTH CAROLINA

Columbia, South Carolina

Department of Distance Education and Instructional Support

University of South Carolina, founded in 1801, is a state-supported university. It is accredited by the Southern Association of Colleges and Schools. It first offered distance learning courses in 1969. In 1996–97, it offered 202 courses at a distance. In the fall of 1996, there was a total of 3,330 students enrolled in distance learning courses.
Course delivery sites Courses are delivered to your home, your workplace, University of South Carolina System (Columbia), high schools, hospitals.
Media Courses are delivered via television, videotapes, audiotapes, e-mail, print. Students and teachers interact via mail, telephone, fax, e-mail. A computer is required for some courses.
Restrictions Programs are available to in-state students only.
Services Distance learners have access to library services, e-mail services, academic advising, tutoring at a distance.
Credit-earning options Students may transfer credits from another institution or may earn credits through examinations.
Typical costs *Undergraduate:* Tuition of $144 per credit hour plus mandatory fees of $4 per credit hour. *Graduate:* Tuition of $144 per credit hour plus mandatory fees of $4 per credit hour. Costs may vary by specific program of study. Financial aid is available to distance learners enrolled full-time or part-time.
Registration Students may register by mail, fax, phone.
Contact Student Services Area, University of South Carolina, Department of Distance Education and Instructional Services, 915 Gregg Street, Columbia, SC 29208. *Telephone:* 800-922-2577. *Fax:* 803-777-6264. *E-mail:* question@deis.sc.edu. *Web site:* http://www.sc.edu/deis.

Special note

For more than 50 years, the University of South Carolina has extended instruction to adult learners who cannot come to campus. Most programs are designed for statewide delivery, using digital satellite technology to transmit programming to viewing sites scattered throughout South Carolina. Master's degrees in business administration, engineering, and library and information science are offered statewide using live, interactive televised instruction combined with on-campus visits.

Some graduate and undergraduate courses offered each semester are available on videocassette. These video courses offer greater scheduling flexibility for students with personal and professional commitments that limit their ability to come to campus.

Undergraduate courses taught through independent learning are available worldwide, but no degree is available from the University of South Carolina. Areas of study include accounting, astronomy, economics, English, finance, French, geography, government and international studies, health promotion and education, history, Latin, management, marine science, marketing, mathematics, music, philosophy, physics, psychology, retailing, sociology, social work, and statistics. Students can take up to 1 year to complete independent learning course work.

Faculty members maintain regular contact with students using toll-free telephone lines and e-mail. Student services staff members are available to help with administrative and testing questions and facilitate application, enrollment, and access to course materials and faculty.

For more information, students should contact Student Services at 803-777-7210 or 800-922-2577 (toll-free within the continental U.S.) or write to USC Distance Education, 915 Gregg Street, Columbia, South Carolina 29208.

DEGREE & CERTIFICATE PROGRAMS

Graduate Degrees

▶ *Business Administration (MBA)*

In the fall of 1996 there were 318 students enrolled in this program. In 1995–96, 124 degrees were earned at a distance through this program.
Restrictions Program is available to in-state students only unless by special agreement.
Application requirements *Prior education:* baccalaureate degree. *Other requirements:* GMAT, college transcripts, an essay or personal statement, letter(s) of recommendation, an application fee of $35, resume.
Completion requirements 54 semester hours are required. 42 semester hours must be completed through the institution. *Maximum time for completion:* six years.
On-campus requirements Saturday sessions in Columbia are required 14 times per year.
Program contact Paul Yazel, Managing Director, University of South Carolina, College of Business Administration, Columbia, SC 29208. Phone: 803-777-7940. Fax: 803-777-9018. E-mail: yazel@darla.badm.sc.edu.

▶ *Chemical Engineering, Civil and Environmental Engineering, Computer Engineering, Electrical Engineering, Engineering, Mechanical Engineering (MS)*

Restrictions Program is available to in-state students and students in parts of Georgia and North Carolina only.
Application requirements *Prior education:* baccalaureate degree. *Other requirements:* college transcripts, letter(s) of recommendation, an application fee of $35.

Completion requirements 30 semester hours are required. 21 semester hours must be completed through the institution. *Other requirements:* thesis. *Maximum time for completion:* six years.
On-campus requirements Four Saturday classes per semester.
Program contact Phyllis Coleman, APOGEE Director, University of South Carolina, College of Engineering, Columbia, SC 29208. Phone: 803-777-4192. Fax: 803-777-3340. E-mail: coleman@sc.edu.

▶ *Chemical Engineering, Civil and Environmental Engineering, Computer Engineering, Electrical Engineering, Engineering, Mechanical Engineering (PhD)*
Restrictions Program is available to in-state students and students in parts of Georgia and North Carolina only.
Application requirements *Prior education:* baccalaureate degree. *Other requirements:* college transcripts, letter(s) of recommendation, an application fee of $35.
Completion requirements 30 semester hours are required. 21 semester hours must be completed through the institution. *Maximum time for completion:* six years.
On-campus requirements Four Saturday classes each semester.
Program contact Phyllis Coleman, APOGEE Director, University of South Carolina, College of Engineering, Columbia, SC 29208. Phone: 803-777-4192. Fax: 803-777-3340. E-mail: coleman@sc.edu.

▶ *Chemical Engineering, Civil and Environmental Engineering, Computer Engineering, Electrical Engineering, Engineering, Mechanical Engineering (ME)*
Restrictions Program is available to in-state students and students in parts of Georgia and North Carolina only.
Application requirements *Prior education:* baccalaureate degree. *Other requirements:* college transcripts, letter(s) of recommendation, an application fee of $35.
Completion requirements 30 semester hours are required. 21 semester hours must be completed through the institution. *Maximum time for completion:* six years.
On-campus requirements Four Saturday classes each semester.
Program contact Phyllis Coleman, APOGEE Director, University of South Carolina, College of Engineering, Columbia, SC 29208. Phone: 803-777-4192. Fax: 803-777-3340. E-mail: coleman@sc.edu.

▶ *Library and Information Science (MLIS)*
Restrictions Program is available to students in South Carolina and West Virginia only.
Application requirements *Prior education:* baccalaureate degree. *Other requirements:* GRE or MAT, TOEFL, college transcripts, an essay or personal statement, letter(s) of recommendation, an application fee of $35, interview.
Completion requirements 36 semester hours are required. 30 semester hours must be completed through the institution. *Maximum time for completion:* six years.
On-campus requirements In South Carolina, 2 Saturday classes per TV course. In West Virginia, 2 Saturday classes at a central WV site per TV course.
Program contact Gayle Douglas, Assistant Dean, University of South Carolina, College of Library and Information Science, Columbia, SC 29208. Phone: 803-777-3538. Fax: 803-777-7938.

INDIVIDUAL COURSE SUBJECT AREAS

Undergraduate
Accounting; astronomy and astrophysics; business; business administration and management; economics; education; English language and literature; history; hospitality services management; human resources management; journalism; liberal arts, general studies, and humanities; nursing; physics; public health; social work

Graduate
Accounting; astronomy and astrophysics; business; business administration and management; computer and information sciences; education; education administration; engineering; English language and literature; health professions and related sciences; history; hospitality services management; human resources management; journalism; library and information studies; nursing; physics; public administration and services; public health; social work; teacher education

UNIVERSITY OF SOUTH DAKOTA

Vermillion, South Dakota

State-Wide Educational Services

University of South Dakota, founded in 1862, is a state-supported university. It is accredited by the North Central Association of Colleges and Schools. It first offered distance learning courses in 1967. In 1996–97, it offered 334 courses at a distance. In the fall of 1996, there was a total of 925 students enrolled in distance learning courses.
Course delivery sites Courses are delivered to your home, your workplace, military bases, Morningside College (Sioux City, IA), Southeast Technical Institute (Sioux Falls), 4 off-campus centers in Aberdeen, Ellsworth AFB, Sioux Falls, Sioux City (IA).
Media Courses are delivered via television, videotapes, videoconferencing, World Wide Web, e-mail, print. Students and teachers interact via videoconferencing, mail, telephone, fax, e-mail.
Services Distance learners have access to library services at a distance.
Credit-earning options Students may transfer credits from another institution or may earn credits through examinations.
Typical costs *Undergraduate:* Tuition of $149.25 per credit. *Graduate:* Tuition of $174 per credit. Costs may vary by campus or location, course delivery options. Financial aid is available to distance learners enrolled full-time or part-time.
Registration Students may register by mail, fax, phone.
Contact State-Wide Educational Services, University of South Dakota, 414 East Clark Street, Vermillion, SD 57069. *Telephone:* 800-233-7937. *Fax:* 605-677-6118. *E-mail:* swes@sundance.usd.edu. *Web site:* http://www.usd.edu/~swes/.

INDIVIDUAL COURSE SUBJECT AREAS

Undergraduate
Abnormal psychology; area, ethnic, and cultural studies; astronomy and astrophysics; biology; business administration and management; developmental and child psychology; educational psychology; English composition; English language and literature; European languages and literatures; health and physical education/fitness; history; human resources management; liberal arts, general studies, and humanities; mass media; philosophy and religion; political science; sociology; teacher education

Graduate
Accounting; biology; business; business administration and management; community health services; education administration; health professions and related sciences; human resources management; law and legal studies; philosophy and religion; sociology; special education; teacher education

Profiles: University of Southern California

UNIVERSITY OF SOUTHERN CALIFORNIA

Los Angeles, California

University of Southern California, founded in 1880, is an independent-nonprofit university. It is accredited by the Western Association of Schools and Colleges, Inc. It first offered distance learning courses in 1972.

Course delivery sites Courses are delivered to your home, your workplace, military bases, other colleges, off-campus center(s).

Media Courses are delivered via television, videotapes, videoconferencing, audiotapes. Students and teachers interact via videoconferencing, audioconferencing, mail, telephone, fax, e-mail. A computer is required for some courses.

Restrictions Students must be able to receive television broadcast or make special arrangements.

Services Distance learners have access to library services, the campus computer network, e-mail services, academic advising, tutoring, career placement assistance at a distance.

Credit-earning options Students may transfer credits from another institution or may earn credits through examinations.

Typical costs Contact university for details. Financial aid is available to distance learners enrolled full-time or part-time.

Contact Central Admissions, University of Southern California, 700 Childs Way - SAS 210, Los Angeles, CA 90089-0911. *Telephone:* 213-740-6753. *Fax:* 213-740-8826.

DEGREE & CERTIFICATE PROGRAMS

Graduate Degrees

▶*Computer Engineering (MS)*

Application requirements *Prior education:* baccalaureate degree. *Other requirements:* GRE, college transcripts, an essay or personal statement, letter(s) of recommendation, an application fee.

Completion requirements 27 semester hours are required. 24 semester hours must be completed through the institution.

On-campus requirements For exams.

Program contact Katherine Collins, Associate Director, Instructional TV, University of Southern California, Engineering — Olin Hall 108 / MC 1455, Los Angeles, CA 90089-1455. Phone: 213-740-0115. Fax: 213-749-3289. E-mail: collins@mizar.usc.edu.

▶*Computer Science (MS)*

Application requirements *Prior education:* baccalaureate degree. *Other requirements:* GRE, college transcripts, an essay or personal statement, an application fee.

Completion requirements 27 semester hours are required. 24 semester hours must be completed through the institution.

On-campus requirements For exams.

Program contact Katherine Collins, Associate Director, Instructional TV, University of Southern California, Engineering — Olin Hall 108 / MC 1455, Los Angeles, CA 90089-1455. Phone: 213-740-0115. Fax: 213-749-3289. E-mail: collins@mizar.usc.edu.

▶*Electrical Engineering (MSEE)*

Application requirements *Prior education:* baccalaureate degree. *Other requirements:* GRE, college transcripts, an essay or personal statement, letter(s) of recommendation, an application fee.

Completion requirements 27 semester hours are required. 24 semester hours must be completed through the institution.

On-campus requirements For exams.

Program contact Katherine Collins, Associate Director, Instructional TV, University of Southern California, Engineering — Olin Hall 108 / MC 1455, Los Angeles, CA 90089-1455. Phone: 213-740-0115. Fax: 213-749-3289. E-mail: collins@mizar.usc.edu.

INDIVIDUAL COURSE SUBJECT AREAS

Undergraduate
Health professions and related sciences

Graduate
Aerospace, aeronautical engineering; computer and information sciences; electrical engineering; engineering/industrial management; industrial engineering; mechanical engineering; teacher education

Noncredit
Aerospace, aeronautical engineering; business administration and management; computer and information sciences; electrical engineering; engineering/industrial management; industrial engineering; mechanical engineering; teacher education

UNIVERSITY OF SOUTHERN COLORADO

Pueblo, Colorado

Division of Continuing Education

University of Southern Colorado, founded in 1933, is a state-supported comprehensive institution. It is accredited by the North Central Association of Colleges and Schools. It first offered distance learning courses in 1987. In 1996–97, it offered 110 courses at a distance. In the fall of 1996, there was a total of 500 students enrolled in distance learning courses.

Course delivery sites Courses are delivered to your home, your workplace, military bases, 8 off-campus centers in Colorado Springs, Altus AFB (OK), McGuire AFB (NJ).

Media Courses are delivered via television, videotapes, videoconferencing, World Wide Web, e-mail, print. Students and teachers interact via videoconferencing, mail, telephone, fax, e-mail. A computer is required for some courses.

Services Distance learners have access to library services, e-mail services, academic advising, career placement assistance at a distance.

Credit-earning options Students may transfer credits from another institution or may earn credits through standardized exams, institutionally developed exams, portfolio assessment, military training, business training.

Typical costs *Undergraduate:* Tuition of $75 per credit. *Graduate:* Tuition of $75 per credit. *Noncredit courses:* $395 per course. Costs may vary by course delivery options. Financial aid is available to distance learners enrolled full-time or part-time.

Registration Students may register by mail, fax, phone, e-mail, World Wide Web.

Contact Office of Continuing Education, University of Southern Colorado, 2200 Bonforte Boulevard, Pueblo, CO 81001-4901. *Telephone:* 719-549-2316. *Fax:* 719-549-2438. *E-mail:* coned@meteor.uscolo.edu. *Web site:* http://www.uscolo.edu/coned.

DEGREE & CERTIFICATE PROGRAMS

Baccalaureate Degrees

▶*Social Sciences (BS)*

In the fall of 1996 there were 105 students enrolled in this program.

Application requirements *Prior education:* some undergraduate course work. *Other requirements:* ACT, SAT (unless a transfer student), high school transcript, college transcripts, an application fee of $125.

Completion requirements 128 semester hours are required. 32 semester hours must be completed through the institution. *Maximum time for completion:* 10 years.

Program contact Lara Van Buskirk, Office of Continuing Education, University of Southern Colorado, 2200 Bonforte Boulevard, Pueblo,

CO 81001-4901. Phone: 719-549-2316. Fax: 719-549-2438. E-mail: coned@meteor.uscolo.edu.

Undergraduate Certificates

▶ *Paralegal*

In the fall of 1996 there were 75 students enrolled in this program. In 1995–96, 125 certificates were earned at a distance through this program.
Application requirements *Prior education:* high school diploma or equivalent.
Program contact Lara Van Buskirk, Office of Continuing Education, University of Southern Colorado, 2200 Bonforte Boulevard, Pueblo, CO 81001-4901. Phone: 719-549-2316. Fax: 719-549-2438. E-mail: coned@meteor.uscolo.edu.

INDIVIDUAL COURSE SUBJECT AREAS

Undergraduate

Accounting; area, ethnic, and cultural studies; art history and criticism; business administration and management; conservation and natural resources; economics; English language and literature; family and marriage counseling; geography; geology; marketing; nursing; political science; social psychology; social work; sociology; substance abuse counseling; teacher education

Graduate

Family and marriage counseling; teacher education

See full description on page 516.

UNIVERSITY OF SOUTHERN INDIANA

Evansville, Indiana

Extended Services

University of Southern Indiana, founded in 1965, is a state-supported comprehensive institution. It is accredited by the North Central Association of Colleges and Schools. It first offered distance learning courses in 1994. In 1996–97, it offered 19 courses at a distance. In the fall of 1996, there was a total of 126 students enrolled in distance learning courses.
Course delivery sites Courses are delivered to your home, your workplace, military bases, over 200 sites throughout Indiana.
Media Courses are delivered via television, videotapes, videoconferencing, computer software, World Wide Web, e-mail, print. Students and teachers interact via videoconferencing, mail, telephone, fax, e-mail. A computer is required for some courses.
Services Distance learners have access to library services, e-mail services, academic advising at a distance.
Credit-earning options Students may transfer credits from another institution or may earn credits through institutionally developed exams, military training.
Typical costs *Undergraduate:* Tuition of $80 per credit hour for in-state residents. Tuition of $195.25 per credit hour for out-of-state residents. *Graduate:* Tuition of $117.75 per credit hour for in-state residents. Tuition of $235.25 per credit hour for out-of-state residents. Costs may vary by course delivery options. Financial aid is available to distance learners enrolled full-time or part-time.
Registration Students may register by mail, fax, phone.
Contact Sandra Hermann, Director of University Division, University of Southern Indiana, 8600 University Boulevard, Evansville, IN 47712. *Telephone:* 812-465-1606. *Fax:* 812-464-1758. *E-mail:* shermann.ucs@smtp.usi.edu. *Web site:* http://www.usi.edu.

INDIVIDUAL COURSE SUBJECT AREAS

Undergraduate

Advertising; American literature; business; computer and information sciences; fine arts; health professions and related sciences; journalism; law and legal studies; liberal arts, general studies, and humanities; nursing; public health; public relations; radio and television broadcasting; special education

Graduate

Nursing

UNIVERSITY OF SOUTHERN MISSISSIPPI

Hattiesburg, Mississippi

Department of Continuing Education

University of Southern Mississippi, founded in 1910, is a state-supported university. It is accredited by the Southern Association of Colleges and Schools. It first offered distance learning courses in 1913.
Course delivery sites Courses are delivered to your home, your workplace, military bases.
Media Courses are delivered via television, videoconferencing, print. Students and teachers interact via videoconferencing, mail, telephone, fax, e-mail.
Services Distance learners have access to library services, the campus computer network, e-mail services, career placement assistance at a distance.
Credit-earning options Students may transfer credits from another institution or may earn credits through standardized exams, institutionally developed exams, military training.
Typical costs *Undergraduate:* Tuition of $283 per course. *Graduate:* Tuition of $367 per course. Costs may vary by course delivery options. Financial aid is available to distance learners enrolled full-time.
Registration Students may register by mail, fax, phone.
Contact Sue Pace, Director, Continuing Education, University of Southern Mississippi, Box 5055, Hattiesburg, MS 39406-5055. *Telephone:* 601-266-4210. *Fax:* 601-266-5839. *E-mail:* pace@whale.st.usm.edu.

INDIVIDUAL COURSE SUBJECT AREAS

Undergraduate

Accounting; algebra; anthropology; bible studies; business; calculus; creative writing; criminal justice; economics; electrical engineering; English language and literature; ethics; genetics; geography; history; logic; management information systems; marketing; mathematics; real estate; sociology; zoology

UNIVERSITY OF SOUTH FLORIDA

Tampa, Florida

Educational Outreach

University of South Florida, founded in 1956, is a state-supported university. It is accredited by the Southern Association of Colleges and Schools. It first offered distance learning courses in 1983.
Course delivery sites Courses are delivered to your workplace, military bases, other colleges.
Media Courses are delivered via television, videotapes, videoconferencing, computer software, computer conferencing.

Profiles: University of South Florida

Services Distance learners have access to library services, academic advising, career placement assistance at a distance.
Credit-earning options Students may transfer credits from another institution or may earn credits through standardized exams.
Typical costs *Undergraduate:* Tuition of $65.35 per semester hour for in-state residents. Tuition of $240.19 per semester hour for out-of-state residents. *Graduate:* Tuition of $120.91 per semester hour for in-state residents. Tuition of $391.65 per semester hour for out-of-state residents.
Contact Dr. Barbara B. Emil, Dean, University of South Florida, 4202 East Fowler Avenue, ADM 226, Tampa, FL 33620. *Telephone:* 813-974-2154. *Fax:* 813-974-5093.

DEGREE & CERTIFICATE PROGRAMS

Baccalaureate Degrees

▶ *Independent Studies (BA)*
In the fall of 1996 there were 145 students enrolled in this program.
On-campus requirements Two weeks in the summer for seminar.
Program contact Dr. Frederick Steier, Director, Interdisciplinary Programs, University of South Florida, 4202 East Fowler Avenue, HMS 413, Tampa, FL 33620. Phone: 813-974-4058. Fax: 813-974-5101.

▶ *Nursing (BSN)*
In the fall of 1996 there were 285 students enrolled in this program.
On-campus requirements One-day orientation.
Program contact Dr. Mary Tittle, Interim Associate Dean, Nursing, University of South Florida, 4202 East Fowler Avenue, MDC Box 22, Tampa, FL 33620. Phone: 813-974-2191. Fax: 813-974-5416.

Graduate Degrees

▶ *Business Administration (MBA)*
In the fall of 1996 there were 631 students enrolled in this program.
Restrictions This program is available to in-state students only. Students must have access to affiliate network.
Application requirements *Prior education:* baccalaureate degree. *Other requirements:* GRE.
Completion requirements 57 credits are required.
Program contact Dr. Richard L. Meyer, Associate Dean, Business Administration, University of South Florida, 4202 East Fowler Avenue, BSN 2102, Tampa, FL 33620. Phone: 813-974-3156. Fax: 813-974-3030. E-mail: meyer@bsn01.bsn.usf.edu.

▶ *Engineering (MSE)*
Restrictions This program is available to in-state students only. Students must work at an affiliate site.
Application requirements *Prior education:* baccalaureate degree. *Other requirements:* GRE, college transcripts, letter(s) of recommendation, an application fee.
Program contact Dr. Andrew J. Barrett, Assistant Dean, Engineering, University of South Florida, 4202 East Fowler Avenue, ETB, Tampa, FL 33620. Phone: 813-974-3783. Fax: 813-974-8010. E-mail: barrett@sunburn.eng.usf.edu.

▶ *Public Health (MPH)*
In the fall of 1996 there were 472 students enrolled in this program.
Restrictions Program is primarily focused in Florida.
Application requirements *Prior education:* baccalaureate degree. *Other requirements:* GRE, college transcripts, letter(s) of recommendation.
On-campus requirements One-week intensive.
Program contact Dr. Kim Blevins, Director, Distance Learning Program, University of South Florida, 4202 East Fowler Avenue, MDC Box 56, Tampa, FL 33620. Phone: 813-974-3623. Fax: 813-974-4718.

INDIVIDUAL COURSE SUBJECT AREAS

Undergraduate
Biology; chemistry; computer and information sciences; creative writing; economics; electrical engineering; English composition; European languages and literatures; geology; history; industrial engineering; liberal arts, general studies, and humanities; mathematics; nursing; physics; political science; sociology

Graduate
Accounting; architecture; business; business administration and management; chemical engineering; civil engineering; computer and information sciences; electrical engineering; engineering/industrial management; environmental engineering; fine arts; geology; human resources management; industrial engineering; library and information studies; mathematics; mechanical engineering; nursing; public health; special education; teacher education

UNIVERSITY OF ST. AUGUSTINE FOR HEALTH SCIENCES

St. Augustine, Florida

Division of Distance Education

University of St. Augustine for Health Sciences, founded in 1978, is a proprietary graduate institution. It is accredited by the Distance Education and Training Council. It first offered distance learning courses in 1979.
Course delivery sites Courses are delivered to your home.
Media Courses are delivered via videotapes, audiotapes, e-mail, print. Students and teachers interact via mail, telephone, fax, e-mail.
Services Distance learners have access to academic advising, tutoring at a distance.
Credit-earning options Students may transfer credits from another institution.
Typical costs Tuition of $795 per course. Financial aid is available to distance learners.
Contact Trish Baker, Coordinator of Distance Education, University of St. Augustine for Health Sciences, 170 Malaga Street, St. Augustine, FL 32084. *Telephone:* 904-826-0084. *Fax:* 904-826-0085.

DEGREE & CERTIFICATE PROGRAMS

Graduate Degrees

▶ *Physical Therapy (DPT)*
Application requirements *Prior education:* be a practicing physical therapist/MPT or have an advanced Masters degree. *Other requirements:* college transcripts, an application fee of $300.
Completion requirements 26 semester hours are required. 6 semester hours must be completed through the institution. *Maximum time for completion:* five years.
On-campus requirements Six-day colloquium in St. Augustine.

▶ *Physical Therapy (MSPT)*
Application requirements *Prior education:* BA in Physical Therapy. *Other requirements:* GRE, an application fee of $50, must pass the Institute of Physical Therapy Certification Exam in Manual Therapy or Sports Physical Therapy for matriculated students.
Completion requirements 36 semester hours are required. 27 semester hours must be completed through the institution. *Maximum time for completion:* five years.
On-campus requirements Two 3-week academic residencies.

INDIVIDUAL COURSE SUBJECT AREAS

Graduate
Health professions and related sciences

THE UNIVERSITY OF TENNESSEE AT MARTIN

Martin, Tennessee

The University of Tennessee at Martin, founded in 1927, is a state-supported comprehensive institution. It is accredited by the Southern Association of Colleges and Schools.
Course delivery sites Courses are delivered to other colleges.
Media Courses are delivered via television. Students and teachers interact via audioconferencing, fax.
Credit-earning options Students may transfer credits from another institution or may earn credits through examinations.
Typical costs *Undergraduate:* Tuition of $258 per course for in-state residents. Tuition of $801 per course for out-of-state residents. *Graduate:* Tuition of $435 per course for local area residents. Tuition of $1155 per course for in-state residents.
Contact Sandy Belote, Director of Evening School, The University of Tennessee at Martin, 109 Gooch Hall, Martin, TN 38238. *Telephone:* 901-587-7080. *Fax:* 901-587-7084. *E-mail:* sbelote@ugn.edu.

INDIVIDUAL COURSE SUBJECT AREAS

Undergraduate
Accounting; business; business administration and management; education administration; educational psychology; nursing; special education; teacher education

Graduate
Accounting; business; business administration and management; education administration; educational psychology; nursing; special education; teacher education

UNIVERSITY OF TENNESSEE, KNOXVILLE

Knoxville, Tennessee

Department of Distance Education and Independent Study

University of Tennessee, Knoxville, founded in 1794, is a state-supported university. It is accredited by the Southern Association of Colleges and Schools. It first offered distance learning courses in 1923. In 1996–97, it offered 150 courses at a distance. In the fall of 1996, there was a total of 2,500 students enrolled in distance learning courses.
Course delivery sites Courses are delivered to your home, your workplace, University of Virginia (Charlottesville, VA), 6 off-campus centers in Kingsport, Nashville, Oak Ridge, Falls Church (VA), Roanoke (VA), Virginia Beach (VA).
Media Courses are delivered via videotapes, videoconferencing, World Wide Web, print. Students and teachers interact via videoconferencing, mail, telephone, fax, e-mail. A computer is required for some courses.
Services Distance learners have access to library services, e-mail services, academic advising, career placement assistance at a distance.
Credit-earning options Students may transfer credits from another institution or may earn credits through standardized exams.
Typical costs *Undergraduate:* Tuition of $84 per semester hour for in-state residents. Tuition of $84 per semester hour for out-of-state residents. *Graduate:* Tuition of $150 per semester hour for in-state residents. Tuition of $407 per semester hour for out-of-state residents. *Noncredit courses:* $100 per course. Costs may vary by number of credits taken, course delivery options. Financial aid is available to distance learners enrolled full-time.
Registration Students may register by mail, fax, phone.
Contact Laurel Thomas, Assistant Director, University of Tennessee, Knoxville, 440 Communications Building, Knoxville, TN 37996. *Telephone:* 423-974-5126. *Fax:* 423-974-6629. *Web site:* http://www.ce.utk.edu.

DEGREE & CERTIFICATE PROGRAMS

Graduate Degrees

▶ *Communications (MS)*
In the fall of 1996 there were 16 students enrolled in this program. In 1995–96, 1 degree was earned at a distance through this program.
Restrictions Program is available to students in Chattanooga and Martin only. Students must have access to a University of Tennessee EDNET teleclassroom is required.
Application requirements *Prior education:* baccalaureate degree. *Other requirements:* GRE, college transcripts, letter(s) of recommendation, an application fee of $15.
Completion requirements 31 semester hours are required. 25 semester hours must be completed through the institution.
Program contact Dr. Herbert Howard, Director, Graduate Studies, University of Tennessee, Knoxville, 426 Communications Building, Knoxville, TN 37996. Phone: 423-974-6651. Fax: 423-974-3896. E-mail: hhoward@utk.edu.

▶ *Engineering Management (MS)*
Application requirements *Prior education:* BS in engineering. *Other requirements:* college transcripts, an application fee of $15, 2 years experience or must be currently employed in engineering or scientific field.
Completion requirements 36 semester hours are required. 24 semester hours must be completed through the institution. *Maximum time for completion:* six years.
Program contact George Garrison, Director, Engineering Management, University of Tennessee, Knoxville, MS19, Tullahoma, TN 37388. Phone: 615-393-7293. Fax: 615-393-7201. E-mail: ggarriso@utsi.edu.

▶ *Industrial Engineering/Engineering Management (MS)*

▶ *Information Sciences (MS)*
In the fall of 1996 there were 83 students enrolled in this program.
Restrictions Students must have access to a University of Tennessee EDNET teleclassroom in Tennessee or Virginia.
Application requirements *Prior education:* baccalaureate degree. *Other requirements:* GRE, college transcripts, letter(s) of recommendation, an application fee of $15.
Completion requirements 43 semester hours are required. 37 semester hours must be completed through the institution. *Maximum time for completion:* six years.
Program contact George Hoemann, Director of Admissions, School of Information Sciences, University of Tennessee, Knoxville, 804 Volunteer Boulevard, Knoxville, TN 37996. Phone: 423-974-5917. Fax: 423-974-4967. E-mail: hoemann@utk.edu.

▶ *Social Work (MS)*

INDIVIDUAL COURSE SUBJECT AREAS

Undergraduate
Abnormal psychology; accounting; agricultural economics; algebra; American (US) history; American literature; anthropology; business administration and management; calculus; child care and development; cognitive psychology; conservation and natural resources; creative writing; criminal justice; curriculum and instruction; developmental and child psychology; English composition; English language and literature; English literature; ethics; European history; forestry; French language and literature; German language and literature; gerontology; Italian language and literature; psychology; religious studies; social psychology; Spanish language and literature; special education; statistics; teacher education; technical writing

Profiles: University of Tennessee, Knoxville

Graduate
Chemical engineering; civil engineering; communications; computer and information sciences; education administration; electrical engineering; engineering mechanics; engineering/industrial management; environmental engineering; human resources management; industrial engineering; information sciences and systems; journalism; library and information studies; mechanical engineering; public relations; radio and television broadcasting; social work

Noncredit
Creative writing; marketing
See full description on page 518.

UNIVERSITY OF TENNESSEE SPACE INSTITUTE

Tullahoma, Tennessee

University of Tennessee Space Institute is a state-supported graduate institution. It is accredited by the Southern Association of Colleges and Schools. It first offered distance learning courses in 1982. In 1996–97, it offered 31 courses at a distance. In the fall of 1996, there was a total of 157 students enrolled in distance learning courses.
Course delivery sites Courses are delivered to your home, your workplace, military bases, other colleges, 4 off-campus centers in Jackson, Kingsport, Nashville, Oak Ridge.
Media Courses are delivered via videotapes, videoconferencing, audioconferencing, interactive television. Students and teachers interact via videoconferencing, mail, telephone, fax, e-mail. A computer is required for some courses.
Services Distance learners have access to library services, e-mail services, academic advising, tutoring, career placement assistance at a distance.
Credit-earning options Students may transfer credits from another institution or may earn credits through institutionally developed exams.
Typical costs Tuition of $526 per semester for in-state residents. Tuition of $1158 per semester for out-of-state residents. Costs may vary by campus or location, course delivery options. Financial aid is available to distance learners.
Registration Students may register by mail, fax, phone, e-mail.
Contact Dr. K. C. Reddy, Dean for Academic Affairs, University of Tennessee Space Institute, 411 B. H. Goethert Parkway, Tullahoma, TN 37388-8897. *Telephone:* 615-393-7318. *Fax:* 615-393-7346. *E-mail:* kreddy@utsi.edu. *Web site:* http://www.utsi.edu.

DEGREE & CERTIFICATE PROGRAMS

Graduate Degrees

▶ *Aviations Systems (MS)*
In the fall of 1996 there were 50 students enrolled in this program. In 1995–96, 33 degrees were earned at a distance through this program.
Application requirements *Prior education:* BS in engineering or science. *Other requirements:* basic knowledge of computer utilization and statistics, understanding of aerodynamic fundamentals, propulsion, performance, economics, and accounting.
Completion requirements 33 semester hours are required. *Maximum time for completion:* six years.
On-campus requirements For presentation of thesis or non-thesis paper to committee.
Program contact Dr. Ralph Kimberlin, Program Chairman, University of Tennessee Space Institute, U.T. Space Institute, MS 39, Tullahoma, TN 37388-8897. Phone: 615-393-7408. Fax: 615-393-7409. E-mail: rkimberl@utsi.edu.

▶ *Industrial Engineering (MS)*
In the fall of 1996 there were 175 students enrolled in this program. In 1995–96, 61 degrees were earned at a distance through this program.
Application requirements *Prior education:* BS in Engineering. *Other requirements:* college transcripts, an application fee of $15.
Completion requirements 36 semester hours are required. 24 semester hours must be completed through the institution. *Maximum time for completion:* six years.
On-campus requirements Students must defend their capstone project on campus.
Program contact Dr. George Garrison, Program Chairman, University of Tennessee Space Institute, U.T. Space Institute, Tullahoma, TN 37388. Phone: 615-393-7529. Fax: 615-393-7201. E-mail: ggarriso@utsi.edu.

INDIVIDUAL COURSE SUBJECT AREAS

Graduate
Aerospace, aeronautical engineering; computer and information sciences; engineering-related technologies; engineering/industrial management; industrial engineering; mathematics; mechanical engineering

THE UNIVERSITY OF TEXAS AT ARLINGTON

Arlington, Texas

Engineering Television Department

The University of Texas at Arlington, founded in 1895, is a state-supported university. It is accredited by the Southern Association of Colleges and Schools. It first offered distance learning courses in 1973.
Course delivery sites Courses are delivered to your home, your workplace, military bases, other colleges.
Media Courses are delivered via videotapes, videoconferencing, print.
Services Distance learners have access to library services, academic advising at a distance.
Credit-earning options Students may transfer credits from another institution. Financial aid is available to distance learners.
Contact Distance Learning Coordinator, The University of Texas at Arlington, 416 Yates Street, Nedderman Hall, Box 19077, Arlington, TX 76015. *Telephone:* 817-272-2352. *Fax:* 817-272-5630.

DEGREE & CERTIFICATE PROGRAMS

Graduate Degrees

▶ *Civil and Environmental Engineering (ME, MS)*
Program contact Dr. Clinton E. Parker, Chairman, The University of Texas at Arlington, Box 19308, Arlington, TX 76015. Phone: 817-272-5055.

▶ *Computer Science and Engineering (ME, MS)*
Program contact Dr. Bill Carroll, Chairman, The University of Texas at Arlington, Box 19015, Arlington, TX 76019. Phone: 817-272-3785.

▶ *Electrical Engineering (MS)*
Program contact Dr. Jack Fitzer, Chairman, The University of Texas at Arlington, Box 19016, Arlington, TX 76015. Phone: 817-272-2671.

▶ *Industrial and Manufacturing Systems Engineering (MS)*
Program contact Dr. G. T. Stevens, Chairman, The University of Texas at Arlington, Box 19017, UTA, Arlington, TX 76015. Phone: 817-272-3092.

▶ *Mechanical and Aerospace Engineering (MS)*
Program contact Dr. Ron Bailey, Chairman, The University of Texas at Arlington, Box 19018, Arlington, TX 76015. Phone: 817-272-2561.

INDIVIDUAL COURSE SUBJECT AREAS

Graduate
Aerospace, aeronautical engineering; civil engineering; electrical engineering; engineering mechanics; environmental engineering; industrial engineering; mechanical engineering

THE UNIVERSITY OF TEXAS AT AUSTIN

Austin, Texas

EIMC: A Distance Education Center

The University of Texas at Austin, founded in 1883, is a state-supported university. It is accredited by the Southern Association of Colleges and Schools. It first offered distance learning courses in 1909. In 1996–97, it offered 195 courses at a distance. In the fall of 1996, there was a total of 15,859 students enrolled in distance learning courses.

Course delivery sites Courses are delivered to your home, your workplace, military bases, The University of Texas System (Austin).
Media Courses are delivered via audiotapes, audioconferencing, World Wide Web, e-mail, print. Students and teachers interact via audioconferencing, mail, fax, e-mail. A computer is required for some courses.
Services Distance learners have access to the campus computer network, e-mail services, academic advising at a distance.
Credit-earning options Students may earn credits through examinations.
Typical costs Tuition of $205 per course. *Noncredit courses:* $75–$1000 per course. Costs may vary by campus or location, specific program of study, number of credits taken, course delivery options.
Registration Students may register by mail, fax, phone, e-mail, World Wide Web.
Contact Jon Griffith, Assistant Director, Independent Learning, The University of Texas at Austin, EIMC-Independent Learning, PO Box 7700, Austin, TX 78713-7700. *Telephone:* 512-471-7716. *Fax:* 512-475-7933. *E-mail:* dec@www.utexas.edu. *Web site:* http://www.utexas.edu/depts/eimc.

INDIVIDUAL COURSE SUBJECT AREAS

Undergraduate
Anthropology; area, ethnic, and cultural studies; business; communications; English language and literature; European languages and literatures; health professions and related sciences; history; mathematics; physical sciences; psychology; social sciences; visual and performing arts

Noncredit
Computer and information sciences

THE UNIVERSITY OF TEXAS AT EL PASO

El Paso, Texas

Information and Telecommunication Services

The University of Texas at El Paso, founded in 1913, is a state-supported university. It is accredited by the Southern Association of Colleges and Schools.
Course delivery sites Courses are delivered to other colleges.
Media Courses are delivered via videoconferencing.
Credit-earning options Students may transfer credits from another institution or may earn credits through examinations, portfolio assessment.

Contact Videoconferencing Coordinator, The University of Texas at El Paso, 500 West University Avenue, El Paso, TX 79968- . 915-747-7709. *Fax:* 915-747-5354.

DEGREE & CERTIFICATE PROGRAMS

Graduate Degrees
▶ *Library and Information Sciences (MA, MS)*
Program contact Brooke Sheldon, Dean, The University of Texas at El Paso, Graduate School of Library and Information Science, Austin, TX 78712-1276. Phone: 512-471-3821. Fax: 512-471-3971. E-mail: bsheldon@uts.cc.utexas.edu.

▶ *Public Health (MA, MS)*
Program contact Gay Robertson, Administrative Coordinator of Distance Education, The University of Texas at El Paso, 1200 Herman Pressler, School of Public Health/UTC, Houston, TX 77225. Phone: 713-792-4448. Fax: 713-794-1612. E-mail: gayr@utsph.sph.uth.tmc.edu.

INDIVIDUAL COURSE SUBJECT AREAS

Undergraduate
Communications

Graduate
Communications

THE UNIVERSITY OF TEXAS AT SAN ANTONIO

San Antonio, Texas

Distance Learning Center

The University of Texas at San Antonio, founded in 1969, is a state-supported comprehensive institution. It is accredited by the Southern Association of Colleges and Schools. It first offered distance learning courses in 1993. In 1996–97, it offered 35 courses at a distance. In the fall of 1996, there was a total of 1,919 students enrolled in distance learning courses.

Course delivery sites Courses are delivered to your workplace, St. Philip's College (San Antonio), The University of Texas at Brownsville (Brownsville), The University of Texas–Pan American (Edinburg).
Media Courses are delivered via videoconferencing, World Wide Web, print. Students and teachers interact via videoconferencing, mail, telephone, fax, e-mail.
Restrictions Courses are available to students enrolled at participating institutions only.
Services Distance learners have access to library services, the campus computer network, e-mail services at a distance.
Credit-earning options Students may transfer credits from another institution or may earn credits through standardized exams, institutionally developed exams, portfolio assessment.
Typical costs *Undergraduate:* Tuition of $408 per semester plus mandatory fees of $647 per semester for in-state residents. Tuition of $2976 per semester plus mandatory fees of $647 per semester for out-of-state residents. *Graduate:* Tuition of $612 per semester plus mandatory fees of $519 per semester for in-state residents. Tuition of $2538 per semester plus mandatory fees of $519 per semester for out-of-state residents. *Noncredit courses:* $25 to audit a class. Costs may vary by term of enrollment. Financial aid is available to distance learners enrolled full-time or part-time.
Registration Students may register by phone.
Contact Bill Angrove, Director of the Distance Learning Center, The University of Texas at San Antonio, 6900 North Loop 1604, W, San

Distance Learning Programs

...ies: The University of Texas at San Antonio

Antonio, TX 78249-0677. *Telephone:* 210-458-5868. *Fax:* 210-458-5872. *E-mail:* wangrove@lonestar.utsa.edu. *Web site:* http://factt.utsa.edu.

INDIVIDUAL COURSE SUBJECT AREAS

Undergraduate
Accounting; area, ethnic, and cultural studies; business; business administration and management; chemical engineering; civil engineering; communications; computer and information sciences; electrical engineering; engineering mechanics; engineering-related technologies; engineering/industrial management; environmental engineering; history; hospitality services management; industrial engineering; journalism; library and information studies; mechanical engineering; political science; public health; Spanish language and literature

Graduate
Area, ethnic, and cultural studies; business; business administration and management; civil engineering; computer and information sciences; electrical engineering; engineering-related technologies; mechanical engineering; political science; Spanish language and literature

Noncredit
Administrative and secretarial services

THE UNIVERSITY OF TEXAS AT TYLER

Tyler, Texas

The University of Texas at Tyler, founded in 1971, is a state-supported upper-level institution. It is accredited by the Southern Association of Colleges and Schools. It first offered distance learning courses in 1991. In 1996–97, it offered 46 courses at a distance. In the fall of 1996, there was a total of 187 students enrolled in distance learning courses.
Course delivery sites Courses are delivered to your home, Kilgore College (Kilgore), Trinity Valley Community College (Athens), 3 off-campus centers in Longview, Mexia, Palestine, hospitals.
Media Courses are delivered via television. Students and teachers interact via videoconferencing, mail, telephone, fax, e-mail.
Services Distance learners have access to library services, the campus computer network, academic advising at a distance.
Credit-earning options Students may transfer credits from another institution or may earn credits through standardized exams.
Typical costs *Undergraduate:* Tuition of $34 per credit plus mandatory fees of $60 per credit for in-state residents. Tuition of $230 per credit plus mandatory fees of $60 per credit for out-of-state residents. *Graduate:* Tuition of $34 per credit plus mandatory fees of $60 per credit for in-state residents. Tuition of $230 per credit plus mandatory fees of $60 per credit for out-of-state residents. Financial aid is available to distance learners enrolled full-time or part-time.
Registration Students may register by phone.
Contact Martha Wheat, Director of Admissions, The University of Texas at Tyler, 3900 University Boulevard, Tyler, TX 75799. *Telephone:* 903-566-7394. *Fax:* 903-566-8368.

DEGREE & CERTIFICATE PROGRAMS

Baccalaureate Degrees
▶ *Nursing (BSN)*
In the fall of 1996 there were 49 students enrolled in this program.
Application requirements *Prior education:* some undergraduate course work.
Completion requirements 120 are required. 30 must be completed through the institution.

INDIVIDUAL COURSE SUBJECT AREAS

Undergraduate
Accounting; area, ethnic, and cultural studies; biology; business administration and management; communications; economics; education administration; English language and literature; health and physical education/fitness; history; liberal arts, general studies, and humanities; mathematics; nursing; political science; protective services; sociology; special education; teacher education

Graduate
Accounting; area, ethnic, and cultural studies; business administration and management; communications; education administration; English language and literature; health and physical education/fitness; history; liberal arts, general studies, and humanities; mathematics; nursing; protective services; public administration and services; special education; teacher education

THE UNIVERSITY OF TEXAS OF THE PERMIAN BASIN

Odessa, Texas

REACH Program Center

The University of Texas of the Permian Basin, founded in 1969, is a state-supported comprehensive institution. It is accredited by the Southern Association of Colleges and Schools. It first offered distance learning courses in 1996. In 1996–97, it offered 25 courses at a distance. In the fall of 1996, there was a total of 160 students enrolled in distance learning courses.
Course delivery sites Courses are delivered to Angelo State University (San Angelo), Howard College (Big Spring), Midland College (Midland), Odessa College (Odessa), 1 off-campus center in Fort Stockton.
Media Courses are delivered via television, videoconferencing, World Wide Web, e-mail. Students and teachers interact via videoconferencing, telephone, fax, e-mail. A computer is required for some courses.
Restrictions Students must be admitted to one of the partner institutions.
Services Distance learners have access to library services, the campus computer network, e-mail services, academic advising at a distance.
Credit-earning options Students may transfer credits from another institution or may earn credits through standardized exams.
Typical costs *Undergraduate:* Tuition of $32 per hour plus mandatory fees of $87.50 per hour for in-state residents. Tuition of $246 per hour plus mandatory fees of $87.50 per hour for out-of-state residents. *Graduate:* Tuition of $50 per hour plus mandatory fees of $87.50 per hour for in-state residents. Tuition of $246 per hour plus mandatory fees of $87.50 per hour for out-of-state residents. Financial aid is available to distance learners.
Registration Students may register by mail.
Contact Dana Deering, Administrative Assistant, The University of Texas of the Permian Basin, 4901 East University, Odessa, TX 79762-0001. *Telephone:* 915-552-2870. *Fax:* 915-552-2871. *E-mail:* deering_d@utpb.edu.

INDIVIDUAL COURSE SUBJECT AREAS

Undergraduate
Business; communications; computer and information sciences; curriculum and instruction; mathematics; Russian language and literature; sociology; visual and performing arts

Graduate
Business; criminal justice; curriculum and instruction; education administration

UNIVERSITY OF THE STATE OF NEW YORK, REGENTS COLLEGE

Albany, New York

University of the State of New York, Regents College, founded in 1970, is an independent-nonprofit four-year college. It is accredited by the Middle States Association of Colleges and Schools. It first offered distance learning courses in 1970.

Course delivery sites Courses are delivered to your home, your workplace, military bases, other colleges.
Media Courses are delivered via World Wide Web. Students and teachers interact via audioconferencing, telephone, e-mail, World Wide Web.
Services Distance learners have access to e-mail services, academic advising, career placement assistance at a distance.
Credit-earning options Students may transfer credits from another institution or may earn credits through standardized exams, institutionally developed exams, portfolio assessment, military training, business training.
Typical costs Contact school for information. Financial aid is available to distance learners enrolled full-time or part-time.
Registration Students may register by mail, fax.
Contact Diane Wild-Smith, Outreach Coordinator, University of the State of New York, Regents College, 7 Columbia Circle, Albany, NY 12203. *Telephone:* 518-464-8611. *Fax:* 518-464-8777. *Web site:* http://www.regents.edu.

DEGREE & CERTIFICATE PROGRAMS

Associate Degrees

▶ *Business, Computer Software, Nuclear Technology (AS)*
Application requirements *Prior education:* none required.
Completion requirements 60 credits are required.

▶ *Electronic Technology (AS)*
Application requirements *Prior education:* none required.
Completion requirements 64 credits are required.

▶ *Liberal Arts (AA, AS)*
Application requirements *Prior education:* none required.
Completion requirements 60 credits are required.

▶ *Nursing (AAS, AS)*
Application requirements *Prior education:* none required.
Completion requirements 66 credits are required.

Baccalaureate Degrees

▶ *Liberal Arts (BA, BS)*
Application requirements *Prior education:* none required.
Completion requirements 120 credits are required.

▶ *Accounting, Computer Information Systems, Computer Technology, Electronics Technology, Finance, General Business, International Business, Management Information Systems, Management of Human Resources, Marketing, Nuclear Technology, Nursing, Operations Management (BS)*
Application requirements *Prior education:* none required.
Completion requirements 120 are required.

INDIVIDUAL COURSE SUBJECT AREAS

Undergraduate

Accounting; biological and life sciences; business; business administration and management; developmental and child psychology; gerontology; history; human resources management; liberal arts, general studies, and humanities; nursing; philosophy and religion; political science; sociology; statistics; teacher education

UNIVERSITY OF TOLEDO

Toledo, Ohio

University College, Division of Distance Learning

University of Toledo, founded in 1872, is a state-supported university. It is accredited by the North Central Association of Colleges and Schools. It first offered distance learning courses in 1996. In 1996–97, it offered 5 courses at a distance.

Course delivery sites Courses are delivered to your home, your workplace, military bases, Lima Technical College (Lima), Michigan State University (East Lansing, MI), The Ohio State University at Lima (Lima).
Media Courses are delivered via television, videoconferencing, World Wide Web. Students and teachers interact via videoconferencing, audioconferencing, mail, telephone, fax, e-mail, site visits. A computer is required for some courses.
Services Distance learners have access to library services, e-mail services, academic advising, tutoring, bookstore at a distance.
Credit-earning options Students may transfer credits from another institution or may earn credits through examinations, portfolio assessment, military training.
Typical costs *Undergraduate:* Tuition of $130 per credit hour plus mandatory fees of $22 per credit hour for in-state residents. Tuition of $360 per credit hour plus mandatory fees of $22 per credit hour for out-of-state residents. *Graduate:* Tuition of $200 per credit hour plus mandatory fees of $22 per credit hour for in-state residents. Tuition of $425 per credit hour plus mandatory fees of $22 per credit hour for out-of-state residents. *Noncredit courses:* $300 per course. Costs may vary by campus or location.
Registration Students may register by mail, fax, phone.
Contact Ruth Meinhart, Director, University of Toledo, Adult Student Assistance Center, 2801 West Bancroft, Toledo, OH 43606. *Telephone:* 419-530-4137. *E-mail:* rmeinha@utnet.utoledo.edu. *Web site:* http://www.utoledo.edu/www/_campus-info/colleges/ucollege.

Special note

The University of Toledo (UT) established University College (UC) in June 1995 to respond to the special needs of adult students and the community. University College performs the University's outreach to geographically dispersed students, businesses, organizations, and other colleges and universities. UC's Adult Student Assistance Center and the Divisions of Continuing Education, Contract Education, Distance Learning, Individualized and Special Programs (including 2+2 programs), and Organization Development work together to promote long-term, proactive partnerships with business, industry, and UT's global community. The College serves as the advocate for lifelong learning at the University of Toledo.

The Division of Distance Learning connects UT and educational opportunities wherever they may exist. This is accomplished by responding to market needs and synergistically joining the instructional design of learner-centered course work with innovative uses of technology and teacher preparation for global instruction. Distance learning courses are taught via compressed video using both T-1 and ISDN lines; via the Internet through University OnLine, Inc.; via cable television; and via satellite downlink. Student-faculty interaction is accomplished through face-to-face or compressed video meetings, telephone, and e-mail.

Profiles: University of Toledo

The University of Toledo is a nationally recognized, comprehensive public university with a broad range of undergraduate and graduate programs that serve more than 22,000 students from all 50 states and 98 countries. Seven colleges award undergraduate degrees: Arts and Sciences, Business Administration, Education and Allied Professions, Engineering, Pharmacy, University College, and the University Community and Technical College. Advanced degrees are offered through the Graduate School and the College of Law. Courses may be offered through University College via distance learning from any of the colleges or the Center for International Studies and Programs.
Contact Karen Rhoda, Interim Director of the University College Division of Distance Learning (telephone: 419-321-5130; fax: 419-321-5137; e-mail: krhoda@utnet.utoledo.edu), for an inventory of current offerings, or students can have their company, school, or agency representative call to discuss how distance learning can meet the educational needs of their organization. World Wide Web: http://www.utoledo.edu/www/_campus-info/colleges/ucollege/

INDIVIDUAL COURSE SUBJECT AREAS

Undergraduate
Algebra; business administration and management; creative writing; developmental and child psychology; English composition; environmental science; history; human resources management; marketing; political science; psychology; sociology; statistics

Graduate
Education; law and legal studies

Noncredit
Continuing education

UNIVERSITY OF UTAH

Salt Lake City, Utah

Distance Education

University of Utah, founded in 1850, is a state-supported university. It is accredited by the Northwest Association of Schools and Colleges. It first offered distance learning courses in 1916. In 1996–97, it offered 122 courses at a distance. In the fall of 1996, there was a total of 1,900 students enrolled in distance learning courses.
Course delivery sites Courses are delivered to your home.
Media Courses are delivered via videotapes, audiotapes, computer software, World Wide Web. Students and teachers interact via mail, telephone, fax, e-mail, in-person meetings. A computer is required for some courses.
Restrictions Some courses are available to in-state students only. Students must have basic command of English language.
Services Distance learners have access to library services, the campus computer network, e-mail services, academic advising, tutoring at a distance.
Credit-earning options Students may transfer credits from another institution.
Typical costs Tuition of $55 per hour plus mandatory fees of $15 per course. *Noncredit courses:* $105 fees and $15 syllabus. Costs may vary by course delivery options.
Registration Students may register by mail, fax, phone, e-mail, World Wide Web.
Contact Cynthia Grua, Director, Distance Education and Curriculum Design, University of Utah, 2180 Annex, Salt Lake City, UT 84112. *Telephone:* 800-INSTUDY. *Fax:* 801-581-6267. *E-mail:* inthing@admin.dce.utah.edu. *Web site:* http://www.dce.utah.edu.

INDIVIDUAL COURSE SUBJECT AREAS

Undergraduate
Area, ethnic, and cultural studies; biology; business; business administration and management; chemistry; creative writing; developmental and child psychology; economics; education administration; educational psychology; English composition; English language and literature; fine arts; health professions and related sciences; history; hospitality services management; journalism; library and information studies; mathematics; music; physics; political science; social psychology; special education; teacher education

See full description on page 520.

UNIVERSITY OF VERMONT

Burlington, Vermont

Distance Learning Network

University of Vermont, founded in 1791, is a state-supported university. It is accredited by the New England Association of Schools and Colleges. It first offered distance learning courses in 1990. In 1996–97, it offered 15 courses at a distance. In the fall of 1996, there was a total of 155 students enrolled in distance learning courses.
Course delivery sites Courses are delivered to your workplace, other colleges, 3 off-campus centers in Brattleboro, Montpelier, Rutland, hospitals, senior centers.
Media Courses are delivered via television, videotapes, videoconferencing. Students and teachers interact via videoconferencing, mail, telephone, fax, e-mail.
Services Distance learners have access to library services, academic advising, tutoring, career placement assistance at a distance.
Credit-earning options Students may transfer credits from another institution or may earn credits through standardized exams.
Typical costs Contact university for details. Financial aid is available to distance learners.
Contact Shari Dike, Information Specialist, University of Vermont, 322 South Prospect Street, Burlington, VT 05401. *Telephone:* 802-656-2085. *Fax:* 802-656-0306. *Web site:* http://uvmce.uvm.edu:443.

DEGREE & CERTIFICATE PROGRAMS

Undergraduate Certificates
▶ *Gerontology*
Restrictions This program is available to in-state students only.
Application requirements *Prior education:* some undergraduate course work. *Other requirements:* application.
Completion requirements 18 credits are required. 18 credits must be completed through the institution. *Maximum time for completion:* five years.
Program contact Deborah Worthley, Director of Student Services, University of Vermont, 322 South Prospect Street, Burlington, VT 05401. Phone: 802-656-2085. Fax: 802-656-0306. E-mail: dworthle@moose.uvm.edu.

INDIVIDUAL COURSE SUBJECT AREAS

Undergraduate
Education administration; electrical engineering; English language and literature; geology; gerontology; law and legal studies; mathematics; nursing; psychology; teacher education

Graduate
Gerontology; nursing

UNIVERSITY OF VIRGINIA

Charlottesville, Virginia

Educational Technology

University of Virginia, founded in 1819, is a state-supported university. It is accredited by the Southern Association of Colleges and Schools. It first offered distance learning courses in 1984. In 1996–97, it offered 11 courses at a distance. In the fall of 1996, there was a total of 309 students enrolled in distance learning courses.
Course delivery sites Courses are delivered to your workplace, 7 off-campus centers in Abingdon, Charlottesville, Fairfax, Hampton Roads, Lynchburg, Richmond, Roanoke, University of Virginia Regional Centers, Commonwealth Graduate Engineering Program Consortium institutions.
Media Courses are delivered via television, videoconferencing, World Wide Web. Students and teachers interact via videoconferencing, audioconferencing, mail, telephone, fax, e-mail. A computer is required for some courses.
Services Distance learners have access to library services, academic advising at a distance.
Credit-earning options Students may transfer credits from another institution.
Typical costs Tuition of $645 per course for in-state residents. Tuition of $1212 per course for out-of-state residents. Costs may vary by term of enrollment. Financial aid is available to distance learners.
Registration Students may register by mail, fax, phone, World Wide Web.
Contact John H. Payne, III, Director, University of Virginia, 104 Midmont Lane, Charlottesville, VA 22911. *Telephone:* 757-982-5254. *Fax:* 757-982-5270. *E-mail:* jdp6m@virginia.edu.

DEGREE & CERTIFICATE PROGRAMS

Graduate Degrees
▶ *Engineering (PhD)*
Restrictions This program is available to local area students only.
Application requirements *Prior education:* graduate degree. *Other requirements:* letter(s) of recommendation, an application fee.
Completion requirements *Other requirements:* comprehensive exam, dissertation or thesis.
Program contact David Chestnutt, Director, University of Virginia, VCES, 303 Butler Farm Road, Suite 101, Hampton, VA 23666. Phone: 757-865-4830. Fax: 757-865-4852. E-mail: dc2d@virginia.edu.

▶ *Engineering (ME)*
In the fall of 1996 there were 282 students enrolled in this program. In 1995–96, 30 degrees were earned at a distance through this program.
Application requirements *Prior education:* baccalaureate degree. *Other requirements:* college transcripts, letter(s) of recommendation, an application fee of $40.
Completion requirements 30 credits are required. 15 credits must be completed through the institution. *Maximum time for completion:* seven years.

Program contact George L. Cahen, Jr., Assistant Dean for Graduate Programs, University of Virginia, Thornton Hall A114, Charlottesville, VA 22903. Phone: 757-924-4051. Fax: 757-924-4086. E-mail: glc@virginia.edu.

INDIVIDUAL COURSE SUBJECT AREAS

Graduate
Aerospace, aeronautical engineering; architecture; chemical engineering; civil engineering; education administration; educational psychology; electrical engineering; engineering mechanics; engineering/industrial management; health professions and related sciences; mechanical engineering; physics; Spanish language and literature; teacher education

Noncredit
Education administration; educational psychology; physics; teacher education

UNIVERSITY OF WASHINGTON

Seattle, Washington

Educational Outreach

University of Washington, founded in 1861, is a state-supported university. It is accredited by the Northwest Association of Schools and Colleges. It first offered distance learning courses in 1915. In 1996–97, it offered 120 courses at a distance. In the fall of 1996, there was a total of 2,500 students enrolled in distance learning courses.
Course delivery sites Courses are delivered to your home, Peninsula College (Port Angeles).
Media Courses are delivered via videotapes, audioconferencing, World Wide Web, e-mail, print. Students and teachers interact via audioconferencing, mail, telephone, fax, e-mail, World Wide Web. A computer is required for some courses.
Services Distance learners have access to library services, academic advising at a distance.
Credit-earning options Students may transfer credits from another institution or may earn credits through examinations, portfolio assessment, military training.
Typical costs *Undergraduate:* Tuition of $77 per quarter credit plus mandatory fees of $15 per quarter. *Graduate:* Tuition of $184 per quarter credit plus mandatory fees of $15 per quarter. Costs may vary by specific program of study, number of credits taken.
Registration Students may register by mail, fax, phone.
Contact University of Washington Distance Learning, University of Washington, 5001 25th Avenue, NE, Seattle, WA 98105. *Telephone:* 800-543-2320. *Fax:* 800-543-0887. *E-mail:* distance@u.washington.edu. *Web site:* http://weber.u.washington.edu/~distance.

DEGREE & CERTIFICATE PROGRAMS

Graduate Degrees
▶ *Pharmacy (PharmD)*
In the fall of 1996 there were 75 students enrolled in this program.
Restrictions This program is available to in-state students only. Portfolio assessment required.
Application requirements *Prior education:* degree from an accredited college of pharmacy. *Other requirements:* college transcripts, an essay or personal statement, letter(s) of recommendation, an application fee of $40, license to practice in state of Washington, portfolio and $400 portfolio assessment fee.
Completion requirements 66 quarter credits are required. 66 quarter credits must be completed through the institution.

Profiles: University of Washington

Undergraduate Certificates

▶ C Programming
In the fall of 1996 there were 53 students enrolled in this program.
Application requirements An application fee of $40, experience with high-level programming language.
Completion requirements 10 continuing education units are required. 10 continuing education units must be completed through the institution.
Program contact Grayson Dyer, Head of Academic Programs, University of Washington, 5001 25th Avenue, NE, Seattle, WA 98105. Phone: 206-543-2320. Fax: 206-543-0887. E-mail: distance@u.washington.edu.

▶ Writing
In the fall of 1996 there were 30 students enrolled in this program.
Application requirements *Prior education:* some undergraduate course work. *Other requirements:* an application fee of $40.
Completion requirements 9 continuing education units are required. 9 continuing education units must be completed through the institution. *Maximum time for completion:* one-and-a-half years.

Graduate certificates

▶ Public Health
Application requirements *Prior education:* baccalaureate degree. *Other requirements:* college transcripts, an essay or personal statement, letter(s) of recommendation, an application fee of $40.
Completion requirements 33 quarter credits are required. 33 quarter credits must be completed through the institution.
On-campus requirements Eight weeks over 15 months.
Program contact Jack Hilovsky, Program Manager, Public Health Graduate Certificate Training, University of Washington, University District Building, Suite 427, 1107 Northeast 45th Street, Seattle, WA 98145-4809. Phone: 206-616-9460. Fax: 206-616-9460. E-mail: jhilov@u.washington.edu.

INDIVIDUAL COURSE SUBJECT AREAS

Undergraduate
Accounting; anthropology; architecture; area, ethnic, and cultural studies; astronomy and astrophysics; business communications; chemistry; communications; creative writing; developmental and child psychology; economics; English as a second language (ESL); English composition; English language and literature; environmental science; European languages and literatures; foods and nutrition studies; French language and literature; geography; geology; gerontology; health professions and related sciences; history; international business; law and legal studies; library and information studies; marketing; mathematics; meteorology; music; oceanography; philosophy and religion; political science; psychology; public health; social psychology; sociology; Spanish language and literature; teacher education; technical writing

Graduate
Health professions and related sciences; social work

Noncredit
Computer and information sciences; creative writing
See full description on page 522.

UNIVERSITY OF WATERLOO

Waterloo, Ontario, Canada

Distance and Continuing Education

University of Waterloo, founded in 1957, is a province-supported university. It is provincially chartered. It first offered distance learning courses in 1968. In 1996–97, it offered 250 courses at a distance. In the fall of 1996, there was a total of 3,500 students enrolled in distance learning courses.
Course delivery sites Courses are delivered to your home.
Media Courses are delivered via videotapes, audiotapes, computer software, World Wide Web, print. Students and teachers interact via mail, telephone, fax, e-mail. A computer is required for some courses.
Restrictions Courses are available to students in the continental US and Canada only.
Services Distance learners have access to library services, the campus computer network, academic advising, tutoring at a distance.
Credit-earning options Students may transfer credits from another institution.
Typical costs Non-Canadian students pay $1106.80 per course. All costs given in Canadian dollars. Costs may vary by number of credits taken. Financial aid is available to distance learners enrolled full-time or part-time.
Registration Students may register by mail, fax.
Contact Reception Area, University of Waterloo, Distance and Continuing Education, Waterloo, ON N2L 3G1, Canada. *Telephone:* 519-888-4050. *Fax:* 519-746-6393. *E-mail:* distance@corr1.uwaterloo.ca. *Web site:* http://www.adm.uwaterloo.ca/infoded/de&ce.html.

DEGREE & CERTIFICATE PROGRAMS

Baccalaureate Degrees

▶ General Science (BS)
In the fall of 1996 there were 500 students enrolled in this program. In 1995–96, 30 degrees were earned at a distance through this program.
Application requirements *Prior education:* high school diploma or equivalent. *Other requirements:* high school transcript, college transcripts, an essay or personal statement.
Completion requirements 30 courses are required. 15 courses must be completed through the institution.

▶ Geography (BES)
In the fall of 1996 there were 175 students enrolled in this program. In 1995–96, 20 degrees were earned at a distance through this program.
Application requirements *Prior education:* high school diploma or equivalent. *Other requirements:* high school transcript, college transcripts, an essay or personal statement.
Completion requirements 30 courses are required.

▶ Humanities, Social Sciences (BA)
In the fall of 1996 there were 2,400 students enrolled in this program. In 1995–96, 160 degrees were earned at a distance through this program.
Application requirements *Prior education:* high school diploma or equivalent. *Other requirements:* high school transcript, college transcripts, an essay or personal statement.
Completion requirements 30 courses are required. 10 courses must be completed through the institution.

INDIVIDUAL COURSE SUBJECT AREAS

Undergraduate
Abnormal psychology; algebra; American literature; anthropology; astronomy and astrophysics; bible studies; biochemistry; biology; calculus; Canadian studies; chemistry; chemistry, organic; comparative literature;

computer programming; criminology; developmental and child psychology; earth science; ecology; economics; educational psychology; English composition; English literature; environmental science; ethics; European history; European languages and literatures; foods and nutrition studies; French language and literature; genetics; geography; geology; German language and literature; gerontology; Greek language and literature; health professions and related sciences; history; Jewish studies; Latin language and literature; logic; mathematics; microbiology; music; organizational behavior studies; philosophy and religion; physics; physiology; plant sciences; psychology; religious studies; Russian language and literature; social psychology; social work; sociology; Spanish language and literature; statistics; technical writing; women's studies

Noncredit
Algebra; calculus; chemistry; mathematics; physics

UNIVERSITY OF WEST FLORIDA

Pensacola, Florida

Libraries/Instructional Technology

University of West Florida, founded in 1963, is a state-supported comprehensive institution. It is accredited by the Southern Association of Colleges and Schools. It first offered distance learning courses in 1988. In 1996–97, it offered 12 courses at a distance. In the fall of 1996, there was a total of 350 students enrolled in distance learning courses.
Course delivery sites Courses are delivered to your home, your workplace, military bases.
Media Courses are delivered via television, videoconferencing, World Wide Web, e-mail. Students and teachers interact via mail, telephone, e-mail. A computer is required for some courses.
Services Distance learners have access to library services, the campus computer network, e-mail services, academic advising at a distance.
Credit-earning options Students may transfer credits from another institution or may earn credits through standardized exams, institutionally developed exams, military training.
Typical costs *Undergraduate:* Tuition of $60.64 per credit hour for in-state residents. Tuition of $235.48 per credit hour for out-of-state residents. *Graduate:* Tuition of $116.20 per credit hour for in-state residents. Tuition of $386.94 per credit hour for out-of-state residents. Costs may vary by campus or location, number of credits taken. Financial aid is available to distance learners enrolled full-time or part-time.
Registration Students may register by mail, e-mail.
Contact Ann Dziadon, Registrar's Office, University of West Florida, 11000 University Parkway, Pensacola, FL 32514. *Telephone:* 904-474-2244. *Fax:* 904-474-3360. *E-mail:* adziadon@uwf.edu. *Web site:* http://www.lib.uwf.edu.

INDIVIDUAL COURSE SUBJECT AREAS

Undergraduate
Advertising; archaeology; computer and information sciences; education; education administration; English language and literature; physics; teacher education

Graduate
Education; education administration; teacher education

UNIVERSITY OF WINDSOR

Windsor, Ontario, Canada

Continuing Education

University of Windsor, founded in 1857, is a province-supported university. It is provincially chartered. It first offered distance learning courses in 1985. In 1996–97, it offered 60 courses at a distance. In the fall of 1996, there was a total of 700 students enrolled in distance learning courses.
Course delivery sites Courses are delivered to your home, 2 off-campus centers in Chatham, Sarnia.
Media Courses are delivered via television, videotapes, videoconferencing, audiotapes, computer software, World Wide Web, e-mail, print. Students and teachers interact via videoconferencing, mail, telephone, e-mail. A computer is required for some courses.
Restrictions Courses are available to students in North America only.
Services Distance learners have access to library services, the campus computer network, e-mail services, academic advising, tutoring at a distance.
Credit-earning options Students may transfer credits from another institution or may earn credits through examinations.
Typical costs Tuition of $305 per course plus mandatory fees of $70 per course. Costs may vary by number of credits taken. Financial aid is available to distance learners enrolled full-time or part-time.
Registration Students may register by phone.
Contact Continuing Education Office, University of Windsor, 401 Sunset Avenue, Windsor, ON N9B 3P4, Canada. *Telephone:* 519-253-3000, Ext. 3305. *Fax:* 519-973-7038. *Web site:* http://www.uwindsor.ca/coned/index.html.

DEGREE & CERTIFICATE PROGRAMS

Baccalaureate Degrees
▶ **Commerce (BComm)**
In the fall of 1996 there were 500 students enrolled in this program.
Restrictions Program is available to students in Canada only.
Application requirements *Prior education:* high school diploma or equivalent. *Other requirements:* high school transcript, college transcripts, an application fee of $25.
Completion requirements 40 semester courses are required. 10 semester courses must be completed through the institution.

▶ **General Science (BS)**
In the fall of 1996 there were 200 students enrolled in this program.
Application requirements *Prior education:* college diploma. *Other requirements:* college transcripts, an application fee of $25, medical lab transcripts.
Completion requirements 13 courses are required. 10 courses must be completed through the institution. This is a degree completion program.

INDIVIDUAL COURSE SUBJECT AREAS

Undergraduate
Accounting; biological and life sciences; biology; business; business administration and management; chemistry; computer and information sciences; economics; English composition; geology; history; human resources management; liberal arts, general studies, and humanities; mathematics; microbiology; philosophy and religion; political science; psychology; social sciences; sociology

Noncredit
Health professions and related sciences

Profiles: University of Wisconsin–Eau Claire

UNIVERSITY OF WISCONSIN–EAU CLAIRE

Eau Claire, Wisconsin

University of Wisconsin–Eau Claire, founded in 1916, is a state-supported comprehensive institution. It is accredited by the North Central Association of Colleges and Schools. It first offered distance learning courses in 1988. In 1996–97, it offered 18 courses at a distance. In the fall of 1996, there was a total of 345 students enrolled in distance learning courses.

Course delivery sites Courses are delivered to Chippewa Valley Technical College (Eau Claire), Northcentral Technical College (Wausau), University of Wisconsin–River Falls (River Falls), University of Wisconsin–Stout (Menomonie).

Media Courses are delivered via television, videoconferencing, audioconferencing, e-mail. Students and teachers interact via videoconferencing, audioconferencing, mail, telephone, fax, e-mail. A computer is required for some courses.

Restrictions Programs are available to in-state students only.

Services Distance learners have access to library services, the campus computer network, e-mail services, academic advising, career placement assistance at a distance.

Credit-earning options Students may transfer credits from another institution or may earn credits through standardized exams, military training.

Typical costs *Undergraduate:* Tuition of $89.25 per credit plus mandatory fees of $18.83 per credit for in-state residents. Tuition of $317 per credit plus mandatory fees of $18.83 per credit for out-of-state residents. *Graduate:* Tuition of $161 per credit plus mandatory fees of $18.78 per credit for in-state residents. Tuition of $530.50 per credit plus mandatory fees of $18.78 per credit for out-of-state residents. Costs may vary by campus or location, specific program of study, number of credits taken, course delivery options, term of enrollment. Financial aid is available to distance learners enrolled full-time or part-time.

Registration Students may register by mail, fax, phone.

Contact Sue E. Shelton, Registrar, University of Wisconsin–Eau Claire, 130 Schofield, Eau Claire, WI 54702. *Telephone:* 715-836-3887. *Fax:* 715-836-3846. *E-mail:* sheltose@uwec.edu.

DEGREE & CERTIFICATE PROGRAMS

Baccalaureate Degrees

▶ *Nursing (BSN)*

In the fall of 1996 there were 21 students enrolled in this program.

Application requirements *Prior education:* associate degree. *Other requirements:* RN license.

Completion requirements 60 credits are required.

On-campus requirements One capstone course.

Program contact Sandra Dirks, RN-BSN Coordinator, University of Wisconsin–Eau Claire, School of Nursing, Eau Claire, WI 54702. Phone: 715-836-5287. Fax: 715-836-5971.

INDIVIDUAL COURSE SUBJECT AREAS

Undergraduate

Accounting; area, ethnic, and cultural studies; business administration and management; engineering; English composition; finance; health and physical education/fitness; history; library and information studies; Middle Eastern languages and literatures; nursing; Russian language and literature

Graduate

Area, ethnic, and cultural studies; health and physical education/fitness; history; library and information studies; marketing; nursing

Noncredit

Business

UNIVERSITY OF WISCONSIN–EXTENSION

Madison, Wisconsin

Continuing Education Extension Division

University of Wisconsin–Extension is a state-supported university extension. It first offered distance learning courses in 1981. In 1996–97, it offered 7 courses at a distance. In the fall of 1996, there was a total of 88 students enrolled in distance learning courses.

Course delivery sites Courses are delivered to your home, your workplace, military bases, other colleges, off-campus center(s), prisons.

Media Courses are delivered via television, videotapes, audiotapes, World Wide Web, e-mail, print. Students and teachers interact via mail, fax, e-mail, computer conferencing. A computer is required for some courses.

Restrictions Students must have access to computer, modem, and browser.

Services Distance learners have access to library services, academic advising, career placement assistance at a distance.

Typical costs Tuition of $110 per semester credit. Students pay a $36 administrative fee. *Noncredit courses:* $125 per course.

Registration Students may register by mail, fax, phone, e-mail, World Wide Web.

Contact Student Services Advisor, University of Wisconsin–Extension, Independent Learning, 432 North Lake Street, Room 104, Madison, WI 53706. *Telephone:* 608-263-2055. *Fax:* 608-262-4096. *E-mail:* ilearn@admin.uwex.edu. *Web site:* http://www.uwex.edu/ilearn/.

DEGREE & CERTIFICATE PROGRAMS

Undergraduate Certificates

▶ *Business*

Application requirements *Prior education:* high school diploma or equivalent.

Program contact Michael D. Wilson, Coordinator, Business and Economics, University of Wisconsin–Extension, 432 North Lake Street, Room 201, Madison, WI 53706. Phone: 608-263-7983. Fax: 608-262-6706. E-mail: wilsonm@admin.uwex.edu.

INDIVIDUAL COURSE SUBJECT AREAS

Undergraduate

Accounting; business; business administration and management; curriculum and instruction; economics; educational psychology; engineering; human resources management; individual and family development studies

Noncredit

Accounting; business; business law; civil engineering; environmental engineering; finance; fine arts; human resources management; international business; mechanical engineering; public administration and services

See full description on page 524.

UNIVERSITY OF WISCONSIN–LA CROSSE

La Crosse, Wisconsin

University of Wisconsin–La Crosse, founded in 1909, is a state-supported comprehensive institution. It is accredited by the North Central Association of Colleges and Schools. It first offered distance learning courses in 1995. In 1996–97, it offered 6 courses at a distance. In the fall of 1996, there was a total of 29 students enrolled in distance learning courses.
Course delivery sites Courses are delivered to your workplace, University of Wisconsin–Eau Claire (Eau Claire), University of Wisconsin–River Falls (River Falls), University of Wisconsin–Stevens Point (Stevens Point), University of Wisconsin–Stout (Menomonie).
Media Courses are delivered via videoconferencing. Students and teachers interact via videoconferencing, mail, telephone, fax, e-mail.
Restrictions Programs are available to in-state students only.
Services Distance learners have access to academic advising, career placement assistance at a distance.
Typical costs *Undergraduate:* Tuition of $89.25 per credit plus mandatory fees of $30 per credit for in-state residents. Tuition of $317 per credit plus mandatory fees of $30 per credit for out-of-state residents. *Graduate:* Tuition of $161 per credit plus mandatory fees of $23 per credit for in-state residents. Tuition of $530.50 per credit plus mandatory fees of $23 per credit for out-of-state residents. Costs may vary by campus or location, number of credits taken, term of enrollment. Financial aid is available to distance learners enrolled full-time or part-time.
Registration Students may register by mail, fax, phone, e-mail.
Contact Diane Schumacher, University Registrar, University of Wisconsin–La Crosse, 1725 State Street, La Crosse, WI 54601. *Telephone:* 608-785-8953. *Fax:* 608-785-6695. *E-mail:* schumach@mail.uwlax.edu.

INDIVIDUAL COURSE SUBJECT AREAS

Undergraduate
Health and physical education/fitness; public health; Russian language and literature; teacher education; women's studies

Graduate
Health and physical education/fitness; public health; teacher education

Noncredit
Health and physical education/fitness; public health

UNIVERSITY OF WISCONSIN–MADISON

Madison, Wisconsin

University of Wisconsin–Madison, founded in 1848, is a state-supported university. It is accredited by the North Central Association of Colleges and Schools. It first offered distance learning courses in 1891. In 1996–97, it offered 45 courses at a distance. In the fall of 1996, there was a total of 672 students enrolled in distance learning courses.
Course delivery sites Courses are delivered to your home, your workplace, University of Wisconsin Centers (Madison), University of Wisconsin–Eau Claire (Eau Claire), University of Wisconsin–Green Bay (Green Bay), University of Wisconsin–Platteville (Platteville).
Media Courses are delivered via television, videotapes, videoconferencing, audioconferencing, World Wide Web, e-mail, print. Students and teachers interact via videoconferencing, audioconferencing, mail, telephone, fax, e-mail. A computer is required for some courses.
Services Distance learners have access to the campus computer network, e-mail services, academic advising at a distance.
Credit-earning options Students may transfer credits from another institution.
Typical costs *Undergraduate:* Tuition of $126 per credit for in-state residents. Tuition of $422 per credit for out-of-state residents. *Graduate:* Tuition of $272 per credit for in-state residents. Tuition of $829 per credit for out-of-state residents. *Noncredit courses:* $25–$600 per course. Costs may vary by specific program of study. Financial aid is available to distance learners enrolled full-time.
Registration Students may register by phone.
Contact Steven Siehr, Outreach Program Manager, University of Wisconsin–Madison, 352 Bascom Hall, 500 Lincoln Drive, Madison, WI 53706. *Telephone:* 608-262-6765. *Fax:* 608-262-2008. *E-mail:* steven.siehr@ccmail.adp.wisc.edu.

DEGREE & CERTIFICATE PROGRAMS

Baccalaureate Degrees
▶*Nursing (BS)*
In the fall of 1996 there were 36 students enrolled in this program.
Restrictions This program is available to in-state students only.
Application requirements *Prior education:* diploma or ADN and Registered Nurse. *Other requirements:* high school transcript, college transcripts.
Completion requirements 124 credits are required. 30 credits must be completed through the institution. This is a degree completion program.
On-campus requirements Weekend and/or consolidated days for capstone course.
Program contact Sharon Nellis, Academic Advisor and Administrative Assistant, University of Wisconsin–Madison, 600 Highland Avenue, K6/230, Madison, WI 53792-2755. Phone: 608-263-5171. Fax: 608-263-5332. E-mail: srnellis@facstaff.wisc.edu.

INDIVIDUAL COURSE SUBJECT AREAS

Undergraduate
Agriculture; American (US) history; electrical engineering; mechanical engineering; physics

Graduate
Electrical engineering; mechanical engineering

Noncredit
Education

UNIVERSITY OF WISCONSIN–OSHKOSH

Oshkosh, Wisconsin

Information Technology

University of Wisconsin–Oshkosh, founded in 1871, is a state-supported comprehensive institution. It is accredited by the North Central Association of Colleges and Schools. It first offered distance learning courses in 1995. In 1996–97, it offered 8 courses at a distance. In the fall of 1996, there was a total of 140 students enrolled in distance learning courses.
Course delivery sites Courses are delivered to University of Wisconsin–Green Bay (Green Bay), University of Wisconsin–Stevens Point (Stevens Point).
Media Courses are delivered via television, videotapes, videoconferencing, audioconferencing, World Wide Web, e-mail, print. Students and teachers interact via videoconferencing, mail, telephone, e-mail. A computer is required for some courses.
Restrictions Programs are available to in-state students only.

Profiles: University of Wisconsin–Oshkosh

Services Distance learners have access to library services, the campus computer network, e-mail services, academic advising, tutoring, career placement assistance at a distance.
Credit-earning options Students may transfer credits from another institution or may earn credits through examinations.
Typical costs Tuition of $2255 per year plus mandatory fees of $272 per semester for local area residents. Tuition of $7285 per year plus mandatory fees of $272 per semester for in-state residents. Costs may vary by specific program of study, number of credits taken. Financial aid is available to distance learners.
Registration Students may register by mail, phone, World Wide Web.
Contact John Berens, Assistant Vice Chancellor, University of Wisconsin–Oshkosh, Information Technology, 800 Algoma Boulevard, Oshkosh, WI 54901. *Telephone:* 414-424-1044. *Fax:* 414-424-7338. *E-mail:* berens@uwosh.edu. *Web site:* http://www.uwosh.edu/it.html.

INDIVIDUAL COURSE SUBJECT AREAS

Undergraduate
Nursing

Graduate
Business; business administration and management; human resources management; nursing; social sciences

UNIVERSITY OF WISCONSIN–PLATTEVILLE

Platteville, Wisconsin

Extended Degree in Business Administration

University of Wisconsin–Platteville, founded in 1866, is a state-supported comprehensive institution. It is accredited by the North Central Association of Colleges and Schools. It first offered distance learning courses in 1979. In 1996–97, it offered 45 courses at a distance. In the fall of 1996, there was a total of 194 students enrolled in distance learning courses.
Course delivery sites Courses are delivered to your home, your workplace.
Media Courses are delivered via videotapes, audiotapes, World Wide Web, e-mail, print, computer conferencing. Students and teachers interact via mail, telephone, fax, e-mail, computer conferencing.
Restrictions Courses are available to US students only.
Services Distance learners have access to library services, the campus computer network, e-mail services, academic advising, career placement assistance at a distance.
Credit-earning options Students may transfer credits from another institution or may earn credits through standardized exams, institutionally developed exams, portfolio assessment, military training, business training.
Typical costs Tuition of $89.75 per credit for in-state residents. Tuition of $317 per credit for out-of-state residents. Costs may vary by number of credits taken, course delivery options. Financial aid is available to distance learners enrolled full-time or part-time.
Registration Students may register by mail.
Contact John Adams, Director, Extended Degree in Business, University of Wisconsin–Platteville, 506 Pioneer Tower, 1 University Plaza, Platteville, WI 53818. *Telephone:* 800-362-3654. *Fax:* 608-342-1466. *E-mail:* adams@uwplatt.edu. *Web site:* http://www.uwplatt.edu/edp.

DEGREE & CERTIFICATE PROGRAMS

Baccalaureate Degrees
▶ *Business Administration/Accounting (BS)*
In the fall of 1996 there were 194 students enrolled in this program. In 1995–96, 13 degrees were earned at a distance through this program.
Application requirements *Prior education:* high school diploma or equivalent. *Minimum age:* 22. *Other requirements:* high school transcript, college transcripts.
Completion requirements 120 quarter credits are required. 32 semester credits must be completed through the institution.

INDIVIDUAL COURSE SUBJECT AREAS

Undergraduate
Accounting; business; business administration and management; finance; human resources management; marketing

UNIVERSITY OF WISCONSIN–RIVER FALLS

River Falls, Wisconsin

Continuing Education Extension

University of Wisconsin–River Falls, founded in 1874, is a state-supported comprehensive institution. It is accredited by the North Central Association of Colleges and Schools. It first offered distance learning courses in 1994. In 1996–97, it offered 8 courses at a distance. In the fall of 1996, there was a total of 70 students enrolled in distance learning courses.
Course delivery sites Courses are delivered to your home, your workplace, University of Wisconsin–Eau Claire (Eau Claire), University of Wisconsin–La Crosse (La Crosse), University of Wisconsin–Platteville (Platteville), University of Wisconsin–Stout (Menomonie), University of Wisconsin–Superior (Superior), 11 off-campus centers in Baldwin, Balsam Lake, Barron, Cameron, Clear Lake, New Richmond, Plum City, Rice Lake, Somerset, Spring Valley, St. Croix Falls.
Media Courses are delivered via television, videotapes, videoconferencing, audioconferencing, computer software, e-mail, print. Students and teachers interact via videoconferencing, audioconferencing, mail, telephone, fax, e-mail. A computer is required for some courses.
Restrictions Programs are available to in-state students only.
Services Distance learners have access to library services, the campus computer network, e-mail services at a distance.
Credit-earning options Students may transfer credits from another institution or may earn credits through institutionally developed exams.
Typical costs *Undergraduate:* Tuition of $89.25 per credit plus mandatory fees of $40 per course. *Graduate:* Tuition of $161 per credit plus mandatory fees of $40 per course. *Noncredit courses:* $40 per course. Costs may vary by campus or location, specific program of study, number of credits taken. Financial aid is available to distance learners enrolled full-time or part-time.
Registration Students may register by mail, fax.
Contact Margo Lessard, Interim Director, University of Wisconsin–River Falls, 410 South Third Street, River Falls, WI 54022. *Telephone:* 715-425-3256. *Fax:* 715-425-0624. *E-mail:* margo.f.lessard@uwrf.edu.

INDIVIDUAL COURSE SUBJECT AREAS

Undergraduate
Education; health and physical education/fitness; liberal arts, general studies, and humanities; teacher education

Graduate
Education; health and physical education/fitness; liberal arts, general studies, and humanities; teacher education

Noncredit
Agriculture; business; business administration and management; education; teacher education

UNIVERSITY OF WISCONSIN–STEVENS POINT

Stevens Point, Wisconsin

University Telecommunications

University of Wisconsin–Stevens Point, founded in 1894, is a state-supported comprehensive institution. It is accredited by the North Central Association of Colleges and Schools. It first offered distance learning courses in 1985. In 1996–97, it offered 16 courses at a distance. In the fall of 1996, there was a total of 134 students enrolled in distance learning courses.
Course delivery sites Courses are delivered to your home, your workplace, University of Wisconsin System (Madison), Wisconsin Technical College System (Madison), high schools.
Media Courses are delivered via television, videoconferencing, audioconferencing, computer software, World Wide Web, e-mail, print. Students and teachers interact via videoconferencing, audioconferencing, mail, telephone, fax, e-mail. A computer is required for some courses.
Restrictions Availability varies by course, program, or delivery means.
Services Distance learners have access to library services, e-mail services at a distance.
Credit-earning options Students may transfer credits from another institution.
Typical costs *Undergraduate:* Tuition of $92.25 per credit plus mandatory fees of $75 per course for in-state residents. Tuition of $320.25 per credit plus mandatory fees of $75 per course for out-of-state residents. *Graduate:* Tuition of $161 per credit plus mandatory fees of $75 per course for in-state residents. Tuition of $531 per credit plus mandatory fees of $75 per course for out-of-state residents. *Noncredit courses:* $40 for 6 hours. Costs may vary by number of credits taken. Financial aid is available to distance learners enrolled full-time or part-time.
Registration Students may register by mail.
Contact Judi Pitt, Scheduling Coordinator, University of Wisconsin–Stevens Point, 1101 Reserve, Room 110, Stevens Point, WI 54481. *Telephone:* 715-346-2647. *Fax:* 715-346-3998. *E-mail:* jpitt@uwsp.edu. *Web site:* http://www.uwsp.edu/acad/uwspext/telecomm/telehome.htm.

INDIVIDUAL COURSE SUBJECT AREAS

Undergraduate
American (US) history; anthropology; art history and criticism; child care and development; communications; computer and information sciences; conservation and natural resources; economics; education; health professions and related sciences; instructional media; special education; teacher education

Graduate
American (US) history; anthropology; child care and development; communications; computer and information sciences; conservation and natural resources; economics; education; instructional media; special education; teacher education

Noncredit
Business; conservation and natural resources

UNIVERSITY OF WISCONSIN–STOUT

Menomonie, Wisconsin

Office of Continuing Education

University of Wisconsin–Stout, founded in 1891, is a state-supported comprehensive institution. It is accredited by the North Central Association of Colleges and Schools.
Course delivery sites Courses are delivered to your home.
Media Courses are delivered via television, videotapes, videoconferencing, audiotapes, radio broadcast, audioconferencing, computer software, print, audiographics conferencing, computer conferencing.
Credit-earning options Students may transfer credits from another institution.
Contact Credit Outreach Program Manager, University of Wisconsin–Stout, Office of Continuing Education, Menomonie, WI 54751. *Telephone:* 715-232-2693. *Fax:* 715-232-3385.

INDIVIDUAL COURSE SUBJECT AREAS

Undergraduate
Biology; business; developmental and child psychology; education; engineering-related technologies; engineering/industrial management; English composition; home economics and family studies

Graduate
Biology; business; developmental and child psychology; education; English composition; home economics and family studies; human resources management; philosophy and religion; social psychology; teacher education

Noncredit
Business; computer and information sciences; education; philosophy and religion; teacher education; visual and performing arts

UNIVERSITY OF WISCONSIN–WHITEWATER

Whitewater, Wisconsin

Graduate Studies, Continuing Education and Summer Session

University of Wisconsin–Whitewater, founded in 1868, is a state-supported comprehensive institution. It is accredited by the North Central Association of Colleges and Schools. It first offered distance learning courses in 1986. In 1996–97, it offered 10 courses at a distance. In the fall of 1996, there was a total of 71 students enrolled in distance learning courses.
Course delivery sites Courses are delivered to University of Wisconsin System (Madison).
Media Courses are delivered via television, videoconferencing, audioconferencing, World Wide Web. Students and teachers interact via videoconferencing, audioconferencing, telephone, fax. A computer is required for some courses.
Restrictions Programs are available to in-state students only. School Business Management courses are for graduate credit only.
Services Distance learners have access to library services, the campus computer network, e-mail services, academic advising, career placement assistance at a distance.
Credit-earning options Students may transfer credits from another institution or may earn credits through standardized exams, military training.

Profiles: University of Wisconsin–Whitewater

Typical costs *Undergraduate:* Tuition of $107.78 per semester hour for in-state residents. Tuition of $335.54 per semester hour for out-of-state residents. *Graduate:* Tuition of $180.96 per semester hour for in-state residents. Tuition of $550.46 per semester hour for out-of-state residents. *Noncredit courses:* $10 per hour. Costs may vary by specific program of study, number of credits taken.
Registration Students may register by mail, phone.
Contact Kathy Gibbs, Distance Education Coordinator, University of Wisconsin–Whitewater, 800 West Main Street, Whitewater, WI 53190-1790. *Telephone:* 414-472-5247. *Fax:* 414-472-5210. *E-mail:* gibbsk@uwwvax.uww.edu. *Web site:* http://www.uww.edu.

INDIVIDUAL COURSE SUBJECT AREAS

Undergraduate
Special education; teacher education

Graduate
Education administration; special education; teacher education

UNIVERSITY OF WYOMING

Laramie, Wyoming

School of Extended Studies and Public Service

University of Wyoming, founded in 1886, is a state-supported university. It is accredited by the North Central Association of Colleges and Schools. It first offered distance learning courses in 1954.
Course delivery sites Courses are delivered to your home, your workplace, military bases, other colleges.
Media Courses are delivered via videotapes, videoconferencing, audioconferencing, print, computer conferencing.
Services Distance learners have access to library services, academic advising, tutoring, career placement assistance at a distance.
Credit-earning options Students may transfer credits from another institution or may earn credits through examinations. Financial aid is available to distance learners.
Contact Office of Off-Campus Credit Courses, University of Wyoming, Box 3106, Laramie, WY 82071. *Telephone:* 307-766-4300. *Fax:* 307-766-3445.

DEGREE & CERTIFICATE PROGRAMS

Baccalaureate Degrees
▶ *Administration of Justice (BA)*
▶ *Nursing (BSN)*
Application requirements Nursing license.
Completion requirements *Other requirements:* some on-site supervision.
▶ *Psychology (BS)*
▶ *Social Sciences (BA, BS)*

Graduate Degrees
▶ *Business Administration (MBA)*
▶ *Public Administration (MPA)*
▶ *Speech Pathology (MS)*

Undergraduate Certificates
▶ *Land Surveying*
Application requirements Experience with land surveying instruments.

INDIVIDUAL COURSE SUBJECT AREAS

Undergraduate
Accounting; agriculture; civil engineering; communications; conservation and natural resources; developmental and child psychology; economics; education; English composition; health and physical education/fitness; health professions and related sciences; history; home economics and family studies; liberal arts, general studies, and humanities; nursing; political science; protective services; social psychology; social sciences; sociology

Graduate
Accounting; business; business administration and management; education administration; educational psychology; health and physical education/fitness; health professions and related sciences; human resources management; nursing; political science; special education; teacher education

UNIVERSITY SYSTEM OF GEORGIA

Athens, Georgia

Independent Study

University System of Georgia is a state-supported university system. In 1996–97, it offered 150 courses at a distance. In the fall of 1996, there was a total of 2,677 students enrolled in distance learning courses.
Course delivery sites Courses are delivered to your home, your workplace.
Media Courses are delivered via videotapes, audiotapes, computer software, World Wide Web, e-mail, print. Students and teachers interact via mail, telephone, fax, e-mail, World Wide Web. A computer is required for some courses.
Services Distance learners have access to library services at a distance.
Credit-earning options Students may earn credits through examinations.
Typical costs Tuition of $63 per quarter hour. Costs may vary by number of credits taken. Financial aid is available to distance learners enrolled full-time or part-time.
Registration Students may register by mail, fax, World Wide Web.
Contact Carmen Shuler, Coordinator for Program Development, University System of Georgia, Division of Academic Credit, University of Georgia, Center for Continuing Education, Athens, GA 30602-3603. *Telephone:* 800-877-3243. *Fax:* 706-542-6635. *E-mail:* usgis@arches.uga.edu. *Web site:* http://www.gactr.uga.edu/usgis

INDIVIDUAL COURSE SUBJECT AREAS

Undergraduate
Accounting; administrative and secretarial services; advertising; agriculture; algebra; anthropology; area, ethnic, and cultural studies; art history and criticism; biological and life sciences; biology; business; business administration and management; calculus; Classical languages and literatures; communications; conservation and natural resources; developmental and child psychology; ecology; economics; education; educational psychology; English composition; English language and literature; European languages and literatures; fine arts; French language and literature; geography; geology; German language and literature; health and physical education/fitness; health professions and related sciences; history; home economics and family studies; horticulture; human resources management; journalism; Latin language and literature; law and legal studies; liberal arts, general studies, and humanities; marketing; mathematics; philosophy and religion; political science; psychology; public health; religious studies; social psychology; sociology; Spanish

language and literature; statistics; teacher education; theological studies; visual and performing arts; women's studies

See full description on page 498.

UPPER IOWA UNIVERSITY

Fayette, Iowa

External Degree

Upper Iowa University, founded in 1857, is an independent-nonprofit comprehensive institution. It is accredited by the North Central Association of Colleges and Schools. It first offered distance learning courses in 1973. In 1996–97, it offered 75 courses at a distance. In the fall of 1996, there was a total of 3,433 students enrolled in distance learning courses.
Course delivery sites Courses are delivered to your home, your workplace, military bases, 13 off-campus centers in Calmar, Des Moines, Manchester, Newton, Waterloo, Fort Irwin (CA), Fort Polk (LA), Fort Riley (KS), Janesville (WI), Madison (WI), Prairie du Chien (WI), Wausau (WI), West Allis (WI).
Media Courses are delivered via videotapes, print. Students and teachers interact via mail, telephone, fax, e-mail.
Services Distance learners have access to library services, e-mail services, academic advising, career placement assistance at a distance.
Credit-earning options Students may transfer credits from another institution or may earn credits through standardized exams, portfolio assessment, military training, business training.
Typical costs Tuition of $145 per semester hour. $35 one-time evaluation fee. Costs may vary by campus or location. Financial aid is available to distance learners enrolled part-time.
Registration Students may register by mail, fax, phone, e-mail.
Contact Kersten Shepard, Director, External Degree Programs, Upper Iowa University, PO Box 1861, Fayette, IA 52142. *Telephone:* 319-425-5283. *Fax:* 319-425-5353. *E-mail:* extdegree@uiu.edu. *Web site:* http://www.uiu.edu.

DEGREE & CERTIFICATE PROGRAMS

Associate Degrees

▶*Business, Liberal Arts (AA)*

Application requirements *Prior education:* high school diploma or equivalent. *Other requirements:* high school transcript, an application fee of $35, external degree application.
Completion requirements 60 semester hours are required. 15 semester hours must be completed through the institution. *Maximum time for completion:* 10 years.

Baccalaureate Degrees

▶*Accounting, Business, Human Resources, Management, Marketing, Public Administration, Social Sciences (BS)*

Application requirements *Prior education:* high school diploma or equivalent. *Other requirements:* high school transcript, an application fee of $35, external degree application.
Completion requirements 120 semester hours are required. 30 semester hours must be completed through the institution. *Maximum time for completion:* 10 years.

INDIVIDUAL COURSE SUBJECT AREAS

Undergraduate

Abnormal psychology; accounting; algebra; American (US) history; art history and criticism; biology; business; business administration and management; business communications; business law; comparative literature; earth science; economics; English composition; English language and literature; European languages and literatures; finance; health professions and related sciences; history; human resources management; industrial psychology; international business; labor relations/studies; law and legal studies; management information systems; marketing; mathematics; physical sciences; psychology; public administration and services; social sciences; sociology; Spanish language and literature; statistics; substance abuse counseling; visual and performing arts

UTAH STATE UNIVERSITY

Logan, Utah

COM-NET

Utah State University, founded in 1888, is a state-supported university. It is accredited by the Northwest Association of Schools and Colleges. It first offered distance learning courses in 1984. In 1996–97, it offered 193 courses at a distance. In the fall of 1996, there was a total of 2,100 students enrolled in distance learning courses.
Course delivery sites Courses are delivered to College of Eastern Utah (Price), Dixie College (St. George), Snow College (Ephraim), Utah Valley State College (Orem), 15 off-campus centers in Blanding, Bluff, Brigham City, Cedar City, Gunnison, Manila, Moab, Ogden, Randolph, Roosevelt, Salt Lake City, Tooele, Tremonton, Vernal, Wendover.
Media Courses are delivered via videoconferencing, radio broadcast, audioconferencing, computer software, World Wide Web, e-mail, print, audiographics conferencing. Students and teachers interact via videoconferencing, audioconferencing, mail, fax, e-mail. A computer is required for some courses.
Restrictions Programs are available to in-state students only.
Services Distance learners have access to library services, the campus computer network, e-mail services, academic advising, tutoring, career placement assistance at a distance.
Credit-earning options Students may transfer credits from another institution or may earn credits through institutionally developed exams.
Typical costs *Undergraduate:* Tuition of $149.16 per credit. *Graduate:* Tuition of $159.48 per credit. Financial aid is available to distance learners enrolled full-time or part-time.
Registration Students may register by mail, fax.
Contact Michele Lyon, Staff Assistant, Utah State University, UMC 3720, Logan, UT 84322-3720. *Telephone:* 801-797-2079. *Fax:* 801-797-1399. *E-mail:* m.lyon@ce.usu.edu.

DEGREE & CERTIFICATE PROGRAMS

Baccalaureate Degrees

▶*Accounting (BS)*

Application requirements *Prior education:* high school diploma or equivalent. *Other requirements:* ACT or SAT, high school transcript.
Completion requirements 186 quarter hours are required.

▶*Business Administration (BS)*

Application requirements *Prior education:* high school diploma or equivalent. *Other requirements:* ACT or SAT, high school transcript.
Completion requirements 186 quarter hours are required.

▶*Business Information Systems and Education (BS)*

Application requirements *Prior education:* high school diploma or equivalent. *Other requirements:* ACT or SAT, high school transcript.
Completion requirements 186 quarter hours are required.

▶*Elementary Education (BA)*

Application requirements *Prior education:* high school diploma or equivalent. *Other requirements:* ACT or SAT, high school transcript.

Profiles: Utah State University

Completion requirements 186 quarter hours are required.

▶ *Psychology (BS)*
Application requirements *Prior education:* high school diploma or equivalent. *Other requirements:* ACT or SAT, high school transcript.
Completion requirements 186 quarter hours are required.

Graduate Degrees

▶ *Business Information Systems and Education (MS)*
Application requirements *Prior education:* baccalaureate degree. *Other requirements:* GMAT.
Completion requirements 54 quarter hours are required.

▶ *Human Resource Management (MSS)*
In the fall of 1996 there were 2,100 students enrolled in this program. In 1995–96, 450 degrees were earned at a distance through this program.
Application requirements *Prior education:* baccalaureate degree. *Other requirements:* GMAT or GRE, college transcripts, letter(s) of recommendation.
Completion requirements 51 quarter hours are required. 24 quarter hours must be completed through the institution.

INDIVIDUAL COURSE SUBJECT AREAS

Undergraduate
Accounting; agriculture; astronomy and astrophysics; biology; business; business administration and management; chemistry; computer and information sciences; conservation and natural resources; creative writing; developmental and child psychology; economics; education administration; educational psychology; English composition; English language and literature; European languages and literatures; fine arts; geology; health professions and related sciences; history; home economics and family studies; human resources management; journalism; liberal arts, general studies, and humanities; mathematics; microbiology; philosophy and religion; physics; political science; social psychology; social work; sociology; special education; teacher education

Graduate
Business; education administration; social psychology

Noncredit
Fine arts

UTAH VALLEY STATE COLLEGE

Orem, Utah

School of Continuing Education–Center for Distance Learning

Utah Valley State College, founded in 1941, is a state-supported primarily two-year college. It is accredited by the Northwest Association of Schools and Colleges. It first offered distance learning courses in 1988. In 1996–97, it offered 30 courses at a distance. In the fall of 1996, there was a total of 700 students enrolled in distance learning courses.
Course delivery sites Courses are delivered to your home, your workplace, 3 off-campus centers in American Fork, Park City, Spanish Fork.
Media Courses are delivered via television, videotapes, videoconferencing, computer software, World Wide Web. Students and teachers interact via videoconferencing, audioconferencing, mail, telephone, fax, e-mail. A computer is required for some courses.
Restrictions Some state areas do not receive broadcasts.
Services Distance learners have access to library services, academic advising at a distance.

Credit-earning options Students may transfer credits from another institution or may earn credits through institutionally developed exams, portfolio assessment.
Typical costs Tuition of $55 per semester hour plus mandatory fees of $20 per course for in-state residents. Tuition of $200 per semester hour plus mandatory fees of $20 per course for out-of-state residents. Costs may vary by number of credits taken. Financial aid is available to distance learners.
Registration Students may register by mail, fax, phone, World Wide Web.
Contact Roger Porter, Director, Off Campus Programs, Utah Valley State College, 800 West 1200 South, Orem, UT 84058. *Telephone:* 801-222-8004. *Fax:* 801-222-8968. *E-mail:* porterro@uvsc.edu.

INDIVIDUAL COURSE SUBJECT AREAS

Undergraduate
Accounting; administrative and secretarial services; biology; business administration and management; chemistry; English composition; European languages and literatures; health professions and related sciences; history; mathematics; philosophy and religion; public health

VALLEY CITY STATE UNIVERSITY

Valley City, North Dakota

North Dakota Interactive Video Network

Valley City State University, founded in 1890, is a state-supported four-year college. It is accredited by the North Central Association of Colleges and Schools. In 1996–97, it offered 14 courses at a distance. In the fall of 1996, there was a total of 50 students enrolled in distance learning courses.
Course delivery sites Courses are delivered to your home, military bases, North Dakota University System (Bismarck).
Media Courses are delivered via television, videotapes, videoconferencing, computer software, World Wide Web, e-mail, print, interactive television. Students and teachers interact via videoconferencing, mail, telephone, fax, e-mail. A computer is required for some courses. The institution provides assistance with acquiring computer equipment.
Services Distance learners have access to library services, the campus computer network, e-mail services, academic advising, tutoring, career placement assistance at a distance.
Credit-earning options Students may transfer credits from another institution or may earn credits through standardized exams, institutionally developed exams, portfolio assessment, military training, business training.
Typical costs Tuition of $121.58 per credit. Tuition capped after 12 credits. *Noncredit courses:* $15–$30 per course. Costs may vary by number of credits taken, term of enrollment. Financial aid is available to distance learners enrolled full-time or part-time.
Registration Students may register by mail, fax.
Contact Jan Drake, North Dakota Interactive Video Network Contact, Valley City State University, 101 College Street, PO Box 1327, Valley City, ND 58072. *Telephone:* 701-845-7302. *Fax:* 701-845-7245. *E-mail:* jdrake@prairie.nodak.edu.

INDIVIDUAL COURSE SUBJECT AREAS

Undergraduate
Accounting; Asian languages and literatures; business; business administration and management; Canadian studies; English language and literature; fine arts; history; journalism; liberal arts, general studies, and humanities; library and information studies; physics; social psychology; Spanish language and literature; teacher education

VICTOR VALLEY COLLEGE

Victorville, California

Victor Valley College, founded in 1961, is a state-supported two-year college. It is accredited by the Western Association of Schools and Colleges, Inc.
Course delivery sites Courses are delivered to your home.
Media Courses are delivered via television.
Restrictions Programs are available to local area students only.
Credit-earning options Students may transfer credits from another institution or may earn credits through examinations, military training. Financial aid is available to distance learners.
Contact Coordinator, Instructional Media Services, Victor Valley College, 18422 Bear Valley Road, Victorville, CA 92392. *Telephone:* 619-245-4271, Ext. 424. *Fax:* 619-245-4373.

INDIVIDUAL COURSE SUBJECT AREAS

Undergraduate
Biology; business; business administration and management; computer and information sciences; developmental and child psychology; history; political science; sociology

VINCENNES UNIVERSITY

Vincennes, Indiana

Extended Instructional Services

Vincennes University, founded in 1801, is a state-supported two-year college. It is accredited by the North Central Association of Colleges and Schools.
Course delivery sites Courses are delivered to your workplace, other colleges.
Media Courses are delivered via television, videotapes, videoconferencing, print.
Services Distance learners have access to library services, academic advising, tutoring, career placement assistance at a distance.
Credit-earning options Students may transfer credits from another institution or may earn credits through examinations, portfolio assessment, military training, business training.
Contact Coordinator, Distance Education, Vincennes University, 1002 North First Street, Vincennes, IN 47591. *Telephone:* 812-888-5343. *Web site:* http://www.vinu.edu.

DEGREE & CERTIFICATE PROGRAMS

Associate Degrees

▶ *Behavioral Sciences (AA, AS)*
Program contact Dr. Christopher Ezell, Professor/Department Chair, Vincennes University, 1002 North First Street, Vincennes, IN 47591. Phone: 812-888-4381. E-mail: cezell@vunet.vwu.edu.

▶ *Business Studies (AS)*
Program contact Rex Cutshall, Associate Professor/Department Chair, Vincennes University, 102 North First Street, Vincennes, IN 47591. Phone: 812-888-5855. E-mail: rcutshal@vunet.vinu.edu.

▶ *General Studies (AS)*
▶ *Law Enforcement Studies (AS)*
Program contact Dan Burgei, Professor/Department Chair, Vincennes University, 1002 North First Street, Vincennes, IN 47591. Phone: 812-888-4588. E-mail: dburgei@vunet.vinu.edu.

▶ *Social Sciences (AA, AS)*
Program contact Dr. Christopher Ezell, Professor/Department Chair, Vincennes University, 1002 North First Street, Vincennes, IN 47591. Phone: 812-888-4381. E-mail: cezell@vunet.vwu.edu.

▶ *Surgical Technology (AS)*
Restrictions Program is available only to certified surgical technologists seeking an associate degree.
Program contact Chris Keegan, Assistant Professor/Department Chair, Vincennes University, 1002 North First Street, Vincennes, IN 47591. Phone: 812-888-5893. E-mail: ckeegan@vunet.vinu.edu.

▶ *Technology Apprenticeship (AS)*
Restrictions Program is designed for non-traditional students who have attained journeyman status in a skilled trade.
Program contact Bryan Douglass, Coordinator, Expert Programs, Vincennes University, 1002 North First Street, Vincennes, IN 47591. Phone: 812-888-5490. E-mail: bdouglas@vunet.vnu.edu.

INDIVIDUAL COURSE SUBJECT AREAS

Undergraduate
Accounting; business administration and management; chemistry; computer and information sciences; creative writing; developmental and child psychology; economics; English composition; English language and literature; geology; health and physical education/fitness; history; liberal arts, general studies, and humanities; mathematics; nursing; political science; protective services; social psychology; sociology

VIRGINIA COMMONWEALTH UNIVERSITY

Richmond, Virginia

Virginia Commonwealth University, founded in 1838, is a state-supported university. It is accredited by the Southern Association of Colleges and Schools. It first offered distance learning courses in 1988.
Course delivery sites Courses are delivered to your home, your workplace, military bases, other colleges.
Media Courses are delivered via computer software, World Wide Web, e-mail. Students and teachers interact via audioconferencing, mail, telephone, fax, e-mail, World Wide Web. A computer is required for some courses.
Services Distance learners have access to library services, the campus computer network, e-mail services at a distance.
Credit-earning options Students may transfer credits from another institution or may earn credits through standardized exams, institutionally developed exams.
Typical costs Tuition of $1905 per semester plus mandatory fees of $1750 per semester for in-state residents. Tuition of $5646 per semester plus mandatory fees of $1750 per semester for out-of-state residents. Costs may vary by specific program of study, number of credits taken.
Contact Dr. Dolores Clement, Associate Professor and Program Director, Virginia Commonwealth University, MCV Campus, PO Box 980203, Richmond, VA 23298-0203. *Telephone:* 804-828-0719. *Fax:* 804-828-

Virginia Commonwealth University

E-mail: dclement@hsc.vcu.edu. *Web site:* http://www.vcu.edu/.../dept.htm.

Special note

The Executive Program is an innovative 2-year course of study that leads to the degree of Master of Science Health Administration (MSHA). The course of study can be completed by individuals residing anywhere and working full-time in health care. It is a distance learning program accomplished mainly over the World Wide Web, with 5 on-campus sessions over a 2-year period of study. The program is designed for self-motivated, mature, experienced professionals who are seeking graduate education in management for continued career advancement. The program is offered by the Department of Health Administration in the School of Allied Health Professions at Virginia Commonwealth University (VCU), on the Medical College of Virginia (MCV) campus in Richmond.

To be considered for admission, an applicant must hold a baccalaureate degree from an institution of higher learning recognized by VCU and have at least a 2.75 grade point average (GPA) for all undergraduate work completed. Applicants with less than a 2.75 undergraduate GPA who have exceptional work experience will be considered for admission on provisional status. The applicant must also submit scores on a standardized aptitude test for graduate studies. Applicants holding professional degrees (e.g., MD, DDS, JD, and PharmD) may have testing requirements waived upon petition to the graduate dean. All applicants must have at least 5 years of increasingly responsible work experience. The specific experience profile depends upon an individual's particular profession or occupation. A résumé should accurately and completely describe an applicant's accomplishments. No specific prerequisite course work is required for application to the program. Upon acceptance, associates complete independent study modules in 3 areas: microeconomics, accounting, and quantitative analysis.

For more information, prospective students can visit the Web site (http://www.vcu.edu/haeweb/had/dept.htm).

DEGREE & CERTIFICATE PROGRAMS

Graduate Degrees

▶ *Health Administration (MSHA)*

In the fall of 1996 there were 58 students enrolled in this program. In 1995–96, 28 degrees were earned at a distance through this program.

Restrictions Students must have five or more years of clinical or managerial/supervisory experience.

Application requirements *Prior education:* baccalaureate degree. *Other requirements:* GRE or GMAT, college transcripts, an essay or personal statement, letter(s) of recommendation, an application fee.

Completion requirements 44 semester hours are required.

On-campus requirements Five on-campus sessions in the two-year program to begin and end each of four semesters of course work.

VIRGINIA POLYTECHNIC INSTITUTE AND STATE UNIVERSITY

Blacksburg, Virginia

Office of Distance Learning

Virginia Polytechnic Institute and State University, founded in 1872, is a state-supported university. It is accredited by the Southern Association of Colleges and Schools. It first offered distance learning courses in 1983.

Course delivery sites Courses are delivered to your workplace, military bases, other colleges.

Media Courses are delivered via television, videoconferencing.

Services Distance learners have access to library services, academic advising, career placement assistance at a distance.

Credit-earning options Students may transfer credits from another institution.

Contact JoAnn Michaels, Executive Secretary, Virginia Polytechnic Institute and State University, Old Security Building, Blacksburg, VA 24061-0445. *Telephone:* 540-231-6664. *Fax:* 540-231-5922.

DEGREE & CERTIFICATE PROGRAMS

Graduate Degrees

▶ *Business Administration (MBA)*

Program contact Ronald D. Johnson, Associate Dean, Virginia Polytechnic Institute and State University, MBA Programs, Pamplin College of Business, 1044 Pamplin Hall, Blacksburg, VA 24061-0209. Phone: 540-231-6152. E-mail: rdjmba@vtvm1.edu.

▶ *Engineering (MS)*

Program contact Benjamin S. Blanchard, Assistant Dean, Virginia Polytechnic Institute and State University, Industrial and Systems Engineering, 302 Whittemore Hall, Blacksburg, VA 24061-0118. Phone: 540-231-9762. E-mail: bsblanch@vtvm1.edu.

INDIVIDUAL COURSE SUBJECT AREAS

Graduate

Business administration and management; civil engineering; electrical engineering; engineering/industrial management; environmental engineering; industrial engineering; mechanical engineering

VISTA COMMUNITY COLLEGE

Berkeley, California

Program for Adult College Education (PACE)

Vista Community College, founded in 1974, is a state and locally supported two-year college. It is accredited by the Western Association of Schools and Colleges, Inc.

Course delivery sites Courses are delivered to your home.

Media Courses are delivered via television, videotapes, computer software, print, computer conferencing.

Restrictions Programs are available to local area students only. Financial aid is available to distance learners.

Contact Dr. Dean of Instruction, Vista Community College, 2020 Milvia Street, Berkeley, CA 94704. *Telephone:* 510-436-2411. *Fax:* 510-841-7333.

INDIVIDUAL COURSE SUBJECT AREAS

Undergraduate

Biology; economics; English language and literature; liberal arts, general studies, and humanities; social psychology; sociology

VOLUNTEER STATE COMMUNITY COLLEGE

Gallatin, Tennessee

Distance Learning/College at Home

Volunteer State Community College, founded in 1970, is a state-supported two-year college. It is accredited by the Southern Association of Colleges and Schools. It first offered distance learning courses in 1991. In 1996–97, it offered 36 courses at a distance. In the fall of 1996, there was a total of 1,700 students enrolled in distance learning courses.
Course delivery sites Courses are delivered to your home, your workplace, other colleges, 2 off-campus centers in Livingston, Nashville, high schools.
Media Courses are delivered via videotapes, videoconferencing, audiotapes, computer software, World Wide Web. Students and teachers interact via videoconferencing, audioconferencing, mail, telephone, fax, e-mail. A computer is required for all courses. The institution provides assistance with acquiring computer equipment.
Restrictions Courses are available to US and Canadian students only.
Services Distance learners have access to library services, the campus computer network, e-mail services, academic advising, tutoring, career placement assistance at a distance.
Credit-earning options Students may transfer credits from another institution or may earn credits through standardized exams, institutionally developed exams, portfolio assessment, military training, business training.
Typical costs Tuition of $497 per semester for in-state residents. Tuition of $1463 per semester for out-of-state residents. All students pay a $5 registration fee. *Noncredit courses:* $100 per course. Costs may vary by number of credits taken. Financial aid is available to distance learners enrolled full-time or part-time.
Registration Students may register by mail, fax, phone, e-mail, World Wide Web.
Contact Daryl Veal, College at Home, Volunteer State Community College, 1480 Nashville Pike, Gallatin, TN 37066. *Telephone:* 615-452-8600, Ext. 409. *Fax:* 615-230-3546. *E-mail:* dveal@vscc.cc.tn.us. *Web site:* http://www.vscc.cc.tn.us.

INDIVIDUAL COURSE SUBJECT AREAS

Undergraduate

Accounting; administrative and secretarial services; astronomy and astrophysics; business; business administration and management; communications; computer and information sciences; creative writing; economics; educational psychology; English composition; English language and literature; European languages and literatures; fine arts; geology; health and physical education/fitness; health professions and related sciences; history; industrial psychology; liberal arts, general studies, and humanities; library and information studies; marketing; mathematics; music; philosophy and religion; physics; public administration and services; social psychology; social work; sociology

WAKE TECHNICAL COMMUNITY COLLEGE

Raleigh, North Carolina

Wake Technical Community College, founded in 1958, is a state and locally supported two-year college. It is accredited by the Southern Association of Colleges and Schools. It first offered distance learning courses in 1986. In 1996–97, it offered 5 courses at a distance. In the fall of 1996, there was a total of 130 students enrolled in distance learning courses.
Course delivery sites Courses are delivered to your home, your workplace.
Media Courses are delivered via television, videotapes, computer software. Students and teachers interact via mail, telephone, in-person meetings. A computer is required for some courses.
Restrictions Programs are available to local area students only.
Services Distance learners have access to library services, the campus computer network, academic advising at a distance.
Credit-earning options Students may transfer credits from another institution or may earn credits through standardized exams, institutionally developed exams.
Typical costs Tuition of $278.25 per semester for in-state residents. Tuition of $2257.50 per semester for out-of-state residents. Part-time tuition: $19.75 per hour, in-state; $161.25 per hour, out-of-state. Costs may vary by number of credits taken.
Registration Students may register by mail, phone.
Contact Pat Richardson, Dean, Educational Support Services, Wake Technical Community College, 9101 Fayetteville Road, Raleigh, NC 27603. *Telephone:* 919-662-3431. *Fax:* 919-779-3360.

INDIVIDUAL COURSE SUBJECT AREAS

Undergraduate

Business; business administration and management; chemistry; computer and information sciences; creative writing; English composition; English language and literature; mathematics; psychology; social psychology; social sciences

WALDEN UNIVERSITY

Minneapolis, Minnesota

Walden University is an independent-nonprofit graduate institution. It is accredited by the North Central Association of Colleges and Schools. It first offered distance learning courses in 1970. In 1996–97, it offered 72 courses at a distance. In the fall of 1996, there was a total of 1,091 students enrolled in distance learning courses.
Course delivery sites Courses are delivered to your home, military bases, 3 off-campus centers in Minneapolis, Bonita Springs (FL), Washington (DC).
Media Courses are delivered via World Wide Web, e-mail, print. Students and teachers interact via audioconferencing, mail, telephone, fax, e-mail. A computer is required for all courses.
Services Distance learners have access to library services, e-mail services, academic advising, tutoring at a distance.
Credit-earning options Students may transfer credits from another institution or may earn credits through portfolio assessment.
Typical costs Tuition of $220 per credit. $285 per credit or $3040 per quarter for the module-based PhD program. Costs may vary by specific program of study.
Registration Students may register by mail, e-mail, World Wide Web.
Contact Office of Student Recruitment, Walden University, 24311 Walden Center Drive, Bonita Springs, FL 34134. *Telephone:* 800-444-6795. *Fax:* 941-498-4266. *E-mail:* request@waldenu.edu. *Web site:* http://www.waldenu.edu.

Special note

Walden University has been a leader in providing distance graduate education to experienced professionals for more than 25 years. Its technology-assisted model of distributed learning includes a

Profiles: Walden University

flexible curriculum, dispersed residencies, and a self-paced approach. Walden's degree requirements allow learners considerable freedom to satisfy professional interests and to do so without foregoing family and career commitments. Household moves, commuting to campus, and extended hours of seat time are not required. Serious attention to growing as a scholar-practitioner committed to making positive changes in one's area of influence, however, is required. Doctoral programs are offered in 5 areas: administration/management, education, health services, human services, and psychology. A master's program is offered in educational change and technology innovation.

Walden University is regionally accredited by the North Central Association of Colleges and Schools. The professional psychology program is accredited by the Consortium for Diversified Psychology Programs.

The Walden Information Network (WIN) facilitates electronic communications among student colleagues and with faculty mentors, as well as access to the rich academic and professional resources of gopherspace and the World Wide Web. One of those rich learning resources is the Indiana University Graduate Library in Bloomington, Indiana, with which Walden maintains a formal agreement for library services.

More than 1,000 students are currently pursuing graduate studies at Walden University. To learn more, students should call 800-444-6795 (toll-free), send e-mail to request@waldenu.edu, or visit the Walden University World Wide Web site at http://www.waldenu.edu.

DEGREE & CERTIFICATE PROGRAMS

Graduate Degrees

▶ *Applied Management and Decision Sciences (PhD)*
In the fall of 1996 there were 349 students enrolled in this program. In 1995–96, 63 degrees were earned at a distance through this program.
Application requirements *Prior education:* graduate degree. *Other requirements:* college transcripts, an essay or personal statement, letter(s) of recommendation, an application fee of $50, three years of professional experience.
Completion requirements 128 hours are required. 128 quarter credits must be completed through the institution. *Maximum time for completion:* eight years.
On-campus requirements 2–3 weeks core residency, 4-day continuing residency.

▶ *Education (PhD)*
In the fall of 1996 there were 226 students enrolled in this program. In 1995–96, 47 degrees were earned at a distance through this program.
Application requirements *Prior education:* graduate degree. *Other requirements:* college transcripts, an essay or personal statement, letter(s) of recommendation, an application fee of $50, three years of professional experience.
Completion requirements 128 hours are required. 128 quarter credits must be completed through the institution. *Maximum time for completion:* eight years.
On-campus requirements 2–3 weeks core residency, 4-day continuing residency.

▶ *Educational Change and Technology Innovation (MS)*
In the fall of 1996 there were 58 students enrolled in this program.
Application requirements *Prior education:* baccalaureate degree. *Other requirements:* college transcripts, an essay or personal statement, letter(s) of recommendation, an application fee of $50, two years of professional experience.
Completion requirements 45 hours are required. 45 quarter credits must be completed through the institution. *Maximum time for completion:* eight years.
On-campus requirements One 2-week summer residency and one 5-day practicum.

▶ *Health Services (PhD)*
In the fall of 1996 there were 109 students enrolled in this program. In 1995–96, 12 degrees were earned at a distance through this program.
Application requirements *Prior education:* graduate degree. *Other requirements:* college transcripts, an essay or personal statement, letter(s) of recommendation, an application fee of $50, three years of professional experience.
Completion requirements 128 hours are required. 128 quarter credits must be completed through the institution. *Maximum time for completion:* eight years.
On-campus requirements 2–3 weeks core residency, 4-day continuing residency.

▶ *Human Services (PhD)*
In the fall of 1996 there were 126 students enrolled in this program. In 1995–96, 26 degrees were earned at a distance through this program.
Application requirements *Prior education:* graduate degree. *Other requirements:* high school transcript, college transcripts, an essay or personal statement, letter(s) of recommendation, an application fee of $50, three years of professional experience.
Completion requirements 128 hours are required. 128 quarter credits must be completed through the institution. *Maximum time for completion:* eight years.
On-campus requirements 2–3 weeks core residency, 4-day continuing residency.

▶ *Professional Psychology (PhD)*
In the fall of 1996 there were 223 students enrolled in this program.
Application requirements *Prior education:* graduate degree. *Other requirements:* college transcripts, an essay or personal statement, letter(s) of recommendation, an application fee of $50, three years of professional experience.
Completion requirements 128 hours are required. 128 quarter credits must be completed through the institution. *Maximum time for completion:* eight years.
On-campus requirements 2–3 weeks core residency, 4-day continuing residency.

INDIVIDUAL COURSE SUBJECT AREAS

Graduate
Business; business administration and management; developmental and child psychology; education; education administration; educational psychology; health professions and related sciences; human resources management; industrial psychology; psychology; public administration and services; social psychology; social sciences; social work; teacher education

WALTERS STATE COMMUNITY COLLEGE

Morristown, Tennessee

Evening and Distance Education Office

Walters State Community College, founded in 1970, is a state-supported two-year college. It is accredited by the Southern Association of Colleges and Schools. It first offered distance learning courses in 1988. In 1996–97, it offered 30 courses at a distance. In the fall of 1996, there was a total of 467 students enrolled in distance learning courses.
Course delivery sites Courses are delivered to your home, 3 off-campus centers in Greeneville, New Tazewell, Sevierville.
Media Courses are delivered via television, videotapes. Students and teachers interact via videoconferencing, mail, telephone, fax, e-mail.

Restrictions Students must be in the broadcast area for telecourses, or capable of getting to the three sites in Tennessee for the interactive video offerings.
Services Distance learners have access to library services, the campus computer network, e-mail services, academic advising, tutoring at a distance.
Credit-earning options Students may transfer credits from another institution or may earn credits through examinations, military training.
Typical costs Tuition of $45 per credit hour plus mandatory fees of $17 per semester for in-state residents. Tuition of $186 per credit hour plus mandatory fees of $17 per semester for out-of-state residents. Costs may vary by number of credits taken. Financial aid is available to distance learners enrolled full-time or part-time.
Registration Students may register by phone.
Contact Dave Roberts, Director, Walters State Community College, 500 South Davy Crockett Parkway, Morristown, TN 37813-6899. *Telephone:* 423-585-6899. *Fax:* 423-585-6853. *E-mail:* droberts@wscc.cc.tn.us. *Web site:* http://www.wscc.cc.tn.us.

INDIVIDUAL COURSE SUBJECT AREAS

Undergraduate
Astronomy and astrophysics; business administration and management; developmental and child psychology; economics; educational psychology; English composition; European languages and literatures; geology; gerontology; health and physical education/fitness; history; hospitality services management; liberal arts, general studies, and humanities; mathematics; philosophy and religion; protective services; social psychology; social work; sociology; teacher education

WASHINGTON AND JEFFERSON COLLEGE

Washington, Pennsylvania

Washington and Jefferson College, founded in 1781, is an independent-nonprofit four-year college. It is accredited by the Middle States Association of Colleges and Schools. It first offered distance learning courses in 1996.
Course delivery sites Courses are delivered to other colleges, libraries, high schools.
Media Courses are delivered via videoconferencing, audioconferencing, World Wide Web, e-mail, print. Students and teachers interact via videoconferencing, audioconferencing, mail, telephone, fax, e-mail.
Typical costs Tuition of $1700 per course.
Contact Dr. G. Andrew Rembert, Vice President for Academic Affairs, Washington and Jefferson College, Washington, PA 15301. *Telephone:* 412-223-6005.

INDIVIDUAL COURSE SUBJECT AREAS

Undergraduate
Business; education

WASHINGTON STATE UNIVERSITY

Pullman, Washington

Extended Academic Programs

Washington State University, founded in 1890, is a state-supported university. It is accredited by the Northwest Association of Schools and Colleges. It first offered distance learning courses in 1992. In 1996–97, it offered 115 courses at a distance. In the fall of 1996, there was a total of 480 students enrolled in distance learning courses.
Course delivery sites Courses are delivered to your home, military bases.
Media Courses are delivered via videotapes, audiotapes, World Wide Web, print. Students and teachers interact via audioconferencing, mail, telephone, fax, e-mail. A computer is required for some courses.
Services Distance learners have access to library services, academic advising at a distance.
Credit-earning options Students may transfer credits from another institution or may earn credits through examinations, military training.
Typical costs Tuition of $163 per credit for in-state residents. Tuition of $245 per credit for out-of-state residents. Flexible enrollment courses (correspondence) in- or out-of-state is $90 per credit. Costs may vary by specific program of study, number of credits taken, course delivery options. Financial aid is available to distance learners.
Registration Students may register by mail, fax, phone, e-mail, World Wide Web.
Contact Cheri Curtis, Program Coordinator, Extended Degree Programs, Washington State University, Van Doren 204, PO Box 645220, Pullman, WA 99164-5220. *Telephone:* 800-222-4978. *Fax:* 509-335-0945. *E-mail:* curtisc@wsu.edu. *Web site:* http://www.eecs.wsu.edu/~edp.

Special note

Washington State University (WSU) has long been an acknowledged leader in developing and delivering distance education programs. Serving the needs of time- and place-bound students in Washington and across the nation, WSU offers traditional correspondence courses and specially produced video courses that support the Extended Degree Program (EDP), a degree completion program begun in 1992.

The Extended Degree Program, leading to a Bachelor of Arts in Social Sciences, is designed primarily for students who have completed the equivalent of the first 2 years of college. The requirements are the same as those for completing degrees on campus; however, students can complete their degrees without coming to a WSU campus.

The Extended Degree Program emphasizes an interdisciplinary approach with possible major and/or minor course concentrations in anthropology, criminal justice, history, human development, political science, psychology, sociology, and women's studies. A formal minor in business administration is also available.

Courses taught by the same instructors as on campus are delivered directly to students' homes through a variety of distance learning technologies: videotape (available for rent), satellite, and cable television. Some courses also include material available on the World Wide Web. Future courses will feature interactive CD-ROM and desktop videoconferencing components.

Access to WSU distance learning staff and faculty members is provided through toll-free telephone, e-mail, and, for students enrolled in EDP video courses, a sophisticated voice mail system. Student services are provided by academic advisers, a student services coordinator, and an EDP librarian.

A 30-minute informational videotape providing details about the Extended Degree Program, advising, and financial aid and presenting short clips from a number of EDP video courses is available from the Students Book Corporation (800-937-4978 toll-free, Ext. 336) for $8.

Profiles: Washington State University

DEGREE & CERTIFICATE PROGRAMS

Baccalaureate Degrees
▶ *Social Sciences (BA)*
Application requirements *Prior education:* some undergraduate course work. *Other requirements:* high school transcript, college transcripts, an application fee of $35.
Completion requirements 120 quarter credits are required. 30 semester credits must be completed through the institution. This is a degree completion program.

INDIVIDUAL COURSE SUBJECT AREAS

Undergraduate
Accounting; American (US) history; American literature; anthropology; architecture; area, ethnic, and cultural studies; Asian languages and literatures; biology; business; business administration and management; Classical languages and literatures; communications; conservation and natural resources; creative writing; developmental and child psychology; economics; English composition; English language and literature; European history; finance; foods and nutrition studies; geology; history; human resources management; insurance; liberal arts, general studies, and humanities; marketing; mathematics; philosophy and religion; political science; psychology; real estate; social psychology; social sciences; sociology; technical writing; women's studies; zoology

See full description on page 526.

WASHTENAW COMMUNITY COLLEGE

Ann Arbor, Michigan

Extension Services and Distance Learning

Washtenaw Community College, founded in 1965, is a state and locally supported two-year college. It is accredited by the North Central Association of Colleges and Schools.
Course delivery sites Courses are delivered to your home.
Media Courses are delivered via television, videotapes, audiotapes, print.
Restrictions Programs are available to local area students only.
Credit-earning options Students may transfer credits from another institution or may earn credits through examinations, portfolio assessment, military training, business training. Financial aid is available to distance learners.
Contact Supervisor, Distance Learning and Extension Service, Washtenaw Community College, PO Box D-1, 4800 Huron River Drive, Ann Arbor, MI 48106. *Telephone:* 313-677-5030. *Fax:* 313-677-5414.

INDIVIDUAL COURSE SUBJECT AREAS

Undergraduate
Area, ethnic, and cultural studies; business administration and management; computer and information sciences; developmental and child psychology; economics; history; sociology

WAUBONSEE COMMUNITY COLLEGE

Sugar Grove, Illinois

Center for Distance Learning

Waubonsee Community College, founded in 1966, is a district-supported two-year college. It is accredited by the North Central Association of Colleges and Schools. It first offered distance learning courses in 1988.
Course delivery sites Courses are delivered to other colleges.
Media Courses are delivered via television, videoconferencing.
Restrictions Programs are available to in-state students only.
Credit-earning options Students may transfer credits from another institution or may earn credits through examinations. Financial aid is available to distance learners.
Contact Instructional Television Programming Manager, Waubonsee Community College, Route 47 at Harter Road, Sugar Grove, IL 60554. *Telephone:* 708-466-4811, Ext. 2641. *Fax:* 708-466-9100.

INDIVIDUAL COURSE SUBJECT AREAS

Undergraduate
Accounting; Asian languages and literatures; biology; business; chemistry; creative writing; developmental and child psychology; economics; English composition; English language and literature; environmental engineering; European languages and literatures; fine arts; health professions and related sciences; history; human resources management; law and legal studies; liberal arts, general studies, and humanities; mathematics; music; philosophy and religion; political science; psychology; social psychology; social work; sociology; special education; statistics; theological studies

WAUKESHA COUNTY TECHNICAL COLLEGE

Pewaukee, Wisconsin

Waukesha County Technical College, founded in 1923, is a state and locally supported two-year college. It is accredited by the North Central Association of Colleges and Schools. It first offered distance learning courses in 1995. In 1996–97, it offered 30 courses at a distance. In the fall of 1996, there was a total of 180 students enrolled in distance learning courses.
Course delivery sites Courses are delivered to your home, your workplace, Blackhawk Technical College (Janesville), Lakeshore Technical College (Cleveland).
Media Courses are delivered via television, videotapes, videoconferencing, World Wide Web, e-mail. Students and teachers interact via videoconferencing, telephone, fax, e-mail. A computer is required for some courses.
Restrictions Broadcast telecourses are available to students in a limited viewing area. Interactive Dental Hygiene program has limited enrollment.
Services Distance learners have access to library services, academic advising, career placement assistance at a distance.
Credit-earning options Students may transfer credits from another institution or may earn credits through examinations, portfolio assessment, military training, business training.
Typical costs Tuition of $51.20 per credit. Mandatory fee of $10 per credit for Internet courses only. Financial aid is available to distance learners.
Registration Students may register by phone.
Contact Registration Office, Waukesha County Technical College, 800 Main Street, Pewaukee, WI 53072. *Telephone:* 414-691-5578. *Web site:* http://www.waukesha.tec.wi.us.

INDIVIDUAL COURSE SUBJECT AREAS

Undergraduate
Accounting; business; business administration and management; business law; economics; English composition; finance; fire science; investments and securities; marketing; mathematics; psychology; real estate; sociology

WAYNE COUNTY COMMUNITY COLLEGE

Detroit, Michigan

Distance Learning

Wayne County Community College, founded in 1967, is a state and locally supported two-year college. It is accredited by the North Central Association of Colleges and Schools. It first offered distance learning courses in 1978. In 1996–97, it offered 60 courses at a distance.
Course delivery sites Courses are delivered to your home, your workplace.
Media Courses are delivered via television, videotapes, computer software. Students and teachers interact via mail, telephone, fax. A computer is required for some courses.
Services Distance learners have access to library services, the campus computer network at a distance.
Credit-earning options Students may transfer credits from another institution or may earn credits through examinations, portfolio assessment, military training.
Typical costs Tuition of $54 per credit plus mandatory fees of $2 per credit for local area residents. Tuition of $70 per credit plus mandatory fees of $2 per credit for in-state residents. Tuition of $89 per credit plus mandatory fees of $2 per credit for out-of-state residents. All students pay an additional $25 per semester. Financial aid is available to distance learners enrolled full-time or part-time.
Registration Students may register by mail.
Contact Deborah Fiedler, District Director, Wayne County Community College, 801 West Fort Street, Detroit, MI 48226. *Telephone:* 313-496-2602. *Fax:* 313-496-0451. *E-mail:* citcdf@admin.wccc.edu.

DEGREE & CERTIFICATE PROGRAMS

Associate Degrees

▶ *Business Administration (AA)*
Application requirements College transcripts.
Completion requirements 65 semester credits are required. 15 credit hours must be completed through the institution.
On-campus requirements An average of four on-campus class sessions are required for each course unless special arrangements have been made.

▶ *General Studies (AGS)*
Application requirements *Prior education:* none required. *Other requirements:* application.
Completion requirements 60 semester credits are required. 15 semester hours must be completed through the institution.
On-campus requirements An average of four on-campus class sessions are required for each course unless special arrangements have been made.

INDIVIDUAL COURSE SUBJECT AREAS

Undergraduate
Accounting; algebra; American (US) history; anthropology; business; business administration and management; business law; child care and development; computer and information sciences; economics; English composition; English language and literature; geography; geology; health professions and related sciences; history; law and legal studies; liberal arts, general studies, and humanities; marketing; mathematics; philosophy and religion; physical sciences; physiology; political science; psychology; sociology

WAYNE STATE UNIVERSITY

Detroit, Michigan

College of Lifelong Learning

Wayne State University, founded in 1868, is a state-supported university. It is accredited by the North Central Association of Colleges and Schools. It first offered distance learning courses in 1967. In 1996–97, it offered 25 courses at a distance. In the fall of 1996, there was a total of 205 students enrolled in distance learning courses.
Course delivery sites Courses are delivered to your home, your workplace, 4 off-campus centers in Detroit, Eastpointe, Farmington Hills, Sterling Heights.
Media Courses are delivered via television, videoconferencing. Students and teachers interact via videoconferencing, mail, telephone.
Restrictions Programs are available to in-state students only.
Services Distance learners have access to library services, the campus computer network at a distance.
Credit-earning options Students may transfer credits from another institution or may earn credits through institutionally developed exams.
Typical costs *Undergraduate:* Tuition of $105 per credit plus mandatory fees of $72 per semester for in-state residents. *Graduate:* Tuition of $153 per credit plus mandatory fees of $72 per semester for in-state residents. Costs may vary by specific program of study. Financial aid is available to distance learners enrolled full-time or part-time.
Contact Paul Fiedler, Telecommunications Coordinator, Wayne State University, 2906 Academic and Administration Building, Detroit, MI 48202. *Telephone:* 313-577-6966. *Fax:* 313-577-7744.

Special note
The Wayne State University/College of Lifelong Learning Instructional Telecommunication (WSU/CLL) unit has broadcast/cablecast 20 telecourses, 4 teleconferences, and 6 live interactive graduate-level credit offerings during the 1995–96 academic year and plans a similar program for 1997–98.

Credit-course lectures are viewed by nearly 1,000 students and attendees, many of whom participate in professionally produced interactive teleconferences from their homes and places of work. Televised presentations are accompanied by in-class workshops and seminars conducted at WSU/CLL off-campus centers.

With newly produced and licensed courses in psychology and gerontology, the WSU/CLL telecourse portfolio has expanded to include 43 high-production quality credit courses offered in 11 academic disciplines.

Wayne State University also delivers a master's degree in electronics and computer control systems by video and 2-way audio to employees of Ford Motor Company. By mid 1997, WSU/CLL will transmit pre-produced and live interactive WSU courses throughout the Detroit metropolitan area to every community within a 40-mile radius of its transmitting facility in Royal Township. This new uninterrupted service will enable Detroit metropolitan area residents to participate in WSU courses from their homes, schools, and places of work. They will communicate with their instructor and fellow students located at remote locations over the University's new television network.

Profiles: Wayne State University

DEGREE & CERTIFICATE PROGRAMS

Graduate Degrees

▶ *Electronics and Computer Control Systems (MA)*
Restrictions This program is available to local area students only. Program is available to Ford Motor Company employees only.
Application requirements *Prior education:* baccalaureate degree. *Other requirements:* college transcripts, an application fee of $50.
Completion requirements 32 credits are required. 32 credits must be completed through the institution.
Program contact Frank Westervelt, Wayne State University, College of Engineering, 3148 Engineering Building, Detroit, MI 48202. Phone: 313-577-3764.

INDIVIDUAL COURSE SUBJECT AREAS

Undergraduate

Area, ethnic, and cultural studies; English language and literature; fine arts; history; liberal arts, general studies, and humanities; nursing; philosophy and religion; political science; psychology; public health; social psychology; social sciences; sociology

Graduate

Computer and information sciences; electrical engineering; engineering; engineering-related technologies

WEBER STATE UNIVERSITY

Ogden, Utah

Distance Learning and Independent Study

Weber State University, founded in 1889, is a state-supported comprehensive institution. It is accredited by the Northwest Association of Schools and Colleges. In 1996–97, it offered 251 courses at a distance. In the fall of 1996, there was a total of 641 students enrolled in distance learning courses.
Course delivery sites Courses are delivered to your home, your workplace, other colleges.
Media Courses are delivered via videotapes, audiotapes, computer software, World Wide Web, print. Students and teachers interact via mail, telephone, e-mail. A computer is required for some courses.
Services Distance learners have access to library services, academic advising, career placement assistance at a distance.
Credit-earning options Students may earn credits through examinations.
Typical costs Tuition of $190 per course. Costs may vary by number of credits taken, cost of materials. Financial aid is available to distance learners.
Contact Distance Learning Customer Services, Weber State University, 4005 University Circle, Ogden, UT 84408-4005. *Telephone:* 801-626-6785. *Fax:* 801-626-8035. *E-mail:* dist-learn@weber.edu. *Web site:* http://www.weber.edu/dist-learn.

DEGREE & CERTIFICATE PROGRAMS

Associate Degrees

▶ *Respiratory Therapy (AAS, AS)*
Completion requirements 30 credits must be completed through the institution.

Baccalaureate Degrees

▶ *Advanced Dental Hygiene, Advanced Respiratory Therapy, Health Administrative Services, Radiological Sciences (BS)*
Completion requirements 183 credits are required. 45 credits must be completed through the institution.

Undergraduate Certificates

▶ *Radiological Sciences, Respiratory Therapy*

INDIVIDUAL COURSE SUBJECT AREAS

Undergraduate

Accounting; anthropology; botany; business administration and management; chemistry; communications; computer and information sciences; creative writing; English composition; English language and literature; finance; geology; health and physical education/fitness; health services administration; history; mathematics; music; philosophy and religion; political science; psychology; social psychology; social work; sociology
See full description on page 528.

WENATCHEE VALLEY COLLEGE

Wenatchee, Washington

Wenatchee Valley College, founded in 1939, is a state and locally supported two-year college. It is accredited by the Northwest Association of Schools and Colleges. It first offered distance learning courses in 1982. In 1996–97, it offered 20 courses at a distance. In the fall of 1996, there was a total of 110 students enrolled in distance learning courses.
Course delivery sites Courses are delivered to your home, 15 off-campus centers in Bridgeton, Cashmere, Chelan, Entiat, Leavenworth, Manson, Okanogan, Omak, Peshatin, Tonasket, Twisp, Wenatchee.
Media Courses are delivered via television, videotapes, audiotapes. Students and teachers interact via mail, telephone, fax, e-mail, on-campus meetings.
Restrictions Programs are available to in-state students only.
Credit-earning options Students may transfer credits from another institution or may earn credits through examinations, portfolio assessment, military training, business training.
Typical costs Tuition of $46.70 per credit plus mandatory fees of $20 per credit for in-state residents. Tuition of $183.70 per credit plus mandatory fees of $20 per credit for out-of-state residents. Financial aid is available to distance learners.
Registration Students may register by mail.
Contact Bruce Swenson, Director, Library Resource Center, Wenatchee Valley College, 1300 Fifth Street, Wenatchee, WA 98801. *Telephone:* 509-662-1651, Ext. 2821. *Fax:* 509-664-2576.

INDIVIDUAL COURSE SUBJECT AREAS

Undergraduate

Astronomy and astrophysics; biology; developmental and child psychology; English composition; English language and literature; geology; health and physical education/fitness; history; political science; social psychology

WESTERN CONSERVATIVE BAPTIST SEMINARY

Portland, Oregon

Department of External Studies

Western Conservative Baptist Seminary, founded in 1927, is an independent-religious graduate institution. It is accredited by the

Northwest Association of Schools and Colleges. It first offered distance learning courses in 1981. In 1996–97, it offered 50 courses at a distance. In the fall of 1996, there was a total of 70 students enrolled in distance learning courses.
Course delivery sites Courses are delivered to your home, your workplace, military bases, other colleges.
Media Courses are delivered via videotapes, audiotapes. Students and teachers interact via mail, telephone, fax, e-mail.
Services Distance learners have access to academic advising, career placement assistance at a distance.
Credit-earning options Students may transfer credits from another institution or may earn credits through examinations.
Typical costs Tuition of $225 per semester hour. *Noncredit courses:* $56.25 per semester hour.
Registration Students may register by mail, fax, phone.
Contact Jon Raibley, Coordinator, Department of External Studies, Western Conservative Baptist Seminary, 5511 Southeast Hawthorne Boulevard, Portland, OR 97215. *Telephone:* 800-547-4546. *Fax:* 503-239-4216. *E-mail:* jlraible@westernseminary.edu.

DEGREE & CERTIFICATE PROGRAMS

Graduate certificates

▶ *Ministerial Studies, Theological Studies (Diploma)*
Application requirements *Prior education:* baccalaureate degree. *Other requirements:* college transcripts, an essay or personal statement, letter(s) of recommendation, an application fee of $35.
Completion requirements 30 semester hours are required. 30 semester hours must be completed through the institution.

▶ *Theological Studies/Biblical Studies/Church Ministries*
In 1995–96, 3 certificates were earned at a distance through this program.
Application requirements *Prior education:* baccalaureate degree. *Other requirements:* an essay or personal statement, an application fee of $20.
Completion requirements 12 semester credits are required. 12 semester credits must be completed through the institution.

▶ *Theological/Ministerial Studies/Biblical Studies (Enrichment Award)*
In 1995–96, 3 certificates were earned at a distance through this program.
Application requirements *Prior education:* none required.
Completion requirements 18 continuing education units are required. 18 continuing education units must be completed through the institution.

INDIVIDUAL COURSE SUBJECT AREAS

Graduate
Theological studies

Noncredit
Theological studies

WESTERN ILLINOIS UNIVERSITY

Macomb, Illinois

School of Extended and Continuing Education

Western Illinois University, founded in 1899, is a state-supported comprehensive institution. It is accredited by the North Central Association of Colleges and Schools. It first offered distance learning courses in 1984. In 1996–97, it offered 135 courses at a distance. In the fall of 1996, there was a total of 1,286 students enrolled in distance learning courses.
Course delivery sites Courses are delivered to your home, your workplace, Black Hawk College (Moline), John Wood Community College (Quincy), Sauk Valley Community College (Dixon), 2 off-campus centers in Moline, Rock Island.
Media Courses are delivered via television, videotapes, videoconferencing, World Wide Web, e-mail, print. Students and teachers interact via videoconferencing, mail, telephone, fax, e-mail. A computer is required for some courses.
Restrictions Courses are available to US students only.
Services Distance learners have access to e-mail services at a distance.
Credit-earning options Students may transfer credits from another institution or may earn credits through standardized exams, portfolio assessment, military training, business training.
Typical costs *Undergraduate:* Tuition of $85 per semester hour. *Graduate:* Tuition of $89.50 per semester hour. Costs may vary by course delivery options. Financial aid is available to distance learners enrolled full-time.
Registration Students may register by mail, fax, phone.
Contact Joyce E. Nielsen, Associate Dean, School of Extended and Continuing Education, Western Illinois University, 1 University Circle, 305 Memorial Hall, Macomb, IL 61455. *Telephone:* 309-298-2182. *Fax:* 309-298-2133. *E-mail:* Joyce_Nielsen@ccmail.wiu.edu. *Web site:* http://www.wiu.edu.

DEGREE & CERTIFICATE PROGRAMS

Baccalaureate Degrees

▶ *General Studies (BA)*
In the fall of 1996 there were 2,850 students enrolled in this program. In 1995–96, 276 degrees were earned at a distance through this program.
Application requirements *Prior education:* some undergraduate course work. *Other requirements:* college transcripts, an essay or personal statement.
Completion requirements 120 semester hours are required. 15 semester hours must be completed through the institution. *Other requirements:* Illinois/United States Constitution Examination, University Writing examination.
Program contact Dr. Hans Moll, Director, Non-Traditional Programs, Western Illinois University, Horrabin Hall 5, Macomb, IL 61455. Phone: 309-298-1929. Fax: 309-298-2226. E-mail: np-bog@wiu.edu.

Graduate Degrees

▶ *Business Administration (MBA)*
In the fall of 1996 there were 30 students enrolled in this program.
Restrictions This program is available to local area students only.
Application requirements *Prior education:* baccalaureate degree. *Other requirements:* GMAT, college transcripts.
Completion requirements 33 semester hours are required. 24 semester hours must be completed through the institution. *Maximum time for completion:* six years.
Program contact Dr. Larry Wall, Associate Dean, College of Business and Technology, Western Illinois University, Stipes Hall 101, Macomb, IL 61455. Phone: 309-298-2442. Fax: 309-298-1039. E-mail: larry_wall@wiu.edu.

INDIVIDUAL COURSE SUBJECT AREAS

Undergraduate
Accounting; administrative and secretarial services; agriculture; American (US) history; American literature; area, ethnic, and cultural studies; astronomy and astrophysics; biology; business; business administration and management; computer and information sciences; creative writing; economics; English language and literature; English literature; European languages and literatures; finance; fire science; fire services administration; French language and literature; geography; geology; history; home economics and family studies; human resources management; international business; law and legal studies; liberal arts, general studies, and humanities; marketing; mathematics; microbiology; organizational behavior studies; philosophy and religion; political science; public health; radio and

Profiles: Western Illinois University

television broadcasting; real estate; social psychology; sociology; Spanish language and literature; special education; teacher education; technical writing; zoology

Graduate
Accounting; administrative and secretarial services; biology; business; business administration and management; creative writing; economics; education administration; health and physical education/fitness; home economics and family studies; instructional media; law and legal studies; liberal arts, general studies, and humanities; microbiology; public health; special education; teacher education; telecommunications; zoology

WESTERN MICHIGAN UNIVERSITY

Kalamazoo, Michigan

Department of Distance Education

Western Michigan University, founded in 1903, is a state-supported university. It is accredited by the North Central Association of Colleges and Schools. It first offered distance learning courses in 1906. In 1996–97, it offered 116 courses at a distance. In the fall of 1996, there was a total of 786 students enrolled in distance learning courses.
Course delivery sites Courses are delivered to your home, your workplace, military bases, other colleges, 4 off-campus centers in Battle Creek, Grand Rapids, Lansing, Muskegon.
Media Courses are delivered via television, videotapes, videoconferencing, audiotapes, audioconferencing, print. Students and teachers interact via videoconferencing, audioconferencing, mail, telephone.
Restrictions Programs are primarily available to in-state students.
Services Distance learners have access to library services, e-mail services, academic advising, career placement assistance at a distance.
Credit-earning options Students may transfer credits from another institution or may earn credits through examinations.
Typical costs Tuition of $124.40 per credit hour. Students must pay a $20 video fee. Costs may vary by campus or location. Financial aid is available to distance learners enrolled full-time or part-time.
Registration Students may register by mail, fax, phone.
Contact Rosemary Nichols, Student Liaison, Western Michigan University, B102 Ellsworth, Kalamazoo, MI 49008. *Telephone:* 616-387-4216. *Fax:* 616-387-4266. *E-mail:* rosemary.nichols@wmich.edu.

INDIVIDUAL COURSE SUBJECT AREAS

Undergraduate
African-American studies; anthropology; biological and life sciences; education; engineering; engineering/industrial management; English language and literature; health and physical education/fitness; history; mathematics; philosophy and religion; physical sciences; psychology; social sciences; social work; substance abuse counseling

Graduate
Business; business administration and management; computer and information sciences; engineering/industrial management

WESTERN MONTANA COLLEGE OF THE UNIVERSITY OF MONTANA

Dillon, Montana

Division of Outreach

Western Montana College of The University of Montana, founded in 1893, is a state-supported four-year college. It is accredited by the Northwest Association of Schools and Colleges. It first offered distance learning courses in 1989. In 1996–97, it offered 2 courses at a distance. In the fall of 1996, there was a total of 15 students enrolled in distance learning courses.
Course delivery sites Courses are delivered to 1 off-campus center in Boulder.
Media Courses are delivered via videoconferencing, World Wide Web. Students and teachers interact via videoconferencing. A computer is required for some courses.
Restrictions Programs are available to in-state students only.
Services Distance learners have access to library services, academic advising at a distance.
Credit-earning options Students may transfer credits from another institution or may earn credits through examinations, military training.
Typical costs Tuition of $430 per course for in-state residents. Tuition of $920.80 per course for out-of-state residents. Costs may vary by number of credits taken. Financial aid is available to distance learners.
Registration Students may register by mail, phone.
Contact Vickie Lansing, Program Assistant, Division of Outreach, Western Montana College of The University of Montana, 710 South Atlantic Street, Campus Box 114, Dillon, MT 59725-3598. *Telephone:* 406-683-7537. *Fax:* 406-683-7809. *E-mail:* v_lansing@wmc.edu.

INDIVIDUAL COURSE SUBJECT AREAS

Undergraduate
Business; computer and information sciences; economics; mathematics; teacher education

Noncredit
Business; computer and information sciences; economics; teacher education

WESTERN NEBRASKA COMMUNITY COLLEGE

Scottsbluff, Nebraska

Information Technologies

Western Nebraska Community College, founded in 1921, is a state and locally supported two-year college. It is accredited by the North Central Association of Schools and Colleges. It first offered distance learning courses in 1994. In 1996–97, it offered 30 courses at a distance. In the fall of 1996, there was a total of 120 students enrolled in distance learning courses.
Course delivery sites Courses are delivered to Central Community College–Hastings Campus (Hastings), 2 off-campus centers in Alliance, Sidney.
Media Courses are delivered via videotapes, videoconferencing, audiotapes, computer software, World Wide Web, e-mail, print. Students and teachers interact via videoconferencing, mail, telephone, fax, e-mail, in-person meetings.

Restrictions Courses are available to students in Sidney and Alliance only.
Services Distance learners have access to library services, e-mail services, academic advising, tutoring, career placement assistance at a distance.
Credit-earning options Students may transfer credits from another institution or may earn credits through examinations, portfolio assessment, military training.
Typical costs Tuition of $37 per credit plus mandatory fees of $5 per credit for in-state residents. Tuition of $41 per credit plus mandatory fees of $5 per credit for out-of-state residents. *Noncredit courses:* $33 per course. Financial aid is available to distance learners enrolled full-time or part-time.
Contact Sally Jahnke, Dean of Instruction, Western Nebraska Community College, 1601 East 27th Street, Scottsbluff, NE 69361. *Telephone:* 308-635-6032. *Fax:* 308-635-6176. *E-mail:* sjahnke@hannibal.wncc.cc.ne.us. *Web site:* http://hannibal.wncc.cc.ne.us.

INDIVIDUAL COURSE SUBJECT AREAS

Undergraduate
Area, ethnic, and cultural studies; business administration and management; developmental and child psychology; English composition; English language and literature; European languages and literatures; liberal arts, general studies, and humanities; mathematics; nursing; protective services; psychology; sociology

WESTERN NEW MEXICO UNIVERSITY

Silver City, New Mexico

Continuing Education and Extension services

Western New Mexico University, founded in 1893, is a state-supported comprehensive institution. It is accredited by the North Central Association of Colleges and Schools. It first offered distance learning courses in 1993.
Course delivery sites Courses are delivered to off-campus sites.
Media Courses are delivered via videoconferencing.
Restrictions Programs are available to in-state students only.
Services Distance learners have access to library services, academic advising at a distance.
Credit-earning options Students may transfer credits from another institution or may earn credits through examinations, military training. Financial aid is available to distance learners.
Contact Director of Continuing Education, Western New Mexico University, PO Box 680, Silver City, NM 88062. *Telephone:* 505-538-6130. *Fax:* 505-538-6155.

INDIVIDUAL COURSE SUBJECT AREAS

Undergraduate
Education; English as a second language (ESL); English language and literature

Graduate
Education; English as a second language (ESL)

WESTERN OKLAHOMA STATE COLLEGE

Altus, Oklahoma

Information Services

Western Oklahoma State College, founded in 1926, is a state-supported two-year college. It is accredited by the North Central Association of Colleges and Schools. It first offered distance learning courses in 1976. In 1996–97, it offered 4 courses at a distance. In the fall of 1996, there was a total of 100 students enrolled in distance learning courses.
Course delivery sites Courses are delivered to your home, military bases, area high schools.
Media Courses are delivered via videotapes, videoconferencing, audioconferencing, print. Students and teachers interact via videoconferencing, audioconferencing, mail, telephone, fax, e-mail.
Services Distance learners have access to library services at a distance.
Credit-earning options Students may transfer credits from another institution or may earn credits through examinations, military training.
Typical costs Tuition of $38.35 per credit hour plus mandatory fees of $20 per credit hour for in-state residents. Tuition of $98.35 per credit hour plus mandatory fees of $20 per credit hour for out-of-state residents. *Noncredit courses:* $35 per course. Financial aid is available to distance learners.
Registration Students may register by mail, phone.
Contact Kent Brooks, Dean of Information Service and Distance Education, Western Oklahoma State College, 2801 North Main, Altus, OK 73521. *Telephone:* 405-477-7764. *Fax:* 405-477-7777. *E-mail:* kent@western.cc.ok.us.

DEGREE & CERTIFICATE PROGRAMS

Associate Degrees
▶ *General Studies (AA)*
In the fall of 1996 there were 13 students enrolled in this program. In 1995–96, 5 degrees were earned at a distance through this program.
Restrictions Program is offered to incarcerated students only.
Application requirements *Prior education:* high school diploma or equivalent. *Other requirements:* high school transcript.
Completion requirements 62 are required.
Program contact Larry Paxton, Director of Admissions and Registrar, Western Oklahoma State College, 2801 North Main, Altus, OK 73521. Phone: 405-477-7720. Fax: 405-477-7777.

INDIVIDUAL COURSE SUBJECT AREAS

Undergraduate
Biology; botany; business; business administration and management; chemistry; developmental and child psychology; economics; English composition; English language and literature; European languages and literatures; fine arts; geology; health and physical education/fitness; history; liberal arts, general studies, and humanities; mathematics; music; philosophy and religion; political science; psychology; sociology; zoology

Profiles: Western Oregon University

WESTERN OREGON UNIVERSITY

Monmouth, Oregon

Division of Continuing Education

Western Oregon University, founded in 1856, is a state-supported comprehensive institution. It is accredited by the Northwest Association of Schools and Colleges. It first offered distance learning courses in 1976.
Course delivery sites Courses are delivered to your home, other colleges.
Media Courses are delivered via videotapes, videoconferencing, World Wide Web, print. Students and teachers interact via videoconferencing, audioconferencing, mail, telephone, fax, e-mail.
Services Distance learners have access to library services, academic advising at a distance.
Credit-earning options Students may transfer credits from another institution or may earn credits through examinations, military training.
Typical costs *Undergraduate:* Tuition of $90 per credit hour. *Graduate:* Tuition of $120 per credit hour. Financial aid is available to distance learners.
Contact Division of Continuing Education and Summer Programs, Western Oregon University, 345 North Monmouth Avenue, Monmouth, OR 97361-1394. *Telephone:* 503-838-8483. *Fax:* 503-838-8473. *E-mail:* cesum@fsa.wou.edu.

DEGREE & CERTIFICATE PROGRAMS

Baccalaureate Degrees

▶ *Fire Services Administration (BA, BS)*
Restrictions Program is available to students in OR, WA, CO, MT, WY, UT, HI, AK, and ID only.
Application requirements 24 quarter credits in Fire Science.
Completion requirements 186 hours are required. 45 hours must be completed through the institution. This is a degree completion program.

Undergraduate Certificates

▶ *Fire Services Administration*
Restrictions Program is available to students in OR, WA, CO, MT, WY, UT, HI, AK, and ID only.
Application requirements 24 quarter credits in Fire Science.
Completion requirements 30 hours are required. 30 hours must be completed through the institution.

INDIVIDUAL COURSE SUBJECT AREAS

Undergraduate

Business communications; computer and information sciences; psychology; social psychology; social sciences; teacher education

Graduate

Psychology; social sciences; teacher education

WESTERN WASHINGTON UNIVERSITY

Bellingham, Washington

University Extended Programs

Western Washington University, founded in 1893, is a state-supported comprehensive institution. It is accredited by the Northwest Association of Schools and Colleges. It first offered distance learning courses in 1912. In 1996–97, it offered 90 courses at a distance. In the fall of 1996, there was a total of 300 students enrolled in distance learning courses.
Course delivery sites Courses are delivered to your home.
Media Courses are delivered via videotapes, audiotapes, computer software, print. Students and teachers interact via mail, telephone, fax, e-mail.
Services Distance learners have access to library services at a distance.
Credit-earning options Students may transfer credits from another institution.
Typical costs Tuition of $60 per credit. $15 registration fee. Costs may vary by number of credits taken.
Registration Students may register by mail, fax, phone.
Contact Independent Learning, Western Washington University, Bellingham, WA 98225-9042. *Telephone:* 360-650-3650. *Fax:* 360-650-6858. *E-mail:* ilearn@cc.wwu.edu. *Web site:* http://www.wwu.edu/~extended/.

INDIVIDUAL COURSE SUBJECT AREAS

Undergraduate

Algebra; American (US) history; American literature; anthropology; Asian studies; calculus; Canadian studies; creative writing; curriculum and instruction; developmental and child psychology; economics; education administration; English language and literature; English literature; history; music; sociology; statistics; women's studies

WESTMORELAND COUNTY COMMUNITY COLLEGE

Youngwood, Pennsylvania

Learning Resources

Westmoreland County Community College, founded in 1970, is a county-supported two-year college. It is accredited by the Middle States Association of Colleges and Schools. It first offered distance learning courses in 1987. In 1996–97, it offered 40 courses at a distance. In the fall of 1996, there was a total of 900 students enrolled in distance learning courses.
Course delivery sites Courses are delivered to your home, your workplace, 4 off-campus centers in Latrobe, Lower Burrell, Penn Township, Rostrauer Township.
Media Courses are delivered via videotapes, videoconferencing, audiotapes. Students and teachers interact via videoconferencing, telephone, fax.
Services Distance learners have access to library services, academic advising, tutoring, career placement assistance at a distance.
Credit-earning options Students may transfer credits from another institution or may earn credits through standardized exams, institutionally developed exams, portfolio assessment, military training.
Typical costs Tuition of $43 per credit for local area residents. Tuition of $86 per credit for in-state residents. Tuition of $172 per credit for out-of-state residents. Financial aid is available to distance learners enrolled full-time or part-time.
Registration Students may register by mail, fax, phone.
Contact Dr. Mary J. Stubbs, Director, Learning Resources/Special Projects, Westmoreland County Community College, 400 Armbrust Road, Youngwood, PA 15697. *Telephone:* 412-925-4097. *Fax:* 412-925-1150. *E-mail:* stubbsms@wccc.westmoreland.cc.pa.us.

INDIVIDUAL COURSE SUBJECT AREAS

Undergraduate

Biology; business; business administration and management; creative writing; developmental and child psychology; economics; educational psychology; English language and literature; geology; health and physical education/fitness; history; law and legal studies; liberal arts, general studies, and humanities; mathematics; philosophy and religion; physical sciences; physics; political science; social psychology; sociology

WEST VALLEY COLLEGE

Saratoga, California

West Valley College, founded in 1963, is a state and locally supported two-year college. It is accredited by the Western Association of Schools and Colleges, Inc. It first offered distance learning courses in 1985.
Course delivery sites Courses are delivered to your home.
Media Courses are delivered via television, videotapes, videoconferencing, computer software, computer conferencing.
Restrictions Programs are available to local area students only.
Credit-earning options Students may transfer credits from another institution or may earn credits through examinations. Financial aid is available to distance learners.
Contact Media Specialist, West Valley College, Instructional Development Services, 14000 Fruitvale Avenue, Saratoga, CA 95070. *Telephone:* 408-867-4711. *Fax:* 408-741-2134.

INDIVIDUAL COURSE SUBJECT AREAS

Undergraduate
Anthropology; business administration and management; developmental and child psychology; English composition; European languages and literatures; fine arts; geology; health and physical education/fitness; health professions and related sciences

WEST VIRGINIA GRADUATE COLLEGE

South Charleston, West Virginia

Information Technology

West Virginia Graduate College, founded in 1972, is a state-supported graduate institution. It is accredited by the North Central Association of Colleges and Schools. It first offered distance learning courses in 1987. In 1996–97, it offered 10 courses at a distance. In the fall of 1996, there was a total of 150 students enrolled in distance learning courses.
Course delivery sites Courses are delivered to your home, your workplace, other colleges, 3 off-campus centers in Beckley, Bluefield, Lewisburg, hospitals.
Media Courses are delivered via television, videotapes, videoconferencing, audioconferencing, e-mail. Students and teachers interact via videoconferencing, audioconferencing, mail, telephone, fax, e-mail. A computer is required for some courses.
Services Distance learners have access to library services, the campus computer network, e-mail services, academic advising at a distance.
Credit-earning options Students may transfer credits from another institution or may earn credits through institutionally developed exams.
Typical costs Tuition of $88 per semester hour for in-state residents. Tuition of $322 per semester hour for out-of-state residents. Costs may vary by campus or location, specific program of study. Financial aid is available to distance learners enrolled full-time or part-time.
Registration Students may register by mail, phone.
Contact Kenneth O'Neal, Director, Admissions and Records, West Virginia Graduate College, 100 Angus E. Peyton Drive, South Charleston, WV 25303-1600. *Telephone:* 304-746-2500. *E-mail:* koneal@wvgc.edu.

INDIVIDUAL COURSE SUBJECT AREAS

Graduate
Education; education administration; environmental engineering; history; history of science and technology; information sciences and systems

WEST VIRGINIA UNIVERSITY

Morgantown, West Virginia

Extended Learning

West Virginia University, founded in 1867, is a state-supported university. It is accredited by the North Central Association of Colleges and Schools. It first offered distance learning courses in 1972.
Course delivery sites Courses are delivered to your home, other colleges.
Media Courses are delivered via television, videotapes, videoconferencing, audiographics conferencing, computer conferencing.
Restrictions Programs are available to in-state students only.
Services Distance learners have access to library services, tutoring at a distance.
Credit-earning options Students may transfer credits from another institution or may earn credits through examinations, portfolio assessment, military training, business training. Financial aid is available to distance learners.
Contact Director, West Virginia University, West Everly Street, PO Box 6800, Morgantown, WV 26506-6800. *Telephone:* 304-293-3852. *Fax:* 304-293-4895. *Web site:* http://www.wvu.edu/~exlearn.

DEGREE & CERTIFICATE PROGRAMS

Graduate Degrees
▶ *Nursing (MSN)*
Program contact Jacqueline Riley, Assistant Dean for Student Affairs, West Virginia University, PO Box 9600, School of Nursing, Morgantown, WV 26506. Phone: 304-293-1386. Fax: 304-293-6826. E-mail: jriley@wvusonl.hsc.wvu.edu.

▶ *Special Education (MA)*
Application requirements 2.75 GPA, teaching certification in early or elementary education.
Program contact Michael Caruso, Assistant Professor, West Virginia University, PO Box 6122, Morgantown, WV 26506-6122. Phone: 304-293-3983. Fax: 304-293-7388.

INDIVIDUAL COURSE SUBJECT AREAS

Undergraduate
Astronomy and astrophysics; biology; developmental and child psychology; economics; English composition; English language and literature; history; liberal arts, general studies, and humanities; mathematics; music; social psychology; sociology

Graduate
Business administration and management; chemical engineering; environmental engineering; European languages and literatures; geology; health and physical education/fitness; public health; social work; special education

Noncredit
Mathematics

Profiles: West Virginia University Institute of Technology

WEST VIRGINIA UNIVERSITY INSTITUTE OF TECHNOLOGY

Montgomery, West Virginia

Extension and Community Service

West Virginia University Institute of Technology, founded in 1895, is a state-supported comprehensive institution. It is accredited by the North Central Association of Colleges and Schools. It first offered distance learning courses in 1978. In 1996–97, it offered 50 courses at a distance. In the fall of 1996, there was a total of 600 students enrolled in distance learning courses.
Course delivery sites Courses are delivered to your home, your workplace, 2 off-campus centers in Charleston, Oak Hill.
Media Courses are delivered via television, videotapes, videoconferencing, e-mail. Students and teachers interact via videoconferencing, telephone, fax, e-mail. A computer is required for some courses.
Restrictions Programs are available to local area students only.
Services Distance learners have access to library services, the campus computer network, e-mail services, academic advising at a distance.
Credit-earning options Students may earn credits through standardized exams, portfolio assessment.
Typical costs *Undergraduate:* Tuition of $230 per course for in-state residents. Tuition of $540 per course for out-of-state residents. *Graduate:* Tuition of $245 per course for in-state residents. Tuition of $565 per course for out-of-state residents. Costs may vary by specific program of study, number of credits taken. Financial aid is available to distance learners enrolled full-time or part-time.
Registration Students may register by mail, fax, phone.
Contact Rodney Stewart, Director, West Virginia University Institute of Technology, Vining Library, Montgomery, WV 25136. *Telephone:* 304-442-3200. *Fax:* 304-442-3090. *E-mail:* rgstew@wvit.wvnet.edu. *Web site:* http://wvit.wvnet.edu.

DEGREE & CERTIFICATE PROGRAMS

Associate Degrees

▶ *Business Technology (AS)*
In the fall of 1996 there were 20 students enrolled in this program. In 1995–96, 5 degrees were earned at a distance through this program.
Application requirements *Prior education:* high school diploma or equivalent. *Other requirements:* ACT or SAT, high school transcript.
Completion requirements 64 credits are required. 15 credits must be completed through the institution. *Other requirements:* 15 of the last 24 credits must be completed through West Virginia University Institute of Technology.

Baccalaureate Degrees

▶ *Engineering (BS)*
Application requirements *Prior education:* high school diploma or equivalent. *Other requirements:* ACT or SAT, high school transcript.
Completion requirements 128 credit hours are required. 21 credit hours must be completed through the institution. *Other requirements:* 21 of the last 30 credits must be completed through West Virginia University Institute of Technology.
Program contact William Gregory, Dean of Engineering, West Virginia University Institute of Technology, Engineering Building, Montgomery, WV 25136. Phone: 304-442-3161. Fax: 304-442-1006.

▶ *Health Services Administration (BS)*
In the fall of 1996 there were 30 students enrolled in this program. In 1995–96, 10 degrees were earned at a distance through this program.
Application requirements *Prior education:* associate degree. *Other requirements:* ACT or SAT, high school transcript, college transcripts.
Completion requirements 128 credit hours are required. 21 credit hours must be completed through the institution. This is a degree completion program. *Other requirements:* 21 of the last 30 credits must be completed through West Virginia University Institute of Technology.
Program contact John David, Chair, Social Services, West Virginia University Institute of Technology, Business and Economics, Montgomery, WV 25136. Phone: 304-442-3157. Fax: 304-442-3285.

INDIVIDUAL COURSE SUBJECT AREAS

Undergraduate
Accounting; business administration and management; chemical engineering; civil engineering; electrical engineering; engineering; English composition; hospitality services management; management information systems; mechanical engineering

Graduate
Chemical engineering; civil engineering; electrical engineering; engineering; mechanical engineering

WEST VIRGINIA WESLEYAN COLLEGE

Buckhannon, West Virginia

Outreach Education

West Virginia Wesleyan College, founded in 1890, is an independent-religious comprehensive institution affiliated with the United Methodist Church. It is accredited by the North Central Association of Colleges and Schools. It first offered distance learning courses in 1975. In 1996–97, it offered 41 courses at a distance. In the fall of 1996, there was a total of 200 students enrolled in distance learning courses.
Course delivery sites Courses are delivered to your home.
Media Courses are delivered via videotapes, audiotapes, audioconferencing, computer software, print. Students and teachers interact via mail, telephone, fax, e-mail. A computer is required for some courses.
Services Distance learners have access to library services, academic advising at a distance.
Credit-earning options Students may transfer credits from another institution or may earn credits through standardized exams, portfolio assessment, military training.
Typical costs Tuition of $90 per credit hour. $180 per credit hour for full-time students. Undergraduate nursing tuition is $250 per credit hour. Financial aid is available to distance learners.
Registration Students may register by mail, fax, phone, e-mail.
Contact Jennifer Bunner, Supervisor of Outreach Education, RN Outreach and Testing, West Virginia Wesleyan College, 59 College Avenue, Buckhannon, WV 26201. *Telephone:* 304-473-8430. *Fax:* 304-473-8429. *E-mail:* outreach@admin.wvwc.edu.

DEGREE & CERTIFICATE PROGRAMS

Baccalaureate Degrees

▶ *Nursing (BSN)*
In the fall of 1996 there were 50 students enrolled in this program. In 1995–96, 3 degrees were earned at a distance through this program.
Restrictions This program is available to in-state students only.
Application requirements *Prior education:* RN license. *Other requirements:* college transcripts, an application fee of $25.
Completion requirements 128 quarter credits are required. 25 semester credits must be completed through the institution.
On-campus requirements One-day seminars for each of the seven nursing courses.

Undergraduate Certificates
▶ *Business Principles*
In the fall of 1996 there was 1 student enrolled in this program.
Application requirements *Prior education:* high school diploma or equivalent. *Other requirements:* high school transcript.
Completion requirements 18 semester hours are required. 18 semester hours must be completed through the institution.
Program contact Brian Williams, Supervisor of Outreach Education, West Virginia Wesleyan College, 59 College Avenue, Buckhannon, WV 26201. Phone: 304-473-8430. Fax: 304-473-8429. E-mail: outreach@admin.wvwc.edu.

INDIVIDUAL COURSE SUBJECT AREAS

Undergraduate
Accounting; area, ethnic, and cultural studies; biological and life sciences; business administration and management; business communications; criminology; English language and literature; fine arts; foods and nutrition studies; health and physical education/fitness; history; liberal arts, general studies, and humanities; marketing; music; nursing; philosophy and religion; physical sciences; political science; social psychology; sociology; women's studies

WHATCOM COMMUNITY COLLEGE

Bellingham, Washington

Whatcom Community College, founded in 1970, is a state-supported two-year college. It is accredited by the Northwest Association of Schools and Colleges. It first offered distance learning courses in 1991. In 1996–97, it offered 10 courses at a distance. In the fall of 1996, there was a total of 200 students enrolled in distance learning courses.
Course delivery sites Courses are delivered to your home.
Media Courses are delivered via videotapes, print. Students and teachers interact via mail, telephone.
Restrictions Programs are available to local area students only.
Credit-earning options Students may transfer credits from another institution or may earn credits through institutionally developed exams, portfolio assessment, military training.
Typical costs Tuition of $48 per credit plus mandatory fees of $20 per credit for in-state residents. Tuition of $185 per credit plus mandatory fees of $20 per credit for out-of-state residents. Costs may vary by number of credits taken. Financial aid is available to distance learners.
Contact Jan Hagan, Associate Dean, Admissions and Registration, Whatcom Community College, 237 West Kellogg Road, Bellingham, WA 98226. *Telephone:* 360-676-2170. *Fax:* 360-676-2171. *E-mail:* jhagan@whatcom.ctc.edu.

INDIVIDUAL COURSE SUBJECT AREAS

Undergraduate
Biology; English composition; English language and literature; geology; history; psychology; social psychology; social sciences; sociology

WHEATON COLLEGE

Wheaton, Illinois

Extension and Continuing Education

Wheaton College, founded in 1860, is an independent-religious nondenominational comprehensive institution. It is accredited by the North Central Association of Colleges and Schools. It first offered distance learning courses in 1972. In 1996–97, it offered 13 courses at a distance. In the fall of 1996, there was a total of 80 students enrolled in distance learning courses.
Course delivery sites Courses are delivered to your home.
Media Courses are delivered via audiotapes, print. Students and teachers interact via mail, fax, e-mail.
Restrictions An undergraduate degree from a regionally accredited college is required.
Services Distance learners have access to academic advising at a distance.
Typical costs Tuition of $165 per semester. *Noncredit courses:* $60 per course.
Registration Students may register by mail, fax, phone, e-mail.
Contact Douglas Milford, Coordinator, Extension Department, Wheaton College, 501 College Avenue, Wheaton, IL 60187. *Telephone:* 630-752-5944. *Fax:* 630-752-5935. *E-mail:* doug.milford@wheaton.edu. *Web site:* http://www.wheaton.edu.

Special note

Distance education courses offered through the Extension Department of the Wheaton College Graduate School can be used to meet the biblical foundations requirement in Old Testament, New Testament, and theology for all of its graduate programs.

Graduate distance education courses are available in biblical/theological studies and in missions/intercultural studies. They include Life and Teaching of Jesus, Life and Teachings of Paul, Principles of Interpretation, Systematic Theology, Contextualization of Theology, Theology of Development in World Perspective, Spiritual Conflict, China and Chinese Ministry, and Christianity and China. Course materials may also be purchased by individuals who do not wish to enroll for credit but who want to benefit from graduate-level study without the academic requirements.

Using carefully designed curricula consisting of audio cassette tapes, instruction manuals, and textbooks, nonresident students may take these courses anywhere with maximum flexibility.

Wheaton's most flexible degree (relative to time in residence) is a 36-semester-hour program leading to an MA in theology. This particular concentration enables students to take 16 hours through distance education, 8 hours through 1-week intensive courses, and 1 full semester in residence to fulfill course requirements. For all other programs, a maximum of 25% may be earned through distance education courses.

Wheaton College Graduate School offers graduate programs leading to the Master of Arts degree in biblical and theological studies, clinical psychology, educational ministries, evangelism, missions/intercultural studies, and interdisciplinary studies, as well as a Doctor of Clinical Psychology program. For further information contact: Extension Department, Wheaton College, Wheaton, IL, 60187-5593. Telephone: 800-325-8718 (toll-free). Fax: 630-752-5935. E-mail: gradexten@wheaton.edu

Profiles: Wheaton College

INDIVIDUAL COURSE SUBJECT AREAS

Graduate
Bible studies; theological studies

Noncredit
Bible studies; theological studies

WICHITA STATE UNIVERSITY

Wichita, Kansas

Media Resources Center

Wichita State University, founded in 1895, is a state-supported university. It is accredited by the North Central Association of Colleges and Schools. It first offered distance learning courses in 1982. In 1996–97, it offered 70 courses at a distance. In the fall of 1996, there was a total of 1,057 students enrolled in distance learning courses.
Course delivery sites Courses are delivered to your home, your workplace, military bases.
Media Courses are delivered via television, videotapes, videoconferencing, World Wide Web, e-mail. Students and teachers interact via videoconferencing, telephone, fax, e-mail. A computer is required for some courses.
Restrictions Programs are available to in-state students only.
Services Distance learners have access to library services, academic advising, tutoring, career placement assistance at a distance.
Credit-earning options Students may transfer credits from another institution or may earn credits through examinations, portfolio assessment.
Typical costs *Undergraduate:* Tuition of $79.30 per credit hour plus mandatory fees of $12 per credit hour for in-state residents. Tuition of $276.75 per credit hour plus mandatory fees of $12 per credit hour for out-of-state residents. *Graduate:* Tuition of $109 per credit hour plus mandatory fees of $12 per credit hour for in-state residents. Tuition of $320 per credit hour plus mandatory fees of $12 per credit hour for out-of-state residents. Financial aid is available to distance learners.
Registration Students may register by phone.
Contact Rebecca S. Wood, Telecourse Coordinator, Wichita State University, 1845 Fairmount, Media Resources Center, Wichita, KS 67260-0057. *Telephone:* 316-978-3575. *Fax:* 316-978-3560. *E-mail:* rswood@twsuvm.uc.twsu.edu. *Web site:* http://www.twsu.edu/~mrcwww.

INDIVIDUAL COURSE SUBJECT AREAS

Undergraduate
Area, ethnic, and cultural studies; astronomy and astrophysics; biology; business; business administration and management; communications; computer and information sciences; English language and literature; fine arts; geology; health professions and related sciences; history; human resources management; liberal arts, general studies, and humanities; music; nursing; physics; sociology

Graduate
Area, ethnic, and cultural studies; business; business administration and management; communications; economics; health professions and related sciences; human resources management; nursing

WILFRID LAURIER UNIVERSITY

Waterloo, Ontario, Canada

Office of Continuing Education

Wilfrid Laurier University, founded in 1911, is a province-supported comprehensive institution. It is provincially chartered. It first offered distance learning courses in 1978. In 1996–97, it offered 57 courses at a distance. In the fall of 1996, there was a total of 813 students enrolled in distance learning courses.
Course delivery sites Courses are delivered to your home.
Media Courses are delivered via television, videotapes, audiotapes, World Wide Web, print. Students and teachers interact via mail, telephone, fax, e-mail, in-person meetings. A computer is required for some courses.
Services Distance learners have access to library services, the campus computer network, e-mail services, academic advising, career placement assistance at a distance.
Credit-earning options Students may transfer credits from another institution or may earn credits through institutionally developed exams.
Typical costs Tuition of $724 per course. Non-canadian students pay $1,400 per course, all students pay $42 to $66 per course in fees. Costs may vary by number of credits taken. Financial aid is available to distance learners enrolled full-time or part-time.
Registration Students may register by mail, fax.
Contact Ms. Lynn Barrett, Office of Continuing Education, Wilfrid Laurier University, 75 University Avenue, W, Waterloo, ON N2L 3C5, Canada. *Telephone:* 519-884-1970. *Fax:* 519-884-6063. *E-mail:* lbarrett@mach1.wlu.ca. *Web site:* http://www.wlu.ca/~wwwconte.

DEGREE & CERTIFICATE PROGRAMS

Baccalaureate Degrees

▶ *Sociology (BA)*
In the fall of 1996 there were 28 students enrolled in this program. In 1995–96, 10 degrees were earned at a distance through this program.
Application requirements *Prior education:* high school diploma or equivalent. *Other requirements:* high school transcript, an application fee of $30.
Completion requirements 15 full credits are required. 5 senior credits must be completed through the institution. This is a degree completion program.
Program contact Ms. Gail Forsyth, Manager of Admissions, Wilfrid Laurier University, 75 University Avenue, W, Waterloo, ON N2L 3C5, Canada. Phone: 519-884-1970. Fax: 519-884-8826. E-mail: gforsyth@mach2.wlu.ca.

INDIVIDUAL COURSE SUBJECT AREAS

Undergraduate
Abnormal psychology; accounting; anthropology; area, ethnic, and cultural studies; biological and life sciences; biology; business; business administration and management; business law; chemistry; criminology; developmental and child psychology; economics; English language and literature; environmental science; European languages and literatures; fine arts; French language and literature; geography; geology; German language and literature; history; investments and securities; philosophy and religion; physical sciences; political science; psychology; religious studies; social sciences; social work; sociology; Spanish language and literature

WILKES COMMUNITY COLLEGE

Wilkesboro, North Carolina

Individualized Studies Department

Wilkes Community College, founded in 1965, is a state-supported two-year college. It is accredited by the Southern Association of Colleges and Schools. It first offered distance learning courses in 1984. In 1996–97, it offered 42 courses at a distance. In the fall of 1996, there was a total of 450 students enrolled in distance learning courses.
Course delivery sites Courses are delivered to your home, 2 off-campus centers in Sparta, West Jefferson.
Media Courses are delivered via videotapes. Students and teachers interact via telephone, in-person meetings. A computer is required for some courses.
Restrictions Programs are available to in-state students only.
Services Distance learners have access to library services, academic advising, tutoring, career placement assistance at a distance.
Credit-earning options Students may transfer credits from another institution or may earn credits through institutionally developed exams.
Typical costs Tuition of $13.25 per credit for in-state residents. Tuition of $107.50 per credit for out-of-state residents. Students taking 14 or more credits pay the price of 14 credits. *Noncredit courses:* $35 per course. Financial aid is available to distance learners.
Contact Nithi Klinkosum, Director, Individualized Studies and Distance Learning, Wilkes Community College, PO Box 120, Wilkesboro, NC 28697. *Telephone:* 910-838-6121. *Fax:* 910-838-6277. *E-mail:* klinkosn@wilkes.cc.nc.us. *Web site:* http://www.wilkes.cc.nc.us.

INDIVIDUAL COURSE SUBJECT AREAS

Undergraduate
Biology; business; business administration and management; economics; history; law and legal studies; liberal arts, general studies, and humanities; mathematics; microbiology; psychology; sociology

WILLIAM PENN COLLEGE

Oskaloosa, Iowa

William Penn College, founded in 1873, is an independent-religious four-year college affiliated with the Society of Friends. It is accredited by the North Central Association of Colleges and Schools. It first offered distance learning courses in 1994. In 1996–97, it offered 4 courses at a distance. In the fall of 1996, there was a total of 53 students enrolled in distance learning courses.
Course delivery sites Courses are delivered to Iowa Communications Network (ICN) sites.
Media Courses are delivered via videoconferencing. Students and teachers interact via videoconferencing, mail, telephone, fax, e-mail.
Restrictions Programs are available to in-state students only.
Services Distance learners have access to library services, the campus computer network, e-mail services, academic advising at a distance.
Credit-earning options Students may transfer credits from another institution or may earn credits through examinations.
Typical costs Tuition of $250 per course. High school students are charged $250 per course. Financial aid is available to distance learners.
Registration Students may register by mail, fax, phone, e-mail.
Contact Jim Knutson, ICN Coordinator, William Penn College, 201 Trueblood Avenue, Wilcox Library, Oskaloosa, IA 52577. *Telephone:* 515-673-1096. *Fax:* 515-673-1098. *E-mail:* knutsonj@wmpenn.edu.

INDIVIDUAL COURSE SUBJECT AREAS

Undergraduate
Computer and information sciences; developmental and child psychology; English composition; European history; geography; history; mathematics; sociology

WILLIAM RAINEY HARPER COLLEGE

Palatine, Illinois

Learning Resource Center

William Rainey Harper College, founded in 1965, is a state and locally supported two-year college. It is accredited by the North Central Association of Colleges and Schools. It first offered distance learning courses in 1984. In 1996–97, it offered 27 courses at a distance. In the fall of 1996, there was a total of 825 students enrolled in distance learning courses.
Course delivery sites Courses are delivered to College of Lake County (Grayslake), Oakton Community College (Des Plaines), hospitals.
Media Courses are delivered via television, computer software, World Wide Web, e-mail. Students and teachers interact via videoconferencing, telephone, fax, e-mail. A computer is required for some courses.
Restrictions Telecourses are available to local area students only.
Services Distance learners have access to library services at a distance.
Credit-earning options Students may transfer credits from another institution or may earn credits through standardized exams, institutionally developed exams.
Typical costs Tuition of $46 per credit hour for local area residents. Tuition of $159.65 per credit hour for in-state residents. Tuition of $205.65 per credit hour for out-of-state residents. *Noncredit courses:* $10 per seminar; $50–$90 for CE. Costs may vary by campus or location, number of credits taken. Financial aid is available to distance learners enrolled full-time or part-time.
Registration Students may register by phone.
Contact Dr. Lee Vogel, Dean, Learning Resource Center, William Rainey Harper College, 1200 West Algonquin Road, Palatine, IL 60067-7398. *Telephone:* 847-925-6550. *Fax:* 847-925-6037. *E-mail:* lvogel@harper.cc.il.us.

INDIVIDUAL COURSE SUBJECT AREAS

Undergraduate
Accounting; administrative and secretarial services; architecture; Asian languages and literatures; business; business administration and management; developmental and child psychology; economics; health and physical education/fitness; history; hospitality services management; law and legal studies; liberal arts, general studies, and humanities; Middle Eastern languages and literatures; philosophy and religion; social sciences; sociology

Noncredit
Nursing

WILSON TECHNICAL COMMUNITY COLLEGE

Wilson, North Carolina

Wilson Technical Community College, founded in 1958, is a state-supported two-year college. It is accredited by the Southern Association of Colleges and Schools. It first offered distance learning courses in

Profiles: Wilson Technical Community College

1989. In 1996–97, it offered 9 courses at a distance. In the fall of 1996, there was a total of 40 students enrolled in distance learning courses.
Course delivery sites Courses are delivered to your home.
Media Courses are delivered via television, videotapes, print. Students and teachers interact via mail, telephone, fax.
Restrictions Students must be able to travel to campus.
Services Distance learners have access to academic advising, career placement assistance at a distance.
Credit-earning options Students may transfer credits from another institution or may earn credits through examinations, portfolio assessment, military training, business training.
Typical costs Tuition of $20.75 per credit hour for in-state residents. Tuition of $163.75 per credit hour for out-of-state residents. *Noncredit courses:* $25–$35 per course. Financial aid is available to distance learners enrolled full-time or part-time.
Contact Lorraine Raper, Business Department Chairperson, Wilson Technical Community College, 902 Herring Avenue, Wilson, NC 27893. *Telephone:* 919-291-1195. *Fax:* 919-243-7148. *Web site:* http://www.wilsontech.cc.nc.us.

INDIVIDUAL COURSE SUBJECT AREAS

Undergraduate
Accounting; administrative and secretarial services; business; business administration and management; business law; economics; English language and literature; human resources management; psychology

WINTHROP UNIVERSITY

Rock Hill, South Carolina

College of Business Administration

Winthrop University, founded in 1886, is a state-supported comprehensive institution. It is accredited by the Southern Association of Colleges and Schools. It first offered distance learning courses in 1994. In 1996–97, it offered 19 courses at a distance. In the fall of 1996, there was a total of 70 students enrolled in distance learning courses.
Course delivery sites Courses are delivered to Coastal Carolina University (Conway), high schools.
Media Courses are delivered via television, videotapes, videoconferencing, audiotapes, computer software, World Wide Web, e-mail, print. Students and teachers interact via videoconferencing, mail, telephone, fax, e-mail.
Services Distance learners have access to library services, e-mail services, academic advising at a distance.
Credit-earning options Students may earn credits through examinations.
Typical costs Contact university for details.
Registration Students may register by mail, fax, phone, e-mail.
Contact Peggy Hager, Director of Graduate Studies, Winthrop University, 227 Thurmond Building, Rock Hill, SC 29733. *Telephone:* 803-323-2186. *Fax:* 803-323-2539.

INDIVIDUAL COURSE SUBJECT AREAS

Undergraduate
Biology; English language and literature; history

Graduate
Accounting; business; business administration and management; business communications; finance; human resources management; management information systems; marketing; organizational behavior studies

WORCESTER POLYTECHNIC INSTITUTE

Worcester, Massachusetts

Advanced Distance Learning Network

Worcester Polytechnic Institute, founded in 1865, is an independent-nonprofit university. It is accredited by the New England Association of Schools and Colleges. It first offered distance learning courses in 1979. In 1996–97, it offered 14 courses at a distance. In the fall of 1996, there was a total of 80 students enrolled in distance learning courses.
Course delivery sites Courses are delivered to your home, your workplace, other colleges.
Media Courses are delivered via videotapes, videoconferencing, World Wide Web, e-mail, print. Students and teachers interact via videoconferencing, audioconferencing, mail, telephone, fax, e-mail. A computer is required for some courses.
Services Distance learners have access to library services, the campus computer network, e-mail services, academic advising, career placement assistance at a distance.
Credit-earning options Students may transfer credits from another institution.
Typical costs *Undergraduate:* Tuition of $1500 per course. *Graduate:* Tuition of $1770 per course. Costs may vary by campus or location. Financial aid is available to distance learners enrolled full-time.
Registration Students may register by mail, fax, phone, e-mail.
Contact Pennie S. Turgeon, Director, Instructional Media Center, Worcester Polytechnic Institute, 100 Institute Road, Worcester, MA 01609. *Telephone:* 508-831-5810. *Fax:* 508-831-5881. *E-mail:* pennie@wpi.edu. *Web site:* http://www.wpi.edu/Academics/ADLN.

DEGREE & CERTIFICATE PROGRAMS

Graduate Degrees

▶ *Business Administration (MBA)*
In the fall of 1996 there were 36 students enrolled in this program. In 1995–96, 5 degrees were earned at a distance through this program.
Application requirements *Prior education:* baccalaureate degree. *Other requirements:* GMAT, TOEFL (for international applicants), college transcripts, an essay or personal statement, letter(s) of recommendation, an application fee of $50.
Completion requirements 49 credits are required. 22 must be completed through the institution. *Maximum time for completion:* eight years.
Program contact Norman Wilkinson, Director, Graduate Management Programs, Worcester Polytechnic Institute, 100 Institute Road, Worcester, MA 01609. Phone: 508-831-5218. Fax: 508-831-5720. E-mail: nwilkins@wpi.edu.

▶ *Marketing and Technological Innovation, Operations and Information Technology (MSM)*
In the fall of 1996 there were 12 students enrolled in this program. In 1995–96, 2 degrees were earned at a distance through this program.
Application requirements *Prior education:* baccalaureate degree. *Other requirements:* GMAT or GRE, TOEFL (for international applicants), college transcripts, an essay or personal statement, letter(s) of recommendation, an application fee of $50.
Completion requirements 30 credits are required. 21 credits must be completed through the institution. *Maximum time for completion:* eight years.
Program contact Norman Wilkinson, Director, Graduate Management Programs, Worcester Polytechnic Institute, 100 Institute Road, Worcester, MA 01609. Phone: 508-831-5218. Fax: 508-831-5720. E-mail: nwilkins@wpi.edu.

Graduate certificates

▶ *Fire Protection Engineering*
In the fall of 1996 there were 25 students enrolled in this program.
Application requirements *Prior education:* Bachelor's degree in any field of engineering or the sciences. *Other requirements:* college transcripts, an application fee of $50.
Completion requirements *Maximum time for completion:* four years.

▶ *Management*
In the fall of 1996 there were 6 students enrolled in this program.
Application requirements *Prior education:* baccalaureate degree. *Other requirements:* college transcripts, an application fee of $50.
Completion requirements 15 credits are required. 15 credits must be completed through the institution. *Maximum time for completion:* four years.
Program contact Norman Wilkinson, Director, Graduate Management Programs, Worcester Polytechnic Institute, 100 Institute Road, Worcester, MA 01609. Phone: 508-831-5218. Fax: 508-831-5720. E-mail: nwilkins@wpi.edu.

INDIVIDUAL COURSE SUBJECT AREAS

Undergraduate
Economics; engineering/industrial management

Graduate
Accounting; business; business administration and management; computer and information sciences; economics; engineering/industrial management; fire science; human resources management; law and legal studies

See full description on page 530.

WRIGHT STATE UNIVERSITY

Dayton, Ohio

Television Center

Wright State University, founded in 1964, is a state-supported university. It is accredited by the North Central Association of Colleges and Schools. It first offered distance learning courses in 1995. In 1996–97, it offered 10 courses at a distance. In the fall of 1996, there was a total of 60 students enrolled in distance learning courses.
Course delivery sites Courses are delivered to military bases, The Ohio State University (Columbus), University of Cincinnati (Cincinnati), University of Dayton (Dayton), branch campus in Celina, OH.
Media Courses are delivered via videoconferencing, audioconferencing, computer software, e-mail. Students and teachers interact via videoconferencing, fax, e-mail.
Restrictions Some courses available to students at branch campus or Ohio Aerospace institutions only.
Services Distance learners have access to library services, the campus computer network, e-mail services, academic advising at a distance.
Credit-earning options Students may transfer credits from another institution or may earn credits through institutionally developed exams.
Typical costs *Undergraduate:* Tuition of $115 per credit hour for in-state residents. Tuition of $230 per credit hour for out-of-state residents. *Graduate:* Tuition of $148 per credit hour for in-state residents. Tuition of $273 per credit hour for out-of-state residents. Costs may vary by specific program of study, number of credits taken. Financial aid is available to distance learners.
Registration Students may register by mail, phone.
Contact George Frey, Director, Television Center, Wright State University, 104 TV Center, Dayton, OH 45435. *Telephone:* 937-775-3685. *Fax:* 937-775-4891. *E-mail:* gfrey@wright.edu. *Web site:* http://www.wright.edu.

INDIVIDUAL COURSE SUBJECT AREAS

Undergraduate
Education; electrical engineering; English language and literature; mechanical engineering; nursing; philosophy and religion

WYTHEVILLE COMMUNITY COLLEGE

Wytheville, Virginia

Division of Business, Humanities and Social Science

Wytheville Community College, founded in 1967, is a state-supported two-year college. It is accredited by the Southern Association of Colleges and Schools. It first offered distance learning courses in 1981. In 1996–97, it offered 30 courses at a distance. In the fall of 1996, there was a total of 425 students enrolled in distance learning courses.
Course delivery sites Courses are delivered to your home, your workplace, 2 off-campus centers in Atkins, Galax, regional sites.
Media Courses are delivered via television, videotapes, videoconferencing, audiotapes, computer software, print. Students and teachers interact via videoconferencing, mail, fax, e-mail. A computer is required for some courses.
Restrictions Courses are available to regional area students only.
Services Distance learners have access to library services, academic advising, tutoring at a distance.
Credit-earning options Students may transfer credits from another institution or may earn credits through standardized exams, institutionally developed exams, portfolio assessment, military training, business training.
Typical costs Tuition of $46.65 per credit plus mandatory fees of $1.50 per credit for in-state residents. Tuition of $156 per credit plus mandatory fees of $1.50 per credit for out-of-state residents. Costs may vary by number of credits taken.
Registration Students may register by mail, fax.
Contact Dr. David N. Johnson, Director of Continuing Education, Wytheville Community College, 1000 East Main Street, Wytheville, VA 24382. *Telephone:* 540-223-4711. *Fax:* 540-223-4716. *E-mail:* wcjohnd@wc.cc.va.us.

INDIVIDUAL COURSE SUBJECT AREAS

Undergraduate
Accounting; American (US) history; biology; business; business administration and management; developmental and child psychology; economics; education; electronics; fine arts; health and physical education/fitness; marketing; philosophy and religion; political science; social sciences

XAVIER UNIVERSITY OF LOUISIANA

New Orleans, Louisiana

Drexel Center for Extended Learning

Xavier University of Louisiana, founded in 1925, is an independent-religious Roman Catholic comprehensive institution. It is accredited by

Profiles: Xavier University of Louisiana

the Southern Association of Colleges and Schools. It first offered distance learning courses in 1989.

Course delivery sites Courses are delivered to your home, your workplace.

Media Courses are delivered via television, videotapes, videoconferencing, print.

Restrictions Programs are available to local area students only. Financial aid is available to distance learners.

Contact Program/Marketing Director, Xavier University of Louisiana, 7325 Palmetto Street, New Orleans, LA 70125. *Telephone:* 504-483-7376. *Fax:* 504-486-2108.

INDIVIDUAL COURSE SUBJECT AREAS

Undergraduate

Area, ethnic, and cultural studies; business; business administration and management; economics; law and legal studies; political science; sociology

YORK TECHNICAL COLLEGE

Rock Hill, South Carolina

Distance Learning Department

York Technical College, founded in 1961, is a state-supported two-year college. It is accredited by the Southern Association of Colleges and Schools. It first offered distance learning courses in 1995. In 1996–97, it offered 18 courses at a distance. In the fall of 1996, there was a total of 200 students enrolled in distance learning courses.

Course delivery sites Courses are delivered to your home, your workplace, other colleges, 3 off-campus centers in Chester, Rock Hill.

Media Courses are delivered via television, videotapes, print. Students and teachers interact via videoconferencing, mail, telephone, fax, e-mail.

Restrictions Students must be close enough for the school to be able to monitor telecourse assessments.

Services Distance learners have access to library services, the campus computer network, e-mail services at a distance.

Credit-earning options Students may transfer credits from another institution or may earn credits through standardized exams, institutionally developed exams.

Typical costs Tuition of $36 per credit for local area residents. Tuition of $47 per credit for in-state residents. Tuition of $128 per credit for out-of-state residents. *Noncredit courses:* $55-$100 per course. Costs may vary by campus or location, number of credits taken. Financial aid is available to distance learners enrolled full-time or part-time.

Registration Students may register by mail, fax, phone, e-mail, World Wide Web.

Contact Anita Armfield, Department Manager, Distance Learning, York Technical College, 452 South Anderson Road, Rock Hill, SC 29730. *Telephone:* 803-981-7044. *Fax:* 803-981-7193. *E-mail:* armfield@york.tec.sc.us.

INDIVIDUAL COURSE SUBJECT AREAS

Undergraduate

Accounting; administrative and secretarial services; business administration and management; developmental and child psychology; electrical engineering; engineering-related technologies; English composition; history; industrial engineering; liberal arts, general studies, and humanities

YUBA COLLEGE

Marysville, California

Learning Resource Center

Yuba College, founded in 1927, is a state and locally supported two-year college. It is accredited by the Western Association of Schools and Colleges, Inc. It first offered distance learning courses in 1975. In 1996–97, it offered 37 courses at a distance.

Course delivery sites Courses are delivered to your home, your workplace, military bases, 2 off-campus centers in Colusa, Live Oak, District high schools/special education centers/elementary schools, branch campuses in Woodland and Clear Lake, California.

Media Courses are delivered via television, videotapes, videoconferencing. Students and teachers interact via videoconferencing, mail, telephone, fax, e-mail.

Restrictions Programs are available to local area students only. Students must be able to receive television signal.

Services Distance learners have access to library services, academic advising, career placement assistance at a distance.

Credit-earning options Students may transfer credits from another institution or may earn credits through institutionally developed exams.

Typical costs *Undergraduate:* Tuition of $13 per unit plus mandatory fees of $11 per semester for in-state residents. Tuition of $138 per unit plus mandatory fees of $11 per semester for out-of-state residents. *Graduate:* Tuition of $13 per unit plus mandatory fees of $11 per semester for in-state residents. Tuition of $138 per unit plus mandatory fees of $11 per semester for out-of-state residents. *Noncredit courses:* $12–$75 per course. Costs may vary by number of credits taken. Financial aid is available to distance learners.

Contact Jeanette O'Bryan, Distance Learning Assistant, Yuba College, 2088 North Beale Road, Marysville, CA 95901. *Telephone:* 916-741-6754. *Fax:* 916-741-6824.

INDIVIDUAL COURSE SUBJECT AREAS

Undergraduate

Algebra; animal sciences; anthropology; area, ethnic, and cultural studies; astronomy and astrophysics; business administration and management; calculus; child care and development; Classical languages and literatures; creative writing; education; electronics; English as a second language (ESL); English language and literature; film studies; fine arts; foods and nutrition studies; health and physical education/fitness; health professions and related sciences; history; home economics and family studies; Japanese language and literature; liberal arts, general studies, and humanities; mass media; nursing; philosophy and religion; physical sciences; political science; radio and television broadcasting; social psychology; Spanish language and literature

IN-DEPTH DESCRIPTIONS

The following two-page descriptions were prepared for this book by the institutions. An institution's absence from this section does not constitute an editorial decision on the part of Peterson's. Rather, it was offered as an open forum for institutions to expand upon the information provided in the previous section of this book. The descriptions are arranged alphabetically by institution name.

Acadia University
The Division of Continuing Education and Centre for Distance Education
Wolfville, Nova Scotia, Canada

Acadia University is a fully accredited institution with a long tradition of offering accessible postsecondary education. Acadia University was founded in 1838 in response to a need to provide educational opportunities to students regardless of religious denomination. It is a member of the Association of Atlantic Universities, the Association of Universities and Colleges of Canada, and the Association of Commonwealth Universities.

Acadia University has embarked on a program that will make it the first university in Canada to apply fully the resources of today's information technology in a liberal education environment. By the year 2000, a high-end laptop computer will be a standard part of every full-time student's admission package, supported by a faculty trained in the latest application of information technology.

DISTANCE LEARNING PROGRAM

Every year, more than 2,000 students access Acadia University through the distance learning program. Acadia offers University credit courses toward degrees in all branches of university work. More than 200 curriculum combinations are available leading to degrees, diplomas, and certificates in the Faculties of Arts, Pure and Applied Science, Professional Studies, and Theology. Students may take courses from anywhere in the world.

DELIVERY MEDIA

Courses make use of the Internet and e-mail, CD-ROMs, audiographics, video conferencing, videotapes, audiocassettes, and print packages. Professors maintain regular contact with distance learners via telephone, e-mail, mail, and discussion forums. Professors are available for consultation throughout a course.

PROGRAMS OF STUDY

Through the Distance Education program, more than eighty degree-credit courses in a variety of disciplines are offered. Certificates are offered in computer science and business administration. A Diploma in Business is offered to students who have completed the Certificate in Business. All courses in diploma and certificate programs can be applied to bachelor's degrees. A description of all the programs and courses may be found at http://conted.acadiau.ca.

SPECIAL PROGRAMS

The Division of Continuing Education and Centre for Distance Education offers specialized personal and professional development programs. Customized courses and programs are developed to meet the specific training requirements of government organizations, business, and industry. Many offered courses can complete requirements for students enrolled in programs such as the Real Estate Institute of Canada, the Canadian Hospital Association, the Atlantic School of Chartered Accountants, and the Institute of Canadian Bankers. Credit and noncredit programs target professional development for teachers, counsellors, nurses, computer scientists, environmental trainers, and other professionals. In addition, a complete summer program for youth that focuses on science, technology, entrepreneurship, and music is offered.

STUDENT SERVICES

The Division of Continuing Education and Centre for Distance Education is the liaison to campus services and an advocate for students studying at a distance. Campus resources available to distance education students include the Vaughan Memorial Library, the Acadia University Bookstore, the Mature Students Association, and the Counselling Centre.

CREDIT OPTIONS

Students may transfer up to 60 credit hours required for a 120-credit-hour degree program. Students may transfer 6 credit hours of the last 60 credit hours required for their intended degree. Transfer credits normally will be given for individual courses that are applicable to the intended undergraduate degree program of study.

FACULTY

There are 250 full-time faculty members at Acadia University. Approximately 20 percent are involved in distance education, with a growing number becoming involved in electronic courseware development.

ADMISSION

Students must have a senior high school diploma or the equivalent, with an average of 70 percent or better to be accepted at Acadia. Students who do not meet published academic admission requirements may be considered for admission on a mature-student basis.

TUITION AND FEES

In 1997–98, undergraduate tuition is Can$407.50 for a 3-hour credit (one semester) and Can$815 for a 6-hour credit. There is a one-time admission fee of Can$25. Fees may be subject to change.

FINANCIAL AID

The Registrar's Office administers the University's financial assistance programs, which include scholarships, bursaries, emergency loans, and alumni awards and acts as a liaison between students and the various provincial student aid offices.

APPLYING

The correspondence and Internet programs are open entry; that is, students may register at any time. The audiographics program and the video program are run on the semester system and are offered in the fall/winter and spring/summer terms.

CONTACT
Dr. Nancy Van Wagoner, Director
Division of Continuing Education and Center for Distance
 Education
Acadia University
Wolfville, Nova Scotia
Canada B0P 1X0
Telephone: 902-585-1434
     800-565-6568 (toll-free in Canada)
Fax: 902-585-1068
E-mail: continuing.education@acadiau.ca

Distance Learning Programs

Antioch University

The McGregor School of Antioch University

Yellow Springs, Ohio

> *Antioch University was founded in 1852 in Yellow Springs, Ohio, as a private liberal arts college. Today, Antioch has evolved into a multicampus university of more than 4,000 students who study at The McGregor School of Antioch University and Antioch College on the Yellow Springs campus and on campuses in Seattle, Washington; Los Angeles and Santa Barbara, California; and Keene, New Hampshire. The McGregor School offers bachelor's, master's, and certificate programs that are designed to accommodate adult lifestyles. Antioch University is accredited by the North Central Association of Colleges and Schools.*

DISTANCE LEARNING PROGRAM

The Individualized Master of Arts (I.M.A.) program offers qualified students the opportunity to pursue graduate education through a limited residency program. Students use resources in their own communities while earning their master's degrees, allowing them to achieve their educational goals while meeting the professional standards of their chosen field.

DELIVERY MEDIA

Students are required to attend a week of orientation at the beginning of the program and one week of residency in the beginning of their thesis year. Both residential sessions are held on campus at The McGregor School, located on the Antioch University campus in Yellow Springs, Ohio. Students must also be prepared to seek additional means of learning within their own community, based on their chosen disciplines.

Courses are delivered to students' homes, workplaces, military bases, or other colleges. Students and instructors interact via mail, telephone, fax, and e-mail.

PROGRAMS OF STUDY

The I.M.A. program is designed specifically for adults who have extensive personal and professional experience. In addition to integrating academic theory with real-world experiences, students are expected to set their own educational and professional goals, collaboratively design programs of study, select relevant faculty members, and conceptualize and write a thesis. Each student works closely with an Antioch faculty adviser to articulate goals and to better understand the nature and standards associated with master's-level study.

The I.M.A. encourages well-formulated plans in most fields and disciplines for which Master of Arts degrees are appropriate. With the help of degree committee members and an adviser, the student designs and implements a degree in his or her professional and/or academic area of interest. I.M.A. students target concentrations within their fields of study that fit their individual backgrounds, interests, and goals and then collaboratively design individualized plans to realize their objectives. Counseling psychology, management, creative writing, environmental studies, marketing, studio art, arts administration, organizational development, gerontology, health-care administration, history, peace studies, literature, women's and men's studies, education, communication, and human resource management are some of the program's more popular fields. In addition to the fully individualized studies, students may pursue master's studies in conflict resolution and intercultural relations.

SPECIAL PROGRAMS

The conflict resolution program provides students with the theory and application of alternative dispute resolution, which they can apply to a range of social issues. By combining two intensive three-week sessions on campus with independent assignments and practica that they complete in their home communities, students master theoretical knowledge while developing and enhancing practitioner skills. Using computer technology, students participate in learning-based discussions with faculty members and other members of their cohort groups.

Intercultural relations is offered jointly with the Intercultural Communication Institute (ICI) in Portland, Oregon. With this program, students reflect upon their own intercultural experiences through the lens of theory and practical application as they explore both domestic and international cultural issues. Except for orientation and three 1- to 2-week sessions in Portland or Yellow Springs, the bulk of this two-year, limited-residency program is individually structured.

STUDENT SERVICES

Distance learners are assigned advisers who work with them to achieve their academic goals. All students of the I.M.A. may be assisted by e-mail, telephone, and fax. The learning community is further expanded, using e-mail conferencing and chat room capabilities.

CREDIT OPTIONS

Students of the I.M.A. and conflict resolution program may transfer a maximum of 15 prior learning credits completed at the graduate level into their program. Intercultural relations students may transfer a maximum of 9 prior learning credits. Credits may be earned at other accredited postsecondary institutions or may be submitted in portfolio form using the guidelines provided by The McGregor School.

FACULTY

There are 15 full-time faculty members and hundreds of adjunct faculty members devoted to the I.M.A. programs. One hundred percent of the full-time faculty members have terminal degrees.

ADMISSION

Applicants must have a bachelor's degree from a regionally accredited U.S. institution of higher learning or its equivalent as recognized by AACRAO, a clear sense of educational direction, and the preparation, skills, and general competence that qualify a student to pursue a chosen program at the graduate level and handle the demands of an individualized, nonresidential program.

TUITION AND FEES

Tuition varies by program. For the I.M.A., it is $1438 per quarter. The conflict resolution program is $2100 per quarter, and the intercultural relations program is $1968 per quarter. Travel, lodging, and materials required for the residential portions of each program are not included in the cost of tuition.

FINANCIAL AID

Students accepted for enrollment who do not have tuition reimbursement available through their employers may be considered for federal subsidized and unsubsidized loans. To be eligible, students must be U.S. citizens or eligible noncitizens, maintain satisfactory academic progress according to the School's policy, and be considered at least half-time students.

APPLYING

Distance education students must submit an application in accordance with each program's requirements, adhering to deadlines published by the program. An educational goals statement, résumé, two letters of reference, and official documentation of the student's bachelor's degree is required. The application fee is $35.

CONTACT

Oscar Robinson, Admissions Officer
The McGregor School of Antioch University
800 Livermore Street
Yellow Springs, Ohio 45387
Telephone: 937-767-6325
Fax: 937-767-6461
E-mail: admiss@mcgregor.antioch.edu

Auburn University
Graduate Outreach Program
Auburn, Alabama

Auburn University was chartered in 1856 as the East Alabama Male College. In 1872, Auburn became a state institution—the first land-grant university in the South to be separate from a state university. Auburn University, ranked by U.S. News & World Report as the twenty-seventh-best value of national universities, is dedicated to serving the state and the nation through instruction, research, and extension. Auburn University is accredited by the Commission on Colleges of the Southern Association of Colleges and Schools.

The campus consists of more than 1,800 acres, with a student body of approximately 21,500. Auburn University, the largest school in the state of Alabama, is located in east-central Alabama. The city of Auburn has a population of about 35,000. Auburn is known for its small-town, friendly atmosphere and is often referred to as "the loveliest village on the Plain."

DISTANCE LEARNING PROGRAM

In response to industry's request, Auburn's College of Engineering began offering courses to off-campus students through the Graduate Outreach Program in 1984. The College of Business made Master of Business Administration (M.B.A.) courses available in 1990. The Graduate Outreach Program allows professionals the opportunity to continue their education while maintaining full-time employment. The program serves more than 500 students in forty states. The engineering programs are fully accredited by the Accreditation Board for Engineering and Technology, and the M.B.A. program is accredited by the American Assembly of Collegiate Schools of Business.

DELIVERY MEDIA

The Graduate Outreach Program makes every effort to ensure that the off-campus students receive the same high-quality education as on-campus students. Live classes are videotaped daily and distributed in standard VHS format. Professors establish telephone office hours and/or e-mail communication so that off-campus students may receive answers to any questions they may have. E-mail accounts are established for the Graduate Outreach Program students. Some faculty members also utilize the Internet to post handouts and class materials.

PROGRAMS OF STUDY

The Graduate Outreach Program offers master's degrees in eight different disciplines in engineering and the Master of Business Administration degree. The Master of Aerospace Engineering, Chemical Engineering, Civil Engineering, Computer Science and Engineering, Industrial and Systems Engineering, Materials Engineering, and Mechanical Engineering are all nonthesis programs without residency requirements. Each candidate must pass an on-campus, comprehensive, oral examination covering the program of study. The examination covers the major and minor subjects, including any research or special projects involved. The Master of Science degree, offered in seven disciplines, requires a formal written thesis and at least one quarter of full-time residence.

In the Master of Business Administration program, students may earn a concentration in either finance, human resource management, marketing, operations management, management information systems, or management of technology. The program consists of 58 to 88 quarter hours of course work, including a minimum of 12 elective hours for the concentration. Applicants are encouraged to complete a course in calculus and statistics prior to entering the program. Incoming students are also advised to have a working knowledge of word processing and spreadsheet software and an elementary understanding of database applications. M.B.A. students must visit the campus for several days during their last quarter prior to graduating for on-campus presentations.

Nondegree professional development courses are available for those who need to meet job requirements or professional certification.

SPECIAL PROGRAMS

Career and job placement assistance is available through Auburn University's Career and Student Development Services. Accessibility to the R. B. Draughon Library is also available. A valid Auburn University student identification card is required to check out resources. The Division of University Computing provides University-wide computing and networking services to students. Computer accounts are free of charge to currently enrolled students.

CREDIT OPTIONS

Graduate credit taken in residence at another approved graduate school may be transferred to Auburn University but is not accepted until the student has completed at least 15 hours of work in the Graduate School at Auburn University. No prior commitment is made concerning whether transfer credit will be accepted. A student must earn at least 35 quarter hours or half of the total hours required for a master's degree (whichever is greater) at Auburn University. No transfer credit is approved without two official transcripts. No course in which a grade lower than B was earned may be transferred.

FACULTY

The Auburn University faculty consists of more than 1,200 members. Eighty percent of the faculty members hold a doctoral degree, and 88 percent hold a terminal degree in their field.

ADMISSION

An applicant to the Graduate School must hold a bachelor's degree or its equivalent from an accredited college or university. The Graduate Record Examinations (GRE) is required for admission to the College of Engineering, and the Graduate Management Admission Test (GMAT) is required for admission to the M.B.A. program. Admission is based on the grade point average of university-level courses, GRE or GMAT scores, and recommendation letters from instructors and supervisors.

TUITION AND FEES

The Graduate Outreach Program fees are $210–$215 per student credit hour. Registration fees for each quarter are $135. Registration schedules and fee bills are mailed to the student prior to the beginning of each quarter.

FINANCIAL AID

Military personnel who have been accepted into the Graduate School may apply for tuition aid through DANTES at their local education office. Many of the Graduate Outreach Program students receive tuition assistance through their employer's tuition reimbursement plan. The Auburn University Office of Student Financial Aid assists in the awarding of grants, loans, and scholarships for qualified full-time students.

APPLYING

To apply for admission, a prospective student must return a Graduate School application, an M.B.A. application (if applicable), a $25 nonrefundable application fee, three letters of recommendation, GRE or GMAT scores, and two official transcripts of all undergraduate and subsequent course work from the respective institutions.

CONTACT

Latisha Durroh
Marketing Coordinator
Graduate Outreach Program
202 Ramsay Hall
Auburn University
Auburn, Alabama 36849-5336
Telephone: 888-844-5300 (toll-free)
Fax: 334-844-2519
E-mail: durrocl@eng.auburn.edu
Web site: http://www.eng.auburn.edu/department/eop/

Distance Learning Programs

Baker College
Center for Graduate Studies
On-Line College
Flint, Michigan

Baker College, founded in the true American tradition as a small business college in 1888, is a private, nonprofit, accredited, coeducational institution. The College has more than a dozen campuses and branch locations in the Midwest and has a total enrollment of more than 13,000 students. The College is uniquely designed for one purpose: to provide high-quality higher education that enables graduates to be successful throughout their challenging and rewarding careers. The College offers diploma, certificate, and associate, bachelor's, and master's degree programs in the fields of business, technical, and health service fields. Total commitment to the students' employment success in uniquely evident in all aspects of the College's operations.

Baker College is accredited by the Commission on Institutions of Higher Education of the North Central Association of Colleges and Schools. Baker College is an equal opportunity affirmative action institution.

DISTANCE LEARNING PROGRAM

Baker College On-Line offers the convenience of classroom accessibility 24 hours a day, seven days a week, from virtually anywhere in the world. Because students do all classroom work off-line, schedules are flexible. A student goes on-line to send and receive completed work and other materials. It is not a self-paced program. Courses begin and end on specific dates, and class work is assigned deadlines.

DELIVERY MEDIA

Students are required to have a computer with the following minimum requirements: a 486 computer system or higher, a 3.5 high-density floppy drive, a 14.4 bps modem (minimum), and a hard drive capacity exceeding the student's current demands by at least 100 megabytes. A CD-ROM is not required but is recommended. Most IBM compatibles or Macintosh computers equipped with a modem are sufficient. The virtual classroom is the common meeting for all students taking classes on-line. Communication is accomplished by sending messages back and forth from the student's computer to the classroom computer. Each classroom has a unique name, and only students taking that class have access to the virtual classroom. This ensures privacy for all students.

PROGRAMS OF STUDY

Baker College On-Line offers the delivery of high-quality, respected courses and programs that enable a student to earn an associate, bachelor's, or master's degree at home, on the road, or anywhere in the world.

The Associate of Business Administration degree has been designed specifically for the On-Line College environment, where students have a variety of choices in filling out the degree plan. The curriculum gives students a good background of business facts and knowledge upon which to build or enhance a career in business.

The Bachelor of Business Administration degree is a program designed for the working professional that combines core course work with independent research and experiential credit to provide a contemporary business degree for today's business environment. Each core course contains focused study in the content area accompanied by independent research.

The Master of Business Administration degree program seeks to combine the best of conventional academic training with the best of field-based learning. Most typical business disciplines are represented in the curriculum because the College believes that a successful manager must be conversant with different aspects of running any of today's organizations or companies. Students may also elect to focus their studies in one of the following areas: computer information systems, health-care management, human resource management, industrial management, integrated health care, international business, leadership studies, or marketing.

SPECIAL PROGRAMS

The On-Line College offers undergraduate courses at all levels to support all of the campuses and their program offerings as a convenience for students who may have trouble commuting to a campus. The On-Line College publishes a listing each quarter showing which classes will be offered.

STUDENT SERVICES

Every Baker College student is assigned an e-mail account on the BakerNet system. Through this system, students can communicate with each other and their instructors and with members of the graduate school staff. Students may also use their accounts to access the World Wide Web. They also have access to the Baker College Library System and FALCON, a consortium of libraries that supports an on-line catalog database of more than 500,000 holdings. Students also have access to InfoTrac periodical indexing databases, the UMI/ProQuest General Periodicals On-Disc full-article imaging station, Books-in-Print with Reviews, and all available Internet and World Wide Web resources.

Baker College offers a renowned Lifetime Employment Service, with access to thousands of career opportunities and employment databases, to all students. This service can be used for the rest of one's life.

CREDIT OPTIONS

Baker College recognizes the expediency of understandable and universally accepted standards related to transfer of academic credit. The College follows the Michigan Association of Collegiate Registrars and Admissions Officers Official Policies and recognizes the College-Level Examination Program (CLEP) or other standardized tests.

FACULTY

The focus of Baker's faculty is somewhat different from that of traditional universities. Instead of placing an emphasis on empirical research, Baker values practitioner-oriented education. Faculty members remain continually active in their professions by consulting, conducting seminars, running their own businesses, writing, volunteering in their communities, and working with other organizations. The faculty-student ratio in distance education is 1:12.

ADMISSION

Graduate program candidates must have a bachelor's degree from an accredited institution and a 2.5 or better GPA in their undergraduate work, be able to display appropriate oral and written communication skills, submit three letters of reference, submit a current résumé, and have completed no less than three years of full-time work. Undergraduates must have graduated from high school, completed a GED, or passed an Ability to Benefit assessment before entering.

TUITION AND FEES

Undergraduate tuition for the 1997–98 school year is $135 per credit hour. Graduate tuition is $205 per credit hour. The cost of books ranges from $150 to $200 per quarter. A one-time access fee of $100 to link with the BakerNet On-Line Classrooms is charged to each student.

FINANCIAL AID

Students who are accepted into Baker College may be considered for several forms of state, federal, and institutional financial aid. Students are requested to complete the Free Application for Federal Student Aid (FAFSA) and return it directly to the College.

APPLYING

Baker College uses a rolling admission process, so there are no deadlines for applications. Students are allowed to begin in any quarter. Once the Admissions Committee receives an application, applicants usually receive a decision in approximately four weeks. Once accepted, students participate in a three-week on-line orientation. They are not required to visit a campus at any time.

CONTACT

Chuck J. Gurden
Director of Development
Center for Graduate Studies
Baker College
1050 West Bristol Road
Flint, Michigan 48507-5508
Telephone: 810-766-4390
            800-469-3165 (toll-free)
Fax: 810-766-4399
E-mail: gurden_c@corpfl.baker.edu
Web site: http://www.baker.edu

Distance Learning Programs

Bellevue University

Bellevue University Online
Bellevue, Nebraska

Bellevue University (BU) is an information-age learning institution that is first and foremost committed to creating optimum learning environments and assisting students in an accelerated process of lifelong learning. Bellevue University provides more diverse access to classes and degrees and is more productive and cost efficient than traditional institutions. Bellevue University's online programs serve the economic development and citizenship development needs of communities locally and nationally. Bellevue University listens, is accountable, and is very flexible and responsive. Bellevue serves students from more than forty countries and is strongly committed to serving international students on campus and online.

DISTANCE LEARNING PROGRAM

Using Internet access, students download online software to open the BU Online classroom, interact with professors and students, and use online library services and advising. Bellevue Online classes are small enough to give the active learning advantage that characterizes Bellevue University. Courses also are offered through self-study, experiential learning, and video and by test.

DELIVERY MEDIA

Online classes are delivered through FirstClass, an Internet-based, server/client groupware application. BU Online is composed of nested conferences and folders, pictures, and icons. Students interact in an asynchronous collaborative environment. Students need to have a computer with 4 MB RAM, 4 MB free space, a modem, and an Internet service provider. Students are provided with client software and instructions for use. Students can preview FirstClass on the University's Web site.

PROGRAMS OF STUDY

The M.B.A. program allows students to gain a broad coverage of tools and methods necessary to effectively run a business. It requires 36 credits and can be completed in eighteen months.

The Master of Arts in Management (M.A.M.), an accelerated program, prepares students to influence behavior, systems, and operations in the business environment. It requires 36 credits and can be completed in sixteen months.

The Bachelor of Science online degree completion programs require 127 credit hours, including the 36-hour major that must be completed through Bellevue University.

The management program is a comprehensive study of the functions of management, including planning, organization, leading, and controlling.

Management information systems focuses on IT issues and applications and is designed for students with computer programming or related associate degrees or course work.

Business information systems is for students without computer technology degrees or course work who want to qualify for management positions in the IT-driven environment. The focus is on effectively using distributed network systems and Internet commerce. The business information systems program begins in 1998.

The program in international business management allows students to become prepared to evaluate international business opportunities, develop action plans for potential business activities, and manage multinational activities.

The program in criminal justice administration is for students employed in the field who are entering management roles. Budgeting, strategic planning, information systems, and facilities issues are covered. This program also begins in 1998.

Detailed program descriptions can be found on the University's Web site.

STUDENT SERVICES

The online library, advising, admissions, transcript requests, and Alumni Services are all part of Bellevue University Online. The online library provides numerous resources, including more than fifty databases on FirstSearch and ProQuest. These databases provide search capabilities that include full-image, full-text materials that can be printed or read at the student's convenience.

CREDIT OPTIONS

Transfer students are welcome at Bellevue University for online baccalaureate degree programs. Associate degrees are accepted in full. In addition, the University accepts CLEP/DANTES tests, allows experiential learning assessment, and accepts corporate and military training using ACE guidelines.

FACULTY

More than 65 percent of the full-time faculty members have terminal degrees. Approximately one third deliver distance courses and programs via the Internet, self-study, and video.

Part-time faculty members are preparing for online/distance delivery.

ADMISSION

B.S. degree applicants must have 60 credit hours or an associate degree and three years of work experience. Graduate applicants need an undergraduate degree, an entrance exam, and work experience. There are no course work prerequisites for M.B.A. or M.A.M. students.

TUITION AND FEES

Graduate tuition is $275 per credit, and undergraduate tuition is $250 per credit. The Online application fee is $100. FirstClass software is provided at no additional charge. Textbook costs vary by program.

FINANCIAL AID

Financial aid and veterans' benefits are available for distance learners. Federal and state grants as well as government guaranteed student loans are available. Students can visit the financial aid Web site at http://bruins.bellevue.edu/FA/finaid.htm for more detailed information. Last year, 60 percent of the students received some form of financial aid. Approximately $8 million in financial aid was disbursed to students during the last academic year.

APPLYING

Applicants must transmit the online application (with fee) and submit transcripts for tentative evaluation. Admissions counselors work with students to complete the official admissions process. An educational degree plan is completed for each student that defines requirements needed to achieve each student's degree goal.

CONTACT
Grady Batchelor, Director of Distributed Learning
Sue Sampson, Associate Director of Distributed Learning
Diane Johnson, Undergraduate Admissions
Elizabeth Wall, Graduate Admissions
Bellevue University Online
Bellevue University
1000 Galvin Road South
Bellevue, Nebraska 68005
E-mail: bellevue_u@scholars.bellevue.edu
Web site: http://bruins.bellevue.edu

Distance Learning Programs

Boston University
College of Engineering
Department of Manufacturing Engineering
Boston, Massachusetts

Boston University, incorporated in 1869, is an independent, coeducational, nonsectarian university, open to women and to members of all minority groups. Its 22,515 full-time students and 2,559 faculty members make it one of the largest independent universities in the world. The Department of Manufacturing Engineering offers B.S., M.S., and Ph.D. degrees and was the first department in the country with an ABET-accredited B.S. program in manufacturing engineering. Interaction with local industry through research and part-time-study corporate programs has created a focus on state-of-the-art educational and research issues.

DISTANCE LEARNING PROGRAM

The Interactive-Compressed Video (ICV) graduate program in manufacturing engineering, comprised of courses identical to those for the on-campus degree, is designed to satisfy the needs of part-time students in industry. The department is a pioneer in distance learning, graduating its first student with an M.S. degree entirely attained by ICV in 1992.

DELIVERY MEDIA

The department maintains three state-of-the-artPictureTelvideoconferencing systems. These systems transmit at speeds ranging from switched 56 to the full-motion video capability of 384 K. PictureTel equipment is compatible with other PictureTel equipment, as well as equipment from other vendors, if those systems meet H.320 standards for video and audio.

PROGRAMS OF STUDY

Courses focus on the technical aspects of design and production. Three concentrations are offered for the master's degree via ICV: manufacturing systems, manufacturing operations management, and process design. While not all of the courses available on campus are offered via ICV, sufficient courses are offered to enable a student to complete all requirements for the M.S. degree in manufacturing engineering, which may be completed in approximately three years.

A limited number of special/nondegree students are admitted each semester. Persons not wishing to pursue a graduate degree may enroll in courses for which they meet prerequisite requirements. Special/nondegree students may apply at any time prior to completing a third course for admission to the degree program. Only three courses taken as a special/nondegree student may be applied to the master's degree.

SPECIAL PROGRAMS

The department encourages all part-time students in industry to visit the campus and become familiar with the resources it can offer. The faculty particularly welcomes the opportunity provided in these visits to develop more significant and lasting relationships with the part-time video students. Matriculated students who wish to visit the campus have access to all facilities, including University libraries and athletic facilities.

Another feature of the program is that each instructor is expected to visit the company at least once during each course offering so that students get to know their instructors firsthand.

Recently, Boston University has developed a substantial collaborative relationship with the Fraunhofer Resource Center Massachusetts. A state-of-the-art laboratory supporting this endeavor houses exceptional equipment for work in high-performance machining and rapid prototyping. The Boston University/Fraunhofer collaboration engages manufacturing engineering students and faculty in programs of contract industrial research directed toward finding practical solutions to actual problems from manufacturing industry customers. Although participation by Fraunhofer personnel in ICV education is limited at present, this interaction is expected to increase.

CREDIT OPTIONS

The master's program in manufacturing engineering consists of 36 credit hours (ordinarily nine courses), of which no fewer than 28 credits must be earned at Boston University and at least 20 credits are from technically oriented courses. A cumulative grade point average of at least 3.0 (B) is required for all courses taken at Boston University and for all courses offered for the degree.

FACULTY

The Department of Manufacturing Engineering has about 20 full-time faculty members. All are actively engaged in industrial problems through writing, consulting, and research.

ADMISSION

Students accepted into the master's program in manufacturing engineering are expected to have earned a bachelor's degree in engineering. Students with strong mathematics backgrounds and aptitudes, but nonengineering degrees, may also apply.

TUITION AND FEES

Tuition for 1997–98 is $687 per credit hour. There is an additional registration fee of $40 per semester. Students may pay as individuals and seek reimbursement from their company, or the University can bill the company.

FINANCIAL AID

No departmental financial aid is offered as students are typically sponsored by their companies.

APPLYING

Students seeking special student status should contact the department. Students seeking admission to the M.S. program should request and complete an application packet.

CONTACT

Jennifer R. Pilton
Department Director
Department of Manufacturing Engineering
Boston University
15 St. Mary's Street
Boston, Massachusetts 02215
Telephone: 617-353-4622
Fax: 617-353-5548
E-mail: jpilton@bu.edu
World Wide Web: http://eng.bu.edu/MFG/

Brigham Young University
Independent Study
Provo, Utah

The University traces its roots to Utah's rich pioneer heritage. The original school, Brigham Young Academy, was established in 1875, on a little over 1 acre of land in what is today downtown Provo. At that time, Brigham Young, the second president of the Church of Latter-day Saints, charged that all secular learning at the institution should be fused with teaching from the scriptures. No longer a primary school in a pioneer town, BYU is a world-renowned center of learning that remains true to that original charge from its namesake.

The mission of Brigham Young University—founded, supported, and guided by the Church of Jesus Christ of Latter-day Saints—is to assist individuals in their quest for perfection and eternal life. That assistance should provide a period of intensive learning in a stimulating setting where a commitment to excellence is expected and the full realization of human potential is pursued. All instruction, programs, and services at BYU, including a wide variety of extracurricular experiences, should make their own contribution toward the balanced development of the total person. Such a broadly prepared individual will not only be capable of meeting personal challenge and change but will also bring strength to others in the tasks of home and family life, social relationships, civic duty, and service to mankind.

DISTANCE LEARNING PROGRAM

Independent Study serves as an extension of the University by providing quality correspondence courses. There are more than 37,000 enrollments in distance education or a nontraditional education. BYU offers 340 college courses and 175 high school courses through Independent Study. BYU Independent Study is fully accredited by the Northwest Association of Schools and Colleges and is a member of the National University Continuing Education Association.

DELIVERY MEDIA

Faculty and students maintain regular contact through mail service, telephone, and electronic mail. Fax and Federal Express services are also available if a student is in a rush to submit assignments or to receive grades. Many courses make use of speedback, cassette tapes, fax, and computer disk. Students are also able to enroll and check grades on the Internet, if they have access to a computer.

PROGRAMS OF STUDY

Up to 36 semester hours of work completed through Independent Study can be used toward a bachelor's degree from BYU, and courses are also available for teacher recertification. Individual high school–level courses, an adult diploma program, a transcript program, and noncredit courses for personal development and enrichment are also available.

Certificate programs are offered for organ and family history research. The organ performance program offers six levels designed to provide motivation for an organist to improve his or her skills by working toward specific goals. A certificate of competence is received for each level completed. The certificate program for family history research provides a solid background in fundamental family history research principles coupled with specialized genealogical training in North American or British research. The certificate requires 18 hours of course work. Through the Department Degrees by Independent Study, a Bachelor of Independent Studies degree is available. It involves study of a broad range of basic and relevant subjects from the fine arts, social sciences, physical sciences, and religion, all under the direction of University faculty and advisers. This degree program, designed especially for the adult student, is a directed program of independent study with no specific major or minor.

SPECIAL PROGRAMS

Brigham Young University's Division of Continuing Education is one of the largest such programs in America. These enrollments are the equivalent of more than 22,000 full-time students. In conjunction with the LDS Church Educational System, the Division provides an extensive schedule of classes, lectures, and seminars—including BYU Campus Education Week, which attracts nearly 30,000 participants. Other learning opportunities include evening classes, conferences, and workshops; independent study; travel study; and youth and family programs. The Division also operates and coordinates programs from centers in Salt Lake City, California, Idaho, and Hawaii.

The purpose of the Division of Continuing Education is to provide educational programs and University services for part-time and off-campus students. These educational opportunities also assist regular daytime students. BYU cooperates with the Continuing Education programs as sponsored by the Church Educational System and its various components. The same University standards required of regular day students apply to those enrolled through the Division of Continuing Education while they are on campus.

CREDIT OPTIONS

Brigham Young University Independent Study does not offer credit options. However, students enrolling for a Bachelor of Independent Study degree, who have previously earned college credits, may request an evaluation of those credits to determine whether they can be considered for satisfaction of some degree by Independent Study course requirements, as applicable.

FACULTY

There are 352 instructors at BYU Independent Study. Fifty-eight percent of the faculty have doctoral or other terminal academic degrees.

ADMISSION

Students are eligible to enroll in Independent Study courses if they are adults with a working knowledge of the English language, are high school juniors or seniors enrolling in University-level courses with the approval of the high school counselor, or have passed the GED. Enrollment in an Independent Study course does not constitute admission to BYU.

TUITION AND FEES

Tuition for University-level courses is $81 per semester hour, unless otherwise stated. Tuition includes the cost of the course manual for each course. It does not include the cost of textbooks, supplemental course materials, handling fees, airmail fees, or fax fees. High school tuition is $79 per ½ unit and $48 per ¼ unit credit.

FINANCIAL AID

Independent Study scholarships and grants-in-aid are awarded four times a year. Awards are made for 1, 2, and 3 University semester hours. Preference is given to applicants who have completed one or more Independent Study courses. Scholarship applicants must have a B+ (3.4) or higher grade point average. Grants-in-aid must show financial need. No federal financial aid is available through BYU Independent Study.

APPLYING

To apply, students must complete an enrollment form and enclose correct fees for tuition, required materials (if any), handling, airmail (if applicable), and the textbooks they wish to purchase from BYU Independent Study. Once enrollment information has been received, all materials ordered for the course will be sent. Enrollments are accepted by telephone when payment of tuition and fees can be made by MasterCard, VISA, or Discover.

CONTACT

Registrar
BYU Independent Study
206 Harman Building
Brigham Young University
P.O. Box 21514
Provo, Utah 84606-1514
Telephone: 801-378-8292
　　　　　 800-914-8931 (toll-free)
Fax: 801-378-5817
E-mail: indstudy@coned1.byu.edu
Web site: http://coned.byu.edu/is/indstudy.htm

Burlington County College

Distance Learning
Pemberton, New Jersey

Since its founding in 1966, Burlington County College has offered more than seventy programs for the citizens of Burlington County. The College provides open access to quality educational programs that meet intellectual, employment, and cultural goals. The College is committed to the best use of instructional technology to enhance learning. Burlington County College has offered a widening array of distance learning opportunities since 1978.

Always seeking new partnerships with business and industry and other institutions of higher education, the College has entered into partnerships with the New Jersey Institute of Technology and the University of Medicine and Dentistry of New Jersey to offer baccalaureate and master's degrees. The College has, first and foremost, a commitment to the motivated adult learner who has to seek alternative means of education.

DISTANCE LEARNING PROGRAM

The Distance Learning program serves 3,000 students each year and offers forty courses and structured programs culminating in A.A. and A.S. degrees. Programs are available by telephone, mail, personal computer, and other media. Any student can obtain a degree via distance without attending classes on campus.

DELIVERY MEDIA

Faculty members maintain regular contact with distance learners via telephone. Many courses make use of video. Videos may be rented or accessed through local cable television stations or the Public Broadcasting System. Some classes provide access through audiotapes and the radio. Several courses utilize electronic mail, which requires the student to have access to a computer with a modem.

PROGRAMS OF STUDY

Burlington County College offers concentrations in liberal arts and sciences leading to the Associate of Arts (A.A.), Associate of Science (A.S.), and Associate of Applied Science (A.A.S.) degrees.

Students design degree programs that include a specific concentration in one area of study as well as the core general education program. There are sixty areas of program concentrations to choose from.

To earn an associate degree, a student must successfully complete 64 credits, with at least 16 of those credits earned through study at Burlington County College.

SPECIAL PROGRAMS

The College offers developmental education courses to provide students with the entry skills needed to succeed in college. Burlington County College's co-operative education program is open to any student. A student majoring in any field may apply for a co-op job related to his or her academic goals. The Educational Opportunity Fund (EOF) Program is primarily geared for first-time students planning to attend Burlington County College full-time. The major goals of this program include increasing access to higher education for financially and academically disadvantaged students. There is also a program in English as a second language for those students whose native language is not English.

CREDIT OPTIONS

Students can transfer credits earned at other postsecondary institutions to Burlington County College and can receive credit for college-level learning acquired through life or work experience by taking the College-Level Examination Program (CLEP). A total of 30 credits can be received under CLEP.

FACULTY

There are 607 full- and part-time faculty members at Burlington County College. Twenty-five percent of the faculty have doctoral or other terminal academic degrees.

ADMISSION

The principal requirement for admission is the applicant's possession of a high school diploma or its equivalent.

TUITION AND FEES

In 1997–98, tuition is $66.50 per credit for residents of Burlington County and $79.50 per credit for out-of-county residents. Full-time students who are in-county residents pay $741 per semester.

FINANCIAL AID

General financial aid programs through Burlington County College include Tuition Aid Grants (TAG), a state program; Federal Pell Grants; Federal Supplemental Educational Opportunity Grants (FSEOG); Educational Opportunity Fund Grant (EOF), a state program; Garden State Scholarships, a state program; and the Federal Direct Student Loan Program (FDSLP).

The Burlington County College Foundation awards scholarships each semester to a selected number of recipients based on academic merit and financial need. Burlington County College awards more than $2 million in financial aid each year.

APPLYING

Burlington County College reviews applications in order of the date received. New distance learners must attend an orientation session in the first semester they are enrolled.

CONTACT

Sue Espenshade
Coordinator of Distance Learning
Burlington County College
  Library
County Route 530
Pemberton, New Jersey 08068
Telephone: 609-894-9311 Ext. 7790
Fax: 609-894-4189

Distance Learning Programs

Caldwell College
External Degree Program
Caldwell, New Jersey

Caldwell College is a Catholic, coeducational, four-year liberal arts institution committed to intellectual rigor, individual attention, and the ethical values of the Judeo-Christian academic tradition.

Founded in 1939 by the Sisters of St. Dominic, the College is accredited by the Middle States Association of Colleges and Universities, chartered by the State of New Jersey, and registered with the Regents of the University of the State of New York.

Located on a 100-acre wooded campus in a quiet suburban community 20 miles from New York City, Caldwell provides a serene and secure environment conducive to study and learning.

Caldwell College offers a 12:1 student-faculty ratio, small classes, and individual attention. Professors know their students by name, challenge them to strive for excellence, and provide the support needed to achieve it. This close relationship between faculty members and students also leads to a spirit of friendship throughout the campus community.

Approximately half of the 1,750 men and women enrolled at the College are adults pursuing degrees part-time or obtaining new skills to compete in the changing marketplace. Through the College's Center for Continuing Education, these adults seek personal growth, professional enrichment, and career advancement. All students find the staff ready to provide the personalized academic planning that will help them succeed in their studies and careers.

DISTANCE LEARNING PROGRAM

Caldwell College pioneered the external degree concept in 1979, becoming the first higher education institution in the state of New Jersey to offer students the option of completing their degrees without attending on-campus classes.

Caldwell designed the program especially for busy adults whose work or family commitments make it difficult to follow a weekly on-campus academic schedule. Traditional course work is presented in a flexible and convenient format. External Degree students are required to be on campus only for the External Degree weekend at the beginning of each semester. Currently, 450 students are pursuing their bachelor's degrees through the External Degree Program. Students use the same textbooks and complete the same course work as their on-campus counterparts.

DELIVERY MEDIA

Students learn with the guidance of an academic mentor and through interaction with the faculty via phone, personal conferences, e-mail, mailing or faxing of assignments, audiocassette, videocassette, and computer technologies. In 1995, the External Degree Program offered its first on-line course in Business Policy to students via the Internet. In fall 1998, the entire business curriculum is scheduled to be available on-line in a multiyear cycle, followed by the entire core curriculum.

PROGRAM OF STUDY

The External Degree Program offers sixteen majors. Bachelor of Science degrees are offered in accounting, business administration, computer information systems, international business, marketing, and management. Bachelor of Arts degrees are offered in art (some on-campus work is required for art majors), communication arts, criminal justice, English, history, political science, psychology, religious studies, sociology, and social studies.

Eligibility for a degree requires completion of 122 credits and a GPA of at least 2.0 (C). This includes completing 60 liberal arts and science core curriculum credits, requirements specific to the student's major, and open electives. Students must also complete major courses with a minimum grade of C and satisfy all other departmental requirements. All majors require a comprehensive examination during the last semester. Overall, a minimum of 45 credits must be taken at Caldwell College, with the last 30 credits of the 122-credit requirement completed at the College before a degree is awarded. Transfer students must complete at least half the total number of credits for a given major at Caldwell College.

SPECIAL PROGRAMS

Students majoring in business administration, English, or psychology who have earned at least 60 prior college credits in courses applicable to their major may apply for Accelerated Degree Completion through the External Degree Program. Students admitted to the Accelerated Degree Completion Program can complete their degrees within two years by taking approximately 27 credits per year (9 credits per term) or an equivalent combination of course credits and College Level Examination Program,

Prior Learning Assessment, internships, and/or cooperative education credits. Each student is expected to work closely with an academic adviser in developing and following a specific course of study.

STUDENT SERVICES

All of the following services are available to External Degree students. The Jennings Library and the Academic Computing Center are open on evenings and weekends. Students have the ability to access the library's vast database from their home computers. The library's home page also provides links to the Internet and other databases and informational resources. The Career Development Center, Campus Minister, Counseling Office, and Learning Center are also available during the evening by appointment. The college bookstore is open evenings and during External Degree Weekend. The Learning Center assists students in academic skill development for all majors through tutoring.

CREDIT OPTIONS

Credit is given for courses completed at an accredited college or university with a grade of C or above, provided it is appropriate to the curriculum chosen at Caldwell College. Students may transfer no more than 75 credits from a baccalaureate institution or 60 credits from a junior college. Students may earn credits by examination through standardized testing (CLEP, DANTES, OHIO, and TECEP). Credit is also awarded for noncollegiate military or corporate training courses accredited by the American Council on Education. Credits may be earned through the Prior Learning Assessment portfolio development process.

FACULTY

Currently 30 full-time and 14 part-time faculty members teach in the Caldwell College External Degree Program, with 69 percent having earned their doctoral or terminal academic degrees.

ADMISSION

Students must be 23 years of age or older, have a strong high school academic record, and have completed at least 12 college credits.

TUITION AND FEES

Tuition for all students is $277 per credit. External Degree students must submit a separate $30 External Degree fee for every semester. The additional cost for books is the responsibility of the student.

FINANCIAL AID

External Degree students are eligible for several of the federal financial aid programs available to full-time students, including Pell Grants and various loans. Approximately 10 percent of External Degree students receive Pell Grants, 70 percent Stafford Loans, 10 percent Caldwell College Grants, and 2 percent Federal Supplemental Educational Opportunity Grants. Tuition Aid Grants are available for full-time External Degree students. Academic advisers of the Center for Continuing Education and the staff of the Financial Aid Office also inform students of special privately funded scholarship opportunities for which they may qualify.

APPLYING

Students wishing to pursue a degree through the External Degree Program must submit the following to the Office of Corporate Education and Adult Admissions: a completed application for part-time admission; a nonrefundable application fee of $25 made payable to Caldwell College (the student's Social Security number should be included on the memo line); official transcripts from high schools, career schools, or colleges previously attended (GED certification may be submitted in place of a high school transcript); and a photocopy of the student's Social Security card.

All application material must be received by the Office of Admissions by the deadline date of each semester, approximately one month prior to the beginning of classes.

Students in the External Degree Program may enroll for a minimum of one and a maximum of five courses per semester, depending on their personal schedules and abilities.

The program offers three semesters: fall, spring, and summer. Students are required to be on campus only for the External Degree weekend at the beginning of each semester. That Friday evening, new students attend an orientation program, socialize with fellow students during a reception and dinner, and participate in workshops designed to enhance their college experience.

On Saturday, students meet with their faculty mentor and receive an overview of the course material, faculty evaluation criteria, and dates that assignments are due. Students also attend department meetings and learn about recent developments and career options in their chosen fields of study. Prior to each semester, students consult with their academic advisers for guidance in selecting courses. Academic counseling is available through the semester as a supportive, ongoing service.

CONTACT

Jack Albalah
Corporate and Adult Admissions
Caldwell College
9 Ryerson Avenue
Caldwell, New Jersey 07006
Telephone: 973-228-4424
    Ext. 500
    800-831-9178 (toll-free)
Fax: 973-364-8453
E-mail: caldadmit@aol.com
    caldwelldj@aol.com
Web site: http://www.caldwell.edu

Distance Learning Programs

Central Missouri State University
Office of Extended Campus–Distance Learning
Warrensburg, Missouri

Founded in 1871, Central Missouri State University is a state university offering approximately 150 areas of study to 11,800 undergraduate and graduate students.

A wide range of academic programs, people with varied backgrounds and experiences, a friendly and inviting environment, skilled teachers, and excellent facilities make Central Missouri State University a great place to go to school. Central offers a wide range of facilities on the 1,050-acre campus.

Central is located in the heart of Warrensburg, a county seat of 15,000 people. Warrensburg is located at the intersection of U.S. Highway 50 and Missouri Highway 13, about 50 miles southeast of Kansas City. Commercial bus services and a main line of Amtrak provide convenient transportation.

Central Missouri State University provides educational and technological leadership for continuously improving distance learning quality and delivery in K–12 education, postsecondary education, and community-based economic development programs.

DISTANCE LEARNING PROGRAM

Central's main Distance Learning Program provides undergraduate- and graduate-level courses through two-way interactive television. The program currently includes two master's degree programs and several undergraduate courses. Dual-credit courses are offered to students in area high schools. From fall 1994 through summer 1997, Central provided instruction to more than 1,000 graduate, undergraduate, and high school students. Central's Distance Learning Program provides an extension for its already diverse degree offerings.

Central is accredited by the North Central Association of Colleges and Schools with additional program-specific accreditation in art, aviation, chemistry, construction science, drafting technology, home economics, industrial science, music, nursing, safety management, social work, speech pathology and audiology, and teacher education. Central's business administration degree programs are accredited by the American Assembly of Collegiate Schools of Business.

DELIVERY MEDIA

Central is a charter member of the Western Missouri Educational Technology (WeMET) Consortium, which uses T-1 compressed video technologies. The network is capable of transmitting audio and video signals at speeds from 56 kbs to full T-1 (1.544 MBS). WeMET uses a quad-split configuration to ensure that teachers, students, and participants have the ability to see and hear each other simultaneously and spontaneously (continuous presences). The network is studio-based, which provides all the dynamics of the traditional classroom. Videotaping of classes is done with instructor approval, enabling students to take the class via videotape. Central is also a charter member of KCEDNet, giving Central the linkage necessary to fulfill its statewide mission.

KMOS-TV, a PBS affiliate, resides on the campus and provides instructional television programming for over 100 Missouri school districts as well as undergraduate and graduate courses for the general public.

PROGRAMS OF STUDY

Three degree programs are currently being offered via I-TV. The distance learning enrollment process is the same as for regular classes.

The Master of Science in Criminal Justice is designed for those students who wish to enter or progress in the criminal justice fields of law enforcement, corrections, and juvenile justice or for those who plan to seek positions in leadership, professional specialization, research, or instruction in criminal justice. Completion of the program requires a minimum of 36 credit hours in required and elective courses.

The Master of Science in Industrial Safety Management prepares graduates to manage the safety of individuals in a variety of occupational environments. A minimum of 36 credit hours is required and elective courses are necessary for the completion of the program.

The Master of Science in Aviation Safety prepares individuals for a career in aviation safety, safety program management, or aviation management. This nonthesis degree program is composed of 32 credit hours in required and elective courses. Aviation safety courses are offered at FAA and Air National Guard sites across the continental United States.

Course work toward completion of the 32-credit-hour Master of Science in Education degree is available via interactive television. Areas of specialization include curriculum and instruction, special education, and education administration.

College-level classes are offered to area high school juniors and seniors. Classes are taken for both high school and college credit. Eligibility for the program is determined by the high school principal or counselor.

SPECIAL PROGRAMS

Central's Distance Learning Program builds upon the existing curriculum offerings at Central as well as offerings that address special distance learning needs. A sampling of such offerings includes technical training and curriculum instruction and design for distance learning, graduate-level special education training for the classroom teacher, police academy training, graduate-level education classes, and educational classes offered over the Internet.

STUDENT SERVICES

All students enrolled at Central are issued a mainframe Internet account. Central's library resources are available via the Internet on Central's Web page at http://cmsuvmb.cmsu.edu.

CREDIT OPTIONS

The University accepts undergraduate transfer students from other accredited colleges and universities and evaluates their credit on the same bases used for other Central students. Thus, admission requires students to be in good standing and to have a grade point average of C (2.0) or better, computed by Central's methods. Students may be considered on an individual basis if their GPA is less than 2.0. For entering graduate students, Central will accept up to 8 hours of transfer credits in graduate work.

FACULTY

Faculty members at Central exemplify the goals of the institution as they balance personal attention with expertise in their respective fields. Approximately 70 percent of the 443 full-time faculty members hold doctoral degrees. The undergraduate student–faculty ratio is 17:1; the graduate student–faculty ratio is 3:1.

ADMISSION

A rolling admission policy is employed at Central. First-time undergraduate students, students returning after an absence of one or more semesters, and students who desire to enroll as visiting students should contact the Office of Admissions at 660-543-4677 or 800-956-0177 (toll-free).

First-time graduate students taking Extended Campus courses may either be admitted by completing the Extended Campus application in person or when calling to enroll in a class. Students must submit official copies of their transcripts to the Graduate Studies Office. Graduate students may enroll in up to 6 credit hours before finalizing their admission.

Students currently attending another university may enroll as visiting students. Graduate students who are not seeking a degree may enroll as non-degree-seeking students.

A nonrefundable application fee of $25 is due upon submission of the application. This applies to first-time applications only.

TUITION AND FEES

For 1997–98, graduate tuition is $182 and undergraduate tuition is $138 per credit hour for interactive television courses.

FINANCIAL AID

Central recognizes a student's continuing need for financial assistance. Undergraduate and graduate students planning to enroll for on-campus, off-campus, and weekend classes may be considered for federal financial aid to help pay education and living expenses. Federal grant and loan funds are available for eligible students who have been accepted for regular degree programs at Central. Application eligibility information may be obtained by contacting the Office of Financial Aid and Veteran Services in person (Administration Building 316) or by calling 660-543-4040.

Students who are veterans may also be considered for VA educational benefits to help with tuition costs. Information and eligibility requirements may be obtained by calling 660-543-4983.

Visiting and nondegree students are not eligible to receive federal financial aid.

Financial aid for graduate students includes graduate assistantships, Regents Scholarships, I. L. Peters Memorial Scholarship, Warren C. Lovinger Graduate Student Scholarship, foundation scholarships, and Presidential Fellowships for Ethnic Minorities. In addition, the University participates in all federal student financial aid grant, loan, and employment programs.

APPLYING

Undergraduate students should contact the Admissions Office at 660-543-4290 or 800-956-0177 (toll-free). Graduate students should contact Graduate Studies and Research at 660-543-4621.

CONTACT

Robyn Criswell-Bloom
Coordinator of Distance Learning
Office of Extended Campus
Humphreys 403
Central Missouri State University
Warrensburg, Missouri 64093
Telephone: 660-543-8480
　　　　　　800-SAY-CMSU (toll-free)
Fax: 660-543-8333

Champlain College
SuccessNet Distance Learning Program
Continuing Education Division

Burlington, Vermont

> *Since 1878, Champlain College has been dedicated to providing education that reflects the realities and needs of the contemporary workplace. It offers professional certificates and two-year and four-year educational programs that are designed to provide sound professional training or updating for careers in today's complex world, as well as to provide broadening education in the humanities and general education. Champlain College is recognized as one of the leading career-building colleges in northern New England, and it has earned the respect of the business, technical, and human services professions for its outstanding career-oriented education.*

DISTANCE LEARNING PROGRAM

Champlain College is a pioneer in the use of computer technologies in distance learning applications. SuccessNet, the College's on-line distance learning program, serves hundreds of students in the United States and is expanding internationally in several areas. Champlain offers complete degree programs and technically oriented, noncredit seminars that may be accessed on-line any time of day.

DELIVERY MEDIA

For Windows users, SuccessNet provides an easy-to-use "point and click" graphical interface. DOS and Mac users are easily supported as well. The minimum configuration needed is an IBM-compatible PC or Macintosh computer with at least one floppy drive and 2400 to 14,400 baud modem. Once connected, students will find messages posted from the instructor and classmates either in the course "forum" or in private e-mail. All communication occurs on-line and includes discussion comments from classmates, lectures, instructional material, and assignments. The material covered in SuccessNet classes is the same as in traditional courses.

PROGRAMS OF STUDY

Champlain College offers an extensive array of traditionally delivered, career-oriented two- and four-year degrees. Through its distance learning program, the College offers both Professional Certificates of Concentrated Study and Associate of Science (A.S.) degrees in accounting, business, computer programming–PC track, and management. The College also offers the Bachelor of Science (B.S.) degree in professional studies, which is designed to complement associate degrees in career areas. Students with liberal arts backgrounds may complete career concentrations in business, computer programming–PC track, and management. Bachelor's degree students must take a lab science course at the College or transfer one from another accredited college. Professional certificates typically require successful completion of 21 credits. Associate degrees require completion of 60 credits, half of which must be taken through Champlain College. The bachelor's degree requires completion of 120 credits, at least 45 of which must be taken through Champlain. Students are also free to take individual courses on a nonmatriculated basis.

In addition to its on-line credit curriculum, the College has a growing on-line noncredit curriculum available as professional development for those employed in computer-related or technical areas.

SPECIAL PROGRAMS

Champlain has several expanding international programs and has also been among the first to make use of computer technology in the international delivery of educational programs. The College is developing on-line courses in connection with programs offered to students in Israel and Russia. In addition, the College is a founding member of WorldLink, a consortium with two other U.S. institutions and three European institutions, which is dedicated to creating virtual exchanges using distance learning technologies. Its Web site is http://www.his.se/his/worldlink/.

Champlain College has a corporate training unit that enters into strategic partnerships with businesses to assist them in the professional development of their employees using a variety of delivery methods, including on-line training.

STUDENT SERVICES

Champlain College provides a number of services to adult learners. Distance learners receive academic advising, services from the Career Development Office, and a full range of on-line library services.

CREDIT OPTIONS

Students may transfer credits earned through other accredited postsecondary institutions. Depending on the program selected, students may also transfer credit for life/work experience or credits from approved testing programs. Champlain accepts credit through approved portfolio assessment programs, CLEP, DANTES, and PONSI.

FACULTY

Champlain's strength lies in its faculty. More than 120 full-time and part-time faculty members focus their primary energies on teaching. Faculty members have completed programs of advanced study, and many have doctoral or terminal degrees.

ADMISSION

The College is experienced in working with adult learners and their diverse backgrounds. Requirements vary for different majors, but there are not any overall tests required for admission. Given the method of instructional delivery, SuccessNet students should possess effective reading and writing skills.

TUITION AND FEES

In 1997–98, tuition is $295 per credit; most courses are 3 credits. There are no additional fees.

FINANCIAL AID

Payment and financial aid options depend on personal circumstances and whether students attend full- or part-time. The College participates in several Federal financial aid programs, including Federal Pell Grant and Federal Stafford Student Loan, and state loan and grant programs.

APPLYING

Students may enroll for on-line courses as nonmatriculating students by registering on-line or by mail, fax, or telephone. The College reviews applications for degree programs when they are received. A short, on-line orientation is required for all SuccessNet students prior to gaining access to their courses.

CONTACT
Renata McAdams
SuccessNet Distance Learning Program
Continuing Education Division
Champlain College
163 South Willard Street
Burlington, Vermont 04502
Telephone: 802-860-2777
Fax: 802-860-2774
E-mail: ced@champlain.edu
Web site: http://www.champlain.edu/success

Distance Learning Programs

Charter Oak State College
Newington, Connecticut

Charter Oak State College was established in 1973 by the Connecticut Legislature to provide an alternate way for adults to earn a college degree. The College offers associate and bachelor's degrees and is regionally accredited by the New England Association of Schools and Colleges. Charter Oak is a Servicemembers Opportunity College.

Charter Oak's degree program was designed to be especially appealing to people who work full-time and have family and financial responsibilities as well. The program is designed for independent adult learners who have the capacity and motivation to pursue a degree program that provides flexibility in how, where, and when they can earn credits. The Charter Oak program assumes that its students possess a basic understanding of the elements of a degree program and that they will seek guidance as often as necessary to progress satisfactorily with their studies.

Charter Oak teaches no classes. Students earn credits based on faculty evaluation of courses transferred from regionally accredited colleges and universities, noncollegiate sponsored instruction, standardized tests, special assessment, Independent Guided Study (IGS), contract learning, and portfolio review.

One of the hallmarks of Charter Oak State College is its individualized professional advisement services. Each student is assigned to an academic adviser, who is a specialist in the student's chosen field of study. That adviser is accessible via telephone, fax, or e-mail and works closely with the student to develop a plan of study for completion of the degree program.

DISTANCE LEARNING PROGRAM

Charter Oak State College offers an external degree program and so, by definition, is a distance learning institution. Students earn their credits "externally" and transfer them into the College; there is no residence requirement. Charter Oak offers more than a dozen IGS courses each semester. Courses run for a period of sixteen weeks but may be completed in less time with the permission of the IGS office.

DELIVERY MEDIA

Students taking IGS courses use textbooks, videotapes, and audiotapes. Textbooks may be purchased from a special mail-order bookstore, and videotapes and audiotapes may be rented from a media production mail-order service. Each student has access to a Charter Oak State College mentor at a designated time each week. Contact may be via telephone, fax, or e-mail.

PROGRAMS OF STUDY

Charter Oak State College offers four degrees in general studies: Associate of Arts, Associate of Science, Bachelor of Arts, and Bachelor of Science. To earn an associate degree, a student must complete at least 60 credits; a bachelor's degree requires at least 120 credits.

A Charter Oak degree is more than an accumulation of the required number of credits. At least one half of the credits toward a degree must be earned in subjects traditionally included among the liberal arts and sciences: humanities, mathematics, natural sciences, and social sciences. Achievement in these areas demonstrates breadth of learning. In addition, students pursuing a baccalaureate degree must complete a concentration, consisting of at least 36 credits, that demonstrates depth of learning.

A concentration plan, in conjunction with an essay, must be submitted to the faculty for approval. Concentrations may be constructed in many areas, including applied arts, applied science and technology, art history, the behavioral sciences, business, child study, communication, computer science, fire science technology, human services, individualized studies, industrial technology, languages, liberal studies, literature, music history, the natural sciences, religious studies, and the social sciences.

SPECIAL PROGRAMS

The College has evaluated a number of noncollegiate courses and programs that can be used in Charter Oak degree programs. Many healthcare specialties from hospital-based programs are included, such as medical laboratory technician, nurse practitioner, physician assistant, radiologic technologist, registered nurse, and respiratory therapist or technician. Other evaluations include the Child Development Associate (CDA) credential; the FAA Airman Certificate; Famous Artists School in Westport, Connecticut; Institute of Children's Literature in West Redding, Connecticut; the National Opticianry Competency Examination; the Contact Lens Registry Examination; and several fire certifications, including Fire Marshal, Deputy Fire Marshal, Fire Inspector, Fire Fighter III, Fire Officer I or II, and Fire Service Instructor I or II.

CREDIT OPTIONS

Students can transfer credits from other regionally accredited colleges and universities; age is not a factor in their transferability. Up to 50 percent of the degree may be earned through prior learning, including ACE-evaluated military credits, ACE, and PONSI-evaluated noncollegiate learning and portfolio. There is no limit to the number of credits that can be earned using standardized examinations. Up to 90 credits may be earned at a two-year regionally accredited college.

FACULTY

Full-time faculty members from public and independent institutions of higher education in Connecticut are appointed to serve as consulting examiners at Charter Oak. They establish credits.

ADMISSION

Admission is open to any person 16 years or older, regardless of level of formal education, who is able to demonstrate college-level achievement. To be admitted, a student must have earned 9 college-level credits from Charter Oak's acceptable sources of credit.

TUITION AND FEES

All students pay a $40 application fee; Connecticut residents pay a first-year enrollment fee of $397, nonresidents pay $595. Active-duty servicemembers pay a special active-duty military fee for all Charter Oak fees and services that is equivalent to the in-state resident fee. All baccalaureate degree candidates pay a Concentration Proposal Review fee of $245 and a $30 technology fee. All students pay a graduation fee of $125. Tuition for IGS courses is $56 a credit for Connecticut residents and $84 a credit for nonresidents.

FINANCIAL AID

Charter Oak State College provides some financial assistance in the form of fee waivers to students who demonstrate both financial need and academic promise. Cash grants-in-aid for testing and service fees and other out-of-pocket costs are occasionally available from private sources. Charter Oak is approved by the Connecticut Department of Higher Education for the education and training of veterans and other eligible U.S. Department of Veterans Affairs beneficiaries.

APPLYING

Charter Oak reviews applications on a rolling basis; students may enroll anytime during the year.

CONTACT

Admissions Office
Charter Oak State College
66 Cedar Street
Newington, Connecticut 06111-2646
Telephone: 860-666-4595
Fax: 860-666-4852
Web site: http://www.cosc.edu

Distance Learning Programs

Chattanooga State Technical Community College

Distance Learning Program

Chattanooga, Tennessee

Chattanooga State Technical Community College, established in 1965, is Tennessee's first comprehensive community college, combining one-year technical vocational training with more than sixty-five career and transfer associate degree programs. Chattanooga State plays a vital and continually changing role in preparing the area's labor force to meet the challenges of the year 2000 and beyond. The many programs of the college are based on continuous assessment of community needs, curricula that respond to the market, faculty members with experience in the fields in which they teach, and state-of-technology labs and equipment.

Providing access and support annually to some 10,000 students, the College offers programs ranging from GED and adult basic education through specialized training in magnetic resonance imaging and sonography, fine and graphic arts, and hazardous materials management. Students may take classes at five campuses, or they may take both credit and noncredit courses through the Distance Learning Program. The College is accredited by the Southern Association of Colleges and Schools, and all academic programs are accredited through the appropriate agencies.

DISTANCE LEARNING PROGRAM

Begun as a lab-based independent studies program in 1979, the program now provides instruction to 3,000–3,500 students annually. Students are eligible for the same services as on-campus students, and the courses mirror traditional courses in content, transferability, credit, and cost. These courses are accepted for full funding by the federal financial aid programs and the Bureau of Veteran's Affairs. Chattanooga State's Distance Learning Program has been named as one of the top twenty distance learning programs in the United States by the League for Innovation in the Community College.

DELIVERY MEDIA

Students may enroll in more than seventy courses each semester through videocassette mailout, cable broadcast, or on-line computer service. Some courses may use a combination of these media. The predominant choice among students has been videocassette delivery, since most homes now have VCRs. However, with an increasing number of families purchasing computers, enrollments in the on-line courses are expected to climb. Students in on-line courses must provide their own computers. Course instructors are expected to be available to these students for the same number of hours as for an on-campus course. Students may contact their instructors in person, by telephone, or via e-mail. All on-line courses also offer synchronous and asynchronous instructor-student and student-student interaction.

PROGRAMS OF STUDY

Chattanooga State offers twenty-two Associate of Arts degrees, forty-four Associate of Science degrees, thirty-eight Associate of Applied Science degrees as well as academic certificates, technical certificates, and noncredit industrial training certificates. Degree programs typically require completion of 65 to 80 hours of semester credits. Degrees are offered in the broad areas of allied health/nursing, business and information systems, engineering technology, environmental science and technology, liberal arts, and mathematics and science. More than forty specialized academic and technical certificates are offered, ranging from American Sign Language to nuclear medicine technology and CAD/CAM technology. Industrial training certificates include air conditioning/refrigeration, machine tool technology, automotive and diesel repair, and fourteen other vocational specialties.

SPECIAL PROGRAMS

The Distance Learning Program offers virtually all of the general education courses for most two-year degrees of the college, but it also includes courses for special populations. Certified Emergency Medical Technologists and Fire Engineers may receive credit for those certifications towards an associate degree in emergency services management and administration. Other unique curricular areas include one-year certificates in forestry for utility personnel who maintain rights-of-way, a business-oriented program for over-the-road truck drivers, and most of the courses for a degree for students majoring in mass communications. The program is also offering a new two-year degree path in maintenance engineering technology, which combines video-based instruction and hands-on laboratory experiences in company locations for employees within the greater metropolitan area of the college. Workers wanting only specific job training without taking the general education required for a degree may also work toward institutional certificates in at least six technical job fields such as electrical maintenance, mechanical maintenance, HVAC, and programmable control systems. Through this new delivery system, workers may receive instruction without leaving their homes or workplace and also receive company-specific hands-on training in the work site.

Students may receive assistance with admissions, course enrollment, and academic advising by telephone. Students who have on-line capabilities may access the College library via the World Wide Web (http://cst.lib) or the Chattanooga State Home Page (http://cstcc.chattanooga.net).

CREDIT OPTIONS

Students may receive transfer credit for work completed at another accredited institution, a maximum of 6 hours of correspondence credit, a maximum of 9 hours of credit for life experience (by presentation of a comprehensive portfolio), credit earned through CLEP and Advanced Placement examinations, credit by departmental examination and credit for appropriate educational experiences through the armed services, as outlined in the ACE guide and through USAFI. Students should call 423-697-2475 for more information.

FACULTY

Chattanooga State has 170 full-time faculty members and 435 adjunct faculty members. Of this total, 19 percent have doctoral or terminal degrees.

ADMISSION

Chattanooga State is a member of the Tennessee Board of Regents System and follows the regulations of that body. Graduation from a regionally accredited high school or a passing grade on the GED test is required. Degree-seeking students under the age of 21 must undergo placement testing (ACT or SAT), followed by the Academic Assessment and Placement Program Exam if the ACT composite score or any subscore is below 19. The Academic Assessment and Placement Program Exam is required of all entering students 21 or over. If the results on any tests indicate deficiencies, those deficiencies must be remediated before students may take college-level courses. However, students over 21 years of age who do not intend to work toward a degree may enroll as "special students" for credit courses, with the exception of English and mathematics courses. Some other requirements may apply in special cases. Students should call 423-697-4404 for more information.

TUITION AND FEES

Tuition for residents of Tennessee and for students working full-time in Tennessee is $45 per credit hour, with approximately $30 in supplementary fees. Out-of-state students who do not work full-time in Tennessee pay $229 per credit hour, plus the $30 in supplementary fees. Fees are subject to change at any time, but Chattanooga State's fees are among the lowest in community colleges.

FINANCIAL AID

Chattanooga State's Financial Aid Program distributes more than $9 million to students each year through a broad variety of College, state, and federal funding sources. Students may apply for Chattanooga State Academic Work Scholarships, Foundation Scholarships, Minority Grants, and selected scholarships funded by businesses, civic groups, and professional organizations. Federal aid may be awarded through Pell Grants, Supplemental Educational Opportunity Grants, Tennessee Student Assistance Awards, Federal Work Program funds, Stafford Loans, and Federal PLUS loans. For information about Financial Aid, students should call 423-697-4402.

APPLYING

Students may apply to the College in any of three ways. They may request, complete, and return an application by mail; they may provide the information by telephone; or they may complete the on-line admission form found on the Chattanooga State World Wide Web home page at the address below.

CONTACT

Sue Y. Hyatt, Director
Distance Learning Program
Chattanooga State Technical
  Community College
4501 Amnicola Highway
Chattanooga, Tennessee 37406
Telephone: 800-207-8202 (toll-free)
Fax: 423-697-4479
E-mail: hyatt@cstcc.cc.tn.us
Web site:
  http://cstcc.chattanooga.net

Distance Learning Programs

City University

Distance Learning Option

Renton, Washington

City University was founded in 1973 on the philosophy that everyone should have access to quality higher education. The University upholds this philosophy by offering programs that are well designed, cost effective, and convenient. The University's progressive approach to education has fueled its growth from a single classroom in downtown Seattle to the largest private university in the state of Washington. It is a private, nonprofit institution and is accredited by the Northwest Association of Schools and Colleges.

City University's programs cover a variety of academic fields ranging from business management and technology to humanities, social sciences, counseling, and teacher preparation. The majority of faculty members actively work in the fields they teach. The combination of innovative program design and outstanding instruction make City University an exceptional higher learning institution.

DISTANCE LEARNING PROGRAM

In keeping with its mission of providing convenient, accessible education, City University offers most of its degree programs through distance learning (DL). The DL option makes degree programs available through traditional correspondence and electronically, through the World Wide Web. City University serves approximately 4,500 students annually through DL.

DELIVERY MEDIA

City University offers standard DL and electronic DL programs. Electronic DL students complete course work through the University's on-line instructional center, using computers and the World Wide Web. In the center, students may access course-specific video, audio, animation, and interactive assignments, as well as instructor notes. DL students communicate with instructors by e-mail or by phone, mail, or fax. Electronic DL students need a computer with a modem and Internet access.

PROGRAMS OF STUDY

City University's undergraduate programs prepare students to compete in today's marketplace. Students may complete an Associate of Science (A.S.), a Bachelor of Science (B.S.), or a Bachelor of Arts (B.A.) degree. Within these degrees, students may pursue one of several areas of study, including business administration, accounting, sociology, management specialty, computer systems, and international studies. Undergraduate courses are 5 credits each; 180 credits are required for completion of a B.S. or B.A. degree.

City University's graduate business and public administration programs prepare management professionals for leadership roles at local, national, and international levels. Students may pursue a graduate certificate or a Master of Business Administration (M.B.A.), with an array of specialties; a Master of Public Administration (M.P.A.); a combined M.B.A./M.P.A.; a Master of Project Management; an Executive M.A. in leadership; or an M.A. in management degree. Most graduate courses are worth 3 credits; total required credits range from 45 to 60. City University also offers programs in education and human services. Students may pursue a Master of Education (M.Ed.) in curriculum and instruction, educational technology, special education, or ESL instructional methods, or they may pursue an M.A. degree in marriage and family counseling, mental health counseling, or vocational rehabilitation counseling. Total required credits for these programs range from 45 to 73.

SPECIAL PROGRAMS

City University has an "open door" admissions policy. Students may begin a distance learning course at the beginning of any month, and there is no application deadline. City University has partnerships with several institutions and organizations worldwide. Through these affiliations, the University offers in-house programs and evaluates prior training for college-level credit.

All of City University's programs are geared for adult students. From its student body to its faculty and staff, City University is a community of professionals. All who are associated with the University understand the needs of adult learners who are seeking quality education that applies to their individual lifestyle.

STUDENT SERVICES

Students may register by touch-tone phone. Academic advising and assistance is available from a distance learning adviser by phone, fax, or e-mail. Students have full access to the library, including an on-line search service; a reference librarian, via a toll-free phone number; and a mailing service for circulation books and articles.

CREDIT OPTIONS

Students may transfer up to 90 approved lower-division and 45 approved upper-division credits from approved institutions for baccalaureate programs. The Portfolio Assessment Program lets students earn credits through documented experiential learning. Students may receive credit for the CLEP or other standardized tests. Graduate students may transfer up to 12 credits from approved programs.

FACULTY

There are more than 250 faculty members included in the distance learning program, 36 of whom are full-time. More than 25 percent of the full-time faculty members have terminal degrees.

ADMISSION

Undergraduate programs are generally open to applicants over 18 years of age who hold a high school diploma or GED. Admission to graduate programs requires that students hold a baccalaureate degree from an accredited or otherwise recognized institution.

TUITION AND FEES

Undergraduate tuition is $150 per credit, and graduate tuition is $268 per credit. The application fee is $75 ($175 for international students).

FINANCIAL AID

For more information, students should contact the Financial Aid Office (telephone: 800-426-5596, toll-free).

APPLYING

DL students may enroll on a rolling admissions basis. Students must speak with an academic adviser to complete the initial enrollment. Students should then submit the application form, nonrefundable application fee, transcripts, and admission documents to the Office of Admissions and Student Affairs.

CONTACT

DL/Online Advisor
Office of Admissions and Student Affairs
City University
919 Southwest Grady Way
Renton, Washington 98055
Telephone: 425-637-1010
　　　　　 800-422-4898 (toll-free)
Fax: 425-277-2437
Web site: http://www.cityu.edu

Distance Learning Programs

Clarkson College
Omaha, Nebraska

Clarkson College is a regionally accredited private institution, with exceptional programs in business, health-care management, nursing, occupational therapy assistant studies, physical therapist assistant studies, and radiography and medical imaging. The College offers the personal qualities of a small institution and the technological advantages found within a larger educational environment. Founded in 1888, it was the first school of nursing in Nebraska and was approved to grant academic degrees in 1984. Clarkson College is accredited by the Commission on Institutions of Higher Education and the North Central Association of Colleges and Schools.

The mission of Clarkson College is to provide education for the future by offering undergraduate and graduate health science degrees. The College provides high-quality education to prepare competent, thoughtful, ethical, and compassionate health-care professionals for service to individuals, families, and communities.

Clarkson College recognizes that all students do not have the opportunity to give up employment and/or move to a college campus to continue their education. Clarkson offers the opportunity for working adults who live more than 100 miles from campus to complete degree programs through a variety of delivery methods.

DISTANCE LEARNING PROGRAM

The Clarkson College Distance Education Program currently serves about 200 students in thirty-four states. Since distance education is an outreach of the College's current programs, it is governed by the academic and administrative policies in effect. Distance students follow the same semester schedule, pay the same tuition, and receive the same support services as on-campus students. Distance Education Programs have the same accreditation as on-campus programs.

DELIVERY MEDIA

Clarkson delivers theory course work to students via mail, videotape and audiotape, fax transmission, computer e-mail, and telephone conferencing. Clarkson advisers help students to access and use the computer system. Syllabi, textbooks, and study questions are mailed to students; follow-up calls are made by faculty members. Tests are mailed to proctors in the students' area who monitor test-taking.

Students must have access to a computer with a modem, a fax machine, a VCR, and an audiocassette player. All students are required to have either a telephone answering machine or voice mail.

PROGRAMS OF STUDY

Registered nurses who hold a diploma or associate degree can complete the Bachelor of Science in Nursing (B.S.N.). All theory courses can be taken by distance education. Students must come to Omaha for a minimum of three weeks and a maximum of nine weeks for clinical sessions during their program. The B.S.N. requires 128 credit hours. Clarkson's Master of Science in Nursing (M.S.N.), which requires 18 credit hours of core courses plus appropriate credit hours in a selected option, allows nurses to enhance their career mobility. Options include nursing administration (additional 18 credit hours), nursing education (additional 18 credit hours), and family nurse practitioner (additional 27 credit hours). All three M.S.N. options and a postgraduate nurse practitioner certificate program can be taken completely through distance education. Clinicals are completed using qualified preceptors in the student's community.

The Bachelor of Science in medical imaging is open to ARRT Registered Technologists and/or board-eligible graduates of an associate degree or diploma program in radiography. Students can earn their bachelor's degree (128 credit hours) in radiography/medical imaging completely through distance education.

The B.S. in business (128 credit hours) and M.S. in health services management (36 credit hours) prepare students to assume leadership roles in the health-care industry. Both programs are available entirely through distance education.

SPECIAL PROGRAMS

There are no special programs offered in distance learning education at Clarkson College.

STUDENT SERVICES

Distance education students have access to many of the same resources as on-campus students. Distance students have regular contact with the Coordinator of Distance Education and Advanced Placement, who serves as a liaison between students and faculty members. The coordinator assists the students in the areas of advisement, registration, and textbook orders, which are accomplished through phone calls, faxes, and e-mail. Distance students' research and informational needs are supported by the College Library Services. Library resources are available via phone, computer, or fax, allowing students the ability to search for articles and books. Distance students have access to the College library loan services. Students also receive an e-mail listing of other students enrolled in the same courses for the semester, which facilitates communication with fellow students to discuss course work and share information.

CREDIT OPTIONS

Students can transfer credits taken at other regionally accredited institutions if the course work is comparable and there is evidence of satisfactory scholarship (at least a C in undergraduate courses and a B for graduate courses). A student may transfer up to 24 of the 48 credit hours in general education. In major course work, up to one third of the total number of credit hours in the major may be transferred. Registered nurses can receive 36 credit hours for their previous nursing education. An ARRT Registered Technologist can receive 42 credit hours for previous radiography education. Students beginning graduate programs may transfer no more than 9 semester credit hours from other institutions. Advanced placement students may take the College-Level Examination Program (CLEP) and/or conduct a portfolio review. The baccalaureate nursing program offers credit by examination through the National League for Nursing (NLN) mobility examinations.

FACULTY

Clarkson College has 31 full-time and 18 part-time faculty members, 13 percent of whom hold doctoral degrees.

ADMISSION

Distance education students are subject to the same admissions requirements as on-campus students. Undergraduate students must have a C+ GPA or higher and an ACT score of 20 or better. Graduate students must have a 3.0 GPA on a 4.0 scale and have completed an undergraduate degree from an accredited college or university. There are certain program-specific admission requirements.

TUITION AND FEES

Distance students pay the same tuition as on-campus students. For the 1997–98 academic year, undergraduate tuition is $272 per credit hour and graduate tuition is $314 per credit hour. There is an additional $17 per credit hour in fees. Students accepted after September 1997 pay a $200 per year distance fee.

FINANCIAL AID

Distance students are eligible for the same financial aid opportunities as on-campus students. Scholarships, grants, and loans are available to meet the individual financial needs of students who qualify.

Scholarships are awarded to outstanding applicants. Students are required to submit the completed Free Application for Federal Student Aid (FAFSA) or the renewal application and the Clarkson College Financial Aid Information Form for eligibility for all forms of aid.

APPLYING

The enrollment policy at Clarkson College allows potential students to apply at any time during the year. A completed application form, accompanied by the $15 application fee, and all official transcripts (high school and previous colleges) should be submitted when seeking admission. Students who have graduated from high school in the past two years must also submit ACT or SAT scores.

CONTACT

Jeff Beals
Director of Enrollment Management
Clarkson College
101 South 42nd Street
Omaha, Nebraska 68131-2739
Telephone: 402-552-3041
   Telephone: 800-647-5500 (toll-free)
      E-mail: admiss@clrkcol.crhsnet.edu
Web site: http://www.clarksoncollege.edu

Colorado Electronic Community College
Aurora, Colorado

Colorado Electronic Community College (CECC) was founded in 1995 as a significant innovation of the Colorado Community College and Occupational Education System (CCCOES), a thirteen-college state system. CECC develops and delivers the excellent degree and certificate programs of the system colleges via communication technologies. Students registering with CECC are awarded their degrees/certificates from one of the CCCOES colleges, which are accredited by the North Central Association of Colleges and Schools.

Colorado Electronic Community College was one of the first of its kind to offer a postsecondary degree completely asynchronously. CECC partners with private communications and multimedia companies and its sister colleges to provide unlimited access to its programs. It has articulated its degree program with all of the public four-year colleges in Colorado and several out-of-state colleges.

DISTANCE LEARNING PROGRAM

CECC has served 495 students in thirty-four states as well as Canada, the Caribbean, Brazil, and Sweden. Students can receive the complete Associate of Arts degree and various occupational certificates from their home or office without ever visiting a campus. All student support services are available at a distance as well.

DELIVERY MEDIA

Course work includes print, videotape, audiotape, broadcast, Internet, and CD-ROM materials, depending on the course of study. Students need only a telephone and a VCR to be able to complete an A.A. degree. Presentations, discussions, and study groups with classmates and faculty members occur through a voice-mail system or via electronic mail. Video components may be rented or accessed via cable. Several courses offer sections through the Internet.

PROGRAMS OF STUDY

CECC offers the entire Associate of Arts degree by distance. This degree is awarded by Arapahoe Community College, one of the thirteen CCCOES Colleges, and includes freshman- and sophomore-level general education courses that transfer toward the completion of a baccalaureate degree. The A.A. degree of the Colorado Community Colleges is a low-cost, high-quality, accredited degree that offers variety, flexibility, and a learner-centered curriculum. Every course guide clearly informs students of the potential learning outcomes they can expect from their investment.

The A.A. degree requires 60 hours, 38 hours of core curriculum and 22 hours of general education electives. Fifteen hours must be completed through CECC. Students completing the core curriculum are guaranteed transferability to Colorado four-year colleges.

Colorado Electronic Community College also brokers the certificates of its thirteen system colleges. Beginning in fall 1997, CECC will offer an advanced farm-ranch management certificate delivered via the Internet through Morgan Community College; an occupational safety and health construction standards certificate via the Internet through Trinidad State Junior College; and a computer programming certificate via the Internet through Aurora Community College. Regardless of the degree awarding college, students need only register at one place with the Colorado Electronic Community College.

SPECIAL PROGRAMS

Colorado Electronic Community College has a state-of-the-art, multimillion-dollar digital video and multimedia production and training facility called the Education Technology Training Center located in Denver, Colorado. It provides training to instructional designers and faculty members as well as business and government in the applications of technology to curriculum. Visitors to the center learn how to produce videos, press CD-ROMs, and create multimedia presentations and Internet applications and other technologies for the enhancement of learning and education access. In addition, the center has videoconferencing capabilities with all of the thirteen colleges in Colorado as well as with sites around the globe. Training, production, and communication can be delivered from the Education Technology Training Center to anywhere in the world.

STUDENT SERVICES

CECC is dedicated to the satisfaction and success of its students. CECC provides easy access to the complete array of student enrollment, academic, financial aid, special support, and career counseling services and provides tutoring to distance learning students. Library access is provided through various Internet library resources, interlibrary loan, and by the Colorado Association for Research Libraries.

CREDIT OPTIONS

Transfer credit and prior-learning portfolio development and assessment are offered toward degree/certificate completion. Credit through the College-Level Examination Program (CLEP) and other standardized tests is also available. Students may transfer up to 45 credits of their 60-hour Associate of Arts degree. College staff members understand that school and work experiences add richness to the education environment for participants. Staff members strive to provide credit for students' experiences.

FACULTY

CECC uses full-time (80 percent) and part-time (20 percent) faculty members from its sister colleges. These faculty members have won regional and national awards for teaching skills and have long experience with a student-centered philosophy.

ADMISSION

Colorado community colleges are open-door institutions, admitting anyone 16 years of age or older. A high school diploma or GED is not required for admission.

TUITION AND FEES

Tuition is $120 per credit hour. Student charges may include a $35 registration fee (once per semester), a $25-per-course voice mail fee, a $45-per-course telecourse license (AV videotape license), and a $15-per-course Internet technology fee.

FINANCIAL AID

General financial aid programs are available through Arapahoe Community College and include the Federal Pell Grant, Federal Supplemental Educational Opportunity Grant, Federal Perkins Loan, Federal Stafford Student Loan, and Federal Work-Study Programs. Approximately 20 percent of CECC's students receive financial aid. Last year, CECC students received a total of $103,619.

APPLYING

Distance learners can enroll by telephone (800-801-5040, toll-free). Admission and enrollment occur simultaneously as CECC is an open-door college. Because of the asynchronous nature of the course, there is always room in every section of every course.

CONTACT

Michael Rusk
Director of Student Services
Colorado Electronic Community College
9075 Lowry Boulevard
Denver, Colorado 80220
Telephone: 303-340-5706
               800-801-5040 (toll-free)
Fax: 303-340-5876
E-mail: sb_mike@cccs.cccoes.edu
Web site: http://www.cccoes.edu

Distance Learning Programs

Colorado State University
Division of Continuing and Distance Education
Fort Collins, Colorado

The University Colorado State University has served the people of Colorado as the state's land-grant university since 1870. Today, the campus in Fort Collins is home to 19,000 students pursuing degrees at all levels in a wide range of subjects in the liberal arts, engineering, business, natural resources, agriculture, and the sciences. The University's instructional outreach activities go far beyond the campus and the state of Colorado.

DISTANCE LEARNING PROGRAM

Colorado State University's distance education courses are designed to begin or to finish a degree, to explore new topics, to enrich life, and to give students an opportunity to develop a level of proficiency in professional development. Approximately 2,000 individuals from all over the country and overseas enrolled in distance education courses from Colorado State University during the 1995–96 academic year.

DELIVERY MEDIA

Colorado State offers courses in both print-base and video-base formats. All courses are supported by Colorado State University faculty members. Students may contact course faculty via telephone, fax, e-mail, or regular mail. Students should contact the Office of Continuing Education for contact information for an instructor.

PROGRAMS OF STUDY

The Colorado SURGE (State Resources in Graduate Education) program provides continuing education opportunities to off-campus graduate students in a flexible, convenient format. The video-based program allows students to take courses or complete a master's degree with no on-campus residence requirements.

Since SURGE began in 1967, more than 470 students have completed their master's degree, and many more have completed courses to advance their career and stay current in their field. SURGE offers degree programs in agricultural, chemical, civil, electrical, environmental, industrial, and mechanical engineering; business administration; computer science; engineering management; human resource development; management; statistics; and systems engineering and optimization. Completion of a degree program through SURGE requires application and admission to the Colorado State Graduate School.

Colorado State also provides other distance education opportunities. These courses are open-entry/open-exit, meaning students may register at any time and take from six to twelve months to complete, depending on the course. Many of the courses can be used for specific programs, such as the Child Care Administration Certificate, the Gerontology Interdisciplinary Studies Program, or the Educator's Portfolio Builder.

The state of Colorado requires certification of all child-care center directors and substitute directors by the State Department of Social Services. Certification requires both experience working with young children and specific education. Colorado State University is proud to offer courses through distance education that satisfy the educational requirements.

Other states may have specific educational requirements. Students should contact the appropriate agency in their area for further information.

The Gerontology Interdisciplinary Studies certificate program assists individuals to increase their knowledge, skills, and effectiveness in working with older adults. The objectives of the program are congruent with standards and guidelines for gerontology programs advocated by the Association of Gerontology in Higher Education (AGHE), of which Colorado State is an institutional member.

The Educator's Portfolio Builder distance education courses are designed for independent, self-paced learning. Students choose an area of interest and focus; they can mix and match and build the portfolio that meets their individual professional development needs. Courses are designed for practicing teachers, with assignments and activities relevant to teachers and students, and they are all college-credit courses. Colorado State University faculty members are the instructors. They are available to answer questions and give feedback via telephone, fax, e-mail, or regular mail.

SPECIAL PROGRAMS

Advising and career counseling services through the University HELP/Success Center are offered to all persons interested in continuing their learning. There is no fee for academic advising services. Students may schedule an appointment with an academic adviser by calling 970-491-0525 or 7095. The Extended University Programs librarian is available to assist students identify and access library materials. Students should call 970-491-6952 to speak with the librarian.

CREDIT OPTIONS

All credits earned through distance education are recorded on a Colorado State University transcript. Distance education courses are the same as on-campus courses and are accredited by each department. A student currently enrolled in a degree program is responsible for checking with the appropriate official at the degree-granting institution to make certain the course will apply.

FACULTY

Distance education faculty members must meet the same high standards any Colorado State University faculty member must meet. All of the distance faculty are faculty members within the department granting the course credit. Faculty members are available to answer questions and give feedback via telephone, fax, e-mail, or regular mail.

ADMISSION

Anyone who has the interest, desire, background, and ability may register for distance learning courses. However, if prerequisites are listed for a course, they must be met. Registration in continuing education courses does not constitute admission to Colorado State University.

TUITION AND FEES

Tuition for the SURGE program for the 1997–98 academic year ranges from $312 to $364 per semester credit hour depending on the student's choice of delivery format and site location. Tuition for other distance education courses for the 1997–98 academic year varies from $94 to $126 per semester credit hour depending on course instruction level and delivery method.

FINANCIAL AID

Colorado State University courses are approved for the DANTES program. Eligible military personnel should process DANTES application through the education office. For information regarding veterans benefits, students should contact the VA office at Colorado State University. With the exception of the SURGE program, distance learning is not a degree-granting program and is therefore not eligible for federal grants. Students are encouraged to seek scholarship aid from organizations and local civic groups that may sponsor such study.

APPLYING

There is no application for distance education. Students should simply register for the course(s) of interest by mail, fax, telephone, or in person and pay the tuition. To complete a degree via SURGE, admittance to the University's Graduate School is required.

CONTACT

For more information about these and other distance courses from Colorado State University or for registration information:
Telephone: 970-491-5288
          800-525-4950 (toll-free)
Fax: 970-491-7886
E-mail: askdede@lamar.colostate.edu
Web site: http://www.colostate.edu/Depts/CE/

Distance Learning Programs

Dallas Community Colleges
Distance Learning Program
Dallas, Texas

More than 200,000 students have enrolled in the Distance Learning Program of the Dallas Community Colleges (DCC) since it began in 1972. Currently, approximately 10,000 students enroll in the program each academic year. The Dallas Community Colleges program is a product of the collaboration of seven colleges, all accredited by the Commission on Colleges of the Southern Association of Colleges and Schools to award the associate degree. The program draws its strength from the full-time faculty members of these colleges and from more than twenty-five years of experience in the development and implementation of distance learning courses, which are used by many colleges worldwide.

DISTANCE LEARNING PROGRAM

The Dallas Distance Learning Program provides greater access to educational opportunities for learners in Dallas County and worldwide through the delivery of flexible, cost-effective courses. These courses are offered through a variety of technologies and may lead to the Associate of Arts and Sciences (A.A.S.) degree or provide opportunities for skill development or enhancement in career fields such as business.

DELIVERY MEDIA

Video-based telecourses include a preproduced video series with print materials. Students may lease videos or view them on television (Dallas area only). Class interaction is offered through the telephone, fax, and mail. Students are required to have a TV, VCR, and telephone.

Video-based telecourses PLUS include the same materials as above with on-line activities. A minimum 486 computer with 8 mb RAM, a 14,400-bps modem, Windows, and Internet access is also required.

Internet courses have the same computer requirements as above. Some courses require additional hardware, software, or telephone resources.

Print-based courses include print materials and participation in specialized activities. Courses may require a VCR or telephone.

PROGRAMS OF STUDY

The Associate of Arts and Sciences degree requires completion of 61 credit hours, a grade of C or better in each of three core courses, and a passing score on all sections of the Texas Academic Skills Program (TASP) test. The A.A.S. degree may be earned in its entirety through the distance learning program of the Dallas Community Colleges.

More than sixty courses are available in a variety of subjects, including business, communications, computer programming, health, humanities and arts, literature, mathematics, office technology and software, sciences, and social sciences.

Students who plan to transfer to a four-year institution should consult the catalog of that institution to ensure that selected courses will both transfer and apply toward the intended major.

SPECIAL PROGRAMS

Dallas participates in the special open-enrollment PACE program that reaches ships, submarines, and remote sites of the U.S. Navy. More than 4,000 military personnel have enrolled in courses through Dallas since 1992. Dallas is also a participant with other community colleges in the International Community College, which offers courses to students in the U.S. and abroad. Dallas Community Colleges also deliver courses to employees of major corporations based in the north Texas area through the AHE Tager network.

STUDENT SERVICES

Distance learners have access to admission and enrollment processes as well as library services, including an on-line search, study skills assistance, and academic advising. These services are available through the Web site or by fax, telephone, or mail.

CREDIT OPTIONS

The DCC transfers many passing grade credits from other colleges accredited through one of the U.S. regional associations. The DCC registrar completes course evaluations as needed for degree planning.

Credits earned through credit-by-examination, military experience, and the U.S. Armed Forces Institute are reviewed by the registrar. Credit may be granted if applicable. The DCC requires that at least 25 percent of the credit hours required for graduation be taken by instruction rather than these methods.

FACULTY

More than 85 percent of the courses in the distance learning program are taught by full-time faculty members who also teach on-campus classes.

Each of the more than 100 faculty members holds credentials approved by the Colleges' accrediting agency. To ensure high-quality instruction, the number of students assigned to a faculty member in a distance learning course is limited.

ADMISSION

Students must have a high school diploma or its equivalent, be at least 18 years of age, or receive special approval for admission as outlined in the DCC catalog. Texas students must also fulfill TASP requirements as mandated by state law.

TUITION AND FEES

Tuition and fees vary with the learner's residence and the number of credit hours. This may range from approximately $80 per 3-credit course for a local Dallas resident to $366 per 3-credit course for an out-of-state student. Other expenses may include tape leasing ($40 plus shipping per course; $20 is refunded if the tapes are returned at the end of the course) and the cost of study guides, textbooks, and course-related software.

FINANCIAL AID

Students accepted for enrollment may be considered for several forms of institutional and federal financial aid. Veterans and financial aid recipients should consult an adviser before enrolling in distance learning courses.

APPLYING

Applicants should submit an official application along with appropriate documentation, such as an official high school transcript, GED scores, or official transcripts from previous colleges, and should complete any required assessment procedures. The DCC application is available on-line or through the mail.

CONTACT
Distance Learning Program
Dallas Community Colleges
9596 Walnut Street
Dallas, Texas 75243
Telephone: 972-669-6400
              888-468-4268 (toll-free)
              972-669-6410 (for recorded information)
Fax: 972-669-6409
Web site: http://ollie.dcccd.edu

Embry-Riddle Aeronautical University
Extended Campus
Daytona Beach, Florida

Embry-Riddle Aeronautical University (ERAU) is an independent, nonsectarian, nonprofit coeducational university with a history dating back to the early days of aviation. The University is accredited by the Commission on Colleges of the Southern Association of Colleges and Schools. Residential campuses in Daytona Beach, Florida, and Prescott, Arizona, provide education in a traditional setting. The Extended Campus network of education centers throughout the United States and Europe and the Distance Learning/Independent Study Program serve civilian and military working adults around the world. Embry-Riddle Aeronautical University has served the public and private sectors of aviation through education for more than sixty-five years and is the only accredited not-for-profit university in the world totally oriented to aviation/aerospace. Alumni are employed in all facets of civilian and military aviation.

DISTANCE LEARNING PROGRAM

Embry-Riddle has developed several innovative methods to extend its education programs to students: a network of resident centers located at or near the students' workplaces; distance and electronic learning technology; and independent study, which provides access to degree programs and courses to students in their homes or at other locations.

Embry-Riddle established an Independent Studies Program in the early 1980s to meet the needs of working professionals. Current yearly enrollments exceed 4,000. Associate, bachelor's, and master's degree courses are offered in several disciplines.

DELIVERY MEDIA

Master's degree courses are delivered via distance learning electronic media. Students, professors, and staff interact through the ERAU private forum established on CompuServe. Students are required to have access to: an IBM/compatible (preferably 386 or later model) or Macintosh personal computer system with monitor, a hard drive system sufficient to load spreadsheet and word processing software, a 3.5" floppy drive, a modem that will support 1200 or higher baud rate, and a VCR and television for video tapes. Undergraduate courses delivered through Independent Study utilize video and/or audio tape and printed material.

PROGRAMS OF STUDY

The Master of Aeronautical Science (M.A.S.) degree with specializations in operations, management, or safety requires 36 semester hours of course work. The M.A.S. program was designed to enable the aviation/aerospace professional to master the application of modern management concepts, methods, and tools to the challenges of aviation and general business. The special intricacies of aviation are woven into a strong, traditional management foundation and examined in greater detail through the wide variety of electives.

M.A.S. core topics (12 credit hours) include air transportation, aircraft and space craft development, human factors in aviation/aerospace, and research methods and statistics. Specialization courses (12 credit hours) provide a strong knowledge base of subject material required. Each of the four courses provides the student with skills needed in the professional arena. Electives and a Graduate Research Project (GRP) (12 credit hours) provide students with the ability to tailor their degrees, adding greater breadth and depth in aviation/aerospace–related intellectual pursuits.

Undergraduate degree offerings include Associate of Science and Bachelor of Science degrees in professional aeronautics; a Bachelor of Science degree in management of technical operations (BSMTO); and an Associate of Science in aviation business administration.

The professional aeronautics degree program was conceived and developed especially for individuals who have already established and progressed in an aviation career. The curriculum is designed to build upon the knowledge and skills acquired through training and experience in one of the many aviation occupations. The combination of aviation experience and required and elective courses in aeronautical science, management, computer science, economics, communications, humanities, social science, mathematics, and physical science prepares graduates for career growth and increased responsibility. The Bachelor of Science in professional aeronautics requires 126 credit hours, and the Associate of Science in professional aeronautics requires 63 credit hours.

The Bachelor of Science in management of technical operations degree requires successful completion of 120 credit hours. Designed for the student who possesses some technical expertise either through previous course work, licensing, or experience, this degree provides the student a flexible yet solid business program.

The Associate of Science in aviation business administration degree requires successful completion of 63 credit hours. This degree provides courses in general education and an introduction to business coupled with some business applications.

SPECIAL PROGRAMS

The Division of Continuing Education is the unit of Embry-Riddle Aeronautical University's Extended Campus that offers quality training programs, including seminars, conferences, and workshops. These programs serve domestic and international aviation professionals, evening/weekend credit and noncredit-seeking adult students, and aviation-oriented youth and educators. Specialized training courses at the customer's site and consulting services to the international education and aviation community are also made available on a contract basis. Seminars are offered through distance learning on a variety of topics.

STUDENT SERVICES

Students are provided on-line library access in addition to a library guide that lists local points of reference for research. Each student is assigned to an admission specialist/academic adviser. The adviser assists students in registering for courses that qualify for their degree program and provides administrative support.

CREDIT OPTIONS

Master's degree applicants may transfer up to 12 semester hours of credit into the University. Credit must be from a regionally accredited institution with a grade of B or better and awarded within seven years of application to ERAU. Courses must be applicable to the M.A.S. degree program.

Undergraduate applicants may transfer credit from regionally accredited institutions with the letter grade of D or better. Advanced standing credit may be awarded for prior learning achieved through postsecondary education, testing, and work or training experience.

FACULTY

The faculty is a blend of traditionally prepared academicians and leaders with significant industry track records. Nearly all faculty members have doctorate or terminal degrees.

ADMISSION

Admission to the master's degree program requires a bachelor's degree from a regionally accredited institution. Admission to the undergraduate programs is unique to each degree.

TUITION AND FEES

Tuition for master's degree courses is $280 per credit hour. Textbook and shipping fees vary from $50 to $125 per course based on textbook prices.

Undergraduate tuition is $130 per credit hour. Other fees vary by course. Each course is 3 semester credit hours.

FINANCIAL AID

Students accepted for enrollment may be considered for several forms of federal financial aid. There are three different federal programs available. Additional information is provided at time of application.

All Embry-Riddle degree programs have been approved by the Department of Veterans' Affairs for enrollment of persons eligible to receive benefits from U.S. Department of Veterans' Affairs (DVA).

APPLYING

Applications must be submitted with appropriate documentation, such as official high school transcripts, GED scores, or official transcripts from previous colleges or universities.

CONTACT
Mr. Thomas W. Pettit, Director
Mr. James T. Gallogly, Graduate Program Manager
Mrs. Linda Dammer, Undergraduate Program Manager
Department of Independent Studies
Embry-Riddle Aeronautical University
600 S. Clyde Morris Boulevard
Daytona Beach, Florida 32114-3900
Telephone: 904-226-6218 (Graduate Program)
   800-866-6271 (toll-free)
   904-226-6363 (Undergraduate Program)
   800-359-3728 (toll-free)
Fax: 904-226-7627
E-mail: indstudy@cts.db.erau.edu
Web site: http://ec.db.erau.edu

Distance Learning Programs

Franklin University

Open Campus
Columbus, Ohio

Franklin University has been offering on-line courses since 1996 and has made the decision to increase its course offerings provided through distance methods. Founded in 1902, Franklin University is located in the heart of downtown Columbus, Ohio. Annually, more than 5,000 students—the majority of whom are working full-time and over 25 years of age—pursue programs leading to Bachelor of Science degrees in seventeen innovative majors. The University also offers a Master of Business Administration degree that focuses on translating theory into practice and enhancing collaborative learning. In 1998, Franklin University also will introduce a Master of Science in human services management and a Master of Science in integrated communication and marketing. Franklin University is an independent, nonprofit institution of higher education and is best characterized by its student-centered philosophy. The University also has a strong commitment to undergraduate open admission and excellence in teaching.

DISTANCE LEARNING PROGRAM

Franklin University's Open Campus is provided as a service to students who are geographically separated from the main campus in central Ohio. Some of the offerings take advantage of a group setting via chat rooms and message centers over the Internet, while others are completely independent study programs.

DELIVERY MEDIA

The University's Open Campus courses are available in several formats: on-line, text-based, and audio/video. On-line courses require the use of a computer, modem, and Microsoft Office software. Students must have an Internet provider with access to the World Wide Web as well as e-mail. Text-based courses require no computers, but students must use the telephone and fax to communicate with instructors. Audio/video courses use tapes and require students to have a TV, VCR, and audio player.

PROGRAMS OF STUDY

Franklin University offers several programs of study through the Open Campus. In 1997, course work leading to the technical administration major program is available on-line for students who have course work equivalent to an associate degree in areas such as automotive management, civil engineering technology, and electronics engineering technology. In addition, business administration, computer science, and health services administration majors will be available in Distance Learning format during the 1997–98 academic year for students who have transfer credit. Student services associates are available to work closely with Open Campus students on planning and evaluating the needed courses.

SPECIAL PROGRAMS

In today's organizations, employees are being asked to take on many responsibilities that cross functional lines. Often, those employees have no formal training for completing those increased responsibilities. In response to these additional educational demands, Franklin University has developed twenty-two professional certificates for those with or without undergraduate degrees. These programs consist of three or four courses that are designed to enhance the knowledge of the business professional who is interested in personal growth or career or business development. Professional certificates are available in distance learning formats in business communication, corporate information systems, cultural studies, international business, investments, process management, and public relations. New certificate programs are also in progress.

STUDENT SERVICES

In Franklin University's student-centered approach, each student is matched with a student services associate (SSA), who becomes an important contact at the University, along with the course instructor. The SSA serves as an initial as well as long-term resource for helping the student with admissions and course scheduling until the academic goals are achieved.

CREDIT OPTIONS

Franklin University students who meet appropriate requirements can earn credit outside the classroom through CLEP (College-Level Examination Program), ACT-PEP (ACT Proficiency Examination Program), FUPE (Franklin University Proficiency Exams), or Prior Learning Portfolios. Any questions pertaining to exam or portfolio requirements and study guides should be directed to Student Services (888-341-6237).

FACULTY

Open Campus faculty members enrich the (virtual) classroom with special talents and abilities drawn from successful careers in business, industry, government, and social service. Franklin University faculty members seek to design and imbue the learning environment with content and methods designed to graduate reflective practitioners.

ADMISSION

Candidates for admission to the technical administration bachelor's degree program should have a high school diploma or its equivalent. A minimum of 26 hours of technical course work from a regionally accredited college or university also is required.

TUITION AND FEES

The standard undergraduate tuition rate for the 1997–98 academic year is $169 per credit hour. A tuition rate of $212 per credit hour is charged for computer science courses, and a surcharge of $20 per hour is charged above other tuition rates for all Open Campus courses.

APPLYING

Anyone who is a graduate of an accredited high school or has passed the GED is eligible for admission as a degree-seeking student. Those seeking a bachelor's degree must complete an admission application and forward an official high school transcript or an official GED test score report. To apply transfer credits from another institution, all official transcripts should be forwarded to Franklin University directly from the previous institution(s). However, a student can begin a distance learning course before the transcripts have been received. Students who would like to take courses as non-degree-seeking students do not need to be high school graduates.

CONTACT

Student Services
Franklin University
201 South Grant Avenue
Columbus, Ohio 43215
Telephone: 614-341-6237
　　　　　 888-341-6237 (toll-free)
Fax: 614-224-8027
E-mail: info@franklin.edu
Web site: http://www.franklin.edu

Distance Learning Programs

Georgia Institute of Technology
Center for Distance Learning
Atlanta, Georgia

Founded in 1885, the Georgia Institute of Technology is the Southeast's largest technological institution. Georgia Tech is located on a 330-acre campus near downtown Atlanta—the financial, communications, and cultural hub of the Southeast. The Institute's mission is to be a leader among those few technological universities whose alumni, faculty, students, and staff define, expand, and communicate the frontiers of knowledge and innovation.

U.S. News & World Report consistently lists Georgia Tech among the fifty best universities in the nation. Georgia Tech also makes their list of the top graduate engineering programs in the country. Ten of the engineering options were ranked in the top fifteen, with several in the top five.

In addition to its high-quality undergraduate and graduate instructional programs, Tech has a world-class research program, with $197 million in new grants and contracts awarded during the 1997 fiscal year. This ranks Tech as the South's largest engineering research university.

DISTANCE LEARNING PROGRAM

Georgia Tech's Center for Distance Learning serves more than 600 distance learning students and is housed within a unit that reports directly to the provost. Georgia Tech is accredited by the Southern Association of Colleges and Schools. Engineering disciplines are accredited by the Accrediting Board for Engineering and Technology.

DELIVERY MEDIA

Video cameras record instructor presentations and student-instructor interaction during regular Georgia Tech graduate classes. The videotapes and supporting materials are sent to off-campus students, who take courses without having to come to the campus. Selected courses are available at some locations via videoconferencing, satellite, and the Internet. Students enrolled in the program communicate with their Georgia Tech professor by telephone, fax, and/or electronic mail. Students have access to the Georgia Tech Electronic Library and the computer system via a business or home computer and a modem. Access is also provided over the Internet.

PROGRAMS OF STUDY

The Georgia Tech video-based distance delivery program provides high-quality graduate-level courses that can be applied to several master's degree programs. The Master of Science in Electrical and Computer Engineering is offered with options in computer engineering, digital signal processing, power, and telecommunications; all options require 50 quarter hours of course work. The Master of Science (M.S.) and the Master of Science in Environmental Engineering (M.S.Env.E.) degrees are offered with concentrations in water quality, surface and subsurface systems, hazardous and solid waste, and air quality; all programs require 50 quarter hours of course work or the equivalent. The Master of Science in Health Physics/Radiological Engineering degree requires 45 quarter hours of course work. The Master of Science in Industrial Engineering is offered with specializations in automation, production and logistics systems, and statistical process control and quality assurance; it requires 48 quarter hours of course work, students must hold an undergraduate degree from an ABET-accredited engineering curriculum. The Master of Science in Mechanical Engineering is offered with specializations in thermal science and mechanical systems; it requires 48 quarter hours of course work.

Specific information on admission and degree requirements can be obtained by calling the academic coordinators for each area. Students should call the contact name for additional information.

SPECIAL PROGRAMS

The Computer Integrated Manufacturing Systems (CIMS) program at Georgia Tech offers an innovative approach to graduate education for students interested in identifying solutions to the manufacturing productivity problems facing U.S. industry. Students enrolled in the CIMS distance learning program pursue graduate degrees in a traditional academic discipline while fulfilling requirements for a CIMS multidisciplinary certificate. The program is designed to strike a balance between technical depth and broad comprehension of the problems facing industry and the current state of art for solving these problems. Elective courses are selected from four main focus areas: Design of Products and Processes, Computer Communication Hardware and Software, System Dynamics and Controls, and Management in Manufacturing.

Students completing a distance learning graduate degree in electrical engineering or in systems analysis offered by the School of Industrial and Systems Engineering may also obtain a Test and Evaluation (T&E) certificate. For students in this category, the T&E certificate is awarded by the College of Engineering and is an enhancement to the degree program. Students enrolled in video-based instruction but not pursuing an M.S. degree may obtain the T&E certificate awarded by the Department of Continuing Education at Georgia Tech.

CREDIT OPTIONS

Students earn credit toward their degree by registering for and completing courses delivered by videotape. Requirements for each course are the same as for on-campus students enrolled in the course. A student may receive transfer credit of up to 9 quarter hours for graduate-level courses (approved by the academic adviser) taken at an accredited institution in the United States or Canada and not used for credit toward another degree.

FACULTY

There are 639 full-time faculty members at Georgia Tech, 93 percent with doctoral degrees. One hundred and five, or 16 percent, teach in the distance learning program.

ADMISSION

Admission requirements vary among the academic disciplines. To apply, individuals should contact the academic adviser or admissions office in the School to which he or she is applying.

TUITION AND FEES

Video enrollment fees for in-state and out-of-state students for the 1997–98 academic year are $297 per credit hour. Fees are subject to change each year. There are no supplemental fees; however, students must purchase their own textbooks.

FINANCIAL AID

There are no financial aid programs available through Georgia Tech for distance learning students. Most employers have programs that will help students pay the course fees. The Department of Veterans Affairs has approved the Georgia Tech Video Program as independent study. Georgia Tech has a memorandum of understanding with DANTES and with the Air Force.

APPLYING

Application materials can be obtained from the School to which the student is applying. Applicants must submit an Application for Admission, three letters of recommendation, a biographical sketch, two official transcripts of all previous college work, and scores from the Graduate Record Examinations (GRE). Decisions are made by the individuals Schools.

CONTACT

Program Coordinator
Center for Distance Learning
Georgia Institute of Technology
Atlanta, Georgia 30332-0240
Telephone: 404-894-0192
Fax: 404-894-8924
Web site: http://www.conted.gatech.edu/distance/cdl-home.html

Distance Learning Programs

GMI Engineering and Management Institute

Graduate Studies Department
Flint, Michigan

In 1919, the Industrial Fellowship League of Flint sponsored a night school for employees of Flint-area industries. General Motors Corporation agreed to underwrite the school in 1926, and General Motors Institute was born. In 1982, GMI became independent of General Motors when the private corporation "GMI Engineering & Management Institute" was established. GMI has maintained a close affiliation with industry throughout its history.

In the fall of 1982 GMI began a video-based, distance learning graduate program leading to a Master of Science in Manufacturing Management degree. In 1990 the Master of Science in Engineering degree was initiated.

GMI's mission is to serve society by preparing leaders to meet the technical and managerial needs of business and industry in both the public and private sectors. World renowned as America's Co-op College, GMI focuses on practice rather than theory. Continuing GMI's long and continuous association with industry and the working student, the Master of Science degrees have a strong orientation toward manufacturing. GMI is accredited by the Commission on Institutions of Higher Education of the North Central Association of Colleges and Schools.

DISTANCE LEARNING PROGRAM

Offering flexibility and convenience, these programs were developed to fit the needs of working professionals. The educational process consists of the on-campus presentation, off-campus communication of the courses via videotape, telephone contact, and evaluation. The video-based program is offered at host companies where the number of prospective students is sufficient. The video-based distance learning program serves approximately 800 students at host companies throughout the United States, Canada, and Mexico. The program, however, is not a correspondence course. It is a rigorous, bona fide graduate program.

DELIVERY MEDIA

GMI's distance learning program is video-based and tapes are delivered to established industrial learning centers throughout the United States. Industrial partners at the centers provide video equipment for classes. Students at the centers have telephone, facsimile, and e-mail access to the professors. A regular schedule of telephone communication is established in the first session of each course. For some courses students may need access to a personal computer for homework.

PROGRAMS OF STUDY

GMI offers a Master of Science in Manufacturing Management degree requiring 54 credit hours and a Master of Science in Engineering degree that requires 45 credit hours. Students in the engineering program can specialize in mechanical design or manufacturing systems engineering.

GMI designed the Master of Science programs to be terminal professional degrees for engineers and managers in industry. The programs are particularly attractive to working professionals who want to extend and broaden their related skills. Although designed as terminal degrees, they also provide preparation for study at the doctoral level.

The M.S. in Manufacturing Management degree is a part-time program designed to be completed in three years. Areas of study include finance and economics, quantitative skills and computer applications, management and administration, and manufacturing engineering. The M.S. in Engineering degree can be completed in one year full-time or two years on a part-time basis. There is no thesis required.

CREDIT OPTIONS

Credits are earned by completing courses; however, students may transfer up to 9 credit hours. Credit may be transferred for grades of B or better upon the recommendation of the candidate's adviser and is granted only for completed graduate study. Credit is not given for experience.

Anyone interested in transfer credit should obtain an application for transfer credit from the Graduate Office.

FACULTY

There are 41 full- and part-time professors teaching in the Graduate Studies program. Ninety-seven percent of the faculty have doctoral or other terminal academic degrees.

ADMISSION

No one is accepted into the program without a bachelor's degree.

A bachelor's degree in engineering is required for the M.S. in Engineering degree program. Requirements include a minimum 3.0 grade point average in undergraduate work, scores on the GMAT or GRE, and two supervisor recommendations. The same requirements apply to on-campus and distance learning students.

TUITION AND FEES

In 1997–98, graduate tuition is $1137 per 3-credit course. All required textbooks and handouts are provided by GMI at no additional cost to the student. There is no application fee, but there is a $45 registration fee per course. The same fees apply to out-of-state students.

APPLYING

GMI accepts applications for fall and winter terms only. The deadline for fall application is July 15 and for winter, November 1.

CONTACT

Betty Bedore
Coordinator of Publicity and Special Projects
Graduate Studies Department
GMI Engineering & Management Institute
Telephone: 810-762-7494
                888-GMI-GRAD (toll-free)
Fax: 810-762-9935
E-mail: bbedore@nova.gmi.edu
Web site: http://www.gmi.edu/official/acad/grad/

Distance Learning Programs

Goucher College
Center for Graduate and Continuing Studies
Baltimore, Maryland

A strong commitment to excellence in liberal arts education has been a hallmark of Goucher College since its founding in 1885. Goucher began as a college for women and became coeducational in 1986. The College is located 8 miles north of Baltimore and 1 hour from Washington, D.C. There are 1,200 undergraduates on campus and more than 300 graduate students in the traditional graduate programs in education and in the distance learning graduate programs in historic preservation and creative writing. A distance learning program in arts administration will begin in August 1998. Goucher College is accredited by the Middle States Association of Colleges and Schools.

DISTANCE LEARNING PROGRAM

The Center for Graduate and Continuing Studies at Goucher College offers the nation's only limited-residency Master of Arts in historic preservation and Master of Fine Arts in creative nonfiction. The new Master of Arts in arts administration will likewise be the only limited-residency program in arts administration in the country. On-campus residency in all of the programs is limited to a maximum of two weeks each summer, with the majority of the course work being conducted electronically, by telecommunication, and/or by mail.

DELIVERY MEDIA

The graduate programs at Goucher take advantage of the College's extensive technological resources, such as the College's Internet services, in order to foster greater student-teacher and peer-to-peer interactions. E-mail lists, Web-based discussion groups, and FTP file transfer services are available to each student. Previous knowledge of the Internet is not required since instruction is offered during the summer residencies. However, the curriculum is not solely based on computer technology; some faculty members, by design or preference, may choose to communicate through mail or other delivery services.

PROGRAMS OF STUDY

The Master of Arts in Historic Preservation Program requires 36 credit hours for graduation, including seven required courses that provide the student with a thorough grounding in the history and philosophy of historic preservation, documentation techniques, and the history and development of American architecture and urban design. Students also choose eight elective courses, ranging from historic preservation as public policy and preservation law to materials conservation and preservation technology. In addition, the program offers students the ability to design their own courses that focus on an area of particular interest. The program culminates in a written thesis, which is orally defended.

The Master of Fine Arts in creative nonfiction at Goucher offers nontraditional students a limited-residency writing program within a single genre that balances critical reading with original writing. Thirty-six credits are required for graduation. Students complete a literary internship and, in their senior semester, submit a final manuscript of "publishable-quality" original work of at least 150 pages. The summer residency is integrated with the annual Mid-Atlantic Creative Nonfiction Summer Writers' Conference held at Goucher College.

The Master of Arts in art administration requires 40 credit hours for graduation. During the first residency, students meet with the program director to finalize the individual program of study and with the faculty members whose courses they take during the first year. During this residency, students also take the required introductory course, Principles of Arts Administration. In the final year, students must complete a 3-credit internship and 3-credit major paper, which will develop from that internship.

CREDIT OPTIONS

Master of Arts in historic preservation students may apply for the transfer of up to 7 credits from approved graduate courses in historic preservation or a related field that have been successfully completed at accredited colleges and universities during the past five years.

The Master of Arts in arts administration and Master of Fine Arts in creative nonfiction do not allow transfer credits because of the uniqueness of these programs.

FACULTY

Faculty members for the programs are drawn from today's leading practitioners in historic preservation, nonfiction writing, the arts, and arts administration and serve as tutors rather than traditional lecturers. To insure individual attention, the programs maintain a low student-faculty ratio.

ADMISSION

A bachelor's degree is required for all programs. Official transcripts of all undergraduate and graduate work must be submitted along with letters of recommendation and an essay that addresses the applicant's ability to undertake the self-directed study that is the foundation of the limited-residency graduate programs. Standardized test scores are not required.

TUITION AND FEES

Tuition for the Master of Arts in Historic Preservation Program is $1400 per course; tuition for the Master of Fine Arts in Creative Nonfiction Program is $4650 per semester; the Master of Arts in Arts Administration Program is $485 per credit hour, regardless of state of residency. A one-time, nonrefundable application fee of $50 is required for all programs.

FINANCIAL AID

To help defray the costs of the programs, students may apply for a Federal Stafford Loan through the Financial Aid Division of Student Administrative Services at Goucher College.

APPLYING

The application deadline for the Master of Arts in Historic Preservation and Master of Arts in Arts Administration Programs that begin in August 1998 is February 13, 1998. The application deadline for the Master of Fine Arts in Creative Nonfiction Program that begins in January 1998 is October 15, 1997; the application deadline for the class beginning August 1998 is May 1, 1998.

CONTACT

Noreen Mack
Center for Graduate and Continuing Studies
Goucher College
1021 Dulaney Valley Road
Baltimore, Maryland 21204
Telephone: 410-337-6200
　　　　　 800-697-4646 (toll-free)

Distance Learning Programs

Heriot-Watt University
Edinburgh Business School
M.B.A. by Distance Learning
Edinburgh, Scotland

Heriot-Watt University was originally established in 1821 and received its Royal Charter (the equivalent of U.S. accreditation) in 1966. The M.B.A. by distance learning was introduced in 1990 and has grown to become one of the largest M.B.A. programs in the world. The thousands of Americans and Canadians who have enrolled include representatives from seventy of the Fortune 100 companies and many government agencies. The textbooks are written specifically for the distance learner by professors at major universities in the U.S. and Europe. Heriot-Watt is widely regarded as one of the preeminent business and technical universities in Europe. Thousands of students study on the 250-acre campus in Scotland's capital city, while many thousands more in more than 130 countries are working on their M.B.A. by distance learning.

DISTANCE LEARNING PROGRAM

The distance learning M.B.A. is designed for motivated adult learners. The degree is earned entirely by passing nine rigorous exams. No interaction with faculty members or other students is required. In 1995, the distance learning M.B.A. merged with the on-campus program so that all students study the same materials and take the same exams.

DELIVERY MEDIA

Students receive a large loose-leaf textbook for each course, which they work through on their own (occasional faculty contact by fax or mail is available but not required). The only requirement for each course is a challenging 3-hour supervised exam. Exams are held twice a year in 120 U.S. and Canadian cities and in more than 130 countries. No computer is required, although optional supplementary software is available for the compulsory courses.

PROGRAM OF STUDY

This M.B.A. by distance learning has no prerequisites: no bachelor's degree, no GMAT exam, and no specific course work in the field. The nine courses may be taken in any order, although some recommendations are given, such as leaving strategic planning until the end. All courses are fully self-contained and designed for the student working alone. No additional reading is required. Students can take as many or as few courses at a time as they wish. Seven of the subjects are compulsory: finance, economics, marketing, organizational behavior, quantitative methods, accounting, and strategic planning. The other two courses are selected from an array of available electives: negotiation; international trade and finance; decision-making techniques; strategies for change; government, industry, and privatization; financial risk management; strategic information systems; and human resource management. Each course contains chapter reviews, practice questions, case studies, and practice examinations so that the students may evaluate their own progress. Each course is equivalent to 4 semester units. A certificate is awarded on completion of each course. When nine certificates are earned, the M.B.A. is awarded. The case study–based courses are designed to prepare students for real business problems and challenges in the increasingly international business world.

SPECIAL PROGRAMS

The M.B.A. by distance learning program is closely linked to the full-time and part-time on-campus M.B.A. programs, and students may transfer between the various modes of study. Six-week on-campus study blocks enable distance learning students to join their on-campus counterparts for one or two courses, while four-day intensive summer school sessions give distance learning students the opportunity to network and to participate in classes.

The University has ties to a host of individual U.S. and European universities through research activities and academic exchanges. Recently these have included Stanford University, Pepperdine University, the State University of New York System, Purdue University, and the University of Tulsa.

The University also offers a unique Consortium M.B.A. in which the curriculum is modified to address the needs of major international corporations, who provide the program to groups of employees. Dozens of executives at two large companies are the pioneers in this effort.

STUDENT SERVICES

The University maintains a help line (by fax or mail) for occasional inquiries. Students can also communicate with each other via the Internet, phone, or mail. Student newsletters are mailed several times a year, and library services are available on-line. Alumni services include an innovative Internet-based Career Advisory

Service, which maintains a sizable employer database.

CREDIT OPTIONS

Up to two compulsory courses may be waived if the student has taken comparable academic courses or has certain professional qualifications such as CPA or CGA accreditation. One compulsory course may be waived if the student holds an acceptable undergraduate degree in business-related subjects. Instructions for applying for course waivers are included in the course catalog.

FACULTY

Courses were written by professors from such schools as Stanford University (U.S.), INSEAD (France), and the London Business School (England). Examinations are graded by the more than 25 current full-time faculty members at Heriot-Watt University and external examiners from other universities.

ADMISSION

Any motivated adult may begin the M.B.A. by distance learning program. No GMAT or TOEFL score is required. Students officially matriculate (become registered) in the program either by holding an acceptable bachelor's degree or by passing two of the compulsory courses. Each course assumes some general business knowledge but begins with chapters designed to start at a basic level and bring the student up to speed in the specific field.

TUITION AND FEES

Courses can be purchased individually as needed. The 1996–97 price was $820 (U.S.) per course, which included tuition and all necessary study materials. There is a £55 fee payable to the University for each examination.

FINANCIAL AID

In the U.S. and Canada, a payment plan is available; those interested should contact the North American Distributor for details. In addition, many students are funded directly by their employers, who range from Fortune 100 companies to small businesses.

APPLYING

Students may start the M.B.A. program at any time by purchasing a course and beginning to study. Although suggestions are given for study order, students may begin with the course or courses that most immediately apply to their work situation or that hold the greatest interest. Exams are held in June and December, with examination sign-up deadlines about three months prior to the exams. For more information in the U.S. or Canada, prospective students should contact the address below.

CONTACT

Student Services
North American Distributor
Heriot-Watt M.B.A. by Distance Learning
6921 Stockton Avenue
El Cerrito, California 94530
Telephone: 800-622-0707 (toll-free)
Fax: 510-528-3555
E-mail: heriotwatt@degree.net
Web site: http://www.degree.net/mba/mba.html

Distance Learning Programs

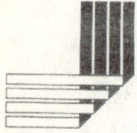

Indiana Higher Education Telecommunication System

Indiana Partnership for Statewide Education
Indianapolis, Indiana

Since 1967, Indiana's colleges and universities have cooperatively managed telecommunications networks through IHETS to share resources and disseminate a wide variety of educational opportunities. In 1992, the institutions established the Indiana Partnership for Statewide Education as the vehicle for collaboration in program planning, delivery of student services, needs assessment and promotion, faculty development, and evaluation. The Partnership's goal is to ensure that lifelong learning is available via distance education to Indiana citizens wherever they may live and work. Technology developments mean that many of the same programs are available on campus and around the world. Consortium members are Ball State University, Independent Colleges of Indiana, Indiana State University, Indiana University, Ivy Tech State College, Purdue University, University of Southern Indiana, and Vincennes University.

DISTANCE LEARNING PROGRAM

Each consortium member is fully accredited and responsible for its own programs. Collectively, enrollments on a statewide basis approach 10,000 per year in high school and college credit courses; hundreds of others are served locally or regionally by distance education, and correspondence programs serve thousands of students around the world. The Partnership has adopted the umbrella label "Indiana College Network" to refer to the comprehensive array of degree programs and learning opportunities provided by Indiana's higher education institutions.

DELIVERY MEDIA

Partnership institutions use a variety of media, including independent study by correspondence, satellite (one-way video with two-way audio), public or cable television, two-way video, videotape, and the Internet. Some degrees are available entirely via satellite to specially equipped learning sites, but most degrees also permit students to take course work in a combination of modes. Most programs with "live" interaction are still available only within Indiana, though more are becoming available at locations throughout the United States and in other countries.

PROGRAMS OF STUDY

Degrees are listed with the name of the institution that offers them: Associate of General Studies (A.G.S.), Indiana University; Associate of Arts (A.A.) (general studies) Ball State University; Associate of Applied Science or Associate of Science (A.A.S. or A.S.) (general studies), Vincennes University; A.S. (labor studies), Indiana University; A.S. (law enforcement option) Vincennes University; A.A. or A.S. (behavioral sciences, social science), Vincennes University; A.S. or A.A.S. (business studies option), Vincennes University; A.G.S. (surgical technology option), Vincennes University (students must be graduates of formal certificate programs as defined by the National Association of Surgical Technology); Bachelor of General Studies (B.G.S.), Indiana University; Bachelor of Science in Nursing (B.S.N.), Ball State University (degree completion for registered nurses who have graduated from an accredited National League for Nursing school); Bachelor of Science (B.S.) (human resource development), Indiana State University (degree completion program); B.S. (labor studies), Indiana University; Master of Business Administration (M.B.A.), Ball State University; Master of Science (M.S.) (computer science), Ball State University; Master of Arts (M.A.) (elementary education, educational administration, or special education), Ball State University (each program requires one summer term in residence on the Muncie campus for two courses currently offered only onsite); Master of Science in Engineering (M.S.E.), Purdue University (includes separate concentrations in electrical, industrial, materials science, and mechanical engineering as well as a multidisciplinary degree); M.S. (human resource development), Indiana State University; Master of Science in Nursing (M.S.N.), Indiana University (available primarily at IU campuses statewide); M.S. (occupational safety management), Indiana State University; and M.S. (recreation therapy), Indiana University.

Several other programs were nearing authorization at the time of publication. Information is available in the separate listings for the institutions or via the World Wide Web.

SPECIAL PROGRAMS

Indiana University offers a certificate program in labor studies, and Vincennes University offers an Associate of Technology Apprenticeship Option by allowing students to receive credit for journeyman training received through a certified Department of Labor apprenticeship program (7,200 hours minimum).

STUDENT SERVICES

All of the partner institutions participate in a library automation network, which makes library catalogs accessible via the Internet. Most professors expect students at a distance to use the Internet for library research and class-related communications. Students are generally expected to obtain Internet access from a local provider, but learning centers in Indiana house computers with dial-up access for students unable to obtain affordable service.

CREDIT OPTIONS

The undergraduate degree programs listed here allow some credit to be transferred from other institutions; the amount varies for each program. The Indiana University general studies degree programs are tailored for adults to permit credit transfer and learning portfolios along with courses to be taken to complete the degree. All other degrees are the same programs as those offered to students on campus; many courses are taken simultaneously by students on and off campus. Graduate degree programs typically allow limited credit transfer.

FACULTY

Faculty members' credentials vary among the institutions, but professors in the university programs are almost exclusively full-time institutional faculty members with terminal degrees.

ADMISSION

Admission requirements are the same as those for on-campus programs, with special flexibility in the IU general studies programs. Older or reentering students are not usually required to take or retake SAT or other standardized tests.

TUITION AND FEES

Fees are highly variable, with a range of $67 to $103 per credit hour for in-state undergraduate students; most institutions charge an additional $15 per credit hour to help cover additional support-service costs for students at a distance.

FINANCIAL AID

Since most distance education students are independent, employed adults attending college part-time, few receive federal or state financial aid, although it is the personal circumstances rather than the delivery methods that reduce or eliminate benefits. Many students are receiving support from Veterans Administration benefits or from employer tuition reimbursement programs.

APPLYING

Application and acceptance processes are approximately the same for on- and off-campus students, although distant students usually apply through special distance education or program coordinators at the offering institutions rather than through the main college or university admissions office.

CONTACT

ICN Student Services Center
2805 East Tenth Street
Bloomington, Indiana 47408
Telephone: 800-426-8899 (toll-free)
Fax: 812-855-9380
TTY: 800-225-8980 (toll-free)
Additional information, including a searchable database of courses and degree programs, is available at the Partnership's Web site: http://www.icn.org

---

Distance Learning Programs

ISIM University
Denver, Colorado

Founded in 1987, ISIM University (International School of Information Management) serves both individuals and organizations in providing its distance education offerings worldwide. ISIM is accredited by the Distance Education and Training Council in Washington, D.C., and recognized by Colorado Commission of Higher Education to offer graduate degree programs, executive education, and continuing education. ISIM University is also a member of the United States Distance Learning Association (USDLA). ISIM brings education and training curricula to individuals over the Internet.

Four times in the last six years, ISIM University has earned top industry honors. In 1991 and 1994, the USDLA conferred on ISIM its "Best Distance Learning Program in Higher Education" award. In 1995, the ISIM and Xerox Management Institute partnership was named "First Place for the Best Distance Learning Program in Corporate Training." In 1996, ISIM was named "Best Distance Learning Program via the Internet—Higher Education."

DISTANCE LEARNING PROGRAM

ISIM University offers graduate degrees in business administration and information management to students worldwide with an eye on the global marketplace. Within the two graduate degree programs, ISIM University provides opportunities for independent study for individuals wishing to focus in a specific field of study. In addition to graduate programs, ISIM offers classes for executive education in finance, project management, C Intranet technology, and other career-enhancing courses for the professional adult.

DELIVERY MEDIA

ISIM University's programs are offered through the Internet and accessible via any Web browser. Individuals who have Internet access can log onto ISIM's electronic classroom. In addition, ISIM University offers its curriculum through its guided self-study approach, in which individuals with limited Internet access may study on their own. ISIM University has no residence requirement; students communicate and exchange information with their instructors and each other through the electronic classroom, e-mail, the postal service, facsimile, or telephone. The ISIM approach to education is very flexible, allowing the student to study on his or her own time from anywhere in the world. This international model attracts students from around the globe, including Asia, the Pacific Rim, Africa, the Middle East, and Europe as well as North, Central, and South America.

PROGRAMS OF STUDY

ISIM University's programs are currently focused around the Master of Business Administration and the Master of Science Information Management. These programs are designed with a specific focus in either management or technology but the student, through the independent study option, can also design a specific focus for his or her area of study. In addition to the standard M.B.A., ISIM provides an M.B.A. Executive-level program for those individuals who do not have a bachelor's degree but have a minimum of twenty years of progressive experience in their industry and are currently at the senior management level.

SPECIAL PROGRAMS

ISIM University provides additional programs for individuals wishing to increase their knowledge. These programs include subjects such as project management, strategic management, and Intranets. ISIM has also designed programs for corporations and organizations who have a diverse employee population and who want to save money on travel. The ISIM model can be tailored to fit the distance training demands of virtually every organization and every type of professional adult. ISIM delivers its programs worldwide and with global relevance and applications.

CREDIT OPTIONS

Students have various options to leverage their learning background. These options include graduate transfer credit, credit by exam, portfolio-assisted assessments (experiential learning), and independent study.

FACULTY

ISIM University's faculty is made up of full-time educators as well as industry experts and business professionals who teach part-time for the university. ISIM's faculty members bring current state-of-the-art information to the programs, providing the student with practical applications of real-business and state-of-the-art information technology. All of the graduate school faculty members have advanced degrees within their respective fields, and most have terminal degrees within their disciplines.

ADMISSION

The principal requirement for admission into ISIM University is an undergraduate degree. However, ISIM does offer an M.B.A. Executive-level program for those individuals who do not have a bachelor's degree (see Program(s) of Study). ISIM does not require a student to take the GMAT or other graduate admission examination.

TUITION AND FEES

ISIM tuition is $375 per credit hour for either the on-line program or for the guided self-study program. On-line fees, mailing costs, and book costs are the responsibility of the student. ISIM University provides a book list so the student can obtain books from other sources if so desired. ISIM University also provides a fee list outlining all the program costs for the student.

FINANCIAL AID

ISIM University does not participate in any government-funded financial aid programs. ISIM University is eligible for tuition reimbursement by many corporations. ISIM University has flexible payment options, and students may apply for financial assistance with an independent educational financing agency.

APPLYING

The principal requirement for admission into ISIM University is an undergraduate degree. Applications are accepted on an ongoing basis with classes starting every ten weeks. There is a $50 nonrefundable application fee. Students must submit an application, the application fee, a current resume, college transcripts, three letters of recommendation, and a goal statement.

CONTACT

Tim Adams
Director of Admissions
501 South Cherry Street
Admissions Office, Room 350
Denver, Colorado 80246
Telephone: 303-333-4224
　　　　　　800-441-ISIM (toll-free)
Fax: 303-336-1144
E-mail: admissions@isimu.edu
Web site: http://www.isimu.edu

Marywood University
School of Continuing Education
Office of Distance Education
Scranton, Pennsylvania

Marywood University prepares students to have a positive impact on society at regional and global levels while providing each student with the foundation for success in an interdependent world. Marywood University is an independent, comprehensive, Catholic institution of more than 3,000 students that is committed to the integration of liberal arts and professional studies in the context of ethical and religious values. Founded by the Congregation of the Sisters, Servants of the Immaculate Heart of Mary in 1915, Marywood offers a wide variety of undergraduate, graduate, and continuing education programs designed to place men and women of all backgrounds and ages at the forefront of service, knowledge, and technology.

Marywood University, located in the scenic Pocono region of northeastern Pennsylvania, is accredited by the Middle States Association of Colleges and Schools.

DISTANCE LEARNING PROGRAM

Marywood University's off-campus degree and certificate programs are designed to make higher education accessible to adult learners who cannot achieve their academic goals in the traditional college setting. For more than twenty years, flexible home study and personalized scheduling have helped hundreds of students earn degrees through Marywood. Bachelor of Science degrees are offered in accounting or business administration (with management, marketing, and financial planning concentrations). Students may also pursue a Certificate in Professional Communications (graduate level), Comprehensive Business Skills (undergraduate), or Office Administration (undergraduate).

DELIVERY MEDIA

Course delivery is primarily through print-based or e-mail-based communication. Upon registration, students receive a shipment consisting of textbook(s), supporting materials, and a study guide, which is authored by Marywood faculty members. The study guide directs the student through each assignment and serves as a supplement to the textbook materials. Particular courses also include audiocassette tapes and/or videotapes. Selected course modules are available via the World Wide Web as of fall 1997. Students are encouraged to take advantage of telecommunications (e.g., fax, e-mail, and phone) for advisement or to submit lesson assignments.

PROGRAMS OF STUDY

Marywood's Bachelor of Science degree programs in accounting and business administration include business core courses (including accounting, business law, economics, management, marketing, and statistics) and advanced courses in the student's chosen major. Business administration majors may concentrate in management, marketing, or financial planning. Accounting majors are encouraged to pursue courses toward earning their CPA. These professional courses are complemented by liberal arts core courses, including literature, fine arts, philosophy, religious studies, sciences, psychology, history, and foreign language. The bachelor's degree consists of 126 total credits in business and liberal arts. To graduate, a minimum of 60 credits must be earned through Marywood, 30 of which must be in the student's major.

At the graduate level, the Certificate in Professional Communications (24 credits) consists of a specialized set of courses in English, advertising, and communication arts. At the undergraduate level, business certificate programs are available in office administration (24 credits) and comprehensive business skills (48 credits). Credits may later be applied toward a degree program. Course work includes areas of accounting, business law, management, and marketing as well as some liberal arts.

For enrichment, students may pursue individual courses tailored to their personal and professional needs. If enrolled at another institution, credits may be earned through Marywood's off-campus program and transferred back to the student's home college (with written approval from the home institution).

SPECIAL PROGRAMS

Specialized residency programs are offered to provide an opportunity for distance learners to visit the campus, earn credits toward graduation, and meet Marywood faculty and staff members and fellow distance learners. A minimum residency requirement of 12 credits through on-campus Marywood instruction is required for the bachelor's degree program. These credits are earned through specially designed adult residency programs, offered in semiannual one- and two-week sessions. Over the duration of the degree program, an estimated four total weeks will earn these required credits. Additional residencies are optional and can accelerate the student's progression toward graduation. There is no residency requirement for certificate programs or enrichment.

STUDENT SERVICES

An academic adviser is available for assistance with course selection, registration procedures, curriculum assessment, and individualized planning. Marywood is a small university, and efforts are made to foster a strong relationship between students, professors, and staff members to create a supportive and encouraging motivation for student progress.

CREDIT OPTIONS

Marywood University recognizes that students learn in a variety of settings and that adult students can often approach the college experience with a wealth of previously acquired college-level learning. Advanced standing may be awarded for transfer credit and through sponsored learning, (i.e., military, business, and industry training), credit by examination (CLEP, AP, and DANTES), or portfolio assessment. While the number of credits awarded may vary, each degree-seeking student must earn a minimum of 60 credits at Marywood, including 30 in the chosen major.

FACULTY

Marywood professors who serve as distance learning faculty members are predominantly on-campus professors at the University. Guest professors from the local business community may also mentor course development and instruction. More than 25 faculty members serve in the Off-Campus Study Program. More than 50 percent of the professors have doctoral degrees or terminal degrees in their disciplines.

ADMISSION

The formal application (for degree-seeking students only) consists of official academic transcripts, a personal/professional goal statement as a letter of introduction, an application form, and the application fee ($40). Current Admissions Committee guidelines suggest a minimum 2.5 GPA on at least 12 credits for transfer students or a strong academic standing (top half of graduating class) in high school for first-time freshmen. However, special consideration is given to assessing the individual's personal and professional development beyond their academic experience.

TUITION AND FEES

For 1997–98, undergraduate tuition is $251 per credit, and graduate tuition is $424 per credit. The text/materials fee is $85 per course (includes shipping), and the registration for each term is $50 (for one course) or $90 (for two or more courses). Accommodation rates for residency programs vary.

FINANCIAL AID

Enrolled students for certificates or degrees may be eligible for Federal Pell Grants or the Federal Stafford Loan program. Regulations governing these programs require that the student be enrolled for at least 6 credits per semester in order to be considered for such funds. Students must file the Free Application for Federal Student Aid as well as a Marywood verification form for each academic year. A monthly deferred payment plan is available for students, as is a deferment for employer-paid tuition.

APPLYING

The enrollment process begins with the above-mentioned application forms. Applications are accepted on a rolling basis. Upon acceptance, students receive their first registration packet and may register at any time thereafter. An orientation is not required for initial enrollments. Students work closely with their academic adviser during initial registrations. The typical term of study is three courses (9 credits) over a six-month semester. However, students can register for one or two courses at a time and have two months to complete each course.

CONTACT
Coordinator of Student Enrollment
Office of Distance Education
Marywood University
2300 Adams Avenue
Scranton, Pennsylvania 18509-1598
Telephone: 800-836-6940 (toll-free)
Fax: 717-961-4751
E-mail: bmcd@ac.marywood.edu
Web site: http://www.marywood.edu

Distance Learning Programs

Massachusetts Institute of Technology
System Design and Management (SDM) Program
Cambridge, Massachusetts

The Massachusetts Institute of Technology is world-renowned as a preeminent technological institution, foremost in engineering and the sciences as well as in management education. MIT's faculty members are among the nation's most reputed and respected leaders in their fields, scientific experts, noted authors, and Nobel laureates. MIT's unique strength lies in its interdisciplinary programs, with more than sixty interdepartmental centers, laboratories, and programs. Founded in 1861 by William Barton Rogers, MIT's pragmatic mission was "to create a new kind of educational institution, relevant to the times and to the nation's need, where students would be educated in the application, as well as the acquisition, of knowledge." A recent study indicates that MIT graduates and faculty members have founded 4,000 firms employing 1.1 million people and generating $232 billion in worldwide sales, equivalent to the GNP of countries such as South Africa and Thailand.

DISTANCE LEARNING PROGRAM

The System Design and Management (SDM) Program permits today's enterprises and practicing engineers to obtain novel systems perspectives and knowledge through a creative new form of education. SDM blends the best of on-campus and distance learning, permitting professionals to pursue advanced education with instruction based at their work sites and with limited interruptions to their careers. SDM classes are live and interactive, with remote students engaged in discussions with faculty members and other students on a weekly or even daily basis. SDM's mission is to educate future technical leaders in architecting, engineering, and designing complex products and systems, preparing them for careers as the technically grounded senior managers of their enterprises, and to set the standards for delivering career-compatible professional education using advanced information and communication technologies.

DELIVERY MEDIA

Distance learning courses are a mixture of real-time MIT courses that are broadcast to company sites via multipoint videoconferencing and videotapes of regular SDM courses, supplemented with regular videoconferencing discussion groups between the professor and the distance learning students. By broadcasting real-time MIT courses to company sites via multipoint videoconferencing, course instructors are able to engage both remote students and live students in a discussion of the subject material and readily integrate remote students into the classroom setting. For certain subjects that are dominated by the lecture format, videotape delivery is optimal. Most students appreciate using videotape in this context because it provides them with the flexibility to view the tape at a convenient time and to take time to absorb more complex material. Live videoconferencing discussion sessions with the course instructor provide ample opportunity for questions and discussion of finer points.

Students participating in distance learning classes are required to have either a Picture-Tel desktop videoconferencing system or a room-based system capable of operating at high end H.320 standards at a minimum of 112 kbps. The Picture-Tel desktop unit is available for approximately $1500 and requires a PC operating system with Microsoft Windows 95, 16 MB RAM, 20 MB of disk space, and an SVGA monitor. Because the latest technology is rapidly changing, students should contact the SDM Program Office before purchasing a new system.

PROGRAM OF STUDY

SDM addresses industry's need for professionals who can tackle the dual challenges of developing and managing complex systems and leading teams of diverse professionals. The program's intellectual content centers on complexity, modeling it, analyzing it, designing with it, and managing it. Students acquire advanced engineering and management skills that practitioners require to develop products and to design and manage large complex systems. They learn about the system development process, requirements, concepts, design, manufacturing, validation, and operations, as well as acquire skills in teamwork and leadership. The SDM curriculum focuses on core competencies identified by industry and government leaders as being essential to the management of systems in enterprises today. A new education track in product development has been designed in partnership with MIT's Center for Innovation in Product Development (CIPD). The product development track features a core curriculum focusing on product development fundamentals and a diverse set of product development electives. In addition, it provides students with a mentored research experience related to product development.

SPECIAL PROGRAMS

The SDM program also offers a full-time, on-campus, thirteen-month degree program and a ten-course Distance Learning Certificate Program. SDM has slightly modified the distance learning program to accommodate Asian and Pacific Rim participants. Although students follow the same curriculum as traditional SDM students, they will have fewer visits to MIT, while retaining all the elements essential to the intellectual content of the program.

CREDIT OPTIONS

The SDM program requires the completion of fourteen subjects (typically 9 or 12 credit units each) and a project-oriented thesis.

FACULTY

The SDM program has approximately 35 affiliated faculty members drawn from throughout the Institute, making it a truly interdepartmental program. Faculty members make contributions to the program as instructors of SDM courses, thesis advisers, and contributors to the program's on-going development.

ADMISSION

The ideal applicant to the SDM program will have an M.S. in engineering and three or more years of experience as a professional engineer, including experience as a team leader (equivalent experience is considered). The TOEFL is required for international students whose native language is not English. Admission to the SDM program is granted by a committee of SDM faculty members. All factors in an applicant's record are considered to be important; therefore, MIT does not have a set minimum number for standardized test scores or GPA. The SDM Program admits the strongest applicants who appear to be qualified for the program in any given year. While an interview is not required, applicants are encouraged to visit the program and/or contact an SDM alumnus in industry.

TUITION AND FEES

Tuition for distance learning students is a total of $50,000 for the two-year program.

FINANCIAL AID

Students who wish to pursue sponsorship through their companies should contact the SDM Program Office. A limited number of research and teaching assistantships are awarded competitively only to full-time in-residence degree students.

APPLYING

Applicants should request materials from the SDM Program Office or download the application forms from the SDM home page listed below. The application deadline for January admission is June 15. SDM will make decisions and notify applicants of their admission status in August.

CONTACT

SDM Program Office
System Design and Management Program
Massachusetts Institute of Technology
Building 20B-040
77 Massachusetts Avenue
Cambridge, Massachusetts 02139-4307
Telephone: 617-253-3799
Fax: 617-258-5229
E-mail: sdm@mit.edu
Web site: http://web.mit.edu/sdm/www/

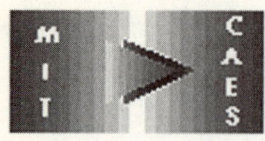

Massachusetts Institute of Technology

Center for Advanced Educational Services (CAES)
Cambridge, Massachusetts

The Massachusetts Institute of Technology (MIT) is one of the world's outstanding universities. MIT is independent, coeducational, and privately endowed. It is organized into five schools that contain twenty-one academic departments, as well as many interdepartmental programs, laboratories, and centers whose work extends beyond traditional departmental boundaries.

The Institute was founded in 1865 by William Barton Rogers. Rogers' philosophy envisioned a new kind of institution relevant to the times and the nation's need, where students would be educated in the application as well as the acquisition of knowledge. A distinguished natural scientist, Rogers stressed the importance of basic research and believed that professional competence was best fostered by the coupling of teaching and research and attention to real-world problems.

MIT's programs in engineering, the sciences, economics, management, linguistics, architecture, and other areas are internationally recognized, and leaders in industry and government routinely draw on the expertise of MIT faculty members.

DISTANCE LEARNING PROGRAM

The Center for Advanced Educational Services (CAES) offers various undergraduate and graduate educational programs via multimodal distance learning. These programs fall into three categories. The first is the Distributed Classroom. In this model, interactive telecommunications technologies extend a classroom-based course from one location to a group of learners at one or more remote locations. These programs are most often delivered in a synchronous manner. The second is Independent Learning. This model frees students from having to be in a particular place at a particular time. Students are provided with a variety of materials, including a course guide and detailed syllabus, and access to a faculty member who provides guidance, answers questions, and evaluates their work. Interaction between the individual student and the instructor is achieved by one or a combination of the following technologies: the World Wide Web, e-mail, and videoconferencing. These programs are most often delivered in an asynchronous manner. The third category is Strategic Partner Relationships. This model involves the redistribution of MIT content through CAES partnerships with leading universities and organizations around the world.

DELIVERY MEDIA

Off-campus learners use a combination of communication technologies for course delivery, including videoconferencing, satellites, the Internet, videotapes, e-mail, and fax machines. The design of MIT's distance learning programs recognizes the benefits of student-professor and student-student interaction. Depending upon the specific programs, students may need access to an e-mail account, the Internet, a videotape player, a satellite downlink, and/or a videoconferencing facility (public videoconferencing facilities are becoming widely available).

PROGRAMS OF STUDY

Programs that exist through the Center for Advanced Educational Services range from entirely asynchronous independent learning to entirely synchronous group-based learning. At present, there is no degree-granting program offered through CAES; however, some of the courses can be taken for MIT credit that may later be applied toward a degree-granting program. Through Strategic Partner Relationships, participants can take MIT courses that earn credit at their home institutions. Several programs exist within CAES for delivery of distance learning courses, including the Advanced Study Program, the primary provider for Distributed Classroom learning, and the Hypermedia Teaching Facility, the primary provider of Independent Learning programs.

The Advanced Study Program (ASP) provides lifelong learning opportunities for working professionals to be a part of the MIT experience through a unique partnership with academia. ASP courses delivered via the MIT Virtual Campus Learning System ™ allow groups of learners to participate at their location instead of coming to the MIT campus. Participants in the virtual campus courses benefit through interaction with other learners in different locations by sharing concepts and ideas through real-time videoconferencing, on-line study groups, and direct e-mail contact with faculty members. The program content is presented through real-time videoconferencing and is supplemented by print, videotape, and Internet activity.

The Hypermedia Teaching Facility (HTF) develops Web-based courses for the MIT community and for distance learning applications. These

Web-based courses are custom designed in collaboration with MIT faculty and staff members to meet the pedagogical and technological requirements of the courses. Web-based courses typically include e-mail, mailing lists, discussion groups, links to Internet and World Wide Web resources, digitized video, animation, photos, figures, charts, and search utilities.

CREDIT OPTIONS

Both credit and noncredit courses are offered through CAES. Distance learners participating in the Advanced Study Program are eligible to receive MIT credit for course work that is successfully completed. In addition, CAES is currently developing a number of distance learning programs that utilize advanced technologies to offer for-credit courses at a distance.

FACULTY

The Center for Advanced Educational Services draws from all faculty members across the Institute. The MIT faculty numbers approximately 1,100, with a total teaching staff of more than 2,000. Most faculty members at MIT teach both graduate and undergraduate students.

ADMISSION

Applicants seeking for-credit courses are admitted based on their official transcripts from the colleges from which they earned their degrees and a record of other graduate work they have completed. A letter of nomination, written by a principle executive in the applicant's organization, confirming approval of their candidacy and the organization's willingness to provide the appropriate support must be included. In addition, a summary of professional experience and a statement indicating the applicant's immediate and ultimate objectives in taking the course are required.

Applicants seeking noncredit courses are accepted based upon their academic training and professional experience. In order to maintain the highest standards, CAES reserves the right to select those applicants whose qualifications and experiences suggest that they will receive the most benefit from a given program.

TUITION AND FEES

Tuition is based on the type of academic credit provided. For-credit courses, delivered live through the Advanced Study Program, carry full MIT tuition for qualified candidates. Academic credit from the Strategic Partner Relationships, with other universities using MIT professors, is based on tuition arrangements established by those institutions.

FINANCIAL AID

There is no financial aid provided for any of the distance learning programs offered through the Center for Advanced Educational Services.

APPLYING

Individuals interested in applying to any of the CAES distance learning programs need to submit an application, along with the required supporting documents.

CONTACT

Kris Kipp
Marketing Manager
Room 9-234
Massachusetts Institute of Technology
Center for Advanced Educational Services
77 Massachusetts Avenue
Cambridge, Massachusetts 02139
Telephone: 617-253-7408
Fax: 617-253-8301
E-mail: caes-courses@mit.edu
Web site: http://www-caes.mit.edu

Distance Learning Programs

Michigan State University
East Lansing, Michigan

Michigan State University (MSU), founded in 1855, is a research-intensive, land-grant university, offering more than 200 programs at the bachelor's through doctoral levels. It is one of only fifty-eight members of the prestigious American Association of Universities and is a member of the Big Ten Conference.

The core of MSU's land-grant tradition is the belief that educational opportunities should be available to the widest possible audience. Six guiding principles reflect the land-grant tradition at MSU: access to quality education, active learning, the generation of new knowledge, problem solving, diversity, and making people matter. A recently announced Technology Guarantee ensures students an intensive, quality-based technological experience (with increased interactive instruction) and lifelong access to MSU technology.

The University's outreach mission, involving all fourteen of its colleges, emphasizes the extension of knowledge to serve the needs of individuals, groups, and communities.

DISTANCE LEARNING PROGRAM

MSU serves more than 6,000 off-campus students per year in Michigan and around the world, about half through distance technology. Offerings expand each year. The University is fully accredited by the North Central Association of Colleges and Schools, and individual programs are accredited, where appropriate, by professional associations. MSU's distance education programs are offered by the individual academic departments, not by a centralized continuing education unit.

DELIVERY MEDIA

MSU uses interactive and satellite television (usually viewed at local sites), the Internet, computer conferencing, and e-mail. Access to a computer with a modem is important. Students are in frequent contact with faculty members by e-mail and/or telephone. A number of courses are fully available on the World Wide Web.

Programs of Study At numerous sites throughout the state, MSU offers master's-level programs in advertising, business, child development, community services, criminal justice, educational administration, family studies, nursing, social work, teacher education, and telecommunications and bachelor's programs in interdisciplinary social science and nursing. MSU also offers courses and master's degree programs available outside of Michigan in engineering via National Technological University and in educational administration, home computing, nursing, physics, security management, social work, and telecommunications via the Internet.

Master's degree programs require a minimum of 30 semester credits (some require more), and bachelor's programs require 120 credits. Students who wish to take courses without or before applying to a degree program may enroll as Lifelong Education students.

SPECIAL PROGRAMS

MSU's off-campus programs are fully equivalent to on-campus programs, follow the same curriculum, have the same entrance and graduation requirements, and charge the same tuition and fees. Courses are almost always taught by the University's regular faculty, not by local adjuncts.

STUDENT SERVICES

All students receive University e-mail accounts and access to the Internet, to MSU and other library catalogs, and to extensive databases. Off-campus students may seek research assistance or request books and articles by telephone, fax, or mail from the MSU libraries.

CREDIT OPTIONS

MSU accepts transfer credit from accredited institutions but does not offer or accept credit through assessment of prior learning. Some College-Level Examination Program (CLEP) and Advanced Placement credits are accepted. For a bachelor's degree, at least 30 semester credits must be earned at MSU; for a master's degree, at least 21 credits of a 30-credit program must be earned at MSU.

FACULTY

MSU has 2,600 faculty members, with 2,000 in the tenure system; about 2,300 are appointed on a full-time basis. Almost all MSU faculty members hold doctoral or other terminal degrees. The regular on-campus faculty members provide 90 percent of the instruction in off-campus programs.

ADMISSION

Distance learners meet the same admission requirements as on-campus students. Admission to undergraduate programs is based on high school grade point average, recent trend of grades, other activities and accomplishments, SAT or ACT scores, and recommendations.

Master's program admission is based on grade point average for the third and fourth years of undergraduate study, other relevant accomplishments, GRE scores, recommendations, and the availability of space in the program.

TUITION AND FEES

Upper-division undergraduate tuition for 1997–98 is $156.75 for Michigan residents and $390 for out-of-state students; graduate tuition is $216 for Michigan residents and $430 for out-of-state students. Matriculation and technology fees are $283 for full-time students (5 or more credits) and $234 for part-time students. Lifelong Education students (those not in a degree program) pay $216 per credit hour (graduate or undergraduate, resident or nonresident), with no additional fees. There is an additional Engineering Program fee of $225 for full-time status and $124 for part-time status.

FINANCIAL AID

Distance learners are eligible for the same federal and state and University financial aid programs as on-campus students, based on part-time or full-time status. However, graduate assistantships are usually not available to students at a distance because they involve on-campus assigned work hours. One fellowship program is targeted specifically for reentry adult students, the Mildred B. Erickson Fellowship.

APPLYING

Applications are accepted all year. However, some programs only accept new students in the fall semester. In some programs, students must attend an orientation program either on campus or at a local site.

CONTACT
Dr. Michael Spurgin
Office of Evening and Off-Campus Programs
49 Kellogg Center
Michigan State University
East Lansing, Michigan 48824
Telephone: 517-353-0791
Fax: 517-432-1327
Web site: http://www.msu.edu

National University

Extended Studies Institute
Global Master's Degree in Business Administration (GMBA)

San Diego, California

Chartered in 1971, National University is a nonprofit, nonsectarian, independent institution of higher education dedicated to providing degree programs for career-oriented adults. Its mission is to serve the adult student by providing meaningful educational opportunities in management, business, computer science, education, and behavioral sciences through a format that maximizes course accessibility and subject relevance. The University is accredited by the Western Association of Schools and Colleges.

Since its inception, National University has become known as a leader in adult education, with nearly 55,000 graduates worldwide working in business, government, and academics. In addition to the main campus in San Diego, the University includes ten other major locations throughout California. To achieve the greatest relevance and quality, National University works cooperatively in strategic alliances with universities and business organizations throughout the world.

DISTANCE LEARNING PROGRAM

National University's unique and innovative distance learning program does not require classroom attendance, and students from all over the world are enrolled in these courses. The program relies on the latest communication and multimedia technologies to achieve unmatched flexibility. Students are able to communicate with professors and classmates in almost any setting at any time.

DELIVERY MEDIA

Case study and research materials are provided on interactive CD-ROM. Students use the Internet, World Wide Web, and videoconferencing to complete research assignments, interact with the faculty members and other students from around the world, and meet experts in the field of study.

PROGRAM OF STUDY

The Global M.B.A. (GMBA) is a preeminent global program offered by one of the world's leading universities for adults. The GMBA is offered through the graduate studies department of the School of Management and Technology. The program is designed to provide future business leaders with the knowledge and skills needed to succeed in the global economy of the twenty-first century. GMBA graduates have the discipline, initiative, and persistence to achieve their goals and the leadership required to motivate others for success. They possess the technical expertise and understand the need to communicate globally through the use of leading-edge technologies.

The twelve-course Global M.B.A. is divided into three modular learning segments that enable students to pursue an M.B.A. while continuing full-time employment or other obligations. The courses incorporate the case study method, which provides a practical, comprehensive model of real-life business management. The course work is developed cooperatively with world-renowned professors from prestigious universities in the U.S. These professors, who are subject matter experts, develop each course specifically for the Global M.B.A. to provide the most current information available and to maintain the highest academic standards. All courses reflect the most current theories, issues, and applications in international management.

SPECIAL PROGRAMS

The Global M.B.A. is also offered in cooperation with international universities in Portugal, Turkey, Mexico, Argentina, and Ecuador. The University provides assistance in acquiring the multimedia hardware required for the Global M.B.A. program.

The University is approved to train veterans under Title 38, U.S. Code (G.I. bill); approved by the California Commission on Teacher Credentialing; approved for student financial aid by the Department of Education; authorized under federal law to enroll nonimmigrant alien students; and approved for Army, Air Force, Coast Guard, Marine Corps, Navy, and U.S. government tuition assistance. Credits are accepted by Peace Officer Standards and Training (P.O.S.T.), and graduates are eligible to apply for federal civil service examinations that require a college degree.

CREDIT OPTIONS

Students at the graduate level may transfer up to 15 quarter units of graduate-level course work from other accredited institutions to be used to satisfy the unit requirements of their master's degrees. In addition to these units, students may also take up to 30 quarter units (six courses) at a distance to fulfill their course/unit requirements in National University's graduate degree programs.

FACULTY

Global M.B.A. faculty members are selected by the School of Management and Technology from National University's full-time and part-time pool and from leading experts in their fields. National University has more than 1,600 full- and part-time faculty members. Of the full-time faculty members, 81 percent have terminal degrees.

ADMISSION

National University accepts applications for admission continuously throughout the year. To qualify for admission to the Global M.B.A. program, candidates must hold a bachelor's degree from an accredited college or university, with a minimum 2.5 grade point average. Under certain conditions, applicants with a grade point average between 2.0 and 2.49 may be granted admission on probation by the Committee on the Application of Standards.

TUITION AND FEES

The Global M.B.A. tuition is $200 per quarter unit. The application fee is $60 ($100 for international students), and there is a graduation fee of $100.

FINANCIAL AID

Students may be eligible for various types of financial assistance: grants, loans, work-study opportunities, and scholarships, as provided by federal, state, and University programs. Application forms are accepted as long as funds are available. The University is approved for the training of veterans and maintains a full-service veterans affairs office.

APPLYING

Each person seeking admission into the Global M.B.A. is interviewed by an admission counselor via mail, telephone, or e-mail. The University takes into consideration a student's previous academic record, professional experience, and educational objectives. National University admits students without regard to race, color, age, sex, religion, or national or ethnic origin.

CONTACT

Pamela Montroy
Academic Advisor
The Global M.B.A.
National University
11255 North Torrey Pines Road
La Jolla, California 92037
Telephone: 619-642-8212
Fax: 619-642-8709
E-mail: gmba@nunic.nu.edu
Web site: http://www.nu.edu

Distance Learning Programs

New Hampshire College
Distance Education Program
Manchester, New Hampshire

New Hampshire College (NHC), founded in 1932, is a private, accredited, coeducational, professional college. The College has a total enrollment of over 8,900 in various divisions—undergraduate day, Continuing Education, Distance Education, the Culinary Institute, and the Graduate School of Business. New Hampshire College maintains Continuing Education undergraduate and graduate centers in Laconia, Manchester, Nashua, Portsmouth, and Salem, New Hampshire; Brunswick, Maine; and Roosevelt Roads, Puerto Rico. Graduate Programs are also offered at the Concord, New Hampshire, center.

New Hampshire College is accredited by the New England Association of Schools and Colleges and the Association of Collegiate Business Schools and Programs (ACBSP).

DISTANCE LEARNING PROGRAM

The Distance Education Program offers students the opportunity to take either undergraduate or graduate courses. Undergraduate certificates in accounting, human resource management, and computer programming are offered, in addition to various courses that are applicable to associate and bachelor's degrees. Graduate courses can be applied to various master's degree programs.

DELIVERY MEDIA

To participate in distance education, the student needs a computer with a modem and access to the Internet, along with a working knowledge of Internet use and applications. A variety of on-line and traditional tools are available for courses, such as e-mail, on-line class conferences, textbooks, and, occasionally, specialized software packages.

PROGRAMS OF STUDY

New Hampshire College provides students with a solid educational foundation and professional training through programs in the Divisions of Business, Liberal Arts, and Hospitality Administration. Degree programs available within the Division of Business include accounting, business administration, business studies, computer information systems, economics/finance, international business, management advisory services, marketing, retailing, sport management, and technical management. Degree programs offered by the Division of Liberal Arts include communication, English language and literature, humanities, psychology, social science, and teacher education (concentrations in business, English, and marketing). Degree programs conferred by the Division of Hospitality Administration include hotel management, restaurant management, and travel and tourism. Associate of Science degree programs are offered in accounting, business administration, computer information systems, liberal arts, marketing, and retailing/fashion merchandising. All associate degree programs are transferable into bachelor's degree programs.

The Graduate School of Business offers programs leading to the Master of Science degree in accounting, business education, community economic development, computer information systems, finance, and international business and to the Master of Business Administration degree. Graduate certificates may be earned in any of twelve areas of concentration, in conjunction with, or independent of, a degree.

SPECIAL PROGRAMS

Cooperative education work experiences are available in all academic programs and range from 3 to 12 credits; all students have the option of participating in work experience abroad. An NHC program in which students live and learn in London, England, is available to selected students through arrangements with the Polytechnic of North London.

Through the College's membership in the New Hampshire College and University Council, New Hampshire College students may take advantage of academic facilities and course offerings at the eleven other four-year colleges and universities in the consortium.

CREDIT OPTIONS

Students can transfer undergraduate credits earned at other postsecondary institutions to New Hampshire College and can receive undergraduate credit by taking the College-Level Examination Program (CLEP) or other standardized tests. A maximum of 90 credits may be transferred toward a bachelor's degree and 30 credits may be applied to an associate's degree. A maximum of 6 semester hours may be transferred into any of the graduate degree programs.

FACULTY

The average faculty-student ratio in distance education is 1:12. Some faculty members are consultants in the Manchester business community, and most have had prior business-related job experience.

ADMISSION

Applicants for undergraduate degrees must have graduated from high school or passed the GED before entering. Admission to the Graduate School requires a bachelor's degree from an accredited institution.

TUITION AND FEES

The tuition for Distance Education undergraduate courses is $471 per course. Tuition for distance education graduate courses is $890 per course. Other general expenses include required textbooks, and some courses require specific software packages.

FINANCIAL AID

Students accepted for enrollment at New Hampshire College may be considered for several forms of institutional and federal financial aid. The College participates in the Federal Work-Study Program, the Federal Perkins Loan Program, and the Federal Supplemental Educational Opportunity Grant Program and is an eligible institution under the Federal Stafford Student Loan Program and the Federal Pell Grant Program.

APPLYING

Distance Education students may enroll in undergraduate or graduate classes on a rolling basis. Applicants must submit an application along with appropriate documentation, such as an official high school transcript, GED scores, or official transcripts from previous colleges. There is no application fee.

CONTACT

Dr. Lee Williams, Director
Victoria Chapman, Coordinator
Distance Education Program
New Hampshire College
2500 North River Road
Manchester, New Hampshire 03106-1045
Telephone: 603-668-2211 Ext. 2270
Fax: 603-645-9706
E-mail: leewil@nhc.edu or vchapman@nhc.edu
Web site: http://www.dist-ed.nhc.edu

Distance Learning Programs

New Jersey Institute of Technology
Division of Continuing Professional Education
Distance Learning—Extension Programs
Newark, New Jersey

Founded in 1881, New Jersey Institute of Technology (NJIT) is New Jersey's technological research university. An international leader in scientific and technological education, NJIT educates students to become frontrunners in the global marketplace. The university seeks students who are seriously committed to education and can bring energy, creativity, and a practical outlook to solving today's pressing problems. The degree programs are demanding, rewarding, and highly regarded by employers.

Since publication in 1978 of The Networked Nation: Human Communication via Computers, *by NJIT's Professors Murray Turoff and S. Roxanne Hiltz, the university has served as a leader in distance education. With four degree programs and six graduate certificate programs offered completely through distance learning, NJIT course work is made available to students regardless of their geographic location. For the adult professional, in particular, ACCESS/NJIT courses provide the flexibility and convenience needed to fit in with work, family, and community responsibilities. NJIT's customer-service orientation allows each student to receive the personal attention that is required for successful completion of a degree program or certificate.*

DISTANCE LEARNING PROGRAM

Via distance learning, ACCESS/NJIT conducts full undergraduate and graduate degree programs, graduate certificates, and individual college courses using today's home electronics to provide the college experience. By virtue of the academic quality, focus, and advanced delivery format, ACCESS/NJIT helps adult men and women cross one bridge to knowledge acquisition leading to gainful employment.

DELIVERY MEDIA

Today's home electronics can be used in a new way to pursue education. Through integration of the personal computer, videocassette recorder (VCR), television, and telephone, the classroom can be a student's home, office, or any place other than the college campus. Each ACCESS/NJIT course consists of two components: a telelecture conducted by NJIT faculty members and an electronic discussion through which students conduct dialogue with a mentor and other classmates at any time of the day or night. The medium of the telelecture is video, furnished as a set of stand-alone leased videotapes that are shipped to the student's home or office for replaying in sequence.

PROGRAMS OF STUDY

The university offers four complete degree programs via ACCESS/NJIT. The 129-credit Bachelor of Arts in information systems program provides students with a solid foundation in applying the principles of computing and information systems to business and industrial problems and managerial decision making.

The 134-credit Bachelor of Science in computer science program provides students with the most comprehensive treatment of computers, with considerable breadth and depth in computer science topics, the sciences, mathematics, and supporting interdisciplinary studies.

The 36-credit Master of Science in Information Systems (M.S.I.S.) program has been designed to train individuals who can assume responsibility for analyzing and organizing the information needs and resources of an organization and develop systems to respond to those needs.

The 30-credit Master of Science in Engineering Management (M.S.E.M.) program has been designed to develop engineers and other technically trained individuals for leadership roles in technology-based, project-oriented enterprises. It provides individuals with the broad-based knowledge and skills to succeed as managers of organizations and of projects from conceptualization through implementation.

In addition, students who wish to complete individual undergraduate or graduate courses in one or more of a dozen academic disciplines may enroll on a nonmatriculated basis.

SPECIAL PROGRAMS

Through the Division of Continuing Professional Education, the administrative unit in which ACCESS/NJIT is housed, NJIT offers several graduate-level certificates that are available in their entirety or in part via distance learning techniques, including continuous process improvement, healthcare information systems, object-oriented design (C++), client/server architecture, project management, practice of technical communications, and telecommunications networking. Each certificate, worth 12 graduate credits, can be used as a springboard to advanced degree study at NJIT or elsewhere. Consisting of four courses, each certificate is in a topic area considered by today's corporations to be employable "hot tracks" through the year 2005.

CREDIT OPTIONS

Students may be awarded transfer credit at the time of admission for courses that were completed at other institutions and are equivalent to courses offered by NJIT. A minimum grade of C must be earned in a course in order to receive transfer credit.

FACULTY

Ninety-eight percent of NJIT's full-time faculty members hold the terminal degree in their field.

ADMISSION

Admission policies for the ACCESS/NJIT distance learning programs follow the same admission criteria as do traditionally delivered NJIT academic programs. In general, admission on a nonmatriculated basis to an undergraduate course requires possession of a high school diploma or General Equivalency Degree. Admission as a nonmatriculated student to a graduate course requires possession, at minimum, of an undergraduate degree from an accredited college or university with a grade point average that meets NJIT academic department standards for regular admission as a Master of Science degree candidate. In general, an acceptable grade point average is no lower than a 2.8 on a 4.0 scale.

TUITION AND FEES

In 1996–97, undergraduate tuition was $172 per credit for New Jersey residents and $357 per credit for nonresidents. Graduate tuition was $326 per credit for New Jersey residents and $451 per credit for nonresidents. Graduate certificate students pay in-state tuition regardless of location. It is expected that tuition will increase approximately 8 percent for the 1997–98 academic year. Required supplemental fees, not including rental of video telelectures, totaled $241 for a 3-credit course taken during the 1996–97 academic year. Updated tuition and fees can be found on-line (http://www.njit.edu/cpe).

FINANCIAL AID

NJIT's Office of Financial Aid provides counseling and administers loans, scholarships, and grants to qualified students. Federal and state programs and private, industrial, and university resources are utilized to support the university's financial aid programs.

APPLYING

Students may apply on a nonmatriculated basis by mail, fax, or on-line (http://www.njit.edu/cpe). To apply for admission on a matriculated basis, students should contact the Office of Admissions at 973-596-3300 or 800-925-6548 (toll-free) to request a degree application or use the on-line matriculated application form (http://www.njit.edu).

CONTACT

Gale Tenen Spak, Ph.D.
Executive Director
Division of Continuing Professional Education
New Jersey Institute of Technology
University Heights, New Jersey 07102-1948
Telephone: 973-596-3063
Fax: 973-596-3203
Web site: http://www.njit.edu/DL

New School for Social Research

The New School

Distance Instruction for Adult Learning (DIAL)

New York, New York

The New School for Social Research was founded in 1919 as America's first university for adults. Over the years, it has grown into an accredited, degree-granting institution comprising seven divisions (the New School, the Graduate Faculty of Political and Social Science, the Robert J. Milano Graduate School of Management and Urban Policy, Parsons School of Design, Mannes College of Music, Eugene Lang College, and the School of Dramatic Arts). About 40,000 students attend the University annually, bringing a wide variety of cultures, perspectives, aspirations, priorities, interests, and talents. But the New School has never neglected its original mission: it continues to serve the intellectual, cultural, artistic, and professional needs and interests of adult students.

DISTANCE LEARNING PROGRAM

The New School's Distance Instruction for Adult Learning (DIAL) program first went on-line with seven noncredit courses in summer 1994. Since then, DIAL has grown into a full cyberspace campus, offering 300 courses each year for credit and noncredit, as well as graduate-level courses and a bachelor's degree on-line. DIAL courses are sections of the same courses that are taught on the Greenwich Village campus and are created and led by the same distinguished faculty. The New School and its programs, including DIAL, are accredited by the Commission on Higher Education of the Middle States Association of Colleges and Schools and chartered as a university by the Regents of the University of the State of New York.

DELIVERY MEDIA

DIAL courses are offered through interactive computer conferencing via the Internet's World Wide Web facility. Programs are asynchronous and fully interactive, meaning that students receive instruction, ask questions of the instructor and each other, discuss issues, and actively participate in the class, all from home or office. It is recommended that students acquire the highest-speed connection that they can afford (14.4 bps modem minimum) from their Internet Service Providers (ISPs), and guidelines are available for those students who need help in identifying and arranging for service from a local ISP. Students and faculty also need computers (PC or Mac) capable of running one of today's graphical Web browsers (Netscape® recommended).

PROGRAMS OF STUDY

Credit, noncredit, and degree courses are offered in many curriculum areas, including the social sciences, humanities, writing, and communication. The New School's Bachelor of Arts degree in liberal arts is offered through DIAL. Students work closely with an academic adviser (on-line) to clarify their educational objectives, assess intellectual strengths and weaknesses, evaluate past academic accomplishments, and then draw on the curriculum available through DIAL to design a program of study reflecting their individual needs and goals. The process of organizing and synthesizing his or her own education is the essential and ongoing responsibility of every New School student. Applicants to the on-line B.A. program must have completed 60 semester credits of course work at an accredited college prior to matriculation. In general, students are required to complete an additional 60 credits to graduate; more information may be obtained by sending e-mail to advisors@dialnsa.edu. In addition to courses offered in fulfillment of B.A. requirements, students may study through DIAL for credits that may be applied to the New School's M.A. in Media Studies and several other graduate degrees (though matriculation into and on-line completion of these degrees is not yet available).

SPECIAL PROGRAMS

Almost all New School courses, including those offered through DIAL, are available for credit or noncredit registration. About half of the students study each semester not for credit but for personal enrichment or intellectual stimulation. A significant proportion of the remaining half study for general credit, which means that the credit earned is transferred to a degree program elsewhere. The balance of the students in DIAL study for credit to be applied to one of the University's degree programs (predominantly the New School B.A. and M.A. in Media Studies). Through its Institute for Professional Development (IPD), the New School's Distance Learning Program seeks to make courses, certificates, and degree programs available to employees through special arrangements with organizations and other employers; for more information, students may send e-mail to dialexec@dialnsa.edu. All New School distance learning students have access to the full range of facilities on the cyberspace campus, including faculty office hours, library support, an orientation center, and 24-hour technical support (on-line and by telephone). There is also a full program of public events, performances, social gatherings—even the New School's unique art collection.

CREDIT OPTIONS

For matriculated students, the academic credits earned upon successful completion of a DIAL course are applied toward degree requirements. Matriculants may earn credit for prior academic and other developmental work; specific information may be obtained by e-mail from advisors@dialnsa.edu. Students who are degree candidates at another college or university or have not yet entered an undergraduate degree program may register for general credit. Students receive academic credit for each course successfully completed. Students at other institutions should make arrangements for transfer of credit at their home institutions prior to registering for New School DIAL courses. Students may also elect to take DIAL courses on a noncredit basis. The University does not maintain a permanent record of noncredit enrollment, although students may request a "Record of Attendance" should verification of enrollment be necessary. Students may send e-mail to advisors@dialnsa.edu for more information or clarification.

FACULTY

Close to 400 of the New School's 1,800 instructors have completed the preparation required to teach on-line. In the core curriculum areas (humanities, social sciences, writing, and communication), about 68 percent of New School faculty members have earned the doctorate or other terminal degree in their fields of specialty.

ADMISSION

General requirements for B.A. matriculants are that they have completed 60 semester credits at an accredited college and that they be at least 24 years of age. Specific information can be obtained by sending e-mail to admissions@dialnsa.edu or calling 212-229-5630. Noncredit and general credit students may simply review course offerings and complete registration on-line at http://www.dialnsa.edu at any time.

TUITION AND FEES

For the 1997–98 academic year, matriculated students enrolled in the B.A. program pay $540 per credit part-time (fewer than 6 credits) and $468 per credit full-time; for those enrolled in the M.A. in Media Studies, $582 per credit part-time (fewer than 9 credits) and $570 per credit full-time. All degree students pay a $95 registration fee per term. General credit students pay $540 per credit for New School courses and $620 per credit for Parsons courses. General credit students pay a $40 registration fee per term. Noncredit tuition varies by course and is listed with each description. Some courses carry additional lab, materials, or other fees; these are also listed with each description. The noncredit registration fee is $15 per term.

FINANCIAL AID

The New School offers a full range of state, federal, and New School–sponsored programs for students enrolled in degree programs, depending on the jurisdiction in which the DIAL student resides. Students at other institutions may be eligible for financial support from those institutions. Applicants must file the FAFSA and PROFILE; these may be obtained from the Financial Aid Office. No student should decide against applying to the New School for financial reasons. For specific information and assistance, students may send e-mail to finance@dialnsa.edu or call 212-229-8930. In the 1995–96 academic year, a total of $1 million in financial aid was distributed to New School students, and 69 percent of all students received some form of aid. Among DIAL students, 53 percent received aid.

APPLYING

Distance students may apply for admission to the New School's B.A. program through DIAL by sending an inquiry to admissions@dialnsa.edu. Students may send e-mail or call 212-229-5630 or 800-862-5039 (toll-free) to find out about on-line "open houses." All new students are required to participate in a week-long, on-line orientation program.

CONTACT

Stephen J. Anspacher
Director of Distance Learning
The New School
68 Fifth Avenue
New York, New York 10011
Telephone: 212-229-5880
Fax: 212-989-2928
E-mail: dialexec@dialnsa.edu
Admissions: admissions@dialnsa.edu
Web site: http://www.dialnsa.edu

New York Institute of Technology

On-Line Campus
Central Islip, New York

New York Institute of Technology (NYIT) is an independent institution of higher learning. Nonsectarian and nonprofit, it is chartered by the Board of Regents of the University of the State of New York and accredited by the Middle States Association of Colleges and Schools. NYIT also enjoys the imprimaturs of various accrediting agencies, including the Accreditation Board for Engineering and Technology, the National Architecture Accrediting Board, the Foundation for Interior Design Education Research, the National Accrediting Agency for Clinical Laboratory Science, the American Dietetic Association for Preprofessional Programs, and the American Osteopathic Association.

Established in 1955, the current roster of students numbers more than 10,000, with more than 40,000 alumni. NYIT maintains three campuses in New York City and Nassau and Suffolk Counties on Long Island. The Islip campus offers dormitory residences.

DISTANCE LEARNING PROGRAM

New York Institute of Technology has been a leader in the delivery of distance education for more than a decade. The college has created a new delivery system that uses technology to maximize the educational potential of each participant. Multimedia, the Internet, fiber optics, ISDN, and other state-of-the-art technologies are woven together in a tapestry that entices, encourages, enables, engages, and empowers the learners.

The On-Line Campus (OLC) of the New York Institute of Technology offers college degrees to students entirely by Web-based computer conferencing. This is an alternative for those who cannot attend a conventional college campus because of personal obstacles and/or time conflicts. NYIT offers custom-tailored college degrees without an on-campus residency requirement.

DELIVERY MEDIA

NYIT utilizes a conferencing system entitled Caucus that is centered in a Web-based environment. Students need a computer, a modem, and Internet access. The system is accessible 24 hours a day, allowing students to access it any time of day or night. The only schedule students must adhere to is the deadlines set for assignments and exams.

Courses require textbooks, which can be ordered directly through the bookstore listed on the NYIT Web page. Books are shipped directly to students. Schedules are posted well in advance of the upcoming semester so that students can order books and be assured of delivery by the beginning of the semester.

PROGRAMS OF STUDY

NYIT's On-Line Campus currently offers degrees in business administration (management) (B.S.); interdisciplinary studies (B.S., B.A.); behavioral sciences with options in criminal justice, psychology, or sociology (B.S.); hospitality management (B.P.S.); and telecommunications management (B.S.). An M.B.A. program with course options in instructional technology for educators and trainers is also offered. Each course has its own "conference."

The Introduction to Computer Conferencing course, a 1-credit required course, enables students to interact with professors and the conference system and prepares them for the course work that follows. It is the first course students need to fulfill. It must be completed before or concurrent with enrolling in any on-line course. It is offered several times a semester.

CREDIT OPTIONS

The Prior Learning Program is designed to evaluate college-level learning relevant to the student's curriculum. All matriculated students with a declared major and at least a 2.0 grade point average are eligible to apply for credit.

NYIT offers a variety of means for recognizing prior learning experiences, including proficiency examinations, noncollegiate course evaluations, and portfolio evaluations (life experience).

A Prior Learning Evaluation Guide that contains more detailed information may be obtained by calling the Office of Prior Learning at 516-348-3312.

ADMISSION

To enroll in the OLC program, students must first meet the admission requirements of NYIT. Each student must submit a completed application form, the $40 application fee, a high school diploma or its equivalent, and official copies of transcripts from all previous colleges and schools.

The application for admission is available on NYIT's Web page (Web address listed below). Three academic semesters are offered each year: fall, spring, and summer.

TUITION AND FEES

Tuition for the 1997–98 school year is $245 per undergraduate credit and $390 per graduate credit.

FINANCIAL AID

NYIT processes and accepts military deferments and vouchers from students' employers. NYIT also offers payment plans for those who qualify. Students may contact the bursar at 516-348-3210 for more detailed information. For more information on how to qualify for financial aid, students should call 516-348-3220.

APPLYING

NYIT/OLC offers a wide range of courses each semester. Formal application to the college may be made. Students are allowed to register as nonmatriculated to jump-start their college careers while NYIT assembles their admissions credentials.

Upon acceptance and evaluation, each student is given a degree map that clearly shows the courses for which the student received credit and which courses he or she needs to take to complete his or her degree. A personal academic adviser is assigned to guide each student through his or her NYIT college career.

Students can register for courses anytime within a week of the start of the semester. Once registered for a course, each student is sent a registration confirmation and a Caucus User Manual Start Guide. Each student is then automatically registered for access to the courses he or she has selected.

CONTACT

Patricia Fenn
NYIT-On-Line Campus
300 Carleton Avenue
P.O. Box 9029
Central Islip, New York 11722-9029
Telephone: 516-348-3058
　　　　　　800-222-NYIT (toll-free)
Fax: 516-348-1107
E-mail: pfenn@acl.nyit.edu
Web site: http://www.nyit.edu/olc

New York University
The Virtual College
New York, New York

New York University was founded in 1831 to enlarge the scope of higher education and to meet the needs of people aspiring to careers in business, industry, science, and the arts, as well as in law, medicine, and the ministry. NYU's School of Continuing Education has grown over the past sixty years to become the nation's largest private university-based adult education provider, offering more than 2,000 credit and noncredit courses to more than 60,000 students annually.

NYU pioneered distance learning in the 1950s with its Sunrise Semester *series, which aired for twenty-five years on national television. In the spirit of* Sunrise Semester, *NYU introduced the Virtual College in 1992 to expand the spatial and temporal boundaries of learning and to respond to the increasing professional education needs of working adults.*

As the infrastructure of the global economy changes from concrete and steel to computers and communications, NYU's teleprogram gives practitioners those collaborative and technical skills necessary for working within (as well as on) decentralized and networked workplaces—in effect, a virtual college preparing employees for tomorrow's virtual organizations.

DISTANCE LEARNING PROGRAM

Created to deliver high-quality, interactive instruction directly to students, the Virtual College is the electronic equivalent of a traditional college and provides learners with a broad range of course, faculty, library, and administrative services. NYU's Virtual College teleprogram is accredited by the Middle States Association of Colleges and Schools.

Through the Virtual College, students receive instruction, ask questions, conduct analyses, manage projects, and complete assignments—all at their own convenience and from practically anywhere. The teleprogram network provides an electronic workplace for students and faculty members, allowing them to go from just talking about course projects to actually completing them. All Virtual College course work is conducted from students' home or office PCs; there are no on-campus sessions.

DELIVERY MEDIA

The Virtual College teleprogram uses Lotus Notes, a powerful groupware package that gives people who work together an electronic environment in which to collect, organize and share information using networked PCs. Coupled with high-speed Integrated Services Digital Network (ISDN) lines, the Virtual College delivers to distance learners the same level of dynamic, hands-on instruction that characterizes the best on-campus lectures, seminars, and laboratories. All Virtual College telecourses employ such advanced technologies as interactive video, on-line laboratories, and hypertext readings. The Virtual College is a unique distance education program in which all instructional materials—video, simulation, laboratories, and reading—are digital and interactively accessible through one common user interface.

During each Virtual College telecourse, students and faculty members collaborate on-line to analyze, design, prototype, and audit case study information systems using Lotus Notes and various software packages. By the second or third week of each course, students are divided into groups of 4 to 5 participants to work asynchronously on various phases of systems projects. Functioning as members of their virtual project teams, students establish discussion guidelines, critique and edit each other's work, and manage on-line workplace responsibilities. During a typical telecourse, each student will create about 200 discussion, analysis, and assignment documents—a level of participation that would be a rare in most on-campus courses.

Virtual College students must have a 486 or Pentium PC with at least 8 MB RAM, a minimum of 100 MB available hard disk space, a 16-bit SoundBlaster or compatible audio board, and an ISDN line and terminal adapter.

PROGRAMS OF STUDY

The Virtual College offers an Advanced Professional Certificate (APC) in information technology. This 16-credit graduate teleprogram consists of four courses—systems analysis, database management, systems auditing, and information security—and prepares managers and professionals to both design and work within on-line information systems that connect people as well as computers. The teleprogram is intended for nontechnical generalists faced with the need to plan and develop systems for their own organizations, and to manage projects and lead teams working within networked environments.

Candidates for the APC in information technology must complete 16 academic credits with an average grade of B or better. The time limit for completion of the APC requirements is two years.

SPECIAL PROGRAMS

To accommodate the schedules of today's busy adult student, the Virtual College teleprogram is offered in an "education-on-demand" format. Once students are admitted to the program, they can register for telecourses anytime and have from four to fourteen weeks to complete each one. Telecourses utilize software agents to track, prompt, and record student progress through the courses. Each on-demand telecourse consists of multiple sessions that contain video, tutorial, laboratory, and reading modules.

While students work mostly independently on these courses, computer conferencing, e-mail, and desktop videoconferencing access to faculty members are available to answer questions, evaluate assignments and examinations, and provide advisement. Throughout each telecourse, the intelligent network identifies and supports groups of students to collaborate on assignments. Faculty-led projects are offered on a scheduled basis throughout the year.

CREDIT OPTIONS

Because of the nature of this program, transfer credits from other colleges or universities cannot be accepted.

FACULTY

There are eight full- and part-time faculty members dedicated to the Virtual College's APC teleprogram. All Virtual College faculty members have doctoral or other terminal academic degrees.

STUDENT PROFILE

More than 150 students have completed Virtual College telecourses. Students range in age from 25 to 50 (with a mean age of 35) and 35 percent are women. Most students are employed as full-time managers or professionals in finance, accounting, and marketing, and study on a part-time basis. All students have a bachelor's degree and 30 percent have advanced degrees (typically an M.B.A.). Two-thirds of all Virtual College students live in the tri-state New York metropolitan region.

ADMISSION

Admission to the APC in information technology teleprogram is open to all qualified applicants holding a bachelor's degree or higher from an accredited undergraduate or graduate institution. Admission is based on a review of the candidate's academic credentials and professional experience. In addition, each candidate must possess strong business writing skills, as the teleprogram requires extensive electronic text communications for all course discussions, analyses, and projects.

TUITION AND FEES

In 1996–97, graduate tuition is $588 for the first credit and $525 for each additional credit. There are no additional charges for teleprogram software, electronic readings, or network connections.

FINANCIAL AID

Financial assistance in the form of Federal Perkins or Stafford Loans is available through the Higher Education Assistance Corporation in New York State and in New Jersey. About 15 percent of APC students receive student loans.

APPLYING

New York University reviews applications in order of date when all materials are received. Students are not required to attend any on-campus orientation sessions.

CONTACT

Richard Vigilante
Director
Information Technologies Institute
New York University
48 Cooper Square
New York, New York 10003
Telephone: 212-998-7190
Fax: 212-995-3550
World Wide Web: http://www.nyu.edu/sce/intechdp.htm

Distance Learning Programs

North Carolina State University
Office of Instructional Telecommunications
Raleigh, North Carolina

Founded in 1887, North Carolina State University (NCSU) is a national center for research, teaching, and extension. As a land-grant state university, it shares the distinctive characteristics of these institutions nationally: broad academic offerings, extensive public service, national and international activities, and large-scale extension and research programs. With an enrollment in excess of 27,000, the University is organized into nine colleges, the School of Design, and the Graduate School. The nine colleges are Agriculture and Life Sciences, Education and Psychology, Engineering, Forest Resources, Humanities and Social Sciences, Management, Physical and Mathematical Sciences, Textiles, and Veterinary Medicine. North Carolina State University is accredited by national and regional accrediting agencies applicable to the University and numerous professional fields.

As the state's only research university in the land-grant tradition, North Carolina State University has the unique mission to serve students through technical assistance, professional development, lifelong education, and technology transfer programs. A primary channel for fulfilling this mission is through the University's existing and emerging distance education technologies.

DISTANCE LEARNING PROGRAM

The Courses by Cable, Internet, and Video programs administered by North Carolina State University's Office of Instructional Telecommunications provide distance learners with access to the excellent faculty and courses of North Carolina State University. The cable and video programs are based on the thesis that good teaching can be captured and delivered without change on the part of the instructor and the instruction—conventional or innovative. The delivery technologies used in the program include cable television and videocassette, both television-based. In fall 1997 the University is offering its first two courses via the Internet. By the nature of the medium, these two courses will require a significant development effort when compared to the cable and video offerings.

The programs began in spring 1987. There were 18 off-campus registrants in the first two courses offered that semester. During 1996–97, the programs offered 114 courses and had 948 registrants. Initially, the program offered College of Humanities and Social Sciences courses and used the studio-classroom facilities of the College of Engineering. In 1990, a VideoClass Room, the heart of the Courses by Cable and Video programs, was built in the College of Humanities and Social Sciences building and became the origin for all Courses by Cable and Video for the next four years. In summer 1994, courses began to be recorded in a second VideoClass Room in the College of Management building. During that time, the program grew and courses were added from the Colleges of Management, Agriculture and Life Sciences, Computer Science (Engineering), Education and Psychology, Physical and Mathematical Sciences, and Textiles. As of spring 1997 the Cable and Video programs have provided courses in 148 communities spread out among sixty-four of the state's 100 counties. In addition, NC State courses have been taken by students in twelve other states and Canada, Germany, Japan, Mexico, Saudi Arabia, and Spain.

Experience with the Courses by Cable and Video programs consistently demonstrates the academic and economic success of this activity. The service mission of the University is well served.

DELIVERY MEDIA

Courses are delivered primarily by cable television, the Internet, or videocassette. Students may select the technology most accessible and appropriate for them and earn credit toward degrees without attending classes on campus.

PROGRAM OF STUDY

Undergraduate degree completion is possible, providing the courses offered are applicable.

A Certificate Program for Training and Development is available at the graduate level. This program is designed as a professional development program of study for people who have been identified by their companies to take on training roles or who are in positions that require competence in skills related to training and development. It was designed to allow students to develop conceptual and process skills through academic study and, at the same time, receive recognition from NCSU for completing a significant program of graduate-level course work (15 hours). The Certificate in Training and Development is a nondegree program offered through the Department of Adult and Community College Education at North Carolina State

University. The program consists of a selected set of courses taken for credit by lifelong learning students. The courses are selected to offer a cohesive continuing education opportunity for people in training roles in business and industry.

CREDIT OPTIONS

All courses offered through cable, Internet, and video can be taken for University credit (undergraduate and graduate), which is considered the equivalent to taking the courses on-campus.

FACULTY

Faculty members and other academic personnel of the University total 1,500. Among the many honors and recognitions received by members of the faculty are six memberships in the National Academy of Science and five in the National Academy of Engineering, forty-eight named professorships, twenty-four University distinguished professorships, eighty-three Alumni Distinguished Undergraduate Professors, and currently more than 307 members of the Academy of Outstanding Teachers.

ADMISSION

The principal requirement for undergraduate admission is a high school diploma. Certificate and graduate admission require a bachelor's degree.

TUITION AND FEES

Tuition for each credit hour depends on the program and whether it is undergraduate or graduate. Tuition ranges between $77 and $150 per semester hour. Supplemental fees typically range from $115 to $120 per course.

FINANCIAL AID

Financial aid is available as long as the student is eligible, that is, taking course work in an NCSU degree program or toward being admitted into an NCSU degree program.

APPLYING

Applications can be handled in person, or at a distance by mail, fax, and e-mail.

CONTACT

Thomas L. Russell
Director
Office of Instructional
   Telecommunications
Campus Box 7401
North Carolina State University
Raleigh, North Carolina 27695-7401
Telephone: 919-515-7730
Fax: 919-515-5778
E-mail: oit@ncsu.edu
Web site: http://www2.ncsu.edu/oit/

Nova Southeastern University
The School of Computer and Information Sciences
Fort Lauderdale, Florida

A major force in educational innovation, the School of Computer and Information Sciences (SCIS) is distinguished by its ability to offer both traditional and nontraditional choices in educational programs and formats that enable professionals to pursue advanced degrees without career interruption. The School offers programs leading to the Master of Science, Doctor of Philosophy, and Doctor of Education in several disciplines. It has more than 800 graduate students from across the United States and other countries and has been awarding graduate degrees since 1980. Nova Southeastern University (NSU) is the forty-seventh-largest private academic institution in the United States and the largest in Florida. It has a 225-acre campus in Fort Lauderdale with more than 6,700 students on campus and 8,500 students in programs elsewhere in Florida, in twenty-four other states, and in several other countries. Other schools of NSU include the undergraduate college and graduate schools of business, education, health professions, law, oceanography, psychology, and social and systemic studies. More than 50,000 NSU graduates contribute with distinction to their businesses and professions worldwide. NSU has enjoyed full accreditation by the Commission on Colleges of the Southern Association of Colleges and Schools since 1971.

DISTANCE LEARNING PROGRAM

SCIS pioneered graduate on-line education and has been offering on-line programs and programs with an on-line component since 1983. All of its programs of study (four master's degree programs, five doctoral degree programs, and the Educational Specialist degree) are offered in distance learning formats. Master's programs require no on-campus classroom attendance. Doctoral programs use one of two formats: cluster or institute. Cluster students attend four cluster meetings per year, held quarterly over an extended weekend (Friday, Saturday, and half-day Sunday) at the University. Cluster terms start in March and September. Cluster weekends take place in March, June, September, and December. Institute students attend a weeklong institute twice a year at the University. Institutes are held in mid-January and mid-July at the start of each five-month term. Doctoral programs also have an on-line component. Clusters and institutes bring together students and faculty members for participation in courses, workshops, and dissertation counseling. Between meetings, students complete assignments, research papers and projects, and participate in on-line activities.

DELIVERY MEDIA

Master's students take courses on-line following an on-campus weekend orientation. Doctoral students participate in a combination of on-campus and on-line activities. On-line connections are made via computer and modem from home, office, or on the road. Students may participate in on-line activities or on-line courses from anywhere in the United States via local call or outside the United States via the Internet. Courses involve a range of on-line activities that facilitate frequent interaction with faculty members, classmates, and colleagues. Teachers and students interact using a variety of on-line techniques and tools such as the real-time electronic classroom, interactive bulletin boards, electronic mail, hypertext menuing systems, and electronic submission of assignments for review by faculty members. Learning is facilitated by the electronic library and NSU's distance library services. The Internet is also used for research.

PROGRAMS OF STUDY

SCIS offers programs leading to the M.S. degree in computer information systems, computer science, computing technology in education, and management information systems. Doctoral-level programs include the Ph.D. in computer information systems, computer science, information systems, and information science, and the Ph.D. and Ed.D. in computing technology in education. The Educational Specialist degree is available is computing technology in education. Combined master's-doctoral degree programs are available. Master's programs, which are offered on campus or on-line, require a minimum of 36 credits of course work (thesis optional) and may be completed in eighteen months. The Ph.D. in computer science and computer information systems are offered in cluster format and require 64 credits, including eight 3-credit courses, four 4-credit projects, and the dissertation. They may be completed in three years. Doctoral programs in information systems, information science, and computing technology in education are offered in cluster and institute formats and require 64 credits, including eight 3-credit courses, four 4-credit projects, and the dissertation. They may be completed in three years.

SPECIAL PROGRAMS

SCIS has four special programs: (1) a graduate certificate program in information resources management for federal employees, (2) a graduate certificate program in information systems for corporations, (3) short course and workshop programs for several companies, and (4) a comprehensive series of technology-oriented courses that have been approved for teacher certification in computer science (grades K–12) by Florida's Bureau of Teacher Certification.

CREDIT OPTIONS

Master's applicants may request transfer of up to 6 graduate credits. Courses proposed for transfer must have grades of at least "B." Credit is not awarded for life or work experience.

FACULTY

SCIS has 20 full-time and 10 part-time faculty members. All faculty members teaching at the graduate level have doctoral degrees.

ADMISSION

The master's applicant must have an undergraduate degree with a GPA of at least 2.5 and a GPA of at least 3.0 in an appropriate major. The doctoral applicant must have a master's degree with an appropriate graduate major and a graduate GPA of at least 3.25. Degrees must be from regionally accredited institutions. All applicants must submit a score report of the GRE or a comprehensive portfolio of appropriate professional experience and credentials. English proficiency is a requirement for admission.

TUITION AND FEES

Tuition is $350 per credit for master's students; for doctoral students, semi-annual tuition is $3925. The registration fee is $30. The application fee is $50.

FINANCIAL AID

To qualify for financial aid a student must be admitted, must be a U.S. citizen or a U.S. immigrant, and must plan on registering for a minimum of 6 credit hours per term. A prospective student who requires financial assistance should apply for financial aid while a candidate for admission. For financial aid information or application forms, students should call 800-522-3243 (toll-free).

APPLYING

Applications, including transcripts and recommendations, should be submitted at least three months before the anticipated starting term. Students who wish to matriculate in a shorter amount of time must contact the SCIS admissions office by telephone to begin the process. Copies of transcripts are acceptable for unofficial early review. Students applying late may be granted provisional acceptance pending completion of the application process. Master's terms start in September, January, April, and July. Doctoral cluster terms start in September and March. Doctoral institute terms start in January and July.

CONTACT
The School of Computer and Information Sciences
Nova Southeastern University
3100 Southwest 9th Avenue
Fort Lauderdale, Florida 33315
Telephone: 954-262-2000
　　　　　　800-986-2247 Ext. 2000 (toll-free)
E-mail: scisinfo@scis.nova.edu
Web site: http://www.scis.nova.edu

Distance Learning Programs

NRI Schools

McGraw-Hill Continuing Education Center
Washington, D.C.

NRI Schools, the pioneer of at-home vocational training, was founded in 1914. Its mission is to provide students who cannot attend residential classes with hands-on instruction in high-growth career fields, including computer repair, computer programming, networking, computer-aided drafting, home inspection, bookkeeping, desktop publishing, building construction, and other fields. All programs cost less than traditional colleges, yet they include real-world equipment, instructor feedback, useful references, and lifetime support services. NRI Schools is fully accredited by the Accrediting Commission of the Distance Education and Training Council. Currently, dozens of companies and government agencies use customized NRI programs to upgrade the skills of their employees.

DISTANCE LEARNING PROGRAM

All NRI Schools' courses are set up in a distance learning format. Each year, approximately 7,000 students graduate from an NRI program and move on to new jobs, promotions, and home-based businesses.

DELIVERY MEDIA

Materials for NRI Schools' courses are sent via the United States Postal Service or the United Parcel Service. Students and faculty members interact by phone, mail, fax, and e-mail. Courses include all the equipment needed to complete the program, including a computer where applicable.

All courses lead to a career diploma. The following represent only a few of NRI Schools' course offerings.

A course in bookkeeping and accounting teaches students traditional and technological bookkeeping methods. Training materials include a solar calculator, a computer, and Peachtree Accounting for Windows software.

The computer-aided drafting course allows students to move from manual drafting techniques to computer-aided shortcuts. Training materials include layout tools, a computer, and AutoCAD LT software.

A computer programming course helps students create working programs in Basic, C, and Visual Basic, which is the language used to create Windows applications. Training materials include a computer and all three compilers.

The desktop publishing with PageMaker course allows students to practice designing by hand and create menus, flyers, and more by using a PC. Training materials include layout tools, a computer, and Adobe's PageMaker software.

The home inspection course teaches students what to look for when inspecting a home and how to prepare a professional report of their findings. Training materials include inspection tools, a computer, and special software.

The microcomputer servicing course teaches students to service all types of computers as they prepare for A+ Certification. Training materials include digital multimeter, a computer, ForeFront diagnostics, and an interactive CD-ROM.

A course in networking with Windows NT prepares students for NT Certification as they learn the secrets of LANs, WANs, and the Windows NT 4.0 server. Training materials include a computer, Windows NT, and special on-line instruction.

Writing courses help students develop their skills in either fiction or nonfiction writing, including how to market manuscripts. Training materials include a computer, Microsoft Works, and detailed instructor feedback.

SPECIAL PROGRAMS

Resources are available to help students make career decisions. NRI Schools gladly writes letters of recommendation upon request.

STUDENT SERVICES

Students may use NRI Schools' 24-hour TeleGrading hotline to find out their grades instantly. Additionally, the Online Connection provides all students with a quick link to their instructor, computer tips, Internet resources, and career-planning sites.

CREDIT OPTIONS

No college credits are awarded for NRI Schools' distance education programs.

FACULTY

At present, there are 12 full-time faculty members and several part-time faculty members. All faculty members hold college degrees and many hold technology certificates.

ADMISSION

There are no admission requirements for NRI Schools' distance education programs, though students must be 18 years of age and a high school diploma is recommended.

TUITION AND FEES

Tuition for NRI Schools' courses ranges from $1000 to $3000 and includes all equipment necessary to complete the program, which in many cases includes a computer.

FINANCIAL AID

Students who have served in the military may be reimbursed for all or part of their tuition through the G.I. bill. NRI Schools also provides necessary information to employers who have tuition reimbursement policies.

APPLYING

Students may call, write, or visit NRI Schools' Web site to request application materials. Enrollment procedures can be handled very quickly by phone, mail, or fax.

CONTACT

Marc Jean-Michel
NRI Schools
4401 Connecticut Avenue, NW
Washington, D.C. 20008
Telephone: 202-244-9792
Fax: 202-244-2047
E-mail: info@mhcec.com
Web site: http://www.mhcec.com

Distance Learning Programs

Ohio University
Lifelong Learning Programs
Athens, Ohio

Ohio University, founded in 1804, was the first institution of higher learning in the Northwest Territory. Today it offers all the resources of a major university—diverse intellectual stimulation and an abundance of social and cultural activities—in a quiet, small-city setting. In addition to the main campus in Athens, the University has six regional centers in the southeast quadrant of Ohio.

Ohio University offers degrees in more than 325 subject areas through its colleges: Arts and Sciences, Business, Communication, Education, Engineering and Technology, Fine Arts, Health and Human Services, Honors Tutorial, Osteopathic Medicine, and University College. The University is accredited by the North Central Association of Colleges and Schools and holds membership in a number of professional organizations; in addition, many academic programs are accredited by their respective associations.

Ohio University has also been a leader in providing learning opportunities for nontraditional students, including more than seventy years of correspondence education, credit for college-level learning from life experience, and the external-student degree program.

DISTANCE LEARNING PROGRAM

The Independent Study Program serves students at a distance through correspondence courses, course credit by examination, and individual learning contracts. Credit earned through one of these options is considered residential credit and may be applied without limit to a degree program at Ohio University or transferred to another institution (subject to any conditions set by the accepting institution). Approximately 350 courses are currently available through Independent Study; the program has about 5,000 course enrollments each year.

The External Student Program (ESP), which operates under the Adult Learning Services Office, assists students at a distance who are working toward Ohio University degrees with such services as transcript evaluation, advising, degree planning, and liaison with other University offices and departments.

DELIVERY MEDIA

Correspondence between students and instructors, using the postal system or fax, is the primary delivery system for Independent Study courses. E-mail lesson service is rapidly being added as an option for many courses; students are required to have access to a computer and modem for this option. Videotape supplements the printed instructional materials in some courses. A few courses use the Internet as a medium for instructional delivery and instructor-to-student and student-to-student communication.

PROGRAMS OF STUDY

Four associate degrees may be earned: Associate in Arts (A.A.), Associate in Science (A.S.), Associate in Individualized Studies (A.I.S.), and Associate in Applied Business (A.A.B.). All associate degrees require the completion of 96 to 105 quarter hours of credit; transfer students must earn at least 30 quarter hours of credit from Ohio University.

The A.I.S. is a self-designed degree; students are required to submit a proposal outlining their course of study and area of concentration (which must consist of a minimum of 30 quarter hours of study). At least 30 of the 96 quarter hours of credit must be completed after admission to the A.I.S. program.

The Bachelor of Specialized Studies (B.S.S.) is offered through University College and offers students the opportunity to design an individual program to meet career or academic goals that cannot be accommodated with a degree currently offered by the University. The B.S.S. degree program is initiated in the form of a proposal that includes a statement of rationale; students must have sophomore rank and a minimum cumulative grade point average of 2.0 before submitting the proposal. The proposal must include an area of concentration that is named and consists of a minimum of 45 quarter hours of related course work that does not duplicate any current major. Students must complete at least 192 quarter hours, with a minimum of 90 hours at the 300–400 (junior/senior) level. At least 45 hours must be earned after the B.S.S. proposal is approved.

SPECIAL PROGRAMS

The M.B.A. Without Boundaries is a structured two-year program offered by the College of Business. Designed for working professionals, it combines several intensive on-site seminar sessions with group and individual projects completed at the student's own location using the OUMBA Intranet to access learning modules, collaborate with other students, and communicate with faculty members. Enrollment is limited.

The Institutes for Adult Learners are held three times a year on the Ohio University campus. These programs offer degree-seeking students the opportunity to earn credit, become acquainted with the campus and faculty, and participate in a residential experience with other nontraditional students. Courses are taught in intensive, one-week classroom formats supplemented by individual work before and after the Institute. Credit for each course is generally 4 quarter hours.

CREDIT OPTIONS

Students at a distance who are interested in completing an Ohio University degree through the External Student Program can use a combination of in-classroom courses, credit for experiential learning documented through a portfolio process, transfer credit (including possible military and professional training equivalencies established by the American Council on Education), and Independent Study options. Students may apply 24 quarter hours of experiential learning credit toward an associate degree; 48 quarter hours may be applied toward a bachelor's degree.

Regularly enrolled students on any Ohio University campus may use Independent Study or experiential learning credit toward their degrees.

FACULTY

All Independent Study courses are taught by permanent Ohio University faculty members; more than 90 percent of the 125 faculty members teaching in the program have a doctorate or other terminal degree.

ADMISSION

Enrollment in Independent Study courses is open to anyone who can profit from the learning. Enrollment in a course does not constitute formal admission to the University. Students must have a high school diploma to be admitted to the External Student program; transfer students must have a minimum 2.0 cumulative grade point average. Admission to the External Student Program does not guarantee on-campus admission to a specific degree program at Ohio University.

TUITION AND FEES

Fees for Independent Study courses in 1997–98 are correspondence courses, $60 per quarter hour plus $15 enrollment fee per course; course credit by examination, $32 per quarter hour; and Independent Study projects, $70 per quarter hour. Fees for the External Student Program are $100 application fee and $60 annual matriculation fee (assessed for a maximum of four years). In 1997–98, students seeking credit for experiential learning pay $295 for the required portfolio development course, plus $135 per course assessment (paid after completion of the portfolio development course).

FINANCIAL AID

Students may use veterans' benefits and employer reimbursement to pay course and program fees. Federal and state financial aid cannot be applied to courses and fees through Independent Study or the External Student Program. Standard tuition and fees paid by on-campus students cannot be applied to Independent Study courses.

APPLYING

Students may enroll in Independent Study courses at any time; enrollment forms are provided in the Independent Study catalog and at the program's World Wide Web site. A separate application process is required for the External Student Program; forms are provided in the External Student bulletin or may be requested from the office of Adult Learning Services.

CONTACT

Independent Study Program
Dr. Richard Moffitt, Director
Independent Study Program
302 Tupper Hall
Ohio University
Athens, Ohio 45701
Telephone: 614-593-2910
Fax: 614-593-2901
WWW: http://www.cats.ohiou.
　　　edu/~indstu/index.htm

External Student Program
Barbra Frye, Coordinator
External Student Program, ALS
301 Tupper Hall
Ohio University
Athens, Ohio 45701
Telephone: 614-593-2150
Fax: 614-593-0452
WWW: http://www.cats.ohiou.
　　　edu/~adullear/index.htm

M.B.A. Without Boundaries
Dr. John Stinson
Copeland Hall
Ohio University
Athens, Ohio 45701
Telephone: 614-593-2073

Old Dominion University
Distance Learning/TELETECHNET
Norfolk, Virginia

Old Dominion University, a state-assisted institution in Norfolk, Virginia, is part of a metropolitan and historic area with a population of approximately 1.4 million. Established in 1930, the University enrolls more than 17,000 students, including 4,000 graduate students, and operates centers in Hampton, Portsmouth, and Virginia Beach as well as TELETECHNET locations throughout the commonwealth of Virginia and southeastern Indiana. Old Dominion students come from all fifty states and 115 countries.

Old Dominion is recognized as an international leader in telecommunications with the creation of TELETECHNET, a distance learning network in partnership with community colleges. TELETECHNET promotes three major objectives: to provide higher education access to students who are place bound due to employment, family obligations, distance, or expense; to provide a cost-effective means of serving the growing number of learners entering the commonwealth's colleges and universities by the year 2000; and to stimulate economic development in the areas where there is a demonstrated shortage of highly trained employees.

All programs are accredited by the Commission on Colleges of the Southern Association of Colleges and Schools. The undergraduate and graduate business programs are fully accredited by the AACSB-International Association for Management Education. The graduate and undergraduate education programs are accredited by the National Council for Accreditation of Teacher Learning Education. The engineering technology programs are fully accredited by the Technology Accreditation Commission of the Accreditation Board for Engineering and Technology (TAC/ABET). The nursing programs are accredited by the National League for Nursing.

DISTANCE LEARNING PROGRAM

Through TELETECHNET, Old Dominion offers degrees through courses televised to off-campus sites across the state and has an enrollment of more than 3,000 students. Students earn baccalaureate degrees from Old Dominion by completing the first two years of course work at their local community college. Old Dominion provides the remaining course work at the community college site primarily through telecourses using audio and video technologies. In addition to sixteen baccalaureate degrees, TELETECHNET also offers seven master's degrees and a certificate in public management.

DELIVERY MEDIA

Old Dominion University courses are delivered by Ku-band satellite with two-way audio for interaction between faculty members and students. The video network is enhanced via a wide area network for e-mail and document exchange.

PROGRAMS OF STUDY

Old Dominion's TELETECHNET program offers baccalaureate degrees in the following areas: business administration (accounting, finance, information systems, management, and marketing), criminal justice, engineering technology (civil, electrical, electrical with a computer emphasis, and mechanical), health sciences, human services counseling, interdisciplinary studies (elementary/middle school math and science, leading to a master's degree, and professional communications), nursing (RN to B.S.N.), and occupational and technical studies (with a specialization in technology).

Master's degrees are offered in the following areas: Master of Business Administration, Master of Engineering (civil engineering/environmental engineering and management), Master of Science in Education (elementary/middle school education, which is tied to the bachelor's program, and special education, which meets certification and endorsement requirements in learning disabilities, mental retardation, and emotional/behavioral disorders), Master of Science in Nursing (family nurse practitioner studies), and Master of Taxation.

In addition to the bachelor's and master's programs, a certificate in public management that leads to a Master of Public Administration is available. Additional programs are in the development stage for TELETECHNET.

Students who wish to take individual courses may enroll on a nonmatriculated basis within many of the programs.

STUDENT SERVICES

TELETECHNET students have the added advantage of checking out videotapes of class presentations if they miss a session due to family responsibilities or job conflicts. Computer labs, which are connected to the main campus and have Internet access, are available at each site for the students' use.

Registration, financial aid, and advising are all available to students through site directors. The directors also help students with testing, program auditing, and course materials.

The Old Dominion University library supports the TELETECHNET students by providing library resources and services and reference assistance that are required for successful completion of course work, research papers and projects, and independent reading and research.

CREDIT OPTIONS

Students can transfer credits earned at other accredited postsecondary institutions to Old Dominion University and can receive credit through taking the College-Level Examination Program (CLEP) for certain courses.

FACULTY

More than 30 percent of Old Dominion University's full-time faculty members have taught on television, and this percentage continues to grow as TELETECHNET expands its degree programs. Specialized training for this unique teaching environment is provided to ensure high-quality instruction for students.

ADMISSION

Prospective students must submit an application accompanied by a $30 fee for degree-seeking admission and request that official transcripts from all previous colleges be sent to the Office of Admissions for evaluation of credits earned (transfer admission generally requires a minimum 2.0 grade point average).

TUITION AND FEES

Old Dominion's TELETECHNET program offers affordable tuition for students. Undergraduate TELETECHNET tuition for the 1997–98 school year is $121 per credit for Virginia residents and $230 per credit for nonresidents. Graduate tuition is $162 per credit for in-state students and $288 for out-of-state students. There is a required general services fee of $10 for each semester.

FINANCIAL AID

Old Dominion University is a direct lending institution and awards financial aid from federally funded and state-funded programs as well as from privately funded sources. All types of aid fall within two categories: need-based and merit-based assistance. Awards are made based on demonstration of financial need, special merit, or both. Between 60 and 80 percent of Old Dominion University's students receive some form of financial assistance.

The University requires all students applying for need-based assistance to complete the Free Application for Federal Student Aid (FAFSA). Those applying for merit-based awards must complete an Old Dominion University Scholarship Application.

APPLYING

The deadline for admission for the fall semester for transfer students and graduate students is July 1; for nursing students, February 1. The deadline for applying for the spring semester is December 1. The summer semester deadline is April 1. Decisions are made on a rolling basis, and applicants are notified of their admission status within four weeks after receipt of all application materials.

CONTACT

Dr. Jeanie P. Kline
Associate Director
TELETECHNET
145 Education Building
Old Dominion University
Norfolk, Virginia 23529
Telephone: 800-YOU-2ODU (toll-free)
Fax: 757-683-5492
E-mail: ttnet@odu.edu
Web site: http://www.odu.edu/~distance_learning/
    TELETECHNET.html

Distance Learning Programs

Rensselaer Polytechnic Institute
RSVP: The Office of Continuing & Distance Education
Troy, New York

> *Rensselaer Polytechnic Institute is America's oldest technological university and is located on a handsome, historic campus high above the Hudson River in Troy, New York. Founded in 1824 by Stephen van Rensselaer "for the purpose of instructing persons...in the application of science to the common purposes of life," Rensselaer has grown into an internationally respected technological university offering graduate and undergraduate degrees in engineering, science, management, architecture, and humanities and social science. Widely respected for the quality of its education, Rensselaer is also a prominent research institution with strong ties to industry and business. In 1995, Rensselaer received the prestigious "Hesburgh Award" and was also named "Educator of the Year" by Boeing Corporation for its pioneering efforts in reengineering undergraduate education to provide for interactive, student-centered learning environments.*

DISTANCE LEARNING PROGRAM

RSVP: The Office of Continuing & Distance Education at Rensselaer provides graduate courses, certificates, degree programs, and noncredit seminars and workshops to working professionals at their work sites. More than 900 working professionals from many of this nation's leading corporations take courses each semester without having to travel.

RSVP is a highly respected program in the field of distance learning. In 1993, it was named "Best Distance Learning Program—Higher Education" by the United States Distance Learning Association. In 1996, it received recognition from the same organization for its partnership with General Motors in the delivery of an M.S. program in the management of technology. RSVP is known for an emphasis on high quality, customer service, and excellent production values.

DELIVERY MEDIA

RSVP delivers courses using a range of technologies that include satellite broadcast, videotapes, and room and desktop videoconferencing. These technologies are integrated so that the same event can be transmitted to multiple locations in different delivery formats. Internet and World Wide Web technology provide support and enhancement to courses, with many faculty members offering "virtual" office hours. Most programs can be received in a live, interactive mode.

PROGRAMS OF STUDY

Working professionals can complete individual courses, four-course certificate programs, or full master's degrees through RSVP. In addition, noncredit seminars and workshops are offered in a range of technical areas. All content is at the graduate level. Full M.S. degrees are available in computer science, engineering science, management and technology (M.S. and M.B.A.), manufacturing systems engineering, mechanical engineering, microelectronics manufacturing engineering, and service systems—industrial and management engineering. Certificates are available in human computer interaction, information science, management and technology, manufacturing systems engineering, mechanical engineering, microelectronics manufacturing, reliability, and service systems. Individual courses come from a range of academic departments at Rensselaer to support the certificate and degree programs listed, and interested students can take single courses for personal and professional development. Seminars and workshops are based on the strengths and talents of Rensselaer faculty members and are offered in a range of technical topics. Custom seminars and workshops can be designed and delivered upon request.

Certificate programs require the successful completion of a four-course sequence of graduate-level courses. All M.S. programs, except the M.B.A., are 30-credit ten-course degrees. The M.B.A. is a 60-credit program with the possibility of waiving from 3 to 12 credits based on prior knowledge and experience. Workshops and seminars can be from one to five days in length.

In the degree area, approximately forty courses are delivered annually via distance learning technology to many of the nation's leading corporations, including AT&T, Consolidated Edison, DuPont, Ford, General Electric, General Motors, Hughes Optical, IBM, Lockheed Martin, Lotus Development Corporation, Lucent Technology, Perkin-Elmer, Pitney Bowes, United Technologies, and Xerox.

In nondegree programming, RSVP has provided approximately twenty programs per year of one to five days in length, either in sequence or over a period of several weeks, depending on content and audience need as well as educational soundness. Over the past few years, programs have been offered in colloid chemistry, vacuum switchgear, computer and information technology, thermophotovoltaic, distributed multimedia, multiphase flow and heat transfer, chemical mechanical planarization, highway capacity, and SIDRA, among other areas. These courses have been attended by working professionals, many Fortune 500 companies, and other leading organizations across the U.S.

SPECIAL PROGRAMS

RSVP works with corporate and government partners who arrange to bring Rensselaer's program on site for their employees. Similar arrangements can be made with regional distribution partners (i. e., community colleges, professional organizations, education centers). Partner sites agree to receive courses and provide all local administrative support, which often includes a library of instructional materials. A minimum number of enrollments (typically ten, depending on individual circumstances) are required to initiate a new site. The credits and degrees that participating students receive through RSVP are identical to those received by campus-based students. Since many RSVP programs have been offered in response to the needs of partners, it is possible to add new courses, certificates, degree programs, or custom seminars based on interest and sufficient enrollments.

CREDIT OPTIONS

In the M.S. program, students can transfer up to two graduate-level courses (6 credits) that have been completed at other institutions, assuming that the courses are approved as acceptable in the plan of study by an academic adviser and have been completed with a grade of B or better. A maximum of 12 credits can be waived in the M.B.A. program based on prior course work and/or work experience. No course work can be transferred into the certificate programs.

FACULTY

Rensselaer's faculty is made up of approximately 400 full-time scholars, teachers, and researchers. Their doctorates or other degrees are from the world's leading universities. The faculty members who teach in the distance learning program are the same who teach on campus, and more than 80 full-time faculty members have taught in the program to date.

ADMISSION

Students interested in credit courses and degree programs must apply to Rensselaer in the same manner as campus-based students, and admission standards are essentially the same. Transcripts of all college-level work and two letters of recommendation must be supplied for degree admission. Transcripts are also required for single courses and certificates. There are no admission requirements for short courses and seminars.

TUITION AND FEES

Tuition for all credit courses is invoiced at the same rate as for campus-based students. For the 1997–98 academic year, that is $600 per credit hour or $1800 per 3-credit course. The only other costs are for the application fee ($35), a transcript fee ($25), and the costs of instructional materials. Costs for noncredit seminars and workshops vary.

FINANCIAL AID

Students enrolled in the credit courses and certificate programs can apply for all state and federal bank loans just as their campus colleagues do. However, the majority of participants have been sponsored by their employers.

APPLYING

Application materials for credit courses and programs are provided to site administrators at participating locations. Application deadlines are typically set at four to six weeks prior to the first day of class, and admission decisions are made as soon as the application is complete. Registration forms for noncredit seminars and workshops are included in the program announcements.

CONTACT

Christine A. Katchmar
Director
RSVP: The Office of Continuing & Distance Education
Rensselaer Polytechnic Institute
Troy, New York 12180
Telephone: 518-276-8351
Fax: 518-276-8026
Web site: http://rsvp.rpi.edu

Distance Learning Programs

Rio Salado College

Distance Learning Program

Tempe, Arizona

In 1978, the Maricopa Community College District approved an intriguing new concept to create a nontraditional college that offered busy, working adults the highest-quality education designed for their total convenience. The result was Rio Salado College.

From the start, Rio Salado College has been recognized for its innovative educational delivery systems. Rio takes college beyond the confines of a traditional campus and provides education wherever a group of students and an instructor can meet to share the adventure of learning. Technology brings courses directly to thousands of students via distance learning. In addition, more than 500 adjunct faculty members teach at approximately 200 existing facilities, including shopping malls, community centers, businesses, and high schools throughout Maricopa County.

For twenty years, Rio Salado College has consistently grown and thrived and has a current enrollment of nearly 24,000 credit and 12,000 noncredit students. Rio Salado College is accredited by the North Central Association of Colleges and Schools.

DISTANCE LEARNING PROGRAM

"Let the College come to you" is the prevailing philosophy at Rio Salado. Rio Salado College makes it possible to earn an associate degree through distance learning, a concept the College has refined over the last fifteen years. As of fall 1997, Rio offers 132 distance learning courses, with seventy-two of those on the Internet. All distance courses encourage maximum interaction between student and instructor. Students choose their own study times and submit assignments by mail, fax, or computer. Instructors are available by phone, fax, and e-mail.

DELIVERY MEDIA

Distance courses are available through different delivery modes that include print-based, mixed media (audiocassette and/or videocassette, teleconference, computer), and the Internet.

Courses delivered on the Internet were first introduced in fall 1996, and, within six months, attracted 900 students. Because of this response, the number of offerings for fall 1997 has quadrupled. Access requires a service provider, Macintosh/Windows capability, and a minimum of 8 MB of RAM.

PROGRAMS OF STUDY

Distance learning classes are primarily academic in nature and include accounting, anthropology, art humanities, biology, business, chemistry, child/family studies, communication, computers, counseling and personal development, economics, education, English, geology, health science, history, humanities, integrated studies, management and supervision, mathematics, office automated systems, philosophy, political science, psychology, Spanish, and theater.

Students can also enroll in the following distance-delivered applied certificate programs: computer usage and technology (electronic workplace/networking/computer Web development), wastewater treatment, water distribution and collection, and water treatment.

Degrees offered are the Associate of Arts, the Associate of General Studies, and the Associate of Applied Science.

SPECIAL PROGRAMS

Rio Salado College provides a variety of accelerated and specialized programs. Among them is the Program for Adult Student Success (PASS). PASS is an accelerated, convenient, high-quality program that reduces the time spent in the classroom. It allows adults to earn an Associate of Arts degree in two years without leaving their jobs, friends, or family behind.

STUDENT SERVICES

All major student services are on-line, including registration, career and academic counseling, tutoring, book orders, and scholarship applications. Two easy-to-follow tutorials assist first-time Internet users. In addition, a technology help desk is available seven days a week.

CREDIT OPTIONS

Because Rio Salado College is accredited by the North Central Association of Colleges and Schools, its credits are recognized nationwide. Students who plan to transfer credits outside Arizona are encouraged to confer with an adviser to obtain specific information as to how the credits will fit into their curriculum or program of study.

FACULTY

In addition to full-time residential faculty members, Rio Salado College capitalizes on the professional career experience and expertise that adjunct faculty members bring to the learning environment. As well as being content specialists, Rio Salado faculty members are specially trained in effective teaching techniques for distance learning.

ADMISSION

With only a few exceptions, students may begin their distance classes any one of twenty-six times throughout the year—new classes start every other week. This open-entry format allows students to enroll anytime and have up to thirteen weeks to complete their courses.

For regular and distance classes, students may be admitted under any of the following classifications: college transfer, high school/GED graduate, or 18 years of age or older. Special admission requirements and forms are available for international students or students who do not qualify for any of these classifications.

TUITION AND FEES

Students pay tuition according to their residency status. Tuition for Arizona residents is $37 per credit hour, plus a $5-per-semester registration fee. Tuition for nonresidents is $62 per credit hour, plus a $5-per-semester registration fee.

FINANCIAL AID

Whether taking regular or distance learning courses, eligible students can apply for grants, work-study, and scholarships. To be eligible for federal financial aid, students must meet application criteria and select a program of study. The application process is approximately eight weeks long, so students should plan ahead.

APPLYING

Registration can be completed by Touch-Tone phone (602-731-8255 or toll-free at 800-729-1197) or via the World Wide Web (http://www.rio.maricopa.edu/). For more information, students should contact Student Services at 602-517-8540. Along with a completed application, students need to provide an official high school transcript, GED scores, or official transcripts from previously attended colleges.

CONTACT

Rio Salado College
2323 West 14th Street
Tempe, Arizona 85281
Telephone: 602-517-8010
For further information:
Debbie Lain
Supervisor of Admissions and Records
Telephone: 602-517-8150
Fax: 602-517-8199

Distance Learning Programs

R·I·T Rochester Institute of Technology
Distance Learning—Educational Technology Center
Rochester, New York

> RIT was founded in 1829 and is accredited by the Middle States Association of Colleges and Schools. A private university in upstate New York, RIT is nationally recognized for the quality of its 230 professional and career-oriented programs. Located on a 1,300-acre suburban campus in Rochester, RIT enrolls 12,600 students in its seven colleges and has an international reputation for programs in technology. It has the nation's only accredited undergraduate program in microelectronic engineering and the only doctoral program in imaging science. Cited among the nation's best comprehensive educational institutions by U.S. News & World Report, RIT is the fifth-largest private college/university in New York State and the seventeenth-largest in the nation.

DISTANCE LEARNING PROGRAM

Since 1979, when RIT offered its first distance learning course, the Institute has been a leader in the use of electronic forms of communication for course interaction. RIT's distance learning courses have the same objectives, rigorous workload, tuition, and academic credit as on-campus courses. Today, there are more than 4,000 annual registrations in distance learning courses.

DELIVERY MEDIA

Most professors have significant course materials on-line; some use on-line testing; and most use on-line conferencing and e-mail for class discussion. In addition to on-line communication, fax and phones are used for contacting faculty members and staff, registering for courses, ordering course materials from the bookstore, and submitting assignments.

Other technologies include audio cassette tapes, electronic blackboards, and the World Wide Web. Videotapes may take the place of classroom lectures, and some use scheduled conference calls for in-class interaction.

Participation requires a video playback unit with a television monitor, a telephone, and a personal computer capable of running programs such as Netscape while connected to the Internet.

PROGRAMS OF STUDY

Several degree programs and certificates are offered to distance learning students worldwide. Bachelor-level programs are designed for students who have some prior college experience or an accredited associate degree. At least 45 quarter-credit hours for a bachelor's degree must be completed through RIT. Master's-level programs require students to have completed a baccalaureate or equivalent degree from an accredited academic institution with a minimum grade point average of 3.0 on a 4.0 scale. GRE scores may also be required from those whose undergraduate GPA is less than 3.0. In addition, a graduate application with two professional recommendations and transcripts must be submitted.

The B.S. in applied arts and science, with concentrations in basic quality, emergency management, environmental management, health systems administration, information technology, management, and telecommunications, requires completion of 190 quarter-credit hours.

The B.S. in electrical/mechanical engineering technology is limited to students located near one of RIT's community college or corporate extension sites. After completing the basic requirements, students choose concentrations in electrical, mechanical, or manufacturing technology until a minimum of 193 quarter-credit hours have been earned.

The B.S. in environmental management requires students to have at least three years of mathematics, including trigonometry, and a minimum of one year of chemistry or physics. Students with a two-year degree in environmental science or a related program may have fulfilled credit requirements similar to those required in the first two years of RIT's program and may be admitted with junior standing.

The M.S. in software development and management consists of 48 quarter-credit hours, comprising the software engineering core foundation, the software engineering project, and electives. A minimal background is required in mathematics (discrete structures, statistics) and computing (programming in a high-level language, data structures, elementary computer architecture, and digital logic).

The M.S. in information technology consists of 48 quarter-credit hours of graduate study in core courses, with a choice of electives and concentrations in telecommunications technology, telecommunications management, and software development and management. Entering students are expected to have programming skills at an intermediate level in an appropriate language and understand the fundamentals of computer hardware.

The M.S. in health systems administration requires that students take two courses per quarter in the sequence in which they are offered and are required to attend three 1-week, on-campus sessions during the twenty-one-month course of study. A GPA under 3.0 will be considered, given superior endorsement and more than three years of management work experience. Students must complete a minimum of 57 quarter-credit hours, maintain a GPA of 3.0 (cumulative) or better, and complete a thesis or other appropriate research or professional achievement.

RIT also offers ten certificates for those wanting to improve or obtain skills in specialized areas. Courses in the certificate programs may be applied toward a degree. Graduate certificates include health systems finance, integrated health systems, and statistical quality. Undergraduate certificates include data communications, emergency management, environmental management science, health systems administration, industrial environmental management and technology, telecommunications network management, and voice communications.

CREDIT OPTIONS

Students have a number of options available for credit, including transfer credit, credit by exam, College-Level Examination Program (CLEP), Regents College exam, credit for educational experiences in the armed forces, credit for educational experiences in noncollegiate organizations, and credit for nontraditional learning. Advisers work with students to evaluate the number of credits that can be transferred, since the number of non-RIT credits accepted varies by program.

FACULTY

More than 100 full- and part-time faculty members teach distance learning courses.

ADMISSION

Requirements for admission and completion of degree or certificate programs vary by academic department. Students should refer to Program of Study descriptions.

TUITION AND FEES

Graduate tuition is the same for all students, $507 per credit hour. Undergraduate tuition is based on program code. All distance learning programs carry an Evening Division program code and are charged Evening Division undergraduate tuition rates of $231 per credit hour for lower-level courses and $253 per credit hour for upper-level courses. Most RIT courses are worth 4 credits.

FINANCIAL AID

RIT offers a full range of traditional financial aid programs as well as a number of innovative financing plans. Scholarships and assistantships are available to matriculated students in most graduate departments. The process of applying for aid should begin during the month of January in the year the student wishes to enroll.

APPLYING

Distance learning students follow the same procedures as all other students attending RIT. Decisions for selection rest within each college. Correspondence between the student and the Institute is conducted through the Admissions Office, which reviews applications as they are received.

CONTACT

Distance Learning
Educational Technology Center
Rochester Institute of Technology
Rochester, New York 14623-5603
Telephone: 716-475-5089
　　　　　800-CALL-RIT
Fax: 716-475-5077
E-mail: ritdl@rit.edu
Web site: http://www.rit.edu

Distance Learning Programs

Rogers University

RUOnline
Claremore and Tulsa, Oklahoma

Rogers University is a unique institution in the Oklahoma State System of Higher Education. Rogers University was created in 1996 through the merger of two of the most innovative institutions in Oklahoma: The University Center at Tulsa and Rogers State College. Rogers State College opened in 1909 as Eastern Oklahoma Preparatory School in Claremore, Oklahoma; the University Center at Tulsa opened in 1982 in downtown Tulsa as a consortium. The academic function of the institution is distinct for each campus.

The function of Rogers University, Claremore campus, is to provide associate-level degree and certificate programs. This includes university-parallel study for those students who plan to complete a bachelor's degree, general education, and programs of technical and occupational education. The Claremore campus carries with it a strong traditional community college foundation.

The Tulsa campus is located in an urban setting that serves mainly part-time students. Rogers University, Tulsa campus, contracts with other universities to bring together seventy-five of the best degree programs from across Oklahoma. Students are able to complete the third and fourth year of a bachelor's degree or choose from a wide selection of master's degree programs.

DISTANCE LEARNING PROGRAM

RUOnline was established in 1992 and now functions at http://www.ruonline.edu. It is fully accredited by the North Central Association. The main mission and goal of RUOnline is to provide a complete university in an on-line form, offering students the courses and traditional university services they want, when and where they need them. RUOnline meets the goals of Rogers University to provide a variety of choices to meet students' personal and divergent goals. The distance learning program serves more than 1,500 students per semester.

DELIVERY MEDIA

Rogers University delivers the bulk of RUOnline courseware over the Internet, including text, hypertext, graphics, audio, and video on-line. Students supplement this courseware with textbooks and videotapes. Additionally, students communicate with faculty members or other students using e-mail, electronic file transfer, threaded discussions, chat rooms, phone, and fax. RUOnline students need the following equipment: Windows 3.1, Windows95, or MacOS with at least a 486-DX or equivalent processor, multimedia capability, a 14.4 bps modem, a full-serve Internet connection, a Java-capable Web browser, and RealPlayer 4.0 (for audio and video).

PROGRAMS OF STUDY

RUOnline students may choose from one of four associate-level degree programs: business administration, computer science, humanities, and liberal arts. Sixty credit hours are required for the completion of each. RUOnline bachelor's- and master's-level degree programs are currently under consideration. Additionally, RUOnline students may choose from more than twenty individual courses in accounting, business management, computer science, economics, English, geography, history, humanities, mathematics, physical science, political science, and psychology. All RUOnline courses are semester courses that begin in August or January and end in December or May. Distance education courses are kept on the same type of schedule as on-campus courses and completion of a course appears on the student's transcript the same as an on-campus course.

SPECIAL PROGRAMS

Rogers University works with both employers and the military in making arrangements for special funding for working or military students. Because RUOnline offers associate degrees in business administration, liberal arts, computer science, and the humanities, special needs students may earn a degree in the convenience of their home, office, or other chosen location. RUOnline has the capacity to offer specialized courses to professionals seeking to complete continuing education requirements.

STUDENT SERVICES

Rogers University provides RUOnline students with the following services via the Internet: counseling and admissions, financial aid, academic advising, bookstore, library, tutoring, career planning and placement, student union, and technical support.

CREDIT OPTIONS

Rogers University accepts transfer credits from other accredited higher education institutions. Students are required to earn a minimum of 12 credit hours at Rogers University (on-line or otherwise). Additionally, students may receive credits for previous military or work experience and through CLEP testing.

FACULTY

Of the 20 Rogers University faculty members working with RUOnline, 80 percent are full-time. Twenty-five percent have doctorates in their fields.

ADMISSION

Applicants must provide proof of high school graduation or GED. To become fully admitted an applicant must also provide an ACT or SAT score. For those only interested in taking individual courses, they may complete up to 9 credit hours without satisfying assessment requirements. Full admission is required for credit hours over 9.

TUITION AND FEES

In-state tuition and fees for the 1997-98 school year are $315 per 3-hour course with video ($265 without video); out-of-state tuition and fees are $495 per 3-hour course, $445 without video. Some courses may not require the use of video instruction. The cost of textbooks and shipping for each course is additional and may vary.

FINANCIAL AID

RUOnline students may apply for federal monies such as the Pell Grant, FSEOG, and Stafford Loans. In addition, vocational-rehabilitation programs such as VA and the G.I. bill and any program covered by the Job Training Placement Act are options for RUOnline students seeking financial aid. It should be noted, however, that indirect costs are not included in any federal Title IV monies. Residents of Oklahoma may apply for an Oklahoma Tuition Aid Grant or ENGA fee-waiver money. RUOnline students may also apply for academic scholarships offered by Rogers University.

APPLYING

Prospective students should contact http://www.ruonline.edu where they can not only apply but also complete the optional new student orientation. RUOnline requires proof of high school graduation or GED before enrollment in any course. Official transcripts should be sent to Rogers University, Office of Admissions, Attention On-line Advisor, 1701 West Will Rogers Boulevard, Claremore, OK, 74017. Rogers University accepts faxed transcripts only when received directly from the college or university.

CONTACT

Mary Sirkel
RUOnline Admissions Director
Rogers University
1701 West Will Rogers Boulevard
Claremore, Oklahoma 74017
Telephone: 918-343-7548
Fax: 918-343-7595
E-mail: online@mail.rogersu.edu

Saint Joseph's College
Distance Education Program
Standish, Maine

Saint Joseph's College was founded in 1912 by the Sisters of Mercy and chartered by the Maine legislature in 1915. The College grants degrees in keeping with the mission of the College and the ministries of the Sisters of Mercy. Saint Joseph's is a liberal arts college that nurtures intellectual, spiritual, and social growth in students of all ages and all faiths within a value-centered environment.

In 1970, Saint Joseph's became a coeducational institution, and in 1976 the Distance Education Program was introduced to serve the needs of the nontraditional adult learner nationwide.

Saint Joseph's is located on the shores of Sebago Lake, 18 miles from Portland. More than 1,000 students attend classes on the 331-acre campus. The beautiful lakefront of the campus faces the White Mountains. The region's natural beauty and the proximity of the College to Maine's popular ski resorts appeal to the outdoor enthusiast in winter. The nearby rocky Atlantic coastline and picturesque New England countryside offer an ideal setting for the summer experience.

DISTANCE LEARNING PROGRAM

Saint Joseph's College offers the adult learner an opportunity to integrate formal education in the liberal arts tradition with professional experience. Saint Joseph's College is accredited by the New England Association of Schools and Colleges. The Distance Education Program provides academic options in a variety of disciplines leading to undergraduate and graduate certificates and to associate, baccalaureate, and graduate degrees. Each option is designed to reflect the special nature of Saint Joseph's College commitment to its students. The Distance Education Program currently enrolls more than 4,000 active students, and approximately 6,500 Saint Joseph's alumni earned their degrees through the distance program. Graduates of Saint Joseph's bachelor's and master's degree programs may take courses at their degree level tuition-free for five years.

DELIVERY MEDIA

Faculty-directed independent study is a highly flexible, accessible mode of education that allows students to study where they are. Upon enrollment, students receive the texts, materials, and study guides for their courses. Some courses require access to a computer or a VCR. Faculty members assist each student with their studies through a combination of written feedback on assignments and telephone consultations. An academic adviser is assigned to work with each student from the first enrollment through to graduation. Undergraduate degree programs require one 2-week summer residency, and graduate degree programs require two 2-week summer residencies at the campus in Maine.

PROGRAMS OF STUDY

The Distance Education Program offers the following degree and certificate programs: a master's degree in health services administration (48 credits) for senior management roles in complex organizations; the Bachelor of Science (128 credits), with majors in health-care administration and long-term-care administration; the Bachelor of Science in professional arts (128 credits), a degree-completion program for licensed health-care professionals with concentrations in education, health-care administration, human services, and psychology; the Bachelor of Science in radiologic science (128 credits), a postcertification baccalaureate degree for radiologic science professionals; the Bachelor of Science in respiratory care (128 credits), a postcertification baccalaureate degree for respiratory care professionals; the Bachelor of Arts in liberal studies (128 credits), an interdisciplinary degree program with concentrations in American studies, women's studies, and the Christian tradition; the Bachelor of Science in Business Administration (128 credits), with concentrations in management and banking (a joint venture with the American Institute of Banking); the Associate of Science in Management (66 credits), a foundation for the Bachelor of Science in Business Administration; graduate certificates (18 credits) in health-care finance, designed to provide nonfinancial health-care managers with an in-depth background in health-care financial management, and medical/dental administration for physicians and dentists; and undergraduate certificate programs (18 credits) in business administration, health-care management, long-term-care administration, Christian tradition, women's studies, American studies, and professional studies (self-designed). Students who would like to take individual courses may enroll as continuing education students.

SPECIAL PROGRAMS

The Department of Nursing offers a Master of Science with a major in nursing (48 credits) and a Bachelor of Science in Nursing with an RN to B.S.N. track (129 credits) for students at a distance.

CREDIT OPTIONS

The Distance Education Program acknowledges the value of certain formal learning and career-based experience. The College follows the American Council on Education guidelines in granting transfer credit for courses of study from accredited colleges or universities with a grade of C or better; ACE/PONSI-approved credit; ACE-approved military training and experience credits; CEUs earned through professional seminars, workshops, internships, and in-service education classes as elective credit; and CLEP, ACT/PEP, and DANTES exams. A maximum of 30 credits can be accepted by exam.

FACULTY

More than 90 full-time and part-time faculty members serve students in the Distance Education Program. Many teach in the traditional program as well as in distance education. All excel in their fields and have experience with nontraditional students.

ADMISSION

Admission requirements vary by program of study. Prospective students should contact the Admissions Office for the Distance Education Program at 800-752-4723 (toll-free) with specific questions about admission requirements.

TUITION AND FEES

In the 1997–98 academic year, tuition is $180 per credit hour ($540 per 3-credit course) at the undergraduate level and $220 per credit hour ($660 per 3-credit course) at the graduate level. Application fees are $50 for degree programs and $25 for certificate programs and continuing education. A complete fee schedule is available in the program catalogs.

FINANCIAL AID

Students may be eligible for the Federal Pell Grant and/or Federal Stafford Student Loan. Applying for financial aid is an individualized process requiring consultation and evaluation. For more information and assistance, students should call the Financial Aid Office at 800-752-1266 (toll-free).

APPLYING

Students are accepted on a rolling admissions basis and, therefore, can apply and begin their studies at any time during the year.

CONTACT

Admissions Office
Distance Education Program
Saint Joseph's College
278 Whites Bridge Road
Standish, Maine 04084-5263
Telephone: 800-752-4723 (toll-free)
Fax: 207-892-7480
E-mail: gcarro@sjcme.edu
Web site: http://www.sjcme.edu

Saint Mary-of-the-Woods College
Women's External Degree Program
Saint Mary-of-the-Woods, Indiana

Founded in 1840, Saint Mary-of-the-Woods College (SMWC) is the nation's oldest Catholic liberal arts college for women and is accredited by the North Central Association of Colleges and Schools. The College offers the rich traditions of academic excellence and dedication to educating women personally and professionally for responsible roles in society. The diverse student community of 1,300 includes traditional resident students, commuters, student mothers and children, and distance learners at both the undergraduate and graduate levels. A hallmark of the College is an emphasis on personalized service.

The general studies curriculum required of all undergraduates is designed to develop the communication and analytical skills needed for success in college and in the professional world.

DISTANCE LEARNING PROGRAM

Since 1973, the Women's External Degree (WED) program has provided the College curriculum to contemporary adult women who juggle multiple responsibilities yet need or want a college degree. This structured but flexible independent study program is based on five-month semesters that begin with in-person appointments with instructors and faculty advisers and leads to a degree in one of more than twenty majors.

DELIVERY MEDIA

Faculty members and students communicate by telephone, voice mail, e-mail, and postal service. All full-time faculty members, some adjuncts, and many students have access to e-mail. Computers with modems are not required, except for accounting and CIS majors, but access to a computer or word processor is strongly recommended. Some courses use videotapes, audiotapes, or optional computer programs.

PROGRAMS OF STUDY

The College is chartered to grant the degrees Associate in Arts, Associate in Science, Bachelor of Arts, and Bachelor of Science to women and the degrees Master of Arts in pastoral theology and Master of Arts in earth literacy to both women and men.

Undergraduates complete the general studies curriculum, courses required for their chosen major, and additional electives to total 125 semester hours for a baccalaureate degree and 65 semester hours for an associate degree; a minimum of 30 hours must be earned at the College.

Associate majors available through WED are early childhood education, general business, gerontology, humanities, and paralegal studies. Baccalaureate majors are accounting, business administration, computer information systems, education (early childhood, elementary, kindergarten-primary, secondary, and special), English, gerontology, human resource management, human services, humanities, journalism, marketing, mathematics, paralegal studies, psychology, social sciences (history concentration), and theology.

There are no geographical restrictions, except that education majors must reside within 200 miles of campus for faculty supervision of field experience and student teaching.

The Master of Arts program in pastoral theology is designed for persons who are or plan to be engaged in ministry and for those seeking personal enrichment in theological study. A total of 36 semester hours of graduate credit is required; up to 15 graduate transfer credits may be accepted.

The Master of Arts program in earth literacy is designed for persons who care for and advocate a sustainable and just earth community. A total of 36 semester hours of graduate credit, including 24 semester hours of interdisciplinary course work and 12 semester hours of practica and projects, is required.

SPECIAL PROGRAMS

Full-time faculty members serve as academic advisers to the WED students in their departments, meeting each semester to monitor progress and plan subsequent semesters. A WED staff of 8 provides additional support, advocacy, registrarial assistance, and information, including a quarterly newsletter for distance learners. One WED staff person provides referral to other campus services, such as career development (available by phone and in person) and library materials by mail.

SMWC offers several learning formats: traditional campus-based study, distance learning, and a third format that combines independent study with intensive weekend seminars on campus. WED students may combine these formats in any semester of study; about 400 choose to enroll in weekend alternative format courses each year. However, all degrees offered through WED may be completed entirely through independent study at home, with the exception of degrees requiring the computers in the law course, which must be taken via alternative format on campus.

CREDIT OPTIONS

Students may transfer credit earned at other accredited colleges and universities, although some credits may be too dated to meet the requirements of a major. WED encourages students to earn credit for previous college-level learning through CLEP and DANTES, ACE/PONSI awards, and portfolio applications documenting other prior learning. At least 30 semester hours of course work must be earned under the direct supervision of SMWC faculty members.

FACULTY

Fifty full-time and 50 adjunct faculty members serve as instructors and academic advisers to WED students. Fifty-five percent of full-time faculty members have doctoral or other terminal degrees.

ADMISSION

Applicants must have earned a high school diploma or GED certificate and demonstrate potential for success in a distance learning program. Academic history, employment and other life experience, writing skills, and stated goals are considered.

TUITION AND FEES

For 1997–98, undergraduate tuition for the WED program is $252 per semester hour. There are a one-time fee of $65 for the initial on-campus residency (not including housing), an annual $46 general fee, and modest materials fees for laboratory courses.

FINANCIAL AID

Available financial aid includes Federal Pell grants, student loans, and, for residents only, Indiana Higher Education grants. In 1996–97 the College processed about $1.6 million from these sources on behalf of WED students. The College awards small WED grants to eligible seniors and offers 10 percent tuition discounts through cooperating employers; this institutional aid totaled $46,000 in 1996–97. Finally, the WED staff maintains a directory of private grants and scholarships and assists WED students in applying for them. Forty-five percent of WED students receive some form of aid.

APPLYING

Applications are reviewed when all materials are received; the evaluation process is usually completed within a month. Two-day orientation residencies are held on campus five times each year and conclude with enrollment in the initial semester.

CONTACTS

Gwen Hagemeyer
WED Admission Director
Saint Mary-of-the-Woods College
Saint Mary-of-the-Woods, Indiana 47876
Telephone: 812-535-5106
          800-926-SMWC
          (toll-free)
Fax: 812-535-5215
E-mail: wedadms@woods.smwc.edu
World Wide Web: http://www.woods.smwc.edu

Mary Lou Dolan, C.S.J.
Earth Literacy Director
Saint Mary-of-the-Woods College
Saint Mary-of-the-Woods, Indiana 47876
Telephone: 812-535-5160
Fax: 812-535-5228
E-mail: mldolan@woods.smwc.edu
elm@woods.smwc.edu

Ruth Eileen Dwyer, S.P.
Pastoral Theology Director
Saint Mary-of-the-Woods College
Saint Mary-of-the-Woods, Indiana 47876
Telephone: 812-535-5170
Fax: 812-535-4613
E-mail: rdwyer@woods.smwc.edu

Skidmore College

University Without Walls

Saratoga Springs, New York

University Without Walls (UWW) is the external degree program for adults at Skidmore College. UWW was in the vanguard in establishing a program for distance learners. The program began in 1971 as an experiment in nontraditional education jointly funded by the Ford Foundation and the U.S. Department of Education. When the funding for this experiment ended in 1975, Skidmore College took over the program as its own. Over the years, UWW has evolved to serve adult students pursuing baccalaureate degrees in a variety of liberal arts, performing arts, and preprofessional fields.

The UWW program is characterized by its flexibility and the high quality of education students receive. The unique advising system at UWW guarantees that each program meets the student's individual needs and the high standards of Skidmore College.

DISTANCE LEARNING PROGRAM

UWW serves 280 full- and part-time baccalaureate students. Student programs may include on-site UWW seminars, UWW on-line courses, independent study with Skidmore faculty members, courses at other accredited institutions, internships, and distance learning courses from major universities. Every program includes a final project in the area of the student's focus.

DELIVERY MEDIA

Independent study courses take place through phone, mail, or e-mail communication. When possible, they may involve meetings on the Skidmore campus. At the present time, UWW's on-line courses are Web-based and require a Web browser and e-mail capability.

PROGRAMS OF STUDY

UWW offers Bachelor of Arts degrees in most traditional liberal arts fields, including American studies, anthropology, art history, biology, chemistry, classics, computer science, economics, English, French, geology, German, government, history, mathematics, philosophy, physics, political economy, psychology, religion, Russian, sociology, Spanish, and women's studies. Bachelor of Science degrees are available in art, business, dance, human services, physical education, and theater. Students can also combine fields to create an interdisciplinary program, such as arts management, Asian studies, communications, environmental studies, health studies, human behavior, Latin American studies, management information systems, nonprofit management, organizational behavior, public administration, and religion and culture. Individually designed majors are welcomed.

All degrees are 120-credit programs. Programs are expected to include at least 12 credits in the humanities, 6 credits in history, 12 credits in the social sciences, and 9 credits in math or science, including laboratory experience. Professional programs must include at least 60 credits in the liberal arts. Courses taken prior to entry of UWW may be considered in satisfaction of these requirements.

SPECIAL PROGRAMS

UWW's flexibility allows many students to take advantage of unusual learning opportunities. Recent UWW students have studied abroad in Austria, Canada, Costa Rica, the Czech Republic, Germany, Ireland, Poland, Spain, Switzerland, and Thailand, among other locations. Business students often have the opportunity to include professional management and banking seminars in satisfaction of their degree requirements.

UWW students are often able to participate in programs sponsored by Skidmore College and the Office of Special Programs, including a summer study program in Florence, the New York State Writers Institute, the Skidmore Jazz Institute, the Summer Dance Workshop, and the Siti Summer Theater Workshop. UWW students are eligible for substantial discounts on courses offered by Skidmore Summer Academic Sessions and the Summer Six Art Program.

UWW business students are eligible to apply for 3/2 M.B.A. programs in cooperation with Rensselaer Polytechnic Institute in Troy and Rensselaer–Hartford.

STUDENT SERVICES

UWW is a small, personal program, and the staff members are happy to assist students in any way possible. Typical services include academic advising, registration assistance, financial aid counseling, and book-order assistance. Local students also enjoy library privileges, career counseling, access to recreational facilities, access to computer labs, and an e-mail account. Some summer housing is available for special program participants.

CREDIT OPTIONS

UWW accepts transfer credit for courses completed with a grade of C or better. There is no limit to the number of credits transferred or the age of the work, provided that the course is appropriate to a liberal arts curriculum. Credit is also available for experiential learning. In addition, students may document knowledge through CLEP, ACT-PEP, DANTES, and Regents examinations. Many college-level courses offered through the military are accepted. Credit from international universities is usually accepted.

FACULTY

There are approximately 200 full- and part-time members of the Skidmore faculty. Most participate as advisers and instructors in the UWW program. Ninety-three percent of the Skidmore faculty members have a terminal degree.

ADMISSION

UWW considers any applicant able to succeed at demanding college-level work. However, the program works best for students who have had some college experience. Applicants must have a high school diploma or the equivalent.

TUITION AND FEES

UWW has an annual enrollment fee of $2400 (exclusive of course costs), a $100 fee for assessment of prior learning, and a $200 final project fee. All courses sponsored by Skidmore are $400.

FINANCIAL AID

Students are eligible for Federal Pell Grants, New York State TAP awards, and all federal loan programs. A small amount of scholarship assistance is available.

APPLYING

Application forms are available from UWW or can be downloaded from the UWW Web site. All students are required to attend a personal admissions interview on the Skidmore campus.

CONTACT

Cornel J. Reinhart, Director
University Without Walls
Skidmore College
Saratoga Springs, New York 12866
Telephone: 518-580-5450
Fax: 518-581-7422
E-mail: uww@skidmore.edu
Web site: http://www.skidmore.edu (click on UWW)

Southern Methodist University
School of Engineering and Applied Science
Dallas, Texas

Founded in 1911, SMU is a private, comprehensive university. SMU comprises six degree-granting schools: the School of Engineering and Applied Science, Dedman College of Humanities and Sciences, Meadows School of the Arts, the Edwin L. Cox School of Business, the School of Law, and Perkins School of Theology. Southern Methodist University is accredited by the Commission on Colleges of the Southern Association of Colleges and Schools.

For more than thirty years, the School of Engineering and Applied Science (SEAS) has been a national pioneer in offering distance education courses for graduate study. In 1964, SEAS established one of the first two regional closed-circuit TV distance learning networks in the nation. In 1978, SEAS instituted its own for-credit videotape program for students living outside the Dallas–Fort Worth area. Today, video-program students are enrolled nationally from coast to coast and in Europe, Asia, South America, and Canada.

DISTANCE LEARNING PROGRAM

The SEAS distance learning programs serve more than 600 graduate students. Degree programs are offered nationally via videotape or, in the north Texas area, via a closed-circuit television network. The Master of Science in Telecommunications program is available via the National Technological University satellite network. No campus attendance is required to complete the degree programs.

DELIVERY MEDIA

Distance learning students are enrolled in classes that are given on the SMU campus. The lectures are videotaped and sent once a week to the distance learning student. North Texas and satellite students may view the lectures live. Distance learning students interact with their professor via telephone or fax or over the Internet. Many courses make course materials available to the student via SEAS's World Wide Web home page.

PROGRAMS OF STUDY

Engineering schools have an obligation to be responsive to challenges and opportunities in a technological society. As a private university, SMU can respond quickly to engineering needs with high-quality academic programs.

SEAS offers Master of Science distance learning programs in engineering management, hazardous and waste materials management, manufacturing systems management, software engineering, systems engineering, and telecommunications. Distance learning programs are also available in the more traditional disciplines of mechanical engineering and electrical engineering.

The Master of Science degree requires 30–36 (depending on the program) semester credit hours for completion, with a minimum 3.0 grade point average on a 4.0 scale. Distance learning students may meet the credit requirement entirely by course work or have the option of preparing a thesis for 6 semester hours of credit.

SPECIAL PROGRAMS

SEAS offers a certificate program in telecommunications. This program is designed for students who have extensive experience but do not hold a bachelor's degree or who do not wish to pursue a master's degree. Admission to the telecommunications certificate program requires 60 semester credit hours of college study with a minimum GPA of 2.0 on a 4.0 scale, three years of related work experience, and three letters of recommendation. Certificate students must complete six courses with a minimum grade of 70 percent in each course. All courses are available to the distance learning student via videotape.

CREDIT OPTIONS

Generally speaking, up to 6 semester hours of graduate courses may be transferred from an institution approved by the SEAS Graduate Division, provided that such course work was completed in the five years prior to matriculation, that the transferred courses carried graduate credit, that those courses were not used to meet the requirements of an undergraduate degree, and that grades of B– or higher were received in the courses to be transferred.

FACULTY

Of the 485 full-time faculty members, 88 percent hold the doctorate or terminal professional degree in their fields. In addition, in the professional degree programs, the School of Engineering and Applied Science utilizes outstanding adjunct faculty members to bring into the classroom valuable experience from industry and government.

ADMISSION

Admission to a Master of Science degree program requires the bachelor's degree appropriate to the program to which the student is applying, as well as a minimum grade point average of 3.0 (on a 4.0 scale) in previous undergraduate and graduate study. The Graduate Record Examinations (GRE) is required for the M.S. in electrical and mechanical engineering. The GRE is not required for the professional M.S. programs.

TUITION AND FEES

Tuition for distance learning students is $600 per credit hour or $1800 for a 3-credit-hour course. In addition, there is a $250 fee per semester to cover the cost of shipping and videotapes. Members of the military and civilian employees of the military should inquire about special tuition rates.

FINANCIAL AID

Financial aid opportunities are available to distance learning students, including Federal Stafford Student Loans. SMU's distance learning programs are approved for Veterans Administration educational benefits.

APPLYING

Distance learning students must complete an application for admission to the Graduate Division of the School of Engineering and Applied Science and submit transcripts of all previous undergraduate and graduate work. Application deadline dates are as follows: for the fall semester, August 1; for the spring semester, December 15; and for the summer term, May 15.

CONTACT

Stephanie Dye
Associate Director, Distance Education
School of Engineering and Applied Science
Southern Methodist University
P.O. Box 750335
Dallas, Texas 75275-0335
Telephone: 800-601-4040 (toll-free)
Fax: 214-768-3778
E-mail: sdye@seas.smu.edu
Web site: http://www.seas.smu.edu

Distance Learning Programs

State University of New York Empire State College

Center for Distance Learning

Saratoga Springs, New York

Since its founding in 1971, SUNY Empire State College has become an international leader in providing innovative models for higher education at the associate, baccalaureate, and master's degree levels throughout the state of New York and beyond. The central purpose of the College is to expand access to students, primarily adults, who prefer alternatives to the fixed schedule, place, program, and structure of campus-based education due to work, family, or other responsibilities.

Empire State College was the first public, nontraditional institution to receive regional accreditation by the Middle States Association of Colleges and Schools and among the first of its kind in the United States. The College has pioneered individualized academic programs, including such innovations as one-to-one instruction, intensive mentoring, learning contracts, undergraduate credit for college-level learning gained from life experience, and distance learning technology and pedagogy.

Empire State College is a statewide institution that serves 10,000 students per year at more than forty locations in New York State, as well as across the nation and the world through distance learning options.

DISTANCE LEARNING PROGRAM

More than 5,000 students are served by the College's Center for Distance Learning, which offers courses and structured external degree programs through the telephone, mail, personal computer, and other media.

DELIVERY MEDIA

The Center for Distance Learning makes use of the latest distance learning technology, as well as standard mail and telecommunications, in working with its students. Students have access to the Empire State College Network, which provides electronic mail, computer conferencing, and an electronic bulletin board to facilitate communication and educational exchange. CAUCUS, an on-line, asynchronous system, allows students and faculty members to share ideas and concepts at any time of the day or night. The SUNY Learning Network, offering on-line degree programs, features Lotus Notes® software for its students.

PROGRAMS OF STUDY

SUNY Empire State College's Center for Distance Learning offers concentrations in the liberal arts and sciences and professional and career studies leading to associate and baccalaureate degrees: Associate in Arts (A.A.), Associate in Science (A.S.), Bachelor of Arts (B.A.), Bachelor of Science (B.S.), and Bachelor of Professional Studies (B.P.S.). Undergraduate students design individualized degree programs in eleven broad areas of study: the arts; business, management, and economics; community and human services; cultural studies; educational studies; historical studies; human development; interdisciplinary studies; labor studies; science, mathematics, and technology; and social theory, social structure, and change. The degree in business, management, and economics includes such concentrations as fire service administration (available only as a bachelor's degree to residents of New York, Rhode Island, Pennsylvania, Vermont, New Hampshire, Massachusetts, Connecticut, Maine, and eastern Canada), criminal justice, and management of health services. A degree in interdisciplinary studies includes concentrations in the social sciences or the humanities. The College also offers four Master of Arts programs, with concentrations in business and policy studies, labor and policy studies, liberal studies, and social policy.

To earn an associate degree, a student must successfully complete 64 credits, with at least 24 earned through study with Empire State College. A bachelor's degree requires successful completion of 128 credits, of which at least 32 must be earned through the College.

The emphasis at Empire State College is on the individual, and the heart of the College's individualized approach to higher education is the one-to-one relationship between a faculty member and student. Each student is assigned a mentor—an Empire State College faculty member—who helps the student plan and coordinate a course of study. The primary mode of instruction at Empire State College is independent study with a mentor or tutor, communicating by computer, telephone, and mail. Independent study is planned and organized through learning contracts that fit within students' overall degree programs and allow students to study at convenient times, places, and paces suited to their needs. Students may also participate in group studies facilitated by computer conferencing. Field experiences, internships, and on-the-job training may be incorporated into learning contracts in many professional areas.

SPECIAL PROGRAMS

The College has a number of specialized programs to serve particular populations of adult learners. FORUM programs in Buffalo, Saratoga Springs, and Syracuse provide undergraduate management education to corporate managers and supervisors. The SUNY Learning Network, a consortium of two arts and science colleges in SUNY (Empire State College and SUNY New Paltz) and several community colleges, offers on-line baccalaureate degrees in business or liberal arts.

CREDIT OPTIONS

Students can transfer credits earned at other postsecondary institutions to Empire State College and can receive credit for college-level learning gained through work and life experience and through the College-Level Examination Program (CLEP) or other standardized tests. A total of 40 prior learning credits may be granted in the associate degree program; 96 credits may be applied to a baccalaureate program.

FACULTY

There are 360 full- and part-time mentors at Empire State College. Eighty-five percent of full-time faculty members and nearly half of part-time faculty members have doctoral or other terminal academic degrees. To supplement the academic expertise of its residential faculty, the College makes use of tutors and adjunct faculty.

ADMISSION

Admission to Empire State College is made without regard to race, sex, handicap, religion, or national origin of the applicant. Two principal requirements for admission are possession of a high school diploma or its equivalent and the ability of the College to meet the applicant's educational needs and objectives.

TUITION AND FEES

In 1995–96, undergraduate tuition and per-credit fees were $140.35. A per-term telecommunications development and support fee of $50 was also charged, which provided access to electronic mail, computer conferencing, the Internet, and other information sources.

FINANCIAL AID

More than $6 million in financial aid was awarded to Empire State College students in 1995–96, with more than 40 percent of the enrolled students receiving some form of financial assistance. General financial aid programs available through Empire State College include the Federal Pell Grant, Federal Supplemental Educational Opportunity Grant, Federal Perkins Loan, and the Federal Work-Study programs. New York State financial aid programs include the Tuition Assistance Program (TAP), Aid for Part-Time Study (APTS), and the SUNY Supplemental Tuition Award. The Empire State College Foundation awards more than $30,000 in scholarships and grants annually.

APPLYING

Empire State College reviews applications in order of date received. The number of new students accepted depends on available space.

CONTACT

Margaret Craft
Assistant Director
Center for Distance Learning
SUNY Empire State College
2 Union Avenue
Saratoga Springs, New York 12866-4390
Telephone: 518-587-2100 Ext. 300
Fax: 518-587-2100 Ext. 356
E-mail: mcraft@sescva.esc.edu
Web site: http://www.esc.edu

Distance Learning Programs

Stephens College
School of Graduate and Continuing Education
Columbia, Missouri

Founded in 1833, Stephens College is a private college nationally known for its innovation in education. The School of Graduate and Continuing Education is built on a history of quality education and academic service to students. Although Stephens is located in Columbia, Missouri, its distance learning programs allow students to complete their degrees as quickly as their schedules allow from home or work. Stephens offers generous transfer credit options, credit for prior learning, one-office registration, and individual advising and degree planning.

Stephens College is nationally known for excellence in teaching and fostering lifelong associations with alumni. Since the first graduating class in 1974, more than 1,300 adult students have completed their degrees through the School of Graduate and Continuing Education.

Stephens College is accredited by the North Central Association of Colleges and Schools.

DISTANCE LEARNING PROGRAM

The School of Graduate and Continuing Education offers graduate, undergraduate, and nondegree programs for adult learners. Flexibility is the hallmark. The External Degree and Weekend College Programs are designed for bachelor's degree candidates, and the Master of Business Administration Program is designed for graduate students seeking to complete a challenging program without relocating or leaving their current jobs.

DELIVERY MEDIA

The External Degree Program is delivered through a variety of methods, including the Internet, telephone, fax, and regular mail. Students are strongly encouraged to have access to a computer with an Internet connection. Internet access and an e-mail address are requirements for M.B.A. students. Certain courses require specific software programs.

PROGRAMS OF STUDY

The adult student is at the heart of Stephens' nontraditional programs. Students are assured of a quality education designed with flexibility that allows them to meet the demands of their busy lives. Faculty members, staff members, and advisers understand the complexities of returning to college and are aware of the many responsibilities adult students must manage. They offer encouragement and support as the students progress through their course work toward graduation.

Working with Stephens College faculty members, students in the External Degree Program study at home or work. This program is designed to complement the student's commitments to career, family, and community, and because courses are taken by independent study, students have some flexibility in completing their courses in less time than the six allotted months. Working with an adviser, each student plans an individual program of study for their degree completion.

Majors available to External Degree Students include business administration; early childhood or elementary education certification; education; English; health information management; philosophy, law, and rhetoric; and psychology. Students who wish to develop an individualized major in two disciplines may combine approved guided study courses from the list of majors.

The Stephens College Master of Business Administration Program utilizes communication technology to deliver a challenging curriculum to students around the globe. With personal attention from instructors and interaction with students from around the world, the program combines theoretical and practical approaches to provide the student with a well-rounded business education at the advanced level. Emphasis areas within the M.B.A. Program include entrepreneurial studies, management, and clinical information systems management. Undergraduate core requirements for the M.B.A. Program are offered through the Stephens College External Degree and Weekend College Programs.

SPECIAL PROGRAMS

Prior learning credit is available for adult undergraduate students who have achieved college-level learning and experience outside the classroom. Evidence of prior learning is presented by the student in a written narrative; oral interview, with supporting materials; and the actual product or demonstrations, if applicable. No letter grades are given.

Dual-disciplinary majors are available for graduates of hospital diploma programs, two-year registered nursing programs, accredited associate degree programs in allied health, or accredited noncollegiate hospital-based programs in allied health. These students may build on their specialized training in health care to earn dual-disciplinary majors such as health care and psychology, health care and business administration, health care and history, health care and philosophy/religion, health science and business administration, health science and psychology, health science and history, and health science and philosophy/religion.

STUDENT SERVICES

Students receive the following services from the College: an individual academic adviser, assistance with prior learning, periodic mailings from the program, course schedules, a course catalog, a student handbook, and maintenance of student records and academic transcripts. Students also may use the College bookstore, Hugh Stephens Library, computer labs, Career Services Office, and the College's lake, golf course, pool, and tennis courts.

CREDIT OPTIONS

The External Degree Program offers many flexible options for earning academic credit, including independent guided study courses, weekend college courses, short-format courses, contract-study courses, transfer credit, noncollegiate professional education or training, prior learning, and credit by standard examination (CLEP tests). Stephens accepts transfer credit from regionally accredited institutions.

FACULTY

Students in the external degree and graduate programs are taught by experienced, qualified faculty members who are dedicated to student learning. With a low student-faculty ratio, students benefit from a high level of interaction with instructors.

ADMISSION

The External Degree Program follows an open admission policy for women and men over 23 years of age who have earned a high school diploma or GED. Students must complete the Liberal Studies Seminar with a grade of C or better to matriculate into the program. The M.B.A. Program admits students with a bachelor's degree from a regionally accredited institution who have met minimum GPA and GMAT requirements.

TUITION AND FEES

Tuition for the External Degree Program is $650 per course ($500 per course for mid-Missouri residents). After completing the first year, students are eligible for substantial tuition discounts when enrolling in two or more courses per year. The M.B.A. Program is $690 per course. Depending on courses selected and the degree sought, other fees may apply. Students should contact the Office of Graduate and Continuing Education for more information.

FINANCIAL AID

A variety of federal, state, and private funds may be available for students who meet specific criteria. Students should contact the Office of Financial Aid for more information (telephone: 800-876-7207, toll-free).

APPLYING

The Stephens College School of Graduate and Continuing Education accepts applications on a rolling basis. Applicants to the External Degree Program must submit an application along with documentation such as transcripts and/or GED scores. Applicants to the M.B.A. program must submit transcripts from an accredited college or university, GMAT scores, three references, and an essay. Students for whom English is a second language must submit a minimum TOEFL score of 550. Application fees are $50 for undergraduate applicants and $25 for graduate applicants.

CONTACT

Mariea Caruthers
Academic Services Coordinator
Stephens College
1200 East Broadway
Columbia, Missouri 65215
Telephone: 573-876-7125
　　　　　　800-388-7579 (toll-free)
Fax: 573-876-7248
E-mail: mc_stu@wc.stephens.edu
Web site: http://www.stephens.edu

Syracuse University
Independent Study Degree Programs
Syracuse, New York

Founded in 1870, Syracuse University is a major private research university of 14,500 residential students and an additional 5,000 part-time adult students located in central New York State. Organized into thirteen separate schools and colleges, each offering a variety of baccalaureate, master's, and doctoral degrees, Syracuse has excellent research facilities, including sophisticated computer networks and a library containing more than 2.4 million volumes. Syracuse is ranked by U.S. News & World Report as one of the top fifty universities in the United States and is one of the select group of American and Canadian universities chosen for membership in the prestigious Association of American Universities.

Syracuse has a long-standing commitment to adult education. The University's innovative Independent Study Degree Programs (ISDP) are a form of nontraditional education in which Syracuse was a pioneer. Offered through nine of the University's academic units, in partnership with Syracuse's Division of Continuing Education and Summer Sessions, ISDP is one of the three oldest external degree programs in the United States. The programs have been active since 1966 and reflect the University's response to the demands for creative educational techniques and programs in a constantly changing society.

DISTANCE LEARNING PROGRAM

Syracuse's Independent Study Degree Programs have a limited-residency structure: they combine short periods of intensive on-site instruction with longer periods of home study, during which students and faculty members communicate at a distance by correspondence, telephone, fax, and computer. There are currently about 1,000 adults actively enrolled in eleven different degree programs through ISDP, approximately one sixth of whom are international students or Americans living abroad. Syracuse degrees earned through ISDP are the same as those earned by traditional Syracuse students in comparable campus programs and have the same accreditation.

PROGRAMS OF STUDY

ISDP offers two undergraduate and nine master's programs by means of the limited-residency, distance education format. Undergraduate degrees include an Associate of Arts and a Bachelor of Arts in Liberal Studies. The Associate of Arts degree is 60 credits. The bachelor's degree is a 120-credit program.

The master's degrees include an M.A. in advertising design or illustration, a Master of Library Science (M.L.S), an M.S. in communications management, an M.S. in information resources management, an M.S. in telecommunications and network management, an M.S. in nursing, a Master of Social Science (M.S.Sc.) with an international studies emphasis, and an M.B.A. The M.A. and M.S.Sc. degrees are 30-credit degrees, the M.L.S. and M.S. in communications management are 36 credits, the M.S. in information resources management and the M.S. in telecommunications and network management are 42 credits, the M.S. in nursing is 45 credits, and the M.B.A. is 54 credits.

In addition to state and regional accreditation, several of the master's programs enjoy professional accreditation appropriate to the field of study. The advertising design and illustration programs are accredited by the National Association of Schools of Art and Design, the nursing program is accredited by the National League for Nursing, the M.B.A. program is accredited by the American Association of Collegiate Schools of Business, and the M.L.S. program is accredited by the American Library Association.

Students may initially enroll in the A.A., B.A., and M.S.Sc. degrees on a nonmatriculated basis. All other degrees require matriculation prior to participation.

SPECIAL PROGRAMS

There are no special programs currently offered through a distance learning format at Syracuse other than the degrees listed above, which are offered through Independent Study Degree Programs. Future plans for additional ISDP master's degrees include an M.S. in engineering management.

STUDENT SERVICES

ISDP students are provided with free computer accounts and have access to the Syracuse University library and mainframe computer facilities.

CREDIT OPTIONS

The associate degree program accepts a maximum of 30 credits to be transferred from another postsecondary institution. The baccalaureate program accepts a maximum of 90 transfer credits, which may include 66 credits from a junior college. Transfer credit is granted for most courses in which a grade of C or better has been earned, provided courses are from an accredited college and fit the ISDP degree requirements. For credit to be accepted from an international institution of higher learning, the institution must be a recognized third-level institution.

A maximum of 30 credits gained through testing or through evaluation of extra-institutional or experiential learning may be applied toward an undergraduate degree program. DANTES, CLEP, and Syracuse advanced credit exams may be used for this purpose. However, credit awarded through testing or experiential evaluation does not count toward the minimum number of credits that must be taken at Syracuse in order to earn a degree. On the graduate level, there is no provision for experiential credit. However, 6 credits may be taken in transfer from other accredited graduate programs, with a grade of C or better. The M.B.A. program also allows students to waive certain core courses by means of testing or documentation of prior academic experience.

FACULTY

ISDP courses are taught by full-time Syracuse University faculty members, who participate in the limited-residency programs in addition to their full-time campus responsibilities. In the case of the M.A. programs in advertising and illustration, additional visiting faculty members are drawn from among the world's most recognized designers and illustrators.

ADMISSION

Candidates for admission to the associate and baccalaureate programs should have a high school diploma or its equivalent. Transfer students must have at least a 2.0 (C) average for the liberal studies program. On the graduate level, candidates must take the GMAT for the M.B.A. program and the GRE for the communications management, information resources management, telecommunications and network management, and nursing programs. Applicants whose primary language is a language other than English must also take the TOEFL. Portfolios of related professional work must be submitted for the advertising design, illustration, and communications management programs.

Applicants for all programs must submit official transcripts of prior academic work, letters of recommendation, and a personal statement that accompanies the application form.

Applicants to the Master of Library Science, communications management, information resources management, telecommunications and network management, and nursing programs must also have a computer with at least a 486 microprocessor, a modem, and Internet access.

TUITION AND FEES

For 1997–98, the undergraduate tuition rate is $320 per credit, and the graduate rate is $529 per credit. Additional expenses for room and board at the on-campus residence average $65–100 per day, depending upon the choice of facility, and book charges average $100 per course. There are additional Internet line charges each semester for programs relying upon that means of communication.

FINANCIAL AID

ISDP students who are U.S. citizens are eligible for all the standard federal grants and loans available to part-time students. Selective institutional aid is available for several of the programs listed above; detailed information is available upon request. Syracuse University awards more than $100,000 to ISDP students each year. International students (non-U.S. citizens) are not eligible for financial aid.

APPLYING

Applicants should request application materials from the address below. The undergraduate programs and the M.B.A. and M.S.Sc. programs admit students on a continuous basis, and students can begin in the fall, spring, or summer terms. The other master's programs require newly admitted students to begin each summer, with the exception of the nursing program, which begins every other summer. In-person interviews are not required, although they can be arranged upon request. Portfolios may be sent to the ISDP office for evaluation.

CONTACT

Roberta S. Jones
Director, Independent Study
  Degree Programs
Syracuse University
610 East Fayette Street
Syracuse, New York 13244-6020
Telephone: 315-443-3480
          800-442-0501
Fax: 315-443-4174
E-mail: suisdp@uc.syr.edu
Web site: http://www.syr.edu/WWW-Syr/AcademicLife/ISDP

Texas Tech University
Extended Learning and College of Engineering
Lubbock, Texas

Created by legislative action in 1923, Texas Tech University (TTU) is a four-year research university composed of seven colleges (Agricultural Sciences, Architecture, Arts and Sciences, Business Administration, Education, Engineering, and Human Sciences), the School of Law, and the Graduate School. Having a residential enrollment of approximately 24,000 students each year, Texas Tech is accredited by the Southern Association of Colleges and Schools and forty other accrediting organizations.

The mission of Texas Tech University is to provide the highest quality of education and instruction in all colleges and to gain national and international recognition in those fields that are designated as areas of excellence; to be a recognized research institution of distinction while maintaining the highest level of commitment to its teaching mission; and to be, above all, a university known throughout the state and the nation as a quality service-oriented institution, as evidenced by its supportive and caring environment and its cordial interactions with all of the people it serves.

DISTANCE LEARNING PROGRAM

Since 1927, Texas Tech has been offering courses at a distance, first as print-based courses and more recently as courses with differing modes of delivery. The mission of distance learning at Texas Tech University is to provide the University and the community with quality educational experiences through distance learning for academic credit, personal enrichment, and professional development opportunities. Each year, Texas Tech serves more than 40,000 students in its distance learning courses; students enrolled last year from each of the fifty states and sixteen other countries.

DELIVERY MEDIA

TTU offers courses at a distance in a rich variety of forms: as traditional print-based courses, through interactive video, via the Internet and World Wide Web, and in a multimedia format. Some courses are synchronous and require students to be present at a remote site for instruction or online for discussions on the Internet; however, most courses are asynchronous and allow students to submit lessons in their most convenient manner—by postage paid envelopes, fax machines, or e-mail. Faculty members and students interact in a timely manner in writing, by phone or fax, or through e-mail.

PROGRAMS OF STUDY

For the past six years, TTU has offered an interdisciplinary, nonthesis Master of Science degree in engineering to students at a distance. Designed primarily for practicing engineers and extremely flexible in its structure, the program allows the opportunity to pursue a graduate degree while continuing to work. The curriculum consists of 36 semester credit hours of coordinated graduate-level course work. Due to its interdisciplinary nature, the degree does not require specific major or minor subjects. Six hours may be taken outside the College of Engineering with approval of the graduate adviser, and there are no language or tool-subject requirements. The University is preparing a program offering a Bachelor of General Studies degree at a distance; the final course should be in place by fall 1998. An interdisciplinary degree program, the Bachelor of General Studies is for students who prefer to pursue a special topic by taking related course work from various departments and colleges. A minimum of 125 credit hours will be required for this degree.

STUDENT SERVICES

Texas Tech's Extended Learning is known for its quality service to students. Counselors are available by phone or by e-mail to assist students with their course choices. Student representatives work with each student to process enrollments, track course progress, handle examination requests, and report grades. Students may contact student service representatives by phone, fax, mail, or e-mail. Some courses require video or audio players, computers, or calculators. Textbooks and other required materials may be purchased through the Distance Learning Bookstore. Courses are designed so that students can use local libraries for their research in most instances; when necessary, students may request materials from the Texas Tech University Library.

CREDIT OPTIONS

Texas Tech University distance learning credit courses are recorded on Texas Tech University or Texas Tech University High School transcripts. Course credits are transferable to any other institution with the receiving institution's approval. Course syllabi are available on the World Wide Web to help determine equivalency at other institutions.

FACULTY

Fifty-one Texas Tech University faculty members teach for Extended Learning; 65 percent of the faculty hold terminal degrees. Eighteen faculty members teach in the Master of Science in engineering degree program; all hold terminal degrees.

ADMISSION

Students may register for most Texas Tech University courses at a distance without being admitted to the University; however, students who are seeking a degree from Texas Tech at a distance must be admitted to the University and the college granting the degree.

TUITION AND FEES

University credit courses offered through Extended Learning cost $53 per credit hour plus a $20 administrative charge. The charge is the same for in-state and out-of-state students. The costs of course materials vary by course. Costs for the College of Engineering's Master of Science in engineering courses are $851 per 3-hour credit course for in-state students and $1469 per 3-hour credit course for out-of-state students.

FINANCIAL AID

Financial aid opportunities are available to distance learning students for college-level courses, including Federal Stafford Student Loans. Texas Tech University's distance learning programs are approved for Veterans Administration educational benefits.

APPLYING

Students applying for high school or college credit courses through Extended Learning may enroll in courses at any time. Students enrolling in a degree program must complete an application for admission to the University and college or school offering the degree. Students may contact the University for application deadlines.

CONTACT

LaNelle Ethridge, Advisor
Extended Learning
Texas Tech University
Box 41002
Lubbock, Texas 79409-1002
Telephone: 800-692-6877 (toll-free)
Fax: 806-742-2318
E-mail: enroll@ttu.edu

Dr. William Marcy, Graduate Advisor
College of Engineering
Texas Tech University
Box 43103
Lubbock, Texas 79409-3103
Telephone: 800-528-5583 (toll-free)
Fax: 806-742-3493
E-mail: scwmm@coe.ttu.edu

Thomas Edison State College
Trenton, New Jersey

Thomas Edison State College is a worldwide community of adult learners. Cited as "one of the brighter stars of higher learning" by the New York Times *and named one of the nation's "Top 20 Cyber-Universities" by* Forbes Magazine, *the College provides quality higher education to adults wherever they live and work. Founded in 1972, Thomas Edison enables adult learners to complete associate, baccalaureate, and master's degrees through distance learning and the assessment of knowledge they already have.*

The College's convenient programs are designed to help learners pursue their educational goals while attending to the challenges and priorities of adult life. Accredited by the Middle States Association of Colleges and Schools, Thomas Edison State College offers a distinguished academic program for the self-motivated adult learner. Many of the College's more than 13,000 alumni have gone on to law, medical, and graduate schools, such as Harvard, Princeton, and Rutgers.

DISTANCE LEARNING PROGRAM

Thomas Edison offers one of the most highly regarded, comprehensive distance learning programs in the United States. Adults can choose from more than 100 distance learning courses, including on-line classes. In addition, learners may take tests and submit portfolios to demonstrate and earn credit for college-level knowledge they already have and transfer credits earned at other accredited institutions.

DELIVERY MEDIA

Distance education courses are provided through several venues, including Guided Study at home or work; the On-Line Computer Classroom™; Contract Learning, a one-on-one learning experience with individual faculty members; telecourses; and approved correspondence courses. Interactive television classrooms with satellite downlinks and cable access are also being developed. The College's distance learning program is administered through its Center for Distance & Independent Adult Learning (DIAL).

Adults may demonstrate and earn credit for knowledge they already have through testing, portfolios, certain licenses and certificates, and courses taken at work or in the military. To facilitate learning, the College has developed the Computer Assisted Lifelong Learning (CALL™) Network, which provides a wide range of educational services to students. CALL™ may be accessed through the College's Web site.

PROGRAMS OF STUDY

The College offers baccalaureate and associate degrees in more than 100 areas of study, including applied science and technology, business, human services, liberal arts, and nursing. There are no residency requirements for undergraduate degrees, except for the Bachelor of Science in Nursing program, which requires that students live or work in New Jersey. Degrees offered are the Associate of Arts (A.A.), Associate of Science in Natural Sciences and Mathematics (A.S.N.S.M.), Associate of Science in Management (A.S.M.), Associate of Science in Applied Science and Technology (A.S.A.S.T.), Associate of Science in Public and Social Services (A.S.P.S.S.), Associate in Applied Science in Radiologic Technology (A.A.S.R.T.), Bachelor of Arts (B.A.), Bachelor of Science in Business Administration (B.S.B.A.), Bachelor of Science in Applied Science and Technology (B.S.A.S.T.), Bachelor of Science in Human Services (B.S.H.S.), and Bachelor of Science in Nursing (B.S.N.).

In addition, the College offers the on-line Master of Science in Management (M.S.M.) degree, which has two brief residency requirements. The M.S.M. degree serves employed adults who have had professional experience in the management field. The degree is designed to have broad appeal for those not served by conventional programs. The program integrates the theory and practice of management as it applies to diverse organizations, educational institutions, and other nonprofit agencies. The emphasis is on theory and practice in the management of organizations.

SPECIAL PROGRAMS

The Office of Corporate–Higher Education Programs brings the resources of Thomas Edison State College to the workplace. Students may be able to earn credit for courses taken at their workplace or through union or professional associations. The College administers the American Council on Education (ACE) College Credit Recommendation Service, a program through which company and other noncollegiate courses are evaluated by faculty experts who determine whether courses meet college-level requirements and who recommend academic credit for each course.

The College's newly established Senior College enables adults in midlife and beyond to complete associate, baccalaureate, and master's degrees with more flexibility and options than any other collegiate program in America. There are no undergraduate residency or time requirements, which means that seniors can take as long as they like to complete a degree at home or quickly earn credit for knowledge gained by living and working.

The Military Degree Completion Program accommodates the special needs of military personnel interested in completing a degree. The program is ideal for the individual who needs 12 semester hours or more of credit to earn a degree and prefers distance learning to classroom-based courses.

The Degree Pathways Program allows students to complete a baccalaureate degree without leaving their home counties and is available to every associate degree graduate from all New Jersey county colleges. Associate degree candidates start to work with Thomas Edison when they send the "intent to transfer" form to the College. Many services to assist students in earning a baccalaureate degree are provided at the county college.

Thomas Edison State College administers the New Jersey State Library, which has nearly 2 million holdings. In addition, the College's John S. Watson Institute for Public Policy provides impartial public policy analysis and review to government and private sectors.

CREDIT OPTIONS

Students at Thomas Edison use several convenient methods of meeting degree requirements, depending upon their individual learning styles and preferences. Guided Study, On-Line Computer Classroom™, Contract Learning, tests, portfolio assessment, corporate or military education, telecourses, approved correspondence courses, and classes transferred from other colleges can be combined in a number of ways to earn credits toward the eleven undergraduate degree programs the College offers.

FACULTY

There are 443 consulting faculty members at Thomas Edison. Drawn from other highly regarded colleges and universities, consulting faculty members provide many services to Thomas Edison, including assessment of prior learning, mentoring, and other special assignments.

ADMISSION

Students can enroll throughout the year at Thomas Edison. The Office of Admissions assists potential applicants in determining whether Thomas Edison suits their particular academic goals.

TUITION AND FEES

Because the College uses efficient distance-learning technologies, Thomas Edison's tuition and fees are among the most affordable in the nation. Students may choose one of the following payment plans: a comprehensive fee paid annually, which includes enrollment, technology services, DIAL courses, testing, and portfolio assessment; or the per-service fee, which enables students to pay for services as they use them. In some cases, fees for out-of-state students are slightly higher since the College is state-assisted. There is also an affordable payment plan for service members enrolled through the Military Degree Completion Program. A complete listing of tuition and fees is included in the College's information packet.

FINANCIAL AID

All applicants for financial aid must complete the Free Application for Federal Student Aid (FAFSA), be an applicant to the College, and have had an evaluation of their previous credits before they can be considered for assistance. Eligible Thomas Edison students who are taking the required number of Guided Study courses per semester can be considered for Federal Pell Grants and federal loans. New Jersey residents who qualify economically and take at least 12 credits per semester may be eligible for the New Jersey Tuition Aid Grant.

APPLYING

Students may apply to Thomas Edison any day of the year by mail, fax, or through the College's Web site. Once a student is enrolled in a specific degree program and has credentials forwarded to the Office of the Registrar, an evaluator determines the number of credits the student has already earned and fits those into the degree program requirements. Orientation is not required at Thomas Edison State College.

CONTACT

Director of Admissions
Thomas Edison State College
101 West State Street
Trenton, New Jersey 08608-1176
Telephone: 609-984-1150
Fax: 609-984-8447
E-mail: admissions@call.tesc.edu
Web site: http://www.tesc.edu

The Union Institute
Distance Learning Program Opportunities
Cincinnati, Ohio

The Union Institute was founded in 1964 by 10 college presidents as a vehicle for educational research and experimentation and was first accredited by the Commission on Higher Education of the North Central Association of Colleges and Schools in 1985. It is a recognized leader in the development and implementation of programs of higher education for strongly motivated adult learners. The Union Institute's individualized programs adhere to the highest intellectual and academic standards. For more than three decades, the Union Institute's programs have met the career and educational needs of men and women from all segments of society, including government, industry, business, education, service, and the health professions.

The Union Institute's distinctive educational system is designed for adults who have the desire and ability to assume a significant measure of personal responsibility for planning and executing their degree programs. Programs are individualized, build upon previous learning, and employ the creative engagement of knowledge through a wide variety of learning resources, under the close guidance and evaluation of the university's highly qualified faculty.

The Union Institute's undergraduate program includes the Center for Distance Learning, administered from the University's headquarters in Cincinnati, Ohio; as well as undergraduate learning centers in Miami, Florida; and San Diego, Sacramento, and Los Angeles, California. The Graduate College functions nationally and internationally and is administered from Cincinnati, Ohio. The University's Washington, D.C., research units include the Office for Social Responsibility, the Center for Public Policy, and the Center for Women.

DISTANCE LEARNING PROGRAM

The College of Undergraduate Studies Center for Distance Learning, founded in 1993, offers courses and structured external baccalaureate degree programs accessible by personal computer and other media. Graduate College learners throughout the United States and in a number of other countries work in individually designed doctoral programs of interdisciplinary research and study. Both of the Union Institute's programs include a requirement for brief face-to-face meetings and seminars, held in locations throughout the United States.

DELIVERY MEDIA

The primary instructional delivery mode for distance learners is individual tutorial-based study, involving a high degree of learner–faculty member interaction supported by computer conferencing. Learners enrolled in the undergraduate Center for Distance Learning are required to have access to and know how to operate a modem-equipped personal computer. All Union Institute learners are provided the opportunity for access to the Internet.

PROGRAMS OF STUDY

The Union Institute offers concentrations in liberal arts and sciences fields leading to the Bachelor of Arts (B.A.), Bachelor of Science (B.S.), and Doctor of Philosophy (Ph.D.) degrees. Doctoral programs are required to be interdisciplinary. Undergraduate learners' individualized degree programs must include a specific concentration in one area (major) as well as a general education requirement ensuring breadth of knowledge. Areas of concentration include business and management, communications, criminal justice studies, education, psychology, social sciences, and the arts and humanities. Other liberal arts and sciences concentrations may also be available.

The baccalaureate degree requires the successful completion of 128 semester credits, of which at least 32 credits must be from sponsored learning at the Union Institute. The doctoral program is not credit-hour based, requiring a minimum of twenty-four months' enrollment for graduation.

SPECIAL PROGRAMS

The Union Institute also provides educational programs designed specifically to meet the needs of particular populations of adult learners, such as programs for substance abuse counselors and criminal justice professionals. Corporate on-site programs are also possible. The Union Institute's mission is to provide innovative yet rigorous educational opportunities to traditionally underserved adult populations; specifically designed programs are one way in which the university fulfills that mission.

CREDIT OPTIONS

The College of Undergraduate Studies accepts academic course credit (grade C or better) earned at regionally accredited postsecondary institutions, when appropriate to the learner's degree plan. The College may also accept credit recommendations from the American Council on Education (ACE) and the College-Level Examination Program (CLEP). Matriculating learners earn credit toward the remaining degree requirements through sponsored learning or the assessment of prior experiential learning. The Graduate College does not accept transfer credits, nor does it grant credit for prior experiential learning.

FACULTY

The Union Institute employs 130 full- and part-time faculty members to work as advisers, mentors, and guides to its learners. Ninety-nine percent of the full-time faculty members and 92 percent of the part-time faculty members have a Ph.D. or the terminal degree in their field.

ADMISSION

Applicants to the College of Undergraduate Studies program are required to have a high school diploma or equivalent. Graduate College applicants are required to hold a master's degree from a regionally accredited college or university. Applicants are not required to submit standardized test scores, but all are required to submit narrative essays as part of the application process. Official college transcripts and three letters of recommendation are also required.

TUITION AND FEES

For academic year 1997–98 (July 1, 1997, through June 30, 1998), undergraduate tuition is $242 per semester credit hour. Graduate tuition is $4090 per semester. Tuition rates are the same for all learners, regardless of state of residence. A one-time, nonrefundable application fee of $50 is required.

FINANCIAL AID

General financial aid programs available through the Union Institute include the Federal Pell Grant, Federal Perkins and Stafford Student Loans, and Federal Work Study programs. Learners may also be eligible for state-based financial aid programs. The Union Institute awards a limited number of scholarships to its learners each year. More than half of all learners received some form of financial assistance in 1996–97.

APPLYING

The Union Institute accepts and reviews applications for admission on a rolling basis. The Center for Distance Learning schedules brief (four-day) orientation seminars for new learners three times a year, in October, February, and June. Graduate College learners matriculate at ten-day entry colloquia that are scheduled monthly. Orientation seminars and entry colloquia are held at locations throughout the United States.

CONTACT

Undergraduate
Timothy Mott
Director, Center for Distance Learning
The Union Institute
440 East McMillan Street
Cincinnati, Ohio 45206-1925
Telephone: 513-861-6400
　　　　　800-486-3116
Fax: 513-861-9026
E-mail: tmott@tui.edu

Graduate
Michael J. Robertson
Associate Registrar-Admissions
440 East McMillan Street
Cincinnati, Ohio 45206-1925
Telephone: 513-861-6400
　　　　　800-486-3116
Fax: 513-861-0779
E-mail: mrobertson@tui.edu
Web site: http://www.tui.edu

The University of Alabama
Division of Distance Education/College of Continuing Studies
Tuscaloosa, Alabama

The College of Continuing Studies' Division of Distance Education upholds the tradition of educational quality with world-class excellence through programs that overcome the obstacles of geography and individual schedules and that limit class size requirements. By recognizing that lifelong learning and technological development are increasingly essential to the lives of individuals and organizations, the following distance learning formats have been developed.

DISTANCE LEARNING PROGRAM

The Division of Distance Education offers various educational formats to students limited by personal circumstances or distance who are seeking high school–, college-, or graduate-level credit. These formats include Independent Study, Quality University Extended Site Telecourses (QUEST), Intercampus Interactive Telecommunications System (IITS), Global Online Academic Learning System (GOALS), and National Technological University (NTU).

DELIVERY MEDIA

Independent Study offers high school and undergraduate college credit through written correspondence. QUEST delivers undergraduate and graduate courses via videotape to a student's place of employment or a QUEST open site. IITS is a network of videoconferencing rooms equipped for full student and teacher live interaction. GOALS features on-line courses delivered over the World Wide Web directly to the student's home or corporate desktop. NTU offers master's degrees in engineering through satellite instruction in ten engineering or engineering-related fields.

PROGRAMS OF STUDY

Through QUEST, a student may obtain a Master of Science degree in aerospace engineering, civil engineering, electrical engineering, engineering, engineering with a concentration in engineering management, environmental engineering, and mechanical engineering. Tapes are made of actual classes and then sent to remote sites the following day to be viewed by students who complete the same requirements as students on campus. QUEST open or corporate sites are easy to establish. There is no fee to become a site. Establishing a site does require a person to serve as site coordinator and be responsible for receiving and returning tapes. Equipment needed at the site includes a television and VCR. Requirements for each degree vary. Students normally must complete their chosen programs in six years. The following colleges offer courses through QUEST: Engineering, Commerce and Business Administration, Nursing, Human Environmental Sciences, and Education.

Master's degrees are available via IITS in advertising and public relations, rehabilitation counseling, and taxation law. Students choose one of several sites located around the state, where they see and hear the instructor and students at all sites in real time. Courses are offered in business, communications, education, engineering, law, library studies, material science, math, and nursing, as well as in other disciplines.

Members from the College of Engineering contribute, via satellite, master's-level course work to nonprofit NTU for business and government agency employees seeking advanced degrees. More than 1,200 courses are available from participating universities in the ten master's programs in engineering. Also available are undergraduate "bridging" courses in computer engineering, computer science, electrical engineering, and software engineering for students wishing to enter the master's programs.

SPECIAL PROGRAMS

Independent Study, the University's oldest distance learning program, offers high school and college credit through written correspondence. Approximately 138 college- and fifty-one high school–level courses are available. Courses may be completed in as little as six weeks and as long as one year. Independent Study is DANTES approved. Students may enroll at any time.

GOALS presently offers undergraduate courses on-line over the World Wide Web directly to the student's home computer or corporate desktop. GOALS has been developed through today's most advanced technology to offer a simple format of study for those in pursuit of academic excellence. Electronic communication reinvents and enhances the student's learning experience. New courses are currently being developed, and these updates can be accessed on the Web site listed below.

CREDIT OPTIONS

Applicability of credit toward an undergraduate degree refers to the prerogative of the respective academic divisions to count specific credit toward a student's degree requirements. A maximum of 64 semester hours of two-year college credit may be applied toward graduation requirements.

At the graduate level, a maximum of 12 semester hours of work taken as a nondegree student may be applied to the credit-hour requirements for a degree.

Responsibility rests with the student to observe the limitations imposed on credit hours, course work, and transfer of credit. Procedures and forms for this type of admission will be furnished upon request.

FACULTY

There are approximately 173 full-time and 10 part-time faculty members involved in these programs. Of this faculty group, 99 percent of the full-time faculty members and 90 percent of the part-time faculty members have doctoral or other terminal academic degrees.

ADMISSION

All undergraduate students enrolling in the QUEST or IITS program must be admitted to the University. Admission to any undergraduate college or division of the University requires acceptable evidence of previous academic performance and scores on a recognized admission test. All graduate students enrolling in QUEST or IITS must also satisfy the University's Graduate School admission criteria. Formal admission is not required of students who enroll in Independent Study or GOALS.

TUITION AND FEES

Independent Study tuition is $75 for a high school course, $185 for a 2-hour college course, $250 for a 3-hour college course, and $315 for a 4-hour college course. QUEST tuition is $150 per semester hour plus a $25 registration fee each term. IITS tuition is the same as on campus tuition. GOALS tuition is $185 for a 2-hour college course, $250 for a 3-hour college course, and $315 for a 4-hour college course. NTU tuition is $263 per credit plus $322 per credit for fees. Tuition is payable in full by check or by VISA, MasterCard, or Discover credit card.

FINANCIAL AID

Loans and work-study are administered through the Office of Student Financial Services. In addition, most academic departments of the Graduate School have teaching or research assistantships that carry a stipend. Teaching and research assistants who are assigned duties of .5 FTE or more may receive a grant equal to their tuition.

APPLYING

Information can be obtained or registration completed by contacting the Division of Distance Education at the address below.

CONTACT

Division of Distance Education
College of Continuing Studies
The University of Alabama
Box 870388
Tuscaloosa, Alabama 35487-0388
Telephone: 205-348-9278
Fax: 205-348-0249
E-mail: disted@ccs.ua.edu
Web site: http://ua1vm.ua.edu/~cstudies/disted.html

Distance Learning Programs

UAH The University of Alabama in Huntsville
College of Engineering, Distance Learning Program

Huntsville, Alabama

The University of Alabama in Huntsville (UAH) is an autonomous campus of the Alabama System dedicated to excellence in teaching, research, and service. Academic programs were initiated in 1950, and the first degree opportunities were established in 1963. UAH is accredited by the Commission on Colleges of the Southern Association of Colleges and Schools to award bachelor's, master's, and doctoral degrees. The College of Engineering has programs in chemical, civil, computer, electrical, industrial and systems, and mechanical engineering, which are accredited by the Accreditation Board for Engineering and Technology.

UAH has a 337-acre campus adjacent to Cummings Research Park, which is the site of numerous companies involved with the space and rocket programs of NASA. The University has an on-campus population of approximately 8,000 students.

DISTANCE LEARNING PROGRAM

UAH's Distance Learning (DL) program was established in 1992 and currently serves an off-campus population of about 250 from Seattle, Washington, to Panama City, Florida, and several foreign countries. UAH contracts with industry to offer graduate degree programs to their qualified employees. Industry Partners agree to serve as facilitators for the course work coming from UAH. Training officers within the companies serve as proctors and points of contact to receive and distribute course material and homework. UAH currently partners with forty-three various industries across the United States and abroad.

DELIVERY MEDIA

Each semester a select number of courses taught live on campus are videotaped and distributed via two-day air to all registered distance learning students. Since the videotapes are available, no student need miss class material. Generally, students view the courses together in a classroom setting, but if on TDY, the tapes are available to be viewed upon the student's return. Faculty members are contacted through telephone, fax, and e-mail. Since the material is taught live each semester, the faculty members keep current and can answer student questions immediately.

The Distance Learning program at UAH has expanded to offer live, interactive capability to industries with compatible computer hardware, software, and phone lines. Classes are scheduled in the early evening to allow working professionals an opportunity to attend the live or remote classes. Video tapes continue to supplement the learning experience should a student be away on TDY.

PROGRAMS OF STUDY

UAH offers programs leading to a master's degree in industrial and systems engineering (ISE), which include engineering management, manufacturing systems, systems simulation, and systems engineering, and in civil and environmental engineering. The majority of the Ph.D. credits in the engineering management option are also offered through the Distance Learning Program. UAH has future plans to offer degree programs in mechanical and electrical engineering at the master's degree level.

SPECIAL PROGRAMS

UAH offers a variety of short courses through the Distance Learning program. These are designed to aid graduate students who have been away from academic study and might need additional instruction before beginning graduate work. These courses have also served as continuing education credit for professional engineers in order to maintain their license.

CREDIT OPTIONS

These graduate programs are full degree-granting programs whose students are subject to the same admission and academic standards as on-campus students. There is a provision to take courses as a nondegree student if the goal is additional knowledge and not ultimately to obtain a degree. A student may choose to audit a course as well. CEU credits are offered for several of the short courses.

FACULTY

The Industrial and Systems Engineering and Engineering Management Department (ISEEM) utilizes 8 full-time faculty members and a number of experienced part-time faculty members to bring real-world applications to the classroom through the Distance Learning program. The 3 faculty members in the Engineering Management (EM) Option have a combined total of more than 40 years of experience teaching through Distance Learning. ISEEM benefits from the contributions of its Executive in Residence, Jim Lewandowski, who is the former vice president for human resources with the Saturn Corporation. The College of Engineering is home to 85 full-time faculty members in chemical, civil and environmental, electrical, industrial, and mechanical engineering.

ADMISSION

Since all degree programs offered are in engineering, the student is required to possess an undergraduate engineering degree from an ABET-credited institution, an undergraduate GPA of 3.0 or better, and a minimum score of 1500 on the GRE. Provisional admission can be granted to students whose GPA is slightly lower but who have shown successful career development. The EM program has the additional requirement that the master's degree student have two full years of engineering experience in a U.S.-based firm and the doctoral student have five years of experience. Students meeting special conditions have been allowed a GRE waiver. An application fee of $20 is required to process the admission form.

TUITION AND FEES

All graduate courses are 3 credit hours, and the fees are determined based on the physical location of the Industry Partner. In 1996–97, the fees for a 3-credit-hour course were $550 in the Huntsville, Alabama, area; $585 in the rest of Alabama, Mississippi, and Tennessee; $630 east of the Mississippi River; $675 west of the Mississippi River and east of the Pacific Coast; $895 along the Pacific Coast; and a minimum of $995 for international students.

FINANCIAL AID

Most students are working full-time as engineers. Financial aid is made available on a limited basis to full-time, on-campus students. Generally, Industry Partners support UAH and students by offering tuition reimbursement for completed course work.

APPLYING

Students should call the EM/DL office at 205-890-6976 for a complete packet of information and forms. Students should return the completed application form, a $20 nonrefundable fee, and a current résumé to the address below. Students may begin taking classes in the same semester in which the application is made. Students are allowed one semester to complete the GRE and request transcripts from all postsecondary institutions attended. The student's file must be complete by the end of the first semester or the student's registration will remain on-hold until time of completion.

CONTACT
Dawn R. Utley, Ph.D., P.E.
Assistant Professor
EB 119
University of Alabama in Huntsville
Huntsville, Alabama 35899
Telephone: 205-890-6075
Fax: 205-890-6608
E-mail: utley@ebs330.eb.uah.edu

University of Alaska Fairbanks
Center for Distance Education Independent Learning Program
Fairbanks, Alaska

In 1917, just fifteen years after the discovery of gold in the heart of the Alaskan wilderness, the Alaska Agricultural College and School of Mines was created by a special act of the Alaska Territorial Legislature. In 1922, the college opened with 6 faculty members and 6 students. Today, the University of Alaska Fairbanks (UAF), whose name was changed in 1931, continues to grow, both in size and stature. In addition to the main campus in Fairbanks, UAF has branch campuses in Bethel, Dillingham, Kotzebue, Nome, and the Interior/Aleutians. UAF is the state's land-, sea-, and space-grant institution. Its College of Rural Alaska has the primary responsibility for Alaska Native education and study, and UAF remains the only university in Alaska that offers doctoral degrees. UAF's colleges and schools offer more than seventy fields of study and a wide variety of technical and vocational programs. All courses are approved and meet the accreditation standards of the Northwest Association of Schools and Colleges Commission on Colleges.

DISTANCE LEARNING PROGRAM

UAF developed a Correspondence Study Program in the late 1950s, but the current Center for Distance Education and Independent Learning (CDE) was created in 1987. It supports close to 200 distance-delivered courses for several certificate and degree programs through the master's level within Alaska each academic year. The Independent Learning Program serves approximately 2,700 students throughout the world each year.

DELIVERY MEDIA

Independent learning courses utilize a wide range of media, including basic written materials, audiotapes, videotapes, CD-ROMs, electronic mail, and the World Wide Web. Not all modes of delivery are available for every course, and students must have access to the appropriate equipment as specified in individual course descriptions. Most interaction between students and instructors is asynchronous in nature.

PROGRAM OF STUDY

The Center for Distance Education and Independent Learning is not a degree-granting organization; however, its approximately 100 independent learning courses can be used to fulfill degree program requirements within the University of Alaska's statewide system or at any other university that accepts the credits.

SPECIAL PROGRAMS

The Center for Distance Education and Independent Learning participates in the Defense Activity for Non-Traditional Education Support (DANTES) programs; information is available from base personnel or education officers. Veterans' educational benefits are also applicable for independent learning courses. DANTES students must complete a UAF enrollment form as well as the DANTES form.

STUDENT SERVICES

Students have access to the state library system and the UAF Rasmuson Library directly or through the Statewide Library Electronic Doorway (SLED). All students can obtain accounts on the University of Alaska Computer Network, which also gives access to the wider Internet and the World Wide Web.

CREDIT OPTIONS

Since the Center for Distance Education and Independent Learning is not a degree-granting organization, there is no transfer of credit or credit for prior learning available.

FACULTY

The Independent Learning Program includes approximately 60 faculty members, about half of whom are also full-time members of the UAF faculty and who have terminal academic degrees.

ADMISSION

Since the Center for Distance Education and Independent Learning is not a degree-granting organization, there are no admissions requirements or procedures. Students may enroll in individual courses any time during the year and have one year to complete the course. An extension of six additional months is available if sufficient progress has been made.

TUITION AND FEES

All students enrolled in UAF independent learning courses are charged the same tuition whether they are Alaska residents or not. Tuition for 100–200-level courses is $71 per credit; 300–400-level courses are $79 per credit; 500-level (professional graduate) courses are $100 per credit; and 600-level (academic graduate) courses are $158 per credit. The only other costs for independent learning courses are materials fees that vary by course and a $20 service fee per course.

FINANCIAL AID

Alaska students who are full-time (enrolled in at least 12 credits per semester) and are taking independent learning courses on a semester basis are eligible for all the types of financial aid available to other students, including Federal Pell Grants, Federal Supplemental Educational Opportunity Grants, State Educational Incentive grants, Bureau of Indian Affairs grants, Federal Stafford Student Loans, and Alaska student loans. Students enrolled in regular yearlong courses are not eligible to receive financial aid.

APPLYING

Since the Center for Distance Education and Independent Learning is not a degree-granting organization, no application is required to take independent learning courses. Completion of a UAF enrollment form and payment of fees are all that is required of students to take courses.

CONTACT

Jim Stricks, Director
Center for Distance Education and Independent Learning
P.O. Box 756700
University of Alaska Fairbanks
Fairbanks, Alaska 99775-6700
Telephone: 907-474-5353
Fax: 907-474-5402
E-mail: racde@aurora.alaska.edu
Web site: http://uafcde.uaflrb.alaska.edu

Distance Learning Programs

University of Bridgeport
Distance Education Program
Bridgeport, Connecticut

> *The University of Bridgeport is an independent, nonsectarian comprehensive university, founded in 1927, offering a wide variety of undergraduate, graduate, and professional degree programs through its several colleges and schools. The University's mission is to teach and search for new knowledge and new solutions to the problems of its social and natural environments. To this end, it offers a central liberal arts experience; high-quality accredited scientific, technical, business, legal, professional, and liberal arts programs; and lifelong learning opportunities. The University is accredited by the New England Association of Schools and Colleges (NEASC).*

DISTANCE LEARNING PROGRAM

The University of Bridgeport's distance learning programs are committed to the larger social mission of education throughout the world. Learning is a lifelong process involving the development of a range of skills for a diversity of learners, which the University provides through advancements in technology. The distance learning program was initiated in 1997 with eight courses offered as part of the Master of Science in human nutrition program.

DELIVERY MEDIA

The on-line program offers a learning environment that is both convenient and instructive. With a computer, modem, and access to the Internet, a student communicates with instructors and classmates from the convenience of the home or office. The student has access to an array of on-line tools for use in the program, such as e-mail, newsgroups, class conferences, informal chat rooms, textbooks, and specially produced software.

PROGRAM OF STUDY

The distance education program provides students with technical and professional training in the health sciences, beginning with the Master of Science in human nutrition. The goal of the human nutrition program is to provide a biochemical and physiological understanding of human nutrition and its role in health and disease. The curriculum, highly relevant to health care, is designed to provide up-to-date graduate-level information, which enables students to acquire an understanding of nutritional issues as applied to their areas of specialization.

SPECIAL PROGRAMS

University of Bridgeport on-line courses and programs are fully equivalent to on-campus programs. They follow the same curriculum, have the same entrance and graduation requirements, and charge the same tuition and fees. All students receive a University login name and password, allowing access to library services, extensive databases, registration, and academic advising.

STUDENT SERVICES

Distance learning students have access to the student resources of a traditional campus, the library, counselors, registration, and financial aid, through the University of Bridgeport's Virtual Campus. Library resources, including books, journals, and other publications within the University library system, are accessible to the students. The University's full-time reference librarians assist students in using resources such as Internet search databases and scholarly indexes, reports, and articles, including special nutrition and medical databases, MedLine, the National Library of Medicine, and the Canadian Science Technical Institute. The reference librarians, academic advisers, and career placement counselors are available to the student through e-mail, fax, or telephone.

CREDIT OPTIONS

Students can transfer undergraduate credits earned at other postsecondary institutions to the University of Bridgeport and can receive undergraduate credit by taking the College-Level Examination Program or other standardized tests. A maximum of

90 credits may be transferred toward a bachelor's degree, and a maximum of 6 semester hours may be transferred into any of the graduate degree programs.

FACULTY

The faculty-student ratio in distance education is 1:15. All instructors hold doctoral or terminal degrees in their field.

ADMISSION

Admission to the graduate programs requires a bachelor's degree from an accredited institution with a minimum GPA of 3.0.

TUITION AND FEES

The tuition for the M.S. in human nutrition degree program is $320 per credit hour. There are 31 credit hours in the complete program. Other general expenses include registration fees and required textbooks, and some courses require specific software packages.

FINANCIAL AID

Students accepted for enrollment at the University of Bridgeport may be considered for several forms of institutional and federal financial aid. The University participates in the Federal Work-Study Program and the Federal Perkins Loan Program and is an eligible institution under the Federal Stafford Student Loan Program.

APPLYING

Distance education students may obtain an application form and other program descriptions from the Office of Distance Education. Applicants must submit a completed application for admission, two letters of recommendation, and official transcripts of all previous college work.

CONTACT

Michael Giampaoli
Office of Distance Education
University of Bridgeport
126 Park Avenue
Bridgeport, Connecticut 06601

University of California

University of California Extension
Center for Media and Independent Learning

Berkeley, California

The University of California (UC) is one of the largest and most acclaimed institutions of higher education in the world, dedicated to excellence in teaching, research, and public service. Chartered in 1868 as California's only land-grant institution, UC began classes in Oakland, with 10 faculty members and 38 students. Today, UC has nine campuses and remains dedicated to excellence and innovation in the pursuit of its fundamental mission.

The UC faculty is internationally respected for its scholarly and scientific achievements. Through the years, 29 faculty members have won the Nobel Prize.

Academic study areas at UC span more than 150 disciplines from agriculture to zoology, giving UC one of the broadest ranges of study of colleges and universities in the nation and the world.

Eight of the nine UC campuses have Extension programs. UC's systemwide distance learning program is administered by UC Berkeley Extension through the UC Berkeley campus, which is accredited by the Western Association of Schools and Colleges (WASC).

DISTANCE LEARNING PROGRAM

The Center for Media and Independent Learning (CMIL) is the distance learning division of UC Extension, the continuing education arm of the University of California. CMIL's independent learning program does not require classroom attendance, and students anywhere in the world may enroll in courses. CMIL was established more than eighty years ago to expand the resources of the University throughout the community, the state, and the nation. More than 3,000 students are served each year.

DELIVERY MEDIA

CMIL offers independent learning courses in which students send and receive written assignments by regular mail, electronic mail, and/or fax, working one-on-one with their instructors. In addition, a number of courses offered via the Internet and America Online™ contain special on-line features for group activities and for research: bulletin boards, chat rooms, an electronic library containing files and software for downloading, and links to other electronic sites.

PROGRAMS OF STUDY

CMIL offers a full on-line certificate program in hazardous materials management. This nine-course program covers the foundations, principles, regulations, and technologies of the field of hazardous materials management. Students receive formal training in the core knowledge needed to make informed and responsible decisions regarding environmental hazards. This certificate program is offered on-line; access to the Internet is required. In addition, CMIL offers courses that can be applied toward UCLA Extension's Certificate in Business, Certificate in General Business Studies, and Award in Accounting.

CMIL and UC Berkeley Extension have developed a joint Certificate in Computer Information Systems. Courses now available through CMIL can be applied toward this certificate, awarded by UC Berkeley Extension.

SPECIAL PROGRAMS

UC Extension Online is an on-line program that is a collaboration between CMIL and UC Berkeley Extension. Extension Online course features include course message boards, e-mail, on-line resources, chat rooms, and course materials that may be either printed or viewed on-line.

CREDIT OPTIONS

Although CMIL does not offer degrees, credit earned for college-level CMIL courses may be accepted at the University of California and at other accredited institutions.

FACULTY

CMIL's approximately 125 instructors include University of California faculty members, UC Extension instructors, and faculty members from other colleges and universities. Nearly half of the instructors have doctorates; the rest have an appropriate combination of higher education and professional experience in their field.

ADMISSION

Enrollment in lower-division courses is open to students who have satisfied any specific prerequisites shown in the course description. Two years of college-level work or the equivalent is required for enrollment in upper-division courses.

TUITION AND FEES

In 1997–98, enrollment fees vary from $150 to $450 per course, with many courses ranging from $375 to $395, depending on the number and type of credit units and course materials supplied. Fees are the same for all students, regardless of their location.

FINANCIAL AID

CMIL students are not eligible for funds originating through grants or loan programs available through the U.S. Department of Education, nor does enrollment in CMIL courses meet federal requirements for loan deferment.

APPLYING

Enrollment is always open—students may apply at any time by mail, fax, telephone, e-mail, or in person. There is no limit to class size, and there are no orientation requirements.

CONTACT

Customer Service
University of California Extension
Center for Media and Independent Learning
2000 Center Street, Suite 400
Berkeley, California 94704
Telephone: 510-642-4124
Fax: 510-643-9271
E-mail: cmil@violet.berkeley.edu
Web site: http://www-cmil.unex.berkeley.edu/

Distance Learning Programs

University of Delaware
FOCUS/Distance Learning
Newark, Delaware

A private university with public support, the University of Delaware is a land-grant, sea-grant, space-grant, and urban-grant institution with a rich 250-year history. Its main campus is located in Newark, Delaware, a suburban community situated between Philadelphia and Baltimore. The University offers more than 100 undergraduate majors. Six of the University's colleges offer both graduate and undergraduate degrees; one college offers only graduate degrees. The University has been fully accredited by the Middle States Association of Colleges and Schools since 1921. There are more than 21,000 students enrolled at the University as undergraduate, graduate, or continuing education students.

DISTANCE LEARNING PROGRAM

The University's FOCUS/Distance Learning system supports more than 2,100 registrations a year in a variety of undergraduate and graduate courses involving twenty-eight academic departments and two degree programs. In 1996, the United States Distance Learning Association gave the University the Most Outstanding Achievement in Higher Education rating for "extraordinary achievements through distance education."

DELIVERY MEDIA

More than ninety University of Delaware courses are available on videotape. Student-faculty interaction is maintained through special telephone office hours and/or e-mail. The University also offers live, interactive courses through a two-way audio, two-way video system to sites in Delaware. A limited number of print-based courses are also available through FOCUS/Distance Learning. In addition, selected undergraduate courses are offered through JEC *College Connection* and selected graduate engineering courses are available through National Technological University (NTU).

The University will soon offer FOCUS/On-Line courses via the Internet.

PROGRAMS OF STUDY

Students can use distance learning to pursue the following degree programs:

Bachelor of Science in Nursing: Baccalaureate for the Registered Nurse major (BRN): Ten of thirteen required nursing courses are offered in a video format, and most of the prerequisites are also offered in a video format. Students are required to enroll in three 1-credit weekend courses held on the Newark, Delaware, campus. The BRN major offers a way for busy professionals to continue their education on a schedule tailored to their particular needs. The BRN major requires 125 credits for program completion.

Bachelor of Science in human resources with a major in hotel, restaurant and institutional management (HRIM): Most of the specialized HRIM core courses as well as the required liberal arts and business courses are available in a distance learning format. Students may pursue a degree or take courses for professional development. Degree-seeking students complete two 10-day resident management institutes at the University's Newark campus. These intensive institutes provide hands-on experience in the state-of-the-art food service laboratory as well as networking with faculty members, other students, and industry mentors. Students must successfully complete 120 credits, with at least 24 credits in University of Delaware HRIM courses.

SPECIAL PROGRAMS

An increasing number of engineering courses are available through distance learning, particularly at the graduate level. Engineering professionals may enroll in individual courses for professional development or may combine distance learning courses with campus courses to pursue a master's degree in a variety of engineering disciplines.

In addition to credit courses, the University offers a variety of noncredit courses through distance learning in topics ranging from art conservation to criminal justice, engineering, nursing, and technical writing.

CREDIT OPTIONS

In order to be eligible for a University of Delaware degree, students must complete either the first 90 or the last 30 credits of the degree program with the University of Delaware.

A credit-by-examination system allows students to demonstrate competence obtained through professional experience. Each University academic department determines the specific courses that may be eligible for credit by examination and the specific requirements for receiving credit.

FACULTY

Eighty percent of the more than 900 faculty members hold the doctoral or terminal degree in their field. In fall and spring semesters, about 10 percent of the faculty participate in distance learning or instructional television activities.

ADMISSION

The Admissions Committee considers all academic credentials, including all previous college work and high school preparation. Students transferring from other schools are normally required to have at least a 2.5 grade point average to be considered for admission.

TUITION AND FEES

Students registering at official FOCUS/Distance Learning work sites may register as site participants and pay $199 per credit hour (undergraduate) or $559 per credit hour (graduate). Students may also register as individual/nonsite participants and pay resident (undergraduate, $172 per credit hour; graduate, $229 per credit hour) or nonresident (undergraduate, $490 per credit hour; graduate, $653 per credit hour) tuition plus a handling fee of $90 per course.

FINANCIAL AID

The Financial Aid Office administers grants and scholarships, which do not have to be repaid; low-interest loans; and student employment. A need-based financial aid package may consist of one or more of the following: Federal Pell Grant, Federal Supplemental Educational Opportunity Grant, Federal Perkins Loan, and Federal Direct Loan. The Federal Direct Parents Loan Program is also available. Delaware residents also may be eligible for need-based funding through General Fund Scholarships and Delaware Right to Education Scholarships. Students must be matriculated and carry at least 6 credit hours per semester.

APPLYING

A completed application consists of the Distance Learning Application for Admission, application fee, and official college and high school transcripts. Due dates for applications are no later than August 1 for fall and no later than December 1 for spring admission. On-campus orientation is not required for distance learners.

CONTACT
Mary Pritchard
Manager
FOCUS/Distance Learning
211 John M. Clayton Hall
University of Delaware
Newark, Delaware 19716
Telephone: 800-833-6287 (toll-free)
Fax: 1-302-831-3292
E-mail: ce@mvs.udel.edu

University System of Georgia Independent Study

University of Georgia Center for Continuing Education

Athens, Georgia

> *University System of Georgia Independent Study (USGIS) is a department of the Division of Academic Credit of the University of Georgia Center for Continuing Education. The mission of University System of Georgia Independent Study is to offer University System academic credit to University System students and individuals with special scheduling or course needs who are interested in earning academic credit through self-directed study.*

DISTANCE LEARNING PROGRAM

Undergraduate academic credit courses are offered through the following University System of Georgia universities: Georgia College and State University, Georgia Southern University, North Georgia College and State University, the University of Georgia, and Valdosta State University. USGIS allows flexibility of registration, permitting students to register at any time and to take several courses simultaneously, with up to 1 year to complete each course. Academic credit is recorded on the student's permanent record in the University of Georgia Registrar's Office and may be used for degree requirements in accord with the regulations of the institution from which the student plans to graduate. Approximately 4,000 students enroll in more than 5,000 courses annually.

When students enroll in an independent study course, they receive a course guide and packet with materials necessary for course completion. Students must purchase required textbooks and materials. Each course consists of lessons (usually between ten and twenty) and examinations. Students complete the lessons and submit assignments at their own pace. Midterm and final examinations must be taken under the supervision of an official test-site proctor of an accredited college or university. Students can submit lessons through the postal service for all courses. Independent study Internet resources and electronic lesson submission options are available.

DELIVERY MEDIA

University System of Georgia Independent Study is developing a Virtual Campus for the academic community it serves. Within the Virtual Campus, students will be able to take independent study courses completely on-line through the World Wide Web and to submit lessons via electronic mail. The Virtual Campus will include links to a vast array of resources useful to the distance education student and faculty member. Services are available to enable students to register for their courses on-line. The Virtual Campus may be accessed via USGIS' World Wide Web site at the address below.

USGIS also offers academic courses via the Internet. Web courses are taught completely on-line, including lesson completion and submission, and may include bulletin boards. Students may also communicate with their professors on-line. Students who have an Internet provider may select the Web course enrollment option on the registration form.

Electronic course guides (e-guides) consist of diskettes containing the course guide and the information and materials required for successful completion of an independent study course. Students may select the e-guide option (as available) on the registration form.

A limited number of independent study courses offer the option of electronic (e-mail) lesson submission. E-mail lesson submission procedures vary little from those for the postal service method but carry the added benefit of eliminating postage costs and delivery delays. Courses offering e-mail lesson submission are identified in the course description. Students may request the e-mail lesson submission option on the registration form.

Lesson submission via fax is available for all courses except those with lessons requiring audiotape or project submissions. There is no charge for submission of ungraded lessons by fax. There is a fee to have graded lessons returned via fax.

Students may choose the fax lesson submission option on the registration form.

PROGRAMS OF STUDY

More than 150 courses are offered in the areas of agricultural and environmental sciences, arts and sciences, business administration, education, family and consumer sciences, forest resources, journalism and mass communication, and veterinary medicine.

TUITION AND FEES

USGIS tuition is $63 per quarter hour ($315 for a five-quarter-hour course). Tuition is payable in full by check, money order drawn on a United States bank or a foreign bank with affiliate branches in the U.S.A., international money order, or credit card (MasterCard, Visa, and Discover). Special fees such as drop/add, extension, special airmail/handling, and return of graded lessons via fax are described in the catalog. All tuition, fees, and other charges are subject to change at the end of any academic term.

APPLYING

Students must submit a completed registration form, which may be obtained from an independent study catalog, with appropriate fees. Students may also enroll on-line via the independent study World Wide Web site, below. Registration in a USGIS course does not require admission tests, transcripts of previous high school or college work, or enrollment in a college or university. High school and home school students enrolled in a college early admission or joint-enrollment program may enroll in USGIS courses. Enrollment is effective for one year and may be extended for an additional three months if the extension fee is received prior to the course expiration date. Students should contact USGIS for more information.

CONTACT
Carmen Shuler or a Student Representative
University System of Georgia Independent Study
University of Georgia Center for Continuing Education
Athens, Georgia 30602-3603
Telephone: 706-542-3243
 800-877-3243 (toll-free in the U.S.)
Fax: 706-542-6635
E-mail: usgis@arches.uga.edu
Web site: http://www.gactr.uga.edu/usgis/

University of Houston
Division of Distance and Continuing Education
Houston, Texas

The University of Houston (UH) is the premier urban teaching and research institution in Texas. Founded in 1927, its activities include a broad range of academic programs encompassing undergraduate, graduate, and professional education; basic and applied research; and public service programs. Its professional schools include law, optometry, pharmacy, hotel, business, engineering, architecture, education, and social work. It is the doctoral degree granting and research-oriented component of the University of Houston System.

Serving 31,000 students, University of Houston educational programs include full-time programs for traditional students and part-time and evening programs for employed individuals. Research laboratories and institutes work directly with area corporations and governments, while public service programs contribute to and enhance the cultural and social climate of the community. UH has placed special emphasis on outreach and access for students, both locally and internationally.

DISTANCE LEARNING PROGRAM

Serving more than 3,000 students annually, UH Distance Education offers junior, senior, and graduate-level credit courses each semester. UH has the highest number of enrollments in distance education courses of any university in the state of Texas. Students may complete degrees through television, videotape, on-line classes, or face-to-face courses at four off-campus sites in the greater Houston area. All courses include ongoing interaction with instructors. Corporate and public sites participate in the UH Professional Training Network for continuing professional education.

DELIVERY MEDIA

UH Distance Education courses are delivered face-to-face at off-campus sites and either live/interactive (compressed video, microwave, or satellite) or asynchronously (tape, cable, or public broadcast, or on-line). For on-line classes, students must be able to access the Internet. Students in asynchronous classes participate in scheduled, real-time sessions with the instructor and/or other class members. Special arrangements must be made for lab requirements in some degree programs. Proctored exams are arranged as needed.

PROGRAMS OF STUDY

UH Distance Education students may complete degrees in thirteen fields of study. All degree program requirements, course work, and prerequisites are the same as for on-campus students. Courses generally carry 3 credits; the number of credits needed for degree completion varies by program. Students can obtain more detailed information through the UH Distance Education Web site.

Undergraduate Distance Education program areas include computer drafting design, computer engineering technology, earth science, English, hotel and restaurant management, industrial supervision, and psychology. Undergraduate courses are available at the junior and senior level. Distance Education students generally transfer courses taken elsewhere (or at the UH campus) for the freshman and sophomore levels.

Graduate degree program areas available through Distance Education include computer science, education (reading and language arts), electrical engineering (computers and electronics), engineering management, hospitality management, and training and development. Most of these programs are 36-hour, nonthesis options.

Students not seeking a degree may enroll in a limited number of selected credit courses.

Additional credit courses outside of these program areas are available each semester, as are noncredit training classes in a variety of subject areas such as computers, environmental safety, food and sanitation services, health-care management, personal enrichment, professional development, and technical field updates.

SPECIAL PROGRAMS

Corporate sites, schools, and libraries may join the University of Houston Professional Training Network to become a receive site for credit and noncredit classes delivered live/interactive. Membership includes special orientations and partnership opportunities with the University of Houston.

STUDENT SERVICES

University of Houston's award-winning Distance Education program provides students access to excellent academic support services. Library support is provided for enrolled students through access to the UH Online Catalog, borrowing privileges, reference services, remote access to electronic databases, guides to research, mail delivery of journal articles on request, and cooperative arrangements with other libraries.

Computer support services available to all enrolled students include a (Houston-area) computer account, e-mail, and World Wide Web browser. Documentation, training, and software are also available.

Student support services for Distance Education students include admission by mail; phone registration; fee payment by mail; book orders by mail; remote-site proctored exams; paper exchange by fax, mail, or courier (corporate and public sites); 24-hour telephone InfoLine; 24-hour fax-on-demand information; and on-line advising.

University of Houston is an equal opportunity institution. Accommodations on the basis of disability are available.

CREDIT OPTIONS

Upon application for admission, students may submit transcripts from work completed at other postsecondary institutions. The amount and types of credit transferable to the University of Houston depend on the degree program that the student is applying for.

FACULTY

The University of Houston has 1,960 full- and part-time faculty members. All UH faculty members teaching Distance Education courses participate in special training programs and ongoing assessment.

ADMISSION

Undergraduate admission is based on graduation from an accredited high school, college transfer, or entrance examination or through a combination of these criteria. Graduate applicants must have an earned bachelor's degree from an accredited institution. Individual programs have additional specific requirements.

TUITION AND FEES

In 1997–98, resident tuition and fees for one 3-credit-hour undergraduate course are $342.50 (nonresident, $960.50); for a graduate course, the cost is $390.50 (nonresident, $960.50). For two courses (6 credit hours), the undergraduate cost is $585.50 (nonresident, $1869.50); the graduate cost is $717.50 (nonresident, $1869.50). In addition, there is a $50 per-semester fee for Distance Education students. Rates are subject to change.

FINANCIAL AID

General financial aid programs through the University of Houston include the Texas Public Education Grant, Texas Public Educational State Student Incentive Grant, Federal Pell Grant, Federal Supplemental Educational Opportunity Grant, Federal Perkins Student Loan, Hinson-Hazlewood College Student Loan, Federal Stafford Student Loan, Federal Parent Loan Program, and other loan and scholarship opportunities based on merit or need. In 1996–97, approximately 50 percent of all University of Houston students received some form of financial assistance.

APPLYING

To enroll in any UH credit course, students must first be admitted to the University of Houston. Complete admission information is available through the UH Distance Education InfoLine or through the UH Distance Education Web site.

CONTACT

Dr. Sandy Frieden
Director
Distance Education
University of Houston
4242 South Mason Road
Katy, Texas 77450
Telephone: 281-395-2810
Distance Ed InfoLine: 800-687-8488 (toll-free)
Fax: 281-395-2629
Fax-on-demand: 800-687-8555, Ext. 1192 (toll-free)
Web site: http://www.uh.edu/academics/de/

University of Idaho

Engineering Outreach

Moscow, Idaho

The University of Idaho, established in 1889, is the land-grant institution for the state of Idaho. The University has a student population of more than 13,000 and offers degree programs in the liberal arts, sciences, agriculture, architecture, engineering, natural resources, mining and metallurgy, and law. Extended program delivery and outreach activities are central to the University's mission. The University of Idaho is a member of the National Association of State Universities and Land-Grant Colleges and the National Commission on Accrediting. The University is accredited by the Northwest Association of Schools and Colleges. The University of Idaho's College of Engineering undergraduate programs are accredited by the Engineering Accreditation Commission of the Accreditation Board for Engineering Technology (EAC/ABET). The computer science program is accredited by the Computer Science Accreditation Commission of the Computing Sciences.

DISTANCE LEARNING PROGRAM

Engineering Outreach has grown from its establishment in 1975 into one of the top providers of graduate off-campus engineering programs, delivering more than ninety courses per semester to more than 400 students in locations around the country and around the world. More than 180 students have received graduate degrees through the Engineering Outreach program.

DELIVERY MEDIA

The Engineering Outreach program uses videotape, microwave, satellite, and videoconferencing technology to deliver graduate-level courses to distant students. Courses are taught by University of Idaho faculty members and simultaneously videotaped in specially equipped studio classrooms. VHS videotapes are sent to students; each tape covers one 50-minute lecture. Both live-taped and previously taped courses are typically offered during a semester.

PROGRAMS OF STUDY

Engineering Outreach courses carry regular University of Idaho resident credit and may be used toward a degree program at the University of Idaho or transferred to other institutions that accept distance-delivered credit from the University of Idaho. By taking courses through Engineering Outreach, a student can obtain a graduate degree from the University of Idaho in biological and agricultural engineering (M.S. and M.Engr.), civil engineering (M.S. and M.Engr.), computer engineering (M.S. and M.Engr.), computer science (M.S. and Ph.D.), electrical engineering (M.S., M.Engr., and Ph.D.), engineering management (M.Engr.), geological engineering (M.S. and M.Engr.), mathematics (Master of Arts in Teaching), mechanical engineering (M.Engr.), metallurgical engineering (M.S.), mining engineering (M.S.), and psychology with an emphasis in human factors (M.S.).

SPECIAL PROGRAMS

The senior faculty members in the College of Engineering at the University of Idaho usually offer a jointly taught course in engineering fundamentals (Civil Engineering 411) through Engineering Outreach each semester. This course is a review of basic engineering and science material covered in the Fundamentals of Engineering exam that each engineering graduate must take to be registered as an engineer-in-training and work toward attainment of professional registration. Another special offering in the Engineering Outreach curriculum is a self-paced short course in the Java programming language.

STUDENT SERVICES

Communication with faculty members is facilitated by e-mail and by use of the program's toll-free telephone number. Current information about the program and courses is available on the World Wide Web. Students may enroll via the Web, as well as by using fax, phone, or mail. All students have access to the University of Idaho Library via the World Wide Web or telephone.

CREDIT OPTIONS

All master's degree programs require a minimum of 30 credits. A combined total of 12 transfer, correspondence, nondegree, or approved overaged (more than 8 years old) credits may be used toward the degree. Credits can be transferred to the University of Idaho, with the consent of the student's committee and the Vice President for Research and Graduate Studies, only from other institutions that grant similar graduate degrees.

FACULTY

Approximately 100 University of Idaho faculty members teach in the program each semester. With few exceptions, these faculty members hold advanced degrees in their fields of expertise; more than 70 percent hold doctorates.

ADMISSION

Requirements for admission vary by department but generally include a bachelor's degree from an accredited college or university, a minimum undergraduate grade point average of 2.8, and a minimum grade point average of 2.8 in subsequent academic work.

TUITION AND FEES

Tuition and fees are $328 per credit hour for students enrolled in a graduate program and for all graduate-level courses and $301 per credit hour for non-degree-seeking students in undergraduate courses. There are no additional fees for nonresidents.

FINANCIAL AID

Engineering Outreach students may be eligible for federal financial aid. Determination of eligibility is made by the University of Idaho Student Financial Aid Office. Financial aid may include scholarships, Federal Pell Grants, and Federal Perkins Loans. Last year, more than $40,000 in financial aid was awarded to Engineering Outreach students. Approximately 5 percent of all students received this aid.

APPLYING

Courses may be taken by non-degree-seeking students or for credit toward a graduate degree. Applications can be completed on the World Wide Web or with forms provided in Engineering Outreach brochures. Students should contact the University of Idaho Graduate Admissions Office at http://www.uidaho.edu/cogs/ or call Engineering Outreach for assistance.

CONTACT

Barry Willis, Director
Engineering Outreach
University of Idaho
Moscow, Idaho 83844-1014
Telephone: 208-885-6373
Fax: 208-885-6165
Web site: http://www.uidaho.edu/evo/

Distance Learning Programs

University of Illinois at Urbana-Champaign

Distance Education Programs
Champaign, Illinois

Since its founding in 1867, the University of Illinois at Urbana-Champaign (UIUC) has earned a reputation of international stature. As a land-grant institution, it serves 36,000 full-time students by providing undergraduate and graduate education in more than 150 fields of study. In addition, another 75,000 Illinois residents participate in conferences, institutes, credit and noncredit courses, and workshops each year. These nontraditional programs are offered statewide and nationally at public and corporate sites.

The University's most significant resource is its talented and highly respected faculty, which includes 10 Nobel laureates and 16 Pulitzer Prize winners. The campus's academic resources are among the finest in the world. The University of Illinois is accredited by the North Central Association of Colleges and Schools.

DISTANCE LEARNING PROGRAM

UIUC's Distance Education programs offer high school seniors, college students, and working professionals undergraduate- and graduate-level credit courses and certificate programs. Working professionals can pursue Master of Science degrees in engineering and library science on a part-time basis. In addition, the campus's Guided Individual Study program offers more than 130 correspondence courses for undergraduate credit.

DELIVERY MEDIA

Most engineering courses are offered via videotaped lectures, textbooks, computer applications, and course notes. There are also some engineering courses that are offered via the Internet. The library and information science courses are all Internet-based. These courses primarily use Moo sessions, e-mail, CD-ROMs, and RealAudio. In addition, NetMath courses and the Math Teacher Link Modules are delivered via the Internet. Guided Individual Study courses use printed study guides, a variety of audiovisual aids, and Internet-based technologies.

PROGRAMS OF STUDY

The College of Engineering at UIUC offers degreed engineers the opportunity to pursue Master of Science degree programs in electrical and computer engineering, general engineering, mechanical engineering, and theoretical and applied mechanics. These programs are designed for engineers who want to improve or update their present competencies, and/or complete a master's degree on a part-time basis. The lectures are taught by regular UIUC engineering faculty members. The programs are offered through the Office of Continuing Engineering Education (http://www.engr.uiuc.edu/OCEE) and are coordinated by the Division of Extramural Programs (http://www.extramural.uiuc.edu). UIUC engineering courses can only be offered at organizations, and a minimum of 3 students must enroll in a course.

The Graduate School of Library and Information Science (http://alexia.lis.uiuc.edu) recently created a distance education scheduling option for its Master of Science degree. This option is called LEEP3, and it combines brief periods of on-campus instruction with independent learning and instruction by using a variety of information technologies, including Groupware and Web-based teaching. Participating students must have technological support either from their workplace or their own resources.

The Guided Individual Study program at UIUC (http://www.extramural.uiuc.edu) provides instruction on an individual basis. Individuals learn at their own pace by using self-instructional course materials, which may include printed study guides, a variety of audiovisual aids, and computer resources. Students contact instructors, submit assignments, and receive feedback on graded assignments by mail and by e-mail. More than 130 courses in a wide range of subjects areas are available for undergraduate credit. Noncredit courses are also available.

SPECIAL PROGRAMS

Illinois NetMath and Math Teach Link combine Internet and computer technology, including the software Mathematica, to teach college-level math courses to qualified high school students, undergraduates, and professionals. Courses in calculus and analytic geometry, differential equations, and matrix theory are available (http://www-cm.math.uiuc.edu/dep). Math Teacher Link offers short modules carrying graduate credit in a variety of topics (http://www-cm.math.uiuc.edu/mtl).

STUDENT SERVICES

Distance learners have access to campus library services, including online searches. They also have access to a toll-free telephone number and campus e-mail addresses. These and other Web-based technologies provide opportunities for the students to interact with their instructors, departmental adviser, and other University personnel. The Illinois NetMath program provides mentors to work with individual students; the engineering programs provide a site coordinator to aid with the use of equipment and proctor examinations.

CREDIT OPTIONS

Many students take courses at other institutions and petition to transfer credit toward a University of Illinois Master of Science degree in engineering. All transfer credit must be approved by the Graduate College and the individual department.

FACULTY

The number of UIUC faculty members involved in distance learning is increasing rapidly. Those faculty members who are involved in the distance learning programs at UIUC are regular faculty members, all of whom hold doctorates.

ADMISSION

Admission to UIUC at both the undergraduate and graduate level must be sought from the individual colleges. Graduate applicants must also be admitted by the UIUC Graduate College. Minimum grade point averages required for admission are set by colleges within UIUC and may vary.

TUITION AND FEES

Tuition and fees for the programs listed vary according to the program. Students should access the desired college's Web page for tuition rates and fees.

FINANCIAL AID

Undergraduate and graduate distance learners must be officially admitted to a degree program at UIUC and must be enrolled at least half time to be eligible for student loans.

APPLYING

Applicants must submit the necessary application materials required by the specific program. Formal admission to UIUC is not necessary to enroll in courses. Application fees vary.

CONTACT

Division of Extramural Programs
Suite 1405
302 East John Street
University of Illinois at
 Urbana-Champaign
Champaign, Illinois 61820
Telephone: 217-333-3060

Distance Learning Programs

University of Maryland University College

Graduate School of Management & Technology
On-Line Degree Programs

College Park, Maryland

Founded in 1947, University of Maryland University College (UMUC) is one of eleven degree-granting institutions in the University System of Maryland. For fifty years, it has fulfilled its principal mission to serve adult, part-time students through high-quality educational opportunities in Maryland and around the world.

The Graduate School of Management & Technology, founded in 1978, offers eight master's degree programs and three executive programs. It enrolls about 3,500 members of the current workforce who are seeking to enhance their competencies in management and technology.

UMUC is accredited by the Commission on Higher Education of the Middle States Association of Colleges and Schools, 3624 Market Street, Philadelphia, Pennsylvania 19104 (telephone: 215-662-5606).

DISTANCE LEARNING PROGRAM

The Graduate School's on-line classes provide the same rigor, structure, requirements, assignments, and tests available in classroom-based courses. The primary differences are that all communication is written, and students may participate at times and from locations convenient to them.

On-line classes are highly structured, requiring students to sign in frequently and participate actively in asynchronous full-class and small-group discussions. Students log-in and participate several times a week.

DELIVERY MEDIA

The Graduate School provides on-line degree programs via Tycho, UMUC's proprietary virtual campus software and via the World Wide Web.

Students taking Tycho on-line classes will require at least a 386, 16-MHz, IBM-compatible computer with a minimum 9600 bps modem. Those taking Web courses will need minimally a 486, 66-MHz computer, a 28.8 Kbps modem, and the ability to run Netscape 3.01. Students living outside the local dialing area or those taking Web courses will need an Internet service provider.

PROGRAMS OF STUDY

UMUC's Graduate School of Management & Technology offers three on-line degree programs and seven specialty tracks. The Master of General Administration (M.G.A.) includes concentrations in applied management, financial management, management information systems, marketing, not-for-profit management, and procurement and contract management. The Master of Science in Computer Systems Management (M.Sc.C.S.M.) is offered in information resources management. The Master of Science in Technology Management (M.Sc.T.M.) is a nontrack option.

The M.G.A. program is designed for professionals who find that the basis for their success has shifted from technological expertise to the knowledge and skills necessary to manage human resources. The M.Sc.C.S.M. degree serves the needs of programmers, developers, engineers, and other knowledge workers who aspire to move upward into technical management positions. The M.Sc.T.M. degree is designed around three competency areas that are important for managers in a technology driven, globally competitive business environment: strategic management, systems management, and operations management. All three programs require students to complete 36–39 credits (twelve to thirteen courses). Students take from eighteen months to about four years to complete their degrees, depending on their personal schedules. The time limit for completion is seven years. Most students who work full-time take two courses in each of the fall and spring semesters and one in the summer.

SPECIAL PROGRAMS

Students who have been away from formal studies for some time often worry about their ability to successfully write academic papers. The Graduate School offers a noncredit on-line graduate writing seminar to assist students in this situation.

For those not wishing to complete a degree, the Graduate School offers 21-credit certificate programs in the three on-line degree areas. Also offered are graduate professional studies programs (tracks only) in finance, management information systems, marketing, procurement and contract management, information resources management, and not-for-profit management.

STUDENT SERVICES

The Graduate School offers full services on-line, including application, pre-entry advising, registration, and ongoing academic advising. All services may be found at UMUC's Web site at the address listed below.

CREDIT OPTIONS

Up to 6 semester hours of graduate credit, if earned at a regionally accredited institution and if applied to the student's program of study, may be transferred to UMUC. Transfer credits must be relevant to the student's area of study and must be approved by the department.

FACULTY

The Graduate School's 28 full-time academic administrators hold doctoral degrees relevant to the on-line degrees. They teach, provide leadership for the Graduate School's approximately 225 adjunct faculty members, and are responsible for the design of the on-line curriculum. More than 85 percent of the Graduate School's faculty members hold terminal degrees in their disciplines and also have many years of practical managerial experience.

ADMISSION

Applicants for all three degrees must have a bachelor's degree from a regionally accredited university or college and an undergraduate GPA of at least 3.0 overall to be accepted as a degree-seeking student. Students with a 2.5 in the major area of study may apply for provisional status. Applicants for the M.Sc.T.M. degree must have a bachelor's degree from a regionally accredited university or college in social science, biological science, physical science, business administration, or engineering.

TUITION AND FEES

Tuition for Maryland residents is $273 per semester hour. For nonresidents, tuition is $353 per semester hour. Schedule adjustments are $15. The fee for withdrawal is $15. The late registration fee is $30.

FINANCIAL AID

UMUC offers a variety of financial aid programs to suit the needs of graduate students. Graduate students are eligible to apply for low-interest loans, state scholarship program funds, the Federal Work-Study Program, and UMUC grants and scholarships. The Federal Direct Loan is available to students regardless of income. While UMUC handles most of the processes involved in delivering federal, state, and institutional funds, students are responsible for completing the Free Application for Federal Student Aid (FAFSA) and adhering to imposed deadlines. For deadlines and further information, students should contact UMUC via e-mail (gradinfo@nova.umuc.edu).

APPLYING

Students interested in applying for admission to one of the three on-line degree programs may find a form at UMUC's Web site (address below) or may request one by e-mail (gradinfo@nova.umuc.edu). The Graduate School accepts and processes applications throughout the year. GRE or GMAT scores are not required for these programs.

CONTACT
Graduate School of Management & Technology
University of Maryland University College
University Boulevard at Adelphi Road
College Park, Maryland 20742-1614
Attn: Distance Learning and Instructional Technology
Telephone: 301-985-7200
Fax: 301-985-4611
E-mail: gradtycho@polaris.umuc.edu
Web site: http://www.umuc.edu

For more information:
Claudine SchWeber, Director, Distance Learning and
  Instructional Technology (e-mail:
  cschwebe@nova.umuc.edu).
Betsy Alperin, Assistant Director, Distance Learning (e-mail:
  balperin@polaris.umd.edu).
Alice Myers, Assistant Director, Instructional Technology
  (e-mail: alice@nova.umuc.edu).

University of Massachusetts Boston
Multi-Site Education (MUSE) Distance Learning Program
Boston, Massachusetts

The University of Massachusetts Boston (UMass Boston) is the urban university of the University of Massachusetts system. UMass Boston comprises five colleges that provide undergraduate and graduate education to residents of metropolitan Boston: the College of Arts and Sciences, the College of Management, the College of Nursing, the College of Public and Community Service, and the Graduate College of Education. All five colleges of UMass Boston share a mission to provide "challenging teaching, distinguished research, and extensive service" and to "sustain a superior faculty dedicated to excellence in undergraduate and graduate teaching; provide innovative and often interdisciplinary programs that can respond in a timely manner to societal issues and problems; meet the needs of both traditional and nontraditional students; continue to promote diversity among students, faculty, and staff; and conduct educational, scholarly, and service activities that contribute to meeting the needs of a diverse society."

UMass Boston offers sixty bachelor's programs, twenty-six master's programs and tracks, seven graduate-level certificate programs, and ten doctoral programs. UMass Boston is a state-supported university established in 1964 and accredited by the New England Association of Schools and Colleges.

DISTANCE LEARNING PROGRAM

The University of Massachusetts Boston operates innovative distance learning programs that use a variety of communication technologies to reach local, UMass system, regional, and national audiences. The programs also support both origination and receipt of videoconferences, which may range from a simple two-way videoconference involving a few people at each site to a complex multipoint videoconference involving hundreds of people at local and remote locations. These operations are known by the general acronym MUSE (MUlti-Site Education). Both distance learning and videoconferencing originations may include computer simulations, videotape and videodisc, computer-mediated application sharing, and other advanced information-sharing capabilities. Both distance learning and videoconferencing may originate and may be received in multiple locations on campus.

DELIVERY MEDIA

The MUSE program relies upon a range of technologies and communication systems, synchronous and asynchronous, that can be mixed and matched to provide richly interactive educational experiences appropriate to specific courses or programs of study. The educational needs identified by students and faculty members drive technology choices within the program.

PROGRAMS OF STUDY

The distance learning programs for K–12 educators and in-service teachers available via cable TV broadcast and Internet data and videoconference communication are information technology in the classroom, introduction to college composition, precalculus, and calculus. The distance learning programs available among UMass campuses via ISDN and/or fiber-optic networks are engineering, graduate biology, international marketing, environmental management, and philosophy of rhetoric. The distance learning programs that are offered via satellite are teacher professional development, marine science, and information technology. The following programs will be offered in the future: management and business, nursing continuing education, multicultural studies, English as a second language, and urban policy.

SPECIAL PROGRAMS

For the past three years, MUSE has been providing college credit courses to Boston Public School (BPS) students and in-service training to BPS K–12 educators via videoconferencing, cable television, the Internet, and other integrated communication systems. In partnership with CableVision of Boston, the MUSE program contributes to UMass Boston's service mission through currently expanding educational teleferencing projects with the Boston Public Schools.

In the near future, UMass Boston's public service to K–12 school systems will be expanding as MUSE becomes partners with the Massachusetts Corporation for Educational Television (MCET) to broaden its base of learners via satellite distribution to twenty-seven states while providing additional course offerings through UMass Boston's Graduate College of Education and the Division of Continuing Education.

MUSE maintains and operates an extensive range of teleconferencing equipment, including PictureTel systems and satellite downlink equipment. The University's Harbor Campus has excellent facilities for hosting on-site teleconference events for groups of various sizes. Moreover, the video redistribution systems make possible the downlinking of satellite transmissions and rebroadcast of those programs (in adherence with established guidelines) over the various video network systems used by MUSE for other distance learning activities.

PictureTel room conferencing equipment maintained by MUSE has provided synchronous classroom learning among students at the five campuses within the UMass system. These five campuses are now being linked by a fiber-optic network. As the room video equipment becomes available, it will be redeployed in a program that will expand UMass Boston's urban service mission to public schools beyond the Boston metropolitan region. MUSE is uniquely equipped to facilitate cross-communication among students and teachers housed in remote locations and their counterparts in schools within the city of Boston.

STUDENT SERVICES

Distance learners enrolled in full-semester credit-bearing courses taught within the MUSE program are eligible to receive electronic accounts that include e-mail services and PPP dial-up access to a modem pool in the 617 area code. In addition, MUSE students have access to some combination of Web-based, password-secured course databases, bulletin boards, chat rooms, virtual office hours, desktop video-conferencing systems, and other collaborative environments. (Specific Web-based course tools vary from course to course, depending upon each instructional designer's or faculty member's selection from among the various communication tools MUSE has developed and/or supports.)

CREDIT OPTIONS

Information regarding credits awarded per course and the number of distance learning courses allowed for credit within a given study program are posted with policy updates at the MUSE Web site listed below.

FACULTY

Instruction within the MUSE program is provided by full and adjunct faculty members from the five colleges of the University and/or from UMass Boston's Division of Continuing Education. UMass Boston is known for the excellence of its faculty members, many of whom are drawn to the challenge of redesigning their most popular courses for delivery over the various media MUSE can provide. Profiles of faculty members associated with specific courses and programs of study can be found at the MUSE Web site listed below.

ADMISSION

Admission requirements for UMass Boston's various programs can be found at the UMass Boston Web site listed below. Prerequisites, including skills tests, may apply for entrance into some MUSE distance learning courses.

TUITION AND FEES

Current information on the tuition and fees for the graduate and undergraduate courses for in-state and out-of-state students can be found at the UMass Boston Web site listed below. Additional technology support fees are applied to most MUSE distance learning courses; support fees vary depending on the delivery systems used, cost of course materials, number of registrants to be admitted, and other factors impacting the cost of course generation.

FINANCIAL AID

Availability of financial aid depends upon the matriculated status of the student. Further information is available at the MUSE Web site listed below.

APPLYING

Students can find information regarding program application and registration for individual courses on the MUSE Web site listed below.

CONTACT
Donald Babcock, Senior Associate Vice Chancellor
University of Massachusetts Boston
100 Morrissey Boulevard
Boston, Massachusetts 02125
Telephone: 617-287-5400
Fax: 617-287-5110
E-mail: babcock@umbsky.cc.umb.edu
MUSE Web site: http://www.muse.umb.edu
UMass Boston Web site: http://www.umb.edu

University of Minnesota, Twin Cities Campus

Independent and Distance Learning

Minneapolis, Minnesota

The University, with its four campuses, is one of the most comprehensive universities in the country and ranks among the top twenty universities in the United States. It is both a land-grant university with a strong tradition of education and public service and a major research institution. It was founded as a preparatory school in 1851 and was reorganized as a university in 1869, benefiting from the Morrill (or Land-Grant) Act of 1862.

The University of Minnesota has campuses in the Twin Cities (Minneapolis and St. Paul), Duluth, Morris, and Crookston, Minnesota. The Twin Cities campus is made up of nineteen colleges and offers 172 bachelor's degrees, 198 master's degrees, 116 doctoral degrees, and five professional degrees.

DISTANCE LEARNING PROGRAM

Independent and Distance Learning offers outstanding university credit courses using mail and electronic technologies. In a recent year, the department received approximately 6,500 registrations from students throughout the United States and abroad. The 340 courses are fully accredited each year by approximately eighty different academic departments of the University. A selection of high school credit courses is also available. Independent and Distance Learning is part of University College (UC), the division of the University of Minnesota that serves adult and part-time learners.

DELIVERY MEDIA

Nearly all courses are available by mail for home study and mail lesson exchange with faculty members. A growing number of courses (approximately ninety) provides the option of e-mail for lesson exchange. Some printed course study guides are also available on the Internet, and several on-line courses are fully interactive. Many courses make use of audiocassettes, videos, and computer disks. In 1997–98, all students who register for college credit with Independent and Distance Learning receive an e-mail and Internet account.

PROGRAMS OF STUDY

Two undergraduate college credit certificates may be earned entirely through Independent and Distance Learning.

The Liberal Arts Certificate program offers students an introduction to a liberal arts education and is equivalent to one year of University study; it can constitute the first 25 percent of a degree program if carefully planned. The Liberal Arts Certificate requires a total of 45 quarter credits, including a minimum of 12 quarter credits earned at the University of Minnesota.

The Science and Quantitative Methods Certificate provides a basic foundation of knowledge in sciences and quantitative methods. It is particularly appropriate for those who want to study health, agricultural, or general sciences or for students who wish to enhance their quantitative skills. It is the equivalent of one year of University study and, if carefully planned, can apply to many bachelor's degrees. The Science and Quantitative Methods Certificate requires a total of 45 quarter credits, including a minimum of 12 quarter credits earned at the University of Minnesota.

SPECIAL PROGRAMS

Group Independent Study (GIS) combines the flexibility of courses by mail with the satisfaction of class meetings in the Twin Cities, providing direct contact with the professor and fellow students. On-line Group Independent Study classes offer students group discussions by computer conferencing, regardless of their location. Several GIS and on-line GIS courses are scheduled for 1997–98.

STUDENT SERVICES

The UC Counseling Office offers academic, financial aid, and career counseling. Academic advising can help students determine prerequisites and academic standing, evaluate transcripts, choose courses, and evaluate the applicability of Independent and Distance Learning credits to specific degree and certificate programs.

If students have a disability, Independent and Distance Learning coordinates efforts to provide accommodations that remove academic and physical barriers to earning credits. Such accommodations may include more time to complete exams or an alternate format for an exam, a separate testing room, audiotaping required materials, and taped rather than written comments from an instructor. Requests for such accommodations should be made well in advance of when they are needed so that necessary documentation may be obtained and accommodations facilitated. Westbrook Hall, where Independent and Distance Learning is located, has an access ramp on the west side of the building (facing Pleasant Street) and an elevator.

CREDIT OPTIONS

Upon review and approval, students may transfer credits earned at other postsecondary institutions and through CLEP tests as credit toward the certificates. Up to 33 quarter credits from prior learning may be applied to the two certificates previously described.

FACULTY

In a recent year, Independent and Distance Learning had 249 faculty members, 100 of whom were University of Minnesota professors, 71 of whom were graduate student teaching assistants, and 78 of whom were adjunct faculty members, lecturers, or others. All professors and many adjunct faculty members hold doctorates or other terminal degrees.

ADMISSION

There are no admission requirements to register in individual courses through Independent and Distance Learning.

For certificate programs, admission requirements vary. They depend on previous educational performance, educational objectives, and patterns of course work completed. Applicants are asked for a written statement outlining how the certificate program will help meet their needs.

TUITION AND FEES

Tuition varies depending on academic college and lower- or upper-level status of the course. For 1997–98, a College of Liberal Arts lower-level course is $89 per credit; an upper-level course is $97.75 per credit. All registrants, regardless of location, qualify for in-state tuition rates. Charges for study guides and other course materials vary.

FINANCIAL AID

Financial aid is available through many employers, the Minnesota State Grant for part-time Minnesota students, University College Tuition Assistance and scholarship programs, state programs for students with disabilities, and military veterans' benefits under the new G.I. bill.

APPLYING

No application is needed to register in individual courses.

CONTACT

Independent and Distance Learning
University of Minnesota
45 Wesbrook Hall
77 Pleasant Street, SE
Minneapolis, Minnesota 55455
Telephone: 612-624-0000
              800-234-6564 (toll-free)
Fax: 612-626-7900
E-mail: indstudy@maroon.tc.umn.edu
Web site: http://www.cee.umn.edu/dis/

For certificate program admission, contact:
University College Counseling
University of Minnesota
314 Nolte Center
315 Pillsbury Drive, SE
Minneapolis, Minnesota 55455
Telephone: 612-625-2500
E-mail: ceeadv@mail.cee.umn.edu

University of Missouri–Columbia
Center for Independent Study
Columbia, Missouri

The University of Missouri (UM) was established in 1839 to serve the economic, social, and cultural needs of the state, but the benefits of its programs and its graduates serve national and international communities as well. As a land-grant institution, the University has a major commitment to the creation of new knowledge through research; it disseminates this knowledge across Missouri and around the world through its extension programs. The University, which provides undergraduate, graduate, and professional programs, offers degrees in a large and diverse group of subject areas. With campuses in Columbia, Kansas City, Rolla, and St. Louis, UM enrolls approximately 55,000 students and employs nearly 3,500 full-time faculty members.

The University of Missouri is accredited by the North Central Association of Colleges and Schools and other accrediting agencies.

DISTANCE LEARNING PROGRAM

Since 1911 the Center for Independent Study (CIS), a unit of the University of Missouri–Columbia Extension, has demonstrated its commitment to lifelong learning by providing individually paced correspondence courses to those students who cannot or choose not to enroll in traditional classes. Today, with more than 15,000 enrollments annually, the center is one of the largest independent study programs in the nation.

In addition to its graduate and undergraduate University courses, the center offers approximately thirty professional continuing education courses and 125 high school courses. It is currently developing an elementary-level curriculum, with courses targeted specifically for home school families.

DELIVERY MEDIA

Students who enroll in a CIS course receive a study guide containing lessons and instructions necessary to complete the course. CIS courses utilize various media, which can include basic written materials, audiotapes, videotapes, and/or computer disks. All required course materials, which are listed in the course description, are available through the center's bookstore.

Most CIS courses are computer-assisted lesson service (CALS) courses. Students may submit CALS course lessons by mail or, if they have access to a computer with a modem and a printer, on-line for immediate lesson response. CIS courses that are faculty evaluated may be submitted by mail, e-mail, or fax, depending on the nature of the assignments. CALS on-line service is also available over the Internet for students who have access to a Web browser.

PROGRAMS OF STUDY

While the Center for Independent Study does not award diplomas or degrees, students may use credit earned through independent study to achieve their specific educational goals.

Independent study courses have been approved by faculty members from the appropriate academic department at one of the four University of Missouri campuses. The center offers more than 175 University courses, graduate and undergraduate level, in a wide range of subject areas, including accountancy; agricultural engineering; animal sciences; anthropology; astronomy; atmospheric science; biological sciences; classical studies; communication; computer science; consumer and family economics; criminology and criminal justice; economics; education; engineering; English; entomology; finance; geography; geology; German and Russian studies; health services management; history; human development and family studies; journalism; management; marketing; mathematics; military science; music; parks, recreation, and tourism; pest management; philosophy; physics and astronomy; plant pathology; plant science; political science; psychology; Romance languages; rural sociology; social work; sociology; statistics; theater; and women's studies.

In addition, the center provides approximately twenty professional continuing education courses in the field of nursing/health care.

SPECIAL PROGRAMS

The Center for Independent Study offers approximately thirty graduate and undergraduate education courses designed to provide assistance and specialized learning to today's teachers, counselors, and administrators. Teachers can generally use graduate-level courses for certification and salary improvement without being admitted to graduate school. Ten education courses are special-topics courses. These courses incorporate textbook materials and videotapes, and in order to successfully complete these courses, students must attend a weekend seminar conducted by the course instructor.

The center provides approximately twenty professional continuing education courses designed for nurses and other health-care professionals; students receive a contact-hour certificate upon satisfactorily completing each of these courses.

The center has been providing courses to military personnel through the Defense Activity for Non-Traditional Education Support (DANTES) program for nearly twenty years. Members of the U.S. Armed Forces, on active duty or in a reserve component, who desire to continue their education on a part-time basis outside of the traditional classroom environment are eligible to enroll in independent study. Information concerning enrollment is available in the DANTES Independent Study Catalog.

STUDENT SERVICES

The center maintains an instructional services office with a toll-free number (800-858-6413) for students needing independent study curriculum information.

By contacting the center's Web site, it is possible to perform many functions over the Internet via the World Wide Web. In addition to submitting their lessons, students may enroll in a course, request a course exam, request a course bulletin, and/or send their comments or questions to the center.

CREDIT OPTIONS

It is possible for students to earn graduate or undergraduate credit, ranging from 2 to 5 hours, for each independent study course they complete. While the Center for Independent Study does not award degrees, University credit earned through independent study can be applied toward a degree or used to achieve any other educational goal a student may have.

FACULTY

Independent study University courses have been written by faculty members from one of the four University of Missouri campuses or by authors who have been approved by the appropriate UM academic department. The center employs approximately 70 instructors to grade its University courses; most of these instructors have doctoral or other terminal degrees.

ADMISSION

There are no admission requirements for students enrolling in a CIS course. Students may enroll at any time of the year and take up to nine months to complete each course; a three-month extension is available to students who request it.

TUITION AND FEES

During 1997–98, tuition at the center is $124.80 per credit hour for undergraduate credit and $157.90 per credit hour for graduate credit. Every enrollment requires payment of tuition and a nonrefundable $10 handling fee. In many cases, textbooks, an audiovisual materials rental/deposit fee, sales tax, and other fees may also be included.

FINANCIAL AID

Scholarships and other forms of financial aid are not available through the Center for Independent Study. However, some business firms and organizations encourage employees to continue their education by paying part or all of their tuition and fees. Individuals should consult their employer to see if funding for independent study is available.

CIS University courses are approved for veterans and other persons eligible under the provisions of the GI Bill. The Veterans Administration reimburses independent study fees to students after it receives a certificate of enrollment from the center.

APPLYING

Students may enroll in a Center for Independent Study course by submitting the completed application and textbook order form by mail, in person, by phone, or by fax. In addition, students may enroll over the Internet via the World Wide Web. Payment for CIS courses must accompany course enrollment and can be made by credit card, check, or money order.

CONTACT

Ellen Wyllie
Instructional Services Advisor
Center for Independent Study
University of Missouri
136 Clark Hall
Columbia, Missouri 65211-4200
Telephone: 800-858-6413 (toll-free)
Fax: 573-882-6808
E-mail: independ@ext.missouri.edu
Web site: http://indepstudy.ext.missouri.edu

Distance Learning Programs

University of Missouri–Kansas City
Interactive Video Network/Kansas City Education Network (KCEDNET)
Kansas City, Missouri

On July 25, 1963, the University of Kansas City became a part of the University of Missouri System, joining the other three campuses located in Columbia, Rolla, and St. Louis. The University of Missouri–Kansas City (UMKC) provides instruction, research, and community service for the improvement of the state and region. As part of the UM System, UMKC is the only university in western Missouri that offers graduate and professional study at the highest academic level. UMKC is responsible for educational programs in three areas: the visual and performing arts, the health sciences, and urban affairs (law, business, education, and similar programs important to the local community). In addition, UMKC aspires to develop programs of eminence in both the basic life sciences and computer science/telecommunications. A partnership with the greater Kansas City community requires UMKC to play a critical role in the economic and cultural development of the region. UMKC emphasizes graduate and professional study, including an interdisciplinary Ph.D. program, to produce scholars prepared for the complex challenges of the twenty-first century. UMKC provides graduate-level courses and noncredit classes to area businesses and to other educational institutions through its video network, and the University's reach extends well beyond the Kansas City metropolitan area. UMKC is active in exchange agreements with more than sixty universities throughout the world.

The University of Missouri–Kansas City is accredited by the North Central Association of Colleges and Schools and numerous specialized accrediting associations.

DISTANCE LEARNING PROGRAM

The University of Missouri–Kansas City, Kansas State University, Central Missouri State University, University of Kansas, and Kansas City Metropolitan Community Colleges have formed the Kansas City Educational Network (KCEDNET). The network provides graduate and undergraduate courses to students via videotape, the Internet, videoconferencing, and television broadcasts.

For those who are unable to attend regular classes on campus, the University offers courses by correspondence. Students who plan to use correspondence course credit as part of a degree program need prior approval from their college, school, or department. Financial aid does not apply to these courses.

DELIVERY MEDIA

Several technologies are used, including commercial cable systems, Instructional Television Fixed Service (ITFS), microwave, satellite (Ku Band), two-way video systems (using compressed video equipment), and the Internet. Depending on the transmission technologies, student-instructor interaction can range from telephone calls to the studio to instant video and audio return when questions are asked.

PROGRAMS OF STUDY

The University of Missouri–Kansas City School of Nursing offers outreach education through a cooperative program with the University of Missouri–St. Louis School of Nursing. Using a combination of telecommunications and on-site faculty members, students jointly participate in master's courses through interactive video. Kansas City provides outreach education to St. Joseph and Joplin and St. Louis provides outreach education to Rolla and Poplar Bluff.

SPECIAL PROGRAMS

UMKC is involved in a number of cooperative or brokered programs. Classes for the Program for Adult College Education (P.A.C.E.) from Longview Community College are produced and broadcast from the Interactive Video Network at UMKC. Students may earn a master's degree in industrial safety or a master's degree in criminal justice from Central Missouri State University; classes are produced at CMSU and sent to the Interactive Video Network for transmission in the Kansas City area. Students also have access to partial degree offerings via technology. The P.A.C.E. program is years three and four college programming for adults. Selected master's-level programming is available and tailored for Kansas City industry. A nursing program from Penn Valley Community College are available to UMKC students via ITFS. Child care and development and fashion design partial degree classes produced at Penn Valley are available to UMKC students via American Cablevision.

STUDENT SERVICES

Students are able to enroll at most KCEDNET colleges or universities via phone. Once an initial account has been set up, future semester enrollments are easy to complete. Telephone advising is also available, along with Internet-based comment/question systems.

CREDIT OPTIONS

Credit transfers differ between KCEDNET member institutions. For accurate information, prospective students should contact the school directly.

FACULTY

Each program selects several faculty members to teach over the network. The majority of faculty members at the University of Missouri–Kansas City Nursing School have Ph.D.'s. Most community professors selected to teach over the network hold master's degrees or Ph.D.'s as well. The UMKC School of Nursing has 22 listed faculty members.

Admissions The Office of Admissions is located in the Administrative center at 5115 Oak Street. Applicants should complete the regular UMKC application for admission as well as a supplemental application to the School of Nursing. Applications and transcripts should be mailed to the UMKC School of Nursing, 2220 Holmes, Kansas City, Missouri, 64108-2676, or to the UMKC Office of Admissions, 5100 Rockhill Road, Kansas City, Missouri, 64110-2499. Applications are welcomed throughout the calendar year. It is recommended, however, that applicants who wish to be enrolled for the fall or winter semester allow adequate time for receipt of transcripts and finalization of the admission process and apply by February 1 and September 1, respectively.

TUITION

For the 1997-98 academic year, total fees for resident undergraduates for classes at UMKC are $172.60. Total fees for resident graduate students are 205.70. The engineering course fee is $34.70 per credit hour; the computer science course fee is $16.50 per credit hour; and the clinical nursing fee is $103.10 per credit hour. Fees are subject to change without notice.

Fees for Longview and Penn Valley classes are $47 per credit hour for in-district residents, $79 per credit our for out-of-district residents, $112 per credit hour for out-of-state residents, and $131 per credit hour for international students.

Fees for classes at Central Missouri State University students taking fewer than 6 credit hours are $88 for undergraduates and $132 for graduate students.

FINANCIAL AID

The School of Nursing offers a range of scholarships, traineeships, and other funds for both full- and part-time graduate and undergraduate nursing students. Funds that may be available for qualified students include the Helen Blond Scholarship, the Laura Larkin Dexter Scholarship, the Hedgepeth Scholarship, the John S. Waggoner Memorial Nursing Scholarship, and the DHHS Public Health Service Professional Nurse Traineeship. Other funds may be available for students who demonstrate financial need. Further information regarding applications and qualifications for any of these funds may be obtained from the School of Nursing Student Services Office, Room 111, 2220 Holmes, Kansas City, Missouri, 64108-2676.

APPLYING

Applicants for the Master of Science in Nursing program must have a Bachelor of Science in Nursing from a National League for Nursing (NLN)–accredited college- or university-based program or from a B.S.N. program comparable to the UMKC School of Nursing B.S.N. program (applicants who have graduated from a non-NLN-accredited baccalaureate program will be considered for admission upon completion of the School of Nursing ENABL Program). Applicants must also have a minimum cumulative grade point average of 3.0 on a 4.0 scale, and they must have at least six months of clinical practice in the area of clinical specialization within the five years prior to admission to the graduate program to be eligible to be admitted in the specified clinical track (adult, women's, or children's health). Nurse practitioner role admission is limited and determined by faculty screening committee selection. An interview is required.

For the community college programs, each candidate for graduation must have on file in the admissions office a transcript of all high school work or scores of performance on the General Education Development (GED) test and transcripts of all prior college work. If a student has successfully completed 15 semester hours of work at an accredited college other than those in the district, high school transcripts are not required.

CONTACT

Thomas Brenneman
Director, Interactive Video Network
301 Fine Arts Building
5015 Holmes
Kansas City, Missouri 64110
Telephone: 816-235-1093
Fax: 816-235-1170
E-mail: tbrenneman@cctr.umkc.edu
Web site: http://www.umkc.edu

University of Southern Colorado
Continuing Education
Pueblo, Colorado

The University of Southern Colorado (USC) has served the changing needs of students for more than sixty years. USC's campus, spanning more than 275 acres, crowns the north end of Pueblo, a historically and culturally rich city of 100,000 located near the Greenhorn Mountains in the colorful Pikes Peak region of southern Colorado. Enrollment exceeds 4,000 students from throughout Colorado, the nation, and several other countries. The University of Southern Colorado is accredited at the bachelor's and master's levels by the Commission on Institutions of Higher Education of the North Central Association of Colleges and Schools.

DISTANCE LEARNING PROGRAM

USC offers a Bachelor of Science in Social Science External Degree completion program. The area of concentration can be tailored to meet the student's needs, such as teaching, business, criminology, law, public and program administration, and evaluation and research. Off-campus credits are nondistinguishable from those earned on campus.

DELIVERY MEDIA

After USC receives the course registration form, a syllabus explaining course requirements is mailed to the student. Completed course work is mailed directly to the instructor. Some courses may require proctored examinations, while others have examinations sent directly to the student. A variety of on-line and traditional tools are available for courses, such as e-mail, textbooks, and videotapes. Instructors are available by telephone, fax, e-mail, and correspondence.

PROGRAM OF STUDY

Requirements for the social science degree are as follows: skills requirements (14 semester hours), knowledge component (13 semester hours), social science core (24 semester hours), specialty core (24 semester hours), area of concentration (20 semester hours), and electives (33 semester hours). A minimum of 128 semester hours are required for graduation, 40 of which must be junior- or senior- (300–400) level credits. Thirty-two semester hours must be completed with USC in order to receive this degree. Sixteen of the last 32 credit hours must be completed with USC. A maximum of 96 semester credits can be transferred. Of those credits, a maximum of 64 semester credits may be from junior/community colleges. Active student enrollment is maintained by enrolling in at least one USC course per year.

Credit is accepted from accredited institutions recommended by the American Association of Collegiate Registrars and Admissions Officers. Credits from a nonaccredited institution may be accepted for transfer after the student has completed at least 24 semester hours at USC with a C (2.0 GPA) average or better. A petition is required. Courses that are not accepted in the transfer process are petitioned by the Continuing Education staff.

SPECIAL PROGRAMS

Legal certificate programs are offered without credit, including legal investigation, victim advocacy, and legal secretary studies. Noncredit enrollment cannot be applied toward academic degree programs. However, a 6-credit-hour paralegal certificate program that can be applied toward the degree program is offered.

STUDENT SERVICES

At the student's request, a preliminary, unofficial evaluation is available. Submittal of unofficial transcripts is reviewed by the Continuing Education staff in an attempt to show the placement of previous college credits against the USC requirements. The unofficial evaluation is subject to change based on the final evaluation and the official acceptance of transfer course work by the Office of Admissions.

CREDIT OPTIONS

A student may earn a maximum of 30 semester hours through the College Level Examination Program (CLEP). A maximum of 6 semester hours may be applied toward credit for life experience. A maximum of 20 semester hours of military service credit is accepted when military service credit is processed and official copies of certificates are received. Twelve credit hours of field experience can also be used to fulfill degree requirements.

FACULTY

Approximately 60 percent of the faculty members in the External Degree Program have a Ph.D. and are full-time professors on campus at USC. The remaining 40 percent are part-time professors. All professors have experience working with distance learners.

ADMISSION

Students should submit the program enrollment fee, applications for External Degree Program and undergraduate admission to Colorado collegiate institutions, and high school transcripts with ACT or SAT scores. Students with at least 30 college credits are not required to submit ACT or SAT scores.

TUITION AND FEES

Tuition, $75 per semester hour for undergraduate credit and $85 per semester hour for graduate credit, must be submitted with the registration for the course. Some courses require videotape fees of $75.

FINANCIAL AID

At the present time, students enrolled in the External Degree Program are not eligible for state or federal financial aid. Company-sponsored tuition and military tuition assistance programs may be used for USC courses. Students are encouraged to seek scholarship aid from local civic groups that may sponsor such study.

USC courses are approved for the Defense Activity for Non-Traditional Educational Support (DANTES) program. Eligible military personnel should process DANTES applications through their education office.

APPLYING

A $125 enrollment fee should be submitted with the applications for admission. Upon acceptance, students receive an acceptance letter followed by an official transfer statement of credits. Shortly thereafter, an official evaluation is issued to the student.

CONTACT

Lara Van Buskirk, Assistant Program Manager
Ronda Rein, Assistant Program Manager
Continuing Education Program
University of Southern Colorado
2200 Bonforte Boulevard
Pueblo, Colorado 81001-4901
Telephone: 800-388-6154 (toll-free)
Fax: 719-549-2438
E-mail: coned@uscolo.edu
Web site: http://www.uscolo.edu/coned/

University of Tennessee, Knoxville
Distance Education and Independent Study
Knoxville, Tennessee

The University of Tennessee, Knoxville (UTK), is a state-supported, land-grant university that traces its roots to Blount College, which was founded in 1794. It is the flagship campus of the University of Tennessee system. It is dedicated to excellence in undergraduate and graduate studies, research and creative activities, and public service. UTK is accredited by the Southern Association of Colleges and Schools.

DISTANCE LEARNING PROGRAM

The University of Tennessee, Knoxville, offers a variety of distance education programs for groups and individuals. The goal is to extend to the off-campus student the unique resources of the University. Undergraduate correspondence and Internet-based courses are available to students throughout the world. Compressed video and videotapes are used to deliver graduate degrees at designated off-campus locations in the South. UTK has more than 3,000 enrollments each year in independent study and more than 700 enrollments in video distance learning degree programs. The program is a unit of the UTK Division of Continuing Studies and Distance Education.

DELIVERY MEDIA

UTK has a state-of-the-art interactive video network in Tennessee that is capable of connecting to similar sites throughout the U.S. Groups of 10–30 students enroll in graduate courses at these sites. Videotapes of selected courses are shipped to individuals and groups. A VCR is the only equipment needed for these courses. Independent study by correspondence courses is available to students throughout the world—wherever mail service or fax are available. E-mail is used in some courses. An Internet-based business simulation course is available to groups and individuals with access to the World Wide Web.

PROGRAMS OF STUDY

The University offers the following degrees: an M.S. in communications, an M.S. in industrial engineering/engineering management, an M.S. in information sciences, and an M.S. in social work.

The M.S. in communications is a broad-based degree with courses in journalism and public relations as well as core communications courses. The nonthesis option requires a minimum of 34 semester hours. This program is available to students at selected locations in Tennessee.

The M.S. in industrial engineering/engineering management is available to students via videotape and at selected sites in Tennessee via interactive compressed video. Students must have a bachelor's degree in engineering or a related scientific or technical field.

The M.S. in information sciences is accredited by the American Library Association. This program is available to students via interactive compressed video at designated sites in Tennessee and Virginia. It requires 43 semester hours of graduate courses; core curriculum consists of six courses. The focus of this program is on electronic as well as traditional print media.

The M.S. in social work is available in Memphis and Nashville, Tennessee. Courses are offered by interactive compressed video and face-to-face classes. The requirements to complete this program include a minimum of 60 semester hours, including completion of foundation courses and field practice, at least five courses and two semesters of field practice in the clinical concentration, or at least five courses in the management and community practice concentration, and one elective.

SPECIAL PROGRAMS

Open Marketplace, an Internet-based business simulation that teaches skills in business planning, budgeting, marketing, and accounting, is offered. Students enroll as individuals or small groups and play a series of rounds against other teams to build a successful business in a competitive, global market.

STUDENT SERVICES

Students registered in UTK distance education master's degree programs have access to University computer resources. A distance education librarian assists off-campus students with reference searches and in obtaining materials through interlibrary loan. Academic advising is provided by telephone and e-mail as well as in group sessions to students in interactive compressed video programs.

CREDIT OPTIONS

Students may transfer up to 6 hours of credit from an accredited university to a UTK master's degree program. In the information sciences program, some elective hours may be earned through directed independent study projects.

FACULTY

Distance education courses are taught by the same full-time and part-time faculty members that teach classes on campus.

ADMISSION

Admission to the Graduate School requires a bachelor's degree with a satisfactory grade point average from an accredited college or university. The Graduate School requires a minimum grade point average of 2.7 (on a 4.0 scale) or a 3.0 during the senior year of undergraduate study. Applicants with previous graduate work must have a grade point average of at least 3.0 or equivalent on all graduate work. The various degree programs may also have additional requirements. Admission is not required to take undergraduate correspondence courses.

TUITION AND FEES

For 1997–98, for in-state students there is a maintenance fee of $150 per semester hour; for out-of-state students, tuition is $258 per semester hour plus a maintenance fee of $150 per semester hour. There is a one-time application fee of $15. Undergraduate correspondence courses cost $84 per semester hour plus $11 postage and handling.

FINANCIAL AID

Financial aid is generally not available to part-time distance education students. Many students are able to secure assistance from their current employer, the Veterans' Administration, or other agencies.

APPLYING

Students interested in applying to one of the master's degree programs should contact the Admission Advisor of the program in which the student is interested at the University of Tennessee, Knoxville, Tennessee 37996. Additional information about programs can be obtained by visiting the UTK Web site at http://www.utk.edu/.

To enroll in a correspondence course, students should contact the University of Tennessee, Knoxville, independent study program as listed below.

CONTACT

Distance Education Graduate Programs: Laurel Thomas
Distance Education Program
108 White Avenue Building
The University of Tennessee, Knoxville
Knoxville, Tennessee 37996-1525
Telephone: 800-325-8657 (toll-free)
Fax: 423-974-6629
E-mail: thomasl@utk.edu
Web site: http://www.ce.utk.edu

Independent Study and Marketplace: Art Cain
118 White Avenue Building
The University of Tennessee, Knoxville
Knoxville, Tennessee 37996-1525
Telephone: 800-670-8657 (toll-free)
Fax: 423-974-4684
E-mail: indstudy@gateway.ce.utk.edu
Web site: http://www.ce.utk.edu/independentstudy/

University of Utah

Continuing Education
Distance Education

Salt Lake City, Utah

The University of Utah, founded in 1850, is the premier research and teaching institution in the Intermountain West. Located just east of downtown Salt Lake City, the University is an urban campus serving more than 20,000 undergraduate and 5,000 graduate students. Students can choose from seventy-one majors at the undergraduate level and more than ninety major fields of study at the graduate level. Minutes from the Wasatch Mountains, Utah offers students a huge array of outdoor activities to complement their academic studies on campus. In keeping with that role, the University will play a central role in hosting athletes and venues for the 2002 Winter Olympic Games.

The Extension Program, now called Continuing Education, was established in 1913. The mission of Continuing Education is to extend the University's educational resources beyond its campus boundaries. This requires creative, flexible delivery routes. Independent study is one of those avenues.

The University of Utah offers more than 100 independent study courses from twenty-nine academic departments ranging from anthropology to writing.

The University of Utah is a member of the Northwest Association of Schools and Colleges.

DISTANCE LEARNING PROGRAM

Independent study is a way to take college classes without entering a classroom. Students use a course manual, textbook, assignments, and exams to learn and to earn college credit. Depending upon the course, students may also use audiocassettes, videos, and/or computer disks. Students communicate with instructors in writing and by phone, fax, or e-mail. Instructors give feedback via written responses to assignments and exams. There is a limit to the number of assignments that can be turned in per week, so it's important to receive the instructor's comments on each assignment before moving on. Grades are typically based on assignments, projects, and exams.

Independent study is a solution for students who require flexibility in the delivery of education. Sixty-one percent of Utah students indicate they are taking an independent study class because it solves a scheduling problem at work, home, or school. Sixty percent of the students work full-time and 18 percent work part-time while attending school. Each year, the University of Utah enables such students to successfully complete college-level courses. Utah's independent study program serves more than 3,300 students per year in all fifty states and more than twenty other countries.

Independent study courses are no different from regular University classes in content. The main differences are that students work from home or some other location, in most cases read information rather than listen to lectures, and have nine months instead of three to complete a course. Upon registration, students receive a manual that explains in detail how the course works; it also includes lessons and assignments. A *Policy and Procedures* brochure covers independent study policies.

Course work can be submitted by phone, fax, e-mail, or mail. Examinations, however, must be proctored. Students may take exams at university or college testing centers. Other independent study programs often have testing facilities. Students who cannot locate such a facility can take exams under the supervision of an approved proctor, such as the head librarian at the city or county library, a high school principal, or the town sheriff, for example.

DELIVERY MEDIA

Independent study can be accessed in many ways, including phone, fax, e-mail, and the Internet. A toll-free phone number (800-INSTUDY) for out-of-town students accesses faculty or office staff. Although U.S. mail is the most common form of delivery, a rapidly growing number of students fax lessons or send them via e-mail.

Courses are enhanced with new forms of technology when appropriate. For example, course manuals or extended syllabi are now available on the Internet. Courses are also being developed to enhance student learning through chat rooms and linking to Web sites.

PROGRAMS OF STUDY

Independent study offers courses in twenty-nine academic departments. The most popular offerings last year were History of Utah, college algebra, and college writing. New courses are developed yearly. One of Utah's largest departments, Educational Studies, offers twenty courses, many of which can be applied toward the teacher continuing education requirements of state education boards all over the U.S. Assignments in these courses often involve researching and writing lesson plans or teaching small groups of K–12 students and reporting outcomes.

The independent study program offers a total of thirty-two general education courses covering behavioral science, fine arts, science, humanities, American history, and college writing. These courses meet many of the graduation requirements for the University of Utah's general education program and may meet similar requirements at other institutions.

CREDIT OPTIONS

The University of Utah does not offer an external degree. Credits can, however, transfer to other schools. Limits on the number of independent study credit hours that may be applied toward an external degree vary from one institution to another. University of Utah undergraduates may apply up to 45 credit hours toward a bachelor's degree. Independent study courses may be audited (fees remain the same); students submit assignments for the instructor's comments but don't have to take the exams. These courses appear on student's transcripts with a "V" for visitor.

In addition, students who prefer to receive credit but not a letter grade may apply for the credit/no-credit option. With this option, the academic transcript reads "CR" for grades of C- or above and "NC" for grades of D+ or below.

Some noncredit classes are offered for Continuing Education Units (CEUs). One CEU is earned for every 10 hours of satisfactory participation in a continuing education course. CEUs are useful when employers or relicensure agencies require study for career advancement.

Many colleges and universities accept credit from University of Utah's independent study courses. Military personnel should consult with their education officer, and teachers seeking endorsements and lane-change credit should speak with their school district or state board of education recertification specialist for details.

FACULTY

Independent study courses are developed and taught by faculty members approved by the academic department. Of the 69 faculty members currently teaching, 33 have doctorates and 26 are working toward a Ph.D.

ADMISSION

Enrollment in an independent study class does not constitute admission to the University of Utah. For admission information, students should write to the Admissions Office, 201 South 1480 E., Room 250, University of Utah, Salt Lake City, Utah 84112-9057 or call 801-581-3096.

TUITION AND FEES

For 1997–98, fees are $55 per quarter credit hour and do not include course materials, textbooks, or postage. The same fees apply for courses taken credit/no-credit or audited. Noncredit course fees vary. Course manuals are $15. Current textbook prices are available either on the University's Web site or in the bulletin. All fees are subject to change without notice.

Payment for all fees and materials is due at the time of registration. Students whose fees are paid by their employers must include an official authorization for billing with their registration.

FINANCIAL AID

Financial aid may be available for independent study. Students should contact their financial aid office for details. Enrollment in independent study courses meets federal requirements for loan deferment only during the term in which the course was completed.

APPLYING

To request a complete listing of all course offerings and registration materials, students can contact the number below. Once students have selected a course, they can enroll by completing both sides of a registration form and sending it, along with payment, by mail, fax, or e-mail. Registration can also be completed by phone. Course materials are sent within 48 hours.

CONTACT

Independent Study
Continuing Education
Annex Room 2180
University of Utah
1901 East South Campus Drive
Salt Lake City, Utah 84112-9364
Telephone: 801-581-8801
  800-INSTUDY (toll-free)
Fax: 801-581-6267
E-mail: inthing@admin.dce.utah.edu
Web site:
  http://www.dce.utah.edu/instudy

Distance Learning Programs

University of Washington
Distance Learning Program
Seattle, Washington

Founded in 1861, the University of Washington (UW) is one of the nation's leading research institutions, with sixteen schools and colleges situated on the main campus in Seattle. Approximately 26,000 undergraduates and more than 9,000 graduate and professional students are enrolled at the University of Washington.

DISTANCE LEARNING PROGRAM

UW Distance Learning began offering fully accredited courses by correspondence in 1915 and today offers more than 120 credit courses. Campus departments approve all courses and faculty members. Courses are both self-paced (students can enroll at any time, and courses are designed to be completed in three months) and group start (students begin as a group and meet specific deadlines). UW Distance Learning serves about 3,500 students annually. UW Distance Learning is a UW Educational Outreach program.

DELIVERY MEDIA

While delivery for most courses centers on a printed course guide, additional technologies such as use of e-mail; the World Wide Web, videotapes, audiotapes, telephone conferencing, on-line discussion groups, and television enhance the learning in many courses. All UW Distance Learning faculty members may be reached by electronic mail and voice mail, as well as by correspondence.

PROGRAMS OF STUDY

UW Distance Learning currently offers more than 120 different courses in areas of computers and engineering, education, health sciences, humanities, natural science, and social sciences. Courses include technical communication, rehabilitation medicine, aging, environmental science, philosophy, C-programming, English, psychology, and American Indian studies.

SPECIAL PROGRAMS

UW Distance Learning currently offers courses leading to a certificate in C-programming (noncredit), Writers' Program, public health (credit), and school library media specialist (credit). Beginning in fall 1997, a certificate program in project management (noncredit) will be offered, and for winter 1998, certificate programs in facilities management and C++ programming will be offered.

STUDENT SERVICES

UW Distance Learning registrants receive student numbers and have library check-out privileges at UW libraries. Students living outside the Seattle area may request specific library materials by mail. The Language Learning Center is open to students studying foreign languages, and the Media Center is open to students in courses that require viewing videotapes. Students who have a Uniform Access Account are eligible to use the Academic Computer center.

CREDIT OPTIONS

Offerings consist primarily of credit courses scheduled regularly by the UW and approved by the faculty curriculum committee. UW Distance Learning credit courses carry University correspondence credit. They parallel undergraduate courses taken on campus and are comparable in content and rigor. Credit is awarded on a quarterly basis, and each credit is equivalent to two thirds of a semester credit.

FACULTY

Most UW Distance Learning courses are designed by the faculty members who teach the same course on the University of Washington campus. Gerald Baldasty, instructor for History and Development of Communication and Journalism, comments, "When I first started a distance learning class, I though I'd miss the in-person contact with students. I've found that the assignments and notes I get from my students seem to bridge that gap. Distance Learning students ask questions that go well beyond the assignments; I find that interchange to be interesting and enjoyable."

The instructors are familiar with the questions and needs of students and, with the help of instructional designers, have developed the appropriate methods to help students achieve the course objectives in the distance learning format. Students can interact with instructors through voice mail and e-mail, receiving prompt, personal instruction and answers to questions. Approximately 80 percent of the faculty members have a Ph.D., and 20 percent have earned a master's degree or higher.

ADMISSION

For most courses, students may enroll without having matriculated into a university degree program. A registration form is included in the UW Distance Learning catalog. To request a catalog, students should call 206-543-2320 or 800-543-2320 (toll-free) or use the e-mail address at distance@u.washington.edu. Students may also view the catalog on the World Wide Web at http://weber.u.washington.edu/~distance.

Prospective students may wish to contact an adviser prior to registering. If the student has questions, he or she should call UW Distance Learning Advising at 206-543-6160 or Arts and Sciences Central Advising at 206-543-2551. Enrollment in UW Distance Learning does not constitute admission to the University of Washington.

TUITION AND FEES

All students must pay a nonrefundable quarterly $15 registration fee at the time of registration. Course fees are $77 per undergraduate quarter credit and $182 per graduate quarter credit. Fees for noncredit courses vary and are listed in the UW Distance Learning catalog, both the printed and on-line versions. Supplementary materials also vary. There is a $60 nonrefundable fee to receive a Uniform Access Account, which provides access to e-mail and the Internet.

FINANCIAL AID

In general, financial aid is not available for UW Distance Learning courses. Enrollment in distance learning courses does not meet federal requirements for loan deferment. Students should explore exceptions with their financial aid office.

APPLYING

Students may register by telephone if VISA or MasterCard is used for fee payment. In the Seattle area, students should call 206-543-2350; outside Seattle, 800-543-2320 (toll-free). To enroll by mail or fax, the student should fill out the registration form found in the UW Distance Learning catalog. To request a catalog, students should call 206-543-2320 or 800-543-2320 (toll-free).

CONTACT
UW Distance Learning
University of Washington Educational Outreach
5001 25th Avenue, NE
Seattle, Washington 98105-4190
Telephone: 206-543-2320
              800-543-2320 (toll-free)
Fax: 206-685-9359
TTY: 206-543-6452
E-mail: distance@u.washington.edu
Web site: http://weber.u.washington.edu/~distance

University of Wisconsin–Extension
Flexible Learning
Madison, Wisconsin

For more than 100 years, the University of Wisconsin (UW) has implemented unique and innovative educational ideas and practices that set the tone for progressive education worldwide. This trend dates back to 1892 with the development of one of the first correspondence study programs in the country. Today, it continues with the creation of a newly established unit in UW–Extension—Flexible Learning.

Flexible Learning provides effective alternative learning environments for people who desire to expand their professional and personal development. Its design strategy focuses on three key elements: the people, the process, and the product.

Flexible Learning emphasizes the variety of unique needs and wants of the learner and meets them with a tailored learning environment that allows individuals to achieve more and to excel in their field. Flexible Learning works for a collaborative learning environment, placing the student's psychological needs and learning styles at the core of the educational experience. UW–Extension's programs are characterized by three distinct qualities: performance-based learning, diverse media- and technology-based instructional strategies, and structured student support.

Flexible Learning uses cutting-edge interactive technology to enrich learning, research, and performance.

DISTANCE LEARNING PROGRAM

Flexible Learning at the University of Wisconsin–Extension links learners to scholars who apply, integrate, and discover knowledge. The self-sustaining program uses the knowledge available regarding learning and teaching, including learning styles, learner needs, student support–learning principles, and teaching processes, and is shaped by the learners' demographics and psychographics (locations, needs, logistics, and subjects). It also uses complementary resources to expand knowledge and strives to maintain high university standards in the quality of learning, learning materials, and programming.

DELIVERY MEDIA

UW–Extension's main delivery method is the Internet, utilizing a central delivery medium that uses collaborative courseware elements, such as discussion areas with e-mail capabilities. The Learning Suite is an innovative learning software environment that allows interaction with interconnected Lotus Notes databases, providing a flexible, dynamic environment for developing, deploying, and delivering courses as well as for supporting and augmenting face-to-face training.

PROGRAMS OF STUDY

The University of Wisconsin–Extension, in partnership with the University of Wisconsin–Platteville, now offers a bachelor's degree in business administration as an extended degree program via print-based materials and the Internet. More information may be obtained via the World Wide Web (http://www.uwex.edu/flexlearn/).

Beginning in spring 1998, the UW–Extension, in partnership with five Wisconsin universities, will offer a Bachelor of Science in Nursing degree via the Internet.

The University of Wisconsin–Extension, in partnership with the University of Wisconsin–La Crosse, offers a certificate in small business management. This five-course program provides certification in finance, marketing, human resource management, and quality and legal issues in partnership with the United States Chamber of Commerce. It is offered via correspondence, the World Wide Web, and the Internet. More information about the program may be obtained via the World Wide Web (http://www.uwex.edu/flexlearn/) or by calling 800-442-6465, toll-free.

A certificate in small business mastery is also offered.

UW–Extension classes are offered in business and economics, including microeconomics, and liberal studies and education, including dance, teaching speaking for oral proficiency, and technical Japanese. HTML-based courses include marketing management, human resources management, and quality management, and Lotus LearningSpace courses include human resources management.

STUDENT SERVICES

Prospective students may contact the Flexible Learning Student Services Office at 800-442-6465 (toll-free) or via e-mail at flexinfo@uwex.edu for course and program descriptions and statuses, explanations of enrollment procedures, delineation of computer system requirements for Web-based courses, and aid in expediting enrollments.

Once enrolled, students may utilize the Flexible Learning Student Services Office for help with contacting instructors, lesson and exam status reports, information regarding completion status, and aid in timely transcript delivery.

CREDIT OPTIONS

College semester credits, generally transferable to other degree-granting colleges and universities, are used. However, students should check with an adviser at their own institution to make sure the credit earned will apply toward their degree.

FACULTY

Faculty members for all Flexible Learning programs are carefully selected for their knowledge, skills, and teaching ability. Each program or course is taught by a faculty member holding an advanced degree in the subject matter area. Faculty members who teach courses on the Internet have participated in advanced training in "Learning and Teaching at a Distance" offered by the Flexible Learning staff. One of the major strengths of the Flexible Learning program is that faculty members are staff members from one of the thirteen 4-year campuses that make up the University of Wisconsin System. The faculty is composed of 32 ad hoc instructors. Ninety-one percent hold advanced degrees, and 63 percent also hold teaching appointments on UW System campuses.

ADMISSION

UW–Extension has an open enrollment and admission policy. If a course has prerequisites, the student is responsible for determining if he or she has met them.

TUITION AND FEES

Tuition for all resident and nonresident students is $110 per credit. A $36 registration fee is also charged per course. Additional fees may apply for special shipping and for transferring from one course to another. Students should consult the cost calculation worksheet on the course enrollment form for details. All costs are subject to change. To get the most current costs, students should call the Flexible Learning program (telephone: 800-442-6460, toll-free).

FINANCIAL AID

Flexible Learning does not offer any financial assistance.

APPLYING

Students must complete the enrollment forms, which are accessible online, via e-mail, by phone, or by surface mail.

CONTACT

Flexible Learning
201 Extension Building
University of Wisconsin–Extension
432 North Lake Street
Madison, Wisconsin 53706-1498
Telephone: 608-265-3645
　　　　　　800-442-6465 (toll-free)
Fax: 608-262-6706
E-mail: flexinfo@uwex.edu
Web site: http://www.uwex.edu/flexlearn/index.html

Washington State University
Extended Academic Programs
Pullman, Washington

Washington State University (WSU), the state's land-grant institution, is dedicated to the preparation of students for productive lives and professional careers, to basic and applied research, and to the dissemination of knowledge. Founded in 1890, the University is a statewide institution with a main campus in Pullman, three branch campuses, six community learning centers, and numerous Cooperative Extension and research facilities throughout the state. WSU is accredited by the Northwest Association of Schools and Colleges.

In addition, the University is an acknowledged leader in developing and delivering distance education programs. Since 1992, WSU's Extended Degree Program (EDP) has been serving students in Washington and across the nation. The University's undergraduate core curriculum, including world civilization courses and expanded writing requirements, is nationally recognized. Money magazine has called WSU a "public ivy" and rated the honors program as one of the nation's best, and in June 1997, Forbes Magazine *rated WSU as one of the top twenty cyber schools in the nation.*

DISTANCE LEARNING PROGRAM

WSU's Extended Degree Program, a degree-completion program leading to a Bachelor of Arts in social sciences, is designed primarily for students who have completed the equivalent of the first two years of college. It is delivered directly to students' homes through a variety of distance learning technologies. It is the same degree offered on three WSU campuses; requirements are the same as those for completing degrees on campus; however, students can complete their degrees without coming to a WSU campus.

A 30-minute informational videotape, providing details about the program, advising, and financial aid and presenting short clips from a number of EDP video courses, is available for $8 from the WSU Students Book Corporation (telephone: 800-937-4978 Ext. 336).

DELIVERY MEDIA

Courses are delivered by videotape (available for rent), satellite, cable television, and print materials. Some courses also include material available on the World Wide Web; others require full Internet connectivity. Future courses will feature interactive CD-ROM and desktop videoconferencing components.

PROGRAMS OF STUDY

WSU's Bachelor of Arts in social sciences is a liberal arts degree that offers students multiple options and emphases in the social sciences and provides a broad background applicable to a variety of careers. It emphasizes an interdisciplinary approach with possible major and/or minor course concentrations in anthropology, criminal justice, history, human development, political science, psychology, sociology, and women studies. A formal minor in business administration is also available.

To earn a bachelor's degree, WSU requires the completion of at least 120 semester credits, 40 at the upper-division level. At least 30 of the 120 credits must be taken through WSU. The 120 credits must include courses that meet WSU General Education Requirements (GER).

More than 30 video courses and nearly 100 correspondence courses are available to students. While the majority of these courses have prerequisites, they have been waived by departments for EDP students. Courses are also available from the National Universities Degree Consortium (NUDC), a group of thirteen land-grant and state universities formed to address the needs of adult and part-time learners.

SPECIAL PROGRAMS

Academic advising is available to all prospective and currently enrolled degree-seeking students through toll-free telephone or electronic mail. The WSU Office of Admissions prepares an official evaluation of a student's transcript when he or she is admitted to the University. An EDP adviser assists EDP students in developing a study plan based on the program options and University requirements. A student services coordinator is available to help students with logistical details.

Students may register via toll-free telephone, fax, or e-mail. Videotapes, lab kits, and other supplementary materials are available through the EDP office. Students may order textbooks and course guides from the WSU Students Book Corporation via toll-free telephone.

All EDP students have access to the WSU libraries. The EDP librarian is available via toll-free telephone to assist students with database searches, in checking out materials, and in copying articles.

CREDIT OPTIONS

Students may transfer to WSU a maximum of 60 semester credits of lower-division credit from community colleges and up to 30 more credits from other four-year institutions.

WSU recognizes there are alternative ways students may gain knowledge and credit. The University has developed a broad program of credit by examination, including Advanced Placement (AP), College-Level Examination Program (CLEP), DANTES, and American Council on Education (ACE). Interested students should check with their advisers for details.

FACULTY

There are 1,206 full-time and 187 part-time faculty members in the Washington State University system. Ninety-three percent of the faculty members have terminal academic degrees.

ADMISSION

Admission to the Extended Degree Program requires at least 27 semester or 40 quarter credits of transferable college course work from an accredited community or four-year college, with at least a 2.0 cumulative GPA.

TUITION AND FEES

In 1997–98, undergraduate tuition is $163 per regular/video credit for Washington residents and $245 per video credit for nonresidents. Videotape rental averages $60 per course. Correspondence course tuition is $90 per credit.

FINANCIAL AID

A financial aid adviser is available to all EDP students. Washington State University students receive aid from all federal programs, such as the Federal Pell Grants and Federal Supplemental Educational Opportunity Grants (FSEOG) and the Federal Perkins, Federal Stafford Student, and Federal PLUS Loans. Washington residents are eligible for institutional and state need grants. In 1995–96, WSU awarded more than $70 million in financial aid. Fifty percent of all WSU students and 52 percent of extended degree students receive financial aid.

APPLYING

WSU degree-seeking students must be admitted to the University. Admission requires that a student submit an admissions form, have official copies of his or her transcript(s) sent directly from the postsecondary institution(s) attended to the EDP office, and pay the $35 application fee.

CONTACT

Cheri Curtis
Program Coordinator
Extended Degree Programs
Washington State University
P.O. Box 645220
Pullman, Washington 99164-5220
Telephone: 509-335-3557
            800-222-4978 (toll-free)
Fax: 509-335-4850
E-mail: edp@wsu.edu
World Wide Web: http://www.eus.wsu.edu/edp

Weber State University
Distance Learning
Ogden, Utah

Weber State University (WSU) provides lifelong opportunities for a spectrum of diverse learners on and off campus. It offers 106 undergraduate degrees through seven colleges and forty departments, including specialized education in allied health sciences. Sited in Ogden, Utah, amid spectacular mountain scenery, it offers year-round outdoor recreation and cultural experiences.

WSU prepares students for immediate employment or further study, offering instruction in formats, places, and times convenient for lifelong learners.

Founded in 1889, WSU became a state junior college in 1933 and a university in 1990. Weber State is dedicated to the realization of human potential through education, so it provides a variety of approaches to the educational process. WSU is accredited by the Northwest Association of Schools and Colleges.

DISTANCE LEARNING PROGRAM

The Distance Learning Program was designed for students remote from the campus and for those who, because of other obligations, cannot attend regular college classes. WSU Distance Learning enrolled 1,805 students in 1996–97.

Distance Learning offers courses from two dozen academic disciplines and degrees in six allied health science areas.

DELIVERY MEDIA

Approved proctors administer exams. Students follow self-paced study guides, read textbooks, view videotapes, hear cassettes, or participate in on-line courses. Instructors and advisers answer questions by mail, telephone, or e-mail. Students may need access to a videocassette player, audiocassette player, computer/word processor, and/or Internet access.

PROGRAM OF STUDY

The Distance Learning degree program evolved from a commitment to providing education for health-care professionals regardless of location. Combining independent study with intensive workshops on campus, a bachelor's degree requires 183 credits (60 upper-division, 45 through Weber State). The University is on the quarter system, but is changing to a semester system in fall 1998.

Bachelor's degrees are available in advanced dental hygiene, advanced respiratory therapy, health administrative services, and radiological sciences (with emphasis in advanced radiography, MRI/CT, mammography, cardiovascular-interventional technology, DMS, radiation therapy, or nuclear medicine).

Associate of Applied Science and Associate of Science degrees in respiratory therapy require 30 credits taken at WSU, completion of the requirements for a major in respiratory therapy, and an overall GPA of at least 2.0.

WSU certificate programs include radiologic sciences and respiratory therapy (entry-level respiratory care practitioner [CRRT] or registered respiratory therapist [RRT]). Radiologic sciences classes can be used toward continuing education units (CEU).

Professional agencies, such as the American Dental Association, the Joint Review Commission for Education in Radiologic Technology, the Commission on Accreditation for Allied Health Education Programs, and the Association of University Programs in Health Administration, accredit specific disciplines.

SPECIAL PROGRAMS

Beginning in fall 1997, Weber State University offers WSU Online. WSU Online is an extension of the University on the Internet. Students with Internet access are not only able to take on-line courses, but they are also able to use on-line support services and participate in on-line discussions and activities with faculty and staff members and other students. WSU Online makes it possible for students with busy schedules and/or long commutes to take advantage of the convenience of an on-line course, with support services that are essential to their success and interpersonal experiences.

STUDENT SERVICES

Weber State University recognizes that most of its students have work, family, and other personal responsibilities that limit their participation in traditional college courses; therefore, convenience is a major factor in the design of the WSU Distance Learning Program.

Students receive academic advisement through the Academic Advisement Center at Weber State University. Degree-seeking students are assigned advisers who review transcripts and past learning experiences to design a program of study specifically for the individual student.

Students may access Stewart Library's catalog, interlibrary loan, and other services electronically.

Textbooks can be purchased directly from the WSU bookstore by mail and eventually on-line for a small handling charge (telephone: 800-848-7770 Ext. 6352 [toll-free]).

CREDIT OPTIONS

WSU may grant credit for active military, National Guard, or reserve experience; 38 or more credits to registered radiographers; a maximum of 45 credits to diploma nursing school graduates; and varying credits to registered respiratory therapy technicians and graduates of accredited therapy/specialty programs. Official transcripts should be sent directly from universities and colleges attended. WSU also grants College-Level Examination Program (CLEP) credits.

FACULTY

WSU Distance Learning has 60 full-time faculty members and 9 part-time faculty members; 85 percent of full-time and 75 percent of part-time faculty members have terminal degrees.

ADMISSION

Distance Learning applicants must meet WSU admission requirements. Departments of Health Administrative Services, Respiratory Therapy, Radiologic Sciences, and Dental Hygiene require a separate application and information specific to their academic areas.

TUITION AND FEES

Distance Learning tuition averages $190 per course, plus materials. Materials may include course modules ($3–$40) and audiotape or videotape deposits ($10–$40).

FINANCIAL AID

Eligible students may apply for federal financial aid such as Pell Grants, Supplemental Educational Opportunity Grants (SEOG), Perkins Loans, and Stafford Loans (telephone: 800-848-7770 Ext. 7003 [toll-free]). Veterans may also be considered for VA educational benefits (telephone: 800-848-7770 Ext. 6042 [toll-free]). Weber State is approved by DANTES. Other educational assistance funds may also be accepted.

APPLYING

Students should send a completed application; an individual program application, if required; official transcripts from previous colleges; and an application fee of $30 (international students, $45) to apply. Distance Learning students need not attend an orientation.

CONTACT

Telephone: 801-626-6785
              800-848-7770 Ext. 6785
Fax: 801-626-8035
E-mail: dist-learn@weber.edu
World Wide Web: http://www.weber.edu/dist-learn

Distance Learning Programs

Worcester Polytechnic Institute
Advanced Distance Learning Network
Worcester, Massachusetts

Worcester Polytechnic Institute (WPI), the third-oldest private university of engineering, science, and management in the United States, has been a pioneer in technological higher education since its founding in 1865. It is fully accredited by the New England Association of Schools and Colleges. WPI's mission is to educate talented men and women in preparation for careers of professional practice, civic contribution, and leadership.

WPI awarded its first advanced degree in 1893. Since then, the university has earned a reputation for academic excellence in technological education, for practical application to the challenges of the marketplace, and for a faculty of renowned academicians and industry experts who are practitioners in their fields. Today, most of WPI's academic departments offer master's and doctoral programs and support leading-edge research in a broad range of fields.

DISTANCE LEARNING PROGRAM

In 1979, WPI's commitment to active, lifelong learning prompted the creation of the Advanced Distance Learning Network (ADLN), a partnership between several academic departments and WPI's Instructional Media Center. ADLN programs empower working professionals to continue to grow within their chosen field without having to make repeated trips to the WPI campus.

DELIVERY MEDIA

ADLN courses consist of the same content and materials as on-campus class meetings. Courses originate in one of WPI's studio classrooms and are delivered via interactive compressed video or videotapes via Express Mail, depending on the facilities available to the student. Materials such as books, handouts, and supplemental readings are sent by Express Mail, fax, or e-mail (e-mail and fax access are required). For convenience, supplemental materials are sometimes posted on the World Wide Web.

PROGRAMS OF STUDY

ADLN offers a Master of Business Administration (M.B.A.) degree and graduate certificate programs in management and fire protection engineering (FPE). An M.S. in FPE is also available, although the number of FPE courses currently offered via ADLN is not sufficient to fulfill the 33-credit requirement. However, with prior approval, students can earn an M.S. in FPE by fulfilling some of the requirements with non-FPE courses.

The newly restructured M.B.A. program focuses on the management of technology and features a highly integrative curriculum that emphasizes leadership, ethics, communication, and a global perspective. Concentration areas include MIS, technology marketing, technological innovation, operations management, and management of technology. This 49-credit M.B.A. program may be reduced to as few as 31 credits with an appropriate academic background. A customized 15-credit graduate certificate program in management is also available.

The fire protection engineering program is oriented toward developing a well-rounded professional who can be successful in a competitive career environment. The curriculum is designed to teach students current standards of practice and expose them to state-of-the-art research literature that will support future practices. In addition to the eleven-course M.S. option, professionals with a B.S. degree in an engineering or science field who complete four thematically related FPE courses can receive a Graduate Certificate in FPE. Master's degree holders may instead opt to complete five thematically related courses for an Advanced Certificate in FPE.

Credits earned in any certificate program can later be applied toward an advanced degree, contingent upon formal admission to graduate study. A maximum of two courses taken as a nondegree-seeking student may be applied for credit to an M.B.A. program; a maximum of four courses taken as a nondegree-seeking student may be applied for credit to an M.S. in FPE.

SPECIAL PROGRAMS

ADLN and appropriate academic personnel are always willing to consider the addition of new programs for which there is sufficient interest.

STUDENT SERVICES

Academic advisers are assigned upon admission. On-line library services are free. Dial-up UNIX accounts (for e-mail, etc.) and career placement and counseling are available for matriculated students. Books can be ordered toll-free from the WPI campus bookstore and are typically delivered one to three days after ordering.

CREDIT OPTIONS

The 49-credit M.B.A. program allows 18 foundation-level credits to be waived for those with appropriate academic backgrounds, either via straight waivers for those with appropriate course work completed within the past six years with a grade of B or better or via waiver exams. Both the M.B.A. program and the M.S. in FPE allow students to transfer up to 9 credits from prior graduate-level coursework. Graduate and advanced certificate programs require all credits to come from WPI.

FACULTY

Management has 19 faculty members (15 full-time members and 4 part-time members), 18 of whom have Ph.D. degrees. FPE has 5 full-time faculty members, all with Ph.D. degrees, and 4 part-time professors.

ADMISSION

To be considered for admission to WPI's M.S. programs or graduate certificate programs, applicants must hold a B.S. degree in an appropriate field of engineering or science and meet department-specific admission standards. Conditional admission is available if all requirements are not met at the time of application.

TUITION AND FEES

Tuition is $612 per credit ($1836 per 3-credit course) for all programs in the 1997–98 academic year. Students wishing to earn CEUs instead of graduate credit may opt to audit courses at half tuition.

FINANCIAL AID

Loan-based aid is available only through special arrangements. Students must be registered on a half-time basis (two courses per semester) or greater.

APPLYING

All departments require standard forms, official transcripts, and a $50 application fee. Management degree programs also require three letters of recommendation and GMAT scores. All international applicants must submit TOEFL scores. GRE scores are not required.

CONTACT

Pennie S. Turgeon, Director, Instructional Media Center
Worcester Polytechnic Institute
100 Institute Road
Worcester, Massachusetts 01609-2280
Telephone: 508-831-5810
Fax: 508-831-5881
E-mail: pennie@wpi.edu
Web site: http://www.wpi.edu/Academics/ADLN

STUDENT PROFILE

Brenda Eades

Personal: Age 38, divorced, mother of three children

Home: Colorado City, Texas

College: The George Washington University, Washington, DC

Distance Learning Accomplishment: completed 12 courses via home computer to earn a Masters of Arts in Education and in Human Development in Educational Technology Leadership.

In an e-mail message to her GW classmates, Brenda says: "Hi everybody! I am proud to announce that I have a new job. I was a fourth grade teacher; now I am an Educational Technology Specialist with the Regional Education Service Center in San Angelo, Texas which means a $10,000 a year raise in pay! I am sharing this information with my GW classmates because my getting this job is a direct result of my involvement in this ETL program. The money is great, but I am really excited to get a chance to be involved in all the kinds of technology I have seen in the classes—we have a brand new teleconference center and all kinds of neat stuff. Anyway, consider this an ETL success story!"

Since Brenda is a single mother, distance learning from her home was the only way she could work, go to school, and care for her children. She notes that the program benefited her in all three areas of her life.

"The class assignments were flexible and directly applicable to work. When I was a teacher I used a multimedia software tutorial I'd created for GW to teach the kids in science class. In my new job, I have been able to turn class assignments into work projects that help support 43 school districts. For example, I produced a brochure for our Teacher's Preview Center and wrote a technology upgrade proposal which otherwise might have been put off."

She notes that, thanks to her salary increase, her master's degree paid for itself in just one year.

INDEX OF INSTITUTIONS OFFERING DEGREE AND CERTIFICATE PROGRAMS

UC=Undergraduate Certificate; GC=Graduate Certificate; A=Associate; B=Bachelor's; M=Master's; D=Doctorate

Accounting
Athabasca University (UC)
Caldwell College (B)
Central Community College–Grand Island Campus (UC, A)
Champlain College (UC, A)
City University (B)
Coastline Community College (A)
Eastern Oregon University (B)
Ivy Tech State College–Wabash Valley (A)
Lake Superior State University (B)
Marywood University (B)
McGraw-Hill World University (A, GC)
New Hampshire College (UC)
St. Cloud Technical College (A)
Saint Mary-of-the-Woods College (B)
University of the State of New York, Regents College (B)
Upper Iowa University (B)
Utah State University (B)

Administrative and Secretarial Services
Central Community College–Grand Island Campus (UC)
City University (A)
The College of West Virginia (UC, A)
Eastern Oregon University (A)
Marywood University (UC)
Ohio University (A)
St. Cloud Technical College (A)
Sinclair Community College (A)
Southwestern Adventist University (A, B)
West Virginia University Institute of Technology (A)

Advertising
Syracuse University (M)

Aerospace, Aeronautical and Astronautical Engineering
Auburn University (M)
Embry-Riddle Aeronautical University, Extended Campus (M)
Illinois Institute of Technology (M)
Stanford University (M)
State University of New York at Buffalo (M, GC)
The University of Alabama (M)
University of Colorado at Boulder (M)

The University of Texas at Arlington (M)

Agricultural Business and Management
Central Community College–Grand Island Campus (UC)
Iowa State University of Science and Technology (B)

Agricultural Engineering
University of Idaho (M)

Agriculture
Iowa State University of Science and Technology (M)
University of Saskatchewan (UC)

Animal Sciences
Kansas State University (B)

Anthropology
Laurentian University (B)

Area Studies
Memorial University of Newfoundland (UC)
Ryerson Polytechnic University (UC)
Saint Joseph's College (UC, B)

Aviation
Central Missouri State University (M)
The College of West Virginia (UC, A)
Embry-Riddle Aeronautical University, Extended Campus (A, B)
University of Tennessee Space Institute (M)

Bible/Biblical Studies
Berean University of the Assemblies of God (A, B, M)
Columbia International University (GC)
International Bible College (B)
Johnson Bible College (M)
LIFE Bible College (A)
Moody Bible Institute (A)
North Central Bible College (UC)
Reformed Theological Seminary (GC)
Temple Baptist Seminary (UC, M)
Tennessee Temple University (A, B)
Trinity International University (UC)

Bilingual/Bicultural Education
California State University, Fresno (UC)

Biology
Ohio University (A)
Southern Christian University (B)

Business
Athabasca University (B)
Caldwell College (B)
Champlain College (UC, A, B)
Charles Stewart Mott Community College (A)
Coastline Community College (A)
Eastern Oregon University (B)
Judson College (B)
Lansing Community College (A)
Liberty University (B)
Marywood University (UC)
New Mexico State University (B)
New York Institute of Technology (B, M)
Northeast Community College (A)
Ohio University–Southern Campus (M)
Pennsylvania State University University Park Campus (UC)
Saint Mary-of-the-Woods College (A)
Salve Regina University (B)
Southwestern Assemblies of God University (B)
Stephens College (B)
University of Hawaii–Maui Community College (UC)
University of the State of New York, Regents College (A, B)
University of Windsor (B)
University of Wisconsin–Extension (UC)
Upper Iowa University (A, B)
Vincennes University (A)
West Virginia Wesleyan College (UC)

Business Administration and Management
Acadia University (UC)
American College (M)
Athabasca University (UC, B, M, GC)
Atlantic Union College (B)
Auburn University (M)
Baker College (A, B, M)
Ball State University (A, M)
Bellevue University (B, M)
Black Hawk College (UC)
Brookdale Community College (A)
Bucks County Community College (A)

Distance Learning Programs

533

Index of Institutions Offering Degree and Certificate Programs

Business Administration and Management (continued)
Burlington County College (A)
Caldwell College (B)
California State University, Dominguez Hills (M)
Catawba Valley Community College (UC)
Central Community College–Grand Island Campus (UC, A)
Central Michigan University (B)
Central Washington University (B)
Chadron State College (M)
Champlain College (UC, A)
City University (A, B, M)
Clarkson College (B)
The College of West Virginia (UC, A, B)
Colorado State University (M)
Columbus State Community College (A)
Dawson Community College (A)
De Anza College (UC)
Duke University (M)
Eastern New Mexico University (B, M)
Fielding Institute (M)
Fitchburg State College (M)
Fort Hays State University (B)
The Graduate School of America (M, D)
Griggs University (B)
Hampton University (B)
Heriot-Watt University (M)
Indiana Wesleyan University (M)
ISIM University (M)
Jackson Community College (M)
Lake Superior State University (B, M)
Laurentian University (M)
Lehigh University (M)
Madison Area Technical College (UC)
Maharishi University of Management (M)
Marywood University (B)
McGraw-Hill World University (A)
Memorial University of Newfoundland (UC)
Mercy College (B)
Mississippi State University (M)
Morehead State University (B, M)
Mount Saint Vincent University (UC, B)
National University (M)
New Jersey Institute of Technology (GC)
New York University (M)
Northampton County Area Community College (A)
Northcentral Technical College (A)
North Dakota State University (M)
Northern Arizona University (B)
Northern Virginia Community College (A)
Northwestern College (A)
Northwood University (B)
Oklahoma State University (M)
Old Dominion University (B, M)
Oral Roberts University (B)
Owens Community College (UC)
Pennsylvania State University University Park Campus (UC, A)
Portland State University (M)
Prince George's Community College (UC, A)
Purdue University (M)
Regent University (M)
Regis University (B, M)
Rensselaer Polytechnic Institute (M, GC)
Rochester Institute of Technology (UC)
Rogers University (A)
Roger Williams University (B)
Rutgers, The State University of New Jersey, Newark (B)
Ryerson Polytechnic University (UC)
Saint Joseph's College (UC, A, B)
Saint Mary-of-the-Woods College (B)
Salve Regina University (UC, M)
San Jose State University (UC)
Southern Illinois University at Edwardsville (M)
Southern Oregon University (B)
Southern Polytechnic State University (B)
Southern Utah University (B)
Southwestern Adventist University (B)
Southwestern Oklahoma State University (M)
Southwest State University (B)
State University of New York Empire State College (A, B)
Stephens College (M)
Stevens Institute of Technology (M)
Syracuse University (M)
Thomas Edison State College (A, B, M)
Universitè Laval (UC)
University of Alaska Southeast (B)
University of Arkansas at Little Rock (M)
University of Great Falls (A, B)
University of Houston (B)
University of Maine at Augusta (A)
University of Mary (B, M)
University of Maryland University College (B, M)
The University of Montana–Missoula (M)
University of Nebraska–Lincoln (M)
University of Nevada, Reno (M)
University of North Dakota (B, M)
University of Notre Dame (UC, M)
University of Phoenix (B, M)
University of Pittsburgh (M)
University of South Carolina (M)
University of South Florida (M)
University of the State of New York, Regents College (B)
University of Wisconsin–Platteville (B)
University of Wyoming (M)
Upper Iowa University (B)
Utah State University (B)
Virginia Polytechnic Institute and State University (M)
Walden University (D)
Wayne County Community College (A)
Western Illinois University (M)
Worcester Polytechnic Institute (M, GC)

Business Communications
International University (B, M)
Marywood University (UC)
Old Dominion University (B)
Southwestern Adventist University (B)

Business Information Services
Bellevue University (B)
ISIM University (M)
Nova Southeastern University (M)
Southwestern Adventist University (B)
University of Alaska Southeast, Sitka Campus (A)
University of Great Falls (A, B)
University of Phoenix (B)
University of the State of New York, Regents College (B)
Utah State University (B, M)

Cell and Molecular Biology
Lehigh University (M)

Chemical Engineering
Auburn University (M)
Colorado State University (M)
Illinois Institute of Technology (M)
Kansas State University (M)
Lehigh University (M)
Mississippi State University (M, D)
National Technological University (M, GC)
Oklahoma State University (M)
University of North Dakota (B)
University of South Carolina (M, D)

Chemistry
Illinois Institute of Technology (M)
Lehigh University (M)

Child Care Services
Metropolitan Community College (A)

Civil Engineering
Auburn University (M)
Colorado State University (M)
Kansas State University (M)
Mississippi State University (M, D)
National Technological University (M, GC)
North Dakota State University (M)
The University of Alabama (M)
University of Idaho (M)
University of South Carolina (M, D)
The University of Texas at Arlington (M)
Worcester Polytechnic Institute (GC)

Civil Engineering Technology
Old Dominion University (B)

Clinical Psychology
Fielding Institute (D)
The Union Institute (D)

Communication Disorders Sciences and Services
California State University, Northridge (B)
Texas Woman's University (M)
University of New Hampshire (M)
University of Northern Colorado (M)
University of Wyoming (M)

Communications
Athabasca University (B)
Atlantic Union College (B)
Caldwell College (B)
California State University, Stanislaus (B)
University of Maryland University College (B)
University of Tennessee, Knoxville (M)

Community Health Services
University of Alaska Fairbanks (UC, A)

Index of Institutions Offering Degree and Certificate Programs

Community Organization, Resources and Services
State University of New York Empire State College (A, B)
The University of Calgary (B)

Comparative Literature
City University (B)

Computer and Information Sciences
Athabasca University (B)
Caldwell College (B)
Central Community College–Grand Island Campus (UC, A)
City University (B)
Florida State University (M)
Illinois Institute of Technology (GC)
McGraw-Hill World University (UC)
New Hampshire College (UC)
New York University (GC)
Nova Southeastern University (M)
Rochester Institute of Technology (M)
Saint Mary-of-the-Woods College (B)
Southwestern Adventist University (A, B)
Southwest Missouri State University (M)
University of California Extension (UC)
University of Maryland University College (B)
University of Phoenix (M)
University of the State of New York, Regents College (A, B)

Computer Engineering
Auburn University (M)
Illinois Institute of Technology (GC)
Kansas State University (M)
National Technological University (M, GC)
Rochester Institute of Technology (M)
Southern Methodist University (M)
University of Houston–Clear Lake (M)
University of Idaho (M)
University of Maryland, College Park (M)
University of Missouri–Kansas City (M)
University of South Carolina (M, D)
University of Southern California (M)
The University of Texas at Arlington (M)

Computer Programming
Champlain College (UC, A)
New Jersey Institute of Technology (GC)
Northeastern University (UC)
University of Washington (UC)

Computer Science
Acadia University (UC)
Atlantic Union College (B)
Ball State University (M)
California State University, Chico (M)
Colorado State University (M)
Illinois Institute of Technology (M, GC)
Mercy College (B)
Michigan State University (M)
National Technological University (M, GC)
New Jersey Institute of Technology (B)
Nova Southeastern University (M)
Oklahoma State University (M)
Rensselaer Polytechnic Institute (M)
Rogers University (A)
Southern Polytechnic State University (M)
Southwestern Adventist University (B)
Stanford University (M)
Stevens Institute of Technology (M)
Universitè Laval (UC)
University of California, Santa Barbara (M)
University of Colorado at Boulder (M)
University of Great Falls (B)
University of Houston (M)
University of Idaho (M)
University of Massachusetts Amherst (M)
University of Southern California (M)

Computer Systems Analysis
University of Maryland University College (M)

Computer Technology
University of the State of New York, Regents College (B)

Counseling Psychology
Fielding Institute (GC)
University of Great Falls (M)
University of Sarasota (D)

Criminal Justice and Corrections
Athabasca University (B)
Bellevue University (B)
Bemidji State University (A, B)
Brevard Community College (A)
Caldwell College (B)
Central Missouri State University (UC, M)
Christopher Newport University (UC, B)
City University (B, M)
The College of West Virginia (A, B)
Colorado Northwestern Community College (A)
Judson College (B)
Lake Superior State University (B)
Michigan State University (M)
Old Dominion University (B)
Pennsylvania State University University Park Campus (UC)
Roger Williams University (B)
Salve Regina University (UC)
Sauk Valley Community College (A)
Taylor University, Fort Wayne Campus (UC)
University of Great Falls (A, B)
University of Hawaii–Maui Community College (UC, A)
University of Wyoming (B)
Vincennes University (A)

Criminology
Memorial University of Newfoundland (UC)
New York Institute of Technology (B)

Curriculum and Instruction
City University (M)
College of St. Scholastica (M)
College of the Southwest (M)
University of Nebraska–Lincoln (M, D)
University of Sarasota (D)

Dental Services
Northcentral Technical College (A)
Weber State University (B)

Design and Applied Arts
Atlantic Union College (B)
Syracuse University (M)

Drafting
Brevard Community College (A)
Ivy Tech State College–Wabash Valley (A)
University of Houston (B)

Economics
Eastern Oregon University (B)

Education
Colorado State University (M)
East Carolina University (M)
Fort Hays State University (M)
The Graduate School of America (M, D)
Metropolitan Community College (A)
Mount Saint Vincent University (M)
New Mexico State University (M)
New River Community College (A)
Southwestern Oklahoma State University (M)
Southwest State University (B)
Texas Wesleyan University (M)
The University of Montana–Missoula (M, D)
University of New England (M)
Walden University (D)

Education Administration and Supervision
Ball State University (M)
California State University, Fresno (M)
City University (M)
College of the Southwest (M)
Fielding Institute (D)
Grand Rapids Baptist Seminary (M)
Indiana State University (GC)
Iowa State University of Science and Technology (GC)
Northern Arizona University (M)
Oklahoma State University (GC)
University of Alaska Southeast (M)
The University of Calgary (M)
University of Kentucky (D)
University of Nebraska–Lincoln (M, D)
University of North Dakota (M)
University of Sarasota (D)

Educational Evaluation, Research and Statistics
University of Kentucky (D)

Educational Psychology
City University (M)
State University of New York at Binghamton (M)
University of Alaska Fairbanks (UC, A)

Educational/Instructional Media Design
Athabasca University (M)
Boise State University (M)
City University (M)
The George Washington University (M)
Indiana University System (UC)
Lesley College (M)
Marywood University (GC)

Distance Learning Programs

Index of Institutions Offering Degree and Certificate Programs

Educational/Instructional Media Design (continued)
Nova Southeastern University (M, D)
Rosemont College (GC)
The University of Calgary (M)
Walden University (M)

Electrical and Electronic Engineering-Related Technology
Central Community College–Grand Island Campus (UC)
Old Dominion University (B)
Rochester Institute of Technology (B)
Saint Mary-of-the-Woods College (UC)
Southern Polytechnic State University (M)
University of Houston (B)
University of the State of New York, Regents College (A, B)
Wayne State University (M)

Electrical, Electronics and Communications Engineering
Arizona State University (M)
Bradley University (M)
Brevard Community College (A)
California State University, Fullerton (M)
California State University, Northridge (M)
Colorado State University (M)
Georgia Institute of Technology (M)
Illinois Institute of Technology (M, GC)
Kansas State University (M)
Michigan State University (M)
Mississippi State University (M, D)
National Technological University (M, GC)
Northeastern University (M)
Oklahoma State University (M)
Purdue University (M)
San Jose State University (M)
Southern Illinois University at Carbondale (B)
Stanford University (M)
State University of New York at Buffalo (M, GC)
The University of Alabama (M)
University of California, Santa Barbara (M)
University of Colorado at Boulder (M)
University of Houston (M)
University of Idaho (M)
University of Illinois at Urbana–Champaign (M)
University of Maryland, College Park (M)
University of Massachusetts Amherst (M)
University of Missouri–Kansas City (M)
University of North Dakota (B)
University of South Carolina (M, D)
University of Southern California (M)
The University of Texas at Arlington (M)

Engineering
Capitol College (B)
GMI Engineering & Management Institute (M)
Michigan Technological University (B)
New Mexico State University (M)
North Carolina State University (M)
Northern Virginia Community College (A)
Pennsylvania State University University Park Campus (M)
Stevens Institute of Technology (GC)
Texas Tech University (M)
The University of Alabama (M)
University of Illinois at Urbana–Champaign (M)

University of Kentucky (M)
University of Michigan (M)
University of South Carolina (M, D)
University of South Florida (M)
University of Virginia (M, D)
Virginia Polytechnic Institute and State University (M)
West Virginia University Institute of Technology (B)

Engineering/Industrial Management
California State University, Northridge (B)
Central Missouri State University (M)
City University (M)
Franklin University (B)
GMI Engineering & Management Institute (M)
Indiana State University (M)
Lake Superior State University (B)
Massachusetts Institute of Technology (M)
National Technological University (M, GC)
New Jersey Institute of Technology (M)
Old Dominion University (M)
Rensselaer Polytechnic Institute (M, GC)
Southern Methodist University (M)
Stanford University (M)
The University of Alabama (M)
The University of Alabama in Huntsville (M)
University of Colorado at Boulder (M)
University of Houston (M)
University of Idaho (M)
University of Maryland University College (B, M)
University of Massachusetts Amherst (M)
University of Missouri–Kansas City (M)
University of Phoenix (M)
University of Tennessee, Knoxville (M)

Engineering Science
Rensselaer Polytechnic Institute (M)

Engineering Technology
Chattanooga State Technical Community College (A)
University of North Carolina at Charlotte (B)
Vincennes University (A)

English
Athabasca University (GC)
Atlantic Union College (B)
Caldwell College (B)
Judson College (B)
Saint Mary-of-the-Woods College (B)
Southwestern Adventist University (B)
Stephens College (B)
University of Houston (B)

English as a Second Language
Seattle Central Community College (UC)
University of Saskatchewan (UC)

English Composition
Pennsylvania State University University Park Campus (UC)

English Creative Writing
Goucher College (M)
University of Washington (UC)

Entrepreneurship
Stephens College (M)

Environmental Control Technologies
Brevard Community College (A)
City University (M)
National Technological University (M, GC)
Scott Community College (UC, A)
Southern Methodist University (M)
University of California Extension (GC)

Environmental Engineering
Colorado State University (M)
Georgia Institute of Technology (M)
Illinois Institute of Technology (M)
Old Dominion University (M)
The University of Alabama (M)
The University of Alabama in Huntsville (M)

Environmental Resources Management
California State University, Bakersfield (UC)
Rochester Institute of Technology (UC, B)
Saint Mary-of-the-Woods College (M)

Environmental Studies
The College of West Virginia (A)

Ethnic and Cultural Studies
Institute of Transpersonal Psychology (UC)
Laurentian University (B)
Metropolitan Community College (A)
Saint Joseph's College (UC, B)
Spertus Institute of Jewish Studies (M, D)

Family and Community Studies
Central Michigan University (B)
Metropolitan Community College (A)

Family and Consumer Sciences
Iowa State University of Science and Technology (M)

Family and Individual Development Studies
City University (M)
Pennsylvania State University University Park Campus (UC, A)
Salve Regina University (M)

Financial Management and Services
American College (UC, M)
Black Hawk College (UC, A)
City University (M)
College for Financial Planning (M)
The College of West Virginia (A)
Universitè Laval (UC)
University of the State of New York, Regents College (B)

Fine Arts and Art Studies
Atlantic Union College (B)
Coastline Community College (A)

Index of Institutions Offering Degree and Certificate Programs

Fire Protection
Brevard Community College (A)
California State University, Los Angeles (B)
Chattanooga State Technical Community College (A)
Chemeketa Community College (A)
University of Cincinnati (A, B)
University of Maryland University College (B)
Western Oregon University (UC, B)

Foods and Nutrition Studies
Auburn University (UC)
Bastyr University (UC)
Kansas State University (UC)
Pennsylvania State University University Park Campus (UC, A)
Universitè Laval (UC)
University of Bridgeport (M)
University of Guelph (UC)
University of Northern Colorado (GC)

Foreign Languages and Literatures
Atlantic Union College (B)
Caldwell College (B)

Forestry
Chattanooga State Technical Community College (UC)
Lakehead University (M)

French
Athabasca University (UC)
Mount Saint Vincent University (UC)

Geography
University of Waterloo (B)

Geological Engineering
University of Idaho (M)

Gerontology
Colorado State University (UC)
Mount Saint Vincent University (UC)
Ryerson Polytechnic University (UC)
Saint Mary-of-the-Woods College (UC, A, B)
University of Vermont (UC)

Health and Medical Administrative Services
California College for Health Sciences (A, B)
Catawba Valley Community College (UC)
Central Community College–Grand Island Campus (UC)
Central Michigan University (B)
City University (M)
Clarkson College (M)
The College of West Virginia (B)
Loma Linda University (B)
Madonna University (M)
Ottawa University (B)
Pitt Community College (A)
Rochester Institute of Technology (UC, M, GC)
Saint Joseph's College (UC, B, M, GC)
Stephens College (B, M, GC)
University of Alaska Southeast, Sitka Campus (A)
University of Dallas (M)
University of Great Falls (B)
Virginia Commonwealth University (M)
Weber State University (B)
West Virginia University Institute of Technology (B)

Health and Medical Assistants
The College of West Virginia (A)
Ivy Tech State College–Northcentral (UC)
Portland Community College (UC)
University of Kentucky (B)

Health and Medical Diagnostic and Treatment Services
Allegheny University of the Health Sciences (B)
California College for Health Sciences (A, B)
Chattanooga State Technical Community College (A)
J. Sargeant Reynolds Community College (A)
Lakeshore Technical College (UC)
Pitt Community College (A)
Saint Joseph's College (B)
Thomas Edison State College (A)
Vincennes University (A)
Weber State University (UC, A, B)

Health and Medical Laboratory Technologies
City University (A)
St. Petersburg Junior College (A)
University of Kentucky (B)

Health and Physical Education/Fitness
United States Sports Academy (M)

Health Professions and Sciences
Athabasca University (UC)
California College for Health Sciences (A)
Lakehead University (UC)
Medical University of South Carolina (B)
Old Dominion University (B)
Saint Francis College (M)
Stephens College (B)
Walden University (D)

Historic Preservation, Conservation and Architectural History
Goucher College (M)

History
Atlantic Union College (B)
Bemidji State University (B)
Caldwell College (B)
California State University, Stanislaus (B)
Judson College (B)
Metropolitan Community College (A)
Reformed Theological Seminary (GC)
Southwestern Adventist University (B)

Horticulture Services Operations and Management
University of Georgia (UC)

Hospitality Services Management
Auburn University (M)
The College of West Virginia (UC, A)
Ivy Tech State College–Wabash Valley (A)
Mount Saint Vincent University (B)
New York Institute of Technology (B)
Northern Arizona University (B)
Peoples College (A)
University of Houston (B, M)

Human Resources Management
American College (UC)
Athabasca University (UC)
Cornell University (M)
Indiana State University (B, M)
Indiana University System (UC, A, B)
New Hampshire College (UC)
North Carolina State University (GC)
Ottawa University (M)
Pennsylvania State University University Park Campus (UC)
Saint Mary-of-the-Woods College (B)
University of Delaware (B)
University of Houston (M)
University of Leicester (M)
University of Nebraska–Lincoln (M)
University of the State of New York, Regents College (B)
Upper Iowa University (B)
Utah State University (M)

Human Services
California Institute of Integral Studies (D)
Dawson Community College (A)
The Graduate School of America (M, D)
Old Dominion University (B)
Saint Mary-of-the-Woods College (B)
Thomas Edison State College (B)
University of Alaska Fairbanks (A)
University of Alaska Southeast, Sitka Campus (A)
University of Great Falls (A, B)
University of Sarasota (M, D)
Walden University (D)

Industrial and Organizational Psychology
Fielding Institute (D)

Industrial Production Technologies
East Carolina University (B)
Ivy Tech State College–Wabash Valley (A)
Roger Williams University (B)
University of Massachusetts Lowell (UC)

Industrial/Manufacturing Engineering
Auburn University (M)
Boston University (M)
California State University, Dominguez Hills (M)
Central Community College–Grand Island Campus (UC)
Colorado State University (M)
East Carolina University (M)
Georgia Institute of Technology (M, GC)
Kansas State University (M)
Lehigh University (M)
Mississippi State University (M, D)
National Technological University (M, GC)

Distance Learning Programs

Index of Institutions Offering Degree and Certificate Programs

Industrial/Manufacturing Engineering (continued)
Purdue University (M)
Rensselaer Polytechnic Institute (M, GC)
Rochester Institute of Technology (GC)
San Jose State University (UC)
Southern Polytechnic State University (M)
Stanford University (M)
State University of New York at Buffalo (M)
Stevens Institute of Technology (M)
The University of Alabama in Huntsville (M)
University of Arizona (GC)
University of Maryland, College Park (M)
University of Michigan (M)
University of Nebraska–Lincoln (M)
University of Tennessee, Knoxville (M)
University of Tennessee Space Institute (M)
The University of Texas at Arlington (M)

Information Sciences and Systems
Athabasca University (UC)
City University (M)
Fairleigh Dickinson University, Teaneck–Hackensack (GC)
New Jersey Institute of Technology (B, M)
Northeastern University (M)
Nova Southeastern University (D)
Rensselaer Polytechnic Institute (GC)
Syracuse University (M)
University of Tennessee, Knoxville (M)

Interdisciplinary Studies
Clayton College & State University (A)
The College of West Virginia (B)
The Graduate School of America (M, D)
Liberty University (B)
New York Institute of Technology (B)
State University of New York Empire State College (A, B)
The Union Institute (D)

International Business
Bellevue University (B)
Brevard Community College (A)
Caldwell College (B)
Christopher Newport University (B)
City University (A)
University of Phoenix (M)
University of the State of New York, Regents College (B)

International Relations and Affairs
Salve Regina University (M)
Southwestern Adventist University (B)

Internet and World Wide Web
McGraw-Hill World University (UC)

Japanese
National Technological University (GC)

Journalism and Mass Communications
City University (B)
Mississippi State University (UC)
Saint Mary-of-the-Woods College (B)
Southwestern Adventist University (B)
The University of Memphis (M)
University of Nebraska–Lincoln (M)

Law and Legal Studies
Black Hawk College (A)
Brevard Community College (A)
Christopher Newport University (B)
The College of West Virginia (A)
Ivy Tech State College–Northcentral (UC)
Pennsylvania State University University Park Campus (UC)
Saint Mary-of-the-Woods College (UC, A, B)
University of Great Falls (A, B)
University of Maryland University College (B)
University of Southern Colorado (UC)

Liberal Arts and Sciences, General Studies and Humanities
Athabasca University (B)
Atlantic Community College (A)
Ball State University (A)
Bellevue Community College (A)
Bemidji State University (A)
Bluefield State College (A)
Brevard Community College (A)
Brookdale Community College (A)
Bucks County Community College (A)
Burlington County College (A)
California State University, Chico (B)
California State University, Dominguez Hills (M)
California State University, Fresno (B)
Central Community College–Grand Island Campus (A)
Central Wyoming College (A)
Charles County Community College (A)
Charles Stewart Mott Community College (A)
Chemeketa Community College (A)
City University (A, B, M)
Coastline Community College (A)
The College of West Virginia (A)
Colorado Electronic Community College (A)
County College of Morris (A)
Cumberland County College (A)
Cuyahoga Community College, Metropolitan Campus (A)
Dallas County Community College District (A)
Daytona Beach Community College (A)
De Anza College (A)
Delta College (A)
DePaul University (B)
Eastern New Mexico University (B)
Eastern Oregon University (B)
Edison Community College (A)
Fort Hays State University (B)
Gadsden State Community College (A)
Galveston College (A)
Governors State University (B)
Greenville Technical College (A)
Hawkeye Community College (A)
Howard Community College (A)
Indiana University System (A, B)
Iowa Western Community College (A)
Jacksonville State University (A)
Lakehead University (B)
Lane Community College (A)
Laurentian University (B, M)
Lesley College (M, GC)
Liberty University (B)
Longview Community College (A)
Louisiana College (B)
Luzerne County Community College (A)
The McGregor School of Antioch University (M)
Mercy College (A)
Metropolitan Community College (A, A)
Milwaukee Area Technical College (A)
Minnesota West Community and Technical College–Worthington Campus (A)
Morgan Community College (A)
Mountain View College (A)
New River Community College (A)
New School for Social Research (B)
Northeast Louisiana University (A)
Northern Arizona University (B)
Northern Virginia Community College (A)
Oakland University (B)
Ohio University (A, B)
Oklahoma City Community College (A)
Oral Roberts University (B)
Oregon State University (B)
Pennsylvania State University University Park Campus (A)
Penn Valley Community College (A)
Pierce College (A)
Portland Community College (A)
Prince George's Community College (A)
Rio Salado College (A)
Rochester Institute of Technology (B)
Rockland Community College (A)
Rogers University (A)
Saint Mary-of-the-Woods College (A, B)
Salve Regina University (B)
Scott Community College (A)
Seattle Central Community College (A)
Sinclair Community College (A)
Skagit Valley College (A)
Skidmore College (B)
Southeast Community College, Lincoln Campus (A)
Syracuse University (A, B)
Tallahassee Community College (A)
Tarrant County Junior College (A)
Thomas Edison State College (A, B)
Troy State University Montgomery (A)
Tulsa Community College (A)
The Union Institute (B)
University of Alaska Anchorage (A)
University of Alaska Fairbanks (A)
University of Alaska Southeast, Sitka Campus (A)
University of Hawaii–Maui Community College (A)
The University of Iowa (B)
University of Kentucky, Ashland Community College (A)
University of Maine (B)
University of Maine at Augusta (A)
University of Maryland University College (B)
University of Minnesota, Twin Cities Campus (UC)
University of Missouri–Kansas City (A)
University of Nevada, Reno (B)
University of Northern Iowa (B)
University of South Florida (B)
University of the State of New York, Regents College (A, B)
University of Waterloo (B)
University of Windsor (B)
Upper Iowa University (A)
Vincennes University (A)
Wayne County Community College (A)

Index of Institutions Offering Degree and Certificate Programs

Western Illinois University (B)
Western Oklahoma State College (A)

Library Assistant
Northampton County Area Community College (UC)
Rose State College (UC, A)

Library Science/Librarianship
Indiana University System (GC)
Memorial University of Newfoundland (UC)
Syracuse University (M)
Texas Woman's University (M)
University of Illinois at Urbana–Champaign (M)
University of Maine at Augusta (A)
University of South Carolina (M)
The University of Texas at El Paso (M)

Marketing Management and Research
Brevard Community College (A)
Caldwell College (B)
City University (B, M)
Northwestern College (A)
Pennsylvania State University University Park Campus (UC)
Saint Mary-of-the-Woods College (B)
University of the State of New York, Regents College (B)
Upper Iowa University (B)

Marketing Operations
Hibbing Community College (A)

Materials Engineering
Auburn University (M)
National Technological University (M, GC)

Mathematics
City University (B)
Saint Mary-of-the-Woods College (B)
Southwestern Adventist University (B)

Mechanical Engineering
Auburn University (M)
Bradley University (M)
California State University, Northridge (M)
Colorado State University (M)
Georgia Institute of Technology (M)
Michigan State University (M)
Michigan Technological University (D)
Mississippi State University (M, D)
Oklahoma State University (M)
Purdue University (M)
Rensselaer Polytechnic Institute (M, GC)
Stanford University (M)
The University of Alabama (M)
University of Idaho (M)
University of Illinois at Urbana–Champaign (M)
University of Maryland, College Park (M)
University of North Dakota (B)
University of South Carolina (M, D)

Mechanical Engineering Technology
Old Dominion University (B)

Mental Health Services
City University (M)
Metropolitan Community College (UC, A)
New York Institute of Technology (B)
University of Great Falls (A)
University of Sarasota (M)

Metallurgical Engineering
University of Idaho (M)

Military Studies
American Military University (B, M)

Mining Engineering
University of Idaho (M)
University of Kentucky (M)

Miscellaneous Health Professions
Clarkson College (B)

Missions/Missionary Studies and Missiology
Berean University of the Assemblies of God (B)
Grand Rapids Baptist Seminary (M)
Reformed Theological Seminary (GC)

Music
Judson College (B)

Neuropsychology
Fielding Institute (GC)

Nuclear and Industrial Radiologic Technologies
University of the State of New York, Regents College (A, B)

Nursing
Athabasca University (UC, B)
Ball State University (B)
Black Hawk College (UC)
California State University, Dominguez Hills (B)
California State University, Fullerton (B)
California State University, Sacramento (M)
Chippewa Valley Technical College (GC)
Clarkson College (B, M, GC)
The College of West Virginia (B)
DePaul University (B, M, GC)
Eastern New Mexico University (B)
Fort Hays State University (B)
Holy Names College (B)
Indiana University System (M)
Jackson Community College (M)
Lakehead University (B)
Lakeshore Technical College (UC)
Lake Superior State University (B)
Laurentian University (B)
Loyola University New Orleans (B)
Michigan State University (B, M)
Mississippi University for Women (B)
Northcentral Technical College (A)
North Dakota State College of Science (A)
Old Dominion University (B, M)
Pennsylvania State University University Park Campus (UC)
St. Cloud Technical College (A)
Saint Francis College (M)
Saint Joseph's College (B, M)
Salve Regina University (B)
Southern Illinois University at Edwardsville (B)
State University of New York at Buffalo (M)
State University of New York College at Plattsburgh (B)
Syracuse University (M)
Texas A&M University–Corpus Christi (M)
Thomas Edison State College (B)
The University of Calgary (B)
University of Cincinnati (B, M)
University of Delaware (B)
University of Kentucky (M)
University of Missouri–Kansas City (M)
University of New Brunswick (B, M)
University of North Dakota (M)
University of Pennsylvania (M)
University of South Florida (B)
The University of Texas at Tyler (B)
University of the State of New York, Regents College (A, B)
University of Wisconsin–Eau Claire (B)
University of Wisconsin–Madison (B)
University of Wyoming (B)
West Virginia University (M)
West Virginia Wesleyan College (B)

Ophthalmic/Optometric Services
J. Sargeant Reynolds Community College (A)

Parks, Recreation, Leisure and Fitness Studies
Eastern Maine Technical College (UC)

Pastoral Counseling and Specialized Ministries
Berean University of the Assemblies of God (B, M)
Oral Roberts University (B)

Pharmacy
The University of Montana–Missoula (D)
University of Washington (D)

Philosophy
Atlantic Union College (B)
Christopher Newport University (B)
City University (B)
Eastern Oregon University (B)
Stephens College (B)

Physical Sciences
University of North Dakota (M)

Plant Sciences
University of Saskatchewan (UC)

Political Science and Government
Caldwell College (B)
California State University, Chico (B)
City University (B)
Eastern Oregon University (B)
Metropolitan Community College (A)

Distance Learning Programs

Index of Institutions Offering Degree and Certificate Programs

Professional Studies
Champlain College (B)
Metropolitan Community College (A)
Saint Joseph's College (UC, B)
Southwestern Assemblies of God University (B)
Troy State University Montgomery (B)

Psychology
Atlantic Union College (B)
Caldwell College (B)
City University (B, M)
Institute of Transpersonal Psychology (UC, M, GC)
Judson College (B)
Laurentian University (B)
Liberty University (B)
Mercy College (B)
Metropolitan Community College (A)
New York Institute of Technology (B)
Saint Mary-of-the-Woods College (B)
Southwestern Adventist University (B)
Stephens College (B)
University of Houston (B)
University of Idaho (M)
University of Maine at Machias (B)
University of Wyoming (B)
Utah State University (B)
Vincennes University (A)
Walden University (D)

Public Administration
Athabasca University (UC)
Christopher Newport University (B)
City University (M)
Iowa State University of Science and Technology (GC)
Lake Superior State University (M)
Memorial University of Newfoundland (UC)
Roger Williams University (B)
Ryerson Polytechnic University (UC)
University of Alaska Southeast (M)
University of Colorado at Colorado Springs (M)
University of North Dakota (M)
University of Wyoming (M)
Upper Iowa University (B)

Public Administration and Services
Chattanooga State Technical Community College (A)
The McGregor School of Antioch University (M)
Memorial University of Newfoundland (UC)
Rochester Institute of Technology (UC)
Thomas Edison State College (A)
University of Alaska Fairbanks (B)

Public Health
California College for Health Sciences (M)
Georgia Institute of Technology (M)
Johns Hopkins University (GC)
Loma Linda University (B)
National Technological University (M, GC)
Ryerson Polytechnic University (UC)
University of South Florida (M)
The University of Texas at El Paso (M)
University of Washington (GC)

Quality Control and Safety Technologies
Scott Community College (A)

Radio and Television Broadcasting
Brevard Community College (A)

Rehabilitation/Therapeutic Services
City University (M)
Indiana University System (M)
University of Kentucky (M)
University of St. Augustine for Health Sciences (M, D)

Religious Education
Berean University of the Assemblies of God (B)
Grand Rapids Baptist Seminary (M)
Griggs University (B)
North Central Bible College (UC, A, B)
Temple Baptist Seminary (M)

Religious Studies
Caldwell College (B)
Christopher Newport University (B)
Griggs University (B)
Judson College (B)
Laurentian University (B)
Liberty University (B, M)
Metropolitan Community College (A)
Southwestern Adventist University (B)
Trinity International University (M)
University of Great Falls (B)

School Psychology
City University (M)

Security Administration
City University (B)

Social Sciences
Bemidji State University (B)
California State University, Chico (B)
Kansas State University (B)
Ohio University (A)
Southwestern Adventist University (B)
Syracuse University (M)
University of Maryland University College (B)
University of Southern Colorado (B)
University of Waterloo (B)
University of Wyoming (B)
Upper Iowa University (B)
Vincennes University (A)
Washington State University (B)

Social Work
California State University, Dominguez Hills (M)
California State University, Long Beach (M)
Cleveland State University (M)
Laurentian University (B)
Madonna University (B)
The McGregor School of Antioch University (M)
Michigan State University (M)
Portland State University (M)
University of Alaska Fairbanks (B)
University of Louisville (D)
University of Maine at Augusta (A)
University of Tennessee, Knoxville (M)

Sociology
Caldwell College (B)
California State University, Chico (B)
City University (B)
Laurentian University (B)
Metropolitan Community College (A)
New York Institute of Technology (B)
Pennsylvania State University University Park Campus (A)
University of Great Falls (B)
Wilfrid Laurier University (B)

Special Education
Ball State University (M)
California State University, Northridge (B)
City University (M)
Eastern New Mexico University (M)
Northcentral Technical College (A)
Northern Arizona University (B, M)
Old Dominion University (M)
Saint Mary-of-the-Woods College (B)
Southern Oregon University (M, GC)
University of Kentucky (M)
University of Louisville (M)
University of Nebraska–Lincoln (M)
University of North Carolina at Charlotte (M)
West Virginia University (M)

Speech and Rhetorical Studies
Stephens College (B)

Statistics
Colorado State University (M)

Student Counseling and Personnel Services
Athabasca University (UC)
City University (M)
Liberty University (M)
McGraw-Hill World University (GC)
Mississippi State University (M)
Northern Arizona University (M)
Southern Christian University (M)
Stephens College (M)
University of Sarasota (M)

Surveying
Michigan Technological University (B)
University of Wyoming (UC)

Systems Engineering
Colorado State University (M)
Iowa State University of Science and Technology (M)
Southern Methodist University (M)
University of Maryland, College Park (M)

Taxation
McGraw-Hill World University (GC)

Teacher Assistant/Aide
The University of Calgary (UC)

Index of Institutions Offering Degree and Certificate Programs

Teacher Education
Atlantic Union College (B)
Ball State University (M)
Brock University (UC, B)
California College for Health Sciences (A)
California State University, Long Beach (B)
Central Washington University (UC, B)
The College of West Virginia (A)
Colorado State University (M)
Fitchburg State College (M)
Fort Hays State University (B)
Grand Canyon University (M)
Indiana University System (M)
Iowa State University of Science and Technology (M)
Marygrove College (M)
Montana State University–Bozeman (M)
Northampton County Area Community College (UC)
Northern Arizona University (B, M)
Oklahoma State University (M)
Old Dominion University (B, M)
Oral Roberts University (B)
Pennsylvania State University University Park Campus (M)
Saint Mary-of-the-Woods College (A, B)
Southern Oregon University (M, GC)
Southwestern Adventist University (B)
University of Alaska Southeast, Sitka Campus (UC, A)
The University of Calgary (M)
University of Colorado at Colorado Springs (UC)
University of Idaho (M)
University of Nebraska–Lincoln (M)
University of Nevada, Reno (UC, M)
University of Pittsburgh (M)
University of Saskatchewan (UC)
Utah State University (B)

Teaching English as a Second Language
City University (M)
The University of Calgary (M)
University of Northern Colorado (GC)

Technical and Business Writing
Judson College (B)
Rensselaer Polytechnic Institute (M, GC)

Telecommunications
City University (M)
Illinois Institute of Technology (GC)
Michigan State University (M)
New Jersey Institute of Technology (GC)
New York Institute of Technology (B)
Oklahoma State University (M)
Rochester Institute of Technology (UC)
Southern Methodist University (M)
Stevens Institute of Technology (GC)
Syracuse University (M)
University of Colorado at Boulder (M)

Textile Studies
North Carolina State University (M, GC)

Theological and Ministerial Studies
Assemblies of God Theological Seminary (M)
Berean University of the Assemblies of God (UC, A, B, M)
Bethel Theological Seminary (M)
Covenant Theological Seminary (M, GC)
Grand Rapids Baptist Seminary (M)
Griggs University (A, B)
International Bible College (B)
Judson College (B)
Lincoln Christian College (UC)
North Central Bible College (UC, A, B)
Northwestern College (B)
Oral Roberts University (UC, B)
Reformed Theological Seminary (GC)
Saint Joseph's College (UC, B)
Saint Mary-of-the-Woods College (UC, B, M)
Southern Christian University (M)
Southwestern Adventist University (B)
Southwestern Assemblies of God University (B)
Taylor University, Fort Wayne Campus (UC)
Temple Baptist Seminary (M, D)
Western Conservative Baptist Seminary (GC)

Visual and Performing Arts, Other
Institute of Transpersonal Psychology (UC)

Distance Learning Programs

STUDENT PROFILE

Gregory Hotchkiss

Personal: Age 42, married with two teenagers

Home: Somerville, NJ

College: Thomas Edison State College

Courses Taken: Computers in society, sociology, religious quest, major philosophers

Academic/Professional Goals: Completed B.A. degree in Religion, a prerequisite for the Master of Divinity from the Philadelphia Theological Seminary that he received in September 1996 and for admission to Princeton's Master of Theology program.

"I am a minister in the Reformed Episcopal Church, which does not require an undergraduate degree if you pass the church exams. But since I was to be made Assistant Bishop, I felt it was important to get my academic credentials in line. Distance learning enabled me to complete several courses in a relatively short amount of time through a program that is really supportive of the family. I could plug into the computer after the kids had gone to bed and still keep commitments to attend their sports and music events.

"I've taken courses on campus, through correspondence study and through electronic distance learning. I found the distance learning experience more enjoyable than independent study because the interaction with classmates on-line prevents you from feeling that you are all alone with your studies. Although taking a course on-line was foreboding at first, I found the group discussions to be even better than those in campus classrooms. Many people who are intimidated to speak up in a classroom of 300 students do not feel that way on-line. This freedom to express yourself helps to create special bonds and friendships between you and you on-line classmates."

INDIVIDUAL COURSES INDEX

Index of individual courses offered by institutions, arranged by subject.
U=Undergraduate; G=Graduate; NC=noncredit

Abnormal Psychology
Brigham Young University (U)
Bucks County Community College (U)
Carleton University (U)
Catonsville Community College (U)
Central Piedmont Community College (U)
Clark State Community College (U)
College of St. Scholastica (U, G)
Colorado Mountain College District (U)
Colorado State University (U)
Columbia Basin College (U)
De Anza College (U)
Delta College (U)
Eastern Washington University (U)
Genesee Community College (U)
The Graduate School of America (G)
Harrisburg Area Community College (U)
J. Sargeant Reynolds Community College (U)
Kansas State University (U, NC)
Lane Community College (U)
McDowell Technical Community College (U)
Mercy College (U)
Moraine Valley Community College (U)
New Hampshire College (U)
New River Community College (U)
Palomar College (U)
Pierce College (U)
Rockland Community College (U)
Seattle Central Community College (U)
Sinclair Community College (U)
Southwest Texas State University (U)
State University of New York at Oswego (G)
State University of New York Empire State College (U)
Tacoma Community College (U)
Taylor University, Fort Wayne Campus (U)
University of Alaska Fairbanks (U)
University of Houston–Clear Lake (G)
University of Illinois at Urbana–Champaign (U)
University of Missouri–Columbia (U)
University of South Dakota (U)
University of Tennessee, Knoxville (U)
University of Waterloo (U)
Upper Iowa University (U)
Wilfrid Laurier University (U)

Accounting
Adams State College (U)
Allegany College of Maryland (U)
Anne Arundel Community College (U)
Athabasca University (U)
Atlantic Community College (U)
Austin Community College (U)
Baker College (U, G, NC)
Ball State University (U, G)
Beaufort County Community College (U)
Black Hills State University (U)
Boise State University (U)
Brevard Community College (U)
Brigham Young University (U)
Broward Community College (U)
Bucks County Community College (U)
Buena Vista University (U)
Cabrillo College (U)
California State University, Bakersfield (G)
California State University, Fullerton (G)
California State University, Hayward (U)
California State University, Los Angeles (U, NC)
California State University, Stanislaus (U, G)
Carleton University (U)
Carl Sandburg College (U)
Catonsville Community College (U)
Central Community College–Grand Island Campus (U)
Central Michigan University (U)
Central Piedmont Community College (U)
Central Wyoming College (U)
Century Community and Technical College (NC)
Chadron State College (U, G)
Champlain College (U)
Charles County Community College (U)
Chattanooga State Technical Community College (U)
Chemeketa Community College (U)
Chesapeake College (U)
Chippewa Valley Technical College (U)
Christopher Newport University (U)
City Colleges of Chicago, Harold Washington College (U)
City University (U)
Clarkson College (U)
Colby Community College (U)
College for Financial Planning (U)
College of DuPage (U)
College of St. Scholastica (U, G)
College of the Southwest (U)
The College of West Virginia (U)
Collin County Community College (U)
Colorado Mountain College District (U)
Colorado Northwestern Community College (U)
Colorado State University (G)
Columbia Basin College (U)
Columbia State Community College (U)
Columbus State Community College (U)
Concordia University (U)
Cornell University (U)
Corning Community College (U)
Cosumnes River College (U)
Cuyahoga Community College, Metropolitan Campus (U)
Dallas County Community College District (U)
Danville Area Community College (U)
Danville Community College (U)
David N. Myers College (U)
De Anza College (U)
DePaul University (G)
Des Moines Area Community College (U)
Drake University (G)
Duke University (G)
Dutchess Community College (U)
Eastern Idaho Technical College (U)
Eastern New Mexico University (U, G)
Eastern Oregon University (U)
Eastern Washington University (U)
Edmonds Community College (U)
El Paso Community College (U)
Embry-Riddle Aeronautical University, Extended Campus (U)
Evergreen Valley College (U)
Fairleigh Dickinson University, Teaneck–Hackensack (G)
Fayetteville Technical Community College (U)
Florida Community College at Jacksonville (U)
Fort Hays State University (U)
Frostburg State University (U, G)
Garland County Community College (U)
Gateway Technical College (U)
Genesee Community College (U)
Georgia Southern University (U, G)
GMI Engineering & Management Institute (G)
Graceland College (U)
The Graduate School of America (G)
Grand Valley State University (U, G)
Greenville Technical College (U)
Hampton University (U)
Harrisburg Area Community College (U)
Heriot-Watt University (G)
Houston Community College System (U)
Howard Community College (U)
Idaho State University (U, G)
Illinois Central College (U)
Illinois Eastern Community Colleges, Olney Central College (U)
Illinois Valley Community College (U)
Indiana University System (U)
Iowa Western Community College (U)
ISIM University (G)
Ivy Tech State College–Wabash Valley (U)
Jamestown Community College (U)
Jefferson Davis Community College (U)

Distance Learning Programs

Individual Courses Index

Accounting (continued)

John A. Logan College (U)
Johnson County Community College (U)
J. Sargeant Reynolds Community College (U)
Kellogg Community College (U)
Kingwood College (U)
Lake Michigan College (U)
Lake Superior State University (U)
Lansing Community College (U)
Lassen College (U)
Laurentian University (U, G)
Lawson State Community College (U)
Lee College (U)
Lehigh Carbon Community College (U)
Liberty University (U)
Longview Community College (U)
Lorain County Community College (U)
Lycoming College (U)
Madison Area Technical College (U)
Marshall University (U)
Marywood University (U)
McCook Community College (U)
McGraw-Hill World University (U)
Memorial University of Newfoundland (U)
Mercy College (U)
Metropolitan Community College (U)
Metropolitan State College of Denver (U)
Michigan State University (U)
Middle Tennessee State University (U)
Midland College (U)
Milwaukee Area Technical College (U)
Milwaukee School of Engineering (G, NC)
Minot State University (U)
Missouri Southern State College (U)
Modesto Junior College (U)
Mohawk Valley Community College (U)
Montgomery County Community College (U)
Morehead State University (U, G)
Mountain View College (U)
Mount Saint Vincent University (U)
National Technological University (G)
New Hampshire College (U)
New Mexico Junior College (U)
New Mexico State University (U, G)
New River Community College (U)
New School for Social Research (U, NC)
New York Institute of Technology (U)
North Carolina State University (U)
Northcentral Technical College (U)
Northeast Community College (U)
Northeastern University (NC)
Northern Arizona University (U)
Northern Oklahoma College (U)
Northern Virginia Community College (U)
North Harris College (U)
North Seattle Community College (U)
Northwestern College (U)
Northwestern Michigan College (U)
NRI Schools (NC)
Oakton Community College (U)
Ohio University (U)
Ohio University–Southern Campus (U)
Oklahoma State University (U)
Owens Community College (U)
Palomar College (U)
Pennsylvania State University University Park Campus (U)
Penn Valley Community College (U)
Phillips Community College of the University of Arkansas (U)

Pikes Peak Community College (U, NC)
Pine Technical College (U)
Portland Community College (U)
Portland State University (U)
Pratt Community College and Area Vocational School (U)
Prince George's Community College (U)
Pueblo Community College (U)
Red Rocks Community College (U)
Regent University (G)
Regis University (U)
Rend Lake College (G)
Rensselaer Polytechnic Institute (G, NC)
Richland Community College (U)
Rio Salado College (U)
Rochester Institute of Technology (U)
Rockland Community College (U)
Rogers University (U)
Roger Williams University (U)
Roosevelt University (U)
St. Cloud Technical College (U)
Saint Joseph's College (U)
St. Louis Community College (U)
St. Petersburg Junior College (U)
Salt Lake Community College (U)
Salve Regina University (G, NC)
San Joaquin Delta College (U)
San Jose State University (U)
Santa Fe Community College (U)
Santa Rosa Junior College (U)
Sauk Valley Community College (U)
Seattle Central Community College (U)
Sinclair Community College (U)
Skidmore College (U)
Southeast Community College, Beatrice Campus (U)
Southeast Community College, Lincoln Campus (U)
Southern Illinois University at Carbondale (U)
Southern Vermont College (U)
Southwestern Assemblies of God University (U)
Southwest Missouri State University (U)
Southwest State University (U)
Southwest Virginia Community College (U)
State Technical Institute at Memphis (U)
State University of New York Empire State College (U)
State University of West Georgia (U, G)
Stephens College (U)
Strayer College (G)
Suffolk County Community College–Ammerman Campus (U)
Syracuse University (U)
Tallahassee Community College (U)
Tennessee State University (G)
Tennessee Technological University (U, G)
Texas Tech University (U)
Thomas Edison State College (U)
Tidewater Community College (U)
Trinity College of Vermont (U, NC)
Troy State University Montgomery (U)
Tulsa Community College (U)
Universitè Laval (U)
The University of Alabama (G)
The University of Alabama in Huntsville (G)
University of Alaska Anchorage (U)
University of Alaska Fairbanks (U)
University of Alaska Southeast, Sitka Campus (U)
University of Baltimore (G)

University of California Extension (U)
University of California, Santa Barbara (NC)
University of Dallas (G)
University of Georgia (U)
University of Great Falls (U)
University of Hawaii–Maui Community College (U)
University of Houston (G)
University of Illinois at Springfield (U, G)
University of Illinois at Urbana–Champaign (U)
University of Maine at Augusta (U)
University of Maine at Fort Kent (U)
University of Maryland University College (U)
University of Minnesota, Twin Cities Campus (U)
University of Missouri–Columbia (U)
University of Missouri–Kansas City (U)
University of Nebraska at Kearney (U)
University of Nebraska–Lincoln (U, G)
University of Nevada, Reno (U, G)
University of New Brunswick (U)
The University of North Carolina at Chapel Hill (U)
University of North Dakota (U)
University of Northern Iowa (U)
University of Notre Dame (NC)
University of Oklahoma (U)
University of Phoenix (U, G)
University of St. Thomas (G)
University of South Carolina (U, G)
University of South Dakota (G)
University of Southern Colorado (U)
University of Southern Mississippi (U)
University of South Florida (G)
The University of Tennessee at Martin (U, G)
University of Tennessee, Knoxville (U)
The University of Texas at San Antonio (U)
The University of Texas at Tyler (U, G)
University of the State of New York, Regents College (U)
University of Washington (U)
University of Windsor (U)
University of Wisconsin–Eau Claire (U)
University of Wisconsin–Extension (U, NC)
University of Wisconsin–Platteville (U)
University of Wyoming (U)
University System of Georgia (U)
Upper Iowa University (U)
Utah State University (U)
Utah Valley State College (U)
Valley City State University (U)
Vincennes University (U)
Volunteer State Community College (U)
Washington State University (U)
Waubonsee Community College (U)
Waukesha County Technical College (U)
Wayne County Community College (U)
Weber State University (U)
Western Illinois University (U, G)
West Virginia University Institute of Technology (U)
West Virginia Wesleyan College (U)
Wilfrid Laurier University (U)
William Rainey Harper College (U)
Wilson Technical Community College (U)
Winthrop University (G)
Worcester Polytechnic Institute (G)
Wytheville Community College (U)
York Technical College (U)

Individual Courses Index

Administrative and Secretarial Services
Allegany College of Maryland (U, NC)
Austin Community College (U)
Baker College (U, G)
Ball State University (U, G)
Black Hawk College (U)
Blackhawk Technical College (U)
Brevard Community College (U)
Burlington County College (U)
Carl Sandburg College (U)
Central Community College–Grand Island Campus (U)
Central Piedmont Community College (U)
Chadron State College (U, G)
Charles County Community College (U)
Charles Stewart Mott Community College (U)
Chemeketa Community College (U)
Chippewa Valley Technical College (NC)
Cleary College (U)
Colby Community College (U)
The College of West Virginia (U)
Columbia State Community College (U)
Dawson Community College (U)
Daytona Beach Community College (U)
Des Moines Area Community College (U)
Drake University (G)
Eastern Oregon University (U)
Florida Community College at Jacksonville (U)
Garland County Community College (U)
Genesee Community College (U)
Hampton University (NC)
Idaho State University (U, G)
Illinois Eastern Community Colleges, Olney Central College (U)
Illinois Valley Community College (U)
Ivy Tech State College–Northcentral (U)
Ivy Tech State College–Wabash Valley (U)
Jefferson Davis Community College (U)
Kingwood College (U)
Marshall University (U)
Memorial University of Newfoundland (U)
Mendocino College (U)
Midland College (U)
Mid-State Technical College (U)
Morehead State University (U, G)
Mount Saint Vincent University (U)
New River Community College (U)
Northcentral Technical College (U)
Northeast Community College (U)
Northern Virginia Community College (U)
North Harris College (U)
Northwestern College (U)
NRI Schools (NC)
Pikes Peak Community College (U, NC)
Portland Community College (NC)
Regis University (U)
St. Cloud Technical College (U)
St. Louis Community College (U)
Santa Rosa Junior College (U)
Southern Arkansas University Tech (U)
Southern Illinois University at Carbondale (U)
Southern Utah University (U)
Southwest State University (U)
State University of New York Empire State College (U)
State University of West Georgia (U)
Technical College of the Lowcountry (U)
University of Alaska Fairbanks (U)
University of Alaska Southeast, Sitka Campus (U)
University of California Extension (U)
University of Georgia (U)
University of Hawaii–Leeward Community College (U)
University of Hawaii–Maui Community College (U)
University of Nebraska at Kearney (U)
University of Nebraska–Lincoln (U, G)
The University of Texas at San Antonio (NC)
University System of Georgia (U)
Utah Valley State College (U)
Volunteer State Community College (U)
Western Illinois University (U, G)
William Rainey Harper College (U)
Wilson Technical Community College (U)
York Technical College (U)

Adult Education
Eastern Idaho Technical College (U)
The Graduate School of America (G)
Indiana University System (G)
Iowa State University of Science and Technology (G)
Lincoln Christian College (U, NC)
Louisiana State University at Eunice (U, G)
Michigan State University (G)
Northern Illinois University (G)
Pratt Community College and Area Vocational School (U)
Rutgers, The State University of New Jersey, Newark (G, NC)
Universitè Laval (U)
The University of Alabama at Birmingham (G)
University of Alberta (G)
University of Arkansas at Little Rock (U)
University of Missouri–Columbia (G)

Advertising
Arizona State University (U)
Ball State University (U)
Brevard Community College (U)
Bucks County Community College (U)
California State University, Fullerton (U)
Catawba Valley Community College (U)
Central Community College–Grand Island Campus (U)
Central Missouri State University (U)
Champlain College (U)
Charles Stewart Mott Community College (U)
Chattanooga State Technical Community College (U)
College of the Southwest (U)
The College of West Virginia (U)
De Anza College (U)
Delaware Technical & Community College, Stanton/Wilmington Campus (U)
Illinois Central College (U)
Illinois Valley Community College (U)
Ivy Tech State College–Northcentral (U)
Jackson Community College (U)
Laurentian University (G)
Lincoln Land Community College (U)
Luzerne County Community College (U)
Marywood University (U, G)
The McGregor School of Antioch University (G)
Michigan State University (G)
Minot State University (U)
Mount Saint Vincent University (U)
New Hampshire College (U)
Northeast Wisconsin Technical College (U)
Northern Arizona University (U)
Northern Virginia Community College (U)
Northwestern College (U)
Northwestern State University of Louisiana (NC)
Polytechnic University, Brooklyn Campus (G, NC)
Rutgers, The State University of New Jersey, Newark (U)
Southwest State University (U)
Tallahassee Community College (U)
Universitè Laval (U)
The University of Alabama (G)
The University of Alabama at Birmingham (G)
University of Alaska Fairbanks (U)
University of Georgia (U)
University of Illinois at Urbana–Champaign (U)
University of Missouri–Columbia (U, G)
University of Nebraska at Kearney (U, G)
University of Oklahoma (U)
University of Southern Indiana (U)
University of West Florida (U)
University System of Georgia (U)

Aerospace, Aeronautical Engineering
Arizona State University (U, G)
California State University, Northridge (U, G)
Georgia Institute of Technology (G, NC)
Illinois Institute of Technology (U, G)
Iowa State University of Science and Technology (G)
Mississippi State University (G)
National Technological University (G, NC)
North Carolina State University (G)
Old Dominion University (G)
Shenandoah University (G)
Southwest Virginia Community College (U)
Stanford University (G, NC)
State University of New York at Buffalo (G)
The University of Alabama (G)
University of Arizona (G)
University of Colorado at Boulder (G, NC)
University of Delaware (G)
University of Oklahoma (G)
University of Southern California (G, NC)
University of Tennessee Space Institute (G)
The University of Texas at Arlington (G)
University of Virginia (G)

African-American Studies
Catonsville Community College (U)
Cuyahoga Community College, Metropolitan Campus (U)
De Anza College (U)
Eastern Washington University (U)
Indiana University System (U)
Metropolitan Community College (U)
Modesto Junior College (U)
The Ohio State University (U, G)
Penn Valley Community College (U)
Pitt Community College (U, NC)
Thomas Edison State College (U)
The University of Iowa (U, G)
University of Missouri–Columbia (U)
The University of North Carolina at Chapel Hill (U)
Western Michigan University (U)

Distance Learning Programs

Individual Courses Index

Agricultural Economics
Iowa State University of Science and Technology (U, G)
Oklahoma State University (U)
Pratt Community College and Area Vocational School (U)
Southern Illinois University at Carbondale (U)
Southwest Texas State University (U)
Texas Tech University (U, NC)
University of Illinois at Urbana–Champaign (U)
University of Tennessee, Knoxville (U)

Agriculture
Bakersfield College (U)
Black Hawk College (U)
Butte College (U)
Carl Sandburg College (U)
Central Community College–Grand Island Campus (U)
Chadron State College (U)
Chattanooga State Technical Community College (U)
Chippewa Valley Technical College (NC)
Colby Community College (U)
Colorado State University (U, G)
Copiah-Lincoln Community College (NC)
Dawson Community College (U, NC)
Dodge City Community College (U)
Eastern Oregon University (U)
Ellsworth Community College (U, NC)
Fort Hays State University (U)
Garrett Community College (U, NC)
Hawkeye Community College (U)
Iowa State University of Science and Technology (U, G)
Joliet Junior College (U)
Kansas State University (U, G, NC)
Kaskaskia College (U, NC)
Louisiana State University and Agricultural and Mechanical College (G)
The McGregor School of Antioch University (G)
Michigan State University (U)
Mississippi State University (G)
Missouri Western State College (G)
Modesto Junior College (U)
North Carolina State University (U)
Northcentral Technical College (U)
North Dakota State University (G)
Northeast Community College (U)
Northeast Wisconsin Technical College (U)
Northwest Iowa Community College (U, G, NC)
Oklahoma State University (U, G)
Pennsylvania State University University Park Campus (U, NC)
Pratt Community College and Area Vocational School (U)
Purdue University (NC)
Rend Lake College (U)
Rogers University (U)
Southwest Missouri State University (G)
Southwest Texas State University (U)
Texas Tech University (U)
Treasure Valley Community College (U)
University of Arizona (U)
University of British Columbia (U)
University of Delaware (U)
University of Georgia (U)
University of Guelph (U, NC)
University of Hawaii–Leeward Community College (U)
University of Hawaii–Maui Community College (U)
University of Idaho (U, G)
University of Kentucky (U, G)
University of Missouri–Columbia (U, G)
University of Nebraska–Lincoln (U, NC)
University of Nevada, Reno (NC)
University of Wisconsin–Madison (U)
University of Wisconsin–River Falls (NC)
University of Wyoming (U)
University System of Georgia (U)
Utah State University (U)
Western Illinois University (U)

Algebra
Brigham Young University (U)
Bristol Community College (U)
Bucks County Community College (U)
Central Arizona College (U)
Central Methodist College (U)
Central Piedmont Community College (U)
City Colleges of Chicago, Harold Washington College (U)
Clayton College & State University (U)
Clovis Community College (U)
Colorado Electronic Community College (U)
Colorado Mountain College District (U)
Colorado Northwestern Community College (U)
Columbia Basin College (U)
Concordia University (U)
Dallas County Community College District (U)
De Anza College (U)
Delaware Technical & Community College, Stanton/Wilmington Campus (U)
Delta College (U)
Eastern Kentucky University (U)
Eastern Oklahoma State College (U)
Floyd College (U)
Genesee Community College (U)
Jefferson College (U)
Kansas State University (U)
Lake Land College (U)
Lane Community College (U)
Lansing Community College (U)
Madison Area Technical College (U)
Manatee Community College (U)
Marywood University (U)
Mercy College (U)
Midland College (U)
Northeastern University (U)
Northern Virginia Community College (U)
NorthWest Arkansas Community College (NC)
Northwestern College (U)
Oklahoma State University (U)
Portland State University (U)
Pratt Community College and Area Vocational School (U)
Richland Community College (U)
San Juan College (U)
Seattle Central Community College (U)
Southern Arkansas University Tech (U)
Southwest Texas State University (U)
State Technical Institute at Memphis (U)
State University of New York Empire State College (U)
State University of West Georgia (U)
Texas Tech University (U, NC)
Thomas Edison State College (U)
Tyler Junior College (U)
University of Alaska Fairbanks (U)
University of Delaware (U)
The University of Iowa (U, G)
University of Nebraska–Lincoln (U)
The University of North Carolina at Chapel Hill (U)
University of Southern Mississippi (U)
University of Tennessee, Knoxville (U)
University of Toledo (U)
University of Waterloo (U, NC)
University System of Georgia (U)
Upper Iowa University (U)
Wayne County Community College (U)
Western Washington University (U)
Yuba College (U)

American (US) History
Bergen Community College (U)
Brigham Young University (U)
Bucks County Community College (U)
Catonsville Community College (U)
Central Arizona College (U)
Central Florida Community College (U)
Central Methodist College (U)
Charles County Community College (U)
Clark State Community College (U)
Clayton College & State University (U)
Clovis Community College (U)
Colorado Northwestern Community College (U)
Community College of Vermont (U)
Concordia University (U)
Crafton Hills College (U)
De Anza College (U)
Eastern Kentucky University (U)
Eastern Michigan University (U)
Eastern Oklahoma State College (U)
Eastern Washington University (U)
El Paso Community College (U)
Floyd College (U)
Fullerton College (U)
Jefferson College (U)
Johnson County Community College (U)
Kansas State University (U, NC)
Kingwood College (U)
Lake Land College (U)
Lake-Sumter Community College (U)
Laramie County Community College (U)
Lee College (U)
Lehigh Carbon Community College (U)
Los Angeles Community College District (U)
Madison Area Technical College (U)
Mercy College (U)
Metropolitan State College of Denver (U)
Midland College (U)
Mount Wachusett Community College (U)
New River Community College (U)
Northern Virginia Community College (U)
Northwestern College (U)
Northwestern Michigan College (U)
Northwest Iowa Community College (U)
Oklahoma State University (U)
Owens Community College (U)
Park College (U)
Pratt Community College and Area Vocational School (U)
Riverland Community College (U)
Roosevelt University (U)
St. Louis Community College (U)
Saint Peter's College (U)

Individual Courses Index

Salve Regina University (U, NC)
San Bernardino Valley College (U)
Sauk Valley Community College (U)
Seattle Pacific University (U, G)
Sinclair Community College (U)
Southeast Community College, Lincoln Campus (U)
Southwest Missouri State University (U)
Southwest Texas State University (U)
State Technical Institute at Memphis (U)
State University of New York Empire State College (U)
State University of West Georgia (U, G)
Sul Ross State University (U)
Taylor University, Fort Wayne Campus (U)
Texas Tech University (U, NC)
Thomas Edison State College (U)
University of Delaware (U)
University of Illinois at Urbana–Champaign (U)
The University of Iowa (U, G)
University of Nebraska–Lincoln (U)
The University of North Carolina at Chapel Hill (U)
University of Tennessee, Knoxville (U)
University of Wisconsin–Madison (U)
University of Wisconsin–Stevens Point (U, G)
Upper Iowa University (U)
Washington State University (U)
Wayne County Community College (U)
Western Illinois University (U)
Western Washington University (U)
Wytheville Community College (U)

American Literature
Austin Community College (U)
Barclay College (U)
Brigham Young University (U)
Bucks County Community College (U)
Central Arizona College (U)
Community College of Vermont (U)
Delaware Technical & Community College, Stanton/Wilmington Campus (U)
Eastern Michigan University (U)
Eastern Washington University (U)
Floyd College (U)
Madison Area Technical College (U)
Marywood University (U)
New River Community College (U)
Northern Virginia Community College (U)
Owens Community College (U)
Pratt Community College and Area Vocational School (U)
Salve Regina University (U, NC)
San Juan College (U)
Seattle Central Community College (U)
State University of West Georgia (U, G)
Stephens College (U)
Taylor University, Fort Wayne Campus (U)
Texas Tech University (U, NC)
University of Houston (U)
University of Illinois at Urbana–Champaign (U)
University of Michigan (U)
University of Nebraska–Lincoln (U)
The University of North Carolina at Chapel Hill (U)
University of Southern Indiana (U)
University of Tennessee, Knoxville (U)
University of Waterloo (U)
Washington State University (U)
Western Illinois University (U)

Western Washington University (U)

American Studies
Christopher Newport University (U)
Indiana University System (U)
Kansas State University (U, NC)
Seattle Central Community College (U)
The University of Iowa (U)
University of Nebraska–Lincoln (U)
The University of North Carolina at Chapel Hill (U)

Anatomy
Central Methodist College (U)
Century Community and Technical College (U)
Dalhousie University (U, G)
Duquesne University (U)
Floyd College (U)
Hocking College (U)
Meridian Community College (U)
Stephens College (U)

Animal Sciences
Brigham Young University (U)
Colorado State University (U)
Columbia State Community College (U)
Iowa State University of Science and Technology (U, G)
Kansas State University (U, G, NC)
Los Angeles Pierce College (U)
Louisiana State University at Eunice (U)
Oklahoma State University (U)
University of Missouri–Columbia (U, G)
The University of North Carolina at Chapel Hill (U)
Yuba College (U)

Anthropology
Atlantic Community College (U)
Austin Community College (U)
Bakersfield College (U)
Blinn College (U)
Brigham Young University (U)
Brookdale Community College (U)
Brown University (NC)
Cabrillo College (U)
California State University, Los Angeles (U, NC)
California State University, Sacramento (U)
California State University, Stanislaus (U)
Carleton University (U)
Carl Sandburg College (U)
Catonsville Community College (U)
Central Arizona College (U)
Central Florida Community College (U)
College of St. Scholastica (U, G)
College of San Mateo (U)
Colorado Electronic Community College (U)
Colorado Mountain College District (U)
Colorado Northwestern Community College (U)
Columbia Basin College (U)
Crafton Hills College (U)
Cuyahoga Community College, Metropolitan Campus (U)
De Anza College (U)
Eastern Kentucky University (U)
El Paso Community College (U)
Genesee Community College (U)
Governors State University (U, G)

Grand Rapids Community College (U)
Hibbing Community College (U)
Indiana University System (U)
Jacksonville State University (U)
Lafayette College (U)
Lane Community College (U)
Long Beach City College (U)
Los Angeles Community College District (U)
Marshall University (U)
MiraCosta College (U)
Mount Wachusett Community College (U)
New York Institute of Technology (U)
Northwestern Michigan College (U)
Oakton Community College (U)
Ohlone College (U)
Palomar College (U)
Pierce College (U)
Portland State University (U)
Rio Salado College (U)
Roger Williams University (U)
St. Louis Community College (U)
San Bernardino Valley College (U)
San Diego City College (U)
Santa Rosa Junior College (U)
Seattle Central Community College (U)
Sinclair Community College (U)
South Puget Sound Community College (U)
Southwest Missouri State University (U)
State Technical Institute at Memphis (U)
Syracuse University (U, G)
Tacoma Community College (U)
Taylor University, Fort Wayne Campus (U)
Texas Tech University (U, NC)
Thomas Edison State College (U)
Triton College (U)
Universitè Laval (U)
University of Alaska Fairbanks (U)
University of Houston (U)
University of Illinois at Urbana–Champaign (U)
The University of Iowa (U, G)
University of Kentucky, Henderson Community College (U)
University of Minnesota, Twin Cities Campus (U)
University of Missouri–Columbia (U)
University of Southern Mississippi (U)
University of Tennessee, Knoxville (U)
The University of Texas at Austin (U)
University of Washington (U)
University of Waterloo (U)
University of Wisconsin–Stevens Point (U, G)
University System of Georgia (U)
Washington State University (U)
Wayne County Community College (U)
Weber State University (U)
Western Michigan University (U)
Western Washington University (U)
West Valley College (U)
Wilfrid Laurier University (U)
Yuba College (U)

Archaeology
Colorado Mountain College District (U)
Cuyahoga Community College, Metropolitan Campus (U)
Lane Community College (U)
St. Louis Community College (U)
Santa Rosa Junior College (U)
Texas Tech University (U, G)

Distance Learning Programs

547

Individual Courses Index

Archaeology (continued)
Thomas Edison State College (U)
The University of Iowa (U, G)
University of Pennsylvania (NC)
University of West Florida (U)

Architecture
Anne Arundel Community College (U)
Arizona State University (U)
Ball State University (G)
Carleton University (U)
Houston Community College System (U)
Howard Community College (U)
Pennsylvania State University University Park Campus (U)
Texas Tech University (NC)
University of Kentucky (U)
University of Maine at Augusta (U)
University of Maine at Fort Kent (U)
University of Minnesota, Twin Cities Campus (U)
University of South Florida (G)
University of Virginia (G)
University of Washington (U)
Washington State University (U)
William Rainey Harper College (U)

Area, Ethnic, and Cultural Studies
Arizona State University (U)
Athabasca University (U)
Austin Community College (U)
Ball State University (U)
Bemidji State University (U)
Blue Mountain Community College (U)
Brevard Community College (U)
Butte College (U)
California State University, Bakersfield (U)
California State University, Dominguez Hills (U)
California State University, Fresno (U)
California State University, Stanislaus (U)
Central Arizona College (U)
Central Community College–Grand Island Campus (U)
Cerritos College (U)
Chadron State College (U)
Charles Stewart Mott Community College (U)
Chemeketa Community College (U)
Chesapeake College (U)
City College of San Francisco (U)
Clackamas Community College (U)
Coastline Community College (U, NC)
College of DuPage (U)
College of San Mateo (U)
College of the Canyons (U)
College of the Southwest (U)
The College of West Virginia (U)
Colorado Mountain College District (U)
Concordia University Wisconsin (U, G)
Cosumnes River College (U)
Cuyahoga Community College, Metropolitan Campus (U)
De Anza College (U)
Des Moines Area Community College (U)
Eastern New Mexico University (U, G)
Eastern Oregon University (U)
Eastern Wyoming College (U)
Edison Community College (U)
Essex Community College (U)
Flathead Valley Community College (U)
Fort Hays State University (U)
Galveston College (U)
Gateway Technical College (U)
Genesee Community College (U)
The Graduate School of America (G)
Grand Valley State University (U, G)
Hampton University (U, NC)
Howard Community College (U)
Idaho State University (U, G)
Illinois Valley Community College (U)
Indiana University System (U, G)
Iowa State University of Science and Technology (U)
Jefferson State Community College (U)
John C. Calhoun State Community College (U)
Kansas State University (U, G, NC)
Kaskaskia College (U, NC)
Kellogg Community College (U)
Lassen College (U)
Lycoming College (U)
Marshall University (U, G)
The McGregor School of Antioch University (G)
Memorial University of Newfoundland (U)
Mendocino College (U)
Metropolitan Community College (U)
Metropolitan State College of Denver (U)
Milwaukee Area Technical College (U)
Minnesota West Community and Technical College–Worthington Campus (U)
Minot State University (U)
Modesto Junior College (U)
Montgomery College–Rockville Campus (U)
Morehead State University (U)
Mt. San Antonio College (U)
Nassau Community College (U)
New School for Social Research (U, NC)
North Carolina State University (U)
Northeast Louisiana University (U)
Northern Arizona University (U)
North Seattle Community College (U)
North Shore Community College (U)
Northwestern State University of Louisiana (NC)
Oakton Community College (U)
The Ohio State University (U)
Ohio State University–Mansfield Campus (U)
Oklahoma State University (U)
Palomar College (U)
Parkland College (U)
Pennsylvania State University University Park Campus (U)
Pima Community College (U)
Portland State University (U)
Prince George's Community College (U)
Quincy College (U)
The Richard Stockton College of New Jersey (U, NC)
Rochester Institute of Technology (U)
Rockland Community College (U)
Sacramento City College (U)
St. Cloud Technical College (U)
Schoolcraft College (U)
Sinclair Community College (U)
Skidmore College (U)
Southeast Community College, Lincoln Campus (U)
Southwestern Assemblies of God University (U)
Southwest State University (U)
Spertus Institute of Jewish Studies (G)
State University of New York Empire State College (U)
Suffolk County Community College–Ammerman Campus (U)
Syracuse University (U)
Tallahassee Community College (U)
Treasure Valley Community College (U)
Tulsa Community College (U)
The Union Institute (U)
University of Alaska Fairbanks (U)
University of Alaska Southeast, Sitka Campus (U)
University of Arizona (U)
University of Baltimore (U)
University of California Extension (U)
University of California, Santa Barbara (U)
University of Delaware (U)
University of Georgia (U, NC)
University of Great Falls (U)
University of Hawaii–Maui Community College (U)
University of Kansas (U, G, NC)
University of Maine (U, G)
University of Maine at Fort Kent (U, G)
The University of Memphis (U)
University of Michigan (U)
University of Minnesota, Twin Cities Campus (U)
University of Missouri–Columbia (U)
University of Missouri–St. Louis (U)
University of Nebraska–Lincoln (U)
University of Nevada, Las Vegas (U)
University of Northern Iowa (U, G)
University of Oklahoma (U)
University of South Dakota (U)
University of Southern Colorado (U)
The University of Texas at Austin (U)
The University of Texas at San Antonio (U, G)
The University of Texas at Tyler (U, G)
University of Utah (U)
University of Washington (U)
University of Wisconsin–Eau Claire (U, G)
University System of Georgia (U)
Washington State University (U)
Washtenaw Community College (U)
Wayne State University (U)
Western Illinois University (U)
Western Nebraska Community College (U)
West Virginia Wesleyan College (U)
Wichita State University (U, G)
Wilfrid Laurier University (U)
Xavier University of Louisiana (U)
Yuba College (U)

Art History and Criticism
Acadia University (U)
Atlantic Community College (U)
Austin Community College (U)
Brigham Young University (U)
Bucks County Community College (U)
Carl Sandburg College (U)
Central Arizona College (U)
Charles County Community College (U)
Clark State Community College (U)
Clayton College & State University (U)
Clovis Community College (U)
Colorado Mountain College District (U)
Colorado Northwestern Community College (U)
Columbia Basin College (U)
Columbia-Greene Community College (U)
Cuyahoga Community College, Metropolitan Campus (U)

Individual Courses Index

Delgado Community College (U)
Delta College (U)
Duquesne University (U)
Edison State Community College (U)
Genesee Community College (U)
Governors State University (U, G)
Greenville Technical College (U)
Lane Community College (U)
Lehigh Carbon Community College (U)
Marywood University (U)
Mercy College (U)
Metropolitan Community College (U)
Northern Virginia Community College (U)
Red Rocks Community College (U)
Richland Community College (U)
Rockland Community College (U)
St. Louis Community College (U)
Salve Regina University (U, NC)
Sinclair Community College (U)
Southern West Virginia Community and Technical College (U)
State University of New York at New Paltz (U)
State University of West Georgia (U)
Sul Ross State University (U)
Thomas Edison State College (U)
University of Alaska Fairbanks (U)
University of Nebraska–Lincoln (U)
The University of North Carolina at Chapel Hill (U)
University of Southern Colorado (U)
University of Wisconsin–Stevens Point (U)
University System of Georgia (U)
Upper Iowa University (U)

Asian Languages and Literatures

Brevard Community College (U)
City Colleges of Chicago, Harold Washington College (U)
College of Lake County (U)
Cuyahoga Community College, Metropolitan Campus (U)
Darton College (U)
Grand Valley State University (U)
Kennesaw State University (U)
Lorain County Community College (U)
The McGregor School of Antioch University (G)
Nassau Community College (U)
New School for Social Research (U, NC)
North Seattle Community College (U)
Oakland University (U)
Oakton Community College (U)
Ohio University–Eastern (U)
Piedmont College (U)
Portland State University (U)
The Richard Stockton College of New Jersey (U, NC)
St. Cloud Technical College (U)
San Jose State University (U)
University of Alaska Anchorage (U)
University of California Extension (U)
University of Hawaii–Leeward Community College (U)
University of Kentucky, Elizabethtown Community College (U)
University of Minnesota, Twin Cities Campus (U)
University of Oklahoma (U)
Valley City State University (U)
Washington State University (U)
Waubonsee Community College (U)
William Rainey Harper College (U)

Asian Studies

Lane Community College (U)
Seattle Central Community College (U)
Thomas Edison State College (U)
The University of Iowa (U, G)
University of Michigan (U)
University of Nebraska–Lincoln (U)
Western Washington University (U)

Astronomy and Astrophysics

Anne Arundel Community College (U)
Athabasca University (U)
Bakersfield College (U)
Ball State University (U)
Bellevue Community College (U)
Bluefield State College (U)
Blue Mountain Community College (U)
Boise State University (U)
Brevard Community College (U)
Brigham Young University (U)
Broward Community College (U)
Bucks County Community College (U)
Burlington County College (U)
Butte College (U)
California State University, Bakersfield (U)
Carleton University (U)
Catonsville Community College (U)
Central Community College–Grand Island Campus (U)
Central Michigan University (U)
Central Piedmont Community College (U)
Charles County Community College (U)
Charter Oak State College (U)
City College of San Francisco (U)
City Colleges of Chicago, Harold Washington College (U)
Coastline Community College (U, NC)
College of San Mateo (U)
College of the Canyons (U)
Colorado Electronic Community College (U)
Colorado Northwestern Community College (U)
Concordia University (U)
Cuyamaca College (U)
Dallas County Community College District (U)
Daytona Beach Community College (U)
Eastern Idaho Technical College (U)
Edison Community College (U)
Essex Community College (U)
Evergreen Valley College (U)
Flathead Valley Community College (U)
Front Range Community College (U)
Garland County Community College (U)
Georgia Southern University (U)
Glendale Community College (U)
Glenville State College (U)
Greenville Technical College (U)
Hibbing Community College (U)
Hillsborough Community College (U)
Illinois Valley Community College (U)
Indiana University System (U)
Jamestown Community College (U)
John Wood Community College (U)
Lake Land College (NC)
Laramie County Community College (U)
Laurentian University (U)
Long Beach City College (U)
Los Angeles Community College District (U)
Luzerne County Community College (U)
Lycoming College (U)
Mendocino College (U)
Milwaukee Area Technical College (U)
Modesto Junior College (U)
Montgomery College–Rockville Campus (U)
Moraine Valley Community College (U)
Morgan Community College (U, NC)
Mt. San Antonio College (U)
New School for Social Research (U, NC)
Northeast Community College (U)
North Seattle Community College (U)
Northwestern College (U)
Oakton Community College (U)
Ohio University (U)
Ohio University–Eastern (U)
Ohlone College (U)
Oklahoma City Community College (U)
Pensacola Junior College (U)
Portland Community College (U)
Prince George's Community College (U)
Pueblo Community College (U)
Rio Salado College (U)
Riverside Community College (U)
Rockland Community College (U)
Rogers University (U)
St. Johns River Community College (U)
St. Petersburg Junior College (U)
Salt Lake Community College (U)
San Bernardino Valley College (U)
San Diego City College (U)
Seattle Central Community College (U)
Sinclair Community College (U)
Skagit Valley College (U)
Southeastern Community College, North Campus (U)
South Florida Community College (U)
South Puget Sound Community College (U)
Suffolk County Community College–Ammerman Campus (U)
Sussex County Community College (U)
Tarrant County Junior College (U)
Thomas Edison State College (U)
Tidewater Community College (U)
Troy State University (U, G)
Troy State University Montgomery (U)
Tulsa Community College (U)
Umpqua Community College (U)
University of British Columbia (U)
University of California Extension (U)
University of Great Falls (U)
University of Hawaii–Leeward Community College (U)
University of Hawaii–Maui Community College (U)
The University of Iowa (U, G)
University of Massachusetts Dartmouth (U)
University of Minnesota, Twin Cities Campus (U)
University of Missouri–Columbia (U, G)
University of Nevada, Reno (U)
The University of North Carolina at Chapel Hill (U)
University of Oklahoma (U)
University of South Carolina (U, G)
University of South Dakota (U)
University of Washington (U)
University of Waterloo (U)
Utah State University (U)
Volunteer State Community College (U)

Distance Learning Programs

Individual Courses Index

Astronomy and Astrophysics (continued)
Walters State Community College (U)
Wenatchee Valley College (U)
Western Illinois University (U)
West Virginia University (U)
Wichita State University (U)
Yuba College (U)

Bible Studies
Bethel Theological Seminary (G)
Brigham Young University (U)
Cincinnati Bible College and Seminary (U)
Denver Conservative Baptist Seminary (G, NC)
Gordon-Conwell Theological Seminary (G, NC)
Indiana Wesleyan University (U)
LIFE Bible College (U)
North Central Bible College (U, NC)
Oral Roberts University (NC)
Pratt Community College and Area Vocational School (U)
Seattle Pacific University (U)
Taylor University, Fort Wayne Campus (U)
Temple Baptist Seminary (G, NC)
University of Southern Mississippi (U)
University of Waterloo (U)
Wheaton College (G, NC)

Biochemistry
Iowa State University of Science and Technology (U, G)
Judson College (U)
University of Waterloo (U)

Biological and Life Sciences
Allegheny University of the Health Sciences (NC)
Athabasca University (U)
Ball State University (U)
Black Hawk College (U)
Brevard Community College (U)
Brigham Young University (U)
Burlington County College (U)
Butte College (U)
California State University, Stanislaus (U)
Calvin College (G)
Carleton University (U)
Central Arizona College (U)
Chattanooga State Technical Community College (U)
Chemeketa Community College (U)
City College of San Francisco (U)
Coastline Community College (U, NC)
Colby Community College (U)
College of DuPage (U)
College of St. Scholastica (U, G)
The College of West Virginia (U)
Community College of Rhode Island (U)
Concordia University (U)
Daytona Beach Community College (U)
De Anza College (U)
East Carolina University (G)
Eastern Oregon University (U)
Ellsworth Community College (U)
Emporia State University (U, G)
Governors State University (U)
Hampton University (U)
Hawkeye Community College (U)
Howard Community College (U)
Idaho State University (U, G)

Illinois Institute of Technology (U, G)
Illinois Valley Community College (U)
John Wood Community College (U)
Lake-Sumter Community College (U)
Loma Linda University (U)
Long Beach City College (U)
Lord Fairfax Community College (U)
Memorial University of Newfoundland (U)
Metropolitan State College of Denver (U)
Missouri Southern State College (U)
Montgomery College–Rockville Campus (U)
North Carolina State University (U)
North Dakota State College of Science (U)
Northeast Community College (U)
Northern Arizona University (U)
Northern Essex Community College (U)
Northern Oklahoma College (U)
North Georgia College & State University (U, G)
Oklahoma City Community College (U)
Parkland College (U)
Pennsylvania State University University Park Campus (U)
Pratt Community College and Area Vocational School (U)
Pueblo Community College (U)
Quincy College (U)
Redlands Community College (U, NC)
Red Rocks Community College (U)
Rogers University (U)
San Bernardino Valley College (U)
Scott Community College (U)
Southwestern Assemblies of God University (U)
Southwest State University (U)
Suffolk County Community College–Ammerman Campus (U)
Tallahassee Community College (U)
Tarrant County Junior College (U)
Troy State University Montgomery (U)
Ulster County Community College (U)
Umpqua Community College (U)
The Union Institute (U)
University of Alaska Fairbanks (U)
University of Alaska Southeast, Sitka Campus (U)
University of California, Davis (U)
University of California Extension (U)
University of Cincinnati Raymond Walters College (U)
University of Georgia (U)
University of Great Falls (U)
University of Hawaii–Maui Community College (U)
University of Minnesota, Twin Cities Campus (U)
University of Missouri–Columbia (U, G)
University of Nebraska–Lincoln (U)
University of North Dakota (U)
University of the State of New York, Regents College (U)
University of Windsor (U)
University System of Georgia (U)
Western Michigan University (U)
West Virginia Wesleyan College (U)
Wilfrid Laurier University (U)

Biology
Adams State College (G)
Alvin Community College (U)
American River College (U)

Arapahoe Community College (U)
Arizona State University (U)
Arizona State University West (U)
Athabasca University (U)
Auburn University (U)
Austin Community College (U)
Bakersfield College (U)
Ball State University (U)
Barclay College (U)
Black Hawk College (U)
Blue Mountain Community College (U)
Brevard Community College (U)
Brigham Young University (U)
Brookdale Community College (U)
Broward Community College (U)
Bucks County Community College (U)
Burlington County College (U)
Butte College (U)
California State University, Bakersfield (U)
California State University, Fresno (U)
California State University, Hayward (U)
California State University, Sacramento (U)
Carleton University (U)
Central Methodist College (U)
Central Michigan University (U)
Central Missouri State University (U)
Central Piedmont Community College (U)
Central Virginia Community College (U)
Central Wyoming College (U)
Charles County Community College (U)
Charles Stewart Mott Community College (U)
Charter Oak State College (U)
Chippewa Valley Technical College (U, NC)
City College of San Francisco (U)
Clovis Community College (U)
Coastline Community College (U, NC)
Colby Community College (U)
College of DuPage (U)
College of St. Francis (U)
College of the Southwest (U)
The College of West Virginia (U)
Colorado Mountain College District (U)
Colorado Northwestern Community College (U)
Concordia University (U)
Concordia University at Austin (U, NC)
Contra Costa College (U)
Crafton Hills College (U)
Cumberland County College (U)
Dallas County Community College District (U)
Dawson Community College (U)
De Anza College (U)
Delta College (U)
Des Moines Area Community College (U)
Eastern Kentucky University (U)
Ellsworth Community College (U)
Fitchburg State College (U)
Florida Community College at Jacksonville (U)
Florida State University (U)
Fort Hays State University (U)
Front Range Community College (U)
Gadsden State Community College (U)
Galveston College (U)
Garland County Community College (U)
Genesee Community College (U)
George C. Wallace State Community College (U)
Georgia Institute of Technology (G, NC)
Glendale Community College (U)
Graceland College (U)
Greenville Technical College (U)

Individual Courses Index

Griggs University (U)
Harrisburg Area Community College (U)
Hillsborough Community College (U)
Idaho State University (U, G)
Illinois Central College (U)
Indiana State University (U)
Indiana University System (U)
Iowa State University of Science and Technology (U)
Iowa Western Community College (U)
Ivy Tech State College–Northcentral (U)
Jefferson College (U)
Johnson County Community College (U)
Joliet Junior College (U)
Judson College (U)
Kankakee Community College (U)
Kellogg Community College (U)
Lakehead University (U)
Laney College (U)
Lansing Community College (U)
Laurentian University (U)
Lawson State Community College (U)
Lee College (U)
Lehigh University (G, NC)
Long Beach City College (U)
Longview Community College (U)
Manatee Community College (U)
Memorial University of Newfoundland (U)
Mercy College (U)
Metropolitan Community College (U)
Metropolitan Community College (U)
Middle Georgia College (U)
Minnesota West Community and Technical College–Worthington Campus (U)
Missouri Southern State College (U)
Missouri Western State College (U)
Morgan Community College (U, NC)
New River Community College (U)
Normandale Community College (U)
North Carolina State University (U)
Northeast Louisiana University (U, G)
Northern State University (U)
Northern Virginia Community College (U)
North Harris College (U)
Northwestern Michigan College (U)
Northwestern State University of Louisiana (U)
Odessa College (U)
Ohio University (U)
Ohio University–Eastern (U)
Oklahoma City Community College (U)
Palo Alto College (U)
Palomar College (U)
Park College (U)
Pennsylvania State University University Park Campus (U)
Penn Valley Community College (U)
Pierce College (U)
Polytechnic University, Westchester Graduate Center (G)
Portland Community College (U)
Portland State University (U)
Pratt Community College and Area Vocational School (U)
Prince George's Community College (U)
Quincy College (U)
Rio Salado College (U)
Rogers University (U)
Roger Williams University (U)
Rutgers, The State University of New Jersey, Newark (U, NC)

St. Louis Community College (U)
St. Petersburg Junior College (U)
Salt Lake Community College (U)
Sauk Valley Community College (U)
Seattle Central Community College (U)
Seattle Pacific University (U)
Shawnee Community College (U)
Skidmore College (U)
Southeastern Community College, North Campus (U)
South Florida Community College (U)
Southwestern Assemblies of God University (U)
Southwest Missouri State University (U)
Southwest State University (U)
State University of New York at Binghamton (U)
State University of New York College of Environmental Science and Forestry (U)
State University of New York Empire State College (U)
Suffolk County Community College–Ammerman Campus (U)
Syracuse University (U)
Tacoma Community College (U)
Tallahassee Community College (U)
Tarrant County Junior College (U)
Taylor University, Fort Wayne Campus (U)
Tennessee Temple University (U)
Texas Tech University (U)
Thomas Edison State College (U)
Trinidad State Junior College (U)
Troy State University Montgomery (U)
Tyler Junior College (U)
University of Alaska Anchorage (U)
University of Alaska Fairbanks (U)
University of Alaska Southeast (U)
University of Alaska Southeast, Sitka Campus (U)
University of Alberta (U)
The University of Calgary (U)
University of California Extension (U)
University of Delaware (U, G)
University of Georgia (U)
University of Great Falls (U)
University of Hawaii–Maui Community College (U)
University of Kansas (U, NC)
University of Kentucky, Henderson Community College (U)
University of Kentucky, Madisonville Community College (U)
University of Maryland University College (U)
University of Minnesota, Twin Cities Campus (U, NC)
University of Missouri–Columbia (U)
University of Nebraska at Kearney (U)
University of Nebraska–Lincoln (U)
University of New Brunswick (U)
The University of North Carolina at Chapel Hill (U)
University of North Dakota (U)
University of Northern Colorado (U)
University of North Texas Health Science Center at Fort Worth (G)
University of Saskatchewan (U)
University of South Dakota (U, G)
University of South Florida (U)
The University of Texas at Tyler (U)
University of Utah (U)
University of Waterloo (U)
University of Windsor (U)

University of Wisconsin–Stout (U, G)
University System of Georgia (U)
Upper Iowa University (U)
Utah State University (U)
Utah Valley State College (U)
Victor Valley College (U)
Vista Community College (U)
Washington State University (U)
Waubonsee Community College (U)
Wenatchee Valley College (U)
Western Illinois University (U, G)
Western Oklahoma State College (U)
Westmoreland County Community College (U)
West Virginia University (U)
Whatcom Community College (U)
Wichita State University (U)
Wilfrid Laurier University (U)
Wilkes Community College (U)
Winthrop University (U)
Wytheville Community College (U)

Botany

Arizona State University (U)
Athabasca University (U)
Austin Community College (U)
Brigham Young University (U)
College of the Southwest (U)
Garland County Community College (U)
Idaho State University (U, G)
Missouri Southern State College (U)
North Carolina State University (U)
Northwestern State University of Louisiana (U)
Ohio University (U)
Rend Lake College (U)
Rockland Community College (U)
Skidmore College (U)
Southwest State University (U)
Texas Tech University (U)
University of California Extension (U)
University of Great Falls (U)
University of Hawaii–Leeward Community College (U)
University of Nebraska at Kearney (U)
Weber State University (U)
Western Oklahoma State College (U)

Business

Acadia University (U)
Allegany College of Maryland (U, NC)
American College (U, G)
Anne Arundel Community College (U)
Arapahoe Community College (U, NC)
Athabasca University (U)
Atlantic Community College (U)
Austin Community College (U)
Baker College (U, G)
Ball State University (U, G)
Berean University of the Assemblies of God (U)
Blackhawk Technical College (U)
Boise State University (U)
Brevard Community College (U)
Brigham Young University (U)
Brookdale Community College (U)
Broward Community College (U)
Bucks County Community College (U)
Burlington County College (U)
California College for Health Sciences (U)
California State University, Fullerton (G)
California State University, Hayward (U)

Distance Learning Programs

Individual Courses Index

Business (continued)

California State University, Stanislaus (U, G)
Camden County College (U)
Carleton University (U)
Carl Sandburg College (U)
Catawba Valley Community College (U)
Catonsville Community College (U)
Central Arizona College (U)
Central Community College–Grand Island Campus (U)
Central Michigan University (U)
Central Piedmont Community College (U)
Central Virginia Community College (U)
Central Wyoming College (U)
Century Community and Technical College (U)
Chadron State College (U, G)
Champlain College (U)
Charles Stewart Mott Community College (U)
Chattanooga State Technical Community College (U)
Chemeketa Community College (U)
Chesapeake College (U)
Chippewa Valley Technical College (U)
City College of San Francisco (U)
City University (U, G)
Clackamas Community College (U)
Clark College (U)
Clatsop Community College (U)
Cleary College (U)
Coastline Community College (U, NC)
Colby Community College (U)
College of DuPage (U)
College of San Mateo (U)
College of the Southwest (U)
The College of West Virginia (U)
Colorado State University (G)
Columbia State Community College (U)
Community College of Philadelphia (U)
Concordia University (U)
Concordia University at Austin (U, NC)
Contra Costa College (U)
Cornell University (U)
Cosumnes River College (U)
Crafton Hills College (U)
Danville Community College (U)
David N. Myers College (U)
Dawson Community College (U)
Daytona Beach Community College (U)
De Anza College (U)
Delaware County Community College (U)
Delaware Technical & Community College, Jack F. Owens Campus (U)
Delgado Community College (U)
Delta State University (U, G)
DePaul University (U, G)
Drake University (G)
Duke University (G)
Duquesne University (U, G, NC)
Eastern Idaho Technical College (NC)
Eastern New Mexico University (U, G)
Eastern Oregon University (U)
Eastern Washington University (U)
Eastern Wyoming College (U)
Edison Community College (U)
Edison State Community College (U)
Embry-Riddle Aeronautical University, Extended Campus (U)
Emporia State University (U, G)
Essex Community College (U)

Fairleigh Dickinson University, Teaneck–Hackensack (G)
Fayetteville Technical Community College (U)
Florence-Darlington Technical College (U)
Florida Atlantic University (G)
Florida Community College at Jacksonville (U)
Franklin University (U)
Fullerton College (U)
Garland County Community College (U)
Gateway Technical College (U)
Genesee Community College (U)
George C. Wallace State Community College (U)
Georgia Southern University (U, G)
Glendale Community College (U)
Governors State University (U)
The Graduate School of America (G)
Grand Rapids Community College (U)
Grand Valley State University (U, G)
Great Basin College (U)
Griggs University (U)
Hampton University (U, NC)
Harrisburg Area Community College (U)
Heriot-Watt University (G)
Hibbing Community College (U)
Hillsborough Community College (U)
Hocking College (U)
Houston Community College System (U)
Howard Community College (NC)
Idaho State University (U, G)
Illinois Eastern Community Colleges, Olney Central College (U)
Illinois Valley Community College (U)
Indiana University System (U)
ISIM University (G)
Ivy Tech State College–Wabash Valley (U)
Jackson Community College (U)
Jefferson College (U)
Jefferson Davis Community College (U)
John C. Calhoun State Community College (U)
Johnson County Community College (U)
Joliet Junior College (U)
J. Sargeant Reynolds Community College (U)
Judson College (U)
Kellogg Community College (U)
Lake Michigan College (U)
Lakeshore Technical College (U)
Lake-Sumter Community College (U)
Lake Superior State University (U)
Lamar University (U)
Lane Community College (U)
Laney College (U)
Laramie County Community College (U)
Lassen College (U)
Laurentian University (U, G)
Lee College (U)
Lehigh University (G, NC)
Lincoln Land Community College (U)
Long Beach City College (U)
Longview Community College (U)
Lycoming College (U)
Madison Area Technical College (U)
Madonna University (G)
Marshall University (U, G)
Massachusetts Institute of Technology (NC)
Mayland Community College (U)
McDowell Technical Community College (U)
The McGregor School of Antioch University (G)
Memorial University of Newfoundland (U)
Mendocino College (U)

Mercy College (U)
Mesa State College (U)
Metropolitan Community College (U)
Michigan Technological University (U, NC)
Middle Tennessee State University (U, G)
Midland College (U)
Mid-Plains Community College (U)
Mid-State Technical College (U)
Milwaukee Area Technical College (U)
Minot State University (U)
Missouri Southern State College (U)
Montana Tech of The University of Montana (U)
Montgomery College–Rockville Campus (U)
Moraine Valley Community College (U)
Morehead State University (U, G)
Mount Saint Vincent University (U)
Nassau Community College (U)
National Technological University (NC)
National University (U, G)
New Hampshire College (U)
New Jersey Institute of Technology (G)
New Mexico Junior College (U)
New Mexico State University (U, G)
New River Community College (U)
New School for Social Research (U, NC)
New York Institute of Technology (U)
New York University (G)
North Carolina State University (U)
North Central Technical College (U)
Northcentral Technical College (U)
Northeast Louisiana University (U)
Northeast Wisconsin Technical College (U)
Northern Arizona University (U)
Northern Essex Community College (U)
Northern Virginia Community College (U)
North Iowa Area Community College (U)
North Seattle Community College (U)
NorthWest Arkansas Community College (NC)
Northwestern College (U)
Northwestern Michigan College (U)
Northwestern State University of Louisiana (NC)
Oakland University (U)
Ohio University (U)
Ohio University–Southern Campus (U)
Oklahoma City Community College (U)
Oklahoma State University (G)
Old Dominion University (U)
Oral Roberts University (U)
Owens Community College (U)
Palomar College (U)
Parkland College (U)
Pennsylvania State University University Park Campus (U, G, NC)
Penn Valley Community College (U)
Pensacola Junior College (U)
Pikes Peak Community College (U, NC)
Pitt Community College (U, NC)
Polytechnic University, Brooklyn Campus (NC)
Portland Community College (U)
Portland State University (U)
Pratt Community College and Area Vocational School (U)
Prince George's Community College (NC)
Quincy College (U)
Redlands Community College (U)
Red Rocks Community College (U)
Regent University (G)
Regis University (U)
Rend Lake College (G)

Individual Courses Index

The Richard Stockton College of New Jersey (U, NC)
Rio Salado College (U)
Rochester Institute of Technology (U)
Rockland Community College (U)
Rogers University (U)
Roosevelt University (U)
Rose State College (U)
Sacramento City College (U)
St. Johns River Community College (U)
Saint Joseph's College (U)
St. Louis Community College (U)
St. Petersburg Junior College (U)
Salt Lake Community College (U)
Salve Regina University (U, G, NC)
San Bernardino Valley College (U)
San Diego City College (U)
San Juan College (U)
Santa Fe Community College (U)
Santa Rosa Junior College (U)
Schoolcraft College (U)
Scott Community College (U)
Scottsdale Community College (U)
Shelby State Community College (U)
Sinclair Community College (U)
Skidmore College (U)
Southeastern Community College, North Campus (NC)
Southeast Missouri State University (U)
Southern Utah University (U)
Southern West Virginia Community and Technical College (U)
Southwestern Assemblies of God University (U)
Southwestern Michigan College (U)
Southwestern Oklahoma State University (U, G)
Southwest Virginia Community College (U)
State Technical Institute at Memphis (U)
State University of New York at Farmingdale (U)
State University of New York at New Paltz (G)
State University of New York Empire State College (U)
Suffolk County Community College–Ammerman Campus (U)
Syracuse University (U)
Tallahassee Community College (U)
Tarleton State University (U)
Tarrant County Junior College (U)
Terra State Community College (U)
Texas A&M University–Commerce (G)
Texas Tech University (NC)
Thomas Edison State College (U)
Tidewater Community College (U)
Treasure Valley Community College (U)
Trinidad State Junior College (U)
Troy State University Dothan (U)
Troy State University–Florida Region (G)
Troy State University Montgomery (U)
Tulsa Community College (U)
Tyler Junior College (U)
The Union Institute (U)
United States Sports Academy (G, NC)
The University of Alabama (U)
The University of Alabama in Huntsville (G)
University of Alaska Fairbanks (U)
University of Alaska Southeast, Sitka Campus (U)
University of Baltimore (G)
University of California Extension (U)
University of California, Santa Barbara (NC)
The University of Charleston (U, NC)

University of Cincinnati (U)
University of Cincinnati Raymond Walters College (U)
University of Dallas (G)
University of Georgia (U)
University of Great Falls (U)
University of Hawaii–Maui Community College (U)
University of Houston (G)
The University of Iowa (U, G)
University of Kentucky, Ashland Community College (U)
University of Maine at Augusta (U)
University of Maine at Fort Kent (U)
University of Mary (U, G)
University of Maryland, College Park (U)
University of Maryland University College (U)
The University of Memphis (U, G)
University of Minnesota, Twin Cities Campus (U, NC)
University of Mississippi (U, G)
University of Missouri–Columbia (U, G)
University of Missouri–Kansas City (G)
The University of Montana–Missoula (G)
University of Nebraska at Kearney (U, G)
University of Nebraska–Lincoln (U)
University of Nevada, Las Vegas (U)
University of Nevada, Reno (U, G)
University of New Brunswick (U)
University of New Hampshire (NC)
University of North Dakota (U)
University of Notre Dame (NC)
University of Phoenix (U, G)
University of St. Thomas (G)
University of Sarasota (G)
University of Saskatchewan (U)
University of South Carolina (U, G)
University of South Dakota (G)
University of Southern Indiana (U)
University of Southern Mississippi (U)
University of South Florida (G)
The University of Tennessee at Martin (U, G)
The University of Texas at Austin (U)
The University of Texas at San Antonio (U, G)
The University of Texas of the Permian Basin (U, G)
University of the State of New York, Regents College (U)
University of Utah (U)
University of Windsor (U)
University of Wisconsin–Eau Claire (NC)
University of Wisconsin–Extension (U, NC)
University of Wisconsin–Oshkosh (G)
University of Wisconsin–Platteville (U)
University of Wisconsin–River Falls (NC)
University of Wisconsin–Stevens Point (NC)
University of Wisconsin–Stout (U, G, NC)
University of Wyoming (U)
University System of Georgia (U)
Upper Iowa University (U)
Utah State University (U, G)
Valley City State University (U)
Victor Valley College (U)
Volunteer State Community College (U)
Wake Technical Community College (U)
Walden University (G)
Washington and Jefferson College (U)
Washington State University (U)
Waubonsee Community College (U)
Waukesha County Technical College (U)

Wayne County Community College (U)
Western Illinois University (U, G)
Western Michigan University (G)
Western Montana College of The University of Montana (U, NC)
Western Oklahoma State College (U)
Westmoreland County Community College (U)
Wichita State University (U, G)
Wilfrid Laurier University (U)
Wilkes Community College (U)
William Rainey Harper College (U)
Wilson Technical Community College (U)
Winthrop University (G)
Worcester Polytechnic Institute (G)
Wytheville Community College (U)
Xavier University of Louisiana (U)

Business Administration and Management

Adams State College (U)
Allegany College of Maryland (U, NC)
American River College (U)
Anne Arundel Community College (U)
Arapahoe Community College (U, NC)
Arizona State University (U)
Assemblies of God Theological Seminary (G, NC)
Athabasca University (U, G)
Atlantic Community College (U)
Auburn University (G)
Austin Community College (U)
Baker College (U, G)
Bakersfield College (U)
Ball State University (U, G)
Bellevue Community College (U)
Bergen Community College (U)
Black Hawk College (U)
Bladen Community College (U)
Boise State University (U)
Brevard Community College (U)
Bristol Community College (U)
Brookdale Community College (U)
Broward Community College (U)
Brown University (NC)
Bucks County Community College (U)
Burlington County College (U)
Butte College (U)
California State University, Bakersfield (U)
California State University, Dominguez Hills (G)
California State University, Fresno (U)
California State University, Fullerton (G)
California State University, Hayward (U)
California State University, Sacramento (U)
California State University, Stanislaus (U, G)
Cape Cod Community College (U)
Carl Sandburg College (U)
Catawba Valley Community College (U)
Catonsville Community College (U)
Central Community College–Grand Island Campus (U)
Central Florida Community College (U)
Central Michigan University (U)
Central Piedmont Community College (U)
Central Virginia Community College (U)
Central Washington University (U)
Chadron State College (U, G)
Champlain College (U)
Charles County Community College (U)
Charles Stewart Mott Community College (U)

Distance Learning Programs 553

Individual Courses Index

Business Administration and Management (continued)

Charter Oak State College (U)
Chattanooga State Technical Community College (U)
Chemeketa Community College (U)
Chesapeake College (U)
Chestnut Hill College (G)
Chippewa Valley Technical College (U, NC)
Christopher Newport University (U)
City College of San Francisco (U)
City Colleges of Chicago, Harold Washington College (U)
City University (U, G)
Clackamas Community College (U)
Clark College (U)
Clarkson College (U, G)
Cleary College (U)
Clovis Community College (U)
Coastline Community College (U, NC)
College of DuPage (U)
College of Lake County (U)
College of St. Francis (G)
College of St. Scholastica (U, G)
College of San Mateo (U)
College of the Southwest (U)
The College of West Virginia (U)
Collin County Community College (U)
Colorado Mountain College District (U)
Colorado State University (G)
Columbia-Greene Community College (U)
Columbia State Community College (U)
Columbus State Community College (U)
Community College of Philadelphia (U)
Community College of Rhode Island (U)
Concordia University (U)
Concordia University at Austin (U, NC)
Corning Community College (U)
Cosumnes River College (U)
County College of Morris (U)
Crafton Hills College (U)
Cumberland County College (U)
Cuyahoga Community College, Metropolitan Campus (U)
Cuyamaca College (U)
Dakota State University (U)
Dallas County Community College District (U)
Danville Community College (U)
David N. Myers College (U)
Dawson Community College (U)
Daytona Beach Community College (U)
De Anza College (U)
Delaware County Community College (U)
Delaware State University (U)
Delaware Technical & Community College, Jack F. Owens Campus (U)
Delaware Technical & Community College, Stanton/Wilmington Campus (U)
Delgado Community College (U)
Delta College (U)
Des Moines Area Community College (U)
Drake University (G)
Duke University (G)
Dutchess Community College (U)
Eastern Idaho Technical College (U)
Eastern Illinois University (U, G, NC)
Eastern Kentucky University (U)
Eastern Oregon University (U)
Eastern Wyoming College (U)
East Tennessee State University (U, G)
Edison Community College (U)

Edison State Community College (U)
Edmonds Community College (U)
El Paso Community College (U)
Embry-Riddle Aeronautical University, Extended Campus (U, G)
Essex Community College (U)
Evergreen Valley College (U)
Fairleigh Dickinson University, Florham-Madison Campus (U)
Fayetteville Technical Community College (U)
Fitchburg State College (U, G)
Florence-Darlington Technical College (U)
Florida Community College at Jacksonville (U)
Fort Hays State University (U)
Front Range Community College (U)
Gannon University (U)
Garland County Community College (U)
Garrett Community College (U, NC)
Gateway Technical College (U)
Genesee Community College (U)
Georgia Southern University (U, G)
Glendale Community College (U)
Glenville State College (U)
GMI Engineering & Management Institute (G)
Governors State University (U)
Graceland College (U)
The Graduate School of America (G)
Grand Valley State University (U, G)
Greenville Technical College (U)
Hampton University (U)
Harrisburg Area Community College (U)
Hawkeye Community College (U)
Hillsborough Community College (U)
Hocking College (U)
Houston Community College System (U)
Idaho State University (U, G)
Illinois Central College (U)
Illinois Eastern Community Colleges, Olney Central College (U)
Illinois Valley Community College (U)
Indiana State University (U)
Indiana University System (U)
Iowa State University of Science and Technology (U, G)
Iowa Wesleyan College (U)
ISIM University (G)
Ivy Tech State College–Northcentral (U)
Ivy Tech State College–Wabash Valley (U)
Jackson Community College (U, G)
Jacksonville State University (U)
Jamestown Community College (U)
Jefferson State Community College (U)
John A. Logan College (U)
John C. Calhoun State Community College (U)
John Wood Community College (U)
J. Sargeant Reynolds Community College (U)
Kankakee Community College (U)
Kansas State University (U, G, NC)
Kellogg Community College (U)
Lackawanna Junior College (U)
Lakeland Community College (U)
Lake Michigan College (U)
Lakeshore Technical College (U)
Lake-Sumter Community College (U)
Lake Superior State University (G)
Laney College (U)
Lansing Community College (U)
Laramie County Community College (U)
Laurentian University (U, G, NC)
Lawson State Community College (U)

Lee College (U)
Lehigh Carbon Community College (U)
Lesley College (G)
Liberty University (U)
Long Beach City College (U)
Longview Community College (U)
Lorain County Community College (U)
Los Angeles Community College District (U)
Louisiana State University and Agricultural and Mechanical College (U, G)
Louisiana State University in Shreveport (U, G)
Luzerne County Community College (U)
Lycoming College (U)
Madison Area Technical College (U, NC)
Madonna University (U, G)
Manatee Community College (U)
Marshall University (U, G)
Marywood University (U)
Massachusetts Institute of Technology (G)
Mayland Community College (U)
McCook Community College (U)
McDowell Technical Community College (U)
McGraw-Hill World University (U)
The McGregor School of Antioch University (G)
Memorial University of Newfoundland (U)
Mendocino College (U)
Mercy College (U)
Metropolitan Community College (U)
Metropolitan Community College (U)
Michigan Technological University (U, NC)
Middle Tennessee State University (U, G)
Midland College (U)
Midwestern State University (U, G)
Milwaukee Area Technical College (U)
Milwaukee School of Engineering (G, NC)
Minot State University (U)
MiraCosta College (U)
Mississippi State University (G)
Missouri Southern State College (U)
Modesto Junior College (U)
Mohawk Valley Community College (U)
Montgomery College–Rockville Campus (U)
Montgomery County Community College (U)
Morehead State University (U, G)
Mountain View College (U)
Mount Saint Vincent University (U)
Mt. San Antonio College (U)
Nassau Community College (U)
National Technological University (NC)
New Hampshire College (U)
New Jersey Institute of Technology (U, G)
New Mexico Junior College (U)
New Mexico State University (U, G)
New River Community College (U)
New School for Social Research (U, NC)
New York Institute of Technology (U, G)
Nicholls State University (U)
Normandale Community College (U)
Northampton County Area Community College (U)
North Central Bible College (U, NC)
North Central Technical College (U)
North Dakota State University (G)
Northeast Community College (U)
Northeast Louisiana University (U)
Northeast Wisconsin Technical College (U)
Northern Arizona University (U)
Northern Illinois University (G)
Northern Kentucky University (U, G)
Northern Oklahoma College (U)

Northern State University (U)
Northern Virginia Community College (U)
North Harris College (U)
North Hennepin Community College (U)
North Seattle Community College (U)
North Shore Community College (U)
Northwestern College (U)
Northwestern Michigan College (U)
Northwestern State University of Louisiana (NC)
Northwood University (U)
Oakton Community College (U)
Odessa College (U)
Ohio University (U)
Ohio University–Southern Campus (U, G)
Ohlone College (U)
Oklahoma City Community College (U)
Oklahoma State University (U)
Old Dominion University (U)
Owens Community College (U)
Palo Alto College (U)
Palomar College (U)
Park College (U)
Parkland College (U)
Pennsylvania State University University Park Campus (U)
Pensacola Junior College (U)
Phillips Community College of the University of Arkansas (U)
Pikes Peak Community College (U, NC)
Pima Community College (U)
Pitt Community College (U, NC)
Polytechnic University, Brooklyn Campus (NC)
Portland Community College (U, NC)
Portland State University (U, G)
Prairie State College (U)
Pratt Community College and Area Vocational School (U)
Prince George's Community College (U, NC)
Pueblo Community College (U)
Purdue University (G)
Quincy College (U)
Redlands Community College (U)
Red Rocks Community College (U)
Regent University (G)
Regis University (U)
Rend Lake College (G)
Rensselaer Polytechnic Institute (G)
The Richard Stockton College of New Jersey (U)
Rio Salado College (U)
Riverland Community College (NC)
Riverside Community College (U)
Rochester Institute of Technology (U)
Rockland Community College (U)
Rogers University (U)
Roger Williams University (U)
Roosevelt University (U)
Rose State College (U)
Rutgers, The State University of New Jersey, Newark (U, G, NC)
Ryerson Polytechnic University (U, NC)
Sacramento City College (U)
St. Johns River Community College (U)
Saint Joseph's College (U)
St. Louis Community College (U)
St. Petersburg Junior College (U)
Saint Peter's College (G)
Salt Lake Community College (U)
Salve Regina University (U, G, NC)
San Bernardino Valley College (U)
Sandhills Community College (U)

San Diego City College (U)
San Joaquin Delta College (U)
San Jose State University (U)
Santa Rosa Junior College (U)
Schoolcraft College (U)
Scott Community College (U)
Seattle Central Community College (U)
Shelby State Community College (U)
Sierra College (U)
Simpson College (U)
Sinclair Community College (U)
Skagit Valley College (U)
Skidmore College (U)
Southeast Community College, Lincoln Campus (U)
Southeastern Community College, North Campus (U, NC)
Southeastern Louisiana University (U)
Southeast Missouri State University (U)
Southern Arkansas University Tech (U)
Southern West Virginia Community and Technical College (U)
South Florida Community College (U)
Southwestern Assemblies of God University (U)
Southwestern Michigan College (U)
Southwestern Oklahoma State University (U, G)
Southwest State University (U, G)
Southwest Virginia Community College (U)
Stanly Community College (U)
State Technical Institute at Memphis (U)
State University of New York Empire State College (U)
State University of West Georgia (U, G)
Stephens College (U)
Stevens Institute of Technology (G)
Strayer College (G)
Suffolk County Community College–Ammerman Campus (U)
Sussex County Community College (U)
Syracuse University (U)
Tallahassee Community College (U)
Tarleton State University (U, G)
Tarrant County Junior College (U)
Technical College of the Lowcountry (U)
Tennessee State University (G, NC)
Texas Tech University (U)
Thomas College (U, G)
Tidewater Community College (U)
Treasure Valley Community College (U)
Triton College (U)
Troy State University Dothan (U)
Troy State University–Florida Region (U)
Troy State University Montgomery (U)
Tulsa Community College (U)
Tyler Junior College (U)
Umpqua Community College (U)
The Union Institute (U)
United States Sports Academy (G, NC)
Universitè Laval (U)
The University of Akron (U, G)
The University of Alabama (U, G)
The University of Alabama in Huntsville (G)
University of Alaska Anchorage (U)
University of Alaska Fairbanks (U)
University of Alaska Southeast (U)
University of Alaska Southeast, Sitka Campus (U)
University of Arkansas (U)
University of Baltimore (G)
University of California, Davis (U)

University of California Extension (U)
University of California, Santa Barbara (NC)
University of Cincinnati (U)
University of Colorado at Colorado Springs (U, G)
University of Dallas (G)
University of Delaware (U)
University of Georgia (U, NC)
University of Great Falls (U)
University of Hawaii–Maui Community College (U)
University of Houston (G)
University of Illinois at Springfield (G)
University of Illinois at Urbana–Champaign (U)
University of Kansas (U, NC)
University of Kentucky, Elizabethtown Community College (U)
University of Kentucky, Hazard Community College (U)
University of Kentucky, Henderson Community College (U)
University of Kentucky, Madisonville Community College (U)
University of Maine at Augusta (U)
University of Maine at Fort Kent (U)
University of Mary (U, G)
University of Maryland University College (U, G)
University of Massachusetts Boston (U)
University of Massachusetts Lowell (U)
The University of Memphis (U, G)
University of Minnesota, Twin Cities Campus (U, NC)
University of Mississippi (U, G)
University of Missouri–Columbia (U, G)
The University of Montana–Missoula (G)
University of Nebraska at Kearney (U, G)
University of Nebraska–Lincoln (U, G)
University of Nevada, Reno (U, G)
University of New Brunswick (U)
University of New Hampshire (U)
University of North Dakota (U, G)
University of Northern Iowa (U)
University of Notre Dame (NC)
University of Oklahoma (U)
University of Pennsylvania (NC)
University of Phoenix (U, G)
University of Pittsburgh (G)
University of Pittsburgh at Bradford (U)
University of St. Thomas (G)
University of Sarasota (G)
University of South Carolina (U, G)
University of South Dakota (U, G)
University of Southern California (NC)
University of Southern Colorado (U)
University of South Florida (G)
The University of Tennessee at Martin (U, G)
University of Tennessee, Knoxville (U)
The University of Texas at San Antonio (U, G)
The University of Texas at Tyler (U, G)
University of the State of New York, Regents College (U)
University of Toledo (U)
University of Utah (U)
University of Windsor (U)
University of Wisconsin–Eau Claire (U)
University of Wisconsin–Extension (U)
University of Wisconsin–Oshkosh (G)
University of Wisconsin–Platteville (U)
University of Wisconsin–River Falls (NC)

Individual Courses Index

Business Administration and Management (continued)
University of Wyoming (G)
University System of Georgia (U)
Upper Iowa University (U)
Utah State University (U)
Utah Valley State College (U)
Valley City State University (U)
Victor Valley College (U)
Vincennes University (U)
Virginia Polytechnic Institute and State University (G)
Volunteer State Community College (U)
Wake Technical Community College (U)
Walden University (G)
Walters State Community College (U)
Washington State University (U)
Washtenaw Community College (U)
Waukesha County Technical College (U)
Wayne County Community College (U)
Weber State University (U)
Western Illinois University (U, G)
Western Michigan University (G)
Western Nebraska Community College (U)
Western Oklahoma State College (U)
Westmoreland County Community College (U)
West Valley College (U)
West Virginia University (G)
West Virginia University Institute of Technology (U)
West Virginia Wesleyan College (U)
Wichita State University (U, G)
Wilfrid Laurier University (U)
Wilkes Community College (U)
William Rainey Harper College (U)
Wilson Technical Community College (U)
Winthrop University (G)
Worcester Polytechnic Institute (G)
Wytheville Community College (U)
Xavier University of Louisiana (U)
York Technical College (U)
Yuba College (U)

Business Communications
Adams State College (U)
California State University, Sacramento (U)
Catonsville Community College (U)
Christopher Newport University (U)
Colorado Mountain College District (U)
Columbus State Community College (U)
Dallas County Community College District (U)
Eastern Michigan University (U)
Gannon University (U)
The Graduate School of America (G)
International University (U, G)
Marywood University (U)
Mercy College (U)
Midland College (U)
Milwaukee School of Engineering (G, NC)
Oklahoma State University (U)
Roosevelt University (U)
Saint Peter's College (G)
Sinclair Community College (U)
State Technical Institute at Memphis (U)
State University of New York Empire State College (U)
Syracuse University (U)
Thomas Edison State College (U)
University of Illinois at Urbana–Champaign (U)

The University of North Carolina at Chapel Hill (U)
University of Washington (U)
Upper Iowa University (U)
Western Oregon University (U)
West Virginia Wesleyan College (U)
Winthrop University (G)

Business Information and Data Processing Services
Roosevelt University (U)

Business Law
Adams State College (U)
Arizona State University (U)
Atlantic Community College (U)
Austin Community College (U)
Bluefield State College (U)
Bucks County Community College (U)
Cabrillo College (U)
Carl Sandburg College (U)
Catonsville Community College (U)
Central Arizona College (U)
Christopher Newport University (U)
Colorado Mountain College District (U)
Columbus State Community College (U)
Community College of Vermont (U)
De Anza College (U)
Delgado Community College (U)
Delta College (U)
Embry-Riddle Aeronautical University, Extended Campus (U)
Greenville Technical College (U)
Lake Land College (U)
Lake-Sumter Community College (U)
Lehigh Carbon Community College (U)
Madison Area Technical College (U)
Marywood University (U)
Mercy College (U)
Midwestern State University (G)
Moraine Valley Community College (U)
New Hampshire College (U)
New River Community College (U)
Northern Virginia Community College (U)
Northwestern College (U)
Oakton Community College (U)
Oklahoma State University (U)
Owens Community College (U)
Palomar College (U)
Roger Williams University (U)
Roosevelt University (U)
Salve Regina University (U, G, NC)
San Diego City College (U)
Sinclair Community College (U)
State Technical Institute at Memphis (U)
State University of New York Empire State College (U)
State University of West Georgia (U)
Stephens College (U)
Strayer College (G)
Texas Tech University (U, NC)
Thomas Edison State College (U)
Treasure Valley Community College (U)
Triton College (U)
Universitè Laval (U)
University of Alaska Southeast (U)
University of Missouri–Columbia (U)
University of Wisconsin–Extension (NC)
Upper Iowa University (U)

Waukesha County Technical College (U)
Wayne County Community College (U)
Wilfrid Laurier University (U)
Wilson Technical Community College (U)

Calculus
Brigham Young University (U)
Bristol Community College (U)
Charles County Community College (U)
Colorado Mountain College District (U)
Cuyahoga Community College, Metropolitan Campus (U)
Delaware Technical & Community College, Stanton/Wilmington Campus (U)
Embry-Riddle Aeronautical University, Extended Campus (U)
Grand Rapids Community College (U)
J. Sargeant Reynolds Community College (U)
Kansas State University (U)
Laramie County Community College (U)
Midland College (U)
Northeastern University (U)
Northern Virginia Community College (U)
Northwestern Michigan College (U)
Oklahoma State University (U)
Portland State University (U)
Rutgers, The State University of New Jersey, Newark (U)
Southwest Texas State University (U)
State University of New York Empire State College (U)
State University of West Georgia (U)
Syracuse University (U)
Texas Tech University (U, NC)
The University of Alabama in Huntsville (NC)
University of Alaska Fairbanks (U)
University of Delaware (U)
The University of Iowa (U, G)
University of Michigan (U)
University of Nebraska–Lincoln (U)
The University of North Carolina at Chapel Hill (U)
University of Southern Mississippi (U)
University of Tennessee, Knoxville (U)
University of Waterloo (U, NC)
University System of Georgia (U)
Western Washington University (U)
Yuba College (U)

Canadian Studies
Ryerson Polytechnic University (U)
Universitè Laval (U)
University of Waterloo (U)
Valley City State University (U)
Western Washington University (U)

Cell Biology
Penn Valley Community College (U)
Universitè Laval (U)

Chemical Engineering
Arizona State University (U, G)
Brevard Community College (U)
Colorado State University (G)
Florida State University (G)
Idaho State University (U, G)
Illinois Institute of Technology (G)

556   Distance Learning Programs

Individual Courses Index

Iowa State University of Science and Technology (G)
Kansas State University (G, NC)
Lehigh University (G, NC)
Michigan State University (G)
Mississippi State University (G)
National Technological University (G, NC)
New Jersey Institute of Technology (G)
New Mexico State University (G)
North Carolina State University (G)
Ohio University–Southern Campus (U)
Oklahoma State University (U, G)
Shenandoah University (G)
Southwest Virginia Community College (U)
Texas Tech University (G)
The University of Alabama (G)
University of Alberta (U)
University of Delaware (U, G, NC)
University of Idaho (U, G)
University of Massachusetts Amherst (G, NC)
University of Missouri–Kansas City (G)
University of North Dakota (U)
University of South Florida (G)
University of Tennessee, Knoxville (G)
The University of Texas at San Antonio (U)
University of Virginia (G)
West Virginia University (G)
West Virginia University Institute of Technology (U, G)

Chemistry
Anne Arundel Community College (U)
Arapahoe Community College (U)
Athabasca University (U)
Bellevue Community College (U)
Bemidji State University (U)
Brigham Young University (U)
Bristol Community College (U)
Bucks County Community College (U)
California College for Health Sciences (U)
California State University, Stanislaus (U)
Carleton University (U)
Catonsville Community College (U)
Central Arizona College (U)
Central Methodist College (U)
Chippewa Valley Technical College (U)
City Colleges of Chicago, Harold Washington College (U)
Coastline Community College (U, NC)
College of DuPage (U)
College of San Mateo (U)
The College of West Virginia (U)
Colorado Mountain College District (U)
Community College of Philadelphia (U)
Concordia University (U)
Concordia University Wisconsin (U, G)
County College of Morris (U)
Daytona Beach Community College (U)
Delaware Technical & Community College, Jack F. Owens Campus (U)
Delaware Technical & Community College, Stanton/Wilmington Campus (U)
Delta College (U)
East Tennessee State University (U)
Edison Community College (U)
Ellsworth Community College (U)
Florida Atlantic University (G)
Florida Community College at Jacksonville (U)
Floyd College (U)
Garland County Community College (U)
Graceland College (U)
Hampton University (U)
Harrisburg Area Community College (U)
Hibbing Community College (U)
Hillsborough Community College (U)
Idaho State University (U, G)
Illinois Institute of Technology (G)
Iowa Western Community College (U)
Jamestown Community College (U)
Johnson County Community College (U)
J. Sargeant Reynolds Community College (U)
Kansas State University (U)
Lakehead University (U)
Lane Community College (U)
Laurentian University (U)
Lehigh University (G, NC)
Metropolitan Community College (U)
Metropolitan State College of Denver (U)
Midwestern State University (G)
Milwaukee Area Technical College (U)
Minnesota West Community and Technical College–Worthington Campus (U)
Missouri Western State College (U)
Modesto Junior College (U)
Montana State University–Bozeman (G)
Montgomery College–Rockville Campus (U)
Morgan Community College (U, NC)
National Technological University (G, NC)
New Jersey Institute of Technology (U)
North Carolina State University (U)
Northcentral Technical College (U)
North Dakota State College of Science (U)
Northeast Community College (U)
Northeast Louisiana University (U)
Northern Virginia Community College (U)
North Seattle Community College (U)
North Shore Community College (U)
Northwestern State University of Louisiana (U)
Ohio University (U)
Park College (U)
Pennsylvania State University University Park Campus (U)
Penn Valley Community College (U)
Pikes Peak Community College (U, NC)
Portland Community College (U)
Pueblo Community College (U)
Rio Salado College (U)
Rochester Institute of Technology (U)
Rutgers, The State University of New Jersey, Newark (U)
Salt Lake Community College (U)
Scott Community College (U)
Seattle Central Community College (U)
Sinclair Community College (U)
Skagit Valley College (U)
South Florida Community College (U)
Southwestern Oklahoma State University (U)
Southwest Missouri State University (U)
Southwest State University (U)
Stephens College (U)
Tallahassee Community College (U)
Thomas Edison State College (U)
Treasure Valley Community College (U)
Troy State University Montgomery (U)
Tyler Junior College (U)
The University of Alabama at Birmingham (G)
University of Alaska Fairbanks (U)
University of Alaska Southeast, Sitka Campus (U)
The University of Calgary (U, G)
University of California Extension (U)
University of Delaware (U)
University of Great Falls (U)
University of Guelph (U)
University of Hawaii–Leeward Community College (U)
University of Mary (U)
University of Massachusetts Dartmouth (U)
University of Massachusetts Lowell (U)
University of Minnesota, Twin Cities Campus (U)
University of Nebraska–Lincoln (U)
The University of North Carolina at Chapel Hill (U)
University of Oklahoma (U)
University of South Florida (U)
University of Utah (U)
University of Washington (U)
University of Waterloo (U, NC)
University of Windsor (U)
Utah State University (U)
Utah Valley State College (U)
Vincennes University (U)
Wake Technical Community College (U)
Waubonsee Community College (U)
Weber State University (U)
Western Oklahoma State College (U)
Wilfrid Laurier University (U)

Chemistry, Inorganic
Pratt Community College and Area Vocational School (U)

Chemistry, Organic
Ellsworth Community College (U)
Thomas Edison State College (U)
University of Waterloo (U)

Child Care and Development
Bakersfield College (U)
Carl Sandburg College (U)
Central Arizona College (U)
Colorado Mountain College District (U)
Colorado State University (U)
Crafton Hills College (U)
Hudson Valley Community College (U)
Iowa State University of Science and Technology (G)
Lane Community College (U)
Northeast Wisconsin Technical College (U)
Northwestern Michigan College (U)
Penn Valley Community College (U)
San Bernardino Valley College (U)
Seattle Central Community College (U)
Southwest Missouri State University (U)
State University of New York Empire State College (U)
Troy State University Montgomery (U)
University of Alaska Fairbanks (U)
University of Delaware (U)
University of Tennessee, Knoxville (U)
University of Wisconsin–Stevens Point (U, G)
Wayne County Community College (U)
Yuba College (U)

Chinese Language and Literature
Rutgers, The State University of New Jersey, Newark (U)

Individual Courses Index

Civil Engineering
Arizona State University (U, G)
Blue Mountain Community College (U)
Brigham Young University (U)
California State University, Northridge (U, G)
Carleton University (U)
Colorado State University (G)
Florida State University (G)
Georgia Institute of Technology (G, NC)
Iowa State University of Science and Technology (G, NC)
Kansas State University (G, NC)
Michigan Technological University (U, NC)
Mississippi State University (G)
Montana State University–Bozeman (G)
National Technological University (G, NC)
New Jersey Institute of Technology (G)
New Mexico State University (G)
North Carolina State University (G)
North Dakota State University (G)
Old Dominion University (G)
Oregon State University (G)
Pennsylvania State University University Park Campus (U, NC)
Shenandoah University (G)
Southern Polytechnic State University (U)
Southwest Virginia Community College (U)
State University of New York at Buffalo (G)
State University of New York College of Environmental Science and Forestry (G)
Tennessee State University (G)
Texas Tech University (G)
The University of Alabama (G)
The University of Alabama in Huntsville (G)
University of Arizona (G)
The University of Calgary (U)
University of California Extension (U)
University of Colorado at Boulder (G, NC)
University of Delaware (G)
University of Idaho (U, G)
University of Maine (U, G)
University of Maine at Fort Kent (U, G)
University of Massachusetts Lowell (G)
University of Missouri–Kansas City (G)
University of Nebraska–Lincoln (U, G)
University of North Dakota (U)
University of North Florida (G)
University of Oklahoma (G)
University of South Florida (G)
University of Tennessee, Knoxville (G)
The University of Texas at Arlington (G)
The University of Texas at San Antonio (U, G)
University of Virginia (G)
University of Wisconsin–Extension (NC)
University of Wyoming (G)
Virginia Polytechnic Institute and State University (G)
West Virginia University Institute of Technology (U, G)

Classical Languages and Literatures
Acadia University (U)
Assemblies of God Theological Seminary (G, NC)
Berean University of the Assemblies of God (U)
City Colleges of Chicago, Harold Washington College (U)
Community College of Rhode Island (U)
Copiah-Lincoln Community College (U)
Corning Community College (U)
Darton College (NC)
Dodge City Community College (U)
Dutchess Community College (U)
Indiana University System (U)
International Bible College (U)
LIFE Bible College (U)
Lycoming College (U)
The McGregor School of Antioch University (G)
Moody Bible Institute (U)
Morgan Community College (U, NC)
New School for Social Research (U, NC)
North Carolina State University (U)
North Central Bible College (U, NC)
Ohio University (U)
Ohio University–Southern Campus (U)
Portland State University (U)
Riverside Community College (U)
Rogers University (U)
San Diego City College (U)
Santa Fe Community College (U)
Skidmore College (U)
Southwest Missouri State University (U)
University of Alaska Fairbanks (U)
University of Delaware (U)
University of Georgia (U)
University of Guelph (U)
University of Kansas (U, NC)
University of Minnesota, Twin Cities Campus (U)
University of Missouri–Columbia (U, G)
University of Nebraska–Lincoln (U)
University of Oklahoma (U)
University of Pennsylvania (U, NC)
University System of Georgia (U)
Washington State University (U)
Yuba College (U)

Cognitive Psychology
California State University, Stanislaus (U)
Carleton University (U)
Clovis Community College (U)
Colorado State University (U)
Community College of Vermont (U)
The Graduate School of America (G)
Northeast Wisconsin Technical College (U)
Salve Regina University (G, NC)
State University of New York at Oswego (U)
Universitè Laval (U)
University of Illinois at Urbana–Champaign (U)
University of Tennessee, Knoxville (U)

Communications
Assemblies of God Theological Seminary (G, NC)
Athabasca University (U)
Berean University of the Assemblies of God (U)
Blackhawk Technical College (U)
Boise State University (U)
Bradley University (U)
Brigham Young University (U)
California State University, Stanislaus (U)
Calvin College (G)
Central Arizona College (U)
Central Community College–Grand Island Campus (U)
Central Piedmont Community College (U)
Chapman University (U)
Chesapeake College (U)
Clovis Community College (U)
College of St. Scholastica (U, G)
The College of West Virginia (U)
Columbia State Community College (U)
Concordia University at Austin (U, NC)
Cosumnes River College (U)
Covenant Theological Seminary (G, NC)
David N. Myers College (U)
Daytona Beach Community College (U)
Edison Community College (U)
Essex Community College (U)
Fairleigh Dickinson University, Florham-Madison Campus (U)
Fairleigh Dickinson University, Teaneck–Hackensack (G)
Gadsden State Community College (U)
Governors State University (U)
Griggs University (U)
Indiana University System (U)
Joliet Junior College (U)
Kellogg Community College (U)
Lakeshore Technical College (U)
Lamar University (U)
Lehigh Carbon Community College (U)
LIFE Bible College (U)
Lord Fairfax Community College (U)
Louisiana State University and Agricultural and Mechanical College (U)
Marywood University (U, G)
Mercy College (U)
Metropolitan State College of Denver (U)
Metropolitan State University (U)
Michigan State University (G)
Milwaukee Area Technical College (U)
Missouri Southern State College (U)
Nassau Community College (U)
New School for Social Research (U, G, NC)
New York Institute of Technology (U)
North Carolina State University (U)
Northeast Wisconsin Technical College (U)
North Harris College (U)
North Iowa Area Community College (U)
North Shore Community College (U)
Oakland University (U)
Odessa College (U)
The Ohio State University (U)
Oklahoma State University (G)
Old Dominion University (U)
Parkland College (U)
Piedmont College (U)
Pikes Peak Community College (U, NC)
Quincy College (U)
Red Rocks Community College (U)
Rensselaer Polytechnic Institute (G, NC)
Rio Salado College (U)
Rochester Institute of Technology (U)
Roger Williams University (U)
Ryerson Polytechnic University (U)
St. Johns River Community College (U)
Santa Rosa Junior College (U)
Simpson College (U)
Sinclair Community College (U)
Skidmore College (U)
Southeast Community College, Lincoln Campus (U)
Southeast Missouri State University (U)
Southern Methodist University (G)
Southwestern Assemblies of God University (U)
Southwestern Michigan College (U)
Southwest Missouri State University (U)

558 Distance Learning Programs

Individual Courses Index

Southwest State University (U)
State University of New York at New Paltz (U)
State University of New York Empire State College (U)
Suffolk County Community College–Ammerman Campus (U)
Sul Ross State University (U)
Tallahassee Community College (U)
Taylor University, Fort Wayne Campus (U)
The Union Institute (U)
Universitè Laval (U)
The University of Akron (U)
University of Alaska Fairbanks (U)
University of Alaska Southeast, Sitka Campus (U)
University of Baltimore (U)
University of California Extension (U)
University of California, Santa Barbara (NC)
University of Cincinnati Raymond Walters College (U)
University of Georgia (U)
University of Great Falls (U)
University of Hawaii–Maui Community College (U)
University of Houston (U)
University of Kentucky (G)
University of Maine at Augusta (U)
University of Mary (U, G)
University of Maryland, College Park (U)
University of Maryland University College (U)
University of Nebraska–Lincoln (U)
The University of North Carolina at Chapel Hill (U)
University of Northern Iowa (U, G)
University of Phoenix (U, G)
University of Pittsburgh at Bradford (NC)
University of Tennessee, Knoxville (G)
The University of Texas at Austin (U)
The University of Texas at El Paso (U, G)
The University of Texas at San Antonio (U)
The University of Texas at Tyler (U, G)
The University of Texas of the Permian Basin (U)
University of Washington (U)
University of Wisconsin–Stevens Point (U, G)
University of Wyoming (U)
University System of Georgia (U)
Volunteer State Community College (U)
Washington State University (U)
Weber State University (U)
Wichita State University (U, G)

Community Health Services

Brigham Young University (U)
Catonsville Community College (U)
Dalhousie University (U, G)
Kansas State University (U, G, NC)
Oklahoma State University (NC)
Salve Regina University (U, NC)
State University of New York Empire State College (U)
University of Illinois at Urbana–Champaign (U)
University of Mary (U, G)
University of Northern Colorado (U)
University of South Dakota (G)

Community Services

Christopher Newport University (U)
Pratt Community College and Area Vocational School (U, G)

Comparative Literature

City University (U)
Clark State Community College (U)
Eastern Kentucky University (U)
Floyd College (U)
Laramie County Community College (U)
Mercy College (U)
Missouri Western State College (U)
Northern Virginia Community College (U)
Saint Peter's College (U)
Salve Regina University (U, NC)
Seattle Pacific University (U)
Syracuse University (U)
University of Waterloo (U)
Upper Iowa University (U)

Computer and Information Sciences

Acadia University (U)
Allegany College of Maryland (U, NC)
Anne Arundel Community College (U)
Arapahoe Community College (U, NC)
Arizona State University (U, G)
Arkansas Tech University (U)
Athabasca University (U)
Austin Community College (U)
Baker College (U, G)
Bakersfield College (U)
Ball State University (G)
Bellevue Community College (U)
Black Hawk College (U)
Bluefield State College (U)
Boise State University (U)
Brevard Community College (U)
Broward Community College (U)
Bucks County Community College (U)
Buena Vista University (U)
Burlington County College (U)
California College for Health Sciences (U)
California State University, Chico (U, G, NC)
California State University, Hayward (U)
California State University, Sacramento (U)
California State University, Stanislaus (U, G)
Central Community College–Grand Island Campus (U)
Central Piedmont Community College (U)
Champlain College (U, NC)
Charles County Community College (U)
Charles Stewart Mott Community College (U)
Chattanooga State Technical Community College (U)
Chemeketa Community College (U)
Chesapeake College (U)
Chippewa Valley Technical College (U, NC)
City University (U, G)
Cleary College (U)
Clovis Community College (U)
Coastline Community College (U, NC)
Colby Community College (U)
College of DuPage (U)
College of San Mateo (U)
The College of West Virginia (U)
Colorado Electronic Community College (U)
Colorado State University (G)
Columbus State Community College (U)
Community College of Vermont (U)
Cuyahoga Community College, Metropolitan Campus (U)
Dakota State University (U)
Daytona Beach Community College (U)
De Anza College (U)
Delaware County Community College (U)
DePaul University (U, G)
Des Moines Area Community College (U)
East Carolina University (U, G)
Eastern Idaho Technical College (U)
Eastern New Mexico University (U, G)
Eastern Oregon University (U)
Edmonds Community College (U)
Embry-Riddle Aeronautical University, Extended Campus (U, G)
Evergreen Valley College (U)
Florida Atlantic University (G)
Florida Community College at Jacksonville (U)
Franklin University (U, NC)
Front Range Community College (U)
Garland County Community College (U)
Garrett Community College (NC)
Genesee Community College (U)
George C. Wallace State Community College (U)
Graceland College (U)
Grand Rapids Community College (U)
Great Basin College (U)
Greenville Technical College (U)
Hampton University (U, NC)
Hillsborough Community College (U)
Houston Community College System (U)
Howard Community College (U)
Idaho State University (U, G)
Illinois Institute of Technology (U, G)
Illinois Valley Community College (U)
Indiana University System (U)
Iowa State University of Science and Technology (U, G)
ISIM University (G)
Ivy Tech State College–Wabash Valley (U)
Jacksonville State University (U)
Jamestown Community College (U)
John C. Calhoun State Community College (U)
Johnson County Community College (U)
J. Sargeant Reynolds Community College (U)
Judson College (U)
Kansas State University (G, NC)
Lakeshore Technical College (U)
Lane Community College (U)
Laney College (U)
Lansing Community College (U)
Laramie County Community College (U)
Laurentian University (U)
Lee College (U)
Longview Community College (U)
Manatee Community College (U)
McGraw-Hill World University (NC)
Memorial University of Newfoundland (U)
Mercy College (U)
Metropolitan Community College (U)
Metropolitan State College of Denver (U)
Michigan State University (U, G)
Midland College (U)
Milwaukee Area Technical College (U)
Minnesota West Community and Technical College–Worthington Campus (U)
Mississippi State University (G)
Missouri Southern State College (U)
Montana State University–Bozeman (U)

Distance Learning Programs

Individual Courses Index

Computer and Information Sciences (continued)
Montgomery College–Rockville Campus (U)
National Technological University (G, NC)
New Hampshire College (U, G)
New Jersey Institute of Technology (U, G)
New River Community College (U)
New School for Social Research (U, NC)
New York University (G)
North Carolina State University (U)
Northeast Community College (U)
Northeastern University (G)
Northeast Louisiana University (U)
Northern Virginia Community College (U)
North Harris College (U)
Northwestern College (U)
Northwestern Michigan College (U)
Northwestern State University of Louisiana (U, NC)
Nova Southeastern University (G)
Oakton Community College (U)
Oklahoma State University (U)
Old Dominion University (U, G)
Oregon State University (U, G)
Owens Community College (U)
Pikes Peak Community College (U, NC)
Pima Community College (U)
Pitt Community College (U, NC)
Polytechnic University, Brooklyn Campus (NC)
Polytechnic University, Westchester Graduate Center (G)
Portland Community College (U)
Portland State University (U, G)
Pratt Community College and Area Vocational School (U)
Prince George's Community College (U, NC)
Pueblo Community College (U)
Redlands Community College (NC)
Red Rocks Community College (U)
Regis University (U)
Rend Lake College (U)
Rensselaer Polytechnic Institute (G, NC)
The Richard Stockton College of New Jersey (NC)
Rio Salado College (U)
Rochester Institute of Technology (U, G)
Rockland Community College (U)
Rogers University (U)
Roger Williams University (U)
Roosevelt University (U)
St. Johns River Community College (U)
St. Louis Community College (U)
St. Petersburg Junior College (U)
Salt Lake Community College (U)
Salve Regina University (G, NC)
Sandhills Community College (U)
San Diego City College (U)
San Diego State University (U)
Santa Fe Community College (U)
Santa Rosa Junior College (U)
Schoolcraft College (U)
Scottsdale Community College (U)
Shawnee Community College (U)
Sinclair Community College (U)
Skagit Valley College (U)
Skidmore College (U)
Southern Arkansas University Tech (U)
Southern Polytechnic State University (G)
Southern Utah University (U)
Southern West Virginia Community and Technical College (U)

Southwestern Assemblies of God University (U)
Southwestern Oklahoma State University (U)
Southwest Missouri State University (G)
Southwest State University (U)
Southwest Texas State University (U)
State University of New York Empire State College (U)
State University of West Georgia (U)
Stevens Institute of Technology (G)
Strayer College (G)
Sul Ross State University (U)
Tallahassee Community College (U)
Tarrant County Junior College (U)
Taylor University, Fort Wayne Campus (U)
Texas Tech University (U)
Thomas Edison State College (U)
Trinidad State Junior College (U)
Tulsa Community College (U)
Tyler Junior College (U)
The Union Institute (U)
Universitè Laval (U)
The University of Alabama (U, G)
The University of Alabama at Birmingham (G)
University of Alaska Fairbanks (U)
University of Alaska Southeast, Sitka Campus (U)
University of Alberta (U)
University of Baltimore (G)
University of British Columbia (U)
The University of Calgary (G)
University of California, Davis (U)
University of California Extension (U)
University of California, Santa Barbara (G, NC)
University of California, Santa Cruz (U, G)
The University of Charleston (U, NC)
University of Colorado at Boulder (G, NC)
University of Great Falls (U)
University of Hawaii–Maui Community College (U, NC)
University of Houston (U, G)
University of Houston–Clear Lake (G)
University of Idaho (U, G)
University of Illinois at Springfield (U, G)
The University of Iowa (G)
University of Kentucky (G)
University of Maine at Fort Kent (U)
University of Mary (U, G)
University of Maryland, College Park (U)
University of Maryland University College (U, G)
University of Massachusetts Amherst (U, G, NC)
University of Massachusetts Lowell (U)
University of Minnesota, Twin Cities Campus (U)
University of Missouri–Columbia (U)
University of Missouri–Kansas City (U, G)
The University of Montana–Missoula (G)
University of Nebraska at Kearney (U, G)
University of Nebraska–Lincoln (G)
University of Nevada, Las Vegas (U)
University of Nevada, Reno (U)
University of New Brunswick (U)
The University of North Carolina at Chapel Hill (U)
University of North Florida (G)
University of Oklahoma (G)
University of Phoenix (U, G)
University of St. Thomas (G, NC)
University of Saskatchewan (U)
University of South Carolina (G)

University of Southern California (G, NC)
University of Southern Indiana (U)
University of South Florida (U, G)
University of Tennessee, Knoxville (G)
University of Tennessee Space Institute (G)
The University of Texas at Austin (NC)
The University of Texas at San Antonio (U, G)
The University of Texas of the Permian Basin (U)
University of Washington (NC)
University of West Florida (U)
University of Windsor (U)
University of Wisconsin–Stevens Point (U, G)
University of Wisconsin–Stout (NC)
Utah State University (U)
Victor Valley College (U)
Vincennes University (U)
Volunteer State Community College (U)
Wake Technical Community College (U)
Washtenaw Community College (U)
Wayne County Community College (U)
Wayne State University (G)
Weber State University (U)
Western Illinois University (U)
Western Michigan University (G)
Western Montana College of The University of Montana (U, NC)
Western Oregon University (U)
Wichita State University (U)
William Penn College (U)
Worcester Polytechnic Institute (G)

Computer Programming
Austin Community College (U)
Central Florida Community College (U)
Charles County Community College (U)
Dallas County Community College District (U)
Kingwood College (U)
Metropolitan State College of Denver (U)
Midland College (U)
Missouri Western State College (U)
National Technological University (G, NC)
New Hampshire College (U)
North Seattle Community College (U)
NRI Schools (NC)
Oklahoma State University (U)
Park College (U)
Pitt Community College (U, NC)
Polytechnic University, Westchester Graduate Center (G)
Roosevelt University (U)
Southern Polytechnic State University (G)
State University of New York at Oswego (U)
Tarleton State University (U, G)
Texas Tech University (G)
Thomas College (U)
Universitè Laval (U)
University of California, Davis (U)
University of Waterloo (U)

Conservation and Natural Resources
Athabasca University (U)
Bellevue Community College (U)
Berean University of the Assemblies of God (U)
Black Hills State University (U)
Burlington County College (U)
California State University, Sacramento (U)
College of San Mateo (U)
College of the Southwest (U)

The College of West Virginia (U)
Colorado State University (U, G)
Community College of Philadelphia (U)
Cosumnes River College (U)
De Anza College (U)
Eastern Maine Technical College (U)
Garland County Community College (U)
Indiana University System (U)
Kansas State University (U, G, NC)
Los Angeles Pierce College (U)
Louisiana State University in Shreveport (U, G)
Luzerne County Community College (U)
The McGregor School of Antioch University (G)
Memorial University of Newfoundland (U)
Mid-State Technical College (U)
Minnesota West Community and Technical College–Worthington Campus (U)
New Jersey Institute of Technology (U, G)
Oregon State University (U)
Owens Community College (U)
Pikes Peak Community College (U, NC)
The Richard Stockton College of New Jersey (U)
Rochester Institute of Technology (U)
San Bernardino Valley College (U)
Scott Community College (U)
State University of New York at Binghamton (U)
Texas Tech University (U)
Tulsa Community College (U)
The University of Alabama in Huntsville (G)
University of Alaska Fairbanks (U)
The University of Calgary (NC)
University of California Extension (U)
University of Georgia (U)
University of Guelph (U)
University of Kansas (U, NC)
University of Michigan (U)
University of Minnesota, Twin Cities Campus (U)
University of Nebraska–Lincoln (U, NC)
University of Nevada, Las Vegas (U)
University of Oklahoma (G)
University of Southern Colorado (U)
University of Tennessee, Knoxville (U)
University of Wisconsin–Stevens Point (U, G, NC)
University of Wyoming (U)
University System of Georgia (U)
Utah State University (U)
Washington State University (U)

Continuing Education
The Graduate School of America (G)
Northern Illinois University (G)
Oklahoma State University (NC)
Pitt Community College (NC)
Pratt Community College and Area Vocational School (U)
Rutgers, The State University of New Jersey, Newark (G, NC)
San Jose State University (U)
Seattle Pacific University (G)
University of Alaska Southeast (G, NC)
The University of Calgary (G)
University of Toledo (NC)

Corrections
Central Florida Community College (U)
Christopher Newport University (U)
Eastern Kentucky University (U)

Hocking College (U)
University of Missouri–Columbia (U)

Counseling Psychology
Columbus State University (G)
Denver Conservative Baptist Seminary (G, NC)
The Graduate School of America (G)
Liberty University (G)
Lincoln Christian College (G, NC)
Oral Roberts University (U)
Rio Salado College (U)
Southern Christian University (G)
State University of New York Empire State College (U)
Taylor University, Fort Wayne Campus (U)
Temple Baptist Seminary (G, NC)
University of Baltimore (G)

Creative Writing
Athabasca University (U)
Bellevue Community College (U)
Bemidji State University (U)
Brigham Young University (U)
Brookdale Community College (U)
Catawba Valley Community College (U)
Catonsville Community College (U)
Central Community College–Grand Island Campus (U)
Central Washington University (U)
Chadron State College (U, G)
Charles County Community College (U)
Chattanooga State Technical Community College (U)
Chemeketa Community College (U)
Chippewa Valley Technical College (U)
Christopher Newport University (U)
City Colleges of Chicago, Harold Washington College (U)
Clark State Community College (U)
Colby Community College (U)
College of the Southwest (U)
Colorado Mountain College District (U)
Columbia Basin College (U)
Concordia University (U)
Cosumnes River College (U)
Cumberland County College (U)
Cuyahoga Community College, Metropolitan Campus (U)
Dallas County Community College District (U)
Dawson Community College (U)
Dodge City Community College (U)
Eastern Washington University (U)
Essex Community College (U)
Fayetteville Technical Community College (U)
Fort Hays State University (U)
Garland County Community College (U)
Genesee Community College (U)
Hampton University (NC)
Hudson Valley Community College (U)
Idaho State University (U, G)
Illinois Central College (U)
Illinois Eastern Community Colleges, Olney Central College (U)
Indiana University System (U)
J. Sargeant Reynolds Community College (U)
Judson College (U)
Kellogg Community College (U)
Laramie County Community College (U)
Laurentian University (U)

Lorain County Community College (U)
Louisiana College (U)
Lycoming College (U)
The McGregor School of Antioch University (G)
Metropolitan Community College (U)
Minot State University (U)
Mississippi Delta Community College (NC)
New Hampshire College (U)
New School for Social Research (U, G, NC)
North Carolina State University (U)
Northeast Community College (U)
Northern Arizona University (U)
Northern Oklahoma College (U)
Northern Virginia Community College (U)
Northwestern College (U)
Northwestern Michigan College (U)
Northwestern State University of Louisiana (NC)
Northwest Iowa Community College (U)
NRI Schools (NC)
Ohio University (U)
Oklahoma State University (U)
Park College (U)
Pennsylvania State University University Park Campus (U)
Portland Community College (U)
Portland State University (U)
Pratt Community College and Area Vocational School (U)
Redlands Community College (U)
Richland Community College (U)
Rogers University (U)
St. Petersburg Junior College (U)
Scottsdale Community College (U)
Sinclair Community College (U)
Skagit Valley College (U)
Skidmore College (U)
Southern Vermont College (U)
Southwestern Assemblies of God University (U)
Southwest State University (U)
Southwest Virginia Community College (U)
State University of West Georgia (U)
Stephens College (U)
Suffolk County Community College–Ammerman Campus (U)
Tallahassee Community College (U)
Tarrant County Junior College (U)
Tennessee Temple University (U)
Texas A&M University–Commerce (U)
Texas Tech University (U)
Thomas Edison State College (U)
The Union Institute (U)
University of Alaska Anchorage (U)
University of Alaska Fairbanks (U)
University of Alaska Southeast, Sitka Campus (U)
University of Arkansas at Little Rock (U)
The University of Calgary (U)
University of California Extension (U, NC)
University of California, Santa Barbara (U, NC)
University of Great Falls (U)
University of Houston (U)
University of Kansas (U, NC)
University of Kentucky, Madisonville Community College (U)
University of Minnesota, Twin Cities Campus (U)
University of Missouri–Columbia (U)
University of Missouri–Kansas City (U)
University of Nebraska at Kearney (U)

Individual Courses Index

Creative Writing (continued)
The University of North Carolina at Chapel Hill (U)
University of Oklahoma (NC)
University of Southern Mississippi (U)
University of South Florida (U)
University of Tennessee, Knoxville (U, NC)
University of Toledo (U)
University of Utah (U)
University of Washington (U, NC)
Utah State University (U)
Vincennes University (U)
Volunteer State Community College (U)
Wake Technical Community College (U)
Washington State University (U)
Waubonsee Community College (U)
Weber State University (U)
Western Illinois University (U, G)
Western Washington University (U)
Westmoreland County Community College (U)
Yuba College (U)

Criminal Justice
Auburn University (U)
Bluefield State College (U)
California State University, Sacramento (U)
Christopher Newport University (U)
City University (U, G)
Clovis Community College (U)
Colorado Mountain College District (U)
Columbia State Community College (U)
Columbus State University (G)
Eastern Kentucky University (U)
Frostburg State University (U)
Kankakee Community College (U)
Lake Land College (U)
Laramie County Community College (U)
Mercy College (U)
Metropolitan State College of Denver (U)
New York Institute of Technology (U)
Northern Virginia Community College (U)
Owens Community College (U)
Park College (U)
Pine Technical College (U)
Pratt Community College and Area Vocational School (U, G)
Rutgers, The State University of New Jersey, Newark (U)
Sauk Valley Community College (U)
State University of New York Empire State College (U)
Taylor University, Fort Wayne Campus (U)
Treasure Valley Community College (U)
Troy State University–Florida Region (U)
The University of Alabama at Birmingham (G)
University of Arkansas at Little Rock (U)
University of Cincinnati (U)
University of Maryland University College (U)
University of Missouri–Columbia (U, G)
University of Southern Mississippi (U)
University of Tennessee, Knoxville (U)
The University of Texas of the Permian Basin (G)

Criminology
Colorado Northwestern Community College (U)
Manchester Community-Technical College (U)
Marshall University (U)
New York Institute of Technology (U)
Northern Virginia Community College (U)
Roger Williams University (U)
Southern Oregon University (U)
Southern West Virginia Community and Technical College (U)
Southwest Texas State University (U)
Treasure Valley Community College (U)
University of Baltimore (U)
The University of Iowa (U, G)
University of Northern Iowa (U, G)
University of Waterloo (U)
West Virginia Wesleyan College (U)
Wilfrid Laurier University (U)

Curriculum and Instruction
Brigham Young University (U)
California State University, Sacramento (G)
Chestnut Hill College (G)
City University (G)
College of St. Scholastica (G)
Columbus State University (U, G)
Eastern Kentucky University (U, G)
Frostburg State University (U, G)
The Graduate School of America (G)
Iowa State University of Science and Technology (G)
Laramie County Community College (U)
Lesley College (G)
Michigan State University (G)
Northern Illinois University (G)
Oral Roberts University (G)
Saint Peter's College (G)
Southwest Missouri State University (G)
Tarleton State University (G)
Texas Tech University (G)
University of Alaska Southeast (U, G)
University of Houston (G)
University of Massachusetts Boston (G)
University of Missouri–Columbia (U, G)
University of Nebraska–Lincoln (U)
University of Tennessee, Knoxville (U)
The University of Texas of the Permian Basin (U, G)
University of Wisconsin–Extension (U)
Western Washington University (U)

Database Management
Kingwood College (U)
Michigan State University (G)
Midland College (U)
National Technological University (G, NC)
Roosevelt University (U)
Salve Regina University (G, NC)
Texas Tech University (G)
Thomas College (U)
Universitè Laval (U)
University of California, Davis (U)

Design
De Anza College (U)
Garland County Community College (U)
Garrett Community College (NC)
Illinois Eastern Community Colleges, Olney Central College (U)
Ivy Tech State College–Wabash Valley (U)
John C. Calhoun State Community College (U)
Manatee Community College (U)
McGraw-Hill World University (NC)
The McGregor School of Antioch University (G)
Moraine Valley Community College (U)
New School for Social Research (U, NC)
Northern Arizona University (U)
Northwestern State University of Louisiana (NC)
Pennsylvania State University University Park Campus (U)
Polytechnic University, Brooklyn Campus (G, NC)
Prairie State College (U)
Southwest Missouri State University (U)
Southwest State University (U)
University of California Extension (U)
University of Hawaii–Maui Community College (U)
University of Minnesota, Twin Cities Campus (U)
University of Nebraska–Lincoln (U)

Developmental and Child Psychology
Adams State College (U)
Allegany College of Maryland (U)
Anne Arundel Community College (U)
Arizona State University (U)
Athabasca University (U)
Atlantic Community College (U)
Auburn University (U)
Austin Community College (U)
Bellevue Community College (U)
Berean University of the Assemblies of God (U)
Bergen Community College (U)
Black Hills State University (U, G)
Bluefield State College (U)
Blue Mountain Community College (U)
Boise State University (U)
Brevard Community College (U)
Brigham Young University (U)
Brookdale Community College (U)
Broward Community College (U)
Burlington County College (U)
Butte College (U)
California College for Health Sciences (U)
California State University, Fresno (U)
Camden County College (U)
Carleton University (U)
Catawba Valley Community College (U)
Catonsville Community College (U)
Central Community College–Grand Island Campus (U)
Central Florida Community College (U)
Central Piedmont Community College (U)
Central Virginia Community College (U)
Central Washington University (U)
Chadron State College (U)
Charles County Community College (U)
Charles Stewart Mott Community College (U)
Chattanooga State Technical Community College (U)
Chemeketa Community College (U)
Chippewa Valley Technical College (U)
City Colleges of Chicago, Harold Washington College (U)
Clark College (U)
Clarkson College (U)
Clayton College & State University (U)
Clovis Community College (U)
Coastline Community College (U, NC)
Colby Community College (U)
College Misericordia (U)
College of DuPage (U)

Individual Courses Index

College of St. Scholastica (U, G)
College of the Canyons (U)
College of the Southwest (U)
The College of West Virginia (U)
Colorado Electronic Community College (U)
Colorado Mountain College District (U)
Colorado Northwestern Community College (U)
Colorado State University (U)
Columbia-Greene Community College (U)
Columbia State Community College (U)
Community College of Philadelphia (U)
Community College of Rhode Island (U)
Concordia University (U)
Concordia University (U)
Concordia University at Austin (U, NC)
Cosumnes River College (U)
County College of Morris (U)
Cumberland County College (U)
Cuyahoga Community College, Metropolitan Campus (U)
Cuyamaca College (U)
Dallas County Community College District (U)
Dawson Community College (U)
Daytona Beach Community College (U)
De Anza College (U)
DeKalb College (U)
Delaware County Community College (U)
Delaware Technical & Community College, Stanton/Wilmington Campus (U)
Delgado Community College (U)
Delta College (U)
Des Moines Area Community College (U)
Dutchess Community College (U)
East Tennessee State University (U)
Edison Community College (U)
Edmonds Community College (U)
Fitchburg State College (U)
Florence-Darlington Technical College (U)
Florida Community College at Jacksonville (U)
Floyd College (U)
Fort Hays State University (U, G)
Fullerton College (U)
Galveston College (U)
Garland County Community College (U)
Genesee Community College (U)
Glendale Community College (U)
Gordon-Conwell Theological Seminary (G, NC)
Governors State University (U, G)
Graceland College (U)
The Graduate School of America (G)
Greenville Technical College (U)
Harrisburg Area Community College (U)
Hillsborough Community College (U)
Houston Community College System (U)
Idaho State University (U, G)
Illinois Central College (U)
Illinois Eastern Community Colleges, Olney Central College (U)
Illinois Valley Community College (U)
Indiana University System (U)
Jacksonville State University (U)
John A. Logan College (U)
J. Sargeant Reynolds Community College (U)
Kansas State University (U, NC)
Kaskaskia College (U)
Lakehead University (U)
Laney College (U)
Laramie County Community College (U)
Laurentian University (U)
Lawson State Community College (U)
Los Angeles Community College District (U)
Luzerne County Community College (U)
Lycoming College (U)
Marshall University (U)
The McGregor School of Antioch University (G)
Memorial University of Newfoundland (U)
Mendocino College (U)
Mercy College (U)
Metropolitan Community College (U)
Metropolitan State College of Denver (U)
Midland College (U)
Midwestern State University (U)
Milwaukee Area Technical College (U)
Minnesota West Community and Technical College–Worthington Campus (U)
MiraCosta College (U)
Missouri Southern State College (U)
Missouri Western State College (U)
Mohawk Valley Community College (U)
Montgomery County Community College (U)
Moraine Valley Community College (U)
Morgan Community College (U, NC)
Morris Brown College (U)
Nassau Community College (U)
New Hampshire College (U)
New Mexico Junior College (U)
New River Community College (U)
New School for Social Research (U, NC)
North Carolina State University (G)
Northcentral Technical College (U)
North Dakota State College of Science (U)
Northeast Community College (U)
Northeast Louisiana University (U, G)
Northern Arizona University (U)
Northern Kentucky University (U)
Northern Virginia Community College (U)
North Harris College (U)
North Iowa Area Community College (U)
North Shore Community College (U)
Northwestern Michigan College (U)
Northwestern State University of Louisiana (U)
Northwest Iowa Community College (U)
Oakton Community College (U)
Odessa College (U)
Ohio University (U)
Ohio University–Eastern (U)
Oklahoma City Community College (U)
Oklahoma State University (U)
Oregon State University (U)
Owens Community College (U)
Palomar College (U)
Parkland College (U)
Pennsylvania State University University Park Campus (U)
Penn Valley Community College (U)
Pensacola Junior College (U)
Pierce College (U)
Portland Community College (U)
Portland State University (U)
Pratt Community College and Area Vocational School (U)
Prince George's Community College (U, NC)
Quincy College (U)
Redlands Community College (U)
Red Rocks Community College (U)
Richland Community College (U)
Riverland Community College (U)
Rockland Community College (U)
Rogers University (U)
Rose State College (U)
St. Johns River Community College (U)
Saint Joseph's College (U)
St. Louis Community College (U)
St. Petersburg Junior College (U)
Salve Regina University (G, NC)
San Antonio College (U)
Sandhills Community College (U)
San Jose State University (U)
Schoolcraft College (U)
Seattle Central Community College (U)
Seattle Pacific University (U)
Shawnee Community College (U)
Shelby State Community College (U)
Sierra College (U)
Sinclair Community College (U)
Skagit Valley College (U)
Skidmore College (U)
Southeastern Community College, North Campus (U)
Southeastern Louisiana University (U)
Southeast Missouri State University (U)
South Florida Community College (U)
Southwestern Assemblies of God University (U)
Southwestern Oklahoma State University (U)
Southwest State University (U)
Southwest Texas State University (U)
Southwest Virginia Community College (U)
Stanly Community College (U)
Suffolk County Community College–Ammerman Campus (U)
Syracuse University (U)
Tallahassee Community College (U)
Tarrant County Junior College (U)
Tennessee Temple University (U)
Texas A&M University–Commerce (U)
Texas Tech University (U)
Thomas Edison State College (U)
Triton College (U)
Troy State University Montgomery (U)
Tulsa Community College (U)
The Union Institute (U)
University of Alaska Anchorage (U)
University of Alaska Fairbanks (U)
University of Alaska Southeast, Sitka Campus (U)
University of Arkansas at Little Rock (U)
University of California Extension (U)
University of California, Santa Barbara (U, NC)
University of Delaware (U)
University of Georgia (U, NC)
University of Great Falls (U)
University of Guelph (U)
University of Hawaii–Maui Community College (U)
University of Houston (U)
University of Illinois at Urbana–Champaign (U)
University of Kansas (U, G, NC)
University of Kentucky, Henderson Community College (U)
University of Maine (U)
University of Maine at Augusta (U)
University of Maine at Fort Kent (U)
University of Massachusetts Lowell (U)
University of Minnesota, Twin Cities Campus (U)
University of Missouri–Columbia (U)
University of Missouri–St. Louis (U)
University of Nebraska at Kearney (U)
University of Nebraska–Lincoln (U)
University of Nevada, Las Vegas (U)

Distance Learning Programs

Individual Courses Index

Developmental and Child Psychology (continued)
University of Northern Iowa (U, G)
University of Oklahoma (U)
University of South Dakota (U)
University of Tennessee, Knoxville (U)
University of the State of New York, Regents College (U)
University of Toledo (U)
University of Utah (U)
University of Washington (U)
University of Waterloo (U)
University of Wisconsin–Stout (U, G)
University of Wyoming (U)
University System of Georgia (U)
Utah State University (U)
Victor Valley College (U)
Vincennes University (U)
Walden University (G)
Walters State Community College (U)
Washington State University (U)
Washtenaw Community College (U)
Waubonsee Community College (U)
Wenatchee Valley College (U)
Western Nebraska Community College (U)
Western Oklahoma State College (U)
Western Washington University (U)
Westmoreland County Community College (U)
West Valley College (U)
West Virginia University (U)
Wilfrid Laurier University (U)
William Penn College (U)
William Rainey Harper College (U)
Wytheville Community College (U)
York Technical College (U)

Drama and Theater
Bakersfield College (U)
Black Hills State University (U)
Boise State University (U)
Brigham Young University (U)
California State University, Dominguez Hills (U)
Colorado Mountain College District (U)
Fairleigh Dickinson University, Teaneck–Hackensack (U)
Kingwood College (U)
Rio Salado College (U)
State University of West Georgia (U)

Earth Science
Bluefield State College (U)
Catonsville Community College (U)
Central Florida Community College (U)
Gannon University (U)
Harrisburg Area Community College (U)
Lane Community College (U)
Lansing Community College (U)
Marywood University (U)
Pierce College (U)
Portland State University (NC)
St. Louis Community College (U)
Stephens College (U)
Syracuse University (U)
Thomas College (U)
Thomas Edison State College (U)
The University of Iowa (U, G)
University of Missouri–Columbia (U)
University of Waterloo (U)
Upper Iowa University (U)

Ecology
Crafton Hills College (U)
San Bernardino Valley College (U)
State University of New York College of Environmental Science and Forestry (U)
University of Nebraska–Lincoln (U)
University of Waterloo (U)
University System of Georgia (U)

Economics
Adams State College (U)
Allegany College of Maryland (U)
Alvin Community College (U)
Anne Arundel Community College (U)
Arapahoe Community College (U)
Athabasca University (U)
Auburn University (U)
Austin Community College (U)
Ball State University (U)
Bellevue Community College (U)
Black Hawk College (U)
Bloomsburg University of Pennsylvania (U)
Bluefield State College (U)
Blue Mountain Community College (U)
Brevard Community College (U)
Brigham Young University (U)
Brookdale Community College (U)
Broward Community College (U)
Bucks County Community College (U)
Burlington County College (U)
California State University, Bakersfield (U)
California State University, Fresno (U)
California State University, Stanislaus (U)
Camden County College (U)
Carleton University (U)
Carl Sandburg College (U)
Catawba Valley Community College (U)
Catonsville Community College (U)
Central Community College–Grand Island Campus (U)
Central Florida Community College (U)
Central Michigan University (U)
Central Piedmont Community College (U)
Central Virginia Community College (U)
Chadron State College (U)
Champlain College (U)
Chapman University (U)
Charles County Community College (U)
Charter Oak State College (U)
Chattanooga State Technical Community College (U)
Chemeketa Community College (U)
Chippewa Valley Technical College (U)
City Colleges of Chicago, Harold Washington College (U)
Clarkson College (U)
Clatsop Community College (U)
Clovis Community College (U)
Colby Community College (U)
College of DuPage (U)
College of the Canyons (U)
College of the Southwest (U)
The College of West Virginia (U)
Colorado Mountain College District (U)
Colorado Northwestern Community College (U)
Colorado State University (U)
Columbia State Community College (U)
Columbus State Community College (U)
Community College of Philadelphia (U)
Community College of Rhode Island (U)
Concordia University (U)
Concordia University (U)
Cosumnes River College (U)
County College of Morris (U)
Crafton Hills College (U)
Cumberland County College (U)
Cuyahoga Community College, Metropolitan Campus (U)
Cuyamaca College (U)
Dakota State University (U)
Dallas County Community College District (U)
Dawson Community College (U)
De Anza College (U)
DeKalb College (U)
Delaware County Community College (U)
Delaware Technical & Community College, Stanton/Wilmington Campus (U)
Delta College (U)
Des Moines Area Community College (U)
Duke University (G)
Dutchess Community College (U)
Eastern Idaho Technical College (U)
Eastern Kentucky University (U)
Eastern Wyoming College (U)
East Tennessee State University (U, G)
Edison Community College (U)
Edison State Community College (U)
El Paso Community College (U)
Embry-Riddle Aeronautical University, Extended Campus (U)
Fayetteville Technical Community College (U)
Fitchburg State College (U)
Florida Community College at Jacksonville (U)
Floyd College (U)
Fort Hays State University (U)
Gadsden State Community College (U)
Galveston College (U)
Gannon University (U)
Garland County Community College (U)
Gateway Technical College (U)
Genesee Community College (U)
Georgia Southern University (U, G)
Glendale Community College (U)
Glenville State College (U)
Governors State University (U)
Graceland College (U)
Grand Rapids Community College (U)
Grand Valley State University (U, G)
Great Basin College (U)
Greenville Technical College (U)
Hampton University (U)
Harrisburg Area Community College (U)
Heriot-Watt University (G)
Hillsborough Community College (U)
Hudson Valley Community College (U)
Idaho State University (U, G)
Illinois Central College (U)
Illinois Eastern Community Colleges, Olney Central College (U)
Illinois Valley Community College (U)
Indiana University System (U)
Ivy Tech State College–Northcentral (U)
Ivy Tech State College–Wabash Valley (U)
Jefferson College (U)
Jefferson Davis Community College (U)
Johnson County Community College (U)
John Wood Community College (U)
J. Sargeant Reynolds Community College (U)
Kaskaskia College (U)

Individual Courses Index

Kellogg Community College (U)
Kingwood College (U)
Lackawanna Junior College (U)
Lakehead University (U)
Lake Land College (U)
Lakeland Community College (U)
Lamar University (U)
Laney College (U)
Lansing Community College (U)
Laramie County Community College (U)
Lassen College (U)
Laurentian University (U)
Lee College (U)
Lehigh Carbon Community College (U)
Lincoln Land Community College (U)
Longview Community College (U)
Los Angeles Community College District (U)
Luzerne County Community College (U)
Lycoming College (U)
Madison Area Technical College (U)
Marshall University (U)
McCook Community College (U)
The McGregor School of Antioch University (G)
Memorial University of Newfoundland (U)
Mercy College (U)
Metropolitan Community College (U)
Metropolitan State College of Denver (U)
Metropolitan State University (U)
Middle Tennessee State University (U)
Mid-State Technical College (U)
Midwestern State University (U)
Milwaukee Area Technical College (U)
Minnesota West Community and Technical College–Worthington Campus (U)
MiraCosta College (U)
Missouri Southern State College (U)
Montgomery College–Rockville Campus (U)
Montgomery County Community College (U)
Moraine Valley Community College (U)
Morgan Community College (U, NC)
Mountain View College (U)
Mount Saint Vincent University (U)
Nassau Community College (U)
National Technological University (G, NC)
New Hampshire College (U)
New Jersey Institute of Technology (U, G)
New River Community College (U)
New School for Social Research (U, NC)
New York Institute of Technology (U)
Normandale Community College (U)
North Carolina State University (U)
Northcentral Technical College (U)
North Central Texas College (U)
Northeast Community College (U)
Northeast Wisconsin Technical College (U)
Northern Kentucky University (G)
Northern Oklahoma College (U)
Northern Virginia Community College (U)
North Harris College (U)
North Iowa Area Community College (U)
North Seattle Community College (U)
Northwestern College (U)
Odessa College (U)
Ohio University (U)
Ohio University–Southern Campus (U)
Oklahoma City Community College (U)
Oklahoma State University (U)
Palo Alto College (U)
Parkland College (U)

Pennsylvania State University University Park Campus (U)
Penn Valley Community College (U)
Pensacola Junior College (U)
Pierce College (U)
Pitt Community College (U, NC)
Polytechnic University, Brooklyn Campus (G, NC)
Portland Community College (U)
Portland State University (U)
Prairie State College (U)
Prince George's Community College (U, NC)
Pueblo Community College (U)
Redlands Community College (U)
Red Rocks Community College (U)
Regis University (U)
Richland Community College (U)
Rio Salado College (U)
Riverside Community College (U)
Rochester Institute of Technology (U)
Rockland Community College (U)
Rogers University (U)
Roosevelt University (U)
Rose State College (U)
Ryerson Polytechnic University (U)
St. Cloud Technical College (U)
St. Johns River Community College (U)
Saint Joseph's College (U)
St. Louis Community College (U)
St. Petersburg Junior College (U)
Salt Lake Community College (U)
Salve Regina University (G, NC)
San Bernardino Valley College (U)
San Diego City College (U)
Schoolcraft College (U)
Scott Community College (U)
Seattle Central Community College (U)
Shelby State Community College (U)
Sinclair Community College (U)
Skagit Valley College (U)
Skidmore College (U)
Southeast Community College, Lincoln Campus (U)
Southern West Virginia Community and Technical College (U)
South Florida Community College (U)
Southwestern Oklahoma State University (U)
Southwest Missouri State University (U)
Southwest State University (U)
Southwest Virginia Community College (U)
State Technical Institute at Memphis (U)
State University of New York at Oswego (U)
State University of New York Empire State College (U)
State University of West Georgia (U)
Stephens College (U)
Suffolk County Community College–Ammerman Campus (U)
Syracuse University (U)
Tarrant County Junior College (U)
Tennessee Temple University (U)
Texas A&M University–Commerce (U)
Texas Tech University (U)
Thomas Edison State College (U)
Tidewater Community College (U)
Trinidad State Junior College (U)
Triton College (U)
Troy State University Dothan (U)
Troy State University–Florida Region (U)
Troy State University Montgomery (U)

Tulsa Community College (U)
The Union Institute (U)
Universitè Laval (U)
The University of Alabama in Huntsville (G)
University of Alaska Anchorage (U)
University of Alaska Fairbanks (U)
University of Alberta (U)
The University of Calgary (U)
University of California Extension (U)
University of California, Santa Cruz (U, G)
University of Cincinnati (U)
University of Delaware (U)
University of Georgia (U)
University of Great Falls (U)
University of Guelph (U)
University of Houston (G)
University of Illinois at Urbana–Champaign (U)
The University of Iowa (U, G)
University of Kansas (U, NC)
University of Kentucky, Elizabethtown Community College (U)
University of Kentucky, Madisonville Community College (U)
University of Maine at Augusta (U)
University of Maine at Fort Kent (U)
University of Maine at Machias (U)
University of Mary (U, G)
University of Maryland University College (U)
The University of Memphis (U)
University of Minnesota, Twin Cities Campus (U)
University of Missouri–Columbia (U, G)
University of Missouri–Kansas City (U)
University of Nebraska at Kearney (U)
University of Nebraska–Lincoln (U)
The University of North Carolina at Chapel Hill (U)
University of Northern Colorado (U)
University of Northern Iowa (U)
University of Oklahoma (U)
University of Phoenix (G)
University of Pittsburgh (U)
University of Saskatchewan (U)
University of South Carolina (U)
University of Southern Colorado (U)
University of Southern Mississippi (U)
University of South Florida (U)
The University of Texas at Tyler (U)
University of Utah (U)
University of Washington (U)
University of Waterloo (U)
University of Windsor (U)
University of Wisconsin–Extension (U)
University of Wisconsin–Stevens Point (U, G)
University of Wyoming (U)
University System of Georgia (U)
Upper Iowa University (U)
Utah State University (U)
Vincennes University (U)
Vista Community College (U)
Volunteer State Community College (U)
Walters State Community College (U)
Washington State University (U)
Washtenaw Community College (U)
Waubonsee Community College (U)
Waukesha County Technical College (U)
Wayne County Community College (U)
Western Illinois University (U, G)
Western Montana College of The University of Montana (U, NC)

Distance Learning Programs

Individual Courses Index

Economics (continued)
Western Oklahoma State College (U)
Western Washington University (U)
Westmoreland County Community College (U)
West Virginia University (U)
Wichita State University (G)
Wilfrid Laurier University (U)
Wilkes Community College (U)
William Rainey Harper College (U)
Wilson Technical Community College (U)
Worcester Polytechnic Institute (U, G)
Wytheville Community College (U)
Xavier University of Louisiana (U)

Education
Acadia University (U)
Assemblies of God Theological Seminary (G, NC)
Ball State University (G)
Black Hills State University (U, G)
Brigham Young University (U)
Brock University (U)
Bucks County Community College (U)
Buena Vista University (U)
California State University, Fresno (U, G)
Central Arizona College (U)
Chattanooga State Technical Community College (U)
Chesapeake College (U)
City University (G)
Cleveland State University (G)
College of DuPage (U)
Concordia College (U)
Daytona Beach Community College (U)
De Anza College (U)
Delaware Technical & Community College, Jack F. Owens Campus (U)
Drake University (G)
Duquesne University (G)
East Carolina University (G, NC)
Eastern New Mexico University (U, G)
Eastern Oregon University (U, G)
Eastern Washington University (U)
Emporia State University (U, G)
Florida Atlantic University (G)
Garden City Community College (U)
The George Washington University (G)
The Graduate School of America (G)
Griggs University (U)
Hampton University (U, G)
Hawkeye Community College (U)
Lassen College (U)
Louisiana College (U)
Louisiana State University in Shreveport (U, G)
Memorial University of Newfoundland (U, G)
Metropolitan Community College (U)
Metropolitan State College of Denver (U)
Morehead State University (U, G)
Northampton County Area Community College (U)
North Carolina State University (G)
Northcentral Technical College (U)
North Dakota State University (G)
The Ohio State University (G)
Old Dominion University (G)
Oral Roberts University (U)
Pacific Oaks College (U, G)
Pima Community College (U)
Pratt Community College and Area Vocational School (U)
Red Rocks Community College (U)
The Richard Stockton College of New Jersey (NC)
Rio Salado College (U)
Rosemont College (G)
Salt Lake Community College (NC)
Savannah State University (U)
Seattle Pacific University (G)
Skidmore College (U)
Southeast Missouri State University (U)
Southern Illinois University at Edwardsville (G)
Southern Oregon University (U, G)
Southwestern Assemblies of God University (U)
Southwestern Michigan College (U)
Southwest State University (U)
State University of New York at Binghamton (G)
State University of New York at Buffalo (G, NC)
State University of West Georgia (U, G)
Stephens College (U)
Texas A&M University–Commerce (U)
Texas Tech University (G)
The Union Institute (U)
The University of Akron (G)
University of Alaska Fairbanks (U)
University of Alaska Southeast, Sitka Campus (U)
University of Arkansas (U)
University of British Columbia (U, G)
The University of Calgary (U, G, NC)
University of Central Oklahoma (U, G)
University of Georgia (U)
University of Great Falls (U)
University of Hawaii–Maui Community College (U)
University of Houston (G)
University of Idaho (U, G)
The University of Iowa (U, G)
University of Maine at Farmington (U)
University of Mary (U, G)
University of Maryland, College Park (U)
University of Massachusetts Lowell (U)
University of Mississippi (U, G)
University of Missouri–Columbia (U, G)
University of Nebraska–Lincoln (U)
The University of North Carolina at Chapel Hill (U)
University of Northern Iowa (U, G)
University of Pittsburgh at Bradford (U)
University of South Carolina (U, G)
University of Toledo (U)
University of West Florida (U, G)
University of Wisconsin–Madison (NC)
University of Wisconsin–River Falls (U, G, NC)
University of Wisconsin–Stevens Point (U, G)
University of Wisconsin–Stout (U, G, NC)
University of Wyoming (U)
University System of Georgia (U)
Walden University (G)
Washington and Jefferson College (U)
Western Michigan University (U)
Western New Mexico University (U, G)
West Virginia Graduate College (G)
Wright State University (U)
Wytheville Community College (U)
Yuba College (U)

Education Administration
Arizona State University (G)
Ball State University (G)
California College for Health Sciences (U)
California State University, Dominguez Hills (G)
California State University, Fresno (U)
Central Methodist College (U, G)
Central Missouri State University (U, G, NC)
Chadron State College (U, G)
Chippewa Valley Technical College (U)
City University (G)
College of the Southwest (U, G)
Columbus State University (G)
Concordia University (U, G)
Delta State University (U, G)
Denver Conservative Baptist Seminary (G, NC)
Drake University (G)
Eastern Kentucky University (G)
Eastern Michigan University (G)
Florida State University (G)
Fort Hays State University (U, G)
Georgia Southern University (U, G)
Gordon-Conwell Theological Seminary (G, NC)
The Graduate School of America (G)
Grand Rapids Baptist Seminary (G)
Grand Valley State University (U, G)
Hampton University (U)
Idaho State University (U, G)
Illinois Eastern Community Colleges, Olney Central College (U)
Indiana State University (G)
Indiana University System (G)
Iowa State University of Science and Technology (G)
Jacksonville State University (G)
Lakehead University (G)
Lamar University (U, G)
Louisiana State University in Shreveport (U, G)
Marshall University (U, G)
The McGregor School of Antioch University (G)
Memorial University of Newfoundland (U)
Michigan State University (G)
Middle Tennessee State University (U)
Mississippi Delta Community College (NC)
Missouri Western State College (G)
Morehead State University (U, G)
New Mexico Junior College (U)
New Mexico State University (G)
North Carolina State University (G)
North Central Bible College (U, NC)
North Dakota State University (G)
Northern Arizona University (U, G)
North Georgia College & State University (U, G)
North Hennepin Community College (U)
Northwestern State University of Louisiana (U, G)
Northwest Iowa Community College (U)
Ohio University–Southern Campus (U)
Oklahoma State University (G)
Oral Roberts University (G)
Oregon State University (G)
Pennsylvania State University University Park Campus (U, G)
Portland State University (U, G)
Rosemont College (G)
Rutgers, The State University of New Jersey, Newark (U, G, NC)
St. Cloud Technical College (G)
Saint Joseph's College (U)

Saint Peter's College (G)
San Diego State University (U, G)
Seton Hall University (G)
Southeast Community College, Beatrice Campus (U)
Southeast Missouri State University (G)
Southern Utah University (U)
Southwestern Oklahoma State University (G)
Southwest Missouri State University (G)
Southwest State University (U)
Southwest Virginia Community College (U)
State University of New York at Buffalo (G, NC)
State University of New York at New Paltz (G)
State University of New York at Oswego (G)
State University of New York College at Plattsburgh (G)
State University of West Georgia (U, G)
Tennessee State University (G)
Tennessee Technological University (G)
Texas A&M University–Commerce (U, G, NC)
Texas Tech University (G)
The Union Institute (U)
United States Sports Academy (G, NC)
Universitè Laval (U)
The University of Alabama (G)
The University of Alabama in Huntsville (G)
University of Alaska Fairbanks (U, G)
University of Alaska Southeast (U)
University of Alberta (U)
University of Arkansas at Little Rock (U)
The University of Calgary (U, G)
University of Central Oklahoma (U, G)
University of Delaware (G)
University of Great Falls (U)
University of Houston (G)
University of Kansas (U, G, NC)
University of Kentucky (G)
University of Maine (G)
University of Maine at Fort Kent (U, G)
The University of Memphis (U, G)
University of Minnesota, Twin Cities Campus (U)
University of Mississippi (U, G)
University of Missouri–Columbia (G)
University of Missouri–St. Louis (U)
The University of Montana–Missoula (G)
University of Nebraska at Kearney (G)
University of Nebraska–Lincoln (G)
University of Nevada, Las Vegas (U)
University of Nevada, Reno (U, G)
University of New Brunswick (U, G)
University of North Dakota (G)
University of Sarasota (G)
University of South Carolina (G)
University of South Dakota (G)
The University of Tennessee at Martin (U, G)
University of Tennessee, Knoxville (G)
The University of Texas at Tyler (U, G)
The University of Texas of the Permian Basin (G)
University of Utah (U)
University of Vermont (U)
University of Virginia (G, NC)
University of West Florida (U, G)
University of Wisconsin–Whitewater (G)
University of Wyoming (G)
Utah State University (U, G)
Walden University (G)
Western Illinois University (G)
Western Washington University (U)

West Virginia Graduate College (G)

Educational Psychology
Arizona State University (U, G)
Athabasca University (U)
Ball State University (G)
Berean University of the Assemblies of God (U)
Brigham Young University (U)
California College for Health Sciences (U)
California State University, Long Beach (U, G)
Carl Sandburg College (U)
Catonsville Community College (U)
Central Methodist College (U, G)
Chadron State College (U)
Chattanooga State Technical Community College (U)
City University (G)
College of DuPage (U)
College of the Southwest (U, G)
Colorado Northwestern Community College (U)
Colorado State University (U)
Columbus State University (G)
Concordia University (U, G)
Drake University (G)
Duquesne University (U)
Eastern Kentucky University (U, G)
East Tennessee State University (U, G)
Edison Community College (U)
Ellsworth Community College (U)
Florence-Darlington Technical College (U)
Fort Hays State University (U, G)
The Graduate School of America (G)
Grand Canyon University (G)
Grand Valley State University (U, G)
Idaho State University (U, G)
Illinois Eastern Community Colleges, Olney Central College (U)
Jackson Community College (U)
Jacksonville State University (G)
Judson College (U)
Kansas State University (G)
Kaskaskia College (U)
Lakeshore Technical College (U)
Lamar University (U, G)
Laurentian University (U)
Lawson State Community College (U)
Lycoming College (U)
Marshall University (U, G)
The McGregor School of Antioch University (G)
Memorial University of Newfoundland (U)
Metropolitan State University (U)
Midwestern State University (G)
Mississippi Delta Community College (U)
Mississippi State University (G)
Mohawk Valley Community College (U)
Moody Bible Institute (U)
Morris Brown College (U)
New Mexico Junior College (U)
New River Community College (U)
North Carolina State University (G)
North Central Bible College (U, NC)
Northeast Louisiana University (U)
Northeast Wisconsin Technical College (U)
Northern Arizona University (U, G)
Northern State University (U)
North Georgia College & State University (U, G)
Northwestern State University of Louisiana (U, G)
Northwest Iowa Community College (U)

Ohio University (U)
Ohio University–Southern Campus (U)
Oklahoma State University (U)
Pennsylvania State University University Park Campus (U)
Portland State University (U, G)
Rosemont College (G)
Saint Joseph's College (U)
Southwestern Assemblies of God University (U)
Southwest Virginia Community College (U)
State University of West Georgia (U, G)
Tarleton State University (U)
Taylor University, Fort Wayne Campus (U)
Tennessee Technological University (G)
Tennessee Temple University (U)
Texas A&M University–Commerce (U, G, NC)
Texas Tech University (U, G)
The University of Alabama at Birmingham (U, G)
University of Alaska Fairbanks (U, G)
University of California, Santa Barbara (U)
University of Delaware (U, G)
University of Georgia (U)
University of Great Falls (U)
University of Houston (U, G)
University of Illinois at Urbana–Champaign (U)
University of Kansas (U, NC)
University of Kentucky (G)
University of Maine at Fort Kent (U)
The University of Memphis (U, G)
University of Minnesota, Twin Cities Campus (U)
University of Missouri–Columbia (U, G)
University of Nebraska at Kearney (U, G)
University of Nebraska–Lincoln (U, G)
University of Nevada, Reno (U, G)
University of New Brunswick (U, G)
University of Northern Iowa (U, G)
University of Sarasota (G)
University of South Dakota (U)
The University of Tennessee at Martin (U, G)
University of Utah (U)
University of Virginia (G, NC)
University of Waterloo (U)
University of Wisconsin–Extension (U)
University of Wyoming (U)
University System of Georgia (U)
Utah State University (U)
Volunteer State Community College (U)
Walden University (G)
Walters State Community College (U)
Westmoreland County Community College (U)

Educational Research
Chestnut Hill College (G)
Cleveland State University (G)
The Graduate School of America (G)
North Georgia College & State University (G)
State University of West Georgia (G)
Texas Tech University (G)

Electrical Engineering
Arizona State University (U, G)
Bradley University (U, G)
Brevard Community College (U)
California State University, Fullerton (U)
California State University, Los Angeles (U, NC)
California State University, Northridge (U, G)
California State University, Sacramento (U)

Distance Learning Programs

Individual Courses Index

567

Individual Courses Index

Electrical Engineering (continued)
Capitol College (U)
Charles County Community College (U)
Chattanooga State Technical Community College (U)
Cleveland State University (G)
Colorado State University (G)
Florida State University (G)
Georgia Institute of Technology (G, NC)
Idaho State University (U, G)
Illinois Institute of Technology (U, G)
Iowa State University of Science and Technology (U, G)
John A. Logan College (U)
Kansas State University (G, NC)
Michigan State University (G)
Michigan Technological University (U, NC)
Mississippi State University (G)
Missouri Western State College (G)
Montana State University–Bozeman (NC)
National Technological University (G, NC)
New Jersey Institute of Technology (U, G)
New Mexico State University (G)
North Carolina State University (G)
Northeastern University (G)
Oklahoma State University (G)
Old Dominion University (G)
Oregon State University (G)
Polytechnic University, Westchester Graduate Center (G)
Rensselaer Polytechnic Institute (G)
Rochester Institute of Technology (U)
San Jose State University (G)
Shenandoah University (G)
Southern Illinois University at Carbondale (U)
Southern Methodist University (G)
Southern Polytechnic State University (G)
Southwest Virginia Community College (U)
Stanford University (G, NC)
State University of New York at Binghamton (G)
State University of New York at Buffalo (G)
Texas Tech University (G)
The University of Alabama (G)
The University of Alabama at Birmingham (G)
University of Alberta (U)
University of Arizona (G)
The University of Calgary (U, G)
University of California Extension (U)
University of California, Santa Barbara (G, NC)
University of Colorado at Boulder (G, NC)
University of Delaware (U, G, NC)
University of Houston (G)
University of Idaho (U, G)
University of Illinois at Urbana–Champaign (U, G)
University of Maine (U, G, NC)
University of Maryland, Baltimore County (U, G)
University of Massachusetts Amherst (U, G, NC)
University of Massachusetts Boston (U)
University of Missouri–Kansas City (G)
University of Nebraska–Lincoln (G)
University of Nevada, Reno (U, G)
University of North Dakota (U)
University of North Florida (G)
University of Oklahoma (G)
University of Southern California (G, NC)
University of Southern Mississippi (U)
University of South Florida (U, G)
University of Tennessee, Knoxville (G)
The University of Texas at Arlington (G)
The University of Texas at San Antonio (U, G)
University of Vermont (U)
University of Virginia (G)
University of Wisconsin–Madison (U, G)
Virginia Polytechnic Institute and State University (G)
Wayne State University (G)
West Virginia University Institute of Technology (U, G)
Wright State University (U)
York Technical College (U)

Electronics
Century Community and Technical College (NC)
Colorado Mountain College District (U)
Community College of the Air Force (U)
NRI Schools (NC)
Oklahoma State University (U)
Stevens Institute of Technology (NC)
Thomas Edison State College (U)
Triton College (U)
Wytheville Community College (U)
Yuba College (U)

Engineering
Arizona State University (U, G, NC)
Auburn University (G)
Boston University (G, NC)
Brigham Young University (U)
Carleton University (U)
East Carolina University (U, G)
Florida Atlantic University (G)
Hibbing Community College (U)
Houston Community College System (U)
Howard Community College (U)
Illinois Institute of Technology (U, G)
Lafayette College (U)
Lakeshore Technical College (U)
Mississippi State University (G)
Moraine Valley Community College (U)
North Carolina State University (G)
Northern Virginia Community College (U)
North Hennepin Community College (U)
The Ohio State University (G)
Pennsylvania State University University Park Campus (U, G, NC)
Penn Valley Community College (U)
Purdue University (G)
Rochester Institute of Technology (U)
Southern Methodist University (G)
Stevens Institute of Technology (G)
Terra State Community College (U)
Texas Tech University (U, G, NC)
The University of Akron (G)
The University of Alabama at Birmingham (G)
University of California Extension (U)
University of Dayton (U)
University of Idaho (U, G)
The University of Iowa (G)
University of Kentucky (G)
University of Maryland, College Park (U, G)
University of Michigan (G)
University of Minnesota, Twin Cities Campus (U)
University of Missouri–Columbia (U)
University of Nebraska–Lincoln (U)
University of New Hampshire (U)
University of North Carolina at Charlotte (U)
University of Oklahoma (U)
University of St. Thomas (G)
University of South Carolina (G)
University of Wisconsin–Eau Claire (U)
University of Wisconsin–Extension (U)
Wayne State University (G)
Western Michigan University (U)
West Virginia University Institute of Technology (U, G)

Engineering Mechanics
California State University, Northridge (U, G)
Colorado State University (G)
Georgia Southern University (U)
Idaho State University (U, G)
Illinois Institute of Technology (U)
Iowa State University of Science and Technology (G)
Michigan Technological University (U, NC)
Mississippi State University (G)
National Technological University (G, NC)
North Carolina State University (G)
Pennsylvania State University University Park Campus (U)
Rochester Institute of Technology (U)
Shenandoah University (G)
Southwest Virginia Community College (U)
State University of New York at Buffalo (G)
State University of New York College of Environmental Science and Forestry (G)
Tarrant County Junior College (U)
Thomas Edison State College (U)
The University of Alabama (G)
University of Arizona (G)
University of Delaware (G, NC)
University of Illinois at Urbana–Champaign (U, G)
University of Missouri–Columbia (U)
University of Nebraska–Lincoln (G)
University of North Dakota (U)
University of Tennessee, Knoxville (G)
The University of Texas at Arlington (G)
The University of Texas at San Antonio (U)
University of Virginia (G)

Engineering-Related Technologies
Arizona State University (U, G)
Austin Community College (U)
Baker College (G)
Central Washington University (U)
Century Community and Technical College (U)
Charles Stewart Mott Community College (U)
Chestnut Hill College (G)
East Carolina University (U, G)
Genesee Community College (U)
Grand Rapids Community College (U)
Howard Community College (U)
Ivy Tech State College–Northcentral (U)
J. Sargeant Reynolds Community College (U)
Lehigh University (G, NC)
Massachusetts Institute of Technology (NC)
Metropolitan State University (U)
Michigan Technological University (U, NC)
National Technological University (G, NC)
New Jersey Institute of Technology (U)
North Carolina State University (G)
Northeastern University (U)
North Hennepin Community College (U)

Ohio University (U)
Oklahoma State University (U)
Old Dominion University (U)
Pennsylvania State University University Park Campus (NC)
Portland State University (U, G)
Rochester Institute of Technology (U)
Roger Williams University (U)
Scott Community College (U)
Sinclair Community College (U)
Southern Methodist University (G)
Southwest Virginia Community College (U)
State University of New York at Farmingdale (U)
State University of New York College of Environmental Science and Forestry (G)
The University of Alabama in Huntsville (G)
University of Colorado at Boulder (G, NC)
University of Delaware (U)
University of Houston (U)
University of Massachusetts Amherst (NC)
University of Massachusetts Lowell (U)
The University of Memphis (U)
University of North Carolina at Charlotte (U)
University of Tennessee Space Institute (G)
The University of Texas at San Antonio (U, G)
University of Wisconsin–Stout (U)
Wayne State University (G)
York Technical College (U)

Engineering/Industrial Management

Abilene Christian University (U)
Arizona State University (U, G)
California State University, Northridge (G)
Central Missouri State University (U, G)
Colorado State University (G)
Grand Valley State University (U, G)
Iowa State University of Science and Technology (G)
Kansas State University (G, NC)
Lake Superior State University (U)
Massachusetts Institute of Technology (NC)
Mississippi State University (G)
Missouri Western State College (G)
National Technological University (G, NC)
New Jersey Institute of Technology (G)
New Mexico State University (G)
North Carolina State University (G)
Northeastern University (G)
Ohio University–Southern Campus (NC)
Polytechnic University, Brooklyn Campus (NC)
Portland State University (U, G)
Rensselaer Polytechnic Institute (G)
Rochester Institute of Technology (U)
Roger Williams University (U)
Shawnee Community College (U)
Shenandoah University (G)
Southern Methodist University (G)
Southwest Virginia Community College (U)
Stanford University (G, NC)
State University of New York at Buffalo (G)
Texas Tech University (U)
The University of Alabama in Huntsville (G)
University of Arizona (G)
University of Colorado at Boulder (G, NC)
University of Idaho (U, G)
University of Maryland University College (G)
University of Massachusetts Amherst (G, NC)
University of Missouri–Columbia (U, G)
University of Missouri–Kansas City (G)
University of Nebraska–Lincoln (G, NC)

University of North Florida (G)
University of Oklahoma (G)
University of Southern California (G, NC)
University of South Florida (G)
University of Tennessee, Knoxville (G)
University of Tennessee Space Institute (G)
The University of Texas at San Antonio (U)
University of Virginia (G)
University of Wisconsin–Stout (G)
Virginia Polytechnic Institute and State University (G)
Western Michigan University (U, G)
Worcester Polytechnic Institute (U, G)

English As A Second Language (ESL)

Athabasca University (U)
Bakersfield College (U)
Butte College (U)
California State University, Dominguez Hills (NC)
California State University, Fresno (U)
Central Missouri State University (U)
Citrus College (U)
City University (G)
Colby Community College (U)
College of DuPage (U)
College of Lake County (NC)
College of the Southwest (U)
Colorado Mountain College District (U)
Cosumnes River College (U)
Dallas County Community College District (U)
Eastern Idaho Technical College (U)
El Paso Community College (U)
Fort Hays State University (U, G)
Fullerton College (U)
Hampton University (U, NC)
Idaho State University (U, G)
Kaskaskia College (U)
Lorain County Community College (U)
The McGregor School of Antioch University (G)
Milwaukee Area Technical College (U)
MiraCosta College (U, NC)
Missouri Western State College (U)
Montgomery College–Rockville Campus (NC)
New School for Social Research (U, NC)
North Carolina State University (U)
Northeast Community College (U)
Oklahoma City Community College (U)
Oral Roberts University (G)
Phillips Community College of the University of Arkansas (U)
Polytechnic University, Brooklyn Campus (NC)
Portland State University (U)
Red Rocks Community College (U)
The Richard Stockton College of New Jersey (NC)
St. Louis Community College (U)
San Bernardino Valley College (U)
Seattle Central Community College (U)
Southeastern Louisiana University (U, G)
State University of West Georgia (U)
Tennessee State University (G, NC)
Texas Tech University (G)
University of Arkansas at Little Rock (U)
University of California, Santa Barbara (NC)
University of Great Falls (U)
University of Houston (G)
The University of Montana–Missoula (G)
University of Nevada, Las Vegas (U)

The University of North Carolina at Chapel Hill (U)
University of North Dakota (U)
University of Washington (U)
Western New Mexico University (U, G)
Yuba College (U)

English Composition

Adams State College (U)
Allegany College of Maryland (U)
Arapahoe Community College (U)
Athabasca University (U)
Austin Community College (U)
Ball State University (U)
Barclay College (U)
Bellevue Community College (U)
Bemidji State University (U)
Berean University of the Assemblies of God (U)
Black Hawk College (U)
Bluefield State College (U)
Brigham Young University (U)
Brookdale Community College (U)
Broward Community College (U)
Bucks County Community College (U)
Burlington County College (U)
Butte College (U)
California College for Health Sciences (U)
Cape Cod Community College (U)
Carl Sandburg College (U)
Catawba Valley Community College (U)
Catonsville Community College (U)
Central Arizona College (U)
Central Community College–Grand Island Campus (U)
Central Florida Community College (U)
Central Missouri State University (U)
Central Piedmont Community College (U)
Central Washington University (U)
Central Wyoming College (U)
Cerritos College (U)
Champlain College (U)
Charles County Community College (U)
Charles Stewart Mott Community College (U)
Chattanooga State Technical Community College (U)
Chemeketa Community College (U)
Chesapeake College (U)
Chippewa Valley Technical College (U)
Christopher Newport University (U)
City Colleges of Chicago, Harold Washington College (U)
Clarkson College (U)
Clark State Community College (U)
Clatsop Community College (U)
Clayton College & State University (U)
Clovis Community College (U)
Coastline Community College (U, NC)
Colby Community College (U)
College of DuPage (U)
College of Lake County (U)
College of the Southwest (U)
The College of West Virginia (U)
Collin County Community College (U)
Colorado Electronic Community College (U)
Colorado Mountain College District (U)
Colorado Northwestern Community College (U)
Columbia Basin College (U)
Columbia State Community College (U)
Columbus State Community College (U)

Individual Courses Index

English Composition (continued)

Community College of Denver (U)
Community College of Rhode Island (U)
Concordia University (U)
Concordia University Wisconsin (U, G)
Corning Community College (U)
County College of Morris (U)
Cumberland County College (U)
Cuyahoga Community College, Metropolitan Campus (U)
Dakota State University (U)
Dallas County Community College District (U)
Danville Area Community College (U)
Danville Community College (U)
Darton College (U)
David N. Myers College (U)
Dawson Community College (U)
Daytona Beach Community College (U)
De Anza College (U)
Delaware State University (U)
Delaware Technical & Community College, Stanton/Wilmington Campus (U)
Delta College (U)
Des Moines Area Community College (U)
Dodge City Community College (U)
Dutchess Community College (U)
Eastern Idaho Technical College (U)
Eastern Kentucky University (U)
Eastern Michigan University (U)
Eastern Oklahoma State College (U)
Edison Community College (U)
Embry-Riddle Aeronautical University, Extended Campus (U)
Fayetteville Technical Community College (U)
Florence-Darlington Technical College (U)
Florida Community College at Jacksonville (U)
Floyd College (U)
Fort Hays State University (U)
Front Range Community College (U)
Gadsden State Community College (U)
Gannon University (U)
Garland County Community College (U)
Garrett Community College (U)
Genesee Community College (U)
Georgia Southern University (U)
Governors State University (U)
Graceland College (U)
Grand Rapids Community College (U)
Great Basin College (U)
Greenville Technical College (U)
Hampton University (U)
Harrisburg Area Community College (U)
Hawkeye Community College (U)
Houston Community College System (U)
Howard Community College (U)
Hudson Valley Community College (U)
Idaho State University (U, G)
Illinois Central College (U)
Illinois Eastern Community Colleges, Olney Central College (U)
Indiana University System (U)
Ivy Tech State College–Northcentral (U)
Ivy Tech State College–Wabash Valley (U)
Jefferson College (U)
John C. Calhoun State Community College (U)
Johnson County Community College (U)
J. Sargeant Reynolds Community College (U)
Judson College (U)
Kellogg Community College (U)
Kingwood College (U)

Lackawanna Junior College (U, NC)
Lakeshore Technical College (U)
Lamar University (U)
Lane Community College (U)
Lansing Community College (U)
Laramie County Community College (U)
Lassen College (U)
Laurentian University (U)
Lee College (U)
Lehigh Carbon Community College (U)
Long Beach City College (U)
Longview Community College (U)
Lorain County Community College (U)
Lord Fairfax Community College (U)
Louisiana College (U)
Loyola University New Orleans (U)
Luzerne County Community College (U)
Lycoming College (U)
Madison Area Technical College (U)
Manatee Community College (U)
Manchester Community-Technical College (U)
Marywood University (U)
McCook Community College (U)
The McGregor School of Antioch University (G)
Memorial University of Newfoundland (U)
Mercy College (U)
Metropolitan Community College (U)
Metropolitan State College of Denver (U)
Middle Georgia College (U)
Mid-Plains Community College (U)
Milwaukee Area Technical College (U)
Minnesota West Community and Technical College–Worthington Campus (U)
Minot State University (U)
Montgomery College–Rockville Campus (U)
Montgomery County Community College (U)
Morehead State University (U, G)
Morgan Community College (U, NC)
Mountain View College (U)
New Hampshire College (U)
New Mexico Junior College (U)
New River Community College (U)
New School for Social Research (U, NC)
New York Institute of Technology (U)
Normandale Community College (U)
North Carolina State University (U)
North Central Bible College (U, NC)
North Dakota State College of Science (U)
Northeast Community College (U)
Northern Oklahoma College (U)
Northern Virginia Community College (U)
North Harris College (U)
Northwestern College (U)
Northwestern Michigan College (U)
Northwestern State University of Louisiana (U)
Northwest Iowa Community College (U)
Oakton Community College (U)
Odessa College (U)
Ohio University (U)
Oklahoma City Community College (U)
Oklahoma State University (U)
Owens Community College (U)
Pennsylvania State University University Park Campus (U, NC)
Penn Valley Community College (U)
Piedmont College (U)
Pierce College (U)
Pima Community College (U)
Portland Community College (U)
Portland State University (U)

Prairie State College (U)
Pratt Community College and Area Vocational School (U)
Prince George's Community College (U, NC)
Pueblo Community College (U)
Redlands Community College (U)
Red Rocks Community College (U)
The Richard Stockton College of New Jersey (U)
Richland Community College (U)
Riverland Community College (U)
Rochester Institute of Technology (U)
Rockland Community College (U)
Rogers University (U)
Roosevelt University (U)
Rose State College (U)
St. Cloud Technical College (U)
St. Johns River Community College (U)
Saint Joseph's College (U)
St. Louis Community College (U)
St. Petersburg Junior College (U)
Salt Lake Community College (U)
San Antonio College (U)
Sandhills Community College (U)
Santa Fe Community College (U)
Sauk Valley Community College (U)
Schoolcraft College (U)
Scott Community College (U)
Seattle Central Community College (U)
Shawnee Community College (U)
Shelby State Community College (U)
Sierra College (U)
Sinclair Community College (U)
Skagit Valley College (U)
Skidmore College (U)
Southeast Community College, Beatrice Campus (U)
Southeast Community College, Lincoln Campus (U)
Southern Utah University (U)
Southwestern Assemblies of God University (U)
Southwestern Oklahoma State University (U)
Southwest State University (U)
State Technical Institute at Memphis (U)
State University of New York Empire State College (U)
State University of West Georgia (U)
Suffolk County Community College–Ammerman Campus (U)
Sul Ross State University (U)
Syracuse University (U)
Tallahassee Community College (U)
Tarrant County Junior College (U)
Technical College of the Lowcountry (U)
Tennessee Temple University (U)
Texas A&M University–Commerce (U)
Texas Tech University (U)
Thomas Edison State College (U)
Tidewater Community College (U)
Treasure Valley Community College (U)
Triton College (U)
Troy State University Dothan (U)
Troy State University Montgomery (U)
Tulsa Community College (U)
Tyler Junior College (U)
The Union Institute (U)
The University of Akron (U)
University of Alaska Anchorage (U)
University of Alaska Fairbanks (U)
University of Alaska Southeast, Sitka Campus (U)

University of Arkansas at Little Rock (U)
The University of Calgary (U)
University of California Extension (U, NC)
University of California, Santa Barbara (U, NC)
University of Cincinnati Raymond Walters College (U)
University of Delaware (U, NC)
University of Georgia (U)
University of Great Falls (U)
University of Guelph (U)
University of Hawaii–Maui Community College (U)
University of Houston–Clear Lake (U)
University of Illinois at Urbana–Champaign (U)
University of Kansas (U, NC)
University of Maine at Augusta (U)
University of Maine at Fort Kent (U)
University of Maryland University College (U)
University of Massachusetts Boston (U)
University of Massachusetts Lowell (U)
The University of Memphis (U, G)
University of Minnesota, Twin Cities Campus (U, NC)
University of Missouri–Columbia (U)
University of Missouri–Kansas City (U, G)
University of Nebraska at Kearney (U)
University of Nebraska–Lincoln (U)
University of Nevada, Las Vegas (U)
University of Nevada, Reno (U)
The University of North Carolina at Chapel Hill (U)
University of Oklahoma (U)
University of Pennsylvania (NC)
University of South Dakota (U)
University of South Florida (U)
University of Tennessee, Knoxville (U)
University of Toledo (U)
University of Utah (U)
University of Washington (U)
University of Waterloo (U)
University of Windsor (U)
University of Wisconsin–Eau Claire (U)
University of Wisconsin–Stout (U, G)
University of Wyoming (U)
University System of Georgia (U)
Upper Iowa University (U)
Utah State University (U)
Utah Valley State College (U)
Vincennes University (U)
Volunteer State Community College (U)
Wake Technical Community College (U)
Walters State Community College (U)
Washington State University (U)
Waubonsee Community College (U)
Waukesha County Technical College (U)
Wayne County Community College (U)
Weber State University (U)
Wenatchee Valley College (U)
Western Nebraska Community College (U)
Western Oklahoma State College (U)
West Valley College (U)
West Virginia University (U)
West Virginia University Institute of Technology (U)
Whatcom Community College (U)
William Penn College (U)
York Technical College (U)

English Language and Literature

Acadia University (U)
Allegany College of Maryland (U)
Arapahoe Community College (U)
Arizona State University (U, G)
Assemblies of God Theological Seminary (G, NC)
Athabasca University (U)
Atlantic Community College (U)
Austin Community College (U)
Ball State University (U)
Bellevue Community College (U)
Bellevue University (U)
Bemidji State University (U)
Berean University of the Assemblies of God (U)
Black Hawk College (U)
Black Hills State University (U)
Bluefield State College (U)
Boise State University (U)
Brevard Community College (U)
Brigham Young University (U)
Brookdale Community College (U)
Broward Community College (U)
Bucks County Community College (U)
Buena Vista University (U)
California State University, Fresno (U)
California State University, Stanislaus (U)
Camden County College (U)
Cape Cod Community College (U)
Carleton University (U)
Catawba Valley Community College (U)
Central Community College–Grand Island Campus (U)
Central Michigan University (U)
Central Piedmont Community College (U)
Cerritos College (U)
Chadron State College (U, G)
Champlain College (U)
Charles County Community College (U)
Charles Stewart Mott Community College (U)
Charter Oak State College (U)
Chattanooga State Technical Community College (U)
Chemeketa Community College (U)
Chesapeake College (U)
Christopher Newport University (U)
City College of San Francisco (U)
City Colleges of Chicago, Harold Washington College (U)
Clarkson College (U)
Coastline Community College (U, NC)
Colby Community College (U)
College of DuPage (U)
College of Lake County (U)
College of St. Scholastica (U, G)
College of the Southwest (U)
The College of West Virginia (U)
Colorado Mountain College District (U)
Columbia Basin College (U)
Community College of Rhode Island (U)
Community College of Vermont (U)
Concordia College (U)
Concordia University (U)
Concordia University at Austin (U, NC)
Concordia University Wisconsin (U, G)
Corning Community College (U)
Cosumnes River College (U)
Cumberland County College (U)
Cuyamaca College (U)
Darton College (U)

David N. Myers College (U)
Dawson Community College (U)
De Anza College (U)
Delaware Technical & Community College, Stanton/Wilmington Campus (U)
Delta State University (U, G)
Des Moines Area Community College (U)
Dodge City Community College (U)
Dutchess Community College (U)
Eastern Idaho Technical College (U)
Eastern New Mexico University (U, G)
Eastern Oregon University (U)
East Tennessee State University (U)
Edison Community College (U)
Embry-Riddle Aeronautical University, Extended Campus (U)
Emporia State University (U, G)
Essex Community College (U)
Flathead Valley Community College (U)
Florence-Darlington Technical College (U)
Florida Community College at Jacksonville (U)
Fort Hays State University (U, G)
Front Range Community College (U)
Gadsden State Community College (U)
Galveston College (U)
Garland County Community College (U)
Genesee Community College (U)
George C. Wallace State Community College (U)
Glendale Community College (U)
Governors State University (U, G)
Graceland College (U)
Greenville Technical College (U)
Griggs University (U)
Hampton University (U)
Harrisburg Area Community College (U)
Hibbing Community College (U)
Houston Community College System (U)
Howard Community College (U)
Illinois Central College (U)
Illinois Eastern Community Colleges, Olney Central College (U)
Illinois Valley Community College (U)
Indiana University System (U)
Iowa Western Community College (U)
Jacksonville State University (U)
Jefferson College (U)
John A. Logan College (U)
John C. Calhoun State Community College (U)
J. Sargeant Reynolds Community College (U)
Judson College (U)
Kankakee Community College (U)
Kansas State University (U, NC)
Kaskaskia College (U)
Labette Community College (U)
Lake Michigan College (U)
Lakeshore Technical College (U)
Lamar University (U)
Lincoln Land Community College (U)
Longview Community College (U)
Lorain County Community College (U)
Los Angeles Community College District (U)
Louisiana College (U)
Luzerne County Community College (U)
Lycoming College (U)
Madison Area Technical College (U)
Marywood University (U)
The McGregor School of Antioch University (G)
Memorial University of Newfoundland (U)
Mendocino College (U)

Individual Courses Index

English Language and Literature (continued)
Metropolitan Community College (U)
Middle Georgia College (U)
Middle Tennessee State University (U)
Midwestern State University (U)
Milwaukee Area Technical College (U)
Minnesota West Community and Technical College–Worthington Campus (U)
Minot State University (U)
MiraCosta College (U)
Mississippi Delta Community College (NC)
Missouri Southern State College (U)
Mohawk Valley Community College (U)
Montana State University–Bozeman (U)
Montana Tech of The University of Montana (U)
Montgomery College–Rockville Campus (U)
Moraine Valley Community College (U)
Morehead State University (U)
Morgan Community College (U, NC)
Mountain View College (U)
Mount Saint Vincent University (U)
Nassau Community College (U)
New Hampshire College (U)
New Jersey Institute of Technology (U)
New Mexico Junior College (U)
New River Community College (U)
New School for Social Research (U, NC)
New York Institute of Technology (U)
North Carolina State University (U)
North Central Bible College (U, NC)
Northeast Community College (U)
Northeast Louisiana University (U)
Northeast Wisconsin Technical College (U)
Northern Arizona University (U)
Northern Essex Community College (U)
Northern Oklahoma College (U)
Northern Virginia Community College (U)
North Harris College (U)
North Shore Community College (U)
Northwestern College (U)
Northwestern Michigan College (U)
Northwestern State University of Louisiana (U)
Northwest Iowa Community College (U)
Oakland Community College (U)
Oakton Community College (U)
Odessa College (U)
Ohio University (U)
Ohio University–Southern Campus (U)
Oklahoma City Community College (U)
Old Dominion University (U)
Oregon State University (U)
Pennsylvania State University University Park Campus (U)
Pierce College (U)
Pima Community College (U)
Portland Community College (U)
Portland State University (U)
Prairie State College (U)
Pratt Community College and Area Vocational School (U)
Prince George's Community College (U, NC)
Pueblo Community College (U)
Redlands Community College (U)
Red Rocks Community College (U)
Rend Lake College (U)
The Richard Stockton College of New Jersey (U, NC)
Richland Community College (U)
Rio Salado College (U)
Rochester Institute of Technology (U)
Rockland Community College (U)
Roger Williams University (U)
Rose State College (U)
Ryerson Polytechnic University (U)
Sacramento City College (U)
St. Johns River Community College (U)
Saint Joseph's College (U)
Salve Regina University (U, G, NC)
San Bernardino Valley College (U)
Schoolcraft College (U)
Scott Community College (U)
Seattle Central Community College (U)
Seattle Pacific University (U)
Shawnee Community College (U)
Sierra College (U)
Skagit Valley College (U)
Skidmore College (U)
Southeast Community College, Lincoln Campus (U)
Southeastern Louisiana University (U)
Southern Utah University (U)
Southern West Virginia Community and Technical College (U)
South Florida Community College (U)
Southwestern Assemblies of God University (U)
Southwestern Oklahoma State University (U)
Southwest Missouri State University (U)
Southwest State University (U)
Southwest Texas State University (U)
State University of New York at Binghamton (U)
State University of New York Empire State College (U)
State University of West Georgia (U, G)
Suffolk County Community College–Ammerman Campus (U)
Syracuse University (U)
Tacoma Community College (U)
Tallahassee Community College (U)
Tarrant County Junior College (U)
Taylor University, Fort Wayne Campus (U)
Technical College of the Lowcountry (U)
Tennessee State University (G)
Tennessee Technological University (U, G)
Tennessee Temple University (U)
Texas Tech University (U)
Thomas Edison State College (U)
Triton College (U)
Troy State University Montgomery (U)
Tulsa Community College (U)
Tyler Junior College (U)
Umpqua Community College (U)
The Union Institute (U)
University of Alaska Fairbanks (U)
University of Alaska Southeast, Sitka Campus (U)
University of Arkansas at Little Rock (U)
University of British Columbia (U)
University of California Extension (U, NC)
University of California, Santa Barbara (U, NC)
The University of Charleston (U, NC)
University of Cincinnati Raymond Walters College (U)
University of Delaware (U)
University of Georgia (U)
University of Great Falls (U)
University of Guelph (U)
University of Hawaii–Maui Community College (U)
University of Houston (U)
The University of Iowa (U, G)
University of Kansas (U, NC)
University of Kentucky, Ashland Community College (U)
University of Kentucky, Elizabethtown Community College (U)
University of Kentucky, Madisonville Community College (U)
University of Maine (U, G)
University of Maine at Augusta (U)
University of Maine at Fort Kent (U)
University of Maine at Machias (U)
University of Maryland University College (U)
The University of Memphis (U, G)
University of Minnesota, Twin Cities Campus (NC)
University of Missouri–Columbia (U, G)
University of Missouri–Kansas City (U)
University of Nebraska at Kearney (U)
University of Nebraska–Lincoln (U)
University of New Orleans (U)
University of Northern Iowa (U, G)
University of Oklahoma (U)
University of Pennsylvania (U, NC)
University of Saskatchewan (U)
University of South Carolina (U, G)
University of South Dakota (U)
University of Southern Colorado (U)
University of Southern Mississippi (U)
University of Tennessee, Knoxville (U)
The University of Texas at Austin (U)
The University of Texas at Tyler (U, G)
University of Utah (U)
University of Vermont (U)
University of Washington (U)
University of West Florida (U)
University System of Georgia (U)
Upper Iowa University (U)
Utah State University (U)
Valley City State University (U)
Vincennes University (U)
Vista Community College (U)
Volunteer State Community College (U)
Wake Technical Community College (U)
Washington State University (U)
Waubonsee Community College (U)
Wayne County Community College (U)
Wayne State University (U)
Weber State University (U)
Wenatchee Valley College (U)
Western Illinois University (U)
Western Michigan University (U)
Western Nebraska Community College (U)
Western New Mexico University (U)
Western Oklahoma State College (U)
Western Washington University (U)
Westmoreland County Community College (U)
West Virginia University (U)
West Virginia Wesleyan College (U)
Whatcom Community College (U)
Wichita State University (U)
Wilfrid Laurier University (U)
Wilson Technical Community College (U)
Winthrop University (U)
Wright State University (U)
Yuba College (U)

English Literature
Brigham Young University (U)
Bucks County Community College (U)

Carl Sandburg College (U)
Catonsville Community College (U)
Christopher Newport University (U)
Clovis Community College (U)
Colorado Northwestern Community College (U)
Columbus State University (U, G)
Concordia University (U)
Crafton Hills College (U)
Delta College (U)
Eastern Kentucky University (U)
Edison State Community College (U)
Essex Community College (U)
Floyd College (U)
Madison Area Technical College (U)
Manchester Community-Technical College (U)
Mercy College (U)
Mesa State College (U)
New Hampshire College (U)
New River Community College (U)
Northern Virginia Community College (U)
Pierce College (U)
Pratt Community College and Area Vocational School (U)
San Bernardino Valley College (U)
Seattle Central Community College (U)
Sinclair Community College (U)
State University of West Georgia (U, G)
Stephens College (U)
Sul Ross State University (U)
Texas Tech University (U, NC)
University of Illinois at Urbana–Champaign (U)
University of Nebraska–Lincoln (U)
The University of North Carolina at Chapel Hill (U)
University of Tennessee, Knoxville (U)
University of Waterloo (U)
Western Illinois University (U)
Western Washington University (U)

Environmental Engineering
Arizona State University (U, G)
Colorado State University (G)
Georgia Institute of Technology (G, NC)
Idaho State University (U, G)
Illinois Institute of Technology (G)
Laurentian University (U)
Michigan Technological University (G)
Mississippi State University (G)
National Technological University (G, NC)
New Jersey Institute of Technology (G)
New Mexico State University (G)
North Carolina State University (G)
Northern Arizona University (U)
Ohio University–Southern Campus (NC)
Oklahoma State University (G)
Old Dominion University (G)
Oregon State University (G)
Owens Community College (U)
Scott Community College (U)
Shenandoah University (G)
Southern Methodist University (G)
Southwest Virginia Community College (U)
State University of New York at Buffalo (G)
State University of New York College of Environmental Science and Forestry (U, G)
Tennessee State University (G, NC)
The University of Alabama (G)
The University of Alabama in Huntsville (G)
University of Colorado at Boulder (G, NC)
University of Delaware (G, NC)

University of Massachusetts Amherst (G, NC)
University of Nevada, Reno (U, G)
University of North Florida (G)
University of South Florida (G)
University of Tennessee, Knoxville (G)
The University of Texas at Arlington (G)
The University of Texas at San Antonio (U)
University of Wisconsin–Extension (NC)
Virginia Polytechnic Institute and State University (G)
Waubonsee Community College (U)
West Virginia Graduate College (G)
West Virginia University (G)

Environmental Health
California State University, Sacramento (U)
Ryerson Polytechnic University (U)
The University of Iowa (U, G)

Environmental Science
Adams State College (U)
Arizona State University West (U)
Catonsville Community College (U)
City University (U)
Duquesne University (U, G)
Genesee Community College (U)
Johnson County Community College (U)
Mercy College (U)
Owens Community College (U)
Rochester Institute of Technology (U)
Salt Lake Community College (U)
Seattle Central Community College (U)
Southern Oregon University (U)
Sul Ross State University (U)
Technical College of the Lowcountry (U)
Thomas Edison State College (U)
Tyler Junior College (U)
University of California, Davis (U)
University of Mary (U)
The University of North Carolina at Chapel Hill (U)
University of Toledo (U)
University of Washington (U)
University of Waterloo (U)
Wilfrid Laurier University (U)

Ethics
Bluefield State College (U)
Bucks County Community College (U)
Charles County Community College (U)
Clayton College & State University (U)
Colorado Electronic Community College (U)
Colorado Mountain College District (U)
Community College of Vermont (U)
Crafton Hills College (U)
Delgado Community College (U)
Delta College (U)
Denver Conservative Baptist Seminary (G, NC)
Duquesne University (U)
Eastern Kentucky University (U)
Gordon-Conwell Theological Seminary (G, NC)
Lake Land College (U)
Laramie County Community College (U)
LIFE Bible College (U)
Marywood University (U)
North Central Bible College (U, NC)
Northern Virginia Community College (U)
Northwestern College (U)
Park College (U)

Regis University (G)
Salve Regina University (U, G, NC)
San Bernardino Valley College (U)
San Jose State University (U)
Seattle Central Community College (U)
Southeast Community College, Lincoln Campus (U)
State Technical Institute at Memphis (U)
Stephens College (U)
Syracuse University (U)
Texas Tech University (U, NC)
Thomas Edison State College (U)
University of Cincinnati (U)
University of Delaware (U)
University of Mississippi (U, G)
University of Missouri–Columbia (U)
The University of North Carolina at Chapel Hill (U)
University of Pennsylvania (NC)
University of Southern Mississippi (U)
University of Tennessee, Knoxville (U)
University of Waterloo (U)

European History
Bluefield State College (U)
Brigham Young University (U)
Bristol Community College (U)
California State University, Sacramento (U)
Charles County Community College (U)
Delgado Community College (U)
East Carolina University (U, G)
Fairleigh Dickinson University, Teaneck–Hackensack (G)
Floyd College (U)
Genesee Community College (U)
Jefferson Community College (U)
Mercy College (U)
Metropolitan State College of Denver (U)
Northwestern Michigan College (U)
Northwest Iowa Community College (U)
Richland Community College (U)
Southeast Community College, Lincoln Campus (U)
Southwest Texas State University (U)
State University of New York at Oswego (U)
State University of West Georgia (U, G)
Texas Tech University (U, NC)
Thomas Edison State College (U)
Troy State University–Florida Region (U, G)
University of Illinois at Urbana–Champaign (U)
The University of Iowa (U)
University of Nebraska–Lincoln (U)
The University of North Carolina at Chapel Hill (U)
University of Tennessee, Knoxville (U)
University of Waterloo (U)
Washington State University (U)
William Penn College (U)

European Languages and Literatures
Acadia University (U)
Alvin Community College (U)
Anne Arundel Community College (U)
Athabasca University (U)
Atlantic Community College (U)
Austin Community College (U)
Bellevue Community College (U)
Brigham Young University (U)
Brookdale Community College (U)

Individual Courses Index

European Languages and Literatures (continued)
Burlington County College (U)
Butte College (U)
California State University, Fresno (U)
Calvin College (G)
Camden County College (U)
Carleton University (U)
Central Florida Community College (U)
Central Missouri State University (U)
Central Wyoming College (U)
Charles County Community College (U)
City College of San Francisco (U)
City Colleges of Chicago, Harold Washington College (U)
Clackamas Community College (U)
Coastline Community College (U, NC)
College of DuPage (U)
College of Lake County (U)
College of San Mateo (U)
Collin County Community College (U)
Community College of Philadelphia (U)
Concordia University Wisconsin (U, G)
Cumberland County College (U)
Cuyahoga Community College, Metropolitan Campus (U)
Dallas County Community College District (U)
Darton College (U)
Daytona Beach Community College (U)
DeKalb College (U)
Dodge City Community College (U)
Eastern Idaho Technical College (U)
Edison Community College (U)
Essex Community College (U)
Evergreen Valley College (U)
Florida Community College at Jacksonville (U)
Garland County Community College (U)
Georgia Southern University (U, NC)
Grand Rapids Community College (U)
Griggs University (U)
Howard Community College (U)
Illinois Eastern Community Colleges, Olney Central College (U)
Indiana University System (U)
John C. Calhoun State Community College (U)
John Wood Community College (U)
J. Sargeant Reynolds Community College (U)
Juniata College (U)
Laney College (U)
Lee College (U)
Louisiana State University at Eunice (U)
Luzerne County Community College (U)
Lycoming College (U)
Madison Area Technical College (U)
The McGregor School of Antioch University (G)
Memorial University of Newfoundland (NC)
Middle Georgia College (U)
Milwaukee Area Technical College (U)
Minnesota West Community and Technical College–Worthington Campus (U)
Montgomery College–Rockville Campus (U)
Mount Saint Vincent University (U)
Nassau Community College (U)
New Mexico Junior College (U)
New School for Social Research (U, NC)
North Carolina State University (U)
Northern Virginia Community College (U)
North Harris College (U)
North Seattle Community College (U)
North Shore Community College (U)
Northwestern Michigan College (U)
Northwest Iowa Community College (U)
Oakland University (U)
Oakton Community College (U)
Ohio University (U)
Ohio University–Southern Campus (U)
Ohlone College (U)
Oklahoma State University (U)
Owens Community College (U)
Pennsylvania State University University Park Campus (U)
Penn Valley Community College (U)
Piedmont College (U)
Pima Community College (U)
Portland State University (U)
Pueblo Community College (U)
The Richard Stockton College of New Jersey (U, NC)
Richland Community College (NC)
Riverland Community College (U)
Rose State College (U)
Sacramento City College (U)
St. Cloud Technical College (U)
St. Louis Community College (U)
St. Petersburg Junior College (U)
Salt Lake Community College (U)
San Antonio College (U)
Santa Rosa Junior College (U)
Skidmore College (U)
Southeast Community College, Beatrice Campus (U)
Southeastern Community College, North Campus (U)
Southwestern Michigan College (U)
Southwest Missouri State University (U)
Southwest State University (U)
Southwest Virginia Community College (U)
Tacoma Community College (U)
Thomas Edison State College (U)
Trinidad State Junior College (U)
Troy State University Montgomery (U)
Tulsa Community College (U)
Tyler Junior College (U)
University of Alaska Anchorage (U)
University of California Extension (U)
University of Central Oklahoma (U)
University of Georgia (U)
University of Houston (U, G)
University of Kansas (U, NC)
University of Maine (U)
University of Maine at Augusta (U)
University of Maine at Fort Kent (U)
University of Minnesota, Twin Cities Campus (U, NC)
University of Missouri–Columbia (U)
University of Nebraska at Kearney (U)
University of Nebraska–Lincoln (U)
University of Nevada, Las Vegas (U)
University of Oklahoma (U, NC)
University of Saskatchewan (U)
University of South Dakota (U)
University of South Florida (U)
The University of Texas at Austin (U)
University of Washington (U)
University of Waterloo (U)
University System of Georgia (U)
Upper Iowa University (U)
Utah State University (U)
Utah Valley State College (U)
Volunteer State Community College (U)
Walters State Community College (U)
Waubonsee Community College (U)
Western Illinois University (U)
Western Nebraska Community College (U)
Western Oklahoma State College (U)
West Valley College (U)
West Virginia University (G)
Wilfrid Laurier University (U)

Family and Marriage Counseling
Eastern Kentucky University (U)
Penn Valley Community College (U)
Tennessee Temple University (U)
Thomas Edison State College (U)
University of Southern Colorado (U, G)

Film Studies
Auburn University (U)
Brigham Young University (U)
Cabrillo College (U)
Charles County Community College (U)
Clark College (U)
Columbia Basin College (U)
Cuyahoga Community College, Metropolitan Campus (U)
Genesee Community College (U)
Kansas State University (U)
Lane Community College (U)
Metropolitan Community College (U)
Moraine Valley Community College (U)
Northern Virginia Community College (U)
San Bernardino Valley College (U)
Seattle Central Community College (U)
Sinclair Community College (U)
Southwestern Michigan College (U)
Southwest Missouri State University (U)
State Technical Institute at Memphis (U)
Thomas Edison State College (U)
Universitè Laval (U)
University of Alaska Fairbanks (U)
University of British Columbia (U)
University of California Extension (U)
University of Houston (U)
Yuba College (U)

Finance
Adams State College (U)
Austin Community College (U)
Bergen Community College (U)
Brigham Young University (U)
Buena Vista University (U)
California State University, Long Beach (U)
Central Michigan University (U)
City University (G)
College for Financial Planning (U, G)
Colorado State University (G)
Columbus State Community College (U)
Delgado Community College (U)
Duke University (G)
Embry-Riddle Aeronautical University, Extended Campus (U)
GMI Engineering & Management Institute (G)
Heriot-Watt University (G)
Marywood University (U)
McDowell Technical Community College (U)
Mercy College (U)
Mesa State College (U)
Metropolitan Community College (U)
Metropolitan State University (U)
Midwestern State University (U, G)

Individual Courses Index

Milwaukee School of Engineering (G, NC)
New Hampshire College (U)
New River Community College (U)
Northern Illinois University (G)
Northern Virginia Community College (U)
Oklahoma State University (U)
Palomar College (U)
Park College (U)
Regis University (G)
Roosevelt University (U)
Salve Regina University (U, G, NC)
Southeastern Louisiana University (U)
State University of New York Empire State College (U)
Stephens College (U)
Texas Tech University (U, NC)
Thomas Edison State College (U)
Universitè Laval (U)
University of Alaska Southeast (U)
University of Dallas (G)
University of Massachusetts Dartmouth (U)
University of Mississippi (U, G)
University of Missouri–Columbia (U)
University of Nebraska–Lincoln (U)
University of Notre Dame (NC)
University of Wisconsin–Eau Claire (U)
University of Wisconsin–Extension (NC)
University of Wisconsin–Platteville (U)
Upper Iowa University (U)
Washington State University (U)
Waukesha County Technical College (U)
Weber State University (U)
Western Illinois University (U)
Winthrop University (G)

Fine Arts
Anne Arundel Community College (U)
Arapahoe Community College (NC)
Arizona State University (U)
Austin Community College (U)
Ball State University (U)
Bellevue Community College (U)
Bluefield State College (U)
Brigham Young University (U)
Butte College (U)
California State University, Bakersfield (U)
California State University, Hayward (U)
Cape Cod Community College (U)
Charles County Community College (U)
Chattanooga State Technical Community College (U)
City Colleges of Chicago, Harold Washington College (U)
Clarkson College (U)
Colby Community College (U)
College Misericordia (U)
College of San Mateo (U)
College of the Southwest (U)
The College of West Virginia (U)
Colorado Mountain College District (U)
Concordia University (U)
Concordia University at Austin (U, NC)
Cosumnes River College (U)
Darton College (U)
Dawson Community College (U)
Daytona Beach Community College (U)
De Anza College (U)
East Carolina University (U, G)
East Central Community College (U)
Eastern Wyoming College (U)

Gadsden State Community College (U)
Garland County Community College (U)
Graceland College (U)
Griggs University (U)
Indiana University System (U, G)
Iowa Wesleyan College (U)
Iowa Western Community College (U)
Jamestown Community College (U)
John C. Calhoun State Community College (U)
Judson College (U)
Kaskaskia College (U)
Lamar University (U)
Lassen College (U)
Loyola University New Orleans (U)
Luzerne County Community College (U)
Lycoming College (U)
Marshall University (U)
The McGregor School of Antioch University (G)
Metropolitan Community College (U)
Minnesota West Community and Technical College–Worthington Campus (U)
Missouri Southern State College (U)
Nassau Community College (U)
New Mexico Junior College (U)
New School for Social Research (U, NC)
North Arkansas College (U)
Northern Virginia Community College (U)
North Shore Community College (U)
Northwestern State University of Louisiana (U)
Portland Community College (U)
Portland State University (U)
Rend Lake College (U)
The Richard Stockton College of New Jersey (U)
Rockland Community College (U)
Saint Joseph's College (U)
St. Louis Community College (U)
Scott Community College (U)
Shelby State Community College (U)
Sierra College (U)
Sinclair Community College (U)
Southeast Arkansas Technical College (U)
Southern Utah University (U)
Southwestern Assemblies of God University (U)
Southwest State University (U)
Suffolk County Community College–Ammerman Campus (U)
Syracuse University (U)
Tarrant County Junior College (U)
Taylor University, Fort Wayne Campus (U)
Triton College (U)
University of California Extension (U)
University of California, Santa Barbara (U, NC)
University of Delaware (NC)
University of Georgia (U)
University of Maine at Augusta (U)
University of Maine at Fort Kent (U)
University of Minnesota, Twin Cities Campus (U)
University of Missouri–St. Louis (U)
University of Oklahoma (U)
University of Southern Indiana (U)
University of South Florida (G)
University of Utah (U)
University of Wisconsin–Extension (NC)
University System of Georgia (U)
Utah State University (U, NC)
Valley City State University (U)
Volunteer State Community College (U)
Waubonsee Community College (U)
Wayne State University (U)

Western Oklahoma State College (U)
West Valley College (U)
West Virginia Wesleyan College (U)
Wichita State University (U)
Wilfrid Laurier University (U)
Wytheville Community College (U)
Yuba College (U)

Fire Science
Catonsville Community College (U)
Copiah-Lincoln Community College (U)
East Central Community College (U)
Louisiana State University at Eunice (U)
Meridian Community College (U)
Missouri Western State College (U)
Oklahoma State University (U)
Owens Community College (U)
Penn Valley Community College (U)
University of Arkansas at Little Rock (U)
University of Cincinnati (U)
University of Maryland University College (U)
Waukesha County Technical College (U)
Western Illinois University (U)
Worcester Polytechnic Institute (G)

Fire Services Administration
Central Florida Community College (U)
Copiah-Lincoln Community College (U)
Penn Valley Community College (U)
St. Louis Community College (U, NC)
State University of New York Empire State College (U)
University of Missouri–Columbia (NC)
Western Illinois University (U)

Foods and Nutrition Studies
Bakersfield College (U)
Bastyr University (U)
Bucks County Community College (U)
Central Arizona College (U)
Central Missouri State University (U)
Clovis Community College (U)
Colorado Mountain College District (U)
Colorado State University (U)
Copiah-Lincoln Community College (U)
Cuyahoga Community College, Metropolitan Campus (U)
Dallas County Community College District (U)
De Anza College (U)
Eastern Kentucky University (U)
Griggs University (U)
Hocking College (U)
Kansas State University (U, G, NC)
Lane Community College (U)
Mount Wachusett Community College (U)
New River Community College (U)
North Dakota State College of Science (U)
Northeast Wisconsin Technical College (U)
Pueblo Community College (U)
Rio Salado College (U)
Santa Rosa Junior College (U)
Seattle Central Community College (U)
Southeast Community College, Lincoln Campus (U)
Southwest Missouri State University (U)
Southwest Texas State University (U)
Syracuse University (U)
Texas Tech University (U, NC)
Troy State University (U)

Distance Learning Programs

Individual Courses Index

Foods and Nutrition Studies (continued)
Universitè Laval (U)
University of Delaware (U)
University of Minnesota, Twin Cities Campus (U)
University of Nebraska–Lincoln (U)
The University of North Carolina at Chapel Hill (U)
University of Northern Colorado (U)
University of Washington (U)
University of Waterloo (U)
Washington State University (U)
West Virginia Wesleyan College (U)
Yuba College (U)

Forestry
Lakehead University (G)
University of British Columbia (U)
University of Tennessee, Knoxville (U)

French Language and Literature
Austin Community College (U)
California State University, Sacramento (U)
Catonsville Community College (U)
Charles County Community College (U)
College of St. Francis (U)
College of St. Scholastica (U, G)
Columbus State Community College (U)
De Anza College (U)
Essex Community College (U)
Jefferson College (U)
Lafayette College (U)
Louisiana State University at Eunice (U)
Marywood University (U)
Metropolitan Community College (U)
Metropolitan State University (U)
Mississippi Delta Community College (U)
Moraine Valley Community College (U)
Oklahoma State University (U)
Pierce College (U)
Southwest Missouri State University (U)
Universitè Laval (U)
University of British Columbia (U)
University of Guelph (U)
University of Illinois at Urbana–Champaign (U)
The University of Iowa (U)
University of Maryland University College (U)
University of Michigan (G)
University of Missouri–Columbia (U)
The University of North Carolina at Chapel Hill (U)
University of Tennessee, Knoxville (U)
University of Washington (U)
University of Waterloo (U)
University System of Georgia (U)
Western Illinois University (U)
Wilfrid Laurier University (U)

Genetics
Black Hills State University (U)
Eastern Michigan University (U)
Emporia State University (U, G)
Iowa State University of Science and Technology (U, G)
Syracuse University (U)
University of Missouri–Columbia (U)
University of Southern Mississippi (U)
University of Waterloo (U)

Geography
Austin Community College (U)
Bellevue Community College (U)
Bluefield State College (U)
Boise State University (U)
Brigham Young University (U)
Bristol Community College (U)
Broward Community College (U)
Cabrillo College (U)
Carleton University (U)
Carl Sandburg College (U)
Central Michigan University (U)
Central Piedmont Community College (U)
Central Wyoming College (U)
Clatsop Community College (U)
Colorado Electronic Community College (U)
Colorado Mountain College District (U)
Copiah-Lincoln Community College (U)
Crafton Hills College (U)
Eastern Kentucky University (U)
Flathead Valley Community College (U)
Florida State University (U)
Governors State University (U)
Grand Rapids Community College (U)
Griggs University (U)
Harrisburg Area Community College (U)
Illinois Valley Community College (U)
Lane Community College (U)
Laramie County Community College (U)
Lehigh Carbon Community College (U)
Manchester Community-Technical College (U)
Marshall University (U)
Mississippi Delta Community College (U)
Moraine Valley Community College (U)
Northern Oklahoma College (U)
Northern Virginia Community College (U)
Oklahoma State University (U)
Portland State University (U)
Pratt Community College and Area Vocational School (U)
Red Rocks Community College (U)
Rio Salado College (U)
Rockland Community College (U)
Roosevelt University (U)
San Bernardino Valley College (U)
San Diego City College (U)
San Jose State University (U)
Seattle Central Community College (U)
Southeast Arkansas Technical College (U)
South Florida Community College (U)
Southwest Texas State University (U)
State Technical Institute at Memphis (U)
Tacoma Community College (U)
Tallahassee Community College (U)
Taylor University, Fort Wayne Campus (U)
Thomas Edison State College (U)
Universitè Laval (U)
University of Alaska Fairbanks (U)
University of Illinois at Urbana–Champaign (U)
The University of Iowa (U, G)
University of Mary (U)
University of Massachusetts Lowell (U)
University of Minnesota, Twin Cities Campus (U)
University of Missouri–Columbia (U)
University of Nebraska–Lincoln (U)
The University of North Carolina at Chapel Hill (U)
University of Northern Colorado (U)
University of Southern Colorado (U)
University of Southern Mississippi (U)
University of Washington (U)
University of Waterloo (U)
University System of Georgia (U)
Wayne County Community College (U)
Western Illinois University (U)
Wilfrid Laurier University (U)
William Penn College (U)

Geology
Alvin Community College (U)
Arapahoe Community College (U)
Athabasca University (U)
Austin Community College (U)
Bakersfield College (U)
Ball State University (U)
Bellevue Community College (U)
Black Hawk College (U)
Bluefield State College (U)
Blue Mountain Community College (U)
Boise State University (U)
Brevard Community College (U)
Broward Community College (U)
Burlington County College (U)
Carleton University (U)
Catonsville Community College (U)
Central Community College–Grand Island Campus (U)
Central Florida Community College (U)
Chemeketa Community College (U)
City Colleges of Chicago, Harold Washington College (U)
Clovis Community College (U)
Coastline Community College (U, NC)
College of DuPage (U)
College of Lake County (U)
College of San Mateo (U)
Colorado Electronic Community College (U)
Colorado Northwestern Community College (U)
Concordia University (U)
Crafton Hills College (U)
Cuyamaca College (U)
Daytona Beach Community College (U)
Dutchess Community College (U)
East Tennessee State University (U)
Edison Community College (U)
El Paso Community College (U)
Emporia State University (U, G)
Essex Community College (U)
Fitchburg State College (U)
Florida Community College at Jacksonville (U)
Floyd College (U)
Fort Hays State University (U)
Front Range Community College (U)
Garland County Community College (U)
Georgia Southern University (U, G, NC)
Glendale Community College (U)
Harrisburg Area Community College (U)
Hibbing Community College (U)
Hillsborough Community College (U)
Idaho State University (U, G)
Illinois Valley Community College (U)
Indiana University System (U)
Iowa Western Community College (U)
Jacksonville State University (U)
Johnson County Community College (U)
Kansas State University (U)
Kaskaskia College (U)
Lake-Sumter Community College (U)

Laurentian University (U)
Los Angeles Community College District (U)
Luzerne County Community College (U)
Marshall University (U)
Metropolitan Community College (U)
Metropolitan State College of Denver (U)
Michigan Technological University (U, NC)
Milwaukee Area Technical College (U)
MiraCosta College (U)
Missouri Southern State College (U)
Modesto Junior College (U)
Montana State University–Bozeman (G)
New River Community College (U)
New School for Social Research (U, NC)
Northeast Community College (U)
Northeast Louisiana University (U)
Northern Illinois University (G)
North Hennepin Community College (U)
North Seattle Community College (U)
Odessa College (U)
Oklahoma City Community College (U)
Oklahoma State University (U)
Pensacola Junior College (U)
Pierce College (U)
Pikes Peak Community College (U, NC)
Portland State University (U)
Pratt Community College and Area Vocational School (U)
Prince George's Community College (U)
Pueblo Community College (U)
Red Rocks Community College (U)
The Richard Stockton College of New Jersey (U)
Rio Salado College (U)
Rochester Institute of Technology (U)
Rose State College (U)
St. Petersburg Junior College (U)
San Bernardino Valley College (U)
San Diego City College (U)
San Jose State University (U)
Scott Community College (U)
Shawnee Community College (U)
Sinclair Community College (U)
Skagit Valley College (U)
Southeast Community College, Lincoln Campus (U)
South Florida Community College (U)
Southwestern Oklahoma State University (U)
State University of New York at Oswego (U)
Syracuse University (U)
Tacoma Community College (U)
Tallahassee Community College (U)
Tarrant County Junior College (U)
Thomas Edison State College (U)
Tidewater Community College (U)
Treasure Valley Community College (U)
Troy State University Dothan (U)
Tulsa Community College (U)
Umpqua Community College (U)
Universitè Laval (U)
University of Alaska Fairbanks (U)
University of Alaska Southeast, Sitka Campus (U)
University of California Extension (U)
University of Colorado at Colorado Springs (U, G)
University of Georgia (U)
University of Great Falls (U)
University of Guelph (U)
University of Hawaii–Leeward Community College (U)

University of Houston (U)
University of Idaho (U, G)
The University of Iowa (U, G)
University of Kansas (U, NC)
University of Maine at Augusta (U)
University of Maine at Fort Kent (U)
University of Minnesota, Twin Cities Campus (U)
University of Missouri–Columbia (U, G)
University of Nebraska–Lincoln (U)
University of Nevada, Las Vegas (U, G)
University of New Orleans (U)
The University of North Carolina at Chapel Hill (U)
University of Oklahoma (U)
University of Saskatchewan (U)
University of Southern Colorado (U)
University of South Florida (U, G)
University of Vermont (U)
University of Washington (U)
University of Waterloo (U)
University of Windsor (U)
University System of Georgia (U)
Utah State University (U)
Vincennes University (U)
Volunteer State Community College (U)
Walters State Community College (U)
Washington State University (U)
Wayne County Community College (U)
Weber State University (U)
Wenatchee Valley College (U)
Western Illinois University (U)
Western Oklahoma State College (U)
Westmoreland County Community College (U)
West Valley College (U)
West Virginia University (G)
Whatcom Community College (U)
Wichita State University (U)
Wilfrid Laurier University (U)

German Language and Literature
Brigham Young University (U)
California State University, Sacramento (U)
Catonsville Community College (U)
Eastern Kentucky University (U)
Joliet Junior College (U)
Oklahoma State University (U)
Rutgers, The State University of New Jersey, Newark (U)
Universitè Laval (U)
University of British Columbia (U)
University of Houston (U)
University of Illinois at Urbana–Champaign (U)
The University of Iowa (U)
University of Kentucky, Elizabethtown Community College (U)
University of Michigan (G)
University of Missouri–Columbia (U)
University of Tennessee, Knoxville (U)
University of Waterloo (U)
University System of Georgia (U)
Wilfrid Laurier University (U)

Gerontology
Bluefield State College (U)
Catonsville Community College (U)
Colorado State University (U)
Columbus State University (U)
Genesee Community College (U)

Lansing Community College (U)
Lehigh Carbon Community College (U)
Mount Wachusett Community College (U)
Nicholls State University (U)
Ryerson Polytechnic University (U)
Sacramento City College (U)
Salve Regina University (U, NC)
Thomas Edison State College (U)
Universitè Laval (U)
The University of Iowa (U, G)
The University of Montana–Missoula (U, G)
University of Northern Colorado (U)
University of Tennessee, Knoxville (U)
University of the State of New York, Regents College (U)
University of Vermont (U, G)
University of Washington (U)
University of Waterloo (U)
Walters State Community College (U)

Greek Language and Literature
Lincoln Christian College (U, G, NC)
Taylor University, Fort Wayne Campus (U)
University of Waterloo

Health and Physical Education/Fitness
Adams State College (U, G)
American River College (U)
Anne Arundel Community College (U)
Arizona State University (U)
Atlantic Community College (U)
Auburn University (U)
Austin Community College (U)
Bakersfield College (U)
Ball State University (U)
Black Hawk College (U)
Blackhawk Technical College (U)
Bluefield State College (U)
Blue Mountain Community College (U)
Brevard Community College (U)
Brigham Young University (U)
Brookdale Community College (U)
Broward Community College (U)
Burlington County College (U)
Butte College (U)
California State University, Fullerton (U)
Camden County College (U)
Catonsville Community College (U)
Central Florida Community College (U)
Central Piedmont Community College (U)
Central Virginia Community College (U)
Central Wyoming College (U)
Chadron State College (U)
Chattanooga State Technical Community College (U)
Chemeketa Community College (U)
Clackamas Community College (U)
Clark College (U)
Clovis Community College (U)
Coastline Community College (U, NC)
College of San Mateo (U)
College of the Southwest (U)
Colorado Mountain College District (U)
Columbia State Community College (U)
Community College of Rhode Island (U)
Concordia University (U)
Contra Costa College (U)
Corning Community College (U)
Cosumnes River College (U)

Individual Courses Index

Health and Physical Education/Fitness (continued)
County College of Morris (U)
Cuyahoga Community College, Metropolitan Campus (U)
Dallas County Community College District (U)
Danville Community College (U)
Dawson Community College (U)
Daytona Beach Community College (U)
De Anza College (U)
DeKalb College (U)
Delta College (U)
Eastern Kentucky University (U)
Eastern Oregon University (U)
Eastern Washington University (U)
Edison Community College (U)
Emporia State University (U, G)
Essex Community College (U)
Floyd College (U)
Fullerton College (U)
Gadsden State Community College (U)
Garland County Community College (U)
Genesee Community College (U)
George C. Wallace State Community College (U)
Glendale Community College (U)
Graceland College (U)
Grand Canyon University (G)
Hampton University (U, NC)
Hillsborough Community College (U)
Idaho State University (U, G)
Illinois Valley Community College (U)
Indiana University System (U, G)
Iowa Wesleyan College (U)
Jacksonville State University (U)
Jefferson College (U)
Jefferson State Community College (U)
John C. Calhoun State Community College (U)
Johnson County Community College (U)
Kingwood College (U)
Lake Land College (U)
Lakeland Community College (U)
Lake-Sumter Community College (U)
Lane Community College (U)
Laney College (U)
Lehigh Carbon Community College (U)
Luzerne County Community College (U)
Marywood University (U)
Middle Tennessee State University (U)
Milwaukee Area Technical College (U)
Minnesota West Community and Technical College–Worthington Campus (U)
Modesto Junior College (U)
Montana State University–Bozeman (G)
Montgomery College–Rockville Campus (U)
Montgomery County Community College (U)
Morehead State University (U)
Morgan Community College (U, NC)
Nassau Community College (U)
New River Community College (U)
New School for Social Research (U, NC)
Nicholls State University (U)
Normandale Community College (U)
North Carolina State University (U)
North Central Bible College (U, NC)
Northeast Community College (U)
Northeast Louisiana University (U)
Northern Kentucky University (U)
North Harris College (U)
North Seattle Community College (U)
North Shore Community College (U)

Northwestern State University of Louisiana (U, NC)
Oakton Community College (U)
Ohio University (U)
Ohlone College (U)
Oklahoma State University (U)
Owens Community College (U)
Pennsylvania State University University Park Campus (U)
Pierce College (U)
Portland Community College (U)
Pratt Community College and Area Vocational School (U)
Prince George's Community College (U, NC)
Redlands Community College (U)
Red Rocks Community College (U)
Rochester Institute of Technology (U)
Rockland Community College (U)
Rose State College (U)
Sacramento City College (U)
St. Louis Community College (U)
St. Petersburg Junior College (U)
San Bernardino Valley College (U)
Scott Community College (U)
Shelby State Community College (U)
Skagit Valley College (U)
Southeast Arkansas Technical College (U)
Southeastern Louisiana University (U)
Southwestern Assemblies of God University (U)
Southwestern Michigan College (U)
Southwest State University (U)
Suffolk County Community College–Ammerman Campus (U)
Tarrant County Junior College (U)
Texas Tech University (U)
Triton College (U)
Troy State University Dothan (U)
United States Sports Academy (G, NC)
The University of Alabama (G)
University of Alaska Anchorage (U)
University of Alaska Fairbanks (U)
University of Georgia (U)
University of Great Falls (U)
University of Hawaii–Leeward Community College (U)
University of Hawaii–Maui Community College (U)
University of Kansas (U, G, NC)
University of Mary (U)
The University of Memphis (U)
University of Missouri–Columbia (U)
University of Nebraska–Lincoln (U)
University of Northern Iowa (U)
University of Oklahoma (U)
University of South Dakota (U)
The University of Texas at Tyler (U, G)
University of Wisconsin–Eau Claire (U, G)
University of Wisconsin–La Crosse (U, G, NC)
University of Wisconsin–River Falls (U, G)
University of Wyoming (U, G)
University System of Georgia (U)
Vincennes University (U)
Volunteer State Community College (U)
Walters State Community College (U)
Weber State University (U)
Wenatchee Valley College (U)
Western Illinois University (G)
Western Michigan University (U)
Western Oklahoma State College (U)
Westmoreland County Community College (U)

West Valley College (U)
West Virginia University (G)
West Virginia Wesleyan College (U)
William Rainey Harper College (U)
Wytheville Community College (U)
Yuba College (U)

Health Professions and Related Sciences
Allegheny University of the Health Sciences (U)
Arizona State University (G)
Athabasca University (U)
Baker College (U, G)
Ball State University (U)
Bastyr University (U)
Blackhawk Technical College (U)
Boise State University (U)
Brigham Young University (U)
Broward Community College (U)
California College for Health Sciences (U, G)
California State University, Hayward (U)
California State University, Sacramento (U)
Calvin College (G)
Catawba Valley Community College (U)
Central Arizona College (U)
Central Michigan University (U)
Century Community and Technical College (U)
Chippewa Valley Technical College (U)
City College of San Francisco (U)
City University (U, G)
Clarkson College (U, G)
Clark State Community College (U)
Coffeyville Community College (U, NC)
Colby Community College (U)
The College of West Virginia (U)
Colorado Northwestern Community College (U)
Copiah-Lincoln Community College (U, G)
Cosumnes River College (U)
Darton College (U)
Daytona Beach Community College (U)
De Anza College (U)
DeKalb College (U)
Delaware Technical & Community College, Stanton/Wilmington Campus (U)
Delta College (U)
Des Moines Area Community College (NC)
East Carolina University (G)
Florida Atlantic University (G)
Garland County Community College (U)
Garrett Community College (NC)
Gateway Technical College (U)
Graceland College (U)
The Graduate School of America (G)
Hampton University (U, G)
Harrisburg Area Community College (NC)
Hocking College (U)
Howard Community College (U)
Idaho State University (U, G)
Illinois Central College (U)
Indiana University System (U, G)
Ivy Tech State College–Northcentral (U)
Jackson Community College (U)
John A. Logan College (U)
J. Sargeant Reynolds Community College (U)
Lakeshore Technical College (U)
Loma Linda University (U)
Louisiana State University at Eunice (U)
Marshall University (U)
Medical College of Georgia (G)

Medical University of South Carolina (U, G)
Metropolitan Community College (U)
Mid-State Technical College (U)
Midwestern State University (U, G)
Mississippi Delta Community College (U)
Missouri Southern State College (U)
Modesto Junior College (U)
Montana Tech of The University of Montana (U)
Moraine Valley Community College (U)
Mountain View College (U)
New Jersey Institute of Technology (G)
North Central Technical College (U)
Northcentral Technical College (U)
Northeast Wisconsin Technical College (U)
Northern Virginia Community College (U)
Northwestern Michigan College (U)
Northwestern State University of Louisiana (NC)
Northwest Iowa Community College (NC)
Ohio University (U)
Oklahoma State University (G)
Old Dominion University (U)
Our Lady of the Lake University of San Antonio (G)
Pennsylvania State University University Park Campus (U, NC)
Pitt Community College (U)
Portland Community College (NC)
Prairie State College (U)
Purdue University (U)
Redlands Community College (U, NC)
Red Rocks Community College (U)
Regis University (G)
The Richard Stockton College of New Jersey (U)
Rio Salado College (U)
Rochester Institute of Technology (U, G)
Saint Joseph's College (U, G)
St. Louis Community College (U)
San Diego City College (U)
San Joaquin Delta College (U)
Shawnee Community College (U)
Southeast Community College, Beatrice Campus (U)
Southwestern Michigan College (U)
Southwestern Oklahoma State University (U)
Southwest Virginia Community College (U)
State University of New York Empire State College (U)
Texas A&M University–Commerce (NC)
Texas A&M University–Corpus Christi (U)
Texas Woman's University (U)
Tidewater Community College (U)
The Union Institute (U)
United States Sports Academy (G, NC)
The University of Alabama (G)
The University of Alabama at Birmingham (G)
University of Alaska Southeast, Sitka Campus (U)
University of California Extension (U, NC)
University of Cincinnati Raymond Walters College (U)
University of Dallas (G)
University of Georgia (U, NC)
University of Great Falls (U)
University of Kentucky (U)
University of Maine (U)
University of Maryland, Baltimore County (U)
University of Massachusetts Lowell (U)
University of Missouri–Columbia (U, G, NC)
The University of Montana–Missoula (G)

University of Nebraska at Kearney (U)
University of Nevada, Reno (NC)
University of New Hampshire (G, NC)
University of North Dakota (G)
University of Northern Colorado (U)
University of Northern Iowa (U)
University of Sarasota (G)
University of South Carolina (G)
University of South Dakota (G)
University of Southern California (U)
University of Southern Indiana (U)
University of St. Augustine for Health Sciences (G)
The University of Texas at Austin (U)
University of Utah (U)
University of Virginia (G)
University of Washington (U, G)
University of Waterloo (U)
University of Windsor (NC)
University of Wisconsin–Stevens Point (U)
University of Wyoming (U, G)
University System of Georgia (U)
Upper Iowa University (U)
Utah State University (U)
Utah Valley State College (U)
Volunteer State Community College (U)
Walden University (G)
Waubonsee Community College (U)
Wayne County Community College (U)
West Valley College (U)
Wichita State University (U, G)
Yuba College (U)

Health Services Administration
Dalhousie University (U, G)
Ottawa University (U)
Park College (U)
Southwest Texas State University (U)
Texas Tech University (U, NC)
Universitè Laval (U)
University of Illinois at Urbana–Champaign (U)
University of Mary (U, G)
University of Missouri–Columbia (U)
The University of North Carolina at Chapel Hill (U)
University of North Florida (U)
Weber State University (U)

Hebrew Language and Literature
Brigham Young University (U)
Concordia College (U)
Lincoln Christian College (U, G, NC)
North Central Bible College (U, NC)
Stephens College (U)
Taylor University, Fort Wayne Campus (U)

History
Acadia University (U)
Adams State College (U)
Allegany College of Maryland (U)
Alvin Community College (U)
Angelina College (U)
Anne Arundel Community College (U)
Arapahoe Community College (U)
Arizona State University (U, G)
Assemblies of God Theological Seminary (G, NC)
Athabasca University (U)
Atlantic Community College (U)

Auburn University (U)
Austin Community College (U)
Bakersfield College (U)
Ball State University (U)
Beaufort County Community College (U)
Bellevue Community College (U)
Bellevue University (U)
Bemidji State University (U)
Berean University of the Assemblies of God (U)
Bergen Community College (U)
Black Hawk College (U)
Blinn College (U)
Bloomsburg University of Pennsylvania (U)
Bluefield State College (U)
Boise State University (U)
Brevard Community College (U)
Brigham Young University (U)
Brookdale Community College (U)
Broward Community College (U)
Bucks County Community College (U)
Buena Vista University (U)
Burlington County College (U)
Butte College (U)
California State University, Bakersfield (U)
California State University, Hayward (U)
California State University, Sacramento (U)
California State University, Stanislaus (U)
Camden County College (U)
Carleton University (U)
Carl Sandburg College (U)
Catawba Valley Community College (U)
Catonsville Community College (U)
Central Community College–Grand Island Campus (U)
Central Florida Community College (U)
Central Piedmont Community College (U)
Chadron State College (U)
Champlain College (U)
Chapman University (U)
Charles County Community College (U)
Charles Stewart Mott Community College (U)
Charter Oak State College (U)
Chattanooga State Technical Community College (U)
Chemeketa Community College (U)
Citrus College (U)
City College of San Francisco (U)
City Colleges of Chicago, Harold Washington College (U)
Clackamas Community College (U)
Clarkson College (U)
Clatsop Community College (U)
Coastline Community College (U, NC)
Colby Community College (U)
College of DuPage (U)
College of St. Francis (U)
College of St. Scholastica (U, G)
College of San Mateo (U)
College of the Canyons (U)
College of the Mainland (U)
College of the Southwest (U)
The College of West Virginia (U)
Collin County Community College (U)
Colorado Mountain College District (U)
Colorado State University (U)
Community College of Denver (U)
Community College of Philadelphia (U)
Community College of Rhode Island (U)
Concordia University (U)
Concordia University Wisconsin (U, G)

Distance Learning Programs

Individual Courses Index

History (continued)

Cosumnes River College (U)
County College of Morris (U)
Crafton Hills College (U)
Cumberland County College (U)
Cuyahoga Community College, Metropolitan Campus (U)
Cuyamaca College (U)
Dallas County Community College District (U)
Dawson Community College (U)
DeKalb College (U)
Delaware County Community College (U)
Delta College (U)
Denver Conservative Baptist Seminary (G, NC)
Des Moines Area Community College (U)
Dutchess Community College (U)
East Carolina University (U, G)
East Central Community College (U)
Eastern Idaho Technical College (U)
Eastern New Mexico University (U, G)
Eastern Washington University (U)
Eastern Wyoming College (U)
East Tennessee State University (U)
Edison Community College (U)
Essex Community College (U)
Evergreen Valley College (U)
Fitchburg State College (U)
Florida Community College at Jacksonville (U)
Florida State University (U)
Fort Hays State University (U)
Franciscan University of Steubenville (U, NC)
Front Range Community College (U)
Fullerton College (U)
Gadsden State Community College (U)
Galveston College (U)
Gannon University (U)
Garland County Community College (U)
Genesee Community College (U)
Georgia Southern University (U, NC)
Glendale Community College (U)
Gordon-Conwell Theological Seminary (G, NC)
Governors State University (U, G)
Graceland College (U)
Grand Rapids Community College (U)
Grand Valley State University (U, G)
Greenville Technical College (U)
Hampton University (U)
Harrisburg Area Community College (U)
Hillsborough Community College (U)
Houston Community College System (U)
Idaho State University (U, G)
Illinois Eastern Community Colleges, Olney Central College (U)
Illinois Valley Community College (U)
Indiana University System (U)
International Bible College (U)
Iowa Western Community College (U)
Jacksonville State University (U)
Jefferson Davis Community College (U)
Jefferson State Community College (U)
John A. Logan College (U)
John C. Calhoun State Community College (U)
Joliet Junior College (U)
J. Sargeant Reynolds Community College (U)
Judson College (U)
Kansas State University (U, NC)
Kaskaskia College (U)
Kellogg Community College (U)
Kennesaw State University (U)
Labette Community College (U)

Lackawanna Junior College (U)
Lakehead University (U)
Lake Land College (U)
Lake Michigan College (U)
Lamar University (U)
Laney College (U)
Lassen College (U)
Laurentian University (U)
Lawson State Community College (U)
Lee College (U)
Lehigh Carbon Community College (U)
LIFE Bible College (U)
Lincoln Land Community College (U)
Long Beach City College (U)
Longview Community College (U)
Lorain County Community College (U)
Lord Fairfax Community College (U)
Los Angeles Community College District (U)
Louisiana College (U)
Louisiana State University and Agricultural and Mechanical College (U)
Louisiana State University in Shreveport (U, G)
Luzerne County Community College (U)
Lycoming College (U)
Manatee Community College (U)
Marshall University (U, G)
McCook Community College (U)
McDowell Technical Community College (U)
The McGregor School of Antioch University (G)
Memorial University of Newfoundland (U)
Mendocino College (U)
Mercy College (U)
Metropolitan Community College (U)
Metropolitan State College of Denver (U)
Midland College (U)
Mid-Plains Community College (U)
Midwestern State University (U)
Milwaukee Area Technical College (U)
Minnesota West Community and Technical College–Worthington Campus (U)
Minot State University (U)
Missouri Southern State College (U)
Modesto Junior College (U)
Montgomery College–Rockville Campus (U)
Montgomery County Community College (U)
Moody Bible Institute (U)
Moraine Valley Community College (U)
Morgan Community College (U, NC)
Mountain View College (U)
Mount Saint Vincent University (U)
Nassau Community College (U)
New Hampshire College (U)
New River Community College (U)
New School for Social Research (U, NC)
New York Institute of Technology (U)
Nicholls State University (U)
North Arkansas College (U)
North Carolina State University (U)
North Central Bible College (U, NC)
North Central Texas College (U)
Northeast Community College (U)
Northeast Louisiana University (U)
Northern Arizona University (U)
Northern Kentucky University (U)
Northern Oklahoma College (U)
Northern State University (U)
Northern Virginia Community College (U)
North Harris College (U)
North Iowa Area Community College (U)
North Shore Community College (U)

Northwestern College (U)
Northwestern College (U)
Northwestern Michigan College (U)
Northwestern State University of Louisiana (U)
Oakland Community College (U)
Oakland University (U)
Oakton Community College (U)
Odessa College (U)
Ohio University (U)
Ohio University–Eastern (U)
Ohio University–Southern Campus (U)
Oklahoma City Community College (U)
Oklahoma State University (U)
Old Dominion University (U)
Oregon State University (U)
Palo Alto College (U)
Parkland College (U)
Pennsylvania State University University Park Campus (U)
Penn Valley Community College (U)
Pensacola Junior College (U)
Phillips Community College of the University of Arkansas (U)
Piedmont College (U)
Pikes Peak Community College (U, NC)
Pima Community College (U)
Polytechnic University, Brooklyn Campus (G, NC)
Portland Community College (U)
Portland State University (U)
Prairie State College (U)
Pratt Community College and Area Vocational School (U)
Prince George's Community College (U, NC)
Redlands Community College (U)
Red Rocks Community College (U)
Richland Community College (U)
Rio Salado College (U)
Riverside Community College (U)
Rochester Institute of Technology (U)
Rockland Community College (U)
Rogers University (U)
Roosevelt University (U)
Rose State College (U)
Rutgers, The State University of New Jersey, Newark (U)
Ryerson Polytechnic University (U)
St. Johns River Community College (U)
Saint Joseph's College (U)
St. Petersburg Junior College (U)
Salt Lake Community College (U)
San Antonio College (U)
San Bernardino Valley College (U)
Sandhills Community College (U)
San Diego City College (U)
Schoolcraft College (U)
Scott Community College (U)
Seattle Pacific University (U, G)
Shelby State Community College (U)
Sierra College (U)
Sinclair Community College (U)
Skagit Valley College (U)
Skidmore College (U)
Southeast Arkansas Technical College (U)
Southeastern Louisiana University (U)
Southern Arkansas University Tech (U)
Southern Utah University (U)
South Florida Community College (U)
South Puget Sound Community College (U)
Southwestern Assemblies of God University (U)

Individual Courses Index

Southwestern Oklahoma State University (U)
Southwest State University (U)
Southwest Virginia Community College (U)
Stanly Community College (U)
State University of New York Empire State College (U)
State University of West Georgia (U, G)
Stephens College (U)
Suffolk County Community College–Ammerman Campus (U)
Sussex County Community College (U)
Syracuse University (U, G)
Tacoma Community College (U)
Tallahassee Community College (U)
Tarrant County Junior College (U)
Taylor University, Fort Wayne Campus (U)
Technical College of the Lowcountry (U)
Tennessee Temple University (U)
Texas A&M University–Commerce (U)
Texas Tech University (U)
Thomas Edison State College (U)
Thomas Nelson Community College (U)
Tidewater Community College (U)
Treasure Valley Community College (U)
Triton College (U)
Troy State University Dothan (U)
Troy State University Montgomery (U)
Tyler Junior College (U)
The Union Institute (U)
The University of Akron (U)
The University of Alabama (U, G)
University of Alaska Anchorage (U, G)
University of Alaska Fairbanks (U)
University of Alaska Southeast, Sitka Campus (U)
University of Alberta (U)
University of Arkansas at Little Rock (U)
University of Baltimore (U)
University of British Columbia (U)
The University of Calgary (U)
University of California Extension (U)
University of California, Santa Barbara (U, NC)
University of California, Santa Cruz (U, G)
University of Cincinnati (U)
University of Georgia (U)
University of Great Falls (U)
University of Guelph (U)
University of Hawaii–Leeward Community College (U)
University of Hawaii–Maui Community College (U)
University of Houston (U)
University of Kansas (U, G, NC)
University of Kentucky, Ashland Community College (U)
University of Kentucky, Elizabethtown Community College (U)
University of Kentucky, Hazard Community College (U)
University of Kentucky, Henderson Community College (U)
University of Kentucky, Madisonville Community College (U)
University of Maine (U)
University of Maine at Augusta (U)
University of Maine at Fort Kent (U)
University of Mary (U)
University of Maryland University College (U)
The University of Memphis (U)
University of Minnesota, Twin Cities Campus (U)
University of Missouri–Columbia (U, G)
University of Missouri–Kansas City (U)
University of Missouri–St. Louis (U)
University of Nebraska at Kearney (U)
University of Nebraska–Lincoln (U)
University of New Brunswick (U)
University of New Orleans (U)
University of Northern Iowa (U, G)
University of Oklahoma (U)
University of Pittsburgh (U)
University of Saskatchewan (U)
University of South Carolina (U, G)
University of South Dakota (U)
University of Southern Mississippi (U)
University of South Florida (U)
The University of Texas at Austin (U)
The University of Texas at San Antonio (U)
The University of Texas at Tyler (U, G)
University of the State of New York, Regents College (U)
University of Toledo (U)
University of Utah (U)
University of Washington (U)
University of Waterloo (U)
University of Windsor (U)
University of Wisconsin–Eau Claire (U, G)
University of Wyoming (U)
University System of Georgia (U)
Upper Iowa University (U)
Utah State University (U)
Utah Valley State College (U)
Valley City State University (U)
Victor Valley College (U)
Vincennes University (U)
Volunteer State Community College (U)
Walters State Community College (U)
Washington State University (U)
Washtenaw Community College (U)
Waubonsee Community College (U)
Wayne County Community College (U)
Wayne State University (U)
Weber State University (U)
Wenatchee Valley College (U)
Western Illinois University (U)
Western Michigan University (U)
Western Oklahoma State College (U)
Western Washington University (U)
Westmoreland County Community College (U)
West Virginia Graduate College (G)
West Virginia University (U)
West Virginia Wesleyan College (U)
Whatcom Community College (U)
Wichita State University (U)
Wilfrid Laurier University (U)
Wilkes Community College (U)
William Penn College (U)
William Rainey Harper College (U)
Winthrop University (U)
York Technical College (U)
Yuba College (U)

History of Science and Technology
Colorado Electronic Community College (U)
Columbus State University (U)
Roger Williams University (U)
University of Missouri–Columbia (U)
West Virginia Graduate College (G)

Home Economics and Family Studies
Acadia University (U)
Anne Arundel Community College (U)
Arizona State University (U)
Ball State University (U)
Blackhawk Technical College (U)
Brevard Community College (U)
Burlington County College (U)
Butte College (U)
California State University, Long Beach (U)
California State University, Sacramento (U)
Central Michigan University (U)
Central Wyoming College (U)
Chadron State College (U)
Chippewa Valley Technical College (U)
Clatsop Community College (U)
Colby Community College (U)
Colorado State University (U)
Copiah-Lincoln Community College (U)
Cosumnes River College (U)
Crafton Hills College (U)
Delaware Technical & Community College, Stanton/Wilmington Campus (U)
Des Moines Area Community College (NC)
Dodge City Community College (U)
East Tennessee State University (U)
Georgia Southern University (NC)
Idaho State University (U, G)
Illinois Valley Community College (U)
Iowa State University of Science and Technology (G)
Kansas State University (U, G, NC)
Lakeshore Technical College (U)
Lamar University (U, G)
Lansing Community College (U)
Lehigh Carbon Community College (U)
Long Beach City College (U)
Los Angeles Community College District (U)
Louisiana State University and Agricultural and Mechanical College (U, G)
Luzerne County Community College (U)
Madison Area Technical College (U)
Marshall University (U)
The McGregor School of Antioch University (G)
Metropolitan Community College (U)
Michigan State University (G)
Mid-State Technical College (U)
Mississippi State University (G)
Missouri Southern State College (U)
Modesto Junior College (U)
Morehead State University (U)
Mount Saint Vincent University (U)
Mt. San Antonio College (U)
Northcentral Technical College (U)
North Dakota State University (U, G)
Northeast Community College (U)
Northwestern State University of Louisiana (U, NC)
The Ohio State University (U, G)
Ohio University (U)
Oklahoma State University (U)
Oregon State University (U)
Palomar College (U)
Pennsylvania State University University Park Campus (U)
Pensacola Junior College (U)
Pima Community College (U)
Redlands Community College (U)
The Richard Stockton College of New Jersey (NC)

Distance Learning Programs 581

Individual Courses Index

Home Economics and Family Studies (continued)
Rio Salado College (U)
Riverland Community College (U)
Riverside Community College (U)
Rose State College (U)
Ryerson Polytechnic University (U)
San Bernardino Valley College (U)
San Diego City College (U)
San Joaquin Delta College (U)
Southwest Texas State University (U)
State University of New York Empire State College (U)
Suffolk County Community College–Ammerman Campus (NC)
Tarrant County Junior College (U)
Tennessee Temple University (U)
Texas Tech University (U, G)
The University of Alabama (U)
University of California, Davis (U)
University of Delaware (U)
University of Georgia (U)
University of Guelph (U)
University of Kansas (U, NC)
University of Kentucky (G)
University of Kentucky, Elizabethtown Community College (U)
University of Maine (U)
University of Minnesota, Twin Cities Campus (U)
University of Missouri–Columbia (U, G)
University of Missouri–Kansas City (U)
University of Nebraska at Kearney (U)
University of Nebraska–Lincoln (U, G)
University of Northern Iowa (U)
University of Wisconsin–Stout (U, G)
University of Wyoming (U)
University System of Georgia (U)
Utah State University (U)
Western Illinois University (U, G)
Yuba College (U)

Horticulture
Auburn University (U)
Central Florida Community College (U)
Kansas State University (U, NC)
Louisiana State University at Eunice (U)
Moraine Valley Community College (U)
University of Missouri–Columbia (U)
University of Nebraska–Lincoln (U)
University System of Georgia (U)

Hospitality Services Management
Anne Arundel Community College (U)
Auburn University (U)
Brevard Community College (U)
Chemeketa Community College (U)
Chippewa Valley Technical College (U)
Clarkson College (G)
College of Lake County (U)
The College of West Virginia (U)
Cornell University (U, NC)
Daytona Beach Community College (U)
Garland County Community College (NC)
Gateway Technical College (U)
Grand Valley State University (U, G)
Hampton University (U)
Idaho State University (U, G)
Illinois Eastern Community Colleges, Olney Central College (U)
Indiana University System (U)
Ivy Tech State College–Wabash Valley (U)
Joliet Junior College (U)
Mount Saint Vincent University (U)
Mt. San Antonio College (U)
New York Institute of Technology (U)
Northeast Wisconsin Technical College (U)
Northwestern State University of Louisiana (U)
Oakton Community College (U)
Peoples College (U)
Pikes Peak Community College (U, NC)
Purdue University (U)
Roosevelt University (U)
Southwest State University (U)
Syracuse University (U)
Tennessee State University (G, NC)
Texas Tech University (U, NC)
University of Alaska Fairbanks (U)
University of Delaware (U)
University of Hawaii–Maui Community College (U)
University of Houston (U, G)
University of Maine at Fort Kent (NC)
University of Nebraska–Lincoln (G)
University of Nevada, Las Vegas (U)
University of South Carolina (U, G)
The University of Texas at San Antonio (U)
University of Utah (U)
Walters State Community College (U)
West Virginia University Institute of Technology (U)
William Rainey Harper College (U)

Human Resources Management
Anne Arundel Community College (U)
Arapahoe Community College (NC)
Atlantic Community College (U)
Austin Community College (U)
Baker College (U, G)
Ball State University (G)
Boise State University (U)
Bucks County Community College (U)
Buena Vista University (U)
California College for Health Sciences (U, G)
Carl Sandburg College (U)
Central Michigan University (U)
Chadron State College (U, G)
Champlain College (U)
Chippewa Valley Technical College (NC)
Christopher Newport University (U)
Cleary College (U)
Coastline Community College (U, NC)
Colby Community College (U)
College of the Southwest (U)
The College of West Virginia (U)
Colorado State University (G)
Community College of Philadelphia (U)
Danville Area Community College (U)
Drake University (G)
Dutchess Community College (U)
Eastern Idaho Technical College (U)
Eastern Illinois University (U, G)
Eastern Oregon University (U)
Eastern Washington University (U)
Eastern Wyoming College (U)
Embry-Riddle Aeronautical University, Extended Campus (U)
Fayetteville Technical Community College (U)
Garland County Community College (NC)
GMI Engineering & Management Institute (G)
The Graduate School of America (G)
Hampton University (U, NC)
Heriot-Watt University (G)
Howard Community College (U)
Idaho State University (U, G)
Illinois Central College (U)
Illinois Eastern Community Colleges, Olney Central College (U)
Indiana State University (U)
Indiana University System (U)
ISIM University (G)
Jamestown Community College (U)
John C. Calhoun State Community College (U)
Laramie County Community College (U)
Lassen College (U)
Laurentian University (U, G)
Marywood University (U)
The McGregor School of Antioch University (G)
Memorial University of Newfoundland (U)
Mercy College (U)
Metropolitan State University (U)
Middle Tennessee State University (NC)
Milwaukee Area Technical College (U)
Minot State University (U)
Missouri Southern State College (U)
Montgomery College–Rockville Campus (U)
Mount Saint Vincent University (U)
National Technological University (NC)
New Hampshire College (U)
New Jersey Institute of Technology (U, G)
New Mexico State University (U, G)
New School for Social Research (U, NC)
New York Institute of Technology (U)
North Carolina State University (G)
North Central Technical College (U)
Northcentral Technical College (U)
Northeast Louisiana University (U)
Northern Illinois University (G)
Northwestern College (U)
Ohio University–Southern Campus (U)
Old Dominion University (U)
Ottawa University (G)
Pennsylvania State University University Park Campus (U)
Pikes Peak Community College (U, NC)
Portland Community College (NC)
Portland State University (U, G)
Prince George's Community College (U)
Regent University (G)
Regis University (U)
Rend Lake College (G)
Rensselaer Polytechnic Institute (G)
Roger Williams University (U)
Rutgers, The State University of New Jersey, Newark (U, G, NC)
Ryerson Polytechnic University (U, NC)
St. Cloud Technical College (U)
St. Johns River Community College (U)
Saint Joseph's College (U, G)
Salve Regina University (U, G, NC)
San Diego State University (NC)
Skidmore College (U)
Southeastern Community College, North Campus (U)
Southern Utah University (U)
Southwestern Assemblies of God University (U)
Southwest State University (U)
State Technical Institute at Memphis (U)
State University of New York Empire State College (U)

Individual Courses Index

Stephens College (U)
Tennessee State University (G, NC)
Texas A&M University–Commerce (G)
Troy State University Montgomery (U)
The Union Institute (U)
United States Sports Academy (G, NC)
Universitè Laval (U)
The University of Alabama (G)
The University of Alabama in Huntsville (G)
University of Alaska Fairbanks (U)
University of Alaska Southeast (U)
University of Alberta (NC)
University of California Extension (U)
University of California, Santa Barbara (NC)
University of Cincinnati Raymond Walters College (U)
University of Dallas (G)
University of Delaware (U)
University of Georgia (U)
University of Hawaii–Maui Community College (U)
University of Kentucky, Elizabethtown Community College (U)
University of Maine at Augusta (U)
University of Maine at Fort Kent (NC)
University of Maryland University College (U)
University of Missouri–Columbia (G)
University of Missouri–Kansas City (G)
The University of Montana–Missoula (G)
University of Nebraska at Kearney (U, G)
University of Nebraska–Lincoln (U, G)
University of New Brunswick (U)
University of Oklahoma (U)
University of Phoenix (U, G)
University of Sarasota (G)
University of South Carolina (U, G)
University of South Dakota (U, G)
University of South Florida (G)
University of Tennessee, Knoxville (G)
University of the State of New York, Regents College (U)
University of Toledo (U)
University of Windsor (U)
University of Wisconsin–Extension (U, NC)
University of Wisconsin–Oshkosh (G)
University of Wisconsin–Platteville (U)
University of Wisconsin–Stout (G)
University of Wyoming (G)
University System of Georgia (U)
Upper Iowa University (U)
Utah State University (U)
Walden University (G)
Washington State University (U)
Waubonsee Community College (U)
Western Illinois University (U)
Wichita State University (U, G)
Wilson Technical Community College (U)
Winthrop University (G)
Worcester Polytechnic Institute (G)

Individual and Family Development Studies
Catonsville Community College (U)
Colorado State University (U)
Iowa State University of Science and Technology (G)
Penn Valley Community College (U)
Southwest Missouri State University (U)

State University of New York Empire State College (U)
Texas Tech University (U, NC)
University of Delaware (U)
University of Wisconsin–Extension (U)

Industrial Engineering
Arizona State University (U, G)
California State University, Los Angeles (U, NC)
Central Community College–Grand Island Campus (U)
Cleveland State University (G)
Colorado State University (G)
Darton College (U)
Florida State University (G)
Georgia Institute of Technology (G, NC)
GMI Engineering & Management Institute (G)
Idaho State University (U, G)
Illinois Institute of Technology (G)
Iowa State University of Science and Technology (G)
Kansas State University (G, NC)
Massachusetts Institute of Technology (NC)
Mississippi State University (G)
National Technological University (G, NC)
New Jersey Institute of Technology (G)
New Mexico State University (G)
North Carolina State University (G)
Northcentral Technical College (U)
Northeastern University (G)
Oklahoma State University (G)
Oregon State University (G)
Polytechnic University, Westchester Graduate Center (G)
Rensselaer Polytechnic Institute (G)
San Jose State University (NC)
Scott Community College (U)
Shenandoah University (G)
Southern Polytechnic State University (U, G)
Southwest Virginia Community College (U)
Stanford University (G, NC)
State University of New York at Binghamton (G)
State University of New York at Buffalo (G)
Texas Tech University (G)
The University of Alabama (G)
The University of Alabama in Huntsville (G)
University of Arizona (G)
University of Houston (G)
University of Kentucky, Elizabethtown Community College (U)
University of Massachusetts Amherst (G, NC)
University of Missouri–Kansas City (G)
University of Nebraska–Lincoln (G, NC)
University of North Florida (G)
University of Oklahoma (G)
University of Southern California (G, NC)
University of South Florida (U, G)
University of Tennessee, Knoxville (G)
University of Tennessee Space Institute (G)
The University of Texas at Arlington (G)
The University of Texas at San Antonio (U)
Virginia Polytechnic Institute and State University (G)
York Technical College (U)

Industrial Psychology
California State University, Hayward (U)
Central Michigan University (U)
College of the Southwest (U)

The Graduate School of America (G)
John Wood Community College (U)
Lawson State Community College (U)
Lycoming College (U)
The McGregor School of Antioch University (G)
Memorial University of Newfoundland (U)
New School for Social Research (U, NC)
Old Dominion University (U)
Owens Community College (U)
Saint Joseph's College (U)
Southwest State University (U)
Southwest Texas State University (U)
Stevens Institute of Technology (G)
The Union Institute (U)
University of California, Santa Barbara (NC)
University of Guelph (U)
University of Illinois at Urbana–Champaign (U)
University of Minnesota, Twin Cities Campus (U)
University of Missouri–Columbia (U)
University of North Dakota (U)
University of Oklahoma (U)
Upper Iowa University (U)
Volunteer State Community College (U)
Walden University (G)

Information Sciences and Systems
Atlantic Community College (U)
Aurora University (U)
Catonsville Community College (U)
Cuyahoga Community College, Metropolitan Campus (U)
Eastern Kentucky University (U)
Fairleigh Dickinson University, Teaneck–Hackensack (G)
Indiana Wesleyan University (U)
Kansas State University (G)
Kingwood College (U)
Lee College (U)
Michigan State University (G)
Midland College (U)
New River Community College (U)
NRI Schools (NC)
Palo Alto College (U)
Riverland Community College (U)
Rochester Institute of Technology (U, G)
Southern Polytechnic State University (G)
Southern Vermont College (U)
State University of New York Empire State College (U)
Stephens College (U)
Texas Tech University (U, NC)
Thomas College (U, G)
University of Maryland University College (G)
University of Tennessee, Knoxville (G)
West Virginia Graduate College (G)

Instructional Media
Arizona State University (G)
Chestnut Hill College (G)
College of St. Scholastica (G)
Marywood University (G)
Michigan State University (G)
New York Institute of Technology (G)
Northern Illinois University (G)
Northern Virginia Community College (U)
Rutgers, The State University of New Jersey, Newark (G, NC)
Southern Illinois University at Carbondale (G)

Distance Learning Programs 583

Individual Courses Index

Instructional Media (continued)
Southwest Texas State University (U)
State University of West Georgia (G)
Texas Tech University (U, G, NC)
University of Delaware (U, G)
University of Houston–Clear Lake (G)
University of Wisconsin–Stevens Point (U, G)
Western Illinois University (G)

Insurance
Roger Williams University (U)
University of Dallas (G)
University of Nebraska–Lincoln (U)
Washington State University (U)

Interdisciplinary Studies
California Institute of Integral Studies (G, NC)

International Business
Baker College (G)
College of St. Scholastica (U, G)
Duke University (G)
GMI Engineering & Management Institute (G)
The Graduate School of America (G)
Heriot-Watt University (G)
Laramie County Community College (U)
Marywood University (U)
Mercy College (U)
Milwaukee School of Engineering (G, NC)
New Hampshire College (U)
Northeast Wisconsin Technical College (U)
Northwestern College (U)
Regis University (G)
Salve Regina University (U, G, NC)
San Diego State University (NC)
State University of New York Empire State College (U)
University of Alaska Southeast (U)
University of Houston (G)
University of Maryland University College (G)
University of Nebraska–Lincoln (U, G)
University of Washington (U)
University of Wisconsin–Extension (NC)
Upper Iowa University (U)
Western Illinois University (U)

International Relations
Bellevue Community College (U)
The Graduate School of America (G)
Kansas State University (U)
Mercy College (U)
Salve Regina University (G, NC)
Syracuse University (U, G)
Troy State University–Florida Region (U, G)
University of Illinois at Urbana–Champaign (U)
University of Mary (U, G)
University of Nebraska–Lincoln (U, G)
University of Northern Iowa (U)

Investments and Securities
College for Financial Planning (U)
Cuyahoga Community College, Metropolitan Campus (U)
Roger Williams University (U)
St. Louis Community College (U)
Waukesha County Technical College (U)
Wilfrid Laurier University (U)

Italian Language and Literature
University of Tennessee, Knoxville (U)

Japanese Language and Literature
Catonsville Community College (U)
Manchester Community-Technical College (U)
National Technological University (G, NC)
Northwestern Michigan College (U)
Stephens College (U)
Yuba College (U)

Jewish Studies
Assemblies of God Theological Seminary (G, NC)
Community College of Vermont (U)
Spertus Institute of Jewish Studies (G)
University of Massachusetts Dartmouth (U)
University of Waterloo (U)

Journalism
Allegany College of Maryland (U)
Arizona State University (U)
Ball State University (U)
Brevard Community College (U)
California State University, Stanislaus (U)
Camden County College (U)
Central Michigan University (U)
Central Missouri State University (U)
Charles County Community College (U)
Chattanooga State Technical Community College (U)
City University (U)
Corning Community College (U)
Cosumnes River College (U)
Cuyahoga Community College, Metropolitan Campus (U)
De Anza College (U)
Delaware Technical & Community College, Stanton/Wilmington Campus (U)
Dutchess Community College (U)
Eastern Idaho Technical College (U)
Eastern Oregon University (U)
Fullerton College (U)
Garland County Community College (U)
Indiana University System (U, G)
John A. Logan College (U)
Judson College (U)
Lehigh Carbon Community College (U)
Louisiana College (U)
Luzerne County Community College (U)
Marshall University (U)
The McGregor School of Antioch University (G)
Metropolitan Community College (U)
New Jersey Institute of Technology (G)
New School for Social Research (U, NC)
North Central Bible College (U, NC)
Northern Arizona University (U)
Northern Kentucky University (U)
North Harris College (U)
Ohio University (U)
Ohio University–Eastern (U)
Ohio University–Southern Campus (U)
Oklahoma State University (U)
Old Dominion University (U)
Polytechnic University, Brooklyn Campus (G, NC)
Pueblo Community College (U)
Quincy College (U)
Rend Lake College (U)
St. Petersburg Junior College (U)
Seattle Central Community College (U)
Taylor University, Fort Wayne Campus (U)
Texas A&M University–Commerce (U)
Texas Tech University (U)
Thomas Edison State College (U)
Tyler Junior College (U)
United States Sports Academy (G, NC)
Universitè Laval (U)
The University of Alabama at Birmingham (G)
University of Alaska Fairbanks (U)
University of Alaska Southeast, Sitka Campus (U)
University of Georgia (U)
University of Houston (U)
The University of Iowa (U, G)
University of Kansas (U, NC)
University of Maryland University College (U)
University of Massachusetts Lowell (U)
The University of Memphis (G)
University of Minnesota, Twin Cities Campus (U)
University of Missouri–Columbia (G)
University of Nebraska at Kearney (U)
University of Nebraska–Lincoln (U)
University of Nevada, Reno (U)
University of Oklahoma (U, NC)
University of South Carolina (U, G)
University of Southern Indiana (U)
University of Tennessee, Knoxville (G)
The University of Texas at San Antonio (U)
University of Utah (U)
University System of Georgia (U)
Utah State University (U)
Valley City State University (U)

Labor Relations/Studies
Embry-Riddle Aeronautical University, Extended Campus (G)
The Graduate School of America (G)
Hudson Valley Community College (U)
Indiana University System (U)
Kansas State University (U, NC)
Salve Regina University (U, G, NC)
San Diego State University (NC)
State University of New York Empire State College (U)
Upper Iowa University (U)

Latin American Studies
Kansas State University (U, NC)
Oakton Community College (U)
Penn Valley Community College (U)
Salve Regina University (G, NC)
Stephens College (U)
Texas Tech University (U, NC)
University of Nebraska–Lincoln (U)

Latin Language and Literature
University of Illinois at Urbana–Champaign (U)
The University of Iowa (U)
The University of North Carolina at Chapel Hill (U)
University of Waterloo (U)
University System of Georgia (U)

Law and Legal Studies
Anne Arundel Community College (U)
Arizona State University (U)

Athabasca University (U)
Berean University of the Assemblies of God (U)
Black Hawk College (U)
Blackhawk Technical College (U)
Brevard Community College (U)
Bucks County Community College (U)
Burlington County College (U)
California College for Health Sciences (U, G)
Camden County College (U)
Carleton University (U)
Central Community College–Grand Island Campus (U)
Chadron State College (U)
Champlain College (U)
Chippewa Valley Technical College (U)
Cleary College (U)
Coastline Community College (U, NC)
The College of West Virginia (U)
Community College of Rhode Island (U)
Community College of the Air Force (U)
Community College of Vermont (U)
Daytona Beach Community College (U)
Delaware County Community College (U)
Duquesne University (G)
Eastern Idaho Technical College (U)
Eastern Wyoming College (U)
Essex Community College (U)
Florida Community College at Jacksonville (U)
Fort Hays State University (U, NC)
Genesee Community College (U)
Georgia Southern University (U)
Hampton University (U)
Houston Community College System (U)
Howard Community College (U)
Illinois Eastern Community Colleges, Olney Central College (U)
Iowa Western Community College (U)
Ivy Tech State College–Northcentral (U)
Jefferson Davis Community College (U)
John C. Calhoun State Community College (U)
Kellogg Community College (U)
Lake Michigan College (U)
Lakeshore Technical College (U)
Lassen College (U)
Laurentian University (U)
Lehigh Carbon Community College (U)
Longview Community College (U)
Los Angeles Community College District (U)
Luzerne County Community College (U)
Marshall University (U)
Memorial University of Newfoundland (U, NC)
Mercy College (U)
Middle Tennessee State University (U)
Mid-State Technical College (U)
Milwaukee Area Technical College (U)
Missouri Southern State College (U)
Montgomery College–Rockville Campus (U)
Moraine Valley Community College (U)
Nassau Community College (U)
New Jersey Institute of Technology (G)
Northeast Wisconsin Technical College (U)
Northern Arizona University (U)
North Iowa Area Community College (U)
Northwestern Michigan College (U)
Northwestern State University of Louisiana (U, NC)
Odessa College (U)
Ohio University–Southern Campus (U)
Oklahoma State University (U)
Palomar College (U)

Parkland College (U)
Pennsylvania State University University Park Campus (NC)
Portland Community College (U)
Pueblo Community College (U)
Redlands Community College (U)
Riverland Community College (NC)
Riverside Community College (U)
Rutgers, The State University of New Jersey, Newark (U, NC)
Saint Joseph's College (U, G)
St. Petersburg Junior College (U)
Santa Rosa Junior College (U)
Sinclair Community College (U)
Southern Illinois University at Carbondale (U)
South Florida Community College (U)
Southwest Virginia Community College (U)
Tallahassee Community College (U)
Technical College of the Lowcountry (U)
Texas Tech University (NC)
Treasure Valley Community College (U)
United States Sports Academy (G, NC)
The University of Alabama (G)
The University of Alabama in Huntsville (G)
University of Alaska Southeast, Sitka Campus (U)
The University of Calgary (NC)
University of California, Santa Barbara (NC)
University of Central Oklahoma (U, G)
University of Georgia (U)
University of Great Falls (U)
University of Kentucky, Elizabethtown Community College (U)
University of Kentucky, Henderson Community College (U)
University of Maine (U)
University of Maine at Fort Kent (U)
University of Mary (U, G)
University of Maryland University College (U)
University of Minnesota, Twin Cities Campus (U)
University of Missouri–Columbia (U, G)
University of Northern Colorado (G)
University of Oklahoma (U)
University of St. Thomas (G)
University of South Dakota (G)
University of Southern Indiana (U)
University of Toledo (G)
University of Vermont (U)
University of Washington (U)
University System of Georgia (U)
Upper Iowa University (U)
Waubonsee Community College (U)
Wayne County Community College (U)
Western Illinois University (U, G)
Westmoreland County Community College (U)
Wilkes Community College (U)
William Rainey Harper College (U)
Worcester Polytechnic Institute (G)
Xavier University of Louisiana (U)

Liberal Arts, General Studies, and Humanities

Allegany College of Maryland (U)
Anne Arundel Community College (U)
Arapahoe Community College (U)
Arizona State University (U, G)
Assemblies of God Theological Seminary (G, NC)

Athabasca University (U)
Atlantic Community College (U)
Ball State University (U)
Bemidji State University (U)
Berean University of the Assemblies of God (U)
Black Hawk College (U)
Bluefield State College (U)
Brevard Community College (U)
Brookdale Community College (U)
Burlington County College (U)
Butte College (U)
California State University, Bakersfield (U)
California State University, Chico (U)
California State University, Dominguez Hills (U)
California State University, Fresno (U)
California State University, Fullerton (U)
California State University, Hayward (U)
California State University, Stanislaus (U)
Calvin College (G)
Camden County College (U)
Carleton University (U)
Central Community College–Grand Island Campus (U)
Central Missouri State University (U)
Central Piedmont Community College (U)
Chadron State College (U)
Champlain College (U)
Chapman University (U)
Charles County Community College (U)
Charles Stewart Mott Community College (U)
Charter Oak State College (U)
Chattanooga State Technical Community College (U)
Chemeketa Community College (U)
Chippewa Valley Technical College (U)
City College of San Francisco (U)
City University (U)
Clarkson College (U)
Cleary College (U)
Coastline Community College (U, NC)
Colby Community College (U)
College of DuPage (U)
College of Lake County (U)
College of the Southwest (U)
The College of West Virginia (U)
Collin County Community College (U)
Colorado Mountain College District (U)
Columbia State Community College (U)
Community College of Rhode Island (U)
Concordia University (U, G)
Concordia University at Austin (U, NC)
Concordia University Wisconsin (U, G)
Corning Community College (U)
Cosumnes River College (U)
Covenant Theological Seminary (G, NC)
Cuyahoga Community College, Metropolitan Campus (U)
Cuyamaca College (U)
Dallas County Community College District (U)
Danville Area Community College (U)
Dawson Community College (U)
Daytona Beach Community College (U)
De Anza College (U)
DeKalb College (U)
Delaware County Community College (U)
Delta College (U)
Des Moines Area Community College (U)
Dodge City Community College (U)
Dutchess Community College (U)
Eastern Idaho Technical College (U)

Distance Learning Programs

Individual Courses Index

Liberal Arts, General Studies, and Humanities (continued)

Eastern Oregon University (U)
Eastern Wyoming College (U)
East Tennessee State University (U)
Edison Community College (U)
Edmonds Community College (U)
Essex Community College (U)
Fitchburg State College (U)
Florida Community College at Jacksonville (U)
Front Range Community College (U)
Galveston College (U)
Garland County Community College (U)
Genesee Community College (U)
George C. Wallace State Community College (U)
Glendale Community College (U)
Governors State University (U, G)
Graceland College (U)
Grand Valley State University (U, G)
Greenville Technical College (U)
Hampton University (U)
Harrisburg Area Community College (U)
Hawkeye Community College (U)
Hibbing Community College (U)
Hillsborough Community College (U)
Houston Community College System (U)
Howard Community College (U)
Idaho State University (U, G)
Illinois Eastern Community Colleges, Olney Central College (U)
Illinois Valley Community College (U)
Indiana University System (U)
Indiana Wesleyan University (U)
International Bible College (U)
Iowa State University of Science and Technology (U)
Iowa Western Community College (U)
Ivy Tech State College–Wabash Valley (U)
Jefferson State Community College (U)
Johnson County Community College (U)
John Wood Community College (U)
Joliet Junior College (U)
J. Sargeant Reynolds Community College (U)
Kansas State University (U, NC)
Kaskaskia College (U)
Kellogg Community College (U)
Lackawanna Junior College (U)
Lakehead University (U)
Lakeshore Technical College (U)
Lamar University (U)
Laney College (U)
Laramie County Community College (U)
Lassen College (U)
Lehigh Carbon Community College (U)
Liberty University (U)
Longview Community College (U)
Lorain County Community College (U)
Los Angeles Community College District (U)
Loyola University New Orleans (U)
Lycoming College (U)
Madison Area Technical College (U)
Manatee Community College (U)
Marshall University (U, G)
The McGregor School of Antioch University (G)
Memorial University of Newfoundland (U)
Mendocino College (U)
Mercy College (U)
Metropolitan Community College (U)
Metropolitan Community College (U)
Middle Tennessee State University (U)
Milwaukee Area Technical College (U)
Minnesota West Community and Technical College–Worthington Campus (U)
MiraCosta College (U)
Montgomery College–Rockville Campus (U)
Montgomery County Community College (U)
Morgan Community College (U, NC)
Morris Brown College (U)
Mount Saint Vincent University (U)
Nassau Community College (U)
New Hampshire College (U)
New Jersey Institute of Technology (U)
New Mexico Junior College (U)
New School for Social Research (U, NC)
New York Institute of Technology (U)
Normandale Community College (U)
Northampton County Area Community College (U)
North Arkansas College (U)
North Carolina State University (U)
North Central Bible College (U, NC)
North Central Technical College (U)
North Dakota State College of Science (U)
Northeast Louisiana University (U)
Northern Arizona University (U)
Northern Essex Community College (U)
Northern Kentucky University (U)
Northern Virginia Community College (U)
North Harris College (U)
North Seattle Community College (U)
Northwestern College (U)
Northwestern Michigan College (U)
Northwestern State University of Louisiana (U)
Northwest Iowa Community College (U)
Oakton Community College (U)
Ohio University (U)
Ohio University–Southern Campus (U)
Oklahoma City Community College (U)
Oklahoma State University (U)
Oregon State University (U)
Owens Community College (U)
Palo Alto College (U)
Palomar College (U)
Pennsylvania State University University Park Campus (U)
Penn Valley Community College (U)
Pensacola Junior College (U)
Pima Community College (U)
Polytechnic University, Brooklyn Campus (G, NC)
Portland Community College (U)
Portland State University (U)
Prince George's Community College (U)
Quincy College (U)
Redlands Community College (U)
Red Rocks Community College (U)
Regis University (U)
The Richard Stockton College of New Jersey (U, NC)
Richland Community College (U)
Rio Salado College (U)
Rochester Institute of Technology (U)
Rockland Community College (U)
Rogers University (U)
Rose State College (U)
Rutgers, The State University of New Jersey, Newark (U, NC)
Ryerson Polytechnic University (U)
St. Johns River Community College (U)
Saint Joseph's College (U)
St. Louis Community College (U)
St. Petersburg Junior College (U)
Salt Lake Community College (U)
Salve Regina University (U, G, NC)
San Bernardino Valley College (U)
San Diego City College (U)
San Jose State University (U)
Schoolcraft College (U)
Scott Community College (U)
Shawnee Community College (U)
Shelby State Community College (U)
Sierra College (U)
Sinclair Community College (U)
Skagit Valley College (U)
Skidmore College (U)
Southeastern Community College, North Campus (U)
Southern Utah University (U)
Southwestern Michigan College (U)
Southwestern Oklahoma State University (U)
Southwest State University (U)
Southwest Virginia Community College (U)
Stanly Community College (U)
State University of New York Empire State College (U)
Suffolk County Community College–Ammerman Campus (U)
Syracuse University (U)
Tacoma Community College (U)
Tallahassee Community College (U)
Tarrant County Junior College (U)
Technical College of the Lowcountry (U)
Tennessee Temple University (U)
Texas Tech University (U)
Thomas Edison State College (U)
Tidewater Community College (U)
Troy State University Montgomery (U)
Tulsa Community College (U)
Tyler Junior College (U)
Umpqua Community College (U)
The Union Institute (U)
The University of Alabama (U, G)
University of Alaska Anchorage (U)
University of Alaska Fairbanks (U)
University of Alaska Southeast, Sitka Campus (U)
University of Alberta (U)
The University of Calgary (U)
University of California Extension (U)
University of California, Santa Barbara (U, NC)
University of California, Santa Cruz (U, G)
University of Colorado at Colorado Springs (U, G)
University of Delaware (U)
University of Georgia (U)
University of Great Falls (U)
University of Hawaii–Leeward Community College (U)
University of Hawaii–Maui Community College (U)
University of Houston (U)
University of Kansas (U, G, NC)
University of Kentucky, Elizabethtown Community College (U)
University of Kentucky, Madisonville Community College (U)
University of Maine (U, G)
University of Maine at Augusta (U)
University of Maine at Fort Kent (U)

Individual Courses Index

University of Maryland, College Park (U)
University of Maryland University College (U)
University of Massachusetts Lowell (U)
The University of Memphis (U)
University of Minnesota, Twin Cities Campus (U)
University of Missouri–Columbia (U)
University of Missouri–Kansas City (U)
University of Nebraska at Kearney (U)
University of Nebraska–Lincoln (U)
University of Nevada, Las Vegas (U)
University of Nevada, Reno (U)
University of New Hampshire (U)
University of New Orleans (U)
University of North Carolina at Greensboro (U, G)
University of North Dakota (U)
University of Northern Iowa (U)
University of Oklahoma (U)
University of Saskatchewan (U)
University of South Carolina (U)
University of South Dakota (U)
University of Southern Indiana (U)
University of South Florida (U)
The University of Texas at Tyler (U, G)
University of the State of New York, Regents College (U)
University of Windsor (U)
University of Wisconsin–River Falls (U, G)
University of Wyoming (U)
University System of Georgia (U)
Utah State University (U)
Valley City State University (U)
Vincennes University (U)
Vista Community College (U)
Volunteer State Community College (U)
Walters State Community College (U)
Washington State University (U)
Waubonsee Community College (U)
Wayne County Community College (U)
Wayne State University (U)
Western Illinois University (U, G)
Western Nebraska Community College (U)
Western Oklahoma State College (U)
Westmoreland County Community College (U)
West Virginia University (U)
West Virginia Wesleyan College (U)
Wichita State University (U)
Wilkes Community College (U)
William Rainey Harper College (U)
York Technical College (U)
Yuba College (U)

Library and Information Studies
Allegany College of Maryland (U)
Anne Arundel Community College (U)
Arizona State University (U)
California State University, Hayward (U)
Central Missouri State University (U)
College of Lake County (U)
Cuyahoga Community College, Metropolitan Campus (U)
Delta State University (U, G)
Eastern Kentucky University (G)
Emporia State University (U, G)
Florida State University (G)
Fort Hays State University (U, G)
Front Range Community College (U)
Idaho State University (U, G)
Indiana University System (G)
Kaskaskia College (U)
Louisiana State University and Agricultural and Mechanical College (G)
Louisiana State University at Eunice (G)
Louisiana State University in Shreveport (U, G)
Memorial University of Newfoundland (U, NC)
New Jersey Institute of Technology (G)
New River Community College (U)
Northampton County Area Community College (U)
Northwestern State University of Louisiana (U)
Pikes Peak Community College (U, NC)
Rose State College (U)
Salt Lake Community College (U)
San Jose State University (G)
Southern Utah University (U)
Southwest Virginia Community College (U)
Texas A&M University–Commerce (U, G, NC)
Texas Woman's University (G)
Ulster County Community College (U)
The University of Alabama (G)
The University of Alabama at Birmingham (G)
University of Alaska Fairbanks (U)
University of Arizona (G)
University of Illinois at Urbana–Champaign (G)
University of Kentucky (G)
University of Maine at Fort Kent (U, G)
University of Missouri–Columbia (G)
University of Nevada, Las Vegas (U, G)
University of Nevada, Reno (U)
University of New Orleans (G)
The University of North Carolina at Chapel Hill (U)
University of North Carolina at Greensboro (G)
University of Oklahoma (U, G)
University of South Carolina (G)
University of South Florida (G)
University of Tennessee, Knoxville (G)
The University of Texas at San Antonio (U)
University of Utah (U)
University of Washington (U)
University of Wisconsin–Eau Claire (U, G)
Valley City State University (U)
Volunteer State Community College (U)

Logic
Brigham Young University (U)
Charles County Community College (U)
Fairleigh Dickinson University, Teaneck–Hackensack (U)
Lake Land College (U)
Mercy College (U)
Northern Virginia Community College (U)
Roger Williams University (U)
Seattle Central Community College (U)
Southwest Texas State University (U)
Stephens College (U)
Syracuse University (U)
Taylor University, Fort Wayne Campus (U)
University of Cincinnati (U)
University of Missouri–Columbia (U)
University of Nebraska–Lincoln (U)
The University of North Carolina at Chapel Hill (U)
University of Southern Mississippi (U)
University of Waterloo (U)

Management Information Systems
Adams State College (U)
California State University, Sacramento (U)
Embry-Riddle Aeronautical University, Extended Campus (G)
GMI Engineering & Management Institute (G)
Heriot-Watt University (G)
Lincoln Christian College (U, NC)
Marywood University (U)
McGraw-Hill World University (NC)
Mercy College (U)
National Technological University (NC)
New York University (G)
Northern Illinois University (G)
Northern Virginia Community College (U)
Oklahoma State University (U)
Salve Regina University (G, NC)
State University of New York Empire State College (U)
State University of West Georgia (U)
University of Alaska Southeast (U)
University of Illinois at Springfield (G)
University of Maryland University College (U, G)
University of Southern Mississippi (U)
Upper Iowa University (U)
West Virginia University Institute of Technology (U)
Winthrop University (G)

Marketing
American River College (U)
Arapahoe Community College (U)
Arizona State University (U)
Austin Community College (U)
Baker College (G)
Boise State University (U)
Brigham Young University (U)
Brookdale Community College (U, NC)
Bucks County Community College (U)
Catonsville Community College (U)
Central Michigan University (U)
Champlain College (U)
Christopher Newport University (U)
City University (U)
Colorado Mountain College District (U)
Colorado State University (G)
Columbus State Community College (U)
Cuyahoga Community College, Metropolitan Campus (U)
Dallas County Community College District (U)
Danville Community College (U)
De Anza College (U)
Delaware Technical & Community College, Stanton/Wilmington Campus (U)
Delta College (U)
Duke University (G)
Eastern Idaho Technical College (U)
Eastern Kentucky University (U)
Edison State Community College (U)
El Paso Community College (U)
Embry-Riddle Aeronautical University, Extended Campus (U)
Essex Community College (U)
Fairleigh Dickinson University, Teaneck–Hackensack (U)
Fullerton College (U)
Gannon University (U)
Genesee Community College (U)
GMI Engineering & Management Institute (G)
Governors State University (U)
The Graduate School of America (G)
Heriot-Watt University (G)

Distance Learning Programs 587

Individual Courses Index

Marketing (continued)
Hillsborough Community College (U)
Hocking College (U)
Houston Community College System (U)
Iowa State University of Science and Technology (U, G)
Johnson County Community College (U)
Joliet Junior College (U)
Lehigh Carbon Community College (U)
Liberty University (U)
Madonna University (U)
Manatee Community College (U)
Marshall University (U)
Marywood University (U)
Mercy College (U)
Metropolitan State College of Denver (U)
Metropolitan State University (U, G)
Midwestern State University (U, G)
Milwaukee School of Engineering (G, NC)
New Hampshire College (U, G)
New River Community College (U)
Northeast Wisconsin Technical College (U)
Northern Illinois University (G)
Northern Virginia Community College (U)
Northwestern College (U)
Oakton Community College (U)
Oklahoma State University (U)
Owens Community College (U)
Pratt Community College and Area Vocational School (U)
Prince George's Community College (U, NC)
Regis University (G)
Roger Williams University (U)
St. Louis Community College (U)
Salve Regina University (U, G, NC)
San Diego State University (NC)
San Juan College (U)
Santa Rosa Junior College (U)
Sinclair Community College (U)
Southern West Virginia Community and Technical College (U)
Southwest Missouri State University (G)
State Technical Institute at Memphis (U)
State University of West Georgia (U)
Stephens College (U)
Tarleton State University (G)
Texas Tech University (U, NC)
Thomas Edison State College (U)
Universitè Laval (U)
University of Alaska Southeast (U)
University of Arkansas at Little Rock (U)
University of Dallas (G)
University of Delaware (U)
University of Illinois at Urbana–Champaign (U)
University of Massachusetts Dartmouth (NC)
University of Mississippi (U, G)
University of Missouri–Columbia (U, G)
University of Nebraska–Lincoln (U)
University of Notre Dame (NC)
University of Southern Colorado (U)
University of Southern Mississippi (U)
University of Tennessee, Knoxville (NC)
University of Toledo (U)
University of Washington (U)
University of Wisconsin–Eau Claire (G)
University of Wisconsin–Platteville (U)
University System of Georgia (U)
Upper Iowa University (U)
Volunteer State Community College (U)
Washington State Courses (U)

Waukesha County Technical College (U)
Wayne County Community College (U)
Western Illinois University (U)
West Virginia Wesleyan College (U)
Winthrop University (G)
Wytheville Community College (U)

Mass Media
Brigham Young University (U)
Colorado Electronic Community College (U)
Eastern Kentucky University (U)
Metropolitan State University (U)
Missouri Southern State College (U)
Oakton Community College (U)
Seattle Central Community College (U)
State University of New York at Oswego (U)
State University of West Georgia
University of Alaska Anchorage (U)
University of Missouri–Columbia (U)
University of South Dakota (U)
Yuba College (U)

Mathematics
Acadia University (U)
Adams State College (U)
Allegany College of Maryland (U)
Alvin Community College (U)
Anne Arundel Community College (U)
Arapahoe Community College (U)
Arizona State University (G)
Athabasca University (U)
Auburn University (U)
Bakersfield College (U)
Ball State University (U)
Beaufort County Community College (U)
Bellevue Community College (U)
Bergen Community College (U)
Black Hawk College (U)
Blackhawk Technical College (U)
Bloomsburg University of Pennsylvania (U)
Bluefield State College (U)
Boise State University (U)
Brevard Community College (U)
Brigham Young University (U)
Bucks County Community College (U)
Burlington County College (U)
Butte College (U)
California College for Health Sciences (U)
California State University, Stanislaus (U)
Cape Cod Community College (U)
Carl Sandburg College (U)
Catawba Valley Community College (U)
Catonsville Community College (U)
Central Arizona College (U)
Central Community College–Grand Island Campus (U)
Central Michigan University (U)
Central Missouri State University (U)
Central Piedmont Community College (U)
Central Virginia Community College (U)
Central Wyoming College (U)
Chadron State College (U)
Champlain College (U)
Chapman University (U)
Charles County Community College (U)
Charles Stewart Mott Community College (U)
Charter Oak State College (U)
Chattanooga State Technical Community College (U)

Chemeketa Community College (U)
Chippewa Valley Technical College (U)
Citrus College (U)
City University (U)
Clarkson College (U, G)
Coastline Community College (U, NC)
Colby Community College (U)
College of DuPage (U)
College of Lake County (U)
College of the Southwest (U)
The College of West Virginia (U)
Collin County Community College (U)
Colorado Mountain College District (U)
Colorado State University (G)
Columbia-Greene Community College (U)
Columbia State Community College (U)
Columbus State Community College (U)
Community College of Rhode Island (U)
Concordia University (U)
Concordia University at Austin (U, NC)
Connors State College (U)
Corning Community College (U)
Cosumnes River College (U)
Cumberland County College (U)
Cuyahoga Community College, Metropolitan Campus (U)
Dallas County Community College District (U)
Danville Area Community College (U)
Danville Community College (U)
Darton College (U)
Dawson Community College (U)
Daytona Beach Community College (U)
De Anza College (U)
Delaware Technical & Community College, Stanton/Wilmington Campus (U)
Des Moines Area Community College (U)
Dodge City Community College (U)
Eastern Idaho Technical College (U)
Eastern New Mexico University (U, G)
Eastern Oregon University (U)
Eastern Washington University (U)
East Tennessee State University (U)
Edison Community College (U)
Embry-Riddle Aeronautical University, Extended Campus (U)
Florence-Darlington Technical College (U)
Florida Community College at Jacksonville (U)
Fort Hays State University (U, G)
Front Range Community College (U)
Garland County Community College (U)
Garrett Community College (U, NC)
Gateway Technical College (U)
Genesee Community College (U)
George C. Wallace State Community College (U)
Georgia Institute of Technology (G, NC)
Georgia Southern University (U, G, NC)
Glendale Community College (U)
Graceland College (U)
Grand Valley State University (U, G)
Greenville Technical College (U)
Griggs University (U)
Hampton University (U)
Harrisburg Area Community College (U)
Hawkeye Community College (U)
Heriot-Watt University (G)
Hillsborough Community College (U)
Hocking College (U)
Howard Community College (U)
Hudson Valley Community College (U)

Individual Courses Index

Idaho State University (U, G)
Illinois Central College (U)
Illinois Eastern Community Colleges, Olney Central College (U)
Illinois Institute of Technology (U, G)
Indiana University System (U)
Iowa State University of Science and Technology (U, G)
Iowa Wesleyan College (U)
Iowa Western Community College (U)
Ivy Tech State College–Wabash Valley (U)
Jacksonville State University (U)
John C. Calhoun State Community College (U)
John Wood Community College (U)
Joliet Junior College (U)
J. Sargeant Reynolds Community College (U)
Kankakee Community College (U)
Kansas State University (U, NC)
Kaskaskia College (U)
Kellogg Community College (U)
Lackawanna Junior College (U, NC)
Lakehead University (U)
Lake Michigan College (U)
Lakeshore Technical College (U)
Lassen College (U)
Laurentian University (U)
Lehigh Carbon Community College (U)
Longview Community College (U)
Lorain County Community College (U)
Luzerne County Community College (U)
Lycoming College (U)
McCook Community College (U)
Memorial University of Newfoundland (U, NC)
Mercy College (U)
Metropolitan Community College (U)
Metropolitan Community College (U)
Metropolitan State College of Denver (U)
Middle Georgia College (U)
Middle Tennessee State University (U)
Midland College (U)
Mid-Plains Community College (U)
Mid-State Technical College (U)
Midwestern State University (G)
Milwaukee Area Technical College (U)
Minnesota West Community and Technical College–Worthington Campus (U)
Minot State University (U)
Mississippi State University (G)
Modesto Junior College (U)
Montana State University–Bozeman (G)
Montgomery College–Rockville Campus (U)
Morehead State University (U)
Morgan Community College (U, NC)
Mountain View College (U)
Mount Saint Vincent University (U)
Mount Wachusett Community College (U)
Nassau Community College (U, NC)
National Technological University (G, NC)
New Hampshire College (U)
New Jersey Institute of Technology (U)
New Mexico Junior College (U)
New River Community College (U)
New School for Social Research (U, NC)
North Carolina State University (U)
North Central Bible College (U, NC)
Northcentral Technical College (U)
Northeast Wisconsin Technical College (U)
Northern Arizona University (U)
Northern Oklahoma College (U)
Northern Virginia Community College (U)

North Harris College (U)
North Iowa Area Community College (U)
Northwestern College (U)
Northwestern State University of Louisiana (U)
Northwest Iowa Community College (U)
Odessa College (U)
The Ohio State University (U, G)
Ohio State University–Mansfield Campus (U)
Ohio University (U)
Ohio University–Eastern (U)
Ohio University–Southern Campus (U)
Oklahoma City Community College (U)
Oklahoma State University (U)
Old Dominion University (U)
Oregon State University (U)
Owens Community College (U)
Parkland College (U)
Pennsylvania State University University Park Campus (U)
Pensacola Junior College (U)
Phillips Community College of the University of Arkansas (U)
Piedmont College (U)
Pikes Peak Community College (U, NC)
Portland Community College (U)
Portland State University (U)
Prairie State College (U)
Pratt Community College and Area Vocational School (U)
Prince George's Community College (U, NC)
Pueblo Community College (U)
Redlands Community College (U)
Red Rocks Community College (U)
The Richard Stockton College of New Jersey (U)
Rio Salado College (U)
Riverside Community College (U)
Rochester Institute of Technology (U)
Rockland Community College (U)
Rogers University (U)
Rose State College (U)
St. Cloud Technical College (U)
St. Johns River Community College (U)
Saint Joseph's College (U)
St. Louis Community College (U)
St. Petersburg Junior College (U)
Salt Lake Community College (U)
San Joaquin Delta College (U)
San Juan College (U)
Santa Fe Community College (U)
Schoolcraft College (U)
Scott Community College (U)
Seminole State College (U)
Shawnee Community College (U)
Shelby State Community College (U)
Shenandoah University (G)
Sierra College (U)
Sinclair Community College (U)
Skagit Valley College (U)
Skidmore College (U)
Southeast Community College, Lincoln Campus (U)
Southeastern Community College, North Campus (U)
Southeast Missouri State University (U, G)
Southern West Virginia Community and Technical College (U)
South Puget Sound Community College (U)
Southwestern Assemblies of God University (U)
Southwestern Michigan College (U)
Southwestern Oklahoma State University (U)

Southwest State University (U)
Southwest Texas State University (U)
Southwest Virginia Community College (U)
State University of New York Empire State College (U)
State University of West Georgia (U)
Suffolk County Community College–Ammerman Campus (U)
Sul Ross State University (U)
Syracuse University (U)
Tallahassee Community College (U)
Tarleton State University (U)
Tarrant County Junior College (U)
Taylor University, Fort Wayne Campus (U)
Technical College of the Lowcountry (U)
Tennessee State University (G)
Tennessee Temple University (U)
Terra State Community College (U)
Texas Tech University (U)
Thomas Edison State College (U)
Thomas Nelson Community College (U)
Treasure Valley Community College (U)
Trinidad State Junior College (U)
Triton College (U)
Troy State University Montgomery (U)
Tulsa Community College (U)
Ulster County Community College (U)
The Union Institute (U)
The University of Alabama (U, G)
The University of Alabama at Birmingham (G)
University of Alaska Anchorage (U)
University of Alaska Fairbanks (U)
University of Alaska Southeast, Sitka Campus (U)
University of Arizona (NC)
University of California Extension (U)
University of Delaware (U)
University of Georgia (U)
University of Great Falls (U)
University of Guelph (NC)
University of Hawaii–Leeward Community College (U)
University of Hawaii–Maui Community College (U)
University of Houston (U)
University of Idaho (U, G)
University of Illinois at Springfield (U)
University of Illinois at Urbana–Champaign (U)
University of Kansas (U, NC)
University of Kentucky (U, G)
University of Maine (U)
University of Maine at Augusta (U)
University of Maine at Fort Kent (U)
University of Mary (U, G)
University of Maryland University College (U)
University of Massachusetts Amherst (U, G, NC)
University of Massachusetts Boston (U)
University of Massachusetts Lowell (U)
University of Minnesota, Twin Cities Campus (U, NC)
University of Missouri–Columbia (U, G)
University of Missouri–Kansas City (U)
University of Nebraska at Kearney (U)
University of Nebraska–Lincoln (U)
University of Nevada, Las Vegas (U)
University of Nevada, Reno (U)
The University of North Carolina at Chapel Hill (U)
University of North Dakota (U)
University of Northern Colorado (U)

Distance Learning Programs

Individual Courses Index

Mathematics (continued)
University of Northern Iowa (U, G)
University of Oklahoma (U, NC)
University of Phoenix (U)
University of Pittsburgh at Bradford (U)
University of Saskatchewan (U)
University of Southern Mississippi (U)
University of South Florida (U, G)
University of Tennessee Space Institute (G)
The University of Texas at Austin (U)
The University of Texas at Tyler (U, G)
The University of Texas of the Permian Basin (U)
University of Utah (U)
University of Vermont (U)
University of Washington (U)
University of Waterloo (U, NC)
University of Windsor (U)
University System of Georgia (U)
Upper Iowa University (U)
Utah State University (U)
Utah Valley State College (U)
Vincennes University (U)
Volunteer State Community College (U)
Wake Technical Community College (U)
Walters State Community College (U)
Washington State University (U)
Waubonsee Community College (U)
Waukesha County Technical College (U)
Wayne County Community College (U)
Weber State University (U)
Western Illinois University (U)
Western Michigan University (U)
Western Montana College of The University of Montana (U)
Western Nebraska Community College (U)
Western Oklahoma State College (U)
Westmoreland County Community College (U)
West Virginia University (U, NC)
Wilkes Community College (U)
William Penn College (U)

Mechanical Engineering
Arizona State University (U, G)
Bradley University (G)
California State University, Northridge (U, G)
Colorado State University (G)
Florida State University (G)
Georgia Institute of Technology (G, NC)
GMI Engineering & Management Institute (G)
Idaho State University (U, G)
Illinois Institute of Technology (U, G)
Iowa State University of Science and Technology (G)
Michigan State University (G)
Michigan Technological University (U, NC)
Mississippi State University (G)
Montana State University–Bozeman (G)
National Technological University (G, NC)
North Carolina State University (G)
Northeastern University (G)
Northern Virginia Community College (U)
NRI Schools (NC)
Oakton Community College (U)
Oklahoma State University (G)
Old Dominion University (G)
Oregon State University (G)
Rensselaer Polytechnic Institute (G)
Rochester Institute of Technology (G)

Shenandoah University (G)
Southern Methodist University (G)
Southwest Virginia Community College (U)
Stanford University (G, NC)
State University of New York at Binghamton (G)
State University of New York at Buffalo (G)
Tarrant County Junior College (U)
Tennessee State University (G)
The University of Alabama (U)
University of Arizona (G)
University of Colorado at Boulder (G, NC)
University of Delaware (U, G)
University of Idaho (U, G)
University of Illinois at Urbana–Champaign (U, G)
University of Maine (U, G)
University of Massachusetts Amherst (G, NC)
University of Missouri–Kansas City (G)
University of Nebraska–Lincoln (G)
University of Nevada, Reno (U, G)
University of North Dakota (U)
University of North Florida (G)
University of Southern California (G, NC)
University of South Florida (G)
University of Tennessee, Knoxville (G)
University of Tennessee Space Institute (G)
The University of Texas at Arlington (G)
The University of Texas at San Antonio (U, G)
University of Virginia (G)
University of Wisconsin–Extension (NC)
University of Wisconsin–Madison (U, G)
Virginia Polytechnic Institute and State University (G)
West Virginia University Institute of Technology (U, G)
Wright State University (U)

Medieval/Renaissance Studies
Arizona State University (U, G)
Kansas State University (U, NC)
Mohawk Valley Community College (U)
Seattle Central Community College (U)
Thomas Edison State College (U)
University of Nebraska–Lincoln (U)

Mental Health Services
City University (G)

Meteorology
Iowa State University of Science and Technology (U, G)
Mississippi State University (U, G)
Oklahoma State University (U)
University of Missouri–Columbia (U)
University of Washington (U)

Microbiology
Brigham Young University (U)
California College for Health Sciences (U)
California State University, Los Angeles (U, NC)
The College of West Virginia (U)
Fort Hays State University (U)
Garland County Community College (U)
Graceland College (U)
Idaho State University (U, G)
Iowa State University of Science and Technology (U, G)
Iowa Western Community College (U)

Lakehead University (U)
North Carolina State University (U)
North Dakota State College of Science (U)
Northwestern State University of Louisiana (U)
Rend Lake College (U)
San Antonio College (U)
Skidmore College (U)
Université Laval (U)
University of Delaware (U, NC)
University of Guelph (U)
University of Maryland University College (U)
University of Minnesota, Twin Cities Campus (U)
University of Nebraska at Kearney (U)
University of New Brunswick (U)
University of Saskatchewan (U)
University of Waterloo (U)
University of Windsor (U)
Utah State University (U)
Western Illinois University (U, G)
Wilkes Community College (U)

Middle Eastern Languages and Literatures
The McGregor School of Antioch University (G)
New School for Social Research (U, NC)
Portland State University (U)
Skagit Valley College (U)
State University of New York at Binghamton (U)
Tennessee Temple University (U)
University of Wisconsin–Eau Claire (U)
William Rainey Harper College (U)

Military Studies
American Military University (U, G)

Music
Assemblies of God Theological Seminary (G, NC)
Bemidji State University (U)
Berean University of the Assemblies of God (U)
Blue Mountain Community College (U)
Brevard Community College (U)
Brigham Young University (U)
Brookdale Community College (U)
Broward Community College (U)
Burlington County College (U)
California State University, Fresno (U)
Central Arizona College (U)
Central Florida Community College (U)
Central Michigan University (U)
Chattanooga State Technical Community College (U)
City College of San Francisco (U)
Clovis Community College (U)
College of DuPage (U)
The College of West Virginia (U)
Colorado Electronic Community College (U)
Concordia University (U)
County College of Morris (U)
Dakota State University (U)
Danville Community College (U)
Darton College (U)
De Anza College (U)
Des Moines Area Community College (U)
Duquesne University (U, G)
Gannon University (U)
Garland County Community College (U)
Governors State University (U, G)

Individual Courses Index

Hampton University (U, G)
Highland Community College (U)
Indiana University System (U)
Jamestown Community College (U)
John C. Calhoun State Community College (U)
Joliet Junior College (U)
Judson College (U)
Kansas State University (U, NC)
Kaskaskia College (U)
Laurentian University (U)
Lorain County Community College (U)
Loyola University New Orleans (U)
Lycoming College (U)
The McGregor School of Antioch University (G)
Mercy College (U)
Metropolitan Community College (U)
Minnesota West Community and Technical College–Worthington Campus (U)
MiraCosta College (U)
Morris Brown College (U)
Nassau Community College (U)
New River Community College (U)
New School for Social Research (U, NC)
North Carolina State University (U)
North Central Bible College (U, NC)
Northern Arizona University (U)
Northern State University (U)
North Iowa Area Community College (U)
North Shore Community College (U)
Northwestern State University of Louisiana (NC)
Oakland University (U)
Ohio University (U)
Old Dominion University (U)
Palomar College (U)
Pennsylvania State University University Park Campus (U)
Portland Community College (U)
Portland State University (U)
Red Rocks Community College (U)
Saint Joseph's College (U)
Salve Regina University (U, NC)
San Diego State University (U)
San Juan College (U)
Scott Community College (U)
Scottsdale Community College (U)
Seattle Central Community College (U)
Shelby State Community College (U)
Sinclair Community College (U)
Southern Utah University (U)
Southwestern Assemblies of God University (U)
Southwest Missouri State University (U)
Southwest State University (U)
State University of West Georgia (U)
Suffolk County Community College–Ammerman Campus (U)
Tarrant County Junior College (U)
Taylor University, Fort Wayne Campus (U)
Texas Tech University (U)
Triton College (U)
Umpqua Community College (U)
University of Alaska Fairbanks (U)
University of British Columbia (U)
University of California, Santa Barbara (U, NC)
University of Guelph (U)
University of Hawaii–Leeward Community College (U)
University of Hawaii–Maui Community College (U)
University of Kansas (U, NC)
University of Maine (U)

University of Maine at Augusta (U)
University of Maine at Fort Kent (U)
University of Mary (U)
University of Minnesota, Twin Cities Campus (U)
University of Missouri–Columbia (U)
University of Nebraska–Lincoln (U)
The University of North Carolina at Chapel Hill (U)
University of North Dakota (U)
University of Northern Iowa (U)
University of Oklahoma (U)
University of Saskatchewan (U)
University of Utah (U)
University of Washington (U)
University of Waterloo (U)
Volunteer State Community College (U)
Waubonsee Community College (U)
Weber State University (U)
Western Oklahoma State College (U)
Western Washington University (U)
West Virginia University (U)
West Virginia Wesleyan College (U)
Wichita State University (U)

Nursing

Arizona State University (U, G)
Athabasca University (U)
Atlantic Community College (U)
Austin Community College (U)
Ball State University (U)
Bemidji State University (U)
Black Hawk College (U)
Bradley University (G)
California State University, Dominguez Hills (U)
California State University, Fresno (U)
California State University, Fullerton (U)
California State University, Hayward (U)
California State University, Sacramento (G)
California State University, Stanislaus (U)
Cape Cod Community College (U)
Carl Sandburg College (U)
Central Community College–Grand Island Campus (U)
Central Methodist College (U)
Central Wyoming College (U)
Charles County Community College (U)
Chippewa Valley Technical College (U)
Christopher Newport University (U)
Clarkson College (U, G)
Colby Community College (U, NC)
The College of West Virginia (U)
Columbia State Community College (U)
Dalhousie University (U, G)
Daytona Beach Community College (U)
De Anza College (U)
Delta College (U)
Delta State University (U, G)
Des Moines Area Community College (U)
Duquesne University (U, G)
Eastern Idaho Technical College (U)
Eastern Kentucky University (G)
Eastern New Mexico University (U, G)
Eastern Oklahoma State College (U)
Eastern Oregon University (U)
East Tennessee State University (U)
Fairleigh Dickinson University, Teaneck–Hackensack (G)
Florida Atlantic University (G)
Floyd College (U)

Fort Hays State University (U, G)
Garland County Community College (U)
Garrett Community College (NC)
Gateway Technical College (U)
Georgia Southern University (U, G)
Graceland College (U)
Grand Valley State University (U, G)
Hampton University (G)
Hocking College (U)
Idaho State University (U, G)
Illinois Central College (U)
Illinois Eastern Community Colleges, Olney Central College (U)
Indiana State University (G)
Indiana University System (U, G)
Iowa Western Community College (U)
Ivy Tech State College–Northcentral (U)
J. Sargeant Reynolds Community College (U)
Lakehead University (U)
Lake Superior State University (U)
Laurentian University (U)
Longview Community College (U)
Loyola University New Orleans (U)
Madison Area Technical College (U)
Marshall University (U, G)
Medical College of Georgia (U)
Medical University of South Carolina (U, G)
Memorial University of Newfoundland (U)
Mesa State College (U)
Metropolitan State University (G)
Midwestern State University (U)
Mississippi University for Women (U)
Missouri Southern State College (U)
Missouri Western State College (U)
Montana State University–Bozeman (G)
Morehead State University (U, G)
Nicholls State University (U)
Northcentral Technical College (U)
North Dakota State College of Science (U)
Northeast Community College (U)
Northern Arizona University (U)
Northern Illinois University (G)
Northern Oklahoma College (U)
North Georgia College & State University (U)
Northwestern Michigan College (U)
Northwestern State University of Louisiana (U, G, NC)
Northwest Iowa Community College (NC)
Odessa College (U)
Ohio University–Southern Campus (U)
Old Dominion University (U, G)
Oregon Health Sciences University (U, G)
Pennsylvania State University University Park Campus (U, G)
Penn Valley Community College (U)
Pine Technical College (U)
Pitt Community College (U)
Pratt Community College and Area Vocational School (U, G)
Rockland Community College (U)
Rogers University (U)
Rutgers, The State University of New Jersey, Newark (U, G, NC)
St. Cloud Technical College (U)
Saint Francis College (G)
Saint Joseph's College (U, G)
Salve Regina University (U, NC)
San Antonio College (U)
San Jose State University (U)
San Juan College (U)

Distance Learning Programs   591

Individual Courses Index

Nursing (continued)
Santa Fe Community College (U)
Shawnee Community College (U)
Southeast Community College, Beatrice Campus (U)
Southeastern Louisiana University (U)
Southern Vermont College (U)
Southern West Virginia Community and Technical College (U)
Southwestern Oklahoma State University (U)
Southwest Missouri State University (U)
Southwest Virginia Community College (U)
State University of New York at Binghamton (G)
State University of New York at Buffalo (G)
State University of New York College at Plattsburgh (U)
State University of West Georgia (U)
Tarleton State University (U)
Tennessee State University (U, G, NC)
Texas A&M University–Commerce (NC)
Texas A&M University–Corpus Christi (G)
Trinidad State Junior College (U)
Troy State University (U, G)
The University of Alabama (U)
The University of Alabama at Birmingham (G)
University of Alberta (G)
University of British Columbia (U)
The University of Calgary (U)
University of Cincinnati (U, G)
University of Delaware (U, G, NC)
University of Hawaii–Maui Community College (U)
University of Illinois at Springfield (U)
The University of Iowa (U, G)
University of Kentucky (U, G)
University of Maine (U)
University of Maine at Augusta (U)
University of Maine at Fort Kent (U, G)
University of Mary (U, G)
University of Maryland, Baltimore (U, G)
University of Massachusetts Lowell (U)
The University of Memphis (U)
University of Michigan (U)
University of Minnesota, Twin Cities Campus (U)
University of Missouri–Columbia (NC)
University of Missouri–Kansas City (G)
University of Nebraska at Kearney (U)
University of Nebraska–Lincoln (U)
University of Nevada, Las Vegas (U)
University of Nevada, Reno (G, NC)
University of New Brunswick (U, G)
University of New Hampshire (U, G)
The University of North Carolina at Chapel Hill (U)
University of North Carolina at Charlotte (G)
University of North Carolina at Greensboro (U, G)
University of North Dakota (U, G)
University of Northern Colorado (U)
University of North Florida (U)
University of Pennsylvania (U, G)
University of Pittsburgh (G)
University of Saskatchewan (U)
University of South Carolina (U, G)
University of Southern Colorado (U)
University of Southern Indiana (U, G)
University of South Florida (U, G)
The University of Tennessee at Martin (U, G)
The University of Texas at Tyler (U, G)
University of the State of New York, Regents College (U)
University of Vermont (U, G)
University of Wisconsin–Eau Claire (U, G)
University of Wisconsin–Oshkosh (U, G)
University of Wyoming (U, G)
Vincennes University (U)
Wayne State University (U)
Western Nebraska Community College (U)
West Virginia Wesleyan College (U)
Wichita State University (U, G)
William Rainey Harper College (NC)
Wright State University (U)
Yuba College (U)

Occupational Therapy
Manchester Community-Technical College (U)
St. Louis Community College (U)
Towson University (U, G)
University of Arkansas at Little Rock (U)

Oceanography
Atlantic Community College (U)
Bellevue Community College (U)
Catonsville Community College (U)
Central Florida Community College (U)
Charles County Community College (U)
Crafton Hills College (U)
Essex Community College (U)
Fullerton College (U)
Johnson County Community College (U)
Lane Community College (U)
Los Angeles Community College District (U)
San Bernardino Valley College (U)
Seattle Central Community College (U)
University of British Columbia (U)
University of Washington (U)

Organizational Behavior Studies
Brigham Young University (U)
Cornell University (G)
Duke University (G)
Embry-Riddle Aeronautical University, Extended Campus (U)
The Graduate School of America (G)
Heriot-Watt University (G)
Laramie County Community College (U)
Mercy College (U)
Mesa State College (U)
Milwaukee School of Engineering (G, NC)
New Hampshire College (U, G)
New River Community College (U)
Oklahoma State University (U)
Owens Community College (U)
Rutgers, The State University of New Jersey, Newark (U, G, NC)
Salve Regina University (U, G, NC)
San Diego State University (NC)
Sinclair Community College (U)
State University of New York Empire State College (U)
Stephens College (U)
Thomas Edison State College (U)
Troy State University–Florida Region (G)
University of Alaska Southeast (U)
University of Dallas (G)
University of Delaware (U)
University of Missouri–Columbia (G)
University of Nebraska–Lincoln (U)
University of Waterloo (U)
Western Illinois University (U)
Winthrop University (G)

Philosophy and Religion
Abilene Christian University (G, NC)
Acadia University (U)
Allegany College of Maryland (U)
American River College (U)
Anne Arundel Community College (U)
Arizona State University (U)
Assemblies of God Theological Seminary (G, NC)
Athabasca University (U)
Austin Community College (U)
Ball State University (U)
Bellevue University (U)
Bemidji State University (U)
Berean University of the Assemblies of God (U)
Black Hawk College (U)
Bloomsburg University of Pennsylvania (U)
Boise State University (U)
Brevard Community College (U)
Brigham Young University (U)
Brookdale Community College (U)
Broward Community College (U)
Bucks County Community College (U)
Butte College (U)
California State University, Bakersfield (U)
California State University, Hayward (U)
California State University, Sacramento (U)
Camden County College (U)
Carleton University (U)
Catawba Valley Community College (U)
Catonsville Community College (U)
Central Michigan University (U)
Central Piedmont Community College (U)
Cerritos College (U)
Chadron State College (U)
Champlain College (U)
Charles County Community College (U)
Charter Oak State College (U)
Chattanooga State Technical Community College (U)
Chemeketa Community College (U)
Christopher Newport University (U)
Cincinnati Bible College and Seminary (U)
City University (U)
Clarkson College (U)
Clovis Community College (U)
Coastline Community College (U, NC)
College of DuPage (U)
College of San Mateo (U)
College of the Southwest (U)
The College of West Virginia (U)
Colorado Mountain College District (U)
Colorado State University (U)
Columbia-Greene Community College (U)
Columbia State Community College (U)
Community College of Philadelphia (U)
Community College of Rhode Island (U)
Community College of the Air Force (U)
Concordia University (U, G)
Concordia University at Austin (U, NC)
Concordia University Wisconsin (U, G)
Contra Costa College (U)
Cosumnes River College (U)
Covenant Theological Seminary (G, NC)
Cumberland County College (U)

Individual Courses Index

Cuyahoga Community College, Metropolitan Campus (U)
Dallas County Community College District (U)
Dallas Theological Seminary (G, NC)
De Anza College (U)
Delaware County Community College (U)
Delta College (U)
Denver Conservative Baptist Seminary (G, NC)
Eastern Oregon University (U)
Eastern Washington University (U)
Eastern Wyoming College (U)
Essex Community College (U)
Florida Community College at Jacksonville (U)
Franciscan University of Steubenville (U, NC)
Front Range Community College (U)
Gannon University (U)
Garland County Community College (U)
Gordon-Conwell Theological Seminary (G, NC)
Governors State University (U)
Graceland College (U)
The Graduate School of America (G)
Grand Rapids Baptist Seminary (G)
Grand Rapids Community College (U)
Greenville Technical College (U)
Hampton University (U)
Harrisburg Area Community College (U)
Hibbing Community College (U)
Indiana University System (U)
Institute of Transpersonal Psychology (G, NC)
International Bible College (U)
Iowa Western Community College (U)
Jamestown Community College (U)
Johnson County Community College (U)
Judson College (U)
Kaskaskia College (U)
Lackawanna Junior College (U)
Lakehead University (U)
Lansing Community College (U)
Lassen College (U)
Laurentian University (U)
Liberty University (G)
Longview Community College (U)
Lorain County Community College (U)
Louisiana College (U)
Luzerne County Community College (U)
Lycoming College (U)
Marshall University (U)
Marywood University (U)
The McGregor School of Antioch University (G)
Memorial University of Newfoundland (U)
Mendocino College (U)
Mercy College (U)
Metropolitan Community College (U)
Metropolitan Community College (U)
Minnesota West Community and Technical College–Worthington Campus (U)
Minot State University (U)
Mississippi State University (U)
Montgomery College–Rockville Campus (U)
Moody Bible Institute (U)
Moraine Valley Community College (U)
Morgan Community College (U, NC)
Mount Saint Vincent University (U)
New Hampshire College (U)
New School for Social Research (U, NC)
New York Institute of Technology (U)
North Carolina State University (U)
North Central Bible College (U, NC)
North Dakota State College of Science (U)
Northeast Louisiana University (U)
Northern Arizona University (U)
Northern Virginia Community College (U)
North Iowa Area Community College (U)
North Shore Community College (U)
Northwestern State University of Louisiana (U)
Northwest Iowa Community College (U)
Ohio University (U)
Oklahoma City Community College (U)
Oklahoma State University (U)
Oregon State University (U)
Parkland College (U)
Pennsylvania State University University Park Campus (U)
Pikes Peak Community College (U, NC)
Polytechnic University, Brooklyn Campus (G)
Portland Community College (U)
Portland State University (U)
Pratt Community College and Area Vocational School (U)
Prince George's Community College (U, NC)
Quincy College (U)
Red Rocks Community College (U)
Regis University (U)
The Richard Stockton College of New Jersey (NC)
Rio Salado College (U)
Rochester Institute of Technology (U)
Rockland Community College (U)
Sacramento City College (U)
Saint Joseph's College (U)
Salve Regina University (U, G, NC)
San Bernardino Valley College (U)
San Jose State University (U)
Santa Rosa Junior College (U)
Schoolcraft College (U)
Scott Community College (U)
Seattle Pacific University (U)
Sinclair Community College (U)
Skagit Valley College (U)
Skidmore College (U)
Southeast Missouri State University (U)
Southern Christian University (U, G, NC)
Southwestern Assemblies of God University (U)
Southwestern Baptist Theological Seminary (U, G, NC)
Southwestern Oklahoma State University (U)
Southwest State University (U)
Southwest Virginia Community College (U)
State University of New York at New Paltz (U)
State University of New York Empire State College (U)
State University of West Georgia (U)
Suffolk County Community College–Ammerman Campus (U)
Syracuse University (U)
Tacoma Community College (U)
Tallahassee Community College (U)
Tarrant County Junior College (U)
Taylor University, Fort Wayne Campus (U)
Temple Baptist Seminary (G, NC)
Tennessee Technological University (U)
Tennessee Temple University (U)
Texas Tech University (U)
Thomas Edison State College (U)
Troy State University Montgomery (U)
The Union Institute (U)
Universitè Laval (U)
University of Alaska Anchorage (U)
University of Alaska Fairbanks (U)
University of Alaska Southeast, Sitka Campus (U)
University of British Columbia (U)
The University of Calgary (U)
University of California Extension (U)
University of California, Santa Barbara (U, NC)
University of Dayton (U, NC)
University of Delaware (U)
University of Georgia (U)
University of Great Falls (U)
University of Hawaii–Leeward Community College (U)
University of Hawaii–Maui Community College (U)
University of Kansas (U, NC)
University of Maine (U)
University of Maine at Fort Kent (U)
University of Mary (U, G)
University of Massachusetts Lowell (U)
The University of Memphis (U)
University of Minnesota, Twin Cities Campus (U)
University of Missouri–Columbia (U)
University of Missouri–Kansas City (U)
University of Missouri–St. Louis (U)
University of Nebraska at Kearney (U)
University of Nebraska–Lincoln (U)
The University of North Carolina at Chapel Hill (U)
University of North Dakota (U)
University of Northern Iowa (U, G)
University of Oklahoma (U)
University of Saskatchewan (U)
University of South Dakota (U, G)
University of the State of New York, Regents College (U)
University of Washington (U)
University of Waterloo (U)
University of Windsor (U)
University of Wisconsin–Stout (G, NC)
University System of Georgia (U)
Utah State University (U)
Utah Valley State College (U)
Volunteer State Community College (U)
Walters State Community College (U)
Washington State University (U)
Waubonsee Community College (U)
Wayne County Community College (U)
Wayne State University (U)
Weber State University (U)
Western Illinois University (U)
Western Michigan University (U)
Western Oklahoma State College (U)
Westmoreland County Community College (U)
West Virginia Wesleyan College (U)
Wilfrid Laurier University (U)
William Rainey Harper College (U)
Wright State University (U)
Wytheville Community College (U)
Yuba College (U)

Photography

Houston Community College System (U)
Lane Community College (U)
San Bernardino Valley College (U)
Thomas Edison State College (U)
University of Mary (U)

Individual Courses Index

Physical Sciences
Acadia University (U)
Athabasca University (U)
Ball State University (U)
Bemidji State University (U)
Berean University of the Assemblies of God (U)
Boise State University (U)
Brigham Young University (U)
Bucks County Community College (U)
Calvin College (G)
Carleton University (U)
Chemeketa Community College (U)
City University (U)
Coastline Community College (U, NC)
Colby Community College (U)
College of DuPage (U)
The College of West Virginia (U)
Cosumnes River College (U)
Daytona Beach Community College (U)
Dutchess Community College (U)
Eastern Idaho Technical College (U)
Eastern Oregon University (U)
George C. Wallace State Community College (U)
Hampton University (U)
Idaho State University (U, G)
LIFE Bible College (U)
Long Beach City College (U)
Longview Community College (U)
Louisiana State University at Eunice (U)
Metropolitan Community College (U)
Missouri Southern State College (U)
North Carolina State University (U)
North Central Bible College (U, NC)
Northeast Community College (U)
Northern Oklahoma College (U)
Northwestern College (U)
Oakton Community College (U)
Oklahoma City Community College (U)
Pennsylvania State University University Park Campus (U)
Penn Valley Community College (U)
Pima Community College (U)
Pratt Community College and Area Vocational School (U)
Redlands Community College (U)
The Richard Stockton College of New Jersey (U)
Rochester Institute of Technology (U)
Rogers University (U)
Roosevelt University (U)
Rose State College (U)
San Bernardino Valley College (U)
Scott Community College (U)
Skidmore College (U)
South Florida Community College (U)
Southwestern Assemblies of God University (U)
Southwest State University (U)
Suffolk County Community College–Ammerman Campus (U)
Tallahassee Community College (U)
Tarrant County Junior College (U)
Taylor University, Fort Wayne Campus (U)
The Union Institute (U)
University of Alaska Fairbanks (U)
University of Alaska Southeast, Sitka Campus (U)
University of California Extension (U)
University of Great Falls (U)
University of Maine at Machias (U)
University of Maryland, College Park (U)
University of Missouri–Columbia (U)
University of Nebraska–Lincoln (U)
University of New Hampshire (U)
University of North Dakota (U, G)
The University of Texas at Austin (U)
Upper Iowa University (U)
Wayne County Community College (U)
Western Michigan University (U)
Westmoreland County Community College (U)
West Virginia Wesleyan College (U)
Wilfrid Laurier University (U)
Yuba College (U)

Physical Therapy
Charles County Community College (U)
Cleveland State University (U)
Medical College of Georgia (G)
Northern Illinois University (G)
St. Louis Community College (U)

Physics
Athabasca University (U)
Ball State University (U)
Brigham Young University (U)
California College for Health Sciences (U)
Carleton University (U)
Central Michigan University (U)
Christopher Newport University (U)
City College of San Francisco (U)
City Colleges of Chicago, Harold Washington College (U)
College of DuPage (U)
The College of West Virginia (U)
Colorado Mountain College District (U)
Colorado Northwestern Community College (U)
Concordia University (U)
Dodge City Community College (U)
Embry-Riddle Aeronautical University, Extended Campus (U)
Garland County Community College (U)
Genesee Community College (U)
Georgia Institute of Technology (G, NC)
Georgia Southern University (U)
Hampton University (U)
Hibbing Community College (U)
Idaho State University (U, G)
Illinois Institute of Technology (U)
Indiana University System (U)
Ivy Tech State College–Wabash Valley (U)
Lansing Community College (U)
Laurentian University (U)
Lorain County Community College (U)
Louisiana State University at Eunice (U)
Midwestern State University (G)
Minnesota West Community and Technical College–Worthington Campus (U)
Missouri Western State College (U, G)
Montana State University–Bozeman (G)
Moraine Valley Community College (U)
National Technological University (G, NC)
New Jersey Institute of Technology (U)
New School for Social Research (U, NC)
North Carolina State University (U)
Northeast Community College (U)
Northeast Louisiana University (U)
Northern Virginia Community College (U)
Oakton Community College (U)
Ohio University (U)
Oklahoma City Community College (U)
Pennsylvania State University University Park Campus (U)
Penn Valley Community College (U)
St. Louis Community College (U)
Salt Lake Community College (U)
San Bernardino Valley College (U)
Sinclair Community College (U)
Southeastern Community College, North Campus (U)
State University of New York at Farmingdale (U)
Syracuse University (U)
Tarleton State University (U)
Thomas Edison State College (U)
Tidewater Community College (U)
Treasure Valley Community College (U)
Troy State University (U)
University of Alaska Fairbanks (U)
The University of Calgary (U)
University of Great Falls (U)
University of Guelph (U)
University of Kentucky, Elizabethtown Community College (U)
University of Maryland, Baltimore County (U, G)
University of Maryland University College (U)
University of Massachusetts Dartmouth (U)
University of Minnesota, Twin Cities Campus (U, NC)
University of Missouri–Columbia (U, G)
University of Missouri–Kansas City (U)
University of Nebraska–Lincoln (U)
University of Nevada, Reno (U)
The University of North Carolina at Chapel Hill (U)
University of North Dakota (U)
University of South Carolina (U, G)
University of South Florida (U)
University of Utah (U)
University of Virginia (G, NC)
University of Waterloo (U, NC)
University of West Florida (U)
University of Wisconsin–Madison (U)
Utah State University (U)
Valley City State University (U)
Volunteer State Community College (U)
Westmoreland County Community College (U)
Wichita State University (U)

Physiology
Central Methodist College (U)
Dalhousie University (U, G)
Delta College (U)
Duquesne University (U)
Floyd College (U)
Meridian Community College (U)
St. Louis Community College (U)
Stephens College (U)
University of Waterloo (U)
Wayne County Community College (U)

Plant Sciences
Colorado State University (U)
Cuyahoga Community College, Metropolitan Campus (U)
Kansas State University (U)
Texas Tech University (U, NC)
Treasure Valley Community College (U)
University of Missouri–Columbia (G)
University of Waterloo (U)

Political Science

Allegany College of Maryland (U)
Alvin Community College (U)
Angelina College (U)
Anne Arundel Community College (U)
Arapahoe Community College (U)
Arizona State University (U)
Athabasca University (U)
Auburn University (U)
Austin Community College (U)
Bakersfield College (U)
Ball State University (U)
Beaufort County Community College (U)
Bellevue Community College (U)
Bemidji State University (U)
Blinn College (U)
Bluefield State College (U)
Boise State University (U)
Brevard Community College (U)
Brigham Young University (U)
Broward Community College (U)
Brown University (NC)
Bucks County Community College (U)
Burlington County College (U)
Butte College (U)
Cabrillo College (U)
California State University, Bakersfield (U)
California State University, Chico (U)
California State University, Hayward (U)
California State University, Los Angeles (U, NC)
Carleton University (U)
Carl Sandburg College (U)
Catonsville Community College (U)
Central Michigan University (U)
Central Piedmont Community College (U)
Central Wyoming College (U)
Cerritos College (U)
Chadron State College (U)
Champlain College (U)
Charles County Community College (U)
Charles Stewart Mott Community College (U)
Chattanooga State Technical Community College (U)
Christopher Newport University (U)
Citrus College (U)
City Colleges of Chicago, Harold Washington College (U)
City University (U)
Clarkson College (U)
Clayton College & State University (U)
Coastline Community College (U, NC)
Colby Community College (U)
College Misericordia (U)
College of DuPage (U)
College of St. Scholastica (U, G)
College of San Mateo (U)
College of the Canyons (U)
College of the Mainland (U)
College of the Southwest (U)
The College of West Virginia (U)
Collin County Community College (U)
Colorado Mountain College District (U)
Community College of Philadelphia (U)
Community College of Rhode Island (U)
Community College of Vermont (U)
Concordia University (U)
Concordia University at Austin (U, NC)
County College of Morris (U)
Crafton Hills College (U)
Cuyamaca College (U)

Dallas County Community College District (U)
Darton College (U)
De Anza College (U)
DeKalb College (U)
Delaware County Community College (U)
Delaware Technical & Community College, Stanton/Wilmington Campus (U)
Delta College (U)
Des Moines Area Community College (U)
Eastern Idaho Technical College (U)
Eastern Kentucky University (U)
Eastern Oklahoma State College (U)
Eastern Washington University (U)
Eastern Wyoming College (U)
Edison Community College (U)
El Paso Community College (U)
Essex Community College (U)
Evergreen Valley College (U)
Florida Community College at Jacksonville (U)
Floyd College (U)
Fort Hays State University (U, G)
Front Range Community College (U)
Frostburg State University (U)
Fullerton College (U)
Galveston College (U)
Garland County Community College (U)
Genesee Community College (U)
Georgia Southern University (U, G)
Glendale Community College (U)
The Graduate School of America (G)
Grand Rapids Community College (U)
Grand Valley State University (U, G)
Griggs University (U)
Hampton University (U)
Harrisburg Area Community College (U)
Hibbing Community College (U)
Hillsborough Community College (U)
Idaho State University (U, G)
Illinois Central College (U)
Illinois Eastern Community Colleges, Olney Central College (U)
Illinois Valley Community College (U)
Indiana University System (U)
Iowa State University of Science and Technology (U, G)
Iowa Western Community College (U)
Jacksonville State University (U)
Jefferson Community College (U)
Jefferson Davis Community College (U)
Jefferson State Community College (U)
John Wood Community College (U)
Joliet Junior College (U)
J. Sargeant Reynolds Community College (U)
Judson College (U)
Juniata College (U)
Kansas State University (U)
Kaskaskia College (U)
Kellogg Community College (U)
Kingwood College (U)
Lafayette College (U)
Lakehead University (U)
Lakeland Community College (U)
Lake Michigan College (U)
Lakeshore Technical College (U)
Lake-Sumter Community College (U)
Lamar University (U)
Laney College (U)
Lansing Community College (U)
Laramie County Community College (U)
Lassen College (U)

Laurentian University (U)
Lawson State Community College (U)
Lee College (U)
Lehigh Carbon Community College (U)
Long Beach City College (U)
Los Angeles Community College District (U)
Louisiana State University and Agricultural and Mechanical College (U)
Louisiana State University in Shreveport (U, G, NC)
Luzerne County Community College (U)
Lycoming College (U)
McCook Community College (U)
The McGregor School of Antioch University (G)
Memorial University of Newfoundland (U)
Mendocino College (U)
Mercy College (U)
Metropolitan Community College (U)
Metropolitan Community College (U)
Midland College (U)
Midwestern State University (U)
Milwaukee Area Technical College (U)
Minnesota West Community and Technical College–Worthington Campus (U)
Missouri Southern State College (U)
Modesto Junior College (U)
Montgomery College–Rockville Campus (U)
Morgan Community College (U, NC)
Mountain View College (U)
New Hampshire College (U)
New School for Social Research (U, NC)
New York Institute of Technology (U)
Nicholls State University (U)
North Arkansas College (U)
North Carolina State University (U, G)
North Central Texas College (U)
Northeast Community College (U)
Northern Arizona University (U)
Northern Kentucky University (U, G)
Northern Oklahoma College (U)
Northern State University (U)
Northern Virginia Community College (U)
North Harris College (U)
North Iowa Area Community College (U)
North Shore Community College (U)
Northwestern College (U)
Northwestern Michigan College (U)
Oakland Community College (U)
Oakton Community College (U)
Odessa College (U)
The Ohio State University (U, G)
Ohio State University–Mansfield Campus (U)
Ohio University (U)
Ohio University–Eastern (U)
Oklahoma City Community College (U)
Oklahoma State University (U)
Old Dominion University (U)
Oregon State University (U)
Palo Alto College (U)
Parkland College (U)
Pennsylvania State University University Park Campus (U)
Phillips Community College of the University of Arkansas (U)
Polytechnic University, Brooklyn Campus (G, NC)
Portland Community College (U)
Prairie State College (U)
Prince George's Community College (U, NC)
Redlands Community College (U)

Distance Learning Programs

Individual Courses Index

Political Science (continued)
Red Rocks Community College (U)
Rio Salado College (U)
Riverside Community College (U)
Rochester Institute of Technology (U)
Rockland Community College (U)
Rogers University (U)
Roger Williams University (U)
Rose State College (U)
Ryerson Polytechnic University (U)
St. Johns River Community College (U)
St. Louis Community College (U)
St. Petersburg Junior College (U)
Salve Regina University (G, NC)
San Bernardino Valley College (U)
San Diego City College (U)
San Jose State University (U)
Schoolcraft College (U)
Scott Community College (U)
Seattle Central Community College (U)
Seattle Pacific University (U)
Shelby State Community College (U)
Sierra College (U)
Skagit Valley College (U)
Skidmore College (U)
Southeast Arkansas Technical College (U)
Southeastern Community College, North Campus (U)
Southern Utah University (U)
Southern West Virginia Community and Technical College (U)
South Florida Community College (U)
Southwestern Michigan College (U)
Southwestern Oklahoma State University (U)
Southwest Missouri State University (U)
Southwest State University (U)
Southwest Texas State University (U)
State Technical Institute at Memphis (U)
State University of New York Empire State College (U)
State University of West Georgia (U)
Suffolk County Community College–Ammerman Campus (U)
Syracuse University (U, G)
Tallahassee Community College (U)
Tarrant County Junior College (U)
Technical College of the Lowcountry (U)
Tennessee State University (G)
Tennessee Temple University (U)
Texas A&M University–Commerce (U)
Texas Tech University (U)
Tidewater Community College (U)
Triton College (U)
Troy State University Dothan (U)
Troy State University–Florida Region (U)
Troy State University Montgomery (U)
Tulsa Community College (U)
Tyler Junior College (U)
The Union Institute (U)
University of Alaska Anchorage (U)
University of Alaska Fairbanks (U)
University of Alberta (U)
University of Baltimore (U)
The University of Calgary (U)
University of California Extension (U)
University of California, Santa Barbara (U, NC)
University of California, Santa Cruz (U, G)
University of Delaware (U, G)
University of Georgia (U)
University of Great Falls (U)
University of Guelph (U)
University of Houston (U)
University of Illinois at Urbana–Champaign (U)
The University of Iowa (U, G)
University of Kansas (U, NC)
University of Kentucky, Madisonville Community College (U)
University of Maine (U)
University of Maine at Augusta (U)
University of Maine at Fort Kent (U)
University of Mary (U)
University of Maryland University College (U)
University of Minnesota, Twin Cities Campus (U)
University of Missouri–Columbia (U, G, NC)
The University of Montana–Missoula (G)
University of Nebraska at Kearney (U)
University of Nebraska–Lincoln (U)
University of Nevada, Reno (U)
University of New Orleans (U)
The University of North Carolina at Chapel Hill (U)
University of North Dakota (U, G)
University of Northern Iowa (U)
University of Oklahoma (U)
University of South Dakota (U)
University of Southern Colorado (U)
University of South Florida (U)
The University of Texas at San Antonio (U, G)
The University of Texas at Tyler (U)
University of the State of New York, Regents College (U)
University of Toledo (U)
University of Utah (U)
University of Washington (U)
University of Windsor (U)
University of Wyoming (U, G)
University System of Georgia (U)
Utah State University (U)
Victor Valley College (U)
Vincennes University (U)
Washington State University (U)
Waubonsee Community College (U)
Wayne County Community College (U)
Wayne State University (U)
Weber State University (U)
Wenatchee Valley College (U)
Western Illinois University (U)
Western Oklahoma State College (U)
Westmoreland County Community College (U)
West Virginia Wesleyan College (U)
Wilfrid Laurier University (U)
Wytheville Community College (U)
Xavier University of Louisiana (U)
Yuba College (U)

Protective Services
Bemidji State University (U)
Black Hawk College (U)
Butte College (U)
Central Arizona College (U)
Central Missouri State University (U)
Chattanooga State Technical Community College (U)
City University (U, G)
Colorado Northwestern Community College (U)
East Tennessee State University (U)
Ellsworth Community College (U)
Garland County Community College (U)
Grand Valley State University (U, G)
Great Basin College (U)
Greenville Technical College (U)
Indiana University System (U)
J. Sargeant Reynolds Community College (U)
Lake Superior State University (U)
Memorial University of Newfoundland (NC)
Metropolitan State College of Denver (U)
Missouri Western State College (U)
Northcentral Technical College (U)
Northeast Community College (U)
Northeast Wisconsin Technical College (U)
Northwestern State University of Louisiana (U)
Ohio University (U)
Pennsylvania State University University Park Campus (U)
Redlands Community College (NC)
Red Rocks Community College (U)
Roger Williams University (U)
Salve Regina University (U, G, NC)
Technical College of the Lowcountry (U)
The Union Institute (U)
University of Delaware (NC)
University of Great Falls (U)
University of Hawaii–Maui Community College (U)
University of Kentucky, Ashland Community College (U)
University of Missouri–Columbia (U, G, NC)
The University of Texas at Tyler (U, G)
University of Wyoming (U)
Vincennes University (U)
Walters State Community College (U)
Western Nebraska Community College (U)

Psychology
Acadia University (U)
Alvin Community College (U)
Arapahoe Community College (U)
Assemblies of God Theological Seminary (G, NC)
Athabasca University (U)
Bakersfield College (U)
Ball State University (U)
Bellevue Community College (U)
Bemidji State University (U)
Bergen Community College (U)
Blackhawk Technical College (U)
Blinn College (U)
Bloomsburg University of Pennsylvania (U)
Blue Mountain Community College (U)
Brigham Young University (U)
Bristol Community College (U)
Bucks County Community College (U)
Buena Vista University (U)
Burlington County College (U)
Cabrillo College (U)
California State University, Fresno (U)
California State University, Stanislaus (U)
Camden County College (U)
Cape Cod Community College (U)
Carleton University (U)
Carl Sandburg College (U)
Catonsville Community College (U)
Central Arizona College (U)
Central Piedmont Community College (U)
Central Wyoming College (U)
Cerritos College (U)
Champlain College (U)
Chapman University (U)

Individual Courses Index

Chattanooga State Technical Community College (U)
Chippewa Valley Technical College (U)
Citrus College (U)
Clackamas Community College (U)
Clark College (U)
Clatsop Community College (U)
Clayton College & State University (U)
Coastline Community College (U, NC)
Colby Community College (U)
College of DuPage (U)
College of St. Scholastica (U, G)
College of San Mateo (U)
The College of West Virginia (U)
Colorado Electronic Community College (U)
Colorado State University (U)
Columbia Basin College (U)
Columbia-Greene Community College (U)
Columbus State Community College (U)
Community College of Denver (U)
Community College of Rhode Island (U)
Concordia University at Austin (U, NC)
Contra Costa College (U)
Corning Community College (U)
Crafton Hills College (U)
Danville Area Community College (U)
De Anza College (U)
Delaware County Community College (U)
Delaware Technical & Community College, Jack F. Owens Campus (U)
Delaware Technical & Community College, Stanton/Wilmington Campus (U)
Delgado Community College (U)
Denver Conservative Baptist Seminary (G, NC)
Des Moines Area Community College (U)
Dutchess Community College (U)
Eastern Idaho Technical College (U)
Eastern Kentucky University (U)
Eastern Michigan University (U)
Eastern New Mexico University (U, G)
Eastern Oregon University (U)
Eastern Washington University (U)
Eastern Wyoming College (U)
Edison Community College (U)
Edison State Community College (U)
El Paso Community College (U)
Embry-Riddle Aeronautical University, Extended Campus (U)
Florence-Darlington Technical College (U)
Front Range Community College (U)
Fullerton College (U)
Gadsden State Community College (U)
Gannon University (U)
Gateway Technical College (U)
Genesee Community College (U)
George C. Wallace State Community College (U)
Governors State University (U, G)
The Graduate School of America (G)
Grand Rapids Community College (U)
Griggs University (U)
Hawkeye Community College (U)
Hibbing Community College (U)
Hillsborough Community College (U)
Hocking College (U)
Houston Community College System (U)
Howard Community College (U)
Hudson Valley Community College (U)
Institute of Transpersonal Psychology (G, NC)
International Bible College (U)
Iowa Wesleyan College (U)
Ivy Tech State College–Northcentral (U)
Jefferson College (U)
Jefferson Community College (U)
Jefferson Davis Community College (U)
Jefferson State Community College (U)
John C. Calhoun State Community College (U)
Johnson County Community College (U)
Joliet Junior College (U)
Judson College (U)
Kankakee Community College (U)
Kellogg Community College (U)
Kingwood College (U)
Labette Community College (U)
Lackawanna Junior College (U)
Lake Land College (U)
Lake Michigan College (U)
Lakeshore Technical College (U)
Lamar University (U)
Laney College (U)
Laramie County Community College (U)
Lassen College (U)
Lee College (U)
Lehigh Carbon Community College (U)
Liberty University (U)
Lincoln Land Community College (U)
Long Beach City College (U)
Longview Community College (U)
Lorain County Community College (U)
Lord Fairfax Community College (U)
Louisiana State University and Agricultural and Mechanical College (U)
Louisiana State University at Eunice (U)
Madison Area Technical College (U)
Manatee Community College (U)
McCook Community College (U)
The McGregor School of Antioch University (G)
Memorial University of Newfoundland (U)
Mendocino College (U)
Mercy College (U)
Metropolitan Community College (U)
Metropolitan Community College (U)
Midland College (U)
Mid-State Technical College (U)
Minnesota West Community and Technical College–Worthington Campus (U)
Missouri Southern State College (U)
Modesto Junior College (U)
Montgomery College–Rockville Campus (U)
Montgomery County Community College (U)
Moraine Valley Community College (U)
Mount Saint Vincent University (U)
Mt. San Antonio College (U)
Mount Wachusett Community College (U)
Nassau Community College (U)
New Hampshire College (U)
New River Community College (U)
New York Institute of Technology (U)
North Carolina State University (U)
North Central Bible College (U, NC)
North Central Texas College (U)
Northeast Wisconsin Technical College (U)
Northern Essex Community College (U)
Northern Oklahoma College (U)
Northern Virginia Community College (U)
North Seattle Community College (U)
Northwestern College (U)
Northwestern Michigan College (U)
Oakland Community College (U)
Oakton Community College (U)
Oklahoma City Community College (U)
Oklahoma State University (U)
Owens Community College (U)
Palomar College (U)
Parkland College (U)
Pennsylvania State University University Park Campus (U)
Pierce College (U)
Pima Community College (U)
Portland Community College (U)
Prairie State College (U)
Pratt Community College and Area Vocational School (U)
Pueblo Community College (U)
Quincy College (U)
Red Rocks Community College (U)
The Richard Stockton College of New Jersey (U)
Rio Salado College (U)
Rochester Institute of Technology (U)
Rogers University (U)
Rose State College (U)
Ryerson Polytechnic University (U)
Sacramento City College (U)
St. Louis Community College (U)
St. Thomas Aquinas College (NC)
Salve Regina University (U, NC)
San Bernardino Valley College (U)
San Diego City College (U)
San Juan College (U)
Sauk Valley Community College (U)
Schoolcraft College (U)
Scott Community College (U)
Shelby State Community College (U)
Sinclair Community College (U)
Skidmore College (U)
Southeast Arkansas Technical College (U)
Southeast Community College, Lincoln Campus (U)
Southeastern Louisiana University (U)
Southeast Missouri State University (U)
Southern West Virginia Community and Technical College (U)
Southwestern Assemblies of God University (U)
Southwestern Michigan College (U)
Southwest Missouri State University (U)
Southwest State University (U)
Southwest Texas State University (U)
State Technical Institute at Memphis (U)
State University of New York at New Paltz (U)
State University of West Georgia (U, G)
Stephens College (U)
Suffolk County Community College–Ammerman Campus (U)
Sul Ross State University (U)
Tacoma Community College (U)
Taylor University, Fort Wayne Campus (U)
Technical College of the Lowcountry (U)
Tennessee Temple University (U)
Tidewater Community College (U)
Towson University (U)
Treasure Valley Community College (U)
Trinidad State Junior College (U)
Triton College (U)
Troy State University Dothan (U)
Troy State University Montgomery (U)
Tyler Junior College (U)
The Union Institute (U)
Université Laval (U)
The University of Alabama at Birmingham (G)
University of Alaska Fairbanks (U)

Distance Learning Programs

Individual Courses Index

Psychology (continued)
University of Alaska Southeast, Sitka Campus (U)
University of Baltimore (U)
University of British Columbia (U)
University of California Extension (U)
University of Georgia (U)
University of Great Falls (U)
University of Hawaii–Maui Community College (U)
University of Houston (U)
University of Idaho (U, G)
The University of Iowa (U, G)
University of Kentucky, Ashland Community College (U)
University of Kentucky, Elizabethtown Community College (U)
University of Kentucky, Madisonville Community College (U)
University of Maine at Augusta (U)
University of Mary (U, G)
University of Maryland University College (U)
University of Michigan (U)
University of Minnesota, Twin Cities Campus (NC)
University of Missouri–Columbia (U, G)
University of Nebraska–Lincoln (U)
University of Nevada, Reno (U)
The University of North Carolina at Chapel Hill (U)
University of North Dakota (U)
University of Northern Iowa (U)
University of Pittsburgh (U)
University of Sarasota (G)
University of Saskatchewan (U)
University of Tennessee, Knoxville (U)
The University of Texas at Austin (U)
University of Toledo (U)
University of Vermont (U)
University of Washington (U)
University of Waterloo (U)
University of Windsor (U)
University System of Georgia (U)
Upper Iowa University (U)
Wake Technical Community College (U)
Walden University (G)
Washington State University (U)
Waubonsee Community College (U)
Waukesha County Technical College (U)
Wayne County Community College (U)
Wayne State University (U)
Weber State University (U)
Western Michigan University (U)
Western Nebraska Community College (U)
Western Oklahoma State College (U)
Western Oregon University (U, G)
Whatcom Community College (U)
Wilfrid Laurier University (U)
Wilkes Community College (U)
Wilson Technical Community College (U)

Public Administration and Services
Athabasca University (U)
Ball State University (U)
California College for Health Sciences (G)
Carleton University (U)
Central Michigan University (U)
Colby Community College (U)
The College of West Virginia (U)
Eastern New Mexico University (U, G)
Grand Valley State University (U, G)
Hocking College (U)
Iowa State University of Science and Technology (U, G)
The McGregor School of Antioch University (G)
Memorial University of Newfoundland (U, NC)
Missouri Southern State College (U)
New York Institute of Technology (U)
North Carolina State University (G)
Northeast Community College (U)
Northern Kentucky University (U, G)
Roger Williams University (U)
Ryerson Polytechnic University (U)
Skidmore College (U)
Southwest State University (U)
State University of New York Empire State College (U)
State University of West Georgia (U, G)
Troy State University–Florida Region (G)
The Union Institute (U)
United States Sports Academy (G, NC)
University of Alaska Fairbanks (U)
University of Alaska Southeast (G)
University of Baltimore (G)
University of Great Falls (U)
University of Guelph (U)
University of Hawaii–Maui Community College (U)
University of Kansas (U, NC)
University of Missouri–Columbia (NC)
University of Nebraska–Lincoln (U)
University of New Orleans (U, G)
The University of North Carolina at Chapel Hill (U)
University of North Dakota (U, G)
University of South Carolina (G)
The University of Texas at Tyler (G)
University of Wisconsin–Extension (NC)
Upper Iowa University (U)
Volunteer State Community College (U)
Walden University (G)

Public Health
Arizona State University (G)
Ball State University (U)
Blue Mountain Community College (U)
Bristol Community College (U)
Brown University (NC)
Carl Sandburg College (U)
Central Michigan University (U)
Colby Community College (U, NC)
The College of West Virginia (U)
Eastern Maine Technical College (NC)
East Tennessee State University (U)
Fort Hays State University (U, G)
Garland County Community College (U)
Governors State University (U, G)
Harrisburg Area Community College (U)
Idaho State University (U, G)
Indiana State University (G)
Indiana University System (U)
Iowa Western Community College (U)
Lincoln Land Community College (U)
Morehead State University (U, G)
New Mexico State University (G)
Northern Arizona University (U)
Northern State University (U)
Northwest Iowa Community College (NC)
Ohio University–Eastern (U)
Old Dominion University (U)
Pennsylvania State University University Park Campus (NC)
Pima Community College (U)
Pine Technical College (U)
Rochester Institute of Technology (U, G)
Saint Joseph's College (U)
Tallahassee Community College (U)
Tennessee Technological University (NC)
Texas A&M University–Commerce (NC)
Thomas Nelson Community College (U)
Universitè Laval (U)
University of Arizona (G)
University of California Extension (U)
University of Georgia (U)
University of Houston (U)
University of Illinois at Urbana–Champaign (U)
University of Kansas (U, G, NC)
University of Minnesota, Twin Cities Campus (U)
University of Nebraska at Kearney (U)
University of New Hampshire (NC)
University of North Dakota (NC)
University of Northern Iowa (U)
University of North Texas Health Science Center at Fort Worth (G)
University of South Carolina (U, G)
University of Southern Indiana (U)
University of South Florida (G)
The University of Texas at San Antonio (U)
University of Washington (U)
University of Wisconsin–La Crosse (U, G, NC)
University System of Georgia (U)
Utah Valley State College (U)
Wayne State University (U)
Western Illinois University (U, G)
West Virginia University (G)

Public Policy Analysis
Christopher Newport University (U)
Duquesne University (G)
Northern Illinois University (G)
Tennessee State University (G)
University of Alaska Southeast (G)

Public Relations
Texas Tech University (U, NC)
University of Southern Indiana (U)
University of Tennessee, Knoxville (G)

Radio and Television Broadcasting
Adams State College (U)
Berean University of the Assemblies of God (U)
Butte College (U)
California State University, Los Angeles (U, NC)
Central Michigan University (U)
Central Missouri State University (U)
Chattanooga State Technical Community College (U)
Cosumnes River College (U)
Daytona Beach Community College (U)
Dodge City Community College (U)
Eastern Kentucky University (U)
Indiana University System (U)
Lawson State Community College (U)
The McGregor School of Antioch University (G)
Metropolitan Community College (U)
Missouri Southern State College (U)
North Carolina State University (U)

Individual Courses Index

Northeast Community College (U)
Northern Arizona University (U)
Oakton Community College (U)
Oklahoma State University (G)
Pikes Peak Community College (U, NC)
Rogers University (U)
San Bernardino Valley College (U)
Southern Methodist University (G)
Southwest State University (U)
State University of New York at Oswego (U)
Texas A&M University–Commerce (U, G)
Texas Tech University (U)
University of Alaska Fairbanks (U)
University of Hawaii–Leeward Community College (U)
University of Kansas (U, NC)
University of Missouri–St. Louis (U)
University of Nebraska–Lincoln (U)
University of Southern Indiana (U)
University of Tennessee, Knoxville (G)
Western Illinois University (U)
Yuba College (U)

Real Estate
Columbus State University (NC)
Eastern Kentucky University (U)
Hocking College (U)
Houston Community College System (U)
Joliet Junior College (U)
Northeast Wisconsin Technical College (U)
North Seattle Community College (U)
Oklahoma State University (NC)
Palomar College (U)
State University of West Georgia (U, G)
Texas Tech University (NC)
Triton College (U)
Universitè Laval (U)
University of Alaska Fairbanks (U)
University of Mississippi (U, G)
University of Nebraska–Lincoln (U)
University of New Orleans (U)
University of Southern Mississippi (U)
Washington State University (U)
Waukesha County Technical College (U)
Western Illinois University (U)

Religious Studies
Barclay College (U)
Bethel Theological Seminary (G)
Concordia University (U)
De Anza College (U)
Eastern Kentucky University (U)
Gordon-Conwell Theological Seminary (G, NC)
Liberty University (U, G)
LIFE Bible College (U)
Manatee Community College (U)
Marywood University (U)
Mercy College (U)
Metropolitan Community College (U)
North Central Bible College (U, NC)
Rutgers, The State University of New Jersey, Newark (U, NC)
Salve Regina University (U, NC)
San Bernardino Valley College (U)
State University of New York Empire State College (U)
Stephens College (U)
Taylor University, Fort Wayne Campus (U)
Temple Baptist Seminary (G, NC)

Thomas Edison State College (U)
University of Delaware (U)
The University of Iowa (U, G)
University of Nebraska–Lincoln (U)
The University of North Carolina at Chapel Hill (U)
University of Tennessee, Knoxville (U)
University of Waterloo (U)
University System of Georgia (U)
Wilfrid Laurier University (U)

Russian Language and Literature
Catonsville Community College (U)
Northern Illinois University (G)
The Ohio State University (U)
State University of New York at Oswego (U)
University of Missouri–Columbia (U)
The University of North Carolina at Chapel Hill (U)
The University of Texas of the Permian Basin (U)
University of Waterloo (U)
University of Wisconsin–Eau Claire (U)
University of Wisconsin–La Crosse (U)

School Psychology
Columbus State University (G)
The Graduate School of America (G)

Sign Language
DeKalb College (U)
Eastern Kentucky University (U)
Floyd College (U)
New River Community College (U)
Palomar College (U)
Pratt Community College and Area Vocational School (U)

Social Psychology
Allegany College of Maryland (U)
Angelina College (U)
Anne Arundel Community College (U)
Athabasca University (U)
Atlantic Community College (U)
Auburn University (U)
Austin Community College (U)
Ball State University (U)
Beaufort County Community College (U)
Berean University of the Assemblies of God (U)
Black Hawk College (U)
Brevard Community College (U)
Brookdale Community College (U)
Bucks County Community College (U)
Butte College (U)
California College for Health Sciences (U, G)
California State University, Fresno (U)
California State University, Hayward (U)
Cape Cod Community College (U)
Carleton University (U)
Catawba Valley Community College (U)
Catonsville Community College (U)
Central Community College–Grand Island Campus (U)
Charles Stewart Mott Community College (U)
Chattanooga State Technical Community College (U)
Chemeketa Community College (U)
City College of San Francisco (U)

City University (U, G)
Clarkson College (U)
Colby Community College (U)
College of DuPage (U)
College of the Southwest (U)
Collin County Community College (U)
Colorado Mountain College District (U)
Concordia University (U)
Concordia University Wisconsin (U, G)
Copiah-Lincoln Community College (G)
Cumberland County College (U)
Cuyahoga Community College, Metropolitan Campus (U)
De Anza College (U)
Delaware Technical & Community College, Stanton/Wilmington Campus (U)
Eastern Washington University (U)
Ellsworth Community College (U)
Evergreen Valley College (U)
Fayetteville Technical Community College (U)
Frostburg State University (U, G)
The Graduate School of America (G)
Grand Rapids Community College (U)
Grand Valley State University (U, G)
Greenville Technical College (U)
Hampton University (U)
Idaho State University (U, G)
Illinois Eastern Community Colleges, Olney Central College (U)
Illinois Valley Community College (U)
Indiana University System (U)
Ivy Tech State College–Wabash Valley (U)
John A. Logan College (U)
John Wood Community College (U)
Kansas State University (U, NC)
Laney College (U)
Lansing Community College (U)
Laurentian University (U)
Lawson State Community College (U)
Lorain County Community College (U)
Los Angeles Community College District (U)
Lycoming College (U)
McDowell Technical Community College (U)
The McGregor School of Antioch University (G)
Memorial University of Newfoundland (U)
Mercy College (U)
Midland College (U)
Milwaukee Area Technical College (U)
MiraCosta College (U)
Missouri Southern State College (U)
Montana State University–Bozeman (G)
Montgomery County Community College (U)
Morgan Community College (U, NC)
New Jersey Institute of Technology (U)
New Mexico Junior College (U)
New River Community College (U)
New School for Social Research (U, NC)
New York Institute of Technology (U)
Northcentral Technical College (U)
Northeast Community College (U)
Northeast Louisiana University (U, G)
Northern Arizona University (U)
North Harris College (U)
North Shore Community College (U)
Northwestern College (U)
Northwestern State University of Louisiana (U)
Northwest Iowa Community College (U)
Odessa College (U)
Ohio University (U)
Old Dominion University (U)

Distance Learning Programs

Individual Courses Index

Social Psychology (continued)
Oregon State University (U)
Park College (U)
Pennsylvania State University University Park Campus (U)
Pensacola Junior College (U)
Phillips Community College of the University of Arkansas (U)
Pikes Peak Community College (U, NC)
Portland State University (U)
Prince George's Community College (U, NC)
Quincy College (U)
Red Rocks Community College (U)
Richland Community College (U)
Riverland Community College (U)
Riverside Community College (U)
Roosevelt University (U)
Rose State College (U)
Saint Joseph's College (U)
St. Petersburg Junior College (U)
Salve Regina University (U, G, NC)
Santa Rosa Junior College (U)
Sierra College (U)
Skagit Valley College (U)
Southeast Community College, Beatrice Campus (U)
Southeast Missouri State University (U)
Southern Illinois University at Carbondale (G)
Southwestern Assemblies of God University (U)
Southwestern Michigan College (U)
Southwest State University (U)
Southwest Texas State University (U)
Southwest Virginia Community College (U)
Stanly Community College (U)
State University of New York Empire State College (U)
Sussex County Community College (U)
Syracuse University (U)
Tacoma Community College (U)
Tallahassee Community College (U)
Tarrant County Junior College (U)
Texas Tech University (U)
Thomas Edison State College (U)
Thomas Nelson Community College (U)
Tulsa Community College (U)
The Union Institute (U)
United States Sports Academy (G, NC)
University of Alaska Fairbanks (U)
University of Alaska Southeast, Sitka Campus (U)
University of Arkansas at Little Rock (U)
University of California Extension (U)
University of California, Santa Barbara (NC)
University of Georgia (U)
University of Great Falls (U)
University of Guelph (U)
University of Hawaii–Maui Community College (U)
University of Houston (U)
University of Illinois at Urbana–Champaign (U)
University of Kansas (U, NC)
University of Kentucky, Elizabethtown Community College (U)
University of Maine (U)
University of Maine at Augusta (U)
University of Maine at Fort Kent (U)
University of Minnesota, Twin Cities Campus (U)
University of Missouri–Columbia (U)
University of Missouri–Kansas City (U)
University of Nebraska at Kearney (U)
University of Nebraska–Lincoln (U)
University of Northern Iowa (U)
University of Oklahoma (U)
University of Southern Colorado (U)
University of Tennessee, Knoxville (U)
University of Utah (U)
University of Washington (U)
University of Waterloo (U)
University of Wisconsin–Stout (G)
University of Wyoming (U)
University System of Georgia (U)
Utah State University (U, G)
Valley City State University (U)
Vincennes University (U)
Vista Community College (U)
Volunteer State Community College (U)
Wake Technical Community College (U)
Walden University (G)
Walters State Community College (U)
Washington State University (U)
Waubonsee Community College (U)
Wayne State University (U)
Weber State University (U)
Wenatchee Valley College (U)
Western Illinois University (U)
Western Oregon University (U)
Westmoreland County Community College (U)
West Virginia University (U)
West Virginia Wesleyan College (U)
Whatcom Community College (U)
Yuba College (U)

Social Sciences
Acadia University (U)
Athabasca University (U)
Ball State University (U)
Bemidji State University (U)
Boise State University (U)
Brigham Young University (U)
Bristol Community College (U)
Buena Vista University (U)
Butte College (U)
California State University, Chico (U)
California State University, Fresno (U)
California State University, Sacramento (U)
California State University, Stanislaus (U)
Carleton University (U)
Central Piedmont Community College (U)
City University (U)
Coastline Community College (U, NC)
Colby Community College (U)
College of DuPage (U)
The College of West Virginia (U)
Concordia University (U)
Copiah-Lincoln Community College (U)
Corning Community College (U)
Danville Area Community College (U)
Daytona Beach Community College (U)
De Anza College (U)
Delaware County Community College (U)
Delta State University (U, G)
Eastern Oregon University (U)
Fullerton College (U)
George C. Wallace State Community College (U)
Grand Rapids Community College (U)
Grayson County College (U)
Great Basin College (U)
Hawkeye Community College (U)
Hibbing Community College (U)
Houston Community College System (U)
Howard Community College (U)
John C. Calhoun State Community College (U)
John Wood Community College (U)
Joliet Junior College (U)
Kellogg Community College (U)
Labette Community College (U)
Lake Michigan College (U)
Lakeshore Technical College (U)
Laurentian University (U)
Long Beach City College (U)
Madonna University (U)
The McGregor School of Antioch University (G)
Memorial University of Newfoundland (U)
Mendocino College (U)
Midwestern State University (U)
Missouri Southern State College (U)
Montgomery County Community College (U)
Mount Saint Vincent University (U)
Murray State University (U)
New School for Social Research (U, NC)
Northampton County Area Community College (U)
North Carolina State University (U)
Northern Essex Community College (U)
North Shore Community College (U)
Oakland Community College (U)
Oakland University (U)
Oklahoma City Community College (U)
Quincy College (U)
Red Rocks Community College (U)
The Richard Stockton College of New Jersey (U)
Rochester Institute of Technology (U)
Roosevelt University (U)
Rose State College (U)
St. Louis Community College (U)
San Bernardino Valley College (U)
San Juan College (U)
Schoolcraft College (U)
Sinclair Community College (U)
Skidmore College (U)
Southwestern Assemblies of God University (U)
Southwestern Michigan College (U)
Southwest State University (U)
State University of New York Empire State College (U)
State University of West Georgia (U)
Syracuse University (G)
Tallahassee Community College (U)
Taylor University, Fort Wayne Campus (U)
Tennessee Temple University (U)
Troy State University Montgomery (U)
The Union Institute (U)
University of Alaska Fairbanks (U)
University of Alaska Southeast, Sitka Campus (U)
University of California Extension (U)
University of Great Falls (U)
University of Hawaii–Maui Community College (U)
University of Kentucky, Ashland Community College (U)
University of Maine at Augusta (U)
University of Maine at Machias (U)
University of Maryland, College Park (U)
University of Minnesota, Twin Cities Campus (NC)
University of Nebraska–Lincoln (U)
University of New Hampshire (U)

Individual Courses Index

University of North Dakota (U)
University of Northern Iowa (U)
The University of Texas at Austin (U)
University of Windsor (U)
University of Wisconsin–Oshkosh (G)
University of Wyoming (U)
Upper Iowa University (U)
Wake Technical Community College (U)
Walden University (G)
Washington State University (U)
Wayne State University (U)
Western Michigan University (U)
Western Oregon University (U, G)
Whatcom Community College (U)
Wilfrid Laurier University (U)
William Rainey Harper College (U)
Wytheville Community College (U)

Social Work

Austin Community College (U)
California College for Health Sciences (G)
California State University, Long Beach (G)
Carleton University (U)
Chadron State College (U)
Charles Stewart Mott Community College (U)
Chattanooga State Technical Community College (U)
City Colleges of Chicago, Harold Washington College (U)
Cleveland State University (G)
Colby Community College (U)
The College of West Virginia (U)
Concordia University (U)
Delaware State University (G)
Dodge City Community College (U)
Florida State University (G)
Fort Hays State University (U, G)
Frostburg State University (U, G)
Garrett Community College (NC)
Governors State University (U, G)
The Graduate School of America (G)
Grand Valley State University (U, G)
Hampton University (U)
Hocking College (U)
Idaho State University (U, G)
Iowa Western Community College (U)
Laurentian University (U)
Lawson State Community College (U)
Loma Linda University (U)
Longview Community College (U)
Marshall University (U, G)
The McGregor School of Antioch University (G)
Memorial University of Newfoundland (U)
Michigan State University (G)
Mississippi Delta Community College (U)
New York Institute of Technology (U)
Northeast Louisiana University (U)
Northern Arizona University (U)
Northwestern Michigan College (U)
Northwestern State University of Louisiana (U)
Pennsylvania State University University Park Campus (U)
Portland State University (U, G)
Rutgers, The State University of New Jersey, Newark (U, NC)
St. Cloud Technical College (U)
Skidmore College (U)
Southeastern Community College, North Campus (U)
Southwestern Oklahoma State University (U)

Southwest State University (U)
State University of New York at Binghamton (G)
Texas A&M University–Commerce (U)
The Union Institute (U)
The University of Akron (G)
University of Alaska Fairbanks (U)
University of Arkansas at Little Rock (NC)
University of Great Falls (U)
University of Hawaii–Maui Community College (U)
University of Houston (G)
The University of Iowa (U, G)
University of Kansas (U, NC)
University of Kentucky (G)
University of Louisville (G)
University of Mary (U)
University of Maryland, Baltimore (G)
University of Minnesota, Twin Cities Campus (U)
University of Missouri–Columbia (U, G)
University of Missouri–Kansas City (U)
University of Nebraska at Kearney (U)
University of North Dakota (U, G)
University of Northern Iowa (U, G)
University of St. Thomas (G)
University of South Carolina (U, G)
University of Southern Colorado (U)
University of Tennessee, Knoxville (G)
University of Washington (G)
University of Waterloo (U)
Utah State University (U)
Volunteer State Community College (U)
Walden University (G)
Walters State Community College (U)
Waubonsee Community College (U)
Weber State University (U)
Western Michigan University (U)
West Virginia University (G)
Wilfrid Laurier University (U)

Sociology

Adams State College (U)
Allegany College of Maryland (U)
Angelina College (U)
Anne Arundel Community College (U)
Arapahoe Community College (U)
Athabasca University (U)
Atlantic Community College (U)
Auburn University (U)
Austin Community College (U)
Bakersfield College (U)
Ball State University (U)
Beaufort County Community College (U)
Bellevue Community College (U)
Bemidji State University (U)
Berean University of the Assemblies of God (U)
Bergen Community College (U)
Black Hawk College (U)
Blinn College (U)
Bloomsburg University of Pennsylvania (U)
Bluefield State College (U)
Boise State University (U)
Brevard Community College (U)
Brigham Young University (U)
Bristol Community College (U)
Brookdale Community College (U)
Broward Community College (U)
Burlington County College (U)
California State University, Chico (U)
California State University, Sacramento (U)

California State University, Stanislaus (U)
Camden County College (U)
Cape Cod Community College (U)
Carleton University (U)
Carl Sandburg College (U)
Catawba Valley Community College (U)
Catonsville Community College (U)
Central Arizona College (U)
Central Community College–Grand Island Campus (U)
Central Florida Community College (U)
Central Michigan University (U)
Central Piedmont Community College (U)
Central Virginia Community College (U)
Central Wyoming College (U)
Cerritos College (U)
Chadron State College (U)
Champlain College (U)
Charles County Community College (U)
Charles Stewart Mott Community College (U)
Charter Oak State College (U)
Chattanooga State Technical Community College (U)
Chippewa Valley Technical College (U)
Christopher Newport University (U)
Citrus College (U)
City Colleges of Chicago, Harold Washington College (U)
City University (U)
Clackamas Community College (U)
Clarkson College (U)
Clatsop Community College (U)
Clayton College & State University (U)
Clovis Community College (U)
Coastline Community College (U, NC)
Colby Community College (U)
College Misericordia (U)
College of DuPage (U)
College of St. Scholastica (U, G)
College of San Mateo (U)
College of the Canyons (U)
College of the Southwest (U)
The College of West Virginia (U)
Collin County Community College (U)
Colorado Electronic Community College (U)
Colorado Mountain College District (U)
Colorado Northwestern Community College (U)
Colorado State University (U)
Columbia Basin College (U)
Columbia-Greene Community College (U)
Community College of Philadelphia (U)
Community College of Rhode Island (U)
Concordia University (U)
Contra Costa College (U)
County College of Morris (U)
Crafton Hills College (U)
Cumberland County College (U)
Cuyahoga Community College, Metropolitan Campus (U)
Cuyamaca College (U)
Dallas County Community College District (U)
Dawson Community College (U)
De Anza College (U)
DeKalb College (U)
Delaware County Community College (U)
Delaware Technical & Community College, Jack F. Owens Campus (U)
Delaware Technical & Community College, Stanton/Wilmington Campus (U)
Delta College (U)

Distance Learning Programs

601

Individual Courses Index

Sociology (continued)

Des Moines Area Community College (U)
East Central Community College (U)
Eastern Idaho Technical College (U)
Eastern Kentucky University (U)
Eastern Michigan University (U)
Eastern New Mexico University (U, G)
Eastern Wyoming College (U)
Edison Community College (U)
Edison State Community College (U)
Ellsworth Community College (U)
El Paso Community College (U)
Essex Community College (U)
Evergreen Valley College (U)
Fayetteville Technical Community College (U)
Fitchburg State College (U)
Florence-Darlington Technical College (U)
Florida Community College at Jacksonville (U)
Floyd College (U)
Fort Hays State University (U, G)
Front Range Community College (U)
Gadsden State Community College (U)
Galveston College (U)
Garland County Community College (U)
Gateway Technical College (U)
Genesee Community College (U)
Georgia Southern University (U, G)
Glendale Community College (U)
Governors State University (U, G)
Graceland College (U)
The Graduate School of America (G)
Grand Rapids Community College (U)
Grand Valley State University (U, G)
Greenville Technical College (U)
Griggs University (U)
Hampton University (U)
Harrisburg Area Community College (U)
Hibbing Community College (U)
Highland Community College (U)
Hillsborough Community College (U)
Houston Community College System (U)
Hudson Valley Community College (U)
Idaho State University (U, G)
Illinois Central College (U)
Illinois Valley Community College (U)
Indiana University System (U)
Iowa Wesleyan College (U)
Iowa Western Community College (U)
Ivy Tech State College–Northcentral (U)
Ivy Tech State College–Wabash Valley (U)
Jacksonville State University (U)
Jamestown Community College (U)
Jefferson College (U)
Jefferson Community College (U)
Jefferson State Community College (U)
John C. Calhoun State Community College (U)
Johnson County Community College (U)
Joliet Junior College (U)
J. Sargeant Reynolds Community College (U)
Judson College (U)
Kansas State University (U, NC)
Kaskaskia College (U)
Kellogg Community College (U)
Lackawanna Junior College (U)
Lafayette College (U)
Lakehead University (U)
Lake Land College (U)
Lakeland Community College (U)
Lake Michigan College (U)
Lakeshore Technical College (U)
Lamar University (U)
Lane Community College (U)
Laney College (U)
Lansing Community College (U)
Laramie County Community College (U)
Lassen College (U)
Laurentian University (U)
Lawson State Community College (U)
Lee College (U)
Lehigh Carbon Community College (U)
Lincoln Land Community College (U)
Long Beach City College (U)
Longview Community College (U)
Lorain County Community College (U)
Lord Fairfax Community College (U)
Los Angeles Community College District (U)
Louisiana College (U)
Louisiana State University and Agricultural and Mechanical College (U)
Louisiana State University at Eunice (U)
Loyola University New Orleans (U)
Luzerne County Community College (U)
Lycoming College (U)
Madison Area Technical College (U)
Marshall University (U, G)
Marywood University (U)
McCook Community College (U)
McDowell Technical Community College (U)
The McGregor School of Antioch University (G)
Memorial University of Newfoundland (U)
Mendocino College (U)
Mercy College (U)
Metropolitan Community College (U)
Metropolitan Community College (U)
Mid-Plains Community College (U)
Mid-State Technical College (U)
Midwestern State University (U)
Milwaukee Area Technical College (U)
Minnesota West Community and Technical College–Worthington Campus (U)
Minot State University (U)
MiraCosta College (U)
Missouri Southern State College (U)
Modesto Junior College (U)
Montgomery College–Rockville Campus (U)
Montgomery County Community College (U)
Moraine Valley Community College (U)
Morgan Community College (U, NC)
Mount Saint Vincent University (U)
Mt. San Antonio College (U)
Mount Wachusett Community College (U)
Nassau Community College (U)
New Hampshire College (U)
New Mexico Junior College (U)
New River Community College (U)
New School for Social Research (U, NC)
New York Institute of Technology (U)
Nicholls State University (U)
North Carolina State University (U)
North Central Bible College (U, NC)
Northcentral Technical College (U)
North Central Texas College (U)
North Dakota State College of Science (U)
Northeast Community College (U)
Northeast Louisiana University (U)
Northeast Wisconsin Technical College (U)
Northern Arizona University (U)
Northern Kentucky University (U)
Northern Oklahoma College (U)
Northern State University (U)
Northern Virginia Community College (U)
North Harris College (U)
North Iowa Area Community College (U)
North Shore Community College (U)
Northwestern College (U)
Northwestern Michigan College (U)
Northwestern State University of Louisiana (U)
Northwest Iowa Community College (U)
Oakland University (U)
Oakton Community College (U)
Odessa College (U)
Ohio University (U)
Ohio University–Eastern (U)
Oklahoma City Community College (U)
Oklahoma State University (U)
Old Dominion University (U)
Oregon State University (U)
Owens Community College (U)
Palomar College (U)
Parkland College (U)
Pennsylvania State University University Park Campus (U)
Pensacola Junior College (U)
Piedmont College (U)
Pikes Peak Community College (U, NC)
Pima Community College (U)
Polytechnic University, Brooklyn Campus (G, NC)
Portland Community College (U)
Portland State University (U)
Prairie State College (U)
Prince George's Community College (U, NC)
Pueblo Community College (U)
Quincy College (U)
Redlands Community College (U)
Red Rocks Community College (U)
Regis University (U)
The Richard Stockton College of New Jersey (U)
Richland Community College (U)
Rio Salado College (U)
Riverland Community College (U)
Riverside Community College (U)
Rochester Institute of Technology (U)
Rockland Community College (U)
Rogers University (U)
Roger Williams University (U)
Rose State College (U)
Ryerson Polytechnic University (U)
Sacramento City College (U)
St. Cloud Technical College (U)
St. Johns River Community College (U)
Saint Joseph's College (U)
St. Louis Community College (U)
St. Petersburg Junior College (U)
Salt Lake Community College (U)
San Antonio College (U)
San Bernardino Valley College (U)
Sandhills Community College (U)
San Jose State University (U)
Santa Fe Community College (U)
Santa Rosa Junior College (U)
Sauk Valley Community College (U)
Schoolcraft College (U)
Scott Community College (U)
Seattle Central Community College (U)
Seminole State College (U)
Shelby State Community College (U)
Sierra College (U)
Sinclair Community College (U)
Skagit Valley College (U)

Individual Courses Index

Skidmore College (U)
Southeast Arkansas Technical College (U)
Southeast Community College, Lincoln Campus (U)
Southeastern Louisiana University (U)
Southern Illinois University at Carbondale (G)
Southern West Virginia Community and Technical College (U)
South Florida Community College (U)
Southwestern Assemblies of God University (U)
Southwestern Michigan College (U)
Southwestern Oklahoma State University (U)
Southwest State University (U)
Southwest Texas State University (U)
Southwest Virginia Community College (U)
State Technical Institute at Memphis (U)
State University of New York at New Paltz (U)
State University of New York Empire State College (U)
State University of West Georgia (U)
Suffolk County Community College–Ammerman Campus (U)
Sul Ross State University (U)
Syracuse University (U)
Tacoma Community College (U)
Tallahassee Community College (U)
Tarrant County Junior College (U)
Tennessee Technological University (U)
Tennessee Temple University (U)
Texas A&M University–Commerce (U)
Texas Tech University (U)
Thomas Edison State College (U)
Thomas Nelson Community College (U)
Tidewater Community College (U)
Towson University (U)
Treasure Valley Community College (U)
Triton College (U)
Troy State University Dothan (U)
Troy State University Montgomery (U)
Tulsa Community College (U)
Tyler Junior College (U)
Umpqua Community College (U)
The Union Institute (U)
Universitè Laval (U)
University of Alaska Anchorage (U)
University of Alaska Fairbanks (U)
University of Alaska Southeast, Sitka Campus (U)
The University of Calgary (U)
University of California Extension (U)
University of California, Santa Barbara (U, NC)
University of Cincinnati (U)
University of Cincinnati Raymond Walters College (U)
University of Delaware (U)
University of Georgia (U)
University of Great Falls (U)
University of Hawaii–Maui Community College (U)
University of Houston (U)
University of Illinois at Urbana–Champaign (U)
The University of Iowa (U, G)
University of Kansas (U, NC)
University of Kentucky, Elizabethtown Community College (U)
University of Kentucky, Henderson Community College (U)
University of Kentucky, Madisonville Community College (U)
University of Maine (U)
University of Maine at Augusta (U)
University of Maine at Fort Kent (U)
University of Mary (U)
University of Maryland University College (U)
University of Massachusetts Lowell (U)
The University of Memphis (U)
University of Minnesota, Twin Cities Campus (U)
University of Missouri–Columbia (U, G)
University of Missouri–Kansas City (U, G)
University of Nebraska at Kearney (U)
University of Nebraska–Lincoln (U)
University of Nevada, Las Vegas (U)
University of New Brunswick (U)
The University of North Carolina at Chapel Hill (U)
University of Northern Iowa (U, G)
University of Oklahoma (U)
University of South Dakota (U, G)
University of Southern Colorado (U)
University of Southern Mississippi (U)
University of South Florida (U)
The University of Texas at Tyler (U)
The University of Texas of the Permian Basin (U)
University of the State of New York, Regents College (U)
University of Toledo (U)
University of Washington (U)
University of Waterloo (U)
University of Windsor (U)
University of Wyoming (U)
University System of Georgia (U)
Upper Iowa University (U)
Utah State University (U)
Victor Valley College (U)
Vincennes University (U)
Vista Community College (U)
Volunteer State Community College (U)
Walters State Community College (U)
Washington State University (U)
Washtenaw Community College (U)
Waubonsee Community College (U)
Waukesha County Technical College (U)
Wayne County Community College (U)
Wayne State University (U)
Weber State University (U)
Western Illinois University (U)
Western Nebraska Community College (U)
Western Oklahoma State College (U)
Western Washington University (U)
Westmoreland County Community College (U)
West Virginia University (U)
West Virginia Wesleyan College (U)
Whatcom Community College (U)
Wichita State University (U)
Wilfrid Laurier University (U)
Wilkes Community College (U)
William Penn College (U)
William Rainey Harper College (U)
Xavier University of Louisiana (U)

Spanish Language and Literature
Austin Community College (U)
Brigham Young University (U)
Cabrillo College (U)
Catonsville Community College (U)
Central Arizona College (U)
Central Community College–Grand Island Campus (U)
Central Florida Community College (U)
Central Michigan University (U)
Christopher Newport University (U)
Clovis Community College (U)
College of St. Francis (U)
Colorado Mountain College District (U)
Colorado Northwestern Community College (U)
Columbus State Community College (U)
De Anza College (U)
Delaware Technical & Community College, Jack F. Owens Campus (U)
El Paso Community College (U, NC)
Essex Community College (U)
Greenville Technical College (U)
Houston Community College System (U)
Iowa State University of Science and Technology (U)
Jefferson College (U)
Joliet Junior College (U)
Kellogg Community College (U)
Kingwood College (U)
Lee College (U)
Madison Area Technical College (U)
Marywood University (U)
Metropolitan Community College (U)
Metropolitan State College of Denver (U)
Northern Virginia Community College (U)
Oakton Community College (U)
Oklahoma State University (U)
Palomar College (U)
Pratt Community College and Area Vocational School (U)
Rio Salado College (U)
Seattle Central Community College (U)
Sinclair Community College (U)
Southeast Community College, Lincoln Campus (U)
Southwest Missouri State University (U)
State Technical Institute at Memphis (U)
Texas Tech University (U, NC)
Thomas Edison State College (U)
Treasure Valley Community College (U)
Troy State University Montgomery (U)
Tyler Junior College (U)
University of Houston (U, G)
University of Illinois at Urbana–Champaign (U)
The University of Iowa (U)
University of Kentucky, Elizabethtown Community College (U)
University of Maryland University College (U)
University of Missouri–Columbia (U)
University of Nebraska–Lincoln (U)
The University of North Carolina at Chapel Hill (U)
University of Tennessee, Knoxville (U)
The University of Texas at San Antonio (U, G)
University of Virginia (G)
University of Washington (U)
University of Waterloo (U)
University System of Georgia (U)
Upper Iowa University (U)
Valley City State University (U)
Western Illinois University (U)
Wilfrid Laurier University (U)
Yuba College (U)

Special Education
Arizona State University West (U, G)
Arkansas Tech University (U)
Ball State University (G)

Distance Learning Programs

Individual Courses Index

Special Education (continued)
California College for Health Sciences (U)
California State University, Sacramento (G)
Central Missouri State University (U, G, NC)
Chadron State College (U)
City University (G)
College Misericordia (G, NC)
College of the Southwest (U)
Colorado Northwestern Community College (U)
Columbus State University (G)
Daytona Beach Community College (U)
De Anza College (U)
Delaware State University (U)
Delta State University (U, G)
Drake University (G)
Eastern Kentucky University (U)
East Tennessee State University (U)
Fort Hays State University (U, G)
Georgia Southern University (U, G)
Governors State University (U, G)
The Graduate School of America (G)
Grand Canyon University (G)
Grand Valley State University (U, G)
Hampton University (U, G)
Idaho State University (U, G)
Illinois Eastern Community Colleges, Olney Central College (U)
Jacksonville State University (U)
Lakehead University (G)
Lamar University (U, G)
Louisiana State University at Eunice (G)
Louisiana State University in Shreveport (U, G)
Marshall University (U, G)
The McGregor School of Antioch University (G)
Memorial University of Newfoundland (U)
Metropolitan Community College (U)
Middle Tennessee State University (U, G)
Mohawk Valley Community College (U)
Morehead State University (U, G)
New Mexico Junior College (U)
New Mexico State University (G)
Nicholls State University (G)
Northeast Louisiana University (U, G)
Northern Kentucky University (U)
North Georgia College & State University (U, G)
Northwestern State University of Louisiana (U, G, NC)
Northwest Iowa Community College (U)
Ohio University–Southern Campus (U)
Old Dominion University (G)
Oral Roberts University (G)
Portland State University (U, G)
St. Cloud Technical College (G)
San Jose State University (U, G)
Seattle Pacific University (G)
Seton Hall University (G)
Shelby State Community College (U)
Southeast Community College, Beatrice Campus (U)
Southeastern Louisiana University (U, G)
Southern Oregon University (G)
Southwest Virginia Community College (U)
State University of New York at Buffalo (NC)
State University of West Georgia (U, G)
Texas A&M University–Commerce (U, G, NC)
Texas Tech University (G)
The University of Alabama at Birmingham (U)
University of Alaska Anchorage (U, G)
University of Alaska Fairbanks (U, G)
The University of Calgary (U, G)
University of Great Falls (U)
University of Kansas (U, G, NC)
University of Kentucky (G)
University of Louisville (G)
University of Maine (U, G)
University of Maine at Farmington (U)
University of Maine at Fort Kent (U, G)
The University of Memphis (U, G)
University of Mississippi (U, G)
University of Missouri–Columbia (G)
University of Nebraska at Kearney (U, G)
University of Nevada, Las Vegas (U)
University of Nevada, Reno (U, G)
University of New Brunswick (U, G)
University of New Orleans (U, G)
University of North Carolina at Charlotte (G)
University of North Dakota (G)
University of Northern Colorado (U, G)
University of Oklahoma (U)
University of Sarasota (G)
University of South Dakota (G)
University of Southern Indiana (U)
University of South Florida (G)
The University of Tennessee at Martin (U, G)
University of Tennessee, Knoxville (U)
The University of Texas at Tyler (U, G)
University of Utah (U)
University of Wisconsin–Stevens Point (U, G)
University of Wisconsin–Whitewater (U, G)
University of Wyoming (G)
Utah State University (U)
Waubonsee Community College (U)
Western Illinois University (U, G)
West Virginia University (G)

Statistics
Adams State College (U)
Atlantic Community College (U)
Brigham Young University (U)
Bucks County Community College (U)
California State University, Sacramento (U)
Central Michigan University (U)
Central Piedmont Community College (U)
Champlain College (U)
Charles County Community College (U)
Christopher Newport University (U)
City Colleges of Chicago, Harold Washington College (U)
Colorado Electronic Community College (U)
Colorado Mountain College District (U)
Colorado Northwestern Community College (U)
De Anza College (U)
Delaware Technical & Community College, Stanton/Wilmington Campus (U)
Duke University (G)
Edison Community College (U)
Embry-Riddle Aeronautical University, Extended Campus (U)
Genesee Community College (U)
Grand Rapids Community College (U)
Jefferson Davis Community College (U)
John C. Calhoun State Community College (U)
Kansas State University (U, G, NC)
Lake Land College (U)
Laramie County Community College (U)
Lassen College (U)
Lehigh Carbon Community College (U)
Loyola University New Orleans (U)
Madison Area Technical College (U)
Manatee Community College (U)
Marywood University (U)
Mercy College (U)
Metropolitan State College of Denver (U)
Midland College (U)
New Hampshire College (U)
New River Community College (U)
New York Institute of Technology (U)
Northwestern College (U)
Oklahoma State University (U)
Owens Community College (U)
Park College (U)
Portland State University (U)
Seattle Central Community College (U)
State University of New York at Oswego (U)
State University of New York Empire State College (U)
Stephens College (U)
Syracuse University (U)
Triton College (U)
The University of Alabama in Huntsville (NC)
University of Alaska Fairbanks (U)
University of Idaho (U)
The University of Iowa (U, G)
University of Minnesota, Twin Cities Campus (U)
University of Missouri–Columbia (U)
University of Nebraska–Lincoln (U)
The University of North Carolina at Chapel Hill (U)
University of Tennessee, Knoxville (U)
University of the State of New York, Regents College (U)
University of Toledo (U)
University of Waterloo (U)
University System of Georgia (U)
Upper Iowa University (U)
Waubonsee Community College (U)
Western Washington University (U)

Student Counseling
City University (G)
Eastern Kentucky University (G)
The Graduate School of America (G)
Michigan State University (G)
Pratt Community College and Area Vocational School (U, G)
State University of West Georgia (U)

Substance Abuse Counseling
Lake Land College (U)
Pratt Community College and Area Vocational School (U)
St. Louis Community College (U)
University of Southern Colorado (U)
Upper Iowa University (U)
Western Michigan University (U)

Surveying
Metropolitan State College of Denver (U)
Michigan Technological University (U, NC)

Teacher Education
Anne Arundel Community College (U)
Arizona State University (G)
Arkansas Tech University (U)
Ball State University (G)
Bemidji State University (U, G)

Individual Courses Index

Black Hills State University (U, G)
Bluefield State College (U)
Boise State University (U)
California College for Health Sciences (U)
California State University, Dominguez Hills (U, G)
California State University, Fresno (U, G)
California State University, Hayward (U)
California State University, Los Angeles (U, NC)
California State University, Sacramento (G)
Calvin College (G)
Carl Sandburg College (U)
Catawba Valley Community College (U)
Central Methodist College (U, G)
Central Missouri State University (U, G, NC)
Central Washington University (U)
Cerritos College (U)
Chadron State College (U, G)
Charles County Community College (U)
Chattanooga State Technical Community College (U)
Chippewa Valley Technical College (U, NC)
Christopher Newport University (U, G)
College Misericordia (G, NC)
College of DuPage (U)
College of St. Francis (U)
College of St. Scholastica (G)
College of the Southwest (U)
The College of West Virginia (U)
Colorado Mountain College District (U)
Colorado Northwestern Community College (U)
Colorado State University (G)
Columbus State University (G)
Concordia College (U)
Concordia University (U, G)
Concordia University (U)
Dakota State University (U)
Dawson Community College (U)
Daytona Beach Community College (U)
Delaware State University (U)
Delta State University (U, G)
Des Moines Area Community College (U)
Drake University (G)
Eastern Idaho Technical College (U)
Eastern Illinois University (G)
Eastern Kentucky University (U)
Eastern Michigan University (G)
Eastern Oregon University (U)
Eastern Washington University (U)
East Tennessee State University (G)
Fairleigh Dickinson University, Florham-Madison Campus (U)
Fairleigh Dickinson University, Teaneck–Hackensack (G)
Fitchburg State College (G)
Florence-Darlington Technical College (U)
Florida State University (G)
Fort Hays State University (U, G)
Front Range Community College (U)
Garland County Community College (U)
Georgia Southern University (U, G)
Governors State University (U)
Grand Canyon University (G)
Grand Valley State University (U, G)
Great Basin College (U)
Hampton University (U, G)
Idaho State University (U, G)
Illinois Eastern Community Colleges, Olney Central College (U)
Indiana University System (U, G)

Indiana Wesleyan University (G)
Iowa State University of Science and Technology (G)
Jacksonville State University (G)
John Wood Community College (U)
Kaskaskia College (G)
Lakehead University (U)
Lamar University (U, G)
Longview Community College (U)
Lorain County Community College (U)
Louisiana State University and Agricultural and Mechanical College (G)
Louisiana State University in Shreveport (U, G)
Lycoming College (U)
Marshall University (U, G)
Marygrove College (G)
The McGregor School of Antioch University (G)
Memorial University of Newfoundland (U)
Metropolitan Community College (U)
Metropolitan State College of Denver (U)
Michigan State University (G)
Middle Tennessee State University (U)
Midwestern State University (G)
Minot State University (G)
Mississippi Delta Community College (NC)
Mohawk Valley Community College (U)
Montana State University–Bozeman (G)
Morehead State University (U, G)
Morris Brown College (U)
Mount Saint Vincent University (U, G)
New Mexico Junior College (U)
New Mexico State University (G)
New School for Social Research (U, G, NC)
North Carolina State University (G)
North Central Bible College (U, NC)
Northeast Community College (U)
Northeast Louisiana University (U, G)
Northern Arizona University (U, G)
Northern Kentucky University (U, G)
North Georgia College & State University (U)
Northwestern State University of Louisiana (U, G, NC)
Northwest Iowa Community College (U)
Ohio University–Southern Campus (U)
Oklahoma State University (U)
Old Dominion University (G)
Oral Roberts University (G)
Oregon State University (G)
Pennsylvania State University University Park Campus (G)
Penn Valley Community College (U)
Portland State University (U, G)
Pratt Community College and Area Vocational School (U, G)
Red Rocks Community College (U)
The Richard Stockton College of New Jersey (NC)
Riverside Community College (U)
Rosemont College (G)
Rutgers, The State University of New Jersey, Newark (U, G, NC)
St. Cloud Technical College (G)
Saint Peter's College (G)
San Diego State University (U, G)
San Jose State University (U, G)
Savannah State University (U)
Seattle Pacific University (G)
Seton Hall University (G)
Shenandoah University (G)

Southeast Community College, Beatrice Campus (U)
Southern Oregon University (G)
Southern Utah University (U, G)
Southwestern Assemblies of God University (U)
Southwestern Oklahoma State University (G)
Southwest Missouri State University (G)
Southwest State University (U, G)
Southwest Virginia Community College (U)
State University of New York at Buffalo (G, NC)
State University of New York at Oswego (U)
State University of West Georgia (U, G)
Stephens College (U)
Temple Baptist Seminary (G, NC)
Tennessee State University (G)
Tennessee Technological University (U, G)
Texas A&M University–Commerce (U, G, NC)
Texas Tech University (U, NC)
Towson University (U, G)
University of Alaska Fairbanks (U, G)
University of Alaska Southeast (U)
University of Alaska Southeast, Sitka Campus (U)
University of Arkansas at Little Rock (U)
The University of Calgary (U, G)
University of Delaware (U, G)
University of Georgia (U)
University of Great Falls (U)
University of Hawaii–Maui Community College (U)
University of Idaho (U, G)
University of Illinois at Springfield (U, G)
University of Kansas (U, G, NC)
University of Maine (U, G)
University of Maine at Fort Kent (U, G)
The University of Memphis (U, G)
University of Minnesota, Twin Cities Campus (U)
University of Missouri–Columbia (G)
University of Missouri–St. Louis (U)
The University of Montana–Missoula (G)
University of Nebraska at Kearney (U, G)
University of Nebraska–Lincoln (U, G)
University of Nevada, Las Vegas (U)
University of Nevada, Reno (U, G)
University of New Brunswick (U, G)
University of New England (G)
University of New Hampshire (NC)
University of New Orleans (U, G)
University of North Dakota (G)
University of Northern Colorado (G)
University of Northern Iowa (U, G)
University of Pittsburgh (G)
University of Saskatchewan (U)
University of South Carolina (G)
University of South Dakota (U, G)
University of Southern California (G, NC)
University of Southern Colorado (U, G)
University of South Florida (G)
The University of Tennessee at Martin (U, G)
University of Tennessee, Knoxville (U)
The University of Texas at Tyler (U, G)
University of the State of New York, Regents College (U)
University of Utah (U)
University of Vermont (U)
University of Virginia (G, NC)
University of Washington (U)
University of West Florida (U, G)
University of Wisconsin–La Crosse (U, G)

Distance Learning Programs

Individual Courses Index

Teacher Education (continued)
University of Wisconsin–River Falls (U, G, NC)
University of Wisconsin–Stevens Point (U, G)
University of Wisconsin–Stout (G, NC)
University of Wisconsin–Whitewater (U, G)
University of Wyoming (G)
University System of Georgia (U)
Utah State University (U)
Valley City State University (U)
Walden University (G)
Walters State Community College (U)
Western Illinois University (U, G)
Western Montana College of The University of Montana (U, NC)
Western Oregon University (U, G)

Technical Writing
Austin Community College (U)
Brigham Young University (U)
Charles County Community College (U)
Charles Stewart Mott Community College (U)
Columbia Basin College (U)
Columbus State Community College (U)
Community College of Vermont (U)
De Anza College (U)
Delaware Technical & Community College, Stanton/Wilmington Campus (U)
East Carolina University (U)
Edison State Community College (U)
Embry-Riddle Aeronautical University, Extended Campus (U)
Genesee Community College (U)
Judson College (U)
Mid-State Technical College (U)
New York Institute of Technology (U, NC)
Northern Virginia Community College (U)
Oklahoma State University (U)
Park College (U)
Polytechnic University, Westchester Graduate Center (G)
St. Thomas Aquinas College (NC)
Texas Tech University (U, NC)
University of Arkansas at Little Rock (U)
University of Illinois at Urbana–Champaign (U)
University of Massachusetts Dartmouth (G)
University of Missouri–Columbia (U)
University of Nebraska–Lincoln (U)
University of Tennessee, Knoxville (U)
University of Washington (U)
University of Waterloo (U)
Washington State University (U)
Western Illinois University (U)

Telecommunications
City University (G)
Hudson Valley Community College (U)
Indiana University System (G)
Michigan State University (G)
National Technological University (G, NC)
New York Institute of Technology (U)
Rochester Institute of Technology (U, G)
Salt Lake Community College (U)
Southern Illinois University at Carbondale (U)
State University of New York Empire State College (U)
Texas Tech University (U, NC)
University of Colorado at Boulder (G, NC)
University of Dallas (G)
University of Maryland University College (G)
University of Massachusetts Dartmouth (NC)
University of Pennsylvania (G)
Western Illinois University (G)

Theological Studies
Acadia University (U)
Assemblies of God Theological Seminary (G, NC)
Berean University of the Assemblies of God (U, G, NC)
Bethel Theological Seminary (G)
Central Baptist Theological Seminary (G, NC)
Chapman University (U)
Cincinnati Bible College and Seminary (U)
Clatsop Community College (U)
Columbia International University (U, G, NC)
Concordia University (U, G)
Concordia University (U)
Concordia University at Austin (U, NC)
Covenant Theological Seminary (G, NC)
Dallas Theological Seminary (G, NC)
Denver Conservative Baptist Seminary (G, NC)
Franciscan University of Steubenville (U, G, NC)
Gordon-Conwell Theological Seminary (G, NC)
Grand Rapids Baptist Seminary (G)
Griggs University (U)
International Bible College (U)
Johnson Bible College (G)
Judson College (U)
Lafayette College (U)
Lassen College (U)
Lincoln Christian College (U, G, NC)
Louisiana College (U)
Loyola University New Orleans (U)
The McGregor School of Antioch University (G)
Moody Bible Institute (U, NC)
Mount Saint Vincent University (U, NC)
North Central Bible College (U, NC)
Northeast Louisiana University (U)
Northwestern College (U)
Oral Roberts University (U)
Oregon State University (U)
Parkland College (U)
Reformed Theological Seminary (G, NC)
Seabury-Western Theological Seminary (G, NC)
Southern Christian University (U, G, NC)
Southwestern Assemblies of God University (U)
Southwestern Baptist Theological Seminary (U, G, NC)
Taylor University, Fort Wayne Campus (U)
Temple Baptist Seminary (G, NC)
Tennessee Temple University (U)
Trinity International University (G)
Universitè Laval (U)
University of Georgia (U)
University of Great Falls (U)
University of Kansas (U, NC)
University of Mary (U)
University of Minnesota, Twin Cities Campus (U)
University of Missouri–Columbia (U, NC)
University System of Georgia (U)
Waubonsee Community College (U)
Western Conservative Baptist Seminary (G, NC)
Wheaton College (G, NC)

Veterinary Science
University of Georgia (NC)

Visual and Performing Arts
Ball State University (U)
Boise State University (U)
Brevard Community College (U)
California State University, Fresno (U)
California State University, Stanislaus (U)
Calvin College (G)
Central Arizona College (U)
Central Michigan University (U)
Central Wyoming College (U)
Colorado Mountain College District (U)
Darton College (U)
Daytona Beach Community College (U)
Eastern Idaho Technical College (U)
Eastern Oregon University (U)
Fairleigh Dickinson University, Florham-Madison Campus (U)
Grand Rapids Community College (U)
Hibbing Community College (U)
Jefferson State Community College (U)
John C. Calhoun State Community College (U)
Labette Community College (U)
Lassen College (U)
Lehigh Carbon Community College (U)
The McGregor School of Antioch University (G)
Minnesota West Community and Technical College–Worthington Campus (U)
Missouri Southern State College (U)
Nicholls State University (U)
North Carolina State University (U)
Northeast Community College (U)
North Shore Community College (U)
Oklahoma City Community College (U)
Oklahoma State University (U)
Palomar College (U)
Pennsylvania State University University Park Campus (U)
Pueblo Community College (U)
The Richard Stockton College of New Jersey (U)
St. Louis Community College (U)
Santa Fe Community College (U)
Sauk Valley Community College (U)
Skidmore College (U)
Southwest State University (U)
Southwest Texas State University (U)
Suffolk County Community College–Ammerman Campus (U)
The Union Institute (U)
University of Central Oklahoma (U, G)
University of Georgia (U)
University of Great Falls (U)
University of Hawaii–Maui Community College (U)
University of Houston (U)
The University of Iowa (U, G)
University of Minnesota, Twin Cities Campus (U)
University of Missouri–Columbia (U)
University of Nebraska–Lincoln (U)
University of North Dakota (U)
University of Oklahoma (NC)
The University of Texas at Austin (U)
The University of Texas of the Permian Basin (U)
University of Wisconsin–Stout (NC)
University System of Georgia (U)
Upper Iowa University (U)

Individual Courses Index

Women's Studies
Arizona State University (U)
Bluefield State College (U)
Christopher Newport University (U)
Cuyahoga Community College, Metropolitan Campus (U)
Eastern Washington University (U)
Genesee Community College (U)
Indiana University System (U)
Judson College (U)
Kansas State University (U, G, NC)
Lane Community College (U)
Laramie County Community College (U)
Memorial University of Newfoundland (U)
Metropolitan State College of Denver (U)
Seattle Central Community College (U)
Thomas Edison State College (U)
The University of Iowa (U, G)
University of Michigan (U)
University of Missouri–Columbia (U)
University of Waterloo (U)
University of Wisconsin–La Crosse (U)
University System of Georgia (U)
Washington State University (U)
Western Washington University (U)
West Virginia Wesleyan College (U)

Zoology
Arizona State University (U)
Central Wyoming College (U)
College of the Southwest (U)
Colorado State University (U)
Garland County Community College (U)
Idaho State University (U, G)
Iowa State University of Science and Technology (U)
Laramie County Community College (U)
Louisiana State University in Shreveport (U, G)
Ohio University–Eastern (U)
Rend Lake College (U)
Shawnee Community College (U)
Skidmore College (U)
Southwest State University (U)
Texas Tech University (U)
University of Nebraska at Kearney (U)
University of Southern Mississippi (U)
Washington State University (U)
Western Illinois University (U, G)
Western Oklahoma State College (U)

Distance Learning Programs

STUDENT PROFILE

Samuel Krosney

Personal: Age 23, single

Home: Tallahassee, Florida

College: University of California-Berkeley

Courses Taken: Critical thinking

Academic Goals: To earn a B.A. in English from University of Northern Colorado

"I had almost given up on the idea of earning a college degree, but thought I'd give it one more try by taking a course over the Internet. Although it was a little difficult at first to learn the techniques for getting on-line, it was well worth it. For one thing, I've learned to write with a word processor, which is a completely different experience than pen and paper. For another thing, it's the most personable class I've ever had. All your contact with your professor is one-on-one, with all his comments addressed directly to you via e-mail. The course itself really challenged me to look at all sides of an issue before forming an opinion.

"Distance learning changed my attitude about going to college. I now want to study creative writing and journalism and hope to attend the University of Northern Colorado as an English major."

GEOGRAPHIC INDEX

Alabama
Auburn University, 9
Community College of the Air Force, 68
Gadsden State Community College, 99
George C. Wallace State Community College, 102
International Bible College, 121
Jacksonville State University, 125
Jefferson Davis Community College, 126
Jefferson State Community College, 127
John C. Calhoun State Community College, 127
Judson College, 130
Lawson State Community College, 141
Southern Christian University, 248
Troy State University, 278
Troy State University Dothan, 279
Troy State University Montgomery, 279
United States Sports Academy, 282
The University of Alabama, 283
The University of Alabama at Birmingham, 284
The University of Alabama in Huntsville, 285

Alaska
University of Alaska Anchorage, 286
University of Alaska Fairbanks, 286
University of Alaska Southeast, 287
University of Alaska Southeast, Sitka Campus, 288

Arizona
Arizona State University, 5
Arizona State University West, 5
Central Arizona College, 38
Grand Canyon University, 107
Northern Arizona University, 189
Pima Community College, 213
Rio Salado College, 222
Scottsdale Community College, 241
University of Arizona, 289
University of Phoenix, 331

Arkansas
Arkansas Tech University, 6
Garland County Community College, 100
North Arkansas College, 183
NorthWest Arkansas Community College, 193
Phillips Community College of the University of Arkansas, 212
Southeast Arkansas Technical College, 246
Southern Arkansas University Tech, 248
University of Arkansas, 289
University of Arkansas at Little Rock, 290

California
American River College, 3
Bakersfield College, 12
Butte College, 27
Cabrillo College, 27
California College for Health Sciences, 28
California Institute of Integral Studies, 29
California State University, Bakersfield, 30
California State University, Chico, 30
California State University, Dominguez Hills, 31
California State University, Fresno, 32
California State University, Fullerton, 32
California State University, Hayward, 32
California State University, Long Beach, 33
California State University, Los Angeles, 33
California State University, Northridge, 34
California State University, Sacramento, 34
California State University, Stanislaus, 35
Cerritos College, 43
Chapman University, 44
Citrus College, 49
City College of San Francisco, 49
Coastline Community College, 55
College of San Mateo, 58
College of the Canyons, 59
Concordia University, 68
Contra Costa College, 70
Cosumnes River College, 71
Crafton Hills College, 73
Cuyamaca College, 74
De Anza College, 77
Evergreen Valley College, 92
Fielding Institute, 93
Fullerton College, 99
Glendale Community College, 103
Holy Names College, 113
Institute of Transpersonal Psychology, 120
Laney College, 139
Lassen College, 140
LIFE Bible College, 144
Loma Linda University, 145
Long Beach City College, 145
Los Angeles Community College District, 147
Los Angeles Pierce College, 147
Mendocino College, 157

MiraCosta College, 166
Modesto Junior College, 169
Mt. San Antonio College, 174
National University, 177
Ohlone College, 201
Pacific Oaks College, 208
Palomar College, 208
Riverside Community College, 223
Sacramento City College, 229
San Bernardino Valley College, 237
San Diego City College, 237
San Diego State University, 238
San Joaquin Delta College, 238
San Jose State University, 238
Santa Rosa Junior College, 240
Sierra College, 244
Stanford University, 259
University of California, Davis, 292
University of California Extension, 292
University of California, Santa Barbara, 293
University of California, Santa Cruz, 294
University of Southern California, 336
Victor Valley College, 355
Vista Community College, 356
West Valley College, 367
Yuba College, 374

Colorado
Adams State College, 1
Arapahoe Community College, 4
College for Financial Planning, 56
Colorado Electronic Community College, 61
Colorado Mountain College District, 62
Colorado Northwestern Community College, 62
Colorado State University, 63
Community College of Denver, 67
Denver Conservative Baptist Seminary, 80
Front Range Community College, 98
International University, 121
ISIM University, 123
Mesa State College, 159
Metropolitan State College of Denver, 160
Morgan Community College, 172
National Technological University, 175
Pikes Peak Community College, 213
Pueblo Community College, 217
Red Rocks Community College, 219
Regis University, 220
Trinidad State Junior College, 277
University of Colorado at Boulder, 296

Distance Learning Programs

Geographic Index

Colorado (continued)
University of Colorado at Colorado Springs, 297
University of Northern Colorado, 328
University of Southern Colorado, 336

Connecticut
Charter Oak State College, 45
Manchester Community-Technical College, 151
University of Bridgeport, 290

Delaware
Delaware State University, 79
Delaware Technical & Community College, Jack F. Owens Campus, 79
Delaware Technical & Community College, Stanton/Wilmington Campus, 79
University of Delaware, 298

District of Columbia
The George Washington University, 102
McGraw-Hill World University, 155
NRI Schools, 197
Strayer College, 265

Florida
Brevard Community College, 22
Broward Community College, 25
Central Florida Community College, 39
Daytona Beach Community College, 77
Edison Community College, 89
Embry-Riddle Aeronautical University, Extended Campus, 91
Florida Atlantic University, 96
Florida Community College at Jacksonville, 96
Florida State University, 96
Hillsborough Community College, 113
Lake-Sumter Community College, 137
Manatee Community College, 151
Nova Southeastern University, 196
Pensacola Junior College, 212
Peoples College, 212
Reformed Theological Seminary, 219
St. Johns River Community College, 231
St. Petersburg Junior College, 234
South Florida Community College, 253
Tallahassee Community College, 268
Troy State University–Florida Region, 279
University of North Florida, 329
University of Sarasota, 333
University of South Florida, 337
University of St. Augustine for Health Sciences, 338
University of West Florida, 347

Georgia
Clayton College & State University, 53
Columbus State University, 66
Darton College, 76
DeKalb College, 78
Floyd College, 96
Georgia Institute of Technology, 102
Georgia Southern University, 103
Kennesaw State University, 133
Medical College of Georgia, 156
Middle Georgia College, 163
Morris Brown College, 172
North Georgia College & State University, 192
Piedmont College, 212
Savannah State University, 240
Southern Polytechnic State University, 251
State University of West Georgia, 263
University of Georgia, 299
University System of Georgia, 352

Hawaii
University of Hawaii–Leeward Community College, 300
University of Hawaii–Maui Community College, 300

Idaho
Boise State University, 20
Eastern Idaho Technical College, 84
Idaho State University, 115
University of Idaho, 303

Illinois
Aurora University, 11
Black Hawk College, 18
Bradley University, 21
Carl Sandburg College, 37
City Colleges of Chicago, Harold Washington College, 50
College of DuPage, 57
College of Lake County, 57
College of St. Francis, 57
Concordia University, 69
Danville Area Community College, 75
DePaul University, 81
Eastern Illinois University, 85
Governors State University, 106
Highland Community College, 112
Illinois Central College, 115
Illinois Eastern Community Colleges, Olney Central College, 115
Illinois Institute of Technology, 116
Illinois Valley Community College, 116
John A. Logan College, 127
John Wood Community College, 129
Joliet Junior College, 129
Kankakee Community College, 131
Kaskaskia College, 133
Lake Land College, 135
Lincoln Christian College, 144
Lincoln Land Community College, 145
Metropolitan Community College, 159
Moody Bible Institute, 171
Moraine Valley Community College, 171
Northern Illinois University, 190
Oakton Community College, 198
Parkland College, 209
Prairie State College, 216
Rend Lake College, 221
Richland Community College, 222
Roosevelt University, 227
Sauk Valley Community College, 240
Seabury-Western Theological Seminary, 241
Shawnee Community College, 243
Southern Illinois University at Carbondale, 249
Southern Illinois University at Edwardsville, 249
Spertus Institute of Jewish Studies, 258
Trinity International University, 278
Triton College, 278
University of Illinois at Springfield, 304
University of Illinois at Urbana–Champaign, 305
Waubonsee Community College, 360
Western Illinois University, 363
Wheaton College, 369
William Rainey Harper College, 371

Indiana
Ball State University, 12
Indiana Higher Education Telecommunication System, 117
Indiana State University, 117
Indiana University System, 118
Indiana Wesleyan University, 119
Ivy Tech State College–Northcentral, 124
Ivy Tech State College–Wabash Valley, 124
Purdue University, 218
Saint Francis College, 230
Saint Mary-of-the-Woods College, 233
Taylor University, Fort Wayne Campus, 269
University of Notre Dame, 330
University of Southern Indiana, 337
Vincennes University, 355

Iowa
Buena Vista University, 26
Des Moines Area Community College, 81
Drake University, 82
Ellsworth Community College, 90
Graceland College, 106
Hawkeye Community College, 111
Iowa State University of Science and Technology, 122
Iowa Wesleyan College, 123
Iowa Western Community College, 123
Maharishi University of Management, 151
North Iowa Area Community College, 192
Northwest Iowa Community College, 196
Scott Community College, 241
Simpson College, 244
Southeastern Community College, North Campus, 247
The University of Iowa, 306
University of Northern Iowa, 329

Distance Learning Programs

Geographic Index

Upper Iowa University, 353
William Penn College, 371

Kansas
Barclay College, 13
Central Baptist Theological Seminary, 38
Coffeyville Community College, 55
Colby Community College, 56
Dodge City Community College, 82
Emporia State University, 91
Fort Hays State University, 97
Garden City Community College, 100
Johnson County Community College, 128
Kansas State University, 131
Labette Community College, 134
Ottawa University, 207
Pratt Community College and Area Vocational School, 217
University of Kansas, 306
Wichita State University, 370

Kentucky
Eastern Kentucky University, 85
Morehead State University, 171
Murray State University, 174
Northern Kentucky University, 190
University of Kentucky, 307
University of Kentucky, Ashland Community College, 308
University of Kentucky, Elizabethtown Community College, 309
University of Kentucky, Hazard Community College, 309
University of Kentucky, Henderson Community College, 309
University of Kentucky, Madisonville Community College, 309
University of Louisville, 310

Louisiana
Delgado Community College, 79
Louisiana College, 147
Louisiana State University and Agricultural and Mechanical College, 148
Louisiana State University at Eunice, 148
Louisiana State University in Shreveport, 148
Loyola University New Orleans, 149
Nicholls State University, 182
Northeast Louisiana University, 188
Northwestern State University of Louisiana, 195
Southeastern Louisiana University, 247
University of New Orleans, 325
Xavier University of Louisiana, 373

Maine
Eastern Maine Technical College, 85
Saint Joseph's College, 231
Thomas College, 274
University of Maine, 311
University of Maine at Augusta, 311
University of Maine at Farmington, 312
University of Maine at Fort Kent, 312
University of Maine at Machias, 313
University of New England, 324

Maryland
Allegany College of Maryland, 2
Anne Arundel Community College, 4
Capitol College, 36
Catonsville Community College, 38
Charles County Community College, 45
Chesapeake College, 47
Essex Community College, 92
Frostburg State University, 98
Garrett Community College, 101
Goucher College, 105
Griggs University, 110
Howard Community College, 114
Johns Hopkins University, 128
Montgomery College–Rockville Campus, 170
Prince George's Community College, 217
Towson University, 276
University of Baltimore, 290
University of Maryland, Baltimore, 313
University of Maryland, Baltimore County, 314
University of Maryland, College Park, 314
University of Maryland University College, 314

Massachusetts
Atlantic Union College, 9
Boston University, 21
Bristol Community College, 24
Cape Cod Community College, 36
Fitchburg State College, 94
Gordon-Conwell Theological Seminary, 105
Lesley College, 142
Massachusetts Institute of Technology, 153
Mount Wachusett Community College, 174
Northeastern University, 188
Northern Essex Community College, 189
North Shore Community College, 193
Quincy College, 218
University of Massachusetts Amherst, 315
University of Massachusetts Boston, 316
University of Massachusetts Dartmouth, 316
University of Massachusetts Lowell, 316
Worcester Polytechnic Institute, 372

Michigan
Baker College, 11
Calvin College, 35
Central Michigan University, 40
Charles Stewart Mott Community College, 45
Cleary College, 54
Concordia College, 68
Delta College, 80
Eastern Michigan University, 86
GMI Engineering & Management Institute, 104
Grand Rapids Baptist Seminary, 108
Grand Rapids Community College, 108
Grand Valley State University, 108
Jackson Community College, 125
Kellogg Community College, 133
Lake Michigan College, 136
Lake Superior State University, 137
Lansing Community College, 139
Madonna University, 150
Marygrove College, 152
Michigan State University, 161
Michigan Technological University, 162
Northwestern Michigan College, 195
Northwood University, 196
Oakland Community College, 197
Oakland University, 198
Schoolcraft College, 240
Southwestern Michigan College, 255
University of Michigan, 317
Washtenaw Community College, 360
Wayne County Community College, 361
Wayne State University, 361
Western Michigan University, 364

Minnesota
Bemidji State University, 15
Bethel Theological Seminary, 17
Century Community and Technical College, 42
College of St. Scholastica, 58
The Graduate School of America, 106
Hibbing Community College, 112
Metropolitan State University, 160
Minnesota West Community and Technical College–Worthington Campus, 166
Normandale Community College, 182
North Central Bible College, 184
North Hennepin Community College, 192
Northwestern College, 194
Pine Technical College, 214
Riverland Community College, 223
St. Cloud Technical College, 230
Southwest State University, 257
University of Minnesota, Twin Cities Campus, 318
University of St. Thomas, 332
Walden University, 357

Mississippi
Copiah-Lincoln Community College, 70
Delta State University, 80
East Central Community College, 84
Meridian Community College, 158
Mississippi Delta Community College, 167
Mississippi State University, 167
Mississippi University for Women, 168
University of Mississippi, 319
University of Southern Mississippi, 337

Missouri
Assemblies of God Theological Seminary, 6

Distance Learning Programs

Geographic Index

Missouri (continued)
Berean University of the Assemblies of God, 16
Central Methodist College, 39
Central Missouri State University, 40
Covenant Theological Seminary, 72
Jefferson College, 126
Longview Community College, 146
Missouri Southern State College, 168
Missouri Western State College, 168
Park College, 209
Penn Valley Community College, 211
St. Louis Community College, 232
Southeast Missouri State University, 247
Southwest Missouri State University, 256
Stephens College, 264
University of Missouri–Columbia, 319
University of Missouri–Kansas City, 320
University of Missouri–St. Louis, 320

Montana
Dawson Community College, 77
Flathead Valley Community College, 95
Montana State University–Bozeman, 169
Montana Tech of The University of Montana, 170
University of Great Falls, 299
The University of Montana–Missoula, 320
Western Montana College of The University of Montana, 364

Nebraska
Bellevue University, 15
Central Community College–Grand Island Campus, 39
Chadron State College, 43
Clarkson College, 52
McCook Community College, 154
Metropolitan Community College, 159
Mid-Plains Community College, 164
Northeast Community College, 187
Southeast Community College, Beatrice Campus, 246
Southeast Community College, Lincoln Campus, 246
University of Nebraska at Kearney, 321
University of Nebraska–Lincoln, 321
Western Nebraska Community College, 364

Nevada
Great Basin College, 109
University of Nevada, Las Vegas, 323
University of Nevada, Reno, 323

New Hampshire
New Hampshire College, 177
University of New Hampshire, 325

New Jersey
Atlantic Community College, 8
Bergen Community College, 17
Brookdale Community College, 24
Burlington County College, 26
Caldwell College, 27
Camden County College, 36
County College of Morris, 72
Cumberland County College, 73
Fairleigh Dickinson University, Florham-Madison Campus, 92
Fairleigh Dickinson University, Teaneck–Hackensack, 93
New Jersey Institute of Technology, 178
The Richard Stockton College of New Jersey, 221
Rutgers, The State University of New Jersey, Newark, 228
Saint Peter's College, 235
Seton Hall University, 243
Stevens Institute of Technology, 265
Sussex County Community College, 266
Thomas Edison State College, 275

New Mexico
Clovis Community College, 54
College of the Southwest, 59
Eastern New Mexico University, 86
New Mexico Junior College, 179
New Mexico State University, 179
San Juan College, 239
Santa Fe Community College, 239
Western New Mexico University, 365

New York
Columbia-Greene Community College, 65
Cornell University, 71
Corning Community College, 71
Dutchess Community College, 83
Genesee Community College, 101
Hudson Valley Community College, 114
Jamestown Community College, 126
Jefferson Community College, 126
Mercy College, 158
Mohawk Valley Community College, 169
Nassau Community College, 175
New School for Social Research, 180
New York Institute of Technology, 181
New York University, 182
Polytechnic University, Brooklyn Campus, 215
Polytechnic University, Westchester Graduate Center, 215
Rensselaer Polytechnic Institute, 221
Rochester Institute of Technology, 223
Rockland Community College, 225
St. Thomas Aquinas College, 235
Skidmore College, 245
State University of New York at Binghamton, 260
State University of New York at Buffalo, 260
State University of New York at Farmingdale, 261
State University of New York at New Paltz, 261
State University of New York at Oswego, 261
State University of New York College at Plattsburgh, 262
State University of New York College of Environmental Science and Forestry, 262
State University of New York Empire State College, 262
Suffolk County Community College–Ammerman Campus, 266
Syracuse University, 266
Ulster County Community College, 281
University of the State of New York, Regents College, 343

North Carolina
Beaufort County Community College, 14
Bladen Community College, 19
Catawba Valley Community College, 37
Central Piedmont Community College, 41
Duke University, 82
East Carolina University, 83
Fayetteville Technical Community College, 93
Mayland Community College, 154
McDowell Technical Community College, 154
North Carolina State University, 184
Pitt Community College, 214
Sandhills Community College, 237
Stanly Community College, 259
The University of North Carolina at Chapel Hill, 325
University of North Carolina at Charlotte, 326
University of North Carolina at Greensboro, 326
Wake Technical Community College, 357
Wilkes Community College, 371
Wilson Technical Community College, 371

North Dakota
Minot State University, 166
North Dakota State College of Science, 186
North Dakota State University, 187
University of Mary, 313
University of North Dakota, 327
Valley City State University, 354

Ohio
Antioch University, 155
Cincinnati Bible College and Seminary, 49
Clark State Community College, 53
Cleveland State University, 54
Columbus State Community College, 66
Cuyahoga Community College, Metropolitan Campus, 73
David N. Myers College, 76
Edison State Community College, 89
Franciscan University of Steubenville, 97
Franklin University, 98
Hocking College, 113

Distance Learning Programs

Geographic Index

Lakeland Community College, 136
Lorain County Community College, 146
The McGregor School of Antioch University, 155
North Central Technical College, 186
Northwestern College, 194
The Ohio State University, 199
Ohio State University–Mansfield Campus, 199
Ohio University, 199
Ohio University–Eastern, 200
Ohio University–Southern Campus, 200
Owens Community College, 207
Sinclair Community College, 244
Terra State Community College, 272
The Union Institute, 281
The University of Akron, 283
University of Cincinnati, 295
University of Cincinnati Raymond Walters College, 295
University of Dayton, 298
University of Toledo, 343
Wright State University, 373

Oklahoma
Connors State College, 70
Eastern Oklahoma State College, 87
Northern Oklahoma College, 190
Oklahoma City Community College, 201
Oklahoma State University, 202
Oral Roberts University, 205
Redlands Community College, 218
Rogers University, 226
Rose State College, 228
Seminole State College, 242
Southwestern Oklahoma State University, 256
Tulsa Community College, 280
University of Central Oklahoma, 294
University of Oklahoma, 330
Western Oklahoma State College, 365

Oregon
Blue Mountain Community College, 20
Chemeketa Community College, 46
Clackamas Community College, 51
Clatsop Community College, 53
Eastern Oregon University, 87
Lane Community College, 138
Oregon Health Sciences University, 206
Oregon State University, 206
Portland Community College, 215
Portland State University, 216
Southern Oregon University, 251
Treasure Valley Community College, 277
Umpqua Community College, 281
Western Conservative Baptist Seminary, 362
Western Oregon University, 366

Pennsylvania
Allegheny University of the Health Sciences, 2
American College, 3
Bloomsburg University of Pennsylvania, 19
Bucks County Community College, 25
Chestnut Hill College, 47
College Misericordia, 56
Community College of Philadelphia, 67
Delaware County Community College, 78
Duquesne University, 83
Gannon University, 100
Harrisburg Area Community College, 111
Juniata College, 131
Lackawanna Junior College, 134
Lafayette College, 135
Lehigh Carbon Community College, 141
Lehigh University, 142
Luzerne County Community College, 149
Lycoming College, 149
Marywood University, 153
Montgomery County Community College, 170
Northampton County Area Community College, 183
Pennsylvania State University University Park Campus, 209
Rosemont College, 227
Saint Francis College, 230
University of Pennsylvania, 331
University of Pittsburgh, 331
University of Pittsburgh at Bradford, 332
Washington and Jefferson College, 359
Westmoreland County Community College, 366

Rhode Island
Brown University, 25
Community College of Rhode Island, 67
Roger Williams University, 226
Salve Regina University, 236

South Carolina
Columbia International University, 65
Florence-Darlington Technical College, 95
Greenville Technical College, 109
Medical University of South Carolina, 156
Technical College of the Lowcountry, 270
University of South Carolina, 334
Winthrop University, 372
York Technical College, 374

South Dakota
Black Hills State University, 18
Dakota State University, 74
Northern State University, 191
University of South Dakota, 335

Tennessee
Chattanooga State Technical Community College, 46
Columbia State Community College, 66
East Tennessee State University, 89
Johnson Bible College, 128
Middle Tennessee State University, 163
Shelby State Community College, 243
State Technical Institute at Memphis, 259
Temple Baptist Seminary, 270
Tennessee State University, 271
Tennessee Technological University, 271
Tennessee Temple University, 271
The University of Memphis, 317
The University of Tennessee at Martin, 339
University of Tennessee, Knoxville, 339
University of Tennessee Space Institute, 340
Volunteer State Community College, 357
Walters State Community College, 358

Texas
Abilene Christian University, 1
Alvin Community College, 2
Angelina College, 4
Austin Community College, 11
Blinn College, 19
College of the Mainland, 59
Collin County Community College, 61
Concordia University at Austin, 69
Dallas County Community College District, 75
Dallas Theological Seminary, 75
El Paso Community College, 90
Galveston College, 100
Grayson County College, 109
Houston Community College System, 114
Kingwood College, 134
Lamar University, 138
Lee College, 141
Midland College, 164
Midwestern State University, 164
Mountain View College, 173
North Central Texas College, 186
North Harris College, 192
Odessa College, 198
Our Lady of the Lake University of San Antonio, 207
Palo Alto College, 208
San Antonio College, 237
Southern Methodist University, 250
Southwestern Adventist University, 254
Southwestern Assemblies of God University, 254
Southwestern Baptist Theological Seminary, 255
Southwest Texas State University, 257
Sul Ross State University, 266
Tarleton State University, 268
Tarrant County Junior College, 269
Texas A&M University–Commerce, 272
Texas A&M University–Corpus Christi, 273
Texas Tech University, 273
Texas Wesleyan University, 274
Texas Woman's University, 274
Tyler Junior College, 280
University of Dallas, 297
University of Houston, 301
University of Houston–Clear Lake, 303

Distance Learning Programs 613

Geographic Index

Texas (continued)
University of North Texas Health Science Center at Fort Worth, 329
The University of Texas at Arlington, 340
The University of Texas at Austin, 341
The University of Texas at El Paso, 341
The University of Texas at San Antonio, 341
The University of Texas at Tyler, 342
The University of Texas of the Permian Basin, 342

Utah
Brigham Young University, 23
Salt Lake Community College, 235
Southern Utah University, 252
University of Utah, 344
Utah State University, 353
Utah Valley State College, 354
Weber State University, 362

Vermont
Champlain College, 43
Community College of Vermont, 68
Southern Vermont College, 253
Trinity College of Vermont, 277
University of Vermont, 344

Virginia
American Military University, 3
Central Virginia Community College, 41
Christopher Newport University, 48
Danville Community College, 76
Hampton University, 110
J. Sargeant Reynolds Community College, 129
Liberty University, 143
Lord Fairfax Community College, 146
New River Community College, 180
Northern Virginia Community College, 191
Old Dominion University, 203
Regent University, 220
Shenandoah University, 243
Southwest Virginia Community College, 258
Thomas Nelson Community College, 276
Tidewater Community College, 276
University of Virginia, 345
Virginia Commonwealth University, 355
Virginia Polytechnic Institute and State University, 356
Wytheville Community College, 373

Washington
Bastyr University, 14
Bellevue Community College, 14
Central Washington University, 41
City University, 50
Clark College, 51
Columbia Basin College, 64
Eastern Washington University, 88
Edmonds Community College, 90
North Seattle Community College, 193
Pierce College, 213
Seattle Central Community College, 242
Seattle Pacific University, 242
Skagit Valley College, 245
South Puget Sound Community College, 253
Tacoma Community College, 268
University of Washington, 345
Washington State University, 359
Wenatchee Valley College, 362
Western Washington University, 366
Whatcom Community College, 369

West Virginia
Bluefield State College, 20
The College of West Virginia, 60
Glenville State College, 104
Marshall University, 152
Southern West Virginia Community and Technical College, 253
The University of Charleston, 294
West Virginia Graduate College, 367
West Virginia University, 367
West Virginia University Institute of Technology, 368
West Virginia Wesleyan College, 368

Wisconsin
Blackhawk Technical College, 18
Chippewa Valley Technical College, 48
Concordia University Wisconsin, 69
Gateway Technical College, 101
Lakeshore Technical College, 136
Madison Area Technical College, 150
Mid-State Technical College, 164
Milwaukee Area Technical College, 165
Milwaukee School of Engineering, 165
Northcentral Technical College, 185
Northeast Wisconsin Technical College, 189
University of Wisconsin–Eau Claire, 348
University of Wisconsin–Extension, 348
University of Wisconsin–La Crosse, 349
University of Wisconsin–Madison, 349
University of Wisconsin–Oshkosh, 349
University of Wisconsin–Platteville, 350
University of Wisconsin–River Falls, 350
University of Wisconsin–Stevens Point, 351
University of Wisconsin–Stout, 351
University of Wisconsin–Whitewater, 351
Waukesha County Technical College, 360

Wyoming
Central Wyoming College, 42
Eastern Wyoming College, 88
Laramie County Community College, 139
University of Wyoming, 352

CANADA

Alberta
Athabasca University, 7
University of Alberta, 288
The University of Calgary, 291

British Columbia
University of British Columbia, 291

New Brunswick
University of New Brunswick, 324

Newfoundland
Memorial University of Newfoundland, 156

Nova Scotia
Acadia University, 1
Dalhousie University, 74
Mount Saint Vincent University, 173

Ontario
Brock University, 24
Carleton University, 37
Lakehead University, 135
Laurentian University, 140
Ryerson Polytechnic University, 229
University of Guelph, 300
University of Waterloo, 346
University of Windsor, 347
Wilfrid Laurier University, 370

Québec
Universitè Laval, 282

Saskatchewan
University of Saskatchewan, 333

UNITED KINGDOM
Heriot-Watt University, 112
University of Leicester, 310

Distance Learning Programs

NOTES